DISORDERS OF CHILDHOOD: DEVELOPMENT AND PSYCHOPATHOLOGY

SECOND EDITION

DISORDERS OF CHILDHOOD: DEVELOPMENT AND PSYCHOPATHOLOGY

ROBIN HORNIK PARRITZ
Hamline University

MICHAEL F. TROY
Children's Hospitals and Clinics of Minnesota

WADSWORTH
CENGAGE Learning

Australia • Brazil • Japan • Korea • Mexico • Singapore • Spain • United Kingdom • United States

Disorders of Childhood: Development and Psychopathology, Second Edition
Robin Hornik Parritz and Michael F. Troy

Publisher: Jon-David Hague

Executive Editor: Jaime Perkins

Developmental Editor: Jessica Alderman

Assistant Editor: Margaux Cameron

Editorial Assistant: Audrey Espey

Media Editor: Mary Noel

Senior Brand Manager: Elisabeth Rhoden

Art and Design Direction: Carolyn Deacy

Production Management and Composition: Lynn Lustberg, MPS Limited

Composition: MPS Limited

Manufacturing Planner: Karen Hunt

Rights Acquisitions Specialist: Roberta Broyer

Text Designer: Kathleen Cunningham

Photo Researcher: Bill Smith Group

Text Researcher: PreMedia Global

Copy Editor: Patricia M. Daly

Illustrator: MPS Limited

Cover Designer: Kathleen Cunningham

Cover Image: ©Colin Anderson/Getty Images

For product information and technology assistance, contact us at
Cengage Learning Customer & Sales Support, 1-800-354-9706

For permission to use material from this text or product, submit all requests online at **www.cengage.com/permissions** Further permissions questions can be e-mailed to **permissionrequest@cengage.com**

Library of Congress Control Number: 2012943575

ISBN-13: 978-1-285-09606-3

ISBN-10: 1-285-09606-1

Wadsworth
20 Davis Drive
Belmont, CA 94002-3098
USA

Cengage Learning is a leading provider of customized learning solutions with office locations around the globe, including Singapore, the United Kingdom, Australia, Mexico, Brazil, and Japan. Locate your local office at **www.cengage.com/global**

Cengage Learning products are represented in Canada by Nelson Education, Ltd.

To learn more about Wadsworth, visit **www.cengage.com/wadsworth**

Purchase any of our products at your local college store or at our preferred online store **www.ichapters.com**

Printed in the United States of America
1 2 3 4 5 6 7 17 16 15 14 13

Brief Contents

Detailed Contents

About the Authors

Robin Hornik Parritz, Ph.D., is a Professor of Psychology at Hamline University in St. Paul, Minnesota. Robin received her undergraduate degree in psychology from Brandeis University in 1983, and her Ph.D. in Clinical Psychology from the University of Minnesota in 1989. Her research and clinical areas of interest include emotional development, developmental psychopathology, and programs designed to increase knowledge and decrease stigma related to children's psychological disorders. Robin teaches Disorders of Childhood, Abnormal Psychology, Theories of Psychotherapy, Psychology of Emotion, and Clinical Psychology. Robin is married to Jon Parritz and has three sons, Ari, Adam, and Jesse.

Michael Troy, Ph.D., is a clinical psychologist and Medical Director of Behavioral Health Services at Children's Hospitals and Clinics of Minnesota. Michael received his undergraduate degree from Lawrence University in 1980 and his Ph.D. in Clinical Psychology from the University of Minnesota in 1988. He completed his internship and fellowship at Hennepin County Medical Center and has been on staff at Children's Hospital of Minnesota since 1988. His clinical and academic interests include diagnostic classification issues in developmental psychopathology, models of therapeutic assessment, and teaching child clinical psychology as part of hospital and community medical education programs. Michael is married to Cynthia Koehler Troy and has two sons, Kevin and Brendan.

Preface

Writing a textbook on the psychological disorders of infants, children, and adolescents involves multiple decisions about content, emphasis, and organization. These decisions reinforce and extend the knowledge base of the field and determine what is distinctive about the authors' approach. The decisions we made while writing this book were influenced by our academic and clinical experiences involving both typical and atypical development. When we made the decision to write this book, we were particularly interested in providing a text that was both relevant and compelling. Our hope was to provide students with the type of meaningful framework and conceptual integration that has come to characterize our field. We also wanted to offer teachers a more practical and more true-to-life approach to organizing their courses. We have built upon and enhanced these strengths in this edition.

In this second edition, we updated all chapters to incorporate changes in the newest edition of the Diagnostic and Statistical Manual, DSM-5 (American Psychiatric Association, 2013). In doing so, we sought to capture not only the changes in organization and nomenclature in DSM-5, but the underlying clinical and research findings that informed those changes as well. We reorganized several chapters to better reflect how disorders, combinations of disorders, and challenging diagnostic issues present in real-world clinical settings. For example, we combined the chapters on oppositional defiant disorder and conduct disorder in order to examine developmental pathways reflecting both continuity and discontinuity. We also included a separate chapter on trauma- and stressor-related disorders, and expanded our review of theoretical and empirical findings on maltreatment in that chapter. We also have a new section on learning disorders in the chapter on intellectual developmental disorder.

Four themes recur throughout the text; together they distinguish our clinical and teaching emphases. Each of these themes is informed by the principles and practices of *developmental psychopathology*, an interdisciplinary approach that asserts that maladaptive patterns of emotion, cognition, and behavior occur in the context of typical development. The first theme emphasizes multifactor explanations. *Multifactor explanations* of disorders encompass biological, psychological, and sociocultural factors. These factors are examined in detailed analyses of etiologies, assessments, diagnoses, developmental pathways, and interventions. Especially distinctive is the way we make sure to discuss the multiple ways that factors at every level of analysis need to be explored for both typically developing and atypically developing children. **In this second edition, for example, we expanded discussions of gene-by-environment processes, an excellent illustration of thinking about development, psychopathology, and pathways across levels of analysis.**

The second theme is focused on *developmental frameworks* and *developmental pathways*, and is reflected in the sequencing of chapters, unique sections that open each chapter and summarize key developmental tasks and challenges, and our descriptions of disorders over time. Disorders that emerge or are diagnosed early in development are presented first, followed by disorders that emerge or are diagnosed in the elementary-school years, followed by those that emerge or are diagnosed in adolescence. This sequencing serves several purposes. First, it allows students to consider specific disorders and sets of disorders that occur in a particular developmental period in proximity and relation to one another. Second, this sequencing allows for an ongoing focus on the constructs of risk and resilience, and provides a basis for coherent discussions of early occurring disorders as risk factors for later occurring disorders. For example, the chapter on disorders of attachment focuses first on understanding the nature and course of these disorders in and of themselves; it also previews the multiple connections that will be made in subsequent chapters between attachment difficulties and later forms of psychopathology. Third, this sequencing emphasizes a more complex understanding of disorders: We think differently, for example, about depression that is identified early and on its own than we do about depression that follows and may be related to an anxiety disorder or attention deficit/hyperactivity disorder.

The sections at the beginning of chapters that summarize the developmental tasks and challenges experienced by typically developing children are especially relevant given the disorders discussed in the chapter. For instance, a detailed summary of the development of self-regulation, effortful control, and executive function is presented before a clinical presentation of attention deficit/hyperactivity disorder. An overview of prosocial behavior is presented at the beginning of the chapter on oppositional defiant disorder and conduct disorder, and a review of stress and coping is provided in the chapter on maltreatment and trauma- and stressor-related disorders. These introductory sections help students to appreciate the developmental contexts of disorders and their core symptoms; to make distinctions among the everyday issues that most children experience, more difficult types of problems, and clinically meaningful psychopathology; and to make comparisons between the factors that influence the multiple pathways of typical development and the multiple pathways of psychopathology.

Discussions of developmental pathways, or descriptions of disorders over time, accurately reflect how each child's psychopathology unfolds over time in real life. This pathway model also emphasizes opportunities for growth and change. For example, we describe age-related experiences, such as the transition to middle school, that are associated with some struggling children getting back on track and certain well-functioning children experiencing distress. **In this second edition, we also provide up-to-date coverage of models describing developmental cascades, the accumulating consequences of multiple transactions across domains, levels, and systems. These new constructs emphasize the integrative and dynamic nature of development and psychopathology.**

The third theme takes into account the *child in context* and calls attention to the multiple settings in which the child is embedded. Discussions throughout the text are intended to highlight the many ways in which children and their disorders are understood in larger social contexts (e.g., families, schools and communities, cultures, and historical eras). **In the second edition, new summaries provide information on children's mental health in global context, as well as additional research findings comparing children's adjustment and maladjustment from diverse cultural backgrounds and in various countries.**

The fourth theme involves a *broad focus on the whole child* rather than a narrow focus on disorder, developmental delay, or impairment. This holistic appreciation of the child emphasizes patterns of interests, abilities, and strengths. We make sure that our case studies include this kind of information, to remind students as often as possible that the diagnosis of a particular disorder does not provide all of the important information about a child. We need to appreciate the everyday joys and special accomplishments that are part of all children's lives. In addition, we believe this holistic focus provides a number of opportunities to talk about the stigma associated with mental illness, and to encourage awareness, tolerance, respect, and compassion for children and adolescents who struggle with disorders.

Our hope is that this book will enable students to think about disorders in the same way that caring adults think about disorders they encounter every day—in terms of an individual child who is coping with distress and dysfunction: a boy or a girl of a certain age with a specific temperament, characteristic strengths, and personal history, with a family and a network of friends, embedded in a community and culture. We believe that we have written a textbook that places the child at the center of comprehensive and meaningful information, reflecting the most up-to-date understandings of child and adolescent psychopathology, in a format designed to support learning and understanding.

Key Features

In addition to the previously discussed case studies woven throughout, our textbook offers a variety of feature boxes that highlight important topics of interest for students. The themes covered in these boxes are (1) The Child in Context, (2) Clinical Perspectives, (3) Risk and Resilience, and (4) Emerging Science. For study and review, each chapter includes a chapter summary and list of key terms that appear in boldface in the text.

Supporting Resources:

Along with this textbook, Cengage Learning offers the following companion resources.

For Instructors

- Online Instructor's Manual with Test Bank. This supplement contains valuable resources for preparing for class, including chapter outlines, lecture topics, class activities, and testing materials.
- Online PowerPoint Lecture Outlines. Prepared by the authors, these lecture outlines are a great starting point to help you prepare for class.

For Instructors and Students

- Companion Website. The book's companion Website contains resources for both students and instructors, helping the professor to prepare for class and enhancing the students' learning experience.

Acknowledgments

We wish to thank the many individuals who have inspired, challenged, encouraged, and supported us from the very beginning of this project to the final revisions of the second edition. Although our two names are on the cover, we are deeply aware that our text reflects the work of countless others whose research studies and clinical insights we have cited and summarized. We thank them for their contributions to this text and to the field of developmental psychopathology.

We are grateful for the exceptional educational, research, and clinical experiences that have motivated us to write this book. We are grateful to teachers and colleagues who have shared their knowledge of child development and psychopathology, along with their vision of sound, compassionate intervention. We especially acknowledge our undergraduate, graduate, and clinical mentors, who exemplify professional accomplishment and generosity and who model passionate commitment to children's well-being: Joe Cunningham of Brandeis University (who has never read anything Robin wrote without scrutinizing, praising, and then improving it), Megan Gunnar and Alan Sroufe of the University of Minnesota, and Ada Hegion and Vivian Pearlman of the Hennepin County Medical Center. We could not be prouder to be their students.

We thank our own students and clients, who have challenged us to be better explainers of theory and more thoughtful models of practice. We also thank our colleagues at Hamline University and at Children's Hospitals and Clinics of Minnesota for their ongoing encouragement and support. Thanks also to Wendy Werdin, the most wonderfully obliging administrative assistant at Hamline University, for typing stacks and stacks of references.

As we prepare to launch this second edition, we wish to thank all those who were so important to the success of the first edition, including the professors and instructors who adopted our textbook and provided us with valuable feedback. In particular, we thank Alan Sroufe and Dante Cicchetti for believing in us and in the value of this endeavor. We are especially grateful for their formal endorsement of the book, which has been key to its widespread acceptance in the field and a source of great pride to the authors.

We have many people to thank at Cengage, especially Jaime Perkins and Jon-David Hague, who provided invaluable advocacy, enthusiasm, know-how, and experience. We thank Jessica Alderman for her careful attention to detail, patient problem solving, and positive attitude. We are grateful to the marketing team for all of their hard work in promoting the first edition and for their excitement about the second edition. We also thank all the individuals on the production team, including Roberta Broyer (Rights Acquisitions Specialist), Elisabeth Rhoden (Senior Brand Manager), and Lynn Lustberg (Project Manager) at MPS Limited.

This text has benefited greatly from the comments and suggestions of many reviewers, including the following:

Jack Bates, *Indiana University–Bloomington*
Michelle Broth, *Georgia Gwinnett College*
Arin Connell, *Case Western Reserve University*
Mary Ann Coupland, *Sinte Gleska University*
Carolyn Fallahi, *Central Connecticut State University*
Bill Frey, *Castleton State College*
Jennifer Green, *Miami University*
Wendy Hart, *Arizona State University*
Steve Lee, *University of California Los Angeles*
Susan Marell, *St. Thomas Aquinas College*
Paul McCabe, *Brooklyn College–City University of New York*
Suzanne Morin, *Shippensburg University*
Casey Tobin, *University of Wisconsin–La Crosse*
Deborah Walder, *Brooklyn College–City University of New York*

Robin Parritz especially thanks Mike Troy, a coauthor whose intellect, passion, and humor have made all aspects of this collaboration rewarding. Robin is fortunate that she is embedded in ever-expanding circles of loving family and wonderful friends. She will always be grateful for their support, encouragement, and friendship. Robin thanks her sons, Ari (and her daughter-in-law Rachel!), Adam, and Jesse for their everyday and exceptional examples of challenge and growth, and for every kind of happiness. Robin is forever indebted to her husband, Jon Parritz, for enormous amounts of love, counsel, and support.

Mike Troy thanks Robin Hornik Parritz for making quite a lot of work, quite a lot of fun. She is the heart and soul of this project and a most generous collaborator. Mike is sustained by the loving memory of his parents, who guide him still, and he thanks his siblings and their families for love and laughter. Mike thanks BGW for the unwavering trajectory of lifelong friendship. Finally, Mike appreciates his wonderful family—his wife, Cynthia, and their sons, Kevin and Brendan—for their support, good humor, and wise counsel. This is a better book for their contributions.

1 Introduction

WHEN WE THINK ABOUT childhood and about growing up, images of wonder, energy, excitement, and joy are common. Babies sharing first smiles and taking first steps. Kindergarteners singing loud songs and looking forward to family vacations. Children reading books, riding bikes, sleeping over with friends. Teens studying for exams, learning to drive, and falling in love. In the midst of all of this growth and change, however, we notice children who are almost always sad, worried, afraid, or angry. We meet children who believe that they are bad, that they have no control over their lives, that the world is an awful place. There are children who lash out at others and some who withdraw from relationships. Some of these children exhibit patterns of feelings, thoughts, and behaviors that are best understood as psychological disorders.

The goal of this textbook is to provide a basic understanding of these children and their disorders, and of the theories, methodologies, and findings of developmental psychopathology. We need to understand so that we may meaningfully describe the psychological disorders of infancy, childhood, and adolescence. We need to understand so that we can identify the numerous factors that increase vulnerability to psychopathology. We need to understand so that we can design appropriate interventions for struggling children. We need to understand so that we can increase awareness and empathy for children who deserve to be treated with dignity and respect. And we need to understand so that we can provide the necessary support and resources to families, schools, and communities.

Our approach in writing and organizing this textbook is based on the central premise of **developmental psychopathology**, which suggests that we gain a better understanding of children's disorders when we think about those disorders *within the context of normal development*. We believe that infant, child, and adolescent psychopathology can only be understood by placing descriptions of disorders against the background of typical emotional, cognitive, and behavioral development. We also believe that it is necessary to acknowledge the everyday problems and difficult phases that characterize normal child development, and to make clear both the connections and the distinctions between adaptation and maladaptation. We present discussions of children's disorders in a sequence that follows the child's own growth from birth through early adulthood, and emphasizes that both children and disorders develop over time.

Defining Disorders of Infancy, Childhood, and Adolescence

Emma is a 5½-year-old girl whose parents are becoming increasingly concerned about her. Emma has always been somewhat quiet and reserved, taking her time to check out unknown situations and new children, but usually warming up to join activities and play. As the time for kindergarten approaches, Emma is exhibiting more anxiety around others, preferring to stay home, close by her mother. She is displaying new fears about the dark, about strangers, and about getting lost in the new school building. Emma is also crying more frequently and seems almost constantly on edge.

Should Emma's parents call the pediatrician? The kindergarten teacher? A child psychologist? Should they wait a few months to see if Emma grows out of this phase and hope that waiting doesn't make things worse?

Understanding psychopathology is complicated. Parents, teachers, and children themselves are often confused about whether a particular pattern of feelings, thoughts, and behaviors reflects an actual disorder, and if so, whether that disorder involves minor, moderate, or major maladjustment. One of the first steps leading to accurate and useful conceptualizations of psychopathology is to recognize the many connections between "normal" and "abnormal" development. In Emma's case, it is important to consider other children's experiences of wariness and fear, differences among children's temperaments, and how much her distress interferes with daily life.

Before making decisions about Emma, we need to review some of the many approaches to the field of child development itself. Models of childhood and child development have been influenced by historical notions of children as miniature adults, blank slates, savages, and innocent beings, as well as more recent images of children as innately and surprisingly competent individuals (Hwang, Lamb, & Sigel, 1996; Mintz, 2006). Depending on the model, our understanding of childhood may lead us to expect that almost all typically developing children will engage in idyllic play, or skill learning, or avoidance of danger. However, we need to think realistically about whether most children amuse themselves for hours on end, or practice piano or take swimming lessons without complaint, or never run into the street without looking for cars.

Most contemporary theorists, researchers, and clinicians emphasize that a useful model of normal development requires a dynamic appreciation of children's strengths and weaknesses. A model like this takes into account the complexities of individual, familial, ethnic, cultural, and societal beliefs about desirable and undesirable outcomes for children and adolescents. Against this multilayered background of normal child development, we are then able to identify children whose distress and dysfunction are exceptional.

What Is Normal?

Common descriptions of normality and psychopathology often focus on (1) **statistical deviance**—the infrequency of certain emotions, cognitions, and/or behaviors;

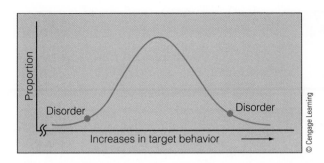

FIGURE 1:1   Statistical deviance model of disorder.

(2) **sociocultural norms**—the beliefs and expectations of certain groups about what kinds of emotions, cognitions, and/or behaviors are undesirable or unacceptable; and (3) **mental health definitions**—theoretical or clinically based notions of distress and dysfunction.

Statistical Deviance

From a statistical deviance perspective, a child who displays too much or too little of any age-expected behavior (such as dependency or assertiveness) might have a disorder. Children of a certain age above the "high number" cutoff, or below the "low number" cutoff would meet the criterion for disorder (see Fig. 1:1). Thinking again about Emma, we will be more concerned about a possible disorder if she is much more anxious and fearful than her peers, and less concerned if many of her peers are also experiencing these difficulties.

Sociocultural Norms

From a sociocultural norm perspective, children who fail to conform to age-related, gender-specific, or culture-relevant expectations might be viewed as challenging, struggling, or disordered. Keep in mind, however, that there is potential for disparity among various sociocultural groups and norms. For instance, pressure in a particular neighborhood or peer group to prove oneself with belligerent or aggressive behavior may contribute to the diagnosis of psychopathology by others outside of that neighborhood or peer group. This time when we consider Emma's fears and anxieties, we are focused on specific social and cultural expectations for a young girl's independence. Are her feelings and behaviors within a generally acceptable range? Depending on the particular social and cultural settings, norms will vary, but there will always be certain patterns of emotion, cognition, and behavior that are considered evidence of psychopathology.

Mental Health Definitions

From a mental health perspective, a child's psychological well-being is the key consideration. The 1999 landmark report of the United States' Surgeon General (U.S. Department of Health and Human Services, 1999) states that "mentally healthy children and adolescents enjoy a positive quality of life; function well at home, in school, and in their communities; and are free of disabling symptoms of psychopathology" (p. 123). Using this criterion, children who have a negative quality of life, or who function poorly, or who exhibit certain kinds of symptoms might have a disorder. Again, we think of Emma. From this perspective, what matters most is how Emma's fears and anxieties make the transition to kindergarten distressing, and whether she is able to participate comfortably in various academic and social tasks.

The Role of Values

Closer examination of these definitions reveals that each raises questions about the role of values in conceptualizations of mental health and psychopathology (Sonuga-Barke, 1998; Wakefield, 2002). Box 1:1 provides an example of a value-informed set of children's needs for psychological well-being. A key value judgment involves distinctions between adaptation and maladaptation, and personal or group standards of *adequate or average* adaptation, or *optimal* adaptation (Offer, 1999). **Adequate adaptation** has to do with what is considered okay, acceptable, or good enough. **Optimal adaptation** has to do with what is excellent, superior, or "the best of what is possible." The following cases illustrate poor adaptation, adequate adaptation, and optimal adaptation.

Poor Adaptation

The Case of Dylan

Dylan is an 8-year-old boy who lives with his mother and two older siblings in an affluent suburb. Dylan is currently struggling in a variety of ways and in a variety of contexts. He is having trouble with the increasingly demanding academics in his private school, and is usually ignored by his classmates. At home, Dylan is angry and withdrawn.

Dylan's mother had a history of depression before having children. After years of healthy functioning, she became depressed following Dylan's birth, a problem she struggled with throughout his early

The Irreducible Needs of Children

Our understanding of children's psychological disorders is continuously informed by our understanding of children's usual development. When we think about what happens in children's lives, we need to remember not only the range and variety of hoped-for outcomes but the basic, bottom-line components of "what every child must have to grow, learn, and flourish." Two prominent children's advocates, T. Berry Brazelton and Stanley Greenspan, have described these essential needs (Brazelton & Greenspan, 2000). They include

- the need for ongoing nurturing relationships
- the need for physical protection, safety, and regulation

- the need for experiences tailored to individual differences
- the need for developmentally appropriate experiences
- the need for limit-setting, structure, and expectations
- the need for stable, supportive communities and cultural continuity

In our descriptions and discussions of children's disorders, we will repeatedly refer to prevention and intervention strategies that are based on these needs. Satisfaction of these needs—from birth through adulthood—is an index of our concern, compassion, and commitment to children's well-being.

childhood. Dylan was described as a "difficult" baby, who cried frequently and slept poorly. As a toddler, he had frequent temper tantrums that often involved biting and scratching. In fact, Dylan's parents were asked to withdraw him from his preschool because of his poor emotional and behavioral regulation. As these issues with Dylan escalated, so did his mother's depression, as well as conflict between his parents, who disagreed on what should be done to manage Dylan's behavior.

With the start of kindergarten, closely followed by his father's death, Dylan's underlying anxiety, always present but overshadowed by his behavior problems, became increasingly evident. Over the next two years, both his first- and second-grade teachers provided Dylan with extra support and encouragement, but with little positive effect. At the beginning of third grade, the school counselor suggested to Dylan's mother that they see a child psychologist. Although Dylan's mother wanted to comply with the referral, she felt overwhelmed by the challenges of single parenting and her depression and never arranged for Dylan to see a therapist. As his classmates became more focused on developing friendships and enjoying academic experiences, Dylan felt increasingly isolated, lonely, and unhappy. ■■

Adequate Adaptation

The Case of Antoine

Antoine is a 6-year-old boy who is currently in his third foster home. Antoine was severely neglected early in his life and was removed from his biological mother's home when he was nine months old by

the county's child protection services. After two brief foster placements, Antoine has been in a stable and nurturing foster home for two years.

Although his teachers have no concerns about his basic academic skills, they note that Antoine does have difficulty paying attention and that he is frequently impulsive. Antoine has several friends who he likes to play with, but he is seldom sought out as a playmate by other children. His feelings are hurt easily and he sometimes misinterprets the intentions of others, feeling that they are out to get him. Consequently, he is quicker than other children to resort to name-calling or shoving when he is upset.

Antoine is more comfortable and relaxed at home with his foster parents, but asks often if he will have to move away from them. While being as reassuring as possible, his foster parents have acknowledged that they do not know how long Antoine will be with them. Antoine clearly worries about leaving his current home, and although his psychotherapist attempts to provide support for his concerns, Antoine is adamant that he does not want to talk about this. ■■

Optimal Adaptation

The Case of Jenna

Jenna is a 6-year-old girl who also suffered an early loss. Jenna's mother was a single parent who died in an automobile accident when Jenna was two. Following her mother's death, Jenna went to live with her maternal grandparents. Although distraught at the loss of their daughter, they dedicated themselves to caring for Jenna to the best of their ability.

In addition to her grandparents, Jenna is also involved with and supported by her many relatives who live nearby and include Jenna in their lives. Jenna's teachers describe her as bright and enthusiastic in the classroom. She is excited about learning to read and seems to have a special aptitude for math. Jenna is well liked by both the girls and the boys in her class, and is often invited to play dates and birthday parties.

At home, Jenna enjoys hearing stories about her mother, and thinking of how loving and proud her mother would be. There are times, of course, when Jenna and her grandparents cry for her mother. And as Jenna gets older she may become more aware of her absent biological father and seek to learn more about him. But Jenna and her grandparents are able to take comfort in each other and in the warm and secure home they have created together. ■■

Even with the traumatic beginnings of their childhoods, both Antoine and Jenna are moving in a positive developmental direction, in contrast with Dylan. Still, Antoine's adequate adaptation is different from Jenna's optimal adaptation in the degree to which each successfully manages past trauma and current challenges, the quality of caregiving and friendship, and the potential for growth in coming years. Neither adequate nor optimal adaptation assumes smooth sailing throughout development. Challenges are inevitable, and struggles themselves are not evidence of disorder. Indeed, challenge and struggle are viewed by most developmental psychologists as forces of growth. Sameroff (1993), in fact, suggests that "all life is characterized by disturbance that is overcome, and that only through disturbance can we advance and grow. . . . In this view, it is the overcoming of challenge that furnishes the social, emotional, and intellectual skills that produce all forms of growth, both healthy and unhealthy" (p. 3).

The Impact of Values on Definitions of Disorder

Other important judgments involving values are tied to specific definitions of disorder. With statistical deviance definitions, it sometimes makes sense to examine *both* extremes of the continuum (e.g., too much intense emotion as well as too little intense emotion), because we have made a judgment that there is a desirable middle course related to emotional intensity (again, see Figure 1:1). At other times, it makes sense to focus only on the "bad" end of the continuum and ignore the "good" end (e.g., too little

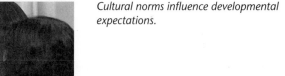

Cultural norms influence developmental expectations.

Digital Vision/Getty Images

empathy, but not too much empathy; too little intelligence, but not too much intelligence). In these specific cases, judgments are made that some types of extreme characteristics are to be accepted or prized.

With sociocultural definitions, value judgments are the very basis of definitions of disorder. Whether casual use of mind-altering substances is tolerated or condemned by a particular sociocultural group influences conceptualizations of pathological addiction. Whether independence or connectedness is more valued influences conceptualizations of pathological dependency. For example, among traditional Hmong families living in the United States after emigrating from Southeast Asia, it would be considered inappropriate or disrespectful for an unmarried child to leave home. So, whereas graduation from high school may be seen as a transition to more independence in traditional Western culture, with young adults moving into their own apartments or going away to college, such behavior would not be viewed as developmentally appropriate or healthy in many Hmong families.

With mental health definitions, the values of psychologists, psychiatrists, and clinical social workers are embedded in both scientific and lay community decision making. Returning to the Surgeon General's description of psychological well-being, clinicians must evaluate whether a young person's life is characterized by a positive quality, adequate functioning, and few symptoms. Whether these particular benchmarks represent the least we can do for children and adolescents, or the best we can hope for, is yet another value judgment. Indeed, recent discussions of models of mental health have emphasized the difference between the absence of mental illness and the presence of flourishing (Keyes, 2007). To enhance individuals' opportunities for flourishing, Keyes argues for increased resources for programs that focus on the promotion of mental health across the lifespan, as well as for programs that focus on the prevention and treatment of mental illness.

Definitions of Psychopathology and Developmental Psychopathology

In this textbook, we will work within the framework provided by the following definitions of disorder. *Psychopathology refers to intense, frequent, and/or persistent maladaptive patterns of emotion, cognition,* *and behavior.* **Developmental psychopathology** *extends this description to emphasize that these maladaptive patterns occur in the context of normal development, and result in the current and potential impairment of infants, children, and adolescents.*

Rates of Disorders in Infancy, Childhood, and Adolescence

If definitions of disorder are problematic, estimates of rates of disorder are even more so. The multipart task of estimating rates of disorder includes (1) identifying children with clinically significant distress and dysfunction, whether or not they are in treatment (and most of them are not); (2) calculating levels of general (e.g., anxiety disorders) and specific (e.g., generalized anxiety, separation anxiety disorder, phobia) psychopathologies and the impairments associated with various disorders; and (3) tracking changing trends in the identification and diagnosis of specific categories of disorder (e.g., autism, attention deficit hyperactivity disorder, and depression) (Costello, Erkanli, & Angold, 2006; Lahey et al., 1996; Maughan, Iervolino, & Collishaw, 2005). Personal, clinical, and public policy implications must be considered when collecting these data. For instance, specific diagnoses may or may not qualify for insurance coverage. Or increases or decreases in the diagnosis of certain disorders may have an impact on the staffing of special education programs in schools.

Frequencies and patterns of distributions of disorders in infants, children, and adolescents can be estimated with varied methodologies and within varied groups. These frequencies and patterns are the focus of the field of **developmental epidemiology** (Costello, Egger, & Angold, 2005; Costello, Foley, & Angold, 2006). Prevalence and incidence rates are both measures of the frequency of psychopathology. **Prevalence** refers to the proportion of a population with a disorder (i.e., all current cases of the disorder); **incidence** refers to the rate at which new cases arise (i.e., all new cases in a given time period). Random sampling of a general population is one option for estimating prevalence (e.g., using surveys, phone questionnaires, and/or detailed psychopathology screening instruments). For example, the investigators in the Great Smoky Mountains Study interviewed over 1,400 participants up to nine times between 9 and 21 years of age (Copeland, Shanahan,

Costello, & Angold, 2011). Sampling in schools, using teachers' assessments, is another option. Or samples can focus on disorders that are seen in children's primary care and mental health clinics.

Whatever method is selected, there can be no doubt that many children struggle with clinically significant disorders. The most recent data from the National Health and Nutrition Examination Study, sponsored by the Centers for Disease Control, estimate that 13% of children between 8 and 15 years of age met the criteria for any disorder (see Figure 1:2) (Merikangas, He, Brody et al., 2010). These rates are comparable to those observed in other studies conducted in the United States (Costello, Mustillo, Erkanli, Keeler, & Angold, 2003; Jaffee, Harrington, Cohen, & Moffitt, 2005) and other countries and regions, including Algeria, Asia, Australia, Great Britain, China, Germany, Greece, Israel, Kenya, the Netherlands, Thailand, and Puerto Rico (Canino et al., 2004; Crijnen, Achenbach, & Verhulst, 1997; Ford, Goodman, & Meltzer, 2003; Kroes et al., 2001; Petot, Petot, & Achenbach, 2008; Sawyer et al., 2001; Srinath, Kandasamy, & Golhar, 2010; Weisz, Sigman, Weiss, & Mosk, 1993).

Allocation of Resources, Availability and Accessibility of Care

Although it is always the case that children's psychopathology deserves our attention, our compassion, and our best clinical responses, a number of critical issues demand renewed and innovative effort. Even

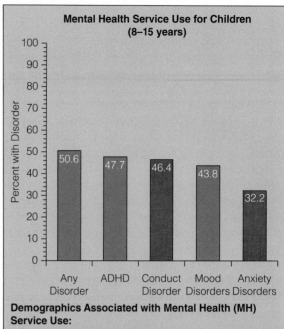

Demographics Associated with Mental Health (MH) Service Use:

• Females are 50 percent less likely than males to use MH services.
• 12–15 year olds are 90 percent more likely than 8–11 year olds to use MH services.
• No differences were found between races for mood, anxiety, or conduct disorders. Mexican Americans and other Hispanic youth had significantly lower 12-month rates of ADHD compared to non-Hispanic white youth.

Data courtesy of CDC

FIGURE 1:3 Percentage of children and adolescents with various disorders who receive mental health services.

with research-based knowledge about ways to promote children's physical and mental well-being that has been available for years (e.g., Weisz, Sandler, Durlak, & Anton, 2005), parents, schools, communities, and policy makers have struggled to allocate often-scarce emotional, social, and financial resources. One continuing difficulty involves access to care. Recent investigations suggest that fewer than half of children and adolescents who need mental health interventions receive them (Merikangas et al., 2011; Simpson, Cohen, Pastor, & Reuben, 2008) (see Figure 1:3). Indeed, "the current state of affairs not only fails to take responsibility for the health and welfare of children, it also fails to recognize the costs and waste in economic and human potential" (Tolan & Dodge, 2005, p. 602).

Barriers to care are widespread and have been extensively summarized by Owens et al. (2002) and Thurston and Phares (2008). Structural barriers

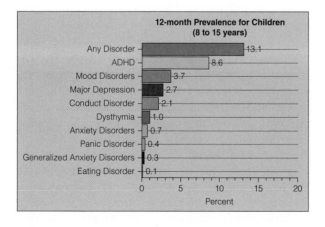

FIGURE 1:2 Prevalence rates for various child and adolescent disorders.

include lack of provider availability, long waiting lists, inconveniently located services, transportation difficulties, and inability to pay and/or inadequate insurance coverage. Barriers related to perceptions about mental health difficulties include the inability to acknowledge a disorder, denial of problem severity, and beliefs that difficulties will resolve over time or will improve without formal treatment. Barriers related to perceptions about mental health services involve a lack of trust in the system, previous negative experiences, and the stigma related to seeking help.

When children do receive psychological care, the cost of appropriate intervention, whether oriented to the individual, the family, or the school, is often prohibitive, and insurance coverage varies widely. Until recently, most health insurance policies placed restrictive limits on reimbursement of mental health coverage. State and federal legislation to eliminate these kinds of restrictions has made progress of late, but many families still face such coverage limits. The availability of effective therapies and treatments for a variety of psychological disorders is significant only if infants, children, and adolescents are able to take advantage of them.

Inadequate money for prevention efforts is also a public policy dilemma, especially given recent estimates that the economic burden of treatment of child and adolescent mental illness surpasses 10 billion dollars (Hsia & Belfer, 2008; National Institute of Mental Health, 2004). There is abundant research, for example, documenting the positive psychosocial impact of early educational programs, but full funding and increased access remain difficult. And for children from minority and disadvantaged backgrounds, access to treatment and prevention programs is even more problematic (Bringewatt & Gershoff, 2010; Merikangas et al., 2011; Thurston & Phares, 2008).

Tolan and Dodge (2005) propose a four-part model for a comprehensive system that "simultaneously promotes mental health within normal developmental settings, provides aid for emerging mental health issues for children, targets high-risk youth with prevention, and provides effective treatment for disorders: (1) Children and their families should be able to access appropriate and effective mental health services directly; (2) Child mental health should be a major component of healthy development promotion and attention in primary care settings such as schools, pediatric care, community programs, and other systems central to child development;

(3) Efforts should emphasize preventive care for high-risk children and families; (4) More attention must be paid to cultural context and cultural competence" (pp. 607–608). These kinds of proposals lay the groundwork for resource allocation and policy implementation that will have longstanding consequences for the well-being of countless children.

The Globalization of Children's Mental Health

Discussions of mental health and mental illness involving resource allocation and public policy increasingly emphasize global perspectives. These global perspectives require careful thinking about Western models of development, disorder and intervention, and the vastly different experiences of children who live in resource-rich versus resource-poor countries. Patel, Flisher, Nikapota, and Malhotra (2008) and Omigbodun (2008) identify rapid social change, urbanization and urban poverty, and inadequate health and educational services as key factors that increase children's vulnerability to psychopathology in resource-poor countries in Eastern and Central Europe, Africa, Asia, Latin America, and the Pacific region. In these countries, awareness of mental illness issues and promotion of mental health is often limited by allocation of scarce resources to urgent medical needs, a lack of formal mental health policies and programs, and too few mental health professionals. The costs of impairment and lost potential are enormous (Belfer, 2008).

We must also emphasize that, across the globe, millions of children are struggling in the face of unimaginable trauma, including exposure to disease and death, armed conflict, abandonment and homelessness, and dislocation (Omigbodun, 2008; Vostanis, 2010). These terrible situations require increased awareness, advocacy, and a responsibility to provide interventions to ensure these children's safety and well-being. Interventions include both prevention efforts and treatment for those with various disorders. To facilitate the success of interventions, mental health professionals must consider how to implement treatments in countries where the health and welfare systems work differently (or are nonexistent), and how to provide treatment to children who are difficult to reach (Morris et al., 2011; Vostanis, 2010). Treatments must take into account local and culture-based approaches, and community

BOX 1:2   THE CHILD IN CONTEXT

The Stigma of Mental Illness

Ignorance and intolerance have long been identified as critical issues for those struggling with mental illness. Much of the available research focuses on adults' limited and inaccurate knowledge and negative attitudes toward other adults with mental illness. In study after study, the data suggest that most adults tend to think primarily in terms of serious psychopathology (such as schizophrenia and bipolar disorder), believe that individuals are responsible for their disorders, and overestimate the likelihood of aggression and violence in adults with mental illness; stigmatization, in terms of ridicule, avoidance, and rejection, is rampant.

Adults also exhibit distorted beliefs and harmful attitudes toward children who are struggling with mental illness and their families. Adults both trivialize the reality of children's distress and dysfunction by suggesting that children are overdiagnosed, overmedicated, and poorly parented, and exaggerate the extent to which these same children are unpredictable, dangerous, and deviant (Giummarra & Haslam, 2005; Pescosolido et al., 2008).

How do children and adolescents compare to their adult counterparts? Sadly, their beliefs and attitudes are all too similar. Surveys of children's labels for those dealing with mental illness—including *crazy, nuts, retarded, psycho,* and *lunatic*—reveal their aversion (Bailey, 1999; Wahl, 2002). Although children

do display increasing knowledge about the causes of mental illness as they age, their attitudes reflect ongoing stigmatization related to views of those struggling with mental illnesses as violent, unpredictable, blameworthy, and hopeless (Coleman, Walker, Lee, Friesen, & Squire, 2009; Corrigan et al., 2007; Watson, Miller & Lyons, 2005). It is not surprising, then, to find that many children and adolescents with disorders "self-stigmatize"; that is, they internalize these negative beliefs and attitudes and exhibit low levels of self-esteem and self-efficacy (Corrigan, Watson, & Barr, 2006; Moses, 2009).

Given that children are exposed to multiple sources of information and attitudes, including parents, peers, and the media, how can stigmatization be prevented or minimized? Many types of programs, from those designed for single classrooms to those intended as national demonstration projects, have shown improvements in knowledge and attitudes (e.g., Corrigan, 2005; Pitre, Stewart, Adams, Bedard, & Landry, 2007; Watson et al., 2004). Successful programs share several emphases. They must begin early; target multiple dimensions of knowledge and attitudes; be developmentally appropriate; and include individuals, families, and communities. Children can learn lies or they can learn facts; they can display ugly attitudes or they can display compassion. The choices are theirs, and ours.

caretaking and service models (Harper & Cetin, 2008; Morris et al., 2011). Holistic approaches with achievable goals, embedded in health, social, and educational networks, have been proposed. These multicomponent treatments focus on children and adolescents, on families, and on communities and systems (Eisenberg & Belfer, 2009; Patel et al., 2007). Finally, the development and implementation of globally useful interventions requires recognition of the current disconnect between where research takes place and where the need is greatest, and a commitment to do better on behalf of the world's children (Patel et al., 2008; Vostanis, 2010).

The Stigma of Mental Illness

A final issue concerns the continued and painfully unnecessary **stigmatization** of individuals with psychopathology (Corrigan, 2005; Hinshaw, 2005;

Pescosolido, 2007). For parents concerned about their children's distress or dysfunction, there is almost always shame, fear, and/or blame (dosReis, Barksdale, Sherman, Maloney, & Charach, 2010). For children, experiences of secrecy and rejection are commonplace. Lack of respect and lack of access to care (again) are often the results of personal, familial, social, and institutional stigma (Heflinger & Hinshaw, 2010). A clinician seeking parental permission to obtain information from a child's teacher is not surprised when a father says, "You know, doctor, we'd prefer that the school not know anything about this. We haven't told his brothers or his grandparents. No one else needs to know." Or a teacher, preparing a child to begin attending a social skills group the following week, is asked, "Why do I have to leave your room, Mrs. Stern? I don't want to go with those kids. They're weird. I'm not weird. I'm not crazy."

Mukolo, Heflinger, and Wallston (2010) identify (a) several dimensions of stigma, including negative stereotypes, devaluation, and discrimination; (b) two targets of stigma, the individual and the family; and (c) two contexts of stigma, the general public and the self/individual. Both Mukolo et al. and Heflinger and Hinshaw (2010) urge researchers to continue to investigate the multiple ways that stigma complicates the experiences of children with mental disorders and their families. Box 1:2 provides additional perspective on this kind of stigma. Understanding the development, course, and treatment of psychopathology in infants, children, and adolescents represents only half the battle. Increasing our tolerance and compassion for the diverse group of those who are diagnosed with psychopathology and believing in the inherent worth of each struggling infant, child, and adolescent makes up the other, far more difficult, half.

Key Terms

Developmental psychopathology (p. 2)
Statistical deviance (p. 2)
Sociocultural norms (p. 3)
Mental health definitions (p. 3)
Role of values (p. 3)
Adequate adaptation (p. 3)
Optimal adaptation (p. 3)
Psychopathology (p. 6)
Developmental epidemiology (p. 6)
Prevalence (p. 6)
Incidence (p. 6)
Barriers to care (p. 7)
Stigmatization (p. 9)

Chapter Summary

- Developmental psychopathology refers to intense, frequent, and/or persistent maladaptive patterns of emotion, cognition, and behavior considered within the context of normal development and resulting in the current and potential impairment of infants, children, and adolescents.
- Prevalence refers to all current cases of a set of disorders, whereas incidence refers to new cases in a given time period. Although specific study results vary, many estimates suggest that significant numbers of children and adolescents struggle with disorders that are associated with serious impairment.
- There are a number of critical issues currently facing the field of developmental psychopathology. For example, too few children who need mental health care have access to that care. Another important issue is the ongoing challenge of overcoming the stigmatization of individuals and families dealing with psychopathology.

2 Models of Child Development, Psychopathology, and Treatment

The Case of Max

Max is 8 years old. He can often be found squirming at his second-grade desk, looking out the window, rearranging his pencils, knocking papers on the floor, poking the girl in front of him. From his teacher's perspective, Max's situation is becoming more and more problematic, and she has referred him for evaluation.

Max's parents describe him as developing normally, although they say that he has always been "on the go." Max lives with his father and mother, both of whom graduated from high school, and his siblings. The family lives in a duplex home; Max's maternal grandparents, who emigrated from Honduras, live in the other half.

In kindergarten, Max was described as active and energetic, but his teacher had no significant concerns. In first grade, his difficulties increased over the course of the year, with most problems involving incomplete classwork and bothering other children. Max's school problems have continued in second grade, where his teacher describes him as generally disorganized and as falling behind in reading and math.

Max's parents provided other information that suggested that Max's struggles were not typical. Beginning in first grade, they noticed some problems at home, including irritability and impulsivity. His parents remembered that these negative emotions and behaviors were more pronounced after the school day. Also, Max began to argue and fight more frequently with his 10-year-old brother and especially his 4-year-old sister. His parents report that Max still enjoys playing with friends in the neighborhood but is becoming increasingly resistant, discouraged, and pessimistic about school. The more stressful family problems coincided with Max's father being laid off from his job as a master electrician. Max's father has spent increasing amounts of time at home, with escalating conflicts between Max's mother (who does not work outside the home) and himself about child care and discipline. ■■

The Case of Maggie

Maggie is 14. She spends a lot of her free time alone in her room, feeling unhappy and not doing much of anything. She rarely gets together with other kids, who have mostly stopped asking her to join them. Maggie's mother is worried about her sadness and withdrawal and has called her family physician for a referral.

Maggie's mother has been a single parent since Maggie's birth and is employed as a customer service representative for a health care company. Maggie's father has a long history of hospitalizations for both major depression and alcohol abuse.

Maggie's mother describes Maggie's infancy and childhood as normal. Throughout elementary school, Maggie was generally quiet and cooperative and received average grades. Although not especially social, she always had a few good friends and was active in sports and with her church youth group. Looking back, Maggie's mother remembers that she seemed to worry more than most other children, but not to the point where it interfered with her schoolwork or social activities. The transition to middle school was difficult. Maggie's mother reports that Maggie seemed somewhat overwhelmed by the size of the school and had difficulty adjusting to changing classes and increased homework. Maggie had less contact with her elementary school friends and had trouble making new friendships.

Although Maggie does not talk much about her situation, her increasing withdrawal, apathy, and occasional irritability are apparent. Maggie no longer participates in athletics, has dropped out of her church youth group, and spends most of her time at home alone. She is increasingly behind in her schoolwork, and her grades have dropped significantly. ■■

The Role of Theory in Developmental Psychopathology

Models of development, psychopathology, and treatment allow us to organize our clinical observations of children and our research findings into coherent, informative accounts. In this chapter, the cases of Max and Maggie will illustrate key concepts related to normal developmental processes, the emergence of disorder, and intervention goals and strategies. For introductory purposes, the sections on Max and Maggie present somewhat simplified examples. In the next chapter, and throughout the rest of this book, the models will be increasingly complex, integrated, and real.

Dishion and Patterson (1999) describe the construction of models as an ongoing process, such that an initial theory is described, followed by observation, definitions, measurements, and experiments, all of which leads to theory revision, and the process begins again. Before the practices and principles of developmental psychopathology are described in Chapter 3, we will summarize the historical models—the "big theories" (Damon & Lerner, 1998)—that have contributed valuable ideas to our contemporary understanding. Although these models are presented separately and are often conceptualized as complete and comprehensive in and of themselves, *they are not mutually exclusive*. It is more useful to think of these models as providing different and complementary perspectives on the complicated phenomena of development, psychopathology, and treatment.

Continuous and Discontinuous Models

To provide additional background for the upcoming summaries, it is useful to consider how various definitions of disorder correspond with continuous versus discontinuous models of psychopathology. **Continuous models of psychopathology** emphasize the ways in which normal feelings, thoughts, and behaviors gradually become more serious problems, which may then intensify and become clinically diagnosable disorders. With continuous models, there are no sharp distinctions between adjustment and maladjustment. Continuous models are also referred to as dimensional or quantitative models. **Discontinuous models of psychopathology,** in contrast, emphasize discrete and qualitative differences in individual patterns of emotion, cognition, and behavior. With discontinuous models, there are clear distinctions between what is normal and what is not. Discontinuous models are sometimes referred to as categorical or qualitative models.

Important differences between continuous and discontinuous models are illustrated by thinking about Max and Maggie. For instance, do the difficulties experienced by Max and Maggie reflect extremes of typical difficulties (continuous examples) or are they problems of a different sort altogether (discontinuous examples)? What do parents, teachers, and clinicians gain from the continuous perspective, which emphasizes the connections between kids who are struggling and kids who are not? And what is gained from the discontinuous perspective, which instead emphasizes the unique patterns of problematic emotions, thoughts, and behaviors that give rise to significant maladjustment?

Physiological Models

Historical and Current Conceptualizations
Physiological models propose that there is a physiological (i.e., structural, biological, or chemical) basis for all psychological processes and events. Historical conceptualizations often focused on the complex ways in which genes, brain structure and function, and early critical periods influenced, directed, and constrained development. Contemporary conceptualizations are even more complex, taking into account new research and clinical data, especially data related to brain development from birth through young adulthood (Nelson, 2011; Pennington, 2009). Using newer technologies that either directly or indirectly image the structure, function, or pharmacology of the brain, we are becoming more knowledgeable about "how a child builds a brain" (Cicchetti, 2002). We are also increasingly focused on brain–behavior relations and how those relations unfold in both typical and atypical development (Pennington, 2009).

Advances in neuroscience have led to the mapping of brain structures over time and to rich descriptions of development: the "exuberant increase in brain connections is followed by an enigmatic process of dendritic 'pruning' and synapse elimination, which leads to a more efficient set of connections that are continually remodeled throughout life" (Toga, Thompson, & Sowell, 2006, p. 148). Toga et al. suggest that some brain areas (such as the frontal cortex) develop under "tight genetic control," whereas other areas are more influenced by the environment. In addition, differing levels of cortical growth are observed, with some regions displaying simpler growth trajectories (e.g., ending earlier) and others more complex trajectories (e.g., ending later) (Nelson, 2011; Shaw, 2008). Sensitive periods in brain development have also been identified, some of which appear domain- or component-dependent (e.g., in the auditory system, or for specific components of language) (Thomas & Johnson, 2008). While these general processes are similar for typically developing children, individual differences have also been observed in "perfectly normally functioning individuals" (Nelson, 2011, p. 52).

Neural plasticity illustrates several key physiological processes related to brain development and brain reorganization. Neural plasticity involves the development and modification of neural (or synaptic) circuits, with "overwhelming" evidence that "both positive and negative experiences can influence the wiring diagram of the brain" (Nelson, 2011, p. 57). Numerous examples of neural plasticity, involving changes in anatomy and neurochemistry, have been described for multiple systems (e.g., visual, motor, language, and learning and memory systems). And whereas we once believed that brain development was relatively complete by age 3, and that any damage was permanent and irreversible, we now understand that plasticity is associated with important growth after the age of 3 and with the lifelong potential for new, improved and recovered function (Nelson, 2011).

With respect to brain–behavior relations, we have shifted from earlier views that emphasized the unidirectional influence of brain structure and function on behavior to models that emphasize bidirectional influences (Stiles, 2009). As one example of brain–behavior relations, Bell and Fox (1996) documented patterns of physiological and electroencephalograph (EEG) activity in groups of 8-month-olds with various crawling histories. Comparisons of noncrawling infants, beginning crawlers, and experienced crawlers provide evidence that brain development specific to crawling involves an initial overproduction of cortical connections that are then "pruned" *with additional crawling experience*. This pattern of production and pruning illustrates how the brain's development responds to environmental feedback,

resulting in increasingly efficient processing. Similar brain–behavior relations can be observed for developmental achievements across the cognitive domain (e.g., in language and learning), the emotional domain (e.g., in emotion regulation), and the behavioral domain (e.g., in sociability).

Genes, as noted, play a critical role in physiological models. We need to understand the complex ways that the genetic make-up of an individual, or **genotype**, influences the observable characteristics of an individual, or **phenotype**. Our understanding of genetics (i.e., genes and heredity) is ever expanding and involves work in both **quantitative** and **molecular genetics**. Some of the numerous contributions of such research are described in Box 2:1; key definitions are provided in Table 2:1. One of the most

---

TABLE 2:1   Some Basic Definitions Related to Physiological Models and Genetics

Additive genetic variance: Individual differences caused by the independent effects of genes that increase the effects of others.

Chromosome: A structure that contains DNA, and resides in the nucleus of cells.

DNA (deoxyribonucleic acid): Double-stranded molecule that encodes genetic information.

Gene: The basic unit of inheritance. A sequence of DNA bases that codes for a particular product.

Gene map: Visual representation of the relative distances between genes or genetic markers on chromosomes.

Genome: All the DNA sequences of an organism. The human genome contains about 3 billion DNA base pairs.

Genomics: Field of study focused on genes and gene functions.

Genotype: The genetic constitution of an individual.

Genotype–environment correlation: Genetic influence on exposure to environments; experiences that are correlated with genetic propensities.

Genotype–environment interaction: Genetic sensitivity or susceptibility to environments.

Heritability: The proportion of phenotypic differences among individuals that can be attributed to genetic differences in a particular population.

Mapping: Linkage of DNA markers to a chromosome and to specific regions of chromosomes.

Molecular genetics: Investigation of the effects of specific genes at the DNA level. Contrast to quantitative genetics, which investigates genetic and environmental components of variance.

Nonadditive genetic variance: Individual differences due to the effects of alternate forms of genes at a particular locus (i.e., dominance), or multiple genes at different loci (i.e., epistasis).

Nonshared environment: Environmental influences that contribute to differences between family members.

Phenotype: An observed characteristic of an individual that results from the combined effects of genotype and environment.

Polygenic trait: A trait influenced by many genes.

Quantitative genetics: A theory of multiple-gene influences that, together with environmental variation, result in quantitative (continuous) distributions of phenotypes.

Shared environment: Environmental factors responsible for resemblance between family members.

Variable expression: A single genetic effect may result in variable manifestations in different individuals.

BOX 2:1 EMERGING SCIENCE

Genomics, Behavior Genetics, and Developmental Psychopathology

Remarkable advances in scientific knowledge and technology have enabled investigators from many disciplines to ask, and begin to answer, questions about the bio-psycho-social nature of human experience. The most comprehensive set of questions and data are provided by the **Human Genome Project**, a collaborative effort by the Department of Energy and the National Institutes of Health to identify the approximately 30,000 genes in human DNA and determine the sequences of the 3 billion chemical base pairs that make up human DNA (genomics.energy.gov). The goals of the project include basic science data on the mapping, sequencing, and analysis of genes, or **genomics** (a term used by Thomas Roderick in 1986), and the application of this data for medical, educational, and technological benefit.

Multiple subfields in genomics include quantitative genetics (i.e., studies of the relative impact of genetic and environmental factors on specific characteristics), a "top-down approach," and molecular genetics (i.e., studies of the effects of specific genes at the DNA level), a "bottom-up approach." According to Plomin (2002), the meeting of the bottom-up and top-down approaches occurs in the brain. The linking of genes, brain, and behavior, with a focus on how genes influence the heritability of disorder and on how genes and environments together influence behavior, is at the heart of developmental psychopathology (McGuffin, 2004; Plomin, DeFries, Craig, & McGuffin, 2003; Plomin & McGuffin, 2003).

Almost all of the information to date suggests that multiple gene systems, rather than single genes, are responsible for the heritable component of both normal and abnormal psychological characteristics. Variations in patterns of DNA, then, provide explanations for the neurological basis of individual differences.

Interacting with a variety of environmental factors, these DNA variations bring us one step closer to understanding the emergence of psychopathology. Even with these exciting data, we need to be cautious about overstating our hypotheses and findings. Kendler (2005) argues that the phrase "X is a gene for Y" is widely used, yet inappropriate for psychiatry and psychology. Kendler states that there are clear criteria for being able to claim that a gene for some psychopathology has been identified. So far, these criteria have not been met; given the nature of individuals and disorders, they are not likely ever to be met. Indeed, many different genetic phenomena may help explain the complexity observed in studies of psychopathology. These include penetrance (i.e., the probability of an observable phenotype in individuals with a particular gene), variable expressivity (i.e., different outcomes associated with a particular gene), gene–environment interaction (i.e., expression of genotype in the presence of specific environments), and genetic heterogeneity (i.e., different genotypes leading to the same phenotype) (Merikangas & Risch, 2003).

Increasingly, new and clinically significant questions are the focus of collaborative investigations by social scientists and genetic researchers. These interdisciplinary efforts are providing data that describe and explain how certain environments expose vulnerability and maladaptation in some children whereas other children demonstrate resilience in the face of similar stressors (Boyce & Ellis, 2008). Other groups of researchers are studying how environments (experience) influence gene expressions at molecular (gene) levels (e.g., Szyf, McGowan, Turecki, & Meaney, 2010). These types of research efforts are the focus of additional discussion in Chapter 3, and throughout the textbook.

important shifts in thinking about genetics involves moving beyond early views on nature *versus* nurture, to current complex descriptions of gene by environment processes. Regarding the reciprocal influences of genes and environments on brain development, Stiles (2009) asserts that "brains do not develop normally in the absence of critical genetic signaling, and they do not develop normally in the absence of essential and contingent environmental input" (pp. 196–197). Stiles explains that "all

children inherit a set of genes very similar to those of every other human, but allelic differences introduce unique genetic variation. All children experience many of the same aspects of the environment (e.g., light, sound, gravity, exposure to language) regardless of where they are born, but each child's specific environments (from the womb to the outside world) are different, exerting different developmental influences" (p. 197). Specific examples of gene-by-environment influences on development are provided in Chapter 3's discussion of complex models.

What we know about psychopathology is also influenced by these physiological models (Cicchetti & Walker, 2003; Nelson, Bloom, Cameron, Amaral, Dahl, & Pine, 2002). For some disorders, psychopathology unfolds according to a "maturational blueprint," with deviance innately and inevitably related to damage or dysfunction (Sameroff, 1993). Certain severe forms of mental retardation are examples of this type of psychopathology. For most disorders of childhood and adolescence, however, this too-simple model of physical cause and psychopathological effect can be dismissed.

Physiological models suggest that there are inborn or acquired vulnerabilities to disorders—including genetic abnormalities, structural pathologies, and biochemical disturbances—that *may* lead to psychological distress and dysfunction. According to this physiological **diathesis–stress model**, structural damage or chemical imbalance does not *by itself* lead to disorder. Rather, diatheses (or predispositions) such as neurological damage at birth or genetic risk for disorder, *in combination with* additional stress (either physiological or environmental), lead to the emergence of a disorder. Diathesis–stress models illustrate the lack of a one-to-one correspondence between the genotype and phenotype for most forms of psychopathology (Merikangas & Risch, 2003).

Two variations of the diathesis–stress model are illustrated in the following cases. In the first case, a child with phenylketonuria (PKU) is born with a particular metabolic dysfunction, an inactive liver enzyme (a physiological diathesis of genetic origin). The presence of phenylalanine (a physiological stressor) in the child's diet and the subsequent metabolic abnormalities result in severe mental retardation. Treatment of this condition involves a diet low in phenylalanine, beginning shortly after birth; this intervention is associated with normal intellectual development. In the second case, a child's physical and psychological well-being may be adversely affected by maternal drug abuse during pregnancy (again, a physiological diathesis, but this one of nongenetic origin). After birth, poor parenting (a psychosocial stressor) may lead to a number of clinical syndromes. High-quality parenting, in contrast, may buffer or protect the child from especially negative outcomes.

We still must consider, of course, the possibility that brain structure or function is, in some clinically

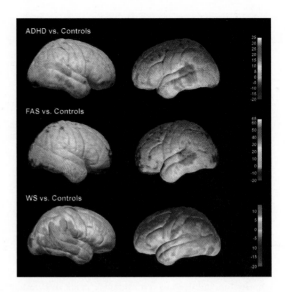

FIGURE 2:1 Differences in gray-matter density between subjects with three neurodevelopmental disorders. The percentage differences in gray-matter density between subjescts with Williams syndrome (WS) (a), attention-deficit hyperactivity disorder (ADHD) (b), fetal alcohol syndrome (FAS) (c), and their respective normally developing control groups are col-orcoded. In all maps, warmer colors represent positive differences, indicating an increase in the patient group (arbitrarily coded as 1) relative to the control group (arbitrarily coded as 0), with red representing the largest group difference. Note that maximum value varies on the three color bars, depending on the maximum group difference from each comparision.
Courtesy of Dr. Arthur Toga, Dr. Elizabeth Sowell and Dr. Paul Thompson of the Laboratory of Neuro Imaging, UCLA, www.loni.ucla.edu

significant way, different in children and adolescents with disorders. For example, differences in gray matter density have been observed in comparisons of typically developing children to children with various neurodevelopmental disorders (see Fig. 2:1). With respect to neural plasticity, gene by environment processes, and brain–behavior relations in psychopathology, current physiological models of psychopathology seek to explain the interplay of physical and biological factors, neurological processes, development, and life experiences in order to understand the emergence, the course, and the treatment of psychopathology.

Thinking About Max

From a physiological perspective, we emphasize the role of brain structure and function and consider the likelihood of abnormal biochemical processes in the development of disorder. Specifically, physiologically oriented clinicians conceptualize Max's difficulties as primarily due to underarousal of key parts of Max's brain; because of this, he lacks sufficient focus and sustained engagement with the environment, resulting in inattentive and impulsive behavior. These difficulties, consistent with a diagnosis of attention-deficit hyperactivity disorder (ADHD), are not typical of other similar-age children.

Because the disorder is physiologically based, the first choice for intervention is physiological in nature. The clinical literature suggests that stimulant drugs such as Ritalin are effective in treating children with ADHD, so a trial of stimulant medication would be prescribed. In addition, although pharmacological treatment is the primary intervention, behaviorally influenced strategies would be routinely included in both the school and home settings.

Advances in neuroimaging techniques are crucial to research into how genetics and environment influence the developing brain.

Thinking About Maggie

Again, from a physiological perspective, we note with special interest Maggie's family history, which includes her father's episodes of clinical depression, and consider the possibility of a genetic vulnerability to depression. Maggie's various problems, then, might be usefully conceptualized as the psychological expression of a biochemical imbalance. For example, Maggie's symptoms may be a result of low levels of the neurotransmitter serotonin.

Although treatment recommendations may include suggestions that Maggie participate in structured social activities in school as a way of helping her to be more active and successful in friendships, the first-step intervention is the initiation of a trial of antidepressant medication designed to correct the biochemical imbalance.

Psychodynamic Models

Historical and Current Conceptualizations

Psychodynamic models have a rich past and a recently revived future and include the classic psychoanalytic explanations set forth by Sigmund Freud, the socially oriented explanations of Erik Erikson and Harry Stack Sullivan, the more recent work of object-relations theorists such as Mahler and Winnicott, and the contemporary perspectives provided by Emde, Stern, and others. Psychodynamic models have historically focused on several themes, including (1) the impact of unconscious processes on normal and abnormal personality development; (2) conflicts among processes and structures of the mind (e.g., id, ego, and superego); (3) stages of development, with different ages associated with distinctive emotional, intellectual, and social challenges; and (4) the lasting impact of more (or less) successful resolutions of stage-related challenges on later outcomes. Indeed, these themes were well appreciated by the novelist and astute observer of human nature, William Faulkner, who wrote (in 1950's *Requiem for a Nun*), "The past is never dead. It's not even past."

Psychodynamic theorists and clinicians usually emphasized a fixation–regression model of psychopathology, which suggested that individuals who failed to work through developmental issues become "stuck" in the past. Disorders themselves were rooted in traumas or conflicts experienced during early childhood (e.g., the oral, anal, and phallic stages). Psychoanalytic interventions for children, such as those developed by Anna Freud and Melanie Klein, made special use of play (using toys and games) and art to bring repressed traumas and unconscious conflicts into therapeutic awareness.

Setting aside some of the more scientifically dubious claims of early psychodynamic models, we are left with much to consider. Contemporary psychodynamic approaches continue to emphasize (1) unconscious cognitive, affective, and motivational processes; (2) mental representations of self, other, and relationships; (3) the meaningfulness of individual (i.e., subjective) experiences; and (4) a developmental perspective focused on the origins of normal and abnormal personality in early childhood and the constantly changing psychological challenges faced by children as they age (Emde, 1992; Fonagy, Target, & Gergely, 2006; Westen, 1998). These emphases are evident in some of today's most significant psychodynamically informed research, such as work on parent–child attachment and attachment's enduring effects on personality and interpersonal functioning.

Although recent psychodynamic models certainly take into account neurophysiology and neurochemistry (Kandel, 1999; Roffman & Gerber, 2009), there is still an emphasis on the importance of psychological contexts, such as relationships, when explaining the development of personality and psychopathology (Blatt & Luyten, 2009). With respect to treatments, today's psychodynamic assessments and treatments continue to rely on play to make connections with troubled children, to identify the specific pathology, and to effect change (Bratton, Ray, Rhine, & Jones, 2005; Harrison & Tronick, 2007).

Thinking About Max

From a psychodynamic perspective, we are concerned that the management of early developmental challenges may have compromised Max's current adjustment. For example, do Max's inattentive and distractible activity and lack of school success reflect unconscious conflicts about autonomy that he failed to resolve in a healthy manner during his preschool years? Or has a somewhat older Max encountered a more troubling set of issues related to competence and achievement? Should we consider the possibility of an underlying identification with his recently unemployed father? And are there connections between problems with family relationships and problems with peer relationships?

With these types of dynamic issues to explore, it will take some time to formulate a clear clinical understanding of Max and a focused intervention plan. Treatment strategies may include exploring such dynamic issues through art, games, and imaginative play and formulating less specific, more open-ended treatment goals.

Thinking About Maggie

From a classic psychodynamic perspective, we wonder about whether the physical and emotional changes associated with early adolescence have stirred up long-dormant conflicts about intimacy and sexuality. Within a more general attachment framework, Maggie may be struggling with a basic sense of insecurity. Early and ongoing experiences with her father's inconsistent emotional availability may contribute to her wariness in relationships and increasingly negative expectations about her ability to manage demanding school and social challenges. In addition, Maggie's mother's insistence on close supervision of her friendships and restrictions on school activities may be making it difficult to express age-appropriate individuality or independence.

Given her age, Maggie's assessment and treatment are more likely to include therapeutic dialogue and discussion, with an emphasis on dynamic strategies of interpretation and clarification. Treatment goals will be focused on intellectual and emotional insight, based on the idea that insight will lead to improved functioning in Maggie's everyday life.

Behavioral and Cognitive Models

Historical and Current Conceptualizations

In contrast to the inward orientation of the physiological and psychodynamic models, the **behavioral models** have an outward orientation, focusing on the individual's *observable behavior within a specific environment*. According to behavioral models, environmental variables have powerful effects on the development of personality and psychopathology, and these effects have been described by major theorists such as Skinner, Mischel, and Bandura.

Behavioral models are based on core concepts of learning theories and share a strong empirical foundation with them. These theories propose that both normal and abnormal behaviors are gradually acquired via processes of learning, including the **classical conditioning** processes described by Pavlov, the **operant conditioning** processes described by Skinner, and the **observational learning** processes described by Bandura. The construct of **reinforcement** (i.e., the idea that positive and negative consequences lead to changes in behavior) is a critical component of all of these learning processes.

According to Thomas's (2001) summary of Skinner's behaviorism, "As a child grows up, two things develop: (a) the variety of behavior options (potential ways of acting) that the child acquires and (b) the child's preferences among those options. As children interact with their environments, they learn to prefer rewarding over nonrewarding actions" (p. 14). Psychopathology, within the behavioral framework, is understood as the result of learning gone awry: the acquisition and reinforcement of maladaptive or undesirable behaviors, the lack of opportunity to learn adaptive or appropriate behaviors, and/or unavailable or inadequate reinforcement of those adaptive or appropriate behaviors. Over many decades, behaviorally oriented treatments have focused on unlearning, relearning, and new learning.

Newer cognitive-behavioral and cognitive approaches correspond to the cognitive revolution of the 1960s, 1970s, and 1980s. Regarding cognitive and behavioral interaction and integration, these approaches emphasize the ways in which children's thinking influences the many varieties of learning, and the ways in which delays or deficits in cognition influence the emergence of disorders. With the more theoretically "pure" **cognitive models**, the focus is on the components and processes of the mind and mental development (Flavell 1982; Keil, 1999). We consider Piaget's and Vygotsky's landmark studies on stages and processes of cognitive development, as well as later information-processing and interactionist models.

Contemporary revisions of Piagetian models focus on the dynamic interaction of tasks, contexts, and emotional states that influence cognition (Rose & Fischer, 2009), whereas probabilistic models focus on innovative interpretations of the *how* and *why* of children's thinking and learning (Gopnik & Tenenbaum, 2007).The **neoconstructivist approach** emphasizes evolutionary contexts, experience–expectant learning (an example of a brain–behavior relation), and both qualitative and quantitative change across development (Newcombe, 2011).

With respect to cognitive variables and psychopathology, "it is becoming increasingly clear that single cognitive deficit models of developmental disorders, like dyslexia, attention deficit/hyperactivity disorder (ADHD), language impairment, or autism, do not work" (Pennington, 2008, p. 76). Instead, an understanding of combinations of cognitive deficits is required (Pennington, 2008). This more complex, and accurate, explanation of disorders depends on understanding the multiple influences of cognitive components, processes, and contexts across development. Effective cognitively-based interventions involve increasing complexity as well.

Thinking About Max

Within the behavioral and cognitive-behavioral frameworks, Max's difficulties may be understood as a reflection of maladaptive learning and/or cognitive deficits. For example, Max's inappropriate classroom behaviors may result in increased displays of adult concern and adult contact. Although negative in tone, these episodes may be positively reinforcing because of the adult attention and proximity they generate. These interactions may be especially salient given his father's change in employment status and the change in his family's focus from children's activities to adult worries. Additional focus on Max's on-task behaviors, such as reading quietly in his seat and completing his math problems within the allotted time, and rewards for homework may be required. Both school performance and peer problems may also be influenced by Max's impulsive decision making. A cognitive-behavioral emphasis on more extensive analysis of situational cues and more deliberate examination of the likely consequences of particular actions may be a key part of Max's treatment plan.

Thinking About Maggie

As with Max, Maggie's problems are viewed from a cognitive-behavioral perspective as a result of maladaptive learning and cognitive distortions. Maggie's social difficulties are conceptualized as rooted in her misinterpretations of the intentions and actions of others. This misreading of benign social cues as signifying rejection has had a negative effect on Maggie's self-esteem and on her belief in her ability to positively influence her environment. These cognitive errors, in turn, have led to avoidant behaviors. These avoidant behaviors, which—in the short term—minimize the distress that Maggie feels, are then reinforced and lead to further isolation.

The intervention designed to ameliorate these behavioral and cognitive deficits includes identifying the cognitive errors Maggie makes and teaching Maggie new ways to interpret and think about social situations. In addition, it is necessary to devise a schedule of positive reinforcements and rewards for increasing adaptive and healthy behaviors.

Humanistic Models

Historical and Current Conceptualizations

Humanistic models have also made valuable contributions to our understanding of development, psychopathology, and treatment. These models, including those of Carl Rogers and Abraham

Maslow, emphasized personally meaningful experiences, innate motivations for healthy growth, and the child's purposeful creation of a self. Within the humanistic framework, psychopathology is usually linked to interference with or suppression of the child's natural tendencies to develop an integrated (or whole) sense of self, with valued abilities and talents. Parents, teachers, social conventions, and children themselves can hinder healthy development. Intervention, then, involves the discovery or rediscovery of internal resources and provision of external support for self-organization, self-direction, and self-righting capacities.

At times criticized as overly optimistic concerning the potential for happiness, creativity, and actualization, the humanistic models are thematically related to recent discussions of the self (Rosenfield, Lennon, & White, 2005), wellness (Cicchetti, Rappaport, Sandler, & Weissberg, 2000; Keyes, 2006) and **positive psychology** (Seligman & Csikszentmihalyi, 2000; Weems, 2009), and renewed emphases on the experiential development of children (DeRobertis, 2006). We see increasing emphasis on "positive subjective experience, positive individual traits, and positive institutions" that seek to promote individual, family, social, and community well-being (Seligman & Csikszentmihalyi, 2000). "Positive youth development" in adolescence, involving identifying opportunities for initiative and engagement, is one application of this model (Bradshaw, Brown, & Hamilton, 2008; Larson, 2000). Although the focus of this textbook is on psychopathology, thinking about "what makes ... life most worth living, most fulfilling, most enjoyable, and most productive" (Seligman & Csikszentmihalyi, 2000) provides us with an essential perspective when considering children's distress and dysfunction.

Thinking About Max

Max has experienced an abrupt shift in educational atmosphere, from activity-centered learning to a teacher-organized approach, with much less time for highly enjoyed art and music. As the classroom expectations for academic achievement become more prominent, Max has struggled to find his place in the classroom setting. It is hard for him to relate what he is expected to learn with what he sees as his abilities and talents. From a humanistic perspective, Max's problems with peers may reflect his dissatisfaction with himself and his feelings of incompetence.

Humanistically-oriented treatment will focus on increasing Max's chances for pleasure and mastery in school. In addition, therapeutic work may include numerous opportunities (talk-based, play-based, art-based) for the creation (and re-creation) of a valued sense of self. With a strong belief in the self-righting tendencies of children, we expect that Max will be able to use these resources for academic and social benefit.

Thinking About Maggie

Maggie, too, is faced with a new school setting and increasing demands from her mother, her peers, and society that she identify special interests and specific goals for her future. Unlike Max, Maggie does not feel that she has any unique gifts that provide personal satisfaction or that make a contribution to others. In fact, over time, Maggie has come to see herself as unintellectual, unartistic, unathletic, and unattractive. These feelings have led to her sadness, irritability, and withdrawal.

Within this framework, psychotherapeutic challenges that require Maggie to take charge of planning, decision making, and her own happiness will be balanced by clear expressions of support and encouragement that she is capable, competent, and indeed uniquely qualified for this responsibility.

Family Models

Historical and Current Conceptualizations

Tolstoy proposed in *Anna Karenina* that "happy families are all alike, but every unhappy family is unhappy in its own way," with much insight into the myriad ways that misery and dysfunction may be experienced and expressed by husbands and wives, parents and children, and brothers and sisters. However, Tolstoy's assertion about the uniformity of happy families is inaccurate, for there are also myriad ways in which joy and compassion may be experienced and expressed. Different families have different beliefs about the essential nature of children (Harold, 2000; Hwang et al., 1996). Different families have different dreams for themselves and their children, as well as different fears, and these different beliefs, dreams, and fears have impacts on the functioning and adjustment of both happy and unhappy families.

In many individually focused models of disorder, we examine the "identified patient" and his or her unique collection of psychologically healthy and unhealthy characteristics (including physiological vulnerabilities, psychodynamic demons, and maladaptive learning). In contrast, **family models** propose that the best way to understand the personality and psychopathology of a particular child is to understand the dynamics of a particular family. In fact, almost from the beginning of our concern with childhood disorders, there has been some recognition that these disorders may reflect, at least in part, family psychopathology. At times, we have correctly recognized the connections between, for example, child and parent anxieties. At other times, with heartbreaking consequences, we have erroneously linked specific child disorders such as autism with alleged parental shortcomings and maladaptive behaviors (Bettelheim, 1967).

Families have a special impact on normal and abnormal development because they are the first context of children's experiences; the influence of families, and parents in particular, is clear and powerful (Collins, Maccoby, Steinberg, Hetherington, & Bornstein, 2000; Davies & Cicchetti, 2004; Parke, 2004a, 2004b). Families are challenged to meet a variety of children's needs, including nurturing and socializing, promoting education, and providing financial support, and they can succeed or fail at any or all of these tasks (Emery & Kitzmann, 1995). A number of family characteristics have received theoretical and empirical attention and require researchers and clinicians to alternate two perspectives on family life: "looking from the inside out and from the outside in" (Fiese & Spagnola, 2007, p. 119). These characteristics include family type (e.g., two-parent, single-parent, blended families), family hierarchies, and family activities, rituals, and narratives (Fiese & Spagnola, 2007). Changes in family relationships over time have also been the focus of research (Cowan & Cowan, 2003; Dunn, 2004). An example of a family variable that has been studied for decades is parental control (Baumrind, 1971; Grolnick & Pomerantz, 2009). Grolnick and Pomerantz emphasize the need for careful description of this construct, contrasting control (e.g., pressure, intrusion, and domination) and structure (e.g., guidance).

When we think about these kinds of family influences on development and psychopathology, we need to consider various intersections of individual and family processes. For example, we might explore how subsystems of the larger family system interact with one another to influence child outcomes (Cummings, 1999) (see Fig. 2:2). Perhaps

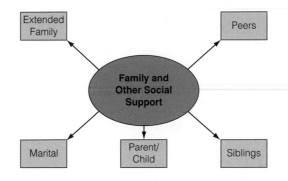

FIGURE 2:2 Subsystems of the family.
Source: From Cummings, E. M. (1999). Some considerations on integrating psychology and health from a life-span perspective. In Whitman, Merluzzi, & White (Eds.), Life-span perspectives on health and illness. Mahwah, NJ: Erlbaum.

the most frequently researched subsystem is the marital relationship. The ways in which this relationship impacts parenting, leading to better and worse outcomes for children, will be repeatedly discussed in upcoming chapters.

The family factors that have been discussed so far are examples of **shared environment**, the aspects of family life and function that are shared by all children in the family. Shared environmental variables are those variables that are often contrasted with genetic variables; that is, what is not explained by genes, or nature, is usually thought to be explained by shared environment, or nurture. In reality, however, **nonshared environment**, the aspects of family life and function that are specific and distinct for each child, has received considerable attention in recent years. Nonshared environmental variables are those that contribute to sibling dissimilarity (McGuire & Shanahan, 2010; Suitor, Sechrist, Plikuhn, Pardo, & Pillemer, 2008; Turkheimer & Waldron, 2000). Siblings are unique, for instance, in terms of gender, age, and temperament and may elicit different types of parenting, affection, and/or material advantages (Jenkins & Bisceglia, 2011). Sibling relationships themselves may be the source of nonshared experiences; how one of a pair of siblings views support, conflict, and respective value within the family may differentially influence adjustment (Brody, 2004). It is also important to consider how siblings respond to a brother or sister who struggles with disorder. Some of these siblings may be more resilient in the face of similar adversity; others may be equally troubled (Kilmer, Cook, Taylor, Kane, & Clark, 2008).

With family models, assessment and treatment of psychopathology addresses the child in the family unit. Interventions include parents and oftentimes siblings. In addition to family- or system-specific treatments, family treatments may be psychodynamically-, behaviorally-, or cognitively oriented. Both individual and family-wide changes are considered when evaluating treatment outcomes.

Thinking About Max

Within the family framework, Max's difficulties are viewed as an expression of family distress and disorganization. In part, Max's school struggles and sibling conflicts may serve as a less-threatening distraction for his parents than their marriage and financial concerns. Even if Max is the identified patient, we cannot ignore the context in which his disorder developed and in which it is maintained.

Other family variables may also contribute to the maladjustment. It may be important that the ideal classroom and school environments for Max are less hierarchical and more egalitarian than his close-knit but highly autocratic family environment. It may also be useful to examine closely Max's parents' beliefs about children's growing-up years, their expectations about his academic success, and their dreams for his future. How do these beliefs support or interfere with his ongoing developmental challenges?

A family-oriented intervention for Max addresses these many variables and capitalizes on his affectionate family bonds. In addition to techniques designed to enhance his sense of self as a valued family member, Max and his parents are likely to be taught specific cognitive and behavioral strategies for his use in school and at home (e.g., keeping records of school assignments, specific folders for completed homework, and schedules of chores posted on the refrigerator). Family sessions will be employed with goals to foster emotional and problem-solving communication skills, to strengthen the parents' alliance, and to diffuse sibling tension. Meetings with just the parents may also address some parenting and marital issues.

Thinking About Maggie

Family-oriented theorists may closely examine Maggie's mother's family values, beliefs, and practices. Perhaps Maggie and her mother are close in unhealthy ways, with Maggie's mother overinvolved in her everyday decisions and Maggie overly responsible for her mother's welfare and happiness. Or perhaps Maggie's mother signals ambivalence or discouragement in response to any signs of Maggie's interest in dating, to the extent that it reminds her of her own romantic unhappiness. As Maggie grows older and begins to explore dating, previous disappointments and current struggles may lead to an exacerbation of Maggie's symptoms.

Identifying the family variables that contribute to Maggie's difficulties will lead to specific hypotheses about the kinds of therapeutic discussions that may be effective; these therapeutic opportunities will include joint mother–daughter sessions as well as individual sessions for both Maggie and her mother.

Beyond Family Relationships: The Role of Peers

Just as relationships within nuclear families are associated with better and worse psychological outcomes, relationship networks outside of families are also related to immediate and long-term consequences (Dishion & Piehler, 2007). For example, many children derive great pleasure from close relationships with extended family members, neighbors, and peers. In addition to pleasure, these relationships serve as rich settings for socioemotional learning (Hartup & Laursen, 1999). Peer relationships, and friendships in particular, provide opportunities for companionship, acceptance, and intimacy. An absence of friendships, because of rejection, conflict, or withdrawal, is associated with maladjustment (Bukowski & Adams, 2005; Dishion & Piehler, 2007). It is important to keep in mind, however, that the benefits and costs of relationships are not always similarly experienced. For example, it appears that peer relationships differentially impact the emotional and behavioral development of boys and girls (Rose & Rudolph, 2006). Several of these specific impacts will be discussed in upcoming chapters.

Sociocultural Models

Historical and Current Conceptualizations

Many early revisions of classic psychoanalytic theory attempted to take into account relevant cultural factors. For instance, Karen Horney, following Freud, argued that Freud's understanding of "penis envy" was mistaken. Rather than girls being envious of the physical fact of maleness, she suggested that they were, instead, envious of the social and cultural rewards associated with being a boy. Decades later, feminist theorists continued to make the case that the identification of disorders and particular interventions was very much influenced by gender-based norms and expectations about desirable personality outcomes.

Fuse/Getty Images

The quality of friendships in childhood is associated with a variety of developmental outcomes.

From this broad historical perspective, we necessarily focus on the ways in which social and cultural factors uniquely disadvantage certain groups in society (e.g., girls, minorities, families from lower socioeconomic status backgrounds) and increase vulnerability to disorders in these groups (Fisher, Jackson, & Villarruel, 1998; Gallay & Flanagan, 2000; Rutter, 1999). One of the most frequently researched variables related to disadvantage and poor outcomes is poverty. Poverty's deleterious impact on the physical and mental health of children and adolescents is well documented (Aber, Jones, & Raver, 2007; Conger & Donnellan, 2007; Keating, 2011) and emphasizes the differing physical health, mental health, and academic outcomes that are associated with social disparities. Over time, **sociocultural models** of development and psychopathology have undergone a *paradigm shift*, in which cultural considerations have moved from the periphery of inquiry to the core (Garcia Coll, 2001; Quintana et al., 2006). Researchers, theorists, and clinicians are now thinking about culture in a very different way. Culture is not only the background for development; rather, it is a major influence on development itself (Bornstein, 2002; Greenfield, Keller, Fuligni, & Maynard, 2003). Understanding the ways in which culture influences adjustment and maladjustment requires the consideration of both cross-cultural variables (e.g., between resource-rich and resource poor countries; between Western and non-Western models of development and psychopathology) and within-culture variables (e.g., among children of different racial or ethnic backgrounds in a city or country; between families of higher socioeconomic status and lower socioeconomic status environments).

Wicker (1992) has described the immediate environments, or "behavior settings," in which children grow and make sense of their lives. These kinds of behavior settings, components of **ecological models**, include homes, classrooms, and neighborhood playgrounds. These behavior settings are, in turn, influenced by broader variables, such as current societal values and norms, political conditions, socioeconomic status, technological changes, demographic conditions, and geographic conditions (Bronfenbrenner, 1986; Rose et al., 2003; Wicker, 1992) (see Fig. 2:3).

Glen Elder and his colleagues have emphasized an even broader perspective that attends to the influence of time and history on children's development. In Elder's model (Modell & Elder, 2002), there are four key assumptions:

1. *Children develop within the social arrangements of a given moment.*
2. *These arrangements are changed by events and trends.*
3. *Developing individuals change history.*
4. *Cultures make sense of the ways of development.*

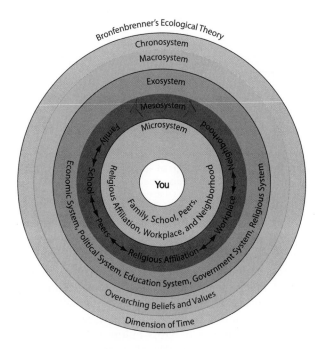

FIGURE 2:3 Children's development is embedded in multiple settings, environments, and systems.
Source: From Bronfenbrenner, U. (1986). Recent advances in research on the ecology of human development. In R. K. Silbereisen, K. Eyferth, & G. Rudinger (Eds.), *Development as action in context: Problem behavior and normal youth development (pp.287-309).* Springer.

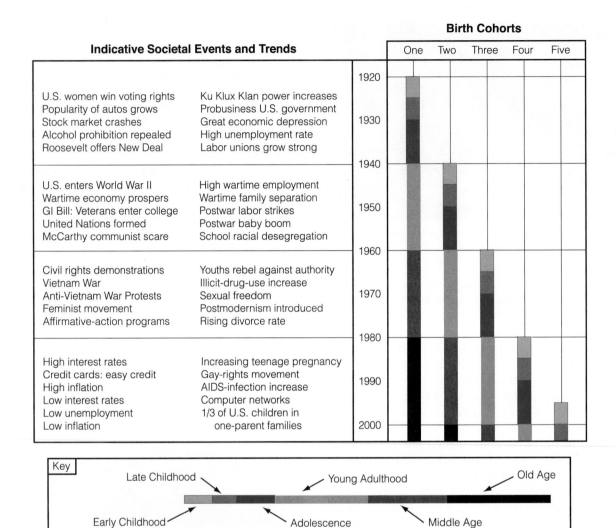

FIGURE 2:4 Relationship of societal conditions and birth cohorts.
Source: Recent theories of human development by THOMAS, R. MURRAY Copyright 2000 Reproduced with permission of SAGE PUBLICATIONS INC BOOKS in the format Republish in a textbook via Copyright Clearance Center.

The construct of **birth cohort** illustrates Elder's approach. A birth cohort includes individuals born in a particular historical period who share key experiences and events. Kids growing up during the Great Depression in the United States belong to a cohort group. Baby boomers are another cohort. So are Generation X and Generation Y (see Fig. 2:4).

Three examples of cross-cultural investigations illustrate the complex role of culture. In the first example, we need to think about how understandings of children and their development are specific cultural contexts. We might focus, then, on one important difference between Western and non-Western

approaches: the "early indulgence of the infant and an orientation toward group identity and spiritual goals" (Timimi, 2009, p. 15). In addition, a greater acceptance of a range of childhood behaviors is more often observed in non-Western cultures (Timimi, 2009); this greater acceptance of a variety of child behaviors may play a part in parent, family, and social conceptualizations of disorder. We might also explore the influence of diverse family contexts on sibling experiences, and the ways in which family factors such as warmth, support, and/or conflict have an impact on children's adjustments (McGuire & Shanahan, 2010).

In the second example, we explore both similarities and differences related to parent discipline practices (e.g., corporal punishment, shaming) in China, India, Italy, Kenya, the Philippines, and Thailand. Most discipline practices, across countries, were associated with similar outcomes (in terms of children's aggression and anxiety). Some differences, however, were observed, depending on perceptions of the normativeness of specific practices (Gershoff et al., 2010).

In the last example, we consider the possibility that transactions among multiple components of culture (e.g., race, family make-up, socioeconomic status, and immigrant status) contribute to individual differences in adolescent well-being. For instance, although adolescents from Asian, Latin American, and European backgrounds report different levels of family obligation, parental authority, and autonomy, levels of family conflict and family cohesion, as well as individual adjustment and academic achievement, are similar (Fuligni, 1998b; Fuligni, Tseng, & Lam, 1999; Fuligni, Witkow, & Garcia, 2005). A more mixed set of findings comes from data comparing the adjustments of children and adolescents from immigrant backgrounds. Fuligni (1997, 1998a) reported that children who moved to the United States from Asian and Latin American countries displayed "remarkable" adjustments, and suggested that strong family values related to cultural identification, family obligations, and education contributed to their success. In contrast, Mirsky (1997) and Birman, Trickett, and Buchanan (2005) observed increased psychological distress and dysfunction in samples of immigrants from the former Soviet Union to Israel and the United States. Various hypotheses have been suggested to explain the disparate findings, including the stressful qualities of migration, poverty and segregation in new destinations, and acculturation and cultural stress (Duarte et al., 2008; SlonimNevo, Sharaga, Mirsky, Petrovsky, & Borodenko, 2006; Suarez-Orozco, Todorova, & Qin, 2006; Vedder & Virta, 2005).

Thinking About Max

Within a sociocultural framework, the assessment of Max will include identification of, for example, the impact of his family's socioeconomic status (previously solidly middle class, now less secure), the balance between assimilation and preservation of Honduran traditions, the embedding of the family in the Honduran/Latino community, and the possibility of faith-based resources. The details, significance, and likely outcome of Max's situation will be interpreted in light of a set of particular cultural values and expectations. A culturally informed intervention will take into account the concern and availability of Max's immediate and extended family and may provide culturally accessible conceptualizations of disorder and intervention.

Thinking About Maggie

Contributions from a sociocultural perspective will also help us understand Maggie's situation. There may be fewer financial resources for Maggie and her mother, but their participation in church-related activities may provide additional support. Perhaps Maggie will become more interested in developing connections to her religious community, or will become more aware of her personal concerns related to gender or politics. In all instances, we expect this perspective to lead to a fuller, more nuanced approach to disorder and intervention.

Over the course of this chapter, it has become abundantly clear that a single model of development, psychopathology, and treatment, no matter how comprehensive, cannot provide all of the necessary information. Depending on the particular child, different aspects of various models, taken together, contribute to better understanding and a greater number of specific options for support and intervention. This emphasis on complexity and integration will naturally lead us, in the next chapter, to consideration of contemporary principles and practices of developmental psychopathology.

Key Terms

Continuous models of psychopathology (p. 13)
Discontinuous models of psychopathology (p. 13)
Physiological models (p. 13)
Neural plasticity (p. 13)
Genotype (p. 14)

Phenotype (p. 14)
Quantitative genetics (p. 15)
Molecular genetics (p. 15)
Human Genome Project (p. 15)
Genomics (p. 15)
Diathesis–stress model (p. 16)

Chapter Summary

- Theoretical models of development, psychopathology, and treatment help to organize clinical observations, direct research efforts, and design treatment programs.
- Continuous models of psychopathology emphasize the gradual transition from the normal range of feelings, thoughts, and behaviors to clinically significant problems.
- Discontinuous models of psychopathology emphasize differences between distinct patterns of emotion, cognition, and behavior that are within the normal range and those that define clinical disorders.
- Physiological models emphasize biological processes, such as genes and neurological systems, as being at the core of human development and experiences, including the development of psychopathology.
- Current physiological models, such as the diathesis–stress model, emphasize the interplay of various physiological factors and stress in order to understand the emergence, course, and treatment of psychopathology.
- Psychological models, such as the psychodynamic, cognitive-behavioral, humanistic, and family models, emphasize intrapersonal or interpersonal factors in the development, course, and treatment of psychopathology.
- Sociocultural models emphasize the importance of the social context, including gender, race, ethnicity, and socioeconomic status, in the development, course, and treatment of psychopathology.

3 Principles and Practices of Developmental Psychopathology

AS WE EXAMINE THE PRINCIPLES and practices of developmental psychopathology, keep in mind the definitions provided in Chapter 1's introduction: **Psychopathology** refers to intense, frequent, and/or persistent maladaptive patterns of emotion, cognition, and behavior; and **developmental psychopathology** extends this description to emphasize that these maladaptive patterns occur in the context of typical development and result in the current and potential impairment of infants, children, and adolescents. We will use these definitions as our cornerstones and will build on them to explore related concepts of distress and dysfunction.

This chapter has three sections. The first section is primarily focused on development; the concept of developmental pathways and notions of child competence and incompetence are summarized. The second section reviews the key constructs of risk and resilience; examples from a variety of empirical and clinical studies make explicit the connections between theoretical constructs and real-life children. The third section provides an overview of research strategies in developmental psychopathology.

The Framework of Developmental Psychopathology

Investigators working to accurately place developmental psychopathology within the broad framework of psychology have variously conceptualized it as a "field" of psychology, a "subfield," a "domain," a "discipline," and a "macroparadigm" (Cummings, Davies, & Campbell, 2000). For our purposes, however, what matters more than terminology is whether developmental psychopathology provides a useful approach for understanding how specific disorders develop, what happens over time to children who develop disorders, and what we can do to help these children.

From a theoretical perspective, developmental psychopathology is *not* associated with a single point of view. Rather, as noted in Chapter 2, developmental psychopathology "integrates and coordinates a wide range of theories (e.g., psychodynamic, behavioral, cognitive, biological, family systems, and sociological)" (Mash & Dozois, 1996, p. 35). From a clinical perspective, developmental psychopathologists assume that a variety of assessment, prevention, and intervention techniques will prove useful. In addition to appreciating multiple psychological perspectives, the contributions of other disciplines are explicitly acknowledged. Numerous researchers and clinicians in psychiatry, social work, education, and public policy provide important hypotheses, data and interpretive insight, and mental health care.

As we review the principles and practices of developmental psychopathology, remember that, like the evolution of general scientific models, understandings of developmental psychopathology also evolve (Cicchetti & Toth, 2008; Sroufe, 2009). Many individuals have contributed to the growth of the field; their seminal reviews have focused the organization and content of this chapter (Achenbach, 1982, 1990, 1997; Cicchetti, 1984, 1990a, 1990b; Cicchetti & Sroufe, 2000; Garmezy & Rutter, 1983; Rutter & Sroufe, 2000; Sameroff, 2000; Sroufe, 1997).

In 1984, a special issue of the journal *Child Development* reviewed the history, theory, research methodologies, and practical applications of developmental psychopathology. At that time, Sroufe and Rutter (1984) defined the domain of developmental psychopathology as "*the study of the origins and course of individual patterns of behavioral maladaptation, whatever the age of onset, whatever the causes, whatever the transformations in behavioral manifestation, and however complex the course of the developmental pattern may be*" (p. 18, italics in original). This broad description takes into account the development of both typical functioning and psychopathology, as well as the relations between patterns of adjustment and maladjustment (Cicchetti, 1984; see Fig. 3:1).

Psychopathology, then, might be understood as a developmental distortion, or a form of unsuccessful adaptation. More specifically, Mash and Dozois (1996) characterize psychopathology in children as an *adaptational failure* that "may involve deviation from age-appropriate norms, exaggeration or diminishment of normal developmental expressions, interference in normal developmental progress, failure to master age-salient developmental tasks, and/or failure to develop a specific function or regulatory mechanism" (p. 5). These types of adaptational failures have, for years, been viewed as either *delay* (e.g., the child acquires language more slowly than other children), *fixation* (e.g., the child continues to suck her thumb long after other children have stopped), or *deviance* (e.g., the child behaves strangely, unlike other children) (Fischer et al., 1997). Understanding children's disorders as delay, fixation, or deviance highlights the difficulties of *a particular child at a particular point in time,* and provides us with one way of thinking about the connection between normal and abnormal development.

Another way of thinking about the connection between normal and abnormal development is to examine the notion of *process.* Sroufe and Rutter's (1984) original definition of developmental psychopathology suggests that adaptation (or maladaptation) is an ongoing activity, with transformations of patterns of thinking, feeling, and behaving at various developmental stages. With respect to process, we can think about disorders as "successions

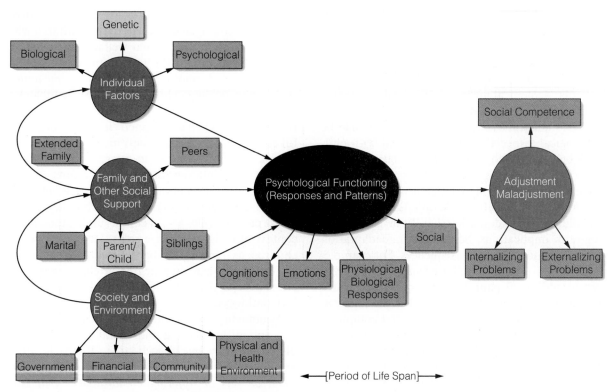

FIGURE 3:1 A framework for developmental psychopathology.
Source: Life-span perspectives on health and illness by Whitman, Thomas L.; Merluzzi, Thomas V.; White, Robert D. Copyright 2003 Reproduced with permission of TAYLOR & FRANCIS GROUP LLC - BOOKS in the format Textbook and Other Book Copyright via Clearance Center.

of deviations over time," with small problems leading to larger problems, or different problems, and so on (Cummings et al., 2000); children's psychopathology, then, does not emerge all of a sudden or out of the blue, but rather unfolds over time. To make these descriptions somewhat less abstract, we can think metaphorically of developmental psychopathologists making difficult choices between taking photographs or videos of troubled children. Single photographs can be compelling in their detail but are time bound. Videos provide a more fluid and dynamic perspective, but wide-angle views may miss some detail. We will have to be creative in our use of both camera lenses and films as we try to capture the essence of children's psychopathology. Acknowledging the ways that the "active, changing" child is embedded in "a dynamic, changing context" makes our understandings of disorders more complicated, but more real (Cummings et al., 2000, p. 24).

Developmental Pathways, Stability, and Change

The concept of **developmental pathways** illustrates the principle that adjustment and maladjustment are points or places along a lifelong map. Considering the stage-salient (age-related) issues that challenge young children (such as the development of trust, or independence, or friendship), we understand that there are a great variety of adaptational efforts and outcomes, which can be grouped according to shared features (what Fischer et al., 1997, refer to as "families" or sets of pathways). There are diverse positive developmental pathways: many different ways for children to grow up safe, happy, and capable. Less happy, less adept children also follow multiple problematic developmental pathways, but these are distinct, different roads.

The 2000 Surgeon General's report on children's mental health and mental illness makes essentially the same point about both normal and abnormal individual development. The report highlights children's active self-organizing and self-righting tendencies, asserting that "a child within a given context naturally adapts (as much as possible) to a particular ecological niche. . . . When environments themselves are highly disordered or pathological, children's adaptations to such settings may also be pathological, especially when compared with children's behaviors within more healthy settings" (U.S. Department of Health and Human Services, Report of the Surgeon General's Conference on Children's Mental Health: A National Action Agenda, 2000).

Children's maladaptation has both short- and long-term implications. Sometimes, maladaptation has immediate negative consequences. For example, one child who is physically abused may, in an effort to prevent additional pain, become aggressive toward other adults or peers. Another child in the same situation may exhibit overly solicitous and compliant behavior in an effort to ensure the approval of others. In the short run, with specific circumstances in place, atypical coping strategies may afford somewhat reasonable (and somewhat useful) accommodations. However, over time, such entrenched patterns of aggression or compliance may lead to a diminished sense of self and difficulties in peer relationships (Fischer et al., 1997).

Developmental pathways can be characterized as broad or as narrow (Holden, 2010). Broad pathways include larger scale goal-directed patterns of feelings, thoughts, and behaviors across multiple domains (e.g., achieving social competence, academic success, overall well-being). Narrow pathways involve more specific goals (e.g., mastering a musical instrument, learning a second language, or maintaining a long-distance friendship). Recent theoretical and empirical work has led to innovative perspectives on developmental pathways, including recognition of the roles of parents in children's pathways.

Developmental pathways, or developmental trajectories, are almost always discussed in terms of individual children or groups of children. But parents have significant impacts on pathways. Holden (2010) describes several ways in which parents influence children's pathways. One way involves *initiating trajectories* by selecting environments and activities. "For example, musical parents immerse their offspring in music and bring them to concerts; political parents expose their children to news reports and discuss politics during meals" (p. 199). Another way

involves *supporting trajectories* by providing attention and encouragement to children. Children who display an interest in animal welfare, for instance, need to be driven to the local humane society to volunteer. And another way involves *mediating trajectories*, helping "children interpret roadblocks, avoid off-ramps, and steer clear of negative trajectories" (p. 199). When unexpected challenges or stressful circumstances (such as chronic illness, exposure to violence, or divorce) occur, parents might actively prepare their children for upcoming events, or talk through difficult events as they happen, or help children understand sad experiences after they occur. These parental roles are, of course, understood in the context of children's active roles. Holden describes children as *reacting* to parent-initiated pathways, as *controlling* their own degree of engagement and effort on a particular pathway, and as *initiating* their own pathways.

Equifinality and **multifinality** refer to similarities and differences in individual pathways to a disordered outcome (Cicchetti & Rogosch, 1996; Sroufe, 1997; see Fig. 3:2). *Equifinality is best understood as sets of differing circumstances that lead to the same diagnosis.* For example, one child may fall behind in school and experience repeated academic failures. Another may be part of a family that is disengaged and hostile. Still another may have a

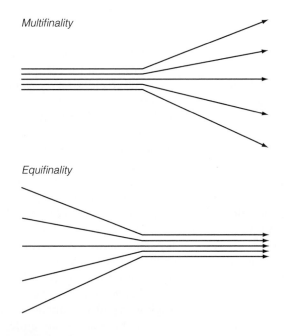

FIGURE 3:2 Illustrations of *equifinality* and *multifinality*.

genetic vulnerability to mood disorder. Equifinality describes the process whereby all three of these children go on to develop major depression in adolescence. With equifinality, different beginnings result in similar outcomes.

Multifinality is best understood as sets of similar beginnings that lead to different outcomes. Here, three children all begin with the same set of circumstances, perhaps involving maternal psychopathology and severe economic disadvantage. One child may struggle and manage to just get by. Another may surpass all expectations. And the last may fail in school, in relationships, and in the job market. With multifinality, similar beginnings result in different outcomes. For both equifinality and multifinality, we are concerned with the kinds of individual, familial, and social variables that influence children's developmental pathways both toward and away from disorder.

So far, our discussion of developmental pathways emphasizes stability, the ways in which maladaptation continues over time and place. We can look at Figure 3:2 and see the straight lines or direct paths

of development and the apparent inevitability of certain outcomes. But developmental pathways also encompass change. The Surgeon General's report (2000) emphasizes this possibility, suggesting that although early maladaptation often leads to later maladaptation, developmental discontinuities also occur and "may reflect the emergence of new capacities (or incapacities) as the child's psychological self, brain, and social environment undergo significant reorganization." The "emergence of new capacities" in a child may lead to numerous instances of change for the better, with difficulties outgrown over time or successfully managed by parents, teachers, and children themselves. There are also, unfortunately, numerous instances of change for the worse, with well-adjusted youngsters developing psychopathologies in later years. The developmental pathways model will need to account for both of these types of trajectories. Figure 3:3 provides additional examples of zigzag, curving, or indirect developmental paths.

Two of the most important things to remember in thinking about the pathways model are that (1) change is possible at many points; however,

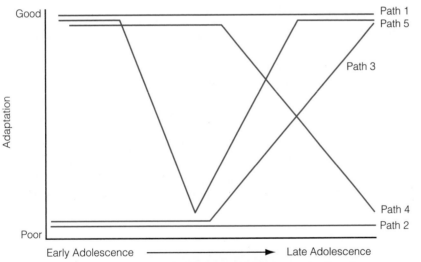

FIGURE 3:3 Zigzag and indirect pathways.
Republished with permission of Annual Reviews Inc., from Adolescent development: Pathways and processes of risk and resilience, Compas, B. E., 46, © 1995; permission conveyed through Copyright Clearance Center, Inc.

Path 1 Stable Adaptation — Few behavior problems: good self-worth. Low risk exposure.

Path 2 Stable Maladaptation — Chronic adversities; little protection. Example: aggressive, antisocial behavior maintained.

Path 3 Reversal of Maladaptation — Important life change creates new opportunity. Example: military carrer affords opportunity.

Path 4 Decline Adaptation — Environmental or biological shifts bring adversity. Example: family divorce contributes to maladaptation.

Path 5 Temporal Maladaptation — Can reflect transient experiment risk taking. Example: use of illegal drugs.

(2) change is constrained or enabled by previous adaptations (Sroufe, 2009). For example, the transition to middle school is often associated with a larger group of peers from which a child may choose new friends; whether a child is able to develop new friendships may depend on his or her self-image, social skills, and earlier successful (or unsuccessful) experiences in elementary school. Depending on a collection of unique factors for any given child—the timing of diagnosis, the specific disorder, the kind of intervention, specific familial and environmental variables—we expect differences in the likely types of change or rates of change.

Rutter (1996) has explored the "transitions and turning points" of developmental pathways, examining the kinds of variables that are associated with change. He identifies both internal, intrinsic factors (such as the acquisition of language or the onset of puberty) as well as external factors (such as a move to a new home or a divorce). Rutter ties these transitions to the shutting down or opening up of opportunities. For example, the decision by an academically struggling adolescent to drop out of school may result in the shutting down of a number of employment options or the closing off of certain aspects of a positive self-image. Or following a move to a new neighborhood, a child with a difficult reputation among peers may be able to develop new and more successful friendships. These transitions and turning points are similar to Holden's (2010) description of "detours, roadblocks, and off-ramps." *Detours* are events or junctures that redirect pathways (e.g., a new school, a change in family structure). *Roadblocks* are events or responses that shut down or slow down positive trajectories (e.g., restricted access to high-quality education, adolescent pregnancy). And *off-ramps* are places where children exit a positive trajectory (although children can reenter at a later point in time).

Throughout the textbook, in discussions of the developmental course of disorders, the mechanisms which are hypothesized to underlie **continuity** (i.e., stability) or **discontinuity** (i.e., change) will be described. At this point, it is important to understand that genes, environments, and development itself all contribute to adaptive and maladaptive pathways (Rutter, Kim-Cohen, & Maughan, 2006; Sroufe, 2009).Whether we describe adaptive or maladaptive pathways, or stable or changing patterns in development, it is important to understand that "the course of development is lawful" (Sroufe & Rutter, 1984). Lawful, or coherent, development is different from stability. Sroufe and Rutter argue that we need to look for connections that make developmental sense. For example, a child's approach to calming herself may look different when she is 8 years old (e.g., talking quietly to herself, breathing deeply) than it did when she was 4 years old (e.g., curling up with a favorite blanket), but her later efforts are meaningfully related to her earlier approach. As another example, some children who are bullied by older siblings at home go on to bully children in younger grades in elementary school. Being maltreated and maltreating others are *not* identical forms of behavior, but they are sometimes connected in terms of ideas about the self, relationships, and power. This notion of **coherence** is the final component of our understanding of both direct and indirect developmental pathways. Coherence reflects our belief that beginnings may be logically linked to outcomes if we carefully evaluate the variables that lead to stability as well as the variables that lead to change.

Competence and Incompetence

Up to this point, we have assumed that children either do well or do poorly. We have assumed that psychological well-being is characteristic of some children, but not others. In reality, of course, well-being is not an all-or-none phenomenon. Most typically developing children do better, or are more competent, in some areas than in others. **Competence,** within the framework of developmental psychopathology, reflects "effective functioning in important environments" (Masten, Morison, Pellegrini, & Tellegen, 1990, p. 239). Competence involves multiple components, including a child's skills and talents, beliefs about his or her effectiveness, personality characteristics, and accomplishments (Harter, 1999; Masten & Coatsworth, 1995).

The Case of Ryan

Ryan is in seventh grade. Although his childhood to date has been relatively happy and uneventful, tensions in the home have increased in the year since his father was laid off from his job. Initially supportive of her husband, Ryan's mother has begun to resent Ryan's father's rejection of several job opportunities that he felt were less than what he deserved. Money has become tight and the family has had to restrict purchases such as new school clothes and supplies.

Ryan, a rather shy individual, is self-conscious and generally uncomfortable around his classmates. He had difficulty making the transition to middle school in sixth grade, and he felt overwhelmed by the large and bustling setting. Ryan is a talented student with an especially strong aptitude in math and science. In fact, his science teacher, Mr. Gordon, invited him to join the middle school math team. Ryan has made a significant contribution there and was asked by several other team members to join them in developing and entering a project for a science competition. Within these more structured social settings, Ryan has begun to relax and develop some genuine friendships. Mr. Gordon has continued to mentor Ryan and has told Ryan's parents that Ryan is his hardest working student and that he is recommending that Ryan switch to the school's accelerated academic track for the following semester. Even with these school achievements, Ryan has become increasingly withdrawn and irritable at home, where the arguments between his parents have become more frequent. ■■

The Case of Jasmine

Jasmine is in the seventh grade. When she was 8 years old, her parents divorced after several turbulent years during which each developed serious chemical dependency problems. Jasmine was sent to live with her grandmother for a year. During that time, Jasmine struggled with a number of anxiety symptoms and sleep disturbances and experienced many problems at school. Her grandmother, however, was patient and supportive of both her granddaughter and her daughter while Jasmine's mother completed a successful course of treatment, found work, and located an apartment close by. After rejoining her mother, Jasmine gradually came to trust the stability of her new home and continued to be very involved with her grandmother.

After several failed attempts to overcome his addictions, Jasmine's father recently found a treatment program that has helped him to make real progress. Although his contact with Jasmine has been limited, he has slowly reentered her life, with the approval and encouragement of Jasmine's mother. In particular, he has taken a strong interest in Jasmine's soccer and basketball teams, attending as many games as possible. Like her father, Jasmine is an outstanding athlete. She has great natural ability, works hard at practice, and loves to compete. All of her close friendships have developed from time spent with teammates. She often says that she is far happier on the soccer field and basketball court than in the classroom.

In fact, school is an increasing challenge for Jasmine. Although her pleasant personality and diligence served her well in elementary school, these qualities have not been enough to make up for her poor reading skills and difficulty comprehending the more abstract and complex content of her middle school courses. She is always behind in her assignments, and her resistance to spending time on her homework is the one major area of conflict between Jasmine and her mother. ■■

Thinking about Ryan and Jasmine, it becomes clear that children's developmental pathways cannot be described as altogether good or altogether bad. And children's developmental outcomes are not altogether competent or altogether incompetent. Ryan displays academic strengths, but struggles to feel comfortable with his family. Jasmine is well liked by peers and is a gifted athlete, but functions poorly in the school setting. As an adult, Ryan may eventually derive great satisfaction from a career as an engineer, but may always feel some discomfort with intimate relationships. Jasmine may believe that her low-paying service job reflects negatively on her overall worth as a person, but feel more accomplished when she thinks about her close-knit family and her several awards for volunteer work in her community. Like Ryan and Jasmine, all children display various **domains of competence,** which involve particular skills and achievements, combined with domains (or areas or types) of incompetence, which involve lack of skill or lack of achievement. Other researchers have referred to similar constructs as **arenas of comfort,** or spaces of relative calm (Simmons & Blyth, 1987): "An arena of comfort provides a context for the individual to relax and rejuvenate so that potentially stressful changes and experiences in another area can be endured or mastered" (Call & Mortimer, 2001, p. 2). Combinations of competencies and incompetencies are as true of children *with* disorders as they are of children *without* disorders. As we present specific psychopathologies in the following chapters, it will be essential to remember that *children's disorders coexist with their talents and successes.* We will emphasize the need to take into account children's strengths during assessment and diagnosis, as well as the need to draw on those strengths in designing effective treatment plans.

Garmezy, Masten, and Tellegen (1984) described three domains of competence in younger school-aged

---

BOX 3:1 THE CHILD IN CONTEXT

Parental Views of Child Competence in a Village Community

All parents in all cultures have ideas about what characteristics make a child successful and well adjusted. As you might expect, many of the hoped-for characteristics are similar across settings and circumstances, such as being well-behaved, getting along with friends, and doing well in school (Durbrow et al., 2001). Other characteristics appear more culture specific. In a study of child competence in the Caribbean, Durbrow (1999) collected data using parent interviews. Parents described less competent children using a variety of mild to moderately negative terms, including *troublesome, miserable, greedy, hardened, lazy,* and *wicked.* In this study, children were viewed as competent if they were respectful and obedient, completed their chores, were satisfactory students, were friendly with peers, and were involved in positive activities outside of home and school. Less salient, but still useful, indicators of competence included attending church, practicing good health habits, and having a content personality. These

adult criteria for competence were similar for younger girls, adolescent girls, and younger boys. Adolescent boys were less likely to be seen as doing well in school, and that criterion was mentioned less frequently for them. For adolescent boys, doing chores well was a more influential indication of competence.

Parents provided a number of explanations for child competence. About half of the parents referred to the extent of firm and responsible caregiving as a factor contributing to child behavior or misbehavior. Other factors included the child's innate characteristics, adequate nutrition and health, and neighborhood characteristics. Some of the differences in parental conceptions of competence likely reflect specific demands of communities and socioeconomic concerns. Multicultural investigations of competence across development will need to continue to address these factors as they explore competence within and across diverse populations.

---

children: academic achievement, behavioral competence, and social competence. Two additional domains appear in adolescence: romantic competence and job competence (Masten et al., 1995). These domains are conceptually distinct, but there is some overlap. Generally, children who are competent in one area are somewhat more likely to be competent in other areas. Even so, competence in one area by no means assures competence in another. By adolescence, there is less overlap than in childhood, with social competence no longer related to academic achievement or behavioral competence (Masten et al., 1995). For instance, many adolescents make increasingly specific decisions about high school coursework (e.g., enrolling in science or language courses that are college prerequisites) and extracurricular activities (e.g., vacations with families or employment opportunities) that lead to increases or decreases in domain-specific skills. Competence in any domain does not emerge full blown, and there are many factors that contribute to the development and maintenance of competence in children. Parents, in particular, may have a variety of views on the personal characteristics used to describe competent children, and a variety of views on the family and social factors linked to children's competence

(Durbrow, 1999; Durbrow, Pena, Masten, Sesma, & Williamson, 2001; see Box 3:1).

Risk and Resilience

We turn now to discussions of some of the multiple factors that enhance or complicate children's development and functioning, and focus first on risk and resilience (Cicchetti & Garmezy, 1993; Garmezy & Rutter, 1983; Rutter, 2009). The constructs of risk and resilience have been investigated for several decades, with much of the early work focused on the developmental outcomes of children of parents with schizophrenia (Garmezy, 1974; Mednick & Schulsinger, 1968). Key observations regarding this group of children were that (1) significantly more of them developed psychopathologies compared to children whose parents were not diagnosed with schizophrenia, and (2) many of these children, despite their difficult family circumstances, had adequate and even excellent outcomes. Why some children struggle and why others prevail are the questions at the heart of risk and resilience research.

Risk is defined as *increased vulnerability to disorder.* **Risk factors** are the individual, family, and social characteristics that are associated with this increased vulnerability. **Resilience** is defined as *adaptation (or competence) despite adversity*. **Protective factors** are the individual, family, and social characteristics that are associated with this positive adaptation.

Risk and Risk Factors

As noted, risk has to do with increased vulnerability to disorder. This vulnerability takes two forms: (1) **nonspecific risk,** which involves increased vulnerability to any, or many, kinds of disorders; and (2) **specific risk,** which involves increased vulnerability to one particular disorder. As an example of specific risk, the inactive liver enzyme that interferes with the metabolism of phenylalanine is associated with a specific type of mental retardation. As an example of nonspecific risk, poverty is associated with a variety of negative outcomes. And just to make things interesting, there are factors that are both somewhat specific and somewhat nonspecific. For example, children whose parents are diagnosed with schizophrenia display increased vulnerability to schizophrenia itself, as well as increased vulnerability to a number of other psychological disorders.

Types of Risk Factors

The most common distinctions made among types of risk factors involve individual, family, and social examples. Individual risk factors are child oriented and include things like gender, temperament, and intelligence. As we will see in upcoming chapters, being a boy or a girl makes one more or less vulnerable to certain psychopathologies. Being very intense, or easily aroused, or difficult to soothe also makes a child more vulnerable to disorder. And being less intelligent is associated with more frequent negative outcomes.

Family risk factors are those associated with the child's immediate caretaking environment and include parent characteristics such as the presence of psychopathology or harsh, punitive styles of parenting, as well as family characteristics such as unusual discord among siblings. Maternal psychopathology is often cited as a nonspecific risk factor. That is, having a mother with a serious psychological disorder is related to children developing disorders; these disorders are sometimes similar to the mother's, but they are also often different. Depressed moms can have depressed kids, but depressed moms can also have anxious kids and kids with conduct problems.

Poverty, lack of access to playgrounds and good schools, and dangerous neighborhoods are all social risk factors that may compromise children's development.

Social risk factors include those associated with the child's larger environment, including neighborhood and socioeconomic niche, school system, and racial, ethnic, and cultural characteristics. Specifically, we want to know if membership in any particular group is associated with increased vulnerability to disorder, and whether poverty or ethnicity makes a child more likely to develop disorders. To further illustrate this idea of social risk, we can think about the connection between neighborhoods and academic performance, and evidence that disadvantaged neighborhoods are associated with children's academic struggles in the elementary school years (Shumow, Vandell, & Posner, 1999).

Certain kinds of family and social risk factors are frequently conceptualized as stressful or adverse life events (e.g., divorce, parental unemployment). Stressful life events also include experiencing natural disasters such as floods or tornadoes. With respect to nonspecific and specific effects of stressful life events, there are recent data that suggest that we look more closely at some particular associations. For example, depression and conduct disorders appear to be more reliably correlated with stressful life events than are attention-deficit hyperactivity disorder and phobias (Tiet et al., 2001).

Another aspect of risk that should be noted is whether the risk is transient or enduring. Transient risk factors are temporary or short lived, such as months-long financial difficulties when a parent is laid off that improve when that parent is rehired. Enduring risk factors are more permanent, such as a child's diminished intellectual ability or marital conflict that lasts for years.

Numbers of Risk Factors

Many researchers have observed that the total number of risk factors that children experience is even more important than the particular type of risk factors. Rutter (1979), Appleyard, Egeland, van Dulmen, and Sroufe (2005), and others have provided convincing data that the more risk factors to which children are exposed, the more negative the developmental outcome. So, even though any risk is unfortunate, we need to be especially watchful over children who experience risk on top of additional risk.

Timing of Risk Factors

Understanding the role of timing is more complicated than understanding the type or the total number of risk factors. Stressors may have no impact, little impact, or profound impact, *depending on the age at which they occur* and whether they occur alone or with other stressors and risk factors. For example, in the disadvantaged neighborhood study mentioned above, the academic struggles of children were observed in the later elementary grades and not the earlier ones (Shumow et al., 1999). If we had only looked at the early grades, we might have missed the later connection and erroneously concluded that poor neighborhoods had little impact on academics. Another example of this differential impact involves divorce, where children's age-related skills and resources interact with the stressful events to produce different outcomes at different ages (Hetherington, Bridges, & Insabella, 1998).

Patterns of Risk Factors

Negative outcomes are also related to whether certain risk factors occur alone or with others; that is, we look to see whether a particular pattern of risk is in place. Some combinations of risk factors may be more problematic than others. For instance, Rutter (1987) observes that boys are more likely than girls to develop particular disorders in the presence of similar risk factors. He hypothesizes that this greater risk may be related to individual risk factors (such as neurophysiological vulnerability), parental risk factors (such as parents arguing more in front of boys than girls), and boys' display of increasingly negative chain reactions to initial difficulties. Understanding the complexities of patterns of risk may help us understand why there are different developmental outcomes for children in the same family, or among children from similar backgrounds (Kohen, Leventhal, Dahinten, & McIntosh, 2008; Morales & Guerra, 2006).

Overall, when we think about risk and risk factors, we are concerned with both immediate and eventual outcomes. The decades-long Kauai study, involving multiethnic children from the Hawaiian island of Kauai, suggests that two-thirds of the children who experience multiple risks, including perinatal stress (an individual factor), dysfunctional families (a family factor), and poverty (a social factor), struggle to adapt, with many of them developing clinically significant disorders (Werner, 1993; Werner & Smith, 1982). These kinds of findings illustrate previously discussed notions of developmental pathways, along with continuities and discontinuities in development. Taken together, these data demonstrate that the construct of risk is complex, and that risk type, number, timing, and pattern all interact to influence children's capacity for weathering the difficulties they encounter.

The Example of Child Maltreatment

Because the construct of risk is so central to the field of developmental psychopathology, we want to take additional time to consolidate our understanding using the example of child maltreatment. (More detailed information about the origins and course of maltreatment is provided in Chapter 13.) **Child maltreatment** is a broad category that includes physical abuse, sexual abuse, psychological abuse, and neglect and reflects the "gross violation of the rights of a vulnerable and dependent child" (Cicchetti & Toth, 1995, p. 541). *Child maltreatment is not a diagnosis that is assigned to a child.* Rather, it is a risk factor that affects hundreds of thousands of children each year, costing billions of dollars and resulting in 1,500 preventable deaths in the United States (U.S. Department of Health and Human Services [DHHS], 2007).

The Department of Health and Human Services (2007) identified the primary form of maltreatment in individual cases and reported that 61% of maltreated children were victims of neglect, with a parent or primary caregiver failing to provide basic shelter, nutrition, medical care, and/or supervision. Nineteen percent of maltreated children were physically abused. Ten percent of maltreated children were sexually abused. Five percent of maltreated children were emotionally abused. Most cases of maltreatment involved combinations of abuse and neglect, an awful example of multiple risks. With respect to age, DHHS reported that infants and toddlers had the highest rates of victimization and the highest fatality rates. With respect to race and ethnicity, African American children, Pacific Islander children, and Native American children exhibited the highest maltreatment rates. Low socioeconomic status and social isolation were frequently correlated with maltreatment. Most maltreatment (79%) was perpetrated by parents, with neglect as the most common form.

Child maltreatment is a nonspecific risk factor, with increased likelihood of immediate, short-term, and long-term negative developmental outcomes. There is widespread evidence of physiological impact (e.g., dysregulation of the stress response), psychological impact (e.g., atypical socioemotional development, poor school performance, increased psychopathology), and relationship impact (e.g., disrupted family relationships, peer difficulties). Advocates for children need to think about maltreatment in multiple ways: as its own risk factor, as one of several co-occurring risk factors, and as a marker of other risk factors. Maltreatment cannot be traced to a single source, such as parent psychopathology, a parent's own history of being maltreated, poverty, or some constellation of difficult characteristics in a child; instead, it is a multiply determined risk, with equal emphasis on family and environmental factors (Belsky, 1993; Cicchetti & Toth, 2003). Although child maltreatment clearly illustrates the construct of risk as involving increased vulnerability to a range of distress and dysfunction, many instances of maltreatment do not inevitably lead to tragic outcomes. That some children manage to stay on track developmentally, and that some children exceed all expectations, leads to our discussion of resilience.

Resilience and Protective Factors

Remember that resilience is a special instance of adaptation; it is *competence in the face of adversity*. Specifically, "*Resilience* refers to the process of, capacity for, or outcome of successful adaptation despite challenging or threatening circumstances" (Masten, Best, & Garmezy, 1990, p. 426). Children who have all of the advantages of life—good health, supportive parents, safe neighborhoods, and effective social institutions—and thrive are not "resilient"; they are skillful, blessed, or lucky, or some combination of those. Resilient children do well *despite* their individual, family, or social circumstances. These are children of adversity who "worked well, played well, loved well, and expected well" (Werner & Smith, 1982). Three types of resilient children have been described: (1) children with many risk factors who have good outcomes; (2) children who continue to display competence when they are experiencing stress; and (3) children who display good recoveries following stress or trauma.

Developmental psychopathologists have argued that resilience is not a trait or characteristic that certain children have and others do not. Instead, they see resilience as a process, a capacity that develops over time (Egeland, Carlson, & Sroufe, 1993; Luthar, Cicchetti, & Becker, 2000; Masten, 2001; Masten & Reed, 2002). Thus some children display certain types of resilience but not others (e.g., keeping up grades while continuing to struggle emotionally) or resilience that is built up over years (e.g., keeping up grades, then mending friendships, then repairing self-image) (see Box 3:2). In addition, children's resilience is embedded in particular contexts. Children and adolescents interact with their families, their social and community groups, and within their culture to achieve individually- and culturally relevant resilience (Ungar, 2010).

Definitions must also take into account the positive developmental outcomes that are the basis of resilience. In Chapter 1, we discussed whether definitions of abnormality should focus on adequate or optimal adaptations; we now consider whether good outcomes are simply the absence of clinically significant disorder, or whether the presence of joy and accomplishment is also important (Benard, 1999; Masten & Reed, 2002). Connections between the study of resilience and the study of positive psychology described in Chapter 2 are also important (Yates & Masten, 2004). From staying out of trouble with the law to achieving award-winning success, we need to acknowledge the range of resilient outcomes we are likely to observe. With these ideas about resilience in mind, we now turn to descriptions of specific protective factors. According to Masten, Morison et al. (1990), *given the presence of risk*, these protective factors make negative outcomes *less likely*. Similar to investigations of risk factors, investigations of protective factors also focus on the various characteristics associated with better outcomes, with most of the research examining types and patterns of factors.

BOX 3:2 RISK AND RESILIENCE

"Ordinary Magic"

The study of risk and resilience is one of the foundations of the field of developmental psychopathology (Anthony, 1974; Garmezy, 1974; Rutter, 1979). The critical issue behind this important area of research is the investigation of the circumstances and mechanisms by which some children thrive and other children falter under conditions of stress and challenge. This has been a rich research vein, mined by many innovative and talented clinical researchers over the decades (Masten & Coatsworth, 1998; Rutter, 1990; Sroufe, 1997). In her seminal article "Ordinary Magic," Ann Masten (2001) highlights several important lessons learned from resilience research. Most important is the somewhat unexpected finding that resilience turns out to be the rule in development rather than the exception.

There is now abundant evidence of how resilience "arises from the normative functions of human adaptational systems" (Masten, 2001, p. 227), and this

resilience is an example of children's self-righting tendencies. Consequently, even under circumstances of extreme stress, resilience is the likely outcome if basic systems are in place and basic needs are met. These needs include consistent caregiving and cognitive, emotional, and social nurturing. Resilience is observed in many children who experience poverty, in many children who struggle with physical illnesses, and in many children who are victims of natural disasters. Of course, if children's needs are compromised, even conditions of very low stress may result in problematic development and psychopathology. Masten concludes: "What began as a quest to understand the extraordinary has revealed the power of the ordinary" (p. 235). As Masten emphasizes, we are finding new reasons to be optimistic about the effectiveness of early interventions and current efforts to strengthen coping and minimize risk for all children and families.

Types of Protective Factors

As with risk, we need to consider individual, family, and social types of protective factors (see Table 3:1). The most frequently noted individual factors have to do with children's personality characteristics. Children who have sunny dispositions, engaging manners, and who are more intelligent fare better (Masten, Morison et al., 1990). Particular kinds of psychological resources also matter. For example, children who have several coping strategies for dealing with stress (e.g., reframing their cognitive explanations for events, or talking about distress with a loving adult) experience more positive adaptations (Murphy & Moriarty, 1976; Rothbaum, Weisz, & Snyder, 1982).

Family factors also serve to protect children in difficult situations, such as children living in impoverished circumstances. Characteristics such as family cohesion and warmth are helpful. Having supportive, emotionally available, and determined parents makes it more likely that at-risk children are able to avoid an ever-increasing string of negative events than children with less capable parents. Having friends also makes a difference. Children who report having a best friend during a

negative experience are buffered from some of the consequences of that experience (Adams, Santo, & Bukowski, 2011).

Social factors are also important. Children whose lives are embedded in ethnic and cultural and religious groups where their well-being is a communal responsibility may have access to support and resources that other children do not (Ungar, 2011). From both theoretical and clinical perspectives, at-risk children with access to economic and political advantages, such as psychological counseling or school-based services, have better outcomes. Keep in mind, however, that research on children living in poverty suggests that resilience is not uncommon and is associated with both genetic and environmental factors (Buckner, Mezzacappa, & Beardslee, 2003; Kim-Cohen, Moffitt, Caspi, & Taylor, 2004).

Patterns of Protective Factors

Again, to appreciate the complexities of patterns of protection, we can look at children in the same family who have similar risks but different outcomes. We expect that, even with siblings, different temperaments will have an impact on

Protective factors, such as positive temperament and a supportive family, promote resilience in the face of stress.

functioning, as will different teachers in school and differences in the timing and number of stressful events (Smith & Prior, 1995). We can also look at the factors that promote better outcomes given particular psychopathologies. How do these protective factors exert their beneficial effects? What are the mechanisms by which they influence the course and direction of children's developmental pathways? Rutter (1987, 1990) suggests that protective factors influence children's outcomes by (1) reducing the impact of risk, (2) reducing the negative chain reactions that follow exposure to risk, (3) serving to establish or maintain self-esteem and self-efficacy, and/or (4) opening up opportunities for improvement or growth.

Reducing the impact of risk involves exposing children to fewer negative events. Reducing the impact may also involve altering the meaning of exposure, so that children think about risk factors in less harmful ways. For example, a child who has experienced physical or sexual abuse can be encouraged to see him- or herself as heroic for reporting the abuse and saving other children from being victimized.

Reducing negative chain reactions has to do with intervening before a series of negative responses or additional negative events occurs. For example, a child who experiences separation anxiety and misses school may be quickly referred for therapy, and a plan may be put into place to return the child to the classroom. With this plan, the consequence of avoiding anxiety by staying home is not reinforced, and academic difficulties resulting from missed class assignments are avoided. As another example,

TABLE 3:1 Child, Family, and Community Protective Factors
Within the Child
Good cognitive abilities, including problem-solving and attentional skills
Easy temperament in infancy; adaptable personality later in development
Positive self-perceptions; self-efficacy
Faith and a sense of meaning in life
A positive outlook on life
Good self-regulation of emotional arousal and impulses
Talents valued by self and society
Good sense of humor
General appeal or attractiveness to others
Within the Family
Close relationships with caregiving adults
Authoritative parenting (high on warmth, structure/monitoring, expectations)
Positive family climate with low discord between parents
Organized home environment
Postsecondary education of parents
Parents with qualities listed as child protective factors (above)
Parents involved with child's education
Socioeconomic advantages
Within Other Relationships
Close relationships with competent, prosocial, and supportive adults
Connections to prosocial and rule-abiding peers
Within the Community
Effective schools
Ties to prosocial organizations (e.g., schools, clubs)
Neighborhoods with high "collective efficacy"
High levels of public safety
Good emergency social services (e.g., 911 or crisis nursery services)
Good public health and health care availability
Source: Masten & Reed (2002).

©iStockphoto.com/Christopher Futcher

children at risk because they or their siblings have a chronic illness such as diabetes may be helped to recognize the range of emotional reactions connected to the waxing and waning of symptoms. Family members or friends may provide support before children become overwhelmed by frustration or panic.

Developing and maintaining self-esteem and self-efficacy is clearly related to our understanding of the role of personality characteristics in moderating distress and dysfunction. As an example, a student with dyslexia who is given the opportunity to meet other students with dyslexia is less likely to view information-processing problems as evidence of personal inferiority, lack of intelligence, or insufficient effort.

As to Rutter's final way that protective factors influence children's outcomes, opening up opportunities for improvement and growth involves the appreciation of turning points in children's lives. Recognizing the particular developmental challenges that children face and then taking advantage of both expected and unexpected bumps in the road of development may have noticeable effects. For a straightforward example, we can consider that a move to a new neighborhood may allow a child to develop other friends. For a more paradoxical example, we can think about Parmelee's (1986) discussion of the beneficial effects of illnesses in children. In his view, relatively minor illnesses such as chicken pox or a broken bone allow children to experience small frustrations that involve coping efforts. This practice sets the stage for later successful coping with more serious or difficult stressors. A child who never experiences frustration or disappointment, then, is actually at a disadvantage; he or she will be easily upset and without well-practiced strategies when the inevitable stressor occurs. As you can see, the possible relations between the experience of stress and the capacity to cope can be very complicated.

The Example of Child Maltreatment

Returning to the example of child maltreatment, concerned adults must focus on ways to promote psychological wellness in at-risk children (Cicchetti et al., 2000). There is both theory and research to guide adults in their efforts. Data suggest that many children and adolescents who experience physical or sexual abuse display resilience throughout their lives (Perkins & Jones, 2004; Rind, Tromovitch, & Bauserman, 1998). *This resilience, of course, in no way minimizes the moral or legal wrongfulness of maltreatment.* Rather, it shows us that parents, teachers, and mental health professionals must work together to identify protective factors at individual, familial, and social levels: resources such as self-esteem, family and peer support, a positive school climate, the presence of other caring adults, and access to both short- and long-term treatments (Cicchetti & Rogosch, 1997; Perkins & Jones, 2004).

Resilience, then, reflects the combined contributions of protective factors from individual, family, and social levels. So a child judged to be resilient in the face of early maltreatment, despite a chaotic and inconsistent home, may have exceptional personal strengths such as an easy temperament, strong intellectual abilities, and a warmth that draws adults and peers close. In addition, factors such as the type, duration, and timing of maltreatment influence resilience as well. Looked at in this way, the construct of resilience is better understood as the probabilistic outcome of multiple dynamic variables rather than as a static condition of the child or the environment (Yates, Egeland, & Sroufe, 2003). With this understanding, researchers are beginning to study, in much greater detail, the interactive influence of biological factors (such as stress-related hormones) and personality characteristics (such as emotional reactivity and self-control) (Cicchetti & Rogosch, 2007). The quality of relationships, from childhood through adolescence and into adulthood, has also been found to mediate the development of psychopathology for individuals maltreated during childhood (Collishaw et al., 2007).

Multicultural Research on Risk and Resilience

Given the concern with the social and cultural variables identified as either risk or protective factors and with data about differing rates of disorder in various groups of children, we must take additional time to consider research findings that ask very specific questions about race and ethnicity. We must also pay special attention to ethical concerns in mental health research focused on minority children in Western cultures as well as children living in various countries around the world (Fisher et al., 2002; Ungar, 2010). For example, do we observe the same kinds, and similar total numbers, of risk and protective factors in diverse groups of children? Are there differences in patterns and outcomes?

There are increasing numbers of both multicultural comparisons (across different cultures) and within-culture investigations of individual, family, and social risk factors. For example, Kilmer, Cowen, Wyman, Work, and Magnus (1998) sampled Hispanic, African American, and European American children from poor neighborhoods and found differences in the kinds of risks experienced. African American and Hispanic children more frequently had a family member arrested or in jail. More African American children were in foster care or living with relatives or friends. Hispanic children struggled more often with parental separations and divorce. European American children encountered family dysfunction more often and were diagnosed more frequently with medical problems.

Although the Kilmer et al. (1998) study reported that different groups of children encountered similar numbers of risks, other studies suggest that differences in numbers may require close attention. José et al. (1998) found similar numbers of major stressors among 10- to 14-year-old Russian and American children, but more daily hassles in the Russian group. This is important because ongoing hassles or small frustrations of everyday life like frequent family arguments, as well as school difficulties such as frequent teacher turnover, are often more strongly associated with poor outcomes than are major events (Lazarus & Folkman, 1984). We also need to think about the possibility that similar risks may lead to different outcomes for various groups of children. Latino children who are maltreated, for example, may fare worse than non-Latino children (Flores, Cicchetti, & Rogosch, 2005).

With respect to resilience and protective factors, research suggests that similar kinds of protective factors are in play for various racial, ethnic, and cultural groups. These include individual factors such as a positive self-image, empathy, a sense of competence, realistic perceptions of control, and family factors such as close relationships with a caregiver (Magnus, Cowen, Wyman, Fagen, & Work, 1999). In their study of maltreated Latino children, Flores et al. (2005) reported that some of the same personality characteristics that protect non-Latino children also serve to enhance Latino children's resilience. However, there may also be some specific differences. Conceptualizing sociocultural approaches as focused on differences rather than deficits, researchers have explored resilience in African American youth (e.g., Taylor et al., 2000), Latino youth (e.g., Reese, Kroesen, & Gallimore, 2000; Taylor et al., 2000), and Asian American youth (e.g., Chao, 2000; McCarty et al., 1999). One noteworthy outcome of an ethnic protective factor is the mental health advantage observed in British Indian children, who display lower levels of externalizing problems (Goodman, Patel, & Leon, 2010). These children benefit, in part, from two-parent families and fewer academic difficulties, but much of the advantage remains to be explained. Overall, resilient outcomes may "transcend racial boundaries" (Magnus et al., 1999, p. 482), but there is still much work to be done on understanding protective factors related to race, ethnicity, and culture.

A Lifespan Approach to Risk and Resilience

Our discussion of risk and resilience has provided numerous examples of both difficult and encouraging outcomes during the developmental periods of childhood and adolescence. However, we continue to be affected by previous and ongoing challenges throughout our lifetimes. We must, again, emphasize the notion of process as we think about the impact of risk and protective factors on adult development and psychopathology.

According to Staudinger, Marisiske, & Baltes (1993), children continue on developmental pathways into adulthood and throughout their lives. Over time, though, we can expect that relatively more of our resources are spent trying to stay on track, and fewer are expended on forging new trails. Some individuals do encounter new risks in their adult years, or discover that adaptations that were effective in childhood no longer work for them as adults. These individuals may, in fact, exhibit novel responses and create new opportunities for growth. Overall, the course of risk and resilience is complex and subject to change and must be considered across the full breadth of our lives.

Research Strategies in Developmental Psychopathology

As in developmental psychology and psychology in general, research in developmental psychopathology takes advantage of all of the core research methodologies, including case studies, correlational approaches, and experimental and quasi-experimental designs. In addition, there are a number of distinctive research methodologies with special importance for investigators in developmental psychopathology. We will focus on three especially relevant issues related to these methodologies: cross-sectional versus longitudinal approaches; complex hypotheses and complex models; and research in real-world settings with practical applications.

Cross-Sectional and Longitudinal Approaches

Cross-sectional research involves the collection of data at a single point in time, with comparisons made among groups of participants. For example, we might ask children in first, fourth, and seventh grades, in the middle of the school year, about their daily hassles. We might compare the children's replies, looking for age-related differences among the younger and older children (e.g., how are the first graders different from the fourth graders; are either or both groups different from the seventh graders?). **Longitudinal research,** in contrast, involves the ongoing collection of data from the same group of participants, or the study of individuals over time. With this approach, we also recruit first graders in the middle of their school year and talk with them about their hassles. But we wait until this same group is in the fourth grade before we collect more data. And then we wait again until the group is in the seventh grade. The longitudinal approach allows us to interpret and discuss data with respect to age (e.g., first versus fourth versus seventh graders) *and* individual differences (i.e., specific children whose hassles increase or decrease over the course of their school years). The research goals for the two types of studies are different. The cross-sectional study focuses on identifying age-related differences (or outcomes at a particular point in childhood). Cross-sectional research has the advantage of providing answers quickly, but the disadvantage of sampling different individuals at different ages. The longitudinal study provides additional data and highlights the developmental processes that occur for the same children across a significant span of time.

Although longitudinal research in developmental psychopathology has occurred for decades, it has become an increasingly common research methodology. Murphy's groundbreaking studies of children's coping (Murphy, 1962, 1974; Murphy & Moriarty, 1976) and Robins's work on deviant children (Robins, 1966) are important early examples of longitudinal investigations of adaptive and maladaptive developmental pathways. Werner's studies of Hawaiian children (Werner, 1993; Werner & Smith, 1977, 1982, 1989; see Box 3:3) and Masten's ongoing investigations of resilience (Masten et al., 1999) provide more contemporary illustrations.

These more recent longitudinal studies are also increasingly complex, given their attempts to address larger developmental questions. Sroufe and Rutter (1984), for example, describe the goals of prospective risk research (i.e., research done over the years *before* psychopathology is evident) as providing valuable data about "not only the different developmental course of at-risk subjects and controls but, especially, the development of those at-risk subjects who do and do not ultimately develop the disorder" (p. 19). Sroufe (1997) has discussed the need for longitudinal data on the factors that are associated with change and continuity once disorder is observed.

Current research on **developmental cascades** provides a number of excellent examples of longitudinal methodologies and goals. Developmental cascades refer to "the cumulative consequences for development of the many interactions and transactions ... that result in spreading effects across levels, among domains at the same level, and across different systems or generations" (Masten & Cicchetti, 2010, p. 491). Because the construct of cascades assumes effects that spread over time, longitudinal research is required. Developmental cascades may be positive or negative. In examples with positive outcomes, "effectiveness in one domain of competence in one period of life becomes the scaffold on which later competence in newly emerging domains develops: in other words, *competence begets competence*" (p. 492). In an example with a negative outcome, "behavior problems arising in the family prior to the school years ... are carried forward into the school context by the child, leading to problems in two new domains of academic and social competence" (p. 492). In another example, multiple measures of competence were linked to various negative outcomes from childhood through young adulthood. Longitudinal analyses provided evidence that "prior successes or failures in social and academic competence had spillover effects on subsequent internalizing symptoms," with especially noteworthy impact of social competence for boys (Obradovic, Burt, & Masten, 2010). In one final example, cascades are observed across generations. In this research, first-generation adolescent problem behavior predicted first-generation lower socioeconomic status, greater family stress,

---

BOX 3:3 RISK AND RESILIENCE

The Kauai Longitudinal Studies

An important example of a longitudinal study of a high-risk population is the Kauai Longitudinal Study (Werner, 1993; Werner & Smith, 1982). Begun in 1955 on the Hawaiian island of Kauai, a group of mental health and medical professionals undertook a prospective study of 201 infants who experienced moderate to significant perinatal distress, lived in poverty, and experienced significant psychosocial stress. Comprehensive data were gathered following the birth of these babies, and their overall developmental progress was tracked at the ages of 1, 2, 10, 18, and 32 years. Although the study began with an emphasis on the effects of vulnerability, over time it became equally focused on issues related to resilience. Much of the study's focus was on a group of 72 children who, despite the early and pervasive challenges they faced, grew into "competent, confident, and caring young adults" (Werner, 1993, p. 504).

Many of the findings point to the fact that, within broad parameters, quality of childrearing appeared to be a more powerful determinant of outcome than biological risk factors. A related finding was that, in general, the impact of reproductive stress diminished over time, presumably as the importance of the child's social world exerted increasing influence. This is not to suggest, however, that the developing children in this study were merely passive recipients of either a negative or a positive environment. Indeed, the investigators note that from a very early age, the most resilient children elicited positive attention from both family members and strangers. They were seen as active, alert, bright, and confident. Their sense of self-efficacy both created and elicited a more supportive social context within which to develop. It is the unique perspective of a longitudinal study such as this one that allows for complex and comprehensive hypotheses to be both designed and answered.

---

and reduced emotional and material investments. These, in turn, predicted next-generation problem behavior in children (Martin et al., 2010).

Complex Hypotheses and Complex Models

It is very clear that our research designs are becoming ever more complicated (again, see Fig. 3:1). With respect to our hypotheses and models, Garcia Coll and Magnuson (1999) summarize: "we begin to ask *new* questions in our research or *old* questions in different ways" (p. 3). We not only stretch our data collection over months, years, and decades, but also examine multiple variables at each particular point in time. In keeping with the interdisciplinary model of developmental psychopathology, researchers are including biological, psychological, and social variables in their studies (Cicchetti & Valentino, 2007). Whereas we once focused our investigations on children and their immediate environments, we now broaden our approaches to include macrosystems such as culture (Boyce et al., 1998). Always, we expect to encounter complex models of causality (Cicchetti & Dawson, 2002), with a "larger number of reciprocally related variables, and the emergence of statistical techniques that permit the analysis of

such complex processes" (Mash & Dozois, 1996, p. 35). The research on developmental cascades, just described, is one example of the combination of complex hypotheses and complex models of investigation.

Current research on child maltreatment provides other examples of complexity. Instead of examining a single variable (such as maltreatment versus no maltreatment) and its association with outcome, investigators account for multiple characteristics of that variable (type of maltreatment, frequency of maltreatment, source of maltreatment), leading to a better understanding of risk and resilience. Danielson, de Arellano, Kilpatrick, Saunders, and Resnick (2005) found that adolescents who had experienced both physical and sexual abuse reported more symptoms of depression than adolescents who had experienced only physical abuse (and adolescents who had no history of abuse). Adolescents who experienced chronic abuse were more depressed than those who experienced single abusive episodes. And girls who were maltreated were more depressed than boys who were maltreated. Another research example involves the impact of childhood trauma on neuroanatomy and neurobiology, the subsequent development of depression, and response to antidepressant treatment in adult women (Heim & Nemeroff, 2001; Kaufman, Plotsky, Nemeroff, & Charney, 2000; Vythilingam et al., 2002). Early maltreatment is hypothesized to sensitize the stress–response system; both genetic factors and subsequent caregiving may ameliorate some of the negative consequences of maltreatment (Kaufman et al., 2000).

Some of the most recent research on maltreatment has focused on the interplay between genes and the environment. In contrast to earlier descriptions of the impact of genes and the environment as separate and independent, current conceptualizations emphasize the ongoing transactions between genetic and environmental factors. These transactions are observed across many levels (e.g., cellular, neural, physiological, psychological) of analysis (Gottlieb, 2007). We now know that, in important and persistent ways, environments direct and guide development (Meaney, 2010; Stiles, 2009) and that environments must be broadly imagined (from intrauterine to cultural environments). We also know that the timing of particular environmental influences (e.g., exposure to neurotoxins, awful rearing circumstances) is important (Rutter, 2011; Sroufe, 2009; Stiles, 2009). Indeed, according to Sonuga-Barke (2010), "serious science is now more than ever focused on the power of the environment to shape neurodevelopmental processes and pathways" (p. 114).

Gene-by-environment (g × e) interactions specify the role of genetics in influencing children's vulnerability to particular risk factors. These interactions are common in both typical and atypical development (Gottlieb, 2007; Moffitt, Caspi, & Rutter, 2006; Rutter, 2011). There are various kinds of g × e interactions. With *passive correlations*, children receive both genes and environments from parents. For example, parents with mental illness may pass on high-risk genes, and they may also provide high-risk environments in which to raise children. With *active correlations*, individuals shape and select their own environments. For instance, different children (as a result of different genetic backgrounds) may choose different after-school activities (reading, playing baseball, coordinating a clothing drive for the homeless). With *evocative correlations*, how children behave (e.g., in prosocial ways, in antisocial ways) influences how others respond to them (e.g., with warmth, with distancing).

Some of the most compelling data on g × e interactions come from investigations of variation in two genes (MAOA and 5-HTT) involved in early brain development and the regulation of mood, behavior, and stress (Kim-Cohen & Gold, 2009; Moffitt et al., 2006). Key findings related to individual differences in outcomes following maltreatment suggest that poor outcomes are more likely if children display certain genetic variations (Moffitt et al., 2006). Even in the presence of both genetic and environmental risk, however, protective factors such as supportive adults may protect children from poor outcomes (Kaufman et al., 2006). In fact, there are data that suggest that the same children whose genetic background makes them vulnerable to poor outcomes in the presence of maltreatment are the same children who are especially responsive to positive environments (Kim-Cohen & Gold, 2009). This is a description of **differential susceptibility,** a construct discussed throughout the text. In addition to the emphasis on complex hypotheses and complex models, we also pay more attention to the variety of available methods for collecting data. Quantitative methods have been the standard for years, but there is renewed interest in qualitative methods such as diaries, narratives, and holistic observations (Oppenheim, 2006; Sullivan, 1998).

Research in Real-World Settings with Practical Applications

One of the more compelling aspects of research in developmental psychopathology is its concern with practical applications and public policy implications, and its focus on child advocacy (Shonkoff & Bales, 2011; Toth, Pianta, & Erickson, 2011). These concerns are at the core of discussions of **translational research,** or research designed, conducted, and interpreted with meaningful applications and social value in mind (Gunnar & Cicchetti, 2009). The goal of translational research is "to move basic findings more rapidly through the pipeline into novel treatments and preventive efforts to reduce or alleviate physical, emotional, and behavioral health problems" (Gunnar & Cichetti, 2009, p. 6). Further, "it is not enough for the basic researchers to hand their findings off to the clinicians and prevention scientists who then develop novel treatments and approaches. The information gleaned from testing those treatments and intervention programs need to feed back to inform basic research" (p. 6). Cooperation and collaboration is required: between researchers who work with animals and researchers who work with humans; between researchers who focus on adults and researchers who focus on children; between researchers who investigate typical development and researchers who investigate atypical developments; and between researchers and clinicians.

One example of such collaboration and cooperation is a research project designed to prevent maltreatment in families with a young mother living in poverty, with the Mt. Hope Family Center, the University of Rochester Medical School Departments of Pediatrics and Social Work, and the Society for the Protection and Care of Children all working together to promote healthy outcomes (Toth et al., 2011).

Key Terms

Psychopathology (p. 27)
Developmental psychopathology (p. 27)
Developmental pathways (p. 29)
Equifinality (p. 30)
Multifinality (p. 30)
Coherence (p. 32)
Competence (p. 32)
Domains of competence (p. 33)
Arenas of comfort (p. 33)
Risk (p. 34)
Risk factors (p. 34)
Resilience (p. 35)
Protective factors (p. 35)
Nonspecific risk (p. 35)
Specific risk (p. 35)
Child maltreatment (p. 36)
Cross-sectional research (p. 42)
Longitudinal research (p. 42)
Developmental cascades (p. 42)
Gene by environment (g × e) interactions (p. 44)
Translational research (p. 44)

Chapter Summary

- Developmental psychopathology focuses on the developmental context within which maladaptive patterns of emotion, cognition, and behavior occur.
- The study of developmental pathways highlights patterns of adjustment and maladjustment over time.
- Equifinality refers to developmental pathways in which differing circumstances lead to the same diagnosis, whereas multifinality refers to developmental pathways in which similar beginnings lead to different outcomes.
- The developmental pathways model emphasizes the ongoing possibility of change over time.

- Coherence in development reflects the logical links between early developmental variables and later outcomes. Continuity is found in understanding the relationship between outcomes and the variables that lead to stability or change.
- Competence, from a developmental perspective, reflects effective functioning in relation to relevant developmental tasks and issues; evaluations of competence are embedded in the environment within which development is occurring.
- Risk is defined as *increased vulnerability to disorder*, whereas risk factors are the individual, family, and social characteristics that are associated with this increased vulnerability.
- Resilience is defined as *adaptation (or competence) despite adversity*, and protective factors are the individual, family, and social characteristics that are associated with this positive adaptation.
- The study of child maltreatment illustrates the varied effects and range of outcomes associated with developmental risk factors.
- Cross-sectional research involves the collection of data from comparison groups at a single point in time. Longitudinal approaches involve the ongoing collection of data from the same individual or group of participants over time.
- The cumulative or spreading effects (both positive and negative) of ongoing developmental processes, across domains, are represented in developmental cascade models.
- Gene-by-environment interactions represent the expression of genetics in the context of life circumstances. This model is commonly used to consider children's vulnerability to particular risk factors experienced in typical and atypical development.
- The purpose of translational research is to facilitate the application of basic research to clinical practice, and to inform research with findings and insights drawn from applied practice.

4

Classification, Assessment and Diagnosis, and Intervention

ON THE ONE HAND, we have infants, children, and adolescents who are struggling, who are distressed, and who are deeply pained. On the other hand, we have theories about typical and atypical development, proposals about risk and resilience, and beliefs about psychotherapy. In this chapter, we are going to make specific and practical connections between the children and the theories. The most basic questions are addressed: What kinds of disorders do children experience? Which disorder best describes a particular child's distress and dysfunction? And what can be done to help?

Classification

Given that it is useful to conceptualize some forms of children's struggle, distress, and pain in terms of disorder, we need to have some reasonably organized way to think about the different kinds of disorders we encounter. We need classification. **Classification** is defined as a system for describing the important categories, groups, or dimensions of disorder. Classification is differentiated from **diagnosis,** which is the method of assigning children to specific classification categories.

A good classification system serves several clinical, research, and theoretical purposes (Clark, Watson, & Reynolds, 1995). It enhances clinical utility; that is, it helps clarify thinking about the expression and emergence of particular disorders, and about prognosis and treatment decisions. For example, if we know that a child's pattern of cognitive, emotional, and behavioral difficulties is consistent with the clinical presentation of autism spectrum disorder, then we know something important about the cause and course of the disorder, and we know something useful about effective interventions. Classification also allows mental health professionals to communicate effectively about their clients and various psychopathologies. If we are working with a child with autism spectrum disorder, then we can discuss the relevant options for treatment with other clinicians, or school personnel, or representatives from insurance companies.

Classification also improves research efforts. Different investigators with similar understandings of disorders are better able to develop theories about the nature of specific psychopathologies, explain hypotheses, recruit participants, and talk about data. As a result, there are many specialized journals, conferences, and institutes focused on single disorders. Finally, efforts to improve classification contribute to the ongoing revisions of the principles and practices of developmental psychopathology discussed in the previous chapter. Across all of these classification purposes, we want to create and/ or increase order and organization.

As we consider various classification schemes, it is important to keep in mind that any classification results in the loss of individual information. Classification in developmental psychopathology is focused on the many ways in which children with particular disorders are *alike.* But we know, of course, that each child is unique in his or her pattern of difficulties (and strengths). Knowing, for instance, that a child displays the distress and dysfunction associated with depression (in contrast to anxiety) is one significant source of information, but it is also important to evaluate each depressed child's unique circumstances.

Categorical (Clinical) Classification

Categorical, clinical classification depends on identifying sets of symptoms that co-occur (or hang together) and that collectively are best understood as distinct, different disorders (similar to the idea of discontinuous models discussed in Chapter 2). **Categorical classification** assumes that there are groups of individuals with relatively similar patterns of disorder. With an ideal categorical scheme, each of the disorders would have its own specific etiology, course, and treatments.

The Diagnostic and Statistical Manual

The best known—although far from ideal—example of such classification is the **Diagnostic and Statistical Manual** (the **DSM**) of the American Psychiatric Association. Introduced in 1952, the DSM was designed as a practical tool for clinicians. Despite that era's pervasive psychoanalytic influence, the DSM was intended to be atheoretical and primarily descriptive, providing useful information about the clinical picture and the course of psychopathology. The DSM is tied, in large part, to the **medical model** of psychopathology. Key assumptions of the medical model are that (1) disorders are categorical (i.e., reflecting clear distinctions between healthy and disordered adjustments); (2) disorders are associated with "constitutional dysfunction" (i.e., the idea that the child somehow fails to display his/her natural function) (Wakefield, 1992, 1997); and (3) disorders are endogenous (i.e., characteristic of the individual, rather than an individual–environment transaction).

The 1952 DSM included only one separate childhood disorder, adjustment reaction of childhood and adolescence, listed in the section on "transient situational disorders." All other classifications of children's disorders were understood as identical to adult disorders, with the same clinical presentation and prognosis. DSM-II, published in 1968, included nine different disorders observed in children, with two of them, mental retardation and childhood schizophrenia, in a separate childhood section. By 1980, with DSM-III (and 1987, with DSM-III-Revised), 44 child and adolescent disorders were described, with a much larger section specifically focused on disorders diagnosed in early development. DSM-III introduced the system of multiple axes, in which individuals were evaluated with respect to clinical symptoms as well as important contextual factors such as physical disease and level of stress. Following extensive literature reviews, data analyses, and field trials, DSM-IV was presented in 1994, with over 350 different categories of adult and child disorders. DSM-IV again increased the number of classification categories for children and made special efforts to incorporate more developmental data. In 2000, DSM-IV-TR (Text Revision) was distributed (with additional information provided about many disorders, but with few changes to diagnostic categories or criteria).

The newest version, DSM-5, published in 2013, includes more significant reorganization and revisions. For example, there is no longer a separate axis for disorders diagnosed in childhood; those disorders are now integrated throughout the manual. For many categories (e.g., autism spectrum disorders and personality disorders), there are important changes to the conceptualization and description of disorder. These changes will be discussed throughout this text.

With any system of classification, we are concerned with indices of reliability and validity. **Reliability** has to do with whether different clinicians, using the same set of criteria, classify children into the same clearly defined categories. **Interrater reliability** is noted when, for example, two or more clinical psychologists, gathering information about one child's developmental history and current difficulties, come to the same decision about the type of disorder. **Cross-time reliability** is noted when a child is similarly classified by the same clinician at two different points in time. Especially for disorders that are understood as chronic, such as intellectual developmental disability (i.e., mental retardation), a classification system that includes descriptions of both continuity and change is important. With a reliable classification system, a child with intellectual developmental disorder would be similarly classified at age 3 and at age 10, even though there would be somewhat different patterns of symptoms and adjustments.

How reliable is the DSM? Given the complexity of the construct of reliability, it is difficult to provide a clear and convincing response. Still, with each successive edition of the DSM, reliability has increased. With increasingly specific criteria for classification, interrater reliability has improved. With more developmental data, cross-time reliability has also improved. But, as always, clinical efforts continue to focus on better applications of the categorical system.

Validity has to do with whether the classification gives us true-to-life, meaningful information. Specifically, **internal validity** tells us something important about the etiology of a disorder, or the core patterns of symptoms or difficulties experienced by children with a particular type or subtype of disorder. **External validity** tells us something important about the implications of the disorder. For example, children with specific disorders might be expected to respond favorably to certain interventions.

How valid is the DSM? Validity, like reliability, is a difficult construct to evaluate. Some categories, such as schizophrenia, have long been presented as types of dysfunction and distress. Other categories, such as disorders of attachment, reflect newer conceptualizations of maladjustment. Ongoing research on some disorders, such as autism spectrum disorders, has led to frequent revision of the general category of disorder as well as the specific diagnostic criteria. Thus, we cannot make definitively positive statements about the internal and external validity of the whole DSM system, although there are categories with better validity support than others. For our purposes, we emphasize the valuable work that continues to address the increasing validity of various child classifications (Beauchaine, 2003; Lahey et al., 2004; Ollendick & Vasey, 1999; Sonuga-Barke, 1998).

Dimensional (Empirical) Classification

The DSM approach initially grew out of the subjective impressions and descriptions of experienced clinicians. Over the years, a more objective strategy for conceptualizing disorder has emerged (for both the DSM and other classification systems). Achenbach (1997) characterizes this empirical approach to classification as a bottom-up process involving (1) the collection of data from children with normal and abnormal adjustments followed by (2) attempts to statistically group the many distresses and dysfunctions into meaningful dimensions (or important characteristics) of disorder. This process contrasts with the top-down approach of clinical classification, which involves (1) the identification of types of disorder and then (2) the specification of symptoms of the disorders. Owing much to

Achenbach's decades-long work, this type of classification is based on statistical techniques that identify key dimensions of children's functioning and dysfunction, with the assumption that all children can be usefully described along these dimensions. Differences among children, then, reflect *differences in degree* (or quantity) of a dimension rather than *differences in kinds* of dimensions. Benefits of this type of classification include reduction of the large number of categories of disorder to fewer dimensions (Clark et al., 1995) and a better reflection of the reality of continuous models of adjustment and maladjustment (Sonuga-Barke, 1998).

The two most commonly identified dimensions of disorder include (1) an **externalizing dimension,** with undercontrolled behaviors such as oppositional or aggressive behaviors that are often directed at others; and (2) an **internalizing dimension,** with overcontrolled behaviors such as anxiety or social isolation that are often directed toward the self. A child would be diagnosed with a disorder when he or she exceeded a certain number of symptoms or presented a pattern of symptoms that reflected significant impairment. In addition to the basic internalizing versus externalizing distinction, more recent descriptions of important narrow dimensions include the following: *withdrawal, somatic complaints, social problems, thought problems, aggressive behavior, delinquent behavior, attention problems,* and *anxious/depressed problems.*

Analyses of these more specific dimensions also take into account age and gender differences in the experience and expression of difficulties. Children may display distress and dysfunction that reflects mostly internalizing difficulties (e.g., a combination of anxious/depressed problems and somatic complaints), mostly externalizing difficulties (e.g., a combination of social problems and aggressive behavior), or a mixture of both (e.g., attention problems, aggressive behavior, and anxious/depressed problems). Figure 4:1 illustrates one way that internalizing and externalizing dimensions might be mapped. Children low on both internalizing and externalizing dimensions would include a variety of typically developing children. Children with moderate scores on either or both internalizing or externalizing dimensions might warrant extra attention but would not necessarily meet clinical or statistical criteria for actual psychopathology. Only those children with extreme scores on either or both dimensions would be diagnosed with a disorder.

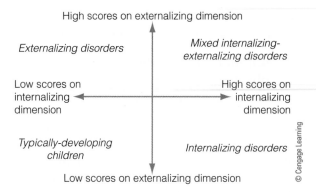

FIGURE 4:1 Children's psychopathology along internalizing and externalizing dimensions.

More recent statistical analyses of the structure of children's psychopathology suggest a combined dimensional–categorical model, with a hierarchical organization that takes into account both genetic and environmental influences (Lahey, D'Onofrio, & Waldman, 2009; Lahey, Van Hulle, Singh, Waldman, & Rathouz, 2011) (see Fig. 4:2). These investigations provide important data that help explain some of the overlapping symptoms in many of the DSM categories, as well as the mixed clinical picture displayed by many children and adolescents (Angold & Costello, 2009; Lahey et al., 2008). Other investigations emphasize identifying the continuity between

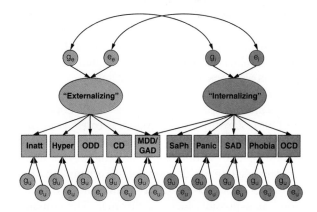

FIGURE 4:2 A testable working model of the hierarchical causal structure of child and adolescent psychopathology. Shared environmental influences are omitted to simplify illustration, but could be included in the model if needed.

Source: Using Epidemiological Methods To Test Hypotheses Regarding Causal Influences On Child and Adolescent Mental Disorders, Lahey, B.B., D'Onofrio, B.M., and Waldman, I.D. Copyright © 2009 The Journal of Child Psychology and Psychiatry. Reproduced with permission of John Wiley & Sons Inc.

child and adult disorder (e.g., along an externalizing dimension of psychopathology) (Tackett, 2010).

Developmental Contributions to Classification Systems

Beginning with early attempts to devise useful descriptions of psychopathology, the focus has been on the classification of adult disorders. For accurate classification of child disorders, it is necessary to integrate a developmental perspective into classification systems, emphasizing salient age- and stage-related concerns as well as continuity and change in clinical difficulties (Achenbach, 1997; Angold & Costello, 2009; Jensen, Knapp, & Mrazek, 2006; Sroufe & Rutter, 1984). This developmental perspective is most frequently observed when, as described in the previous chapter, clinicians conceptualize children's disorders as delay, fixation, or deviance (Fischer et al., 1997). These kinds of conceptualizations depend on a clear understanding of what is typical during particular periods of development and provide one important way to describe development that is off track. But there are other frameworks for examining the way in which children's disorders are embedded in a developmental context.

One example of a classification scheme that illustrates the connections between typical and atypical development is the Diagnostic Classification of Mental Health and Developmental Disorders of Infancy and Early Childhood, published by the Zero to Three Association (1994, 2005). Unlike the DSM, a product of mainly one group of mental health professionals (i.e., psychiatrists), the Zero to Three manual reflects the contributions of multiple disciplines, including psychology, social work, nursing, early education, as well as medical specialties (Egger & Emde, 2011). Like the DSM, Zero to Three's system is categorical. But the Zero to Three system, focused exclusively on the earliest manifestations of psychopathology, is much more explicit in its developmental orientation. For example, the child–caregiver relationship is understood as a possible locus of disorder. The clinician considers (a) the behavioral quality of the relationship between the child and caregiver, (b) the emotional tone of the relationship, and (c) the degree of psychological involvement. This approach recognizes that very young children's "sense of self and of their place in the world is shaped at its very core by the interactions with those who have major responsibility for their care" (Lieberman, Wieder, & Fenichel, 1997, p. 11). Although a number of analyses of the reliability

Developmental contributions to classification emphasize the ways in which relationship factors influence the development of problems and disorders.

© Knauer/Johnston/Getty Images

and validity of the Zero to Three system have been completed, much more remains to be done (Egger & Emde, 2011).

Another perspective on developmental approaches to classification involves explicit appreciation of the principles and practices of developmental psychopathology (summarized in Chapter 3). Yates, Burt, and Troy (2011) describe several ways to improve classification efforts. The first is an emphasis on *developmental pathways* and increased focus on the timing of the disorder's onset. Whether a disorder has an early versus a later onset may point toward different etiological factors or provide information about well-timed interventions. The second way to improve classification is to focus on *age-salient references*, with better understanding of the expression and meaning of disorder given a child's age, developmental challenges, and available resources. Another way to improve classification is to include *multilevel analyses*, with consideration of genetic, physiological, psychological, familial, and sociocultural influences on the emergence and maintenance of disorder.

Cultural Contributions to Classification Systems

In Chapter 2, sociocultural models of child development, psychopathology, and treatment were described. Culture also influences systems of classification. There are many reviews of the impact of culture on adult disorder, but our emphasis is on work related to child and adolescent classification (Harkness & Super, 2000; Weisz, McCarty, Eastman, Chaiyasit, & Suwanlert, 1997; Weisz, Weiss, Suwanlert, & Chaiyasit, 2006). The major concern is how well the classification categories or dimensions of disorder account for children's distress and dysfunction in different cultures or subcultures. A review by Verhulst and Achenbach (1995) suggests that current classifications are, in fact, both relevant and robust across different cultures. Verhulst and Achenbach conclude that, with respect to a variety of cultures, there are only small differences in both the estimates of disorder and the underlying dimensions of disorder in children, and there is overall similarity associated with gender and SES factors. One recent investigation of 30 societies confirmed the overall similarity of the eight dimensions previously described in the section on dimensional approaches (Ivanova et al., 2007). Still, we need to be aware of ongoing research in the area of cultural variations and make refinements in classifications as necessary (Alarcon et al., 2002; Pine et al., 2002; Weisz et al., 2006).

The Phenomenon of Comorbidity

So far, our discussion has implicitly assumed that a classification system involves such distinctive categories that any particular child at a particular point in time can be reliably and validly described as having one—and only one—disorder. But the reality is otherwise. For multiple reasons, we must consider comorbidity. **Comorbidity,** a phenomenon that has received much attention in recent years, can be defined in several related ways. The simplest, most straightforward definition of comorbidity involves the co-occurrence of two or more disorders in one individual. Here, a child might be struggling with *any* two disorders: a mood disorder *and* a substance abuse disorder, or an anxiety disorder *and* an eating disorder.

Another way that researchers and clinicians have defined comorbidity involves the co-occurrence of two or more disorders where the co-occurrence is greater than chance (Costello, Foley, & Angold, 2006; Cramer, Waldorp, van der Maas, & Borsboom, 2010; Lilienfeld, Waldman, & Israel, 1994). That is, we are not looking for *any* two disorders, but rather two disorders that are frequently observed together. This definition makes explicit the idea that comorbid conditions are not random. In fact, there are many "systematic comorbidities." Common, nonrandom pairings in children include attention deficit/hyperactivity disorder and conduct disorder, autism and intellectual developmental disorder, and depression and anxiety.

Just to make the definitional issues as interesting (or as complicated) as possible, there are a few other variations on the basic definitions (Angold, Costello, & Erkanli, 1999). The first variation takes into account whether there is **homotypic comorbidity,** or two or more diagnoses within a classification group (for example, two different anxiety disorders), or **heterotypic comorbidity,** or diagnoses from different classification groups (for instance, depression and conduct disorder). Finally, we might consider whether disorders are experienced at the same time, as with **concurrent comorbidity,** or whether disorders are experienced sequentially, one after the other, as with **successive comorbidity.**

No matter what definition we use, "Comorbidity is the rule, not the exception" (Sroufe, 1997, p. 257). In community samples of adults, half of persons with one disorder also have another disorder (Clark et al., 1995). And the picture is similar for children and adolescents. Pure, unmixed cases are infrequent occurrences. Given this situation, we need to look closely at the factors that are related to decisions about comorbidity.

Inaccurate Decisions About Comorbidity

Comorbidity is affected by a number of factors related to classification issues, methodological considerations, and developmental concerns. These factors can be sources of error, or they can be sources of valid information. Childhood disorders may be difficult to differentiate because of the imperfections of all classification schemes (Clark et al., 1995). That is, given that all classification emphasizes group similarities rather than unique variations, some children are not going to match up well with strictly defined categories. The clinical picture for these children may include a mix of symptoms from different disorders. Clinicians may then diagnose two disorders, neither of which is quite right (or quite wrong). These kinds of errors occur because of categories that do not allow for much individual variation. Alternatively, categories that are too loosely or vaguely defined, with lots of symptom overlap among categories, also contribute to the appearance of comorbidity (Clark et al., 1995). So some children may meet multiple sets of criteria. These errors occur because there is not enough detail or specification.

For methodological considerations, we are chiefly concerned with the people who are filling out forms (i.e., informant-related factors) and the forms themselves (i.e., instrument-related factors). Informant-related factors have to do with whether individuals (children, parents, or teachers) who report particular patterns of symptoms are more likely to also report other negative symptoms. The tendency to report any and all negative symptoms may lead to many additional—and inaccurate—instances of comorbidity. Instrument-related factors have to do with whether the tools of assessment, rather than the disorders themselves, contribute to the number of cases.

Accurate Decisions About Comorbidity

In contrast to factors related to error, there are factors that influence valid instances of comorbidity. Krueger, Silva, Caspi, and Moffitt (1998) suggest that comorbidity may reflect "core psychopathological processes." In other words, the same underlying vulnerability may be a general risk factor for a number of disorders. For example, a child might be deficient in the ability to interpret emotional signals from other people. This deficiency may hinder the child's early relationships with parents and with peers. The later emergence of oppositional defiant disorder, depression, and/or conduct problems directed at peers might all relate back to the initial psychopathological process.

Nottelmann and Jensen (1995) present a different set of hypotheses related to comorbidity. They first propose that comorbid disorders "may reflect amorphous, nonspecific expressions of psychopathology in younger children" (p. 110). That is, younger children appear to have multiple difficulties because they are observed at a point in time when particular patterns of symptoms have not yet coalesced. In these cases, we expect that specific problems will become more differentiated with age. So a 6-year-old child exhibiting angry, defiant behavior, numerous fears, and problems with friends may become

the 10-year-old child whose presenting symptoms are organized more coherently and consistently as generalized anxiety disorder. More recent investigation of this hypothesis suggests that, although some differentiation of psychopathology over development occurs for some disorders, differentiation does not contribute much to explanations of comorbidity (Sterba et al., 2010).

Nottelmann and Jensen also suggest that comorbid disorders "could be a developmentally influenced, transient phenomenon. . . . Thus, one disorder may be the early manifestation of another" (pp. 110–111). For example, some adolescent girls with conduct disorder eventually are diagnosed with depression in adulthood. Many investigators have hypothesized that these women are still dealing with the same underlying difficulties with which they struggled in adolescence, but that time and experience may alter the "surface variation" of the disorder (Waldman & Lilienfeld, 2001).

Nottelmann and Jensen provide one additional possibility, that comorbid disorders may come about because one disorder compromises functioning in such a way that a second disorder also develops (successive comorbidity). For instance, disorders of attachment in the early years increase the likelihood that other types of psychopathology will emerge in later years, including conduct disorders, personality disorders, and depression. Given that the long-term effects of comorbidity include greater severity of disorder, more complicated courses, and more negative outcomes, it is encouraging that ongoing research continues to refine the methods and systems of classification.

Assessment and Diagnosis

Definitions of Assessment and Diagnosis

In order to evaluate a child, we need some orderly way of gathering information. **Assessment** involves the systematic collection of relevant information and is used to solve two kinds of practical problems described by Costello and Angold (1996): (1) differentiating everyday problems or transient difficulties from clinically significant psychopathology, and (2) classifying and caring for those who have been identified as having disorders.

The first practical problem for assessment involves a decision about whether diagnosis is necessary or appropriate, and necessitates thinking about disorder within a developmental framework (Emde, Bingham, & Harmon, 1993). After collecting information about a child's various difficulties (and strengths), current distress and dysfunction (and achievements), and likely outcomes, a clinician may conclude that a child is functioning within the normal range or is experiencing a "bump-in-the-road" kind of problem. In these cases, although advice or support may be provided, a diagnosis might not be made. In other cases, a clinician may become convinced that the child displays more serious maladaptation. Assessment, then, would likely result in a specific diagnosis.

The second practical problem involves the method of assigning individuals to specific classification categories, or diagnosis. Diagnosis becomes particularly important when psychologists or other mental health professionals talk to parents about the nature of their child's disorder, when clinical decisions about treatments have to be made, or when insurance companies require verification of a disorder in order to approve reimbursements for the cost of care. With respect to these practical issues, assessment certainly depends on gathering information about the specific distress and dysfunction experienced by a child, but it also must include information about a child's strengths and accomplishments. We need to know what a child does well, not only to help with accurate diagnosis, but also to provide valuable insights about more effective plans for treatment.

After evaluating the intensity, frequency, duration, and pattern of difficulties in a developmental context, we need to decide what the best fit is between the clinical presentation and available classification categories. When choosing the correct category, it is also important to consider whether a child's clinical presentation reflects a single case of disorder, an atypical or mixed symptom case, or a combination of comorbid conditions. At times, DSM-5 classification requires clinicians to make **differential diagnoses:** decisions about mutually exclusive categories of disorder. For example, a child would not receive a diagnosis of oppositional defiant disorder *and* disruptive mood dysregulation disorder, because the defining symptoms of the former are subsumed in the larger symptom set of the latter. Overall, researchers and clinicians are concerned with **diagnostic efficiency,** the degree to which clinicians maximize diagnostic hits and minimize diagnostic misses.

With all of these diagnostic issues in mind, it is important to remember that we will always have more children with more kinds of problems than we have categories in which to place them. But as we continue to improve classification and diagnosis, we must emphasize that naming a disorder, or diagnosing a child, is not the same thing as understanding the disorder or the child. Naming is the first step, not the only step. In addition, we need to remember that assigning a particular child's disorder to a classification category is accomplished at *a moment in time.* Because children change and continue to develop after a diagnosis is made, diagnoses must be periodically reviewed and reevaluated.

A final concern about diagnosis relates to the effects of labeling. As discussed at the end of Chapter 1, the stigmatization of mental illness is difficult for children and their families to manage. According to Lieberman et al. (1997, p. 12), "It is essential to remember that people are not defined by their psychiatric diagnoses. Individuals may have a disorder, but they also possess a core human dignity as well as areas of experiences where they function flexibly, competently, and creatively." The effects of labeling are often viewed as damaging. For example, we are concerned with the self-fulfilling prophecy of children who internalize adult expectations for struggle or failure given a particular diagnosis (such as autism spectrum disorder or attention deficit/hyperactivity disorder), or with the potential for adults to mischaracterize them as "alphabet children" who receive diagnosis (ADHD) after diagnosis (LD) after diagnosis (ODD) (Baum & Olenchak, 2002).

We must also recognize, however, that labels may have some positive impact (Egger & Emde, 2011). Parents who have been confused and upset by their children's behavior, who have questioned their own competence, and who have despaired over their children's futures may view labels as providing "validation and legitimation of their experience" (Klasen, 2000). Labels may also provide both parents and children with knowledge about ways to deal with the difficulties of disorders. Given these multiple perspectives, negotiation among professionals, parents, and children for particular labels with particular meanings is an ever-present issue.

Methods and Processes of Assessment

The Case of Alicia

Alicia is a 9-year-old fourth grader referred for a psychological evaluation by her parents at the suggestion of her teacher. Alicia began to experience school difficulties in third grade that continued into fourth grade and that have gotten considerably worse as the school year goes on. She has difficulties with work completion, especially on long-term projects, and often fails to turn in assignments; her grades are consistently lower than what either her parents or her teachers believe she is capable of. ■■

The Case of David

David is a 12-year-old sixth grader referred by his parents for evaluation. David currently resists going to school in the mornings due to his extreme and disabling anxiety. He also experiences severe headaches before leaving home. Socially, David has become increasingly isolated from his classmates, and generally plays alone or with a neighbor who is 2 years younger than David. ■■

The Case of Tyler

Tyler is a 4½-year-old boy referred for assessment and therapy by his pediatrician after noting that Tyler and his mother's interactions in the office were characterized by frustration and conflict. Additional concerns expressed by Tyler's mother and his day care provider included oppositionality, frequent temper tantrums, and occasional physical aggression. There have been several instances when Tyler has kicked and bitten others at preschool and at home. ■■

In the real world, clinical assessments begin with a specific concern, question, or problem. In the above cases, we think about whether Alicia's school difficulties are the result of anxiety, attention deficit/hyperactivity disorder, or a learning disorder. We think about whether David's distress is best characterized as anxiety or depression, whether it is going to resolve on its own, and available options for treatment. We think about whether Tyler's dysfunction reflects the emergence of a more severe psychopathology such as disruptive mood dysregulation disorder, which requires intensive intervention, or whether we are dealing with less severe psychopathology, such as oppositional defiant disorder, which calls for treatment focused on temperament and parenting issues.

These specific concerns influence the assessment strategy that is devised, but most assessments also include a more general overview of the child's circumstances. Clinicians should, of course, respond to the presenting concern, but need to remain alert to many kinds of contextual information, other possible problems, and the child's positive characteristics. A narrow focus early on in the assessment process may lead to diagnostic error, with a quick confirmation of the initial hypothesis without consideration of alternatives.

Assessment Technique: The Interview

Assessments usually begin with **interviews**. Initial interviews allow parents and children to explain their concerns and, more broadly, to tell their stories. Interviews also provide opportunities to start to build the helping relationship, an especially important consideration when a clinician knows that he or she will be working closely with various family members. There are many potential informants for interviews, with different perspectives and agendas. Each informant provides "unique and indispensable" information (Verhulst, Dekker, & van der Ende, 1997), even when the information varies somewhat from person to person. Clinicians are interested in the areas of agreement among informants as well as areas of disagreement; both kinds of information can be useful. Whenever possible, interviews are conducted with both parents. Parents are able to provide helpful data about their children and, in many cases, are the ones most likely to detect problems in their early stages (Glascoe, 1995, 2000). Parental and family characteristics, such as psychopathology and life events, are important to keep in mind, however, because these kinds of characteristics appear to affect their ratings of their children's functioning. Parents who struggle with their own mental illnesses or with economic hardship, for instance, have lower thresholds for identifying behavior as problematic (Verhulst & van der Ende, 1997; Youngstrom, Loeber, & Stouthamer-Loeber, 2000). And again, clinicians would do well to attend to the parents' and families' strengths as well as their limitations, because they may have important implications for diagnosis and treatment. Keep in mind that, as with all health care relationships, children and parents "mostly want us to tell them what is wrong, what to do to suffer less, and to listen and speak with kindness and respect" (March, 2009, p. 171).

Research suggests that mothers and fathers provide somewhat different data. For example, Achenbach, Howell, Quay, and Conners (1991) found that mothers report more problems than do fathers. In another study, mothers and fathers reported similar numbers of problems, but different types of problems, with fathers more concerned with cognitive difficulties (Hay et al., 1999). In the Hay et al. study, mothers' and fathers' reports were associated with different kinds of adjustments years later, with fathers' reports correlated with school problems and mothers' reports correlated with difficult parental and family relationships.

Accurate assessment of children may also need to take into account the cultural background of parents and families (Achenbach & Rescorla, 2007; Hoagwood & Jensen, 1997). Parents from certain cultures may be more sensitive to internalizing or externalizing kinds of problems in children (Achenbach & Rescorla, 2007; Weisz, Sigman, Weiss, & Mosk, 1993). Parents may also differ with respect to the levels of concern they display, with some parents more likely to believe that their children will improve over time (Weisz et al., 1988, 1991). As noted, some of the most important aspects of communication between mental health professionals and parents are to help them make sense of their situation and to keep them engaged with and supportive of their children. According to Yates et al. (2011), the "developmental formulation paints a hopeful picture in which there is an enduring capacity for change and, even in the midst of extreme maladaptation, a shared humanity in which we are all more alike than we are different" (Yates et al., 2011, p. 256).

In the interview with Alicia's parents, they emphasized that school is becoming increasingly stressful for both Alicia and for them, with much more time spent closely monitoring assignments, homework, and teacher concerns. In addition, Alicia has begun to complain about stomach aches and has missed school as a result. Alicia's mother and father are particularly upset about the fact that Alicia has lied to them about schoolwork because they have always felt that they could trust their daughter. Alicia's parents also provided information about the extended family, noting that two of Alicia's cousins have been diagnosed with attention deficit/hyperactivity disorder. They believe that Alicia does not display the increased activity or impulsiveness observed in these other children. In contrast to these recent difficulties, her parents report that Alicia seemed relaxed and happy during the summer and enjoys playing with her younger sister and in community sports programs. When the focus is not on school, Alicia can be very pleasant and is able to entertain herself for long periods of time coloring and doing crafts.

David's parents noted that, in addition to seeming anxious, he is increasingly irritable at home, and angry and aggressive when frustrated. They described David as having a "short fuse" and as being both oppositional and inflexible. They also reported that

the summer prior to this school year, David seemed to lose interest and enjoyment in his usual activities.

Tyler's mother reported that he had been a difficult infant, easily upset and difficult to comfort. His infancy was a challenging time for her because she was in the middle of ending an abusive relationship. She reported that by the age of 2, Tyler was consistently aggressive with others and seemed especially stressed in social situations. She talked about feeling very guilty about her current anger and resentment toward Tyler. She said that although she does love Tyler, she no longer expects to have a pleasant and easy time with him and is resigned to the belief that each day with him will be a struggle. She also acknowledged that she feels exhausted and impatient, and despairs of finding anything helpful in dealing with her son.

Interviews with children are also critical sources of information, although the types of interviews conducted with David, Alicia, and Tyler are going to be very different. The format of child interviews ranges from structured play to highly planned sets of questions to open-ended conversations, and takes into account characteristics such as age and whether the child is comfortable interacting with a clinician apart from parents (Angold & Fisher, 1999). Even the youngest children with limited verbal skills can be expected to provide unique assessment data through, for example, their behavioral and play patterns (Sessa, Avenevoli, Steinberg, & Morris, 2001). And, again, areas of agreement and disagreement between parents and their children provide an important perspective (Hope et al., 1999; Jensen et al., 1999; see Box 4:1).

In the interview with 9-year-old Alicia, she was subdued and reluctant to talk at first, but was easily reassured and quickly became more open and communicative. Alicia is very aware of her current school difficulties and said she thinks she needs to try harder. Alicia said that she tries to pay attention in class, but when she later tries to complete assignments at home, she has forgotten what the teacher talked about. She acknowledges that she has sometimes told her parents that she does not have homework because the work is too hard and she wants to have more free time at home. Alicia was able to describe a number of activities she enjoys, including time spent with a best friend, and talked excitedly about a planned trip with her family. Alicia did describe trouble falling asleep at night because she is worried about things such as upcoming tests and about someone breaking into the house. When this happens, she leaves her room and crawls into bed with her parents.

BOX 4:1 THE CHILD IN CONTEXT

Agreement and Disagreement Between Parents and Children

When thinking about the assessment of a child or adolescent, it makes sense that gathering data from multiple sources provides a more accurate clinical picture than gathering data from a single source. That is, the pieces of information provided by a child, coupled with those provided by a parent, accompanied by additional pieces from a teacher, should—like a puzzle—result in a meaningful, interlocking whole. Unfortunately, this is not a common outcome. Indeed, one of the most consistent research findings related to assessment is that individuals who provide information seldom agree with one another about the type, scope, or cause of the difficulties (De Los Reyes & Kazdin, 2005; Hawley & Weisz, 2003; Youngstrom, Findling, & Calabrese, 2003). Parents disagree with children, mothers disagree with fathers, and teachers disagree with students.

Given the fact that few children and adolescents refer themselves for psychotherapy, it is hardly surprising that when they find themselves in the office of a mental health professional they rarely agree with adult perceptions of themselves or their difficulties. We might hope that once more formal assessment takes place, some of the disagreements might be resolved. However, at this time, "there is no single measure or method of assessing psychopathology in children that provides a definitive or 'gold standard' to gauge which children are experiencing a given set of problems" (De Los Reyes & Kazdin, 2005, p. 483). These circumstances contribute to a pervasive clinical dilemma: *over three-quarters of parent–child–therapist triads fail to agree about a single target problem* (Hawley & Weisz, 2003). Disagreements must be acknowledged and addressed because failure to agree about the nature of

the problems or the goals of treatment is likely associated with poor outcomes (Ferdinand, van der Ende, & Verhulst, 2004).

Both child and parent factors influencing lack of agreement have been investigated. Lack of agreement is *not* reliably associated with either child age or gender; and although there is some evidence that children and adolescents attempt to portray themselves and their adjustments in the most positive light, these data are also not always replicated (De Los Reyes & Kazdin, 2005). The Attribution Bias Context (ABC) Model detailed by De Los Reyes and Kazdin hypothesizes that parents, in general, focus more on child dispositions, whereas children focus more on external explanations for current difficulties. Other parent factors are associated with additional complications. Parental psychopathology (such as depression), for example, may lead to more negative ratings of children and their struggles (Chi & Hinshaw, 2002). The type of disorder also plays a part. Better rates of agreement between parents and children, and between mothers and fathers, are documented for observable, externalizing problems (De Los Reyes & Kazdin, 2005; Duhig, Renk, Epstein, & Phares, 2000; Yeh & Weisz, 2001).

Clinicians tend to agree with parents more often than with children or adolescents (De Los Reyes & Kazdin, 2005; Hawley & Weisz, 2003). Even so, they must actively reconcile conflicting information, perspectives, and motives. This reconciliation must occur during the initial phases of the assessment and treatment process in order to facilitate engagement and cooperation from all participants and to prepare for the development of the therapeutic alliance.

In the interview with 12-year-old David, he acknowledges that he does not like to go to school, which he describes as "mostly boring." He says he used to do well in school but does not talk about his accomplishments with any sense of pride or joy. He disputes his parents' description of his behavior at home, saying that he would prefer to be left alone but that his parents are "always bugging me about everything" and that he gets upset. David said that he frequently worries that he will get sick in school and throw up in the classroom. This worry has led him to go to the school nurse almost every day and to resist going to school at all if he thinks he might be feeling

ill. In response to questions about his interests, David said that he used to like playing baseball and practicing piano. Now, however, he describes these as "boring and dumb" and has dropped both activities.

In the interview with 4½-year-old Tyler, he was briefly seen alone, and then with his mother. Tyler had no difficulty separating from his mother and played enthusiastically but impulsively with various toys in the office. He generally ignored the clinician and rebuffed attempts to engage in shared play activities. When joined by his mother, Tyler became somewhat more active, impulsive, and aggressive. At one point, he hit his mother with a toy car and laughed. Tyler's mother told him that he had hurt her, and that if he did it again, she would not allow him to watch television when they got home.

Assessment Technique: The Standardized Test

In addition to the rich information that can be gathered from interviews, data from **standardized tests** are almost always part of an assessment. Standardized tests are assessments in which the data from a particular child can be compared to data gathered from large samples of children, including normally developing children and children with a variety of diagnoses. Results from standardized tests are often evaluated with respect to specific age and gender characteristics. That is, a result from a 5-year-old girl is compared to the results of other young girls, and a result from a 14-year-old boy is compared to the results of other adolescent boys. The most common standardized tests are rating scales, checklists, and

Psychological assessments of children often include standardized tests.

basic questionnaires completed by parents and adolescents. These are global measures of personality functioning and problem areas, such as the widely used Child Behavior Check List (Achenbach & Edelbrock, 1983; Achenbach, 1991), which has many forms and numerous translations (see Box 4:2).

Other common standardized tests include measures of general cognitive or intellectual functioning such as the Wechsler Intelligence Scales for Children or the Stanford-Binet. Neurological and neuropsychological evaluations are sometimes part of the standardized assessment plan. There are also tests that are domain specific, focusing on a particular disorder such as depression or anxiety. The Reynolds Child Depression Scale and the Reynolds Adolescent Depression Scale are examples of self-report tests that take the age of the child into account when asking particular types of questions and in phrasing the questions.

Other traditional measures of personality and clinical symptoms would include **projective measures** such as the Rorschach inkblots and the Thematic Apperception Test (TAT), a story-telling task. Projective measures are based on the assumption that, given an ambiguous stimulus, individuals' responses will reflect the *projection* of unconscious conflicts. Although academic researchers frequently decry the continued use of projective measures, given the relatively poor data on their reliability and validity (Garb, Wood, Lilienfeld, & Nezworski, 2002), clinicians counter that these measures often allow us to engage children in ways that enable them to talk about difficult feelings or experiences indirectly, and in ways that are developmentally more familiar and appropriate.

Assessment Technique: Observation

Another source of valuable information comes from **observations** made by the clinician. Clinicians usually observe children in clinical settings such as offices but may also observe children in naturalistic settings such as the home or school. These behavioral observations can provide specific sorts of contextual data, including analyses of what comes before, and what follows, a child's dysfunctional behavior. Observations may also be more encompassing. For example, a clinician might focus on evaluating children's relationships to determine whether the relationship is itself the cause of disorder, or how it plays a part in the maintenance of a child's disturbance.

A number of structured observations make use of an explicit developmental framework (Yates

BOX 4:2 CLINICAL PERSPECTIVES

Summary of Information Provided by the CBCL

The Child Behavior Checklist (CBCL) (Achenbach, 1991) is a common measurement instrument used to assess the clinical significance of a wide range of potentially problematic behaviors. The 112 items on the CBCL were factor analyzed to empirically generate scales representing a variety of clinical problems. These scales are organized into two larger dimensions: internalizing and externalizing problems. The accompanying table shows these two broad dimensions and the specific scales that contribute to each of them.

It is important to note that the names of the specific scales are simply descriptive labels for the group of items that clustered together in the factor analysis. They are not diagnostic labels for underlying psychopathology. For each scale, both a raw score and a T-score are generated. The T-score provides a way of considering the extent of a problem as a point on a continuous scale, whereas cutoff points (reflecting normal, borderline, and clinical scores) allow for more discrete judgments to be made.

In addition to the CBCL, which is typically completed by a parent, there are teacher report and youth self-report forms of the checklist as well. These different forms allow for the consideration of various perspectives on the youth's functioning.

INTERNALIZING	EXTERNAL-IZING	TOTAL SCORE
Withdrawn	Delinquent	Composite of All Scales
Somatic Complaints	Aggressive Behavior	
Anxious/Depressed		

et al., 2011). For example, the Disruptive Behavior Diagnostic Observation Schedule (Wakschlag, Tolan, & Leventhal, 2010) is intended to distinguish the "terrible twos and threes" from more serious behavior difficulties in young children. As a developmentally informed assessment, it is designed to elicit atypical examples of problem behavior. Structured observations also address the context *specificity* of problem behaviors, problem behaviors that appear in one context and not another (e.g., at home and not at preschool; or at preschool and not at home) (Yates et al., 2011).

Because many of the initial concerns about children are related to school functioning, teachers and schools can be important sources of clinical data. In some cases, teachers complete parallel forms of parent questionnaires. Many times, teachers' information is consistent with that provided by parents and children; other times, different information becomes available. Youngstrom et al. (2000) report that teachers identify fewer and somewhat different problems than do parents (see also Offord et al., 1996). Teacher characteristics may influence the information provided about children. Mash and Dozois (1996) suggest that these influences may reflect bias or error on the part of the teacher. For instance, both Sbarra and Pianta (2001) and Youngstrom et al. (2000) report that teacher ratings of students can be influenced by the students' racial backgrounds, with African American children rated as having more difficulties compared to similar European American children. Other differences in teacher ratings may be tied to actual differences in children's behaviors in various settings (at home versus in school). In addition to teacher ratings and school records, a large armamentarium of possible tests is available, designed to examine many different aspects of ability and achievement as well as to measure cognitive functioning, such as inattention and memory, that might affect learning.

Another perspective on the central roles of the school classroom, teachers, and school psychologists emphasizes the need to coordinate diagnoses of children using the DSM with the special education categories delineated in the **Individuals with Disabilities Education Improvement Act** (IDEA) of 2004 (Wodrich, Pfeiffer, & Landau, 2008). Because the special education categories are broad and the criteria are general, the students in any category have "decidedly heterogeneous problems and diverse educational needs" (p. 627). For example, children diagnosed with attention deficit/hyperactivity disorder often improve with a combination of medication and classroom interventions; this information should be part of school-based planning. Another example of necessary coordination and planning involves the identification of children whose disorders place them at higher risk for poor outcomes and in greater need of limited-availability school services (Wodrich et al., 2008). Finally, from a developmental view, children's functioning in school (both academic and social) is a key marker of well-being. Understanding children's school adaptation or impairment is a necessary component of any comprehensive assessment.

For Alicia, the set of tests included the parent version of the CBCL; the teacher version of the CBCL; two self-report questionnaires, including the Depression Self-Rating Scale and the Children's Manifest Anxiety Scale; the Wechsler Intelligence Scale for Children; the Woodcock-Johnson III Tests of Achievement; and the Integrated Visual and Auditory Continuous Performance Test, which is designed to measure one's ability to inhibit response, remain vigilant, demonstrate consistency of attentional focus, and respond quickly.

Alicia's diagnostic summary: Alicia's current difficulties are most consistent with a DSM-5 diagnosis of attention deficit/hyperactivity disorder (ADHD). The diagnosis of ADHD with a predominant clinical presentation of inattention is often made later in the elementary school years when demands for organization and independent functioning in school begin to increase. Alicia's academic achievement is generally consistent with her intellectual functioning, and there is no evidence that she responds poorly to instruction, so there is no strong case to be made for a learning disorder. Clearly, Alicia is a somewhat anxious child, and the school problems she is experiencing have exacerbated this vulnerability. Although a case can be made for also diagnosing an anxiety disorder, it may be most reasonable to monitor the anxiety symptoms as the ADHD is addressed.

For David, a set of tests similar to Alicia's was used. However, because there were no concerns about academic problems, the cognitive and attentional measures were not administered. Because the underlying emotional state was problematic, along with social adjustment, some projective techniques were used during the assessment. The Rorschach and the TAT provided additional ways to understand David's subjective experience of the world around him. In completing the self-report measures of emotional functioning, David denied most of the obvious symptoms of depression and anxiety, with the exception of anxiety related to being physically ill. Projective data (e.g., repeated sad and discouraging themes in David's TAT stories), however, suggested depressed mood, relative developmental immaturity, and a poor sense of self-efficacy. David's parents independently completed the CBCL. There were striking consistencies in their reports, with highly significant elevations on the three internalizing scales reflecting symptoms of social withdrawal, anxiety, and depression.

David's diagnostic summary: Taken together, the data provided suggest that David is experiencing both an anxiety disorder and a depressive disorder. His symptoms meet the DSM-5 criteria for both classification categories, both disorders contribute to current distress and dysfunction, and both disorders appear to require immediate intervention.

For Tyler, age and presenting concerns influence a different selection of tests. Because of his age, Tyler did not complete any assessment measures himself. His mother did complete the CBCL. The resulting profile had extremely high scores on all of the externalizing scales, indicating that aggression, impulsivity, and hyperactivity were all significant problems. Because some of the initial concerns reflected a high level of discomfort in social situations and some other atypical behaviors and developmental patterns, the Children's Autism Rating Scale was completed by the psychologist. The score on this scale was not in the clinically significant range.

Tyler's diagnostic summary: Although ADHD is a reasonable diagnosis given the clinical presentation, it is a difficult diagnosis to make confidently given Tyler's very young age, the high level of stress he and his mother have experienced, and their relative lack of social support. A diagnosis of oppositional defiant disorder was made as a way of capturing the most important concern at this time, which centers on Tyler's difficulty internalizing developmentally appropriate self-control and his mother's difficulty managing day-to-day routines and interactions with him.

Intervention

Classification, assessment, and diagnosis are most practical when they provide information about what can be done to help children who are experiencing clinically significant distress and dysfunction. This section provides a general introduction to the topic of interventions for children and adolescents, with an emphasis on the progress that has already been made, as well as the potential that has yet to be fully achieved (Huang et al., 2005; March, 2009; Shonkoff, 2010; Tolan & Dodge, 2005). The contributions of a developmental psychopathology framework to intervention efforts are noteworthy, including the basic notion that age-related norms and expectations must be taken into account when designing any intervention strategy. This framework informs decisions about whether and when to intervene, the goals of intervention, and simple versus more complex treatments and techniques (Ialongo et al., 2006; Masten & Cicchetti, 2010). The developmental perspective emphasizes the unique context of treatment for each child, with respect to the factors that have contributed to the child's disorder, factors that contribute to the child's improvement, factors related to the network of peers and friends, factors related to the school setting, and cultural contributions. Interventions must include more effective use of translational research (described in Chapter 3) and efforts that target "genomics to social policy" (Leckman & Yazgan, 2010). Nontraditional interventions, such as those provided by paraprofessionals and those delivered in new formats (e.g., Internet based) may become increasingly prevalent (Kazdin & Blasé, 2011). No matter the provider or format, ethical issues related to child and adolescent psychotherapy, including issues involving autonomy, confidentiality, protection, and communication (with parents, with teachers, with other mental health professionals), must always be addressed (Ascherman & Rubin, 2008; Koocher, 2003).

The Efficacy of Psychotherapy for Children and Adolescents

Research on psychotherapy can be generally sorted by whether it is focused on outcome or process. **Outcome research** has to do with whether children and adolescents have improved at the end of treatment relative to their pretreatment status and compared to others who have not received treatment. Results of numerous meta-analytic studies confirm that psychotherapy works, with statistically significant and clinically meaningful effects for infants, toddlers, children, and adolescents (Shonkoff & Meisels, 2000; Weisz, Doss, & Hawley, 2005; Weisz & Kazdin, 2010; Zeanah, 2009). Therapies that focus on helping children by working with their parents and families have also received much research support (Cummings, Davies, & Campbell, 2000; Weisz & Kazdin, 2010; Zeanah, 2009).

Process research deals with the specific mechanisms and common factors that account for therapeutic change (Kazdin & Nock, 2003). Process-related discussions have focused on shifts from a one-size-fits-all model of treatment to models that emphasize specific pairings (or matching) of disorders and treatments (Chorpita & Daleiden,

In order to be effective, therapeutic interventions must reflect developmentally appropriate norms and expectations.

Michael Newman/PhotoEdit

2009; Chorpita, Bernstein, & Daleiden, 2011) and the realities of "clinic therapy" (i.e., what happens every day in the real world of children, families, and schools), in contrast to the very regularized therapy of research studies (Karver, Handelsman, Fields, & Bickman, 2005; Yates et al., 2011).

Primary, Secondary, and Tertiary Interventions

Interventions can be characterized in a variety of ways, from the target of intervention (child, parent, or school) to the timing of intervention. Differences in primary, secondary, and tertiary interventions are related to timing. **Primary prevention** involves reducing or eliminating risks as well as reducing the incidence of disorder in children. Cowen (1994, 1996; Cowen & Durlak, 2000) identifies two types

of primary prevention strategies. The first involves the identification of risk factors plus early treatments intended to minimize their impact. The second is a more inclusive approach, emphasizing the enhancement of psychological wellness as a general protective factor, as illustrated in Figure 4:3.

Following Gordon's (1983, 1987) work, Fonagy (1998) distinguishes three types of preventive measures: (1) **universal preventive measures,** which are provided for entire populations (e.g., mandatory immunizations for children); (2) **selective preventive measures,** provided for groups at above-average risk (e.g., Head Start programs for preschoolers from disadvantaged backgrounds); and (3) **indicated preventive measures,** provided for groups with specific risk factors that include more extensive interventions (e.g., packages of services for families with

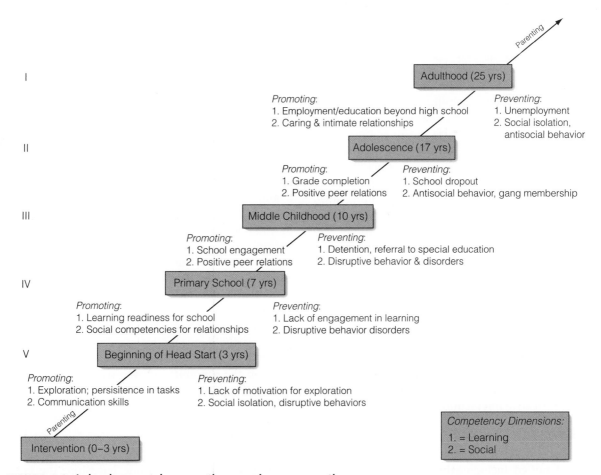

FIGURE 4:3 A developmental perspective on primary prevention.
Source: From J. P. Shonkoff and S. J. Meisels (Eds.), Handbook of Early Childhood Intervention, 2/e, p. 160. Copyright © 2000 Cambridge University Press. Reprinted with the permission of Cambridge University Press.

prematurely born infants). The principles of prevention associated with the most positive results have been summarized by Cummings et al. (2000): Primary interventions that begin early, last longer, and are more intensive are more likely to be effective. More effective programs target the child. And the initial positive effects of comprehensive and multifaceted intervention programs require continued environmental support.

Secondary prevention has to do with interventions that are implemented following the early signs of distress and dysfunction, before the disorder is clearly established in the child. Recent discussions of this kind of prevention have emphasized the potential benefit of including biological processes in the design and evaluation of interventions (Beauchaine, Neuhaus, Brenner, & Gatzke-Kopp, 2008; Cicchetti & Gunnar, 2008). A number of barriers to prevention have been identified (Rapee, 2008). For example, both children and their parents are motivated to seek treatment and to become engaged in treatment because they are distressed. To the extent that prevention programs are designed to alleviate difficulties before they become very distressing or impairing, participation in prevention programs may be lessened. Sustainability and access are also issues. Many prevention programs are demonstration programs conducted within a research framework, and continued availability and support for these programs is intermittent at best. Finally, social and policy implications must be taken into account. At times, popular but ineffective programs (such as the Drug Abuse Resistance Education program, DARE) are funded, whereas other education- and community-oriented programs with demonstrated efficacy are not (Rapee, 2008).

Tertiary prevention has to do with responding to already present and clinically significant disorders. The goals of secondary and tertiary prevention include restoring healthy functioning and minimizing future impairments. Most of what clinicians do when working with children and adolescents involves secondary and tertiary prevention. As with primary prevention, research and clinical data suggest that these are effective interventions.

Working with Children

Several key influences on current services for children can be identified, including the mental hygiene movement of the early 20th century, primarily related to concerns about the poor treatment of adults in state mental hospitals; the child guidance clinics, focused on the reform and rehabilitation of juvenile offenders; and the emergence of psychoanalysis, emphasizing the etiology of psychopathology during childhood (Morris & Kratochwill, 1998; Weisz, Sandler, Durlak, & Anton, 2005). Noteworthy recent trends include the strengthening of connections between research and clinical practice; the introduction of pharmacological interventions for children (Brown & Sammons, 2002; Vitiello, 2008); the implications of social policies such as mental health parity in insurance coverage; and intervention guidelines that emphasize short-term and evidence-based therapies (Chambers, Ringeisen & Hickman, 2005; Mash & Hunsley, 2005; Weisz & Kazdin, 2010). Changes in patterns of inpatient care, involving shorter stays for evaluation and treatment ("despite higher apparent rates of serious illness and self-harm") are also documented (Case, Olfson, Marcus, & Siegel, 2007).

Working with Parents and Families

Different parents require different helping strategies (Hoagwood et al., 2010; Svanberg, 1998). Family support might include education and instruction, emotional support, and/or advocacy information. And there are parents who need psychological treatment themselves. For all parents, the overall goals are similar: to help caregivers create and provide environments conducive to children's physical, emotional, intellectual, and social growth. One key issue, already noted, is the timing of intervention. Svanberg (1998) argues that efforts that coincide with parent-related transitions (e.g., prebirth, entrance to toddlerhood) are particularly efficacious. One example of a home-based interventions targeted multirisk urban families with young children and emphasized the development of positive parent–child relationships (Lowell, Carter, Godoy, Paulicin, & Briggs-Gowan, 2011).

Because parents are usually responsible for recognizing the need for intervention and following through on intervention efforts, the relationship between the therapist and the parent or parents is critical. General agreement about the goals of therapy, the expectations for the child and his or her family, and financial considerations will all play important roles in children's access to mental health care. Numerous actual and perceived barriers to treatment, such as economic hardship, the belief that therapy is irrelevant, or the therapist blaming the parent for the child's difficulties, are related to dropping out of the treatment process (Farmer, Burns, Phillips, Angold, & Costello, 2003; Kazdin, Holland, & Crowley, 1997; Owens et al., 2002).

Working with Schools and Communities

Because teachers frequently refer children and adolescents for assessment and treatment, and because difficulties are often displayed in the school setting, it makes sense that many interventions are attempted in schools with the cooperation of school personnel. For these interventions to be successful, it is important for therapists to pay attention to the ecological context of schools and the central role of teachers. As described in the diagnosis and assessment section, therapists must also be well versed in relevant legislation, with the many federal and state laws, regulations, and requirements related to access to school services for children with various kinds of disabilities (Wodrich et al., 2008). For example, therapists are often consulted by school personnel during the design of an Individualized Education Plan (IEP), which the school is required to formulate whenever a child's academic performance is impaired by an identified disability.

School-based mental health services can include services designed to promote learning, services designed to mitigate the effects of adversity on brain development, or services designed to bridge high-risk "home and neighborhood ecologies" (Atkins, Hoagwood, Kutash, & Seidman, 2010; Cappella, Frazier, Atkins, Schoenwald, & Glisson, 2008; Shonkoff, 2011). Schools can also be the place where other kinds of interventions (e.g., family-based interventions) begin, such as the "Family Check-Up" intervention aimed at engaging at-risk families in the middle school years in order to decrease rates of antisocial behavior and substance use (Stormshak et al., 2011).

Community-centered approaches, such as the Carolina Abecedarian project, are often system-wide interventions (targeting families, child care settings, schools, and communities) (Campbell & Ramey, 2010). After-school and summer school programs, often located in recreational settings, are other examples of community intervention efforts (Frazier, Chacko, Van Gessel, O'Boyle, & Pelham, 2011). Two final, and most unfortunate, settings for child and adolescent interventions are found in child welfare and juvenile justice settings (Ungar, 2005a, 2005b).

Overall, our consideration of clinical intervention efforts reflects our consideration of developmental principles and practices. The focus of intervention must be on developmentally salient tasks and issues, and it must focus on multiple levels of development—from within the individual, the individual as part of a family system, and the individual in context of school, community, and culture.

Key Terms

Classification (p. 47)
Diagnosis (p. 47)
Categorical classification (p. 47)
Diagnostic and Statistical Manual (DSM) (p. 47)
Medical model (p. 47)
Reliability (p. 48)
Interrater reliability (p. 48)
Cross-time reliability (p. 48)
Validity (p. 48)
Internal validity (p. 48)
External validity (p. 48)
Dimensional classification (p. 48)
Externalizing dimension (p. 49)
Internalizing dimension (p. 49)
Comorbidity (p. 51)
Homotypic comorbidity (p. 51)
Heterotypic comorbidity (p. 51)

Concurrent comorbidity (p. 51)
Successive comorbidity (p. 51)
Assessment (p. 52)
Differential diagnosis (p. 53)
Diagnostic efficiency (p. 53)
Interviews (p. 54)
Standardized tests (p. 57)
Projective measures (p. 57)
Observations (p. 57)
Individuals with Disabilities Education Improvement Act (IDEA) (p. 58)
Outcome research (p. 60)
Process research (p. 60)
Primary prevention (p. 61)
Universal preventive measures (p. 61)
Selective preventive measures (p. 61)
Indicated preventive measures (p. 61)
Secondary prevention (p. 62)
Tertiary prevention (p. 62)

Chapter Summary

- Diagnostic classification systems group individuals with similar patterns of disorder. Effective classification systems help to organize symptom patterns into meaningful groups, facilitate communication among professionals, and inform research and treatment efforts.

- The most commonly used categorical (clinical) classification system with adults and children is the Diagnostic and Statistical Manual of the American Psychiatric Association (DSM-5). This type of classification identifies types of disorders and then specifies the defining symptoms of the disorders.

- Dimensional (empirical) classification systems have been an especially useful way to consider the development of psychopathology. This approach is based on statistical techniques that identify key dimensions of children's functioning and dysfunction, with the assumption that all children can be meaningfully described along these dimensions.

- The two clinically useful and well-researched clinical dimensions are the externalizing dimension, with undercontrolled behaviors such as oppositional or aggressive behaviors, and the internalizing dimension, with overcontrolled behaviors such as anxiety or depression.

- The integration of developmental perspectives with classification systems is an ongoing concern in the field of developmental psychopathology. A number of efforts emphasize the integration of information about typical development, age-salient challenges and expectations, and developmentally informed assessment and diagnosis.

- Comorbidity is the co-occurrence of two or more disorders in one individual. Systematic comorbidities reflect the fact that certain disorders are likely to often occur together (e.g., ADHD and oppositional defiant disorder).

- Psychological assessment involves the systematic collection of relevant information in order to differentiate everyday problems from psychopathology and to accurately diagnose disorders.

- Assessment methods, including interviews, standardized tests, projective measures, and observation, all contribute to a diagnosis; making a decision about which of several diagnoses best describes an individual is called differential diagnosis.

- Research on psychotherapy generally focuses on either outcome or process. Outcome research has to do with whether, at the end of treatment, children and adolescents have improved relative to their pretreatment status and compared to others who have not received treatment. Process research has to do with the specific mechanisms and common factors that account for therapeutic change.

- Interventions can vary in their focus (child, parent, or school) and timing (primary, secondary, or tertiary) depending, in part, on whether they are designed to prevent or treat psychopathology.

5 Disorders of Early Development

FOR MANY DECADES, the mental health and psychopathology of infants were discussed almost exclusively by psychodynamically oriented clinicians, who focused their attention on problems in the caregiving relationship. Conceptualizations of infant disorders within a broader biopsychosocial framework are fairly recent, owing much to theory and research focused on neurobiological development, temperament, and attachment. Taking the pioneering work of the psychiatrist Stanley Greenspan and the longitudinal studies of Stella Chess and Alexander Thomas as a point of departure, most clinicians and researchers now accept the need to identify and respond to infant distress and dysfunction, and to increase the numbers of programs devoted to infant mental health (Harmon, 2002; Shonkoff & Phillips, 2000; Zeanah, 2009).

In the chapter, we examine the earliest manifestations of adjustment and maladjustment. We describe several clinical presentations that many mental health professionals believe reflect distinct disorders. We also present evidence that certain early patterns of development are risk factors for many different kinds of later psychopathology.

Developmental Tasks and Challenges Related to Physiological and Emotional Functioning

From birth onward, infants interact with their personal and material worlds in ways that promote physical, emotional, intellectual, and social development. This growth is marked by three *biobehavioral shifts* that signal important intra- and interpersonal changes (Emde, 1985); Brazelton (1994, 2006) has referred to these periods as "touchpoints." The first of these biobehavioral shifts occurs between 2 and 3 months of age, after infants and caregivers have negotiated the transition from intrauterine to extrauterine experience through their rhythmic routines of feeding, dressing, and comforting (Hofacker & Papoušek, 1998). Later in the first year, between 7 and 9 months, another shift takes place. By this time, most babies communicate their feelings and intentions through gestures and vocalizations, play with toys, and have a number of daily and nightly schedules. The third shift occurs between 18 and 20 months. By then, toddlers are walking and talking and are increasingly independent explorers of their many environments. These accomplishments—involving new, challenging, and sometimes stressful events—are no less astounding because they are common outcomes. Indeed, these achievements reflect the remarkable capacities of the average newborn.

Temperament

In addition to these normative developments, there are important individual differences that are quickly noted by parents and others. Mary Rothbart and her colleagues have described variations in newborns' styles of attention, activity, and distress. These "constitutionally based individual differences in reactivity and self-regulation" make up the construct of **temperament** (Rothbart, 1991; Rothbart & Bates, 2006). **Reactivity** involves the infant's excitability and responsiveness. For instance, some infants may become quite agitated while being passed from relative to relative during a family reunion. Other infants may accept strangers' kisses, hugs, and peek-a-boo games in stride. **Regulation** involves what the infant does to control his or her reactivity. Some upset infants seek and receive comfort from a parent and quickly settle down; others may wail and thrash about and take a much longer time to recover. Infant temperament has been and continues to be the focus of many scientists and clinicians. This brief overview is intended to introduce important ideas and findings, especially those that are relevant to the upcoming discussion of disorders of regulation as well as discussions of disorders in later chapters.

The nature of temperamental reactivity and regulation has been widely discussed, with proposals for both categorical and continuous models. Kagan and his colleagues identified two general categories or types of temperament that distinguish some babies from others (Kagan & Snidman, 1991; Kagan, Snidman, Arcus, & Reznick, 1994). The first type is highly reactive and inhibited, and the second type is less reactive and uninhibited.

Current continuous, or dimensional, models of temperament emphasize **surgency** (i.e., extraversion),

Temperamental characteristics, such as negative affectivity, are significant factors in later child and adult personality.

negative affectivity (i.e., predispositions to experience fear and frustration/anger), and **effortful control** (i.e., infant attempts to regulate stimulation and response) (Rothbart & Bates, 2006). Each of these dimensions reflects, in part, **infant emotionality**, including the latency to respond to emotional stimuli and the average and peak intensities of emotional response. Individual infants possess varying amounts of each characteristic, leading to many different combinations. Other researchers have combined aspects of the categorical and continuous approaches. For example, Fox and Henderson (1999) have differentiated very reactive children, who are also highly negative in their emotional responses (the inhibited group), from very reactive children, who are highly positive in their responses (the exuberant group) (see also Polak-Toste & Gunnar, 2006).

Research on gender and temperament is plentiful. Data suggest that boys are more likely to score higher on scales measuring surgency, whereas girls score higher on measures of effortful control; there are few differences related to negative affectivity (Else-Quest, Hyde, Goldsmith, & Van Ulle, 2006). Research on culture and temperament is less plentiful, although there are data suggesting some differences in Eastern versus Western cultures and among various Western cultures (Gartstein et al., 2006, 2010; Porter et al., 2005).

Overall, there is agreement that it is helpful to think about temperament as the foundation of later child and adult personality (Bates, Schermerhorn, & Goodnight, 2010; Clark, 2005; Eder & Mangelsdorf, 1997; Rothbart, 2007). Consistent with this idea, Graziano, Jensen-Cambell, and Sullivan-Logan (1998) have creatively described temperament as a "hard ice ball, around which the softer snowball of personality" develops (p. 1267).

Newborn Characteristics

Looking more closely at the origins of temperament, we must first take into account the biology–behavior links, including contributions of genetics, neurophysiology, and the maturation and increasing coordination of physiological and psychological systems (Bates et al., 2010; Rothbart & Bates, 2006). Individual differences in negative affectivity and effortful control are also important, with developments in neurophysiology and other physical domains related to changes in the infant's ability to attend and respond to incoming stimuli. Differences in effortful control are frequently

discussed in the context of arousal and emotion (Cole, Martin, & Dennis, 2004; Stifter, 2002). Arousal is an adaptive phenomenon, alerting individuals to potential threats as well as potentially rewarding stimuli. But some infants and children experience too much arousal, or too frequent arousal, or arousal without purpose; many of these experiences are related to the management of fear and anger (Rothbart & Bates, 2006). Although negative emotions are central to the construct of temperament, we cannot overlook the part that positive emotions play. Well-adjusted children have access to the full range of positive *and* negative emotions, as well as mild, moderate, and strong intensities of experience. Developmental psychopathologists emphasize the variety of normal positive and negative emotional responses and the "strong, self-righting properties of the healthy newborn" (Gunnar, Porter, Wolf, & Rigatuso, 1995, p. 1).

Caregiver Characteristics

Even as theorists and researchers focus primarily on the role of nature (genetic predispositions or inborn tendencies), there is also a place for nurture (parents and families) in almost all temperament models (Bates & Pettit, 2007). The influence of the caregiver on measures of both infant reactivity and infant regulation is frequently observed. With respect to reactivity, there is evidence that sensitive caregiving, in both everyday and adverse circumstances, is associated with positive changes in infants' stress-reactive hormones (Calkins & Hill, 2007; Gunnar, 1998; Gunnar & Donzella, 2002). Sensitive caregiving includes a variety of parenting behaviors that support and promote development. Less sensitive parenting is correlated with ongoing negative affectivity (Blandon, Calkins, Keane, & O'Brien, 2010; Lipscomb et al., 2011).

Caregivers also influence regulation, including the ways that infants depend on active regulation by others and the ways that caregivers support infants' own attempts at self-regulation (Bates & Pettit, 2007; Calkins & Hill, 2007; Eisenberg, 2002). Caregivers regulate their infants by responding to their signals of discomfort, such as changing wet diapers or rocking tired babies to sleep. Mothers and fathers help babies by providing the shoulders to cry on, the blankets to cuddle in, and the soothing lullabies at bedtime. In each of these instances, infants, caregivers, and their relationships benefit from successful regulation. In contrast, some parents may exhibit more frequent

Goodness of fit refers to the complementary relationship between infant temperament and parenting.

overcontrolling or intrusive behavior. Over time, these behaviors may have a negative impact on children's own effortful control (Graziano, Keane, & Calkins, 2010).

In addition to actual caregiving behaviors, parental beliefs about temperament also influence the infant's emerging personality (Gartstein et al., 2010; Graziano et al., 1998; Porter et al., 2005). Cultural variability in such beliefs leads to cultural differences in parental responses. For example, parents who believe that babies should be able to control their emotions and behaviors quickly and quietly are likely to respond differently than parents who believe that babies should be allowed to be loud and active at all times in all places. Also, particular behaviors associated with temperament may be consequential for some caregivers but not others, again eliciting different responses. Certain parents, for instance, might be more accepting of less active girls than less active boys.

Goodness of Fit

Thomas and Chess (1977; Chess & Thomas, 1984) describe **goodness of fit** as the interplay between infant temperament and parenting. Some of the more frequently mentioned combinations include the well-matched pairs (e.g., easygoing babies with easygoing parents and exuberant babies with exuberant parents), and the less well-matched pairs (e.g., easygoing babies with exuberant parents and exuberant babies with easygoing parents). But it is important to understand that the goodness of fit between infants and their caregivers is not an all-or-nothing situation. Within any infant–caregiver

pair, there are both matches and mismatches, with some mismatches associated with growth and the broadening of the infant's set of experiences (Stern, 1985). For example, a parent might offer an encouraging smile to a wary baby as she struggles to approach a lamb at the petting zoo. Indeed, according to Bates et al. (2010), children who are high in negative affectivity are likely to "benefit from being at least moderately challenged by their parents, perhaps because well-managed exposure to stress helps such children to develop effective emotion-regulation skills" (p. 229). More problematic are the infant–caregiver pairs with more frequent or more extreme mismatches (Seifer & Dickstein, 2000). For instance, we expect frequent or ongoing conflict to occur if a very gregarious parent is regularly insisting that a behaviorally inhibited child approach unfamiliar children and adults with enthusiasm.

When discussing goodness of fit, "difficult" temperaments are often highlighted, with descriptions of babies who are quickly aroused, emotionally intense, and hard to soothe. The assumption is that temperamentally difficult, demanding babies are challenging for any kind of parent, and that is almost certainly so (Ganiban, Ulbricht, Saudino, Reiss, & Neideriser, 2011; Calkins, Hungerford, & Dedmon, 2004; Williford, Calkins, & Keane, 2007). Infants with difficult temperaments, for example, influence trajectories of parenting over time, with a variety of outcomes. Recent investigations of temperament characteristics have emphasized **differential susceptibility**; that is, "the hypothesis that some individuals are more susceptible than others to both negative (risk-promoting) and positive (development-enhancing) environmental conditions" (Ellis, Boyce, Belsky, Bakermans-Kranenburg, & van IJzendoorn, 2011, p. 7) (see Box 5:1).

Temperament over Time

At about 3 or 4 months of age (following that first biobehavioral shift), various aspects of temperament appear to come together in meaningful ways. With the idea that temperament characteristics provide many of the building blocks of personality, we would then expect to see evidence of temperamental **consistency** across a variety of situations and **stability** across time. Numerous longitudinal studies provide this evidence, suggesting clear associations between early temperament and later child and adolescent personality

BOX 5:1 EMERGING SCIENCE

Differential Susceptibility: Interactions among Genes, Temperament, and Parenting

We have understood for a number of years that individual differences, including genetic differences, interact with environments, and these interactions result in varied outcomes in terms of adjustment or maladjustment. This perspective, exemplified by the **diathesis–stress model**, has focused on the identification of specific risks for psychopathology; the additional stressors that trigger, or interact with, those risks; and the pathways that lead to various disorders. The diathesis–stress model is based on the idea that some individuals are at greater risk for developing disorders due to the negative impact of innate characteristics (e.g., difficult temperament). Although the greater risk may not lead to disorder under conditions of low stress, poor outcomes are more likely under conditions of high stress. Diathesis–stress research has led to a rich and enlightening literature on the origins and development of psychological disorders such as schizophrenia, depression, and anxiety.

In recent years, researchers have taken the basic premise of this model—that genetic profile and other biological factors interact with environmental influences to produce individual differences—and extended it. This new approach, called **differential susceptibility** (Belsky, Bakermans-Kranenburg, & van IJzendoorn, 2007; Belsky & Pluess, 2009), suggests that although it is true that some children are differentially vulnerable to stressful environments, it is also true that some children thrive in a differentiated way with developmentally appropriate and encouraging environments. Indeed, the "individuals most adversely affected by many kinds of stressors may be the very same ones who reap with most benefit from environmental support and enrichment" (Belsky & Pluess, 2009, p. 886). A number of specific genetic markers

that influence neurotransmitter systems (including serotonin and dopamine) are proposed to underlie differential susceptibility.

In the differential susceptibility model, difficult temperament is not necessarily viewed as a negative characteristic, but rather as a marker of the potential to be influenced by a "for-better-and-for-worse pattern of parenting effects" (Belsky & Pluess, 2009, p. 889). In other words, better quality parenting predicts fewer problems (and poorer quality parenting predicts more problems) for children with difficult temperaments. The strength of effects diminishes for children with intermediate levels of difficult temperament and is weaker still for children with easy temperaments (Belsky & Pluess, 2009).

Boyce and colleagues (Boyce & Ellis, 2005; Obradovic & Boyce, 2009) have described a related gene-by-environment model, **sensitivity to context**, in which individual differences in genetic sensitivity, physiological sensitivity, and behavioral sensitivity to environments help to explain better versus worse adaptations. Much of the research on sensitivity to context involves stress reactivity (one measure of a difficult temperament). One such study (Obradovic, Bush et al., 2010) showed how stress reactivity interacted with family adversity in a group of 5- to 6-year-old children. Results revealed that the children who demonstrated the most sensitive physiological stress reactivity showed the most social and emotional problems under conditions of high adversity, as well as the highest levels of adaptive functioning under conditions of low adversity. Boyce (2007) asserts that each of these better and worse outcomes can have a multiplying effect over time, leading to compromised (or enhanced) physical, psychological, and social consequences over the course of children's lives.

(Bates et al., 2010) (see Table 5:1). Genetic factors certainly help to explain stability, but (as noted in Box 5:1) gene-by-environment (g × e) interactions are also essential to descriptions of developmental pathways. Shiner and Caspi (2003) describe several ways in which children's temperaments interact with environments. For example, temperament characteristics may influence learning processes. Temperament characteristics may elicit varied responses from the environment (especially in important relationships).

These characteristics may also lead some children to seek out certain environments, and to alter or modify those environments.

Temperament and Psychopathology

For some infants and children, temperament characteristics are not the source of interesting variations in personality but the roots of later child and

TABLE 5:1   Temperament and Personality Characteristics over Time

BIG FIVE DIMENSION	CHILDHOOD	ADOLESCENCE	ADULTHOOD
Extraversion	Increases over the first year, and then decreases from early to middle childhood	Social dominance increases and shyness decreases; other aspects of extraversion show stability	Mixed findings, but in general, extraversion decreases over the course of adulthood
Negative Emotionality and Neuroticism	Negative emotionality decreases	Mixed findings	Neuroticism decreases beginning in late adolescence/early adulthood
Agreeableness	–	Stable over adolescence	Increases across adulthood
Effortful Control and Conscientiousness	Effortful control increases	Mixed findings for conscientiousness	Conscientiousness increases across adulthood
Openness to Experience	–	Mixed findings	Increases in early adulthood, and decreases in later adulthood

From Bates et al. (2010)

adult psychopathology. As discussed in Chapter 3, **risk** is conceptualized as one or more factors that make it more likely that a child will develop or experience psychopathology. A **general risk factor** is associated with increased vulnerability to any, or many, possible disorders. A **specific risk factor** is associated with increased vulnerability to a particular disorder. Much of the work on temperament as a *general risk factor* has focused on children with difficult temperaments and problems with either under- or overregulation (Cole & Deater-Deckard, 2009; Nigg, 2006), as well as the specific combination of high levels of negative affectivity and low levels of effortful control (Calkins & Fox, 2002; Muris & Ollendick, 2005; Oldehinkel, Hartman, Ferdinand, Verhulst, & Ormel, 2007). This combination of high negative affectivity and low effortful control has been associated with externalizing disorders in both the United States and China (Zhou, Lengua, & Wang, 2009). Low positive emotionality is associated with internalizing disorders in both cultures (Zhou et al., 2009). Discussions of *specific risks* have focused on connections between highly reactive, inhibited children and later internalizing disorders such as anxiety, and between less reactive, uninhibited children and later externalizing disorders such as conduct disorder.

In order to better explain the connection between early temperament type and specific disorder, a number of researchers have examined the role of caregivers' responses to their inhibited children. These researchers report poorer outcomes—meaning more consistent and more extreme inhibition and anxiety—for children who have parents who are overinvolved, controlling, or intrusive (Booth-LaForce & Oxford, 2008; Feldman, 2007; Nachmias, Gunnar, Mangelsdorf, Parritz, & Buss, 1996). Of course, not all shy or exuberant children go on to struggle with anxiety or conduct disorders, and not all adults with anxiety or conduct disorders were shy or exuberant as children; there are multiple developmental pathways to both adjustment and maladjustment. The pathways to early instances of maladjustment are the focus of the rest of the chapter.

Disorders of Early Development

The organization of the following sections is similar to discussions of psychopathology in all subsequent chapters. The clinical characteristics and course of various disorders are presented, followed by discussions of developmental course, etiology, assessment and diagnosis, and treatments. The focus in this chapter is on disorders involving basic physiological functioning and patterns of dysregulation. Problems with feeding and sleeping can be very distressing, for caregivers as well as their children. Two types of diagnostic categories are fairly dramatic but infrequently observed (Benoit, 2009): **pica**, or the ingestion of nonfood substances such as paint, pebbles, or dirt; and **rumination**, or the repeated regurgitation of food. More common are feeding disturbances related to not eating enough for normal growth and development. A brief overview of this kind of problem, **avoidant/restrictive food intake disorder**, is presented below. **Sleep–wake disorders** are also disruptions of basic functioning. Both DSM-5 and the Zero to Three classification systems summarize several kinds of these disorders observed across development.

Regarding dysregulation, we describe patterns of atypical development characterized by difficulties in sensory, sensorimotor, or organizational processing, and problems achieving and maintaining calm, alert, emotionally pleasant moods (Zero to Three, 2005). These early patterns of distress and dysfunction, including *hypersensitivity*, *underreactivity*, and *motor disorganization*, have been the subject of much theoretical speculation by Greenspan and DeGangi and their colleagues (DeGangi et al., 2000; Greenspan & Weider, 1993) and by Dunn (1997). Whether these patterns are best characterized as actual clinical syndromes relates to the validity of (a) diagnosing disorders in very young infants, and (b) diagnosing disorders in infants rather than infant–caregiver pairs. In fact, although these specific syndromes are described in detail in the Zero to Three classification system, they are *not* included in the DSM-5. However, with the developmental framework of this textbook and the emphasis on risk in developmental psychopathology, it is important to become familiar with these early unusual and/ or extreme presentations.

Avoidant/Restrictive Food Intake Disorder

Although the organization of efficient and effective feeding is an especially salient developmental task in infancy and early childhood, there are few uniformly accepted categories of feeding disorders. In part, this is because it is not easy to determine when feeding quirks become feeding problems, and when feeding problems become disorders (Benoit, 2009). According to recent estimates, 25% to 45% of typically developing children and up to 80% of developmentally delayed children experience some type of feeding problem (Bryant-Waugh, Markham, Kreipe, & Walsh, 2010). Current research and clinical efforts attempt to identify subtypes that differentiate difficulties on the basis of cause, course, and treatment (Bryant-Waugh et al., 2010; Chatoor & Ammaniti, 2007). The following cases provide some perspective.

The Case of Alex

Alex is a 6-month-old infant referred by his pediatrician to a feeding clinic in a children's hospital. Alex recently experienced a severe gastrointestinal illness that led to decreased appetite and repeated refusal to drink from his bottle. After growing concerned about possible weight loss, Alex's parents began to feed him by bottle while he was sleeping. Consequently, even as Alex recovered from his illness, he lost interest in feeding when awake. From the behavioral viewpoint, Alex has lost the positive connection between the act of sucking and relief from hunger. From a psychodynamic perspective, the cuddling and play that often accompanied feeding have been replaced by tension. In this case, the feeding clinic provided both reassurance and education to the parents regarding the problematic pattern that has been established, as well as the steps necessary to change the behavioral patterns and emotionally unpleasant interactions. Specifically, the staff worked with the parents to set up a feeding schedule designed to heighten Alex's experience of hunger when he is awake, and to foster an appreciation of the feeding interaction's positive emotional and social consequences. ■

The Case of Jessica

Jessica is a 3-year-old girl who experienced in-utero drug and alcohol exposure. She was born prematurely and suffered extensive neglect in her first year before being removed from her home and placed in foster care. Significant developmental delays, particularly in the areas of cognition and speech, have been documented. Although always a fussy eater, Jessica's diet has become progressively more restricted, and she is now at the point of subsisting almost entirely on apple juice and french fries. Intervention efforts involving Jessica's foster parents and early childhood special education services centered on gradually introducing new foods and reinforcing Jessica for tasting them. Providing more structured mealtimes, with social stimulation and clear reinforcement, was also helpful in expanding the range of Jessica's food options. Equally important was the focus on promoting reciprocity and decreasing conflict within the caregiver relationship. ■

Developmental Course

From the start, feeding involves the integration and coordination of internal processes (such as orienting, sucking, and swallowing) and relational processes (such as communication and reciprocity). By the time infants make the transition to solid foods, typically between 4 and 6 months of age, pleasant patterns of interactions between most infants and their parents have evolved. Benoit (2009) summarizes the infant characteristics that underlie this process, including the ability to experience hunger and satiety, oral–sensory and oral–motor functioning, developmental readiness, and past feeding experiences. Over the early years, many young children display peculiar food behaviors: eating macaroni and cheese every meal, making sure that different foods do not touch, or refusing previous favorites. Almost always, these are temporary situations and are not cause for alarm.

Sometimes, however, as with Alex and Jessica, the process goes awry. When it does, the responses of caregivers may exacerbate the situation. Even though Alex's parents were well intentioned, feeding Alex while he was sleeping made daytime feeding more difficult. Because being able to successfully nourish infants is a notable early parenting achievement, ongoing feeding problems may also have an increasingly negative impact on the caregiver. Feelings of personal incompetence, and anger toward the child, may create additional distress and dysfunction, with increasing difficulties related to amounts of food, choices of food, and mealtime behavior. More serious situations may be associated with poor growth and compromised development (Benoit, 2009; Bryant-Waugh et al., 2010).

Etiology

Feeding difficulties may be the result of developmental delays, genetic conditions, or abnormalities of oral anatomy. Some infants may be less sensitive to feelings of hunger or may present signals that are unclear or difficult to read by their caregivers. Temperamental differences may also come into play, with children who are highly reactive to new stimuli responding more negatively to the introduction of new tastes and textures. Infants who, for a variety of reasons, may be "too sleepy, excited or distressed to feed are at risk" (Chatoor, 2002, p. 166). For certain children, including Jessica, the issue of control may be important. For other children, such as Alex, a traumatic event like serious illness, with associated physical discomfort and stomach pain, may interfere with normal developmental pathways.

Parents who are insecure, controlling, or hostile, or who have poor parenting skills, may also contribute to the emergence of feeding disorders (Davies et al., 2006). In addition, parents who struggle with mental health issues (such as an eating disorder) or live in chaotic environments are more likely to have children who struggle with feeding (Davies et al., 2006; Micali, Simonoff, Stahl, & Treasure, 2010).

Assessment and Diagnosis

For all of the disorders of early development, useful assessments depend on establishing a therapeutic alliance with the child's caregiver. Parents whose infants are struggling with basic developmental tasks often feel confused and guilty. Recognizing the role of parental factors in the etiology and/or maintenance of disorder does not equate with focusing blame on parents. Given the primary goal of improving the child's well-being, mental health professionals and parents need to work together to improve children's current and future adaptations.

Basic assessments involve multiple sources and multiple types of data. The first step is usually focused on gathering data about children's overall health and development, including prenatal care, birth complications, and early experiences. With feeding disorders, detailed feeding histories are obtained, and diagnostic tests of physiological functioning such as swallowing are common. Specific rating scales may be completed by parents, nurses, or therapists. Actual observation of parent–child feeding interactions may be most helpful.

Intervention

Intervention is always focused on the interplay of physiological, psychological, and environmental factors and is tied to the alliance developed during the assessment process. Depending on the particular constellation of symptoms and infant–caregiver pairs, treatments range from empirically supported behavioral interventions (Kerwin, 1999; Larue, Patel, Piazza, Stewart, Volkert, & Zeleny, 2011) to more psychodynamically informed approaches

© Jose Luis Pelaez, Inc./Bridge/CORBIS

Effective infant feeding involves the coordination of physiological skills of the infant and relational processes between the infant and caregiver.

focused on relationships, vulnerability, and conflict (Chatoor, 2002). Benoit and Coolbear (1998) describe a three-part treatment designed for children who struggle with feeding following a trauma. They suggest that physiological and environmental changes be made to address the dysfunction in cycles of hunger and satiety. In Alex's case, the parents needed to stop feeding Alex while he was sleeping so he could reexperience hunger when awake. The second part of treatment involves nutritional monitoring. In Alex's case, careful measurement of intake and weight gain is required. The third part of treatment focuses on behavioral techniques. For Alex, this involved emphasizing the positive social and emotional aspects of feeding situations in order to make these interactions more rewarding.

Sleep–Wake Disorders

Several sleep–wake disorders diagnosed in both adults and children are described in DSM-5, including insomnia (e.g., difficulties falling and staying asleep), disorders of arousal (e.g., sleep terrors or sleepwalking), and nightmare disorder. Anders, Goodlin-Jones, and Sadeh (2000) suggest a more differentiated set of categories that takes into account severity of disorder, relationship factors, infant factors, and contextual factors. In the early years of life, for typically developing children, difficulties going to sleep and difficulties staying asleep are the most commonly observed, with estimates of incidence ranging from 10 to 30% in families with young children (Anders & Dahl, 2007). For atypically developing children, estimates of sleep problems are much higher (Goodlin-Jones, Tang, Liu, & Anders, 2008). Nightmares are also a fairly common experience. From a clinical perspective, it is important to understand the pathways by which sleep problems lead to sleepiness, which leads to daytime impairment (Goodlin-Jones, Tang, Liu, & Anders, 2009). The following case, summarized from Dahl (1996), provides a more personal view.

The Case of Cassandra

Cassandra was a 16-month-old girl brought in by her mother for chronic difficulties with night waking. For months, Cassandra would awaken several times each night and would often require hours of interaction with her parents to get back to sleep. She was also resistant to daytime naps (except when falling asleep during car rides). Other aspects of her health, growth, and development were completely normal. Cassandra's behavior during the day, however, showed extreme irritability, fussiness, and very low frustration tolerance. She cried frequently and was difficult to console when upset. Also, her attention span was very short and she changed activities rapidly. Her parents, equally fatigued and frustrated at their inability to get Cassandra to sleep, dreaded the nighttime hours. Cassandra's sleep problems responded well to a behavioral program focused on self-comforting and cessation of parental involvement at sleep onset. The change in daytime behavior was equally positive, with decreases in negative emotions and improved attention. Cassandra is now a more pleasant, happy child with much better relationships. ■

Cassandra's situation is appropriately characterized as a disorder because it reflects marked and persistent difficulties settling down and falling asleep as well as maintaining sleep through the night. These ongoing difficulties are associated with impaired daily functioning and increasingly distressed relationships with her caregivers.

Developmental Course

Although many sleep difficulties and disorders resolve over time, many persist. Night waking problems tend to decrease over time, whereas sleep onset problems such as bedtime resistance and bedtime struggles remain stable or increase in frequency or severity (Gaylor, Burnham, Goodlin-Jones, & Anders, 2005). It is important to understand that the course of infant and toddler sleep disorders is superimposed on the changing course of sleeping during the first 3 years of life. Observing that over half of these years are spent sleeping, Dahl (1996) states that sleep is the *primary* activity of the brain" during infancy (p. 3), and that understanding sleep is the key to understanding early brain development. With respect to time spent sleeping, kinds of sleep, and physiological and interpersonal regulation of sleep, these years involve great changes in the patterns of sleep–wake organization and the varieties of sleep rhythms (stages of sleep) (Anders et al., 2000; Meltzer & Mindell, 2006). Throughout early childhood, adequate sleep is essential for cognitive, emotional, and social development (Anders & Dahl, 2007; Bernier, Carlson, Bordeleau, & Carrier, 2011). And across childhood and adolescence, longitudinal studies of sleep continue to emphasize the critical role of sleep in brain–behavior relations and overall well-being (Feinberg & Campbell, 2010; Jenni & Carskadon, 2007; Reid, Huntley, & Lewin, 2009).

The immediate consequences of sleep disorders are observed in both children and their families. Children's daytime emotions and moods, attention and cognitive activities, and social relationships are all likely to be negatively affected. Tired and distressed children are also likely to have tired and distressed parents. Investigators have documented negative impacts on parents' self-efficacy, parents' marital satisfaction, and overall family climate (Fiese, Winter, Sliwinski, & Anbar, 2007; Meijer & van den Wittenboer, 2007). Long-range consequences have also been described, including behavioral difficulties such as acting out, academic difficulties, and ongoing family conflict (El-Sheikh, Buckhalt, Cummings, & Keller, 2007; Hall, Zubrick, Silburn, Parsons, & Kurinczuk, 2007). Even more problematic outcomes, such as the development of other forms of psychopathology and the exacerbation of already diagnosed disorders, have been identified (Alfano & Gamble, 2009).

Etiology

Individual variations in the ability to self-regulate and self-soothe are frequently mentioned as contributing to sleep difficulties and are tied to underlying differences in the neurophysiological systems related to arousal and attention (Anders et al., 2000; Gaylor et al., 2005). Difficult temperament has also been cited as a risk factor (Anders & Dahl, 2007); the temperament characteristic of resistance to control seems particularly important (Goodnight, Bates, Staples, Pettit, & Dodge, 2007).

Parent factors such as problematic cognitions related to setting limits (e.g., thinking that enforcing a bedtime reflects controlling or mean parenting) and anxiety and/or depression increase the likelihood of sleep disorders (Morrell & Steele, 2003; Sadeh, Flint-Ofir, Tirosh, & Tikotzky, 2007). Marital difficulties may increase sleep problems (Mannering et al., 2011). Relationship factors such as inconsistent or insensitive caregiving are also risk factors. Racial, ethnic, and cultural values and practices are also important to take into account (Anders & Dahl, 2007; Milan, Snow, & Belay, 2007). Co-sleeping provides one example. Whether co-sleeping is viewed by the family and/or by the clinician as a negative consequence of child awakening or as a positive family experience is a clinically relevant factor.

Many investigators emphasize the distinction between factors that influence the *emergence of sleep disorders* and factors that influence the *maintenance of disorders* (Minde, 2002). For instance, transient disturbances such as ear infections or teething may lead to parents offering high levels of physical comforting during bedtime; continuing these bedtime interactions may reinforce maladaptive patterns for non-self-soothing infants and toddlers and may exacerbate already-observable sleep difficulties.

Assessment and Diagnosis

Because we expect to see many changes in patterns of infant sleep, it is difficult to know exactly when to diagnose a sleep disorder. In addition to general overviews of health and development, sleep diaries are often requested from parents (Meltzer & Mindell, 2006). Sleep diaries provide quantitative data related to the frequency and intensity of symptoms. Using these criteria, we can distinguish among perturbations (i.e., one episode per week for at least 1 month), disturbances (i.e., two to four episodes per week for at least 1 month), and disorders (i.e., five to seven episodes per week for at least 1 month) (Anders & Dahl, 2007). Additional issues in this kind of assessment include: "Does an infant's schedule conform to the family's schedule in a socially appropriate way, and does it meet the infant's need for sleep?" (Anders et al., 2000, p. 332). Here, the degree of parent tolerance for sleep disruptions may influence whether and when parent concerns lead to seeking help. Sometimes lab assessments, in which babies are directly observed and physically monitored while they sleep in the hospital, are necessary to rule out physiological complications, such as sleep apnea (Anders et al., 2000).

Intervention

Behavior therapies and other dynamically oriented approaches (focused on relationships and parental adjustments) have all been used to treat infants with sleep disorders, although drug treatments are sometimes included. These approaches are associated with significant improvements. Although nightmares and night terrors are usually transient and outgrown without specific interventions, children often appreciate reassurance and comfort following a nightmare (Anders et al., 2000); when nighttime fears are associated with significant distress and/or impairment, psychosocial treatments are often quickly effective (Gordon, King, Gullone, Muris, & Ollendick, 2007).

Disorders of Regulation

Keeping in mind the need for much more empirical work to help us understand both how effective regulation unfolds and how dysregulation develops, the following sections make use of the hypersensitive, underreactive, and disorganized classifications of the Zero to Three diagnostic system, and are summarized and adapted from the cases presented by Black (1997), Kalmanson (1997), and Ahrano (1997) in the Zero to Three casebook (Lieberman, Wieder, & Fenichel, 1997).

The Case of Sara

Sara is a first-born 1-year-old girl who was referred for evaluation by her parents following several months of waiting for Sara to "grow out of a difficult phase." Sara's parents describe her as extremely reactive to both sounds and lights, and they contrast her overly negative responses to other babies they know. Sara's mother reports that she cannot turn on the television or the radio without Sara starting to cry. Switching on lights also results in loud and prolonged protests. So far, Sara's parents have managed to keep their home relatively quiet and dark, but it is getting more and more difficult to anticipate Sara's reactions when they visit a friend or go on errands, where Sara displays wary and fearful behaviors. In addition, Sara's parents say that she has always had a hard time feeding, often gagging, with the transition to solid food especially problematic. Sara also has a history of sleep problems. She continues to wake several times each night, and fusses whenever she is laid down for a nap. At this point, Sara's parents are increasingly concerned about their daughter's overall development and wonder whether they waited too long to seek professional help and whether Sara will ever be happy. ■

The characteristics of this type of **hypersensitive regulatory disorder** consist of heightened or exaggerated sensitivity to both auditory and visual stimulation. When aroused, Sara is very difficult to soothe, and what works at one time does not necessarily work at another. Sara's parents also describe feeding and sleeping irregularities and note that this pattern of discomfort has been evident since birth. Of the two common subtypes of this regulatory disorder, Sara's clinical presentation is more consistent with the highly inhibited and fearful subtype, although she does display some features of the negativistic and defiant subtype.

The Case of Noah

Noah is a 32-month-old boy whose parents are concerned about his combination of unusual physiological and behavioral responses. Noah prefers to play alone, is physically awkward, and displays peculiar patterns of attention and language. Noah's parents described him as an easy baby, although somewhat "floppy," who was often content to lie alone and look around. They did report some sound sensitivities and fears connected to, for example, the noise of the vacuum. As a toddler, Noah appears to respond slowly to requests and demands, whether the tone is positive or negative. Both at home and at preschool, Noah is often distracted and disengaged from other children and group activities. ■

Noah's history and presentation are characteristic of **underreactive regulatory disorder**, with poor motor tone and coordination, self-absorption, and lagging skills in organizational processing. Although reminiscent in some ways of other developmental disorders such as autism spectrum disorder (discussed in Chapter 8), Noah's social and emotional interactions with his mother and father are more positive and more animated than the kinds of interactions usually observed in children with autism spectrum disorder.

The Case of Amanda

Amanda is a loud, high-spirited 2-year-old girl, adopted at birth, who demonstrates irregular attention, delayed language, and impulsive—often reckless—behavior. Amanda previously received speech and language therapy but remains highly active, intrusive, and undercontrolled. Amanda is frequently nonresponsive to attempts to direct or control her. Amanda's parents are most worried about increases in negative behaviors, such as hitting others, and engaging in dangerous activities, such as climbing and jumping from heights. Her parents are inconsistent in their interactions with Amanda, with her mother sometimes able to help Amanda organize herself and her behaviors, and her father often distant or angry in his responses. They are seeking psychological advice to better understand and help their daughter. ■

Amanda's experiences are best categorized as a **motorically disorganized, impulsive regulatory disorder,** with displays of significant disruptive activity and frequent sensation-seeking behavior. Similar to Sara and Noah, Amanda is usually unable to soothe or control herself when she becomes aroused; others' attempts to manage her difficult moods and behaviors are unpredictable.

At this point, we want to emphasize that these subtypes are based mainly on theoretical assumptions, although there are data providing initial support for these constructs (DeSantis, Harkins, Tronick, Kaplan, & Beeghly, 2011; Tirosh, Bendrian, Golan,

Tamir, & Dar, 2003). That is, it makes sense that different patterns of reactive and regulatory dysfunction are extreme examples of different types of normal variations. However, there is not much empirical data that support these particular subtypes; indeed, the **mixed category of regulatory disorder** in the Zero to Three classification scheme suggests the current lack of clinical consensus in this area.

Developmental Course

Given the rocky start of infants and toddlers with regulatory disorders, we expect to see evidence of ongoing problems related to reactivity and regulation. And, in fact, we do. In two longitudinal studies, DeGangi and colleagues observed poorer developmental outcomes for infants who displayed early dysregulation (DeGangi et al., 2000; DeGangi, Porges, Sickel, & Greenspan, 1993). In the later study, 40% of 4-year-olds diagnosed with a mild regulatory disorder in infancy and 95% with a history of moderate to severe regulatory disorder experienced later developmental delays and/or parent–child difficulties. The persistent nature of this disorder is summarized well by Hofacker and Papoušek (1998), who state that "the longer dysfunctional reciprocities are maintained in a kind of a vicious cycle the more likely they become automated, ritualized, and rigid" (p. 185).

Etiology

The characteristic disturbances in sleep, feeding, self-calming, and the self-regulation of emotion that appear very early in life suggest a neurophysiological basis to disorder. Data that support the notion of physiological risk come from numerous studies of infants with histories of prematurity and low birth weight, maternal substance abuse, and early adverse experiences; these types of infant difficulties are associated with many disruptions in early regulation (infant arousability, intensity, and soothability—taken together, the "difficult temperament") all appear to be involved. Additional support for this hypothesis comes from genetic and biologically based investigations of temperament, with an emphasis on the far ends of normally distributed characteristics.

We have already summarized studies of normal temperament and developmental outcome where, for all babies, parental beliefs, parental behaviors, and goodness of fit are important. These parent and caregiving factors are even more salient for the baby who struggles with extremes of reactivity and regulation. To the extent that caregivers recognize and respond to the special needs of certain infants, the emergence of disorder may be prevented or delayed. Once the disorder is present, caregivers' behaviors may either aggravate or improve symptoms.

Assessment and Diagnosis

For the most part, the assessment of regulatory disorders depends on interviews and observations. Given that parental concerns about infant and toddler development are the reason for most early referrals to clinics (Keren, Feldman, & Tyano, 2001), developmental and medical histories are key sources of information. Interview instruments designed to assess regulatory disorders can also be used (Dunn & Westman, 1997; Eppright et al., 1998). In addition to parents, other informants, such as day care providers, preschool teachers, and pediatricians, may provide valuable data. Observations by clinicians can be done in the office or during home visits. These multiple perspectives on child functioning are evident in the assessments of Sara, Noah, and Amanda, where parents identify, and other adults confirm, abnormal patterns early on.

Depending on the age of the child, different rating forms for temperament are available, along with numerous reviews of the reliability and validity of such data (Rothbart & Hwang, 2002). And for some children, various neuropsychological tests might be appropriate. In addition to information about distress and dysfunction, descriptions of the infant's strengths and competencies should also be included.

Intervention

Many different successful interventions have been documented for regulatory disorders, with the majority of families reporting significant improvement after three sessions (Cohen et al., 1999). Stern (1995) suggests that serial brief therapy might be especially useful, with sets of treatment sessions offered at several times during the first few years for infants and caregivers to deal with continuing development and change.

The meaningful impact of sensitive parenting has been emphasized throughout this chapter, and it has been a major focus of treatment efforts (Barton & Robins, 2000; VanFleet, Ryan, & Smith, 2005). As always, parent-centered interventions depend on the alliance established during the assessment process. Hofacker and Papoušek's (1998) interaction-centered infant–parent psychotherapy and VanFleet et al.'s (2005) filial therapy are two approaches that include treatment tasks geared to the infant, the mother (regular relief from stress, distress), and the father (increasing involvement and support), with the intention of increasing positive interactions between parents and babies. Other parent-oriented treatments focus on psychodynamic therapy for the parents (Baradon, 2002).

Another common intervention involves occupational therapy, with the primary goal of increasing infants' and toddlers' sensory adaptation (Barton & Robins, 2000). Examples of these occupational techniques include rubbing fuzzy blankets, engaging in water play, and listening to loud and soft music. Another close look at the intervention plans for Sara (Black, 1997), Noah (Kalmanson, 1997), and Amanda (Ahrano, 1997) provides additional detail.

Some Cases Revisited

The Case of Sara

A better understanding of Sara's deficits and abilities allows the clinician and her parents opportunities to compensate for her weaknesses and play to her strengths. Sara's parents, like many parents of poorly regulated children, felt responsible and incompetent. They needed education, support, and specific intervention techniques, such as increasing predictability and structure and anticipating difficult events. Learning to follow Sara's lead was accomplished by having mom and dad spend "floor time" with her, a structured form of play in which parents align their responses to those of the child (Greenspan, 1992). Musical instruments were also found to be calming for Sara, who enjoyed both listening and playing.

The Case of Noah

A parent and family approach to treatment was planned, in coordination with speech and language specialists. For Noah's parents, reciprocity in play was emphasized, so that Noah might experience positive, self-directed activity. In addition, the clinician suggested that increased involvement on the part of Noah's father would benefit both Noah and the family.

The Case of Amanda

A more comprehensive intervention was indicated for Amanda. The first step was enrolling Amanda in a therapeutic day treatment program for young children, where a more structured, calmer setting proved beneficial. In addition, Amanda began swimming and dancing lessons designed to improve her sensorimotor integration. Finally, Amanda's parents received education and support to boost their confidence and skills in dealing with their daughter's development.

Key Terms

Temperament (p. 66)
Reactivity (p. 66)
Regulation (p. 66)
Surgency (p. 66)
Negative affectivity (p. 67)
Effortful control (p. 67)
Infant emotionality (p. 67)
Goodness of fit (p. 68)
Differential susceptibility (p. 68)
Consistency (p. 68)
Stability (p. 68)
Diathesis–stress model (p. 69)
Sensitivity to context (p. 69)
Risk (p. 70)
General risk factor (p. 70)
Specific risk factor (p. 70)
Pica (p. 70)

Rumination (p. 70)
Avoidant/restrictive food intake disorder (p. 71)
Sleep–wake disorders (p. 71)
Hypersensitive regulatory disorder (p. 75)
Underreactive regulatory disorder (p. 75)
Motorically disorganized, impulsive regulatory disorder (p. 75)
Mixed category of regulatory disorder (p. 76)

Chapter Summary

- There is widespread acceptance of the need to identify and respond to infant and toddler distress and dysfunction.
- The interaction of infant temperament with the caregiver's response to that temperament is related to both adjustment and maladjustment in later development.

- Recent research in areas such as neurobiological development, temperament, and attachment is contributing to the emerging field of infant mental health.

- The sleep disorders most common in early development are those that involve significant difficulties falling or staying asleep. Other common problems are night terrors and nightmare disorder.

- Disorders of sleeping and feeding represent problems with basic physiological functioning.

- The assessment of both feeding and sleep disorders requires careful consideration of general health and developmental history, as well as current behavioral and relationship patterns.

- Feeding disorders represent an impairment of efficient and effective feeding—an especially salient developmental task in infancy and early childhood. Feeding disorders may be the result of developmental delays, genetic conditions, abnormalities of oral anatomy, caregiver difficulties, or combinations of those factors.

- Disorders of regulation include several patterns of dysregulation that interfere with the measured and efficient processing of sensory stimuli in early childhood.

6

Disorders of Attachment

THE HISTORICAL CONTEXT for current conceptualizations of disorders of attachment is provided, in large part, by Rene Spitz's (1945, 1946) compelling studies of institutionalized infants; by John Bowlby's (1953, 1961) reviews of maternal deprivation and infant mourning; and by Tizard's reports on children in residential nurseries (Tizard & Hodges, 1978; Tizard & Rees, 1975). Indeed, as models of developmental psychopathology would suggest, much of what we know about attachment in clinical samples of children is based on what we know about attachment in normally developing children.

Developmental Tasks and Challenges Related to Attachment

We already know that there are all kinds of babies. Affable, cuddly babies. Cranky, demanding babies. Babies who are into everything. Babies who are content to observe. Some babies are temperamentally difficult, and some babies are temperamentally easy. For all of these babies, there are also many kinds of caregivers and many kinds of caregiving relationships. By the end of the first year, most infants—together with their caregivers—have accomplished several key tasks and challenges. These include the development of an *attachment relationship*, a rudimentary *sense of self*, and a basic *understanding of others and the world*. Attachment relationships include caregivers and infants and reflect the degree to which infants experience safety, comfort, and affection. Sense of self involves the earliest set of cognitions and emotions focused on the infant as a separate being (e.g., Who am I? Am I likeable? Am I good?). An understanding of others and the world involves early beliefs about unfamiliar adults and children, along with the new situations in which infants so often find themselves. For most infants, whose early caregiving is characterized by sensitivity, consistency, and warmth, these early challenges are positively resolved.

As described in the previous chapter, much of the first year of life is devoted to the establishment of routines that promote physical, intellectual, emotional, and social growth. During this year, most infants thrive in homes that provide for their needs and desires in ways that are *mostly* sensitive, *reasonably* consistent, and *usually* warm. Over time, most infants come to understand, in a fundamental way, that they will be cared for, that they are worthy of care, and that the world around them is a pleasant place with interesting people, objects, and activities. This understanding—experienced and expressed emotionally, cognitively, and behaviorally—is the basis of attachment. According to attachment theorists (Ainsworth, 1969, 1979; Bowlby, 1982; Main, Kaplan, & Cassidy, 1985; Sroufe & Waters, 1977), the development of an attachment relationship is *the significant psychological achievement* of late infancy.

Most infants and toddlers are able to use the caregiver for several important purposes, in everyday settings as well as in difficult circumstances. The most critical advantage of attachment, from an evolutionary perspective, is to ensure the protection and the survival of the young infant (Bowlby, 1982). Protection and survival are linked to several defining features of caregivers: (1) providing a *safe haven*, a person to whom the infant can turn to for comfort and support; (2) allowing for *proximity maintenance*, for an infant who seeks closeness and resists separation; and (3) establishing a *secure base*, a person whose presence serves as a source of security from which a child ventures out to explore the world, and to which he or she can reliably return.

In their daily interactions with caregivers, infants and toddlers process a variety of positive and negative experiences, and exchange relevant emotions and appraisals (e.g., moving closer to a parent for comfort during a thunderstorm, or sharing surprise when a jack-in-the-box pops up). Infants and toddlers also balance their wishes to explore with their ongoing concerns for maintaining interpersonal connections. For example, very young children may play with other children and toys in an unfamiliar home as long as a parent is nearby. When a parent moves farther away or leaves the room, keeping the parent within view or reestablishing closeness may become more important than exploration. In more challenging or stressful circumstances, such as the birth of a sibling, a difficult illness, or parental stress after losing a job, attachments provide a deeply rooted sense of safety and security. Although a young child may struggle (and struggle mightily) with adults who fuss over a new brother or sister, with painful medical procedures, or with a move to a different apartment, attachment relationships are instrumental in terms of children's abilities to keep hold of feelings of worth and love.

Individual Differences in Attachment

Whereas the normative processes of attachment can be described as they unfold over months of caregiving (Ainsworth, Blehar, Waters, & Wall, 1978; Bowlby, 1982), there are also distinctive patterns in the attachments of particular children. Individual differences emerge from particular caregiving and relationship histories that become internalized early in development; similar patterns are observed in all countries and cultures (see Box 6:1). Caregiver sensitivity, availability, and responsiveness—or insensitivity, unavailability, or unpredictability—contribute to infants' and toddlers' emotionally salient beliefs and expectations related to self ("I am worthy/not worthy of care," "I am/am not lovable"),

BOX 6:1 THE CHILD IN CONTEXT

Attachment Across Cultures

There are several approaches to the classification of attachment. Much of the work has been accomplished in the laboratory. Mary Ainsworth's development of the **Strange Situation Procedure** is an example of the way in which a carefully designed lab assessment provides rich data about life outside the lab. In this procedure, the child and caregiver are observed in a playroom as they engage in a series of brief but increasingly upsetting separations and reunions. In these episodes, infants and toddlers are challenged to regulate themselves and use their caregivers or an unfamiliar adult for assistance and support. Young children's patterns of emotions and behaviors are interpreted to reflect attachments that are classified as secure, insecure-avoidant, insecure-resistant, and disorganized.

Keeping in mind that Ainsworth's original investigations were conducted in Uganda and then replicated in Baltimore, Maryland, continuing cross-cultural research suggests that babies around the world exhibit very similar kinds of attachment. In the United States, using the Strange Situation Procedure, approximately two-thirds of babies are classified as having a secure attachment. Similar percentages are observed in Northern European countries, in Japan, in China, in parts of Africa, and in Israel. The relative percentages of insecure-avoidant and insecure-resistant attachments appear to vary more relative to cultural context. For example, avoidant attachments are more frequent in the United States and Europe, whereas resistant attachments are more frequent in Japan, Indonesia, Korea, and Israel (Jin, Jacobvitz, & Hazen, 2010; Van IJzendoorn, 1995). Similarities in attachment processes and behaviors are thought to reflect evolutionary (i.e., functional) adaptations (Grossmann, Grossmann, & Keppler, 2005; Posada & Jacobs, 2001).

Even with abundant data supporting many aspects of similarity across cultures, a number of investigators have focused more specifically on cultural relativism related to the development and consequences of attachment. These investigators have described multiple instances of culturally specific caregiving practices and attachment behaviors, with a focus on differences in Western and Japanese samples (Rothbaum, Kakinuma, Nagaoka, & Azuma, 2007; Weisner, 2005). Ongoing research will undoubtedly provide additional examples of the impact of culture; whether these examples lead to subtle refinements or more significant revisions remains to be seen.

---

significant others ("I can/cannot trust that you will respond to me in appropriate ways"), and the world ("The world is/is not safe and pleasant"). These specific patterns of attachment can be broadly characterized as **secure** or **insecure**.

Patterns of secure attachment, in general, reflect caregiving histories in which the caregiver responds sensitively, consistently, and appropriately to an infant's physical, emotional, and social needs. In contrast, patterns of insecure attachment develop over time as a result of inconsistent, inadequate, or unavailable care, with such caregiver inadequacies sometimes interacting with difficult infant characteristics and/or environmental stressors. Patterns of infant insecurity are usually interpreted in terms of resistant, avoidant, and disorganized attachments (Ainsworth et al., 1978; Cassidy & Shaver, 1999; Main et al., 1985; see Fig. 6:1).

Resistant (or **anxious/ambivalent**) **attachment** is generally related to inconsistency or unpredictability. Mothers may respond to an infant's signals for affection on some days and not others. Fathers may feed a hungry baby at certain times and misread the discomfort of hunger at other times. Fears may be sensitively addressed or they may be ignored. These types of on-again, off-again caregiving environments

Although specific child-rearing practices may vary across cultures, the importance of a secure attachment relationship to healthy psychological development is universal.

Yann Layma/The Image Bank/Getty Images

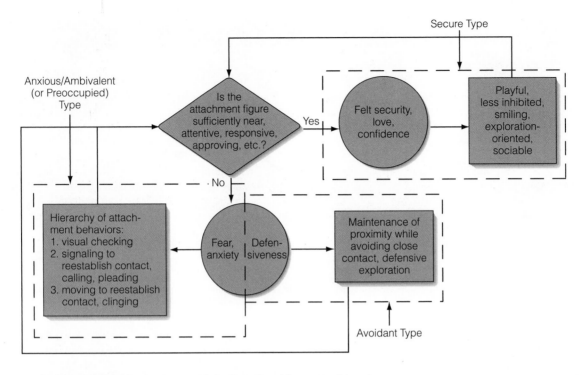

FIGURE 6:1 Patterns of secure, resistant, and avoidant attachments.
Source: From C. Hazan and P.R. Shaver (1994), "Attachment as an organizational framework for research on close relationships", 'Psychological Inquiry', 5(1), 1-22. Reprinted by permission of Taylor & Francis Ltd, http://www.tandf.co.uk/journals

are confusing and frustrating. Depending on the kind and the degree of inconsistent care, very young children with resistant attachments often appear unsure and anxious about themselves, their caregivers, and their situations. These children may or may not feel comfortable enough to explore a new playground. These children may or may not settle down with a familiar babysitter when mom runs a few errands. And these children may or may not happily reconnect with mom when she returns.

Avoidant (or **anxious/avoidant**) **attachment** is generally related to inadequate care. Caregivers who are less competent or overwhelmed or resentful may repeatedly fail to protect or nurture their children. Intrusive, excessively controlling care may also influence the development of an avoidant attachment. With inadequate care, very young children appear emotionally constricted and distant, with a sense of themselves as less worthy of care and concern. Individuals in the child's immediate and wider social settings may be perceived as unfriendly and not especially responsive. With intrusive care, children may avoid overstimulating interactions, blunt their emotional displays, attempt to care for themselves,

and look to persons other than their caregivers for play and comfort.

Disorganized attachment signals a pattern of care in which the caregiver is perceived as frightening, frightened, or malicious (Hesse & Main, 2006; Van IJzendoorn, Schuengel, & Bakermans-Kranenburg, 1999). Solomon and George (1999a, 1999b) report that this pattern may also be observed in young children who have experienced long or repeated separations from a caregiver. There are instances, however, where disorganized attachment has been identified in the presence of sensitive parenting (Hesse & Main, 2006; Rutter, Kreppner, & Sonuga-Barke, 2009). With disorganized attachment, the attachment conflict is centered on the caregiver, who is experienced as both a source of comfort and a source of anxiety. Unable to resolve the conflict, the child displays—especially in times of stress—behaviors and emotions that are disorganized with regard to establishing or maintaining a sense of safety or security. The absence or breakdown of a set of attention-, emotion-, and behavioral strategies is reflected in undirected or misdirected behaviors, behavioral "freezing" or stereotyped movements, and/or expressions of fear and apprehension (Hesse & Main, 2006). A number of researchers have suggested that the pattern of disorganization is more reflective of dysregulation than insecurity (e.g., Rutter et al., 2009).

Factors Influencing the Development of Attachment

Numerous factors have been identified that influence the kind of care that infants receive. Parental sensitivity is usually viewed as the single most important factor (Bakermans-Kranenburg & van IJzendoorn, 2007). Some of the other factors receiving theoretical and empirical attention include interactions of infant temperament and parenting variables, the role of the father, nonpaternal care, the attachment histories of the parents, marital relationships, parents' psychological well-being and/or psychopathology, and sociocultural factors. In addition, genetic factors have also been investigated, with findings supporting the differential susceptibility hypothesis (described previously in Chapter 5, in Box 5:1). That is, more negative outcomes have been observed for susceptible children in unfavorable environments, and more positive outcomes for susceptible children in favorable environments (Bakermans-Kranenburg & van IJzendoorn, 2007; Barry, Kochanska, & Philibert, 2008). A different pattern of genetic effects has been hypothesized for disorganized attachment (Rutter et al., 2009).

It is important to understand that it is not the presence or absence of any one particular factor that determines relative security or insecurity. Instead, it is *the additive or cumulative effect* of positive or negative factors—including child variables, parent variables, interaction variables, and contextual variables—that underlies attachment in any particular child. An even more complex process is suggested by De Wolff and Van IJzendoorn (1997) and Sroufe, Carlson, Levy, and Egeland (1999), who argue that we should consider not only the numbers of positive and negative factors, but the *dynamic interplay* of child, parent, interaction, and contextual factors.

Although stability and coherence over time in attachment-related emotions, cognitions, and behaviors is expected (Fraley, 2002), there is also a real possibility for change (from secure to insecure, or vice versa). Changes in parental expectations or behaviors and/or changes in social support for the caregiver are associated with changes in infants' attachment classifications (Thompson, 1997; Vaughn, Egeland, Sroufe, & Waters, 1979).

Outcomes of Early Attachment

Attachment is a critical challenge and meaningful achievement for several reasons. First, the process of attachment may positively or adversely influence neurological development (LeDoux, 1995; Schore, 2001; Swain, Lorberbaum, Kose, & Strathearn, 2007). Second, the attachment relationship influences the emergence and organization of emotion regulation and highlights the central role of emotion in early personality development (DeKlyen & Greenberg, 2008; Eder & Mangelsdorf, 1997; Sroufe, 1995). Third, the attachment relationship provides a relationship prototype, and a way to model how to behave in relationships (Bretherton, 1990; Sroufe & Fleeson, 1986). Finally, by providing children with internalized representations (or "working models") of the self and the world, attachment influences current and later personal and social adaptation (Thompson, 1998, 1999). It is important to keep in mind, however, that although attachment security is a key component of the caregiver–young child relationship, there are additional components of early relationships. In addition, the links among child–caregiver relationships and internal working models, and later friendships and romantic relationships, continue to be the focus of theoretical and empirical work (Rutter et al., 2009).

Attachment and Psychopathology

It is necessary to emphasize that *not all insecure patterns are, in and of themselves, clinical disorders* (DeKlyen & Greenberg, 2008; Rutter et al., 2009; Zeanah & Smyke, 2009). Remember that in typical, nonclinical samples approximately two-thirds of babies are classified as secure (see Box 6:1); it simply does not make sense that one-third of babies in normal samples have a diagnosable attachment disorder (Rutter, 2008). Data related to the prevalence of disorganized attachment are also important to consider. The prevalence of disorganized attachment in nonclinical samples is approximately 15%; in high-risk (e.g., maltreated or institutionalized) samples, prevalence estimates range from 50 to 80% (Bakermans-Kranenburg & van IJzendoorn, 2007; Rutter et al., 2009).

Here, again, we need to think about the concept of **risk**. Infants with insecure attachments are at *a higher risk* for the development of certain kinds of difficulties than infants with secure attachments. Babies with disorganized attachments are at *even greater risk* than insecure babies characterized as

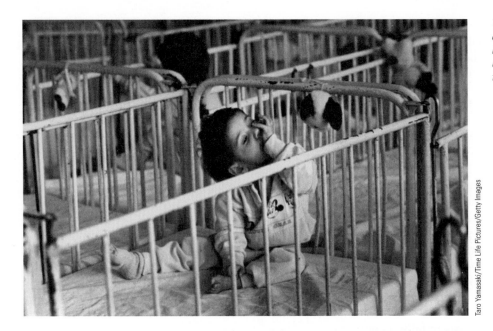

The absence of consistent and competent care provided by a reliable attachment figure is a significant risk factor for later psychopathology.

Taro Yamasaki/Time Life Pictures/Getty Images

avoidant or resistant (Rutter et al., 2009; Solomon & George, 1999b). Recent data suggest that insecure attachment and disorganization is more likely to be associated with later externalizing symptoms compared to internalizing symptoms; this association is stronger for boys than for girls (Fearon, Bakermans-Kranenburg, van IJzendoorn, Lapsley, & Roisman, 2010; Groh, Roisman, van IJzendoorn, Bakermans-Kranenburg, & Fearon, 2012).

It is certainly true that many young children with either relatively transient or subclinical difficulties would benefit from early recognition of their problems and early intervention (DeKlyen & Greenberg, 2008). Still, just as secure attachments do not always lead to trouble-free childhoods, we *cannot* assume that all insecure attachments lead to inevitably negative outcomes. Instead, it is useful to view these kinds of early relationship difficulties as a possible "marker of a beginning pathological process," with a focus that shifts from problems within a particular relationship to problems within a particular child (Sroufe et al., 1999). Over time, what was mostly characteristic of a child and his or her primary relationship may become characteristic of that child in multiple relationships, and this shift signals increasing difficulties.

Disorders of Attachment

Some young children exhibit such extreme attachment-related distress and dysfunction that they are best understood as having a clinically significant

disorder (Zeanah & Smyke, 2009). However, as with disorders of regulation in early development, there are different approaches to identification and classification of this category of disorder. The Zero to Three (2005) classification scheme calls attention to various etiologies and emphasizes that these types of disorders are best understood as *disorders of relationships*. Zero to Three identifies atypical attachments related to (a) the young child's never having a specific or special attachment with any caregiver, (b) the young child's experience of inadequate or abusive care, and (c) the young child's loss of an already-established attachment. DSM-5 describes two categories of attachment disorders, **reactive attachment disorder** and **disinhibited social engagement disorder.** The most recent research on disorders of attachment supports the validity of the DSM classifications (Gleason et al., 2011), and the rest of this chapter will summarize that work. Comparisons of the two categories of disorder are provided in Table 6:1.

The Case of Andreas: Reactive Attachment Disorder

Andreas is 30 months old. He and his mother were referred by staff at Andreas's day care center, who described Andreas as almost never seeming to be settled and calm. Unlike most of the other children around his age, he seemed to have no preferred activities or real connection with specific

TABLE 6:1   Similarities and Contrasts between Reactive Attachment Disorder and Disinhibited Social Engagement Disorder

	REACTIVE ATTACHMENT DISORDER	DISINHIBITED SOCIAL ENGAGEMENT DISORDER
Etiology	Links to social deprivation and neglect	Links to social deprivation and neglect
Maltreatment	Readily identifiable in maltreated children	Identifiable in maltreated children
Institutional care	Identifiable in children raised in institutions	Identifiable in children raised in institutions
Children adopted out of institutions	Not identified	Identifiable in children adopted out of institutions
Quality of caregiving	Related to quality of caregiving	Not necessarily related to quality of caregiving
Intervention	Responsive to enhanced caregiving	Less responsive to enhanced caregiving

Adapted from Zeanah & Smyke, 2009, Handbook of Infant Mental Health (3rd ed.)

caregivers. They described him as nervous, wary, easily upset and difficult to comfort. One of the day care staff noted that "Andreas just doesn't seem to find anything delightful. He seldom smiles, almost never laughs, and when we try to comfort him, he often becomes even more agitated." When these concerns were reported to Andreas's mother, she did not seem to realize that Andreas's behaviors were unusual or concerning. As part of the clinical intake, Andreas's mother acknowledged that she had spent very little time with Andreas after his birth. She described Andreas's first 18 months as a time when she struggled to get out of an abusive relationship with Andreas's biological father. She noted that she frequently fled from their apartment and would stay away for up to a month at a time without Andreas. She acknowledged fearing that Andreas was likely neglected, and possibly abused, by his father and his friends, who spent most of their days and evenings in the apartment using and selling drugs. Andreas's mother reported that when Andreas was 2, she finally found a way to leave the abusive relationship and move in with her mother, who has been supportive. She notes that while life feels safer and more stable, she also feels that she is just now learning how to be a good mother to Andreas. ■

As described in the case of Andreas, reactive attachment disorder involves a lack of organized attachment behaviors, reduced social engagement, and emotion regulation difficulties (such as excessive inhibition and hypervigilance). Children with reactive attachment disorder do not seek comfort when distressed and are not easily soothed by others (Rutter et al., 2009; Zeanah & Smyke, 2009).

Reactive attachment disorder is rare and is almost always diagnosed in children with very adverse experiences (e.g., institutionalization, maltreatment) (Zeanah & Smyke, 2009).

The Case of Julia: Disinhibited Social Engagement Disorder

Julia is 36 months old. She and her parents were referred by a county social worker who has worked with the family for years. The social worker, having observed Julia during home visits and in her early childhood day care program, expressed concern about Julia's indiscriminate and overly affectionate engagement of nearly every adult she encounters. These behaviors are not only evident at day care, away from her parents, but in the home as well, when her parents are present. The social worker also notes that when Julia becomes frustrated or upset, she often seems to prefer comfort and help from adults relatively unfamiliar to her, rather than from her parents.

Both of Julia's parents have documented cognitive delays and major mental illnesses. Two of Julia's older siblings were removed from the home and have been in long-term foster care after child protection services were alerted to conditions of severe neglect. Although Julia's parents have had more support since her birth and are functioning better than in years past, they struggle with a broad range of daily care activities in their own lives and as parents. They rightly count as progress their ability to better feed and clothe Julia, but they provide very little developmentally appropriate stimulation for her. For example, they generally choose to leave

Children in Romanian Orphanages: Risks, Interventions, and Outcomes

Concerns over breakdowns in early caregiving predated research on the attachment process. In fact, prior to his work on attachment theory, John Bowlby, as well as other psychiatrists working in the 1940s and 1950s, called attention to the devastating developmental impact of early psychological deprivation. In orphanages, hospitals, and residential nurseries, clinicians observed infants and young children whose basic physical requirements were met but whose emotional and social needs went unrecognized and unfulfilled. Whereas some orphanages, for example, provided babies with both nutrition and nurturance, others—because of overcrowding, lack of resources, and lack of knowledge—provided only the barest essentials: a crib, bottles of milk, and rigid feeding and changing schedules. Caregivers changed from morning to evening; intimate and enduring relationships were impossible.

We know now that a cheerful, stimulating environment, with warm and consistent caregiving, is the foundation for psychological growth. But this knowledge has not eliminated the poor institutional care that was blamed for the intellectual, emotional, and social struggles of so many deprived children during and following World War II. We have only to look at the more recent experiences of children in Romanian and other Eastern European orphanages to see that—for multiple reasons—basic needs for contact, care, and comfort from a familiar adult are too often unmet.

The experiences of Romanian babies abandoned to poor quality institutions and later adopted (or fostered) by well-functioning families have been described in several longitudinal research programs, including the English and Romanian Adoptees study (ERA) in the United Kingdom (e.g., Rutter, Sonuga-Barke, & Castle, 2010) and the Bucharest Early Intervention Program (BEIP) in the United States (e.g., Smyke, Zeanah, Fox, & Nelson, 2009). The ERA study, which has followed Romanian children adopted by English families from infancy to adolescence, documented marked improvement in physical health and psychological functioning for many children following adoption, as well as continuing cognitive and mental health difficulties for a substantial minority of children. A finding of particular interest

is that several distinctive patterns of compromised development, called *deprivation-specific psychological patterns* (DSPs), are evident among these children (Kumsta et al., 2010). These patterns include "quasi-autism," "disinhibited attachment," "cognitive impairment," and "intervention/overactivity." Whereas the specific problems described by these patterns are common in clinical populations, the ERA researchers believe that the DSPs reflect patterns of maladaptive development that are directly linked to early deprivation.

The BEIP study represents a unique "natural experiment" in which infants and toddlers from Romanian institutions were placed in high-quality Romanian foster homes and compared, over time, with children who continued to be institutionally raised. Factors ranging from genetic sensitivity to caregiving (Drury et al., 2011) to varied psychiatric outcomes (Bos et al., 2011) are being carefully considered in a set of longitudinal studies. These studies provide data about wide-ranging developmental delays and patterns of maladjustment, as well as frequent instances of resilience and the possibility of remarkable recovery. BEIP research has shown, for example, that children in foster care who displayed greater attachment security developed fewer internalizing disorders (McLaughlin, Zeanah, Fox, & Nelson, 2012). And, more generally, that children raised in foster care displayed significantly greater gains in cognitive functioning, especially if they entered foster care before they were 2 years old (Nelson et al., 2007).

Both the ERA and BEIP research have documented the powerfully negative impact of early deprivation on physical, cognitive, emotional, social, and behavioral development. As salient as these negative consequences of early deprivation are, it is equally impressive to note the dramatic turnarounds that may occur with family placements. Improvements have been described for all types of physiological, psychological, and social functioning, with normalization of some domains and the diminishment of severity of disorder in others. Even with these positive outcomes, we need to keep in mind that many children continue to struggle; appropriate interventions for all of the children remain the focus of ongoing study.

her alone in front of the TV for hours rather than play with her or take her to the nearby playground. At times, when prompted by county case workers involved with the family, they make a greater effort to engage Julia, but they are generally unable to sustain these interactions. They have been observed to overreact to Julia's attempts to get attention and, at other times, to ignore these types of behaviors altogether until Julia finally gives up. Although they continue to accept help from the county in an effort to head off Julia's removal from their home, it is clear that more intensive services are necessary. ▬

Children with disinhibited social engagement disorder, as seen in the case of Julia, display little if any reticence with unfamiliar others and wander off without checking back. This social behavior is noteworthy given typically developing children's wariness around strangers and in unfamiliar settings. Children with disinhibited social engagement disorder also exhibit socially superficial behavior and attention seeking; inappropriate physical contact (e.g., hugging, climbing into laps) is also observed (Rutter, 2009; Zeanah & Smyke, 2009). This indiscriminate sociability may be understood as part of a larger pattern of dysregulation (Pears, Bruce, Fisher, & Kim, 2010). Compared to reactive attachment disorder, disinhibited social engagement disorder is more frequently diagnosed (Zeanah & Smyke, 2009).

Developmental Course

Young children diagnosed with disorders of attachment may follow a number of developmental pathways; these pathways include both resilience and psychopathology. With respect to various short- and long-term outcomes, it is important to keep several things in mind: (1) Most of the longitudinal research has been done with samples of young children who were classified as insecure, rather than with young children diagnosed with disorders of attachment; (2) there are no clear associations between specific classifications (i.e., resistant vs. avoidant vs. disorganized) and specific disorders; and (3) although specific links are not well described, increased risk for both internalizing and externalizing disorders has been well documented (Sroufe, 2005; Zeanah & Smyke, 2009). An especially compelling review of the developmental course of attachment disorders is provided in Box 6:2, a summary of contemporary studies that focus on children from Romanian orphanages.

Many children with insecure attachments and disorders of attachment exhibit ongoing difficulties in physiological, emotional, behavioral, and cognitive domains. The most salient effect of disordered attachment is on the parent–child relationship, and the ways in which children and parents play together, learn together, and work together. In many different studies, children with insecure attachments display less positive, less agreeable, and less competent interactions than children with secure attachments (Sroufe, 1983, 2005; Thompson, 1999).

With respect to physiological correlates of attachment, there are abundant data that caregiving influences the development and organization of stress systems, with a variety of impacts on infant sensitivity to stress, infant arousal, and infant responsivity (Luecken & Lemery, 2004; Nachmias, Gunnar, Mangelsdorf, Parritz, & Buss, 1996; Oosterman, De Schipper, Fisher, Dozier, & Schuengel, 2010). One particularly problematic consequence involves "hyperactivation strategies in the face of anxiety," a result of earlier "dysfunctional co-regulation of fear and stress states" (Nolte, Guiney, Fonagy, Mayes, & Luyten, 2011).

Intrapersonal experiences and interpersonal expressions of emotions are also problematic. Insecurely attached children frequently exhibit negative emotion (e.g., fear, anger, sadness) in multiple situations (e.g., both in and out of the home) (Nolte et al., 2011; Sroufe, 2005). Feelings of security are often diminished or absent. In addition, the development of emotional dispositions or styles, including competencies related to the signaling and interpretation of emotion, are tied to early attachment patterns (Magai, 1999).

The emphasis on cognitive components of attachment and the development of internal models and mental representations provide a theoretical basis for the association between attachment difficulties and cognitive difficulties. With respect to cognitive content, Greenberg, Speltz, and DeKlyen (1993) have observed that insecure children have cognitive models "in which relationships are ... characterized by anger, mistrust, chaos and insecurity" (p. 201); these investigators link these negative cognitions to the aggressive behavior exhibited by insecure children. A 6-year-old child's story of what happens in playing with dolls illustrates this point: "And see, and then, you know what happens? Their whole house blows up. See. . . . They get destroyed and not even their bones are left. Nobody can even get their bones. Look. I'm jumping on a rock. This rock feels rocky. Aahh! Guess what? The hills are alive, the hills are shakin' and shakin'. Because the hills are alive. Uh huh. The hills are alive. Ohh! I fall smack off a hill. And get blowed up in an explosion. And then the rocks tumbled down and smashed everyone. And they all died" (Solomon & George, 1999b, p. 17).

With respect to cognitive skills, Fonagy and Target (1996, 1997) highlight the compromised capacity of insecurely attached children for "mentalizing," or understanding others in terms of their own mental states. Further, Fonagy (1998) suggests that children with insecure attachments have inadequate "mind-reading skills." Children with mind-reading difficulties exhibit, for example, less acceptance of personal responsibility, a lack of appreciation for others, and less concern with distress in others. (Significant difficulties with mind-reading are also evident in children with autism spectrum disorder, discussed in Chapter 8.) Atypical conscience development has also been noted (Kochanska, 1995). For children with disorganized attachments, troubling indications of early dissociation, such as spacing out or being unaware of what just happened, are sometimes observed (Ogawa, Sroufe, Weinfield, Carlson, & Egeland, 1997; Solomon & George, 1999b). Dissociation is an especially concerning symptom because it reflects disrupted integration of the core functions of consciousness, including memory, identity, and awareness of the environment.

With respect to peer relationships in childhood, social skills and social outcomes are clearly affected (Sroufe, 2005; Thompson, 1999). Patterns of withdrawal and victimized children, and patterns of aggression and bullying children, are frequently noted (Sroufe, 2005; Troy & Sroufe, 1987). And across the lifespan, relationship difficulties involving friends, romantic partners, and, later, children may be observed (Sroufe, 2005; Waters, Merrick, Treboux, Crowell, & Albersheim, 2000).

For children diagnosed with reactive attachment disorder, improvements occur when children are placed in better caregiving environments. For example, institutionalized children who are adopted or fostered display positive attachment behaviors fairly quickly. For children diagnosed with disinhibited social engagement disorder, difficulties persist, sometimes into adolescence. This is the case even with more favorable caregiving environments (Rutter et al.., 2009; Zeanah & Smyke, 2009).

Etiology

Much of what is known about the etiology of disorders of attachment is based on what we know about the development of insecure patterns in normal and at-risk children. According to Zeanah and Smyke (2009), "[t]he propensity for human infants to form selective attachments is believed to be so strong that only in highly unusual and maladaptive caregiving environments do attachments fail to develop. For infants raised in species-atypical rearing conditions, however, seriously disturbed and developmentally inappropriate ways of relating may evolve. Examples of atypical environments include institutions (i.e., orphanages), frequent changes of caregivers (as sometimes happens in foster care), neglectful or abusive caregivers, or being raised by insensitive or unresponsive caregivers" (p. 421). All of these factors are discussed in the following sections.

Caregiving Factors

For both categories of attachment disorders, the causal role of caregiving (i.e., caregivers and the caregiving environment) is primary. Inadequate, inattentive, inconsistent, and intrusive care has been repeatedly associated with insecure attachment in children. Neglectful and abusive parenting leads to insecurity and disorders of attachment, with more neglect and more abuse associated with increasingly negative outcomes. Extremely adverse caregiving environments include institutions and problematic foster care and settings that are characterized by maltreatment and domestic violence (Bernier & Meins, 2008; Zeanah & Smyke, 2009). The length of time that children spend in institutional care is specifically related to disinhibited social behavior (Bruce, Tarullo, & Gunnar, 2009). In addition to attachment disorders, institutional rearing is also related to a variety of other poor psychiatric outcomes (Zeanah et al.., 2009).

Parent Factors

Reviews of parent factors include personality and psychopathology, attachment history, and other contextual variables. Mental illness in parents has received a lot of attention (Seifer & Dickstein, 2000). Maternal depression, bipolar disorder, anxiety, substance abuse, and schizophrenia have all been associated with greater frequency of insecurity in children. With respect to disorganized attachment, pathological parenting (e.g., frightening and fearful behaviors) is hypothesized to reflect unresolved conflicts related to the caregiver's attachment (Hesse & Main, 2006; Lyons-Ruth, Yellin, Melnick, & Atwood, 2005; van IJzendoorn, 1995). Pathological parenting is often, but not always, coupled with insensitive parenting (Bernier & Meins, 2008; Rutter et al.., 2009).

Child Factors

Attachment research is primarily focused on caregiving and parental factors. There is evidence, however, that particular infant characteristics do have some effect on attachment variables. For example, for some babies and caregivers, difficult temperament is associated with higher rates of insecure attachment, with more negative, more intense, and more difficult-to-soothe babies making sensitive and consistent caregiving less likely. For the most part, though, many different kinds of babies—easy, demanding, happy, and cranky—are observed in both secure and insecure categories of attachment.

With respect to genetic influence, results from various molecular genetic investigations suggest increased differential susceptibility to poor parenting (i.e., insensitivity and/or frightening or other atypical behavior) (Bernier & Meins, 2008; Drury et al., 2011). Genetic effects may be particularly important for boys (Minnis et al.., 2007). Atypical populations (i.e., babies with special medical histories or needs) provide additional perspective on the contributions of infants to the development of normal and maladaptive attachment. For example, infant prematurity by itself does not lead to higher rates of insecure attachment (Crnic, Greenberg, & Slough, 1986; Easterbrooks, 1989). But with added stressors and few resources or additional medical complications, there is an increase in insecurity (Plunkett, Meisels, Steifel, & Pasik, 1986; Wille, 1991). Empirical reviews of other atypical developments report somewhat lower rates of security in infants with various congenital or medical conditions compared to normal samples (50% versus 65%) (Van IJzendoorn, Goldberg, Kroonenberg, & Frenkel, 1992; Barnett et al.., 1999).

There is also evidence that children with certain neurological difficulties, such as Down syndrome or autism, may display unusual attachments (Zeanah & Smyke, 2009). Babies diagnosed with cystic fibrosis and congenital heart defects are later classified as disorganized at higher rates than typically developing babies (Goldberg, Gotowiec, & Simmons, 1995); this is also the case with babies diagnosed with epilepsy

(Marvin & Pianta, 1996). Diagnostic differentiation of overlapping clinical presentations is a difficult task (Barnett et al., 1999; Pipp-Siegel, Siegel, & Dean, 1999). Regarding the development of attachment in atypical infants, it appears that a combination of factors is critical, including parental acceptance and understanding of a child's medical condition and needs, personal and family demands, and child characteristics that present caregiving challenges.

Assessment and Diagnosis

In contrast to much of the research-oriented assessment of attachment in normal and at-risk samples of young children, the clinically oriented assessment of disorders of attachment involves more naturalistic data collection (O'Connor & Zeanah, 2003). Home visits or assessments in homelike settings are preferable, and in some cases may be necessary. An assessment of the child's attachment(s) will also depend, in a very significant way, on fostering a therapeutic alliance with the parent (or other primary caregiver). This particular therapeutic alliance may be more problematic than other parent–professional collaborations, because the child's core distress and dysfunction relate to issues of caregiving (Hirshberg, 1993). Managing to collect information that may reflect poorly on actual caregiving attitudes and behaviors of parents or that may exacerbate parental beliefs about incompetency is often difficult. Highlighting shared parental and clinical concerns about improvements in the child's well-being may help smooth the assessment process.

History Taking and Interviews

Basically, the initial assessment must provide relevant data on the attachment struggles of a particular child; what kind of caregiver is involved; and what match there is between this particular baby and this particular caregiver. The characteristics of the child that are most frequently addressed include birth variables (such as prematurity or peri- and postnatal complications), temperament, patterns of early regulation, and timetables for developmental milestones (such as crawling and talking).

The characteristics of parents that are often addressed include general perceptions and specific knowledge about infants and caregiving, available support and resources, personalities, parental attachment histories, and associated family dynamics. If we think about the possibility that parental attachment issues are reenacted and rene-gotiated in the new caregiving relationship, it may be especially important to gain perspective on parents' own attachment experiences. Still, because parents usually come to therapy because of difficulties with a child and *not* to explore their own issues, it makes sense to keep the focus of the assessment on "the past as it is active in the present" (Hirshberg, 1993, p. 177). That is, clinicians may need to emphasize the specific ways in which unresolved or intensely experienced parental attachment contributes to the current child or family difficulties. Valuable context for such information might be provided by having parents talk about the ways in which their tempera-ments, their personalities, and their preferences for activities and goals do and do not mesh with their child's, and the ways in which particular caregiv-ing attitudes and behaviors may have compromised their child's attachments.

Questionnaires and Structured Tasks

Other sources of assessment data in clinical settings include a variety of instruments and procedures originally designed for use with normal samples of young children. One of the more widely used instru-ments, developed as an alternative to the Strange Situation Procedure, is the Attachment Q-Sort for children between 1 and 5 years (Waters, 1995). Bretherton, Ridgeway, and Cassidy (1990) devel-oped an attachment-relevant story completion task for preschoolers, using doll play and story situations designed to tap challenging parent–child experiences (e.g., child injury, separation, fear of monsters). Their data suggest that 3-year-olds are capable of produc-ing coherent story narratives in which parents are described as supportive and empathic. For assess-ments related to disorders of attachment, we would expect less coherent narratives and more descrip-tions of parents as unable to protect the child, as less warm and more punitive. This assessment hypoth-esis requires additional research.

Observations

Perhaps the most important contributions to the accurate assessment of disorders of attachment are observations of the infant in his or her everyday envi-ronment. Clinical interpretations of real-life parent–child interactions are essential for understanding the dynamics of attachment. In all of the clinical cases presented earlier in the chapter, direct observation

of the children contributed to making the correct diagnosis. The rating and analysis of observed parental behaviors in everyday and challenging situ-ations may provide additional perspective.

Assessments in Older Children and Adolescents

Although much of the theoretical and clinical atten-tion currently paid to disorders of attachment is focused on the first few years of life, it is likely that many instances of these disorders will be identified and assessed in older children. As already discussed, in terms of the normative processes of attachment, we expect coherence and stability in the years beyond infancy and preschool, as well as salient differences in the experience and expression of attachment. For example, by the age of 6, there is a new emphasis on language-mediated information (Main et al., 1985). Main and her colleagues suggest that children's more-developed language abilities allow for mean-ingful assessments of emotional openness in dis-cussions of parent–child separations and/or other aspects of relationships.

With increasing age, it becomes more difficult to assess and diagnose specific disorders of attachment. Older children and adolescents often exhibit multiple problems, including aggression, anxiety, and depres-sion, with a number of children meeting the diagnostic criteria for several disorders. Some of these disorders have their etiological roots in disorders of attachment, and some do not. A comprehensive assessment—whether simple and straightforward or messy and complicated—will always keep the child in full view.

Intervention

Within the framework of developmental psychopa-thology, it is both theoretically and practically eas-ier to prevent the development of disorder than it is to intervene effectively. However, children, parents, and mental health professionals must deal with real-life circumstances. Real life demands that we design and validate therapeutic interventions for disorders of attachment.

Prevention Strategies

Prevention strategies related to disorders of attach-ment can be usefully categorized as **universal mea-sures** for the general population, **selective measures** for groups at above-average risk, and **indicated mea-sures** for groups with specific risk factors requiring more extensive help. One example of a universal measure designed to promote infant and parent well-being is the early child education program, delivered before and after the baby is born (Feinberg & Kan, 2008). Home-based strategies provide illustrations of selected and indicated preventive measures. Overall, it is difficult to enhance parental sensitivity; effective interventions have clear goals and, often, a behavioral emphasis (Bakermans-Kranenburg, Van IJzendoorn, & Juffer, 2003). Clinicians have also been successful in strengthening parent–child relationships using psychodynamically informed filial therapy (VanFleet, Ryan, & Smith, 2005). Erickson's Steps Toward Effective, Enjoyable Parenting (STEEP) model (Erickson, Korfmacher, & Egeland, 1992), based on the Minnesota Mother–Child Project, targets at-risk parents. Individual and group sessions during the mother's pregnancy and through the child's first year, exploring the mother's feelings, attitudes, and behaviors related to caregiving, are designed to influence the mother's internal working model of attachment. Changes in the mother's working model positively influence children's security. Another ambitious, multidisciplinary, home-based model was developed by Cicchetti and Toth (1987, 1995) in Rochester, New York, involving social workers, psychologists, psychiatrists, special educators, and other health professionals, and focuses on parent, child, and environmental variables.

Prevention-oriented intervention can also be provided to caregivers at high risk for maltreatment. The Attachment and Biobehavioral Catch-up (ABC) program is a brief, manualized intervention that targets three key behaviors: providing nurturant care when children are distressed; following children's leads when they are not upset; and not exhibiting frightening behavior. Young children whose parents participated in the program displayed more secure and more organized attachments (Bernard et al., 2012).

An ambitious approach to prevention via institutional change was conducted by McCall and colleagues in Russia (St. Petersburg–USA Orphanage Research Team, 2008). In orphanages where training on sensitive caregiving was provided and where attempts were made to enhance positive relationships by reducing the number of children per caregiver, young children displayed more positive patterns of emotions and behaviors. Finally, to the extent that at-risk children (in all sorts of extremely adverse environments) are quickly placed in positive caregiving settings, the prevalence of disorders of attachment would certainly decrease (Zeanah & Smyke, 2009).

Child Treatment

With respect to therapeutic approaches for children already diagnosed with problematic or disordered attachments, meaningful improvement depends on the duration and degree of disorder, particular etiology, age of the child, and the scope of environmental change. Zeanah and Smyke (2009) make clear that "the first priority of treatment is to establish a safe and stable caregiving environment with a warm and consistent caregiver" (p. 429), with the goals of enhancing adaptive behaviors and decreasing maladaptive behaviors. Further, they suggest that optimism is warranted, because "it is so crucial for children to form and sustain attachments to caregiving adults that they retain the capacity to do so once environments improve" (p. 430). McDonough (1993) describes "interaction guidance" therapy that builds on the skills and strengths (however fleeting or minimal) that caregivers display. In each therapeutic session, caregivers and their infants are videotaped, with opportunities for immediate processing and feedback. Consider a mother who displayed distant, emotionally constricted care for her young son, saying "I just don't seem to matter to him. No one does" (p. 423). Viewing a just-videotaped interaction of the child's smiling in response to the mother's brief imitation of the child's vocalizations allowed the mother to see her child's actual happiness. Changing the caregiver's perceptions and behaviors, little bit by little bit, leads to changes in the attachment relationship.

A noteworthy example of the repair of attachment relationships is provided by Stovall and Dozier's (2000) case studies of new attachments in very young children placed in foster care. Stovall and Dozier explored the effects of early versus later placement and the attachment status of the foster parent. New, secure attachments developed over the course of 2 months for those children placed early with autonomously attached foster parents. Children placed later, or those placed with adults with unresolved or dismissive attachments, exhibited insecure patterns of attachment. Foster parents who responded to their children's difficult and often alienating behaviors with nurturant caregiving were more likely to have securely attached children.

Infant–Parent Psychotherapy

In other clinical approaches, Lieberman (Lieberman & Pawl, 1993; Lieberman & Van Horn, 2009) describes infant–parent psychotherapy, based on Fraiberg's work (Fraiberg, Adelson, & Shapiro, 1980). In infant–parent psychotherapy, there is a joint emphasis on what the parent and the child each bring to the difficult relationship, as well as the subjective experiences of both parent and child. This psychotherapy is a collaborative endeavor, with the therapist and parent working together to create agendas, determine goals, and establish procedures for evaluation. Acknowledging complex parent motivations and feelings, including "anger, relief, reluctance, and hope" (Lieberman & Pawl, 1993, p. 429), is important. Lieberman and Zeanah (1999) further note that the therapist's positive regard for the parent(s) and his/her empathy and attention during difficult moments illustrate adaptive and positive ways of relating, which the parent can—over time—both internalize and express in attachment relationships. Infant–parent psychotherapy has proven useful for varied clinical samples, including infants in maltreating families (Cicchetti, Rogosch, & Toth, 2006; Lieberman & Van Horn, 2009).

The therapist–child relationship, and the ways in which the relationship serves as a template or a substitution for the actual parent–child relationship, requires special attention. In particular, therapists must be wary of the following situation: "When the parent blames the baby, the therapist blames the parent. In this therapeutically damaging parallel process, parent and therapist both forget that the situation at hand is only the immediate and concrete representation of a tormented emotional landscape where both parent and baby are being victimized. Blame does not help. Only understanding holds hope…" (Lieberman & Pawl, 1990, p. 438).

With respect to the efficacy of various interventions, results are mixed. Treatment outcome research provides some support for the infant–parent psychotherapy approach to disorders of attachment (Lieberman & Van Horn, 2009). Reviews of the empirical data suggest that strategies designed to improve maternal sensitivity, and thereby attachment status, sometimes do and sometimes do not achieve expected outcomes (Cohen et al., 1999; Lieberman & Van Horn, 2009), suggesting that additional work on specific and efficacious treatments is clearly needed.

Finally, as repeatedly discussed, it is absolutely critical to understand that there is no clear professional consensus related to the assessment, diagnosis, and treatment of attachment disorders. Theoretical accounts remain speculative, and much empirical work remains to be done before we can achieve a reliable understanding of these phenomena. In the interim, it is important that our working formulations do not lead us to pathologize children excessively. For example, we must take care to ensure that adults do not misperceive children diagnosed with attachment disorders as permanently damaged or impaired. To the contrary, as described in Box 6:1, the evidence to date suggests that the earlier at-risk children are provided with healthy emotional and social support, the better their prospects for reduced developmental delay and recovery of emotional and cognitive well-being.

Key Terms

Secure attachment (p. 81)
Insecure attachment (p. 81)
Strange Situation Procedure (p. 81)
Resistant (anxious/ambivalent) attachment (p. 81)
Avoidant (anxious/avoidant) attachment (p. 82)
Disorganized attachment (p. 82)
Risk (p. 83)
Reactive attachment disorder (p. 84)
Disinhibited social engagement disorder (p. 84)
Universal measures (p. 90)
Selective measures (p. 90)
Indicated measures (p. 90)

Chapter Summary

- The development of a secure attachment relationship between infant and caregiver is the critical task in the first year of life.
- Secure attachment relationships are the result of consistent, appropriate responsiveness by the caregiver to the infant's physical, emotional, and social needs.

- Resistant attachment relationships stem from inconsistent caregiving behavior.
- Avoidant attachment relationships result from ineffective or inappropriate caregiving.
- Disorganized attachment relationships occur when the caregiver is associated with frightening or malicious events. They involve a distinctive pattern of both approach and avoidance in infants.
- Early attachment relationships impact neurological and personality development and provide models for future relationships.
- DSM-5 describes two kinds of attachment disorders: reactive attachment disorder and disinhibited social engagement disorder.
- Attachment disorders may compromise a number of developmental domains, including social, cognitive, and emotional development. These outcomes can reverberate throughout childhood, adolescence, and adulthood.
- Caregiving, parental, and some child-based factors influence the etiology of attachment disorders.
- Assessment takes a variety of forms, including clinical and naturalistic observation as well as standardized interviews and questionnaires with parents and children.
- Prevention strategies range from universal measures for the general population to more selective measures, which target more specific risk factors and high-risk groups.
- Child-oriented, parent-oriented, and joint therapeutic approaches have met with mixed empirical success, meriting further study of treatments for attachment disorders.

7

Intellectual Developmental Disorder and Learning Disorders

"**ADAM DEALS WITH MANY** things more graciously than I do. Take illness, for example. My first clue that he isn't feeling well is usually a polite knock on my door in the middle of the night. After a pause, just as I'm telling myself that I didn't hear anything and should go back to sleep, a small, gruff voice will rasp, 'Mom, U'm gick.'

"I'll drag myself awake to find him standing by my bed, fraught with some horrific assortment of symptoms: blazing fevers, rashes that turn his usually flat little face into a topographical map of Nepal, chest coughs that sound like gang warfare between two prides of lions. Adam's immune system is weaker than a normal nine-year-old's, and every germ he catches rollicks gaily through his body, holding orgies of self-reproduction and sending enthusiastic invitations to others of its kind. When Adam gets gick, he gets really, really gick.

"Gick, if you haven't figured it out by now, is Adam's word for sick. He has learned to speak fairly well in the last few years, but the muscles of his mouth aren't formed for our language, so he often uses his own. Adamic, we call it. It is a strange dialect, in which syllables are often reversed or replaced with random consonants, sound effects, and gestures. . . .

"Eventually I get out of bed, and we go down the hall together, Adam holding my hand in his small, dry, stubby fingers. We stand in the doorway of his room and assess the damage. This is what always amazes me: if he's thrown up, he will have done his best to clean the room before involving me. 'Bleah,' he will explain, flipping his hand from his mouth outward, as though the smell alone weren't enough to tell me what happened. 'I keen.' 'Yes,' I'll say. 'You cleaned up. Thanks, buddy. Good boy.'

"Then Adam, ill and weary as he is, helps me spray the rug with cleanser, scrub out the stain, and change his sheets. He gamely swallows a dose of Tylenol, says 'Unkoo, Mom'—and flops down on his pillow, already asleep. The genetic weakness of his muscles (hypotonia, the doctors call it) lets his body fall into strange shapes, as though he has been dropped out of a plane to his death; legs twisted under him, undersize head bent too far back, chunky little arms flung wide. His small, slanted eyes flicker beneath their lids as he begins to dream. Watching him, I think he is the most beautiful child I have ever known." (from Martha Beck's *Expecting Adam*, pp. 20–21) ■

There have always been children like Adam: children with intellectual developmental disorder who have been the causes of bewilderment, the targets of ridicule and institutionalization, and the focus of parents' love and care. Any historical perspective on intellectual developmental disorder must include the centuries of mistaken beliefs and woeful attempts at intervention (see Box 7:1); it must also include the longstanding concern expressed for children with intellectual developmental disorder by parents, teachers, and mental health professionals, and the recent developments related to progress in mapping the human genome (www.genome.gov). With interest and research at an all-time high, intellectual developmental disorder has gone from the "Cinderella" of child psychiatry to the "belle of the biopsychosocial ball" (State, King, & Dykens, 1997, p. 1664).

Developmental Tasks and Challenges Related to Intelligence and Cognition

"A child's IQ is more closely related to the child's later occupational success than is the socioeconomic status of the family within which the child grows up, the family's income, the school the child attends, or

---

BOX 7:1   THE CHILD IN CONTEXT

A Look Back at History—The Eugenics Movement

Over the past two centuries, public attitudes and policies related to the treatment of individuals with intellectual developmental disorder have undergone dramatic shifts (Baumeister & Baumeister, 1995; O'Brien, 1999). Mesibov (1976) describes the mid-19th century as a time when individuals with mild or moderate intellectual developmental disorder probably blended into the mostly unschooled, agrarian American landscape. Over time, physicians and other professionals became increasingly interested in training persons with intellectual developmental disorder so that they could become active, productive members of a more complex society characterized by changing forms of labor and sociocultural organization. Intensive training took place, primarily in residential settings, designed to prepare individuals with intellectual developmental disorder for successful adjustment to their communities. These plans were overly optimistic, and many advocates of change became discouraged. Residential programs "slowly became places of refuge for mentally retarded people who were now thought to be unable to live in modern society" (Mesibov, 1976, p. 27).

By the late 19th and early 20th centuries, attitudes and policies took an alarming turn. With new knowledge about heredity and the development of intelligence tests, scientists, mental health professionals, and government officials accepted the premises of eugenics—that social control of reproduction could and would improve the species—and began to view individuals with intellectual developmental disorder with scorn and disapprobation. Sensationalistic concerns about the impact of the "feeble-minded," the "morons," and the "degenerates" on crime rates and every other social ill were widespread. Two solutions seemed reasonable to the overwrought citizens: segregation and sterilization. Segregation involved the forced separation of men and women in residential care; sterilization laws were passed in many states. Even the extreme option of euthanasia was discussed, but it did not receive widespread support. With more data, and moral and practical reflection, segregation and sterilization came to be seen as unethical and unnecessary. Recent decades have been characterized as focused on advocacy and support for those who struggle with intellectual developmental disorder.

---

any other variable that has been studied" (Siegler, 2003, p. 314). Siegler's appraisal of the empirical data underscores the need to understand the complex construct of intelligence and its contribution to normal and pathological aspects of development. Given the many controversies surrounding the nature and assessment of intelligence, the following summaries are necessarily brief. They are organized around several key issues: (1) What are the underlying components and mechanisms of intelligence? (2) How does cognitive and intellectual development unfold over time? (3) What kinds of individual differences are observed? (4) What are the roles of heredity and the environment in the development of intelligence?

Components and Mechanisms of Intelligence

The most basic question involves the nature of intelligence. Our working definition of intelligence is "cognition comprising sensory, perceptual, associative, and relational knowledge" (Das, 2004). A theoretically broader, more empirically driven definition, based on a research review by an American Psychological Association's task force, asserts that "individuals differ from one another in their ability to understand complex ideas, to adapt effectively to the environment, to learn from experience, to engage in various forms of reasoning, to overcome obstacles by taking thought. Although these individual differences can be substantial, they are never entirely consistent: a given person's intellectual performance will vary on different occasions, in different domains, as judged by different criteria" (Neisser et al., 1996). Hypotheses about the components of intelligence range from a single, unitary competence that influences almost all that we do (and that each of us possesses to a greater or lesser degree), to unique collections of particular talents and skills that exhibit little overlap, to hierarchically organized sets of both general and specific abilities.

Most theorists agree that intelligence involves the performance of basic mental tasks, including perception of the environment, communication and language, and higher-level tasks such as reasoning, problem solving, and planning. Although traditional models emphasize the components or capacities of intelligence that are related to academic, educational, and occupational outcomes (i.e., verbal and mathematical abilities), these models may also include capacities for music, art, mechanics, and relationships (Gardner, 1993; Siegler, 2003). In addition to these components, mechanisms such as speed (or efficiency) of mental processing and working memory must be accounted for in models of intellectual functioning (Anderson, 2001; Kail, 2003). Motivational aspects such as curiosity and exploration must also be understood (Wentworth & Witryol, 2003).

Development of Cognitive and Intellectual Functioning

To understand the slowed and atypical pathways for children with intellectual developmental disorder, and the ways in which learning is accomplished for typically developing children and compromised for children with learning disorders, we must appreciate both **cognitive development**, or general age-related trends, and **intellectual development**, or individual differences observed among normally developing children at every age. With respect to cognitive development, we need to take into account the components and processes of cognition (e.g., perception, attention, memory, concept formation). As described in Chapter 2, contemporary research focuses on the dynamic interaction of tasks, contexts, and emotional states that influence cognition (Rose & Fischer, 2009), as well as interpretations of the *how* and *why* of children's thinking and learning (Gopnik & Tenenbaum, 2007). The neoconstructivist model of cognition emphasizes evolutionary contexts, experience–expectant learning (an example of a brain–behavior relation), and both qualitative and quantitative change across development (Newcombe, 2011). In general, it is well accepted that there is steady, linear progress in cognitive achievements, with occasional reorganizations, or qualitatively distinct "developmental leaps." For example, children learn and remember more information as they age, but they also become faster and more efficient at manipulating that information; the pace of progress is greater through the preschool and elementary school years and slows somewhat during adolescence (Kail, 2000, 2003).

With respect to intellectual development, there is a general emergence of intellectual functioning, as well as specific patterns of strengths and weaknesses in both components and mechanisms, reflected in individual differences in various intellectual domains (Anderson, 2001; Flavell, 1982a, 1982b; Gardner, 1983). Components and mechanisms include factors such as reasoning, complex problem solving, speed of processing and learning. Patterns of individual differences appear relatively stable from 4 or 5 years of age through adulthood, with both growth and decline observed throughout the lifespan.

Heredity and the Environment

There is overwhelming evidence that both heredity and the environment contribute to children's cognitive and intellectual development (Anderson, 2007; Gray & Thompson, 2004; Newcombe, 2002). Data from numerous twin, family, and adoption studies suggest that genes influence about 50% of the variation in intelligence (with overlapping genetic effects on specific cognitive abilities), and that the genetic influence increases with age. That is, "the genetic contribution to intelligence becomes larger, not smaller, as children develop" (Siegler, 2003, p. 314). This is associated with some of the genetic impact expressed after infancy, with some genes becoming active later in development, along with children's increasingly active role in choosing particular tasks and environments for themselves (Haworth et al., 2010; Scarr, 1997, 1998). The Colorado Adoption Project provides support for both increased genetic influence and the role of nonshared environmental factors (Alarcon, Plomin, Fulker, Corley, & DeFries, 1998; Petrill et al., 2004).

Much of the genetic influence on intelligence is associated with brain structure and function. Brain size is correlated with intelligence (Gray & Thompson, 2004), and multiple (and networked) brain regions (such as the prefrontal cortex) linked to intelligence become fine-tuned over development (Casey, Tottenham, Listen, & Durston, 2005; Choi et al., 2008; Shaw et al., 2006). Differences in the dopamine system have also been hypothesized to underlie the tendency to be imaginative, curious, and intellectual (DeYoung et al., 2011).

The child's immediate and larger environments also have considerable impact (Gray & Thompson, 2004; Siegler, 2003). Pre- and postnatal environments have demonstrable impacts. Maternal drug or alcohol use, or exposure to toxins, negatively impacts intelligence. Factors such as parental stimulation and/or responsiveness, education, parental interest in academics, and parental beliefs about children's intelligence have been associated with more positive outcomes (Roberts, Bornstein, Slater, & Barrett, 1999). Many researchers have also described within-family, nonshared effects on children's intelligence related to siblings' differing expectations, roles, and birth order positions (Siegler, 2003).

The most frequently mentioned influence from the larger environmental milieu is poverty, with damaging effects on intellectual development and achievement. According to Siegler (2003), "poverty exerts its negative effects on intellectual development through several mechanisms: inadequate diet, lack of timely access to health services, parental preoccupation with other problems, and insufficient intellectual stimulation and support in the home" (p. 316; see also Lawlor et al., 2005). He continues, "In 1998, 26% of African American and Hispanic children lived in families with incomes below the poverty line versus 8% of European American children (U.S. Census Bureau, 2000). This means that the effects of poverty are not randomly distributed among families in the United States; they are concentrated in African American and Latino families" (p. 316). Interventions involving early enrichment promote typical development by preventing adverse impacts on cognitive ability and other characteristics (Gottlieb & Blair, 2004). How our society addresses these kinds of inequalities and provides (or fails to provide) effective interventions are ethical issues with far-reaching consequences.

Learning, of course, depends on intellectual and cognitive development. With respect to academic tasks, there are a myriad of learning-related capacities and skills, each with its own maturational and practice timeline (Barkley, 1997a, 1997b; Brocki & Bohlin, 2004). The development of self-regulation is critical (Blair, 2002; Eisenberg, Valiente, & Eggum, 2010; Morrison, Ponitz, & McClelland, 2010). These capacities and skills underlie children's expected mastery and progress in early school skills, such as reading and mathematics, with individual variations in the timing and nature of children's learning (Blair, 2002; Li-Grining, Votruba-Drzal, Maldonado-Carreno, & Haas, 2010). In addition, there are well-documented changes in the ways in which children appraise themselves, their cognitive and academic abilities, and their progress toward their own and others' goals. During the elementary school years, for example, children view their reading and math skills as increasingly stable and pay more attention to performance evaluations, especially those related to competence or incompetence (Pomerantz & Altermatt, 1999; Pomerantz & Eaton, 2001).

The sociocultural context of academic pathways, with an emphasis on cultural values related to education and achievement, must be considered. For instance, studies of immigrant families, and American Indian and Alaska Native youth, illustrate the ways in which parents and communities, and factors such as socioeconomic status and access to quality educational practices, influence children's academic outcomes (Marks & Coll, 2007; Mitchell, Croy, Spicer, Frankel, & Emde, 2011; Szalacha, Marks, Lamarre, & Coll, 2005). Across all cultures and backgrounds, children's learning occurs in the context of transactions among individuals (children, parents, teachers), settings (home, school, child care), and institutions (communities, schools, governments) (Mashburn & Pianta, 2006).

Intellectual Developmental Disorder

Intellectual developmental disorder (IDD) involves deficits in **intellectual functioning** and deficits in **adaptive behavior,** both of which emerge early in development (American Association on Intellectual and Developmental Disabilities [AAIDD], 2002; DSM-5, 2013). Deficits in intellectual functioning are evaluated with respect to the range and distribution of intelligence (IQ) scores in typically developing individuals (see Fig. 7:1). The most important distinction related to the clinical presentation of intellectual developmental disorder is level of severity. *Mild, moderate, severe,* and *profound* levels of severity indicate the degree of impairment in adaptive functioning. According to the AAIDD and DSM-5, adaptive functioning refers to how well an individual negotiates everyday tasks and challenges in conceptual, social, and practical domains. Some children with poor adaptive functioning exhibit significant problems with basic activities of daily living such as getting dressed and maintaining hygiene; others do well with basic tasks but struggle with more complex activities such as preparing snacks or performing household chores.

Although both the DSM-5 and AAIDD conceptualizations of IDD recognize the interdependent

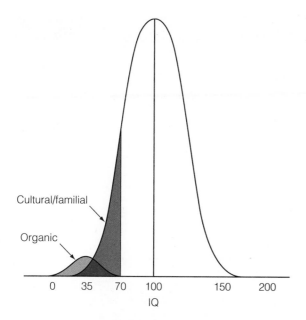

FIGURE 7:1 Bimodal distribution of IQ scores.
Source: From E. Zigler & R.M. Hodapp, "Understanding Mental Retardation", p. 73 (New York, NY: Cambridge University Press, 1986). Copyright © 1986 Cambridge University Press. Reprinted with the permission of Cambridge University Press.

nature of intellectual and adaptive functioning, as well as multiple etiologies and outcomes, the AAIDD emphasizes a more holistic perspective. In this view, IDD is not a physical or mental disorder, but "a disability characterized by significant limitations both in intellectual functioning and in adaptive behavior as expressed in conceptual, social, and practical adaptive skills." Each area of dysfunction includes a corresponding description of the support necessary for maximizing the individual's well-being: *intermittent*, *limited*, *extensive*, or *pervasive support*. Rather than emphasizing the degree of deficit, the AAIDD emphasizes the possibility of adaptation. Whether the definition of IDD emphasizes deficits or supports, it is also important to acknowledge the impact that the actual name of a disorder or a disability has on individuals who are diagnosed, on family members, and on society (see Box 7:2).

The Case of Katherine

Katherine is 8 years old, the fourth of seven brothers and sisters, but her mother Mary always refers to her as "my baby, because she never fusses." Mary and her family live with her mother in the cramped three-bedroom apartment where Mary grew up. She dropped out of high school when she became pregnant with her first baby at age 15. Katherine's grandmother cleans houses for a living, and Mary cares for the children, who range from 2 to 14 years of age. Katherine's father Philip is a food services worker at the local hospital, but he only sees the children on occasion.

When Katherine neared the end of first grade, Mary was surprised to hear her teacher's concern that Katherine wasn't making adequate progress at school. Katherine's three older brothers had been a handful, each of them experiencing discipline problems ahead of Katherine in the same public school. Mary had noticed that Katherine seemed to lag a little behind her brothers in learning to walk and talk, but she just figured that she would eventually catch up. Mary didn't usually make it to parent nights at school, but she had heard no bad reports on Katherine from the kindergarten teacher, and she was always pleased by how Katherine played so well with her younger sisters. But the teacher told Mary that Katherine wasn't making progress in letter and word recognition, had a hard time following directions, and seemed to be getting more and more anxious and disconnected from the other children as the year went on. It didn't help that some of the other children had started to tease Katherine about her reading struggles.

The school psychologist's assessment of Katherine revealed that she had an IQ of 65 and adaptive skill deficits in the sensorimotor, communication, and self-help areas. Katherine's functioning in all of those areas was more than 2 standard deviations below the norm for her peers, which led to her diagnosis of intellectual developmental disorder of mild severity. An Individualized Education Plan (IEP) was developed in which Katherine remains in the regular classroom for about half the day, with the support of a teacher's aide to guide her work more closely. She also leaves the classroom periodically to participate in specialized classes dedicated to more intensive work on her reading, fine motor, and auditory processing abilities. The IEP contains very specific goals in each skill area, along with a timetable for evaluating Katherine's progress toward each of the goals several times a year. Like any child, Katherine has individual strengths and weaknesses in different areas, and the learning goals are continually readjusted over time to reflect her differential rates of progress. Katherine's classroom teacher has also adopted a curriculum unit that addresses disability stereotyping and helps the children to both understand and be more supportive of Katherine.

The school psychologist met with Mary to help her better understand the nature of Katherine's disability and her future expectations. She explained

BOX 7:2 THE CHILD IN CONTEXT

Changing Names, Changing Stigma?

The names that professionals and lay people use to describe psychopathology provide important information about historical and current attempts to balance scientific knowledge and the social construction of mental illness. Over the years, the terms *moron, idiot, imbecile, changeling,* and *feebleminded* have been used to refer to individuals with particular kinds of intellectual and adaptational limitations. More recently, descriptive concepts such as *mild, moderate, severe,* and *profound mental retardation* are being replaced by terms such as *intellectual developmental disorder* and *developmental disabilities.* Because the language we use depends, in part, on time and context, we must be careful about assumptions related to the similarity of underlying conceptualizations (Gelb, 2002; Goodey, 2001; Smith, 2002; Stainton & McDonagh, 2001). In some important ways, what we identify and understand about intellectual developmental disorder is the same across generations; in other equally important ways, what we identify and understand is very, very different.

Still, a few general trends emerge. First, with every new name, we see an attempt to clarify the essential nature of a specific psychopathology (Smith, 2002). Each attempt takes place within a specific historical milieu and has a variety of functions. These functions include selecting appropriate interventions and designing prevention programs, as well as assigning the individual some status reflecting moral, legal, and social standards. The powerful roles of religion, class, race, and gender that are associated with these functions remain to be fully explored and insistently challenged (Goodey, 2001; Stainton & McDonagh, 2001).

The second trend involves the rethinking of the typological approach to intellectual developmental disorder (Gelb, 1997; Smith, 2002). That is, we see a clear shift in our understanding from (1) an emphasis on the distinction between normal and abnormal, with a de-emphasis on differences among individuals with intellectual developmental disorder, to (2) an emphasis on the continuity between typical and atypical, with a heightened appreciation of "people with very diverse needs and characteristics" (Smith, 2002, p. 64).

The third trend involves the attempt to address the stigma that is quickly attached to terms used for psychopathological diagnosis. Whether we name a disorder in order to segregate, protect, or treat struggling individuals, the names we use often become pejorative words used to mock and ridicule vulnerable persons (Gelb, 2002). Remember how awful it was (and is) to be called a "retard" in school. Many have argued that the label *mental retardation* should be abandoned for a more descriptive and more general label. And, in DSM-5, the term *intellectual developmental disability* replaces *mental retardation.* According to the editors of DSM-5, the change was made to increase standardization (with AAIDD, and with the International Classification of Diseases system) and to distinguish the disorder from declines and/or degeneration in intellectual and cognitive functioning that is associated with dementia). The new label allows for an increasingly accurate, less stigmatizing approach to understanding and treating the disorder in children and adolescents. The historical record suggests, unfortunately, that any new term is likely to have limited success in countering misconception and prejudice.

---

that Katherine's development in many ways follows the same sequence and growth pattern as other children, but progresses more slowly and will not continue as far in terms of her ability to think abstractly and process complex information. As she matures, her caregivers will need to pay increasing attention to the level of support Katherine requires, in line with the standards established by the American Association of Intellectual and Developmental Disabilities (AAIDD, 2002). It is likely that Katherine's necessary support level as she moves into adulthood will fall somewhere between Intermittent (e.g., as needed, such as following a job loss or health crisis) and Limited (e.g., consistent support in areas like vocational training and housing assistance that varies in intensity). ■

Taking into account various definitions of intellectual developmental disorder and the difficulties associated with accurate calculations, epidemiological estimates of the prevalence of IDD range between 1% and 2% of the population (Durkin, 2002; Leonard & Wen, 2002; Maulik et al., 2011; National Institute of Child Health and Human Development [NICHD], 2009). Most individuals (85%) with intellectual developmental disorder are diagnosed with mild levels of severity (as described here in the case of Katherine). Approximately 10% are diagnosed with moderate levels, 3%–4% with severe levels, and 1%–2% with profound levels (Singh, Oswald, & Ellis, 1998). Intellectual developmental disorder is observed more frequently in boys.

Zigler's Developmental Approach to IDD and the Developmental–Difference Debate

Several of the most important and affirming proposals about children with intellectual developmental disorder were put forth by Edward Zigler (1969, 1971). Zigler proposed that, in many respects, the majority of children with intellectual developmental disorder are similar to children without intellectual developmental disorder. Although delayed in their mastery of most motor, cognitive, emotional, and social tasks and stopping short of the eventual achievements of their normal peers, children with intellectual developmental disorder display the same kinds of sequences and coherent growth that are characteristic of most children. That is, children with intellectual developmental disorder develop slowly, but in organized ways. Broadening his concern beyond deficits and dysfunctions, Zigler also emphasized a holistic perspective, and the need to understand the motivations and personalities of children with intellectual developmental disorder (see also Cicchetti & Pogge-Hesse, 1982).

The **developmental–difference debate** focused specifically on the nature of cognitive disability. Zigler and his colleagues suggested that children with intellectual developmental disorder possess similar cognitive structures and slowly progress in a similar cognitive sequence to that of their typically developing peers (the developmental side of the debate). Others argued that children with IDD think in qualitatively distinct (and deficient) ways (the difference side of the debate); an emphasis on difference is often presented along with data on the genetic etiologies of IDD (discussed next). As with most complex issues, there is evidence to support both hypotheses (M. Anderson, 1998; Bennett-Gates & Zigler, 1998; Burack, 1997; Hodapp, 1997; Pennington, 2002).

Genotypes and Behavioral Phenotypes

Alternative classification models have focused on identifying and understanding children with intellectual developmental disorder by grouping them according to etiology, with much of the attention focused on various **genotypes**—the underlying genetic causes— associated with IDD (Hodapp & Dykens, 2003). These genetic subtypes are medical diagnoses rather than psychiatric or psychological categories; the genotype assumption is that different etiological explanations are reflected in differences in specific dysfunction and disability, differences in the course of IDD, and differences in family backgrounds and adjustments (Dykens & Hodapp, 2001). The related construct of **behavioral phenotypes** emphasizes the increased probability that a child will display a particular set of behaviors or symptoms given a particular genetic etiology. In other words, many children—but not all children—with a particular genetic background will display similarities related to physical characteristics, cognitive and linguistic profiles, perceptual skills and deficits, socioemotional patterns, and overall outcomes (Hodapp & Dykens, 2005).

Genetic disorders appear to influence subsequent behaviors in two ways (Hodapp & Dykens, 2005): First, a genetic disorder may be linked to a unique symptom or pattern observed in all children with the diagnosis. This type of link is observed in the extreme eating behaviors observed in individuals with Prader-Willi syndrome, and is relatively rare. A second, more commonly observed link is when two or more genetic disorders lead to shared outcomes. This type of link is confirmed by findings that, for example, many forms of IDD are associated with similar attention and/or hyperactivity difficulties.

Down Syndrome

Three brief descriptions of behavioral phenotypes associated with specific genotypes illustrate this classification approach to IDD. **Down syndrome,** caused by an extra chromosome 21 (i.e., trisomy 21), is among the most widely known genetically influenced forms of IDD. As with many forms of IDD, there are accompanying physical characteristics, including distinctive facial features, heart problems, and poor muscle tone. Intellectual challenges almost always involve language difficulties, with expressive speech more problematic than receptive speech (Abbeduto, Warren, & Conners, 2007). Visual short-term memory is often a relative strength. Intelligence estimates range from mild to severe. With respect to personality and psychopathology, parents often report that their children with Down syndrome are happy and outgoing; indeed, Down syndrome is sometimes referred to as "Prince Charming" syndrome (Dykens, 2000). Compared to others with IDD, children with Down syndrome display relatively few maladaptive behaviors during childhood, although both internalizing and externalizing symptoms occur in some children (Dykens, Shah, Sagun, Beck, & King, 2002; Fidler, 2006; Fidler, Most, Booth-LaForce, & Kelly, 2006).

Williams Syndrome

Williams syndrome, caused by a microdeletion on chromosome 7, is associated with its own distinctive pattern of IDD (Braden & Obrzut, 2002; Semel & Rosner, 2003; Stromme, Bjornstad, & Ramstad, 2002). The syndrome is characterized by deficits in general cognitive function and visual–spatial skills and relative strengths in language and music domains (Mervis & Becerra, 2007; Semel & Rosner, 2003). Even though the language of children with Williams syndrome seems relatively unaffected in comparison with children with other types of IDD, many studies provide data suggesting that there are specific language difficulties that have an impact on reading and require educational interventions (Clahsen & Temple, 2003; Laing, 2002; Temple, Almazan, & Sherwood, 2002; Vicari, Caselli, Gaglirdi, Tonucci, & Volterra, 2002). Children with Williams syndrome exhibit "sparkling dispositions" and "a remarkable and contagious zest for life" (Dykens, 2006, p. 190). That said, social disinhibition is a frequent concern for children with Williams syndrome, who "crave attention and interaction" and who frequently display overly friendly and talkative behaviors (Dykens, 2006). Children with Williams syndrome usually demonstrate a special facility for facial and emotion recognition and are known for their displays of empathy (Garfield & Perry, 2001; Pearlman-Avnion & Eviatar, 2002). The most common psychopathological symptoms include numerous fears and anxieties (Dykens, 2003).

In addition, many individuals with Williams syndrome display a particular affinity for music. Individuals with Williams syndrome are more engaged and accomplished than individuals with other forms of intellectual developmental disability, and similar in many ways to typically developing individuals (Levitin et al., 2004). Levitin et al. provide this example of the experience of music: "As the parent of a WS child reported, her daughter began weeping after a couple of notes were played at a Mozart concert. The girl's reaction was so strong that she left the concert and after returning, once again burst into tears. After hearing a more uplifting Mozart song some months later, she explained to her mother, 'there are two kinds of Mozart: the kind that hurts and the kind that does not hurt' " (p. 238).

Fragile X Syndrome

Fragile X syndrome, caused by a mutation on the *FMR1* gene, is the most common type of inherited IDD in boys, affecting 1 in 4,000 boys and 1 in 8,000 girls; it is seen in all racial and ethnic groups. Boys, who have only a single fragile X gene, are likely to be more severely affected and are more frequently diagnosed with moderate IDD. Girls usually are diagnosed with mild IDD. There are fewer physical characteristics of fragile X syndrome, although some babies do have large head circumferences, somewhat unusual facial features, and loose joints (Koukoui & Chaudhuri, 2007; Schwarte, 2008). Speech and communication difficulties underlie the fragile X cognitive profile (Abbeduto, Brady, & Kover, 2007; Abbeduto & Hagerman, 1997). Psychopathological symptoms associated with fragile X syndrome range from difficulties relating to others to autism; boys are more likely to experience severe behavioral difficulties such as high activity, poor attention, and low adaptability (Bailey, Hatton, & Skinner, 1998; Dykens, 2000; Roberts, Boccia, Hatton, Skinner, & Sideris, 2006; van Lieshout et al., 1998).

Researchers describe several benefits to an approach emphasizing genetic etiology. The most important of these benefits include the potential for prevention and early diagnosis (Huang, Sadler, O'Riordan, & Robin, 2002). Taking into account different patterns of strengths and weaknesses, treatments might be able to be more effectively specialized (Fidler, Hodapp, & Dykens, 2002; Hodapp & Des-Jardin, 2002). Others note the drawbacks to this kind of approach. These include the possibility that with increasing numbers of subtype classifications (numbering now in the hundreds), clinicians and others may overlook key similarities among children with IDD, with negative implications for both diagnosis and intervention (Burack, 1997). Given the current variety of outcomes for individuals with the same etiologies, Pennington (2002) suggests that for "any psychopathology, there is no doubt that etiological definitions will help focus medical interventions, but short of a medical cure, we will also need behavioral definitions to guide treatments" (p. 250).

So far, our emphasis has been on describing several genotypes associated with IDD, each of which is usually associated with a diagnosis of moderate to severe IDD. We must keep in mind that the majority of cases of children diagnosed with IDD are, in fact, diagnosed with mild IDD, as the case of Katherine illustrates. Children with mild IDD are not readily identified by genetic assays, physical characteristics, unique language or social presentations, or other sets of difficulties. These children must not be overlooked; indeed, efforts to identify and support these children must be renewed and reinvigorated.

Comorbid Disorders

Depending on the etiology and severity of IDD, estimates of comorbid conditions range widely, from 10% to 70% (Dykens, 2000; State et al., 1997). Common medical conditions include epilepsy, heart problems, sensory disorders, deafness, and physical abnormalities. Psychopathological complications are also frequent. For children diagnosed with mild IDD, internalizing symptoms (such as anxiety and mood disturbances) and externalizing problems (such as oppositional defiant disorder and attention deficit hyperactivity disorder) are frequently observed (Baker, Blacher, Crnic, & Edelbrock, 2002; Burack, Evans, Klaiman, & Iarocci, 2001; Dykens, 2000). For children diagnosed with more severe forms of IDD, autistic symptoms and self-injurious behaviors are frequently reported (Dykens, 2000).

Etiology

The most common distinction in discussions of etiology is between **organic** and **nonorganic causes.** Organic causes of IDD are associated with a specific physiological or physical origin; organic causes are usually associated with more severe forms of IDD and are observed across all family and socioeconomic status backgrounds. Organic explanations may be either genetic or environmental (see Table 7:1), and there are hundreds of possibilities. Genetic causes, such as those just described, include relatively rare dominant gene disorders, recessive gene disorders resulting in errors in metabolism (e.g., treatable phenylketonuria [PKU] and nontreatable Tay-Sachs), X-linked disorders, and chromosomal abnormalities (Winnepenninckx, Rooms, & Kooy, 2003; Simonoff, Bolton, & Rutter 1996). Figure 7:2

For most children with developmental delays, feelings of individual competence and social connection are key to a positive and resilient developmental trajectory.

provides information about the relative incidence of various genetic causes. Environmental causes include infectious diseases (such as in-utero exposure to rubella, cytomegalovirus, and HIV/AIDS), prenatal exposure to toxic substances (such as alcohol or other drugs that may lead to fetal alcohol syndrome),

TABLE 7:1 Selected Etiological Explanations for Intellectual Developmental Disorder

1. Prenatal causes
   a. Chromosome disorders (e.g., Down syndrome)
   b. Syndrome disorders (e.g., Tuberous sclerosis)
   c. Inborn error of metabolism (e.g., Phenylketonuria)
   d. Developmental disorders (e.g., spina bifida)
   e. Intrauterine malnutrition (e.g., fetal alcohol syndrome and other prenatal toxicants)
   f. Unknown

2. Perinatal causes
   a. Intrauterine disorders (e.g., prematurity)
   b. Neonatal disorders (e.g., intracranial hemorrhage)

3. Postnatal causes
   a. Head injuries (e.g., cerebral concussion)
   b. Infections (e.g., pediatric HIV)
   c. Demyelinating disorders (e.g., Schilder disease)
   d. Degenerative disorders (e.g., Rett syndrome)
   e. Seizure disorders (e.g., myoclonic epilepsy)
   f. Toxic metabolic disorders (e.g., lead exposure)
   g. Malnutrition (e.g., protein caloric deficiency)
   h. Environmental deprivations (e.g., psychosocial disadvantage)

Source: Pennington (2002).

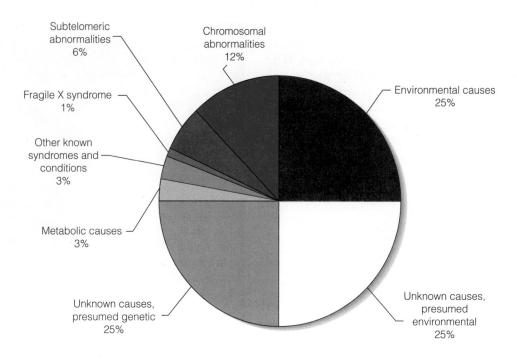

FIGURE 7:2 Overview of causes of mental retardation.
SOURCE: From Winnepenninckx Birgitta, Rooms Liesbeth, Kooy Frank, "Mental retardation: A review of the genetic causes", 'The British Journal of Developmental Disabilities, 49 (2003), pp. 29–44.

exposure to neurotoxins following birth (such as lead and methylmercury) (Mendola, Selevan, Gutter, & Rice, 2002), and physical trauma (such as birth complications, encephalitis, or head injury) (Dammann & Leviton, 1997; Ornoy, 2002).

Nonorganic causes of IDD are also referred to as familial or cultural–familial and are generally understood to reflect the outcome of multiple risks, including the normal variability of intelligence in the general population (i.e., there are always going to be some children at the very far ends of the distribution) coupled with adverse life situations (such as poverty and economic deprivation). Unlike IDD associated with organic causes, this type of intellectual developmental disorder is observed more often in groups of individuals with disadvantaged backgrounds (Siegler, 2003; Simonoff et al., 1996). This type of IDD also runs in families. To the extent that the components and processes of intelligence are genetically transmitted, we expect that a family's other children, who share some of the same genes as their parents and their sibling with IDD, display below average intelligence, and they do (Pennington, 2002; Plomin & Kovas, 2005). This family pattern

can be compared to organic forms of IDD, where, for example, a genetic error is a one-time mutation and not part of a parent's genetic make-up passed on to other children; in these families, the siblings of the affected child display near average intelligence (Pennington, 2002). The organic–nonorganic distinction is also explored in connection with Zigler's developmental–difference hypothesis; there, nonorganic etiologies are associated with slowed or delayed intellectual functioning that reflects the similar sequences and coherent growth observed in typically developing children.

As one might expect, much of the research on etiology is focused on cognitive domains and processes. Karmiloff-Smith (2009) examines a number of issues related to cognitive functioning in individuals with intellectual developmental disorder. For instance, comparisons among various organic etiologies often involve descriptions of impaired domains and other domains, with emphasis on the most severely impaired domains. In research on Williams syndrome, face perception is often understood as a relatively intact function, with scores on tests of facial processing similar to typically developing individuals. But in her own work, Karmiloff-Smith and colleagues have shown that the processing of faces by children with Williams syndrome involves distinctive differences at both cognitive and brain levels of functioning, suggesting that "scores in the normal range do not necessarily entail normal developmental trajectories" (p. 57). It will be increasingly important to take into account various types of delays and deviance, as well as data that help explain the positive consequences of plasticity, compensation, and remediation.

Developmental Course

Given the number and range of etiologies, marked differences in children's developmental trajectories are expected and observed (Dykens & Hodapp, 1999; Hodapp & DesJardin, 2002). In general, poorer prognoses are associated with organic etiologies. Not only are the organic etiologies related to more severe intellectual developmental disorder, but many are also associated with life-threatening physical disease and dysfunction. For the most impaired children, outcomes may include institutionalization, total dependence on others for care, and briefer lives. More positive outcomes tend to be observed in children with mild or moderate degrees of intellectual developmental disorder, with organic, nonorganic, mixed, or unclear etiologies. For all of these children, keeping in mind the holistic approach favored by Zigler and others, we can examine the course of disorder as it plays out in various domains of development.

Physical and Neurological Domains

As already described, for many types of intellectual developmental disorder, there are physical abnormalities associated with the disorder. Although both immediate and long-term growth and health are often compromised, medical advances have made a lifespan approach to IDD essential (Hodapp & Burack, 2006). In fact, longevity has increased so dramatically that researchers are now focused on identification, assessment, and treatment for a variety of specific complications, such as Alzheimer's disease in individuals with Down syndrome emerging in middle to later years (Zigman et al., 2004).

With respect to neurological development, brain structure and brain development have been the focus of much recent attention. Researchers have described microcephaly and reduced volumes in the frontal lobes and cerebellum in adults with Down syndrome, microcephaly in Williams syndrome, and structural abnormalities in individuals with fragile X syndrome (Pennington, 2002). The various functions of the prefrontal cortex and the hippocampus have also been examined (Pennington, Moon, Edgin, Stedron, & Nadel, 2003). In addition, abnormalities in the genetic regulation of dendritic and synaptic growth and neuronal pruning have been identified (Dierssen & Ramakers, 2006; Pennington, 2002). These types of defects have direct and indirect and short- and long-term consequences for the overall development of the child. These investigations of brain development and function reflect contemporary trends involving longitudinal perspectives and provide essential data illustrating the brain pathways that underlie the many patterns of deficits, dysfunctions, and relative strengths observed in various forms of IDD.

Intelligence, Language, and Communication

Although issues remain with conceptualizing intelligence as a general competence or as multiple abilities and understanding the deficits in intellectual developmental disorder as delays or differences, we still must describe the paths and outcomes related to the cognitive domain of functioning. As Pennington (2002) states, "there is the fact that individuals with MR [IDD] do develop, that they follow a normal sequence of developmental acquisitions much more often than not, and that their performance on most, but not all tasks is well predicted by mental age" (p. 264). Against this changing background, there are various cognitive and intellectual impairments displayed by children with intellectual developmental disorder, with specific etiological patterns of relative strengths and weaknesses in language, memory, and information processing (M. Anderson, 1998; Pennington, 2002).

Children with intellectual developmental disorder exhibit different trajectories of intellectual development relative to the rate and timing of growth for normally developing children (Pennington, 2002; see Figs. 7:3A and 7:3B). In addition, children with IDD show "less solid, more 'fragile' developments of their highest stages" (Hodapp & Zigler, 1995, p. 311). These changes are likely tied to innate characteristics, but are also influenced by the interaction of the child's abilities and environmental factors. For many children with IDD, cognitive and linguistic profiles

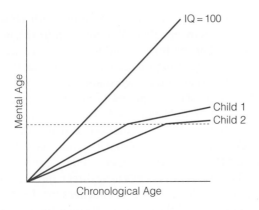

FIGURE 7:3A Task-related slowing of development.
Republished with permission of American Association on Intellectual Developmental Disabilities, from Mental Retardation by Hodapp, © 1993; permission conveyed through Copyright Clearance Center, Inc.

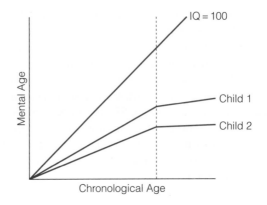

FIGURE 7:3B Age-related slowing of development.
Republished with permission of American Association on Intellectual Developmental Disabilities, from Mental Retardation by Hodapp, © 1993; permission conveyed through Copyright Clearance Center, Inc.

of strengths and weaknesses also change over time, with strengths becoming stronger and weaknesses becoming weaker (Hodapp & Burack, 2006).

One particularly relevant environmental variable is education. In the United States, the Individuals with Disabilities Education Act mandates diagnostic, educational, and support services from birth to age 21, with individual education plans developed with input from parents, teachers, and mental health professionals. Educational approaches have changed over previous decades and now emphasize inclusion of children with developmental disabilities in age-appropriate classrooms. Success in these classrooms depends on many variables, and behavior difficulties are often the main reason for lack of success in mainstream placements. Inclusion strategies designed to enhance children's success make use of self-monitoring, behavioral contracts, and peer-mediated interventions (Matts & Zionts, 1997; Simpson, Myles, & Simpson, 1997).

Because the mild forms of IDD are often identified in the early school years, with increasing demands for academic performance in each successive year (State et al., 1997), it is not surprising that eventual educational accomplishments are, in part, related to teachers' attitudes toward inclusion (see Box 7:3). The school milieu also includes other children, and their beliefs and behaviors are also important (Heiman, 2000). Although some negative biases are common (Nowicki & Sandieson, 2002), we can be encouraged by the slightly more positive attitudes of high school students toward their peers

with IDD over the last several decades (Krajewski, Hyde, & O'Keefe, 2002).

Social, Emotional, and Personality Development

The general course of adaptive functioning is variable. Some groups of children with IDD show improvements over time, others display up-and-down patterns of adjustment, and still others exhibit declines (Hodapp & Burack, 2006; Pennington, 2002). For all groups, however, the emphasis remains on supporting personality development and functioning (Zigler, 1999; Zigler & Bennet-Gates, 1999) and achieving a positive quality of life (Dykens, 2006; Schalock, 1996, 1997, 2000). As we have already discussed, Zigler's "approach was aimed at understanding the 'whole child' with intellectual developmental disorder, in all of that child's psychological complexity" (Hodapp & Zigler, 1995, p. 316). And many investigators since Zigler have focused on identifying essential similarities and differences in children with and without intellectual developmental disorder. Research on emotion, attachment, and play in children with Down syndrome, for example, supports Zigler's position that children with IDD exhibit basic emotion skills, appreciate humor, and experience complex emotional relationships (Cicchetti & Serafica, 1981; Marcell & Jett, 1985; Motti, Cicchetti, & Sroufe, 1983; Reddy, Williams, & Vaughan, 2001). With increasing age, however, children with Down syndrome also exhibit fewer positive emotions and increased withdrawal (Dykens, 2006).

BOX 7:3 THE CHILD IN CONTEXT

Teachers' Attitudes Toward Inclusion

There is a complicated historical and legal background to the discussion of inclusion of children with special needs into regular classroom settings. In general, we see a move from demands for the "least restrictive environments" for children with IDD to more recent efforts that emphasize both inclusion and integration for children and educational curricula (Kavale, 2002; Kavale & Forness, 2000; Lowenthal, 1999; Miller, Fullmer, & Walls, 1996). With a diversity of parent and teacher beliefs and attitudes about inclusion (Palmer, Borthwick-Duffy, Widaman, & Best, 1998), research evidence is necessary to make informed and valued policy decisions (Kavale, 2002; Kavale & Forness, 2000; Miller, Fullmer, & Walls, 1996).

Many discussions of inclusion presume that successful outcomes depend, in part, on teacher attitudes, and reviews of the literature suggest that teachers have positive attitudes about inclusion and integration. However, their attitudes and beliefs are influenced by the nature and severity of children's special needs, as well as their own needs for personal and educational support for their work (Avramidis & Norwich, 2002).

Teachers' positive attitudes are countered by their lack of confidence in their abilities to manage classrooms with special needs children (Avramidis, Bayliss, & Burden, 2000; Buell, Gamel-McCormick, & Hallam, 1999). This lack of confidence may underlie their reluctance to fully embrace the notion of inclusion. Many investigators have observed that knowledge about specific disabilities, along with training, experience, and collaborative work with other teachers, has an impact on teachers' perceived competence (Avramidis et al., 2000; Buell, Hallam, Gamel-McCormick, & Scheer, 1999; Snell & Janney, 2000), although there are some data suggesting that experience may be related to some teachers' greater hostility toward inclusion (Soodak, Podell, & Lehman, 1998). It seems clear that additional work remains to document both the benefits and costs related to inclusion for both children and teachers, and that the acceptance and translation of policy into practice is ongoing (Carrington & Elkins, 2002).

Children also display characteristic patterns of social competence and peer relationships, depending on their etiological backgrounds and surrounding environments (Rosner, Hodapp, Fidler, Sagun, & Dykens, 2004; Sigman & Ruskin, 1999). Compared to typically developing children, for instance, children with intellectual developmental disorder appear more motivated to seek and obtain approval and positive reinforcement from others and to look more frequently to others for information and guidance (Hodapp & Zigler, 1995). With respect to leisure activities, etiology-associated patterns are again observed, with differences in the selection and practice of social activities, television and computer activities, musical activities, and physical activities (Buttimer & Tierney, 2005; Sellinger, Hodapp, & Dykens, 2006). With age, individuals with Down, Williams, and Prader-Willi syndromes all increased social activities; other increases and decreases in specific activities were also observed (Sellinger et al., 2006).

It is important to understand that children with IDD are not just occupying themselves or following others' directives related to various activities.

In many cases, selection and pursuit of specific activities appear related to a number of positive internal strengths (Dykens, 2006). Individuals with Williams syndrome, for instance, may be assisted in their drive for relationships to make safe, appropriate, and reciprocated overtures to others. Given their pleasure, skill, and deep engagement in music, they may also be encouraged, challenged, and supported in their musical journeys (Dykens, 2006).

Maladaptive Behavior and Psychopathology

The prevalence and types of comorbid symptoms and disorders were already summarized. In this section, we explore why children with IDD are at increased risk for various psychopathologies and how these psychopathologies play out over time (Hodapp & Dykens, 2005). Certainly shared genetic and physiological vulnerabilities contribute to overlapping psychopathologies (Dykens, 2000). But Dykens (2000) suggests that another reason that children with IDD struggle in multiple ways is related to the nature of lower intellectual functioning. That is, children with IDD generate fewer problem-solving strategies and have fewer cognitive resources, leading to unrealistic appraisals of tasks and abilities and less successful outcomes for a variety of intellectual and social challenges. Distress is likely, along with increasingly negative self-evaluations. Over time, particularly for children and adolescents with mild IDD, anxiety, mood, and behavioral symptoms may exacerbate intellectual and adaptive functioning. These kinds of difficulties also increase the cost of care for children (Einfeld et al., 2010). Another example of developmental complications involves the consequences of problematic peer relationships. According to Dykens (2000), many individuals with IDD are at increased risk for physical abuse and sexual exploitation, given histories of sociability and failed social overtures. Additional research investigating the emergence and maintenance of additional maladaptation is essential in order to decrease poor outcomes and increase the likelihood of physical and mental well-being.

Adult Outcomes

With emphases on quality of life and appropriate support for individuals with IDD, we look to the future with hope. For some individuals with mild intellectual developmental disorder, leaving the school system, with its focus on academic skills and achievement, leads to improvements in adaptation. Many advocates for individuals with IDD have documented numerous instances of persons with a diagnosis of intellectual disability who essentially disappear into society and function well enough that they no longer meet the diagnostic criteria for intellectual developmental disorder. Most, however, continue to struggle with many of the tasks of daily living. As these individuals move into early adulthood, they and their families may look for community activities or employment opportunities. Interest and success in these endeavors is likely related to the productive and/or dysfunctional career beliefs observed in adults with disabilities (Lustig & Strauser, 2002).

Other predictable developmental challenges are also observed. One of the most difficult challenges involves adult sexuality. Historically, both mental health professionals and the general public exhibited strong negative attitudes about sexual behavior in adults with IDD; sexual freedom was rarely permitted (Kempton & Kahn, 1991; Rhodes, 1993). Although recent surveys continue to reveal negative perceptions (Lunsky & Konstantareas, 1998), sexuality is increasingly understood as an important aspect of life satisfaction for persons with intellectual developmental disorder. Sex education, therefore, is essential (Lumley & Scotti, 2001; McConkey & Ryan, 2001; Valenti-Hein & Dura, 1996). Of course, specific concerns about the sexual abuse of vulnerable adults and unwanted pregnancies must also be addressed (Sundram & Stavis, 1994).

Adults with intellectual developmental disorder live in a variety of environments, from family homes to group settings. Very few adults (and even fewer children) reside in institutions; those who do are likely to exhibit comorbid psychopathology (Szymanski et al., 1999). Reviews of studies published following deinstitutionalization suggest that long-term community placements are associated with increases in overall adaptive behavior (Kim, Larson, & Lakin, 2001), with more positive outcomes in smaller, less restrictive settings (Gardner, Carran, & Nudler, 2001).

The Role of the Family

As children with intellectual developmental disorder develop, so do their families. Many patterns of emotional response and eventual adjustment to babies with disabilities have been described, with differences depending on family characteristics, the perception and meaning of the individual child, and the type of intellectual developmental disorder; the particular maladaptive behaviors associated with specific etiologies are especially important to consider in this respect (Fidler, Hodapp, & Dykens, 2000; Glidden, 2002; Hodapp, 2002). These factors may underlie what has been described as the "Down syndrome advantage," the tendency for families of children with Down syndrome to cope better than families of children with other forms of IDD (Hodapp, 2007). Despite the financial and social difficulties of raising a child with IDD in the home, parents want to be responsible for their children's care (Hadadian & Merbler, 1995b). Effective care depends, in part, on the information provided to families. Information that includes both general overviews of disorder, specific descriptions of a child's weaknesses and strengths, and concrete, lifespan support strategies is essential (Fidler, Hodapp, & Dykens, 2002; Hodapp, 2007). There are many different types of informal and professional support available; this may vary by culture or country (Shin, 2002).

Early on, different roles for mothers and fathers are often observed, with mothers taking a more active role in caregiving, and fathers more preoccupied with financial and practical concerns (Hadadian & Merbler, 1995a). Outcomes for children and their families are related to individual and parent variables. For example, young children with mothers who are both highly sensitive and highly directive have better prognoses (Hodapp & Zigler, 1995). Family well-being is associated with the extent of help and cooperation achieved by parents (Simmerman & Baker, 2001).

Considering the many unique family contexts, many stress-and-coping models of ongoing family adjustment discuss both positive and negative aspects of having a child with IDD (Gerstein, Crnic, Blacher, & Baker, 2009; Hodapp & Zigler, 1995). With respect to stress, for instance, there are difficulties associated with children's transitions and milestones. According to Hodapp and Burack (2006), families of children with IDD attend to developmental issues (such as the first smile), chronological issues (such as entrance into school), and familial issues (such as a younger child passing the first) that may all be problematic; each event may lead to parents reexperiencing sadness. Chronic stress is related to poor health outcomes for parents (Miodrag & Hodapp, 2010; Seltzer, Floyd, Song, Greenberg, & Hong, 2011).

With respect to coping and resilience, many researchers have documented effective personal, familial, and environmental strategies (Heiman, 2002; Lustig, 2002). Some of the most positive rewards of having a child with IDD families describe include the joy that the child brings to the family, a sense of purpose, expanded personal and social networks, personal growth, and increased tolerance (Dykens, 2005). Overall, our understanding of parents has shifted to "a more positive, coping perspective" (Hodapp & Zigler, 1995, p. 314).

The role of siblings of individuals with intellectual developmental disorder is a recent focus of investigation. Many siblings, early in their own development, report increased caregiving responsibilities as well as expectations for greater responsibilities and additional support as they age (Hodapp, Urbano, & Burke, 2010; Seltzer, Greenberg, Orsmond, & Lounds, 2005). Siblings also report many benefits, including closer relationships with their siblings with intellectual developmental disorders; closeness was associated with their own well-being (Seltzer et al., 2005).

Assessment and Diagnosis

The American Association on Intellectual and Developmental Disabilities (AAIDD, 2002) sets forth a number of assumptions that must be considered before a diagnosis of intellectual developmental disorder is made: "(1) limitations in present functioning must be considered within the context of community environments typical of the individual's age, peers, and culture; (2) valid assessment considers cultural and linguistic diversity as well as differences in communication, sensory, motor, and behavioral factors; (3) within an individual, limitations often coexist with strengths; (4) an important purpose of describing limitations is to develop a profile of needed supports; (5) with appropriate personalized supports over a sustained period, the life functioning of the person with intellectual developmental disorder generally will improve." With these assumptions in mind, we can examine the ways in which assessments and diagnoses are made.

Background Information

Medical and developmental histories are a key component of the assessment of intellectual developmental disorder. Almost always, clinicians rely on parents and others for these types of reports and observations, although there is evidence that interviews and self-reports may also be useful with some individuals with IDD (Finlay & Lyons, 2001; Levitas, Hurley, & Pary, 2001). Clinicians must evaluate whether the presence of more specific developmental delays in speech, language, and reading account for intellectual and adaptive delays; in those cases, DSM-5 diagnoses such as Language Disorder or Speech Disorder would be appropriate. Physical concerns such as hearing difficulties or hearing loss may also have an impact on cognitive and language development.

Assessment of Intellectual Functioning

Standardized tests of intelligence, such as the Stanford-Binet (Roid, 2003) or one of the Wechsler tests (Wechsler, 2003), are administered individually. In addition to a general evaluation of intellectual functioning, evaluations of particular cognitive processes may also be included. It is important to note that these types of tests have both technical and nontechnical concerns. With respect to technical issues, there is one clear advantage to current instruments:

"A score of 130 at age 5 means that a child's performance exceeds that of 98% of age peers; a score of 130 at age 10 means exactly the same thing" (Siegler, 2003, p. 313). And, although they provide no information about etiology or course, scores on intelligence tests do allow comparisons among groups of children with IDD. Other assessment concerns involve the focus on formal academic skills and predicting school achievement in standardized tests, and the comparability of scores for children of different ethnic and racial backgrounds on traditional and nontraditional intelligence tests.

A final issue is raised by differing definitions. Depending on the particular cutoff score (e.g., 70 versus 75), various percentages of the population might be diagnosed with intellectual developmental disorder. Given the distribution of IQ scores in the general population, raising the cutoff score to 75 from 70 doubles the number of individuals who would be eligible for a diagnosis of IDD, with multiple consequences, both positive and negative (Kanaya, Scullin, & Ceci, 2003; Pennington, 2002). Decisions and recommendations related to scores reflecting deficits in intellectual functioning need to be understood in the context of the "Flynn effect," the gradual increase in IQ scores over the past several decades (Flynn, 1987, 2007). Fluctuations in IQ scores, coupled with restrictive notions of low intellectual functioning, may have serious impacts on children and adolescents who are repeatedly tested throughout their school lives (Kanaya & Ceci, 2007).

Assessment of Adaptive Functioning

Of the various standardized scales for assessment of adaptive functioning, the most common are the Vineland Social Maturity Scale and the AAIDD Adaptive Behavior Scale (Sparrow, Cicchetti, & Balla, 2005). These instruments are designed to measure basic skills in different developmental domains, including communication, self-care and health, social skills, and leisure and work, at various ages. They are usually completed by adults who know the child well. Although most often conceptualized as tapping separate areas of functioning, there are data to support the notion of an underlying, general factor of adaptation (Hodapp & Dykens, 1996; Pennington, 2002). Given the somewhat variable course of intellectual and adaptive functioning for different groups of children with intellectual developmental disorder,

repeat assessments throughout the growing years are important.

Following the collection of information on significant deviations in intellectual and adaptive functioning, and after the diagnosis of intellectual developmental disorder, additional assessment may be especially valuable. Information about maladaptive behaviors and psychopathology must be included. Specific behavioral assessments, socially oriented assessments, and personality measures such as happiness may provide a more complete picture of a whole child. Plans for supporting physical and psychological well-being depend on this more comprehensive approach.

Intervention

When considering intervention for children and adolescents with intellectual developmental disorder, two points are worth emphasizing. First, in general, we are not trying to treat the condition as we would most episodes of psychopathology. Rather, we are attempting to maximize the potential of the individual to meet developmental demands while at the same time modifying the environment to better match the individual's deficits and strengths. Consequently, the majority of mental health professionals, educators, and advocacy groups stress the importance of intervention plans that target multiple points along the developmental continuum, as well as a range of relevant social and educational systems within which the child functions. These include, for example, early screening and identification, early intervention for the child and the family, appropriate school programming, and coordination of the various persons and agencies involved in the child's care.

The second point to emphasize in the context of this textbook is that mental health is an important issue for everyone, regardless of level of intellectual functioning. We must be careful not to define a person by a single, if salient, attribute like intellectual developmental disorder (or, for that matter, being intellectually gifted or a star athlete). Psychological variables such as emotion, social relationships, and impulse control are every bit as relevant for individuals diagnosed with intellectual developmental disorder as for those who are not. Intervention strategies, then, must be designed to address all relevant problem areas. Finally, although exceptional progress in the treatment of mental illness has been made in recent years, these advances are often delayed in their applications to special needs populations such as children and adolescents with intellectual developmental disorder. The mental health field has a clear obligation to improve its efforts to apply emerging treatment approaches to all groups, including the mentally retarded.

Genetic Screening and Prevention Strategies

Genetic screening of parents, prenatal testing, and **genetic counseling** afford many specific intervention opportunities (Durand, 2001; Simonoff, 1996; Stainton, 2003). However, with "technology … advancing more rapidly than the ethical and practical guidelines for its use" (Simonoff et al., 1996, p. 273), we must be careful to respect many different perspectives (see Box 7:4). Broad-based prevention approaches, such as public information campaigns discouraging drinking while pregnant, are also possible (see Box 7:5). In addition, measures including supplementing women's diets with folic acid to reduce neural tube defects and removing lead from the environment reduce rates of IDD (Szymanski et al., 1999).

Pharmacological Treatment

Once intellectual developmental disorder has been diagnosed, there are a variety of treatment options sharing similar goals: to develop and maintain skills, increase positive attributes, and decrease negative characteristics of IDD. Pharmacological treatments of associated maladaptive behaviors are common, with the majority of individuals with intellectual developmental disorder who reside in institutions on some sort of psychotropic medication, with multiple medications increasingly prescribed (Howerton et al., 2002). Available data on outcome are mixed,

---

BOX 7:4 | EMERGING SCIENCE

Ethical Issues in Prenatal Genetic Counseling

Advances in our abilities to detect abnormalities during prenatal development are associated with a host of pragmatic and ethical issues for parents, medical and mental health providers, and society (Bower, Veach, Bartels, & LeRoy, 2002; Okasha, 2002; Veach, Bartels, & LeRoy, 2001, 2002). For parents, prenatal decision making is a multipart process. For some parents, genetic screening is routine; for others, it involves the first of many practical and moral decisions (Rice, 2001; Santalahti, Hemminki, Latikka, & Ryynaenen, 1998). Deciding what to do with available information, especially given the high false positive rates of some genetic screening techniques, is the next difficult step, and diverse parental values and beliefs are among the most important factors that have an impact on these decisions (G. Anderson, 1998; Copel & Bahado-Singh, 1999; Rice, 2001). Parents who are making these kinds of multiple eventful decisions require accurate information and support (Santalahti et al., 1998; Williams, Alderson, & Farsides, 2002).

Medical and mental health providers also encounter many ethical and professional challenges. Determining what conditions to screen for, and when and how to screen for them, are among the immediate decisions to be made (Copel & Bahado-Singh, 1999; Williams et al., 2002). Veach et al. (2001, 2002) and Bower et al. (2002) describe a number of other challenges that underlie and follow these first ones. Among the most demanding are the following: obtaining informed consent, dealing with uncertainty, providing upsetting feedback, respecting value conflicts, and maintaining professional identity and expertise. The extent to which a genetic counselor is directive or nondirective may require special ethical attention (Bower et al., 2002; Veach et al., 2001, 2002; Weil, 2003).

From a societal standpoint, there is much to be addressed. First, we need to recognize that there are many perspectives in this multidisciplinary field (Pelletier & Dorval, 2004). There are parents, physicians, psychologists, bioethicists, advocates for disabled children and adults, and others who have reasoned and passionate beliefs that are at odds with one another. Keeping all of these people and the many social consequences of genetic counseling in mind, we need to be able to anticipate the various ethical issues that confront diverse populations (Parker & Gettig, 1997). We need to discuss the personal, community, and economic costs and benefits of genetic counseling. And we need to develop practice recommendations for counselors (Bennett, Pettersen, Niendorf, & Anderson, 2003). For all of these tasks, ethically informed decision making depends on our commitment to engage in respectful dialogue, as individuals and as a society.

Prevention and Fetal Alcohol Syndrome

Fetal alcohol syndrome (FAS), one of the fetal alcohol spectrum disorders (FASD), is caused by maternal drinking during pregnancy. FAS is characterized by persistent physical, cognitive, and socioemotional impairments and psychopathology in infants, children, and adults (Olson, 2002; Sokol, Delaney-Black, & Nordstrom, 2003). FAS has been identified around the world in various populations (Riley et al., 2003). Given recent U.S. Supreme Court and state court cases and legislative attempts to criminalize drug and alcohol use during pregnancy (Marshall, Menikoff, & Paltrow, 2003), as well as the enormous impact of FAS in personal, social, economic, and political spheres (Greenfield & Sugarman, 2001), FAS requires scientific scrutiny and thoughtful response.

Although information about FAS has become much more available in recent years (due, in part, to public awareness campaigns), much more remains to be done (Murphy-Brennan & Oei, 1999; Sokol et al., 2003). FAS is an "entirely preventable disorder" (Murphy-Brennan & Oei, 1999). Intervention efforts geared to decreasing the rates of FAS are widespread, although they achieve mixed results. Hankin (2002) describes universal, selective, and indicated prevention efforts, including education, screening, and treatment (Greenfield & Sugarman, 2001). Universal efforts include media messages about drinking while pregnant and posters and labels on alcoholic beverages. Price increases are a pragmatic attempt to reduce drinking; they appear to have an impact on heavy and binge drinkers (Abel, 1998a, 1998b).

Selective efforts include education and support directed specifically at at-risk groups, such as Native American women and adolescents (Ma, Toubbeh, Cline, & Chisholm, 1998a, 1998b, 2002), although a lack of resources hinders some of these prevention

attempts (Clarren & Astley, 1997; Ma et al., 2002). Risk factors also extend beyond group status. Identifying women at risk involves understanding the ways in which at-risk women respond to messages about drinking and pregnancy (Branco & Kaskutas, 2001). What do these women understand about the nature and course of FAS? Do they believe that some drinks are safer than others? How much drinking is too much? What peer, family, and social pressures are there related to drinking or not drinking during pregnancy (Branco & Kaskutas, 2001)? And, are some prevention messages (such as failing to distinguish between alcohol use and alcohol abuse) actually counterproductive (Abel, 1998a, 1998b)? We need to think carefully about the factors that promote abstinence in at-risk women, such as higher intelligence, higher household incomes, and the availability of social support, and the ways in which these factors might be mobilized (Astley, Bailey, Talbot, & Clarren, 2000).

Targeting women who are already drinking is the most problematic of prevention and intervention efforts and is fraught with complicated ethical and legal issues. For example, the Supreme Court has ruled that nonconsensual drug screening is unlawful (*Ferguson vs. City of Charleston et al.,* 2001), and punitive policies such as incarceration or forced treatment may scare some women away from seeking help (Marshall et al., 2003). This is especially distressing given that there are data indicating that brief, focused interventions do reduce alcohol use in mothers-to-be who drink heavily (Hankin, 2002). We will need to be cautious as we balance responsibility, blame, rehabilitation, and punishment, so that we emphasize healthy pre- and postnatal development as among the most important—and achievable—goals.

but the most frequently used drugs associated with behavioral improvements are methylphenidate (Ritalin), antipsychotics, and mood-related medications (Dosen, 2001; Tyrer & Hill, 2001). There is also interest in nutritional and hormonal treatments to support better outcomes (Ellis, Singh, & Ruane, 1999). The evaluation of side effects and adverse drug reactions is especially important to consider in a population of children and adolescents who may have difficulty communicating (Dosen, 2001; Kalachnik, 1999). Indeed, accepted

practice parameters suggest that individuals with IDD be prescribed psychotropic medications cautiously, given difficulties related to informed consent, enhanced sensitivity to drugs and their side effects, and poor monitoring of outcomes (Szymanski et al., 1999).

Psychological Treatment

Psychological treatments are complex and comprehensive, and there is research and clinical consensus that children and adolescents with IDD benefit from individual, family, and group therapies. Better outcomes are associated with therapeutic practices that take into account cognitive, communication, and behavior skills (Szymanski et al., 1999). Therapies include behavioral treatments (Berkson, 1993; Gardner, Graeber-Whalen, & Ford, 2001), cognitive treatments (Benson & Valenti-Hein, 2001), and socioemotional programs (Dosen, 2001; Hollins, 2001) as well as family, educational, and vocational planning (Day & Dosen, 2001; Rotthaus, 2001; Thompson et al., 2002). Educational interventions often have dramatic impact, depending on the factors underlying impaired intellectual functioning (Rutter et al., 2004; Rutter & the ERA Study Team, 1998). Increasing attention is paid to matching treatments to etiologies (Hodapp & DesJardin, 2002). As with many other treatment strategies, early intensive efforts are associated with better outcomes (Pennington, 2002; Ramey, Campbell, & Blair, 1998).

Following educational interventions, behavior modification therapies are among the most frequently used. The goals of behavioral strategies include enhancing adaptive skills and teaching appropriate behaviors. Given that maladaptive behaviors are a major source of difficulty at home and at school, these strategies are essential (Szymanski et al., 1999). Behavioral treatments utilizing aversive techniques such as restraint or punishment are rarely used today; alternatives such as token reinforcement strategies are almost always available (Singer, Gert, & Koegel, 1999). When aversive techniques are used, serious self-harm or aggression toward others is a concern (Szymanski et al., 1999).

Family Education and Support

Given the lifelong nature of intellectual developmental disorder, the family's role in treatment is a prime concern. Parents often serve as co-clinicians (Baker, 1996), and both direction and support are necessary. For instance, some parents are reluctant to set strict behavioral limits for their children with intellectual developmental disorder. Although based in empathy or sympathy, this reluctance may also reflect a lack of understanding about the need for structure and clear expectations (Hodapp, 2004). For children and adolescents with intellectual developmental disorder, eventual adjustments and outcomes depend on integrated, collaborative efforts that provide as much information, support, and optimism as is possible.

Learning Disorders

The Case of Ethan

Ethan is 10 years old and in fifth grade. He was referred for neuropsychological assessment at the request of his parents, who are concerned about his difficulty completing tasks and academic underachievement. Language processing difficulties were identified early in Ethan's development, and he received speech and language therapy before entering elementary school.

Ethan's parents note that although they have no current concerns about his language skills, Ethan is reluctant to initiate writing tasks, often getting upset and claiming that "it's impossible!" This is true even when the writing is not related to his schoolwork (for example, making cards or writing notes to family members). He loves to have books read to him, but argues when his parents try to encourage him to read on his own. His parents are concerned that an underlying learning disorder might be contributing to his increasing resistance to school. Although respectful of their concerns, Ethan's teacher feels his issues are more likely related to anxiety and his tendency to procrastinate.

The neuropsychologist assessing Ethan noted that he struggled with writing tasks. He had difficulty forming letters, which were printed awkwardly. Additionally, his spelling and written output appeared slow and labored. Ethan made frequent erasures as he worked and, on an untimed test involving math problems, he appeared reluctant to use a paper and pencil to work on the problems, preferring to do them in his head. Test results showed Ethan's general cognitive abilities to be in the high average range, with processing speed (measured by timed tests with pencil and paper) to be the one area of relative weakness. Ethan's executive functioning skills were generally typical for his age, although his parents state that he has difficulty controlling his emotions at home, especially in regard to completing his homework, when he can quickly become frustrated and angry.

Achievement testing showed that Ethan had strong math reasoning ability and good reading comprehension scores. However, his writing skills were more problematic and discrepant from most of his other abilities. Ethan needed considerably more time than average on writing tasks. He appeared to struggle as he thought about how to form each letter as he wrote it. He showed poor visual–motor control, but his fine motor speed and coordination were not delayed. On standardized tests, Ethan scored below age expectations in terms of his ability to write conventionally (e.g., use of paragraphs and punctuation) and had even more difficulty with his contextual language skills (e.g., with fragmentary sentences, run-on sentences, absence of compound sentences). However, with a topic of his choosing, Ethan was able to show good story construction, with sequence and plot, and scored in the average range.

The neuropsychologist concluded that Ethan met criteria for Learning Disorder of Written Expression as evidenced by his differentiated difficulties with handwriting, conventional writing skills, and clarity of written expression. With this understanding, Ethan's teachers worked with his parents to develop a plan that included decreasing the amount of written work required of Ethan while at the same time providing him with greater support in an effort to improve his writing skills, increase his confidence in his writing, and decrease his feelings of frustration and inadequacy. Additional strategies, such as reducing unnecessary copying, providing additional time for tasks requiring written work, and increasing the use of keyboarding and dictating for longer written assignments, were also recommended. ■

Children, adolescents, and adults with learning disorders (LDs) display persistent difficulties in the acquisition and application of academic skills. These difficulties are associated with significant impairment in school, work, and/or everyday living. Given the dimensionality of learning (i.e., the continuity between typical and atypical performance) and the inferences involved in making a diagnosis of learning disorder (e.g., how to make a decision related to lack of skills), it is not surprising that definitions of learning disorders change over time. The

Specific learning disorders in areas such as written expression may contribute to academic underachievement.

most common approach to conceptualizing learning disorders, over the past several decades, emphasized the discrepancy between an individual's aptitude (usually measured with an intelligence test) and achievement. According to Fletcher, Lyon, Fuchs, and Barnes (2007), this approach lacks external validity because it does not specify what exactly is disordered in learning disorders. Alternative models that focus solely on low achievement or on intraindividual patterns (e.g., unevenness in academic skills, with particular patterns of cognitive strengths and weaknesses) are also problematic. Response to intervention (RTI) models focus on students who do not respond to appropriate instruction and high-quality interventions. Fletcher et al. suggest that an integrated model of learning disorders is more useful. In their model, students' responses to appropriate instruction, low achievement, and intraindividual differences in academic skills all contribute to the construct of learning disorders.

DSM-5 describes several domains of **specific learning disorder**: in reading, written expression, and mathematics. Disorders are associated with "unexpected underachievement" (Fletcher et al., 2007). Exclusionary factors that might compromise learning include problems involving sensory or perceptual skills, low intelligence, emotional and behavioral difficulties, economic disadvantage, and inadequate instruction. Children may display one or more specific learning disorders. Descriptions of specific learning disorders overlap somewhat with the related constructs of verbal learning disabilities and nonverbal learning disabilities. Verbal learning disabilities are similar to the language-based reading and writing learning disorders. Nonverbal learning disabilities include atypical difficulties involving motor skills, visual–spatial skills, and social skills. These specific descriptions are not included in DSM-5, although DSM-5 does include categories for social communication disorder and motor disorders.

Specific learning disorders involving reading include difficulties related to *word recognition, reading fluency*, and *reading comprehension*. Each of these difficulties is associated with an academic skill deficit and a core cognitive process (Fletcher et al., 2007). The academic skill deficit in word recognition (i.e., dyslexia) involves single-word decoding. The core cognitive process is phonological awareness (i.e., the metacognitive understanding that the words we hear and read have internal structures based on sound). Other processes related to word recognition are the rapid naming of letters and digits, and working memory for verbal and/or acoustic information. The academic skill deficit in reading fluency is reading speed (i.e., accuracy and automaticity). The core cognitive deficit is rapid automatized naming. Compared to other languages (e.g., German, Dutch, Swedish, French, Spanish, and Finnish), the English language is especially difficult to master (Aro & Wimmer, 2003). The academic skill deficit in reading comprehension involves extracting meaning from text. The core cognitive deficits (in children who are typical with respect to decoding) include language skills, working memory, and inferencing (making interpretations and/or integrations).

For learning disorders related to mathematics, the academic skills deficits include computation and problem solving. Although there is much less research compared to reading problems, core cognitive deficits are observed in working memory, executive functions, and language (Butterworth, Varma, & Laurillard, 2011; Fletcher et al., 2007). For disorders related to written expression, the academic skills deficits include handwriting, spelling, and composition. The core cognitive processes include fine motor skills, the automaticity of handwriting, and spelling (Fletcher et al., 2007).

Prevalence rates for learning disorders involving reading range from 10% to 15% in school-age populations, and from 80% to 90% of those in special education programs in the United States. Boys are somewhat more frequently diagnosed (Fletcher et al., 2007; President's Commission on Excellence in Special Education, 2002). Rates are similar for learning disorders involving mathematics in samples of school-aged children; there do not appear to be gender differences in these rates (Fletcher et al., 2007). There is not much data on rates of learning disorders involving written expression. Learning disorders are frequently diagnosed with other disorders, including attention deficit hyperactivity disorder, autism, and mood disorders (Mayes & Calhoun, 2006).

Because languages and writing systems differ (often in significant ways) and various countries and societies have particular ways of understanding learning, education, and individual differences in children, it is important to examine learning disorders in sociocultural context. Learning disorders are common in many countries. For example, approximately half of children receiving special education services in Guatemala and Spain are children with LDs (Jimenez & de la Cadena, 2007). Rates are much lower in Taiwan and South Korea, which may reflect differences in the writing system, emphasis on education and academic performance, and a reluctance on the part of parents to label their children as disabled (Tzeng, 2007).

Developmental Course

Even when special education efforts are taken into account, learning disorders involve persistent difficulties rather than developmental delays in acquisition and use of academic skills. Indeed, the learning and achievement gaps between typically developing children and children with LDs often widen over time, although some children with LDs do display compensatory cycles of growth (Morgan, Farkas, & Wu, 2011).

Problematic learning experiences have many outcomes, including poor achievement and poor personal and social adjustment (Blair & Dennis, 2010). LDs are also associated with the development of both internalizing and externalizing disorders in the elementary school years (Halonen, Aunola, Ahonen, & Nurmi, 2006). The role of parents in influencing children's developmental pathways of achievement and adjustment is noteworthy. Related to special education efforts, parents are involved in identification of learning problems, collaboration with school professionals (homeroom teachers, special education teachers, aides), and issues related to equity and advocacy (Valle, 2011).

Certainly many children and adolescents diagnosed with LDs demonstrate success in school and in life. The *New York Times* essay "Words Failed, Then Saved Me" by the poet Philip Schultz illustrates the not-to-be-missed potential of students with LDs (see Box 7:6).

Etiology

Fletcher et al. (2007) provide a model of multiple influences on the development of learning disorders (see Fig. 7:4). These influences include genetic factors, neurobiological factors, child factors, and environmental factors. With respect to genetic factors, there is evidence for a strong heritable component. Children whose parents have dyslexia are at much higher risk for the development of an LD (i.e., rates of 30%–60%); rates of disorders are higher in fathers, compared to mothers, of children with LDs

BOX 7:6   RISK AND RESILIENCE

"Words Failed, Then Saved Me"

I was well into middle I was well into middle age when one of my children, then in the second grade, was found to be dyslexic. I had never known the name for it, but I recognized immediately that the symptoms were also mine. When I was his age I'd already all but given up on myself.

Repeating third grade at a new school, after having been asked to leave my old one for hitting kids who made fun of my perceived stupidity, I was placed in the "dummy class." There were three of us, separated from our classmates at a table in the corner of the room. One day, the teacher, who seldom spoke to us since it was understood that most of what she taught was beyond the reach of our intelligence, placed books in our hands and whispered that we should sit there quietly "pretending to read." The principal was coming.

It was not the most outlandish thing she might've said, given how little was known about learning disabilities in the early 1950s, and how little training a teacher in the poorest section of Rochester would have received. And her request seemed reasonable to me. I couldn't tie my shoes, tell time or left from right, or recreate musical notes or words. I not only couldn't read but often couldn't hear or understand what was being said to me—by the time I'd processed the beginning of a sentence, the teacher was well on her way through a second or third. When I did have something to say I couldn't find the words with which to say it, or if I could, forgot how to pronounce them.

My situation then seemed hopeless; I had no idea what a learning disability was, or that it had nothing to do with intelligence. Being asked to pretend I wasn't as stupid as I feared made perfect sense. Only in recollection does the pain of such a moment make itself felt.

So this summer's news that research is increasingly tying dyslexia not just to reading, but also to the way the brain processes spoken language, was no surprise to me. I found many ways around my dyslexia, but I still have trouble transforming words into sounds. I have to memorize and rehearse before reading anything aloud, to avoid embarrassing myself by mispronouncing words. And because learning a foreign language is sheer torture to dyslexics (even though it's a requirement in many schools), to this day I can't attend a High Holy Day service at my synagogue without feeling I don't belong there, because I can't speak Hebrew and must pretend to read my prayer book.

When I did finally learn to read, my teachers didn't have much to do with it. I was 11, and even my school-appointed tutors had given up on me. My mother read the one thing I would listen to—Blackhawk comics—over and over again, hoping against hope that by some leap of faith or chance I would start to identify letters and then learn to arrange them into words and sentences, and begin the intuitive, often magical process of turning written language into spoken language.

One night, lying in bed as she read to me, I realized that if I was ever going to learn to read I would have to teach myself. The moon glowing outside my window, I remember, seemed especially interested in my predicament. Was it a dummy, too? I wondered. If only I could be another boy, a boy my age who could sound out words and read and write like every other kid I knew.

I willed myself into being him. I invented a character who could read and write. Starting that night, I'd lie in bed silently imitating my mother read, imagining the taste, heft and right of each sound as if it were coming out of my mouth. I imagined being able to sound out the words by putting the letters together into units of rhythmic sound and the words into sentences that made sense. I imagined the words and their sounds being a kind of key with which I would open an invisible door to a world previously denied me.

And suddenly I was reading. I didn't know then that I was beginning a lifelong love affair with the first person voice and that I would spend most of my life inventing characters to say all the things I wanted to say. I didn't know that I was to become a poet, that in many ways the very thing that caused me so much confusion and frustration, my belabored relationship with words, had created in me a deep appreciation of language and its music, that the same mind that prevented me from reading had invented a new way of reading, a method that I now use to teach others how to overcome their own difficulties in order to write fiction and poetry. (It's perhaps not surprising that many famous writers are said to have struggled with dyslexia, including F. Scott Fitzgerald and W. B. Yeats.)

We know now that dyslexia is about so much more than just mixing up letters—that many dyslexics have difficulty with rhythm and meter and word retrieval, that they struggle to recognize voices and sounds. It's my profound hope that our schools can use findings like these to better teach children who struggle to read, to help them overcome their limitations, and to help them understand that it's not their fault.

We knew so much less when I was a child. Then, all I wanted and needed, when I learned so painstakingly to read and then to write, was to find a way to be less alone. Which is, of course, what spoken and written language is really all about. But poetry should be a passion, not survival.

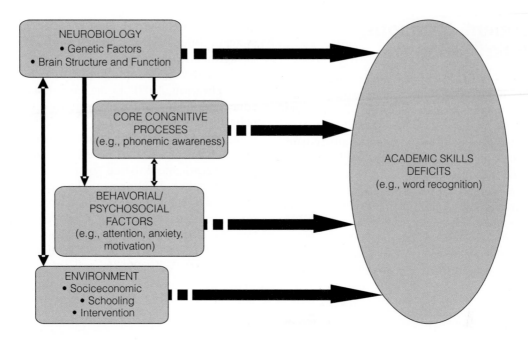

FIGURE 7:4 **Framework representing different sources of variability that influence academic outcomes in children with learning disorders.**
Source: From Fletcher et al. (2007).

(Fletcher et al., 2007; Pennington, 2009). Genetic influences are also documented for mathematics ability and disability (Docherty et al., 2010). In fact, recent analyses suggest that the genes that influence the development of LDs are "generalists"; that is, the same genes influence individual differences in multiple cognitive domains (Kovas et al., 2007; Petrill & Justice, 2007). The continuity over time in display of LDs is also genetically mediated (Kovas et al., 2007). Gene-by-environment interactions are also evident, with poor outcomes for children with genetic and environmental risks (Docherty, Kovas, & Plomin, 2011). There are also data that suggest that there is overlap in the genetic influences on LDs and attention deficit hyperactivity disorder (Pennington, 2006).

Differences in brain structure and function have been described, with involvement of larger neural networks (i.e., the left hemisphere regions) associated with the language system (Collins & Rourke, 2003; Fletcher et al., 2007). The parietal lobes are the focus of research on mathematics-related LDs (Butterworth et al., 2011).

Child factors are also important to consider. As noted earlier in this chapter, individual

approaches to learning and school readiness likely influence early academic success (Blair, 2002; Li-Grining et al., 2010). Other cognitive factors that have an impact on the emergence of LDs include executive functions (Best, Miller, & Jones, 2009; Blair & Dennis, 2010). Multiple cognitive deficits, and specific deficits that have cascading effects, have also been described (Anderson, 2008; Pennington, 2006).

Environmental factors, usually discussed in combination with genetic risk, also influence the development of LDs. As already noted, children with LDs often have parents with LDs. Parents who are poor readers are less likely to read to their children, and so provide less frequent and lower quality reading experiences (Fletcher et al., 2007). Economically disadvantaged families and families experiencing significant stressors are also less likely to provide and support learning-related activities (Docherty et al., 2011; Morgan et al., 2011). School factors such as teacher expectations, teaching practices, and class size are also key factors. With respect to the course of LDs, environments appear to contribute to change over time (in contrast to the continuity effect of genes) (Kovas et al., 2007).

Assessment, Diagnosis, and Intervention

Early models of LD assessment began with diagnosis and testing of struggling children, and then progressed to treatment. Recent models of assessment emphasize that large-scale screenings and instruction implementation should be provided to all students. Those who do not learn on typical timetables can then be provided with increasingly intensive interventions (Fletcher & Vaughn, 2009). The goals of this type of assessment and intervention plan include preventing disabilities and enhancing educational opportunities for all children (Fletcher & Vaughn, 2009).

Advances in intervention research and practice are taking place around the world, in Africa, in Israel, and in Europe, and take into account educational systems, differences in ethnicity and socioeconomic backgrounds, and access to effective services (Abosi, 2007; Correia & Martins, 2007; Gumpel & Sharoni, 2007; Thygesen, 2007). In the United States, special education and remediation efforts are often based on **individualized education plans** (IEPs) designed for students with LDs. Individual and small group lessons are often a component of an IEP and are focused on specific academic skill and cognitive deficits (Wills, 2007). Empirically informed adaptive software is a relatively recent innovation (Butterworth et al., 2011). Related characteristics, such as self-regulation abilities, are also targets of change (Blair, 2002; Raver et al., 2011). The earlier the interventions, the better the outcomes (Wills, 2007).

Key Terms

Cognitive development (p. 97)
Intellectual development (p. 97)
Intellectual developmental disorder (p. 98)
Intellectual functioning (p. 98)
Adaptive behavior (p. 98)
Developmental–difference debate (p. 101)
Genotypes (p. 101)
Behavioral phenotypes (p. 101)
Down syndrome (p. 101)
Williams syndrome (p. 102)
Fragile X syndrome (p. 102)
Organic causes (p. 103)
Nonorganic causes (p. 103)
Genetic counseling (p. 111)
Specific learning disorder (p. 114)
Individualized education plan (p. 118)

Chapter Summary

- Individual patterns of intellectual development are relatively stable by 4 or 5 years old.
- Intellectual developmental disorder (IDD) involves significant deficits in intellectual functioning and adaptive functioning.
- The classification levels of mild, moderate, severe, and profound intellectual developmental disorder describe the degree of compromise in intellectual and adaptive functioning present in an individual diagnosed with IDD.
- Adaptive behavior refers to the ability to master age-appropriate tasks of daily living.
- An alternative classification approach focuses on the relation between genetic causes (genotype) and specific behaviors and symptoms (phenotype). Examples of this approach include Down syndrome, Williams syndrome, and fragile X syndrome.
- Both organic (physiological) and nonorganic (other risk factors, such as normal range variability of intelligence and environmental challenges) causes may contribute to intellectual developmental disorder. In general, poorer prognoses are associated with organic etiologies.
- In addition to careful consideration of all relevant medical and developmental background information, standardized assessment of both intellectual and adaptive functioning is critical to the valid and reliable diagnosis of intellectual developmental disorder.
- In contrast to most forms of psychopathology, the focus of treatment for intellectual developmental disorder is not the condition itself. Rather, the focus of intervention is the maximization of the individual's potential functioning.

8 Autism Spectrum Disorder

The Case of Mark

Four-year-old Mark was referred for a psychological evaluation 2 years ago after his parents and pediatrician became concerned about his significantly delayed language development. Mark's parents described him as an extremely fussy baby who was hard to settle. Unlike his older sister, he was not very cuddly and, much to his parent's dismay, actually seemed to become more distressed when he was held. Although Mark's motor milestones were all achieved at expected times, his language and communications skills lagged far behind. Not only did he speak much later than expected, he seemed to show little interest in any kind of communication. For example, he did not respond to his name and did not seek his parents' attention.

Mark is very dependent on fixed and predictable routines. He plays with only a few toys and always in the same order. When playing, Mark often uses toys in unusual ways that disregard their intended purpose, such as using a doll to hammer in a peg or repeatedly spinning a horse on its side. He becomes extremely upset if these favorite toys are moved or rearranged on the shelf in his room where he keeps them. Mark also has difficulty engaging in imaginative or pretend play. Even on Halloween, he had difficulty with the idea of pretending to be a character, finding the idea confusing and upsetting.

When Mark speaks, which isn't often, his speech is atypical in rhythm and volume, and he frequently reverses his pronouns (saying, for example, "Would you like the ball?" when he wants someone to give him a ball). When his parents or the evaluators attempt to speak directly to Mark, he quickly looks away and sometimes even turns his back on them. Mark has always been extremely active and easily frustrated; at times when he is upset he bangs his head against the wall. He is described as being generally fearful and anxious in new situations and settings, and has been observed engaging in lots of hand-flapping and other self-stimulating behaviors. Mark's parents are quite worried about his starting kindergarten in a few months, knowing that he will be reluctant to be away from home and does not seem at all interested in the school setting or in meeting or playing with other children. ■

The Case of Will

Will is 9 years old and having considerable difficulty at school. Although Will's early motor and cognitive development were typical, he began to show both communication and social disturbances as a preschooler. For instance, Will can be very affectionate and engaging, but he can also be intrusive and overwhelming when interacting with other children. Although quite talkative from an early age, Will often talks at length about his own interests and is quite resistant to sharing in the interests or responding to the questions of others. By the time he entered elementary school, he had developed clear, specific, and obsessive interests. This characteristic first manifested itself in his keen interest in weather and meteorology and now includes weather radar equipment. All of his reading and nearly all conversations he initiates with others are on these topics. Although his parents, teachers, and older siblings have all explained to him that his intensity and relentlessness make others uncomfortable, he has not modified this behavior at all.

In the primary grades, the major concerns expressed by his teachers were his poor attention, impulsivity, and poor work completion. Although these problems have continued, it is his poor social skills that are currently causing the most difficulties. Will was mostly ignored and somewhat isolated in the early school years, but now he has become the target of teasing and rejection. Recently, his classmates have goaded him into doing things that have gotten him into trouble and resulted in his being ridiculed by classmates. Will is quite sensitive to the trouble he is having in regard to schoolwork and friendships, but he shows little insight into either the causes or solutions to these problems. ■

Historical and Current Conceptualizations of Autism Spectrum Disorder

Both Mark and Will exhibit a pattern of emotional, cognitive, and behavioral characteristics that reflect atypical development associated with clinically significant impairment. *What we call these patterns is important*, because names of disorders facilitate research on causes and treatments, allow mental health professionals to communicate with parents and teachers, and help children and adolescents make sense of their challenges and strengths. The disorders displayed by Mark and Will have, at various times, been called *autistic disorder*, *Asperger syndrome*, *high-functioning autism*, *atypical autism*, and/or *pervasive developmental disorder*; they are now called **autism spectrum disorder**. The change in nomenclature in DSM-5 must be understood in the context of continuing work focused on the complex etiology of autism, the varied developmental pathways, and the best interventions for Mark and Will and children like them.

Current conceptualizations of autism spectrum disorder are based on decades of work following clinical summaries provided by Leo Kanner (1943) and Hans Asperger (1944/1991) (Mesibov, Adams, & Schopler, 2000; Volkmar, Chawarska, & Klin, 2005; Wing, 1997, 1998). Both Kanner, in his descriptions of children with "early infantile autism," and Asperger, in his portrayals of boys with "autistic psychopathy," emphasized the children's profound lack of social awareness. Asperger, however, described better language skills and more social interest in his small sample (Asperger, 1944/1991). Much of the theory and research on autism in the United States, at least up until the 1990s, was based on Kanner's work. A picture of autism emerged that highlighted three areas of deviance: social isolation, impaired language and communication, and stereotypical behaviors. Some children, of course, did not fit the classic presentation. These children usually had better cognitive and language skills and were thought to have "high-functioning autism." More recently, clinicians and researchers hypothesized that some of the children diagnosed with high-functioning autism might be better understood (and better treated) if their symptoms and struggles were conceptualized as a related, but distinct, disorder: Asperger syndrome. Asperger syndrome was included as a separate diagnosis in DSM-IV.

Fifteen years of research, clinical work, and discussion and debate later, the overwhelming evidence is that autism and Asperger syndrome are best understood as part of a continuum (i.e., a spectrum) of disorder, and that is how these disorders are presented in DSM-5. Complicated and still-unresolved issues related to the nature, identification, and classification of autism spectrum disorder still exist (Georgiades et al., 2007; Volkmar, State, & Klin, 2009) and will be discussed later in the chapter.

One last point: Neither Mark nor Will, in the cases presented at the beginning of this section, displays intellectual developmental disorder. The rate of comorbidity between autism and intellectual developmental disorder is the focus of current research, with recent estimates ranging between 30% and 70% (Edelson, 2006; La Malfa, Lassi, Bertelli, Salvini, & Placidi, 2004). Varying estimates also depend on whether investigators begin with samples of children with autism and then look for IDD, or whether they begin with children with IDD and then look for autism (de Bildt et al., 2003), as well as on specific measures of intellectual functioning (Edelson, 2005; Edelson, Schubert, & Edelson, 1998).

Developmental Tasks and Challenges Related to the Coordination of Social, Emotional, and Cognitive Domains

The sections on typical development in the three previous chapters have described many of the remarkable achievements of young children, including the emergence of physiological and emotional regulation, attachment, and intellectual functioning, in order to provide useful comparisons and contrasts for specific psychopathologies. In this chapter, rather than focusing on a single domain of functioning, we emphasize the interdependent, coordinated nature of early development.

Social Cognition

This more integrative overview begins with a focus on **social cognition,** a construct at the intersections of self and other, emotion and cognition, and language and meaning. Social cognition refers to the many ways that people think about themselves and their social worlds. We are especially concerned with the ways in which young children take in and meaningfully process socially relevant information from the vast amounts of information available to them. An appreciation of social cognition in the typically developing child is essential in order to understand what goes wrong for children with autism spectrum disorder.

Two of the most important features of social cognition are the distinctions between (a) what is more and less important, and (b) what is social and nonsocial. According to Landa (2000), almost all children "pay attention to what is important. This awareness of salience is reflected in children's first words, which typically represent a salient person, place, thing, or action such as 'ball, kitty, cookie' rather than inanimate objects having little relevance in their lives such as 'wall'" (p. 133). Among salient people, places, and things, people receive the most attention. Almost all children recognize that the caregiver is worthy of notice and behave as if emotional and social engagement with the caregiver is special, pleasant, and informative. Indeed, "infants have many opportunities to observe people acting on objects, interacting with other people, and emotionally responding to these events. Thus, there is the potential for infants to acquire a rich set of social knowledge from observation alone." And, typically developing children are "well-equipped to engage in 'socially guided' learning" (Repacholi & Meltzoff, 2007, p. 503).

Social learning tasks include both *learning from others* (e.g., imitation of action, mirroring of emotion) and *learning about others* (e.g., others' desires, beliefs, intentions); learning begins early in development and extends throughout childhood and adulthood (Frith & Frith, 2012). According to Meltzoff (2007), the *"like me* nature of others is the starting point for social cognition" (p. 126). In order to acquire important social information while interacting with others and while observing others, infants must appreciate (at some basic level) that others are like themselves. This "salient recognition experience" provides the basis for the first of many interpretations of the social world and allows children "to imbue the behavior of others with felt meaning" (p. 132).

There are numerous investigations of the role of brain structure and function related to social cognition. The research on "building a social brain" is focused on identifying various brain regions implicated in the processing of important social stimuli (e.g., faces, human movement) and describing the development of increasingly organized networks of activity (Johnson, Grossman, & Kadosh, 2009; Perlman, Vander Wyk, & Pelphrey, 2010). This development is the result of ongoing "interactions between different brain regions and between the whole brain and its external environment" (Johnson et al., 2009, p. 151).

Theory of Mind

In addition to recognizing the salient and social aspects of one's surroundings, Landa (2000) discusses how simple but essential behaviors also contribute to interdependent, coordinated development. In Landa's view, "communicative intentions" such as eye contact, pointing, and shared attention smooth out the processes of social interaction and facilitate and reward participation in the social world. Investigations of these kinds of communicative intentions, or **joint attention,** provide strong evidence for its role in fostering development in several domains. Joint attention is the capacity to coordinate one's visual attention with the attention of another person (Mundy & Jarrold, 2010). It is both "a consequence and an organizer" of brain development that serves to "respond to and direct the behavior of other people in order to share experience" (p. 985). Joint attention is an example of social perception that precedes social cognition (Perlman et al., 2010).

One important developmental achievement dependent on joint attention involves the child's theory of mind. **Theory of mind** (ToM) refers to an ability to attribute mental states to others (Baron-Cohen, 1989, 1995, 2001), to see others as "bodies animated by minds" (Griffin & Baron-Cohen, 2002). Theory of mind develops from infancy through late childhood and beyond (Brune & Brune-Cohrs, 2006; Peterson, Wellman, & Slaughter, 2012) and is composed of various processes and skills (Ahmed & Miller, 2011). With ToM, children "learn to follow another's gaze, engage in pretend play, understand that another person can hold a different belief than oneself, [and] comprehend jokes and irony" (Ahmed & Miller, 2011, p. 668). The perspective taking that underlies ToM is essential for "successful social interactions in everyday functioning" (p. 668). We see evidence of ToM in all sorts of social exchanges, such as when babies look first to parents for information before approaching a large puppy, and then again when they share their delight in puppy licks and kisses.

Affective Social Competence

The development of social cognition over the early years also depends on increasingly complex emotion skills. Halberstadt, Denham, and Dunsmore's (2001) construct of affective social competence provides an important example of integrated functions. **Affective social competence** involves the coordination of the capacities to experience emotion, send emotional messages to others, and read others' emotional signals. The dynamic interaction of these types of emotion abilities with emerging cognitive abilities provides yet another way that children are able to glean salient information from their social partners. Overall, then, the developmental transition from the sensorimotor experiences of infancy to the symbolic experiences of toddlerhood and later years is marked by ever-increasing coordination among various developmental domains and processes. This in turn leads to an emphasis on the idea of the child as a social being in a social world and the recognition that this is of central importance throughout development.

Autism Spectrum Disorder

Autism spectrum disorder (ASD) is characterized by deficits and significant impairment in two domains: (a) social and communication deficits and (b) repetitive behaviors and fixated interests.

For a diagnosis of autism spectrum disorder using DSM-5, children must display three kinds of social and communication deficits: deficits in social–emotional reciprocity; deficits in nonverbal communication during social interactions; and deficits in developing and maintaining relationships. Each of these deficits is evaluated against developmental norms. In addition to these social and communication deficits, children must also display at least two types of repetitive behaviors and fixated interests. These might include stereotyped or repetitive speech, motor movements, or use of objects; excessive adherence to routines or ritualized patterns or resistance to change; highly restricted interests that are atypical with respect to intensity or focus; or atypical sensitivity to sensory stimulation or atypical interest in aspects of the sensory environment. In addition to the core symptoms described in DSM-5, the level of severity of the symptom picture is noted, from *requiring support*, to *requiring substantial support*, to *requiring very substantial support*. This severity index reflects the newly emphasized dimensional conceptualization of autism spectrum disorder.

The validity of the revised DSM-5 criteria has been the subject of much research and debate. The key issues include sensitivity (i.e., do the revised criteria capture all children who struggle with ASD?), specificity (i.e., do the revised criteria differentiate children with ASD from children with other disorders and from typically developing children?), and service eligibility (i.e., do the revised criteria make it more difficult for children who struggle with significant impairment to continue to receive mental health and education services?). A number of large-scale studies of the new criteria suggest that the two-factor model (social and communication deficits + repetitive behaviors and fixated interests) exhibits superior specificity (compared to DSM-IV) in distinguishing children with ASD from other groups of children (Frazier et al., 2012; Mandy, Charman, & Skuse, 2012; Mattila et al., 2011). The new criteria are perhaps somewhat less sensitive, particularly in relation to children who display less severe symptoms (Mattila et al., 2011). It is not yet clear how the new DSM will affect the numbers of children diagnosed with ASD or the services available to children along the autism spectrum. These last concerns will be explored more fully in upcoming sections on assessment, diagnosis, and intervention.

Social and Communication Deficits

Children with autism spectrum disorder display a heterogeneous set of **social and communication deficits.** Their socioemotional development is both quantitatively and qualitatively different from typically developing children and children with other disorders (Carr & Lord, 2009; Hobson, 1999; Klin, Jones, Schultz, Volkmar, & Cohen, 2002a, 2002b; Klin & Volkmar, 1997). Atypical behaviors displayed by children with autism spectrum disorder, all evidence of difficulties with social perception or social cognition, include a lack of social orienting; a failure to respond to social sounds and signals, such as the parent's voice or clapping hands; a lack of social reciprocity, or the turn-taking of social interactions; and fewer and more deviant social behaviors (Bruinsma, Koegel, & Koegel, 2004; Dawson et al., 2004; Klin & Volkmar, 1997). Each of these atypical behaviors reflects a relative lack of differentiation between social and nonsocial stimuli.

Ongoing research is focused on identifying the specific social mechanisms that underlie complex social behaviors (Klin, 2002). One hypothesis connects social interaction and language learning (Kuhl, Coffey-Corina, Padden, & Dawson, 2005). Kuhl and her colleagues investigated *motherese*, the sounds and melody of mothers' speech to very young children. In the Kuhl study, normally developing children preferred the baby talk and display specific patterns of brain activity when exposed to it. Children with autism, however, preferred computer-generated nonspeech. Other work related to joint attention summarizes data that suggest that children with autism do attend to persons and events; however, their unusual resistance to distraction, their skill at parallel perception, and their atypical display of certain actions make typical instances of joint attention unlikely (Hamilton, Brindley, & Frith, 2007; Gernsbacher, Stevenson, Khandakar, & Goldsmith, 2008; Iarocci & Burack, 2004; Sebanz, Knoblich, Stumpf, & Prinz, 2005).

In addition to atypical social development and adaptation, there are also difficulties related to the experience, perception, and processing of emotion (Hobson, 1991, 1993) (see Box 8:1). In contrast to long-held beliefs that children and adolescents with autism spectrum disorder lack emotion or emotion skills, many studies provide compelling evidence of emotional experiences. Children with autism spectrum disorder display more negative emotion and less well-regulated emotion (Mazefsky,

BOX 8:1 EMERGING SCIENCE

The Role of the Face

Researchers in the United States and Canada are using innovative eye-tracking technology to gain new insights into how individuals with autism view their socioemotional and interpersonal worlds. Data from multiple studies (Klin et al., 2002b; Ristic et al., 2005) document the distinctive patterns of focusing and shifting attention displayed by individuals with autism. Compared to individuals without autism, who look frequently and for relatively longer periods of time at the eyes of others, individuals with autism are more likely to gaze at the mouths and bodies of others, and at extraneous objects. Not only is this pattern of face scanning unusual, but the information gleaned from such scanning is likely to be incomplete and less meaningful. Differences between the gaze patterns of individuals with autism and individuals without autism are illustrated in the accompanying photo.

These findings are especially interesting in light of some of the hallmark symptoms of autism, such as lack of eye contact and poor recognition of faces. In related research, also conducted at Yale (Schultz, Grelotti, Klin et al., 2003), functional magnetic resonance imaging (MRI) studies showed that research participants with autism perceived faces as if they were objects. The 3-year study provided evidence of reduced activity for those with autism in the area of the cerebral cortex dedicated to face recognition. At the same time, they showed increased activity in an adjacent area of the brain that processes information regarding objects. Recent reviews of the perceptual, cognitive, and motivational–affective hypotheses related to impaired facial processing include descriptions of deficits in initial stages of face processing and later stages of face recognition (Dawson, Webb, & McPartland, 2005; Perlman, Hudac, Pegors, Minshew, & Pelphrey, 2011; Ristic et al., 2005). In addition, there is evidence that some of the abnormalities in the "social brain" circuitry may be observed in first-degree relatives of children with autism (Dawson, Webb, Wijsman, et al., 2005; McCleery, Allman, Carver, & Dobkins, 2007).

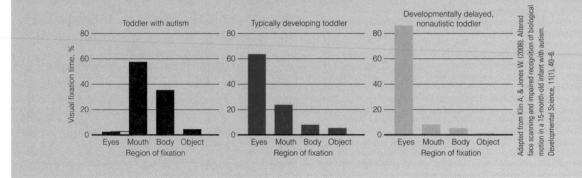

Adapted from Klin A, & Jones W. (2008). Altered face scanning and impaired recognition of biological motion in a 15-month-old infant with autism. *Developmental Science,* 11(1), 40–6.

Pelphrey, & Dahl, 2012), although a wide range of emotions are described by children and adolescents themselves (Losh & Capps, 2006). Individuals with autism spectrum disorder recognize and express basic emotions (such as happiness, anger, and sadness), although they have difficulties with more complex emotions (such as embarrassment, pride, and guilt) (Hobson, Chidambi, Lee, & Meyer, 2006; Jones et al., 2011). Many individuals with autism spectrum disorder make use of compensatory strategies (e.g., using better developed cognitive resources) in emotionally demanding situations, but most individuals clearly struggle. "Even exceedingly intelligent adults with autism seem to lack the necessary tools for successfully traversing the convoluted emotional landscapes that undergird affective interactions and relationships" (Losh & Capps, 2006, p. 810).

However, it is equally important to emphasize that key aspects of important relationships may be intact. Studies of attachment in children with autism spectrum disorder suggest that many children exhibit secure attachments; that is, "the children's relationships with their caregivers are clearly special, even though their qualities of relatedness are atypical" (Hobson et al., 2006, p. 23). In a study that provides evidence of both typical and atypical emotional development, children with autism spectrum disorder displayed laughter at rates similar to typically developing peers, but their laughs were expressed in response to positive internal states, in contrast to peers who laughed in response

Face scanning by toddlers with autism (left column), typically-developing toddlers (middle column), and developmentally-delayed toddlers (right column).

to positive states *and* to negotiate social interactions (Hudenko, Stone, & Bachorowski, 2009).

Basic social and emotional deficits influence multiple domains of typical development. Children with autism display deficits in pretend play and imitation (Charman et al., 1997, 2000). For instance, "children with autism do not want to use their miniature snow shovel to shovel snow just like daddy or use a screwdriver to repair a toy when mommy is doing the same" (Harris, 1995, p. 306). Other children never deviate from a particular play routine. Filipek et al. (1999) provide an example of a "verbal autistic preschooler who 'plays' by repeatedly reciting a soliloquy of the old witch scene verbatim from Beauty and the Beast while manipulating dollhouse characters

in precise sequence according to the script. When given the same miniature figures and dollhouse, but instructed to play something other than Beauty and the Beast, this same child is incapable of creating any other play scenario" (p. 445).

Children with autism also display an overall lack of social "style" (Hobson & Lee, 1998, 1999). The difficulties are perhaps most obvious in reciprocal relationships such as peer friendships, where expectations for social and emotional skills are higher, and are observed even in the highest functioning groups of children with autism (Lord & Volkmar, 2002). In some cases, children do better when interacting with much older or younger children, where they can adopt the clearly defined role of follower or leader (Filipek et al., 1999). This is certainly true for Mark, the 4-year-old described at the beginning of the chapter, who has the most social difficulties with other children around his age. He is somewhat more comfortable when interacting with his 13-year-old sister or his parents, who understand his routines and rituals and can adjust their behaviors to what he most needs.

With a dimensional perspective, we expect that children with autism spectrum disorder vary in their social and emotional functioning. Some children (e.g., those previously diagnosed with Asperger syndrome and now likely diagnosed with autism spectrum disorder with fewer supports required) appear to be more aware of others as social beings and more interested in social interactions (Klin & Volkmar, 1997). However, although the desire and motivation are present, these children are still somewhat stymied by the seemingly intuitive give-and-take of social exchange (Klin & Volkmar, 1997; Volkmar & Klin, 2001). Relying on the formal rules of social behavior, these children make more overtures to other children but often appear awkward, rigid, and insensitive in their interactions (Volkmar & Klin, 1997). Their general social ineffectiveness, and the ridicule of their peers, may lead later to the withdrawal and isolation more characteristic of children with more severe autism spectrum disorder (Filipek et al., 1999).

With respect to individual differences in emotional development and adaptation, the children previously diagnosed with Asperger syndrome can and do talk about emotions and relationships. But the more time one spends in such conversations with these children, the more it is apparent that the talk is concrete and intellectualized (Klin, Volkmar et al., 2000). One of the authors works with a young adolescent who is preoccupied with violent "slasher" movies. In therapy, it has become clear that he responds to the highly exaggerated (and more easily perceived) emotional states of the characters. Similarly, Will, the 9-year-old presented at the beginning of the chapter, is fascinated by comic books. Will can talk endlessly about the clearly outlined conflicts, resolutions, and emotional states of the characters, although he never even comes close to expressing these feelings himself.

With respect to communication, children with autism display both delay and deviance. There are impairments in the forms of speech, with slowed babbling and delayed use of words, later onset (or lack of onset) of intentional communication such as pointing, lack of imitation, and abnormalities in the nonverbal components of speech such as tone and prosody (Filipek et al., 1999; Klin & Volkmar, 1997;

Lord & Pickles, 1996). The content of speech is also unusual, with both immediate and delayed echolalia (inappropriate or uncommunicative repetition of words or phrases). For example, in addition to the pronoun reversals of Mark (asking "would you like the ball?" when he wants a ball), he also frequently repeats the last word spoken to him in a conversation.

There are even more pronounced difficulties with the social use of language, or pragmatics (Filipek et al., 1999; Landa, 2000). Children with autism use language for instrumental reasons such as getting a dessert, rather than for social purposes such as sharing one's pleasure in completing a puzzle (Wetherby, 1986). Mark's family, for example, came to realize that he never initiates a conversation unless it is about something he wants or needs. Consequently, they look for these opportunities to engage with him and broaden, by very small increments, the scope of their communication with him.

Some children with autism spectrum disorder (again, those previously diagnosed with Asperger syndrome) engage in pedantic, one-sided conversations. In addition, they do not self-censor their speech. One child in treatment greeted a therapist with "Hi … hey did you know your eyes bug out, like you have some medical problem or something?" Klin (2002) provides another example of a college student with Asperger syndrome who asked a student if he would be willing to trade his girlfriend for a watch (note here the very thin line between things and people). Will (in the case described earlier), for example, was often preoccupied with issues of fairness at home, where he often complained bitterly about his baby sister getting new clothes when he did not. Although he was able to keep track of her entire wardrobe, he was not comforted by explanations that he was treated similarly as an infant, or by the fact that babies grow more rapidly than 9-year-olds.

An especially compelling perspective on the development and experience of the self in children and adolescents with autism spectrum disorder is provided by Hobson et al. (2006). In their monograph, Hobson et al. describe the emotional, cognitive, and motivational factors that contribute to the development of self-awareness. This emerging awareness takes into account several aspects of self-experience and self-knowledge. First, there is a "relational" or "interpersonal" self, a self embedded in relationships. There is also a "reflective" self, dependent on the ability to understand one's own perspective as person specific and different from others' perspectives. In typical early development, the process of identifying with others supports the trajectory of self awareness. In that process, "there is both connectedness and differentiation" (p. 16). Thinking back to Meltzoff's description of the basis of social cognition as the "like me" phenomenon, it is clear that children with autism spectrum disorder are likely to display an atypical and/or compromised sense of self.

Repetitive Behaviors and Fixated Interests

Most children with autism spectrum disorder exhibit **restricted, repetitive behaviors** and/or stereotyped body movements such as rocking, hand-flapping, and twirling (Leekam, Prior, & Uljarevic, 2011). These atypical behaviors are sometimes observed in children with other disorders, but the collective pattern of behaviors is unique for those with autism spectrum disorder. Children with more severe ASD display more restricted and repetitive behaviors (Leekam et al., 2011). Repetitive behaviors in children with ASD appear to be associated with anxiety, both the direct experience of anxiety and attempts to manage or minimize the experience of anxiety (Rodgers et al., 2012). Recent research is focused on understanding the ways in which the repetitive behaviors displayed by children with ASD are different from those displayed by typically developing children, as well as identifying emotional and motivational triggers (in addition to anxiety) for repetitive behaviors (Leekam et al., 2011).

Some children with autism spectrum disorder also display **fixated interests** and/or strong attachments to certain objects, but their attachment is often unusual. For instance, a child may be focused only on the wheel mechanisms of toy cars rather than their ability to move across the floor. A different child may

Children with autism spectrum disorder display fixated interests and/or strong attachments to certain objects.

©iStockphoto.com/UrsaHoogle

be absorbed by the smell of a toy. Many young children with autism spectrum disorder are intrigued by water (Filipek et al., 1999). These obsessions in children are almost always associated with "folk physics" (an interest in how *things* work) rather than in "folk psychology" (how *people* work) (Baron-Cohen & Wheelwright, 1999). In some children with autism spectrum disorder, specialized interests or skills lead to the display of unusual giftedness (see Box 8:2).

Most children with autism spectrum disorder also insist on sameness in their environments and routines, protesting vehemently when this sameness is disturbed (Klin & Volkmar, 1997). Filipek et al. (1999) describe instances of children needing to have furniture in exact places or clothes in a single color. According to Klin (2002), this insistence on sameness in the environment is a powerful and meaningful symptom, reflecting the individual's concern and struggle with control of his or her surroundings. Additional investigations have emphasized the role of executive dysfunction (i.e., cognitive rigidity) in children's insistence on sameness (South, Ozonoff, & McMahon, 2007; Szatmari et al., 2006). Some children with less severe autism spectrum disorder may assert control in the verbal and language domain, through dominating conversations and continuing to discuss topics long after conversational partners have wearied.

In addition to repetitive behaviors and fixated interests, many children with autism spectrum disorder display sensory sensitivities or unusual curiosity about sensory aspects of the environment. Children may exhibit either underreactivity or overreactivity, and these difficulties are likely to influence the activities in which children participate and the numbers of others with whom they interact (Ben-Sasson et al., 2009; Boyd et al., 2010; Hilton, 2011). One final category of behavioral difficulties includes aggression. Children with autism spectrum disorder display aggressive behavior at much higher rates than typically developing children (Kanne & Mazurek, 2011; Mayes et al., 2012).

Prevalence and Related Information

Estimates of the prevalence of autism vary widely. Using data from 14 sites around the United States, the Centers for Disease Control and Prevention of the U.S. Department of Health and Human Services (2012) estimate current prevalence at 1 in 88, up from 1 in 150 in 2007. Rates vary depending on site and by racial/ethnic group. The lowest rates were observed in Alabama, and the highest rates in New Jersey and Utah. Higher rates were observed

BOX 8:2 CLINICAL PERSPECTIVES

Splinter Skills and Savant Talents

One of the most unusual attributes of certain individuals diagnosed with autism is the extraordinary development of a single skill or talent. Although most children and adolescents with autism struggle with intellectual impairments and display uneven performances in various intellectual domains, there are some individuals who possess relatively preserved sets of skills ("splinter skills") as well as others whose exceptional abilities in language, drawing, music, or mathematics ("savant talents") capture our attention (Hermelin, 2001). Dustin Hoffman, in the 1989 movie *Rain Man*, portrays an adult with autism who has an amazing facility with numbers. One of Clara Park's books about her daughter Jessy, *Exiting Nirvana*, is illustrated with Jessy's brightly colored, intricately detailed architectural drawings (see Fig. 8:1). For the most part, these special skills are not used for practical or constructive ends.

What explains this phenomenon? As we have discussed in this chapter, there is evidence that individuals with autism process information in fragments or segments (ignoring available holistic information). Some investigators believe that this tendency is even more developed in those who display special skills (Heaton, Hermelin, & Pring, 1998; Hermelin, 2001; O'Connor & Hermelin, 1994; Pring & Hermelin, 2002), although there are also lesser roles for practice and instruction (Pring, Hermelin, Buhler, & Walker, 1997). As we try to make sense of observations that reflect multiple connections among intelligence, autism, and giftedness, we need to acknowledge—again—the essential connections between typically developing and atypically developing children.

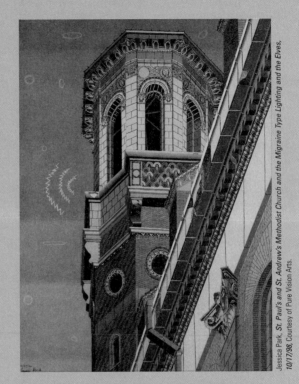

FIGURE 8:1 *St. Paul's and St. Andrew's Methodist Church and the Migraine Type Lighting and the Elves, 10/17/98,* drawing by Jessy Park. From *Exiting Nirvana: A Daughter's Life with Autism,* by C. Claiborne Park, 2001, New York: Little, Brown.

Jessica Park, St. Paul's and St. Andrew's Methodist Church and the Migraine Type Lighting and the Elves, 10/17/98, Courtesy of Pure Vision Arts.

for children of European American backgrounds, and lower rates for children of African American and Latino American backgrounds. Three to four times as many boys are diagnosed as girls, but girls with autism have higher rates of intellectual developmental disability. Some researchers believe that "fewer females with normal IQ are diagnosed with autism because they may be more socially adept than males with similar IQ" (Filipek et al., 1999, p. 440). Various hypotheses related to dramatic increases in prevalence rates, and varied rates across regions and ethnic groups, include the widening of diagnostic criteria (prior to DSM-5), greater (and lesser) awareness among parents and mental health

professionals, better and earlier identification, as well as the possibility of a true increase in prevalence (Chakrabarti & Fombonne, 2005; Fombonne, 2007; Holburn, 2008; Lord & Volkmar, 2002; Wing & Potter, 2002, 2009). Although many mental health professionals predict some decline in rates following the revisions to the diagnostic criteria in DSM-5, whether and by how much rates will change remain empirical questions requiring careful investigation.

One of the most important consequences of any change in the conceptualization and identification of autism spectrum disorder involves access to mental health and educational services. Klin et al. (2000) observed years ago that "decades of effective parent action in autism on the one hand and learning disabilities on the other hand have resulted in a relatively rich infrastructure of services for children with these conditions and their families, including better special education resources, entitlement programs, and more generally, increased awareness in the mental health and educational communities" (p. 5). With the DSM-5 changes, parent advocacy and organization (e.g., in Autism Speaks, autismspeaks.org), including children from one end of the autism spectrum to the other, continue to keep the research and clinical focus on appropriate and adequate services that enhance the well-being of children.

In addition to prevalence rates and access to services, it is also important to consider comorbid disorders. As already discussed, we must keep in mind that three-quarters of children with autism spectrum disorder also meet the diagnostic criteria for intellectual developmental disorder, with 30% in the mild to moderate range and 45% in the severe to profound range; one-half of children with autism and intellectual developmental disorder are without functional speech (Pennington, 2002). The strong association between autism and intellectual developmental disorder is undeniable. The reasons for the association will be discussed in the upcoming section on etiology but remain to be fully explained. Other disorders are also frequently observed in children with autism spectrum disorder, including attention-deficit hyperactivity disorder, tic disorder, mood disorders, and anxiety disorders (Deprey & Ozonoff, 2009; Tager-Flusberg & Dominick, 2011).

Developmental Course

For almost all children, autism spectrum disorder is a lifelong disorder. Many cases of autism are identified in the first year of life, although the mean age of initial evaluation in a recent population sample was 48 months, with diagnosis at 61 months (Wiggins, Baio, & Rice, 2006). Although most researchers suggest that precursors to the characteristic symptoms of autism are present from birth onward, there is evidence of a subgroup of children who develop relatively normally for the first year and then show significant regression, with a loss of verbal and social skills (e.g., Luyster et al., 2005; Richler et al., 2006). Home videos of children provide additional information about such regression (see Box 8:3).

The characteristic symptoms of autism are in place and often at peak frequency between 2 and 4 years of age (Bryson et al., 2007; Chawarska et al., 2007; Muratori & Maestro, 2007; Werner, Dawson, Munson, & Osterling, 2005; Zwaigenbaum et al., 2005). From then on, a number of developmental trajectories have been identified, with substantial heterogeneity observed in communication, social, and behavioral domains (Carr & Lord, 2010; Fountain, Winter, & Bearman, 2012) (see Fig. 8:2). Please note that, as shown in Figure 8:2, improvement is more likely in the social and communication domains, with much of the improvement occurring early. Also note that there were groups of children, labeled "bloomers," who displayed major, rapid improvement. Children who were higher functioning at the time of diagnosis were those who are most likely to show significant improvement. Children who were also diagnosed with intellectual developmental disorder were much less likely to improve.

According to numerous studies, which often rely on parental reports, between 15% and 30% of children diagnosed with autism spectrum disorder display regression. That is, some parents report that their children exhibit either an abrupt loss of skills (particularly communication skills) or a more gradual change over months (Ozonoff, Williams, & Landa, 2005; Yirmiya & Charman, 2010). The phenomenon of regression, whether it follows genuinely typical development, and its documentation by parents and professionals, requires additional study (Ozonoff et al., 2010). A minority of individuals with autism show a decline beginning in adolescence, usually associated with the onset of seizures (Bolton et al., 2011; Canitano, Luchetti, & Zappella, 2005). Even with recent advances in early identification and early intervention, many adults with autism continue to have significant difficulties, living with their parents and experiencing ongoing social and vocational struggles (Howlin, Goode, Hutton, & Rutter, 2004; Rutter, Kim-Cohen, & Maughan, 2006). Indeed, in one study comparing adults with autism spectrum disorder and adults with intellectual developmental disorder, adults with ASD were less independent, had fewer social contacts, received fewer services, and had more unmet needs than adults with IDD (Esbensen et al., 2010).

Social and Communication Pathways
Given that early language abilities and language competence are related to better outcomes (Bennett et al., 2008; Pry, Petersen, & Baghdadli, 2005), it is lamentable that about half of children with autism

BOX 8:3   THE CHILD IN CONTEXT

Early Home Videos of Children with Autism Spectrum Disorder

Retrospective reporting by parents is sometimes difficult to evaluate. By the time a diagnosis of a autism spectrum disorder is made, parents have often struggled for years to sort through medical opinions and hypotheses offered by well-meaning relatives and friends. Understanding the history of parental concerns is important, because information about rates of development and their specific pathways has predictive value that is useful for parents, clinicians, and children (Klin, 2002).

The validity of parents' early concerns is supported by several creative investigations of early home videos. Family videos of infants and toddlers provide a rich source of data about social development, language and communication, and unusual behaviors. By 1 year of age, raters can distinguish children who will later be diagnosed with autism from typically developing children (Osterling & Dawson, 1994; Osterling, Dawson, & Munson, 2002; Werner, Dawson, Osterling, & Dinno, 2000). One salient difference is that children who will later be diagnosed with autism fail to respond to their names when called (Werner et al., 2000). Another difference is an intense interest in objects (rather than people) (Maestro et al., 2006). In fact, the atypical social,

language, and behavior patterns observed not only differentiate children with autism spectrum disorder from typically developing children, but also provide information about differences between the development of autism and intellectual developmental disorder, and the onset of regression in subset of children later diagnosed with autism spectrum disorder (Osterling, Dawson, & Munson, 2002; Ozonoff et al., 2010; Werner & Dawson, 2005).

Another study focused on the early course of autism, comparing videos of children across 6-month intervals (i.e., birth–6 months, 6–12 months, 12–18 months, and 18–24 months) (Bernabei, Camaioni, & Levi, 1998). The most common pattern observed in this study was one in which babies made developmental progress during the first or second periods, and then regressed between the second and third periods or the third and fourth periods, with the most significant deterioration in the domain of social behaviors. In addition to providing compelling information about the early nature of autism, each of these investigations provides support for the often underappreciated usefulness of parent reports and concerns about their children's development.

never develop useful speech. Of course, many of these nontalking children also are diagnosed with intellectual developmental disorder, which complicates the clinical picture. Early display of joint attention and immediate imitation contribute to language and communication ability at diagnosis, and better toy play and deferred imitation predict better language and communication outcomes (Toth, Munson, Meltzoff, & Dawson, 2006).

For individuals who do develop language, the "pragmatic impairment may be the most stigmatizing and handicapping aspect of these disorders. From school age onward, individuals with Asperger syndrome report that their social language vulnerabilities give rise to anxiety, avoidance of some social situations, and self-image challenges and are a source of great concern to them. Adults with Asperger syndrome report having difficulty at jobs and establishing friendships due to their social communication impairment, despite being professionally productive and otherwise quite capable" (Landa, 2000, p. 125).

The poignancy of the situation is clear for individuals with autism spectrum disorder, who, at each successive stage, are further compromised in their ability to deal with new challenges. This situation also illustrates in a very real way the notion of a *developmental disorder*, with different deficits and difficulties coming to the fore at various ages (Tantam, 2000, 2003).

With deficits in social perception, social cognition, and communication, we expect that children with autism spectrum disorder will struggle with establishing and maintaining rewarding relationships. For instance, only half of children with autism spectrum disorder who are in inclusive classrooms are involved in the social networks of their classrooms. Children with ASD are more likely to be isolated across all grade levels, and this difference is increasingly dramatic in later grades (Rotheram-Fuller, Kasari, Chamberlain, & Locke, 2010). However difficult interactions, friendships, and relationships may be, it is clear that children and adolescents with ASD desire connections with

A Communication trajectories

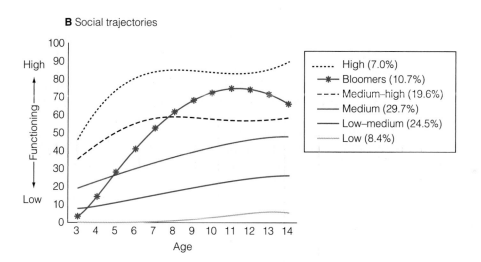

FIGURE 8:2 Multiple developmental pathways for autism spectrum disorder.
Fountain, C., Winter, A. S., & Bearman, P. S. (2012), "Six developmental trajectories characterize children with autism." Pediatrics volume 129 pp. e1112–e1120. Reproduced with permission from Pediatrics, Copyright © 2012 by the AAP.

B Social trajectories

C Repetitive behavior trajectories

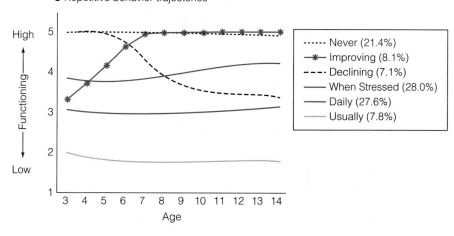

others (Causton-Theoharis, Ashby, & Cosier, 2009). Causton-Theoharis et al. provide this example from a journal of an individual with Asperger syndrome: "I was gradually becoming more and more aware of my loneliness and began to long for a friend. All my classmates had at least one and most had several. I would spend hours at night awake in bed looking up at the ceiling and imagining what it might be like to be friends with somebody" (Tammet, 2006, p. 74). Klin (2002) recalls a student who asked a young woman, "Can I touch your crotch?" It is easy to see how craving social contact, combined with developing sexuality and lack of insight and self-censorship, might lead quickly to social conflict and confusion. Over time, ongoing lack of success in connecting with others, especially peers, may elicit sadness, anxiety, and withdrawal for many older children and adolescents with ASD (Ghaziuddin, Ghaziuddin, & Greden, 2002). It may happen, however, that the transition to adolescence provides an opportunity for more rewarding social interactions for some (Tantam, 2000).

Behavior Pathways

Repetitive behavior pathways display more stability than the social and communication pathways (Fountain et al., 2012). Most children (about 85%) continue to struggle from their diagnosis forward. Half of the children who do change significantly improve, and half deteriorate (Fountain et al., 2012). Children with higher nonverbal IQ scores show more improvement (Richler, Heurta, Bishop, & Lord, 2010). With respect to fixated interests over time, it is possible that "circumscribed interests involving particular expertise can sometimes be an asset, as older more able individuals find a niche in employment that makes good use of their special interests and expertise, for example high-level computer skills" (Leekam et al., 2011, p. 564).

The Role of the Family

Parenting children with autism spectrum disorder is an obviously difficult task. Parents report a number of major stressors, with somewhat different patterns of stress described by mothers and fathers (Bloch & Weinstein, 2010; Sivberg, 2002). There are different stressors associated with various times (e.g., at diagnosis, entrance to school, transition to adulthood) and with various tasks (e.g., identifying available services, accessing such services) (Barker et al., 2011; Bloch & Weinstein, 2010; Taylor & Seltzer, 2011).

Siblings also are affected, and they display a range of emotions and responses to a brother or sister with ASD (Aronson, 2009). In the book *The Siege: A Family's Journey Into the World of the Autistic Child*, Clara Clairborne Park, the mother of a child with autism, describes the adjustment required of the child's siblings: "It was hard for a little boy six and little girls nine and ten to put all their minds to choosing a Christmas present for their two-year-old sister's first real Christmas and know that in all probability she wouldn't look at it or them" (1967/1995, p. 105). As time went on, however, the siblings of Park's daughter accepted their sister for who she was and became an integral part of her increasing engagement with the world: "The best thing they could do for Elly, as she entered the world by slow degrees, was to be children with her, to play naturally and with enjoyment the games that came to me, at forty, with such difficulty and awkwardness. They carried her about, dressed her in clothes from the dress-up chest, rode her in the wagon, chased her on the grass." Given the difficulties that children and adolescents with ASD experience, sibling relationships across the lifespan, including into and throughout adulthood, are especially important to consider. The degree of involvement and support offered by siblings may have an especially meaningful impact on the well-being of individuals with ASD (Beyer, 2009; Orsmond & Seltzer, 2007).

Etiology

Early Hypotheses

Although the earliest etiological hypotheses of Kanner and Asperger suggested physiological origins for autism, these were quickly displaced by psychosocial explanations more in tune with the psychoanalytic era. Most frequently associated with Bruno Bettelheim, as well as other psychoanalysts, these explanations focused on poor parenting and the cool, distant "refrigerator mothers," whose infants intuitively understood that they were being rejected and so withdrew from contact and relationships. The consequences of being blamed for a pervasively debilitating disorder in one's own child were devastating. In time, although much too late for many parents, these theories were completely discredited.

Genes and Heredity

Autism spectrum disorder has been described as "probably the most heritable of the psychopathologies" observed in children (Pennington, 2002, p. 226). Comparisons of monozygotic (MZ) and dizygotic (DZ) twins document clear genetic effects, with estimates of the proportion of risk attributable to genetic factors at about 90% (Gupta & State, 2007; Pennington, 2002; Yirmiya & Charman, 2010). Family data support this notion of genetic transmission (Pennington, 2002). Additional review of genetic investigations highlights a number of theoretical and empirical advances. Various models of genetic vulnerability have been documented (Yirmiya & Charman, 2010). In the polygenic model, the risk is the result of interactions among several different genes (e.g., Bartlett, Gharani, Millonig, & Brzustowicz, 2005; Schellenberg et al., 2006). These investigations are consistent with evidence that autism is sometimes associated with other genetically transmitted disorders, including fragile X syndrome and tuberous sclerosis (Filipek, 1999; Pennington, 2002); they may also provide useful information about the origins of the sex difference in prevalence rates. In addition, genetics likely explain much of the association between autism and intellectual developmental disorder. An alternative to the polygenic model asserts that risk is associated with rare mutations (*de novo* mutations) in any number of genes (e.g., Sanders et al., 2012). These mutations appear to be more frequently observed with older parents, especially older fathers (Kolevzon, Gross, & Reichenberg, 2007; Lundstrom et al., 2010). This *de novo* model is supported by very high concordance rates in MZ twins and very low concordance rates in DZ twins. It may be that there are "more and less familial forms of autism" (Yirmiya & Charman, 2010).

Interactions between genetic vulnerability and environmental factors are also being examined (Croen, Grether, & Selvin, 2002). Prenatal and perinatal complications are the focus of ongoing research (Hallmeyer et al., 2011; Kolevzon et al., 2007). Childhood vaccines and immunizations have also been repeatedly and convincingly ruled out as causes of autism (Madsen et al., 2002, 2003; Offit, 2008; Schreibman, 2005).

Physiological Factors

Physiological factors associated with brain structure, brain function, and brain chemistry are likely to help explain the multiple domains of impairment observed in children with autism spectrum disorder. The regions of the brain most often identified in studies of autism include the frontal lobes, the amygdala, and the cerebellum (Amaral, Schumann, & Nordahl, 2008). Studies of areas involved in the processing of emotion (i.e., the amygdala) (Monk, 2008; Schultz, 2005) and the processing of social stimuli (i.e., the superior temporal sulcus and other areas) have provided important information (Dawson, Carver et al., 2002; Perlman et al., 2010). Impaired connectivity between the brain hemispheres has also been described (Minshew & Williams, 2007). Elevated levels of the neurotransmitter serotonin have been described in about one-fourth of those with autism; the consequences of this are yet unclear (Chandana et al., 2005; Scott & Deneris, 2005; Whitaker-Azmitia, 2005).

The **mirror neuron system** has also been investigated. Mirror neurons are located in the cortical motor system and respond to the observation of others' motor acts. Mirror neuron activity is believed to underlie understanding of motor acts done by others as well as the intentions behind the actions (Rizzolatti, Fogassi, & Gallese, 2009). In children with autism spectrum disorder, dysfunction in the mirror neuron system may help explain the deficits in social cognition that are a core component of the disorder (Bernier & Dawson, 2009). According to the mirror neuron theory of autism, dysfunction "precludes the individual with autism from having an immediate, direct experience of the other through this internal representation. Social impairments, including impairments in imitation, empathy, and theory of mind, are hypothesized to cascade from this lack of immediate, experiential understanding of others in the social world" (Bernier & Dawson, 2009, p. 261).

Many studies suggest that brain development over time is atypical. Unusual brain growth patterns have been described for children with autism, in what Courchesne calls "growth without guidance." The **growth dysregulation hypothesis** proposes that the normally well-controlled process of brain growth and organization goes awry, leading to the clinical symptoms of autism (Courchesne, Campbell, & Solso, 2011; Courchesne & Pierce, 2005; Courchesne, Redclay, Morgan, & Kennedy, 2005). It appears that early brain overgrowth during infancy and early childhood is followed by an accelerated rate of decline in size and possible further deterioration from adolescence forward (Courchesne et al., 2011) (see Fig. 8:3).

A

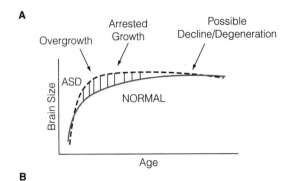

B

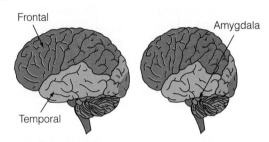

FIGURE 8:3 Three phases of atypical growth in autism spectrum disorder.
Reprinted from Brain Research, 1380, Courchesne, E.,Campbell, K., and Solso, S., Brain Growth Across the Lifespan In Autism: Age-Specific Changes In Anatomical Pathology, p. 138–145, Copyright 2011, with permission from Elsevier.

Another model that integrates genetics and brain function is the **extreme male brain theory** (Baron-Cohen, 2002a; Baron-Cohen, Wheelwright, Lawson, Griffin, & Hill, 2002). Baron-Cohen and his co-investigators emphasize the evolutionary role of sex-linked dimensions of brain functioning (such as the logical, systematic thinking characteristic of men, and the relational empathy characteristic of women) and suggest that autism may be an extreme example of the "normal" male profile. With this model, autism spectrum disorder might even be understood as a *developmental difference* rather than a *developmental disability* (Baron-Cohen, 1997, 2000, 2002b). This model, and the empathizing–systemizing theory, is explored in additional detail in the following section.

Child Factors

The child factors that have been most frequently investigated are cognitive factors. Investigators have long attempted to identify an essential cognitive deficit that would explain the atypical development and impairment observed in children with autism spectrum disorder. One very well-researched possibility involves theory-of-mind deficits. As previously defined, theory of mind (ToM) refers to an ability

to attribute mental states to others. Children and adults with autism are sometimes described as having *"mindblindness"* (Baron-Cohen, 1989, 1995, 2001), and the vast majority of them fail even simple theory-of-mind tests (see Fig. 8:4). Children and adolescents who understand very basic ToM tasks often do poorly on more sophisticated ones (Peterson, Wellman, & Slaughter, 2012). A strength of the mindblindness theory is that it explains many of the social and communication difficulties in autism spectrum disorder. A drawback of the theory is that it does not account very well for the nonsocial difficulties

FIGURE 8:4 Diagram of Sally Ann theory-of-mind task: Dark-haired Sally watches Ann, the light-haired girl, place the doll in the basket and leave. Sally then moves the doll to the box. Children are asked where Ann will look for the doll when she returns. Children with theory-of-mind abilities understand that Ann does not know that Sally moved the doll and so Ann will look in the basket. Children with theory-of-mind deficits perform poorly on these types of perspective-taking tasks.
Source: Axel Scheffler. Copyright © Cengage Learning, Illustrator: Macmillan Publishing Solutions.

(i.e., the repetitive behaviors and fixated interests) (Baron-Cohen, 2010).

Baron-Cohen (2010) describes a newer approach, the **empathizing–systemizing (E–S) theory,** which includes below-average empathy (indexed by poor performance on ToM tasks) and above-average systemizing. Systemizing is "the drive to analyze or construct systems" (p. 129). Rules define systems, and these rules can be identified or discovered. Examples include mechanical systems (e.g., locks), numerical systems (e.g., timetables or calendars), natural systems (e.g., weather patterns), or abstract systems (e.g., musical notation). The E–S theory is related to the extreme male brain theory in that there are clear sex differences in empathizing (women score higher than men on empathizing tasks) and in systemizing (men score higher than women on systemizing tasks). Autism spectrum disorder, then, is a reflection of an extreme male profile (Baron-Cohen, 2010).

Another possibility has to do with the **central coherence hypothesis** (Frith & Happe, 1994). The central coherence hypothesis is based on the idea that most individuals attempt to perceive and construct meaning from information that is part of an environmental whole. Information makes sense, or is coherent, because it is part of something larger than itself. Children and adolescents with autism are at a disadvantage because they process information piecemeal, in a more fragmented fashion (Frith & Happe, 1994; Jolliffe & Baron-Cohen, 2001a, 2001b). Interestingly, when cognitive tasks involve attention to detail, such as identifying embedded figures in a drawing, individuals with autism do better than individuals without autism (Baron-Cohen, 2010). Indeed, the perceptual functioning of children with autism has sometimes been described as "enhanced"; this is an example of a strength-based understanding of autism (Gernsbacher et al., 2008; Mottron, Dawson, Soulieres, Hubert, & Burack, 2006). How this particular ability may be related to the infrequent appearance of specially developed, relatively isolated skills is an unanswered question (Hermelin, 2001; Mottron et al., 2006).

We want to emphasize again that the cognitive deficits and differences are most obvious in children with autism who are not also diagnosed with intellectual developmental disorder. Indeed, when researchers compare the cognitive performances of children with autism and children with IDD, matched for mental age, children with IDD often do better than children with autism on ToM, central coherence, and social cognition tasks. That is, children with IDD are better at understanding the mental states of others and at perceiving the environment in a holistic manner (Dyck, Ferguson, & Shochet, 2001; Leffert & Siperstein, 2002; Yirmiya, Erel, Shaked, & Solomonica-Levi, 1998).

Although the structure of intelligence appears to be similar in children with and without autism spectrum disorder, children with autism spectrum disorder (without intellectual developmental disorder) exhibit a number of difficulties (Goldstein et al., 2008). These include a variety of specific problems with verbal learning; there appear to be fewer difficulties with nonverbal skills, rote and rule-based learning, and memory tasks (Joseph, Tager-Flusberg, & Lord, 2002; Klinger & Dawson, 2001); increasingly complex tasks reveal greater impairment (Williams, Goldstein, & Minshew, 2006a, 2006b). More global deficits are noted in executive functioning such as planning and organizational abilities (Keehn, Lincoln, Muller, & Townsend, 2010; Luna, Doll, Hegedus, Minshew, & Sweeney, 2007; O'Hearn, Asato, Ordaz, & Luna, 2008).

Assessment and Diagnosis

As with many other diagnoses, there have been important changes in the classification and diagnosis of autism spectrum disorder over time. This is a time of transition for children and adolescents previously diagnosed with autistic disorder or Asperger syndrome or pervasive developmental disorder. The DSM-5 revisions to the diagnostic criteria are intended to more meaningfully reflect what we currently understand about autism spectrum disorder. These revisions will also impact children, families, teachers, and mental health professionals as they strive to understand particular children and their particular needs. Tony Attwood (1998) provides a useful analogy involving plaid fabrics. He says that almost everyone agrees that many different patterns are plaid but acknowledges that each specific pattern is unique. Children with autism spectrum disorder may all be thought of as wearing plaid clothes, yet each child's pattern of plaid is unique. However we come to understand the tremendous variability in this spectrum, we are ultimately responsible for understanding and treating *the child*, not his or her diagnostic label.

In evaluating the autism spectrum disorder, the first consideration is whether the core symptoms related to social and communication deficits and repetitive behaviors are present, and the degree of impairment associated with these deficits. Given that complex diagnoses require complex assessments, interdisciplinary teams including medical, psychological, speech and language, and other professionals provide the most effective evaluations (Filipek et al., 1999; Klin, Sparrow, et al., 2000). Most children with ASD can be reliably diagnosed by age 2 (Carr & Lord, 2009). With this group of children, "the keywords are *experience* and *skill*" (Carr & Lord, 2009, p. 306). The positives of early identification and immediate initiation of treatment outweigh the negatives (Carr & Lord, 2009; Romanczyk et al., 2005). Brief assessment as a part of well-child visits to general practitioners and pediatricians is one way to address parent questions and concerns, and the American Academy of Pediatrics now calls for screening for autism spectrum disorders as part of well-child checkups at 18 and 24 months of age (Johnson, Myers, & the Council on Children with Disabilities, 2007; Robins, 2008). Early screening of high-risk children (e.g., younger siblings of children with autism spectrum disorder) presents special challenges related to ethical-, clinical- and evidence-based assessment and intervention (Yirmiya & Charman, 2010; Zwaigenbaum et al., 2009).

Parent Interviews

Parent interviews are often the source of very useful information, including information about early development, medical history, and family background. A careful history involves much reliance on parent recall of past events, and retrospective data are sometimes unreliable. However, parental concerns must be taken very seriously (Glascoe, 1997, 2000; Goin & Myers, 2004; Goin-Kochel & Myers, 2005) because "parents *usually are correct* in their concerns about their child's development" (Filipek et al., 1999, p. 450). Further, "parents rarely complain of social delays or problems, so any and all such concerns should be immediately investigated" (Filipek et al., 1999, p. 452). In addition to interviews, there are several parent-oriented diagnostic questionnaires available.

Checklists, Rating Scales, and Observations

Autism spectrum disorder assessments have also been developed to aid the often difficult diagnostic process, and the design and refinement of valid, reliable, and practical measures is the focus of much current research. For example, the Modified Checklist for Autism in Toddlers (M-CHAT) is designed for early identification and consists of 23 yes/no questions; the Autism Observation Scale for Infants is also designed for early assessments (Bryson, Zwaigenbaum, McDermott, Rombough, & Brian, 2008; Dumont-Mathieu & Fein, 2005). The Autism Diagnostic Interview (Lord, Rutter, & LeCouteur, 1994) is a more extensive protocol in which the child's caregiver provides a detailed description of behaviors reflecting the diagnostic criteria for autism. Similarly, the Childhood Autism Rating Scale (Schopler, Reichler, & Renner, 1988) is a scale commonly used by clinicians to assess autism spectrum symptoms throughout childhood. The Autism Diagnostic Observational Schedule (Lord et al., 2000) is an assessment instrument in which the examiner engages the child directly in a series of semistructured interactions designed to elicit behaviors associated with autism. For example, examiners may attempt to make eye contact or play cooperatively. Observational assessments require training and practice, but they are essential components of a comprehensive evaluation (Carr & Lord, 2009).

Differential Diagnosis and Comorbid Disorders

With changing conceptualizations of autism spectrum disorder, the various ways in which children present symptoms, and the latest revision of diagnostic criteria, clinicians are likely to have a very difficult time with differential diagnosis. Language disorders must be ruled out (Carr & Lord, 2009). The diagnosis of intellectual developmental disorder requires special attention because some children are best diagnosed with IDD alone, autism spectrum disorder alone, or both. As noted earlier, attentiondeficit/hyperactivity disorder, tic disorder, mood disorders, and anxiety disorders are also frequently diagnosed in children with autism spectrum disorder (Deprey & Ozonoff, 2009; Tager-Flusberg & Dominick, 2011).

Intervention

Think about the clinical picture of autism spectrum disorder and how important it is to make the right treatment decisions. Now consider how parents and teachers of children with autism must feel as they consider the multitude of treatment options, some offering slow and steady progress and others promising miraculous improvements. Parents in particular may have limited sources of information (Mackintosh, Myers, & Goin-Kochel, 2006); they are often desperate for help and confused about their options, leading them to embrace popular yet useless strategies such as facilitated communication, chelation (i.e., the removal of heavy metals from the bloodstream), and oxygen therapy (Mesibov, 1995; Offit, 2008; Schreibman, 2005). With these considerations and Koenig et al.'s (2000) assertion that "in the absence of a definitive cure there are a thousand treatments" (p. 306) in mind, we will emphasize the imperative for *evidence-based intervention* (Schopler, Yirmiya, Shulman, & Marcus, 2001).

Pharmacological Treatment

Given the evidence for genetic involvement in autism spectrum disorder, it is reasonable to examine pharmacological interventions. Those with autism are a "heavily medicated clinical population," with older individuals, individuals living in out-of-home settings, and individuals with mental retardation most likely to receive medications (Martin, Patzer, & Volkmar, 2000, p. 217). The most frequently prescribed drugs include antidepressants, stimulants, and neuroleptics; none of these drugs is specific to autism (Esbensen, Greenberg, Seltzer, & Aman, 2009; Martin et al., 2000). For the most part, these pharmacological efforts have been ineffective in treating the core symptoms of autism (Pennington, 2002). As with intellectual developmental disorder, there are data that support the use of medications for frequently occurring comorbid disorders (Erickson, Posey, Stigler, & McDougle, 2007; Nickels et al., 2008; Parikh, Kolevzon, & Hollander, 2008).

Psychological Treatment

The most effective treatments, based on years of clinical and empirical data, are the psychological treatments that emphasize social and behavioral techniques. Early and intensive interventions appear critical for meaningful improvements (Carr & Lord, 2009). Common features of these interventions include significant time commitments (often more than 20 hours per week) and highly structured efforts to facilitate the acquisition of basic language and social skills (Carr & Lord, 2009; Smith, 2010). With this kind of time and effort, parents frequently serve as cotherapists, working with their children along with mental health professionals and aides (Schreibman & Koegel, 2005). Interventions designed to alter the developmental pathways of high-risk infants and toddlers are the focus of much research and clinical attention (Dawson, 2008; Wallace & Rogers, 2010).

One of the most widely applied intervention strategies is **applied behavior analysis,** developed by Ivar Lovaas (Lovaas, 1987, 1993, 2003; Lovaas & Buch, 1997). This is an intensive behavioral approach, with near constant control and direction of the child and his/her environment. The approach begins as early as possible and involves more than 40 hours of intervention per week for two or more years. The focus is first on decreasing negative behaviors and then on increasing language and peer interaction. The introduction of new behaviors must take into account the positive, enjoyable aspects of prosocial actions (Smith, 2010). Finally, for some children, school readiness skills are included. The Lovaas approach is based on the discrete trial format, with a specific single behavior presented to the child by the therapist, then an immediate reward for response and imitation. In this way, complex behaviors are built from simple ones.

Some theorists believe that the strictly behavioral approach of Lovaas fails to demonstrate an appreciation for the unique developmental status of young children (Rogers & DiLalla, 1991; Rogers & Lewis, 1988). Rogers and his colleagues suggest that the social deficits that are at the core of autism spectrum disorder must be addressed within social relationships that the child controls. This is in contrast to the approach of Lovaas, whose strategies are based on the idea that the child with autism does not easily interact with his or her environment and so needs adults to direct learning opportunities. Other experts, like Farran (2000), emphasize the importance of integrating these two perspectives. Work by Schreibman and her colleagues that focuses on key deficits or dysfunctions in autism spectrum disorder, individual differences in response to treatments, and integration of multiple perspectives provides an excellent example of cutting-edge intervention (Sherer & Schreibman, 2005). Another new approach to comprehensive intervention includes using apps for computers and smart phones (Joshi, 2011).

One of the key deficits in social cognition that has received a lot of research and clinical focus is joint attention. Joint attention, as already discussed, is believed to underlie a number of later-emerging social–communication problems. Early attention-related interventions are thought to change the developmental trajectories for children with autism spectrum disorder by reducing these later-emerging problems. Joint attention interventions using behavioral techniques have led to increases in joint attention as well as improvements in positive emotion, play, and spontaneous speech (Kasari, Paparella, Freeman, & Jahromi, 2008; Kasari, Freeman, & Paparella, 2006; Whalen & Schreibman, 2003; Whalen, Schreibman, & Ingersoll, 2006). It is also the case, however, that researchers and clinicians are increasingly focused on adapting to children's competencies. Several intervention studies have documented the positive outcomes of adults' joining with the focus of attention of children with autism rather than attempting to redirect that attention (Aldred, Green, & Adams, 2004; Gernsbacher et al., 2008).

Much of the current work on treatment of autism spectrum disorders involves broadening the behavioral approach to include the natural aspects of the child's world. With respect to communication, for instance, repetition of words and skills is done in the most natural context to strengthen the pragmatic impact of learning. Social interventions might require children to focus on peers and to practice their skills in real-life settings of home and school (Krasny, Williams, Provencal, & Ozonoff, 2003; Paul, 2003). In addition, some of the specific deficits associated with autism spectrum disorder require very creative techniques. One such technique involves using "thought bubbles" (used in cartoons and comic strips to indicate a character's thinking)

to teach children with autism about the mental states of others (Wellman et al., 2002). Another approach makes use of nonsocial reinforcers to increase social behaviors (Ingersoll, Schreibman, & Tran, 2003). The Treatment and Education of Autistic and related Communication-Handicapped Children (TEACCH) model is a comprehensive intervention with convincing empirical support (Mesibov, 1994, 1997; Schopler, 1998). The intervention has seven components: (1) improved adaptation, (2) parent collaboration, (3) individualized assessment, (4) teaching structure, (5) emphasis on skills, (6) usefulness of cognitive and behavior therapy, and (7) a generalist training model (see Box 8:4).

School-Based Programs

School-based services are limited by time, resources, and trained personnel. Still, access to such services is one of the most frequently debated issues related to the change in the DSM-5 criteria for autism spectrum disorder. All children who struggle, with autism spectrum disorder and without, should be supported in their educational goals. Many have suggested that school services be decoupled from DSM diagnoses so that the child's particular learning, social, and behavioral problems guide eligibility and individual planning.

With respect to mainstream classrooms, there is little actual evidence that shows large or sustained benefits of inclusion for children with autism spectrum disorder (Klin & Volkmar, 2000; Mesibov & Shea,

---

BOX 8:4   CLINICAL PERSPECTIVES

The TEACCH Model of Intervention

The TEACCH program, originally developed by Eric Schopler and colleagues at the University of North Carolina in the 1970s, is a broad-based treatment program for autism that has become a major intervention approach used in communities throughout the world (Schopler, Mesibov, & Hearsey, 1995). This program is distinctive in its emphasis on careful individual assessment; its structured teaching program is based on that assessment and integrated into all aspects of the autistic person's day-to-day life. The structured teaching plan includes careful organization of the physical environment and daily schedule, as well as clear expectations and rules. Additionally, this approach advocates for an increased respect for

what is called the "culture of autism." Understanding this culture involves recognizing the unique ways individuals with autism view their environment and experience the physical and social world. Interventions, then, are designed to be consistent with this sensibility. Methods that emphasize the relative strengths of autism—such as strong memory, good visual processing skills, and recognition of details— are utilized and promoted wherever possible. These treatment principles are then integrated across systems and settings, including home and school, through comprehensive services such as social skills training, vocational training, and parent counseling and training.

1996). It may be that, unlike children with intellectual developmental disorder, children with autism display a range and severity of social deficits that make integration less likely to succeed. Intervening early to promote the development of social skills may have both short- and long-term benefits. That is, promoting the participation of children with ASD "in popular activities to share with peers in early childhood may be a key preventive intervention to protect social relationships in late elementary school grades" (Rotheram-Fuller et al., 2010).

Long-Term Treatment

Although psychological treatments for the autism spectrum disorders necessarily target the child, the needs of the family must also be addressed (Carr & Lord, 2009; Steiner, 2011). Because in almost all cases of child disorder the "family is the child's best resource" (Filipek et al., 1999, p. 466), an assessment of the family's functioning and resources is important. Information and supportive services make a difference. As children with autism spectrum disorder age, intervention strategies and goals are likely to be revised, with specific treatments and supports designed for adolescents and adults (Van Bourgondien, Reichle, & Schopler, 2003). Residential options and vocational training are necessary components of developmentally appropriate plans that are geared toward maximizing each individual's potential and well-being (Hewitt et al., 2012; Mesibov, 1992; Van Bourgondien et al., 2003).

Key Terms

Autism spectrum disorder (ASD) (p. 120)
Social cognition (p. 121)
Joint attention (p. 122)
Theory of mind (p. 122)
Affective social competence (p. 122)
Social and communication deficits (p. 123)
Restricted, repetitive behaviors and fixated interests (p. 127)
Mirror neuron system (p. 133)
Growth dysregulation hypothesis (p. 133)
Extreme male brain theory (p. 134)
Empathizing–systemizing theory (p. 135)
Central coherence hypothesis (p. 135)
Applied behavior analysis (p. 137)

Chapter Summary

- Autism spectrum disorder (ASD) is a broad term, used in a variety of contexts, reflecting compromised development in social functioning and communication as well as restricted, repetitive behaviors and fixated interests.
- Social cognition refers to the many ways that people think about themselves and their social worlds. Children with ASD display atypical social cognition.
- Theory of mind refers to the ability to understand that others have their own mental state or perspective; it is an example of an important psychological process compromised in the development of autism spectrum disorders.
- Affective social competence—the coordination of emotional perception, experience, and communication—is another developmental achievement that is compromised in children with ASD.
- Although children with autism spectrum disorder are a heterogeneous group, all display quantitative and qualitative deficits in social and communication adaptation, and repetitive, restricted behaviors and fixated interests.
- Although the core symptoms of autism spectrum disorder are generally evident between 2 and 4 years of age, there are a number of developmental pathways that children exhibit.
- The core symptoms of autism spectrum disorder generally present lifelong challenges and compromised social functioning.
- A variety of physiological factors, including genetics, brain structure and function, and brain chemistry, are all being actively researched in an effort to identify causes of autism spectrum disorder.
- Child factors reflecting differences in the perception and processing of socially salient information are another set of factors that are being investigated in order to better explicate the etiology and course of autism spectrum disorder.
- The broad array of symptoms and varied degree of compromised functioning necessitates multiple assessment and intervention strategies. The most successful interventions are those that are delivered early and intensively across a variety of domains of functioning.

9

Attention Deficit/Hyperactivity Disorder

ATTENTION DEFICIT/HYPERACTIVITY DISORDER (ADHD) is a disorder that is complexly determined, both over- and underdiagnosed, and often inadequately treated. With its prevalence and readily recognizable symptoms of impulsivity, restlessness, and inattentiveness, as well as the fact that evaluations for ADHD account for a large proportion of referrals to children's primary care and mental health clinics (Brown et al., 2001; DuPaul & Barkley, 2008), ADHD is a focus of controversy. In part, controversy results from the difficulty in distinguishing between *patterns of normally distributed childhood characteristics*, including behavioral characteristics such as self-control, emotional characteristics such as temperament traits, and cognitive characteristics such as information-processing style, and a *clinically significant pattern* of behavioral, emotional, and cognitive characteristics. For individuals, families, and mental health professionals, ADHD is presumed to reside a few steps across a fuzzy boundary toward disorder and impairment. Ongoing debates related to ADHD include the nature of children (boys in particular) and of schooling, the widespread use of psychotropic medication, and the extent to which those diagnosed with ADHD are "responsible" for their disorder. Given its significant impact on the development of self, relationships, and academic and vocational success, and the social and moral overtones of some discussions, ADHD requires thoughtful investigation.

Developmental Tasks and Challenges Related to Self-Regulation, Effortful Control, and Executive Function

Because ADHD is frequently diagnosed in the early school years, it makes sense to examine the normally occurring developmental challenges that children encounter as they make the transition to more structured school environments. We would not expect, for example, any 6-year-old child to sit attentively through a 90-minute university lecture. A young child who fidgeted and was distracted in such a situation would not be showing evidence of ADHD. On the other hand, it is reasonable to expect a 10-year-old child to listen to a teacher's directions before beginning a classroom assignment, or to refrain from interrupting a classmate's comments. The child's consistent failure to do so might indeed be cause for concern. In order to differentiate typical from atypical patterns, it is essential to understand the development of self-regulation, effortful control, and executive function.

Self-regulation, involving one's own control of emotion, cognition, and behavior, includes both automatic and controlled processes (Dale & Baumeister, 1999). Automatic responses, such as putting one's hands over one's ears in a very noisy room, are exhibited almost immediately and without much thought. Controlled responses, such as waiting one's turn on a crowded playground, require more effort. According to Cole and Deater-Deckard (2009), self-regulation strikes "a balance between protecting the self from

misfortune and promoting opportunity for positive experiences" (p. 1327). Physiological, emotional, cognitive, and behavioral regulation develop across the lifespan, are associated with both consistency and stability, and are influenced by a host of factors, including brain development and relationships (Calkins, 2009; Lewis, Todd, & Xu, 2010; McCabe & Brooks-Gunn, 2007). Depending on individual factors (e.g., genes, age, experiences) and environmental factors (e.g., parental support, specific types of academic or social challenges), a child may display appropriate self-regulation, underregulation, or overregulation. Sets of skills underlying various sorts of regulation are interdependent and dynamic (Bell & Deater-Deckard, 2007; Calkins & Marcovitch, 2010) (see Fig. 9:1). These skill sets also contribute

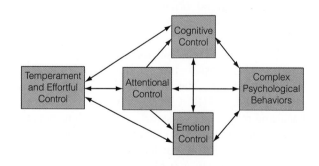

FIGURE 9:1 Dynamic interplay among behavior, genetics, and psychophysiology with respect to self-regulation.
Source: Bell, M.A. & Deater-Deckard, K, Biological Systems and the Development of Self-Regulation: Integrating Behavior, Genetics, and Psychophysiology. Journal of Developmental and Behavioral Pediatrics, 28, 5, p. 409–420.

to ongoing ego development related to *ego control* (i.e., the ability to modulate thoughts, feelings, and behaviors) and *ego resiliency* (i.e., the ability to respond flexibly and adaptively to new or stressful situations) (Block & Block, 2006; Eisenberg et al., 2003; Troy, 1989).

Effortful control (already discussed briefly in Chapter 5) is an especially important mechanism of self-regulation. Increases in young children's effortful control and declines in impulsivity and distractibility are well described (Kochanska, Murray, & Harlan, 2000; Kopp, 1982, 1989). A number of factors influence the development of effortful control. Data suggest that genes, temperament, parent factors, sociocultural factors, and gene-by-environment interactions are all important (Deater-Deckard & Mullineaux, 2010; Karreman, van Tuijl, van Aken, & Dekovic, 2008; Kochanska, Philibert, & Barry, 2009; Li-Grining, 2007). In terms of temperamental style, for example, less angry and more inhibited children display higher levels of effortful control (Kochanska & Aksan, 2004). Higher levels of effortful control are also observed in girls (Kochanska et al., 2000).

One of the most frequently cited examples of effortful control occurs during Walter Mischel's "marshmallow test." In that procedure, how long a child resists a small, immediate reward (one marshmallow) for a later, larger reward (two marshmallows) is a measure of the child's ability to delay gratification (i.e., his or her "willpower"). Better delay-of-gratification abilities are associated with immediate and long-term psychological and social benefits (Mischel et al., 2011). In related work, other longitudinal studies of children's self-regulation suggest that such regulation also predicts physical health, personal wealth, and fewer criminal offenses (Moffitt et al., 2011). With respect to self-regulation, effortful control, and ADHD, closer examination of the cognitive domain is important. **Executive function** (EF) includes those "cognitive processes that underlie goal-directed behavior and are orchestrated by activity within the prefrontal cortex" (Best & Miller, 2010); there are both basic and more complex forms of EF. With respect to basic forms, three interrelated but distinct components have been identified: inhibition, working memory, and shifting (Best & Miller, 2010; Miyake et al., 2000). *Inhibition* involves delay (i.e., withholding a dominant or habitual response), conflict (i.e., making a response that is incompatible with the prepotent response), or termination (of a response already initiated or executed). *Working memory* involves maintaining and manipulating information over relatively brief periods of time and is the component that is most closely related to intelligence (Friedman et al., 2006). *Shifting* involves attentional control and/or conscious changes in mental states, rule sets, or tasks. Each of these EF components displays its own trajectory, from infancy through adulthood; these trajectories are linked to the "extremely protracted" development and maturation of the prefrontal cortex (PFC), especially the anterior attention system (Best, Miller, & Jones, 2009; Posner & Rothbart, 2007; Zelazo & Muller, 2011). There is ample evidence for strong genetic influence on each component (Miyake & Friedman, 2012).

Planning, decision making, and deliberate problem-solving are examples of more complex forms of EF. Zelazo and Muller (2011) distinguish "hot" and "cold" EF by emphasizing the different degrees of emotion and motivation involved in types of problem solving and the connections to different areas of the prefrontal cortex. Most of the literature on EF involves relatively abstract tasks and reflects cold (or cool) EF; the marshmallow procedure reflects hot (or warm) EF. Hot contexts are more likely to undermine EF (Zelazo & Muller, 2011).

Executive function is critical for success in a variety of child, adolescent, and adult domains. Diamond and Lee (2011) describe four EF qualities that underlie success: creativity, flexibility, self-control, and discipline. They assert that "children will need to think creatively to devise solutions never considered before. They'll need working memory to mentally work with masses of data, seeing new connections among elements. They'll need flexibility to appreciate different perspectives and take advantage of serendipity. They'll need self-control to resist temptations, and avoid doing something they'd regret. Tomorrow's leaders will need to have the discipline to stay focused, seeing tasks through to completion" (p. 959). External support and training can enhance the development, display, and successful implementation of EF (Conway & Stifter, 2012; Miyake & Friedman, 2012). Among the effective interventions are computerized training, aerobics, mindfulness, and school programming (Diamond & Lee, 2011).

With the increasingly frequent diagnosis of ADHD, there have been repeated suggestions that the very nature of children, especially boys, places them at higher risk for the misidentification of disorders such as ADHD. Young children are active, boisterous, distractible, and willful. Many young

Care must be taken to differentiate the active, often physical play of boys from the behavioral symptoms of ADHD.

Design Pics/Kristy-Anne Glubish/Getty Images

boys exhibit very strong needs for extended periods of play, including rough-and-tumble play (Panksepp, 1998). These children often require parents and teachers to creatively, patiently, and repeatedly provide direction, redirection, assistance, and control. In combination with the requirements of early schooling, some adults may perceive some children's demanding characteristics as evidence of psychopathology. The accuracy or inaccuracy of these perceptions must be carefully evaluated with respect to the many varieties of developmentally *appropriate,* developmentally *meaningful,* and developmentally *necessary* challenges and struggles (Panksepp, 1998).

Attention Deficit/ Hyperactivity Disorder

The Case of Christopher

Christopher is an 11-year-old boy in the fifth grade referred for a psychological evaluation by his parents following several meetings with school teachers and the assistant principal. Major concerns included Christopher's distractibility, difficulty completing tasks, verbal impulsivity, and restlessness. Christopher is a very bright, creative child who loves to read. His parents and teachers agree that he is happiest when he is busy, and "always wants to do more." Christopher has a good sense of humor. And his teachers note his long attention span in some situations, such as when he is absorbed in reading, which he especially enjoys.

But most of the time Christopher does not listen or pay close attention to what is expected of him, is very easily distracted, and has difficulty organizing and following through with tasks. Christopher often forgets to bring needed items home from school and back to school from home. Christopher is also very fidgety and restless and has difficulty sitting still. As he gets up and moves about the room, sometimes making noises, he is distracting and disruptive to the other students. He sometimes carries toys with him and plays with them at inappropriate times. Christopher needs frequent reminders to stay focused, although he is usually cooperative when teachers intervene. He is proud of his excellent reading skills, but has been discouraged by his struggles with math and his difficulty completing schoolwork in a timely way.

Christopher's behaviors with others are also troublesome. He talks "incessantly" and often socializes when he should be doing schoolwork. Christopher is verbally impulsive, frequently blurting out remarks that are hurtful. He sometimes gets into conflicts with peers because of his impulsivity and his wish to be in charge. At home, Christopher and his brother "get each other going" and can together become "wild and crazy." His 14-year-old brother has been diagnosed with ADHD and has responded well to stimulant medication. ■

The Case of Tamara

Tamara is an 8-year-old girl in the second grade who was referred for an evaluation by her parents after consultations with school staff and her pediatrician. Her parents described Tamara's difficulty with schoolwork and chores, distractibility, and "spacing out." At the end of the previous school year, her report card included this teacher comment: "Tamara is easily distracted, though her off-task behaviors don't disturb others, only herself. She sometimes appears to daydream or be in her own little world. Tamara's distractions may be preventing her from working to her full potential." At the beginning of this school year, Tamara's new teacher also noticed her classroom difficulties, discussing with her parents her tendency to "drift off" and the slow pace of her work (Tamara is always the last to finish any assignment).

When asked about school, Tamara is positive, saying that she likes school, her teacher, and music class. Tamara says that she often needs extra time to complete assignments and acknowledges having difficulty listening, paying attention, and concentrating. She feels that this is particularly difficult when it is noisy in the classroom. Tamara also agrees that she frequently becomes frustrated with her own performance on school projects. At times, she may give up in disgust when she does not meet her own high standard.

Her parents describe Tamara as an affectionate, sensitive child who is usually cheerful and cooperative. She is "fun to be around." Tamara enjoys art and music and loves to sing. She is a very social child who has many friends. She may hang back briefly in new situations but warms up quickly. Tamara is occasionally fidgety but has never seemed hyperactive. Her parents agree that Tamara is easily distracted and needs frequent reminders to complete everyday tasks such as picking up her room or doing her homework. She often forgets or misplaces her belongings, is critical of herself for forgetting things, and worries about doing things right. Her parents believe that these behaviors are more problematic at school than at home. ■

Not all children present with identical clinical difficulties. There are differences in the particular symptoms displayed, the combination and severity of symptoms, and the range and depth of impairments. In all cases of ADHD, however, the child's abilities to meet the day-to-day tasks and demands that depend on attention and impulse control—at school, at home, and during baseball or piano practice—are compromised. ADHD is characterized by a variety of specific behavioral and cognitive symptoms involving both developmental delays and developmental deficits in the areas of inattention, impulsivity, and hyperactivity. Although many individuals have the impression that ADHD is a uniquely American phenomenon, this is simply *not* the case (Faraone, Sergeant, Gillberg, & Biederman, 2003). In surveys of North America, South America, Europe, Africa, Asia, Oceania, and the Middle East, the worldwide prevalence of ADHD is estimated at 5.2% (Polanczyk, de Lima, Horta, Biederman, & Rohde, 2007). Differences in prevalence were most often associated with methodological factors (e.g., combinations of diagnostic criteria); few differences in prevalence were observed in comparisons between North America and Europe (Polanczyk et al., 2007). Interpretation of these data suggests that ADHD is a real disorder, not a social construct tied to permissiveness, and not a product of a profit-motivated pharmaceutical industry (Moffitt & Melchior, 2007; Rohde et al., 2005). Still, differences in worldwide prevalence rates and within the United States (see Fig. 9:2) suggest that diagnosis may well be influenced by varied social and cultural expectations, values, and goals (Singh, 2008).

Core Characteristics

Attention deficit hyperactivity disorder involves compromised functioning in two underlying dimensions: inattention and hyperactivity/impulsivity. The formal diagnosis of ADHD is based on atypical frequency, intensity, and impairment in *either one or both* dimensions. In Christopher's case, he meets the DSM-5 criteria for multiple symptoms of inattention, including failure to pay close attention to details, difficulty in sustaining attention, not listening, not finishing schoolwork, difficulty organizing, distraction, and forgetfulness. Tamara also meets the DSM-5 criteria for problems with attention. Although inattention is more likely to be a problem with boring or repetitive tasks, it is also commonly observed in other contexts. For example, "once children begin to play on organized sports teams, parents and coaches often note that children with ADHD have trouble focusing on their own activity and, instead, are distracted by the game on the next field, the dog walking by, or the bees on the clover in right field" (Mayes, Bagwell, & Erkulwater, 2008, p. 154). With respect to

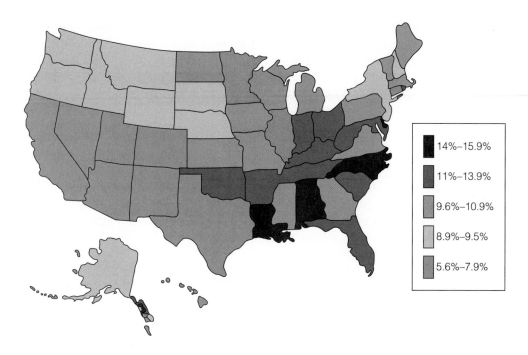

FIGURE 9:2 State-based Prevalence Data of ADHD Diagnosis.
SOURCE: Percent of Youth 4-17 ever Diagnosed with Attention-Deficit/Hyperactivity Disorder: National Survey of Children's Health, 2007 (http://www.cdc.gov/mmwr/preview/mmwrhtml/mm5944a3.htm?s_cid=mm5944a3_w).

hyperactivity/impulsivity, only Christopher meets the DSM-5 requirement. Christopher's symptoms include his need to be busy, fidgeting, leaving his seat in the classroom, excessive talking, blurting out remarks, and intrusive interactions. In addition, both Christopher and Tamara display their difficulties at school and at home. And both Christopher and Tamara have struggled since their early elementary years with these problems. That these symptoms are exhibited in multiple settings and have been apparent for several years meets the additional DSM-5 criteria for pervasiveness, impairment, and age of onset.

Current conceptualizations of ADHD no longer emphasize different subtypes (or distinct categories) of disorder (Marcus & Barry, 2011). Using the **two-factor model of ADHD,** descriptions of children as having predominantly hyperactive/impulsive difficulties, predominantly inattentive difficulties, solely inattentive difficulties, or combined difficulties reflect "a convenient clinical shorthand" and index their current presentations rather than any empirically valid distinctions related to etiology, functioning, or response to treatment (Willcutt et al., 2012).

Another issue related to validity depends on the degree to which the particular symptoms of ADHD can be differentiated from the symptoms of other disorders, for example, oppositional defiant disorder or conduct disorder. Again, there are data that support the notion that the particular cluster of disruptive symptoms is different in children diagnosed with ADHD compared to children diagnosed with oppositional defiant disorder (Barkley, Murphy, DuPaul, & Bush, 2002; Berlin, Bohlin, Nyberg, & Janols, 2004; Martin et al., 2010).

Associated Difficulties and Domains of Impairment

There are many associated difficulties related to ADHD and many domains in which ADHD compromises achievement and well-being. Problems in school are almost always evident. Academic struggles include reading problems, difficulties with homework, and overall lack of achievement (Biederman et al., 2004; McGee, Prior, Williams, Smart, & Sanson, 2002). For many children, multiple classes with multiple teachers overwhelm limited coping skills (Cantwell, 1996). "Difficulties are especially conspicuous upon entry into the fourth and seventh grades, when classroom demands and academic assignments become increasingly more complex, take longer to complete, and rely heavily on one's ability to work independently" (Rapport, 1995, p. 357). For teachers, students with ADHD pose many challenges, with stressors related to student achievement, student behavior, and various forms of treatment for ADHD (Greene, 1996; Greene, Beszterczey, Katzenstein, Park, & Goring, 2002). Given the short- and long-term consequences of school-related difficulties, it is essential that children's opportunities for learning be fully supported.

Family disturbances are also frequent complications. As noted in a National Institutes of Health (NIH) (1994) report, "It's especially hard being the parent of a child who is full of uncontrolled activity, leaves messes, throws tantrums, and doesn't listen or follow instructions" (p. 27). A child's impulsive, oppositional, and sometimes destructive behaviors may require near constant supervision and tax many parents' abilities and sympathies. Given the on-again, off-again self-control displayed by children with ADHD, common parenting practices such as reasoning and scolding do not usually help, resulting in many instances and various intensities of parent–child conflict (DuPaul & Barkley, 2008). Sibling relationships may also be affected because of frequent conflicts with each other or because of difficulties with family routines or outings.

Some of the most common and most distressing difficulties associated with ADHD are related to social dysfunction (Hoza et al., 2005). Inattention, restlessness, and impulsivity make it difficult for children with ADHD to establish rapport with other children, to pay heed to other children's emotional and behavioral messages, and to negotiate disagreements in thoughtful ways. The most significant social skills deficits appear in three areas: communication, poor emotional regulation, and cognitive biases (i.e., routinely interpreting ambiguous information as negative) (Saunders & Chambers, 1996). For some children, these deficits lead to conflictual and ineffective peer relationships; for others, social withdrawal and/or rejection occurs (Paulson, Buermeyer, & Nelson-Gray, 2005). Overall, Hoza et al. report that children with ADHD are less well liked and have fewer friends.

Recent investigations have documented specific behaviors that may help explain the origin of some social difficulties. Ronk, Hund, and Landau (2011) report that, although children with ADHD sometimes use competent strategies to enter peer groups, they rely more often on incompetent strategies (e.g., disruptive attention getting) that interfere with entry and lead to negative peer reputations. In addition to the negative impact on the child's place in the culture of playgrounds, birthday parties, and friendships, there is also a negative impact on collaborative learning situations, where academic success depends on smooth working relationships (Saunders & Chambers, 1996).

Gender, Ethnicity, and Age

One of the most replicated and controversial findings in ADHD research is the striking gender difference in diagnosis. Boys receive diagnoses of ADHD *four to five times more often* than do girls. One explanation of the gender difference is that many more boys are diagnosed with the predominantly hyperactive subtype because parents and teachers misperceive boys' greater activity levels and impulsivity as evidence of psychopathology. Even in the case of roughly similar behaviors, boys may be the focus of heightened concern, increased control, and earlier interventions.

Although there is continuing research on the clinical characteristics of ADHD in girls and children of various ethnic backgrounds, there are data that suggest that, for the most part, all children diagnosed with ADHD struggle in similar ways with the core symptoms of the disorder (Bauermeister et al., 2007; Biederman et al., 2005). In a review of 18 studies comparing the clinical presentations of girls and boys with ADHD, Gaub and Carlson (1997) reported overall similarity. In studies of ADHD in African American children, data suggest that African American children display somewhat more symptoms but are diagnosed *less frequently* than European American children. This pattern may be related to African American parents' beliefs about ADHD and lack of treatment access or utilization (Miller, Nigg, & Miller, 2009). It is important to explore more fully "how aspects of African American culture, identity, and experience influence perceptions of ADHD and its treatment" (Miller et al., 2009, p. 84).

Adolescents, like the younger boys and girls of diverse ethnic backgrounds, present a similar

Some children with ADHD struggle primarily with problems with inattention, but not impulsivity or hyperactivity.

Brad Wilson/Stone/Getty Images

picture of symptoms, impairments, and comorbid disorders (Seidman et al., 2005). There are no data that support the hypothesis that individuals diagnosed earlier in childhood have more severe clinical difficulties than those diagnosed in later in childhood (Kieling et al., 2010). It is likely that other factors contribute to the timing of diagnosis in certain children and adolescents. For instance, many clinicians recognize that higher levels of cognitive functioning and the display of predominantly inattentive characteristics are associated with later diagnoses, when there are greater demands placed on children's organizational skills, efficiency, and autonomy. Finally, two recent patterns of diagnosis are noteworthy. First, ADHD is being identified at earlier ages, with many preschoolers meeting the diagnostic criteria (Greenhill, Posner, Vaughan, & Kratochvil, 2008). Second, ADHD is also increasingly identified at later ages, into adulthood, with adults displaying similar (although somewhat age-adjusted) patterns of symptoms (Fayyad et al., 2007; Kessler et al., 2006; Wilens, Faraone, & Biederman, 2006).

Comorbid Disorders

As children with ADHD get older, there are increasing rates of comorbid diagnoses, including both internalizing and externalizing disorders (Blackman, Ostrander, & Herman, 2005; Mannuzza, Klein, Abikoff, & Moulton, 2004; Rommelse et al., 2009; Waschbusch, 2002). Some of the most frequent psychiatric disorders seen along with ADHD, with estimated prevalence, include the following: oppositional defiant disorder, conduct disorder, mood and anxiety disorders, learning disabilities, language disorders and other learning problems, tic disorders, and fine motor difficulties (Biederman, Faraone et al., 1998; Bloch, Panza, Landeros-Weisenberger, & Leckman, 2009; Singh, 2008) (see Fig. 9:3). Patterns of comorbidity appear similar for boys and girls and for children and adolescents (Biederman et al., 1999). Hypotheses about the frequency of overlapping disorders include shared genetic etiologies, interactions between children with ADHD and their environments (parents, teachers, and peers), and complications from unrecognized or undertreated ADHD (Rommelse et al., 2009).

Several recent investigations have focused on the pathways between ADHD and later depression and have emphasized the role of academic struggles, parent management strategies, and family environment in the development of depression (George, Herman, & Ostrander, 2006; Herman, Lambert, Ialongo, & Ostrander, 2007). A major longitudinal

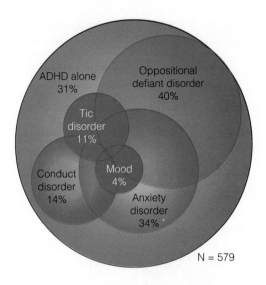

FIGURE 9:3 Co-occurring disorders in the Multimodal Treatment Study of children with ADHD. Participants in the National Institute of Mental Health Multimodal Treatment Study for attention deficit/hyperactivity disorder(ADHD) reflect the complex mental-health profiles of US children with ADHD. Only a third of the children in the study had a diagonisis of ADHD alone. More than half of the children had conduct or oppositional defiant diagnoses in addition to having ADHD, and a significant proportion of those with conduct and oppositional diagnoses also had an anxiety disorder.
Reprinted by permission from Macmillan Publishers Ltd: Nature Reviews: Neuroscience, from ref 18, copyright 2008.

investigation of ADHD and mood disorders (Biederman, Faraone et al., 1998) found that major depression occurred more frequently in their sample of 11-year-olds with ADHD (29%) compared to 11-year-olds in their comparison group (2%). Four years later, when the study participants were 15 years old, the rates of depression had risen to 45% for those with ADHD versus 6% for those without ADHD. A similar pattern was evident for the co-occurrence of anxiety disorders: 27% of the 11-year-olds with ADHD also were diagnosed with an anxiety disorder (35% at 15 years), whereas 5% of the comparison group were so diagnosed (9% at 15 years).

The comorbidity of ADHD and substance abuse has long been a research and clinical focus because of concerns that adolescents will abuse stimulants (especially if, for example, they have access to Ritalin). In fact, however, stimulant treatment of ADHD reduces the likelihood of later substance abuse (Kollins, 2007). For adolescents with diagnoses

of both ADHD and substance abuse, the most frequently abused substance is marijuana (Spencer et al., 1996), although adolescents are also at risk for alcohol abuse and dependence (Biederman, Wilens et al., 1998).

Developmental Course

Although there is a great deal of individual variability in clinical presentation and patterns of chronicity, a diagnosis of ADHD demonstrates significant stability over time both in clinical samples (75%–85%) and in large school samples (70%) (Faraone, Biederman, & Mick, 2006; Mannuzza, Klein, & Moulton, 2003b; Willcutt et al., 2012). Measures of quality of life, from both parent and child perspectives, illustrate the lasting negative impact of ADHD on multiple domains of functioning (Danckaerts et al., 2010). Cantwell (1985, 1996) describes three kinds of long-term outcomes: (1) *developmental delay,* with gradual improvement in symptoms and with no significant impairment in functioning by late adolescence or adulthood (30%); (2) *continual display,* with ongoing impairment throughout adolescence and adulthood (40%); and (3) *developmental decay,* with ongoing impairment plus the development of other serious psychopathology (30%). As Cantwell summarizes, most individuals do not outgrow ADHD, but many do learn to manage the disorder and adapt to varying levels of impairment. It is also important to keep in mind that some of the apparent age-related decline in the number of ADHD diagnoses may be due, in part, to "outgrowing the DSM item set" rather than more meaningful improvement. That is, we need to consider whether the current diagnostic criteria are appropriately sensitive to ADHD symptoms across the lifespan. In any case, even with the most optimistic forecasts, the wide-ranging impact of ADHD (particularly untreated ADHD) on children, families, and society is something that must be fully appreciated.

Early Childhood Precursors

Babies with difficult temperaments who exhibit excessive activity, poor sleeping and eating, and more emotional negativity are at greater risk for development of ADHD (Barkley, 1997a). Deficits in the development of self-regulation are fairly stable in the early years, with the majority of children who will later be diagnosed with ADHD displaying poor inhibition and inattention in their preschool years (Berlin, Bohlin, & Rydell, 2003; von Stauffenberg & Campbell, 2007). These preschoolers are also described as "on-the-go, "into everything," very curious, and disobedient. Tantrums, aggression, and fearless behaviors are particularly noteworthy (Jester et al., 2005). Although only a subset of children with early attention and activity difficulties continues to struggle throughout childhood, there is clear evidence of stability between the preschool and the early school years for those children with the most severe symptoms (von Stauffenberg & Campbell, 2007). Indeed, most preschoolers who exhibit significant struggles early on continue to display impairment years later (Lee, Lahey, Owens, & Hinshaw, 2008).

Three kinds of impairment are observed for early emerging ADHD: developmental delays, deficient preacademic skills, and problems with social skills and relationships (Sonuga-Barke & Halperin, 2010). Several developmental trajectories of disruptive disorders have been described for children with early emerging difficulties (Lahey et al., 2004; Sonuga-Barke & Halperin, 2010). One type involves a pattern in which early difficulties are not clinically significant but become so over time (as a result of some combination of genetic and/or environmental factors). Another type involves a "preschool-limited" pattern, in which early difficulties that are clinically significant improve over time (as a result of some combination of protective factors). Yet another type, with more severe early problems, persists and in some cases deteriorates over time. For some children, symptoms and impairment appear later. School entry, with its increased structure and demands, may be "an especially important provoking factor" (Sonuga-Barke & Halperin, 2010, p. 378). These various types reflect the heterogeneity of ADHD phenotypes and pathways.

Child, Adolescent, and Family Outcomes

For many adolescents first diagnosed as children, struggles continue with the core symptoms of ADHD, with estimates ranging between 30% and 80% (DuPaul & Barkley, 2008). There are conflicting data about the relative expression of specific symptoms. In some reports, inattention and impulsivity remain problematic whereas overactivity diminishes. In other reports, hyperactivity and impulsivity decline at a higher rate than inattention (Biederman, Mick, & Faraone, 2000). Even when excessive activity declines, an "internal sense of restlessness" may remain (Cantwell, 1996).

As noted, in addition to the disorder-related difficulties, ADHD also influences multiple domains of functioning; these effects continue to be evident over time. With respect to their academic and educational status, children and adolescents with ADHD use more school-based services and experience more frequent suspension and expulsion (Loe & Feldman, 2007; Murphy et al., 2002). Overall, poor educational outcomes are more common (Biederman et al., 2004; Loe & Feldman, 2007).

In family settings, noncompliant and negative behaviors often occur more frequently, particularly related to issues of responsibility (e.g., chores), rights and privileges (e.g., driving), and social activities (DuPaul & Barkley, 2008). Risky behaviors are also more prevalent, with a variety of problematic outcomes, including driving accidents, substance abuse, and teen pregnancy (Barkley, DuPaul et al., 2002; DuPaul & Barkley, 2008). For families, the personal and economic costs of ADHD may be especially burdensome. The costs of treatment for children with ADHD, often not fully covered by insurance plans, can be significant (NIH, 1998).

Peer problems remain especially significant. Murray-Close et al. (2010), building on the work of Masten and Coatsworth (1998), describe "developmental cascades and vicious cycles" related to the negotiation of several typical developmental challenges; these include engaging in socially appropriate conduct, forming a coherent sense of self, and forming friendships. Murray-Close and colleagues assert that children with ADHD often fail to develop appropriate social skills, which increases the risk for peer rejection. Peer rejection then impairs the ongoing development of additional social skills, leading to further rejection. At the same time, children with ADHD, like all children, are evaluating their personalities and abilities as they construct a sense of self. Children with ADHD may internalize the negative views of peers, or they may compensate by developing overly positive self-perceptions. These self-perceptions may lead to other difficulties. "For example, children with behavioral problems and poor social skills who nonetheless maintain positive self-perceptions in these domains will likely be unmotivated to alter their behavior, leading to sustained problems across development" (p. 787).

Adult Outcomes

Approximately one-half to two-thirds of adults continue to experience difficulties related to the core symptoms of ADHD and related disorganization, poor concentration, procrastination, and negative mood (Cantwell, 1996; Rapport, 1995). The additional deficits associated with ADHD, including poorly developed academic/vocational and social skills, also contribute to a variety of negative experiences (Murphy et al., 2002; Weiss & Hechtman, 1999). In one longitudinal study, Mannuzza, Klein, Bessler, Malloy, and LaPadula (1998) followed over 100 boys diagnosed with ADHD. When the boys were 24-year-old men, investigators observed higher rates of antisocial personality disorder and substance abuse, but no differences in rates of anxiety or mood disorders. In another study of individuals first diagnosed with ADHD as adults, somewhat higher rates of anxiety and mood disorders were noted, but most adults had made reasonable adjustments. Even though many adults continue to experience the negative impact of ADHD, it is also important to understand that "many people with ADHD … feel that their patterns of behavior give them unique, often unrecognized, advantages. People with ADHD tend to be outgoing and ready for action. Because of their drive for excitement and stimulation, many become successful in business, sports, construction, and public speaking. Because of their ability to think about several things at once, many have won acclaim as artists and inventors. Many choose work that gives them freedom to move around and release excess energy" (NIH, 1994, p. 33). In fact, Brooks (2002) suggests that "changing the mindset" of children, adolescents, and adults with ADHD may go a long way toward supporting more positive outcomes across the lifespan.

Etiology

There are multiple etiological factors leading to ADHD, with the disorder as the **"final common pathway"** of combinations of different types of predisposing conditions and events. Recent investigations of the causes and course of ADHD highlight the complex interplay of genetic vulnerability, brain processes, cognitive functioning, environmental factors, and maintenance factors in order to provide explanations for the heterogeneity in phenotypes and trajectories.

Genes and Heredity

The high heritability of attention deficit/hyperactivity disorder is well established in numerous family studies, twin studies, and adoption studies. Family studies, for instance, provide data that the risk of ADHD is eight times higher in first-degree relatives of children with ADHD, and that 40% to 60% of children of parents with ADHD also have ADHD (Coghill & Banaschewski, 2009). Heritability estimates for ADHD are similar to those for height and higher than those for intelligence (Coghill & Banaschewski, 2009). Across many studies, a **polygenic model** of ADHD is proposed. It is clear that "many genes of small effects are implicated in ADHD," "with effects operating in different ways in different individuals" (Sonuga-Barke & Halperin, 2010, p. 374).

New meta-analytic studies suggest that the genetic influences are distinct for the core symptom dimensions of ADHD, with 71% of the genetic variance explained for inattention and 73% of the genetic variance explained for hyperactivity/impulsivity (Nikolas & Burt, 2010). Dominant genetic effects were larger for inattention, and additive effects were larger for hyperactivity/impulsivity (Nikolas & Burt, 2010). Related research provides additional data that genetic influences are also important for components of self-regulation, effortful control, and executive function (Bell & Deater-Deckard, 2007).

Molecular genetic analyses are currently focused on the identification of specific gene locations (Neale et al., 2010) and also provide information related to the frequent comorbidity observed in children and adolescents with ADHD (Asherson, Kuntsi, & Taylor, 2005; Doyle et al., 2005; Faraone et al., 2005). Given numerous associations between ADHD and other internalizing and/or externalizing psychopathology, contemporary approaches emphasize the likelihood of shared genetic influences and a common physiological risk factor (Dick, Viken, Kaprio, Pulkkinen, & Rose, 2005). Gene-by-environment research has identified several promising interactions. For example, genotypes that have an effect on the regulation of dopamine and serotonin interact with psychosocial factors to influence the severity of ADHD symptoms (Nigg, Nikolas, & Burt, 2010; Sonuga-Barke et al., 2009).

Physiological Factors

With increasingly sophisticated neuroimaging techniques, areas and processes of the brain that are implicated in ADHD can be identified. Areas of the brain that have been examined include the frontal lobes, the anterior cingulate cortex (a key area for coordinating top-down and bottom-up processing, associated with the attention system), the corpus callosum, the temporal lobes, and the striatal regions. With respect to brain development, children with ADHD show a several-years-long delay in cortical maturation, most prominent in the prefrontal cortex (Shaw et al., 2007, 2009). Both gray matter and white matter differences in structure and development have been identified (Nagel et al., 2011; Proal et al., 2011). These kinds of pathophysiological evidence provide extremely valuable information about possible etiologies, developmental trajectories, and interventions.

Given the widespread influence of neurotransmitters on prefrontal functions, many studies have focused on neurotransmitter dysfunction in the development and maintenance of ADHD (Arnsten, Berridge, & McCracken, 2009). Investigations of dopamine, serotonin, and noradrenaline are ongoing. Dysfunction of the dopamine reward pathway appears to be associated with motivational deficits (Volkow et al., 2011). Serotonin variations are linked to delay aversion (Sonuga-Barke et al., 2011).

Other aspects of neurophysiological functioning are also implicated. Recent research has identified atypical processing related to emotional reactivity, self-regulation, and effortful control (Bell & Deater-Deckard, 2007; Musser et al., 2011; Posner et al., 2011; Wiersema & Roeyers, 2009). Pre- and postnatal complications and low birth weight are associated with many aspects of physiological regulation (Mill & Petronis, 2008; Nigg, 2006). In addition, the role of sleep disturbances, and its effects on efficient self-regulation, is important to consider (Alfano & Gamble, 2009). Overall, genetic, neuropsychological, and psychopharmacological research provides strong converging evidence that a central nervous system dysfunction may underlie the disruptions in a multicomponent self-regulatory system and the development of ADHD (Durston & Konrad, 2007; Nigg, 2005).

Psychological Factors

Among the most widely researched variables underlying the development of ADHD are cognitive factors, especially those related to executive function. Meta-analyses suggest that children with ADHD exhibit weaknesses in several aspects of EF, with the strongest effects related to response inhibition, vigilance, working memory, and planning (Willcutt et al., 2005). Other EF work has focused on the distinction between hot and cold EF and the "cognitive heterogeneity" and multiple pathways of ADHD (Castellanos, Sonuga-Barke, Milham, & Tannock, 2006). It may be that "some individuals with ADHD will manifest primarily 'hot' EF dysfunction, whereas others will show mainly 'cool' EF deficits and others will have both types" (Castellanos et al., 2006, p. 119). The worse the EF deficits, the more likely it is that a child with ADHD also has accompanying learning disabilities (Mattison & Mayes, 2012). Some adolescents and young adults with ADHD who show recovery over time display improvements in EF, whereas others continue to exhibit EF impairment (Halperin, Trampush, Miller, Marks, & Newcorn, 2008; Miller, Ho, & Hinshaw, 2012).

Research on *sluggish cognitive tempo*, the inconsistent alertness and orientation displayed by some children (including Tamara), provides additional information about ADHD (Bauermeister et al., 2005; Hartman, Willcutt, Rhee, & Pennington, 2004; Todd, Rasmussen, Wood, Levy, & Hay, 2004). Children diagnosed with the inattentive subtype of ADHD who also exhibit symptoms of sluggish cognitive tempo are a relatively homogenous group with higher levels of anxiety and depression, withdrawn behavior, and social dysfunction (Carlson & Miranda, 2002).

Temperament, personality, and age of the child also appear to have an impact on the development of ADHD. As noted previously, temperamental reactivity and regulation may increase a child's risk for ADHD. Two processes may be particularly important: "bottom-up" processing, which is adversely affected by immediate emotional incentives, and "top-down" processing, which is less responsive to new information. Impulsivity–hyperactivity is related to the incentive response systems, and inattention to the effortful control system (Nigg, 2010) (see Fig. 9:4). Motivational deficits, related to sensitivity to reward and punishment, have also been observed (Sonuga-Barke & Halperin, 2010). Finally, with respect to relative age in classroom settings, rates of ADHD in the youngest children in elementary school grades are 8.4%, compared to 5.1% of their older peers. This suggests that teacher ratings of problematic behaviors in developmentally less-mature children may influence the diagnostic process (Elder, 2010).

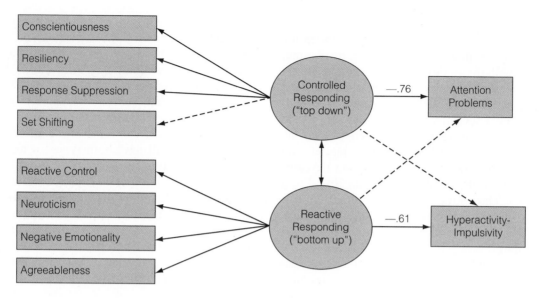

FIGURE 9:4 "Top-down" and "bottom-up" psychological processes hypothesized to influence ADHD.
Nigg, J. T., Current Directions in Psychological Science, 19(1), pp. 24-29, copyright © 2010 by Sage. Reprinted by Permission of SAGE Publications.

Russell Barkley, who views ADHD as "a developmental delay in internalization and self-regulation" (Barkley, 1997b, p. 313), offers a perspective on the core symptoms that integrates cognitive and personality factors. Barkley argues that the core behavioral deficit observed in children with ADHD is impulsivity, reflecting a basic impairment in the ability to delay responding to stimuli. In this model, the inattention and excessive motor activity are both accounted for by this impaired responding capacity. The executive functions of children with ADHD are also implicated, with differences in deficits and severity across children (Barkley, 2004). According to Barkley, the behavior of children with ADHD "will be less directed at maximizing the future and more directed at maximizing the moment. Being less internally guided and rule-governed, their behavior will seem to others as more chaotic, reactive, ill considered, and emotional, and as less organized, purposive, reflective, and objective" (p. 314).

Family and Environmental Factors

There is almost no empirical evidence supporting the hypothesis that family or environmental factors alone contribute to the *development* of ADHD; however, numerous studies have described ways in which these factors have a role in the *maintenance and exacerbation* of the disorder. With respect to the development of disorder, the gene by environment

interactions discussed previously suggest that certain parent or family factors may influence the emergence of disorder in at-risk children. With respect to the maintenance or exacerbation of the disorder, Johnston and Freeman (1997) compared the attitudes of parents of children with ADHD and parents of children without behavior disorders. In general, most parents tended to rate children's behaviors as internally caused and controllable. However, parents of children with ADHD accepted less responsibility for child behaviors and rated impulsivity and oppositional behaviors as more internally caused and controllable than parents of children without behavior disorders did. Parents of children with ADHD viewed impulsivity as more persistent across time, and prosocial behaviors as less consistent than parents of children without ADHD. All parents responded negatively to oppositional behaviors, but parents of children with ADHD responded even more negatively. In addition to these cross-family data, there are also data suggesting that parent–child interactions differ within families (i.e., nonshared environmental influence), depending on a particular child's ADHD status (Cartwright et al., 2011). These results suggest that parental beliefs about ADHD and about their children may contribute to an increasingly destructive cycle of negative interpretations and blame, as well as harsh and intrusive parenting, making it difficult to intervene effectively

(Sonuga-Barke & Halperin, 2010). These types of family factors may, in fact, tell us more about the risk for the development of comorbid disorders such as oppositional defiant disorder or conduct disorder than about the ADHD (Barkley, 1997b; Patterson, DeGarmo, & Knutson, 2000).

Environmental factors have also received renewed attention. In addition to the many pre- and perinatal environmental risks such as maternal smoking and alcohol use and exposure to stress (Mill & Petronis, 2008), children with ADHD have higher levels of lead in their blood (Froehlich et al., 2009; Nigg, Nikolas, Knottnerus, Cavanagh, & Friderici, 2010). Exposure to lead is linked to lower IQ and more ADHD symptoms (mainly the impulsive/hyperactive domain). The "near universal exposure is important because it means lead can function as a widely shared environmental trigger," that in combination with other measures of genotype and stress, may help to explain rates of ADHD (Nigg, 2010).

Assessment and Diagnosis

We know that ADHD is a disorder that is often mistaken for a child's lack of ability or effort, stubborn willfulness, or the result of lackadaisical parenting. In addition, perhaps more so than any other childhood disorder, ADHD is a disorder that frequently co-occurs with other disorders. Given these circumstances and the fact that *there is no specific psychological or neurological test for ADHD,* we must pay careful attention to the particular criteria that lead to an accurate diagnosis of ADHD. As already emphasized, ADHD reflects deficits and/or delays in key behavioral, cognitive, and emotional abilities. Assessment of children, adolescents, and adults depends, first and foremost, on appropriate knowledge of typical development. Thus, a clinician may observe a child who exhibits distractibility, excessive activity, and less-than-optimal decision making, but these behaviors are observed in all kinds of children for all kinds of reasons. In the case of ADHD, the clinician must look for *more frequent behaviors, more intense behaviors,* and *more impairment.* In addition to the continuity between typical and atypical patterns, onset-related and developmental transitions also must be taken into account. The "dynamic nature of symptom expression" means that symptom levels and patterns may differ within individuals and may fluctuate over time (Sonuga-Barke & Halperin, 2010).

Diagnostic Interviews

Interviews are often conducted with children, parents, and teachers. Parents and teachers usually provide more useful data because children (and even adolescents) are not always aware of or able to describe their difficult behaviors (Smith, Pelham, Gnagy, Molina, & Evans, 2000). And although the information provided by parent and teacher reports is almost never exactly the same, research suggests that clinical diagnoses of ADHD that are based on parent reports are likely to be confirmed by teacher reports (Biederman, Faraone, Milberger, & Doyle, 1993). That said, it is essential to appreciate the factors that may influence parent and teacher descriptions of problem behaviors. For instance, parents of preschoolers may perceive certain problem behaviors as normal and put off seeking help (Maniadaki, Sonuga-Burke, Kakouros, & Karaba, 2007). Teachers may respond differently to similar behaviors in boys versus girls and refer boys for evaluation more often than girls (Sciutto, Nolfi, & Bluhm, 2004). As noted previously, teachers may be strongly influenced by the relatively less mature functioning of the younger children in their classes (Elder, 2010). Lastly, it is important to take into account cultural variations in mental health attitudes and knowledge (Bussing, Gary, Mills, & Garvan, 2007).

Comprehensive interviews, in addition to providing baseline data, may reveal information about a family history of ADHD or the presence of additional disorders. In addition, careful review of the relations between the particular patterns of deficits and the demands of particular settings is important. With ADHD, the assumption is that the core difficulties are present from early childhood and are *not* the result of a specific stressor. Diagnosis of adult ADHD remains clinically problematic, given that there is no consensus on the criteria for adult ADHD. According to McGough and Barkley (2004), "the DSM criteria have never been validated in adults, do not include developmentally appropriate symptoms and thresholds for adults, and fail to identify some significantly impaired adults who are likely to benefit from treatment" (p. 1948). Additional work in this area is essential.

Another consideration in judging the presence of ADHD and making differential diagnoses is whether or not the identified symptoms are better accounted for by another disorder. Many disorders, such as depression, generalized anxiety disorder, or schizophrenia, can disrupt the basic cognitive and behavioral processes that are the core features of ADHD. In the case of these other disorders, however, symptoms such as poor concentration and impulsivity are secondary problems relative to the primary disorder.

A final consideration is that, most often, primary care physicians (such as pediatricians) rather than mental health professionals (e.g., clinical psychologists or psychiatrists) assess and diagnose ADHD in children and adolescents and prescribe medications as treatment. It may be that diagnosis occurs with "less than full rigor because of the intense economic and time constraints they face, coupled with their training (or lack thereof) in the area of mental disorders" (Mayes et al., 2008, p. 157). Programs that are designed to increase primary care providers' standardization, accuracy, and consultation are promising (Foy & Earls, 2005; Mayes et al., 2008)

Rating Scales

In addition to interview data, there are a number of available rating scales for parents and teachers, specifically designed to assess the symptoms of ADHD and provide information about the degree to which an individual deviates from well-established norms. For the most part, these scales provide reasonably accurate and, in some cases, compelling information about the likely presence of ADHD. The widespread use of teacher rating scales, however, has been the focus of several investigations concerning the assessment of students of various racial and ethnic backgrounds. Reid et al. (1998) reviewed comparisons of teacher rating scales between American and Thai children, mainland American and Puerto Rican children, and Anglo-American and Mexican American children. In all cases, children of minority backgrounds were rated as more symptomatic. In another study, conducted in Britain, even when the objectively measured behaviors of children were identical, teachers' ratings of Asian children identified more ADHD symptoms than their ratings of non-Asian children (Sonuga-Barke, Minocha, Taylor, & Sandberg, 1993). In several studies, consistent differences have been observed in comparisons between teacher ratings of African American and European American children, with African American children receiving more negative ratings (DuPaul et al., 1998). More recently, however, there are data that suggest that teacher ratings of students from minority backgrounds are *more consistent* with direct observations (Hosterman, DuPaul, & Jitendra, 2007). Given these

Continuous Performance Tests such as this one make use of computers to assess selective attention and impulse control.

data, the increased presence and expanding role of school psychologists provides valuable perspective on school-based referrals and treatments (Demaray, Schaefer, & Delong, 2003).

Observations

Given possible bias, it becomes even more important to balance parents' and teachers' reports and ratings with actual observations. Most observations are done in the school, because some children's abilities to exhibit self-control and maintain attention in the structured office setting may not reflect typical behavior (Dulcan et al., 1997). Ideally, observations should be made in a variety of settings, with different environmental demands, with the expectation that symptoms will be more pronounced in circumstances that are not interesting or stimulating (Rapport, 1995).

Other Sources of Information

Although not definitive by themselves, a variety of continuous performance tests are often used as part of an ADHD assessment (Nichols & Waschbusch, 2004). These tests generally involve monitoring stimuli (visual, auditory, or both) and responding selectively to instructions. For example, letters might be presented on a computer screen and the child told to respond to a certain target letter but not to others. These tests measure various attention and impulse control skills, including the ability to remain vigilant, to demonstrate consistency of attentional focus, to respond quickly, and to inhibit responding. In many cases, additional assessment related to academic achievement is often conducted, including intelligence testing and assessment of learning disabilities (Dulcan et al., 1997). Medical evaluations are also sometimes included as part of the assessment plan.

Differential Diagnosis

As described earlier, an important consideration in the assessment and treatment of ADHD involves differential diagnosis and identification of comorbid problems. These tasks are especially important because many of the symptoms of ADHD, such as executive function and attention deficits and poor self-regulation, are also observed in other disorders (e.g., oppositional defiant disorder, anxiety disorders, autism spectrum disorders, motor coordination problems, and learning disabilities) (Rommelse et al., 2009). Whether the child or adolescent presentation best fits a single diagnosis of ADHD or multiple diagnoses has implications for treatment planning. For example, more comprehensive treatments for ADHD combined with oppositional defiant disorder are indicated (Hechtman et al., 2005). It is also critical to determine if an anxiety or mood disorder complicates the clinical presentation and must be addressed in treatment.

Intervention

DuPaul and Barkley (1998) assert that "ADHD is a developmental disorder of self-control and social conduct that is chronic and without cure. An attitude of *coping* rather than *curing* is a reasonable clinical position" (p. 135). Thinking about the possibilities for coping with the core deficits and the many additional difficulties with which children with ADHD struggle, the need for cooperation and coordination across treatment modalities, professionals, and settings is clear (DuPaul & Barkley, 1998; Waschbusch & Hill, 2003; Hechtman et al., 2005). Given the many comorbid psychopathologies associated with ADHD, it becomes essential to address *the whole child* rather than one or several clinical disorders.

Given children's ADHD-related experiences and impairment, many different interventions have been proposed, with varying success. Interventions for preschoolers, elementary-school-aged children, adolescents, and adults have all been investigated. Medications and psychosocial treatments receive the most empirical and clinical support (Fabiano et al., 2009; Hoza, Kaiser, & Hurt, 2008; Pliszka, 2009). Even with data suggesting that combined treatments are more effective for many children, the cost effectiveness of treatments certainly comes into play. Medication treatments are the least expensive, followed by psychosocial treatments, and then combined treatments (Jensen et al., 2005). There is considerable variation in treatment strategies and implementation in countries around the world, depending, in part, on economic and sociocultural factors. Some countries, for example, display more antipsychiatry and antimedication attitudes; others are more likely to use a combination of treatments (Hinshaw et al., 2011). One necessary aspect of all treatments involves parent and child education, including information about medication and psychosocial interventions; available special educational services; and access to mental health resources such as parent support groups and individual counseling. Much of our current understanding of treatment has been enhanced by one of the most impressive and comprehensive longitudinal studies of the treatment of ADHD: the National Institute of Mental Health's Collaborative Multisite Multimodal Treatment Study of Children with ADHD, which combines rigorous experimental protocols with particular attention to individual differences (see Box 9:1).

Pharmacological Treatment

In hundreds of studies with thousands of children, the use of central nervous system (CNS) stimulants, as well as newer nonstimulant medications to treat ADHD has received significant support (Daughton & Kratochvil, 2009). This is why medication is often viewed as a first-line intervention. The majority of children who are treated with long-used medications such as methylphenidate (Ritalin) and newer types of long-acting stimulants (such as Adderall and Cylert) show real and substantive improvement, with improvement measured by parent–teacher ratings, direct observations, and performance in lab tasks. Worldwide use of methylphenidate varies widely and has significantly increased over several decades (Singh, 2008) (see Fig. 9:5). ADHD medications have been shown to work for girls as well as boys, for African American youth, and for youth from a

BOX 9:1 CLINICAL PERSPECTIVES

The MTA Cooperative Group Study

There are frequent criticisms that research in developmental psychopathology often fails to take into account the realities of actual children in complicated circumstances. In ADHD outcome-oriented research, such criticism has focused on studies of the short-term impact of stimulant medications (neglecting possible long-range negative consequences) and the inadequate consideration of multi-component intervention strategies (neglecting the whole child to focus on problematic symptoms). The Multimodal Treatment Study of Children with Attention Deficit/Hyperactivity Disorder (MTA) Cooperative Group Study is an effort to comprehensively address previous research shortcomings (Jensen et al., 2007; MTA Cooperative Group, 2004; Molina et al., 2009).

The MTA Cooperative Group Study included six independent research teams (in San Francisco; Los Angeles; Durham, North Carolina; New York; and Pittsburgh, Pennsylvania) working in collaboration with the National Institute of Mental Health and the U.S. Department of Education. Comparisons of long-range efficacy of a 14-month-long intervention (i.e., 14-month, 24-month, 36-month, and 8-year outcomes) in 579 children with ADHD were conducted for medication management, intensive behavioral treatment, a combined approach, and community care. Numerous outcome measures were identified, including reduction in the core ADHD symptoms, personal adjustment, academic achievements, and improvements in social skills and relationships.

Across multiple settings and a diverse sample of children, strong support for medication management was demonstrated at the 14-month evaluation, with some additional benefits observed for the combined medication/behavioral treatment strategy. At this first assessment, peer-related functioning continued to be very problematic, although treatment appeared to reduce additional diagnoses of oppositional defiant disorder, conduct disorder, and anxiety disorder (Hechtman et al., 2005; Hoza et al., 2005). By 36 months, many of the advantages of the combined treatment had diminished, although all treatment groups maintained improvements over baseline. Many of the children showed clinically significant improvements across five domains of functioning; others showed improvements that were less dramatic and less far reaching (Karpenko et al., 2009). Certain types of treatments were associated with particular outcomes. For example, behavioral treatments were associated with better homework performance (Langberg et al., 2010). At the 8-year follow-up, the adolescents' current status was best predicted by their early symptom trajectories. That is, those "children with behavioral and sociodemographic advantage, with the best response to any treatment, will have the best long-term prognosis" (Molina et al., 2009, p. 484). Overall, however, the adolescents, in comparison with typically developing peers, continued to display significant impairments.

This type of research collaboration is expensive and difficult to coordinate. It is, however, absolutely necessary if we as researchers, clinicians, parents, teachers, and others want to be able to describe and offer optimal care to individuals with ADHD.

variety of socioeconomic status (SES) backgrounds, as well as for preschoolers, adolescents, and adults (Arnold et al., 2003; Ghuman, Arnold, & Anthony, 2008; Rieppi et al., 2002). A relatively recent trend in ADHD treatment is combined pharmacotherapy, using combinations of medications to treat the disorder. Explanations for this trend include the higher rates of comorbid psychopathologies, better symptom control, and the synergy of combined medications.

Positive effects of stimulant treatments are observed for relationships with parents, teachers, and peers, although parents and teachers report different patterns of benefits and side effects (Pomeroy &

Gadow, 1998). Whether improvements are evaluated with respect to a reduction in symptoms or with respect to the "normalization" of a child's cognitive and behavioral performance remains a tricky issue (Karpenko et al., 2009). However, even with a variety of improvements, there are children who will continue to display higher-than-normal levels of inattention, activity, and impulsivity (Karpenko et al., 2009). Families' varied beliefs about medication use may provide clinicians with valuable information related to communication, decision making, and long-term responses to children's treatment (Krain, Kendall, & Power, 2005; Leslie, Plemmons, Monn, & Palinkas, 2007).

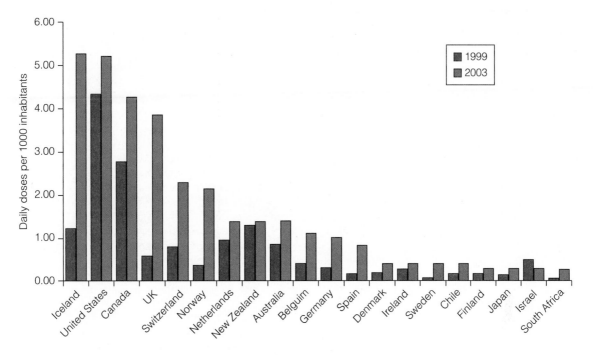

FIGURE 9:5 Worldwide consumption of methylphenidate. In 2003, iceland and the United States had the highest per capita consumption of methylphenidate in the world. Growth in consumption between 1999 and 2003 was highest in european countries. The only country in which methylphenidate consumption decreased during this period was Israel. figure reproduced, with permission, from REF.115 © (2005) INTERNATIONAL NARCOTICS BOARD.

SOURCE: Adapted from ref 115 © 2005 from International Narcotics board

There are, however, a number of cautions. Improvements in ADHD symptoms last as long as medication continues and, in some cases, do not persist (Jensen et al., 2007; Sonuga-Barke & Halperin, 2010). This lack of sustained improvement may reflect poor adherence and early termination related to medication use (Pappadopulos et al., 2009). Adherence and termination may be influenced by adverse effects (e.g., poor sleeping and poor appetite) as well as small decreases in growth rates (Sonuga-Barke, Coghill, Wigal, DeBacker, & Swanson, 2009; Swanson et al., 2007). In addition, critics of medication management hypothesized that children would attribute improvements, when they did occur, to the pills rather than themselves or their efforts; this does not appear to be the case (Pelham et al., 2002). Finally, most researchers, clinicians, parents, and teachers believed that general academic improvements would follow any change for the better in specific ADHD symptoms. Contrary to hopeful hypotheses, however, it appears that the use of most ADHD medications alone results in little improvement in long-range academic achievement. According to DuPaul and Barkley

(1998), the "most prudent conclusion" is that medication is helpful in the short term, but is not sufficient; additional interventions are necessary to address the multiple difficulties associated with core deficits. Discussions related to the history and current use of medications for children and adolescents are ongoing (see Box 9:2).

Psychosocial Treatment

Psychosocial interventions include **behavioral parent training,** cognitive-behavioral interventions for children, behaviorally oriented peer interventions, social skills training, and summer programs. Positive effects are described for multiple domains, but amount, intensity, and generalization all need to be taken into account (Pelham & Fabiano, 2008). Positive outcomes are most often related to the amelioration of problems related to self, school, families, and peers. Although there are mixed results from studies of social skills training, such training may be particularly important given the data on negative developmental cascades related to peer dislike and peer rejection (Aberson, Shure, & Goldstein, 2007;

BOX 9:2 CLINICAL PERSPECTIVES

Medication and Children

Currently, approximately 8% of youth between 4 and 17 are diagnosed with ADHD, and 4.5% of youth both have an ADHD diagnosis and are using medication (Mayes, Bagwell, & Erkulwater, 2008). The upsurge in diagnosis and medication use is a result of "a confluence of *trends* (clinical, economic, educational, political), an alignment of *incentives* (among clinicians, educators, policymakers, health insurers, the pharmaceutical industry), and the sizable growth in scientific *knowledge* about ADHD and stimulants, all of which converged in the first half of the 1990s" (Mayes et al., 2008, p. 152).

With rapidly rising rates of psychopharmacological interventions for very young children, school-aged children, adolescents, and adults, we must thoughtfully address various public health and ethical concerns. With respect to the youngest group, are actual disorders increasing in younger samples? Are our methods of detection and diagnosis improving, or are we confusing normal behavioral, emotional, and cognitive variations in preschoolers with deviant behavioral, emotional, and cognitive displays in older children and adolescents? What are the costs and benefits of using drugs that have not been investigated or approved for young children? And what are the societal, clinical, and personal meanings associated with the prescription of Ritalin, or any other psychotropic medication, to a very young child?

As we have repeatedly emphasized throughout this textbook, taking a developmental view of distress, dysfunction, and disorders provides us with valuable perspective. Children experience the "terrible twos," the "often still thorny threes," and the "formidable fours." Some of their worrisome behaviors fade with time, and some continue. We must acknowledge that developmental bumps in the road are inevitable and that there are no alternatives to patient, loving, and individualized caregiving. But we also acknowledge that psychopathology does occur in the early years.

We know that, for example, troubled preschoolers often present with a mix of clinical difficulties in many psychological domains. Whether a child is appropriately understood as anxious, depressed, learning disabled, or as having ADHD is difficult to determine. Parents are often desperate to find out exactly what is "wrong" with a child, and do something to "fix" that child as fully and as quickly as possible. It is a public policy shame that in many ways mental health professionals cannot offer the kinds of educational services, family support, and nonmedical interventions that may be exactly what many families need.

Of course we must also consider the very small number of young children with well-defined ADHD that results in significant impairments; these children might be suitable candidates for what is clearly an effective intervention strategy in older children. But even when medication might be appropriate, the ethics of medicating children remain (Singh, 2008). Safety concerns involve testing protocols that focus on older children, adolescents, and adults and whether the effects of medication on still-developing brain–behavior systems are well understood. With increasing use of multiple medications (i.e., "polypharmacology"), concerns become even more compelling. Some have expressed reservations about threats to children's autonomy and everyday experiences of childhood. But, according to Singh (2008), children with ADHD would choose to take medication, and "they successfully negotiate the stigma around drug treatment." Further, "ADHD diagnosis and stimulant drug use have been shown to affect children's concepts of identity and personal authenticity, but the available evidence suggests that these effects are largely positive for most children, at least until they reach adolescence" (p. 962). Adolescence also presents another opportunity for addressing clinical and ethical issues, as the abuse potential (mainly for youth who are *not* diagnosed with ADHD) becomes more relevant (Kollins, 2007).

Antshel & Barkley, 2008; Murray-Close et al., 2010). Even with improvements, however, children with ADHD often remain impaired in their peer relationships (Hoza et al., 2005). With adolescents, psychotherapy takes a somewhat different approach given the developmental challenges related to independence and self-control, especially if there are more negative, more pronounced oppositional behaviors

and conduct problems (DuPaul & Barkley, 1998). Overall, the data suggest that psychosocial treatments, like medications, may be usefully understood as a primary intervention (Pelham & Fabiano, 2008).

A number of child factors that might influence treatment efficacy and outcome have been investigated. Severity of ADHD symptoms, below-average

IQ, and parent psychopathology all had a negative impact on treatment; ethnicity did not (Hinshaw, 2007; Jones et al., 2010; Owens et al., 2003). Psychosocial interventions that are focused on the particular challenges of adolescents are increasingly implemented (e.g., Evans, Schultz, DeMars, & Davis, 2011).

As we consider the variety of ADHD interventions, we must grapple with underlying concerns about personal responsibility. For many adults (parents, teachers, and others), it seems that children and adolescents (especially those who are already being treated with medications) have more control over their behaviors and emotions than children and adolescents with other kinds of psychological difficulties. The question of how much accountability is appropriate to expect from individuals with ADHD is hard to answer, but Barkley (1997b) points out that diagnosis and intervention does not excuse children and adolescents with ADHD from personal accountability. "Consequences must be made more immediate, increased in their frequency, made more 'external' and salient, and provided more consistently than is likely to be the case for the natural consequences associated with one's conduct" (Barkley, 1997b, p. 316). Within this framework, as children and adolescents become better at self-reflection and self-regulation, we might eventually, and appropriately, expect increases in personal responsibility for their own well-being.

School Interventions

Most children with ADHD are placed in mainstream classes, but some may require individual tutoring and specialized plans to support academic achievement (Cantwell, 1996). Both the National Rehabilitation Act and the Individuals with Disabilities Education Act (IDEA) are legislative efforts requiring appropriate educational services for children with ADHD. Special accommodations such as having children with ADHD sit in a place with fewer distractions (e.g., in the front of the class, next to the teacher's desk), receiving written as well as oral instructions, and providing visual aids and reminders are common.

Among the most effective school-based interventions involve **behavior contingency management** in the classroom (Antshel & Barkley, 2008; Pelham & Fabiano, 2008). These interventions include reward programs, point systems, and time outs for inappropriate behavior. They are designed to target multiple difficulties, including academic, behavioral, and social functioning (DuPaul, Helwig, & Slay, 2011). Participation, collaboration, and coordination among service providers, teachers, and parents are essential (Nadeem & Jensen, 2009). The Family–School Success model is one example of a successful intervention that combines psychosocial approaches across settings for improved child outcomes (Power et al., 2012).

Interventions with Adults

As previously noted, medications are effective in treating the symptoms of ADHD in adults. Improvements in occupational and marital functioning have also been observed with medication management (Castle, Aubert, Verbrugge, Khalid, & Epstein, 2007). With regard to ongoing relationship problems, workplace/career difficulties, and self-esteem issues, Nadeau (1998) suggests an increased therapeutic emphasis on life management skills. For example, Nadeau focuses on "thing management" (papers, personal objects), "time management," and "to do management" (lists of tasks), as well as money management.

Future Trends

New forms of treatment are also being discussed, with renewed emphasis on cognitive training interventions, complementary and alternative treatments (such as aerobics and mindfulness), and earlier interventions (Nigg, 2011). There are also efforts to design prevention protocols that target underlying causes, alter developmental trajectories, and improve outcomes (Sonuga-Barke & Halperin, 2010). Implementation of these protocols involves identifying risk profiles, differentiating children who require intervention from those who don't, and matching children with individualized treatments (e.g., medication, cognitive interventions, parenting programs) (Sonuga-Barke & Halperin, 2010).

We expect, and hope, that in the coming years, children, adolescents, and adults will receive more careful evaluations of ADHD, with an increased appreciation for the developmental context of ADHD, the overlap of normal and disruptive behaviors, and the varied clinical presentations in diverse samples. We recognize that some children whose behavior is problematic but not actually disordered will be misdiagnosed with ADHD; we also recognize that some children with ADHD will fall through the cracks and will struggle without any kind of intervention or supportive services.

Key Terms

Attention deficit/hyperactivity disorder (p. 140)
Self-regulation (p. 141)
Effortful control (p. 142)
Executive function (p. 142)
Two-factor model of ADHD (p. 145)
Final common pathway (p. 150)
Polygenic model (p. 150)
Behavioral parent training (p. 157)
Behavioral contingency management (p. 159)

Chapter Summary

- Attention deficit/hyperactivity disorder (ADHD) is characterized by a combination of the symptoms of impulsivity, restlessness, and inattentiveness.
- Self-regulatory, effortful control, and executive functioning skills are important developmental milestones that are compromised by ADHD.
- The diagnosis of ADHD reflects compromised functioning in the domains of inattention and/or hyperactivity/impulsivity.
- Boys receive diagnoses of ADHD four to five times more often than do girls.
- In general, ADHD is an exceptionally stable diagnosis over time.

- Rates of co-occurring internalizing and externalizing disorders increase for children with ADHD over time.
- Diagnoses most commonly occurring along with ADHD include oppositional defiant disorder, mood and anxiety disorders, and learning problems.
- Genetic and neurological factors are central to the development of ADHD, whereas psychosocial factors play an important role in the maintenance and exacerbation of the disorder.
- Extensive research into the cognitive deficits that tend to characterize ADHD points, in particular, to weaknesses in effortful control.
- Because the core symptoms of ADHD (e.g., distractibility and impulsivity) are present in many children, variable, and continuous with typical behavior, it is especially important that assessment include multiple data sources from multiple settings.
- The majority of children treated with stimulant medication show significant improvement.
- Although medication is especially helpful in the short term, psychological interventions, such as behavioral parent training, and environmental interventions, such as classroom adaptations, are important for sustained improvement in functioning.

10

Oppositional Defiant Disorder and Conduct Disorder

FOUR-YEAR-OLD MARISSA yells at her mother when her mother reminds her to brush her teeth. Six-year-old Jonah sits in time-out for hours because he refuses to apologize for disrespectful behavior at the dinner table. For the third time in a week, 11-year-old Luis is sent to the principal's office, this time for ignoring his teacher's repeated requests for him to sit down and complete his math assignment.

Are these children headstrong, or spoiled, or bad? Are their parents and teachers too lenient or too harsh? Is anyone to blame in these battles for control? And why do some argumentative and disobedient children grow up into adolescents who lie, cheat, and steal? How do we explain adolescents who flout rules and exploit others? How can we comprehend the heartbreaking episodes of adolescent rage and violence that destroy families, schools, and communities? Understanding oppositional defiant disorder and conduct disorder involves thinking carefully and critically about "bad" behavior throughout history and the apparent increases in externalizing behaviors in recent decades (Collishaw, Maughan, Goodman, & Pickles, 2004; Robins, 1999; see Box 10:1). As we think about the various pathways toward and away from externalizing behaviors, it is essential that we continue to make use of a developmental framework (Hartup, 2005; Koops & de Castro, 2004); with such a framework, bridges among research, treatment, and public policy may be built (Coie & Dodge, 1998; Pettit & Dodge, 2003).

BOX 10:1 THE CHILD IN CONTEXT

Historical Perspectives on Bad Behavior

Over the centuries, adults have sought to teach, control, and socialize children, and to respond appropriately to children's bad behaviors. Costello and Angold (2001) summarize multiple historical approaches to dealing with deviant behaviors and deviant children. Each of these perspectives has something to say about the nature of children and about the emergence of responsibility for one's own behaviors, the relations between the family and the larger social group with respect to control of children, and institutions for out-of-control individuals.

With respect to the nature of children, Costello and Angold describe approaches that focus on the children's behavior as the result of disease (e.g., genetic and hereditary explanations), disposition, motivation, lack of knowledge (e.g., malice-related or ignorance-related explanations), or problematic environments (e.g., distressed families or dysfunctional neighborhoods). Hostile, oppositional, defiant, and aggressive behavior is at times the sole responsibility of the child, sometimes the responsibility of the parents, and sometimes the responsibility of society. Blame and recriminations are pervasive.

In various eras, adults have alternately viewed children as similar to adults (judging them accordingly) and as different from adults (responding with leniency and mercy). And societies have struggled to balance their obligations to children and to the communities in which children live. Many societies have developed separate legal and physical systems for dealing with difficult children. The consequences of unacceptable behaviors have ranged from education and rehabilitation through punishment, ostracism, and isolation.

Other, more recent discussions of children's behavior have held out the possibility that some types of bad behavior may in fact be adaptive for some children. The benefits of bad behavior may be understood within an evolutionary context (Pinker, 2002) or within more circumscribed settings including socioeconomic status [SES], ethnic background, and family environments (Underwood, 2003a, 2003b). The role of developmental level and the impact of specific developmental challenges remain to be fully explored. And whether we are concerned about girls or boys also influences our definitions of bad behavior, our expectations, and our responses to such behavior (Underwood, 2003a, 2003b; Underwood, Galen, & Paquette, 2001). As we grapple with our concerns, we need to remind ourselves that the questions we frame about children will need to be as complex, difficult, and genuine as they are.

Developmental Tasks and Challenges Related to Prosocial Behavior

Prosocial behaviors are behaviors that benefit self, others, and society. Young children who are prosocial cooperate with their parents, share with their peers, and help in their communities. As children age, their prosocial repertoires expand in a variety of ways, involving achievements related to self-control and rule-based behavior. The development of prosocial behavior depends on individual, relationship, and environmental factors. This brief overview summarizes information about typical patterns of prosocial behavior and provides a framework for comparison and contrast for upcoming discussions of oppositional defiant disorder and conduct disorder.

The development of **conscience** is the key child factor underlying prosocial behavior. According to Kochanska and Aksan (2006), the child's conscience is the "inner guiding system responsible for the gradual emergence and maintenance of self-regulation" (p. 1587). The construct of conscience includes both moral emotions (guilt, discomfort following transgressions) and moral conduct (behavior compatible with rules and standards). While early forms of moral emotions and moral conduct are observed in young children, mature forms develop over a lifetime (Blasi, 1983; Frimer & Walker, 2009; Hardy & Carlo, 2011; Kohlberg, 1969).

Kochanska and Aksan describe the early form of conscience as the "child's eager, willing stance toward parental socialization" (p. 1587) and identify two components of temperament, fearfulness and effortful control, that influence that stance. In related temperament–conscience research, Stifter, Cipriano, Conway, and Kelleher (2008) report that inhibited (more reactive, more fearful) children exhibited more prosocial behavior than exuberant and less highly aroused children. The exuberant and less highly aroused children appeared less responsive to the discomfort associated with violating rules.

Children's ongoing emotional, cognitive, and behavioral development also contributes to the development of conscience. With respect to emotion, experiences of empathy underlie prosocial behavior. With respect to cognition, better perspective-taking abilities lead to increases in prosocial behavior. With respect to behavior, improved self regulation influences cooperation and compliance. Taken together over time, a prosocial orientation—a "moral self"—can help organize a child's pattern of thinking, feeling and behaving (Eggum et al., 2011; Kochanska, Koenig, Barry, Kim, & Yoon, 2010).

Of course, children do not develop prosocial orientations on their own. In the early years of childhood, the quality of the parent–child relationship and parental discipline style are important influences on children's prosociality (Karreman, van Tuijl, van Aken, & Dekovic, 2006; Spinrad et al., 2012). Kerr, Lopez, Olson, and Sameroff (2004) report that warm responsiveness, parental induction (e.g., reasoning, reminders about rules, encouraging perspective taking), and less frequent use of physical punishment are associated with higher levels of moral regulation in children and fewer externalizing problems. In research on prosociality, there is an emphasis on the *parent–child mutually responsive orientation* (MRO) (Kochanska, Barry, Aksan, & Boldt, 2008). With MRO, "parents and children become responsive to each other, smoothing the way for successful parental socialization efforts" (p. 1225). This responsiveness toward parents is enduring and generalized, consistently associated with children's internalization of parental values, and evident in rule-based behavior. According to Kochanska and colleagues, responsiveness is the link between the parent's behaviors and the child's conscience and prosocial behavior (Kochanska, Koenig, Barry, Kim, & Yoon, 2010).

There are a number of studies that illustrate interactions between child factors and parent factors. Cornell and Frick (2007) observed that, for uninhibited children, inconsistent discipline was associated with lower levels of guilt and empathy. Inhibited children displayed more guilt and empathy irrespective of parenting behavior. In other research, effortful control predicted the development of conscience for inhibited children, whereas parental socialization predicted conscience for exuberant children (Stifter et al., 2008). Differential susceptibility models related to parenting and child compliance have also been proposed, with some children (depending on genetic factors) showing greater reactivity to both supportive and unsupportive environments (Sulik et al., 2011).

As noted, prosociality develops throughout childhood and adolescence. And the parent–child relationship that supports (or hinders) prosociality also changes over time. Relationships in general, and close relationships in particular, are characterized by dimensions of permanence, power, and gender (Laursen & Bukowski, 1997). Permanence has to do with the stability of the relationship. Parent–child and sibling relationships are among the most enduring, although there are certainly individual differences in the degree of closeness in family relationships. Power has to do with control and responsibility. Parents and children provide a good example of a *vertical relationship*, where parents are typically invested with most of the power. Sibling and peer relationships tend to be *horizontal*, characterized by more egalitarian roles and shared control and responsibility. Gender plays an important role in almost all relationships; understanding the differential impact of mothers and fathers, and same-sex and opposite-sex peers, on boys' and girls' experiences across childhood and adolescence is essential. Although cultural factors (such as those influencing the interactions of adolescent boys and girls) must always be taken into account, important similarities in relationships across various ethnicities and nationalities (e.g., between Dutch and Japanese adolescents, and between Chinese and American adolescents) have also been documented (Chen, Greenberger, Lester, Dong, & Guo, 1998; Claes, 1998; Dekovic, Engels, Shirai, De Kort, & Anker, 2002).

Less hierarchical relationships are observed in adolescence, and adolescents increasingly influence their relationships with their parents (Laursen & Collins, 2009; McGue, Elkins, Walden, & Iacono, 2005). Conflicts increase, and the topics of parent–adolescent conflicts differ by age and gender (Renk, Liljequist, Simpson, & Phares, 2005). For example, younger adolescents are more likely to argue about separation–individuation issues, rules and responsibilities, and school issues; older adolescents are more likely to argue over peer group issues. Conflicts appear similar across ethnicity and culture (Daddis & Smetana, 2005; Smetana & Gettman, 2006; Yau & Smetana, 2003). Some of these conflicts seem superficial, but in fact may be "proxies for arguments over more serious issues such as substance use, automobile driving safety, and sex" (Arnett, 1999, p. 320). Levels of warmth and supportiveness may also change, in ways that may be particularly problematic for some adolescents. For instance, Hafen and Laursen (2009) note that struggling adolescents often report that they experience less support from their parents. Even

after considering changes related to conflict and warmth, however, most adolescents and parents report continuing positive relationships (Arnett, 1999; McGue et al., 2005).

Patterns of prosocial behavior across childhood and adolescence increasingly involve peer-related behaviors, and bidirectional influences on prosociality are frequently described (see Fig. 10:1). Although overlapping somewhat with relationships with parents, relationships with peers offer unique experiences. Citing Piaget's and Kohlberg's theories, Parker, Rubin, Price, and DeRosier (1995) provide the example of moral development as a domain wherein what you learn from peers can be very different from what you learn from parents and other adults.

Positive peer relationships reflect a critical developmental achievement, with both individual and social consequences (Bukowski & Adams, 2005; Rose & Rudolph, 2006). Some of the most important aspects of adolescent life involve the density and diversity of social networks. Over the years of childhood and early adolescence, the availability of peers increases with, for instance, entrance into larger schools and involvement in sports, clubs, extracurricular lessons, and community activities. Over the school years, "the peer group also becomes increasingly segregated by sex, and to a lesser extent, race, and organized into more discernable hierarchies of power and popularity" (Parker et al., 1995, p. 101). Across adolescence, we see some loosening of cliques and clique behavior and a shift to peer subcultures. These are larger groups of "similarly stereotyped individuals" and include "jocks, brains, loners, rogues, druggies, populars, and nerds" (Parker et al., 1995, p. 104). Other investigators have examined adolescent groups and friendships using different methods, measures, and classifications. Coie, Dodge, and Coppotelli (1982) described four extreme status groups of children, based on peer nominations. The *popular* children were those who received lots of positive responses and few negative ones. The *rejected* children received many negative responses and few positives. The *neglected* children received few positive or negative responses. And the *controversial* children had both positive and negative responses. Although 60% to 65% of children were classified as average (i.e., not in any of the extreme groups), the results from many studies suggest that the extreme classifications are relatively stable. Keep in mind, however, that there are important differences among acceptance,

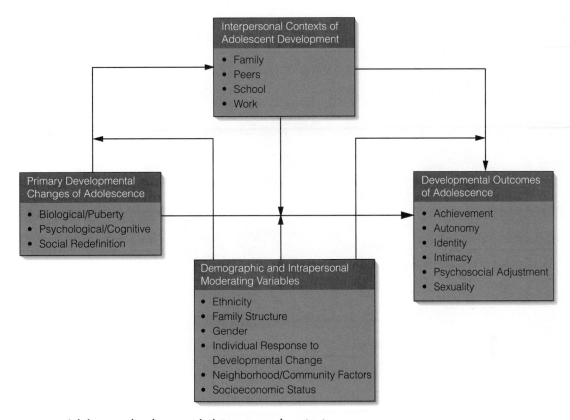

FIGURE 10:1 Adolescent development in interpersonal context.
Source: Handbook of Research Methods in Clinical Psychology, Phillip C. Kendall, James N. Butcher and Grayson N. Holmbeck. Copyright © 1999 John Wiley & Sons, Inc. Reproduced by permission of John Wiley & Sons, Inc.

popularity, and friendships, as well as differences between objective and subjective indices of peer relationships (Parker et al., 1995). The "reality" observed by others does not always match the "reality" felt by an adolescent.

In addition to understanding the availability and classifications of peer relationships, the nature and continuity of relationships must also be addressed (Poulin & Chan, 2010). School transitions from elementary to middle school or middle school to high school can disrupt longstanding friendships (Parker et al., 1995). Indeed, "different environments present different challenges to individuals. For example, the maintenance of friendships may be less difficult in the well-structured environments of elementary school than in the expansive environments of secondary schools" (Laursen & Bukowski, 1997, pp. 748–749). These changes can be almost as upsetting to parents, who may for the first time not know their children's friends, as it is to young adolescents themselves. Related to

the nature of adolescent relationships, the positive qualities (e.g., intimacy, loyalty, trust) appear more important than the quantity of friendships, especially for boys (Demir & Urberg, 2004). And positive experiences in one type of relationship, such as with friends, may buffer negative experiences in others, such as with parents (and vice versa) (Laursen & Bukowski, 1997).

Understanding the impact of gender on healthy and unhealthy peer relationships is critical (Rose & Rudolph, 2006; Underwood, 2004a), and the ways in which adolescent boys and girls conceptualize and manage negative emotion and various forms of aggression provide relevant developmental information. Both boys and girls exhibit physical and nonphysical aggression, but the frequency and intensity of aggression differ; for both boys and girls, individual differences also need to be taken into account (Archer, 2004; Card, Stucky, Sawalani, & Little, 2008; Zimmer-Gembeck, Geiger, & Crick, 2005). Relational (or social) aggression is thought

Peer group relationships become an increasingly important influence on moral and behavioral development during adolescence.

Peter Cade/The ImageBank/Getty Images

to be more common in girls and is focused on harm caused in relationships. Examples include exclusion, gossip, and friendship manipulation (e.g., exploiting one's friends or having friends lie to parents or teachers) (Crick & Grotpeter, 1995; Underwood, 2004b). A recent meta-analysis of nearly 150 studies, however, suggests that the gender difference may be relatively trivial (Card et al., 2008). Physical aggression is more typical of boys and, like relational aggression, needs to be understood in the broader context of emotional development.

A developmental perspective on bullying

Around the world, there is increased attention paid to the phenomenon of **bullying** and the sometimes tragic consequences for bullied children and adolescents. A developmental perspective is especially useful for understanding the prevalence, origins, and outcomes of bullying and victimization and allows for informed discussion of prevention, treatment, and public policy. Definitions of bullying emphasize negative actions intended to hurt or harm (e.g., fighting, harassing, excluding) that are repeated over time and that involve a power differential between the bully and the victim. Cyberbullying is an increasingly problematic form of bullying

(Williams & Guerra, 2007). Some bullying behaviors (e.g., nasty teasing) have more typical developmental counterparts (e.g., friendly teasing).

Bullying is a globally pervasive problem in families, schools, and neighborhoods. In schools, bullying is observed at all grade levels, including kindergarten (Pepler, Jiang, Craig, & Connolly, 2008; Perren & Alsaker, 2006), with the roots of some forms of bullying interactions observed even earlier in development (Georgiou, 2008; Troy & Sroufe, 1987). Both boys and girls bully, and both boys and girls are victims. Cross-country estimates of the prevalence of bullying vary widely, from 10% to 50%, with cross-country differences noted in adult sensitivities to different forms of bullying (Smorti, Menesini, & Smith, 2003). Rates are highest in the middle school years: for boys in eighth grade, and for girls in ninth grade. Specific forms of bullying change over time, with more aggression related to emerging sexuality and sexual identity in middle school and high school (Pepler et al., 2006). Overall, bullying decreases from childhood to adolescence (Monks et al., 2009; Pepler et al., 2006).

Bullies are a heterogeneous group of children and adolescents. Researchers have identified a number of factors that are associated with being a bully. Both poor social skills (being an "oaf") (Crick & Dodge, 1994) and well-developed social skills (the "Machiavellian" view) (Sutton, Smith, & Swettenham, 1999) have been described (Arsenio & Lemerise, 2001). Other research has focused on deficits in empathy and in the internalization of values (Arsenio & Lemerise, 2001). Increased risk for bullying is also associated with child maltreatment, parent monitoring (relevant for both bullies and victims) and parent hostility, domestic violence, and hostile neighborhood interactions (Bowes et al., 2009). School factors such as teacher attitudes, degree of supervision, school ethos, and school policies are also important (Monks et al., 2009). The motivations for bullying are also complex and include status, psychological gratification, and material rewards. Various trajectories are possible, including high levels of bullying over time and decreasing levels over time (Pepler et al., 2008). Whereas some bullies desist, others go on to display other forms of antisocial behavior and conduct disorder; still others go on to adult forms of bullying such as sexual and workplace harassment and violent relationships (Pepler et al., 2006).

Victims, too, are a mixed group. Factors associated with increased risk include minority status, low peer status, low socioeconomic status, being gay or lesbian, having special needs or a psychological disorder, or being seen as "provocative" by bullies.

A "vicious cycle" has been described, with some of the immediate consequences of bullying (e.g., withdrawn and internalizing behaviors) leading to further victimization (Biggs et al., 2010). Individual reputations as victims are stable (in peers), but there is significant variability in self-perceptions (Biggs et al., 2010). Poor outcomes include short- and long-term consequences related to psychological, physical, and social adjustment. One of the most poignant involves suicidality, which is related to social hopelessness (Bonanno & Hymel, 2010).

Antibullying programs have been adopted in most states in the United States. The U.S. Department of Education has listed 16 components of legislation, and ranks states' laws and policies accordingly. However, antibullying programs are only associated with modestly positive outcomes and, too often, not enough meaningful impact; there is an urgent need for better research (Merrell, Gueldner, Ross, & Isava, 2008; Ryan & Smith, 2009). Research-to-date suggests that both universal and individual (victim-oriented) interventions are necessary, targeting schools, families, and communities (Biggs et al., 2010; Bowes et al., 2009). Adult support (from both parents and teachers) is critical (Conners-Burrow et al., 2009). Well-timed interventions (e.g., at late elementary-school, before the transition to larger schools) are also important.

Bullying behavior, including threatening and harassing more vulnerable classmates, is increasingly recognized as a serious problem warranting the development of school- and community-based prevention and intervention initiatives.

SW Productions/Getty Images

Oppositional Defiant Disorder

Oppositional defiant disorder (ODD) is a sustained pattern of anger, irritability, and defiant or vindictive behavior. The disorder is differentiated from the more severe conduct disorder (CD), which involves the violation of social norms and rules as well as the rights of others. The following two cases illustrate common ODD presentations.

The Case of Brad

Brad is a 6-year-old child who exhibits noncompliance, frequent temper tantrums, and physical aggression at home and at school. These aggressive behaviors include throwing objects, biting, punching, and kicking. Brad's mother, a single parent, reported that his difficulties began at age 3 and emerged during a period of multiple life changes, including moving to a new home and enrolling in a different school. Because of the disruptive behaviors, Brad had been asked to leave several day care centers before starting kindergarten. In addition to being frustrated with Brad, Brad's mother is also upset with herself because she has no idea how to handle Brad's increasingly loud and obnoxious interactions with her and with his siblings at home and in public. She is also concerned that, despite Brad's enjoyment of all things related to nature and interest in science, Brad's disrespectful attitude and behaviors in school will lead to teachers labeling him a troublemaker, and to peers rejecting him on the playground and in the neighborhood. ■

The Case of Nick

Nick is an 11-year-old referred for a diagnostic assessment by his mother and father because of his "horrible" behavior and school difficulties. Nick is in sixth grade. His parents describe him as disrespectful, disobedient, and spiteful. At times they are taken aback by his loud and threatening behavior, especially when directed at his younger brother. Grounding Nick and withholding money and other privileges has had little impact, even though there are times when Nick seems distressed by his own actions. Nick has been suspended twice this school year for disruptive behavior, including yelling at a teacher. His few close friends are increasingly frustrated with his mean-spirited teasing and his blaming them for some recent classroom misbehavior. Academically, Nick is struggling to keep his grades high enough to pass, although he had little trouble in school prior to this year. ■

Negativistic, hostile, and defiant behavior are the core features of oppositional defiant disorder.

Both Brad and Nick exhibit mixes of typical and atypical behaviors that require closer study. Developmentally, Brad displays disruptive behaviors that are more frequent and more intense than expected; indeed, his repeated dismissals from day care settings suggest clinically significant disturbance. Nick displays externalizing behaviors that complicate his personal agenda and ruin family activities. For the boys, the transition to new school situations that require additional self-control also seems more problematic than for most of their peers. Both Brad and Nick meet the diagnostic criteria for oppositional defiant disorder.

Early descriptions of oppositional defiant disorder mainly focused on its role as an early or milder expression of conduct disorder. Researchers and clinicians have since come to conceptualize ODD as a distinct entity associated with significant impairments (Burke, Waldman, & Lahey, 2010; Drabick, Gadow, & Loney, 2007; Rowe, Maughan, Costello, & Angold, 2005; Stringaris & Goodman, 2009; Wakschlag, Tolan, & Leventhal, 2010). Stringaris and Goodman identify three dimensions of oppositionality in children: irritability, being headstrong, and being hurtful. According to the researchers, each dimension is associated with different developmental pathways, different etiologies, and differentially focused treatments.

In related research, Wakschlag, Tolan, and Leventhal (2010) described four dimensions that underlie oppositional defiant disorder, emphasizing that problematic behaviors need to be distinguished from typical misbehavior in children. The dimensions in the Wakschlag et al. model are as follows:

1. Aggression, the "tendency to respond aggressively including multiple forms, triggers, and targets" (p. 6). Normative aggression is common, but not frequent; a predictable developmental pathway is observed (i.e., increasing in the second year, decreasing across the preschool period). Stable or increasing aggression is nonnormative. Reactive (compared to proactive) aggression is more common (Dodge, 1991; Dodge & Coie, 1987).

2. Noncompliance is the "resistance to, and failure to comply with, directives, rules, and social norms" (p. 7). Noncompliance is present in 2-year olds and then increases across preschool years, reflecting age-appropriate expressions of independence. As children get older, with advances in cognition and better language skills, there are changes in the forms and skillfulness of noncompliant behaviors (e.g., verbal negotiation instead of direct noncompliance). An important distinction is that assertiveness is more typical than defiance. Also important is the degree to which the child is able to modulate the noncompliant response.

3. Temper loss involves "problems in regulation of anger, including intensity, frequency, and modulation" (p. 8). The most studied form of temper loss is tantrums. The key differences in normative versus nonnormative tantrums relate to the intensity of tantrums, the destructiveness of tantrums, and the difficulty in recovering from tantrums. Although the overall frequency of tantrums decreases significantly over the preschool years, destructive tantrums, when present, increase in frequency between 3 and 5 years of age and are strongly associated with later clinical disorder (Egger, in press).

4. Low concern for others is a "disregard of others' needs and feelings ranging from mild insensitivity to more active and pervasive disregard as well as efforts to cause distress" (p. 10). Low concern, and a lack of empathy, can be understood as deviations from typical conscience development (think back to Kochanska and Aksan's descriptions of moral emotions and moral conduct, discussed in the opening section of this chapter).

Oppositional defiant disorder has been documented in many different cultures and countries (Robins, 1999). Estimates of prevalence in community samples vary from 2% to 16% (Barrickman, 2003; Maughan, Rowe, Messer, Goodman, & Meltzer, 2004; Nock, Kazdin, Hiripi, & Kessler, 2007). Estimates of prevalence in clinical samples of children are much higher, between 28% and 65% (Loeber, Burke, & Pardini, 2009). Some suggest that the diagnostic criteria seriously underidentify the number of children with ODD who struggle with significant impairments (Burke, Waldman, & Lahey, 2010). Although usually diagnosed before age 8, ODD can be seen in preschoolers and in adolescents. Almost all investigations of ODD report that it is more common in boys, but there is increasing work on descriptions of disruptive disorders in girls. Oppositional defiant disorder is frequently discussed in tandem with conduct disorder, and although there is significant overlap in risk factors, etiology, and clinical presentation, many children diagnosed with conduct disorder *do not* meet the diagnostic criteria for ODD (Burke, Waldman, & Lahey, 2010; Loeber, Burke, & Pardini, 2009; Rowe, Costello, Angold, Copeland, & Maughan, 2010).

Conduct Disorder

The Case of Lucas

Lucas is a 14-year-old referred for evaluation by his mother and school principal due to concerns about escalating behavior problems, school difficulties, and suspected substance abuse. He gets in trouble at school nearly every week: sometimes for disobeying school rules, sometimes for rude comments to teachers, and occasionally for fighting with other students. Recently Lucas was suspended for stealing a cell phone and money from another student's locker. He was also suspended last year, when he punched and kicked a younger student who accidentally ran into him in the hallway. Although Lucas is not involved in any school teams or organizations and most other students avoid him, he does have a small group of friends who have also been in considerable trouble. Some of them have been arrested for property-related criminal behavior.

Lucas's problems at school are compounded by defiant, reactive, and disruptive behavior at home, dating all the way back to his preschool years. When younger, Lucas was hard to manage at home and at school, and by middle school Lucas's parents felt that they had very little control over him. Now, Lucas's parents tend to steer clear of him and are grateful for the occasional periods of uneasy truces. ■■■

The Case of Elena

Elena is a 15-year-old referred for evaluation at the suggestion of her pediatrician. She is in the tenth grade and currently failing most of her classes. She skips school several times a week and hangs out with a group of older teens who have dropped out of high school. Elena has been stealing money from her parents and has also been arrested twice for shoplifting. She has recently come home intoxicated, and her parents have found drug paraphernalia in her room.

This is not how life has always been for Elena. Elena's parents report a relatively uneventful childhood. They began to be concerned about her, however, during eighth grade. At the time, Elena dropped out of sports and her grades fell dramatically. Eventually Elena was diagnosed with depression, participated briefly in therapy, and began taking an antidepressant. Although Elena's mood and behavior improved somewhat, she continued to struggle throughout the year. After a period of social isolation, she began to hang out with a group of girls who prided themselves on their alienation from mainstream school and family experiences. ■■

Conduct disorder (CD) involves a persistent pattern of very problematic behavior in which there are serious violations of social norms and rules. As described in DSM-5, these violations include aggression or mistreatment directed toward people or animals, property destruction, deceitfulness or theft, and other serious rule violations. In addition to these behavioral criteria, children and adolescents who receive a diagnosis of conduct disorder are also evaluated with respect to **callous–unemotional (CU) characteristics.** These characteristics include lack of empathy, lack of guilt or remorse, shallow emotions, and a lack of concern about performance (Frick & Moffitt, 2010).

There are two subtypes of conduct disorder: **child-onset subtype** and **adolescent-onset subtype.** With childhood onset, the individual diagnosed with conduct disorder has a long history of negative personal and interpersonal behaviors, and the behaviors deteriorate over time. With onset in adolescence, the individual's problem behavior emerges more abruptly. Adolescent-onset conduct disorder is three times as common as childhood-onset (Frick, 1998). The data on prevalence by age is mixed, with some studies showing increases in conduct disorder from middle childhood to adolescence, whereas other studies do not. For child-onset CD, boys outnumber girls

10 to 1; for adolescent-onset CD, boys outnumber girls 5 to 1 (Moffitt & Caspi, 2001). The diagnosis is more common in youth from lower SES backgrounds (Loeber, Burke, Lahey, Winters, & Zera, 2000). Ethnicity also appears to influence prevalence rates (Bird et al., 2001; Hishinuma et al., 2005).

Child-onset and adolescent-onset conduct disorder differ not only in their timing, but also in their symptom patterns, severity, and outcomes. Moffitt's (2003) theory of CD describes a **life-course trajectory** (LCP) (similar to child-onset CD) and an **adolescence-limited trajectory** (AL). The AL form of CD is somewhat less problematic over time than the child-onset form, although there is still evidence of significant impairment in daily functioning and risk for poor outcomes (Cicchetti & Rogosch, 2002; Moffitt, 2003). LCP individuals are more likely to have a history of ODD and a family history of antisocial behavior and are more likely to display aggression and have worse outcomes than AL individuals (Lahey et al., 1998; Loeber et al., 2000). As noted in prevalence data, more boys exhibit the early onset, more severe CD pathway. However, some researchers hypothesize that certain girls display a "delayed onset," with similar underlying factors; this hypothesis is based, in part, on similar poor adult outcomes for girls diagnosed later with CD compared to boys diagnosed earlier (Silverthorn & Frick, 1999). Given recent increases in the diagnosis of girls, negative consequences such as early pregnancy and later antisocial behavior, and the fact that much of our CD data is based on samples of boys, we will need to look more carefully at girls in coming years (Keenan, Stouthamer-Loeber, & Loeber, 2005). It may also be prudent to pay attention to the "subclinical" range of problem behaviors, given long-term individual and social consequences (Cicchetti & Rogosch, 2002).

Because aggression is common in both typical and atypical development, it makes sense to step back and carefully consider the forms and functions of aggression (Hawley & Vaughn, 2003; Robins, 1995) and the ways in which aggression predicts later antisocial outcomes (Burt, Donnellan, Iacono, & McGue, 2011). **Aggression** involves behaviors that are carried out with an immediate goal of causing harm to another. Many investigators have attempted to understand why aggression occurs and what it involves (Dodge, 1991; Little, Jones, Henrich, & Hawley, 2003) (or proactive) or reactive. **Instrumental aggression** is aggression that is premeditated or planned. In most cases, instrumental aggression is a means to a particular end. A bully who plans to wreck another child's science project exhibits instrumental aggression. **Reactive aggression** is aggression that occurs in response to a provocation. It is more angry and impulsive. A child who is thrown out at first base displays reactive aggression by cursing at the umpire. Although this instrumental–reactive distinction is useful in many ways, it is important to remember that aggression often has multiple motives and multiple goals; these include attempts to reestablish self-esteem or public image, attempts to express grievances, or attempts to obtain benefits such as money or information (Bushman & Anderson, 2001).

The *whats* of aggression have to do with whether aggression is direct or indirect (Card et al., 2008). Direct, or **overt aggression**, involves harmful physical behaviors or overt behaviors such as name-calling. Direct aggression is more often associated with low levels of prosocial behavior, emotional dysregulation, externalizing problems, and poor peer relationships. Indirect, or **covert aggression**, may include the externalizing behaviors observed in CD, such as property damage or theft; it may also involve behaviors that harm the target by rejection or exclusion (Crick's "relational aggression") or alternative strategies (such as manipulation) employed when the costs of direct aggression are high. Indirect aggression is associated with higher levels of prosocial behavior and internalizing problems.

In addition to ongoing theoretical and empirical work focused on aggression, recent research has emphasized the need to better understand the callous–unemotional construct in order to "attempt to identify a group of conduct-disordered youth who are at greatest risk for developing severe and persistent forms of antisocial behavior" (Loeber et al., 2009, p. 136). Callous–unemotional characteristics include, as noted previously, shallow affect, a lack of empathy, guilt and/or remorse, and a failure to accept responsibility for antisocial acts. In combination with interpersonal features such as manipulativeness, deceitfulness, superficial charm, and grandiosity, this early form of psychopathy is linked to a number of deleterious outcomes (Frick & Moffitt, 2010; Loeber et al., 2009). Recent work on girls with conduct disorders, for example, suggests that girls with CU traits display more serious aggression and more global impairment than conduct-disordered girls without these traits (Pardini, Stepp, Hipwell, Stouthamer-Loeber, & Loeber, 2012).

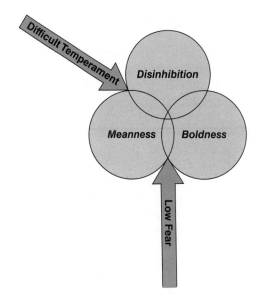

FIGURE 10:2 **A presentation of hypothesized relations among constructs of disinhibition, boldness, and meanness (circles) and influences of difficult temperament and low fear (arrows) on each construct.**
SOURCE: From Patrick, Fowles, & Krueger (2009).

Patrick, Fowles, and Krueger (2009) describe a three-part, developmentally informed conceptualization of psychopathy. The first component is disinhibition, involving a propensity toward impulse-control problems, a lack of planfulness, an insistence on immediate gratification, and deficient behavioral restraint; disinhibition is "at the nexus of impulsivity and negative affectivity" (p. 925). The second component is boldness, involving the capacity to remain calm in stressful situations, high self-assurance and social efficacy, and a tolerance for danger. The third component is meanness, with deficient empathy, a disdain for others, exploitativeness, and empowerment (see Fig. 10:2). Overall, the research on callous–unemotional characteristics and psychopathy suggests that it will be necessary to make explicit the developmental connections among ODD, CD, and antisocial personality disorder (Frick & Moffitt, 2010; Loeber et al., 2009).

Developmental Course

There are several predictable pathways for children with early externalizing disorders. For oppositional defiant disorder, it is important to keep in mind the continuous nature of oppositional and disruptive behaviors (i.e., the connections between typically- and atypically-developing children) (Wakschlag et al., 2010). However, early patterns of disruptive difficulties are frequently and strongly associated with later patterns of difficulties, and children with clinically significant disorders do not "grow out" of their problems (Burke, Waldman, & Lahey, 2010; Caspi et al., 2003). For conduct disorder, the historical framework for understanding developmental pathways is provided by Lee Robins's (1966) classic book, *Deviant Children Grown Up*. Robins documented the potential stability of conduct disorder, finding that many troubled children and adolescents display antisocial personalities as adults along with other types of psychopathologies. However, he also observed the possibility of positive change and better outcomes in some individuals. Robins's findings have been replicated many, many times in other longitudinal studies; the stability of conduct-disordered behavior, especially related to aggression and callous–unemotional characteristics, is abundantly clear across individuals and across generations.

Oppositional Defiant Disorder

With respect to oppositional defiant disorder, one developmental pathway is for ODD to continue without much improvement or deterioration, resulting in years of conflict, hostility, and disappointment. Without intervention, this pathway is the most common, especially for girls. For both girls and boys, the more severe the ODD symptoms, the more stable the disorder. There is, however, evidence that supports the notion of a possible reorganization, with some improvement, during early adolescence (Granic, Hollenstein, Dishion, & Patterson, 2003; van Lier, van der Ende, Koot, & Verhulst, 2007).

One of the factors that most strongly predicts stability of disorder is age of onset. Those with childhood-onset ODD—the early starters—display more persistent patterns of difficulty (Keenan, Shaw, Delliquadri, Giovannelli, & Walsh, 1998). Gender also plays an important role. Beginning in preschool, boys exhibit more disruptive behaviors with more negative impact. In the Great Smoky Mountains community study, boys diagnosed with ODD displayed worse outcomes involving externalizing disorders, although girls later developed more internalizing disorders (Rowe et al., 2002). Combinations of other factors, such as early temperamental difficulties, poor self-regulation, certain forms of

aggression, and low SES, also appear to influence gender-specific pathways (Hill, Degnan, Calkins, & Keane, 2006; Silverthorn & Frick; 1999).

Parent, family, and peer factors also influence the ways in which ODD plays out over time. Adult patience and tolerance for oppositional behavior varies widely; similar child misbehaviors may evoke very different responses in different individuals (Calzada, Eyberg, Rich, & Querido, 2004). Compared to most parents' experiences of managing extremes of oppositional and defiant behavior for discrete periods of time, for parents of children with ODD, the prospect of chronic conflict may be overwhelming (Williford, Calkins, & Keane, 2007). Negative parenting, involving either hostility and harsh discipline or timid discipline, is associated with poorer outcomes (August et al., 1999; Burke, Pardini, & Loeber, 2008). Conversely, parental warmth, coupled with active monitoring of children's activities, is associated with better outcomes (Buckner, Mezzacappa, & Beardslee, 2003).

The case of Brad provides many examples of the influence of parents and parenting on the course of ODD. Brad's mother recalls how many times she has felt embarrassed over the last year as Brad has misbehaved loudly in the grocery store, the discount store, and the entrance lobby of his school. She is positive that other parents believe that she is either unfit or stupid, and these concerns have led her to withdraw from many of her regular social activities. Her parents have tried to help with babysitting and financial support, but they have also repeatedly criticized her for not being strict enough with Brad. At this point, Brad's mother is discouraged and ready to give up on Brad to focus on her other children.

Another common pathway for children with ODD is progression to conduct disorder (Burke et al., 2010; Loeber et al., 2009). A diagnosis of ODD is a stronger predictor of CD for boys (Rowe et al., 2010). And lower SES and higher levels of parent hostility also increase the risk of a later diagnosis of CD (Loeber et al., 2009). In longitudinal research, ODD is identified as "a pivotal developmental disorder," especially in boys (Burke et al., 2005). This is because ODD is not only linked to later externalizing disorders; it is also linked to later internalizing problems such as anxiety and depression (Loeber et al., 2009). With respect to depression, Capaldi and her colleagues have hypothesized that the disruptive symptoms of

ODD underlie academic and interpersonal failures, which then lead to depression (Capaldi, 1991, 1992; Capaldi & Stoolmiller, 1999). Stringaris and Goodman (2009), in contrast, assert that the irritability dimension of ODD predicts anxiety and depression; the headstrong and hurtful dimensions predict CD.

The combination of oppositional defiant disorder and attention deficit hyperactivity disorder is of special concern. Lahey, Loeber, and their colleagues have proposed a model of externalizing disorders in which only those children who are diagnosed with *both* ODD and ADHD go on to develop conduct disorders, with ADHD often preceding ODD as a specific risk factor (Burke, Loeber, Lahey, & Rathouz, 2005; Lahey et al., 2004; Lahey & Loeber, 1997). In this model, there are three deviant pathways, each with its own set of developmental challenges (although these may overlap): (a) the **overt pathway**, with minor aggression leading to more serious aggression that tends to be unconcealed and blatant; (b) the **covert pathway**, with minor misbehaviors leading to more serious delinquent acts that tend to be more concealed or secretive; and (c) the **authority conflict pathway**, with stubborn relationship-oriented behaviors leading to more serious disobedience and hostility. Trajectories specific to delinquency have been presented: one involving arrests occurring before age 13 and progressing to serious and chronic adult criminal behavior, and the other involving later arrests and less frequent adult crime (Clingempeel & Henggeler, 2003; Loeber & Farrington, 2000; Patterson & Yoerger, 2002).

One of the most problematic pathways is from oppositional defiant disorder to conduct disorder to antisocial personality disorder, with increases in aggression, violence, and substance abuse along the way (Burke et al., 2002; Burke, Loeber, & Lahey, 2003; Frick & Viding, 2009). Aggression, in particular, exhibits very stable trajectories. However, it is important to emphasize that, with age, fewer and fewer individuals are diagnosed with the increasingly severe and persistent disorders.

The Coercion Model

The **coercion model** described by Gerald Patterson and his colleagues is a developmental model that provides a framework for understanding the emergence, maintenance, and treatment of oppositional defiant disorder. In this model, often referred to as the Oregon model (where much of the research was

conducted), the primary focus is on social interaction learning and patterns of parental characteristics that lead to negative parent–child interactions. Chamberlain and Patterson (1995) and Patterson, Forgatch, and DeGarmo (2010) describe these characteristics in detail: (1) inconsistent discipline, with parents only sometimes enforcing limits and rules; (2) irritable, explosive discipline, with parents enforcing limits and rules in harsh and angry ways; (3) inflexible, rigid discipline, with parents enforcing limits and rules without regard to individual child attributes or special circumstances; and/or (4) low supervision and involvement.

The basic assumption of the coercion model is that parents and children struggle for control over a number of everyday tasks and activities, and that maladaptive parenting leads to children's externalizing behavior; the coercion model specifically examines a conditioning sequence in which children are inadvertently reinforced for their problematic behaviors (Patterson, Reid, & Eddy, 2002). If parents are ineffective and rigid, children's initial misbehavior and disobedience (which may be typical and not always a major concern) escalates. The child's escalating opposition is met by the parent's increasingly punitive responses, again and again and again. Over time, children's externalizing behaviors generalize to other settings. In school settings, for example, oppositional behavior leads to struggles with teachers and increased risk for academic failure. In peer settings, the child's negative behaviors lead to rejection by their typically developing, more prosocial peers. This rejection leads to increased association with other deviant peers and increasingly antisocial behavior.

The Transactional Model

Green and Doyle and their colleagues have described a somewhat more expansive model, the **transactional model**, which asserts that parent–child incompatibility is multiply determined, with multiple pathways to both externalizing and internalizing disorders, multiple interventions, and multiple outcomes. The coercion model is focused mainly on the primary role of the parents and, according to Greene and Doyle (1999), is one possible pathway among many. The transactional model emphasizes the investigation of several domains of risk factors, including child characteristics, maladaptive parenting, gene-by-environment interactions, peer influences, and sociocultural context, each of which may be tied to the diagnosis of externalizing problems. As with other psychopathologies, the more risk factors an individual experiences, the more likely the emergence of ODD.

Conduct Disorder

Estimates of the stability of conduct disorder over time range between 44% and 88% (Loeber et al., 2009). With respect to adolescent-onset conduct disorder, Moffitt (2003) and Frick and Viding (2009) suggest that for many, the externalizing problems reflect a "misguided attempt to obtain a subjective sense of maturity and adult status in a way that is maladaptive (e.g., breaking societal norms) but encouraged by an antisocial peer group. Given that their behavior is viewed as an exaggeration of a process specific to adolescence, and not because of an enduring vulnerability, their antisocial behavior is less likely to persist beyond adolescence" (Frick & Viding, 2009, p. 1114). For most adolescents with CD, this is a time-bound, albeit difficult and upsetting, phase characterized by impairment in most domains of functioning. For others, this is the beginning of an ongoing or deteriorating pathway involving other psychopathologies such as substance abuse and other negative outcomes such as school dropout (Loeber et al., 2009).

With respect to child-onset CD, stable externalizing trajectories are already evident in the early school years (Lahey & Waldman, 2003; Shaw, Gilliom, Ingoldsby, & Nagin, 2003). According to Lahey and Waldman, children with the highest level of early problems experience more maladjustment. In addition, researchers have reported that the externalizing behaviors exhibited by boys on the life-course path do not change over time; rather, their repertoire of externalizing behaviors expands to include new overt and covert problem behaviors (Frick, 1998; Lahey, Loeber, Burke, & Applegate, 2005; Patterson, Dishion, & Yoerger, 2000).

In comparisons of conduct-disordered youth with callous–unemotional characteristics and conduct-disordered youth without those characteristics, those with CU characteristics exhibit particularly severe and violent patterns over time (Byrd, Loeber, & Pardini, 2012; Frick & Viding, 2009; McMahon, Witkiewitz, Kotler, & Conduct Problems Research Group, 2010). Youth without CU traits display higher levels of anxiety and appear distressed by the effects of their problematic behaviors.

Family and peer factors also contribute to deteriorating (or improving) pathways. Family instability and conflict are associated with children's worsening externalizing behaviors (Burt, McGue, Krueger, & Iacono, 2005; Milan, Pinderhughes, & Conduct Problems Prevention Research Group, 2006). Parents of conduct-disordered youth appear to become disengaged over time, with less monitoring of their children's behaviors and activities (Dishion, Nelson, & Bullock, 2004; Hafen & Laursen, 2009). The breakdown in family management leads some adolescents to associate more frequently with deviant peers, and this leads to an escalation of CD behaviors. Groups of deviant peers experience more negative emotion and exhibit more support for rule breaking and aggression (Bagwell & Coie, 2004; Monahan, Steinberg, & Cauffman, 2009). The greatest increases in problem behaviors are seen in less well-accepted adolescents whose peers display higher levels of delinquency (Laursen, Hafen, Kerr, & Stattin, 2012). Sexual activity, sexually transmitted diseases, and unplanned pregnancies are primary health concerns for adolescent girls with CD. Connections between problem behaviors and disengagement from school have also been observed; symmetrically, staying in school despite problem behaviors has a protective benefit (Henry, Caspi, Moffitt, Harrington, & Silva, 1999; Steinberg & Avenevoli, 1998).

Developmental Cascade Models

Recent conceptualizations of developmental pathways focused on conduct disorder and antisocial behavior have emphasized the likelihood that there are differences in the underlying patterns and pathways of CD. With child-onset CD, for example, research has suggested the following: a difficult and vulnerable child experiences inadequate or dysfunctional parenting that leads to disruptions in conscience development and socialization. Poor socialization leads to problematic relationships in and out of the home and negative impacts on a variety of psychological and social domains (Frick & Viding, 2009). Other research on **developmental cascade models** (summarized earlier in Chapter 3) has emphasized the cross-domain, spreading effects observed over time in children with externalizing behaviors. In these studies, researchers have documented that difficulties with social information processing, peer rejection, and aggression "compound and exacerbate one another" (Lansford, Malone, Dodge, Pettit, & Bates, 2010) and that antisocial behavior and poor peer relations become

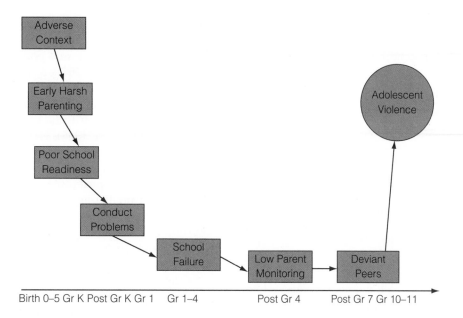

FIGURE 10:3 Hypothesized developmental cascade model of violent behavior.
Source: Testing an Idealized Dynamic Cascade Model of the Development of Serious Violence in Adolescence, Dodge, K.A., Greenberg, M.T., Malone, P.S. & Conduct Problems Prevention Research Group. Copyright 2008 Child Development. Reproduced with permission of John Wiley & Sons Inc.

"entangled" over time, with cascading effects from externalizing to internalizing problems over time (van Lier & Koot, 2010). In a detailed model of the development of violent behavior, Dodge, Greenberg, Malone, and Conduct Problems Prevention Research Group (2008) described the progression from an adverse early environment to harsh parenting, to poor school readiness, to conduct problems, to school failure, to poor parent supervision, to deviant peer relationships, to adolescent violence (see Fig. 10:3), with each successive risk building and expanding on previous risk and poor adjustment.

Etiology

Genes and Heredity

With respect to the role of genetic factors, the picture is complicated, with evidence for genetic, shared, and nonshared environmental influences on oppositional defiant disorder, conduct disorder, and antisocial behavior. Researchers have repeatedly observed that externalizing disorders aggregate in families; the often-overlapping clinical presentations of ODD with ADHD and CD suggest the possibility of shared genetic risks (Arseneault et al., 2003;

Dick, Viken, Kaprio, Pulkkinen, & Rose, 2005; Lahey & Waldman, 2003). Both additive and interactive models of genetic influence are documented (Frick & Viding, 2009; Pérusse & Gendreau, 2005). There appear to be differences related to gender (Derks, Dolan, Hudziak, Neale, & Boomsma, 2007; DiLalla, 2002) and differences related to the subtypes of antisocial behavior (Burt, 2009; Frick & Viding, 2009). There are also differences related to the timing (i.e., during childhood or during the pubertal transition) of genetic effects on antisocial behavior (Van Hulle et al., 2009).

Much of the research on genes and heredity is focused on specific characteristics that are part of the clinical presentation of ODD and CD. For example, there are ample data on the heritability of prosociality, negative emotionality, and daring (Waldman et al., 2011); inhibitory control (Gagne & Saudino, 2010); disinhibition, boldness, and meanness (Patrick et al., 2009; Young et al., 2009); and callous–unemotional and psychopathic personality characteristics (Bezdjian, Tuvblad, Raine, & Baker, 2011; Frick & Viding, 2009). As discussed in other chapters, recent research is often focused on models of vulnerability and differential susceptibility. Several investigations provide evidence that gene-by-environment interactions are essential to understanding the development of externalizing disorders (Buckholtz & Meyer-Lindenberg, 2008; Lahey et al., 2011; Latendresse et al., 2011).

Physiological Factors

Brain imaging studies have reported both structural and functional impairments (Davidson, 2000; Frick & Viding, 2009). Individual differences in brain areas and processes include those related to frontal lobe activation, the amygdala, the hypothalamic-pituitary-adrenal (HPA) axis, the behavioral inhibition system, and the workings of neurotransmitters and hormones (such as testosterone). Biological mechanisms that underlie sex differences in conduct disorder have also been investigated (Eme, 2007). The findings from many studies emphasize the underarousal of the autonomic nervous system, cortisol dysregulation, and important differences in the brain regions involved in the processing of emotional stimuli (Beauchaine, Gatzke-Kopp, & Mead, 2007; Fairchild et al., 2011; van Goozen, Fairchild, & Harold, 2008). Although many of these difficulties are hypothetically tied to genetics, prenatal and perinatal problems such as maternal smoking and substance abuse have also been implicated (Burke et al., 2002).

Child Factors

Child factors that have an impact on the development of oppositional defiant disorder, conduct disorder, and antisocial behavior include neuropsychological factors, emotion factors, cognitive factors, and temperament and personality factors. Among the most common findings are that children diagnosed with ODD or CD exhibit deficits in the processing of negative emotional stimuli (e.g., they do not respond in typical ways to others' fear and distress) (Frick & Viding, 2009; Loeber et al., 2009) and differences in sensitivity to reward and punishment (Fairchild et al., 2009). In addition to these types of neuropsychological deficits, high negative emotionality and poor emotion regulation are risk factors (Calkins & Keane, 2009; Cole, Hall, & Radzioch, 2009). Eisenberg and Fabes (1992) present a causal model (of aggression) focused on the interaction of emotionality and emotion regulation. In their model, reactive aggression is the result of high negative emotionality and problematic regulation, whereas proactive aggression is the result of low emotionality and problematic regulation.

Increased risk is also associated with a number of cognitive factors. These include lower overall intelligence, language deficits, and poor executive functions (Barker et al., 2011; Frick & Viding, 2009; Pajer et al., 2008; Raine et al., 2005). The often comorbid diagnosis of ADHD, however, makes executive function deficits difficult to tie specifically to ODD (Crick & Dodge, 1994, 1996). Deficits in moral reasoning have also been noted (Arsenio & Lemerise, 2004). With respect to aggression in particular, Bandura (1986) identified three components of social cognition that predict aggression: self-efficacy (i.e., the belief in one's ability to be aggressive); outcome expectations (i.e., belief that aggression will result in positive outcomes); and outcome values (i.e., the perceived desirability of outcomes).

As noted in the earlier section on bullying, we need to take into account cognitive factors that reflect impairment as well as cognitive factors that are associated with an ability to exploit the social environment. Most research to date has focused on deficits in social information processing and **impaired social cognition**, with less accurate and more hostile/aggressive interpretations of everyday social information (Card, 2011; Crick & Dodge, 1994). Other research, consistent with recent efforts to understand callous–unemotional traits, emphasizes that some children and adolescents "perceive their social worlds quite accurately, and use that knowledge to their personal advantage" (Arsenio & Lemerise, 2001, p. 60; Sutton et al., 1999).

Behavior-related risks involve impulsivity and deficits in the domain of effortful control (Burke et al., 2002; Frick & Morris, 2004). The negative consequences of impulsivity are heightened by the presence of characteristics such as being daring (i.e., the enjoyment of exciting, risky, and possibly dangerous activities) (Farrington & West, 1993; Lahey & Waldman, 2003) or being disinhibited (Iacono et al., 2003; Kagan, Reznick, & Snidman, 1988). Effortful control appears especially important for boys (Karreman, van Tuijl, van Aken, & Dekovic, 2009) and for less guilt-prone children (Kochanska, Barry, Jimenez, Hollatz, & Woodard, 2009). Coupled with high negative emotionality, or angry rumination, self-control becomes even more important (Denson, DeWall, & Finkel, 2012; Eisenberg, 2009). Overall, these are youth with fewer coping skills and resources.

Temperament and personality factors are also associated with increased risk. Investigators have identified a combination of emotionality and high

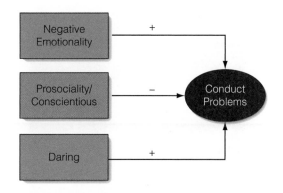

FIGURE 10:4 Temperament dimensions and disruptive behavior problems.
Source: Lahey and Waldman (2003).

activity levels as potentially problematic (Stringaris, Maughan, & Goodman, 2010); others have argued that "the temperamental deficits in different aspects of emotional reactivity could make it more difficult for a child to develop appropriate levels of guilt, empathy, and other dimensions of conscience" (Frick & Viding, 2009, p. 1117). Lahey and his colleagues have presented temperament data in a straightforward model, with negative emotionality and daring positively associated with externalizing behavior, and prosociality negatively associated (see Fig. 10:4). A dual-pathway model has also been described, in which two dimensions of temperament—poor emotional and behavioral control and low reactivity to fear—contribute to the emergence of psychopathy (Fowles & Dindo, 2009).

The personality characteristic receiving the most theoretical and empirical attention is the callous–unemotional construct. Callous–unemotional traits are associated with significant stability over time and more severe and more aggressive conduct disorder (Frick & Viding, 2009; Kroneman, Hipwell, Loeber, Koot, & Pardini, 2010; Obradovic, Pardini, Long, & Loeber, 2007; Waschbusch, Walsh, Andrade, King, & Carrey, 2007). Related to callousness is the personality construct of psychopathy (Lynam et al., 2005; Salekin et al., 2005). Several dimensions of psychopathy have been observed in adolescents: the callous–unemotional trait, impulsivity, and narcissism (Frick, Bodin, & Barry, 2000; Pauletti, Menon, Menon, Tobin, & Perry, 2012), with different studies suggesting various relations among psychopathy, conduct disorder, and normally developing personality (Espelage, Mebane, & Adams, 2004; Lynam et al., 2005; Lynam & Gudonis, 2005).

Another individual characteristic associated with externalizing problems is early puberty (Graber, Lewinsohn, Seeley, & Brooks-Gunn, 1997; Keenan et al., 1999). Adolescents who experience early puberty in the context of harsh parenting and in an at-risk neighborhood are more likely to exhibit conduct problems (Burt, McGue, DeMarte, Krueger, & Iacono, 2006; Ge, Brody, Conger, Simons, & Murry, 2002). Witnessing domestic violence and being exposed to community violence are also important risk factors for CD (Jaffee, Moffitt, Caspi, Taylor, & Arseneault, 2002; Pearce, Jones, Schwab-Stone, & Ruchkin, 2003).

The impact of gender has been repeatedly discussed in connection with oppositional defiant disorder and conduct disorder. Boys are overrepresented in conduct-disordered populations for a variety of reasons, including lower levels of prosociality, higher levels of impulsivity, and genetic influences on the timing of puberty (Cross, Copping, & Campbell, 2011; Lahey & Waldman, 2003). In early childhood, measures of decreased sociability predict externalizing behaviors for boys; measures of low compliance are predictive for girls (Lahey et al., 2006).

Overall, in general terms, Lahey and Waldman (2003) focus on the notion of **antisocial propensity** to explain the collection of child characteristics that increases the likelihood of conduct disorder. The factors that underlie antisocial propensity in the early years include emotion variables, cognitive abilities, and temperament styles. Those that become more important during adolescence include peer relationships and other social variables.

Parent and Family Factors

Parent and family factors include parent characteristics (e.g., genetic background, personality, and psychopathology), parenting attitudes and practices, and relationship variables. The direct and indirect impact of parents on the development of most instances of early and later externalizing disorders cannot be overestimated. Keeping in mind that genetic and environmental factors exert ongoing influences on children, adolescents, and relationships (Elkins, McGue, & Iacono, 1997; Neiderhiser et al., 2004), we can begin to think carefully about the continuity of antisocial behavior, aggression, and conduct problems across multiple generations (Smith & Farrington, 2004) and the "double whammy" of high-risk genes and high-risk environments (Jaffee, Moffitt, Caspi, & Taylor, 2003, p. 109).

Depression in either mothers or fathers increases the risk for conduct disorder (Kim-Cohen, Moffitt, Taylor, Pawlby, & Caspi, 2005; Ohannessian et al., 2005). Antisocial personality disorder (ASPD) and/or substance abuse in fathers are frequently cited risks (Frick & Loney, 2002; Loukas, Zucker, Fitzgerald, & Krull, 2003). Depression in mothers coupled with ASPD in fathers is another high-risk combination (Marmorstein & Iacono, 2004). Parental psychopathology has both direct (e.g., genetic) and indirect effects (e.g., marital conflict, family dysfunction and instability, and poor parenting) that impact child and adolescent adjustment (Becker, Stuewig, Herrera, & McCloskey, 2004; Jester et al., 2005). Some children and adolescents appear to be even more harmed than others by marital and family conflict and chaos (Button et al., 2005; Klahr, McGue, Iacono, & Burt, 2011); being a girl and positive relationships with siblings or friends may moderate this risk (Schwartz, Dodge, Pettit, Bates, & Conduct Problems Prevention Research Group, 2000). However, siblings may also collude together to "promote deviance and undermine parenting" (Bullock & Dishion, 2002).

Parenting practices such as harsh and coercive punishments have also been identified as causal factors (Deater-Deckard & Dodge, 1997; Stormshak, Bierman, McMahon, Lengua, & Conduct Problems Prevention Research Group, 2000). Data on physical punishment suggest that the association between physical punishment and child aggression is somewhat moderated by cultural norms, but even so, more frequent, more intense physical punishments are tied to both aggression and anxiety (Lansford et al., 2005; Lansford, Wager, Bates, Dodge, & Pettit, 2012). The kinds of negative parenting described in the coercive model emphasize the frequent coercive practices, infrequent positive parenting, and rigid, noncontingent environments that at-risk children experience. Indeed, Patterson et al. (2010) assert that there is "a direct path from antisocial parent to antisocial child behavior; this path was fully mediated by ineffective parenting practices" (p. 957).

Neglectful or indulgent parenting has also been associated with externalizing problems (Steinberg, Blatt-Eisengart, & Cauffman, 2006). These forms of negative parenting, including lack of warmth and regard, have been observed throughout the child's early and later years and are similar for groups of conduct-disordered European American and

Lack of parental monitoring is one link to adolescent conduct problems.

African American children (Campbell, Shaw, & Gilliom, 2000; Caspi et al., 2004; Kim et al., 2003).

Parental permissiveness and poor monitoring of adolescents and their activities have received growing theoretical and research attention (Brody, 2003; Burke et al., 2008; Dishion & Bullock, 2002), with links observed between lack of monitoring and conduct disorder (Laird, Pettit, Dodge, & Bates, 2003). Conversely, parental involvement has been identified as a protective factor; so has religiosity (Pearce et al., 2003). In fact, "adolescents from authoritative homes are more susceptible to prosocial peer pressure (e.g., pressure to do well in school) but less susceptible to antisocial peer pressure (e.g., pressure to use illicit drugs and alcohol)" (Collins et al., 2000, p. 227). Appropriate monitoring may be especially important in problematic, high-risk neighborhoods (Beyers, Bates, Pettit, & Dodge, 2003). Differences in parenting practices related to ethnicity have also been correlated with CD (Lansford, Deater-Deckard, Dodge, Bates, & Pettit, 2004). Finally, the community context of parenting is a key variable in the emergence or prevention of CD (Broidy et al., 2003; Pinderhughes, Nix, Foster, Jones, & Conduct Problems Prevention Research Group, 2001).

Interactions between child characteristics (such as gender or temperament) and parent characteristics may also contribute to the emergence of disruptive and conduct-disordered behavior. For example, sons and daughters who display challenging behaviors may elicit differentially effective discipline from parents (Burke et al., 2002; Burt, Krueger, McGue, & Iacono, 2003; Keiley, Lofthouse, Bates, Dodge, & Pettit, 2003). In another example, the experience of marital conflict may be especially problematic for children high on physiological reactivity (El-Sheikh et al., 2009). And, as noted earlier in the chapter, several investigations have explored the bidirectional influences of parenting and the development of conscience. According to Frick and Viding (2009), uninhibited preschoolers display well-developing conscience if they experience consistent discipline. In contrast, the "underarousal exhibited by fearless children may require parents to incorporate stronger methods of socialization that bring arousal levels into an optimal range for the child to internalize parental norms for prosocial behavior" (p. 1116). This approach is consistent with Blair's (1997, 2005) work on moral socialization. However, parental use of power assertion needs to be understood in the context of parent–child relationships. For instance, children with insecure attachments respond with resentment and oppositional behavior to coercive parenting; this resentment may itself predict externalizing behavior (Kochanska, Barry, Stellern, & O'Bleness, 2009). It is also important to keep in mind that there are some data suggesting that the impact of child behaviors on parenting may be greater than the impact of parenting on child behaviors (Burke et al., 2008).

Peer Factors

Peers and peer relationships have a notable impact on both the development and the later improvement or deterioration of oppositional defiant disorder, conduct disorder, and antisocial behavior (Adams, Bukowski, & Bagwell, 2005; Kupersmidt & DeRosier, 2004; Lansford, Criss, Pettit, Dodge, & Bates, 2003). Various forms of peer difficulties need to be considered, including difficulty forming and keeping relationships, aggression and bullying, and peer rejection. Related to the emergence of psychopathology, some common factors underlie many types of peer difficulties. For example, deficits in social cognition are likely to negatively influence relationships; these deficits are reflected in children and adolescents who misinterpret others' social intentions, who display more incompetent problem solving during peer conflicts, or who are inaccurate in predicting the outcomes of their own negative behaviors.

Laursen, Hafen, Rubin, Booth-LaForce, and Rose-Krasnor (2010) describe the distinctive difficulties of disagreeable youth (who are different from aggressive, victimized, and withdrawn youth). Disagreeable youth display an inability to get along with others, because they are high in negative emotions, stubborn, self-centered, and argumentative. Stated directly, "the rude and the obnoxious make poor friends" (p. 96). As expected, disagreeableness is associated with poor individual and interpersonal adjustment.

Peer dislike, rejection, and victimization often begin early and are a key predictor of later problems (Dodge et al., 2003; Miller-Johnson, Coie, Maumary Gremaud, Bierman, & Conduct Problems Prevention Research Group, 2002; Rose, Swenson, & Carlson, 2004). One of the most common reasons for rejection is angry or aggressive behavior. Hughes et al. (2001) describe children who "act nasty" when frustrated. Other rejected children behave aggressively following exclusion or ridicule (Werner & Crick, 2004). Boys with histories of externalizing problems are more reactive than other boys and appear to hold grudges longer (Waschbusch et al., 2002). And some rejected boys become even more aggressive with ongoing rejection (Guerra, Asher, & DeRosier, 2004).

One of the most negative consequences of peer rejection is that rejected children and adolescents associate with other rejected children and adolescents. Deviant groups emerge, and pathways to conduct disorder evolve (Brendgen, Vitaro, & Bukowski, 2000a, 2000b). Coercion and deviancy training are two processes that explain deteriorating pathways (Snyder et al., 2008); these are examples of **peer contagion**. There may be important gender differences. Both antisocial boys and girls experience rejection by peers, but boys end up associating with more deviant peers with somewhat different developmental outcomes (Van Lier, Vitaro, Wanner, Vuijk, & Crijnen, 2005). Friendships with deviant peers do not substitute for friendships with typically developing adolescents. The quality of the relationships is different (Dishion, Eddy, Haas, & Li, 1997; Poulin, Dishion, & Hass, 1999), and being part of a delinquent group exacerbates one's own delinquent tendencies (Lacourse, Nagin, Tremblay, Vitaro, & Claes, 2003). Violent behavior and gang activity are further steps on a worsening trajectory (Lahey, Gordon, Loeber, Stouthamer-Loeber, & Farrington, 1999). Gang association and gang membership are related to aggression, conduct problems, drug-related activity, and violent crime; this is a "powerful social influence" to understand and address (Lahey & Waldman, 2003).

Sociocultural Factors

Many studies of larger environmental variables such as ethnicity, socioeconomic status, and neighborhoods provide context to current conceptualizations of ODD and CD. For example, once SES and neighborhood factors (such as neighborhood disadvantage) are accounted for, there is little or no influence of race or ethnicity (Burke et al., 2002; Goodnight et al., 2011; Stouthamer-Loeber, Loeber, Wei, Farrington, & Wikstroem, 2002). SES is inversely related to CD, even though the majority of youth from financially disadvantaged backgrounds do not exhibit disorders (Lahey & Waldman, 2003). Combinations of risk factors dramatically increase the likelihood of CD. Hypotheses exploring the social learning of conduct disorder emphasize the transactions among high-crime neighborhoods, poor parenting, delinquent peer groups, and lack of economic resources (Chung & Steinberg, 2006; Guerra, Huesmann, & Spindler, 2003; Lahey & Waldman, 2003; Lynam et al., 2000). For some adolescents, neighborhood cohesion buffers the effects of poor parenting (Silk, Sessa, Sheffield Morris, Steinberg, & Avenevoli, 2004). Examining gene-by-environment interactions provides a last source of data on the etiology of ODD and CD. According to Lahey and Waldman (2003), "genetic influences on conduct problems can be muted by favorable social learning environments." Studies of children adopted by well-adjusted parents show lower levels of CD. Also, "different individuals respond in different ways to the social factors that encourage conduct problems." Some adolescents move toward problematic behaviors, peers, and activities; others move away.

Assessment and Diagnosis

Although there have been changes in diagnostic criteria for ODD and CD, patterns of externalizing behavior are usually observed more quickly compared to patterns of internalizing behavior (Delligatti, Akin-Little, & Little, 2003). Given the individual impairment associated with ODD and CD and the effects of externalizing children and adolescents on their families, teachers, peers, neighborhoods, and society, it is imperative to identify early and identify correctly. Indeed, early screening in kindergarten, with ratings made by parents and teachers, can identify children at risk; this makes early prevention efforts possible (Jones et al., 2002). Before ODD or CD is diagnosed, careful distinctions need to be made between more common and developmentally expected problems and more severe psychopathology (Willoughby, Chalmers, & Busseri, 2004). Multiple instruments and evidence-based assessments, including observations, parent and teacher ratings, self-reports, and lab tests, are essential (Collett, Ohan, & Myers, 2003; Malone, 2000; McMahon & Frick, 2005).

Parents, teachers, and children provide data in a variety of ways and for a variety of purposes. Correlations among these different informants are sometimes low, but each contributes information that helps to illustrate the clinical picture (Owens & Hoza, 2003; Youngstrom, Loeber, & Stouthamer-Loeber, 2000). Taking note of the different settings in which symptoms are displayed—at home or school, in the clinic or the community—is also necessary (Gadow & Nolan, 2002). Parent reports must sometimes be interpreted cautiously, but parental perspectives on functioning in the home and on especially problematic behaviors such as aggression can be very useful. Teacher ratings are also important and are sometimes better predictors of degree of impairment (Flanagan et al., 2003; Mattison, Gadow, Sprafkin, & Nolan, 2002) and are better predictors of impairment in children (Hart et al., 1994).

Children and adolescents themselves should also be routinely included in the assessment process. Self-reporting by children and adolescents about behavioral difficulties seems an unlikely source of good data. However, young children and adolescents provide useful information (Arseneault, Kim-Cohen, Taylor, Caspi, & Moffitt, 2005; Gadow et al., 2002; Hartung, McCarthy, Milich, & Martin, 2005). Keep in mind that even though most adolescents do not refer themselves for treatment, many with difficulties, particularly peer difficulties, do want help (Asher & Paquette, 2003).

The most salient issues related to differential diagnosis focus on distinctions among CD, ODD, and ADHD. It is possible to differentiate CD from each of these other disorders, but clinicians must understand that ODD, CD, and ADHD may co-occur, with appropriately separate diagnoses (Beauchaine, Hinshaw, & Pang, 2010; Burt et al., 2003; Kim & Miklowitz, 2002; Waschbusch, 2002). CD may also be comorbid with either anxiety or depression (Boylan, Vaillancourt, Boyle, & Szatmari, 2007; Loeber et al., 2009). Questioning about depression is especially important because the combination of CD and depression involves much higher risk for substance abuse and suicidality; girls are more likely to display this combination (Loeber et al., 2000).

Intervention

Because oppositional defiant disorder, conduct disorder, and antisocial behavior are so disturbing to adults and so debilitating for children and adolescents, there has been significant work focused on prevention and treatment for many years (Eyberg, Nelson, & Boggs, 2008; Reid, Patterson, & Snyder, 2003). Given the preceding sections, it may seem as if poor outcomes for struggling youth are inevitable. But Dodge et al. (2008) insist otherwise, stating "it is premature to conclude that an early-starting antisocial 5-year-old is unequivocally destined for a life-persistent path toward violent outcomes. Although the risk is substantial, it is by no means certain. Trajectories can be deflected at each subsequent era in development, through interactions with peers, schools, and parents along the way" (p. 1922). There are compelling data that well-timed, individualized, and comprehensive interventions for externalizing disorders are both successful and cost effective (Burke et al., 2002; Frick & Viding, 2009). Comprehensive interventions such as the Incredible Years program, the Fast Track model, and the Early Risers program include several components and take into account both child-treatment compatibility and adult-treatment compatibility (Bierman et al., 2002; Greene & Doyle, 1999; Jensen & MTA Cooperative Group, 2002; Webster-Stratton & Herman, 2010; see Box 10:2). Interventions are most likely to be useful when there is a reasonable match between the clinical presentation and various treatment components. Examples of such matches include children's social skills deficits paired with cognitive-behavioral techniques, poor parenting

skills paired with parent training and support, and damaged parent–child relationships paired with family therapy.

Child Treatments

Given the difficulties observed in children and adolescents struggling with externalizing disorders, it is not surprising that willingness to participate in treatment must be addressed. Adolescents especially may be reluctant to become engaged in psychotherapy (Cicchetti & Rogosch, 2002; Weisz & Hawley, 2002). It is essential, then, to quickly address the motivation for change and personal responsibility for change. For example, in designing treatments, clinicians may want to allow an adolescent some responsibility for goal setting, and decisions about discipline and rule breaking (DeRoma, Lassiter, & Davis, 2004). These efforts may foster motivation, attendance, and treatment adherence (Nock & Kazdin, 2005). In addition, a strong therapeutic alliance must be established that includes both the child and/or adolescent and his or her parents; the roles and responsibilities of all participants must be clear (Kazdin, Marciano, & Whitley, 2005).

Child treatment targets emotional, cognitive, and behavioral difficulties. Specific cognitive-behavioral interventions address deficits in the child's information-processing and problem-solving repertoires, including executive function impairments, problematic peer relationships, and difficulties at home. Greene et al.'s (2004) Collaborative Problem Solving and Kazdin's (2005) problem-solving skills training are examples of effective cognitive-behavioral treatments. Problem-solving skills training involves a focus on cognitive skills such as interpreting normal peer behavior as less threatening (Thomas, 2006) and social skills such as learning scripts for how to join a group of peers already interacting (DeRosier & Marcus, 2005). The Stop Now and Plan (SNAP) Program also emphasizes cognitive behavioral strategies, with separate groups for boys and girls (Koegl, Farrington, Augimeri, & Day, 2008). The goals of all of these programs involve improving social competency and enhancing prosociality. Developing and supporting new relationships with prosocial peers is also important (Frick & Viding, 2009).Understanding the impact of neurological dysfunction on adolescent problem-solving abilities may enhance cognitively based treatment outcomes (Coolidge, DenBoer, & Segal, 2004).

BOX 10:2 CLINICAL PERSPECTIVES

The Early Risers Program

The Early Risers program, originally developed at the University of Minnesota and now implemented in communities across the country, is a multi-component, high-intensity intervention program that targets aggressive elementary school children at risk for developing significant conduct problems (August, Lee, Bloomquist, Realmuto, & Hektner, 2004; Bernat, August, Hektner, & Bloomquist, 2007). This innovative program is based on the premise that early, comprehensive intervention, sustained over time and across settings, can change the developmental pathway for at-risk children from one characterized by destructive and maladaptive behaviors to one characterized by resilience and success. The intervention includes social skills training; tutoring in reading and math; behavioral group therapy for aggressive, disruptive, and noncompliant behavior; and parent support services, including consultation and brief intervention for acute family problems. Sessions are based in schools or community centers and emphasize communication, consistency, and coordination of the intervention approach throughout the child's environment (school, community, and home). The enhanced sense of general competence the children develop in the program has been shown to improve their self-image, decision-making, and problem-solving skills. Outcomes for individuals completing 5 years of continuous intervention show sustained improvement (Bernat et al., 2007). Barriers to effective treatment and positive outcomes include poor collaboration between agencies and schools, transportation difficulties, and high staff turnover; these factors must be accounted for and addressed in planning and treatment stages (August, Bloomquist, Lee, Realmuto, & Hektner, 2006). Predictors of more effective implementation of the Early Risers Program include the use of Web-based technologies to monitor adherence to the treatment protocol (Lee et al., 2008) and specific clinician characteristics such as confidence in the program, conscientiousness, and flexible coping skills (Klimes-Dougan et al., 2009). The Early Risers Program is included in the U.S. Department of Health and Human Services list of effective, evidence-based interventions for disruptive behavior disorders (HHS, 2011).

For young children with temperamental vulnerabilities, these risks can be offset by either the development of emotion regulation skills or emotional aspects of conscience. Matching child temperament and parenting style to therapeutically exploit individual differences may be key to reducing negative outcomes (Frick & Morris, 2004; Kochanska, 1995, 1997). Anger management strategies for older children emphasize identifying emotion triggers, learning how to cope with intense emotion, engaging in role playing, and achieving stress inoculation (Lochman, Boxmeyer, Powell, Barry, & Pardini, 2010; Weisz, 2004). Recent research has focused on cognitive perspective taking, in order to foster empathy (Frick & Viding, 2009). With respect to treatment focused on personality characteristics, such as callous–unemotional traits, researchers have emphasized that these characteristics are at least somewhat malleable (Frick & Viding, 2009; Kolko & Pardini, 2010). Overemphasizing the unchangeable nature of personality characteristics and behaviors may lead to a focus on punishment and segregation rather than psychotherapy (Tolan & Titus, 2009).

For children and adolescents diagnosed with conduct disorder, there is some data suggesting that mood stabilizers may be useful, but overall there is not a lot of work on medication management for CD (Burke et al., 2002; Donovan et al., 2003). When additional disorders (such as ADHD) are present, medication plus therapy improves outcomes (Burke et al., 2002). However, even with successful treatments, with meaningful decreases in externalizing behaviors, many children and adolescents still struggle (Kolko & Pardini, 2010). The hurtful dimension of ODD predicts ongoing severe problems following treatment (Kolko & Pardini, 2010).

Parent Treatments

For decades, most of the interventions focused on parent training—particularly behaviorally oriented parent training, frequently referred to as parent management training (PMT). There is overwhelming support for the role of this training in the treatment of externalizing disorders in children and adolescents (Forgatch & Patterson, 2010). The goals of PMT, across all variations of PMT, involve decreasing coercive interactions, increasing positive parenting, and increasing compliant behavior and prosociality. The Oregon model is based on social interaction learning processes and "includes two contingency mechanisms for change. The first mechanism describes interaction within the family, primarily negative reinforcement provided to children for deviant behavior. The second mechanism involves contingencies in the social environment outside the home, primarily from peers" (Patterson et al., 2010, p. 950). According to Patterson et al., "strengthening parenting sets in motion an avalanche of enduring effects that generalize throughout and beyond the family" (p. 949). That is, changes in target behaviors lead to changes in other behaviors, change in one family member (parent or child) leads to change in other family members, and changes in families' social interactional patterns lead to new social communities.

Greene and colleagues' Collaborative Problem Solving therapy provides detailed feedback to parents about their behaviors. For instance, parents can respond to children's defiance by asserting their power, by removing their request or expectation, or by collaborative problem solving. Even when parents recognize that the last option is a better choice, they may not know how to act effectively (Greene et al., 2003). Parents may need to learn how to give instructions to their children (e.g., employing a firm directive rather than a pleading question) and how to create after-school schedules to prevent nightly battles over homework. Monitoring the whereabouts and well-being of children is another specific skill that may need to be taught (Jones et al., 2003).

Eyberg's (1988, 2005) Parent–Child Interaction Therapy (PCIT) is an empirically supported, developmentally informed intervention for children with disruptive behavior problems and their parents. PCIT recognizes that the parent–child relationship provides a powerful context for understanding and changing behavioral patterns in young children. Using a variety of techniques, the parent and therapist collaborate to understand the nature and effects of the parent's behavior on the child, to discover and practice new ways of interacting with the child, and to acknowledge both the problematic aspects of the parent's behavior and her/

his capacity to modify those behaviors to change the child's behavior and experience of the world. Together, the parent and therapist work to create specific improvements in the child's behavior as well as a broader foundation of security and satisfaction in the parent–child relationship upon which the child can organize a more adaptive and competent developmental trajectory (Yates, Burt, & Troy, 2011).

In addition to treatment components that focus on parents' interactions with their children, some parents will require other types of individual support. The treatment of parent psychopathology is especially important. Less immediately compelling, but no less essential, are efforts to increase positive parenting characteristics such as optimism and warmth in order to promote good outcomes for both children and parents (Jones et al., 2002a; Patterson & Fisher, 2002; Sheeber, Biglan, Metzler, & Taylor, 2002).

As noted, there is clear empirical support for these interventions for both children and adolescents.Indeed, "effective parenting is the most powerful way to reduce adolescent problem behaviors" (Kumpfer & Alvarado, 2003, p. 457), although improvements do not always bring adolescents into the normal range of functioning (Burke et al., 2002; Thomas, 2006). Both parents and families in treatment have high drop-out rates; designing one-session interventions, therefore, may be a meaningful therapeutic approach (Lim, Stormshak, & Dishion, 2005).

Comprehensive, Peer, School, and Residential Programs

The research is overwhelming that intensive, multimodal approaches work best. One example of such an approach is multisystemic therapy, based on Henggeler's research (Henggeler & Lee, 2003; Weisz, 2004). The mechanisms and direction of change in multisystemic therapy include the following: adherence to treatment model → improved family relationships → decreased delinquent associations → decreased delinquent behavior. Good outcomes have been repeatedly demonstrated with multisystemic therapy, including 18 months following the end of treatment (Butler, Baruch, Hickey, & Fonagy, 2011). The benefits of multidomain interventions are that achievements in specific domains can mitigate risks in others. In other words, risks associated with adverse neighborhood contexts can be lessened by positive parenting; risks related to harsh and inconsistent parenting can be lessened by success at school; and risks due to difficult early school experiences can be lessened by parents who communicate and support their children (Dodge et al., 2008).

Peer groups for conduct-disordered youth are common. One critical caveat about treatments that involve groups of conduct-disordered adolescents relates to peer contagion. **Peer contagion** involves the sharing of information about conduct problems, including drugs, weapons, targets of negative behaviors, and immediate and powerful reinforcement of deviancy (Boxer, Guerra, Huesmann, & Morales, 2005; Burke et al., 2002; Dodge et al., 2006; Gifford-Smith, Dodge, Dishion, & McCord, 2005). Thinking back to descriptions of the role of deviant peers in eliciting and maintaining conduct-disordered behavior, it is not hard to imagine the likely effects of including deviant peers in treatment settings. Although "proponents believe that deviant youth can empathize with each other, learn valuable lessons from each other, and provide real-life interactions for each other that are grist for intervention," numerous clinical trials indicate not only a lessening of positive impact but also increasing adverse impacts, with worse outcomes compared to control groups (Dodge et al., 2006). Participants with lower initial levels of delinquent behavior are at particular risk (Dishion, Bullock, & Granic, 2002; Macgowen & Wagner, 2005).

Well-intentioned adults need to be increasingly cautious about who to include in treatment groups (which include residential interventions, group homes, and group therapies such as social skills training), because "perversely, much of what we do as public policy is to segregate deviant youth from their mainstream peers and assign them to settings with other deviant youth" (Dodge et al., 2006, p. 3). "The best empirical evidence suggests that the first solutions are to eliminate the routine practices of tracking low-performing youth into isolated classrooms, mandatory grade retention, self-contained classrooms for unruly students in special education, group in-school suspension, placement into alternative schools, and expulsion" (Dodge et al., 2006, p. 11). In order to support children and adolescents with conduct disorders, prevention and treatment programs must be reworked to focus on adults (parents and teachers) and nondeviant peers, and changes must be made across disciplines, in mental health clinics, educational and school settings, the juvenile justice system, and community organizations (Dodge et al., 2006).

School-based programs are very important for some children and have shown success in reducing coercive and antisocial behaviors (Barrera et al., 2002; Leff, Costigan, & Power, 2004; Webster-Stratton, Reid, & Stoolmiller, 2008). Community interventions designed to promote effective discipline techniques and decrease parent–child conflicts supplement individual, family, and school plans (Bradley et al., 2003).

Out-of-home treatments are increasing, with family-style residential care and token economies showing good outcomes for some adolescents (Field, Nash, Handwerk, & Friman, 2004). Specialized foster care may be an option (Dodge, Dishion, & Lansford, 2006). Military-style residential programs ("boot camps") can work, but their efficacy may depend on adolescent willingness to participate (Weis, Wilson, & Whitemarsh, 2005). Both boys and girls improve in these settings, but they appear less useful to girls with a history of maltreatment and comorbid internalizing disorders (Weis, Whitemarsh, & Wilson, 2005).

Prevention

In the hopes of minimizing future treatment needs, prevention efforts allow for the possibility of reducing the rates and/or severity of ODD, CD, and antisocial behavior; universal, targeted, and individual strategies have been pursued (Burke et al., 2002). One example of a universal measure that has been effective in decreasing disruptive behaviors in the classroom is the school-based part of the Fast Track intervention. Other school-based interventions focus on self-control, problem solving, and peer relationships (Bierman et al., 2007; Greenberg et al., 2003; Van Lier, Vuijk, & Crijnen, 2005). In many of these school-based programs, parents and families choose to participate, and levels of engagement in the therapeutic process differ. Programs designed to prevent bullying, as described earlier in the chapter, are increasingly incorporated in school curricula in many countries and cultures (Olweus, 2005); specific components of such programs focus on social competence and a positive school environment (Orpinas & Horne, 2006a).

An example of a targeted measure involves screening high-risk children in preschool and primary grades before ODD problems have become entrenched (Jones, Dodge, Foster, Nix, & Conduct Problems Prevention Research Group, 2002). Targeted prevention might also be directed at promoting social competence and social skills in young children, thereby lessening the peer problems that are elicited by children's early externalizing behaviors. The younger the children, the more likely it is that negative cascades are minimized (Bornstein et al., 2010; Shaw, Dishion, Supplee, Gardner, & Arends, 2006; Van Lier & Koot, 2010). Parents are also the recipients of targeted interventions, with programs designed to enhance maternal responsiveness and positive parenting in at-risk groups (Kochanska et al., 2008). To be especially useful, these efforts also should be well-timed, with programs related to parent discipline offered during the child's preschool years.

Several prevention programs emphasize the need to promote child competence in as many ways as possible (Brody, Kim, Murry, & Brown, 2004).

Youth development programs, designed to foster adolescent–adult relationships, also show long-term positive outcomes (Roth, Brooks-Gunn, Murray, & Foster, 1998). Combining these types of programs with child, parent, school, and community programs, with multiple options for maximum effect, is a further improvement. One example of a community prevention program is the "Overcoming the Odds" study, which compares African American adolescents' participation in gangs versus community organizations. One key aspect of this successful effort is connecting developmental strengths displayed by the adolescents with supports from their ecological contexts (Taylor et al., 2005). Overall, there are nine characteristics associated with effective prevention efforts: a comprehensive approach, a theory-driven model, a well-trained staff, varied methods, sufficient intervention intensity, opportunities for positive relationships, appropriate timing, sociocultural relevance, and outcome evaluation (Nation et al., 2003).

Key Terms

Prosocial behaviors (p.163)
Conscience (p.163)
Bullying (p.166)
Oppositional defiant disorder (p.168)
Conduct disorder (p.170)
Callous–unemotional characteristics (p.170)
Child-onset subtype (p.170)
Adolescent-onset subtype (p.170)
Life-course persistent trajectory (p.170)
Adolescence-limited trajectory (p.170)
Aggression (p.170)
Instrumental aggression (p.170)
Reactive aggression (p.171)
Overt aggression (p.171)
Covert aggression (p.171)
Overt pathway (p.173)
Covert pathway (p.173)
Authority conflict pathway (p.173)
Coercion model (p.173)
Transactional model (p.173)
Developmental cascade models (p.174)
Impaired social cognition (p.176)
Antisocial propensity (p.177)
Peer contagion (p.179)

Chapter Summary

- Important developmental tasks across emotional, cognitive, and behavioral domains are critical to the formation of typical self-regulatory and prosocial skills.
- The social context for the development of self-regulatory and prosocial skills is anchored in the parent–child relationship, especially in early development, and then widens over time to include peer- and other social relationships. This broadening social context can serve as either a protective or risk factor in relation to the development of disruptive behavior problems.
- Bullying is characterized by negative actions intended to cause harm, that are repeated over time, and that involve a power differential between bully and victim.
- Oppositional defiant disorder (ODD) is characterized by a sustained pattern of negativistic, hostile, and defiant behavior. Irritability and impaired social cognition are also common symptoms of ODD.
- Although most children diagnosed with ODD do not go on to develop more severe forms of the disorder, ODD does significantly increase the risk for later conduct disorder.

- The presence of ADHD along with ODD is associated with a more negative prognosis.
- Conduct disorder (CD) is differentiated from ODD by the severity of the externalizing behaviors and the degree of impairment associated with the disorder.
- Conduct disorders are further differentiated by patterns of externalizing behaviors and whether the onset of the disorder occurs during childhood or adolescence.
- Callous–unemotional characteristics, such as lack of empathy or remorse, are associated with greater continuity of problems throughout development.
- Adolescence onset of conduct disorder is significantly more common than childhood onset.
- A number of etiological risk factors may contribute to the development of ODD and CD, including characteristics of the child (such as temperament), quality of parenting, genetics, and environmental factors.
- The etiological complexity of ODD and the overlap with normal range negative behavior in childhood make assessment and diagnosis of ODD challenging.
- Because externalizing symptoms are usually identified more easily and earlier by observers, early diagnosis and intervention efforts are especially relevant for both ODD and CD.
- Differential diagnosis often focuses on the commonalities and distinctions among ODD, CD, and ADHD. Additionally, both ODD and CD may be comorbid with either anxiety or depression.
- Intervention approaches that are intensive, comprehensive, multimodal, and implemented early have been shown to be most effective.

11 Anxiety Disorders, Obsessive-Compulsive Disorder, and Somatic Symptom Disorders

IN A WORLD THAT can be realistically frightening (with adversity, violence, and natural disasters) and unpredictably threatening (with germs, spiders, or pain), many children and adolescents are diagnosed with anxiety-based disorders. Discussion of these disorders provides a useful illustration of the distinction between childhood problems and clinically significant disorders. Many children struggle with fears and worries that have a real, negative impact on daily functioning. For some children, taking a bath is a sudsy disaster because they are afraid of the water or of going down the drain. For other children, thunderstorms ruin a family's evening. Parents and mental health professionals need to take into account a variety of factors, including developmental context, the specific stimuli that elicit fear, and the degree of impairment, as they recognize, diagnose, and respond to children's anxiety-related problems and disorders.

Developmental Tasks and Challenges Related to Fears, Worries, and Emotion Regulation

We know that children feel, express, and control a variety of emotions and that emotional arousal is an integral component of emotional experiences. Ideally, emotional arousal is accompanied by emotion regulation, or emotion control, which involves the "modulation, toleration and endurance of emotions" (Denham, 1998, p. 148; see also Campos, Frankel, & Camras, 2004; Cole, Martin, & Dennis, 2004; Gross & Thompson, 2007). The regulation of difficult, negative, or intense emotions takes many forms, including emotion-focused strategies, cognitive strategies, and behavioral strategies. With age and experience, these strategies become more differentiated and more organized, and individual differences in children's capacity for emotion regulation become increasingly apparent (Cole & Hall, 2008; Southam-Gerow & Kendall, 2002; Thompson, 2001). Some of these individual differences must be understood in the context of psychological variables such as control (Chorpita, 2001) and sociocultural variables such as family socialization of emotion regulation, ethnicity, and poverty (Raver, 2004; Thompson & Meyer, 2007).

The process of **emotion regulation** (ER) itself unfolds over time. From birth, there is an ongoing balance of independent and coordinated ER (Campos et al., 2004; Cole et al., 2004). Although we think of infants and toddlers as mostly supported in their ER efforts by their caregivers (so that a mother may pick up and soothe a frightened child), babies also initiate ER by physically turning away from overwhelming stimulation or by cuddling with a special blanket. Preschoolers and young children are often ER partners with adults, as when a teacher and a child work together through an episode of anger. Older children and adolescents are usually expected to manage ER independently, so that an athlete on a team having a bad day might distract himself from looming fear or sadness in order to keep playing well during an important basketball game.

It is important to keep a couple of things in mind about the development of ER. First, as new strategies emerge, earlier strategies are not lost. We accumulate and organize strategies over the years, but sometimes (like the baby with the blanket) we still crawl under the covers for comfort. And, the simple idea that we move from dependency on others to independent ER, and that independent ER reflects optimal adjustment, is somewhat inaccurate. A more complex notion includes older children's and adolescents' capacities for independent ER but emphasizes the flexible use of a variety of ER strategies in different situations. Even well-adjusted adults sometimes seek comfort from others when afraid or anxious. Prominent child psychologists such as David Elkind (1994) suggest that ever-increasing demands for autonomy and self-reliance in youngsters are tied to changing cultural perspectives on childhood and childhood disorders. Earlier conceptions of children as innocent and in need of protection and direction have been replaced by current views of children as inherently skilled and competent. Elkind says, "While some of these demands have allowed children to demonstrate formerly unrecognized competencies, many others are age-inappropriate, overwhelming, and stressful" (p. 119) and increase risks for vulnerable youth.

Finally, with respect to normal development, it is important to emphasize the useful and adaptive nature of much of the anxiety experienced by children (Beesdo, Knappe, & Pine, 2009; Thompson, 2001). Wariness in the presence of strangers or on an unfamiliar bike path, or apprehension before an exam or a performance, provides children and adolescents with important information about the possibility of harm or the need to prepare for challenging activities. When signals are perceived and adjustments are made, anxiety usually diminishes quickly. Children who experience little or no anxiety may place themselves in risky or unsafe situations or fail to plan for upcoming events. So, in line with the fundamentally adaptive function of emotion, we are looking for a healthy balance in the amounts of anxiety experienced and in the situations in which anxiety is elicited and supports adaptation.

With this background information, we are able to better understand the fears and worries that are part of almost every child's life. The variety of fears and worries range from the relatively minor (such as getting poor grades, being sent to the principal, and having parents argue), to the more troubling (such as falling from high places or not being able to breathe), to the truly awful and dangerous (such as being hit by a car, getting burned in a fire, dying or seeing dead people, and being bombed or attacked) (Ollendick, Matson, & Helsel, 1985). Although discussions of anxiety do not always differentiate between fears and worries, the distinction provides added clarity. **Fears** are defined as anxieties elicited *in the presence of a specific stimulus*. **Worries** are defined as anxieties *about possible future events*.

Most children exhibit one or more fears during normal development (Bronson & Pankey, 1977; Lieberman, 1993; see Table 11:1). A predictable sequence can be observed, with initial increases in fears and worries related to the cognitive capacity to understand risk and imagine potential harm (Holaway, Rodebaugh, & Heimberg, 2006; Westenberg, Drewes, Goedhart, Siebelink, & Treffers, 2004; Muris, Merckelbach, Meesters, & van den Brand, 2002). With the growth of knowledge, self-confidence, and ER strategies, most fears decline with age (Craske, 1997; Gullone, King, & Ollendick, 2001). Both age-related changes and individual differences influence the number and nature of children's fears. Cognitive development is perhaps the most relevant. Children's increasing abilities to make distinctions between fantasy and reality and to recognize, understand, and control danger are noteworthy achievements (Gordon, King, Gullone, Muris, & Ollendick, 2007).

Biologically based sensitivity to certain kinds of emotional information (e.g., threat-related signals) is associated with both age-related changes and individual differences in brain–behavior relations (Leppanen & Nelson, 2012). Individual differences in overall temperament, shyness, and behavioral inhibition are also key factors related to the emergence of fears (Fox, Henderson, Marshall, Nichols, & Ghera, 2005). Gender also plays a role, with girls exhibiting more fears than boys (Craske, 1997; Gordon et al., 2007). Factors such as race, ethnicity, religion, and ecological context influence children's fears as well (Ingman, Ollendick, & Akande, 1999; Safren et al., 2000). Children from Africa, for instance, report higher levels of fears than children from the United States, China, or Australia; children from Christian backgrounds report higher

TABLE 11:1   Fears in Childhood
Toddlerhood Thunder, lightning, fire, water Darkness Nightmares Animals
4–5 years Death, dead people
6–7 years Strange, loud, or abrupt noises (e.g., animal noises, wind, and thunder) Ghosts, witches, or other supernatural beings Bodily injury Separation from parents and being lost Being alone at night Being hurt or rejected at school
7–8 years The dark and dark places Real-life catastrophes (e.g, kidnapping, floods, fires, war) Not being liked Being left out of family or school events Being hurt or rejected at school
8–9 years Personal humiliation Failure in school or play Being caught in a lie or misbehavior Being the victim of physical violence Parents fighting, separating, or being hurt
9–11 years Failure in school or sports Becoming sick Heights and sensations of vertigo (i.e., dizziness) Sinister people (e.g., killers and molesters)
11–13 years Failure in school, sports, or popularity Looking or acting strange Life-threatening illnesses or death Sex (attracting others, repelling others, being attacked) Being fooled or humiliated
Adapted from Philadelphia Child Guidance Center (1993) and Beesdo et al. (2009).

levels of fears than children from Muslim backgrounds (Ingman et al., 1999). Latino children, especially younger Latino children, report more fears compared to children of European American backgrounds (Varela & Hensley-Maloney, 2009). Exposure to media accounts of frightening events is another variable that may need to be taken into account.

In contrast to fears, worries involve somewhat more vague concerns about possible threats. The three most common types of worries are tied to health, school, and personal harm (Silverman, La Greca, & Wasserstein,

1995). In a sample of typically developing children, almost 70% reported worrying "now and then" (Muris, Meesters, Merckelbach, Sermon, & Zwakhalen, 1998). Preschoolers are worried most about imaginary and supernatural events, 5- and 6-year-olds by their physical well-being, and 8- to 12-year-olds by social and behavioral competence and psychological well-being (Muris et al., 1998). As with fears, age-related changes and individual differences are important. Girls, again, worry more than boys (Craske, 1997; Silverman et al., 1995). Latino children and African American children worry more than European American children (Silverman et al., 1995; Varela & Hensley-Maloney, 2009). Children who describe themselves as very inhibited also report more worries (Muris, Merckelbach, Wessel, & van de Ven, 1999).

In order to deal with their everyday fears and worries, children display a variety of effective and ineffective coping strategies. Emotional strategies (e.g., minimizing or maximizing facial expressions), cognitive strategies (e.g., thinking of something else, talking with others), and behavioral strategies (e.g., avoidance, asking for help) are all common (Denham, 1998; Gordon et al., 2007). The coordination and regulation of negative experiences also becomes more manageable over time (Zahn-Waxler, Klimes-Dougan, & Slattery, 2000).

For most children, specific fears and worries are distressing; now and then, they may make relationships, activities, and routines more difficult. In general, though, most anxieties are transient. Individual coping efforts, support from others, and time itself eventually lead to good adaptations. For some children, however, fears and worries are more problematic. For these children, fears and worries signal an anxiety disorder that is both painful and disabling. These children are the focus of the rest of the chapter.

Anxiety Disorders

Anxiety disorders are ubiquitous and are among the most frequently diagnosed psychopathologies in children, adolescents, and adults. Juxtaposed with these high rates of anxiety and impairment are relatively low rates of treatment (Chavira, Stein, Bailey, & Stein, 2004; Ollendick, Shortt, & Sander, 2005). These disorders have received considerable theoretical and empirical attention, and there are many excellent reviews available (Beesdo et al., 2009; Craske, 1997; Southam-Gerow & Chorpita, 2007; Walkup & Ginsburg, 2002). Anxiety disorders are internalizing disorders in which

Occasional anxiety and distress are normal-range responses to novelty and new situations for most children.

anxiety has gone from adaptive to pathological in terms of its intensity, duration, and pervasiveness. All of the anxiety disorders are characterized by inhibition and withdrawal, exaggerated and unrealistic fears and worries, overcontrol, and somatic symptoms; each also has detection of danger and/or avoidance of danger as a key feature. Most cases involve mild to moderate impairment in daily functioning (Beesdo et al., 2009; Langley, Bergman, McCracken, & Piacentini, 2004). Although there is underlying similarity, there are distinctive perceptions, thoughts, emotions, levels of arousal, behaviors, somatic symptoms, and effects on relationships that are associated with particular types of anxiety disorders (see Table 11:2).

In addition to the primary symptoms of anxiety, many children and adolescents also exhibit **anxiety sensitivity,** involving hypervigilance and attention to bodily sensations, a tendency to focus on weak or infrequent sensations, and a disposition to react to somatic sensations with distorted cognitions (Eley, Stirling, Ehlers, Gregory, & Clark, 2004). Anxiety sensitivity may be understood as a kind of distress tolerance, "where high anxiety sensitivity involves a decreased capacity to tolerate anxiety states and sensations and, conversely low anxiety sensitivity involves an increased tolerance" (Weems, 2011, p. 28). Developmental and sociocultural factors are important influences on individual differences in anxiety sensitivity (Weems, 2011).

Various epidemiological estimates of anxiety disorders in children range from 3% to 18%; rates in adolescence approach 20% (Albano, Chorpita, & Barlow, 2003; Cartwright-Hatton, McNicol, & Doubleday, 2006; Essau, Conradt, & Petermann, 1999a, 2000a,

TABLE 11:2	Clinical Comparison Of Anxiety Disorders			
	SEPARATION ANXIETY	PHOBIAS	GENERALIZED ANXIETY DISORDER	PANIC DISORDER
Perception	• Separation is perceived as threatening	• Specific objects, events or situations are perceived as threatening	• The whole environment is perceived as threatening • The child is hypervigilant, scanning the environment for threats to well-being	• The recurrence of a panic attack is seen as threatening • Attention is directed inward and benign somatic sensations are perceived but misinterpreted as threatening
Cognition	• The child believes that harm to the parent or the self will occur following separation	• The child believes that contact with the phobic object or entry into the phobic situation will lead to catastrophe	• The child catastrophizes about many minor daily events	• The youth believes that the panic attacks may lead to death or serious injury
Affect	• Intense fear or anger occurs when separation is anticipated, during separation or following separation	• Intense fear or anger is experienced if contact with the feared object or situation is anticipated or occurs	• A continual moderately high level of fear is experienced, often called free floating anxiety	• During panic attacks intense fear occurs and between attacks a moderate level of fear of recurrence is experienced
Arousal	• Episodes of hyperarousal • Sleep problems	• Episodes of hyperarousal • Sleep problems	• Continual hyperarousal • Sleep problems	• Episodes of extreme hyperarousal against a background of moderate hyperarousal • Sleep problems
Behavior	• Separation is avioded or resisted • The child refuses to go to school • The child refuses to sleep alone	• The phobic object or situation is avoided	• As worrying intensifies social activites become resticted	• The youth may avoid public places in case the panic attacks accur away from the safety of homes. This is secondary agoraphobia
Interpersonal adjustment	• Peer relationships may deteriorate • Academic performance may deteriorate	• With simple phobias interpersonal problems are cofined to phobic situations • Agoraphobia may lead to social isolation	• Peer relationships may deteriorate • Acadmic performance may deterioate	• If agoraphobia develops secondary to the panic attacks, social isolation may result

2000b; Southam-Gerow & Chorpita, 2007). Prevalence increases with age, with overall rates of 7.5%, 10.7%, 19.7%, and 20.3% observed at 11, 15, 18, and 21 years of age, respectively (Beesdo et al., 2009; Costello, Egger, & Angold, 2005). In both childhood and adolescence, girls are diagnosed with anxiety disorders more frequently than boys (Beesdo et al., 2009). Anxiety disorders are among the earliest appearing psychopathologies. High-risk phases for the initial onset of anxiety disorders vary by specific anxiety disorder (Beesdo et al., 2009).

Current descriptions appear to be both internally and externally valid, although research continues in this area (Dhossche, van der Steen, & Ferdinand, 2002; Saavedra & Silverman, 2002). Between 40% and 60% of children and adolescents with one anxiety disorder also meet the diagnostic criteria for another (Rapee, Schniering, & Hudson, 2009). Comorbidity with other psychopathology is also essential to consider, as children and adolescents with multiple disorders (e.g., anxiety and depression) experience more severe symptoms and have more psychosocial risk factors (Beesdo et al., 2009; Franco, Saavedra, & Silverman, 2007).

There are also topics that require additional investigation, such as the nature of anxiety in ethnic minority youths (McLaughlin, Hilt, & Nolen-Hoeksema, 2007; Pina & Silverman, 2004; Raver, 2004; Wren et al., 2007). Findings from these investigations include, for instance, data about higher levels of somatic symptoms of anxiety in Latino youth and higher levels of physical symptoms of anxiety in African American boys and adolescents (McLaughlin et al., 2007; Varela & Hensley-Maloney, 2009). The cultural context in which anxiety is experienced and expressed is the topic of many recent studies. According to Varela and Hensley-Maloney (2009), the impact of culture is observed in perceptions of physical versus mental illness, the interpretation and/or meaning of symptoms, and the manner in which struggling individuals cope and are supported by family and community.

The Case of Sophie: Separation Anxiety Disorder

Sophie is a 6-year-old girl and is starting first grade. Sophie enjoyed kindergarten and was in the same class as her close friend and neighbor. Early in the summer, her mother had surgery and was hospitalized for several days. Although she made a good recovery, the event was stressful for Sophie. As the summer progressed, Sophie became increasingly concerned about her mother's well-being, despite frequent reassurances. Sophie also began to have difficulty staying with her babysitter and needed her mother to call frequently if she was away from home. The first several days of first grade were uneventful for Sophie, but she was unhappy about the fact that her best friend was in a different classroom. Late in the first week of school, Sophie refused to get on the school bus and her mother drove her to school. The following morning, Sophie said she felt too sick to go to school. By the following week, Sophie was upset about going to school every morning, often crying and pleading to stay home. On days she was allowed to stay home, she seemed quite happy and content. If forced to go to school, she was quite agitated, though she tended to calm down over the course of the day. The daily struggle has continued for months, and Sophie, her mother, and her teacher are all upset, exhausted, and hoping for some relief. ∎

Sophie's symptoms are consistent with a DSM-5 diagnosis of **separation anxiety disorder** (SAD). The symptoms include both significant distress when separated from the caregiver and clingy behaviors in the presence of the caregiver. The key developmental criterion is that the anxiety must be age inappropriate. In younger children like Sophie, anxiety is often focused on the caregiver's well-being or possible harm that may befall the caregiver. In older children and adolescents, anxiety is also frequently related to difficulties being away from home and is expressed in a reluctance or refusal to go to school (Kearney & Albano, 2004; Suveg, Aschenbrand, & Kendall, 2005). In fact, SAD is the most common cause of school refusal and associated impairments in academic and social domains (King et al., 1998).

Sophie's struggles with somatic problems are also common; headaches and stomach aches are frequent complications of SAD. Nightmares and panic symptoms may also occur with SAD. Estimates of SAD range between 3% and 8% (Beesdo et al., 2009). SAD is most common in children, and is one of the earliest appearing anxiety disorders (Beesdo et al., 2009). Girls are more likely to be diagnosed with SAD. Compared to children with other anxiety disorders, children with SAD have the highest number of comorbid diagnoses (Verduin & Kendall, 2003).

The Case of Jack: Phobic Disorder

Jack is a 7-year-old boy who has developed an intense and pervasive fear of dogs. Jack has never had a pet and has never been very comfortable around animals. Recently, while playing in the backyard, he was surprised by his neighbor's dog, which had gotten out of its fenced yard. The dog barked aggressively at Jack, though it did not approach him. Jack was quite frightened and ran into his house crying. Following this incident, Jack began to refuse to play outside if the neighbor's dog was out. This progressed to refusing to play outdoors at all. Jack soon begged to be excused from visiting family friends if they had dogs at their home, unless the dog was kept out of sight. If Jack is out with his parents and sees a dog, he becomes upset and agitated and cries and clings to his mother. ■■

Phobic disorders involve excessive and exaggerated fears of particular objects or situations, intense anxiety in the presence of such objects or situations, and avoidant behaviors; the fears and anxieties are associated with significant impairment (Beesdo et al., 2009; Ollendick, King, & Muris, 2002). DSM-5 lists three general types of phobias: **specific phobias** (like Jack's) (e.g., animals, injury or blood, natural phenomena); **social phobia** (e.g., fear of scrutiny or evaluation by others); and **agoraphobia** (i.e., intense anxiety in places where individuals feel insecure, trapped, or not in control). Prevalence estimates are about 10% for specific phobias in children and adolescents, and about 7% for social phobia (Bessdo et al., 2009). Agoraphobia is rare in childhood and adolescence. Girls are at higher risk. As with other anxiety disorders, developmentally informed assessment is important. Many children exhibit fears; we want to differentiate those children for whom fears are mild or moderate and short lived from those children for whom fears are intense and long lasting.

The Case of Aisha: Social Phobia

Aisha is an 11-year-old girl and is in sixth grade at a large suburban middle school. Aisha has always had some difficulty adjusting to new situations and has been described as "slow to warm up" when meeting new people. But neither her parents nor her teachers had expressed significant concerns until this year—her first in middle school. Aisha's parents note that at home she is generally energetic and fun loving. And although she is seen as quiet and reserved at her elementary school, Aisha enjoys close friendships with several other girls and never resists going to school. However, whether she described herself as enjoying school depended on how comfortable she was with her homeroom teacher. Aisha has struggled in several noteworthy ways since starting middle school. From the start of

the year, she seemed to be anxious and distressed from the time she woke up in the morning until her return home at the end of the day. She complained that not only was she not making new friends at middle school, but her best friends from elementary school were developing new groups of friends that she believed were excluding her. Her school work suffered, and she seemed to lose confidence in her abilities as a student. Aisha struggled, in particular, with the increasing focus on group projects, where she was reluctant to offer ideas for fear that the other students would "think they were stupid." On those occasions where groups were required to meet outside of school, Aisha would often neglect to tell her parents in order to avoid having to go to another student's home. In fact, Aisha was beginning to miss a considerable amount of school because of frequent stomach aches and occasional headaches. In elementary school, Aisha enjoyed participating in music concerts and having small parts in class plays. Thinking it might help her adjustment to middle school, her parents encouraged her to try out for the all-school musical production. Reluctantly, Aisha signed up. But when the day came to audition, she called her mother, crying, and told her that she didn't feel well and couldn't perform in front of other students and teachers. Confused and distressed, Aisha's parents talked with her about her increasing avoidance of activities she had previously enjoyed. Aisha, with tears welling up in her eyes, insisted that she was no longer interested in the same things as when she was younger, noted that the kids and teachers at the middle school were mean and did not like her, and said that she would be fine if she could simply come home after school and do her homework on her own. ■■

Social phobia is not just shyness or inhibition. Shyness is a complex psychological construct, and it is sometimes difficult to distinguish between normal and abnormal social anxieties. It may be useful to think about a continuum, with groups of shy children followed by groups of socially anxious children followed by groups of socially phobic children (Albano & Hayward, 2004; Rapee & Sweeney, 2005). Shy children are those who may be slow to warm up at a friend's birthday party but who eventually join in the fun; socially anxious children are those who stay huddled next to a parent for the party's duration; and socially phobic children cannot attend a party at all.

One of the most compelling manifestations of social phobia is displayed by children and adolescents

For children experiencing social phobia, anxiety symptoms often prevent them from enjoying developmentally important group activities.

with performance anxiety. Studies of talented young musicians suggest that distress and impairment related to performance anxiety are quite common and are accompanied by a range of coping strategies (Fehm & Schmidt, 2006; Osborne & Kenny, 2005; Osborne, Kenny, & Holsomback, 2005). Other forms of social anxiety are observed in adolescents who cannot complete certain school projects that require oral presentations or adolescents who cannot eat with their friends in restaurants. Compared to the other anxiety disorders, social phobia usually has its onset in later childhood or adolescence (Beesdo et al., 2009).

The Case of Miranda: Generalized Anxiety Disorder

Miranda is a 9-year-old girl presenting with a high level of general distress. She was originally referred for evaluation because of concerns raised at school about some learning difficulties and problems related to extreme avoidance behavior. These problems included not talking in class, not turning things in, not going to her locker, and not interacting with other kids on the playground. For several months Miranda has refused to ride the school bus, so her mother has driven her to school. Although Miranda has always liked sports, she will only play soccer and softball with her parents or her older brother, and only in their yard. Her parents have tried several times to encourage her participation on a team, but Miranda became so anxious and upset before games that she would become nauseated and refuse to get out of the car at the playing fields. Recently, Miranda has been

unable to use public restrooms because she says that they scare her. After witnessing a classmate vomit in class on a hot spring day, Miranda has become preoccupied with a fear that she will also vomit if she becomes too warm. Consequently, she has come to associate being hot with being nauseated and insists on always being in air-conditioned buildings during the summer.

Miranda has difficulty sleeping because of her tendency to ruminate. She describes this as being "unable to shut my brain off." She also worries at night that she will be kidnapped. Miranda is interested in theater and would like to participate in school plays and summer community theater programs, but says she is too nervous to try out. When asked if she could change one thing about her life, Miranda says that she would most want to be able to be in a play. Miranda's mother describes her as "afraid of her own shadow." ■

Miranda's presentation is consistent with the DSM-5 criteria for **generalized anxiety disorder** (GAD), with excessive and unrealistic worries and fears about a variety of stimuli and situations. That Miranda is a girl is also consistent with data suggesting higher rates of GAD in girls than in boys. Because of changes to the description of GAD in children in the last two versions of the DSM, prevalence is difficult to estimate (Beesdo et al., 2009; Bittner et al., 2007). GAD is observed throughout the childhood years, although it is more commonly diagnosed in older children, adolescents, and adults (Beesdo et al., 2009). There are conflicting data about whether children diagnosed with GAD report more somatic symptoms than children with other anxiety disorders (Ginsburg, Riddle, & Davies, 2006; Hofflich, Hughes, & Kendall, 2006). Children with GAD do receive comorbid diagnoses of obsessive-compulsive disorder and mood disorders more frequently than children with other anxiety disorders (Verduin & Kendall, 2003).

The Case of Lauren: Panic Disorder

Lauren is 15 years old and in ninth grade. Lauren's parents have accompanied her for a consultation following several panic attacks that happened during the school day. Lauren's parents describe her during her early years as bright, friendly, and somewhat reserved. Although Lauren has always been somewhat anxious in new situations, she has a number of close friends and is a talented musician. At home, Lauren is talkative and even mildly argumentative at times; at school she is seen as quiet and serious. Lauren's parents first became concerned about her in sixth grade when she transitioned from elementary school to junior high. At the start of that school year, Lauren began to complain of stomach aches and to frequently miss school. Her symptoms gradually receded as she became more comfortable with her new environment. Lauren acknowledges that the start of each school year has been a struggle for her, although never quite as severe as in sixth grade.

Lauren was nervous about high school but also looked forward to the new school and new experiences. Overall, Lauren's parents were pleased with her adjustment. Lauren found her classes challenging but engaging, and she was enjoying new opportunities provided by an expanded music program. Socially, she stayed close to junior high friends and said that she found it difficult to venture out and make new friends. One day while eating lunch alone in the cafeteria, Lauren began to feel ill. She felt her pulse racing and became short of breath. She was light-headed and nauseated. She made it to the first class after lunch, where her teacher immediately asked her if she was all right. Lauren said she felt as if she might pass out and was sent to the nurse's office. Once there, she began to cry and told the nurse that she was afraid she would die. After lying down for a short time, Lauren began to feel better and had largely recovered by the time her mother came to pick her up. The next morning, Lauren complained of a headache and expressed anxiety about returning to school. Her mother encouraged her to go, reassuring her that she would come and get her if she became ill. After several days without incident, Lauren had a second attack during which she felt dizzy, nauseated, felt her heart pounding, and had trouble breathing. This occurred at a football game just after performing in the band's halftime program. Again Lauren reported feeling a sense of panic that she might be dying. Lauren has not been able to return to school since the second panic attack. ■■■

Lauren meets the DSM-5 criteria for **panic disorder**. Recurrent, somewhat unpredictable panic attacks are the primary component of panic disorder. Panic attacks are extremely intense and uncomfortable episodes of anxiety. Sometimes panic occurs in normally developing children without other symptoms and with few negative consequences. Although certainly distressing, these isolated attacks are not necessarily cause for alarm. When panic attacks are associated with one of the other anxiety disorders, such as separation anxiety disorder, phobias, or generalized anxiety disorder, they are more likely to be understood as a complication of that specific disorder rather than as a separate disorder.

Panic disorder is usually diagnosed in adults but may be observed in adolescents (Ollendick, Birmaher, & Mattis, 2004). Girls are more frequently diagnosed than boys, but the gender difference in rates increases further over the course of adolescence and young adulthood (Beesdo et al., 2009). Preliminary investigations of personality characteristics in adolescents with panic disorder identify three subtypes: high functioning/dysphoric, emotionally dysregulated, and avoidant (Powers & Westen, 2010). These subtypes are similar to those observed in adults and suggest the early appearance of specific patterns of personality and impairment (Powers & Westen, 2010). Comorbid disorders include other anxiety disorders, major depression, and bipolar disorder and are observed more frequently in girls than boys with panic disorder (Diler et al., 2004).

Obsessive-Compulsive Disorder

The Case of Danny

Danny is a 13-year-old boy referred because of concerns noted by both his parents and teachers about some of his increasingly unusual behaviors. Danny has been an excellent student throughout his school years until this term, in eighth grade, when he began to fall behind in his classes. His parents also reported that he has dropped several favorite activities and become increasingly socially isolated. During the initial assessment, Danny took an unusually long time to complete some simple questionnaires. When asked about this, Danny admitted that he felt compelled to count the words in each sentence before reading the sentence. He said that this has become a real problem because he can no longer complete his homework on time. Danny also described counting steps and feeling that he always needed to finish climbing stairs with his right foot. In fact, he has memorized the number of steps throughout his school, church, and home so that he always knows which foot to start with. If he does finish climbing stairs with his left foot, he feels compelled to go back down the stairs and start over. Although he has never worried about germs before, he is now very concerned about them and has begun carrying a cloth with him so that he does not have to touch things like door knobs or public telephones. He also finds himself washing and rewashing his hands as often as he can throughout the day. He also said that after he showers, he often still feels dirty and so immediately takes another shower. This has recently caused him to be late getting to school on many mornings. ■■

This description of Danny reflects the acute distress and level of impairment associated with **obsessive-compulsive disorder** (OCD). Danny's intrusive concerns about germs and contamination and his repetitive counting behaviors are among the most common symptoms. Other characteristic obsessions involve fear of harming others, death, or sex; prevalent rituals include hand washing, checking, and avoidant behaviors. In previous editions of the DSM, obsessive-compulsive disorder was included with the anxiety disorders. In DSM-5, obsessive-compulsive disorder is in its own section, with related disorders, including hoarding disorder (a new category), body dysmorphic disorder, hair-pulling disorder (trichotillomania), and skin picking disorder (another new category). Although these related disorders are sometimes observed in children and adolescents, this summary will focus on developmental pathways of OCD.

It is important to evaluate children's **obsessions** (i.e., persistent and intense intrusions of unwanted thoughts or images) and **compulsions** (i.e., persistent and intense impulses to perform a specific behavior) within a developmental framework, because many children display specific preferences and rituals that are not pathological (Evans, Gray, & Leckman, 1999; Rassin, Cougle, & Muris, 2007). For instance, prescribed sequences of separation behaviors at day care centers or bed-time routines are common; most of these kinds of rituals fade by later childhood, when OCD is setting in (Thomsen, 1994a). It is also important to consider the distinctions between the obsessions observed in OCD and the pathological worrying that is more consistent with a diagnosis of generalized anxiety disorder (Comer, Kendall, Franklin, Hudson, & Pimentel, 2004).

Four distinct symptom dimensions of OCD in children have been identified: compulsions, sexual and aggressive obsessions, superstitions, and hoarding/ordering/somatic concerns (McKay et al., 2006). These dimensions do not correspond entirely to the dimensions identified in adults with OCD (McKay et al., 2006). A number of additional features of OCD have been described. These include poor insight (associated with early onset and severity), avoidance (also associated with severity), indecisiveness (associated with impairment), sense of responsibility, pervasive slowness (i.e., excessive amounts of time to complete simple tasks), and pathological doubting (Lewin, Caporino, Murphy, Geffken, & Storch, 2010). New research has also focused on the phenomenology and correlates of rage in children with OCD. Rage outbursts were associated with additional impairment and family accommodation to the OCD symptoms (Storch et al., 2012).

Prevalence rates for OCD are difficult to provide, with many investigators arguing that the disorder is underestimated and underdiagnosed (Heyman et al., 2001). There are data that suggest that boys are at higher risk than girls, but more research remains to be done on both gender and multicultural variables. Age of onset for OCD is difficult to pin down. Some researchers have subtyped children with earlier onsets (between 5 and 9 years) and those with later onsets (after 17 years). Early onset children are more likely to be boys, to have family members with OCD, and to display comorbid tic disorders (Busatto et al., 2001; Diniz et al., 2004; Farrell, Barrett, & Piacentini, 2006). OCD is frequently diagnosed in combination with other disorders, including anxiety disorders, tic disorders, depression, and externalizing disorders (Canavera, Ollendick, May, & Pincus, 2010; Langley, Lewin, Bergman, Lee, & Piacentini, 2010; Lewin, Chang, McCracken, McQueen, & Piacentini, 2010). Sleep-related problems are also frequently observed (Storch et al., 2008).

Somatic Symptom Disorders

The Case of Estella

Estella is a 14-year-old girl, a good student who is well liked by her teachers. Although not rejected by peers, she is rather shy and spends most of her time with just a few friends. Estella reports feeling ill frequently, and each year she has missed many school days, including field trips and special events. Estella's older sister had an emergency appendectomy several years ago. Ever since this event, Estella's parents have been especially vigilant about her health. Estella's parents have extremely high expectations for their children's academic achievement; any problems with academic performance are viewed with great concern, and doing well is highly reinforced. Estella's older sister is a top student at her high school, where Estella is currently enrolled as a ninth grader. In the spring of eighth grade, Estella began to show a pattern of frequent headaches and stomach aches in the morning that sometimes led to her being late to, and occasionally missing, school.

Beginning the second week of ninth grade, Estella began complaining of severe, debilitating abdominal pain. After being called on several occasions to bring Estella home from school because of pain, Estella's parents became alarmed and brought her first to her pediatrician and then, after a particularly severe episode, to the emergency room. Preliminary assessments in each case could find no obvious cause for Estella's symptoms. Finally, the specialist the family consulted recommended hospitalization for more extensive and intrusive diagnostic procedures. After all of the findings from these tests proved negative, a psychology consult was requested. Although initially skeptical of the involvement of the psychologist, Estella and her mother were cooperative. The psychologist observed that although Estella verbalized concern about missing school, she appeared relaxed and calm. Additionally, although she reported no lessening of her pain, she showed none of the obvious symptoms generally associated with extreme discomfort. When asked if she felt stressed or anxious about starting high school, Estella denied having any worries about this other than those related to falling behind in her work since being hospitalized. ▬▬

Recurrent complaints of somatic (physical) symptoms are quite frequent among children and, under certain conditions, in adolescents. **Somatization** refers to a variety of processes in which aspects of psychological distress are manifest in physical symptoms (Gledhill & Garralda, 2006). Somaticizing persons generally do not differentiate between emotional and physical experiences and have difficulty using emotion language to express anxiety. Rather, they use somatic language to describe both physical and emotional problems. Although clinically significant **somatic symptom disorders** (called somatoform disorders in the previous DSM) are at the severe end of a continuum, occasional somatization (at least in mild and transient forms) is extremely common (Dell & Campo, 2011; Garralda, 2010). Indeed, it is the rare adult who does not have a childhood memory of the early morning stomach ache on the day of a big test. For some children and families, however, this process of somatization leads to clinically significant distress and impairment. Discussion of these disorders is included as part of this chapter on anxiety-based psychopathology because the somatic symptoms, like the compulsive and avoidant behaviors of OCD, serve to moderate the direct experience of anxiety; this moderation comes with a very high cost.

Some of the most common somatic symptoms include headaches, fatigue, pain, sore muscles, and abdominal distress. Girls report more symptoms than boys (Vila et al., 2009). An especially common and well-studied somatic symptom disorder involves recurrent abdominal pain (Dorn et al., 2003), as seen in the case of Estella. Recurrent abdominal pain involves three or more episodes over a 3-month period of severe pain that compromises a child's functioning. Studies of recurrent abdominal pain suggest that it tends to occur in families where illness is a central concern and where there is both somatic and emotional distress (Fritz et al., 1997; Garralda, 2010).

Conversion disorder (functional neurological symptom disorder; DSM-5) is characterized by unexplained deficits in voluntary motor or sensory function that cannot be adequately accounted for by known pathophysiological mechanisms; psychological factors are clearly associated with the emergence of symptoms. Typical motor dysfunctions include paralysis, problems with balance, or difficulty swallowing. Typical sensory dysfunctions include loss of touch or pain sensation, double vision or vision loss, deafness, or hallucinations. Children and adolescents may display pseudoseizures (i.e., a nonepileptic seizure, one that is not associated with abnormal firing of neurons), muscle weakness, or extreme sensory sensitivity (Fritz et al., 1997).

Developmental Course
Continuity and Course of Anxiety Disorders

Anxiety in children and adolescents is associated with diverse outcomes, from clear improvement for some, to persistent struggles for others (Beesdo et al., 2009; Weems, 2008). As Craske (1997) emphasizes, "childhood anxiety does not guarantee the development of adult anxiety, nor is it necessary for adult anxiety" (p. A13). While keeping the diversity of outcomes in mind, it is important to emphasize that there is strong evidence for the continuity of anxiety disorders from early childhood through adulthood (Bittner et al., 2007; Goldstein, Olfson, Wickramaratne, & Wolk, 2006; Hale, Raaijmakers, Muris, van Hoof, & Meeus, 2008). That is, anxious and internalizing preschoolers remain anxious and internalizing children, who remain anxious and internalizing adolescents. The stability of specific diagnoses over time (e.g., social phobia diagnosed at 9, and again at 14) reflects **homotypic continuity.**

From a developmental psychopathology perspective, however, we also need to keep in mind the expected changes in the kinds of anxiety experienced over time. For instance, Weems (2008) suggests that separation anxiety and animal fears are predominant between 6 and 9 years of age, generalized anxiety and danger and death fears between 10 and 13 years, and social anxiety between 14 and 17 years. If specific anxiety diagnoses change over time, these changes are likely related to developmental challenges and reflect **heterotypic continuity** (i.e., underlying similarity despite differences in observed patterns of emotion, cognition, and behavior). *Maladaptive anxious emotion* is the core feature that contributes to heterotypic continuity.

More specific outcome-related questions concern whether subsets of children with anxiety disorders can be identified who are at higher risk for continuity of psychopathology. Factors associated with these higher risks include being a girl and displaying more severe symptoms early in development (McCracken, Walkup, & Koplewicz, 2002; Pfeifer, Goldsmith, Davidson, & Rickman, 2002). A developmental chronology of anxiety more often than not involves comorbidity. Many children with one anxiety disorder also meet the diagnostic criteria for another anxiety disorder (Bittner et al., 2007). Many others who are diagnosed with anxiety disorders later develop depression, substance use disorders, and suicidality (Beesdo et al., 2009; Bittner et al., 2007). Beesdo et al. (2009) state that "the 'load' of anxiety seems to contribute to the development of secondary psychopathological complications" (p. 8). Gender, again, appears to be an important variable, with girls more likely to display two or more anxiety disorders as well as comorbid anxiety and depression (Egger, Costello, Erkanli, & Angold, 1999). Sometimes, externalizing disorders such as substance abuse or conduct problems also emerge; this pattern is observed more often in boys (Egger et al., 1999). For those children whose anxiety is coupled with missing school, academic achievement may also be compromised (Ialongo et al., 1995).

With respect to the continuity of specific anxiety disorders over time, the highest rates of stability are observed for specific phobias and panic disorder. Among the most unstable is social phobia (Beesdo et al., 2009). Even with relatively unstable trajectories, social phobia has been the focus of many investigations. Early behavioral inhibition has been identified as a key factor in the development of social phobia (Hirshfeld-Becker et al., 2007). These early markers are important because there are data that show that peers dislike children with social phobia more than children with generalized anxiety disorder or separation anxiety disorder (Verduin & Kendall, 2008). Peer difficulties may be one reason why children with social phobia are at substantial and higher risk for later depression (Beesdo et al., 2007).

Continuity and Course of Obsessive-Compulsive Disorder

As with anxiety disorders, there are a number of developmental pathways observed for children and adolescents diagnosed with OCD. In a 22-year long investigation, four pathways of about equal size were described: a group with improvement (no ongoing OCD), a group with subclinical OCD symptoms, a group with chronic and disabling OCD, and a group with episodic OCD (Thomsen, 1994b). A meta-analysis of 16 study outcomes revealed that about 40% of children with OCD continued to display the full syndrome at various follow-up assessments, and another 19% continued to display subclinical symptoms. Early onset and increased duration of OCD predicted persistence (Stewart et al., 2004).

A number of problematic consequences are associated with ongoing OCD. In addition to negative personal effects (e.g., poor self-image, isolation), family life is negatively impacted. Coercive and disruptive behaviors are often displayed by children and adolescents with OCD and are associated with attempts to impose rules and prohibitions on family members (Lebowitz, Vitulano, & Omer, 2011). Parents of children with OCD expressed high levels of distress and helplessness in the face of OCD symptoms and attempts at control (Lebowitz et al., 2011). Children with OCD are also more likely to be victimized by peers. Similar to children with anxiety disorders, peer difficulties are associated with later depression (Storch et al., 2006).

Continuity and Course of Somatic Symptom Disorders

Somatic symptom disorders interfere with family, peer, and school functioning (Dell & Campo, 2011; Garralda, 2010). One of the factors that appears to contribute to ongoing difficulties involves the social consequences of physical symptoms. For example, when children's pain is associated with positive attention and activity restriction, symptom maintenance is more likely (Walker, Claar, & Garber, 2002). However, "children's success in their normal social roles may affect the extent to which they identify with the sick role and find it a rewarding alternative to other social roles" (Walker et al., 2002, p. 689). Once established, a somaticizing pattern is generally chronic and resistant to both psychological and medical treatment. Individuals with somatic symptom disorders are subject to more frequent and more invasive medical procedures, leading to increased medical costs and potential medical problems. Children and adolescents with these disorders are also at increased risk for other psychopathology (e.g., anxiety, depression) (Campo, Jansen-McWilliams, Comer, & Kelleher, 1999).

Etiology

With so many types of anxiety-based psychopathology, this discussion of etiology is organized around the well-known observation that anxiety runs in families, and the multipart explanation of why and how it does (Dadds, 2002; Manassis, Hudson, Webb, & Albano, 2004). Before summarizing the long list of factors that influence the development and maintenance of anxiety (across anxiety disorders, obsessive-compulsive disorder, and somatic symptom disorders), it is necessary to take a few steps back in order to view anxiety in evolutionary perspective. As previously discussed, much of the anxiety experienced by children and adolescents is useful and adaptive. But this understanding needs to be balanced with Pennington's (2002) more contemporary insight that "evolution has prepared us to be more anxious than we need to be, especially given the relative safety of modern life" (p. 142). With this in mind, we can appreciate the many pathways that lead to anxiety-based disorders.

Genes and Heredity

Clearly, genetics has a significant impact on the development of both normal and pathological anxiety (Beesdo et al., 2009; Muris, 2006; Rapee et al., 2009). Twin and family studies have provided ample evidence that anxious parents are more likely to have anxious children, and that the fears of MZ twins are more similar than the fears of DZ twins (Beesdo et al., 2009; Ehringer, Rhee, Young, Corley, & Hewitt, 2006). For the most part, the genetic role appears to involve a general

vulnerability rather than a disorder-specific risk, although there may be important gender and environmental contributions. Estimates of heritability are in the range of 30% to 40% (Beesdo et al., 2009). Current neuroscience research is focused on identifying gene locations associated with increased risk for anxiety disorders.

An especially important finding involves the many connections between vulnerability to anxiety-based disorders and vulnerability to mood disorders. Over and over, the data suggest clear overlap between genetic influences on the development of anxiety and the development of depression (Eley & Stevenson, 1999a, 1999b, 2000; Grillon et al., 2005; Pennington, 2002). Children with both of these internalizing disorders exhibit negative emotion and emotion dysregulation; there are several models described by Eley and Stevenson (1999a, 1999b, 2000) that may explain the connections. First, the two types of disorders may share the same underlying etiologies. Second, there may be a temporal association, with anxiety usually preceding depression. Third, anxiety and depression may be distinct psychopathologies, each one increasing the risk that the other will develop. Other explanations involve specific environmental events that, coupled with underlying vulnerability, lead to the expression of either anxiety or depression (Eley, 1999; Eley & Stevenson, 2000; Pennington, 2002).

Physiological Factors

Hypotheses about genetically transmitted predispositions to anxiety-based disorders in children are numerous and likely involve multiple mechanisms. Understanding global and specific aspects of neuroanatomy, neurophysiology, and neurochemistry are important for explaining both normal and pathological anxiety. Many investigations involve the study of the brain's right hemisphere, prefrontal cortex, or cerebellum (De Bellis & Kuchibhatla, 2006; Richert, Carrion, Karchemskly, & Reiss, 2006). Given its central role in the fear circuit and the processing of threat, the limbic system, particularly the amygdala, is another important research focus (Pine, 2007). Amygdala abnormalities such as hyperactivation have been documented (Beesdo et al., 2009). There are extensive connections between cortical regions and the amygdala that develop over time; additional investigation of typical and atypical development is warranted (Pine, 2007). The autonomic nervous system and the hypothalamic-pituitary-adrenal (HPA) axis system are other contributors to risk (Pervanidou et al., 2007; Shea et al., 2005). In addition, neurotransmitter dysfunctions have also been observed (Feder et al., 2004; Hooper & Tramontana, 1997). From the physiological perspective, then, hyperarousal and dysregulation are key contributors to increased risk for anxiety disorders. Specific models of vulnerability for various anxiety disorders have been proposed (Cummins & Ninan, 2002; Pine, 2007). For OCD, the roles of the prefrontal cortex and the thalamus are noteworthy (Maia, Cooney, & Peterson, 2008). Certain infections may lead to Pediatric Autoimmune Neuropsychiatric Disorder associated with Streptococcus (PANDAS), an OCD-like presentation (Gause et al., 2009).

Child Factors

With the emphasis on arousal and dysregulation described in the previous section, it makes sense that temperament is one of the child variables that is associated with anxiety disorders (Buss, 2011; Moehler et al., 2008; Muris et al., 2007). The temperamental trait most associated with anxiety is inhibition. Inhibition involves a unique mix of wariness, arousal, and emotional and behavioral preferences for any given child (Fox, Henderson, Marshall, Nichols, & Ghera, 2005; Hirshfeld-Becker et al., 2007; Muris & Dietvorst, 2006). This mix is part of a developmental profile that also includes parents, peers, and cultural context (Degnan, Almas, & Fox, 2010; Kagan & Fox, 2006; West & Newman, 2007). The many investigations by Kagan and his colleagues describe children at risk for later anxiety as highly inhibited and highly reactive. Pennington (2002) emphasizes a distinction between genotype and phenotype and suggests that there are two groups of inhibited children: those who have no family history of anxiety disorders and are not themselves at increased risk for disorders; and those who do have a family history of anxiety and are at risk.

The experience of emotion and emotion regulation is also a primary factor in the etiology of anxiety disorders. Weems (2008) describes a developmental trajectory organized around the construct of *anxious emotion*. Anxious emotion reflects "dysregulation of the normal anxiety response system" (Weems, 2008, p. 492). It involves intense worries that are not useful in terms of anticipating upcoming

danger, or intense fears in the absence of real threat, as well as resulting impairment in functioning. Another way to think about emotion is to recognize the heterogeneity of fearful behavior and attempt to identify which dimensions of fearful behavior (e.g., increased distress or avoidance) underlie increased risk (Buss, 2011). In Buss's research, toddlers who displayed high fear in low-threat circumstances exhibited high physiological reactivity and less flexibility (i.e., more dysregulation). The hypothesis is that, as children encounter increasingly varied environmental opportunities and challenges (e.g., during the transition to school), fear dysregulation increases wariness and withdrawal, and later anxiety disorders.

Another important emotion factor to do with individual differences in positive and negative affectivity, with negative affectivity (or emotionality) related to the emergence of internalizing disorders, including anxiety disorders (Anthony, Lonigan, Hooe, & Phillips, 2002; Lahey et al., 2004; Lonigan, Phillips, & Hooe, 2003; Ollendick, Seligman, Goza, Byrd, & Singh, 2003). The complex psychological construct of affectivity is the basis of the **tripartite model of anxiety and depression** (see Box 11:1). The model's three core concepts are as follows: (1) anxiety and depression share a common causal factor of negative affectivity; (2) along with negative affectivity, low levels of positive affectivity are associated with depression; and (3) along with negative affectivity, high levels of physiological arousal are associated with anxiety. Emotion regulation or dysregulation is another key component in the development of anxiety disorders. Children who experience frequent or intense negative emotions, *and who lack the skills to regulate these emotions or the confidence that their efforts will have meaningful effects*, are most vulnerable (Suveg & Zeman, 2004; Thompson, 2001). Especially poor emotion regulation skills may differentiate children with obsessive-compulsive disorder from other anxiety disorders (Jacob, Morelen, Suveg, Jacobsen, & Whiteside, 2012). The influence of cognitive variables on the development of anxiety disorders is also salient. Cognitive and attentional biases to perceive and attend more closely to threatening stimuli, cognitive appraisals of ambiguous situations as negative and threatening, and specific cognitive distortions related to the self and others all contribute to increased risk for anxiety disorders (Alfano, Beidel, & Turner, 2002; Cannon & Weems, 2010; Muris, 2006; Pine, 2007).

BOX 11:1 EMERGING SCIENCE

Tripartite Model of Anxiety and Depression

The study of the relationship between anxiety and depression has a long and interesting history. Anxiety and depression frequently occur together, though not always. Although the categorical structure of the DSM diagnostic system defines each domain of disorder independently, anxiety and depression are often difficult to differentiate empirically. Most people recognize intuitively the ways in which both types of disorders are expressions of a negative emotional state while at the same time seeming distinct from one another. These were among the observations and questions addressed by David Watson, LeAnn Clark, and others over 20 years ago in innovative research into the underlying structure of anxiety and depression. The model they developed— the tripartite model of emotion—continues to guide research efforts today.

The tripartite model (Watson & Clark, 1991) identifies three groups of symptoms that combine to define disorders of anxiety and depression. According to this model, anxiety and depression share a common core symptom of general emotional distress (i.e., negative affect). Anxiety disorders are differentiated by the additional prominence of physiological hyperarousal, whereas depression is characterized by a low positive emotional state (i.e., low positive affect). This conceptual model led to research efforts to develop valid and reliable assessment measures of the common factor (negative affect), as well as specific symptoms of anxiety and specific symptoms of depression (Watson et al., 1995a, 1995b).

Although originally derived from research with adults, the tripartite model of emotion has been investigated in adolescents and children as well. As the model began to be considered from a developmental perspective, it was suggested that anxiety and depression may be part of a single, more global factor of psychopathology that becomes more differentiated over time. However, this does not appear to be the case. Instead, the basic three-factor structure of the tripartite model can

be measured early in life and is relatively stable over time (Turner & Barrett, 2003). The preponderance of research of children with anxiety and depressive disorders generally supports the tripartite model among youth populations (Anderson & Hope, 2008; Cannon & Weems, 2006; Jacques & Mash, 2004), though anxiety and mood disorders show greater co-occurrence earlier in life, somewhat obscuring the underlying three-factor structure.

A broader developmental perspective may help further clarify the clinical and research findings that have made some of these developmental questions difficult to answer. Research integrating the broad underlying structure of emotion, emerging neuroscience, cognitive development, and psychopathology may provide especially useful insights (Posner, Russell & Peterson, 2005). Research integrating findings from several areas has shown that although the neurophysiology underlying the tripartite model may be in place early in development, the cognitive ability to label a variety of subjective emotional states takes time to emerge. In other words, perhaps what develops over time is not the differentiated core symptom domains but the individual's ability to conceptualize and describe his or her symptoms.

In addition to considering the tripartite model across the developmental continuum, studies have also validated the model across diverse cultural groups. For example, validating studies have been conducted with an urban youth sample (Lambert, Joiner, McCreary, Schmidt, & Ialongo, 2004), European youth (de Beurs, den Hollander- Gijsman, Helmich, & Zitman, 2006), and children and adolescents in South Korea (Yang, Hong, Joung, & Kim, 2006). Even though some differences and inconsistencies exist, anxiety and depression are both consistently characterized by negative emotion, with anxiety also associated with physiological hyperarousal and depression also associated with low positive affect.

Level of cognitive development and the ability to correctly identify problematic physical symptoms may be especially important to consider for certain anxiety and somaticizing disorders (Muris, Mayer, Vermeulen, & Hiemstra, 2007). And metacognitive variables may be equally important for disorders involving worry and obsessive thinking (de Bruin, Muris, & Rassin, 2007).

Anxiety sensitivity may further complicate cognitive processing as well as interfere with effective emotion regulation (Eley, Gregory, Clark, & Ehlers, 2007; Weems, Taylor, Marks, & Varela, 2010). To the extent that children and adolescents are predisposed to immediately focus on and overreact to uncomfortable body sensations, high levels of anxiety sensitivity may be conceptualized as a diathesis; coupling this diathesis with significant or multiple stressors may explain the development of panic disorder in some youth.

Early experiences with control, and lack of control, may contribute to a lack of security and a cognitive predisposition to assume that one does not control events or outcomes; this predisposition underlies a sense of helplessness and increases a child's general vulnerability (Weems & Silverman, 2006) and may be particularly relevant as a predictor of psychosomatic problems (Hagekull & Bohlin, 2004). In the integrative model proposed by Weems and Silverman (2006), understanding the relations between control and anxiety disorders involves clearly describing the kinds of control that children and adolescents actually have, as well as their perceptions of control. That these kinds of experiences occur in certain developmental periods is important. According to Pynoos et al. (1999), "the peak incidences (and surprisingly high prevalence) of serious near-drownings, burns, and dog bites are between infancy and five years of age" (p. 1550) and underlie a number of neurobiologically based cognitive changes in children. Intolerance of uncertainty has been documented to increase levels of adolescent worry; given the unsettled nature of adolescence, this may be particularly problematic (Laugesen, Dugas, & Bukowski, 2003). Adolescents who are ignored or rejected by their peers experience, as one might expect, more social anxiety (Inderbitzen, Walters, & Bukowski, 1997).

Behavioral models of risk and psychopathology emphasize that children's learning is at the root of anxiety. Rachman's (1977) theory of fear acquisition presented three pathways to disorder: direct conditioning, modeling, and/or instruction or information. There are data to support both direct and indirect pathways (Field, Argyris, & Knowles, 2001; King, Eleonora, & Ollendick, 1998). Contemporary explanations of behavioral risk also include aspects of neuropsychology and temperament (Mineka & Zinbarg, 2006; Rapee et al., 2009).

Insecure attachments lead to both short- and long-term outcomes involving anxiety disorders (Elizabeth et al., 2004; Nolte et al., 2011; van IJzendoorn & Bakermans-Kranenburg, 1996; Warren, Huston, Egeland, & Sroufe, 1997). The heightened risk involves not only more frequent experiences of anxiety, but difficulties engendered by the caregiver's problematic and often ineffective attempts to manage the child's distress (Thompson,

2001). Adverse life events experienced by children also influence risk and vulnerability. Loss of parents, parental divorce, and maltreatment all increase the risk for the development of anxiety disorders (Beesdo et al., 2009). Particular types of events, such as threat or loss, are differentially associated with the development of anxiety or depression (Eley & Stevenson, 2000), but other types of events may be linked to specific anxiety subtypes (Beesdo et al., 2009). Chronic stressors such as discrimination, schoolwork, family problems, and friendship problems have also been identified as both syndrome specific (tied to either anxiety or depression) and child specific (related to nonshared environmental causes) (Asbury, Dunn, Pike, & Plomin, 2003; Szalacha et al., 2003).

Although discussion of etiologies necessarily emphasizes risk factors, Muris (2006) identifies a number of protective factors that may buffer children and adolescents. These include the temperamental characteristic of effortful control, and a child's sense of perceived control and self-efficacy. Friendships may also protect anxious children from rejection and other peer difficulties (Degnan et al., 2010).

Parent Factors

The family context in which children's genetic inheritance and psychological make-up is embedded is critical to the development of anxiety-based disorders. The transactional approach to psychopathology, discussed in many other chapters, emphasizes the connections among child variables, parent and relationship variables, and larger ethnic and cultural variables (Hughes, Hedtke, & Kendall, 2008; Suarez-Morales & Bell, 2006; Vendlinski, Silk, Shaw, & Lane, 2006). Parental psychopathology is associated with increased vulnerability (Colletti et al., 2009; Knappe et al., 2009). Two types of parenting have been identified as risk factors: overprotective/overcontrolling parenting, and negative/critical parenting; the most consistent results and the largest effects are observed for overprotective/overcontrolling parenting (Rapee et al., 2009). A related construct, intrusive and controlling parenting, is also linked to child anxiety (Degnan et al., 2010). In combination with insecure attachments, insensitive parenting is especially problematic (Degnan et al., 2010).

The impact of fathers, distinct from mothers, is important. Numerous studies have shown that fathers' roles involve challenges, risk taking, and encouraging independence; these activities support overall well-being (Bogels & Phares, 2008). Fathers' control, lack of affection, problematic parenting, and psychopathology are all associated with anxiety in children (Bogels & Phares, 2008). Parenting behaviors and styles must be understood in cultural contexts. In communities and cultures where controlling behavior is more frequent and widely accepted, it is less predictive of children's anxiety (Varela & Hensley-Maloney, 2009; Varela, Sanchez-Sosa, Biggs, & Luis, 2009).

Parent fears and worries, modeling of avoidant behavior, and acceptance or accommodation of children's anxiety and avoidance are all potentially related to both the development and the maintenance of anxiety disorders (Barrett, Shortt, & Healy, 2002; Berg-Nielsen, Vikan, & Dahl, 2002; Bogels, van Dongen, & Muris, 2003; Hastings et al., 2008; Rapee et al., 2009). These kinds of parental characteristics and parenting behaviors, understood in the broad context of emotion socialization, may contribute to a child's sense of fragility and incompetence in a scary world (Suveg, Zeman, Flannery-Schroeder, & Cassano, 2005).

Assessment and Diagnosis

There are two main tasks of assessment: (1) to determine whether children's anxiety reflects normal or pathological adjustment, and (2) to discriminate among anxiety disorders. Comprehensive assessment includes interviews, self-reports, rating scales, physiological assessments, and clinical observations, and evidence-based assessment is increasingly emphasized (Hunsley & Mash, 2007; Rapee & Sweeney, 2005; Silverman & Ollendick, 2005; Southam-Gerow & Chorpita, 2007).

There are many self-report questionnaires for children and adolescents, for many different types of anxiety disorders. Many of these questionnaires allow mental health professionals to differentiate between anxiety and mood disorders as well as among anxiety subtypes (Brotman, Kamboukos, & Theise, 2008; Muris, Merckelbach, Ollendick, King, & Bogie, 2002). For younger children, narrative stories may be used to elicit anxiety themes (Warren, Emde, & Sroufe, 2000). Parent and teacher forms of anxiety rating scales are also used frequently (Aschenbrand, Angelosante, & Kendall, 2005; Kendall et al., 2007; Nauta et al., 2004). Parent attitudes and expectancies can also be assessed (Eisen,

Spasaro, Brien, Kearney, & Albano, 2004). A developmental systems framework focused on child–family transactions may also be useful (Mash & Hunsley, 2007).

Even with abundant data, interpretation is often difficult. That's because agreement between children's reports and parents' reports of anxiety symptoms and avoidant behavior is usually poor (Comer & Kendall, 2004; Meiser-Stedman, Smith, Glucksman, Yule, & Dalgleish, 2007; Safford, Kendall, Flannery-Schroeder, Webb, & Sommer, 2005). Discrepancies among parent, teacher, and clinician ratings of adolescent disorders have also been reported, and these discrepancies are associated with poor outcomes (Ferdinand, van der Ende, & Verhulst, 2004). Reasons for lack of agreement include children's abilities (or inabilities) to describe their anxiety, children's willingness (or lack of willingness) to disclose their anxiety, parental awareness (or lack of awareness), parental distress, and parental motivations; these reasons underscore the need to gather data from both children and parents (Wren, Bridge, & Birmaher, 2004; Youngstrom, Findling, & Calabrese, 2003, 2004; Youngstrom et al., 2004). Especially when making decisions about internalizing disorders, clinicians also need to take into account the cultural backgrounds of children and their families (Garralda & Raynaud, 2008; Varela et al., 2004). Finally, as with every disorder, it is important to take into account a child's strengths and resources (Beaver, 2008). These positive characteristics allow the clinician (as well as parents and teachers) to be reminded that children are more than their disorders. Further, these positive characteristics may be incorporated into a treatment plan that maximizes therapeutic engagement.

Assessment and diagnosis of obsessive-compulsive disorder, as with anxiety disorders, must take into account typical development (e.g., the routines and rituals of young school-aged children). Structured interviews and child- and parent reports are all part of a comprehensive clinical intake. Assessment of OCD severity and impairment must be addressed. Comorbid and differential diagnoses are likely to focus on tic disorders, anxiety disorders, and autism spectrum disorder (Lewin & Piacentini, 2010).

Perhaps more than any other physical or psychiatric diagnosis, the somatic symptom disorders require an integrated approach involving combined medical and psychological perspectives. The critical starting point is to rule out known physical causes. In pediatric settings, high rates of medically unexplained symptoms should prompt physicians to explore internalizing psychopathologies (Dhossche et al., 2002; Gledhill & Garralda, 2006). This can then be followed by a consideration of how well symptoms meet the criteria for a somatic symptom disorder (Meesters, Muris, Ghys, Reumerman, & Rooijmans, 2003), although it is again important to understand symptoms in the context of culture (Varela et al., 2004). Because the child, and often the family as well, has a considerable psychological investment in the physical symptoms, both are likely to respond with frustration and even distrust when confronted by an inadequate medical explanation. Also, these children and adolescents are, by definition, resistant to an attribution focused on emotional functioning. Consequently, they are unlikely to accept a referral for psychological intervention. At least for the more severe somatization cases, then, collaboration between the psychologist and pediatrician is crucial.

Intervention

As with all psychopathologies, the prevention or reduction of anxiety disorders is the goal of mental health professionals. A number of prevention programs have demonstrated success, and new ideas related to prevention are also promising (Dadds & Roth, 2008; Lock & Barrett, 2003; Rapee et al., 2009; Rapee, Kennedy, Ingram, Edwards, & Sweeney, 2010). These programs have been implemented in preschools and in elementary schools. Some of these programs (as we would predict in the field of developmental psychopathology) have also enhanced our understanding of typical development (Hudson, Kendall, Coles, Robin, & Webb, 2002). When prevention is not possible, early interventions become very important, not only for the immediate relief of symptoms but also for the reduction of later disorders such as depression.

Psychological Treatment

Given the nature of internalizing disorders, many children and adolescents become the focus of intervention efforts only after an anxiety disorder is firmly rooted; many others who struggle remain undiscovered and untreated. Effective treatments for the wide range of anxiety disorders are available (Barrett, Farrell, Pina, Peris, & Piacentini, 2008; Silverman & Ollendick, 2005; Rapee

et al., 2009). The treatment of choice is clearly cognitive-behavioral therapy. **Cognitive-behavioral therapy** (CBT) is based, in large part, on the work of Kendall and his colleagues (e.g., Albano & Kendall, 2002; Kendall, 2012) and is associated with both immediate and long-term improvements. Both individual and group formats do very well (Barrett, Healy-Farrell, & March, 2004; Silverman, Pina, & Viswesvaran, 2008); CBT is also helpful for children who have been diagnosed with anxiety and additional internalizing or externalizing disorders (Flannery-Schroeder, Suveg, Safford, Kendall, & Webb, 2004; Tsao, Mystkowski, Zucker, & Craske, 2002). Relaxation training is often a key component of CBT (Gosch, Flannery-Schroeder, Mauro, & Compton, 2006). Internet-based treatments, with various educational and experiential components presented in interactive formats, have also been effective and are well received by both children and parents (Elkins, McHugh, Santucci, & Barlow, 2011; Spence, Holmes, March, & Lipp, 2006). School-based interventions are another promising option; relaxation exercises, for example, have had positive impacts when taught to groups of children with asthma as well as entire classrooms (Bernstein, Layne, Egan, & Tennison, 2005). Overall, much progress has been made to make sure that effective interventions are "transportable" from the university clinic to the community clinic and beyond (Elkins et al., 2011).

Summarizing dozens of investigations, Velting, Setzer, and Albano (2004) have identified the six

Cognitive-behavioral therapy approaches, such as the Coping Cat program, have been adapted for use in treating childhood anxiety disorders.

TABLE 11:3	Main Components of Cognitive-Behavioral Therapy	
COMPONENTS	**FOCUS/GOALS**	**ASSOCIATED TECHNIQUES**
Psychoeducation	Provide corrective information about the nature of anxiety and feared stimuli	Didactic instruction; self-monitoring (diaries); assigned reading
Somatic management	Target autonomic arousal and related physiological symptoms; focus attention away from anxiety-arousing physical sensations; break the association between physiological arousal and anxiety	Breathing retraining (deep and slow diaphragmatic breathing); relaxation training (progressive muscle/cue controlled/applied relaxation); meditation; exercise
Cognitive restructuring	Identify maladaptive (unhelpful) thoughts, beliefs, and images and teach realistic, coping-focused thinking	Monitoring of thought processes (diaries); identification of automatic thoughts (ATs); teaching rational disputation of ATs; use of behavioral experiments to gather evidence to refute ATs; age-appropriate methods for younger children (e.g., Kendall's FEAR steps)
Problem solving	Develop a variety of active methods for coping with specific problem situations and a system for testing the potential solutions	Identify the specific problem; generate multiple alternative actions for improving the situation; explore costs and benefits of each potential solution; determine and implement the preferred or most feasible alternative; evaluate outcomes
Exposure	Graduated, systematic, and controlled exposure to feared situation(s) to provide experience with using anxiety management skills and consolidation of psychoeducation material	Behavioral exposure to feared situations; interoceptive exposure to feared bodily sensations (such as in panic disorder); exposure should be direct (in vivo) but may begin with imaginal or symbolic exposure (e.g., use of photos of feared object instesd of actual stimulus)
Relapse prevention	Focus on consolidating anxiety management skills and generalizing treatment gains over time; decrease reliance on therapist and others (e.g., parents) for managing anxiety	Fading of sessions (from weekly to biweekly); role reversal (child acts as therapist for a session); videotape commercial of therapy program; planned booster sessions

SOURCE: From Velting et al. (2004).

main components of effective CBT: psychoeducation, somatic management, cognitive restructuring, problem-solving, exposure, and relapse prevention (see Table 11:3). *Psychoeducation* involves providing children and their families with information about normal anxiety and the emergence and maintenance of pathological anxiety, and about theoretical and practical aspects of CBT. *Somatic management* involves targeting the distressing physiological symptoms and is usually focused on relaxation and breathing techniques. In addition, children and adolescents learn how to predict and tolerate the anxiety that accompanies challenging and stressful events. *Cognitive restructuring* has to do with the identification and modification of negative thoughts that elicit and prolong anxiety. Thinking about emotions and emotional biases may also be important and is in some instances the focus of treatment efforts (Suveg, Southam-Gerow, Goodman, & Kendall, 2007). *Problem solving* is a step-by-step, active, behaviorally oriented approach for coping. *Exposure* to the stimuli and situations that are associated with anxiety is systematic and controlled, with in vivo (real-life) practice preferred. *Relapse prevention* involves laying the groundwork for the maintenance and generalization of improvements. With all CBT treatments, the therapeutic alliance and developmental considerations in the design and implementation of all aspects of individual interventions must be emphasized.

Given the salient role of the parents in etiology and maintenance, it makes sense to work within a treatment framework that includes parents and recognizes the impact of culture on parents (Barrett & Shortt, 2003; Kendall, 2012). Family approaches to anxiety disorders are often used and are often very effective (Ginsburg & Schlossberg, 2002; Weisz, 2004; Wood, Piacentini, Southam-Gerow, Chu, & Sigman, 2006). In particular, treatments for OCD that address family conflicts, parent accommodation of the child's coercive behavior, and poor family cohesion are associated with better outcomes (Lebowitz et al., 2011; Peris et al., 2012). Family approaches are also highly effective for the somatic symptom disorders (Garralda, 2010).

Designing various treatments for several of the children presented earlier in the chapter provides examples of these psychological treatments. In helping Sophie with separation anxiety disorder and school refusal, it was important to first clarify for her parents and family that it was not school that was upsetting Sophie. Rather, it was anxiety about separating from her mother that was interfering with her entry into first grade. Consequently, intervention efforts were aimed at restoring Sophie's confidence in her relationship with her mother as well as her own self-confidence (see also Heyne et al., 2002). To help with the transition to a calmer start to the school day, a picture of her mother was taped to the inside of her desk as a reminder that her mother was fine and would be waiting for her at home at the end of the day. For several days, Sophie was also allowed to call her mother after lunch if she wished. By the end of four weeks of these efforts, Sophie was again looking forward to her school day and separated from her mother easily in the morning.

For Jack's dog phobia, any of four classic treatments for fears (or combinations of these treatments) might be used, including modeling, systematic desensitization, reinforced exposure, and self-talk (Weisz, 2004), with attention paid to the individual response pattern and developmental status (Davis & Ollendick, 2005; King et al., 2005; Muris, 2005). **Modeling** treatments are based on the impact of observational learning. With this approach, Jack might participate in symbolic modeling (using videos of children displaying nonfearful behavior) or live modeling (using in-person observation of nonfearful children) or participant modeling (pairing Jack with

a nonfearful child). Depending on the child, modeling treatments may achieve good outcomes quite quickly. **Systematic desensitization** involves teaching an anxious child how to relax and how to maintain relaxation when exposed to the feared stimulus. Exposure is done gradually (i.e., systematically, from stuffed dogs to videos of dogs to real dogs), building on the child's successes over time. **Exposure** involves rewarding a child for desired behavior. In Jack's case, he might receive tokens for more functional dog-related behaviors. **Self-talk** is a cognitive technique focused on providing positive self-statements, such as "I am brave," to enhance appropriate behaviors. All of these treatment approaches depend on establishing a trusting relationship with a therapist, because children need to believe (and feel deep down) that this adult will keep them safe.

Miranda, the girl diagnosed with generalized anxiety disorder, needed to spend several sessions becoming accustomed to, and comfortable with, the therapeutic setting, the therapist, and the therapeutic relationship. Miranda and her parents discussed the age-related expectations and tasks that were important to her and the ways that it would be advantageous (and even fun) to meet them. Miranda spent many of the sessions engaged in role playing and in practicing self-talk strategies that would help her manage her base levels of anxiety and her specific anxiety symptoms. Danny, who struggled with OCD, received an intervention that first involved education for Danny and his parents about the disorder. During these discussions, Danny's father also revealed that he had experienced a variety of significant anxiety symptoms, including some marginal obsessive-compulsive behaviors, as well. A cognitive-behavioral treatment plan was developed and a referral for a medication consultation was made. Cognitive techniques were used to identify patterns of thoughts and behaviors that had become maladaptive and new, more effective strategies for dealing with anxiety were developed. Behavioral plans to limit compulsive behaviors were also created. These included techniques that exposed Danny to triggering stimuli while preventing the compulsive response. In this way, Danny became desensitized to anxiety-provoking stimuli and no longer felt the urgent need to engage in the compulsive behaviors.

After several meetings with Estella and her parents, the hospital team working with her diagnosed a somatoform pain disorder. In discussing this with Estella and her parents, it was emphasized that no one thought

Estella was "faking." Rather, the facts that Estella very much wanted to do well in high school and also please her parents were noted, and the suggestion made that although Estella was not feeling directly anxious about this, the pressure to perform had begun to interfere with her ability to manage her daily demands. As part of this suggestion, the therapist mentioned that there were many ways in which bodies and minds work together, in both positive and negative ways. A plan was developed with input from the family, physician, and psychologist, in which medical monitoring would be combined with help from the psychologist in returning to school. It was emphasized that although they would continue to investigate physiological factors, most truly dangerous possibilities had already been ruled out and it was medically safe for Estella to return to school. Gradually, the psychologist helping Estella became more involved in coaching her to develop more adaptive and effective ways of managing stress in her life. Mind–body pain management strategies were an important component of ongoing treatment (Kuttner, 1997).

Pharmacological Treatment

Many effective treatments combine psychological and pharmacological techniques, with anxiety medications prescribed most frequently for children and adolescents with anxiety disorders and obsessive-compulsive disorder (March, Entusah, Rynn, Alvano, & Tourian, 2007; Liebowitz & Ginsberg, 2005; Mancini, van Ameringen, Bennett, Patterson, & Watson, 2005; Walkup et al., 2008). Although much more research work remains to be done, these combined therapies seem especially appropriate for older children and those with more severe symptoms, and for complex cases that involve comorbidity. In the future, it is likely that the recent growth in the pharmacological treatment of anxiety disorders in young people will become more refined as a result of ongoing clinical trials of medications that include children and adolescents. Advances in imaging research, such as functional magnetic resonance imaging (fMRI) techniques, will also likely provide a more precise understanding of the brain mechanisms and brain activity that are implicated in the development of anxiety disorders. These kinds of advances will also improve the precision with which medications are prescribed for children (Storch & McKay, 2010). But even with such improvements, it is important to keep in mind that cognitive-behavioral psychotherapies will continue to play a central role in providing the most effective treatment strategies for helping children cope with anxiety.

Key Terms

Emotion regulation (p. 188)
Fears (p. 189)
Worries (p. 189)
Anxiety disorders (p. 190)
Anxiety sensitivity (p. 190)
Separation anxiety disorder (p. 192)
Phobic disorders (p. 193)
Specific phobias (p. 193)
Social phobia (p. 193)
Agoraphobia (p. 193)
Generalized anxiety disorder (p. 194)
Panic disorder (p. 195)
Obsessive-compulsive disorder (p. 196)
Obsessions (p. 196)
Compulsions (p. 196)
Somatization (p. 197)
Somatic symptom disorders (p. 197)

Conversion disorder (functional neurological symptom disorder) (p. 197)
Homotypic continuity (p. 197)
Heterotypic continuity (p 198)
Tripartite model of anxiety and depression (p. 200)
Cognitive-behavioral therapy (p. 204)
Modeling (p.206)
Systematic desensitization (p. 206)
Exposure (p. 206)
Self-talk (p. 206)

Chapter Summary

- Although some fears and worries are a normal and expected part of childhood, when they consistently interfere with healthy development, an anxiety disorder may be present.
- Emotional regulation, the ability to modulate and organize emotions, follows a developmental

course that must be considered when determining whether or not normal-range anxiety crosses over to pathological anxiety.

- Anxiety disorders represent the maladaptive experience of anxiety in terms of intensity, duration, and pervasiveness.
- Anxiety disorders are also characterized by inhibition and withdrawal, exaggerated and unrealistic fears and worries, and overcontrol.
- Anxiety disorders are among the most frequently diagnosed disorders in children, adolescents, and adults.
- Some of these disorders, such as generalized anxiety disorder, represent an anxious reaction to a wide array of stimuli, whereas others, such as separation anxiety disorder and specific phobias, are rooted in more specific anxiety-producing situations.
- In some anxiety disorders, including obsessive-compulsive disorder and conversion disorder, the behaviors used to block the direct experience of anxiety (i.e., avoidance) are the primary symptoms.
- Posttraumatic stress disorder is the only anxiety disorder to specify a cause (traumatic experience) as part of the clinical description.
- Somatization and somatoform disorders involve the experience of physical symptoms that appear

related to the moderation of emotions, especially anxiety. Anxiety sensitivity is often exhibited.

- Genetic and other physiological risk factors are clearly linked to the development of anxiety disorders.Research suggests that anxiety and mood disorders result from closely related risk factors.
- Parenting behaviors that may potentially contribute to the development of anxiety disorders include an anxious style of parenting, such as overinvolvement and overprotection, as well as the modeling of anxious and avoidant behavior.
- One of the assessment challenges in regard to the anxiety disorders is the fact that agreement between parents' and children's reports of anxiety symptoms is relatively low.
- Comprehensive assessment, including clinical interview, self-report measures, and clinical observations, are used to differentiate normal from pathological levels of anxiety and discriminate among anxiety disorders.
- A variety of psychological interventions (cognitive-behavioral therapy in particular), often in combination with pharmacological approaches, have proven effective in the treatment of anxiety disorders.

12 Mood Disorders and Suicidality

THERE ARE MANY MYTHS about depression in children. Some people believe that children cannot experience genuine depression. But children can. Some people believe that, even if children can be clinically depressed, few are. But depression is not rare. Others believe that childhood depression is short lived, or a typical developmental phenomenon. It is neither. Depression is a common and serious psychopathology with lasting negative consequences; it is underrecognized and undertreated in both children and in adolescents (Cicchetti & Toth, 1998; Coyle et al., 2003; Garber, 2007). Issues related to the diagnosis and treatment of mood disorders in children and adolescents are receiving increased attention from mental health professionals, from researchers, and from special interest groups, including pharmaceutical companies and parent advocacy organizations. Much of the focus has been on the use (and overuse) of antidepressant medications and the impact of medication on youth suicidality (Bridge & Axelson, 2008). Suicidality refers to the risk of suicidal ideation (thinking about suicide) as well as the risk for suicidal behavior (attempted or completed suicide); these topics are discussed in a later section of this chapter. Another focus has been on the ever-increasing numbers of both children and adolescents diagnosed with bipolar disorder (Blader & Carlson, 2007; Moreno et al., 2007) and on a new category of disorder introduced in DSM-5, disruptive mood dysregulation disorder (Leibenluft, 2011). Our goal for this chapter is to provide an up-to-date overview and a compassionate analysis of the many forms of mood disorders in children and adolescents.

Developmental Tasks and Challenges Related to the Construction of Self and Identity

Given the myriad physiological, psychological, and social changes associated with the transition from late childhood to adolescence, the development of a coherent *sense of self* (i.e., "the set of attributes, abilities, attitudes, and values that an individual believes defines who he or she is," Berk, 2009, p. 451) and a *positive identity* (i.e., an individual's understanding, acceptance, and prizing of his or her self, roles, relationships, and responsibilities) becomes critical for ongoing healthy adjustment (Call & Mortimer, 2001; Thoits, 1999); well-differentiated and integrated experiences of self and identity underlie all of the various types of autonomy and achievement that adolescents seek (Blasi & Milton, 1991; Cicchetti & Rogosch, 2002; Harter, 1999, 2003; Robins & Trzesniewski, 2005). Taking into account the "torturous self-consciousness" of adolescence (Crystal, Watanabe, Weinfurt, & Wu, 1998, p. 715), the hoped-for outcome is a "balanced, stable, and accurate view of self" (Jacobs, Bleeker, & Constantino, 2003, p. 43). Indeed, according to the pioneering lifespan developmental psychologist Erik Erikson (1968), developing a mature psychological identity is *the primary achievement* of adolescence.

The construction of self is a process that begins in infancy and stretches across a lifetime. As just described, this construction is an individual achievement, but one that is accomplished within a particular family, in a particular culture, and in a particular era (Crystal et al., 1998; Lerner, Lerner, von Eye, Bowers, & Lewin-Bizan, 2011; Roberts et al., 1999). The convergence of such late-childhood challenges as puberty, academic demands, romantic involvements, and vocational interests means that the constructs of self and identity become increasingly important in adolescence (Graber & Brooks-Gunn, 1996). One important factor that requires emphasis is that older children and adolescents are increasingly active agents in their own development. That is, they are more likely than younger children to influence their development by selecting their environments (e.g., peer groups and peer activities) and then "optimizing" or "compensating" for challenges, opportunities, and risks (Gestsdottir, Lewin-Bizan, von Eye, Lerner, & Lerner, 2009). A key component of this developmental process involves adolescents' abilities to cope with increases in both daily hassles (e.g., homework difficulties, disagreements with siblings) and larger stressors (e.g., economic uncertainty, domestic violence). In the absence of psychopathology, typical age-related increases in sadness, frustration, and anger are responses to particular situations and transient. For most children and adolescents, the experience of these negative emotions supports the acquisition of various and flexible coping strategies (e.g., talking over problems, changing behaviors, avoiding conflict) that are more likely to result in positive outcomes (Compas, 1987; Compas, Malcarne, & Fondacaro, 1988). But for some, as a result of biological predisposition and/or traumatic experience, such negative emotions can become predominant, diminishing self-esteem and contributing to a negative self-identity and the emergence of mood disorders.

In earlier chapters we have discussed **domains of competence** as areas of challenge and resolution that have an impact on the ways in which children perceive themselves. Researchers have described domain categories—including academics, behavior and conduct, and friendships—that have an impact on younger children's developing sense of self. Others have identified domains related to sports and appearance. In adolescence, additional domains such as romantic relationships and the world of work emerge (Roisman, Masten, Coatsworth, & Tellegen, 2004). We do not expect that children and adolescents exhibit similar achievements in each and every domain at the same time. Some kids excel in sports early and display academic accomplishments later. Other kids become more physically or interpersonally attractive and socially comfortable as they

age. Domains involve multiple tasks with their own patterns of "emergence, ascendancy and decline" (Roisman et al., 2004, p. 123). Adolescents can be characterized as more or less comfortable in each important domain of development, and, during adolescence, domains related to academics, friendships and relationships, and appearance all become increasingly salient (Crystal et al., 1998; Roisman et al., 2004).

Arenas of comfort are the domains in which adolescents express relative satisfaction with themselves and their accomplishments (Call & Mortimer, 2001; Simmons, 2001). For instance, some adolescents who value relationships may spend time and effort developing multiple connections with others; success is tied to a sense of one's worth. Other adolescents focus on academic achievement and school activities, and successful experiences enhance well-being (Call & Mortimer, 2001). Typically developing adolescents experience comfort in at least one arena, and two-thirds report feeling comfortable in two or more arenas (see Table 12:1). Comfort appears to increase slightly over the course of adolescence and varies by gender, ethnicity, and SES background.

There are important connections between arenas of comfort and the adolescent's sense of self and

TABLE 12:1 Arenas of Comfort in Adolescence						
	9th GRADE		**10th GRADE**		**11th GRADE**	
Arena	*Percent*	*n*	*Percent*	*n*	*Percent*	*n*
Family Comfort						
Comfort with mother	57.9	921	59.0	918	59.5	881
Comfort with father	35.4	856	34.8	865	33.9	844
Peer Comfort						
Peer support	57.5	921	60.7	853	65.7	944
School Comfort						
Teacher support	57.9	993	56.2	949	57.8	892
Low time pressures	68.2	996	65.8	949	61.2	891
Work Comfort						
Supervisor support	41.3	269	34.1	337	35.6	491
Support from coworker	40.3	447	46.0	337	39.1	476
Work satisfaction	84.7	503	85.4	446	87.9	554
Low work stress	89.6	491	86.6	440	83.9	547
Work is interesting	73.8	504	71.0	451	69.3	554

From Call and Mortimer (2001).

identity. First, participation in multiple arenas is associated with an adolescent having more chances to experiment with identities and skills, and these chances are tied to increased opportunities for success and enhanced esteem (Barber, Stone, Hunt, & Eccles, 2005; Eccles et al., 2006). It is important, however, to balance changes in various arenas, because some adolescents may be overwhelmed if change occurs in every domain simultaneously (Costa et al., 2005; Simmons, 2001). Another connection involves the degree of commitment to a particular identity or arena (Barber, Eccles, & Stone, 2001). An adolescent who plans a career in theater may feel especially proud of a leading role in a school play; another adolescent whose parents were immigrants may seek an internship focused on immigration reform or international economics.

For both domains of competence and arenas of comfort, evidence of individual achievement and the accompanying respect and/or liking of peers contribute to a sense of competence, development of self-esteem, and the creation of social relationships that serve as protective factors. In fact, in the same way that developmental cascades have been described for various psychopathologies and for poor outcomes, a developmental cascade model can also describe "how one good thing leads to another," with interactive and expanding effects for positive outcomes for children and adolescents (Lewin-Bizan, Bowers, & Lerner, 2010). In contrast, lack of success in valued domains, lack of confidence in one's abilities, and feelings of social isolation may predispose a child or adolescent to a preponderance of negative emotions and negative moods; these are risk factors for current and later maladjustment.

Over the years of adolescence, most typically developing individuals come to construct a coherent autobiography (McLean & Pasupathi, 2010). Habermas and Bluck (2000) refer to this emergence of one's story as "getting a life" and emphasize that it depends on certain cognitive and social advances. Weaving together personal events (e.g., idiosyncratic family relationships) with normative cultural events (e.g., religious milestones or graduation from high school) and making sense of both continuity and discontinuity in personality are complicated tasks. The development of a life story may have particular significance for those who have struggled with psychopathology as children and for those who struggle during adolescence. As we move into a discussion of mood disorders, we will need to think carefully about the many

Nacivet/Getty Images

As with adults, sad mood and loss of pleasure are primary characteristics of childhood depression.

meanings of psychopathology and how they fit (or do not fit) into developing life stories.

Depressive Disorders

There are many excellent reviews of mood disorders in children and adolescents that provide historical perspectives (Cicchetti, Rogosch, & Toth, 1997; Fristad, Shaver, & Holderle, 2002; Garber & Smith, 2006; Zahn-Waxler, Klimes-Dougan, & Slattery, 2000). These reviews refute earlier theoretical models that proposed that children lacked the necessary psychological structures and processes to experience adult-like depression, and later beliefs that children's depression was often "masked" by irritability and aggression. The reviews also recall the poignant observations of René Spitz (1946), who described long-hospitalized infants displaying sadness, withdrawal, developmental delays, and maladaptation. These reviews also describe contemporary conceptualizations of children's mood disorders. Against the background of children's rapid developmental growth and change, researchers and clinicians agree that it is useful to think about a **mood-related continuum** (i.e., a range of distress and impairment) (Hankin, Fraley, Lahey, & Waldman, 2005) and to distinguish among children and adolescents who exhibit periods of sadness and/or irritability, those who struggle with longer episodes of depression and dysfunction, and those who are appropriately diagnosed with clinically significant mood disorders (Cicchetti & Toth, 1998; Garber & Smith, 2006).

The Case of Rebecca

Rebecca is an 8-year-old girl referred by her parents and pediatrician. Although Rebecca has always been somewhat shy, neither her parents nor the school had any serious concerns until she started third grade. Rebecca began to complain about difficulty falling asleep, and her teachers noted that she appeared tired in class. She began to have problems completing homework. Rebecca had been on the volleyball team for the past year; she loved the sport and was an excellent player and popular teammate. This year, however, she said she did not want to play because she felt she wasn't very good and that volleyball was "boring."

Always a cooperative child at home, Rebecca's parents are distressed by the fact that she has recently become argumentative and irritable. She is easily frustrated and cries often. Recently, Rebecca's mother was looking through Rebecca's schoolwork and found several notes written by Rebecca saying that she wished she were dead. When confronted with this, Rebecca refused to talk about it and sobbed at her parents that they didn't understand her at all. ■

The Case of Jacob

Jacob is a 9-year-old boy in the fourth grade referred because of concerns raised by his parents and teachers. Specifically, they describe him as irritable, hypersensitive, and sullen. Standardized testing suggests above-average intellectual ability, but Jacob struggles in class. He is easily discouraged and gives up quickly when he does not immediately understand a lesson. In these situations, he sometimes describes the assignments as "stupid," whereas at other times he says he cannot do them because he is "dumb." Jacob tends to play on his own on the playground and generally avoids group activities unless they are organized and supervised by an adult.

Jacob's parents note that school reports were generally more positive in his first year or two in elementary school. They say he was often described as bright, active, and friendly. Although he tended to be overly reactive to conflict and limit setting, he had several good friends that he enjoyed playing with during recess, and occasionally outside of school. His parents have difficulty pinpointing when his difficult moods began to worsen and linger, but they say the current problems have been present for at least the past year. Now Jacob seems to expect the worst in himself and others, fights frequently with his younger brother, and spends as much time as possible playing video games by himself. School reports make clear that Jacob struggles behaviorally and socially to a much greater extent than in past years. Jacob's parents have tried to talk to him about their concerns, but he rejects the idea that he is having any real difficulties. Jacob does say that he is frustrated with what he believes is near-constant nagging by his parents and the annoying behavior of his brother.

At home, Jacob's moodiness, negativity, and quick temper are upsetting to his parents. In particular, they are distressed by his severe and frequent temper outbursts. They note that several times a week Jacob will react to some small frustration, request, or correction with verbal, and sometimes physical, rage. At such times, Jacob will usually scream at his parents, throw and kick things, and occasionally hit them. Over the years, they have referred to these episodes as Jacob's "emotional storms" and assumed that he would outgrow such out-of-control behavior as he got older. That there has been such little change in his temper outbursts is especially discouraging to them and confusing to Jacob himself. ■

The Case of Zoey

Zoey is 15 years old and in tenth grade. She has been a good student, though her grades have recently slipped from mostly Bs to mostly Cs. Zoey's guidance counselor met with her after noticing the drop in her grades and hearing that she had quit the school's speech team. Zoey had been an enthusiastic and successful member of the team for her first 2 years of high school. Her closest friends were on the speech team; after quitting, she has become increasingly withdrawn. After confiding to the counselor that she was crying for no apparent reason and had lost interest in activities she used to enjoy, her counselor spoke to Zoey's parents and suggested they schedule an appointment with a psychologist.

The psychologist met with Zoey and her parents, both individually and as a family. Zoey's parents described her as an active, social, and fun-loving teenager who enjoyed everything about high school. In addition to speech, she was a member of a number of clubs and community service organizations. Although she liked the activities themselves, it was the opportunity to be with the other kids that seemed to give her the most pleasure. Zoey's parents reported that she was not an especially gifted student, but she was conscientious and worked very hard. Teachers recognized and appreciated this, and Zoey was proud of her B average. Looking back, her parents noted that things began to change the summer before eleventh grade. They recalled that she began to sleep more and more and was much less active during the day. Although she had planned on finding a job at the local mall, she never actually applied anywhere. She seemed to prefer to stay home and watch TV in the evening, and she began to gain weight. At first her friends called her often, but after Zoey repeatedly declined their invitations, they began to make plans without her. She appeared to regain some energy and enthusiasm when school started, but soon did poorly on some quizzes and tests and fell behind in her schoolwork. For the first time, she began to complain that the work was too hard and often fell asleep when trying to do homework. When her parents asked if she was using drugs, Zoey become extremely angry and agitated. She accused her parents of never trusting her and always being critical.

When informed that her parents had spoken about how well the first 2 years of high school had gone, Zoey seemed surprised and annoyed, saying that she had never liked school or most of the people there. She said she had participated in activities to make her parents happy, but that nothing she did was good enough so she quit. She talked at length about a group of friends that she felt had turned against her, and also that she felt "different" from the other students. She said that she last remembered being happy "maybe when I was a kid in grade school." Zoey told the psychologist that she had decided to ask for help because she had begun to experience repeated and intrusive thoughts about dying. She said that she did not have a plan for killing herself but was finding it increasingly difficult to manage these feelings of dread. She also said that she felt her guidance counselor was the only person she could really trust. She worried, however, that referring her to a psychologist was the counselor's way of getting rid of her. ■

There are several kinds of child and adolescent mood disorders, with different causes, courses, and outcomes. **Major depressive disorder** in children and adolescents is characterized by sadness and a loss of pleasure and is accompanied by cognitive, behavioral, and somatic symptoms. Cognitive symptoms include problems with attention and concentration, rumination, and thoughts of worthlessness and guilt. Behavioral and somatic symptoms include social withdrawal, fatigue and insomnia, and changes in appetite and/or weight. The case of Rebecca illustrates major depressive disorder in a child, whereas the case of Zoey illustrates major depressive disorder in an adolescent. Single or repeated episodes of depression in a child can be contrasted with his or her more usual, more adaptive functioning. The average length of episodes of major depression is between 7 and 9 months, and these episodes are often recurrent. **Dysthymia** involves a longstanding disturbance of mood, with ongoing sadness, irritability, and lack of motivation; other symptoms involving emotion, cognition, and behavior may also be observed. Childhood dysthymia lasts an average of 4 years, and about 70% of children with dysthymia eventually develop major depression (Birmaher et al., 1996a; Cicchetti & Toth, 1998). Compared to depressive disorder, dysthymia is underresearched and requires additional child- and adolescent-specific investigation (Masi, Millepiedi et al., 2003).

Although there is much similarity in the clinical presentation of depressive disorders in children and adolescents (and from childhood through adulthood), it is still important to consider the impact of age and development (Garber, 2007; Weiss & Garber, 2003). Younger children like Rebecca often have a more depressed appearance, display more somatic difficulties and anxiety symptoms, and struggle with externalizing behaviors. Adolescents are more likely to exhibit guilt and hopelessness, substance abuse, psychotic symptoms, and suicidality (Birmaher et al., 1996; Garber, 2007). Both children and adolescents struggle with rest–activity cycles, and many of them display sleep disturbances (Alfano & Gamble, 2009; Dahl & Lewin, 2002). Sleep disturbances are worrisome because they have been associated with worse outcomes (Armitage et al., 2004). It may be, however, that some of the sleep problems reported by adolescents are more likely to be associated with anxiety disorders than major depressive disorder (Forbes et al., 2008). Of course, for both children and adolescents, we need to keep in mind the possibility of atypical presentations of depression (Williamson et al., 2000).

With respect to depressive disorders in adolescence, we need to emphasize that even typically developing adolescents experience more extreme moods (especially negative ones) and more mood fluctuations than they did in childhood (Arnett, 1999; Garber, 2007); therefore, it is important to be very careful about identifying a pattern of symptoms that reflects clinically significant distress, dysfunction or impairment, or a pattern that includes subthreshold symptoms (Georgiades, Lewinsohn, Monroe, & Seeley, 2006). We also need to consider distinctions between an episode of major depressive disorder emerging for the first time in adolescence (that is, as initial psychopathology) and depression that emerges in adolescence following another disorder (that is, as a complicating comorbid disorder). This distinction may have even more relevance given the earlier discussion of the development of self and identity during adolescence. Adolescents diagnosed with depression may have difficulties reconciling joyful and successful childhoods with their current struggles, and may have a much more difficult time constructing a sense of self characterized by self-worth and self-efficacy.

Disruptive mood dysregulation disorder is a new type of depressive disorder introduced in DSM-5. The conceptualization of disruptive mood dysregulation disorder is the result of considerable research and clinical work. This work was, in large part, related to a previous broadening of the symptoms used to diagnose bipolar disorder in DSM-IV in children and in adolescents, dramatic increases in the diagnosis of bipolar disorder in children and adolescents, and a lack of continuity observed between clinical presentation in childhood and later in adulthood (American Psychiatric Association, 2010). In addition, important treatment implications related to access to mental health services and medications were taken into account; these will be discussed further in the intervention section.

Disruptive mood dysregulation disorder involves severe, recurrent temper tantrums that are atypical with respect to intensity and frequency. In between tantrums, the mood of the child is persistently and pervasively irritable or angry. The case of Jacob is an example of this disorder. Keep in mind that typically developing children display tantrums. As noted in the summary of oppositional defiant disorder in

Chapter 10, the key differences in normative versus nonnormative tantrums relate to the intensity of tantrums, the destructiveness of tantrums, and the difficulty in recovering from tantrums (see Figs. 12:1a, 12:1b, and 12:1c). Whereas the overall frequency of tantrums decreases significantly over the preschool years, destructive tantrums, when present, increase in frequency between 3 and 5 years of age and are strongly associated with later clinical disorder (Egger, 2011; Egger & Angold, in press). Nondestructive tantrums are those that involve, for example, crying, stamping, nondirected kicking, and holding one's breath. Destructive tantrums include aggression against others or the self (such as hitting, kicking, or biting) or breaking things. The DSM-5 diagnostic criteria specify that the diagnosis *should not* be given to a child younger than 6. Although the rationale for this cutoff is not provided in DSM-5, it is likely that this criterion reflects an attempt to emphasize the atypical presentation and associated impairment of high-frequency, destructive tantrums that persist with age and that occur in multiple settings with a variety of others (in addition to parents) (Egger, 2011).

Also keep in mind that many typically developing children and adolescents are intermittently irritable, and irritability is observed in a variety of childhood disorders (such as oppositional defiant disorder and the anxiety disorders) (Stringaris, 2011). In disruptive mood dysregulation disorder, the chronic irritability is atypical and is associated with significant impairment (Leibenluft, 2011). Children who displayed this chronic irritability in previous years might have been diagnosed with bipolar disorder. Whereas the earlier set of diagnostic criteria allowed for nonepisodic irritability as part of the clinical presentation of bipolar disorder in children, the new diagnosis makes clear that persistent, nonepisodic irritability is part of the distinct pattern of difficulties and impairment in disruptive mood dysregulation disorder.

Because only a small percentage of children and adolescents with mood disorders are seen at mental health facilities, it is important to make use of population studies that calculate the prevalence of depressive disorders (Avenevoli, Knight, Kessler, & Merikangas, 2008). Several investigations have estimated that these disorders are relatively uncommon in preschoolers and increase in following years, from 2% to 3% in 6- to 12-year-olds, to 10% to 20% in adolescents (Essau & Dobson, 1999; Kessler,

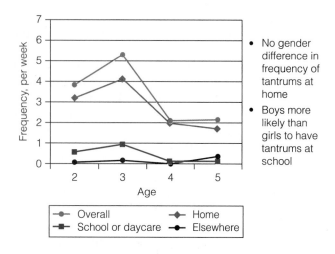

FIGURE 12:1a Mean frequency of tantrums by age.
Source: From Egger (2011).

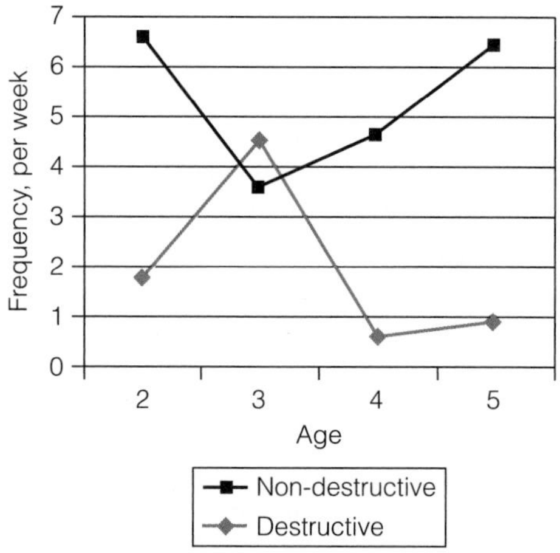

FIGURE 12:1b Relative frequency of destructive and non-destructive tantrums.
Source: From Egger (2011).

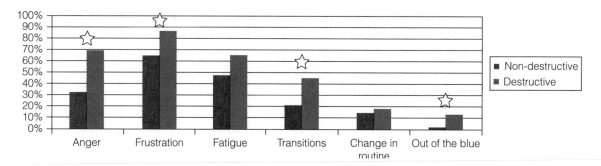

FIGURE 12:1c Triggers of tantrums.
Source: From Egger (2011).

Avenevoli, & Merikangas, 2001; Lewinsohn & Essau, 2002). Gender differences in rates of disorder are notable, with gender ratios approximately equal before adolescence; girls' levels of depression increase rapidly in early adolescence (Essau, Lewinson, Seeley, & Sasagawa, 2010; Garber, 2007; Hankin, Wetter, & Cheely, 2008; Nolen-Hoeksema, 2002; see Box 12:1). There also appear to be group cohort differences in rates of disorder, with successive increases in recent years (Pennington, 2002; Twenge & Nolen-Hoeksema, 2002), although there are also data suggesting relative stability (Costello, Erkanli, & Angold, 2006). With respect to ethnic differences, rates are lower for youth of Chinese background and higher for youth of Mexican background and boys of African American backgrounds (Kistner, David-Ferdon, Lopez, & Dunkel, 2007; Roberts, Roberts, & Chen, 1997); adolescents in Hong Kong display rates similar to European American adolescents (Stewart, Lewinsohn et al., 2002). Other differences related to ethnicity and SES require additional investigation, particularly as they relate to larger groups of Hispanic American children and immigrant youth (Roberts et al., 1997; Yearwood, Crawford, Kelly, & Moreno, 2007).

The presence of other comorbid disorders is a frequent phenomenon. The most common categories of comorbid disorders include all types of anxiety disorders, attention-deficit hyperactivity disorder, substance abuse disorders, and eating disorders (Rohde, 2009). As noted in Chapter 4, the sequence in which disorders develop is important. For most examples of comorbidity that involve major depressive disorder, the depressive disorder follows the other disorder (Rohde, 2009). For individuals with a comorbid disorder, the duration of a major depressive episode is likely to be longer; this is particularly true for boys (Essau et al., 2010).

BOX 12:1 RISK AND RESILIENCE

Gender Differences in Depression in Adolescence

One of the most striking examples of developmental psychopathology can be found in the relations among depressive disorder, age, and gender. Depressive disorder occurs in childhood at relatively equal rates in boys and girls. However, as children move through puberty and into adolescence, girls develop depression at an accelerated rate until they are twice as likely to develop depression as boys. This finding is so striking and so well replicated that it is sometimes referred to as "the big fact" (Galambos, Leadbetter, & Barker, 2004; Hankin & Abramson, 2001). Whereas this developmental pattern is clear, the reasons for the shift in the prevalence of depression are more elusive.

A number of hypotheses have been investigated. Some researchers have examined differences in risk factors prior to adolescence that may make depression more likely within the context of the challenges of adolescence. One such risk factor is the sexual abuse of preadolescent children. A history of sexual abuse is known to predispose an individual to later depression, and girls are far more likely than boys to have been sexually abused (Weiss, Longhurst, & Mazure, 1999). We also know that genetic factors influence the onset of depression. It may be that genetic risk is unevenly distributed in girls and boys and is not fully expressed until adolescence and in combination with environmental stressors (Silberg et al., 1999).

Gender differences in cognitive variables have also been considered. For example, research has shown that boys tend to judge the physical changes they experience in puberty more positively than girls view the physical changes they undergo (Rierdan & Koff, 1997). Also, during early adolescence girls tend to show a greater need for approval and success, lower levels of positive thinking, and more self-focused negative cognitions; all of these are associated with depressive symptoms (Calvete & Cardenoso, 2005; Papadakis, Prince, Jones, & Strauman, 2006). Other researchers have investigated the roles of biological factors interacting with social development. It may be that both hormonal and social factors promote affiliative needs during puberty for girls, and that these drives create certain vulnerabilities that lead to greater risk for depression (Hazler & Mellin, 2004).

The **cognitive vulnerability–stress model** of depression is an example of a multifactorial risk model

focused on gender differences (Hyde, Mezulis, & Abramson, 2008; Mezulis et al., 2010). In this model, biological risk factors, affective risk factors, and cognitive risk factors interact with stressors, leading to the development of major depressive disorder. With respect to gender, the model suggests that greater cognitive vulnerability in girls coupled with increased numbers of stressors in adolescence explains the differences in rates of depression in adolescent girls.

The link between risk-taking behaviors and adolescent depression has been a recent focus of study. In an extensive National Institutes of Health–sponsored study, the development and correlates of depressive symptoms in nearly 19,000 teens were examined (Waller et al., 2006). Risky behaviors such as the use of tobacco, alcohol, and other drugs, and sexual activity, as well as level and severity of risk taking, were considered. Boys and girls who abstained from these risky behaviors showed no differences in the development of depressive symptoms. The same was true (i.e., equivalent rates of depression) for teens who engaged in very high-risk behaviors such as intravenous drug use. However, the clinical picture was much different for those teens in the low and moderate risk categories. Girls who engaged in low to moderate levels of risky behaviors were significantly more likely than boys to develop depressive symptoms. The specific mechanisms leading to this correlation are not known, but researchers' hypotheses will guide further studies. It may be, for instance, that behaviors such as substance abuse and sexual activity alter girls' social contexts more than boys' and so are associated with greater risk. Or it may be that the use of drugs and alcohol affects the developing brains of adolescent boys and girls differently, which then affects cognitive and emotional development in ways that link to later depression. Of course, it is also possible that these risk behaviors are actually the result, rather than the cause, of developing depression. It is important to remember that there is no reason to assume that there is a single explanation for these findings. As with many interesting and challenging aspects of developmental psychopathology, new data on gender and the course of depressive disorders lead to new questions that, in turn, lead to innovative new research designs capable of addressing complex interactions.

The Case of Kareem

Kareem is 17 years old and in twelfth grade. He is a gifted runner and was recently voted captain of the track team. Throughout high school, Kareem has been active and popular. In addition to being on the track and cross country teams, he is also vice president of the student council, plays trumpet in the jazz band, and has been in several school plays. Kareem experienced some difficulties in elementary and middle school, where he struggled academically and got in trouble for being impulsive and somewhat oppositional. In sixth grade, a school counselor suggested that he might have ADHD. At his parents' urging, Kareem's pediatrician started him on a trial of medication typically used to treat ADHD. The trial was discontinued, however, when the medication seemed to exacerbate rather than help the problem. Despite these challenges, a combination of classroom modifications and some individual counseling allowed Kareem to finish middle school on a more positive note. Kareem appeared to thrive in high school, where his energy, extraversion, and enthusiasm found many positive outlets.

The first signs that Kareem would not end his high school career as well as he had started came early in his senior year. Kareem became preoccupied with a new girl in his English class. Although he had never spoken with her before, he came to class one day with flowers and a necklace he had bought for her. Although flattered, the girl felt uncomfortable with the attention and let Kareem know this. Kareem's reaction was to profess his undying love for her and assure her that he was certain she was secretly in love with him. At first, other students found this odd but funny and said it was just "Kareem being Kareem." This perception began to change when the girl and her parents went to the principal with a stack of sexually explicit notes that Kareem had sent by e-mail. Kareem was suspended briefly and moved to a different English class.

Kareem's behavior became more erratic and bizarre. He would get up and pace during classes, and he became increasingly impatient with other students, teachers, coaches, and his family. He often responded belligerently to questions and also pushed a coach following a difficult track practice. Two days after the track incident, Kareem took a history exam, ignoring all questions but one. His essay was an elaborate and difficult-to-follow argument that all of human history was culminating in the emergence of a superior individual with psychic powers, and that the time was right to reveal the fact that he was that person. Later that same day, Kareem walked into the staff lounge, where he propositioned a teacher. Kareem became angry when told to leave, overturned furniture, and threatened those who tried to intervene. Eventually the police were called and he was taken to a local hospital. Along the way, Kareem began to weep. By the time he arrived at the emergency room, Kareem was exhausted and despondent. After an initial interview revealed that he was suicidal, Kareem was admitted to the adolescent psychiatric unit. ◼

Bipolar Disorder

Bipolar disorder is an especially severe form of mood disorder. It has been extensively researched in the adult population, and its presentation, etiology, and treatment are fairly well understood. Bipolar disorder in adults usually involves periods of depression alternating with periods of severe or moderate **mania**. Manic episodes are characterized by unusual and persistent mood elevation, including decreased need for sleep, increased irritability, extremely impulsive and risky behaviors, and sometimes even psychotic thinking. Manic symptoms in adolescents, as described in the case of Kareem, may also include grandiose delusions (related to current and later success, or great wealth), increased nighttime activity (such as rearranging furniture in bedrooms or leaving the house to be with friends), pressured speech (i.e., the tendency to speak rapidly and urgently), hypersexuality, and risk-taking behaviors (Geller & Luby, 1997; Geller, Zimerman, et al., 2002). **Hypomania** involves unusual and dysregulated emotions, thoughts, and behaviors similar to mania, although there are no psychotic symptoms and the degree of impairment is less severe. For some adolescents, it may be difficult to identify discrete episodes of disorder because there may be a gradual worsening of distressing and dysfunctional behavior. There are also some reports of "model" adolescents with an abrupt onset (Geller, Zimerman et al., 2002; Lewinsohn et al., 2003). Suicidality is a critical concern. Overall, these clinical symptoms and diagnostic criteria are very similar for both adolescents and adults.

The picture is more complicated, however, when the issue is bipolar disorder in children. Like earlier debates over whether children actually experience major depression, the question of whether (and how often) bipolar disorder is accurately diagnosed in children remains controversial. "For prepubertal children especially, the devil has been in the details in defining episode, euphoria, grandiosity, decreased need for sleep, and distinguishing the other symptoms of bipolar disorder from various childhood conditions, especially attention deficit/hyperactivity disorder" (Meyer & Carlson, 2010, p. 36). The current consensus is that bipolar disorder can emerge in childhood but that it is difficult to diagnose and complicated to treat (Brotman et al., 2006; Meyer & Carlson, 2010). When bipolar disorder is observed and diagnosed in children and young adolescents, the revised DSM-5 criteria emphasize the similarities in clinical presentation among children, adolescents, and adults, with an increased focus on the *episodic nature* of mania. This is in contrast, as already discussed, to the chronic display of irritability in disruptive mood dysregulation disorder.

Because conceptualizations of bipolar disorder in childhood and adolescence have undergone revision, rates of disorder are difficult to estimate. Rates in late adolescence are assumed to be similar to rates observed in adult populations (Geller & Luby, 1997; Lewinsohn, Seeley, & Klein, 2003); rates of admission to adolescent inpatient units for bipolar disorder more than doubled between 1995 and 2000 and continued to increase until 2004 (Blader & Carlson, 2007; Harpaz-Rotem, Leslie, Martin, & Rosenheck, 2005). But these rates likely reflect the broadened symptom set that has been recently revised. Although the clinical picture appears similar for both boys and girls, more boys are diagnosed in adolescence (Biederman et al., 2003; Moreno et al., 2007).

Developmental Course

Continuity of Depressive Disorders

As with all types of child psychopathology, developmental continuity is often observed for youngsters with major depressive disorder. That is, struggles in childhood are associated with struggles in adolescence, and struggles in adolescence are associated with struggles in adulthood (Costello, Foley, & Angold, 2006; Garber, 2007; Rutter et al., 2006). Although continuity is common, other pathways are also possible, including the emergence of difficulties in adolescence without previous symptomatology, subthreshold symptoms that increase in severity and contribute to the emergence of major depressive disorder, and the emergence of adult depression preceded by anxiety disorders in childhood and adolescence (Garber, Keiley, & Martin,

2002; Georgiades et al., 2006; Rutter et al., 2006). According to Cole et al. (2002), there are several "destabilizing factors" that influence developmental continuity versus discontinuity during late childhood and early adolescence. Some of the destabilizing factors that may be coupled with either significant improvement or deterioration include changes in emotional lability, improving (or deteriorating) relationships, and educational transitions. By late adolescence, individual patterns are more stable.

Individual differences in developmental pathways and outcomes depend on a variety of factors. Repeat episodes and worse outcomes are linked to gender, early diagnosis, severity of depression, history of sexual abuse, parent psychopathology, and poor peer relationships (Barbe, Bridge, Birmaher, Kolko, & Brent, 2004; Birmaher et al., 2004; Essau et al., 2010; Kovacs, Obrosky, & Sherrill, 2003). Thinking back to the case of Rebecca earlier in the chapter, there are several risk factors that portend long-term difficulties. First, she is a girl. Whereas gender ratios for depression are relatively equal in early and middle childhood, being a girl may further complicate the clinical presentation as she transitions into adolescence. Rebecca's depression is also identified before puberty. And her depression is severe, accompanied by suicidal ideation. But there are also protective factors that may balance or moderate the developmental course of the disorder. Rebecca's parents are aware and involved, and she has a history of good friendships (Brendgen, Wanner, Morin, & Vitaro, 2005). With this mixed clinical picture, either better or worse outcomes for Rebecca are possible.

Most children and adolescents who experience depression deal with multiple episodes. In addition to the chronic struggling with depressive psychopathology itself, it is also necessary to understand how repeat episodes of depression interfere with everyday challenges. For example, major depressive disorder has a negative impact on school achievement, especially for boys. To the extent that children take pride in academic success and value themselves less when they do poorly, additional cycles of depression, failure, and despair may exacerbate the initial psychopathology and contribute to a poor self-image that lasts years longer than treated, time-limited episodes of depression (Ialongo, Edelsohn, & Kellam, 2001; Rapport, Denney, Chung, & Hustace, 2001; Street et al., 2004).

Data on the developmental course of children diagnosed with disruptive mood dysregulation disorder are, of course, limited (given its recent description). However, there are longitudinal data that contributed to the conceptualization of the new disorder, as well as to its differentiation from childhood-onset bipolar disorder. These data suggest that the chronic irritability component of disruptive mood dysregulation disorder predicts later depressive disorders (Leibenluft, 2011; Stringaris & Goodman, 2009).

With respect to the ongoing impact of children's depressive disorders on parents and families, there are many studies, a lot of data, and various conclusions. Children's depression is often accompanied by difficult communication, conflict, disturbed relationships, and decreases in nurturant parenting (Brody, 1998; Kim et al., 2003; Slesnick & Waldron, 1997). Intact, better functioning families are predictive of more rapid rates of recovery (Geller, Craney et al., 2002).

A number of professionals have noted that mood disorders in children and adolescents may also be linked with special strengths. For example, some children "may learn to be especially attuned to others' feelings and sensitivities, which in some contexts may be especially adaptive and valuable" (Cummings, Davies, & Campbell, 2000, p. 335). These children may focus their talents on animal care, or artistic endeavors, or volunteering and community involvement.

Comorbidity Across Time

Comorbidity is another influential factor. Major depressive disorder combined with other psychopathologies is associated with increased impairment, substance use and abuse, and suicidality (Costello, Foley, & Angold, 2006; Fombonne et al., 2001a, 2001b). Depressed adolescents with substance abuse disorders are more likely to be later diagnosed with personality disorders (i.e., inflexible, maladaptive personality patterns together with serious personal and social distress and impairment), such as borderline personality disorder (Grilo, Walker, Becker, Edell, & McGlashan, 1997). Clinicians have hypothesized that some adolescents may attempt to "self-medicate" with either drugs or alcohol. Given that depression usually precedes substance abuse by several years, Cicchetti and Toth (1998) have described a window of opportunity (between the onset of the major depression and the later onset of substance abuse) where mental health professionals might focus specific prevention efforts.

Continuity of Bipolar Disorder

With respect to bipolar disorder, a chronic pattern has been observed for children and adolescents. Ongoing difficulties include both subthreshold symptoms and full episodes (Birmaher et al., 2009). Relapse rates are high and often occur during medication management treatments (Geller, Craney, et al., 2002; Jairam, Srinath, Girimaji, & Seshadri, 2004). There are also variations in some of the associated difficulties of mania, depending on whether the manic symptoms are more intermittent or chronic (e.g., depression and suicidality for episodic subtype versus violent behavior for chronic subtype) (Bhangoo et al., 2003). Again, early diagnosis, more severe symptoms, and comorbid disorders are associated with poor outcomes (Craney & Geller, 2003a; DelBello, Hanseman, Adler, Fleck, & Strakowski, 2007; Geller et al., 2004; Meyer & Carlson, 2010). There are also data that suggest that for individuals at high risk (because their parents were diagnosed with bipolar disorder), there was variability in disorders in adolescence (e.g., anxiety disorders) that preceded later onset bipolar disorder (Meyer & Carlson, 2010). Other data suggest that cultural factors have an impact on outcome. For example, adolescents from Taiwan fare better than adolescents in the United States (Strakowski et al., 2007). Better outcomes for adolescents in Taiwan were explained, in part, by lower levels of depression and substance abuse, earlier help seeking, and longer hospitalizations (Strakowski et al., 2007).

Etiology

Depressive Disorders

There are many causes, many pathways, and many outcomes for children and adolescents with depressive disorders. As with other types of psychopathology, it is necessary to construct risk models that include multiple factors, in various combinations, that lead to disorder. One such model is provided by Goodman and Gotlib (1999, 2002), who describe several major causal mechanisms, including (1) the heritability of depression, (2) innate dysfunctional neuroregulatory mechanisms, (3) exposure to negative parental personality and parenting, and (4) the general stressful context of children's lives. Another model provides a multilevel, developmental framework, with both direct and interactive effects (Garber, 2007) (see Fig. 12:2).

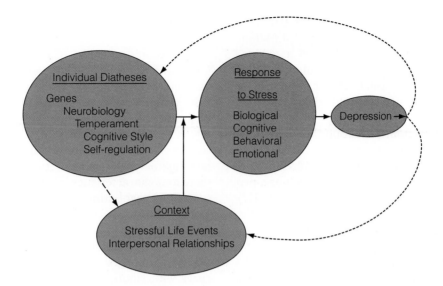

FIGURE 12:2 A multilevel biopsychosocial model of depression.

Source: Multilevel dynamics in developmental psychopathology: pathways to the future by MINNESOTA SYMPOSIUM ON CHILD PSYCHOLOGY Copyright 2007 Reproduced with permission of TAYLOR & FRANCIS GROUP LLC - BOOKS in the format Textbook and Other Book via Copyright Clearance Center.

Genes and Heredity

Estimates of heritability for mood disorders for children and adolescents are moderate and are similar to those observed for adults; there is some evidence for higher heritabilities in boys (Birmaher et al., 2004; Ehringer et al., 2006; Elizabeth, King, & Ollendick, 2004). The genetic impact on depressive symptoms appears to increase as children age (Rutter et al., 2006; Scourfield et al., 2003). This increase in heritability appears linked to gene-by-environment interactions, with individuals at high risk because of genetics experiencing more negative life events (Garber, 2007; Rutter et al., 2006). Family studies of depressive disorder indicate that "having a depressed parent is one of the most powerful predictors of depression in children, which likely is due to both genetic and environmental influences" (Garber, 2007, p. 202).

Physiological Factors

Neurophysiological investigations have identified a number of structural and biochemical differences that contribute to the emergence of depressive disorders (Kaufman & Charney, 2003). Abnormalities have been observed in mood-regulating areas of the brain, such as the amygdala (Forbes & Dahl, 2005; Del-Bello, Zimmerman, Mills, Getz, & Strakowski, 2004;

Leibenluft, Charney, & Pine, 2003). There are also data depicting decreased blood flow and reduced activation patterns in the left frontal regions of the brain (Dawson et al., 2003; Rao et al., 2002), and these EEG asymmetries continue into adulthood (Miller et al., 2002). Pennington (2002) brings these sets of findings together and describes an "imbalance between top-down (prefrontal) and bottom-up (amygdala) components of the affect regulation system" (p. 117).

Additional research highlights the dysregulation of neurotransmitters, norepinephrine and serotonin in particular (Pennington, 2002). This dysregulation may, in turn, lead to chronic overactivity of the hypothalamic-pituitary-adrenal (HPA) axis (Ashman, Dawson, Panagiotides, Yamada, & Wilkinson, 2002). Abnormalities in the secretion of growth hormones are also consistently observed in children and adolescents at risk for major depression (Birmaher & Heydl, 2001; Dahl et al., 2000). Overall, the neural pathways that lead to depressive disorders appear to be distinct from neural pathways to bipolar disorder (Rich et al., 2011).

The physiological bases of temperament also likely play an etiological part. Infants and children with difficult temperaments, who show decreases in flexibility and increases in negative moods, are at higher risk for the development of mood disorders (Austin & Chorpita, 2004; Hirshfeld-Becker et al., 2003; Lonigan, Phillips, & Hooe, 2003). Sleep disturbances are also commonly described (Alfano & Gamble, 2009). Decreased sleep is associated with increases in negative mood and risk-taking behaviors (Holm et al., 2009). Better sleep may be a protective factor in children and adolescents (Silk et al., 2007).

Pennington (2002), investigating the neural consequences of social stress, emphasizes the roles of "behavioral sensitization and electrophysiological kindling" and states that "social stress causes a permanent vulnerability in the HPA axis" (pp. 116–117). He suggests that over time the increasingly sensitive neurological response system requires lower thresholds of stimulation to trigger a new episode. This **kindling model** explains, in part, why later episodes of depression occur in the context of less severe stress. The kindling model may be further understood in the *social context of brain development*. That is, changes in the microstructures of the brain take place in continuous transaction with the environment. With the rapid production of neurons in early life, followed by neuronal pruning, stabilization, and sensitization, the experience of social distress and dysfunction has both immediate and long-term negative impacts (Bhangoo & Leibenluft, 2002; Curley et al., 2011; Dougherty, Klein, Rose, & Laptook, 2011). Finally, given the dramatic increases in rates of depressive disorders in adolescence, puberty changes and the timing of puberty are the frequent focus of study (Angold, Worthman, & Costello, 2003; Ge et al., 2003; Twenge & Nolen-Hoeksema, 2002). Early pubertal transitions are associated with greater stress, particularly for girls (Dorn et al., 2003; Garber, 2007). Physiological challenges include changes in hormone levels and endocrine functioning; the worrisome notion of "raging hormones" is now understood to be somewhat exaggerated (Weisz & Hawley, 2002). Still, there is clear evidence that neural systems do undergo significant change in brain regions associated with emotion, motivation, and decision making (Forbes et al., 2011; Forbes & Dahl, 2010; Pine, 2009). For some girls, physical development outpaces cognitive and emotional development. Social pressures may also increase, as peers and adults expect more adult-like behavior from those whose appearance suggests greater maturity. For boys, early maturity has a mix of positive and negative impacts, with higher levels of self-esteem balanced by engaging in more frequent risk behaviors.

Child Factors

Cicchetti and others (Cicchetti et al., 1997; Cicchetti & Toth, 1998) have described four individual characteristics of infants and young children, problems that increase risk for depression: (1) physiological regulation, (2) emotion differentiation and regulation, (3) the attachment relationship, and (4) the emergence of self and self-awareness. These investigators suggest that deficits or problems with these four characteristics influence children's lack of success in negotiating early age-related challenges, and this lack of success leads to poor outcomes.

Zahn-Waxler (2000) believes that emotion dysregulation is the core deficit. According to Zahn-Waxler, intense, prolonged, and poorly controlled experiences with emotion lead to the development of an affective bias. The bias or tendency to feel sad is usually most prominent, but there may also be biases related to anxiety, guilt, and shame. Having fewer emotion-regulation strategies, less effective strategies, or believing that strategies are ineffective contributes to the development of mood disorders (Brent & Maalouf, 2009; Cole, Luby, & Sullivan, 2008; Garber, 2007).

Attachment status has far-reaching impact, with an emphasis on the association between insecure attachment patterns and the emergence of internalizing disorders such as depression (Duggal, Carlson, Sroufe, & Egeland, 2001; Herring & Kaslow, 2002; Lyons-Ruth, Lyubchik, Wolfe, & Bronfman, 2002). Feelings of emotional security are the primary concern. According to Cummings et al. (2000), *emotional security* is central to the regulation of many kinds of behavior and is tied to three underlying processes: the child's emotional reactivity; representations of family relationships (i.e., the internalized working models); and regulation of exposure to family emotion. In addition, attachment security appears to moderate the child's response to later stress (Nachmias, Gunnar, Mangelsdorf, Parritz, & Buss, 1996). Lack of emotional support in early development may also lead to cognitive consequences, including negative self-concept and negative beliefs about the self. Dysfunctional cognitions that develop early may become entrenched because of ongoing or additional negative events (Garber et al., 2002; Nolen-Hoeksema, 1998; Tram & Cole, 2000).

Cognitive theories that emphasize self-efficacy, including Aaron Beck's (1987) information-processing theory of depression, Bandura's work on self-efficacy (e.g., Bandura, Pastorelli, Barbaranelli, & Caprara, 1999), and Seligman's (1975) theory of learned help-lessness, provide additional details about how cog-nitive factors influence developmental pathways to depression. Cognitions that increase the risk for depression include negative beliefs about the self, negative beliefs about the world, and negative beliefs about the future (Beck, 1987). In numerous studies, children who display negative automatic thoughts, dysfunctional attitudes, and low self-efficacy and self-esteem are more likely to develop depressive dis-orders (Garber, 2007). Negative beliefs may develop because of problematic early experiences, additional life stressors, difficult interpersonal relationships (e.g., with peers), or as a result of modeling others' beliefs (Garber, 2007). For adolescents, low self-efficacy in more than one domain of competence (e.g., academic, social, athletic, romantic) may have cumulative effects; higher levels of self-efficacy in any domain may have protective effects (Seroczynski, Cole, & Maxwell, 1997). These efficacy hypotheses have received support in studies of adolescents in both the United States and in Hong Kong (Stewart et al., 2004).

One cognitive characteristic that has received a lot of research attention is **rumination**. Rumination is a "relatively stable maladaptive coping strategy" involves repeated focus on problems or symptoms and causes and consequences of those problems or symptoms (Burwell & Shirk, 2007, p. 56; Nolen-Hoeksema, 2000). Rumination appears to prolong episodes of depression, especially in girls and young women (Burwell & Shirk, 2007; Essau et al., 2010). Further, a "cost of caring" has been described in girls' friendships, in which the rumination of one friend is associated with increased empathic distress in the other (Smith & Rose, 2011).

Psychological characteristics that *decrease the likelihood of externalizing disorders* may ironically *increase the likelihood of other disorders*. Particu-lar personality types, such as being overcontrolled, illustrate this paradoxical situation (Robins, John, Caspi, Moffitt, & Stouthamer-Loeber, 1996; Zahn-Waxler et al., 2000). That is, a child who is over-controlled is less likely to display problematic externalizing behaviors such as defiance or aggres-sion but is more likely to display problematic inter-nalizing behaviors such as worrying or withdrawal. Individual differences in coping must also be con-sidered, because short-term strategies for deal-ing with stress and pain often become either more

positive or more negative long-term traits. So, for example, "avoidance takes the form of moving out of the house. Escapes become enduring dedications, such as 'working like a lion' in school, excelling in sports, [or] becoming 'spiritual'" (Radke-Yarrow & Klimes-Dougan, 1997, p. 386).

Parent and Family Factors

There have been numerous investigations of children of depressed parents. Longitudinal data provides clear evidence that depressed parents, *in addition to their genetic and physiological impact*, have chil-dren who struggle with a variety of internalizing and externalizing disorders (Dawson & Ashman, 2000; Diego et al., 2004; Goodman et al., 2011; Hammen, Shih, & Brennan, 2004). According to Radke-Yarrow and Klimes-Dougan (1997), "being born to and reared by a depressed parent carries the expectation of problems" (p. 374). But not all chil-dren with depressed parents are depressed them-selves. If they do have problems, not all of them are similar. Most research on depressed parents focuses on mothers. Results of research with fathers are mixed. There are data that document the negative impact of depressed fathers, and other data suggest-ing that a father's depression is less strongly related to child depression than a mother's depression (Kane & Garber, 2004; Jacob & Johnson, 1997).

Three **pathways of parental impact** have been described (Cummings et al., 2000):

1. Parent depression affects parent–child rela-tionships and interactions and leads to child psychopathology.
2. Parent depression affects family relationships and interactions and causes family disruptions, which lead to child psychopathology.
3. Parent depression affects marital satisfaction, and this leads to child psychopathology.

With respect to the parent–child relationship, Cicchetti et al. (1997) note that depressed mothers are "affectively asynchronous" with their infants. That is, the sadness, social withdrawal, and reduced activ-ity that are hallmarks of adult depression interfere with the typical positive emotional and behavioral exchanges that characterize mother–infant interac-tions (Tronick & Gianino, 1986). Some depressed parents express irritability or hostility or hold neg-ative beliefs about their children (Goodman et al., 2011). The timing, severity, and chronicity of parent depression may moderate or intensify these patterns.

© iStockphoto.com/YazolinoGirl

Along with other risk factors, having depressed parents significantly increases the likelihood that a child will develop depression or other forms of psychopathology.

The emotional unavailability and insensitivity sometimes seen in depressed parents hinder the development of secure attachment relationships (Cicchetti, Rogosch & Toth, 1998; Cummings et al., 2000). Depressed mothers with comorbid psychopathology (such as personality disorders) have even more negative impact (Ellenbogen & Hodgins, 2004; Radke-Yarrow & Klimes-Dougan, 1997).

Parenting practices of depressed parents are also frequently inconsistent and ineffective (Davis, Sheeber, & Hops, 2002; Koenig, Ialongo, Wagner, Poduska, & Kellam, 2002; Sagrestano, Paikoff, Holmbeck, & Fendrich, 2003). Family conflict is another risk factor (Duggal, Carlson, Sroufe, & Egeland, 2001). But specific family factors may have differential impact, depending on ethnicity. High levels of family conflict appear to be particularly problematic for European American adolescents, whereas lack of family cohesion appears to be especially problematic for African American adolescents (Herman, Ostrander, & Tucker, 2007).

Overall, many of these risk factors are consistent with a **reinforcement model** of depression (Pennington, 2002), in which parents offer fewer rewards and more punishments to their children. This reinforcement model is sometimes viewed as more consistent with the maintenance of depression in children rather than the emergence of depression. Mental health services that support effective parenting for mothers and fathers with depression are essential (Lyons-Ruth, Wolfe, & Lyubchik, 2000).

Even as we discuss the caregiving difficulties experienced by depressed parents, we need to remember that many depressed parents exhibit average or even excellent parenting. "For example, a girl's father, despite being alcoholic and depressed, may remain very loving and caring toward her. While she may experience the negative sequelae of the father's problems, she may also firmly understand that she is loved and may treasure and benefit from those experiences that are supportive and special" (Cummings et al., 2000, p. 301). It is also the case that there is specificity observed in children's interactions with a depressed parent, so a child's relationships with nondepressed adults may serve as important protective factors.

Certain child factors moderate or exacerbate the impact of parent depression. The age and developmental stage of a child may interact with various symptoms of parental depression (Radke-Yarrow & Klimes-Dougan, 1997). Or, for instance, "a child may have an easy temperament, with a high capacity to adapt, or even profit, from adversity" (Cummings et al., 2000, p. 301). Gender again plays a role. In a recent meta-analysis, maternal depression was more strongly associated with internalizing disorders for girls (Goodman et al., 2011). "In contrast, pathways to externalizing problems in children of depressed mothers" were not gender specific (p. 15). For the girls, hypotheses about greater vulnerability included more genetic impact, gendered patterns of socialization, more interpersonal stressors and greater sensitivity to those stressors, and specific parenting practices (Goodman et al., 2011).

Another recent investigation described a "launch and grow" model of depression (Garber & Cole, 2010). In that model, a set of cascading effects (related to self-worth, family environment, and stressful life events) was set into motion for children who experienced maternal depression by age 12 and predicted the trajectory of depression across adolescence.

With respect to family relationships and family atmosphere, parental psychopathology has varied consequences (Duggal et al., 2001; Zahn-Waxler et al., 2000). It helps to keep in mind that all families experience stress and conflict. But families with a depressed adult often experience more atypical stressors and less competent coping. According to Radke-Yarrow and Klimes-Dougan (1997), in well-functioning families, "severe stress is generally severe in ways that are 'normal' (e.g., illness, death, loss of job, husband-wife incompatibility). In the depressed families, there is a compounding of stress, not only of the 'normal' sort but also of a less normal nature (e.g., husband throws the family out of the house; the depressed mother disappears and neighbors and church members take over the running of the family; the children are abused by a live-in uncle; mother cannot manage the daily routines, so the 8-year-old takes over)" (p. 383).

Finally, parent psychopathology influences child psychopathology via mechanisms related to marital conflict. Depressed parents are negative and critical toward their spouses as well as their children. Warmth and emotional support from the well spouse is critical in helping the struggling spouse both with the disorder and with parenting. However, "the tiresome, chronic reassurance seeking and frustrating inconsistency … may lead to eventual rejection by significant others" (Cummings et al., 2000, p. 313). At times, marital violence may aggravate an already tense situation (Fainsilber Katz & Low, 2004).

Environmental Factors

Even with the myriad factors related to genes, individual characteristics, and family functioning, we should not overlook the impact of larger events (such as trauma) and larger environments (such as culture and socioeconomic background) on the development of mood disorders (Cicchetti & Toth, 1998; Rutter, 1998). However, we should also be thinking about the emergence of psychopathology in more complex ways. For example, children at high genetic risk may be more sensitive to the effects of adverse environments (Birmaher et al., 1996b). Also, individual children, even those in the same family, may respond differently to a stressor; distinctions need to be made between shared risk factors (affecting all siblings) and nonshared risk factors (affecting only one sibling, or affecting one or more siblings disproportionately) (Eley, 1999; Pennington, 2002).

Both specific **negative life events** (such as a parent losing a job or a serious illness in the family) and

chronic hassles have been associated with depression in children, especially in the early years (Birmaher et al., 1996b; Nolen-Hoeksema et al., 1992). With increasing age, interactions between negative events and the child's cognitive abilities and tendencies (such as pessimistic explanatory styles) become more important (Nolen-Hoeksema et al., 1992; Weisz, Sweeney, Proffitt, & Carr, 1993), as well as interactions between environmental factors (negative events and social support) (Petti et al., 2004).

In addition to major life events, chronic hassles can also contribute to high levels of stress (Garber & Little, 1999). Problematic peer relationships, and romantic difficulties in particular, may also be extremely stressful for adolescents (Furman & Shaffer, 2003; Nolan, Flynn, & Garber, 2003). Evidence suggesting that girls are exposed to more episodic stressors, and more total stressors, may provide additional perspective on observed gender differences in rates of depression (Hankin, Mermelstein, & Roesch, 2007; Shih, Eberhart, Hammen, & Brennan, 2006). As an everyday, environmental risk factor, poverty exerts a number of deleterious effects. In addition, it appears to "be a broad-scale enhancer of risk in relation to depression in mothers" (Goodman et al., 2011, p. 15). That is, findings related to the effects of maternal depression on children are magnified in the presence of poverty. Neighborhood adversity also constrains the benefits of available protective factors (Silk et al., 2007).

Maltreatment, including physical abuse, sexual abuse, emotional abuse, and neglect, long understood to be precursors of insecure attachment, are also predictably related to later mood disorders in children and adolescents (Cicchetti & Toth, 1995, 2003; Putnam, 2003). Individual and developmental factors; the specific form, severity, and chronicity of abuse; and other environmental factors all influence children's outcomes (Barbe, Bridge, Birmaher, Kolko, & Brent, 2004; Nolen-Hoeksema, 2002).

Bipolar Disorders

As with major depressive disorder, genes are important determinants of risk for bipolar disorder (Faraone, Glatt, & Tsuang, 2003; Potash et al., 2007; Rende et al., 2007); in fact, bipolar disorder is second only to autism in terms of familiality and heritability (Pennington, 2002). Genes also appear to have an impact on age of onset (Faraone, Lasky-Su, Glatt, Van Eerdewegh, & Tsuang, 2006). There are also data that suggest partial overlap between bipolar disorder and major depression (Pennington, 2002).

Neuroimaging studies reveal multiple anatomical and functional abnormalities related to the amygdala and emotion processing and regulation (Chang et al., 2005; Frazier et al., 2005; Sanches et al., 2005; Singh, DelBello, Adler, Stanford, & Strakowski, 2008) as well as some unique patterns of abnormality in children and adolescents relative to adults (DelBello, Adler, & Strakowski, 2006). Physiological and neuropsychological patterns of both overlap and distinction between bipolar disorder and ADHD have also been identified (Galanter & Leibenluft, 2008; Henin et al., 2007; Moore et al., 2006). Neurodegeneration is increasingly likely with successive episodes of disorder (Pennington, 2002). Prodromal descriptions and specific markers (e.g., physiological or temperamental characteristics) of bipolar disorder are the focus of recent investigations (Luby & Navsaria, 2010).

Physiologically based explanations of bipolar disorder must account not only for episodes of both depression and mania but also for the mechanisms linked to cycling; the brain systems involving goals and rewards provide a promising focus for research (Pennington, 2002). Early, severe temperamental difficulties have also been identified as a marker for emerging bipolar disorder (Chang et al., 2003; Kochman et al., 2005). Sleep dysregulation may also contribute to symptoms of bipolar disorder (Rao et al., 2002).

Child factors include cognitive problems such as impaired executive functioning (Dickstein et al., 2004; Meyer et al., 2004) and difficulties with emotion regulation (Muralidharan et al., 2010). Parent and family factors such as high negativity, low warmth, and conflict predict early onset and a more negative course (Meyer & Carlson, 2010). For those at genetic risk, stressful life events also contribute to the development and recurrence of bipolar disorder (Hillegers et al., 2004; Tillman et al., 2003). A developmental cascade model has been described that links genetic risk to externalizing difficulties, internalizing difficulties, and thought problems; considerable variability in individual pathways was observed (Klimes-Dougan et al., 2010).

Assessment and Diagnosis

Assessment and Diagnosis in Children

With children, assessment of mood disorders is complex because agreement between parents and children about the presence of depression is often low (Cole, Hoffman, Tram, & Maxwell, 2000) and many of the symptoms of depression are also observed in children with other psychopathologies. Irritability, for example, is a common complaint of parents and teachers and may be characteristic of many internalizing and externalizing disorders (Craney & Geller, 2003a; Weller, Calvert, & Weller, 2003). Comprehensive assessments, then, must include multiple measures such as self-report, parent report, medical exams, and observations. There are many standardized interviews and checklists; among the most frequently used is the Children's Depression Inventory (Kovacs, 1985, 1992). Consistent with the recent emphasis on early signs of developing disorder, there is also a preschooler checklist (Luby, Heffelfinger, Koenig-McNaught, Brown, & Spitznagel, 2004). For disruptive mood dysregulation disorder, careful assessment involves close attention to typical development in preschoolers and older children (Egger & Emde, 2011). Children who meet the diagnostic criteria for both disruptive mood dysregulation disorder and oppositional defiant disorder are diagnosed *only with* the more severe disruptive mood dysregulation disorder (DSM-5, 2013).

For children at risk for bipolar disorder, well-known inventories of child and adolescent symptoms may provide useful information (Faraone, Althoff, Hudziak, Monuteaux, & Biederman, 2005; Holtmann et al., 2007); brain imaging and other lab measures may also provide important data (Davanzo et al., 2003; Garber & Kaminski, 2000). There continues to be considerable diagnostic confusion when trying to differentiate mania (and bipolar disorder) from ADHD. Impulsivity and hyperactivity are certainly part of the clinical presentation of both disorders. However, the same core symptoms that define adult mania can be applied, in general, to children and adolescents if appropriate developmental considerations are taken into account, such as age of onset (Tillman et al., 2003). Early onset bipolar disorder can be differentiated from ADHD by the presence of typically manic symptoms such as elated mood, flight of ideas, and grandiosity (Geller, Zimerman et al., 2002), and children themselves are often accurate reporters of such symptoms (Tillman et al., 2004). A child with *elated mood* might laugh hysterically in inappropriate situations with no obvious reason. *Flight of ideas* may be evident in rapid and continuous jumping from one topic to another, often with loud, pressured speech. Children presenting with *grandiosity* often believe that they have superior knowledge and abilities and behave as if rules do not apply to them. In extreme instances, they may state that they have supernatural powers.

Comorbid psychopathology is a critical aspect of assessment and diagnosis, because 40% to 70% of children with major depressive disorder also have other psychopathologies. The most frequent are dysthymia and anxiety disorders, with anxiety disorders usually preceding the mood disorder. Externalizing disorders are also common (Birmaher et al., 1996a; Zahn-Waxler et al., 2000). For children with bipolar disorder, anxiety disorders (in particular, obsessive-compulsive disorder) and externalizing disorders are frequently observed (Masi et al., 2003, 2004).

Assessment and Diagnosis in Adolescents

With adolescents, assessment of mood disorders is even more complicated. Parents and clinicians, and adolescents themselves, need to consider possible symptoms in the context of a developmental period characterized by emotional and personal challenges. In addition, with increases in child and adolescent suicide attempts and completions over recent years, it is imperative to screen for suicidality (Birmaher et al., 1996a). The selection of evidence-based instruments is absolutely critical, given that there is often little agreement among adolescents, parents, teachers, and clinicians about the presence of psychopathology (McClure, Kubiszyn, & Kaslow, 2002; Silverman & Ollendick, 2005); these discrepancies are associated with poorer outcomes (Ferdinand, van der Ende, & Verhulst, 2004). There are data that suggest that adolescents underreport their own symptoms and that parent judgments are more accurate (Youngstrom, Findling, & Calabrese, 2003, 2004; Youngstrom et al., 2004). However, as noted, adolescents seem better able to identify symptoms that differentiate bipolar disorder from ADHD (Tillman et al., 2004), though progress has been reported related to increased validity of parent-report screening (Tillman & Geller, 2005). Multiple informants may provide valuable perspective (Thuppal, Carlson, Sprafkin, & Gadow, 2002).

Bipolar disorder is more frequently misdiagnosed than anxiety disorders or major depressive disorder. There are many reasons for confusion. Parents with their own histories of bipolar disorder may not recognize symptoms in their children, whereas parents without psychopathology may tolerate early episodes of mania or hypomania because they believe they are adolescent phases and expect their children to improve (Geller & Luby, 1997). Mental health professionals may struggle with accurate diagnosis because the clinical picture of bipolar disorder is especially complex. Irritability and belligerence are more common than euphoria, and the pattern may be more erratic than persistent; with the addition of dramatic mood swings, marked deterioration, the possibility of psychotic symptoms, and many atypical presentations, accurate diagnosis is even more problematic (McClellan et al., 1997).

Diagnostic accuracy must also take into account differential diagnosis and comorbidity. Clinicians want to find the best explanation of the presenting symptoms while still recognizing that some adolescents will be appropriately diagnosed with more than one disorder. As already noted, many of the symptoms of bipolar disorder overlap with both internalizing and externalizing disorders such as anxiety, ADHD, substance abuse, and personality disorders (Geller & Luby, 1997; Tillman & Geller, 2005). Early onset schizophrenia must also be considered and ruled out; adolescents from minority backgrounds must be evaluated carefully because there is evidence that they are more frequently misdiagnosed with schizophrenia (McClellan et al., 1997; Pavuluri, Janicak, Naylor, & Sweeney, 2003).

Comorbidity, especially involving externalizing disorders, is a common complication (Masi, Toni et al., 2003; Wozniak et al., 2004). Conduct disorder needs to be separately assessed and addressed (Biederman et al., 2003). Eating disorders, with their accompanying dysregulation of moods and eating, impulsivity, and cravings for activity, require careful consideration (McElroy, Kotwal, Keck, & Akiskal, 2005). And substance abuse is even more common and more problematic for adolescent-onset bipolar disorder than earlier emerging bipolar disorder (Wilens et al., 2004).

Intervention

As we think about the variety of efforts mobilized to treat and prevent mood disorders, and the fact that many of those treated and targeted are children and adolescents, it is essential to take into account the developmental context of intervention (Holmbeck & Kendall, 2002). Weisz and Hawley (2002) have argued that treatments for adolescents must address their distinctive physiological, psychological, and social functioning. For instance, motivation is a key contributor to treatment success.

BOX 12:2 CLINICAL PERSPECTIVES

Developmental and Ethical Issues Related to the Use of Antidepressant Medication in Children and Adolescents

By any measure, depression occurring during childhood and adolescence is a major clinical concern and the cause of considerable distress for youth and families. For very good reasons, parents of children and adolescents with depression, along with medical and mental health professionals working with these populations, are eager for efficacious and efficient ways to treat these disorders. It is not surprising, then, that the most recently developed and most common pharmacological approaches used for treating adults with depression have been applied to treating children and adolescents (Jureidini et al., 2004). Indeed, for a number of years, clinicians have recognized that medications used to treat adult depression were often similarly effective with adolescents and even children. This was especially true of the newer class of antidepressants known as the SSRIs. These medications have also been shown to be helpful in treating other disorders, including obsessive-compulsive disorder and other anxiety disorders.

For a time, the relatively manageable side-effect profile and good clinical effect obscured the fact that careful trials on the use of these medications in children had not been done. Consequently, clinicians were caught off guard when anecdotal and case reports began to suggest that the use of SSRIs with youth might be associated with an increase in suicidality. In 2004, the Food and Drug Administration (FDA) conducted a summary review of a number of smaller studies considering these reports. The FDA review study indicated that antidepressants did, indeed, increase the risk—slightly but significantly—of suicidal thinking and behavior. In contrast to placebo samples with a 2% risk of suicidality, the use of antidepressants was associated with a 4% risk of suicidality during the first few months of treatment (USFDA, 2004). It is important to note that no completed suicides occurred during the trials.

These findings stimulated considerable controversy. Initially, a rash of media reports focused on the potential dangers of medication and the lack of standardized trials with children. However, a more balanced discussion soon took place, in which the small but real risks associated with the use of medications for depressed children was weighed against the well-documented risks associated with untreated depression. The primary risks of using SSRIs with children include the fact that such medications have an as yet unknown effect on the developing nervous system. Additionally, there is some evidence that, in children predisposed to the development of bipolar disorder, the use of the wrong medications may actually induce the onset of mania. There is also evidence that, at least temporarily, children may exhibit greater disinhibition and impulsivity while on antidepressant medication. On the other hand, there are real risks in not treating depression in youth with all of the available tools, including medications. If left untreated or inadequately treated, depression in children and adolescents may lead to poor family and peer relationships, poor academic performance, compromised health, increased risk of substance abuse, and significant rates of suicidality.

In response to these competing concerns, the U.S. FDA issued guidelines that require prescribing physicians to more closely monitor patients during the first 4 months of medication use. Clinically, many mental health providers suggest a trial of psychotherapy for mild to moderate levels of depression and anxiety disorders before starting medication. The combination of psychotherapy and medication is generally emphasized, along with more aggressive assessment of suicide risk throughout treatment for those patients on medication (March et al., 2004).

More generally, the issues surrounding the use of antidepressant medications with youth illustrate two important trends. First, as our understanding of the interplay among genetics, developmental neurobiology, and experience grows, so does the complexity of intervention strategies and the demand for more nuanced and integrated research into the safety and effectiveness of those interventions. Second, the role of pharmaceuticals in the treatment of mental health problems continues to expand. Indeed, it was the relatively good side-effect profile of the SSRIs that contributed to the explosion of prescriptions for children and teens with psychiatric diagnoses. Although medications are likely to continue to be an important tool in the treatment of psychopathology, they are not a panacea and must be used carefully after consideration of all available data.

Most struggling adolescents do not refer themselves to therapy; once there, many remain reluctant to participate. So immediately addressing motivational issues is important to help adolescents develop a strong therapeutic alliance and engage with specific therapy techniques. Adolescents also appear to prefer active, psychological interventions; selecting such interventions (or including components of these in pharmacological treatments) may increase commitment and follow-through (Jaycox et al., 2006). Finally, Hinshaw (2002) has emphasized the need to convey an understanding of the adolescent's integrity and agency throughout the course of treatment.

The treatment of both depressive disorders and bipolar disorder involves a number of goals, implemented over time. First, acute symptoms need to be managed. Then, attention must be paid to the maintenance of improvements (Kowatch et al., 2005). The reduction of long-term complications (such as suicidality) and the promotion of non-disorder-related growth and development also contribute to treatment success. With these concerns in mind, it will be as important to design an integrative plan of intervention as it was to think about development of mood disorders in the context of an integrative model of risk factors (Goodman & Gotlib, 2002). This task is complicated by the fact that there are fewer well-controlled treatment studies for childhood and adolescent depression than, for example, for anxiety disorders (Compton, Burns, Egger, & Robertson, 2002; Coyle et al., 2003; Olfson, Gameroff, Marcus, & Waslick, 2003). Even so, meta-analytic studies reveal the immediate positive impact of treatment for mood disorders, with possible long-term benefits (Compton et al., 2002; Domino et al., 2008).

Pharmacological Treatment

As stated, we know that many, many children and adolescents are presenting for treatment of mood disorders at outpatient clinics (Moreno et al., 2007). We also know that these individuals are prescribed medications *more frequently* and are provided psychotherapy *less frequently* than youth with other disorders (Ma, Ky-Van, & Stafford, 2005). These data are both cause for optimism and cause for concern. Many researchers and clinicians are appropriately optimistic that previously underserved groups are receiving mental health services and responding well to pharmacological treatments (Brent & Maalouf, 2008; Lock, Walker, Rickert, & Katzman, 2005; Sewitch, Blais, Rahme, Bexton, & Galarneau, 2005). Others are more cautious about the use of medication in children and adolescents, whose brains and nervous systems continue to develop (El-Mallakh, Peters, & Waltrip, 2000), and call for additional research into commonly used drugs and the factors that influence their prescription (Bridge & Axelson, 2008; Sewitch et al., 2005; Weller, Calvert, & Weller, 2003).

Research also continues on the multiple physiological, psychological, and clinical factors that influence a child's response to drug intervention (Birmaher et al., 2007; Emslie, Mayes, Laptook, & Batt, 2003; Emslie et al., 1997; Kowatch & DelBello, 2005). In addition to thinking about what kinds of medications are effective for children of different ages (Emslie et al., 1997, 2008), there are also important ethical issues involved (see Box 12:2). Preferences for particular forms of treatment, informed consent, and issues related to confidentiality are especially important when working with adolescents (Jaycox et al., 2006; McClellan et al., 1997).

The goals of pharmacological treatments include ameliorating the distress and dysfunction of children and preventing or limiting relapse (Birmaher & Brent, 2002; Hughes et al., 2007; Pine, 2002). The most common medications used with children are the selective serotonin reuptake inhibitors (SSRIs) (Brent & Maalouf, 2009). Symptom improvement usually takes about 8 to12 weeks, longer than the 3 to 4 weeks observed in adults (Pennington, 2002), but complete remission is rare (Emslie et al., 1997). In a meta-analytic review of treatment outcome studies, the benefits of antidepressant treatment appeared to be much greater than the risks from increased suicidality (Bridge et al., 2007). With increasing empirical data on the efficacy and long-term outcomes of antidepressant treatment for children and adolescents, informed and well-monitored use of antidepressants is often a key component of comprehensive interventions (Emslie et al., 2008; Hughes et al., 2007).

For both children and adolescents with bipolar disorder, mood stabilizers such as lithium appear to be the most effective intervention, with combinations of drugs for children who do not respond to a single mood stabilizer (Kowatch, Sethuraman, Hume, Kromelis, & Weinberg, 2003; Patel et al., 2006; Weller, Danielyan, & Weller, 2002). Using lithium requires multiple appointments to check kidney, thyroid, and heart functioning; children and adolescents from "chaotic" families are likely to present special challenges with this type of treatment regimen (Geller & Luby, 1997; McClellan et al., 1997). Because the diagnosis of bipolar disorder in children is relatively recent, there are fewer long-term data available; consensus related to clinical trials and medication management of bipolar disorder is necessary (Carlson et al., 2003; Craney & Geller, 2003b; Kowatch et al., 2005). Hospitalization for those in crisis is an important clinical option, although many children and adolescents experience a range of difficulties following discharge. Only 35% of those in outpatient treatment following hospitalization displayed full medication adherence; complicating factors include comorbidity, lower SES, and lack of a psychotherapy component (DelBello et al., 2007).

Child Treatment

Psychosocial interventions for children with mood disorders are effective (Birmaher et al., 1996a; Brent & Maalouf, 2009; Sheffield et al., 2006), with **cognitive-behavioral therapies** and **interpersonal therapies** (i.e., relationship-focused approaches) appearing equally useful (Kaufman, Rohde, Seeley, Clarke, & Stice, 2005; Klomek & Mufson, 2006; Mufson et al., 2004). Individual and group approaches are both associated with good outcomes (Goldberg-Arnold & Fristad, 2003; Sherrill & Kovacs, 2002). With respect to cognitively oriented therapies, we need to remember that adolescents "span a broad range of cognitive ability and cognitive sophistication" and to take these differences into account as we design individual interventions or use available treatment manuals (Weisz & Hawley, 2002, p. 29). Even with attention appropriately focused on cognitive variables, the impact of therapist empathy and the therapeutic alliance must also be appreciated (Kaufman et al., 2005). Psychosocial therapies that are combined with pharmacological approaches are also effective for depression and bipolar disorder (Ginsburg, Albano, Findling, Kratochvil, & Walkup, 2005; Lofthouse & Fristad, 2004; Pavuluri et al., 2004). A recent large-scale review of treatment outcome studies affirmed the efficacy of psychotherapy in the treatment of major depression, but noted that the gains made by children and adolescents were more modest compared to children with other disorders (Weisz, McCarty, & Valeri, 2006). Another large-scale, multisite project examining the relative strengths and weaknesses of medication, cognitive-behavior therapy (CBT), combined medication-CBT, and placebo, called the Treatment for Adolescents with Depression Study (TADS), is ongoing (Curry et al., 2006;

Kennard et al., 2006; Kratochvil et al., 2005). Early results suggest the combination of medication and CBT is superior to either single therapy (March, Silva, & Vitiello, 2006).

A specific example of cognitive and cognitive-behavioral interventions for children is the program Kevin Stark and his colleagues have designed. The empirically supported treatment addresses many of the factors presumed to contribute to both development and maintenance of the disorder (Stark, Ballatore, Hamff, Valdez, & Selvig, 2001; Stark et al., 2005; Weisz, 2004). Among the treatment components are emotion-focused tasks designed to help children learn to identify basic emotions and depression symptoms, the scheduling of pleasant activities, personal and interpersonal problem solving, and altering negative cognitions. Therapists work with both children and families over time to develop and strengthen new cognitive and behavioral coping skills.

Examples of cognitive and cognitive-behavioral interventions for adolescents include Weisz and colleagues' primary and secondary control enhancement training (Weisz, Southam-Gerow, Gordis, & Connor-Smith, 2003), Lewinsohn's Adolescent Coping with Depression Course (Rohde, Lewinsohn, Clarke, Hops, & Seeley, 2005), and the Adolescent Depression Empowerment Project (ADEPT), focused on helping African American girls with depression (McClure, Connell, Zucker, Griffith, & Kaslow, 2005). For adolescents in psychosocial treatments, ongoing assessment of suicidality is imperative (Bridge, Barbe, Birmaher, Kolko, & Brent, 2005).

Interpersonal therapies (IPT) for both children and adolescents address the salient age-related personal, social, and developmental issues in the context of topics such as loss, grief, and relationship difficulties (Jacobson & Mufson, 2010; Mufson et al., 2004) and work well in both individual and group settings (Mufson, Gallagher, Dorta, & Young, 2004). Interpersonal approaches have also paid particular attention to cultural differences (Rossello & Bernal, 2005). Both CBT and IPT treatments must include mechanisms designed to maintain improved functioning; in several studies initial gains were not maintained at 6-month follow-up (Horowitz, Garber, Ciesla, Young, & Mufson, 2007; Young, Mufson, & Davies, 2006).

Family Treatment

Both mothers and fathers may be especially powerful agents of change (Schock, Gavazzi, Fristad, &

Goldberg-Arnold, 2002; Sherrill & Kovacs, 2002), with parent advocacy a key factor in new research and treatment (Hellander, 2003). Parents may be somewhat more helpful for depressed children than for depressed adolescents (Cottrell, 2003). Parent involvement in CBT treatment is one aspect of the successful protocol of the previously described TADS (Wells & Albano, 2005). Psychoeducational support and family-specific techniques are associated with decreases in children's distress and dysfunction (Fristad, Goldberg-Arnold, & Gavazzi, 2002, 2003). Education may be especially critical for parents of children and adolescents with bipolar disorder (Miklowitz et al., 2004). The role of the family is also emphasized as we consider the ongoing need for maintenance treatment after initial improvements (Danielson, Feeny, Findling, & Youngstrom, 2004; Morris, Miklowitz, & Waxmonsky, 2007; West, Henry, & Pavuluri, 2007). In addition, given the impact of poor marital relations on children's adjustment, marital therapy may be a useful adjunct intervention (Cummings et al., 2000). Finally, recognizing that parents of children with mood disorders also struggle to remain optimistic and effective, caregiver support is critical. There are many ways to provide that support, from individual counseling to internet groups (Hellander, Sisson, & Fristad, 2003).

Prevention Efforts

Prevention efforts have included studies targeting children of depressed parents as well as samples of children with more general high-risk profiles (e.g., children of low-income families). The Penn Resiliency Program (PRP), which focuses on the cultivation of optimism and coping skills in middle schoolers, has shown benefits (Gillham & Reivich, 1999, 2004). Other types of prevention emphasize the timing of therapeutic techniques to coincide with developmental milestones; the hypothesis is that children and their families may be more accepting of change-related opportunities when a transition period is underway (Gladstone & Beardslee, 2002). Another type involves going where at-risk children and adolescents gather and providing resources in community centers (Weersing & Weisz, 2002). In some prevention research, ethnicity and culture appear to moderate effects, with data from a recent study suggesting that low-income Latino fifth and sixth graders exhibited more improvements than African American children; these findings highlight a need for more culturally specific therapy and strategies (Cardemil, Reivich, & Seligman, 2002).

Suicidality

"The young boy scrawled a note and pinned it to his shirt. Then he walked to the far side of the family Christmas tree and hanged himself from a ceiling beam. The note was short—'Merry Christmas'—and his parents never forgot or understood it" (Redfield Jamison, 1999, p. 73).

One of the saddest developmental trajectories ends with suicide. For most of us, the idea that death is preferable to even the most difficult of life's struggles is hard to understand. It is even more awful when the individual who thinks about, or attempts, or completes suicide is a child or adolescent. Although suicide in adolescence is relatively rare, with estimates ranging from 0.04% to 0.2% (Diekstra, 1995), suicide attempts and completions have quadrupled since 1950 (Birmaher et al., 1996b); these higher rates are most dramatically observed in adolescent males (Rutz & Wasserman, 2004) and in some developing countries (Aaron et al., 2004). National suicide statistics provide much of the information, although these are somewhat complicated by sociocultural factors such as religiosity and ethnicity (Diekstra, 1995; Goldston et al., 2008). Adolescents attempt suicide ten times as often as they complete suicide; that is, one in ten adolescent suicide attempts results in death (Apter & Wasserman, 2003). Rising rates have leveled off in the past decade, plausibly connected to increases in prescribing antidepressant medication to adolescents (Gould, Greenberg, Velting, & Shaffer, 2003).

In order to understand some of the factors that predispose an adolescent to consider suicide, it is important to be clear about definitions related to suicidality. **Suicidal ideation** involves a variety of cognitions from "fleeting thoughts that life is not worth living" to "very concrete, well-thought out plans for killing oneself" (Diekstra, 1995, p. 214). Depending on the specific research definition, estimates of suicidal ideation in adolescence range from 3.5% when narrowly defined to 53% when broadly defined; throughout adolescence, more girls report suicidal thoughts than boys. **Parasuicide** includes many behaviors, from less dangerous gestures to serious but unsuccessful suicide attempts. The term *parasuicide* is increasingly preferred over *attempted suicide* because the motives and intentions of individuals are often difficult to identify: "Since parasuicide, particularly during adolescence and young adulthood, is usually carried out at the height of an interpersonal crisis by an individual feeling desperate and confused, such obscurity of intent is not at all surprising" (Diekstra, 1995, p. 215). Estimates of parasuicide range between 2.4% and 20%; again, more girls than boys exhibit this behavior (Diekstra, 1995). **Self-injurious behavior**, or **self-harm**, overlaps with many kinds of parasuicide but can also be considered a distinct phenomenon (Joiner, Conwell et al., 2005). Compared to adolescents who exhibit parasuicidal behavior, adolescents who display self-harm report different attitudes toward life and death and use different means of injury (e.g., cutting versus overdosing) (Hjelmeland & Groholt; 2005; Muehlenkamp & Gutierrez, 2004; Rodham, Hawton, & Evans, 2004; see Box 12:3).

Suicide is "any death that is the direct or indirect result of a positive or negative act accomplished by the victim" (Diekstra, 1995, p. 215). In contrast to the impact of gender on suicidal ideation and parasuicide (with girls outnumbering boys), boys far outnumber girls when the focus is on actual death (Conner & Goldston, 2007). Many suicide experts believe that rates of suicide are underestimated and point, for example, to single car accidents with young male drivers as possible, unreported, instances of suicide. **Suicidality** is the construct that includes suicidal ideation, parasuicide, and suicide.

Many different variables increase the risk for suicidality in adolescents (Bridge, Goldstein, & Brent, 2006; Van Orden, Witte, Selby, Bender, & Joiner, 2008). Genetic effects on persistent suicidal thinking, suicide attempts, and completed suicides are observed, with concordance rates for monozygotic twins higher than rates for dizygotic twins, even after the impact of genetics on adolescent psychopathology is taken into account (Brent et al., 2004; Joiner, Brown, & Wingate, 2005). The heritability of neurobehavioral disinhibition and impulsive aggression is the focus of current research, with investigations of abnormalities in the serotonin system and the HPA axis (Apter, 2003; Joiner, Brown, et al., 2005; Tarter, Kirisci, Reynolds, & Mezzich, 2004). Entering puberty at younger ages has also been associated with increased risk. Possible explanations for the increase in risk are the "disjunction of biological development on the one hand and psychological and social development on the other" (Diekstra, 1995, p. 231) and the connections between early puberty and risk taking.

Psychological factors are among the most frequently investigated factors. One factor that has received a great deal of clinical and research attention is child or adolescent psychopathology. Psychopathologies linked to suicide include the mood disorders (especially when they are severe or comorbid with personality disorders), anxiety disorders, and externalizing disorders such as conduct disorder (Barbe et al., 2005; Joiner, Brown, et al., 2005; Rudd, Joiner, & Rumzek, 2004). Substance abuse disorders may present a special risk, with most parasuicidal behavior preceded by alcohol use (Conner & Goldston, 2007; Rossow, Groholt, & Wichstrom, 2005; Sher & Zalsman, 2005). Adjustment disorders (i.e., disorders associated with a specific traumatic event from which an adolescent doesn't recover) are also critical risk factors (Oquendo et al., 2005; Pelkonen, Marttunen, Henriksson, & Lonnqvist, 2005). Gender-specific patterns of risk have also been identified (Fennig et al., 2005; Rudd et al., 2004). Overall, three diagnostic clusters predict most of the adolescents who attempt suicide: adjustment disorders, major mood disorders, and externalizing behavior disorders combined with a mood disorder (Spirito, Kurkjian, & Donaldson, 2003).

There are mixed data on the impact of risk-taking behaviors. Some investigators argue that general indices of risk taking are not related to suicidality (Stanton, Spirito, Donaldson, & Boergers, 2003). Others suggest that drinking, smoking, and sexual activity do increase adolescent vulnerability (Bae, Ye, Chen, Rivers, & Singh, 2005; Cerel, Roberts, & Nilsen, 2005; Hallfors et al., 2004). Impulsivity, then, becomes an important variable to track (Conner, Meldrum, Wieczorek, Duberstein, & Welte, 2004).

Variables related to identity, self-image, and self-esteem are also noteworthy contributors to increased risk, particularly with respect to lack of self-efficacy and hopelessness (Rutter & Behrendt, 2004; Wilburn & Smith, 2005; Wild, Flisher, & Lombard, 2004). Hopelessness is significant both for the development and maintenance of suicidality; shame and guilt, as well as a sense of being a burden to others, often exacerbate hopelessness (Barbe et al., 2005; Joiner, Conwell, et al., 2005; Stewart et al., 2005). According to Habermas and Bluck (2000), "the drastic increase in suicide rates during adolescence may be a sign that adolescents start thinking about their whole life and its quality" (p. 754). To the extent that adolescents cannot envision their own continuity through time, or that they believe that

BOX 12:3   CLINICAL PERSPECTIVES

Self-Harm in Adolescence

Self-injurious behavior (SIB), also called self-harm or self-mutilation, is the deliberate, self-inflicted destruction of body tissue, outside of cultural norms, and without suicidal intent (Gratz, Dukes, & Roemer, 2002; Yates, 2004). Self-injurious behaviors include cutting, scratching, and burning. Broadly conceived, SIB is thought to be a compensatory strategy for regulating emotional states and a maladaptive coping skill displayed in response to stress. SIB likely serves a variety of psychological functions, such as reducing or blocking anxiety, as well as communicating with and engaging others (Brown, Comtois, & Linehan, 2002; Gratz, 2007). Although incidence rates vary considerably, it is clear that SIB is a surprisingly common clinical problem, with lifetime prevalence for repeated SIB estimated to be between 5% and 10% (Yates, 2004). These self-destructive behaviors peak in late adolescence and early adulthood, especially in psychiatric samples of individuals; as many as 21% of teens with a psychiatric diagnosis have been found to display SIB (Cleary, 2000). SIB is frequently observed in connection with borderline personality disorder, eating disorders, and dissociative disorders, although there has been recent discussion of the possibility that SIB is better understood as a distinct diagnostic category (Gratz et al., 2012; Muehlenkamp, 2005).

As noted in Yates's (2004) comprehensive review, strong associations have been established among early trauma, dissociative processes, and later SIB. Although not the only pathway to SIB, considerable research has demonstrated that child sexual abuse is a powerful risk factor. Yates notes that sexual abuse readily evokes dissociative defenses, involves specific trauma to the body, and is generally accompanied by a lack of competent parenting. In a more recent review, Yates (2009) describes three possible pathways toward self-injurious behavior. In the first, *the representational pathway*, children and adolescents develop representations of the self as defective, of others as malevolent, and of relationships as dangerous. In this pathway, SIB is a means of self-punishment or a means of self-soothing in the absence of positive relationships. In the second, *the regulatory pathway*, maltreatment leads to

poor integration of emotion and cognitive processing in children and adolescents and decreased capacity to self-regulate. In this pathway, SIB involves dissociation and somatization as ways to regulate arousal or stress. In the third, *the reactive pathway*, underlying physiological systems related to arousal and regulation are negatively impacted by early maladaptive experiences. In this pathway, SIB is associated with positive physiological responses.

One of the most compelling aspects of SIB is that it usually occurs in absence of physical pain (Nock & Prinstein, 2005). It is thought that SIB may release neurochemicals (endorphins) that block pain and promote reinforcing feelings. This, along with the impulsive nature of the act, makes SIB especially challenging to treat. Careful research (Nock & Prinstein, 2004, 2005) into the functions of SIB indicates that it most often acts as an automatic negative reinforcer (stops unwanted feelings) but sometimes as an automatic positive reinforcer (relieves feelings of numbness by eliciting other feelings).

There may be important group differences between individuals who tend to engage in mild SIB and do so in the context of social groups, and those who engage in more severe SIB and for whom it is a more solitary behavior. Although a history of child abuse is strongly associated with all forms of SIB, child abuse and neglect are even more likely to lead to more severe forms of disturbance (Yates, 2004). In recognition of how widespread and varied the clinical presentation of SIB is, therapeutic approaches are becoming more targeted and differentiated. For example, if SIB is primarily serving a regulatory function, then alternative methods of managing the awareness and experience of emotions may be a focus of intervention. If the self-harming behavior is primarily maintained by social reinforcement, then therapeutic efforts focused on more appropriate and effective interpersonal communication may be utilized (Gratz, 2007; Nock & Prinstein, 2005). Also, as the neurophysiology of SIB is better understood, the potential role for pharmacological treatments is being more aggressively explored (Villalba & Harrington, 2003).

their continued existence will involve unremitting psychological pain, extreme decisions may occur. Adolescents' inability to communicate their ongoing struggles and their deeply felt pain, combined with

hesitation about seeking help from others, further complicates difficult situations (Gould et al., 2004; Horesh, Zalsman, & Apter, 2004). Adolescents who do turn to peers may not always receive appropriate help. Peers may misperceive intent or misjudge lethality (Dunham, 2004). Even when a friend is clearly struggling, peers do not always try to connect with parents or mental health professionals; peer support and assistance may be compromised by their own history of psychopathology (Dunham, 2004).

Previous suicidal behavior is a strong predictor of future suicidality (D'Eramo, Prinstein, Freeman, Grapentine, & Spirito, 2004; Joiner, Conwell, et al., 2005; Van Orden et al., 2008). Past behavior appears to habituate individuals to the fear and pain of self-injury (Joiner et al., 2005) and underlies Joiner's (2002, 2005) **interpersonal–psychological theory of suicidality**. The theory proposes two general categories of risk: dysregulated impulse control and intense psychological pain. The idea is that adolescents "gradually acquire the ability to enact lethal self-injury through prior experience with self-injury (which in turn is encouraged by impulsive behavior underlain by serotonergic dysregulation) ... ability not acted upon unless the desire for death is instantiated by a strong sense of perceived burdensomeness coupled with a sense of failed belongingness" (Joiner, Brown et al., 2005, p. 305). In other words, in the context of adolescent impulsivity and psychological anguish, self-destructive behavior may escalate over time, culminating in suicide.

Environmental, familial, and sociocultural contexts of suicidal behavior are also noteworthy variables (Melhem et al., 2007; Smalley, Scourfield, & Greenland, 2005; Wagner, Silverman, & Martin, 2003). Negative life events, such as loss, physical or sexual abuse, or failing academic performance, may necessitate immediate attention (Evans, Hawton, & Rodham, 2005; Horesh, Sever, & Apter, 2003; Richardson, Bergen, Martin, Roeger, & Allison, 2005). The historically relatively lower rates for African Americans and Latinos have been increasing in recent years (O'Donnell, O'Donnell, Wardlaw, & Stueve, 2004; Zayas, Lester, Cabassa, & Fortuna, 2005). Latina girls are an especially high-risk group (O'Donnell et al., 2004). Another high-risk group that has received significant amounts of research and clinical attention is American Indian adolescents. We see differences in suicidality for those living in urban areas versus those living on reservations (Freedenthal & Stiffman, 2004).

The presence of suicidal "models" must also be considered. Models of parasuicidal behavior may include close relatives, a peer, or a celebrity. The role of the media in presenting information on suicide, particularly when news reports include details about specific individuals and/or methods, requires scrutiny (Shoval et al., 2005; Stack, 2005). Internet chat rooms are a more recent phenomenon that also requires careful study (Becker & Schmidt, 2004).

Reducing adolescent suicidality involves multiple, coordinated efforts designed to identify at-risk individuals so that (1) suicide attempts and completions decline in frequency, and (2) adolescents who do attempt suicide receive immediate and ongoing treatment. With respect to prevention, general school-based education programs and staff training are viewed as more acceptable than school-wide screening (Scherff, Eckert, & Miller, 2005). Whereas universal screening may be interpreted as intrusive, there are also legal issues related to consent, confidentiality, and malpractice that must be taken into account (Judge & Billick, 2004). For adolescents contemplating suicide, telephone counseling has been shown to have an immediate positive impact (King, Nurcombe, Bickman, Hides, & Reid, 2003); publicizing such help lines in high schools, shopping malls, community centers, and on billboards may alert suicidal youth to easily accessible (and anonymous) support services. Informational campaigns that raise adult awareness are also essential and may include lists of behaviors that increase adolescent risk (see Table 12:2). Programs designed to address the individual, family, and social factors that limit access to mental health services are critical

TABLE 12:2 Warning Signs of Suicidality
Change in eating and sleeping habits
Withdrawal from friends, family, and regular activities
Violent actions, rebellious behavior, or running away
Drug and alcohol use
Unusual neglect of personal appearance
Marked personality change
Persistent boredom, difficulty concentrating, decline in schoolwork
Frequent complaints about physical symptoms
Loss of interest in pleasurable activities
Not tolerating praise or rewards

From the American Academy of Child and Adolescent Psychiatry (2000).

components of any prevention plan and might usefully target the young men who are less likely to seek help and more likely to employ lethal means (Spirito, Boergers, Donaldson, Bishop, & Lewander, 2002; Suominen, Isometsa, Martunen, Ostamo, & Lonnqvist, 2004). These types of resources are absolutely necessary, given that many studies report rates of up to 50% for suicide completions on a first attempt (Joiner, Conwell et al., 2005).

Emergency management plans for adolescents who do attempt suicide are a priority (Stewart, Manion, & Davidson, 2002). Inpatient admission is an option that should be considered. Successful outpatient treatments that bridge the crisis and recovery stages have been documented for both physiological and psychosocial therapies (Donaldson, Spirito, & Esposito-Smythers, 2005; Donaldson, Spirito, & Overholser, 2003; Fristad & Shaver, 2001; Macgowan, 2004), although the kinds of meta-analyses that have demonstrated the efficacy of cognitive-behavioral approaches for adults in preventing suicide have

yet to be conducted for adolescents (Tarrier, Taylor, & Gooding, 2008). Lack of long-term treatment plans and noncompliance with treatment plans are problems that seriously hinder positive outcomes (Stewart et al., 2002). Adolescents who repeatedly attempt suicide require even more aggressive care. Compared to those who attempt suicide only once, repeat attempters experience more anger, depression, and emotional dysregulation; these symptoms must be specifically targeted in treatment plans (Esposito, Spirito, Boergers, & Donaldson, 2003; Spirito, Valeri, Boergers, & Donaldson, 2003). Connections between programs that seek to prevent both youth suicide and youth violence also require additional support and resources (Lubell & Vetter, 2006). What we do for the desperately troubled adolescents who are in every community is a reflection of our basic humanity. Providing school-based coping skills training, better screening, and the restriction of lethal means are first steps to lowering suicide rates.

Key Terms

Domains of competence (p. 211)
Arenas of comfort (p. 211)
Mood-related continuum (p. 213)
Major depressive disorder (p. 214)
Dysthymia (p. 214)
Disruptive mood dysregulation disorder (p. 215)
Cognitive-vulnerability stress model (p. 217)
Bipolar disorder (p. 218)
Mania (p. 218)
Hypomania (p. 218)
Kindling model (p. 222)
Pathways of parental impact (p. 223)
Reinforcement model (p. 224)
Negative life events (p. 225)
Chronic hassles (p. 225)
Cognitive-behavioral therapies (p. 230)
Interpersonal therapies (p. 230)
Suicidal ideation (p. 231)
Parasuicide (p. 231)
Self-injurious behavior/self-harm (p. 232)
Suicide (p. 232)
Suicidality (p. 232)
Interpersonal–psychological theory of suicidality (p. 234)

Chapter Summary

- Depression in childhood occurs frequently, can have long-term consequences, and is generally underrecognized and undertreated.
- The transition from childhood to adolescence is marked by the development of a coherent psychological identity that includes a sense of competence and self-esteem. These are among the core domains adversely affected by child and adolescent depression.
- Major depressive disorder in childhood and adolescence is characterized by sadness and loss of pleasure and is accompanied by cognitive, behavioral, and somatic symptoms.
- Dysthymia is a longstanding disturbance of mood and places the child or teen at significantly greater risk for developing major depression.
- Disruptive mood dysregulation disorder is a new type of depressive disorder included in DSM-5. It involves developmentally atypical and severe temper tantrums and chronic negative mood and irritability.
- In younger children, depression often manifests itself in depressed appearance, somatic

complaints, anxiety symptoms, and externalizing behaviors. In teens, hopelessness, substance abuse, suicidality, and other serious symptoms are more common.

- Before adolescence, the rate of depressive disorders is generally the same for boys and girls. However, beginning in adolescence the rate of depression is much greater for girls.
- Bipolar disorder is a severe form of mood disorder involving alternating periods of depression and mania. In adolescence, the bipolar disorder generally presents as it does in adulthood.
- There is significant developmental continuity of depressive disorders occurring in childhood, through adolescence, and into adulthood.
- Researchers are considering a range of genetic, neurological, life stress, and parenting risk factors in the development of depression.
- Genetic impact on the development of depressive disorders increases as children get older due, most likely, to gene by environment interaction effects.

- Parent depression is an especially important and researched risk factor for the development of depression in childhood.
- Many children and adolescents with major depression have other psychopathologies as well, especially dysthymia and anxiety disorders.
- Recent research suggests the combination of cognitive-behavioral therapy and medication is generally the most effective intervention approach in the treatment of more severe mood disorders in childhood and adolescence.
- Although still rare, adolescent suicide attempts and completions have steadily increased in recent decades.
- Although adolescent girls are more likely to experience suicidal ideation and to attempt suicide, boys far outnumber girls in terms of completed suicides.
- In addition to mood disorders, substance abuse is a significant risk factor for suicide among youth.

13

Maltreatment and Trauma- and Stressor-Related Disorders

"**IN THE UNITED STATES** alone, over 900,000 children are maltreated every year, more than 13 million children live in poverty, and millions of children are raised in homes in which one or both parents suffer from some form of serious psychopathology. . . . All of these events and circumstances are characterized by stress and adversity in the daily lives of children" (Compas, 2009, p. 88). Given the high-risk status of these children and the potential for poor developmental outcomes, Compas declares, "the stakes are high," and he is absolutely correct in his assessment. Further, countless more children and adolescents, in the United States and around the world, encounter the kinds of traumatic events that overwhelm adult capacities for coping and adaptation. This chapter is focused on children and stress, including discussions of typical and atypical experiences of stress, disorders related to stress and trauma, and prevention and treatment efforts.

Developmental Tasks and Challenges Related to Stress and Coping

Stress occurs when the demands of the individual exceed his or her available resources. **Coping** involves the "regulatory processes enacted in response to stress" (Compas, 2009). From birth onward, stressors abound. They include everyday events such as parents leaving infants to go to work, physical exams and inoculations, playground mishaps, homework that is too difficult, conflicts with friends, and forgetting one's lines in a school play. They also include not-so-everyday events such as the birth of a sibling, a move to a new state, failing a grade, and breaking up with one's first romantic partner. Each of these events requires some kind of response from a child or adolescent. Whether these coping efforts are successful or unsuccessful influences a number of important developmental outcomes.

The stress–response system is an evolutionarily influenced, hierarchically organized, and integrated brain-based system (Ellis, Jackson, & Boyce, 2006; Gunnar & Quevedo, 2007). Brain regions involved in stress responses include the hippocampus, the amygdala, and the prefrontal lobes, as well as the circuitry that connects those regions (Lupien, McEwen, Gunnar, & Heim, 2009). Stress triggers the activation of the hypothalamus-pituitary-adrenal (HPA) axis and the release of stress hormones. Receptors for these stress hormones are located throughout the brain. The stress hormones initiate a coordinated physiological response involving autonomic, neuroendocrine, metabolic, and immune system components. Following activation of the system, feedback loops signal for regulation and shutdown of the HPA axis and a return to homeostasis (Lupien et al., 2009). Two constructs help describe this process: **allostasis,** "meaning the process of maintaining stability (homeostasis) by active means, namely, by putting out stress hormones and other mediators," and **allostatic load** (or allostatic overload), "meaning the wear and tear to the body and the brain by use of allostasis, particularly when the mediators are dysregulated, i.e., not turned off when the stress is over or not turned on adequately when they are needed" (McEwen, 2007, p. 874). Key contributions made by the constructs of allostasis and allostatic load involve understanding the role of the brain in the regulation of feedback, understanding that biological set points

are dynamic (in that they respond to changing contexts), and understanding that there are predictable variations in stress sensitivity across development (Ganzel & Morris, 2011).

The stress system is organized to expend both physiological and psychological energy as it attempts to meet typical (or expected) and atypical (or unexpected) demands (Flinn, 2006; Gunnar & Loman, 2011). According to Gunnar and Loman, "If there is an immediate threat to our survival, we do not need to put energy into fighting off a virus, digesting our lunch, or growing an extra inch. We need that energy to fuel the mental and physical processes that increase our chances of surviving to face tomorrow. As this example suggests, stress is not necessarily detrimental. The capacity to mount an effective stress response allows us to adapt to the changing and sometimes extreme demands of our daily existence, to stretch our abilities, and to achieve more than we might were we to avoid situations of high demand" (p. 97). These high-demand circumstances need to be followed by periods of rest and repair. If they are not, there may be negative short- and long-term consequences.

The effects of stress are observed across the lifespan, from the prenatal period, across infancy and childhood, and through adolescence and adulthood. A "life cycle" model of stress describes changes in various brain structures related to the timing of stress (see Fig. 13:1). Exposure to prenatal and postnatal stress has "programming effects" on the developing brain and HPA axis (Fox, Levitt, & Nelson, 2010; Lupien et al., 2009). These programming effects involve changes in gene function (i.e., not in the genetic code or composition, but in the way in which the genetic information operates). These effects are examples of **epigenetics,** or the environmental regulation of gene expression (Meaney, 2010). Early adversity appears to alter the magnitude of the stress response (usually in the direction of hyperreactivity, but also sometimes hyporeactivity) and the poor regulation of that response (Blair, 2010; Meaney, 2010). The experience of stress in early development may be buffered by responsive caregiving. "Beginning early in the first year, when the HPA system of the infant is quite labile, sensitive parenting is associated with either smaller increases in or less prolonged activations of the HPA axis to everyday perturbations" (Lupien et al., 2009, p. 436). Indeed, Gunnar and Donzella (2002) describe the suppression of stress hormones as evidence of the "social regulation" of the stress system.

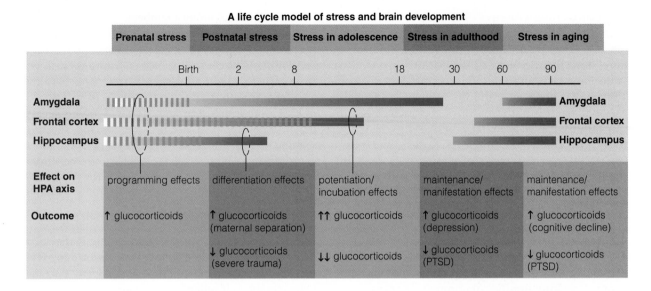

FIGURE 13:1 Changes in various brain structures are influenced by the timing of stressful experiences.
Source: Lupien, S.J., McEwen, B.S., Gunnar, M.R., and Heim, C. (2009). Effects of stress throughout the lifespan on the brain, behaviour, and cognition. Nature Reviews/Neuroscience, 10, 434–445. Reprinted by permission from Macmillan Publishers Ltd: Nature Reviews/Neuroscience, copyright © 2009.

One key development in the emergence of a well-functioning stress–response system is the dissociation between behavioral and physiological indices of the stress–response system. One example of this is observed "in secure relationships where even the temperamentally fearful toddler does not show increases in cortisol when confronted by events that scare him or her. . . . The dissociation between distressed behavior and activation of the stress system probably allows the infant to recruit parental attention at less biological cost. That is, she can cry and gain adult protection from threat, without putting the future on hold through the activation of her stress system" (Gunnar & Loman, 2011, p. 103).

Adolescence is associated with heightened responses of the HPA axis, and adolescent brain development (especially in the frontal cortex) is likely affected by this activity (Romeo & McEwen, 2006). In addition, compared to early childhood, there is relatively less buffering of the stress–response system (Gunnar & Quevedo, 2007). Adolescence is also a period in which the cumulative effects of early adversity are observed (Lupien et al., 2009). Across development, the stress–response system appears highly attuned to social challenges. For example, children who receive inconsistent or inadequate care and preschoolers who are rejected by their peers produce higher levels of stress hormones (Gunnar & Quevedo, 2007). The resolution of these types of stressful

experiences may be particularly meaningful (Flinn, 2006).

Individual differences in stress reactivity and regulation are linked to both genes and experience. As noted, one very important contributor to individual differences in the pathways and organization of the stress–response system is early caregiving (and attachment security). Gunnar and Quevedo explain that "responsive caregiving allows children to elicit help by expressing negative emotions, without triggering the endocrine component of the stress response" (p. 158). Temperament is another factor that influences the development and functioning of the stress response system. Individual differences in temperament are linked to both hyper- and hyporeactivity (Gunnar & Quevedo, 2007). "Risky" families, in which dysfunctional relationships and conflict are present, are another source of individual variation (Repetti, Taylor, & Seeman, 2002; Repetti, Robles, & Reynolds, 2011). One environmental factor with significant impact is poverty. Growing up in impoverished circumstances is associated with chronic stress and increased allostatic load (Blair, 2010; Blair et al., 2011). These adverse environments may be especially challenging for highly reactive children (who are more responsive than less reactive children to both highly supportive and highly stressful environments) (Boyce, 2007).

It is important to emphasize that children are not just passive recipients of stress. They are also active agents in dealing with stress. Zimmer-Gembeck and Skinner (2011) provide a developmental framework for thinking about coping. In their framework, they describe age-related transitions in twelve "families of coping and adaptive processes" (see Table 13:1). Their descriptions "allow the identification of healthy pathways through which children can acquire robust resources for dealing constructively with challenges, obstacles, failure, and loss" (p. 1). The various types of coping responses in each family are constrained by age and ability; each is also linked to more- and less-likely positive outcomes (Eisenberg, Valiente, & Sulik, 2009). For each family of coping responses, a developmental progression can be described. Examples of this developmental progression are provided in Figures 13:2a and 13:2b for the problem-solving and support-seeking families of coping responses.

According to Zimmer-Gembeck and Skinner, age-related transitions in coping occur from infancy to toddlerhood (about age 2); between ages 5 and 7; from late childhood to early adolescence, from ages 10 to 12; from early to middle adolescence, from ages 14 to 16; and from middle to late adolescence, from ages 18 to 22. Among the most common types of coping, across much of development, are problem solving, support seeking, distraction, and escape. Escape is the most common maladaptive strategy. There are certainly developmentally influenced changes in the frequency of use. In the preschool period, for instance, "young children seek support from adults or use overt behaviors to get what they want." Support seeking seems to be an "all-purpose strategy," and escape is the "primary alternative" when other strategies are ineffective (p. 12). In middle childhood, children "become increasingly self-reliant and their coping strategies become more differentiated and sophisticated" (p. 12). Cognitive strategies are increasingly deployed and support seeking appears more focused. In adolescence, there is an overall increase in coping repertoires, with more planful problem solving and better emotion regulation, as well as matching of coping strategies to types of stressors.

There are several key distinctions related to coping. The first is the distinction between *automatic* and *controlled processes*. In the memory system, for example, biases to attend to threatening information are automatic, whereas the purposeful shifting of attention observed in distraction is controlled (Compas, 2009). Another distinction involves *antecedent regulation* (i.e., coping that anticipates a psychologically demanding event) and *response-focused regulation* (i.e., coping that follows the psychologically demanding event) (Ochsner & Gross, 2008). Differences in the motives and goals associated with coping, such as those related to personal well-being and/or the well-being of others, must also be considered. Differences in goals may also be linked to whether stress is controllable or uncontrollable (Compas, 2009).

Many factors influence individual differences in coping repertoires and coping success. These include physiological factors (like brain development), psychological factors (such as temperament and the development of the self), and social factors (including parent and peer relationships) (Compas, 2009; Kopp, 2009; Gunnar & Donzella, 2002). Parent support of children's coping, as well as parent assistance, may be especially important when high levels of stress are encountered and/or when the child's coping resources

TABLE 13:1 Families of Coping Strategies	
Problem Solving Strategizing Instrumental action Planning	**Delegation** Maladaptive help seeking Complaining Whining Self-pity
Information Seeking Reading Observation Asking others	**Social Isolation** Social withdrawal Concealment Avoiding others
Helplessness Confusion Cognitive interference Cognitive exhaustion	**Accommodation** Distraction Cognitive restructuring Minimization Acceptance
Escape Behavioral avoidance Mental withdrawal Denial Wishful thinking	**Negotiation** Bargaining Persuasion Priority setting
Self-Reliance Emotion regulation Behavior regulation Emotional expression Emotion approach	**Submission** Rumination Rigid perseveration Intrusive thoughts
Support Seeking Contact seeking Comfort seeking Instrumental aid Social referencing	**Opposition** Other-blame Projection Aggression

Source: Zimmer-Gembeck, M.J. and Skinner, E.A, International Journal of Behavioral Development, 35, pp. 1–17, copyright © 2011 by Sage Publications. Reprinted by permission of SAGE.

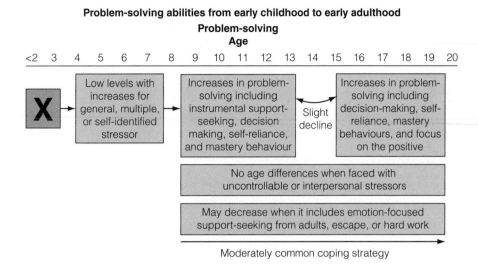

FIGURE 13:2a Summary of key achievements in the developmental progression of problem solving.
Source: Zimmer-Gembeck, M.J. and Skinner, E.A, International Journal of Behavioral Development, 35, pp. 1–17, copyright © 2011 by Sage Publications. Reprinted by permission of SAGE.

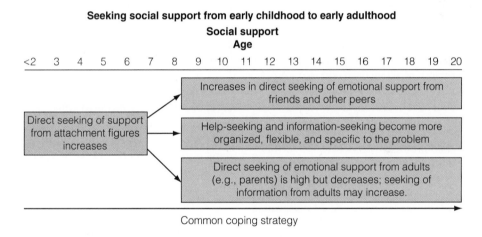

FIGURE 13:2b Summary of key achievements in the developmental progression of seeking social support.
Source: Zimmer-Gembeck, M.J. and Skinner, E.A, International Journal of Behavioral Development, 35, pp. 1–17, copyright © 2011 by Sage Publications. Reprinted by permission of SAGE.

are taxed (Abaied & Rudolph, 2010; Pomerantz & Thompson, 2008). Abaied and Rudolph (2010) provide a detailed description of the role of parents in the socialization of children's coping. In their description, parents both instruct and model a variety of coping strategies. Engagement strategies include problem solving, support seeking, and positive thinking. Disengagement strategies include avoidance and denial. Parents can also reinforce or redirect children's coping. And, of course, parents' contributions to children's coping can be helpful or ineffective.

Overall, across development, the ongoing interactions of stress and coping are evident every day. For many children, whose stressful experiences are typical and whose coping is supported by concerned adults, these interactions contribute to a sense of self-efficacy, accomplishment, and well-being. For other children, whose stressful experiences are unusually frequent and severe and whose coping is not adequately supported, developmental outcomes are more likely to include significant distress and dysfunction. These children and their experiences are the focus of the rest of this chapter.

Maltreatment

The Case of Kyle

Kyle is a 4-year-old boy recently removed from his home and placed in foster care along with his younger sister. Until recently, Kyle and his sister lived with his mother and her current boyfriend in a somewhat isolated rural community. Kyle's mother has struggled with polydrug addiction, including alcohol and methamphetamine, since before Kyle's birth. Although not physically abusive of her children, Kyle's mother's cycle of addiction, recovery, and relapse has led to multiple periods of physical neglect and emotional unavailability. Kyle was removed from the home by child protective services when he was one year old, when a visiting county social worker found him suffering from severe neglect—including untreated eye and ear infections and signs of malnutrition. He spent several months in a foster home while his mother completed a rehab program and gave birth to his sister. Kyle was then returned home, where he and his sister lived for the next three years. During this time Kyle's mother continued to cycle through periods of active drug and alcohol abuse followed by brief periods of sobriety.

While assessing Kyle as part of a pre-kindergarten screening program, the evaluator noted multiple bruises on Kyle's face and legs. A follow-up evaluation by child protective services found further bruising on Kyle's back and buttocks. Kyle told the child protection worker that his mother's boyfriend routinely struck him with his hand or a stick in response to any behaviors of which he disapproved. This included even mild oppositional behavior, as well as unintentional behaviors such as wetting the bed or spilling a drink. Kyle's mother confirmed that the abuse had been occurring, but defended her boyfriend by noting that he only behaved violently when drunk or high and was otherwise kind to her and provided for her family. Following the investigation, both Kyle and his sister, who was not physically abused, were removed from the home and placed in separate foster care homes. Kyle's mother again entered into a residential treatment program, and her boyfriend was arrested and charged with multiple counts of child abuse.

Kyle now lives with experienced and loving foster parents and is enrolled in a therapeutic preschool. Kyle's foster parents express surprise that he almost never mentions his mother or sister. They report that he settled quickly into his new surroundings and

routine. Both at home and at preschool, Kyle is noted to be acutely aware of and reactive to even mild disapproval. In fact, he quickly recognizes frustration or anger in his environment even when it is not directed toward him. Over time, Kyle has become more trusting of his foster parents, though he also becomes anxious if he is not in the same room as them. Kyle has struggled to manage the complexity and energy typical of a preschool classroom. He has difficulty joining in with other children and becomes easily frustrated and emotionally reactive to even minor frustrations and problems. At such times, he may exhibit either internalizing behaviors such as hiding or crying, or externalizing behaviors such as throwing toys or hitting other children.

Further assessment indicates that Kyle is experiencing mild-to-moderate delays in general cognitive functioning and expressive language ability. Kyle's teachers are developing a comprehensive plan combining structured, small group play opportunities with speech therapy and remedial school readiness training. All those currently working with Kyle remain both hopeful that he can continue to make progress and concerned about whether or not his mother will choose for Kyle to continue the current therapeutic program if he returns home to live with her. ▬

As described in Chapter 3, **maltreatment** is a broad category including physical abuse, sexual abuse, psychological abuse, and neglect, reflecting the "gross violation of the rights of a vulnerable and dependent child" (Cicchetti & Toth, 1995, p. 541). *Child maltreatment is not a diagnosis* that is assigned to a child. Rather, as emphasized in many other chapters, it is a risk factor that is associated with the increased likelihood of immediate, short-term, and long-term negative developmental outcomes (Belsky, 1980, 1993; Cicchetti & Toth, 1995, 2003). Indeed, "although the thought of a maltreated child conjures up images of head trauma, bruises, broken bones, malnutrition, and the like, it appears that emotional damage, not physical damage, may exert the most long-term harmful effect" (Cicchetti & Toth, 2003, p. 190).

Definitions of maltreatment vary, depending on context, professional background, and purposes of definition (e.g., involving lawmakers and legal issues or mental health professionals and treatment issues). Even so, basic definitions can be provided (Cicchetti & Valentino, 2006). **Sexual abuse** involves sexual contact or attempted sexual contact between an adult and a child. **Physical abuse** refers to injuries that are inflicted by nonaccidental means. **Neglect** involves

becky rockwood/Vetta/Getty Images

Although physical signs are frequently evidence of maltreatment, long-term emotional damage is an especially concerning outcome of all types of abuse.

failure to provide minimum standards of care (e.g., regarding shelter, safety or supervision, nutrition) that leads to harm or endangerment. **Emotional (or psychological) abuse** refers to ongoing and extreme disregard or thwarting of basic emotional needs. Additional classification considerations include the frequency, severity, and timing of maltreatment.

Maltreatment has been conceptualized as a "failure of the average expectable environment" (Cicchetti & Valentino, 2006). "For infants, the expectable environment includes protective, nurturant caregivers and a larger social group to which the child will be socialized, whereas for older children, the normative environment includes a supportive family, a peer group, and continued opportunities for individuals to dynamically engage in the construction of their own experiences" (Cicchetti & Valentino, 2006, p. 129). Maltreatment, then, reflects

the breakdown of the most basic set of expectations for safety and security.

Children are most vulnerable in the first five years of life, with high rates of victimization and death related to maltreatment (DHHS, 2007; Lieberman, Chu, Van Horn, & Harris, 2011). As noted in Chapter 3, child neglect is the most common form of maltreatment and parents are the most frequent perpetrators (Cicchetti & Valentino, 2006; DHHS, 2007). Many cases of maltreatment involve both abuse and neglect. Although it is imperative to account for sociocultural factors (described in more detail in the etiology section), higher rates of maltreatment are reported for African American, Native American, and multiracial children; for children from single-parent families; and for children living in poverty (Cicchetti & Valentino, 2006; Lieberman et al., 2011). Once maltreatment reports are made to child protective services, children from minority backgrounds are more likely to be placed out of home and stay longer in foster care. They are also less likely to be reunited with parents (Lieberman et al., 2011).

Trauma- and Stressor-Related Disorders

The Case of Natasha

Natasha is 8 years old and in third grade. Up until recently, she lived with her mother in an apartment in the city. Natasha's parents had a highly conflictual relationship and had been separated for several months following an incident in which police responded to a domestic dispute call and found her mother badly bruised and reporting that her husband had hit her. Frightened and confused by her husband's erratic behavior, Natasha's mother obtained a restraining order in an effort to keep herself and Natasha safe. Natasha, aware of her parents' conflict, was becoming increasingly anxious and protective of her mother. After a quiet period of several weeks, Natasha woke one night to a loud argument and realized that her father was in the house. Eventually, Natasha fell back asleep. In the morning, she went looking for her mother after calling to her but receiving no answer. Natasha found her mother's body on the kitchen floor in a pool of blood. Slowly realizing that her mother was dead, Natasha, confused and in shock, remained alone with her mother's body for several hours until a concerned neighbor, who had heard the argument the night before, let herself into the apartment, called the police, and took Natasha to stay with her in her nearby apartment.

In the weeks following this traumatic incident, Natasha went to live with her maternal grandmother. Her grandmother reports that, prior to the murder of Natasha's mother, Natasha was a generally shy, quiet, and guarded girl. Although she tended to be somewhat anxious in new situations, Natasha would usually become comfortable after a short time and enjoyed being with friends, both at school and in the neighborhood. However, since the day she found her mother's body, Natasha has been especially withdrawn, resists going to school, and has been unable to answer questions about finding her mother's body. Natasha now complains of frequent nightmares and insists on sleeping with her grandmother. She appears tired most days, is emotionally reactive, and reports experiencing frequent stomach aches.

Natasha has recently begun seeing a therapist who specializes in working with children who experience trauma. Although still unable to describe the events surrounding her mother's death, Natasha has begun to draw pictures that include her mother. These pictures likely represent initial attempts to work through the complex psychological effects of the trauma. For example, Natasha has drawn a series of pictures of her mother encountering threatening creatures such as ferocious dinosaurs and monsters. Proceeding slowly and carefully, Natasha's therapist has begun to help Natasha talk about these drawings in some detail. Although a tentative and indirect process at this point, Natasha has begun to organize and acknowledge some of the thoughts and feelings related both to the sudden loss of her mother and the traumatic experience of finding her body. Some of Natasha's more challenging symptoms—such as emotional volatility and sleep disturbance—have begun to lessen in intensity and frequency. However, others—such as difficulty separating from her grandmother—have shown little change. ◼

"Bad things happen. As much as we might wish otherwise, close friends and relatives die, painful things happen to our bodies, there are natural disasters and war, and sometimes people do senselessly horrible things to other people" (Bonanno & Mancini, 2008, p. 369). When traumatic events occur, many children and adolescents experience distress and dysfunction. There are a number of types of trauma- and stressor-related disorders in DSM-5. Reactive attachment disorder and disinhibited social engagement disorder, already presented in Chapter 6, are included in this category. And, as described in Chapter 6, maltreatment is the key factor in the development of disorders of attachment. **Acute stress disorder** involves the display of multiple symptoms from any combination of categories (e.g., related to intrusion, dissociation, avoidance, and arousal) following exposure to a traumatic event. Acute stress disorder is diagnosed when the duration of symptoms lasts up to one month. **Posttraumatic stress disorder** (PTSD) involves the experience of trauma and the display of symptoms from each category; PTSD is diagnosed when symptoms last longer than one month. Intrusion symptoms include recurrent memories of the trauma, frightening dreams, or flashbacks. Avoidance symptoms include efforts to avoid people, places, or situations that are associated with the trauma. Alterations in cognition or mood include dissociative symptoms (such as difficulties with memory), negative beliefs about the self or others or the world, or persistent negative mood (such as fear, anxiety, or shame). Alterations in arousal and reactivity include hypervigilance, irritability, and extreme responses.

For many years, young children were not diagnosed with PTSD; their developmental status was thought to be associated with forgetting and "bouncing back" from terrible events. We now know that even infants and toddlers display some of the symptoms of PTSD and that these may be appropriately conceptualized as PTSD (De Bellis & Van Dillen, 2005; Scheeringa, Zeanah, & Cohen, 2011). In DSM-5, there are no differences in the set of diagnostic criteria for children and adolescents (compared to adults). However, there is a subtype of PTSD for preschool children, with fewer symptoms in the set of diagnostic criteria and some developmentally informed adjustment in the descriptions of symptoms. It is important to recognize that children frequently display subclinical symptoms, particularly connected to more common and lower magnitude stressors such as interpersonal loss. Many of these children displaying subclinical symptoms have experienced other recent stressful events (Copeland, Keeler, Angold, & Costello, 2010).

PTSD is more likely to be diagnosed in children and adolescents if there are repeated, multiple, or prolonged experiences of trauma, more direct or severe exposure, and/or a perceived lack of protection (e.g., trauma perpetrated by caregiver or trusted adult, or trauma experienced when a child is separated from parents) (Masten & Narayan, 2012). PTSD is a disorder that unfolds over time. In the immediate wake of the trauma, all aspects of children's adjustment are likely to be affected (Masten & Narayan, 2012; Pynoos et al., 1999; Scheeringa et al., 2011). During the acute stress period, emotions such as terror, helplessness, shame, and sadness are common; intense physiological responses and behaviors are additional complications (De Bellis & Van Dillen, 2005; Meiser-Stedman et al., 2007). Pynoos and colleagues (1999) describe a 7-year-old who reported, "My heart was beating so fast I thought it was going to break" (p. 1544). Cognitive functioning is disrupted, with confusion, uncertainty, and misunderstanding. Younger children, for instance, are less likely to appreciate the uncontrollable nature of intrusive thoughts (Sprung & Harris, 2010). Appraisal and misappraisal of ongoing events and their likely causes and consequences are particularly important developmental constructs to consider (Dalgleish, Meiser-Stedman, & Smith, 2005). For example, changing expectations of responsibility for personal safety, as well as individual differences in appraisal processes and stress responses, may exacerbate children's reactions to trauma (Bryant, Salmon, Sinclair, & Davidson, 2007; Ehlers, Mayou, & Bryant, 2003; Stallard & Smith, 2007).

Adjustment to the trauma, or lack of adjustment, is related to many child factors, including developmental status and neurobiological maturation, temperament and attachment, and anxiety sensitivity; outcomes are also influenced by external factors related to the nature of the trauma itself, parents and families, other life events, and schools and larger social communities (Furr, Comer, Edmunds, & Kendall, 2010; Masten & Narayan, 2012; Scheeringa et al., 2011). The elements of trauma include the frequency, intensity, and duration of exposure, and the specific form of trauma (e.g., natural disaster versus parental abuse), with longer, more intense trauma and trauma involving human perpetrators associated with more severe and persistent PTSD. Trauma details and reminders are often upsetting; they may come from unexpected sources such as media reports (Masten & Narayan, 2012). Children's adjustments are sometimes embedded in the adjustments of others, as they witness the distress and horror of loved ones and their continuing struggles to recover; indeed, there may be cascades of additional stressful experiences that continue to negatively impact children (Masten & Narayan, 2012; Pynoos et al., 1999; see Fig. 13:3).

PTSD has been documented in children and adolescents around the world: following hurricanes in New Orleans, the Carolinas, and Hawaii; earthquakes in California, Athens, Taiwan, and Turkey; and tsunamis in Sri Lanka (Asarnow et al., 1999; Catani et al., 2010; Giannopoulou, Strouthos, Smith, Dikaiakou, Galanopoulou, & Yule, 2006; Hamada, Kameoka, Yanagida, & Chemtob, 2003; Hsu, Chong, Yang, & Yen, 2002; Kronenberg et al., 2010; Sahin, Batigun, & Yilmaz, 2007). PTSD has also been described in children and adolescents exposed to war trauma in the Middle East, in Bosnia, and in Africa (Husain, Allwood, & Bell, 2008; Kithakye, Morris, Terranova, & Myers, 2010; Morgos, Worden, & Gupta, 2008; Solomon & Lavi, 2005; Thabet, Tawahina, El Sarraj, & Vostanis, 2008); in child refugees from Tibet and Latin America and in children adopted from Romania (Hoksbergen et al., 2003; Kinzie, Cheng, Tsai, & Riley, 2006; Servan-Schreiber, Lin, & Birmaher, 1998); and in children and adolescents who experienced the 9/11 attacks on the World Trade Center in New York City (Brown & Goodman, 2005; Mullett-Hume, Anshel, Guevara, & Cloitre, 2008).

A recent review of child development in the context of "mass trauma" experiences such as disaster, war, and terrorism provides much-needed perspective on the scope and impact of this awful global phenomenon (Masten & Narayan, 2012). Across countries and investigations, several findings are clear. First, children's exposure to danger and disaster varies widely, depending on geography, socioeconomic status, and politics and institutions. Most analyses suggest that older children and adolescents experience more adversity than younger children, and that there are cumulative effects with multiple stressful and traumatic experiences. Increased risks are associated with separation from parents, proximity to threat, severity of threat, dislocation, greater exposure to death of family and friends, and rape (Furr et al., 2010; Masten & Narayan, 2012). Understanding gender differences in risk and outcome is complex. Girls often report more symptoms of PTSD, but the effects of gender may be stronger for older youth (Furr et al., 2010). The most salient protective factor is the availability of an attachment figure. Indeed, "the buffering effect of proximity to parents and other attachment figures for children in the midst of terrifying experiences is one of the most enduring findings in the literature on war and other life-threatening disasters" (Masten & Narayan, 2012, p. 229).

TRAUMATIC STRESS
- Context
- Complexity
- Objective features
- Subjective experience
- Coping strategies
- Loss

PROXIMAL TRAUMA REMINDERS
- External and Internal Cues
- Constellation
- Pattern of Occurrence
- Pattern of Reactivity
- Challenge to Regulation of Aggression
- Trauma & Loss Reminders
- Reminders of Prior Trauma

PROXIMAL TRAUMA REMINDERS
- Changes in Family Living Circumstances-Resources
- Change in Community Resources
- Change in Family Constellation & Function
- Change in Availability & Utilization of Social Support
- Need to Assume New Responsibilities
- Medical/Surgical Care-Rehabilitation
- Altered Role Performance
- Issues of Accountability
- Acquisition of New Social Skills
- Intercurrent Trauma, Loss, Life Adversity

APPRAISAL & RESPONSE TO DANGER

RESISTANCE & VULNERABILITY

ECOLOGY OF THE CHILD

FAMILY
  Parental Factors
- Similar grouping as Child Intrinsic Factors
- Parental physical illness
- Parent past exposure to trauma & loss
- Reactivity to reminders
- Loss and secondary stresses
- Current responsiveness
- Current trauma and loss-generated psychopathology
DEVELOPMENTAL CYCLE OF THE FAMILY
  Family structure and function
SCHOOL MILIEU AND RESPONSIVENESS
PEER MILIEU AND RESPONSIVENESS
SOCIAL ECOLOGY AND RESPONSIVENESS

CHILD INTRINSIC FACTORS
- Genetic history
- Temperament
- Alarm propensity
- Anxiety Sensitivity
- Organization of stress response systems
- Acquired developmental competencies
- Phase-specific concerns
- Pre-existing psychopathology
- Prior experience
  - Threats to attachment
  - Trauma and Loss
  - Coping with prior danger
- Modes of attachment
- Coping repertoire

ACUTE DISTRESS
- Acute post-trauma reactions
- Registration of personal consequence
- Attributions to self and others
- Failure of developmental expectancies
- Other categories of reactions
- Early efforts at adjustment directed at:
  1. Environmental
  2. Internal state

RESILIENCE

FIGURE 13:3 Developmental psychopathology model of PTSD.
Source: Reprinted from Biological Psychiatry, 46, Pynoos, R.S., Steinberg, A.M., & Piacentini, J.C., A Developmental Psychopathology Model of Childhood Traumatic Stress and Intersection With Anxiety Disorders, p. 1524–1554, Copyright 1999, with permission from Elsevier.

In addition to these types of natural disasters and manmade horrors, everyday tragedies are also associated with the emergence of PTSD. Serious car accidents, for example, are a common cause (Schafer, Barkmann, Riedesser, & Schulte-Markwort, 2006). Interpersonal trauma (such as maltreatment or exposure to family violence) is also clearly associated with high-risk status (Margolin & Vickerman, 2007; Scott, 2007). Co-occuring maltreatment and exposure to family violence is common (Gewirtz & Edleson, 2007). For children who experience repeated interpersonal trauma, it is important to keep in mind that events intended to provide safety are also often upsetting. Given the literature on the development of attachment in maladaptive relationships, and that "parents provide children's primary protection from real or perceived

danger, and thus, children's and young adolescents' perceptions of danger and how to stay safe," it is not

WILLIAM WEST/AFP/Getty Images

Children surviving severe trauma, such as natural disasters, are at increased risk to develop symptoms of PTSD.

surprising, then, that children who were placed in foster care following maltreatment reported that the most frightening event they experienced was "placement in foster care" (Scheeringa et al., 2011, p. 776).

Recent studies of children and adolescents who experience multiple and complex interpersonal trauma (e.g., recurrent or chronic physical or sexual abuse) suggest that a new diagnostic category be included in upcoming editions of the DSM: **developmental trauma disorder,** a disorder involving both exposure and adaptation to chronic trauma, with exposure often occurring in the context of a child's caregiving environment (Cook et al., 2005; Spinazzola et al., 2005; van der Kolk, 2007; van der Kolk, Roth, Pelcovitz, Sunday, & Spinazzola, 2005; see Box 13:1).

Exposure to traumatic events is not uncommon, with estimates ranging from one-fourth to two-thirds of children reporting some traumatic history by age 16 (Copeland, Keeler, Angold, & Costello, 2007; Costello, Erkanli, Fairbank, & Angold, 2002; Scheeringa et al., 2011). Although we usually think of trauma in terms of the direct and life-threatening experiences just described, indirect forms of exposure (such as living in dangerous environments or exposure to domestic or gun violence) are increasingly frequent (Berman, Silverman, & Kurtines, 2002; Hanson et al., 2006; Margolin & Vickerman, 2011; Pynoos, Steinberg, & Piacentini, 1999). Because increased risk is associated with additional exposure, the experience of both direct and indirect forms of trauma in ethnic minority children from disadvantaged backgrounds is especially troubling (Foster, Kuperminc, & Price, 2004; Lieberman et al., 2011; Richards et al., 2004).

Developmental Course

Maltreatment

Short-term outcomes

As emphasized, maltreatment is not a disorder for which a developmental course can be described. Instead, it is a risk factor whose impact may be experienced in multiple domains and in various pathways over time. In the physiological domain, a number of negative consequences of maltreatment have been identified. With respect to brain structures, maltreatment is associated with reduced volume in the hippocampus and frontal lobes and increased volume in the amygdala (Lupien et al., 2009). This is likely related to disruptions in the typical process of overproduction and pruning of neuronal connections. Further, "besides slowing down the development of the brain during times of adversity, leading to reduced brain volumes in adulthood, stress in early life could modify the developmental trajectory of the brain" (Lupien et al., 2009, p. 441). Additional effects are observed on the HPA axis, the dysregulation of the stress response, and the functioning of the serotonin system (Cicchetti & Rogosch, 2012; Gunner & Quevedo, 2007; Tarullo & Gunnar, 2006).

These atypical physiological patterns may be associated with both short-term advantages and long-term disadvantages (Gunnar & Loman, 2011; Meaney, 2010). For example, one aspect of disrupted neurological function has to do with regions of the brain involved in emotion experience and regulation, and the processing of others' facial emotions. Abused children exhibit enhanced sensitivity to angry faces; their perceptions are fine-tuned to respond to salient aspects of their social environments (Pollak, 2008). Although these perceptions are exceedingly important to attend to, especially in environments with ongoing threats, this hypersensitivity often interferes with the development of effective and flexible self-regulation in later, less threatening contexts (Pollak, 2008).

In the psychological domain, abundant data document the maladaptive consequences of maltreatment. Difficulties with negotiating typical developmental challenges (such as those involving attachment, autonomy, peer relationships, play, and learning) are also observed (Cicchetti & Valentino, 2006). As noted in the example of the processing of facial emotions, emotional development is often negatively impacted. Both emotional overreactivity and underreactivity have been observed (Cicchetti & Valentino, 2006; Pollak, 2008). With respect to cognition, attention, memory, and problem solving are all affected. Although basic memory processes in children who have been maltreated appear generally similar to children who have not been maltreated, there is evidence of difficulty in recalling specific autobiographical memories. These difficulties may be related to the avoidance of negative emotion associated with painful memories (Howe, Cicchetti, & Toth, 2006; Valentino, Toth, & Cicchetti, 2009; Williams et al., 2007). Negativity bias, deficits in social information processing, and impaired problem solving have all been described (Ayoub et al., 2006). As might be expected, academic achievement

BOX 13:1 CLINICAL PERSPECTIVES

Developmental Trauma Disorder

In recent years, many researchers and clinicians working with children exposed to ongoing trauma have proposed a new diagnosis to better capture the unique characteristics and effects of complex trauma occurring in childhood (DeAngelis, 2007). Although not included in DSM-5, the proposed diagnosis—developmental trauma disorder (DTD)—has been considered as a way to more accurately describe, treat, and study both the specific symptoms of this early and repeated pattern of trauma and the effect of early trauma on the children's neurological development (Spinazzola et al., 2005).

The diagnosis of PTSD describes the pattern of pathological response that sometimes develops following acute trauma. Although the diagnosis of PTSD was developed primarily with adults in mind, DSM-5 does include PTSD in Preschool Children as a subtype of the PTSD diagnosis (Scheeringa et al., 2011). Typically, PTSD refers to a constellation of emotional, cognitive, physiological, and behavioral symptoms experienced following a traumatic episode. In contrast, the type of trauma to which children are often exposed is repetitive and chronic and occurs in the context of the very relationships that should provide a protective buffer to threat and stress (Spinazzola et al., 2005). Examples of this type of complex stress include physical and emotional abuse, witnessing domestic violence, and ongoing exposure to community violence. Although children who struggle in the face of such stressors are given a variety of diagnoses to account for their emotional and behavioral problems, proponents of the DTD diagnosis believe these generally fail to adequately describe the core etiology and distinctive cluster of symptoms these children experience (D'Andrea et al., 2012).

Additionally, there is increasing evidence that experiencing this kind of trauma during childhood leads not only to immediate clinical symptoms but to more pervasive and long-term neurobiological and psychological consequences resulting from specific structural and functional changes in brain development (Gabowitz, Zucker & Cook, 2008; van der Kolk, Roth, Pelcovitz, Sunday, & Spinazzola, 2005). Long-term difficulties associated with early trauma include problems with regulation of emotions and behavioral impulses, as well as problems with memory and attention, self-perception, and relationships.

The National Child Traumatic Stress Network is a group of over 70 child mental health centers dedicated to the study and treatment of children experiencing complex trauma. This consortium is developing an extensive database based on the over 50,000 children per year who are seen at these centers, where they are studied and treated. The resulting research and clinical findings are generating a range of compelling findings that support the scientific basis for the DTD diagnosis (National Child Traumatic Stress Network, 2011).

Work on refining the diagnostic criteria for developmental trauma disorder continues. At this point, the current formulation includes the following criteria (van der Kolk et al., 2005):

Exposure: Exposure to one or more forms of developmentally adverse interpersonal traumas, such as abandonment, betrayal, physical or sexual abuse, and emotional abuse. May also experience subjective feelings in relation to this trauma such as rage, betrayal, fear, resignation, defeat, and shame.

Dysregulation: Dysregulated development in response to trauma cues, including disturbances in emotions, health, behavior, cognition, relationships, and self-attributions. Behavioral manifestations could involve self-injury; cognitive manifestations might appear as confusion or dissociation.

Negative attributions and expectations: Negative beliefs in line with experience of interpersonal trauma. May stop expecting protection from others and believe that future victimization is inevitable.

Functional impairments: Impairment in any or all arenas of life, including school, friendship, family relations, and the law.

is often compromised (Schelble, Franks, & Miller, 2010). With respect to behavior, both internalizing and externalizing behaviors have been observed (Cicchetti & Toth, 2003; Jaffee, Caspi, Moffitt, & Taylor, 2004).

Deficits in the self system (i.e., self-concepts, self-regulation, autonomy) are notable (Cicchetti & Valentino, 2006). Some children and adolescents exhibit dissociation, including atypical experiences of perception, memory, and identity (Carlson,

Yates, & Sroufe, 2009). These dissociative experiences are distinct from more typical dissociative states displayed by children (often involving imaginative play, and more permeable boundaries between fantasy and reality). Dissociation following maltreatment is related to severe and multiple episodes of trauma and reflects the "collapse" of coping and regulation (Carlson et al., 2009).

In the relationship domain, negative effects are described in both family and peer systems. Because "young children's sense of safety and well-being is organized around the availability and responsiveness of the caregiver," traumatic experiences "may damage the child's trust in the reliability of the attachment figure as a protector" (Lieberman et al., 2011, p. 399). Maltreated children are much more likely to display insecure attachments than non-maltreated children (Cicchetti & Valentino, 2006; Stronach et al., 2011). Peer difficulties have also been repeatedly observed. Maltreated children are at increased risk for both bullying and victimization (Cicchetti & Valentino, 2006). Some findings suggest that physically abused boys are more likely to display physical aggression toward peers, whereas sexually abused girls are more likely to display relational aggression (Cullerton-Sen et al., 2008). Kim and Cicchetti (2010) hypothesize that peer difficulties are explained by emotion dysregulation that lead to negative behaviors in social interactions and peer rejection.

Poly-victimization, the experience of high levels of many types of victimization, is a particularly distressing outcome (Finkelhor, Ormrod, Turner, & Holt, 2009). Children who endure poly-victimization "experience physical and emotional abuse by caregivers, assaults and harassment by peers, sexual victimizations by acquaintances and strangers, and are exposed to crime and violence in their communities and neighborhood—all this over the course of a relatively short period of time" (p. 316). There are four pathways to becoming a poly-victim. *Living in a dangerous community* involves exposure to violence and crime, neighborhood chaos, and a lack of social ties and support, all of which contribute to an individual's vulnerability in multiple contexts. *Living in a dangerous family* involves intrafamily maltreatment that leads to emotional dysregulation and problematic peer interactions, which in turn lead to an individual being the target of bullies. *Having a chaotic, multiproblem family environment* may include parental illness, unemployment, psychiatric disorders,

and poor supervision and neglect, all of which are associated with vulnerability in both family and peer contexts. *Having emotional problems that increase risky behaviors and compromise adaptation* is a pathway possibly related to temperament; characteristics perceived as "annoying, frustrating, disruptive, passive, and difficult to relate to or weak" lead to heightened risk for maltreatment in family and peer contexts. This last pathway is associated with earlier onset of poly-victimization. Two periods are linked with spikes in onset: entry into elementary school and entry into high school.

Long-term outcomes

There is a continuum of outcomes related to personality and psychopathology. In other chapters, maltreatment is linked to both internalizing disorders and externalizing disorders, including PTSD, anxiety disorders, mood disorders, conduct disorders, substance abuse disorders, eating disorders, and personality disorders (Battle et al., 2004; Hilarski, 2004; Jaffee et al., 2005; Lansford et al., 2007; Lee & Hoaken, 2007). Children from minority backgrounds appear to be at higher risk for negative outcomes (Cicchetti & Valentino, 2006). Gene-by-environment effects are increasingly described (Cicchetti, 2010; Nikulina, Widom, & Brzustowicz, 2012; Nugent, Tyrka, Carpenter, & Price, 2011; Uher et al., 2011). Much of the research and clinical attention has focused on the trajectory from maltreatment to mood disorders (see Box 13:2).

The results of a longitudinal investigation of the impact of sexual abuse on the development of girls provide compelling data on outcome variability (Trickett, Noll, & Putnam, 2011). Three patterns of abuse and outcome were observed. The first pattern of abuse involved sexual abuse by the biological father, early onset, and longer duration. The second pattern involved abuse by the stepfather/mother's boyfriend or other relative, later onset, shorter duration, and less frequent violence. The third involved abuse by multiple perpetrators, short duration, and severe violence. The first pattern of abuse, involving the biological father, was associated with the poorest outcomes. Across all of the patterns of abuse, poor outcomes included atypical physical development (e.g., early puberty, more obesity); more psychological and psychiatric symptoms (dysregulated stress–response system, atypical cognitive development and academic underachievement, atypical sexual attitudes and beliefs and risky

---

BOX 13:2 EMERGING SCIENCE

Maltreatment and Mood Disorders

As researchers in the field of childhood psychopathology come to take a developmental perspective, they are increasingly interested in the links between early risk and protective factors and later disorder. One of the most consistently demonstrated findings from these efforts is the relation between maltreatment in childhood and the development of depressive disorders (Cicchetti & Valentino, 2006). Child maltreatment, including all forms of abuse and neglect, compromises development in many domains. For example, we have previously discussed the importance of the early attachment relationship that develops between the infant and the primary caregiver in the first year of life. If that relationship is characterized by either consistent abuse or an unpredictable pattern that includes abuse, important aspects of children's expectations of themselves, of others, and of their ability to effectively manage their environment may be disrupted or disturbed. The significant relations among abuse, attachment, and depression are especially strong for emotional abuse (Lieberman et al., 2011; Liu, Alloy, Abramson, Iacoviello, & Whitehouse, 2009; van Harmelen et al., 2010).

There is much emphasis in developmental psychopathology on the integration of different levels of analysis. A number of researchers have asserted the necessity of specifying how the effects of early adverse experiences may cascade across levels and lead to the development of psychopathology. For example, in addition to considering how the relation between abuse and depression is mediated by the attachment relationship, recent research has also focused on how genes, the brain, the family, and the larger social context all provide links between early maltreatment and later depression.

One such link, or pathway, being studied involves the effects of abuse on critical neuroendocrine systems. For some time now, we have understood that stressful life events can affect certain neurocircuits and that these changes in neurocircuitry can be reliably measured. Further, there is extensive evidence linking specific neurological and endocrine pathways to the development of depressive and anxiety disorders (Gunnar & Loman, 2011; Heim et al., 2000). Past research has demonstrated that the neurobiological alterations resulting from early abuse may, in many cases, be permanent and significantly increase the risk for depression in childhood, adolescence, and adulthood (Carpenter et al., 2004; Gunnar & Quevedo, 2007). Specifically, stress early in development is associated with poor regulation of the HPA axis. This complex neuroendocrine system helps the body to mobilize in the presence of stress and helps to reestablish equilibrium after the threat has passed. Prolonged or repeated and unpredictable stress, as is the case with many instances of child maltreatment, may lead to later emotional and behavioral problems. The pathway from maltreatment to disorder may be especially relevant for those at genetic risk for disorders like depression.

It is important to note that not all children who are maltreated develop depression. And by no means does a diagnosis of depression necessarily imply a history of abuse. However, by better understanding the relation that does exist between maltreatment and depression, more targeted and effective approaches to prevention and treatment can be designed to help many children, adolescents, and adults. Also, the models developed to understand the pathways across physiological, psychological, and social levels that may lead from maltreatment to depression will inform other investigations of developmental psychopathology.

---

sexual behaviors); more disorders; ongoing victimization and sexual violence; and later domestic violence. Intergenerational consequences (such as less frequent secure attachment relationships with their own children) were also noted.

Resilience

Not all maltreated children display maladaptive outcomes. Many maltreated children exhibit resilience. Resilience is a dynamic construct that encompasses many levels of adaptation (e.g., physiological, psychological, and social levels) (Cicchetti, 2010; Masten, 2011). In addition, each child's resilience is embedded in larger systems (e.g., families, communities, and cultures) that are themselves more or less adaptive (Masten & Narayan, 2012). When conceptualized in this way, resilience, as noted many times previously, is not an all-or-nothing phenomenon.

A number of protective factors that promote resilience following maltreatment have been identified. These protective factors include genetic predispositions (Bradley et al., 2011; Gunnar &

Quevedo, 2007); child characteristics such as average or above-average intelligence, positive emotionality and optimism, and perceived self-efficacy and better self-regulation; and relationship characteristics such as secure attachment and friendships (Cicchetti, 2010; Lieberman et al., 2011; Masten & Narayan, 2012; Seeds, Harkness, & Quilty, 2010). "Taken together, it seems that self-reliance and self-confidence, in concert with interpersonal reserve, may bode well for the development of resilient adaptation in maltreated children" (Cicchetti & Valentino, 2006, p. 167).

The Case of Deion

Deion is currently enjoying a productive, busy, and fun college career at a large state university. He is consistently on the Dean's List, he helped to establish a tutoring program with inner-city youth in several nearby elementary schools, and, along with a number of his good friends, he is an enthusiastic participant in several intramural sports. Deion's life, however, was not always so positive and hopeful. In August of 2005, Deion had just begun his final year of junior high in New Orleans, where he lived with his mother, older brother, and younger sister, when Hurricane Katrina struck. With water rising quickly, streets closed, and no way to get to safety, Deion's family found themselves trapped in their home with little drinking water or food. Eventually rescued by resourceful neighbors who gained access to a small boat, Deion and his family made it to the New Orleans Superdome, where tens of thousands of others found shelter. Over the next several days, however, conditions steadily deteriorated, along with the health of Deion and his siblings. Deion's mother managed to keep the family together, garnered resources where she could, and created a sense of safety and hopefulness for her children. Unable to return to their destroyed home, Deion's mother reached out to family and church contacts. In time, she got her family out of the city and into a small home outside of Houston, where she had supportive relatives and found a welcoming church.

Initially, Deion struggled in the aftermath of his family's traumatic and abrupt dislocation. He felt lonely and angry. He had difficulty making the transition to his new school and missed the friends he had grown up with. Although generally understanding and patient with Deion, his mother noticed that his grades had begun to slip and that he was spending an increasing amount of time alone in his room. She insisted that he work to his potential in the classroom and encouraged him to join at least one co-curricular activity each semester of that school year. Initially resentful and resistant, Deion soon found himself making new friends and receiving positive feedback from teachers and coaches. The following year Deion started high school with a small but close circle of friends and with newly developed interests in debate and track. Deion proved to be an excellent student and was passionate in his commitment to debate and track. In his college applications Deion wrote movingly about his experiences during and after the Hurricane Katrina tragedy. He was open and clear about the ongoing sense of loss he felt and about the generosity of those who helped his family start a new life in a new community. Finally, he wrote about the personal strengths he discovered in himself and his confidence in the future as he prepared to leave home and begin college. With excellent grades, varied accomplishments, strong recommendations, and a memorable essay, Deion was an attractive applicant and eagerly pursued by several highly regarded colleges and universities. Taking advantage of generous scholarship support, Deion enrolled in his adopted state's major public university, where he is currently thriving. ■

Trauma- and Stressor-Related Disorders

Short-term outcomes

The developmental course of PTSD varies. For some, symptoms improve over time; for others, symptoms go from bad to worse. Many children and adolescents display a "mixed picture of resilience and lingering vulnerability and harm" (Masten & Narayan, 2012, p. 229). Several PTSD pathways have been described, including a *resilient (i.e., stress-resistant) pathway,* a *response and recovery pathway,* a *delayed breakdown pathway,* and a *chronic dysfunction (i.e., breakdown without recovery) pathway* (Bonanno, 2004; Bonanno & Mancini, 2008; Masten & Obradovic, 2008; see Fig. 13:4). One of the most consistent outcome-related findings is that the parent's own response to trauma and his or her ability to function is linked to the child's symptom severity and outcome (Masten & Narayan, 2012; Scheeringa & Gaensbauer, 2000).

For those children and adolescents who struggle, the effects of stress and trauma are noted across multiple levels and in multiple domains. PTSD is linked to physiological changes involving both structure and function (De Bellis & Kuchibhatla, 2006; Perkonigg et al., 2005; Pervanidou et al., 2007; Shea, Walsh, MacMillan, & Steiner, 2005; van der

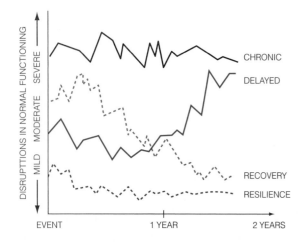

FIGURE 13:4 Developmental pathways for children with PTSD.
Source: From Bonanno, G. A. (2004), "Loss, trauma, and human resilience: Have we underestimated the human capacity to thrive after extremely aversive events?", *American Psychologist*, 59(1), 20–28. Copyright © 2004 American Psychological Association.

Kolk, 2003). Damage to the hippocampus, as well as atypical frontal lobe anatomy and volume, has been documented (Carrion et al., 2009; Carrion, Weems, & Reiss, 2007). In fact, as summarized in the first section of this chapter, the "effects of experience can become biologically embedded in a developing organism," and "bad timing ... can disrupt development, with long-lasting implications for adaptive capacity, health, and vulnerability to later trauma experiences" (Masten & Narayan, 2012, p. 241).

Psychological maladaptation is also frequently observed. For example, trauma appears to have lasting effects on both the content and organization of memory, and on cognitive appraisal processes (Ehlers & Clark, 2000). When trauma reminders are present in the everyday lives of children and adolescents, these additional stressors may complicate recovery efforts (Pynoos et al., 1999). The unusual, repeated experiences of intense negative emotion can make emotion regulation more difficult; the development of certain personality characteristics, such as independence, may also be affected (Scheeringa & Gaensbauer, 2000). Sleep disturbances are also common (Brown, Mellman, Alfano, & Weems, 2011). As with maltreatment, PTSD may also disrupt a child's management of age-related tasks and challenges (Briggs-Gowan et al., 2010). Children who experience family violence in early childhood, for instance, display disrupted and atypical development

related to attachment, self-regulation, and social and peer competence (Gewirtz & Edleson, 2007). To the extent that trauma is related to disaster or war, and homes, neighborhoods, schools, and economies are damaged or destroyed, a range of other childhood experiences are also likely to be affected (Masten & Narayan, 2012; Moore & Varela, 2010).

Long-term outcomes

Although there are several factors that appear to moderate outcomes, PTSD is associated with later emergence of both internalizing and externalizing disorders. Non-interpersonal trauma appears to be linked more often with anxiety disorders (Briggs-Gowan et al., 2010; Lieberman et al., 2011; Mrug & Windle, 2010; Pine, 2003). Chronic exposure to stress and trauma is associated with worse outcomes, and gene-by-environment effects are implicated in worse outcomes for girls and young women (Gewirtz & Edleson, 2007; Hammen, Brennan, Keenan-Miller, Hazel, & Najman, 2010). Children who live embedded in multirisk environments are likely to display cascading effects of trauma, involving both atypical resolutions of developmental challenges as well as internalizing or externalizing disorders (Gewirtz & Edleson, 2007; Masten & Narayan, 2012). In addition to a range of mental health outcomes, physical health may also be adversely affected across the lifespan (De Bellis & Van Dillen, 2005). The construct of allostatic load may be especially useful in thinking about mental and physical health trajectories (Danese & McEwen, 2012; Juster et al., 2011; Rogosch, Dackis, & Cicchetti, 2011).

One issue that remains unresolved is whether exposure to stress and adversity involves *inoculation* versus *sensitization* effects (Masten & Narayan, 2012). With inoculation effects, early exposure to stress allows children and adolescents to develop and practice a variety of coping responses and may provide one kind of protective effect. With sensitization effects, early exposure leads to physiological and psychological changes that likely increase risk. Research suggests that moderate stress (*not* the kind experienced in PTSD) may have beneficial effects, whereas "exposure to overwhelming or capacity-depleting levels of adversity" is more likely to lead to increased vulnerability. To take advantage of any stress-related benefits, "interventions designed to build capacity for resilience would need to scaffold or in other ways ensure an adaptive response in order to avoid risk of breakdown or depletion of resilience capacity" (Masten & Narayan, 2012, p. 242).

Resilience

Many researchers and clinicians have suggested that resilience in the face of trauma is more common than we might think (Bonanno, 2004; Hoge, Austin, & Pollack, 2007). As previously described, two of the PTSD pathways involve adaptation (see Fig. 13:4).

Bonanno differentiates resilience (i.e., the maintenance of pretrauma trajectories) from recovery (i.e., a trajectory characterized by maladaptation following trauma, followed by gradual improvement). Keep in mind, though, that "even resilient individuals may experience at least some form of transient stress reaction; however these reactions are usually mild to moderate in degree, are relatively short-term, and do not significantly interfere with their ability to continue functioning" (Bonanno & Mancini, 2008, p. 371).

Factors that are associated with resilience and recovery include child characteristics, family and relationship characteristics, and sociocultural characteristics. Child factors include intelligence, positive personality characteristics, and religious and spiritual beliefs (Masten & Narayan, 2012). Relationship factors include the availability and quality of attachment figures (Gewirtz & Edleson, 2007; Lieberman et al., 2011; Masten & Narayan, 2012). As with the findings related to maltreatment, parenting is a key source of support for children, even when the trauma involves domestic violence in which the parent is the victim (Gewirtz, DeGarmo, & Medhanie, 2011). Peer support is also important. Children who were able to receive support from classmates following Hurricane Katrina displayed better outcomes; these better outcomes were likely related, in part, to the effects of shared experiences (Moore & Varela, 2010). Community support has also been described as helpful. Former child soldiers who were exposed to harrowing trauma displayed better outcomes in the presence of community acceptance and social reintegration; opportunities for schooling were particularly important (Betancourt et al., 2010; Masten & Narayan, 2012).

In addition to resilience and recovery, **posttraumatic growth** is also possible. Posttraumatic growth involves positive changes following trauma. These changes include identification of personal strengths, appreciation for life, enhanced spirituality, better relationships with others, and new possibilities for change and growth (Levine, Laufer, Stein, Hamama-Raz, & Solomon, 2009; Tedeschi & Calhoun, 2004). Posttraumatic growth "only occurs if trauma has been upsetting enough to drive the survivor to (positive) meaning-making of the negative event" (Levine et al., 2009, p. 285). Additional research focused on the characteristics of children and their environments that might support such meaning-making following significant trauma would complement the resilience research already underway.

Etiology

Maltreatment

Single-factor explanations of maltreatment (e.g., related to parent psychopathology, parent's own history of abuse, poverty) have given way to more complex models, such as the ecological–transactional model of child maltreatment (Cicchetti & Valentino, 2006). In that model, for example, multiple factors contribute to high-risk outcomes. Many characteristics of parents increase the likelihood of maltreatment. Many studies identify parents' own histories of maltreatment as an important risk factor, although rates of subsequent maltreatment vary widely (Berlin, Appleyard, & Dodge, 2011; see Fig. 13:5). Additional parent factors include younger-aged parents, history of psychiatric disorders, and parenting beliefs and attitudes (such as those related to discipline) (Azar, 2002). The youngest and poorest caregivers display the most negative parenting strategies. Parents with intellectual disabilities are also more likely to neglect their children (Azar, Stevenson, & Johnson, 2012).

As described earlier in the chapter, maltreatment is especially problematic in early childhood. Increased risk may be due, in part, to the types of parenting stressors experienced by caregivers. For instance, Kopp (2009) notes that toddlers most annoy their mothers when they persistently whine, act aggressively, and fail to listen, whereas preschoolers are most upsetting when they argue or talk back. "For some parents, positive interludes are sufficiently satisfying to encourage their own coping, whereas for others, the combination of rapid developmental change, child negatives, and unpredictability promotes harsh, withdrawn, or imprudent childrearing" (p. 37).

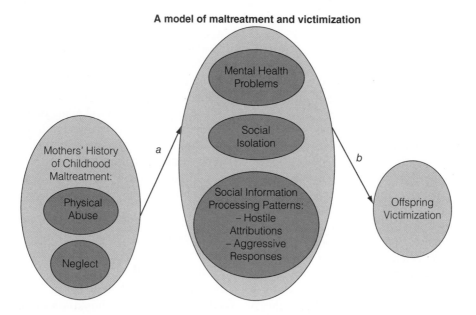

FIGURE 13:5 Hypothetical relations among mothers' history of childhood maltreatment, mental health problems, social isolation, social information processing patterns, and offspring victimization.
Source: Intergenerational Continuity In Child Maltreatment: Mediating Mechanisms and Implications For Prevention, Berlin, L.J., Appleyard, K. and Dodge, K.A. Copyright © 2011 Child Development. Reproduced with permission of John Wiley & Sons Inc.

Family factors such as angry, conflictual, and violent relationships between adults, chaotic and unstable home lives, and social isolation also increase the risk for maltreatment. Sociocultural factors, including poverty and communities and cultures that accept violence as normative, also contribute to higher rates of maltreatment.

Trauma- and Stressor-Related Disorders

Explaining the emergence of trauma- and stressor-related disorders begins with exposure to traumatic experiences. We need to understand children's distress and dysfunction in the context of particular traumatic events. Then, we need to account for the specific factors that, in combination with trauma, lead to disorder.

Genes and Heredity

Pretrauma factors, such as individual differences in genes that are involved in the experience and regulation of stress, are likely to interact with environmental factors to increase risk for some children exposed to acute or chronic trauma (Gunnar & Quevedo, 2007). Several of these gene-by-environment effects have been described. For example, children and adolescents with certain alleles are at higher risk for poor outcomes following maltreatment compared to those

without these alleles (Bradley et al., 2011; Cicchetti, Rogosch, & Sturge-Apple, 2007; Uher et al., 2011). Another example of gene-by-environment impact involves the "biology of misfortune," in which stress reactivity combined with chronic stressors such as low socioeconomic status and impoverished circumstances lead to uneven distributions of mental and physical illness and disorder (Boyce, 2007).

Physiological Factors

Neurodevelopmental models of early abuse and posttraumatic stress provide details about changes in brain systems associated with threat perception and threat response. In these models, physiological dysfunction is conceptualized first as an underlying vulnerability (i.e., present in some children before the experience of trauma) and second as a consequence of noxious experiences that disrupt normal functioning (i.e., resulting in additional, perhaps permanent, dysfunction) (Gunnar & Loman, 2011; Kalin, Shelton, & Davidson, 2007; Vermetten & Bremner, 2002a, 2002b). The "chronic destabilization of neuronal networks in the hippocampus or cerebral cortex, combined with enhanced fear circuits in the amygdala" may lead to the development of disorders such as PTSD (Flinn, 2006, p. 151). The trajectories underlying various disorders may depend on the timing of brain development and stress. "Exposure to adversity at the time of hippocampal development could lead to hippocampus-dependent emotional disorders, which would be different from disorders arising from exposure to adversity at times of frontal cortex development" (Lupien et al., 2009, p. 441).

Child Factors

As noted in earlier sections, child age and gender have varied effects, depending on the type of trauma. Other child factors such as temperament have been investigated, with data indicating increased risk for children with difficult temperaments. Temperamental characteristics are genetically influenced and associated with the reactivity and regulation of emotionality and stress, so this increased risk is not surprising (Gunnar & Quevedo, 2007). In addition, trait anxiety and anxiety sensitivity are each associated with the increased frequency of the somatic symptoms of PTSD (Hensley & Varela, 2008). Protective roles for child and adolescent coping, intelligence, and positive personality characteristics that reduce risk in the presence of atypical stressful experiences have already been described in the previous section on the developmental course of PTSD.

Parent Factors

Parents can influence the development of PTSD, for example, via the "shotgun effect," the "lack of protective shield effect," and/or a "toxic family effect" (Scheeringa & Gaensbauer, 2000, p. 375; Ostrowski, Chrisopher, & Delahanty, 2007; Punamaki, Qouta, El Sarraj, & Montgomery, 2006). The "shotgun effect" involves trauma that is so overwhelming that it produces anxiety symptoms in all family members. In other words, parents as well as children struggle to deal with the aftermaths of awful experiences such as the loss of a home in a fire or flood. The "lack of protective shield effect" involves parents who, for varied reasons, cannot provide the comfort, support, and security necessary for recovery. In these cases, parents may not recognize or they may minimize the impact of a particular trauma on children, believing that children are less affected by stress or that ignoring distress and dysfunction will help a child move on. And the "toxic family effect" has to do with the ways in which parent responses to trauma actually elicit and maintain anxiety symptoms in their children. In some cases, for instance, parents may exacerbate their children's distress by having their children repeatedly recall the traumatic experience or consider the possibility of new or repeat trauma.

Parents also contribute to children's risk or resilience via socialization of coping. Abaied and Rudolph (2010) describe two models that predict varied outcomes. The first, the *amplification-effects model*, suggests that there are "stronger risk effects for maladaptive coping suggestions and stronger protective effects for adaptive coping suggestions." The second, the *differential effects model*, suggests that "socialization of coping has different, but equally significant, effects of risk for psychopathology in the context of high versus mild stress" (pp. 2–3). Abaied and Rudolph also note that girls and boys may respond to socialization of coping differently. Girls are often more socially competent than boys and may be better prepared to implement coping suggestions that require social skills.

Environmental Factors

Availability and access (or lack of availability or access) to a range of resources and support may influence the development of trauma- and stressor-related disorders. Following natural or human-made disasters, or in war-torn regions, economic factors (e.g., continued employment, and costs for food, housing, and other essentials), political factors (e.g., discrimination, marginalization), and community-based factors (e.g., schools and religious institutions) come into play and may exacerbate or improve children's and adolescents' initial functioning (Masten & Narayan, 2012).

Assessment and Diagnosis

Special clinical skills are very important when assessing children who have been traumatized. Depending on the type of trauma, various accommodations related to developmental and physical status, or legal requirements, may be necessary (Scheeringa et al., 2011; Stover & Berkowitz, 2005; Strand, Sarmiento, & Pasquale, 2005). Assessment and diagnosis in very young children is especially challenging (Lieberman et al., 2011). Sociocultural factors (such as family and cultural norms, values, and available supports) must be appropriately addressed (Fontes & O'Neill-Aran, 2008). In most cases, it will be useful to expand assessments beyond a focus on the symptoms of disorder to include coping resources and social supports; at times, crisis intervention will need to take place immediately (Bal et al., 2009).

The American Academy of Child and Adolescent Psychiatry (AACAP) (2010) recommends routine screening for PTSD during all initial mental health assessments. Parents should be included in evaluation whenever possible. Questions related to exposure to traumatic events and children's responses should be specific. For instance, AACAP suggests that asking "When you went past the house where the event occurred, did you get upset?" is more likely to elicit useful information than open-ended, more general questions.

Assessments related to maltreatment are often multidisciplinary, involving mental health professionals, physicians, and individuals from police and law agencies. These assessments are often initiated by social service agencies such as child protection units. Knowledge of best practices and ethical issues related to privacy and informed consent is essential (Jent et al., 2009; Manley & Chavez, 2008). Age- and gender-sensitive techniques as well as the use of multiple informants for sexually abused children and for children who have witnessed family violence are recommended (King et al., 2003).

Few children and adolescents report maltreatment. Patterns of disclosure in youth range from no disclosure at all, to seeking help from peers, to seeking help from adults (neighbors, teachers, school counselors, police officers), to displaying internalizing or externalizing behaviors (Unger, Barter, McConnell, Tutty, & Fairholm, 2009). Reticence to disclose may be related to anxiety about disclosure, loss of control following disclosure, unpredictability of events following disclosure, negative personal consequences (e.g., physical harm), or worries about jail or legal consequences for the perpetrator (Malloy, Brubacher, & Lamb, 2011; Ungar, Tutty, McConnell, Barter, & Fairholm, 2009). A close victim–perpetrator relationship is associated with delayed disclosures (Foynes, Freyd, & DePrince, 2009). Children and adolescents who have suffered because of natural disasters such as earthquakes and hurricanes or because of terror attacks, or who live in war zones amid widespread violence, also benefit from knowledgeable and compassionate assessments (Masten & Narayan, 2012).

Issues related to differential diagnosis and comorbidity are likely to involve decisions about anxiety disorders, mood disorders, ADHD, or externalizing disorders, and whether clinical presentations are consistent with single or multiple diagnoses (AACAP, 2010; De Bellis & Van Dillen, 2005; Margolin &

Vickerman, 2011). Because of the frequent display of somatic symptoms in children and adolescents who experience trauma, physical examinations are always important (AACAP, 2010).

Intervention

Treatment

"In an ideal world, treatment would be readily available and strongly encouraged at the time of disclosure" (Trickett et al., 2011, p. 469). Meta-analyses of psychological interventions for maltreatment indicate positive results with medium-size effects (Skowron & Reinemann, 2005). Observer-rated gains were somewhat smaller than parent-rated gains. Similar effects were noted for both individual and group formats. The findings emphasize the need to target multiple aspects of maltreatment (e.g., both sexual abuse and neglect) and comorbid disorders. There was some evidence for better outcomes associated with nonbehavioral interventions (e.g., psychodynamic treatment), but these better outcomes may be more closely linked to longer treatments. Individualized treatment plans, including both medication and psychotherapy, are also recommended (Saveanu & Nemeroff, 2012).

Comprehensive, multilevel interventions that comprise both child-focused and family-centered treatments are also recommended. These interventions include risk-focused strategies (that reduce or prevent further risk), protection-focused strategies (that add resources to counterbalance risk), and process-focused strategies (that promote the development of well-being in domains of self-regulation and relationships) (Gewirtz & Edleson, 2007). For children and adolescents dealing with multiple kinds of maltreatment and victimization, timely identification and treatment is necessary before any additional traumas are experienced (Finkelhor et al., 2009).

For young maltreated children, the goals of child–parent interventions include amelioration of symptoms and support for ongoing development. Beneficial effects related to secure attachment, the development of positive self-systems, and improved parenting have all been described (Cichetti, 2011). In addition, there are multiple treatment studies that suggest that "interventions designed to improve caregiving following experiences of early adversity can reverse or prevent disruptions in HPA functioning" (Cicchetti, Rogosch, Toth, & Sturge-Apple, 2011; see also Fischer, Gunnar, Dozier, Bruce, & Pears, 2007). "The fact that interventions are able to bring about beneficial effects beyond the early years of life suggests that there is a psychobiology and neuropsychology of hope and optimism for maltreated children that can minimize or eradicate the adverse effects of their histories" (Cicchetti, 2011, p. 448).

With respect to the treatment of posttraumatic stress disorder, there is clear need for both acute, crisis-oriented interventions and ongoing support (Layne et al., 2011; Masten & Narayan, 2012). Crisis management often includes the debriefing of traumatized children and facilitated discussions about the traumatic event; whether these techniques are effective, ineffective, or possibly harmful requires additional investigation. The central components of PTSD treatment involve reestablishing a sense of safety for the child, processing and eventually reducing the intensity of emotional experiences, helping the child to understand the impact of the traumatic event on him- or herself, addressing secondary stresses, and providing support and guidance to the child's caregivers (De Bellis & Van Dillen, 2005; La Greca & Silverman, 2009). For experiences related to mass trauma, five principles are at the core of intervention efforts: promote a sense of safety, promote calming, promote a sense of self- and collective efficacy, promote connectedness, and promote hope (Hobfoll et al., 2007). Especially when working with children, adolescents, and families from diverse backgrounds and cultures, it is imperative to be mindful of when treatments may interfere with natural or typical recovery processes (Bonanno & Mancini, 2008; Watters, 2010).

Cognitive and cognitive-behavioral approaches for PTSD have received the most empirical support (De Bellis & Van Dillen, 2005; Scheeringa, Weems, Cohen, Amaya-Jackson, & Guthrie, 2011; Taylor & Weems, 2011). Trauma-focused cognitive behavior therapy is a multicomponent model that includes parent treatment, psychoeducation, relaxation and stress management skills, cognitive coping skills, emotion regulation skills, trauma narrative and cognitive processing of the traumatic experience, in vivo desensitization to trauma reminders, joint parent–child sessions, and enhancement of safety and future development (Cohen & Mannarino, 2008; Cohen, Mannarino, Kliethermes, & Murray, 2012).

Individual, group, and family formats all appear to be successful; group treatment may be especially useful in situations in which social and economic resources are limited (Amaya-Jackson et al., 2003; Giannopoulou, Dikaiakou, & Yule, 2006; Silverman et al., 2008; Smith et al., 2007). Pharmacological additions to psychotherapy may also be useful (Cohen, Mannarino, Perel, & Staron, 2007). For PTSD that follows abuse, there are a number of comprehensive, structured interventions that are efficacious (Cicchetti & Toth, 2003; Cohen et al., 2007; Osofsky, 2003); these interventions target the many domains of development that have been adversely affected by ongoing trauma (Deblinger, Mannarino, Cohen, & Steer, 2006; Kinniburgh, Blaustein, Spinazzola, & van der Kolk, 2005; Spinazzola et al., 2005; Vickerman & Margolin, 2007).

Prevention

Prevention of maltreatment is a high-priority effort. Increasing public awareness of maltreatment, providing support for at-risk children and families, and ensuring widespread availability and access are essential components of maltreatment prevention initiatives (Cicchetti & Valentino, 2006). Effective prevention programs include empirically supported treatments and account for developmental considerations and cultural relevance. In addition, they recognize the many challenges to implementation of prevention programs, such as outreach and buy-in from various stakeholders (e.g., families, communities, and health agencies) (Toth, Manly, & Nilsen, 2008).

A number of prevention programs target at-risk parents and families with home visits and parenting education and support (e.g., Gunnar, Fisher, & The Early Experience, Stress, and Prevention Network, 2006; Mikton & Butchart, 2009), with the greatest benefits observed for lower income, first-time adolescent mothers (Howard & Brooks-Gunn, 2009). Parent–child interaction therapy for at-risk families is associated with a reduction in rates of maltreatment and significant improvements in parenting and child well-being (Thomas & Zimmer-Gembeck, 2011). Identifying unmet needs in at-risk populations (such as formerly homeless mothers living in community housing) is another important part of the prevention process (Gewirtz & August, 2008; Lee et al., 2010). Mobilizing adults (such as teachers and other school staff) during transition periods (such as entry into elementary and high school) when already-vulnerable children are at risk for additional victimization is another prevention strategy (Finkelhor et al., 2009).

Key Terms

Chapter Summary

- Stress occurs when the demands on the individual to adjust to the environment exceed available coping resources. Allostasis refers to the natural process of maintaining physiological and psychological stability in response to environmental demands. Allostatic load refers to the cumulative physiological and psychological wear and tear caused by ongoing, and sometimes maladaptive, allostatic processes.
- Coping involves the child's active attempts to respond to stress and adversity.
- Child maltreatment, including physical, sexual, and emotional abuse, as well as neglect, is a significant risk factor for immediate, short-term, and long-term negative developmental outcomes.
- Acute stress disorder involves the development of multiple psychologically based symptoms that last up to one month following exposure to a traumatic event. Posttraumatic stress disorder (PTSD) involves significant, specific symptoms that develop after a traumatic experience and last longer than one month.
- Maltreatment, and other forms of trauma, has both short- and long-term negative effects on neurological, psychological, and social development.
- A parent's own response to trauma has a significant effect on his or her child's symptom development, severity, and outcome.
- Resilience and recovery following trauma is related to health-promoting child, family, and sociocultural factors.
- Posttraumatic growth refers to positive changes following trauma.
- Multiple etiological factors, including genetic, physiological, individual, family, and environmental factors, interact in complex ways and lead to pathological responses to stress and trauma.
- Although a variety of treatment approaches are effective in treating symptoms related to maltreatment, trauma, and stress, prevention programs targeting at-risk families are especially important to the reduction of child maltreatment.

14

Substance Use and Addictive Disorders

COMPARED TO THEIR YOUNGER SELVES, adolescents can get into trouble in a number of new and more dangerous ways. Driving recklessly, becoming sexually active, gambling, and using drugs and alcohol are common forms of risk taking that are frequently observed as adolescents explore adult behaviors and adult roles. Some of these behaviors are associated with the three leading causes of mortality in adolescents: accidental death (including car accidents), homicide, and suicide

(Kelley, Schochet, & Landry, 2004; Windle & Windle, 2006). Given this increased vulnerability, it is often difficult for concerned adults to keep a developmental perspective in mind as adolescent challenges play themselves out. Even so, it is essential to understand that adolescent health and development are embedded in evolutionary, historical, and cultural contexts (Crockett, 1997), and that "risk taking and novelty seeking are hallmarks of typical adolescent behavior" (Kelley et al., 2004, p. 27).

Developmental Tasks and Challenges Related to Brain Development and Risk Taking

Of all the myriad events that occur during adolescence, brain development is one of the most significant. Advances in MRI and fMRI technologies make it clear that the brain continues to develop throughout adolescence and early adulthood, with increases in overall brain size and the thickness and number of neuronal connections (Ernst & Hardin, 2010; Giedd et al., 1999; 2004; Spear, 2011) (see Fig. 14:1). This development is a dynamic, nonlinear process, with frontal lobe maturation progressing in a back-to-front direction; more complex cognitive processes (e.g., difficult decision making with multiple options, with each option having mixed positive and negative consequences) mature later than more basic cognitive processes (e.g., straightforward decision making with few options and clear consequences) (Gogtay et al., 2004; Luna & Sweeney, 2004).

A related developmental phenomenon involves transformations in adolescent sleep patterns. As a result of biologically based changes in sleep–wake cycles, many adolescents experience inadequate sleep (increased need for sleep coupled with decreased time sleeping), with cognitive, emotional, and behavioral consequences (Brown et al., 2011; Carskadon, Acebo, & Jenni, 2004). High levels of sleepiness seen in high school students are exacerbated by incompatible weekday and weekend schedules (Dahl & Lewin, 2002). As described in Chapter 5 on infant and toddler disorders, sleep is an active process that promotes early physiological development. Sleep serves similar purposes in adolescence, so adequate sleep is essential.

Connections between physiological development and cognitive development affect decision-making abilities and strategies, impulsivity and novelty seeking, and motivation and emotion (Brown et al., 2011; Dahl, 2004; Ernst & Hardin, 2010). Ongoing change in these processes and characteristics is a result of "a genetically based internal clock and is shaped by

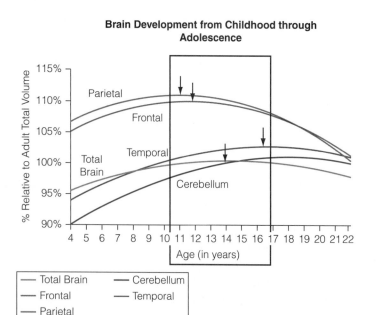

FIGURE 14:1 Developmental changes of regional brain percentage of total brain volumes between the ages of 4 and 22 years. This figure is based on a combination of cross-sectional and longitudinal data from 243 MRI scans from 145 children and adolescents. The adolescent period is highlighted by a rectangle that includes the ages between 10 and 17 years.
Source: Developmental social cognitive neuroscience by Zelazo, Philip David; Chandler, Michael J.; Crone, Eveline Copyright 2010 Reproduced with permission of TAYLOR & FRANCIS GROUP LLC - BOOKS in the format Textbook and Other Book via Copyright Clearance Center.

the interaction of biological and environmental factors" (Ernst & Hardin, 2010, p. 168).

What are the implications of all of this brain-related information? One critical implication is that we will need to think carefully about adolescents' tendencies to use and misuse alcohol and drugs because substance use may have detrimental effects on the developing brain (Brown et al., 2011; Spear, 2002a; Spear, 2011). Another important implication involves the biologically based disjunction between novelty seeking and competent self-regulation; in other words, *the development of good judgment lags behind expanding opportunities for risk taking* (Masten, 2004; Steinberg, 2004).

Risk taking is the product of a competition between the brain-based socioemotional and cognitive-control networks, each of which displays its own developmental trajectory (Albert & Steinberg, 2011; see Fig. 14:2). Risk taking must be understood in the context of adolescent identity formation, the sampling of adult behaviors coupled with freedom from adult responsibilities, and the increasing influence of peers (Arnett, 2000; Ernst & Hardin, 2010; Gardner & Steinberg, 2005). The social primacy of peers, for instance, is evident in the increased risk taking that occurs in social contexts (Albert & Steinberg, 2011; Ernst & Hardin, 2010). Protective factors with a positive impact on adolescent health behavior and risk taking include personal variables such as the adolescent's concern with health and conventionality, family variables such as modeling of healthy behaviors, and social factors such as positive peer relationships and school involvement (Jessor, Turbin, & Costa, 1998a, 1998b).

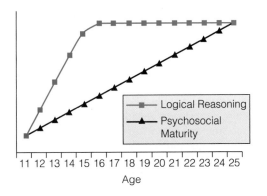

FIGURE 14:2 The development of logical reasoning and psychosocial maturity.
Source: Steinberg, L., Current Directions in Psychological Science, 16(2), pp. 5, copyright © 2007 by Sage Publications. Reprinted by Permission of SAGE Publications.

It is important to distinguish risk taking from impulsivity. *Impulsivity* includes reward hypersensitivity, punishment hyposensitivity, and inadequate effortful control (Cross, Copping, & Campbell, 2011). Impulsivity and risk taking are not interchangeable constructs. "Many impulsive actions are harmless. Hugging someone out of happiness, buying a treat on the spur of the moment, or opting for a new dish at a restaurant are hardly dangerous actions, for the most part. Parachuting, rock climbing, or skiing, although risky, are not generally impulsive. They require planning, training, and a measured consideration of risk. Yet some actions may clearly be both impulsive and risky: running across a road, having sex with a stranger, or accepting an offer of drink or drugs" (Cross et al., 2011, p. 122). In addition to alcohol and drug experimentation and use described in this chapter, other types of risk taking are widespread in adolescence. Given the possibility of grave threats to self and others, reckless driving is one of the most frightening examples. Such driving is often the result of lower levels of parental modeling and peer pressure from teen male passengers (Bina, Graziano, & Bonino, 2006; Simons-Morton, Lerner, & Singer, 2005). Increasing parental and community limits on teen drivers have positive impacts on driving safety (Simons-Morton, Hartos, Leaf, & Preusser, 2006).

Gambling is another risk-taking behavior that is increasingly viewed as a public health issue, with adolescents at the highest risk for pathological gambling (Chambers & Potenza, 2003; Messerlian, Derevensky, & Gupta, 2005). Early onset of gambling is associated with other problems such as substance abuse; girls display more of these symptomatic behaviors (Desai, Maciejewski, Pantalon, & Potenza, 2005). Many instances of adolescent gambling occur on the Internet, and this and other types of Internet addiction are observed across countries and cultures (Johansson & Gotestam, 2004; Kaltiala-Heino, Lintonen, & Rimpela, 2004; Ko, Yen, Chen, Chen, & Yen, 2005).

Sexual activity in adolescence often has serious and unintended consequences such as sexually transmitted diseases and pregnancy (Snyder, 2006). Like other risky behaviors, the timing and extent of sexual activity are related to individual, family, and social factors, with self-regulation particularly important (Meschke, Zweig, Barber, & Eccles, 2000; Raffaelli & Crockett, 2003).

Each of these high-risk behaviors, on its own, can lead to challenging circumstances. In combination, these behaviors set in motion pathways that end in very negative outcomes. According to the **problem behavior syndrome** described by Jessor (1998; Jessor et al., 2003), if adolescents are at risk for one problem behavior, they tend to be at risk for others. In fact, adolescents at risk for negative outcomes report involvement in approximately 4 out of the following 10 categories of problem behaviors: alcohol use, smoking, marijuana use, other drug use, sexual activity, minor delinquency, major delinquency, direct aggression, indirect aggression, and gambling (Willoughby, Chalmers, & Busseri, 2004). Typically developing adolescents, at relatively low risk for clinical disorders, report involvement in one or two activities; adolescents at higher risk report more frequent and persistent involvement in greater numbers of activities (Willoughby et al., 2004). Problem behavior syndrome has been investigated in Asian, Eastern and Western European, North American, and Eurasian/Muslim cultures. Even with very diverse cultures, overall similarity with respect to risk factors, protective factors, and domains of problematic behavior has been observed (Vazsonyi et al., 2010).

Although we have so far emphasized the challenges and risks associated with adolescence, it is important to keep in mind the everyday experiences of most adolescents and the research related to adolescents' knowledge and behavior. The "stereotype of adolescents as irrational individuals who believe they are invulnerable and who are unaware, inattentive to, or unconcerned about the potential harms of risky behavior" are unsupported by data (Steinberg, 2007, p. 55). With respect to better understanding of the physiological, psychological, and social determinants of risk taking, empirical and clinical research continues to be focused on complex models of aspects of cognitive development (e.g., the mix of logical analysis, quick intuitive processing, and bias), the role of experience, adolescents' perceptions of benefits and risks, and the strength of the links between knowledge and behavior (Albert & Steinberg, 2011; Steinberg, 2007).

Substance Use and Addictive Disorders

The Case of Elijah

Elijah is a 15-year-old high school sophomore in the largest town in a rural area. Elijah moved to this community as a ninth grader when his father started a new job. Elijah was an average student through junior high school, although his impulsivity and sporadic oppositional behavior created conflict with his teachers. Elijah left behind a large network of friends and family when he moved, and he found himself somewhat isolated in his new school. There were fewer peers who appreciated his quirky sense of humor and fewer opportunities to share his appetite for ethnic foods and music. Toward the end of ninth grade, Elijah began working at a local movie theater and met several boys about to graduate from high school. Over the summer, Elijah hung out with these friends after work and drank beer with them. When school started in the fall, Elijah quit his job but continued to get together with these friends for parties that included drinking and, occasionally, other drug use. Although Elijah did not try these other drugs, which he viewed as dangerous, he did drink heavily. During the first semester of school, Elijah slept through several morning classes and two exams after late-night parties.

Although uncomfortable with his spending time with these older teens and concerned by his poor school performance, Elijah's parents hesitated to limit his contact because these seemed to be the only friends he had. When they first suspected that Elijah was drinking with this group, Elijah's mother was quite upset. His father saw the behavior as "normal teenage guy stuff." However, when they began to notice liquor missing from their home, they agreed that Elijah's drinking was a problem. They told Elijah that he could not get his driver's license until he agreed to see a counselor and stop drinking. ■■

The Case of Nora

Nora is an 18-year-old senior attending an alternative high school for students who have struggled in traditional school environments. Nora began high school at a large, very competitive suburban high school. Both of her parents are successful professionals; her older brother was class valedictorian and currently attends a prestigious university.

Nora was not only a bright and engaging child but also very strong willed and stubborn. Nora began smoking cigarettes with her friends in seventh grade and was caught drinking with these same friends several times in eighth grade. Upset by these discoveries and Nora's insistence that nothing was wrong, Nora's parents sought mental health counseling several times (with individual sessions for Nora as well as family sessions), but a pattern emerged in which either Nora or her parents came to view the therapists as either unhelpful or incompetent. Multiple therapies were ended without much positive change. By the time Nora started high school, she was smoking marijuana as well as drinking. By the end of ninth grade, however, many of her friends decreased their drug use as they became more involved in academics and co-curricular activities. Nora's drug use, in contrast, increased in both severity and variety. Although unaware of her escalating drug use, Nora's parents became increasingly concerned as her grades dropped and the school administrator contacted them about repeated truancy.

Nora was skipping school and driving to the apartment of friends who attended a local college. In addition to alcohol and marijuana, Nora was beginning to experiment with synthetic psychoactive drugs such as Ecstasy and prescription narcotics such as Oxycontin. Midway through her junior year, Nora was failing almost all of her classes and her health was deteriorating. With the combined insistence of her parents and a therapist, Nora again began—but never completed—several outpatient drug treatments. Typically, Nora would initially cooperate, but she found staying sober physically and psychologically intolerable; she would quickly fall back into a pattern of drug and alcohol use. Late one night, returning from a dance club, Nora was driving erratically and had a minor accident. Nora had been drinking before going to the club and had later taken Ecstasy. The police were called; in addition to determining that Nora was driving while intoxicated, they found other drugs in her car and filed further charges. Nora agreed to enter an inpatient drug treatment program for adolescents. She started at the alternative high school when she was discharged. Nora likes the school, attends regularly, and feels understood and supported by the staff. She is actively attempting to avoid another relapse, but she acknowledges that it is extremely difficult, because she still feels that "the only time I am really happy and alive is when I'm high." ▄▄

The cases of Elijah and Nora illustrate just two of the many clinical presentations of adolescent substance abuse and dependency that depend on definitions of use, abuse, tolerance, dependence, and addiction. *Use* is defined as ingestion of a substance. *Experimental substance use* involves trying a drug once or a few times, often related to curiosity or peer influence. *Social substance use* occurs during social events with one or more peers; parties, concerts, dances, and athletic events are common settings for this type of use (Arnett, 2007). *Abuse* is defined as excessive use of or dependence on an addictive substance. Individual differences in the progression from use to abuse

are noteworthy, with some adolescents transitioning slowly, others rapidly, and still others not at all.

Tolerance occurs when the central nervous system (CNS) gradually becomes less responsive to stimulation by particular drugs. Individuals then need to ingest higher and higher doses to achieve the same CNS effects. **Physical dependence** involves susceptibility to withdrawal symptoms; it occurs only in combination with tolerance. **Withdrawal symptoms** are noxious physical and psychological effects caused by reduction or cessation of substance intake (e.g., sleep disturbances, headaches, nausea and vomiting, tremors, restlessness, anxiety, and depression); these symptoms can range from relatively mild to life threatening. **Psychological dependence** involves a craving or compulsion to use despite significant harm, and it is not always accompanied by withdrawal symptoms. Distinctions between abuse and dependence are often tied to specific substances and their CNS effects. Impairment provides another key diagnostic criterion, with the presence of immediate negative consequences and secondhand effects (such as interrupting the sleep and study of others, or damaging property) (Windle & Windle, 2006). **Addiction** is defined as a chronic disorder characterized by compulsive drug seeking and abuse, physiological effects, loss of control over the urges to use drugs, and impairment.

DSM-5 describes many categories of substance use and addictive disorders. They include alcohol-related disorders, cannabis-related disorders, hallucinogen-related disorders, inhalant-related disorders, opioid-related disorders, stimulant-related disorders, and tobacco-related disorders. Depending on the specific substance, there are subtypes related to use, intoxication, and withdrawal. Gambling disorder is another category in this group of disorders. Additional research is recommended for the provisional category of Internet use disorder.

There are multiple ongoing surveys of adolescent alcohol and drug use in the United States. Some of the most recent data disseminated by the National Institute on Drug Abuse (NIDA; www.nida.nih.gov) and the Substance Abuse and Mental Health Services Administration (SAMHSA; www.samhsa.gov), based on the 2010 National Survey on Drug Use and Health and the 2011 Monitoring the Future study (www.monitoringthefuture.org), show that rates of substance use declined from the late 1990s until the mid-to-late 2000s, but have recently increased, largely due to the increasing popularity of marijuana (see Figs. 14:3a and 14:3b). Positive trends include lower

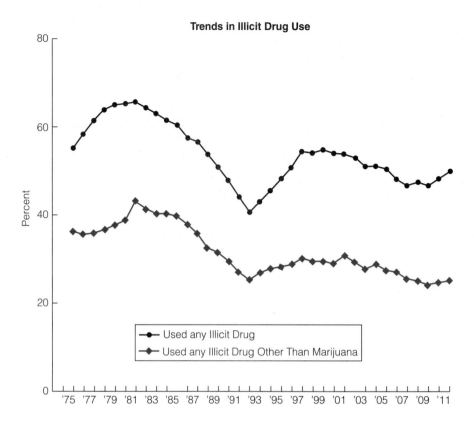

FIGURE 14:3a Lifetime prevalence for illicit drug use by Grade 12 (1975–2011).
Source: www.monitoringthefuture.org, National Survey Results on Drug Use. 1975–2011.

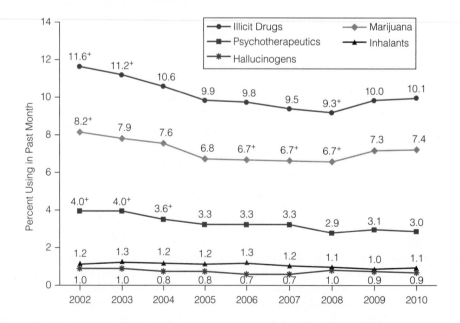

FIGURE 14:3b Past month use of illicit drugs among youth aged 12 to 17 (2002–2010).
Source: Substance Abuse and Mental Health Services Administration, Results from the 2010 National Survey on Drug Use and Health: Summary of National Findings, NSDUH Series H-41, HHS Publication No. (SMA) 11-4658. Rockville, MD: Substance Abuse and Mental Health Services Administration, 2011.

rates of alcohol use, inhalant use, and cocaine use. Specific populations at very high risk for substance abuse are runaway and homeless adolescents (Johnson, Whitbeck, & Hoyt, 2005). Across countries and cultures, there is similarity in age of onset of substance use, but differences in lifetime rates of substance abuse disorders (Vega et al., 2002). Within the United States, rates of disorder vary across states (see Fig. 14:4). Between 7% and 10% of adolescents in the United States are in need of treatment; few receive it (Kaminer & Bukstein, 2005).

Alcohol Use and Alcohol-Related Disorders

Although the legal drinking age in the United States is 21, survey results reveal that the majority of adolescents have drank alcohol by age 18. Prevalence rates are higher for boys compared to girls. African Americans and Asian Americans have lower rates, and European Americans and Latino Americans

have the highest rates (Brown et al., 2011; Kaminer & Bukstein, 2005); among Latino groups (Mexican Americans, Puerto Ricans, Cuban Americans, and others), differences in rates of disorder are observed and are hypothesized to have some connection to degree of acculturation (Delva et al., 2005; Guilamo-Ramos, Jaccard, Johansson, & Tunisi, 2004). Mean age of onset for alcohol use is 14 years (National Institute on Alcohol Abuse and Alcoholism [NIAAA], 2005), although there is increasing concern about access to alcohol and use in elementary school children (Donovan et al., 2004). Figure 14:5 displays the rates of alcohol use between the ages of 12 and 20 over the last decade.

The transition to young adulthood does not signal a lessening of alcohol misuse. Drinking in college students, for instance, is widespread and often problematic; indeed, binge drinking has been investigated as a developmental phenomenon (King,

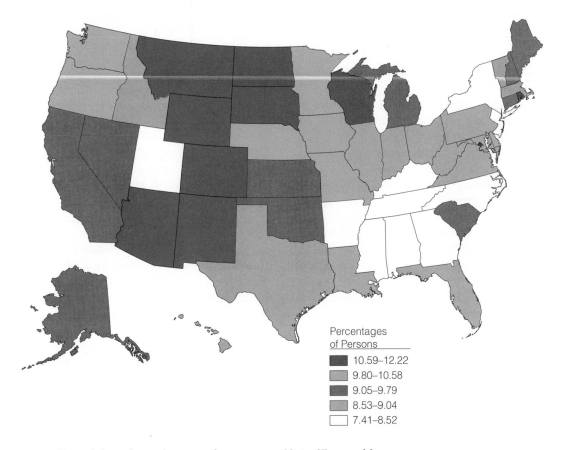

Percentages
of Persons

- 10.59–12.22
- 9.80–10.58
- 9.05–9.79
- 8.53–9.04
- 7.41–8.52

FIGURE 14:4 Map of drug dependence or abuse among 12- to 17-year-olds.
Source: Substance Abuse and Mental Health Services Administration (SAMHSA), Office of Applied Studies, *National Survey on Drug Use and Health,* 2003 and 2004.

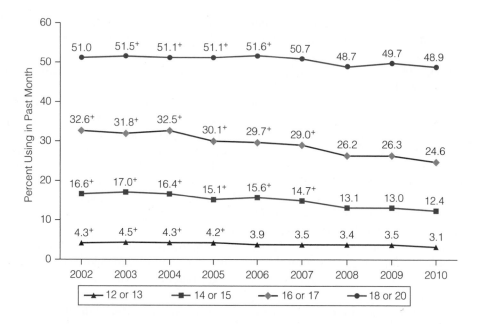

FIGURE 14:5 Current alcohol use among persons aged 12 to 20, by age: 2002–2010.
Source: From Substance Abuse and Mental Health Services Administration, *Results from the 2010 National Survey on Drug Use and Health: Summary of National Findings*, NSDUH Series H-41, HHS Publication No. (SMA) 11-4658. Rockville, MD: Substance Abuse and Mental Health Services Administration, 2011.

Burt, Malone, McGue, & Iacono, 2005; Masten, Faden, Zucker, & Spear, 2008) and is linked with poor academic performance and later alcohol dependence and abuse (Brown et al., 2011; Jennison, 2004; Wechsler & Wuethrich, 2002).

Several studies focus on the locations and contexts of adolescent drinking (Windle, 2003). Most adolescents report purchasing their own alcohol, suggesting that access to alcohol is not particularly difficult; girls are challenged less frequently by retailers than boys (Willner & Hart, 2001). Often-cited reasons for drinking include curiosity, the pleasurable effects of alcohol, and social drinking with friends. Many adolescents use alcohol and other drugs in outdoor or out-of-the-way settings that are associated with dangers such as walking home alone and driving while intoxicated (Coleman & Cater, 2005).

Many adolescents are drinking to get drunk (Johnston et al., 2008). Twenty-eight percent of twelfth graders report **binge drinking** (more than five drinks) in the previous two weeks (NIAAA, 2005). Twelfth graders who drink frequently and heavily report many alcohol-related difficulties, including behaving in ways they later regret, poor decision making, and reckless driving. For athletes with a "jock identity," binge drinking has been associated

with violent behavior in young men (Miller, Melnick, Farrell, Sabo, & Barnes, 2006).

Smoking and Tobacco-Related Disorders

Although less dramatic than the substance use and abuse described in the cases of Elijah and Nora, adolescent tobacco smoking is a major public health problem, with the long-term complications of smoking presenting a somewhat different set of clinical concerns than the immediate dysfunction and distress seen with other substance use and abuse (Chassin, Presson, & Sherman, 2005). Nicotine is one of the most frequently used drugs, and "the cigarette is a very efficient and highly engineered drug-delivery system," with nicotine reaching the brain within 10 seconds (NIDA, 2001b). Nicotine has both stimulant and sedative effects, with a nearly immediate release of adrenalin that many individuals perceive as pleasurable. Cigarettes and other tobacco products are highly available and sophisticatedly marketed. Although cigarette smoking has declined in recent years, the popularity of other forms of smoked tobacco (such as hookah water pipes) has increased (NIDA, 2012). Adolescent smoking is correlated with a host of other problem behaviors, including alcohol use, early sexual activity, and

Binge drinking by college students is a significant risk factor for both academic problems and later alcohol abuse.

© ACE STOCK LIMITED/Alamy

delinquency (Turbin, Jessor, & Costa, 2000). With repeated use, tolerance develops. Of every five adolescent smokers, between one and three are dependent on nicotine; the withdrawal symptom described most frequently is *craving*, or "drug wanting" and a strong desire to use (Colby, Tiffany, Shiffman, & Niaura, 2000).

Marijuana and Cannabis-Related Disorders

Marijuana use has increased slightly over the last several years (see Figs. 14:3a and b). In 2011, 7.2% of eighth graders (up from 5.7% in 2007), 17.6% of tenth graders (up from 14.2%), and 22.6% of twelfth graders (up from 18.8%) used marijuana in the previous month. More adolescents now smoke marijuana than smoke cigarettes (NIDA, 2012). The increasingly frequent use of synthetic marijuana is a major concern because it is wrongly perceived as a safe alternative (NIDA, 2012).

The active chemical in marijuana is delata-9-tetrahydro-cannabinol (THC), and the amount of THC in marijuana has risen dramatically over recent decades. THC attaches to cannabinoid receptors in many brain areas (see Table 14:1). Its use is associated with both short- and long-term physical impairments. Smoking marijuana leads to addiction in some users, who display compulsive use and impaired functioning (NIDA, 2005c). Findings related to the effects of marijuana use are mixed. Some studies show decreases in executive functioning (related to attention, memory, and learning) and brain abnormalities, and lower rates of school achievement and high school graduation; other data suggest few, if any, long-term impairments (Carlson, 2007; Lyons et al., 2004; Windle & Wiesner, 2004). Investigators have attempted to describe subtypes of marijuana users and have found the most useful distinctions related to age of onset, difficult temperament, and whether other psychopathology is present (Babor, Webb, Burleson, & Kaminer, 2002).

Other Commonly Abused Substances and Disorders

Inhalants are substances that produce chemical vapors that can be inhaled to produce psychoactive, or mind-altering, effects. These include solvents (e.g., paint thinner, gasoline, glue), aerosols (e.g., spray paint), gases (e.g., nitrous oxide), and nitrites (e.g., "poppers," "snappers"); they achieve their effects via suppression of the central nervous system. "Within seconds of inhalation, the user experiences intoxication along with other effects similar to those produced by alcohol. Alcohol-like effects may include slurred speech, an inability to coordinate movements, euphoria, and dizziness" (NIDA, 2005b, p. 4). The effects are short lived, and "because intoxication lasts only a few minutes, abusers frequently seek to prolong the high by continuing to inhale repeatedly over the course of several hours, a very dangerous practice" (p. 4). Inhalant use peaks

TABLE 14:1 Marijuana's Effects on the Brain	
BRAIN REGION	**FUNCTIONS ASSOCIATED WITH REGION**
Brain regions in which cannabinoid receptors are abundant	
Cerebellum	Body movement coordination
Hippocampus	Learning and memory
Cerebral cortex, especially cingulate, frontal, and parietal regions	Higher cognitive functions
Nucleus accumbens	Reward
Basal ganglia Substantia nigra pars reticulata Entopeduncular nucleus Globus pallidus Putamen	Movement control
Brain regions in which cannabinoid receptors are moderately concentrated	
Hypothalamus	Body housekeeping functions (body temperature regulation, salt and water balance, reproductive function)
Amygdala	Emotional response, fear
Spinal cord	Peripheral sensation, including pain
Brain stem	Sleep and arousal, temperature regulation, motor control
Central gray	Analgesia
Nucleus of the solitary tract	Visceral sensation, nausea and vomiting

Source: NIDA (2005c).

between seventh and ninth grades, with sustained use more frequent in boys. Indeed, the most serious inhalant abuse is exhibited by children and adolescents who have little access to alcohol or other drugs, and is particularly awful in children from impoverished cultures who "live on the streets completely without family ties" (NIDA, 1995). Inhalant abuse has neurotoxic consequences, with immediate short-term and long-term physical and psychological complications, including progressive, permanent declines in cognitive functioning and heart arrhythmias that can lead to heart failure and death ("sudden sniffing death") (Cairney, Maruff, Burns, & Currie, 2002; NIDA, 2005b).

Cocaine has been used and abused for centuries (NIDA, 2004); following the peak in the 1980s and 1990s, cocaine use has declined. Cocaine has two chemical forms, hydrochloride salt and freebase (one type of which, crack, is processed for smoking), and is ingested in a variety of ways, including inhaling, smoking, and injecting. Cocaine acts on the brain's reward systems and the neurotransmitter dopamine. Cocaine is a powerfully addictive drug;

tolerance and craving are frequently observed. Single or repeated use may result in cardiovascular, respiratory, and neurological complications.

Methamphetamine is a potent stimulant drug that has become increasingly widespread and extraordinarily problematic. It has a similar drug structure to amphetamines, but more dramatic and more toxic effects on the CNS (NIDA, 2002). Users often display "binge and crash" patterns; "after the initial 'rush,' there is typically a state of high agitation that in some individuals can lead to violent behavior" (NIDA, 2002, p. 2). "In contrast to cocaine, which is quickly removed and almost completely metabolized in the body, methamphetamine has a much longer duration of action and a larger percentage of the drug remains unchanged in the body" (p. 5).

Hallucinogens (such as LSD) cause hallucinations—distortions of a person's perception of reality and disruption of nerve cell interaction and the serotonin system—with unpredictable effects (NIDA, 2001a). There can be long-lasting psychological complications, including flashbacks. Dissociative drugs (such as PCP) affect the neurotransmitters glutamate and dopamine, also with unpredictable effects. With characteristics and effects overlapping stimulant and psychedelic drugs, MDMA (i.e., Ecstasy) is another abused substance, often used in combination with alcohol or marijuana. Originally used in night clubs and at dance parties (McCaughan, Carlson, Falck, & Siegel, 2005), its use is associated with increases in feelings of well-being, increases in emotional and sensory perception, and decreases in anxiety. Ecstasy's effects occur via neurotransmitter systems, with immediate life-threatening consequences for some and long-term complications (such as damage to serotonin-containing neurons) (NIDA, 2006).

Heroin is another highly addictive substance; it is the most rapidly acting and most abused of the opiate class of drugs (although fewer than 2% of eighth–twelfth graders have tried heroin) (NIDA, 2005a). Heroin users exhibit high degrees of tolerance and dependence. "Once they are addicted, the heroin abuser's primary purpose in life becomes seeking and using drugs. The drugs literally change their brains and their behavior" (NIDA, 2005a, p. 3).

Prescription drugs are also increasingly abused by adolescents; increased initiation rates for nonmedical use of prescription drugs are second only to initiation rates for marijuana (SAMHSA, 2011). The most commonly abused prescription drugs are pain medications, medications that depress the central nervous system (such as those prescribed for anxiety and sleep disorders), and stimulants (such as those prescribed for ADHD) (NIDA, 2012). Approximately 10% to 15% of high school seniors used prescription drugs for nonmedical reasons in 2011 (NIDA, 2012; SAMHSA, 2011).

Anabolic steroids were originally developed to treat certain medical conditions; they promote growth and strength. Their primary use and abuse are related to improvements in sports performance. Steroidal supplements such as androstenediol and other "pro-hormones," sold in many health food stores, are also widely used. Steroids can be taken orally, injected, or rubbed on skin. Steroid abusers often take combinations of steroids ("stacking") or make use of "pyramid" doses, slowly increasing and then decreasing intake. There are many adverse physical and psychological effects; these occur immediately and over the long run. Connections between steroid use and irritability and aggression have been made; however, "the most dangerous of

the withdrawal symptoms is depression, because it sometimes leads to suicide attempts" and suicide completion (NIDA, 2000).

Comorbid Disorders

Many connections between substance abuse disorder and other psychopathologies have been documented. In community studies, approximately two-thirds of adolescents who use or abuse substances also meet the diagnostic criteria for another psychiatric diagnosis (Lansford et al., 2008). Externalizing disorders are more common, although internalizing disorders are also frequently observed (Beesdo et al., 2009). Externalizing disorders, depression, and histories of abuse are common in both adolescent boys and girls; anxiety disorders and suicidality are more frequent in girls, with current research emphasizing especially vulnerable groups of adolescents at risk for multiple psychopathologies (Deas, St. Germaine, & Upadhyaya, 2006; Giaconia, Reinherz, Paradis, & Stashwick, 2003; O'Brien et al., 2004). This emphasis is consistent with work related to the problem behavior syndrome previously discussed (Jessor et al., 2003; Langhinrichsen-Rohling, Rohde, Seeley, & Rohling, 2004).

Developmental Course

Substance abuse disorders rarely resolve on their own (Maggs & Schulenberg, 2005). It is necessary, then, to understand the developmental context of use and abuse: *How and why do adolescents begin to use drugs, and what factors underlie continued use?* There are multiple pathways and multiple outcomes of adolescent substance use and abuse. For most classes of drugs, there is often a progression from exposure and opportunity to use, to experimentation, to repeat and regular use, to abuse and dependence, with different probabilities marking the transitions between stages for different drugs (Tsuang et al., 1999; Turner, Mermelstein, & Flay, 2004). That is, we can describe a common sequence, but we also need to keep in mind that the likelihood that an individual moves from one stage to the next varies depending on personal and drug characteristics.

With respect to initial use, there are two periods of highest vulnerability: during early adolescence and during the transition to young adulthood. Early users are at higher risk for poor outcomes. Substance use in early adolescence often involves immediate negative consequences, including less successful resolution of developmental challenges related to self and identity (D'Amico, Ellickson, Collins, Martino, & Klein, 2005). Early substance use also predicts substance abuse in later adolescence and adulthood, and a range of negative personal and social long-term outcomes (Armstrong & Costello, 2002; Merline, O'Malley, Schulenberg, Bachman, & Johnston, 2004; Tucker, Ellickson, Orlando, Martino, & Klein, 2005). Substance abuse is also associated with suicidality, with increases in risk observed in both clinical and community samples of adolescents (Esposito-Smythers, 2004; Goldston, 2004).

Pathways Involving Alcohol

The general trend in alcohol use involves a gradual increase throughout adolescence, a peak in early adulthood, and then a decrease (Brown et al., 2011; Harford, Grant, Yi, & Chen, 2005; Maggs & Schulenberg, 2004–2005). Focusing on the years of adolescence, however, provides a somewhat different perspective. Brown et al. (2011) describe the following trajectory groups: *abstainers/light drinkers* (with stable low use or nonuse); *stable moderate drinkers* (with stable moderate use, limited heavy use); *fling drinkers* (with time-limited periods of heavy use); *decreasers* (early onset, but declining use); *chronic heavy drinkers* (early onset and stable heavy drinking); and *late-onset heavy drinkers* (late onset, rapid escalation, heavy use).

The immediate, short-term, and long-term effects of drinking depend, in part, on age and developmental status (Brown et al., 2011; Masten et al., 2008). Early drinking results in a variety of negative consequences. Age at first use is the key variable. Those who begin drinking at age 11 or 12 have higher rates of substance abuse (13.5%) and dependence (14.9%) a decade later; rates are lower for those who began drinking at 13 or 14 (13.7% and 9%, respectively), and lowest for those who began at 19 or older (2% and 1%, respectively) (DeWit, Adlaf, Offord, & Ogborne, 2000; Grant, Stinson, & Harford, 2001). Early drinking is also associated with higher rates of binge drinking, risky sexual activity, aggression and violence, and poor adult outcomes (Stueve & O'Donnell, 2005; Wells, Horwood, & Fergusson, 2004). Initiation of drinking usually precedes initiation of smoking in adolescents (Jackson, Sher, Cooper, & Wood, 2002). Early onset alcohol abuse is also associated with suicidality; hypotheses suggest links among impulsivity, disinhibition, and comorbid psychopathology (especially mood disorders) (Kelly, Cornelius, & Clark, 2004; Nishimura, Goebert, Ramisetty-Mikler, & Caetano, 2005; Sher & Zalsman, 2005).

Important differences in alcohol use emerge in middle school and become more distinct in high school (Guo, Collins, Hill, & Hawkins, 2000). Frequent and heavy drinking that continues through adolescence is accompanied by problems including poor academic functioning, family and peer difficulties, and varied deviant behaviors (Windle, 2003; Windle, Mun, & Windle, 2005). Frequent and heavy drinking is also linked to damage in alcohol-susceptible brain regions (Brown et al., 2011; Masten et al., 2008). Frequent drinking, like early drinking, is related to fighting and injuries to self and others; this outcome is sometimes part of a wider pattern involving school misbehavior and participation in sports (Masten et al., 2008; Swahn & Donovan, 2005). Transitional life events (e.g., changes in education setting or employment) may provide opportunities for some adolescents to grow out of alcohol use and abuse (Dawson, Grant, Stinson, & Chou, 2006; Masten et al., 2008).

With respect to ongoing developmental challenges, it is important to remember that "underage drinking arises not in a passive organism, but in one that is thinking, motivated, self-regulating, and in many other ways actively and dynamically interacting with the people and objects in the environment. The development of planning, decision-making, risk-taking, friendship, and other manifestations of agency are important aspects of the development of alcohol use and its consequences. It also is important to understand how alcohol use may alter the processes of agency in development, altering the quality or nature of decision-making or actions that could have great consequences for the future" (Masten et al., 2008, p. S248). In other words, we must consider the way in which the disorder plays out over time as well as the way in which the course of the disorder influences the overall trajectory of an individual's development.

Pathways Involving Smoking

Multiple trajectories and patterns of smoking in adolescence have been described (Abroms, Simons-Morton, Haynie, & Chen, 2005; Orlando, Tucker, Ellickson, & Klein, 2004; Stanton, Flay, Colder, & Mehta, 2004). These include early onset stable smokers, late-onset stable smokers, experimenters, and

Prescription drugs, relatively easy to obtain, are increasingly abused by adolescents.

quitters (Chassin, Presson, Pitts, & Sherman, 2000; White, Pandina, & Chen, 2002). Factors related to smoking in adolescence include alcohol use, peer influence, and a history of depression (Lloyd-Richardson, Papandonatos, Kazura, Stanton, & Niaura, 2002; Windle & Windle, 2001). Young smokers are frequently young drinkers. It is relatively common to both smoke and drink, and to drink and not smoke; it is relatively rare to smoke and not drink (Hawkins, Hill, Guo, & Battin-Pearson, 2002; Orlando, Tucker, Ellickson, & Klein, 2005). Early onset smoking and combined patterns of smoking and drinking predict later substance abuse and dependence as well as more deviance (Hanna & Grant, 1999; Orlando et al., 2005).

Pathways Involving Other Drugs

Patterns of marijuana use are varied; adolescents have been described as *abstainers*, *experimental users*, *decreasers*, *increasers*, and *high chronic users* (Schulenberg et al., 2005; Windle & Wiesner,

2004). Cigarette smoking often precedes marijuana use (Ellickson, Tucker, Klein, & Saner, 2004). Conduct problems in childhood predict marijuana use in adolescence; the connection is stronger for girls (Pedersen, Mastekaasa, & Wichstrom, 2001). Compared to other drugs, marijuana is associated with the highest probability documented for the transition between exposure and use. Heroin is associated with the highest probability for transitions between repeated use and regular use, and cocaine with the highest probability for transitions from regular use to abuse/dependence (Tsuang et al., 1999).

The Gateway Hypothesis, Common Factors Model, and Developmental Cascade Models

The **gateway hypothesis** is an inclusive stage theory of drug involvement that proposes that the use of alcohol or marijuana acts as a "gateway" to the use of "harder" drugs such as cocaine, heroin, or methamphetamines (Kandel, 2002; Kandel & Yamaguchi, 2002). Data suggest that nicotine may also be a gateway drug that leads to marijuana use (Hawkins et al., 2002; Tullis, DuPont, Frost-Pineda, & Gold, 2003). Drug use trajectories of many adolescent boys and girls provide support for this model, although there are adolescent subgroups that illustrate other pathways (George & Moselhy, 2005).

There are alternatives to the gateway hypothesis. The **common factors model** assumes that there is a nonspecific propensity to use drugs. This propensity is correlated with both opportunities to use various drugs and the actual use of drugs given an opportunity (Agrawal, Neale, Prescott, & Kendler, 2004;

The gateway hypothesis proposes that early use of alcohol, tobacco, or marijuana may create a pathway to the use of "harder" drugs.

Morral, McCaffrey, & Paddock, 2002; Vanyukov, Tarter et al., 2003). Shared individual and social factors, then, contribute to the use and abuse of multiple substances. More complex explanations suggest that shared factors (such as social norms) increase an adolescent's overall risk to use any drug, and personality factors influence decisions about use of particular drugs. Pharmacological effects of particular drugs (such as marijuana) may then lead an adolescent to use other drugs (Agrawal, Neale, Jacobson, Prescott, & Kendler, 2005; Hall & Lynskey, 2005; Schenk, 2002).

Developmental cascade models of substance use and abuse have also been described. In a dynamic cascade model of the initiation of substance use, various indices of problematic functioning at particular points in time predict later problematic functioning (Dodge et al., 2009, see Fig. 14:6). The indices include biological factors, parenting factors, peer factors, and environmental factors. Findings related to this model include multiple modest effects of various factors, the importance of early development, continuity over time, ongoing transactions among domains of functioning, and opportunities for change at various time points in various domains (Dodge et al., 2009). Other cascade models of substance use and abuse highlight individual and interpersonal risk factors that influence high-risk trajectories (Haller, Handley, Chassin, & Bountress, 2010; Lynne-Landsman, Bradshaw, & Ialongo, 2010), specific experiences such as maltreatment that lead to internalizing and/or externalizing disorders that increase the risk for substance abuse (Rogosch, Oshri, & Cicchetti, 2010), and the ways in which changes in school, family, and/or work roles may precipitate changes in substance use during the transition to adulthood (Staff et al., 2010).

Substance Abuse and Other Problematic Behaviors

Previous discussion of the problem behavior syndrome emphasized how connected various forms of adolescent distress and dysfunction can be. These connections remain as we consider the more serious

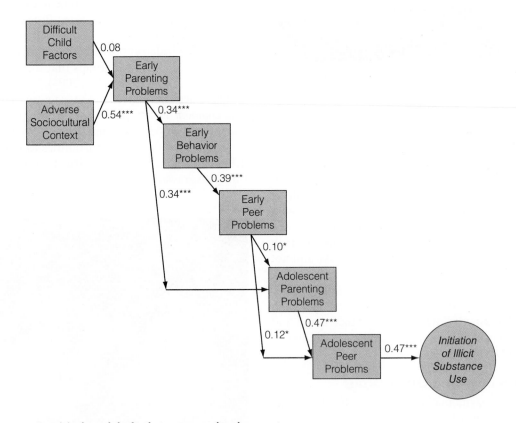

FIGURE 14:6 Empirical model of substance-use development.
Source: A Dynamic Cascade Model of the Development of Substance-Abuse Onset, Dodge et al. Copyright © 2009 Monographs of the Society for Research in Child Development. Reproduced with permission of John Wiley & Sons Inc.

clinical picture observed for substance abuse disorders. For instance, there are common pathways described for alcohol, marijuana, and gambling, and the earlier the onset, the greater the involvement and the more persistent the problems (Wanner, Vitaro, Ladouceur, Brendgen, & Tremblay, 2006; Winters, Stinchfield, Botzet, & Slutske, 2005). One of the most pressing problems involves associations among substance abuse, illegal activity, and violence. Correlations between substance abuse and illegal activities are complex, with offenses usually linked with serious substance abuse, impulsivity, and deviant peer relationships (Cuellar, Markowitz, & Libby, 2004; White, Tice, Loeber, & Stouthamer-Loeber, 2002). Correlations between heavy alcohol and marijuana use and violence have been documented, although most substance abusers do not display aggressive behavior (Wei, Loeber, & White, 2004). Substance abuse has also been tied to escalations in antisocial behavior and later antisocial personality disorder (Hussong, Curran, Moffitt, Caspi, & Carrig, 2004; Malone, Taylor, Marmorstein, McGue, & Iacono, 2004). Lack of anger control appears to be the variable that accounts for the connections between drug use and violence (Weiner et al., 2004).

Etiology

Models of etiology need to explain initial experimentation and drug use, drug abuse, and drug addiction, with various factors coming into play at different points along the trajectory of use (Clark, Cornelius, Kirisci, & Tarter, 2005; Dodge et al., 2009; Haller et al., 2010). For most adolescents, combinations of risk factors (such as maturational factors; emotional and cognitive development; and family, peer, and social variables) lead to disorder; for others, a single risk may be enough to set psychopathology in motion (Cicchetti & Rogosch, 1999; Clark et al., 2005).

Genes and Heredity

Genetic contributions to substance abuse disorders must be understood in the context of clear environmental impact (Dick, 2011; Knopik et al., 2004; Walden, McGue, Iacono, Burt, & Elkins, 2004). That said, twin studies, family studies, and adoption studies provide overwhelming evidence of a moderate to high inherited vulnerability (Agrawal, Madden et al., 2005; Goldman, Oroszi, & Ducci, 2005; Prescott, Maes, & Kendler, 2005). The genetic impact on drug abuse and addiction is both general (related to the use of any substance) and specific (related to the use of a particular substance), with the most unique variance observed for heroin (Tsuang et al., 1998; Vanyukov, Tarter et al., 2003). Genetic influence varies depending on age (with increasing influence over the course of adolescence) and appears differentially related to initiation and to continued use or dependence (Dick, 2011). In general, the data suggest that "the environment plays a strong role in influencing a person to try a drug and perhaps continue to use it recreationally, but genetics plays a stronger role in determining whether the person becomes addicted" (Carlson, 2007, p. 636).

The role of genetics in alcohol use and abuse has been extensively researched. The Stockholm Adoption Study is one example of a large-scale longitudinal investigation providing valuable data (Cloninger, Bohman, & Sigvardsson, 1981; Sigvardsson, Bohman, & Cloninger, 1996). Multiple alcohol problems are genetically influenced, including motivation to drink, alcohol sensitivity, the amount of alcohol consumed, steady drinking, and eventual dependence (Dick, 2011; Prescott, Cross, Kuhn, Horn, & Kendler, 2004; Whitfield et al., 2004). Age of first drink is also influenced by genes, but environmental factors and gene-by-environment interactions are even more influential (McGue & Iacono, 2004; Rose, Dick, Viken, Pulkkinen, & Kaprio, 2001). Sibling concordance rates are higher for brothers than sisters for alcohol dependence (Bierut et al., 1998). In most of the studies of genes and alcohol, the genetic impact of fathers is most significant; some studies, however, show contributions of both fathers and mothers (Dawson & Grant, 1998; Dierker, Merikangas, & Szatmari, 1999).

Genetic explanations for combinations of substance abuse and other psychopathology have also been set forth (Krueger et al., 2002; Pickens, Svikis, McGue, & LaBuda, 1995). Specific connections between alcohol use and conduct disorder appear more likely to be influenced by environmental factors (Dick, 2011; Rose, Dick, Viken, Pulkkinen, & Kaprio, 2004), although evidence suggests genetic overlap between alcohol dependence at age 17 and antisocial personality disorder at age 20 (Malone et al., 2004). Future studies in search of more real-life validity may need to focus on more complex models of gene-by-environment interaction (Dick, 2011).

Physiological Factors

Animal studies illustrate many of the potential mechanisms of drug use and abuse, with different brain pathways underlying drug reinforcement, tolerance, dependence, and addiction (Booze, 2004; Kelley & Rowan, 2004; Kosten, George, & Kleber, 2005; Rezvani & Levin, 2004). The adolescent brain, in and of itself, is a risk factor, with age-related changes in sensitivity to the effects of alcohol and drugs (Andersen & Navalta, 2004; Casey & Jones, 2010; Spear, 2011). The initial stages of drug use and drug liking are associated with the brain's reward centers, which are embedded in the mesolimbic system. Activation of the mesolimbic pathway, particularly the dopamine receptors, depends on the particular substance; the most addictive drugs have the most rapid effects (Carlson, 2007; Kosten et al., 2005). Individual differences in sensitivity to these immediate effects and the ability to digest or metabolize substances (likely attributable to genetic influences) may relate to individual differences in the levels of pleasure or aversion that accompany drug experimentation (Goldman et al., 2005).

For some adolescents, the immediate pleasurable consequences of drug use "overpower the recognition of long-term aversive effects" (Carlson, 2007, p. 617). Chronic use leads to neurobiological changes that may underlie tolerance (Brown & Tapert, 2004; Kosten et al., 2005); further, "repeated exposure to escalating dosages of most drugs alters the brain, so that it functions more or less normally when the drugs are present and abnormally when they are not" (Kosten et al., 2005, p. 7). With tolerance, transitions to dependence may occur, with cravings, compulsive drug seeking, and urgent attempts to escape withdrawal (Kosten et al., 2005).

Going beyond the hedonic view that emphasizes the pleasure associated with drug use (i.e., drug liking) and the need to avoid withdrawal symptoms, the **incentive-sensitization theory** is a multistage explanation of addiction (Berridge, 2007). First, various substances alter brain organization and function. Second, these altered brain systems affect behavior in situations involving motivation and reward. The dopamine system that usually signals that certain stimuli will lead to positive reinforcement becomes hypersensitized to drugs and drug stimuli; this is referred to as *incentive salience*. At this stage, drug cues are increasingly difficult to ignore, and craving may become a more important factor in continued drug use than pleasurable effects. To understand craving as an essential aspect of drug use, researchers must address both physiological and psychological factors (Berridge, 2007; Bruijnzeel, Repetto, & Gold, 2004; Koob, 2002; Willner, James, & Morgan, 2005).

Child Factors

A history of childhood psychopathology is one important influence on the development of substance abuse disorders in adolescence (Costello, Erkanli, Federman, & Angold, 1999; White, Xie, Thompson, Loeber, & Stouthamer-Loeber, 2001). Conduct problems are perhaps the most strongly linked to substance use and abuse (Cicchetti & Rogosch, 1999; Putnins, 2006; Sung, Erkanli, Angold, & Costello, 2004). Depressed adolescents, especially those with additional social impairments, are also at higher risk (Cicchetti & Rogosch, 1999; Rao et al., 1999; Sung et al., 2004). Child maltreatment is another key risk factor (Agrawal et al., 2005; Bailey & McCloskey, 2005; Moran, Vuchinich, & Hall, 2004; Rogosch et al., 2010). Insecure attachment, posttraumatic stress disorder, and learning disorders are all also associated with increased vulnerability to substance use and abuse (Giaconia et al., 2003; Kilpatrick et al., 2003; Vungkhanching, Sher, Jackson, & Parra, 2004).

Many externalizing disorders as well as panic attacks are related to smoking in particular (Agrawal et al., 2005; Lambert, 2005; Ramsey et al., 2003). Higher rates of smoking have also been noted in adolescents prior to the emergence of schizophrenia (Weiser et al., 2004). These connections raise the issue of **self-medication**, and whether some adolescents are smoking or using other drugs to improve mood, increase cognitive function, and deal with difficulties or symptoms of other disorders. Data related to self-medication hypotheses are mixed (Beesdo et al., 2009; Lansford et al., 2008; Putnins, 2006; Triplett & Payne, 2004; Valentiner, Mounts, & Deacon, 2004).

Many of the associations between childhood disorders and adolescent substance abuse are likely mediated by individual variables such as deficits in executive function, high levels of negative emotion and emotional dysregulation, and poor self-control (Fishbein et al., 2006; Habeych, Charles, Sclabassi, Kirisci, & Tarter, 2005; Iacono, Malone, & McGue, 2003; Kirisci, Tarter, Reynolds, & Vanyukov, 2006; Nigg et al., 2004). Disinhibition (or behavioral undercontrol) is a key construct underlying increased risk (Hirsh, Galinsky, & Zhong, 2011; Zucker, Heitzeg, & Nigg, 2011). Integrating physiological and cognitive factors, the **cognitive-deficits model** of addiction is based on the idea that repeat, chronic drug use results in abnormalities in the prefrontal cortex, impairing judgment, decision making, and impulse control (Kosten et al., 2005).

Motivations, expectancies, and attitudes are cognitive variables associated with drug use. Positive attitudes and expectancies about alcohol (e.g., that recreational drug use is acceptable; that use leads to individual pleasure and social rewards) increase with age; the most dramatic increase occurs between third and fourth grades (Miller, Smith & Goldman, 1990). Positive expectancies are moderated by parent expectations (Simons-Morton, 2004). Younger children of alcoholics have more negative expectations (hypothetically related to aversive learning); in contrast, and somewhat surprisingly, adolescents with family histories of alcoholism have more positive expectations (Wiers, Gunning, & Sergeant, 1998). Perceptions of risk related to binge drinking are highest in eighth graders, somewhat lower in tenth graders, and lower still in twelfth graders; these perceptions are associated with decreases in rates of disapproval across the upper grades (Johnston et al., 2008). There appears to be a balance between adolescent perceptions of risk and benefits, on the one hand, and personal experiences of drinking, on the other hand (Hampson, Severson, Burns, Slovic, & Fisher, 2001).

Attitudes about smoking are complex. Beginning smokers emphasize social motives (e.g., related to peer approval) and environmental factors (e.g., positive media portrayals) that influence decisions about smoking; regular and dependent smokers emphasize the automatic nature of smoking, and that smoking helps to control mood and reduce stress (Piper et al., 2004; Wetter et al., 2004). Many adolescent girls focus on the belief that smoking helps to manage weight (Austin & Gortmaker, 2001; Klesges, Elliott, & Robinson, 1997). Interactions among individual intentions and beliefs, powerful external cues, smoking escalation, and nicotine dependence require careful study (Baker, Brandon, & Chassin, 2004; Wahl, Turner, Mermelstein, & Flay, 2005; Wakefield et al., 2004). For many adolescents, continued smoking coincides with increasingly positive recall of early smoking experiences (Riedel, Blitstein, Robinson, Murray, & Klesges, 2003). Perceptions of risk related

to smoking must be appreciated in the context of adolescent beliefs about overall health, the immediate impact of smoking, and future harm (Baker et al., 2004; Rubinstein, Halpern-Felsher, Thompson, & Millstein, 2003; Slovic, 2000). For instance, Baker et al. (2004) state that adolescents' "value on health as an outcome declined during the high school years and did not begin to increase until early adulthood. These data suggest that adolescence is a period of increased cognitive vulnerability to smoking, based both on decreasing perceptions of the personalized risks of smoking and decreasing values on health as an outcome" (p. 469).

Adolescent ideas related to marijuana reflect increases in perceived risk coupled with increases in disapproval and somewhat declining rates of use (Johnston et al., 2008). Permissive beliefs are related to marijuana use; relief-oriented beliefs are related to dependence (Chabrol, Massot, & Mullet, 2004). Marijuana attitudes are more positive in adolescents who drink than in adolescents who do not drink (Willner, 2001). Adolescents' perceptions of risk are moderately high for methamphetamines, inhalants, cocaine, Ecstasy, and heroin; perceived risks of amphetamine use are lower (Johnston et al., 2008). Rates of disapproval are generally higher (over 80%) than perceptions of risk across all categories of drugs (Johnston et al., 2008).

Several studies describe two personality profiles that are linked to substance abuse: one related to a tendency toward social deviance, and the other related to an excitement- or pleasure-seeking path (Crawford, Pentz, Chou, Li, & Dwyer, 2003; Finn, Sharkansky, Brandt, & Turcotte, 2000), with similar personality profiles predicting both substance abuse and gambling problems (Slutske, Caspi, Moffitt, & Poulton, 2005). Adolescents with a "smoker" self-image that includes "toughness, sociability and precocity" are also at risk (Baker et al., 2004). Girls who both smoke and binge drink display different personality characteristics and risk profiles than girls who either smoke or drink, and girls who do neither (Pirkle & Richter, 2006). For example, girls who smoke but do not binge drink, and girls who smoke and binge drink report more symptoms of depression than do girls who only binge drink. Girls who only binge drink report greater popularity as well as a belief that drinking leads to less inhibited behavior (Pirkle & Richter, 2006).

Other adolescent factors related to drug experimentation and use include early puberty (Lanza

& Collins, 2002), academic struggles (Bryant, Schulenberg, O'Malley, Bachman, & Johnston, 2003), and social impairment (Greene et al., 1999). A desire to improve self-image and obtain social approval may also lead to experimentation (Amaro, Blake, Schwartz, & Flinchbaugh, 2001). Deviance acceptance is another risk factor (Abroms et al., 2005).

Parent and Family Factors

Parents influence adolescent substance use and abuse in a variety of ways (Barnes, Welte, Hoffman, & Dintcheff, 2005; Walden et al., 2004). The first way is through exposure. One in four children is exposed to alcohol abuse or dependence in family settings (Grant, 2000), with African American and Latino American children disproportionately affected (Ramisetty-Mikler & Caetano, 2004). Parental use increases adolescent use; parental nonuse moderates adolescent use, even when peer use is taken into account (Li, Pentz, & Chou, 2002). Combined with genetic predispositions, heavy drinking in families leads to binge drinking in adolescents (Carlson, 2007). In some studies, fathers' alcohol abuse is more predictive of adolescent abuse than mothers' use (Ohannessian et al., 2005; Rohde et al., 2001); in other studies, fathers' alcohol problems predict drinking in daughters, whereas mothers' use predicts drinking in both daughters and sons (Coffelt et al., 2006). In addition, fathers' gambling problems predict adolescent gambling problems (Vachon, Vitaro, Wanner, & Tremblay, 2004). Marijuana use and abuse appear especially influenced by parent and family factors (Tsuang et al., 1998). Parental smoking is less consistently associated with adolescent smoking (Baker et al., 2004). Parents who quit decrease their children's risk, but that risk is still higher than risk for children whose parents never smoked (Bricker et al., 2003). Siblings also have an important role to play, legitimizing, promoting, or discouraging various forms of substance use (Pomery et al., 2005). For example, even after adjusting for parent smoking, older siblings who smoke increase rates of adolescent smoking (Rajan et al., 2003). Other types of parent and family psychopathologies likely influence all of these associations (Ohannessian et al., 2004; Yu, Stiffman, & Freedenthal, 2005).

Parenting expectations and parenting practices also influence substance use and abuse. Although parents differ in their perceptions of their ability to prevent drug use (Redmond, Spoth, Shin, & Hill, 2004), parents who convey expectations that drug use will not occur and who monitor their adolescents' activities do provide protective benefits (Cleveland, Gibbons, Gerrard, Pomery, & Brody, 2005; Simons-Morton, 2004; Simons-Morton & Chen, 2005). African American and Asian American adolescents receive more antismoking messages from their parents; African American parents report their clear impact on their adolescents' decisions to smoke (Baker et al., 2004; Mermelstein, 1999).

Although family structure, such as single-parent status, is frequently associated with increased substance abuse, family structure is better viewed as "a marker of the unequal distribution of factors" such as exposure to stress and connections with deviant peers that lead to substance abuse (Barrett & Turner, 2006). Authoritative parenting further reduces adolescent risk (Chassin, Presson, Rose, et al., 2005; Wang, Matthew, Bellamy, & James, 2005; Wills, Resko, Ainette, & Mendoza, 2004). Adolescents' perceptions of parental support are crucial (Beitchman et al., 2005). Overall, positive parent–child relationships have a "conventionalizing effect"; that is, positive relationships enable adolescents to adopt perspectives on the choices they make that are more informed, mature, and in line with what parents value (Brody, Flor, Hollett-Wright, McCoy, & Donovan, 1999).

Social and Cultural Factors

Whether friends drink, smoke, or use drugs influences adolescent beliefs and behaviors, although there are gender and cultural variations (Jaccard, Blanton, & Dodge, 2005; White et al., 2002). In mixed-sex friendships, for example, boys have influence over girls' drinking; girls do not have a similar influence over boys (Gaughan, 2006). And African American adolescents seem less influenced by peer smoking than European American adolescents (Mermelstein, 1999). Being a member of certain peer groups, such as sports teams or performing arts groups, increases vulnerability (Barber, Eccles, & Stone, 2001; Eccles & Barber, 1999). Relationships with deviant peers are another key risk factor (Dishion & Owen, 2002; Iervolino et al., 2002; Moss, Lynch, & Hardie, 2003; Walden et al., 2004). The transition to high school appears to be a turning point. At this time, peers who support deviance and rule breaking lead to increases in adolescent substance use (Dishion, Capaldi, Spracklen, & Li, 1995; Ellickson et al., 2004). Researchers describe a pattern of reciprocal influence, from peers, to substance use, to more exclusive selection of deviant peer groups, and then to more frequent and more serious substance use and abuse (Dishion & Owen, 2002).

The school setting is also extremely important. School policies that involve more monitoring of students reduce substance use (Kumar, O'Malley, & Johnston, 2005). The norms of the student and staff population, and the social image of smokers, are also influential factors (Evans, Powers, Hersey, & Renaud, 2006; Kumar et al., 2005). Other environmental factors that increase or decrease risk include neighborhoods and community norms, ease of access, economic factors, and advertising and the media (Jessor et al., 2003; Johnston, O'Malley, & Terry-McElrath, 2004; Wagenaar, Lenk, & Toomey, 2006). Numbers of life stressors are also important (Wills, Sandy, & Yaeger, 2002b; Wills, Sandy, Yaeger, Cleary, & Shinar, 2001). Cohort effects related to *generational forgetting* of the potential harm associated with particular drugs also seem related to increases and declines in substance use (Johnston et al., 2008).

Assessment and Diagnosis

As with every other form of psychopathology, comprehensive assessment of substance abuse disorders is critical (Winters, Latimer, & Stinchfield, 2001). And given physiological complications such as tolerance or withdrawal, medical evaluations are an important component of complete assessments (Dekker, Estroff, & Hoffmann, 2001). With respect to the substance abuse itself, patterns of use (whether episodic or continuous), availability and accessibility of drugs, perceived importance of drugs, the effects of drugs, and family histories of alcohol and drug abuse are key criteria (Tarter, 2005).

The multifactorial etiology of substance abuse requires a full assessment of psychological functioning, including deficits or maladjustment related to cognition, emotion, or behavior (Tarter, 2005). Cognitive assessments include neuropsychological testing and tests of skills frequently impaired by drug use, such as abstract thinking and memory. Cognitive difficulties related to attributional style, perceptions of risk, and mistaken beliefs must also be considered. The emotionality and emotional flare-ups observed in adolescents with substance abuse disorders must also be carefully assessed.

Clinicians must collect information about behavioral maladjustment in personal, family, peer, school, and employment domains. The extent to which an adolescent has access to social support from family or friends (or is connected to deviant or delinquent groups) is another important piece of data.

In addition, an adolescent's underlying personality and other comorbid psychopathologies require review and appreciation. Even though many adolescents do not see connections between substance abuse and other problems or disorders, mental health professionals need to encourage disclosure (Medeiros et al., 2005). Another critical component of assessment involves the appraisal of the adolescent's "developmental assets" or strengths (Leffert et al., 1998). Given that few adolescents seek treatment for substance abuse on their own, acknowledgment of these strengths may lay the foundation for initial rapport and allow for discussions about readiness for intervention.

Self-report inventories have demonstrated utility (Crowley, Mikulich, Ehlers, Whitmore, & Macdonald, 2001; Miller & Lazowski, 2005). Brief screening and preliminary interventions in primary care clinics are another source of information about substance use and abuse (Babor, Higgins-Biddle, Dauser, Higgins, & Burleson, 2005).

Intervention

Prevention

Avoidance of drugs is a developmental challenge (Brown et al., 2011; Simons-Morton & Haynie, 2003), with theoretical and practical issues complicating prevention research, design, program delivery, and evaluation (Nation et al., 2003; Sussman, Stacy, Johnson, Pentz, & Robertson, 2004). But even with multiple viewpoints and assorted difficulties, prevention efforts aimed at reducing substance use and abuse can be successful (Derzon, Sale, Springer, & Brounstein, 2005; Masten et al., 2008; Skara & Sussman, 2003; Toumbourou, Williams, Waters, & Patton, 2005). Universal prevention programs cast a very wide net and often promote healthy lifestyles and healthy choices to adolescent populations (He, Kramer, Houser, Chomitz, & Hacker, 2004; Williams, Holmbeck, & Greenley, 2002). Many mental health and public health professionals point out that declines in drug use in recent years parallel the widespread use of prevention efforts in early and middle adolescence (Pentz, 2003). Even so, there is ample evidence of their ineffectiveness, in addition to data that prevention programs *increase interest* in drug use for certain adolescents (Kaminer & Bukstein, 2005). One of the important aspects of prevention efforts, and one of the more controversial, is whether to acknowledge that most adolescents will at some time use mood-altering substances, and whether and how to include harm reduction (i.e., non–abstinence based) approaches as well as abstinence messages (MacMaster, Holleran, & Chaffin, 2005).

One example of harm reduction for older adolescents involves emphasizing safe or sensible drinking with some adult supervision (Coleman & Cater, 2005). The "social norms" approach addresses the inclination of college students to believe that their peers drink much more than they actually do. It has been demonstrated to reduce levels of alcohol consumption and high-risk drinking in many campus communities (Dejong et al., 2006). Using public and institutional policies to change the environment is another prevention option (Hallfors & Van Dorn, 2002; Pentz, Mares, Schinke, & Rohrbach, 2004; Wagenaar et al., 2006). Restricting the availability of alcohol and enforcing limits on alcohol use are examples of these types of policies (Markowitz, Chatterji, & Kaestner, 2003; Wagenaar, Toomey, & Erickson, 2005).

Selective prevention efforts are more focused. Several effective programs converge on developmental transitions that are associated with increased risk (Botvin, Scheier, & Griffin, 2002; Furr-Holden, Ialongo, Anthony, Petras, & Kellam, 2004; Petry, 2005). For example, family-centered programs that begin in middle school can delay the initiation of substance use for both typical and at-risk adolescents (Dishion, Kavanagh, Schneiger, Nelson, & Kaufman, 2002; Stormshak et al., 2011). Parent training can also be effective (Mason, Kosterman, Hawkins, Haggerty, & Spoth, 2003). Collaborative, community-based efforts have also shown promise (Flewelling et al., 2005); community interventions require attention to variables such as rural versus urban settings and homogeneous versus diverse groups of adolescents (Komro et al., 2004).

Targeted prevention is even more specifically directed, and is based on ideas that risk and vulnerability can be reliably measured in individuals and subgroups of adolescents (Vanyukov, Kirisci et al., 2003). Although there are many risk factors and individual differences in vulnerability to those factors, it is imperative to design programs that will reach those most in need. For example, embedding prevention programs in early, related services such as Head Start might involve fostering the personality characteristics that are associated with later drug avoidance (Kaminski, Stormshak, Good, & Goodman, 2002). Paying attention to children's gender, personalities, social challenges, and environmental contexts maximizes prevention outcomes (Brown et al., 2011; Masten et al., 2008; Simons-Morton & Haynie, 2003).

Prevention efforts frequently target at-risk youth, including American Indian and Alaskan Native adolescents (Hawkins, Cummins, & Marlatt, 2004). Cultural and ethnic differences related to exposure, norms, risk, and vulnerability must, of course, be taken into account. For instance, African American adolescents are exposed to many more risk factors than European American adolescents; prevention efforts must be tailored to the specific risks that are encountered (Wallace & Muroff, 2002). Other targeted groups include children who have already been diagnosed with other psychopathologies (Compton, Burns, Egger, & Robertson, 2002).

Treatment

The treatment of substance abuse disorders involves outpatient therapies, inpatient programs, day treatment placements, special school environments, and, for some, the juvenile justice system. Treatments vary widely across settings, and outcome statistics are mixed (Henggeler, Clingempeel, Brondino, & Pickrel, 2002; Stevens & Morral, 2003). Still, treatment is superior to no treatment, although the adolescents who succeed are often those with the least serious disorders (Kaminer & Bukstein, 2005). Reviews of outcome studies suggest that relapse is common and multiple therapeutic attempts are likely (Cornelius et al., 2003; Dasinger, Shane, & Martinovich, 2004; Kaminer & Bukstein, 2005).

There are many adolescent variables that cut across types of problems and therapies. Adolescent motivation for substance abuse treatment is a primary concern, because most adolescents enter treatment due to external pressure. Incentive to change in adolescents abusing substances is modest; the strongest predictors of incentive are the negative consequences attributed to drug use (Battjes, Gordon, O'Grady, Kinlock, & Carswell, 2003; Breda & Heflinger, 2004; Sommers-Flanagan, Richardson,

& Sommers-Flanagan, 2011). Individual differences related to incentives to quit (such as girls who smoke to manage weight) need to be specifically addressed (Meyers, Klesges, Winders, & Ward, 1997; Turner & Mermelstein, 2004). Adolescents who recognize that change is necessary do better in treatment than those who do not (Callaghan et al., 2005), even though some help-seeking adolescents look for help from individuals who may not be well trained or knowledgeable (or even supportive of their efforts, in the case of troubled peers) (Stiffman, Striley, Brown, Limb, & Ostmann, 2003).

Therapeutic alliances are essential to establish. Many adolescents come into therapy with various negative beliefs: "My therapist may try to force me to do things I don't like." "This therapy may do more harm than good." "He probably thinks he knows everything." "She'll think I'm a failure if I use again." "I'm better off without therapy" (Beck, Liese, & Najavits, 2005, p. 490); these must be identified and refuted. Parents, too, may enter therapy with erroneous beliefs related to confidentiality and process. Because alliances with adolescents and their parents are both related to treatment success, ongoing attention to trust and rapport is needed (Hogue, Dauber, Stambaugh, Cecero, & Liddle, 2006; Shelef, Diamond, Diamond, & Liddle, 2005; Tetzlaff et al., 2005). Paying close attention to ethnic and culturally relevant factors may enhance alliances for some adolescents (Austin & Wagner, 2010; Cunningham, Foster, & Warner, 2010; Wintersteen, Mensinger, & Diamond, 2005). Retention and premature drop-out are constant concerns; addressing these concerns early and often is important (Beck et al., 2005). Adolescents who view the therapist more positively are more likely to stay in treatment; they also display less severe substance-related impairments and have fewer deviant friends (Battjes, Gordon, O'Grady, & Kinlock, 2004).

One of the first treatment decisions for adolescents involves level of care (e.g., outpatient versus inpatient). Specialty care is often needed for those who have previously failed in outpatient programs, those with comorbid psychopathologies, those experiencing suicidality, those in need of medical supervision for withdrawal, and those requiring isolation from family, friends, or communities (Kaminer & Bukstein, 2005; Vandrey, Budney, Kamon, & Stanger, 2005). Crisis situations require immediate placements (Fishman, Clemmey, & Adger, 2003). Sadly, racial and ethnic disparities exist in terms of access to specialty care and involvement in the justice system (Aarons, Brown, Garland, & Hough, 2004). For some adolescents, drug courts are more effective than family courts in reducing substance use and externalizing behavior (Belenko & Dembo, 2003; Henggeler et al., 2006).

Individual Approaches

Individual treatment is a common intervention paradigm. Variations include behavior therapy, cognitive-behavioral therapy, 12-step programs, and pharmacotherapy, with modifications for particular drugs (e.g., alcohol versus heroin) (Clemmey, Payne, & Fishman, 2004). New pharmacological treatments show promise (Dawes & Johnson, 2004). Positive outcomes associated with 12-step programs are often dependent on adolescent motivation and severity of disorder (Kelly, Myers, & Brown, 2002). Among the most well-defined, well-studied, and well-supported treatments for substance abuse are the cognitive-behavioral approaches (Beck et al., 2005; Deas & Thomas, 2001; Lochman & van den Steenhoven, 2002; Waldron & Kaminer, 2004). Working with adolescent beliefs is core to the cognitive model of psychotherapy. Beliefs about self (such as negative beliefs about worth, lovability, and vulnerability), beliefs about life experiences, and substance-related beliefs are all important. The process by which change occurs involves the identification of automatic thoughts and the eventual understanding by the adolescent that these thoughts are not completely accurate or valid. Modification of these thoughts must take place at both surface and deep levels for sustained improvement (Beck et al., 2005).

Motivational interviewing is another individual therapy that shows potential. Motivational interviewing is a brief intervention incorporating aspects of motivational psychology, client-centered therapy, and stages-of-change theory (Lawendowski, 1998; O'Leary Tevyaw & Monti, 2004). One unique contribution of motivational approaches is their attempt to capitalize on some of the most pertinent adolescent characteristics and control for others (Metrik, Frissell, McCarthy, D'Amico, & Brown, 2003; Neal & Carey, 2004).

Individual psychotherapies that account for neurocognitive and emotional deficits related to drug abuse are likely to produce better results (Fishbein et al., 2006). Psychotherapy for adolescents with substance abuse disorders must, in many cases, include treatment for additional psychopathologies (Esposito-Smythers, 2004, 2005; Funk, McDermeit,

Godley, & Adams, 2003; Sakai, Mikulich-Gilbertson, & Crowley, 2006; Titus, Dennis, White, Scott, & Funk, 2003). Pharmacotherapy, and combinations of individual, family, and milieu therapies, may be beneficial for these adolescents (Kaminer & Bukstein, 2005; Randall, Henggeler, Cunningham, Rowland, & Swenson, 2001).

Family and Group Approaches

With the role of parents and families in the development and maintenance of substance abuse disorders, it makes sense that family approaches would be an important source of therapeutic impact (Brody et al., 2004; Lochman & van den Steenhoven, 2002; Thompson, Pomeroy, & Gober, 2005). For some subgroups, it appears particularly important. For instance, parents have different roles in different cultural groups (Kim, Zane, & Hong, 2002). There are differences, for example, in the degree to which families display connectedness or involvement in their adolescents' lives, as well as in the amount and type of supervision. In Latino families, with high rates of substance abuse disorders and a family-oriented culture, family therapy is effective (Sale et al., 2005); for Latina girls, family connectedness is an especially salient factor leading to delayed or reduced alcohol use. Mental health professionals working with diverse families need to account for variables such as ethnic orientation, level of acculturation, and ethnic mistrust in order to provide culturally competent treatments (Gil, Wagner, & Tubman, 2004; Stewart-Sabin & Chaffin, 2003; Strada, Donohoe, & Lefforge, 2006).

Group approaches can also be effective, particularly those based on cognitive-behavioral principles (Waldron & Kaminer, 2004) and those focused on reducing marijuana use (Battjes et al., 2004). The role of peers is again an issue. As with treatments for conduct disorder, group treatment for substance abuse is related to both improvement and deterioration (Macgowan & Wagner, 2005; O'Leary et al., 2002), because peers often provide "deviancy training," as well as support and modeling of varieties of substance abuse (Dishion, Poulin, & Burraston, 2001; Dishion, McCord, & Poulin, 1998; Kaminer, 2005; Wagenaar et al., 2006). Managing the peer environment in group therapy is critical to treatment success (Dishion & Medici Skaggs, 2000), with "denormalization" of risk behaviors essential (Messerlian et al., 2005). School-based quitting programs are another treatment option; adolescent awareness of and access to such programs are necessary first steps (Balch et al., 2004). Students who display higher motivation to change, who have previously attempted to quit, and who experience fewer stressors are more likely to attend school programs (Turner, Mermelstein, Berbaum, & Veldhuis, 2004). Residential treatments often report the most marked improvements, but meaningful reductions in drug use must be understood in the context of the more distressed and dysfunctional adolescents who enter residential programs and who frequently relapse when discharged (Dasinger, Shane, & Martinovich, 2004).

Given that relapse is a fairly common occurrence, relapse prevention must be incorporated and emphasized in individual, family, and group treatments. Research has identified the variables most associated with relapse; these include comorbid psychopathology, negative emotion, withdrawal symptoms, and peer pressure (Cornelius et al., 2003; Kaminer & Bukstein, 2005; McCarthy, Tomlinson, Anderson, Marlatt, & Brown, 2005). The likelihood of drug exposure and renewed drug use must be addressed. It is essential to learn to manage cravings and urges, to deal with high-risk situations, and to make necessary lifestyle changes (Beck et al., 2005; Wills et al., 2001). For many adolescents leaving inpatient programs, specific and detailed aftercare plans are crucial components of ongoing success.

Key Terms

Risk taking (p. 261)
Problem behavior syndrome (p. 262)
Tolerance (p. 263)
Physical dependence (p. 263)
Withdrawal symptoms (p. 263)
Psychological dependence (p. 263)

Addiction (p. 263)
Binge drinking (p. 266)
Gateway hypothesis (p. 271)
Common factors model (p. 271)
Incentive-sensitization theory (p. 274)
Self-medication (p. 274)
Cognitive-deficits model (p. 275)
Motivational interviewing (p. 279)

Chapter Summary

- Adolescent brain development is characterized by continuing growth, increased risk taking, and evolving self-regulation.
- Substance use and abuse in adolescence carries particular risk for the still-developing adolescent brain.
- Substance abuse is defined as excessive use of or dependence on an addictive substance. Addiction is defined as a chronic disorder characterized by compulsive drug seeking and abuse.
- Alcohol use and abuse by adolescents is of particular concern because of its relatively high incidence and its specific detrimental effects on adolescent brain development.
- Although less dramatic than some other forms of substance abuse, tobacco use is the source of extensive health problems and is associated with a variety of other substance abuse and behavioral problems.
- Other substances abused by adolescents include marijuana, inhalants, cocaine, methamphetamine, hallucinogens, and anabolic steroids.
- For most classes of drugs, developmental trajectories involve a progression from exposure, to experimentation, to regular use, and, potentially, abuse and dependence.

- In general, early substance abuse predicts later use and a range of negative physical and psychological outcomes.
- The gateway hypothesis is a stage theory of drug involvement that proposes that the use of drugs such as alcohol or marijuana act as a "gateway" to the use of "harder" drugs such as cocaine, heroin, or methamphetamines. The common factors model assumes there is a nonspecific propensity to use drugs. Developmental cascade models emphasize that early maladjustment in a particular domain leads to later maladjustment in multiple domains.
- Genetic studies indicate that a strong heritable vulnerability exists for substance abuse problems.
- Conduct problems and depression occurring in childhood are both significant risk factors for the development of substance abuse during adolescence.
- Parental expectations and practices are a powerful influence on whether or not adolescents abuse substances during adolescence.
- Peer attitudes supporting substance use, especially as teens enter high school, lead to an increase in substance abuse.
- Assessment of, and treatment for, comorbid psychopathologies is particularly important when treating substance abuse in adolescence.
- Relapse prevention is an important aspect of an effective substance abuse treatment program.

15

Eating Disorders

IN PREVIOUS CHAPTERS, we have considered how biological and psychological processes interact and how they contribute to the challenges and achievements of normal development, as well as to the nature, progression, and treatment of disorders. This interplay between biology and psychology is particularly salient as we focus attention on relations between healthy and unhealthy eating, safe and dangerous practices for weight management, and clinically significant eating disorders. Because of the developmental status of older children and adolescents, their increasing independence, increased autonomy in food choice, and still not fully mature cognitive abilities, they are vulnerable to an array of eating problems. Given the significant public health issues related to eating disorders (Chavez & Insel, 2007), it is absolutely crucial to understand the unique circumstances of adolescence and the ways in which eating disorders emerge and are maintained, because struggles with eating disorders may involve ongoing distress and impairment as well as life-threatening crises.

Developmental Tasks and Challenges Related to Eating and Appearance

The physical development that occurs throughout later childhood and adolescence has multiple impacts on psychological development and functioning, with the onset of puberty signaling many of the most dramatic changes. Significant growth involves proportional increases in the food intake of nutrients and energy (Stang & Story, 2005). For girls, average weight gain is approximately 38 pounds over the course of adolescence, with associated increases in body fat levels. For boys, average weight gain is about 50 pounds, with a decrease in body fat levels. There are, of course, individual and group differences related to the beginning of puberty and weight gain; African American girls, for example, enter puberty earlier than European American girls (Stang & Story, 2005). Keep in mind, however, that the prevalence of weight issues and dieting in ever-younger samples suggests that body-related concerns are not exclusive to a particular age or stage of development.

One of the keys to understanding eating disorders depends on understanding issues related to **body image** (i.e., a person's perception of his or her own physical appearance) and **body satisfaction** (i.e., the degree to which a person is accepting of, or pleased with, his or her physical appearance). Concerns about body image do not appear suddenly in adolescence. These concerns are present in elementary school and increase significantly from fifth to eighth grades (Lynch & Eppers-Reynolds, 2005; Pine, 2001). Body concerns have been studied mostly in girls and women; more recent studies include boys and men. Body satisfaction is relatively similar in younger girls and boys, with most children reporting satisfaction. By early adolescence, however, **body dissatisfaction** increases (Littleton & Ollendick, 2003; Wiseman, Peltzman, Halmi, & Sunday, 2004). Girls become more preoccupied with appearance and weight (Jones, 2004; Phares, Steinberg, & Thompson, 2004). Girls who are underweight are more satisfied with their bodies (Kelly, Wall, Eisenberg, Story, & Neumark-Sztainer, 2005). Dissatisfied boys are divided between wanting to lose weight and wanting to gain weight (or muscle) (Jones & Crawford, 2005; McCabe & Ricciardelli, 2004b). For both girls and boys, there is a need to explore cognitive and

Body image and body satisfaction are important developmental issues emerging in middle childhood and early adolescence.

Peter Dazeley/Photographer's Choice/Getty Images

emotional evaluations related to negative body image and dissatisfaction (Bearman, Presnell, Martinez, & Stice, 2006; Bornholt et al., 2005).

There are, of course, links between perception and reality. For instance, heavier body shapes and weights for girls, and both thinner and heavier shapes and weights for boys, have been associated with lower levels of popularity (indexed by peer reports of status and reputation); likeability (indexed by peer reports of who they want to spend time with) is not affected (Wang, Houshyar, & Prinstein, 2006). Although it is somewhat reassuring that, in the immediate context of friendships, body shape and weight do not impact how likeable one is, we must emphasize that, in the larger social context of peer relationships, shape and weight do influence perceptions of popularity. Body weight also has some impact on dating: "for each one point increase in body mass index, the probability of having a romantic relationship decreased by 6%" (Halpern, King, Oslak, & Udry, 2005). So, although girls underestimate the body size that boys find attractive, boys do regard thinness as important in rating the attractiveness of girls (Paxton, Norris, Wertheim, Durkin, & Anderson, 2005). Overall, because of various combinations of personal and social factors, negative body image is associated with poor opposite-sex relationships (Davison & McCabe, 2006).

In the United States, differences in body image and body satisfaction are related to race and ethnicity. Body satisfaction is highest (about 40%) among African American girls (Kelly, Wall et al., 2005; Nishina, Ammon, Bellmore, & Graham, 2006). This may be because descriptions of ideal body size are larger; this is the case for both African Americans and for Latina Americans (Perry, Rosenblatt, & Wang, 2004). Although African American and Latina girls are aware of culturally prevalent (i.e., Western, European American, secular) ideals that emphasize thinness, these ideals appear to be internalized less frequently compared to European American and Asian American girls (Hermes & Keel, 2003; Shaw, Ramirez, Trost, Randall, & Stice, 2004; White, Kohlmaier, Varnado-Sullivan, & Williamson, 2003). Ethnicity is also important for boys, with reviews of the data suggesting that boys from a range of ethnic groups (e.g., African Americans, Latino Americans, Native Americans) display more disordered eating and body change strategies than boys from European American backgrounds (Ricciardelli, McCabe, Williams, & Thompson, 2007).

Negative body image, body dissatisfaction, and concerns related to weight and appearance are observed across many countries and cultures, including Argentina, Australia, Chile, China, Cuba, Denmark, Guatemala, India, Iran, Israel, Norway, Panama, Peru, Taiwan, Tibet, and Turkey (Canpolat, Orsel, Akdemir, & Ozbay, 2005; Latzer, 2003; Li, Hu, Ma, Wu, & Ma, 2005; McArthur, Holbert, & Pena, 2005; Nobakht & Dezhkam, 2000; Page, Lee, & Miao, 2005; Ricciardelli, McCabe, Ball, & Mellor, 2004; Shroff & Thompson, 2004; Storvoll, Strandbu, & Wichstrom, 2005; Waaddegaard & Petersen, 2002; Wang, Byrne, Kenardy, & Hills, 2005; Ying & Hong, 2005). Rapid social transformation in some countries (such as Fiji, Belize, and the countries of East Africa) has been tied to increasing concerns. It is hypothesized that among the social changes are a profusion of media images that spread Western, European American, secular ideals of beauty and thinness (Eddy, Hennessey, & Thompson-Brenner, 2007). Findings from a large-scale comparative study suggested that a combination of body-mass index and exposure to Western media predicted body dissatisfaction among women. Noteworthy cross-cultural differences were observed related to socioeconomic status, with body dissatisfaction and desire for thinness more frequently reported in high SES settings (Swami et al., 2010). Research designed to investigate sets of risk and protective factors is taking place around the globe (Anderson-Fye, 2004; Becker, 2004).

The influence of society and the media on body image and body attitudes has been extensively researched (Derenne & Beresin, 2006; Levine & Murnen, 2009; Wiseman, Sunday, & Becker, 2005), and researchers have described the ways in which television, movies, magazines, and Internet sites glamorize specific, narrow, and often unrealistic versions of beauty (e.g., very slender women's bodies and muscular men's bodies). Harrison and Hefner (2008) suggest that media exposure "(1) normalizes dieting and excessive thinness, and (2) encourages young people to repeatedly evaluate their bodies, to find them wanting, and to engage in extreme dieting, overexercising, and other health-compromising behaviors" (p. 381).

Many investigations have distinguished between the awareness of ideas and attitudes about appearance, thinness, and beauty, and the *internalization* of such ideas and attitudes (Cafri, Yamamiya, Brannick, & Thompson, 2005; Harrison, 2001; Jones, Vigfusdottir, & Lee, 2004). Studies of younger (11–12 years) and older girls (15–16 years) show that both groups are aware of sociocultural images and ideals; the older girls, however, are more likely to have internalized these images and ideals (Clay, Vignoles, & Dittmar, 2005; Hermes & Keel, 2003; see Fig. 15:1). According to Sherwood and Neumark-Sztainer (2001), "media exposure does not cause, but reinforces, an unhealthy body image among vulnerable women" (p. 228). In other words, *internalization is more important than awareness.*

How these sociocultural factors relate to dieting (and the kinds of harmful and extreme dieting characteristic of eating disorders) is complex. This topic will be more fully explored in upcoming sections. For now, examples of some of the connections between these factors and dieting include findings that link body image, dieting, and smoking (Austin & Gortmaker, 2001; Stice & Shaw, 2003) and findings that adolescents from higher socioeconomic status backgrounds are more aware of body ideals related to thinness and have more family and friends who are trying to lose weight (Wardle et al., 2004). Dieting also appears to be related to different sets of variables (such as friends' and families' weight concerns) for

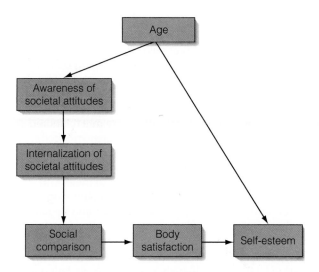

FIGURE 15:1 A conceptual model of proposed mediators of age trends in body satisfaction and self-esteem. *Source:* Body Image and Self-Esteem Among Adolescent Girls: Testing the Influence of Sociocultural Factors, Clay, D., Vignoles, V.L., & Dittmar, H. Copyright © 2005 Journal of Research on Adolescence. Reproduced with permission of Blackwell Publishing Ltd.

adolescent girls and boys (Presnell, Bearman, & Stice, 2004; Saling, Ricciardelli, & McCabe, 2005; Thompson, Rafiroiu, & Sargent, 2003).

Eating Disorders

The Case of Elizabeth

Elizabeth is 17 years old and in eleventh grade. She is a successful student, in leadership positions on several service clubs, and student editor of her high school's literary magazine. Elizabeth's grades have been outstanding, and her teachers consider her a bright and extremely conscientious student. Elizabeth is the only child of two affluent, professional parents who are both very involved in her academic and extracurricular activities. Elizabeth reports that she gets along well with her parents, but that she would like more independence than they seem comfortable with. Elizabeth's parents have noted that she has become increasingly withdrawn and even secretive, especially toward them, in the past year.

Although Elizabeth has had a very successful high school career thus far, junior high was a much more difficult time for her. Although she performed well academically, she had few friends and described feeling lonely and alienated. Her parents became concerned about her sad mood and noticeable weight gain in eighth grade and brought her to her pediatrician, who started her on an antidepressant. Within a few months of taking the medication and starting high school, Elizabeth was clearly happier, more energetic, and making more friends. Because of lingering concern over her weight, she began a very disciplined diet and program of running, resulting in the loss of 30 pounds over several months. Elizabeth received considerable attention and praise for these efforts from her parents and friends.

Elizabeth's sophomore year was successful, and her parents described her as happy and busy. The summer before her junior year, Elizabeth and her parents visited several colleges and she enrolled in a course to help her prepare for the SAT and ACT tests she would be taking in her junior year. Her parents also hired a consultant to begin working with Elizabeth in preparation for applying to colleges in the fall of her senior year. The consultant helped Elizabeth plan her upcoming schedule, including advising her on what extracurricular activities would look best to the selective colleges her parents were encouraging her to apply to.

Early in her junior year, Elizabeth's parents began to notice that her diet was increasingly restricted and that she seemed to avoid eating while out in public. Already quite thin when the school year started, Elizabeth began to lose weight at an alarming rate. She continued to run early in the morning before school and began to miss most family dinners. Her parents became increasingly worried as Elizabeth's appearance became gaunt and she admitted to them that she had not had her period in several months. Throughout this time, Elizabeth continued to excel in school and her energy level seemed especially high. At home, however, Elizabeth was isolated, seldom speaking to her parents except to argue about her refusal to eat the food her mother prepared. The only foods her parents ever saw her eat were yogurt and raw vegetables such as carrots and cauliflower. Also, despite being told by her parents and friends that she was too thin, she insisted that she was fat. Over Elizabeth's objections, her parents brought her to their physician for a checkup. There they learned that her weight had fallen to a dangerously low level and that she was experiencing clinically significant anemia and cardiac symptoms. Elizabeth was admitted directly to a medical inpatient unit for eating disorders. ■

The Case of Kayla

Kayla is 19 years old and a first-year student at a local community college. She lives in an apartment with several of her high school friends who are also students. Kayla's time in high school was characterized by considerable variability in her academic performance. She did well early in high school but, following her parents' divorce in the middle of her sophomore year, she began to disengage from school. This was a stressful time for the family as Kayla's mother made the transition to working full time while continuing to care for Kayla and her two younger siblings. Kayla began to skip classes occasionally, failed to complete homework, and began hanging out with a new group of friends who smoked and drank and did not value academic activities. After her promising start in high school, her guidance counselor became concerned about Kayla's missed classes and dropping grades, and met with Kayla and her mother toward the end of the year. That meeting led to a referral to her family physician and a mental health counselor. Kayla was treated for depression with medication and psychotherapy. She felt better, reconnected with old friends, and returned to school in the fall feeling more settled and focused. Over the next two years, Kayla did somewhat better, but continued to have intermittent academic and social problems, although never to the extent that she did in tenth grade.

Early in her senior year of high school, Kayla became concerned about her body size and shape. She was slightly overweight and a boy she was dating made some joking but rude comments about her "full and curvy" appearance. Kayla was very upset and made several unsuccessful attempts to lose weight. During this time, she also began to induce vomiting after hearing several friends talk about this as a way of controlling their weight. Soon Kayla was vomiting several times a day, generally at home but occasionally at school as well. Kayla found herself thinking about food often; this made her feel very anxious. She found that the anxiety lessened considerably when she ate, although the relief did not last. In fact, once the initial pleasure wore off, eating made her feel more anxiety and more shame. These feelings led her to induce vomiting to calm herself and keep from gaining more weight. Multiple times per day, Kayla was repeating a cycle in which she would binge on foods high in carbohydrates, such as cookies and ice cream, feel anxiety and guilt, and vomit. She began to buy food and hide it in her bedroom so that she could binge late at night when everyone else was sleeping. Although the girls at school often talked about various ways of purging (e.g., vomiting, using laxatives, exercising), Kayla kept her behavior secret. Her weight fluctuated considerably, although always returning to approximately the same weight she was when the difficulties began. Although Kayla continued to meet periodically with her therapist throughout high school to talk about her parents' divorce and to get help with symptoms of mild depression, she never mentioned her binge eating and purging behaviors.

Once she was living in an apartment, Kayla found it more difficult to hide her binge eating and purging from her roommates. Although two of the women she lived with pretty much ignored the unusual behavior, one roommate expressed her concern and told Kayla that she was currently being treated for bulimia in a group program at the college. She encouraged Kayla to meet with an eating disorders specialist in the counseling department. Eventually, Kayla agreed and began both individual and group therapy. ■

Eating disorders are psychopathologies characterized by severe disturbances in eating behaviors, disturbed perceptions of body size and shape, fear of being fat, and compensatory behaviors to lose weight or to prevent weight gain. Eating disorders are not a contemporary phenomenon. Descriptions of eating-disordered behavior have been documented for centuries (Halmi, 2009). Halmi asserts that it is unlikely that earlier descriptions of individuals (mostly women) "were starving themselves in order to be beautiful but rather fasting for a variety of different reasons. The common denominator in these cases is that severe food restriction spiraled out of control" (p. 163). DSM-5 describes several types of eating disorders: **anorexia nervosa** (illustrated in the case of Elizabeth), **bulimia nervosa** (the case of Kayla), and **binge eating disorder**. Anorexia nervosa includes two subtypes: restricting type (without binge eating or purging) and binge eating/purging type (with recurrent episodes of binge eating and purging). DSM-5 also includes a residual category for eating disorders with atypical, mixed, or below-threshold presentations.

Disturbed eating behaviors include severe restricting of food intake or limiting food to particular types. Distorted body perceptions involve distorted body image or denial of the seriousness of weight loss. Compensatory behaviors include excessive exercising, vomiting, and/or laxative use (Reba et al., 2005; Shroff et al., 2006); laxative use is associated with increased severity of eating disorders (Tozzi et al., 2006). Other associated symptoms, such as obsessions and compulsions, are often described. Typical obsessions include concerns with symmetry and somatic functioning; typical compulsions include rituals involving order and control (Halmi et al., 2003). Although most of the research on the clinical picture of eating disorders has involved girls and women, there are data indicating that some aspects of the disorder may differ by gender (Anderson & Bulik, 2004; Muise, Stein, & Arbess, 2003; Robb & Dadson, 2002). For instance, the nature and function of compensatory behaviors appear to be different for adolescent boys and adolescent girls.

Although there is both heterogeneity and considerable overlap in the clinical presentations of the various eating disorders, there are distinctive patterns of symptoms, pathways, and outcomes. Anorexia nervosa is characterized by restriction of food and energy intake and significantly low weight, an intense fear of gaining weight, and disturbed or distorted perceptions of weight or shape. Bulimia nervosa involves recurrent episodes of binge eating, a sense of lack of control over binge eating, recurrent problematic compensatory behaviors, and poor self-evaluations of body shape and weight. Binge eating disorder is characterized by repeated episodes of binge eating, a sense of lack of control, and significant distress.

Research into the subtypes of eating disorders continues, with important implications for assessment and treatment. Key issues include whether these subtypes are best understood as continuous or discontinuous examples of disorder; as multiple, distinct disorders; or as varied manifestations of underlying common pathology (the *transdiagnostic* approach) (Fairburn & Cooper, 2011; Gleaves, Brown, & Warren, 2004; Gordon, Holm-Denoma, Smith, Fink, & Joiner, 2007; Williamson, 2007). At this point, the data provide some support for the two subtypes of anorexia nervosa. The binge/purging subtype of anorexia associated with higher rates of impulsivity, self-harming and suicidal behavior, and more negative outcome (Peat, Mitchell, Hoek, & Wonderlich, 2009). There are few, if any, data supporting any subtypes of bulimia nervosa (there are no subtypes in DSM-5) (van Hoeken, Veling, Sinke, Mitchell, & Hoek, 2009). Compared to anorexia and bulimia, binge eating disorder appears distinctive, although there are issues related to its relation to obesity (Wonderlich, Gordon, Mitchell, Crosby, & Engel, 2009). These findings must be understood in the context of many other findings highlighting the significant *crossover* observed in individuals with eating disorders (e.g., being diagnosed at one point with anorexia nervosa and later with bulimia nervosa). These data suggest that the common experiences, symptoms, and impairment may be more important than the differences observed in individuals diagnosed with eating disorders (Fairburn & Cooper, 2011).

Peterson et al. (2011) provide a model of eating disorders with three classes of symptoms: binge eating and purging, binge eating, and low body-mass index (see Fig. 15:2). This model maps mostly on to the DSM-5 categories, except that the binge eating/purging subtype of anorexia more often falls into the binge eating and purging class rather than the low body-mass index class. If individuals who binge eat and purge are grouped together, crossover frequency may be reduced and classification may improve (Peterson et al., 2011). However the classification process unfolds, both scientific (e.g., whether the underlying genetic and physiological vulnerabilities are similar across eating disorders) and clinical usefulness (e.g., whether the treatments for eating disorders have better outcomes if they are specialized) need to be considered (Wonderlich, Crosby, Mitchell, & Engel, 2007).

Additional research is focused on atypical or partial eating disorders, which are subclinical presentations in adolescents and adults who meet some, but not all, of the diagnostic criteria. These problems include multiple physical and psychological symptoms and reflect a range of severity. Some individuals who present with atypical or partial eating disorders

Anorexia nervosa can lead to dangerous levels of weight loss.

Christopher LaMarca/Redux

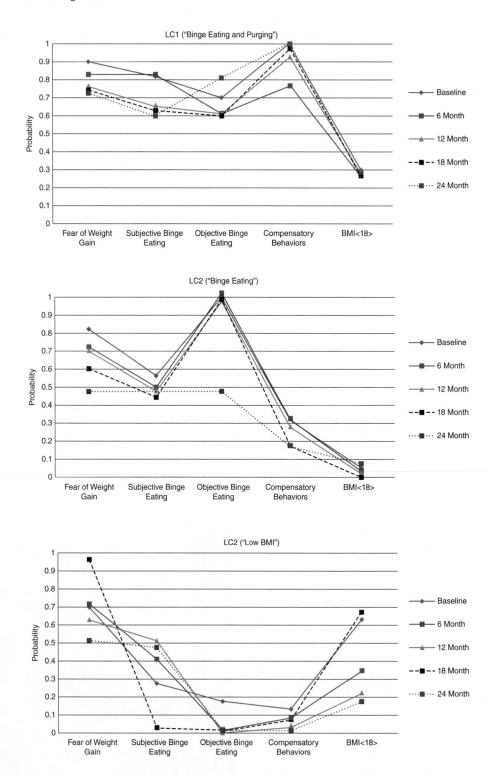

FIGURE 15:2 Latent class (LC) structures (LC1, LC2, LC3) for each time assessed (baseline, 6 month, 12 month, 18 month, 24 month) with probability estimates for each indicator: Fear of Weight Gain, Subjective Binge Eating, Objective Binge Eating, Compensatory Behaviors, Body Mass Index (BMI) less than 18.5.

Source: From Peterson et al. (2011). Examining the stability of DSM-IV and empirically-derived eating disorder classification: Implications for DSM-5. *Journal of Consulting and Clinical Psychology, 79,* 777–783.

will go on to develop full-blown disorders; most will display remission (Chamay-Weber, Narring, & Michaud, 2005).

The prevalence of eating disorders has increased over the past 50 years. Estimates of eating disorders are, for girls, approximately 1% for anorexia nervosa, 1% for bulimia nervosa, 1.5–3.5% for binge eating disorder, and 14% for the residual category of eating disorders; for boys, the corresponding percentages are 0.2% for anorexia, 0.4% for bulimia, 1–2% for binge eating disorder, and 6.5% for the residual category (Hudson, Hiripi, Pope, & Kessler, 2007; Kjelsas, Bjornstrom, & Gotestam, 2004). Lifetime prevalence data for the United States vary widely, from 1–4% for anorexia nervosa and bulimia nervosa, to almost 3% for all eating disorders, to 7% for binge eating disorder (Hoek & van Hoeken, 2003; NIMH, 2008). Binge eating disorder is more common than anorexia or bulimia (Wonderlich et al., 2009). Prevalence rates are relatively high, despite the fact that most individuals with bulimia nervosa or binge eating disorder are very likely to *not be recognized, diagnosed, or treated* (Hudson et al., 2007). It is generally accepted that adolescents from African American and Latina backgrounds have lower rates of eating disorders, but evidence suggests that rates are increasing in these groups (Granillo, Jones-Rodriguez, & Carvajal, 2005; Shaw, Ramirez, Trost, Randall, & Stice, 2004). There are data that suggest that European American women are more likely to display any eating disorder, whereas African American women are more likely to display bulimia or binge eating disorder (Wonderlich et al., 2009). The cross-cultural data are relatively similar. Across a 6-year European study, almost 9% were diagnosed with all types of eating disorders (Patton, Coffey, & Sawyer, 2003).

Adolescents diagnosed with eating disorders are also frequently diagnosed with other psychopathologies; depression is the most common comorbid disorder (Reijonen, Pratt, Patel, & Greydanus, 2003). This comorbidity is reflected in Elizabeth's case. There is also considerable overlap between eating disorders and bipolar disorder, and symptom similarities in terms of eating dysregulation, mood dysregulation, impulsivity, and compulsions (McElroy, Kotwal, Keck, & Akiskal, 2005). Anxiety disorders, including obsessive-compulsive disorder and social phobia, are also frequently observed (Kaye, Bulik, Thornton, Barbarich, & Masters, 2004). Self-harm and suicidality are primary concerns. Sansone and Levitt (2002) note that between 15% and 39% of inpatients and outpatients with eating disorders report suicide attempts; 54% of those with bulimia who are also struggling with alcohol abuse report such attempts. Connections between eating disorders and substance abuse disorders are widely described (Halmi, 2009); these have led some researchers to hypothesize that, for some, eating disorders are addictions, with food as a mood-altering substance, and food preoccupation, craving, and abuse despite negative consequences (Gold, Frost-Pineda, & Jacobs, 2003).

Developmental Course

As with all of the disorders discussed in this textbook, developmental pathways, courses, and outcomes of eating disorders are variable. In general, most adolescent syndromes are "brief and self-limiting" (Patton et al., 2003, p. 125) and approximately 70% have good recoveries. Other adolescents exhibit fluctuating courses of weight loss and gain, whereas still others deteriorate over time and are repeatedly hospitalized (Denda et al., 2002; Patton et al., 2003; Peterson et al., 2012; Steinhausen, Boyadjieva, Griogoroiu-Serbanescu, & Neumarker, 2003). There are continuities between adolescent and adult eating disorders as well. For example, bulimia in early adolescence predicts a 9-fold increase in risk for bulimia in late adolescence; bulimia in late adolescence (as illustrated in the case of Kayla) predicts a 35-fold increase in risk for bulimia in adulthood (Fairburn et al., 2003; Kotler, Cohen, Davies, Pine, & Walsh, 2001).

Age of onset peaks at two times: early adolescence and late adolescence. And these peaks represent key transition points, from childhood to adolescence, and from adolescence to adulthood (Doyle, Smyth, & le Grange, 2012). Younger adolescents are more likely to present with symptoms of anorexia nervosa, and older adolescents are more likely to present with symptoms of bulimia (Reijonen et al., 2003). The first transition involves puberty, and increased weight concerns may lead to compensatory and other problematic behaviors, including smoking and drinking (Field et al., 2002; Stice, 2003). Both early- and late-maturing girls are more likely to engage in risky body change behaviors such as purging, laxative use, and exercise dependence (McCabe & Ricciardelli, 2004a). Compared to anorexia or bulimia, binge eating disorder has a later onset (Wonderlich et al., 2009). When identification and intervention occur earlier, the course of the disorder may be less severe and less chronic (Doyle et al., 2012; le Grange & Loeb, 2007). Although most eating disorders emerge during adolescence, recent reports suggest that instances of middle- and late-life eating disorders are increasing; this phenomenon warrants additional attention (Scholtz, Hill, & Lacey, 2010; Zerbe, 2003b).

As noted earlier, although many adolescents are diagnosed with one form of eating disorder and remain so diagnosed, there is some evidence of crossover from anorexia to bulimia, and from bulimia to anorexia (Fairburn & Cooper, 2011; Peat et al., 2009; Tozzi et al., 2005). Personality and family characteristics may influence the change (Tozzi et al., 2005). Alcohol abuse, for example, is associated with a trajectory from bulimia to anorexia; parental criticism is associated with a trajectory from anorexia to bulimia (Tozzi et al., 2005).

The psychological consequences of eating disorders include impairments in self-image, health, and social functioning (Graber, Tyrka, & Brooks-Gunn, 2003; Johnson, Cohen, Kasen, & Brook, 2002; Striegel-Moore, Seeley, & Lewinsohn, 2003), and, as described above, the development of depressive disorders and substance abuse (Measelle, Stice, & Hogansen, 2006; Perez, Joiner, & Lewinsohn, 2004; Stice, Burton, & Shaw, 2004). Substance abuse may or may not be related to anxiety modulation (Bulik et al., 2004; Patton et al., 2003; Burton, Stice, Bearman, & Rohde, 2007) and is lower in adolescent women with restricting symptoms (Stock, Goldberg, Corbett, & Katzman, 2002). For those with severe and prolonged courses, suicidality is especially problematic (Stein et al., 2003).

There are, as well, immediate and long-term medical complications such as biochemical, endocrine, hematological, and bone-related difficulties (Chavez & Insel, 2007; Reijonen et al., 2003; Rome & Ammerman, 2003; see Table 15:1). The mortality rate for eating disorders is high. For those admitted to hospitals, rates are approximately 10%. Across ages, estimates range from 5.9% to 7.4% for anorexia, and from 2.4% to 3% for bulimia (Reijonen et al., 2003). The mortality rate for eating disorders is about 5% per decade (Chavez & Insel, 2007).

Etiology

Two of the most prominent explanations of eating disorders are related to (1) family factors and (2) sociocultural factors. Critical analyses of these explanations are necessary in order to separate fact

---

TABLE 15:1 Medical Complications of Eating Disorders

Medical complications of anorexia nervosa:

- Severe dehydration, possibly leading to shock
- Electrolyte imbalance (such as potassium insufficiency)
- Cardiac arrhythmias
- Severe malnutrition
- Thyroid gland deficiencies that can lead to cold intolerance and constipation
- Appearance of fine baby-like body hair (lanugo)
- Bloating or edema
- Decrease in white blood cells, which leads to increased susceptibility to infection
- Osteoporosis
- Tooth erosion and decay
- Seizures related to fluid shifts, due to excessive diarrhea or vomiting

Medical complications of bulimia nervosa:

- Type 2 diabetes
- High blood pressure
- High blood cholesterol levels
- Gallbladder disease
- Heart disease
- Certain types of cancer

Source: From MedlinePlus (2009) and National Institute of Diabetes and Digestive and Kidney Diseases (2008).

---

from fiction and to examine empirical data that support or refute these hypotheses. The idea that families create or foster eating disorders is most fully explored in psychodynamic explanations and is often associated with the psychodynamic theorists Hilde Bruch (1973, 1982) and Salvador Minuchin. Bruch observed eating disorders in "good girls," girls who were char-acteristically compliant, achievement oriented, and attuned to pleasing others. Bruch asserted that the daughters in these families with indulgent, overinvolved parents lacked many of the basic skills of early childhood, such as the ability to distinguish among physical sensations, the ability to differentiate emotional experiences, and the ability to feel confident in one's body and oneself. Minuchin's book *Psychosomatic Families* (Minuchin, Rosman, & Baker, 1978) described families who were "enmeshed," or too closely involved and covertly controlling. These dysfunctional families allowed little opportunity for children's autonomy, a stressful situation exacerbated by an atmosphere of overt nurturing and affection. With the developmental press for independence and self-definition associated with early adolescence, crises were inevitable. Without a well-defined sense of self, and without the ability to appropriately identify their own needs and desires, daughters sought control over themselves in any way possible; for some, the struggle played out in the form of eating disorders.

As might be expected, parents of adolescent girls diagnosed with eating disorders were "bewildered, blamed and broken-hearted" (MacDonald, 2000) as they sought help for their children. And their confusion and upset was warranted, because there is little or no empirical support in prospective studies for the causal impact of these psychodynamic family factors (Stice, 2002). Indeed, as we will review in a moment, if families of eating-disordered adolescents "tend to be perfectionistic, rigid, achievement-oriented and controlling, that may simply be a result of the fact that they have a genetic tendency toward obsessionality. The parents' controlling personalities aren't causing their daughters' anorexia; they are simply proof of the genetic disposition that they all share" (Lott, 1998). A recent position paper from the Academy for Eating Disorders (le Grange, Lock, Loeb, & Nicholls, 2010) is quite clear: "It is the position of the Academy for Eating Disorders (AED) that whereas family factors can play a role in the genesis and maintenance of eating disorders, current knowledge refutes the idea that they are the exclusive or even the primary mechanisms that underlie risk. Thus, the AED stands firmly against any etiologic model of eating disorders in which family influences are seen as the primary cause of anorexia nervosa or bulimia nervosa, and condemns generalizing statements that imply families are to blame for their children's illness" (p. 1). More recently, sociocultural models of eating disorders have become prominent (Markey, 2004). These explanations, briefly discussed in the opening section of this chapter on developmental challenges associated with eating and appearance, begin with the near-constant presentation of images of actresses and fashion models with impossibly thin bodies and shapes. Internalization of this thin ideal, coupled with pressure to be thin (coming from oneself, family, peers, and society), leads to body dissatisfaction, negative emotions, problematic dieting behaviors, and eating pathology. Indeed, research suggests that exposure to media images of the thin ideal and peer pressure to be thin immediately increase levels of body dissatisfaction (Groesz, Levine, & Murnen, 2002; Stice, Maxfield, & Wells, 2003). This is especially the case if girls are vulnerable in

terms of already-present body dissatisfaction, perceived pressure to be thin, and lack of social support (Stice et al., 2001). According to Harrison and Hefner (2008), the "thin-ideal media exposure may coax body image disturbance and disordered eating into expression by activating related cognitions and emotions" (p. 381). Given that the vast majority of adolescent girls and young women *do not* develop clinically significant eating disorders, however, a single-factor model is unlikely to capture the real-life complexity of eating disorders.

A biopsychosocial, multifactorial risk model provides a more nuanced explanation of the development of eating disorders (Keery, van den Berg, & Thompson, 2004; le Grange et al., 2010; Steiner et al., 2003). As we review the genetic and environmental factors, keep in mind that both the number and pattern of risk factors likely influence an individual's vulnerability (Stice, 2002). In addition, it is important to know that many of the studies summarized here do not differentiate among subtypes of eating disorders; given the distinct symptom profiles of the various subtypes, it is probable that some of the patterns of risk and maintenance factors differ (Stice, 2002).

Genes and Heredity

The first factors to examine are the genetic factors, which are investigated using family studies, twin studies, and molecular genetic analyses. Family and twin research suggests strong heritabilities for both anorexia and bulimia (Bulik et al., 2006; Halmi, 2009; le Grange et al., 2010). There are data that are consistent with explanations that highlight common genetic factors underlying eating symptoms, anxiety and depression, as well as explanations that emphasize distinct genetic factors for early symptoms of eating disorder. Evidence for shared environmental factors for eating symptoms and depression, gene-by-environment interactions, and gender specificity have also been described (Bulik, Reba, Siega-Riz, & Reichborn-Kjennerud, 2005; Silberg & Bulik, 2005; Wade, Bulik, Prescott, & Kendler, 2004). One example of a gene-by-environment interaction involves a biologically determined susceptibility to binge eating coupled with an environment that provides good-tasting food that is very accessible (Williamson, 2007). Current research is also examining various candidate genes for their roles in the etiology of eating disorders (Ribases et al., 2005; Slof-Op't Landt et al., 2005).

Physiological Factors

Physiological studies provide additional perspective on the brain structures and mechanisms involved in appetite, food intake, and associated pleasure and reward (Berridge, 2009; Frank et al., 2006; Södersten, Bergh, & Zandian, 2006; Vanderlinden et al., 2004). Data suggest abnormal activity in various regions of the brain, including the prefrontal and temporal lobes (Chowdhury et al., 2003; Frank et al., 2004; Uher et al., 2004). Related research focuses on the role of the vagus nerve, dysregulation of the serotonin and dopamine systems, and elevated pain thresholds observed in adolescents with eating disorders (Faris et al., 2006; Frank et al., 2004; Halmi, 2009; Papezova, Yamamotova, & Uher, 2006; Steiger, 2004). Some of the physiological factors that appear to be implicated are similar to those observed in individuals with certain mood disorders and substance abuse disorders, including dysregulation of eating and mood, impulsivity, and craving responses after exposure to food cues (Berridge, 2009; Halmi, 2009; Kelley, Schiltz, & Landry, 2005; McElroy et al., 2005). These factors may be particularly salient for those adolescents and adults with more severe psychopathology.

Halmi (2009) describes a physiological model that emphasizes allostasis. Extending a model originally designed to explain drug addiction (Koob & LeMoal, 1997), Halmi suggests that individuals diagnosed with anorexia or bulimia experience "a dysregulation of reward circuits with activation of brain and

hormonal stress responses" (p. 163). These "changes in the entire brain-body system" underlie ongoing risk, chronic distress and impairment, and frequent relapses (p. 164).

Child Factors

Individual factors that influence the emergence of eating disorders have received much clinical and empirical attention. A cluster of biologically influenced personality characteristics has been identified that increases vulnerability. These include temperament (Martin et al., 2000), negative emotionality and emotion dysregulation (Crosby et al., 2009; Vanderlinden et al., 2004), impulsivity (Favaro et al., 2005; Wunderlich, Connolly, & Stice, 2004), stress reaction and harm avoidance (Peterson et al., 2010), and reward and punishment sensitivity (Loxton & Dawe, 2006). **Perfectionism,** as part of a constellation of features of obsessionality, appears to run in families and leads to the "relentless pursuit of the thin ideal" (Bruch, 1973); this factor is central to both etiology and maintenance processes (Castro-Fornieles et al., 2007; Halmi et al., 2005; Tozzi et al., 2004). Perfectionism is also associated with increased risk for a chronic pathway (Nilsson, Sundbom, & Hagglof, 2008). The role of sexual orientation requires further exploration: gay and bisexual adolescents are at increased risk (Austin et al., 2004; Feldman & Meyer, 2010). Cognitive schema that overlap with those observed in adolescents who are depressed, such as the belief that one is ugly or stupid, have also been identified as risk factors (Cooper, Rose, & Turner, 2005, 2006).

Another cluster of personality characteristics is more psychodynamically informed (Caparrotta & Ghaffari, 2006). These include variables related to self (Bers, Blatt, & Dolinsky, 2004; Eliot, 2004; Huprich, Stepp, Graham, & Johnson, 2004). For example, with respect to levels of agency, reflectivity, differentiation, and relatedness, Bers et al. report that individuals with anorexia described lower levels of agency and relatedness, as well as a heightened and harsh self-reflectivity; these self-descriptions distinguish between psychiatric patients with anorexia and nonpsychiatric patients, as well as between patients with anorexia and patients with other disorders. Other variables in the psychodynamic framework involve atypical emotional development and functioning (such as a reluctance to express emotion or a tendency to restrict emotional experiences), with difficulties often traced back to early relationship

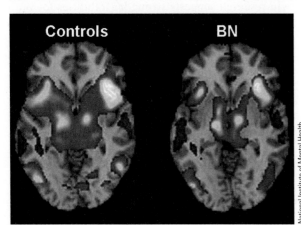

Women with bulimia nervosa (BN), when compared with healthy women, showed different patterns of brain activity while doing a task that required self-regulation. This abnormality may underlie binge eating and other impulsive behaviors that occur with the eating disorder.

SOURCE: Marsh et al. (2009). Deficient activity in the neural systems that mediate self-regulatory control in bulimia nervosa. *Archives of General Psychiatry, 66,* 51–63.

National Institute of Mental Health

interactions (Clinton, 2006; Sim & Zeman, 2004). Various personality patterns also increase the risk of eating disorders (Cassin & von Ranson, 2005; Sansone, Levitt, & Sansone, 2005). Overall neuroticism, as well as combinations of a sense of incompetence, avoidant coping style, and a lack of reciprocity with parents, are examples of these factors (Bulik et al., 2006; Holliday, Landau, Collier, & Treasure, 2006; Wheeler, Wintre, & Polivy, 2003).

Body-related characteristics and attitudes are another set of risk factors, with body dissatisfaction at the nexus. According to Stice and colleagues (Stice, 2002; Stice & Whitenton, 2002), body dissatisfaction results from either a history of being overweight or pressure to be thin, or both. Higher body-mass index predicts teasing from others that leads to body dissatisfaction; dissatisfaction then leads to eating pathology and impaired psychological functioning (Johnson & Wardle, 2005; Striegel-Moore et al., 2005). Teasing appears to be a particularly important factor for both girls and boys (Barker & Galambos, 2003; Eisenberg, Neumark-Sztainer, Haines, & Wall, 2006). A different type of body risk factor involves participation in weight-focused sports, such as gymnastics or running (Sherwood, Neumark-Sztainer, Story, Beuhring, & Resnick, 2002). Puberty has also received research scrutiny, with current hypotheses related to gender-specific interactions of pubertal status and other variables such as social comparison (Morrison, Kalin, & Morrison, 2004; Ricciardelli & McCabe, 2004).

Another type of risk factor involves the motivation underlying food choices and dieting. According to Lindeman and Stark (2000), low-risk dieters enjoy food more, are less depressed, and have fewer body-image issues. High-risk dieters experience less pleasure in eating, are more depressed, and have more body-image disturbances. High-risk dieters appear to use food more ideologically. For instance, those who see food as an expression of self (as do some vegetarians or vegans) are at higher risk for the development of eating disorders.

A history of negative events or psychopathology also increases an individual's risk of developing an eating disorder. Early health problems, physical and sexual abuse, date violence and rape, and both internalizing and externalizing disorders increase vulnerability (Ackard & Neumark-Sztainer, 2002; Fonseca, Ireland, & Resnick, 2002; Moorhead et al., 2003; Perkins, Luster, & Jank, 2002). The impact of internalized racism and acculturative stress (i.e., the difficulties associated with attempts to assimilate

to the majority culture) for women of color has also been emphasized (Gilbert, 2003).

Parent and Family Factors

Parent and family factors have long been implicated in the development and maintenance of eating disorders. As noted, however, we need to be very careful how we evaluate and address these factors. It may turn out that an appreciation of bidirectional influences provides the most useful information. It is also likely that specific family factors are more salient for already vulnerable adolescents (le Grange et al., 2010; Stice, 2002). One basic risk variable involves general family dysfunction. For instance, families with more problematic communication, more psychopathology, and more financial difficulties have adolescents at higher risk (Moorhead et al., 2003; Steinberg & Phares, 2001). Perceptions of family functioning (versus actual family functioning) provide additional perspective. Daughters with eating disorders, for example, perceive more family dysfunction than their mothers, and this may be because of their feelings of inadequacy and distrust of others (Dancyger, Fornari, & Sunday, 2006).

Examining some of the specific aspects of maternal and paternal behaviors may elucidate some of these more general findings. The relationships of mothers and daughters are a frequent clinical focus. Mothers' critical comments about weight and shape and the frequency of such comments appear to be more influential than family conflict (Cooley, Toray, Wang, & Valdez, 2008; Hanna & Bond, 2006).

Encouragement of dieting is also related to body dissatisfaction and drive for thinness (Cooley et al., 2008; Wertheim, Martin, Prior, Sanson, & Smart, 2002). The data on mothers' own modeling of eating pathology (e.g., emotional eating or restrictive eating) and negative body image are mixed (Cooley et al., 2008; Elfhag & Linne, 2005).

Fathers who emphasize attractiveness and control food intake increase the risk of eating pathology (Dixon, Gill, & Adair, 2003). Fathers, as well as mothers and siblings, who tease daughters increase negative outcomes (Keery, Boutelle, van den Berg, & Thompson, 2005). Paternal rejection is an especially poignant risk factor (Rojo-Moreno, Livianos-Aldana, Conesa-Burquet, & Cava, 2006). There are, of course, protective family factors as well. Family connectedness, positive family communication, and parental monitoring all decrease the risk of eating disorders in adolescents (Fonseca et al., 2002).

Environmental Factors

Negative life events (e.g., school transitions, death of a family member, relationship changes, home and job transitions, illness/hospitalization, and maltreatment) increase the risk for eating disorders and may trigger the onset of an eating disorder (Berge, Loth, Hanson, Croll-Lampert, & Neumark-Sztainer, 2012). As already described, media influences are also important risk factors.

The **tripartite influence model of eating disorders** incorporates several of the psychosocial risk factors (Keery et al., 2004; Shroff & Thompson, 2006). This model proposes that three factors (i.e., parents, peers, and media) influence the development of body dissatisfaction and eating problems through two mechanisms: the internalization of the thin ideal and appearance comparison processes. Investigations focused on Japanese adolescents and French and Australian young women have increased empirical support for the model (Rodgers, Chabrol, & Paxton, 2011; Yamamiya, Shroff, & Thompson, 2008).

Assessment and Diagnosis

Assessment and diagnosis of eating disorders can be especially problematic because most adolescents with eating disorders deny difficulties (often vehemently) and avoid contact with medical or mental health professionals (Becker et al., 2009; Collins & Ricciardelli, 2005). Therefore, therapeutic engagement and alliance processes, to be addressed more fully in the following section, are of the utmost priority.

There are a number of well-validated structured interview and self-report measures for screening and diagnosis, although instruments need to be designed and interpreted with regard for differences in the clinical presentation of adolescents versus adults and in ethnicity and gender (Anderson, Lundgren, Shapiro, & Paulosky, 2004; Franko et al., 2004; Stice, Fisher, & Martinez, 2004). Because several of the diagnostic criteria for eating disorders involve cognitive symptoms (e.g., negative evaluations of weight and shape; motivation for restricted eating), the diagnostic process must take into account age-related and cultural considerations (Becker et al., 2009). For example, "body experience and weight concerns may be difficult to formulate and express, in part because they are highly subjective, and in part because they are relative to social norms" (p. 616). In addition, given the different perspectives of adolescents and parents, particularly related to family functioning,

parent reports should always be solicited (Dancyger, Fornari, Scionti, Wisotsky, & Sunday, 2005). It is, of course, absolutely necessary for a comprehensive medical examination to be part of the assessment process.

Differential diagnosis most often involves making a decision regarding the presence of body dysmorphic disorder (involving an excessive preoccupation with imagined or actual slight defects in physical appearance) (Sobanski & Schmidt, 2000), obsessive-compulsive disorder, and the anxiety disorders. Clinicians must also decide whether eating disorders are present by themselves or in combination with depression or other forms of psychopathology.

Intervention

Prevention

Interventions for eating disorders include both prevention and treatment. Prevention strategies frequently target some of the more malleable risk factors, including body dissatisfaction, negative emotion, and internalization of the thin ideal, and seek to strengthen some of the protective factors, such as self-esteem and social support (Durkin, Paxton, & Wertheim, 2005; Neumark-Sztainer et al., 2006; Stice, Shaw, Burton, & Wade, 2006). Key components of effective interventions include interaction, multiple sessions, and programs focused on selected groups (such as older adolescent girls) (Stice & Shaw, 2004). School-based programs in both middle schools and high schools, and across ethnic groups, can be effective. These may focus on components of healthy eating and healthy dieting, self-esteem and perfectionism, and critical analysis of media images and may specifically address teasing and harassment related to body weight and shape (Larkin & Rice, 2005; McVey, Tweed, & Blackmore, 2007; Rodriguez, Marchand, Ng, & Stice, 2008; Scime, Cook-Cottone, Kane, & Watson, 2006; Wliksch, Durbridge, & Wade, 2008). Internet-oriented school programs have also been designed (Brown, Winzelberg, Abascal, & Taylor, 2004). Peer-led prevention programs for older adolescents and college students have also received empirical support (Becker, Bull, Schaumberg, Cauble, & Franco, 2008; Becker, Smith, & Ciao, 2006). Several of these programs have more positive, immediate impacts for high-risk girls (Becker et al., 2008; McVey et al., 2007; Weiss & Wertheim, 2005).

Treatment

Treatment models include inpatient hospitalization, partial hospitalization, intensive outpatient settings, and traditional outpatient settings (Stewart & Williamson, 2004a, 2004b). Current approaches provide multidisciplinary, comprehensive, and integrated treatments that address the medical and psychological issues of adolescents and their family and peer contexts (Haines & Neumark-Sztainer, 2006; Södersten et al., 2006). Even with excellent and effective models, there continues to be a need for more good research focused specifically on children and adolescents, related to developmental course and outcomes (Couturier & Lock, 2006; Gowers & Bryant-Waugh, 2004). Ongoing research on treatment is especially important for several reasons. First, compared to adults with eating disorders, treatments for adolescents with eating disorders are more effective (Halmi, 2009). Second, early treatment may decrease rates of more chronic and treatment-resistant forms of eating disorders (le Grange & Loeb, 2007). Third, the presence of family members may provide sources of support that enhance treatment (Doyle et al., 2012).

Hospitalization remains essential for those with severe and life-threatening disorders. Both inpatient and partial hospitalization are aggressive forms of treatment that require considerable clinical skills on the part of mental health professionals who work with therapeutically challenging adolescents. With accumulating data on empirically supported outpatient treatments for eating disorders, it is increasingly the case that the primary function of hospitalization is medical stabilization.

As noted, adolescents rarely initiate or compliantly accept treatment (Halmi, 2009; Sommers-Flanagan et al., 2011). Even if treatment begins, dropout rates are high. Halmi et al. (2005) emphasize the need to study the personality characteristics of eating-disordered adolescents to identify those that may predict difficulty (e.g., obsessionality) or engagement (e.g., self-esteem). Readiness to recover may be key (Ametller, Castro, Serrano, Martinez, & Toro, 2005). Characteristics of the therapist, and the therapeutic alliance, also take on added significance (Constantino, Arnow, Blasey, & Agras, 2005). As with all therapists working with children and adolescents with all kinds of psychopathologies, Stewart (2004) suggests that therapists who are nonjudgmental, neutral, and accepting are more likely to engage their eating-disordered clients.

Pharmacological treatments are relatively unexplored with adolescents (compared to adults), but there are numerous research projects underway. Most of the research is focused on the use of antidepressants and mood stabilizers. There is little evidence that pharmacological treatments are effective for restoring weight for individuals diagnosed with anorexia, and mixed data on the role of pharmacological treatments for reducing relapse rates and improving core features of eating disorders (Chavez & Insel, 2007).

Psychosocial interventions are much more prominent and include individual and family psychotherapies. In general, current treatment trends include the use of family-based treatments for older children and adolescents and the use of cognitive-behavioral therapy for young adults. Family therapies are effective for adolescents with both anorexia and bulimia (Keel & Haedt, 2008; Loeb, Lock, Greif, & le Grange, 2010; Tierney & Wyatt, 2005). In fact, "family involvement appears to be useful in reducing both psychological and medical morbidity, especially for younger patients with a short duration eating disorder" (le Grange et al., 2010, p. 3). Parent participation is also associated with lower rates of dropout for adolescents (le Grange et al., 2010).

The **Maudsley model of family therapy** (le Grange, 2005), in which parents have a central role in treatment, has been the focus of much current research and has received much empirical support (Lock & le Grange, 2005; Wallis, Rhodes, Kohn, & Madden, 2007). The Maudsley model is a "highly practical approach, which initially focuses exclusively on problems related to improving eating and promoting weight gain" (Lock & le Grange, 2005, p. S64). In the early phase of treatment, parents have significant control over the adolescent's eating; problems in family structure that make improvements in eating more difficult are addressed quickly. When eating and weight have improved, adolescents take more responsibility and control over eating. The last part of treatment focuses on the typical developmental challenges of adolescence (e.g., autonomy, sexuality) that may have an impact on continued progress.

Compared to individual treatments for adolescents with anorexia, family-based treatments were more effective in maintaining full remission of symptoms over time (Lock et al., 2010). Also, the more severe the clinical presentation, the greater the benefit associated with family-based treatments compared

Regardless of the specific approach, successful treatment of eating disorders depends on changing the individual's attitude toward eating.

Susan Rosenberg/Science Source/Photo Researchers

to individual treatments (le Grange et al., 2012). In addition to family-based treatments, groups of parents whose adolescents are diagnosed with eating disorders benefit from parent training programs that provide both information and support for their own struggles (Holtkamp, Herpertz-Dahlmann, Vloet, & Hagenah, 2005; le Grange et al., 2010; Zucker, Marcus & Bulik, 2006).

The most common, empirically supported individual approach is cognitive-behavioral psychotherapy (Burton et al., 2007; Chavez & Insel, 2007; Gowers, 2006; Williamson, White, York-Crowe, & Stewart, 2004; Wilson, 2005). A specialized version, **cognitive behavioral therapy for eating disorders (CBT-E)**, is designed to address various forms of eating disorders and to match adolescents' and young adults' personalities and psychopathologies (Fairburn, 2008; Fairburn et al., 2009). The focus of CBT-E treatment involves identifying factors that maintain the eating disorder (in contrast to factors that influenced the development of the disorder) and helping individuals step back or distance themselves from their disorder so that they can understand it better. The initial stage of treatment involves engaging the patient, assessing the nature and severity of the disorder, education about eating disorders, and working together to devise an individualized treatment plan. The second and third stages involve reviewing progress and compliance and identifying ongoing barriers to change. Examples of work in these stages might include exploring the overevaluation of shape and weight and developing strategies to (a) reduce the importance of shape and weight and (b) develop other domains for self-evaluation. Additional work might focus on dealing with dietary rules, dietary restraint, or negative moods. The final phase emphasizes understanding and minimizing relapse and devising plans for dealing with setbacks.

Other common treatments for adolescents with bulimia focus more specifically on dieting and dietary restraint strategies. For those with bulimia, who often relapse and struggle with repeat cycles of binge eating and purging, and for those with binge eating disorder, dieting must be appreciated as a complex phenomenon (Stice, Martinez, Presnell, & Groesz, 2006; Wonderlich et al., 2009). Although once thought to exacerbate the symptoms of bulimia, dieting actually improves the clinical picture (Stice, Presnell, Groesz, & Shaw, 2005). To the extent that early progress can be made, initial improvement often predicts eventual outcome (Fairburn, Agras, Walsh, Wilson, & Stice, 2004). Relapse prevention can be addressed by having therapists pay special attention to an adolescent's higher level of initial preoccupation with food, greater ritualization of eating, and lower motivation for change (Halmi et al., 2002).

Less prevalent, with fewer data to support them, are the psychodynamic treatments for eating disorders. These tend to center on providing a safe space to explore painful emotions, construct self and identity, and explore early and current family relationships (Bryant-Waugh, 2006; Caparrotta & Ghaffari, 2006; Murphy, Straebler, Basden, Cooper, & Fairburn, 2012; Zerbe, 2003a). Finally, given the reluctance of many adolescents to avail themselves of help, alternative individual resources such as telephone hotlines are essential (Latzer & Gilat, 2000).

Group interventions have also been widely used, with both positive and negative outcomes (Davies, 2004; Dishion & Stormshak, 2007; McGilley, 2006;

Wolf & Sefferino, 2008). Groups enable children and adolescents to explore similar psychological factors underlying the emergence and maintenance of eating disorders (e.g., related to dysregulated emotion, distorted cognitions, problematic behaviors) as well as parent, peer, and media influences on eating disorders. Peers in groups also provide specific kinds of support for recovery and examples of successful treatment. However, as with other forms of psychopathology (e.g., conduct disorders, substance abuse disorders), negative influences are also observed, with peers providing information about noncompliance and strategies for treatment sabotage (Dishion & Stormshak, 2007). This kind of negative influence is especially important to counter, because it may be reinforced by numerous websites that promote eating-disordered behavior as a lifestyle choice (Lapinski, 2006; Mulveen & Hepworth, 2006). In the end, individual, family, and group treatments may each contribute to improvements in the clinical presentation and better long-term outcomes. As with all psychopathologies, the overriding goal of treatment of eating disorders is to enable children and adolescents to capitalize on their strengths, to cope with inevitable difficulties, and to move forward with confidence and hope.

Key Terms

Body image (p. 283)
Body satisfaction (p. 283)
Body dissatisfaction (pg. 283)
Eating disorders (p. 286)
Anorexia nervosa (p. 286)
Bulimia nervosa (p. 286)
Binge eating disorder (p. 286)
Perfectionism (p. 292)
Tripartite influence model of eating disorders (p. 294)
Maudsley model of family therapy (p. 295)
Cognitive behavioral therapy—E (CBT-E) (p. 296)

Chapter Summary

- Adolescence is a time of increased risk for all types of eating disorders.
- Weight gain in adolescence is generally accompanied by an increase in body fat for girls and a decrease in body fat for boys. Attitudes of body dissatisfaction increase during adolescence for both boys and girls.
- Core eating disorder symptoms include disturbed eating behaviors, body dissatisfaction and negative body perceptions, as well as compensatory behaviors to lose weight or prevent weight gain.
- Key symptoms of anorexia nervosa include a fear of fatness and extreme behaviors leading to weight loss. Binge eating and compensatory behaviors to prevent weight loss characterize bulimia nervosa, whereas binge eating disorder does not include the compensatory behaviors.
- The prevalence of eating disorders has increased in recent decades.
- Depressive disorders and anxiety disorders commonly occur along with eating disorders.
- The peak onset of eating disorders is early adolescence for anorexia and late adolescence for bulimia. Compared to anorexia or bulimia, binge eating disorder has a later onset.
- The biopsychosocial model of eating disorders emphasizes the interaction of genetic, physiological, personality, and family factors in the development and maintenance of eating disorders.
- Negative emotionality and emotional dysregulation are temperament characteristics with particular salience for eating disorders.
- Negative life events increase the risk for eating disorders and may also precipitate the onset of an eating disorder.
- Once established, many forms of eating disorders are relatively resistant to treatment. Severe and life-threatening forms often require hospital-based programs for medical stabilization.
- Current treatment trends include the use of family-based treatments for older children and adolescents and the use of cognitive-behavioral therapy for young adults.
- An important component of all treatment models is a focus on healthy attitudes toward food and eating, as well as improved coping skills.

Glossary

A

Acute stress disorder A disorder involving the development of multiple psychologically-based symptoms that last up to one month following exposure to a traumatic event.

Adaptational failure Deviation from age-appropriate norms; exaggeration or diminishment of normal developmental expressions; interference in normal developmental progress; failure to master age-salient developmental tasks; and/or failure to develop a specific function or regulatory mechanism.

Adaptive behavior A reflection of an individual's ability to manage daily living tasks, including self-care and household tasks.

Addiction A disorder characterized by compulsive drug seeking and abuse, accompanied by neurophysiological changes.

Adequate adaptation With respect to children's functioning, adequate adaptation refers to functioning that is okay, acceptable, or "good enough."

Adolescence-limited trajectory (AL) From Moffitt's model of conduct disorder (CD), related to adolescent-onset CD. The AL form of CD is somewhat less problematic over time than the child-onset form, although there is still evidence of significant impairment in daily functioning and higher risk for poor outcomes.

Adolescent-onset subtype (conduct disorder) With onset in adolescence, the individual's problem behavior emerges more abruptly than with childhood onset, and is more often time limited. Adolescent-onset CD is three times as frequent as child-onset.

Adverse drug effects Harmful, undesired, and sometimes unpredictable effects of medications.

Affective social competence The coordination of the capacities to experience emotion, send emotional messages to others, and read others' emotional signals.

Aggression Behaviors that are carried out with an immediate goal of causing harm to another.

Agoraphobia A type of anxiety disorder characterized by the experience of intense anxiety in places where individuals feel insecure, trapped, or not in control, most often associated with avoidance of such places.

Allostasis The process of actively maintaining physiological and psychological stability in response to environmental demands.

Allostatic load The cumulative physiological and psychological wear and tear caused by ongoing, and sometimes maladaptive, allostatic processes.

Anorexia nervosa A type of eating disorder characterized by a refusal to maintain body weight, intense fear of gaining weight or becoming fat, disturbance in the way in which one's body weight or shape is experienced, and denial of the seriousness of the current low body weight.

Antisocial propensity The factors that increase the risk for conduct disorder, including temperament style and cognitive abilities; those that become more important during adolescence include negative peer relationships and other social variables.

Anxiety disorders Internalizing disorders in which anxiety has gone from adaptive to pathological in terms of its intensity, duration, and pervasiveness; characterized by exaggerated and unrealistic fears and worries, overcontrol, inhibition, withdrawal, avoidance, and somatic symptoms.

Anxiety sensitivity The degree to which an individual focuses on signals of anxiety; involving hypervigilance and attention to bodily sensations, a tendency to focus on weak or infrequent sensations, and a disposition to react to somatic sensations with distorted cognitions.

Applied behavior analysis One of the most widely applied intervention strategies for autism spectrum disorder; an intensive behavioral approach, with near constant control and direction of the child and his/her environment.

Arenas of comfort The domains in which children express relative satisfaction with themselves and their accomplishments.

Assessment The systematic collection of relevant information in order to both differentiate everyday or transient difficulties from clinically significant psychopathology and classify a child's particular disorder(s).

Attention deficit/hyperactivity disorder (ADHD) A disorder characterized by a combination of impulsivity, hyperactivity, and inattentiveness.

Authority conflict pathway One of three potential developmental pathways for oppositional defiant disorder and conduct disorder, with stubborn and negativistic behaviors leading to more serious disobedience and hostility.

Autism spectrum disorder A broadly conceptualized category of disorder reflecting compromised development in social functioning and communication, as well as restricted patterns of activities or interests.

Avoidant (anxious/avoidant) attachment Form of insecure attachment that usually reflects ineffective or inappropriate caregiving.

Avoidant/restrictive food intake disorder Eating disturbance involving the lack of interest in or avoidance of food.

B

Barriers to care Factors that impede access to mental health services, including structural barriers such as lack of provider availability, inconveniently located services, transportation difficulties, inability to pay and/or inadequate insurance coverage; individual barriers such as denial of problems or lack of trust in the system; and sociocultural barriers such as the stigma of psychopathology or mental illness.

Behavior contingency management A school-based intervention of ADHD, utilizing behavioral techniques, designed to target multiple difficulties, including academic, behavioral, and social functioning.

Behavioral models Psychological models that emphasize the individual's observable behavior within a specific environment.

Behavioral parent training A psychosocial intervention for ADHD that focuses on parent-managed reinforcement of child behavior, especially in regard to core ADHD symptoms.

Behavioral phenotypes The outwardly observable behaviors (such as physical characteristics, cognitive and linguistic profiles, perceptual skills and deficits, socioemotional patterns, and overall outcomes) associated with an underlying genetic condition. Hypotheses about links between genotypes and phenotypes must be carefully investigated.

Binge drinking Heavy consumption of alcohol in a relatively short period of time with the primary intention of becoming intoxicated.

Binge eating disorder An eating disorder characterized by repeated episodes of binge eating, a sense of lack of control, and significant distress.

Bipolar disorder A mood disorder characterized by alternating periods of depression and mania, or hypomania.

Birth cohort Individuals born in a particular historical period who share key experiences and events.

Body dissatisfaction The degree to which a person is concerned or displeased with his or her physical appearance.

Body image A person's perception of his or her own physical appearance.

Body satisfaction The degree to which a person is accepting of, or pleased with, his or her physical appearance.

Bulimia nervosa A type of eating disorder characterized by recurrent episodes of binge eating, a sense of lack of control over eating during the episode, and recurrent inappropriate compensatory behavior in order to prevent weight gain, such as self-induced vomiting; misuse of laxatives, diuretics, enemas, or other medications; fasting; or excessive exercise. Self-evaluation is unduly influenced by body shape and weight.

Bullying The intentional infliction of physical or emotional harm through physical aggression, harassment, intimidation, teasing, or psychological coercion.

C

Callous–unemotional characteristics A set of personality traits characterized by a lack of empathy, concern, guilt, or remorse.

Categorical classification A clinical classification approach based on the identification of co-occurring symptoms reflecting distinct disorders.

Central coherence hypothesis A hypothesis based on the idea that most individuals attempt to perceive and construct meaning from information that is part of an environmental whole; information makes sense, or is coherent, because it is part of something larger than itself.

Child maltreatment *Not* a diagnosis that is assigned to a child, but a broad category including physical abuse, sexual abuse, psychological abuse, and neglect.

Child-onset subtype (conduct disorder) With childhood onset, the individual is usually diagnosed early and has a long history of negative personal and interpersonal behavior; this behavior deteriorates over time. With onset in adolescence, the individual's problem behavior emerges more abruptly and is more often time limited.

Chronic hassles Everyday, ongoing problems, such as struggles with homework or being teased at school, that are associated with depression and other disorders.

Classical conditioning A form of associative learning in which certain stimuli become paired with other stimuli resulting in the reliable elicitation of a response.

Classification A system for describing the important categories, groups, or dimensions of disorders.

Coercion model Model of ODD and CD, focused on the assumption that parents and children struggle for control over a number of everyday tasks and activities and that maladaptive parenting leads to children's externalizing behavior. The coercion model specifically examines a conditioning sequence in which children are inadvertently reinforced for their problematic behaviors.

Cognitive-behavioral therapy (CBT) A psychotherapy approach that attempts to remedy dysfunctional emotions, cognitions, and behaviors through goal-oriented, systematic, empirically based treatment techniques. CBT is based on the principles and empirical findings of learning theories and cognitive psychology.

Cognitive behavioral therapy—enhanced (CBT-E) A therapeutic approach to eating disorders focusing on identifying cognitions and behaviors that maintain the eating disorder and working with individuals to objectively consider their disorder and develop an individualized treatment plan.

Cognitive development The developmental course of internal mental processes such as perception, attention, memory, and concept formation.

Cognitive models Psychological models that focus on the components and processes of the mind and mental development.

Cognitive restructuring A main component of cognitive-behavioral therapy. The identification and modification of negative thoughts.

Cognitive-deficits model A model of addiction that integrates physiological and cognitive factors, this model is based on the idea that repeat, chronic drug use results in abnormalities in the prefrontal cortex, impairing judgment, decision making, and impulse control.

Cognitive-vulnerability stress model of depression A model that proposes that an individual's negative attributional style coupled with negative life events leads to depression.

Coherence From a developmental perspective, reflects the logical and meaningful links between early developmental variables and later outcomes.

Common factors model An alternative to the gateway hypothesis of drug use; the model assumes that there is a nonspecific propensity to use drugs.

Comorbidity The co-occurrence of two or more disorders in one individual.

Competence From a developmental perspective, reflects effective functioning in relation to relevant age-related tasks and issues; evaluations of competence are embedded in the environment within which development occurs.

Compulsions Persistent and intense impulses to perform a specific behavior.

Concurrent comorbidity When two or more disorders are experienced at the same time.

Conduct disorder (CD) A disorder characterized by a more severe pattern of negativistic, hostile, and defiant behavior that involves the violation of social norms and rules as well as the rights of others.

Conscience The internal guide to prosocial behavior, rooted in self-regulation, including both moral emotions and moral behavior.

Consistency The degree to which an individual characteristic or pattern is similar across situations.

Continuous models of psychopathology Models that emphasize the gradual transition from normal range of feelings, thoughts, and behaviors to clinically significant problems.

Continuous performance tests Tests often used as part of an ADHD assessment. These tests generally involve monitoring stimuli (visual, auditory, or both) and responding selectively to instructions; these tests measure various attention and impulse control skills, including the ability to remain vigilant, to demonstrate consistency of attentional focus, to respond quickly, and to inhibit responding.

Conversion disorder (Functional neurological symptom disorder) A type of anxiety disorder characterized by unexplained deficits in voluntary motor or sensory function that cannot be adequately accounted for by known pathophysiological mechanisms; psychological factors are clearly associated with the emergence of symptoms.

Coping Cognitive, emotional, and behavioral regulatory responses to manage stress.

Covert aggression Also called indirect aggression, it may include the externalizing behaviors observed in conduct disorder such as property damage or theft.

Covert pathway One of three potential developmental pathways for oppositional defiant disorder and conduct disorder, with minor misbehaviors leading to more serious delinquent acts that tend to be concealed or secretive.

Cross-sectional research Research that collects data at a single point in time, with comparisons made among groups of participants (e.g., 4-year-olds versus 8-year-olds versus 12-year-olds).

Cross-time reliability Measure of whether a child is similarly diagnosed by the same clinician at two different points in time.

D

Developmental cascades The cumulative consequences of interactions and transactions that spread across domains and over time.

Developmental cascade models For various forms of psychopathology, the multiple pathways that reflect the consequences of interactions and transactions that spread across domains and over time.

Developmental epidemiology Frequencies and patterns of distributions of disorders in infants, children, and adolescents.

Developmental pathways Trajectories that reflect children's adjustment and/or maladjustment in the context of growth and change over a lifetime.

Developmental psychopathology Intense, frequent, and/or persistent maladaptive patterns of emotion, cognition, and behavior considered within the context of normal development, resulting in the current and potential impairment of infants, children, and adolescents.

Developmental trauma disorder A disorder involving both exposure and adaptation to chronic trauma, with exposure often occurring in the context of a child's caregiving environment.

Developmental – difference debate A debate on the nature of cognitive disability. Proponents of the developmental side of the debate suggest that children with intellectual developmental disorder (IDD) possess similar cognitive structures and slowly progress in similar cognitive sequence to children without IDD. Proponents of the difference side of the debate propose that children with IDD think in qualitatively distinct (and deficient) ways; an emphasis on difference is often presented along with data on genetic etiologies of IDD.

Diagnosis The method of assigning children to specific classification categories.

Diagnostic and Statistical Manual (DSM) Published by the American Psychiatric Association, the DSM, now in its fifth edition, provides a listing of forms of mental illness along with diagnostic criteria.

Diagnostic efficiency The degree to which clinicians maximize diagnostic hits and minimize diagnostic misses.

Diathesis-stress model A model that emphasizes the combination of underlying predispositions (risk factors related to, for example, structural abnormalities or early occurring trauma) and additional factors (such as further physiological or environmental events) that lead to the development of psychopathology.

Differential diagnosis Decisions about mutually exclusive categories of disorder.

Differential susceptibility Differentiated vulnerability to stressful environments, as well as differentiated benefit from enriched and encouraging environments.

Dimensional classification A clinical classification system based on statistical techniques that identifies individuals along dimensions of adaptive and maladaptive functioning.

Discontinuous models of psychopathology Models that emphasize distinctive and/or qualitative differences between patterns of emotion, cognition, and behavior that are within the normal range, and those that exemplify clinical disorders.

Disinhibited social engagement disorder An attachment disorder characterized by an unusual lack of reticence with unfamiliar others or wariness in unfamiliar settings. Children with disinhibited social engagement disorder also exhibit socially superficial behavior and attention seeking and may initiate inappropriate physical contact (e.g., hugging, climbing into laps) with strangers.

Disruptive mood dysregulation disorder A childhood mood disorder involving severe, recurrent temper tantrums that are atypical with respect to intensity and frequency. In between tantrums, the mood of the child is persistently and pervasively irritable or angry.

Domains of competence Particular areas of skills and achievements such as academic achievement, behavioral competence, and social competence.

Down syndrome A developmental disorder caused by an extra chromosome 21 (i.e., trisomy 21), Down syndrome is among the most widely known genetically influenced forms of intellectual developmental disorder. Accompanying physical characteristics including distinctive facial features, heart problems, and poor muscle tone. Intellectual challenges almost always involve language difficulties; socioemotional functioning is often characterized by positive affect and extraversion.

Dysthymia A mood disorder characterized by long-standing disturbance of mood, with ongoing sadness, irritability, and lack of motivation; other symptoms involving emotion, cognition, and behavior may also be observed.

E

Eating disorders Psychopathologies characterized by severe disturbances in eating behaviors, disturbed perceptions of body size and shape, fear of being fat, and compensatory behaviors to lose weight or prevent weight gain.

Ecological models Models that emphasize the immediate environments, or "behavior settings," in which children grow and make sense of their lives including homes, classrooms, neighborhoods, and communities.

Effortful control Attempts by infants to regulate their own stimulation and response; an individual characteristic described in current continuous, or dimensional, models of temperament.

Emotional (or psychological) abuse A type of child maltreatment involving ongoing and extreme disregard or thwarting of basic emotional needs.

Emotion regulation Emotional control, involving the "modulation, toleration and endurance of emotions."

Empathizing-systemizing theory An etiological model of autism that suggests that the combination of below-average empathy skills and a high level of systemizing (reliance on analyzing and constructing systems) may underlie the characteristic symptoms of autism.

Epigenetics The effect of experience and environment on the regulation of gene expression. The resultant changes in gene expression can be transmitted across generations.

Equifinality Refers to developmental pathways in which differing beginnings and circumstances lead to similar outcomes.

Executive functions A set of processes that include working memory, internalization of speech, and self-regulation of emotion, which contribute to children's increasing control over their thoughts, feelings, and behaviors, and their interactions with others and their environments.

Exposure A main component of cognitive behavioral therapy for anxiety disorders. Exposure to the stimuli and situations that are associated with anxiety is systematic and controlled, with in vivo (real-life) practice preferred.

Extensive support (intellectual developmental disorder) Consistent and more comprehensive assistance in most life settings to maximize an individual's well-being, usually provided over one's lifetime.

External validity In the context of classification, external validity reflects the degree to which a diagnosis provides useful information about the implications (i.e., likely outcomes, effective treatments) of a disorder.

Externalizing dimension In the empirical, dimensional classification system, the externalizing dimension involves problematic patterns that are directed outward, toward others (e.g., disruptive or aggressive behavior).

Extreme male brain theory A genetic hypothesis for autism spectrum disorders; highlights the role of evolutionary sex-linked dimensions of brain functioning (such as the logical, systematic thinking characteristic of men and the relational empathy characteristic of women) and proposes that autism spectrum disorders may be an extreme example of the "normal" male profile.

F

Family models Models that emphasize that the best way to understand the personality and psychopathology of a particular child is to understand the dynamics of a particular family.

Fear of fatness, with compensatory behaviors A dimension of some types of eating disorders; combinations of this dimension with binge eating and drive for thinness correspond to the discrete syndromes of anorexia, bulimia, and binge eating disorder.

Fears Anxieties elicited in the presence of a specific stimulus.

Final common pathway There are multiple etiological factors leading to disorder, with the disorder as the result, or final common pathway, of combinations of different types of predisposing conditions and events.

Fixation–regression model Usually emphasized by psychodynamic theorists and clinicians, this model suggests that individuals who fail to work through developmental issues become stuck in the past.

Fragile X syndrome A developmental disorder caused by a mutation on the *FMR1* gene, fragile X syndrome is the most common type of inherited MR in boys, affecting 1 in 4,000 boys and 1 in 8,000 girls. Cognitive and language difficulties, as well as behavioral problems, are important features of the fragile X profile.

G

Gateway hypothesis A stage theory of drug involvement that proposes that the use of alcohol or marijuana acts as a gateway to the use of "harder" drugs such as cocaine, heroin, or methamphetamines.

General risk factor A risk factor associated with increased vulnerability to any, or many, possible disorders (see *nonspecific risk*).

Gene-by-environment (g × e) interactions The interactive effect between genetic and environmental factors, including the influence of genes on vulnerability to risk factors.

Generalized anxiety disorder A type of anxiety disorder characterized by excessive and unrealistic worries and fears about a variety of stimuli and situations.

Genetic counseling Process by which individuals at higher risk for inherited disorders are educated about the probabilities of having a child with the disorder; the medical, psychological, and family implications of the disorder; testing options; and resources for prevention, management, and/or family planning.

Genomics The mapping, sequencing, and analysis of genes and application of this data for medical, educational, and technological benefit (term coined by Thomas Roderick in 1986).

Genotype The genetic make-up of a cell, an organism, or an individual.

Goodness of fit The interplay between infant temperament and parenting.

Growth dysregulation hypothesis A hypothesis that proposes that the normally well-controlled process of brain growth and organization goes awry, leading to the clinical symptoms of autism spectrum disorders.

H

Heterotypic comorbidity Diagnoses from different classification groups (for instance, depression and conduct disorder).

Heterotypic continuity The underlying similarity of symptoms, relative to developmentally salient issues and tasks, over time despite changes in specific diagnoses.

Homotypic comorbidity Two or more diagnoses within a classification group (for instance, generalized anxiety disorder and specific phobia).

Homotypic continuity The stability of specific diagnoses and symptom patterns over time. For example anxious and internalizing symptoms present during preschool, childhood, and adolescence for the same individual.

Human Genome Project A collaborative effort by the Department of Energy and the National Institutes of Health to identify the approximately 30,000 genes in human DNA and determine the sequences of the three billion chemical base pairs that make up human DNA.

Humanistic models Psychological models that emphasize personally meaningful experiences, innate motivations for healthy growth, and the child's purposeful creation of a self.

Hypersensitive regulatory disorder Clinically significant difficulties and/or impairment related to heightened or exaggerated sensitivity to auditory, visual, and tactile stimulation.

Hypomania A mood disorder symptom characterized by problematic emotions, thoughts, and behaviors similar to mania, although there are no psychotic symptoms and the degree of impairment is less severe.

I

Individuals with Disabilities Education Act (IDEA) A federal law that defines and governs the provision of special education services.

Impaired social cognition Deficits and/or delays in the processing of social and emotional information and events.

Incentive-sensitization theory A two-stage explanation of addiction: (1) various substances alter brain organization and function and (2) these altered brain systems affect behavior in situations involving motivation and reward.

Incidence New cases of a type (or types) of disorder in a given time period.

Indicated preventive measures Type of preventive measure provided for groups with specific risk factors that include more extensive interventions (e.g., packages of services for families with premature infants).

Individualized education plans (IEPs) Educational plans designed for students with learning disabilities to improve specific academic skills and cognitive deficits.

Infant emotionality The latency to respond to emotional stimuli and the average and peak intensities of emotional response; a broad concept that encompasses aspects of *surgency*, *negative affectivity*, and *effortful control*.

Insecure attachment Forms of attachment (including resistant, avoidant, and disorganized) that reflect inconsistent, ineffective, or harmful caregiving behavior.

Instrumental aggression Aggression that is premeditated or planful. In most cases, instrumental aggression is a means to a particular end.

Intellectual development The general emergence of intellectual functioning, including specific patterns of strengths and weaknesses in cognitive functioning, resulting in individual differences.

Intellectual developmental disorder (IDD) A developmental disorder reflecting significant deficits in intellectual functioning and adaptive functioning.

Intellectual functioning A reflection of an individual's cognitive ability, including everyday and academic problem-solving abilities.

Internal validity In the context of classification, internal validity reflects the degree to which children with the same diagnosis have similar developmental histories and current symptom pictures.

Internalizing dimension In the empirical, dimensional classification system, the internalizing dimension involves problematic patterns that are directed inward, toward the self (e.g., anxiety or depression).

Interpersonal psychological theory of suicidality A theory of suicidality that postulates two general categories of risk: dysregulated impulse control and intense psychological pain.

Interpersonal therapies A relationship-focused therapeutic approach that focuses on salient age-related personal, social, and developmental issues in the context of topics such as loss, grief, and relationship difficulties.

Inter-rater reliability Measure of whether two or more clinicians, gathering information about one child's developmental history and current difficulties, come to the same decision about the type of disorder.

Interviews Either structured evaluations or unstructured conversations about adjustment and maladjustment, allowing parents and children to explain their concerns and, more broadly, to tell their stories. Interviews also provide opportunities to start to build the helping relationship, an especially important consideration when a clinician knows that he or she will be working closely with children and various family members.

J

Joint attention "Communicative intentions" such as eye contact, pointing, and shared attention, all of which smooth out the processes of social interaction and make it easier and more rewarding to participate in the social world.

K

Kindling model A hypothesis that explains why later episodes of depression often occur in the context of less severe stress: initial stress leads to vulnerability in the hypothalamic-pituitary-adrenal axis; and, over time, the increasingly sensitive neurological response system requires lower thresholds of stimulation to trigger a new episode.

L

Life-course persistent trajectory (LCP) From Moffitt's model of conduct disorder (CD) related to childhood-onset CD. Those with this trajectory are more likely to have a history of ODD and a family history of antisocial behavior, are more likely to display aggression, and have worse outcomes.

Longitudinal research The ongoing collection of data from the same group of participants, or the study of individuals over time.

M

Major depressive disorder A mood disorder in children, adolescents, and adults characterized by sadness and a loss of pleasure, with multiple cognitive, behavioral, and somatic symptoms, and impaired functioning.

Maltreatment *Not* a diagnosis that is assigned to a child, but a broad category including physical abuse, sexual abuse, psychological abuse, and neglect.

Mania Distinct periods characterized by unusual and persistent mood elevation, high activity levels, decreased need for sleep, increased irritability, extremely impulsive behaviors, and sometimes psychotic thinking.

Maudsley model of family therapy A therapeutic approach to eating disorders, generally used with adolescents, in which parents have a central role in treatment. Family structure and adolescent issues related to eating and weight gain are the focus of different phases of treatment.

Medical model of psychopathology Key assumptions of this model are that disorders are (1) categorical (i.e., reflecting clear distinctions between healthy and disordered adjustments), (2) associated with "constitutional dysfunction" (i.e., the idea that the child somehow fails to display his/her natural function), and (3) endogenous (i.e., characteristic of the individual, rather than an individual–environment transaction).

Mirror neuron system Mirror neuron activity is believed to underlie understanding of motor acts done by others as well as the intentions behind the actions. In children with autism spectrum disorder, dysfunction in the mirror neuron system may relate to deficits in social cognition.

Mixed category of regulatory disorder Clinically significant difficulties and/or impairment related to combinations of features of hypersensitive, underreactive, and motorically disorganized regulatory disorders.

Modeling A classic treatment for fears, based on the principles of observational learning, modeling involves watching, practicing, and imitating adaptive behavior.

Molecular genetics Studies of the effects of specific genes at the DNA level.

Mood-related continuum A range of distress and dysfunction related to problematic emotions, from short periods of sadness with minimal impairment, to longer periods with moderate impairment, to ongoing episodes of clinically significant depression with severe impairment.

Motivational interviewing A brief intervention for substance abuse incorporating aspects of motivational psychology, client-centered therapy, and stages-of-change theory.

Motorically disorganized, impulsive regulatory disorder Clinically significant difficulties and/or impairment related to impulsivity, frequent sensation-seeking behavior, or high-risk or destructive activity.

Multifinality Refers to developmental pathways in which similar beginnings and circumstances lead to different outcomes.

N

Negative affectivity Predispositions to experience fear and frustration/anger; an individual characteristic described in current continuous, or dimensional, models of temperament.

Negative life events Major stressful events, such as a parent losing a job or a serious illness in the family, associated with depression and other disorders.

Neglect A type of child maltreatment involving a failure to provide for physical, emotional, and/or educational needs of a child.

Neoconstructivist approach An emphasis on evolutionary contexts, experience–expectant learning, and both qualitative and quantitative change across development.

Neural plasticity The ability of the brain to flexibly respond to physiological and environmental challenges and insults.

Nonorganic causes (intellectual developmental disorder) Also referred to as familial or cultural-familial intellectual developmental disorder that involve multiple factors, including variations in the normal distribution of intellectual functioning and risk variables such as poverty.

Nonshared environment The aspects of family life and function that are specific and distinct for each child.

Nonspecific risk Increased vulnerability to any, or many, kinds of disorders.

O

Observational learning A form of learning that occurs by watching, remembering, and/or imitating others.

Observations A source of valuable information involving careful watching by a clinician. Clinicians usually observe children in clinical settings such as offices, but may also observe children in naturalistic settings such as the home or school.

Obsessions Persistent and intense intrusions of unwanted thoughts or images.

Obsessive-compulsive disorder A type of anxiety disorder characterized by intrusive thoughts that lead to anxiety and ritual behaviors that are intended to reduce anxiety.

Operant conditioning A form of learning in which consequences (negative or positive) lead to changes (decreases or increases) in behavior.

Oppositional defiant disorder (ODD) A disorder characterized by a sustained pattern of negativistic, hostile, and defiant behavior.

Optimal adaptation With respect to children's functioning, optimal adaptation refers to functioning that is excellent, superior, or "the best of what is possible."

Organic causes (intellectual developmental disorder) Associated with a specific physiological or physical origin, usually associated with more severe forms of intellectual developmental disorder, and observed across all family and socioeconomic status backgrounds. Organic explanations may be either genetic or environmental.

Outcome research Studies of whether, at the end of treatment, children and adolescents have improved relative to their pre-treatment status compared to others who have not received treatment.

Overt aggression Also called aggression, involves harmful physical behaviors.

Overt pathway One of three potential developmental pathways for oppositional defiant disorder and conduct disorder, with minor forms and consequences of aggression leading to more serious forms and consequences of aggression.

Overt/covert dimension A continuum that reflects the degree to which a particular behavior or pattern of behavior is observable (i.e., overt) or secret (i.e., covert).

P

Panic disorder A type of anxiety disorder characterized by recurrent, somewhat unpredictable panic attacks (i.e., extremely intense and often frightening episodes of anxiety).

Parasuicide Includes many behaviors, from less dangerous gestures to serious but unsuccessful suicide attempts; this term is increasingly preferred over *attempted suicide* because the motives and intentions of individuals are often difficult to identify.

Pathways of parental impact Three ways in which parents influence the development of child depression: (1) parent depression affects parent–child relationships and interactions and leads to child psychopathology; (2) parent depression affects family relationships and interactions and family disruptions, and these lead to child psychopathology; (3) parent depression affects marital satisfaction, leading to child psychopathology.

Peer contagion A drawback of group adolescent treatments, peer contagion involves the sharing of information about conduct disorders, substance abuse disorders, as well as providing immediate and powerful reinforcement of deviancy.

Perfectionism A personal standard or attitude that involves setting unrealistic goals and a sense of failure and/or worthlessness when those goals are not met; in individuals with eating disorders, perfectionism often accompanies obsessionality and leads to the "relentless pursuit of the thin ideal."

Phenotype The observable characteristics of an individual.

Phobic disorders Types of anxiety disorders characterized by excessive and unrealistic fears of particular objects or situations, intense anxiety in the presence of such objects or situations, and avoidant behaviors.

Physical abuse A type of child maltreatment involving physical aggression that results in pain, injury, or bodily harm.

Physical dependence Susceptibility to withdrawal symptoms; occurs only in combination with tolerance.

Physiological models Models of psychopathology that emphasize biological processes, such as genes and neurological systems, as being at the core of human experience; physiological models explain the development of psychopathology, its course, and its treatment in terms of biological factors.

Pica The ingestion of nonfood substances such as paint, pebbles, or dirt.

Polygenic model An etiological model of disorders based on the cumulative and additive effect of multiple genes.

Poly-victimization The experience of children exposed to high levels of many types of victimization.

Positive psychology A field of psychology focusing on "positive subjective experience, positive individual traits, and positive institutions" that seeks to promote individual, family, social, and community well-being.

Posttraumatic growth An adaptive response to trauma characterized by positive changes.

Posttraumatic stress disorder (PTSD) A disorder characterized by a severe and ongoing pattern of anxiety and avoidance, lasting longer than one month, following exposure to a traumatic event.

Prevalence All current cases of a type (or types) of disorder.

Primary prevention Reducing or eliminating psychopathology-related risks, thereby reducing the incidence of disorder in children.

Problem behavior syndrome Described by Jessor, the proposition that adolescents who are at risk for one problem behavior are likely to be at risk for others, and the observation that problem behaviors tend to cluster in adolescence.

Problem solving A main component of cognitive-behavioral therapy. A step-by-step, active, behaviorally oriented approach for coping.

Process research Studies of the specific mechanisms and common factors that account for therapeutic change.

Projective measures Measures such as the Rorschach inkblots and the Thematic Apperception Test that are based on the assumption that, given an ambiguous stimulus, individuals' responses will reflect the projection of unconscious conflicts.

Prosocial behaviors Behaviors that benefit self, others, and society.

Protective factors The individual, family, and social characteristics that are associated with the positive adaptation of resiliency.

Psychodynamic models Psychological models that emphasize unconscious cognitive, affective, and motivational processes; mental representations of self, others, and relationships; the subjectivity of experience; and a developmental perspective on individual adjustment and maladjustment.

Psychoeducation A main component of psychotherapy, psychoeducation provides children and their families with information about symptoms of disorders, about the emergence and maintenance of disorder, and about the theoretical and practical aspects of various interventions.

Psychological dependence A craving or compulsion to use a substance despite significant harm.

Psychopathology Intense, frequent, and/or persistent maladaptive patterns of emotion, cognition, and behavior that are associated with significant distress and/or impairment in functioning.

Q

Quantitative genetics Studies of the relative impact of genetic and environmental factors on specific characteristics.

R

Reactive aggression Angry and impulsive aggression that occurs in response to a provocation.

Reactive attachment disorder A rare attachment disorder involving lack of organized attachment behaviors and reduced social engagement. Diagnosed in children with very adverse childcare experiences.

Reactivity An infant's excitability and responsiveness, including individual variations in emotions and behaviors.

Regulation What an infant does to control his or her reactivity, as well as the degree to which a distressed infant accepts comfort from others.

Reinforced exposure The application of reward following desired behavior.

Reinforcement The idea that positive and negative consequences lead to changes in behavior; a critical component of all learning processes.

Reinforcement model Based on the principles of operant conditioning, behavior is maintained, or changed, in response to positive or negative consequences.

Reliability Measure of whether different clinicians, using the same set of criteria, classify children into the same clearly defined categories.

Resiliency Adaptation (or competence) despite adversity.

Resistant (anxious/ambivalent) attachment Form of insecure attachment that usually reflects inconsistent caregiving.

Risk Increased vulnerability to disorder.

Risk factors The individual, family, and social characteristics that are associated with increased vulnerability, or risk.

Risk taking A disregard or indifference to the consequences of a behavior or situation; in less problematic terms, the disjunction between novelty seeking and competent self-regulation.

Restricted, repetitive behaviors and fixated interests Among the core, defining symptoms of autism spectrum disorder. These behaviors and focused interests appear to be associated with anxiety—both the direct experience of anxiety and attempts to manage or minimize the experience of anxiety.

Rumination The repeated chewing and regurgitation of food.

S

Secondary prevention Interventions that are implemented following the early signs of distress and dysfunction, before the disorder is clearly established in the child.

Secure attachment Form of attachment that results from consistent, sensitive responsiveness by the caregiver to the infant's physical, emotional, and social needs.

Selective preventive measures Type of preventive measures; provided for at-risk groups (e.g., Head Start programs for preschoolers from disadvantaged backgrounds).

Self-injurious behavior/self-harm Deliberate infliction of pain or injury to oneself, without suicidal intent.

Self-medication The use of drugs to improve mood, increase cognitive function, and deal with difficulties or consequences of other disorders; not specifically prescribed, directed, or supervised by a psychiatrist or physician.

Self-regulation Control of one's emotions, cognitions, and behaviors, involving both automatic and controlled processes.

Self-talk A cognitive technique focused on providing positive self-statements such as "I am brave" to enhance appropriate behaviors.

Separation anxiety disorder A type of anxiety disorder characterized by intense age-inappropriate distress when separated from the caregiver, as well as clingy behaviors in the presence of the caregiver; associated with significant impairment in a child's daily functioning.

Sexual abuse A type of child maltreatment involving sexual contact or attempted sexual contact between an adult and a child.

Shared environment The aspects of family life and function that are shared by all children in the family.

Sleep–wake disorders Clinically significant difficulties related to falling and staying asleep, or sleep dysfunctions, associated with impairment in development and functioning.

Social and communication deficits Deficits in social–emotional reciprocity, in nonverbal communication, and in developing and maintaining relationships.

Social cognition Psychological construct involving the processing of social and emotional information and events; this processing is observed at the intersections of self and other, emotion and cognition, and language and meaning.

Social phobia A type of anxiety disorder characterized by an intense fear of scrutiny or evaluation by others.

Sociocultural models Models that emphasize the importance of the social context, including gender, race, ethnicity, and socioeconomic status, in the development, course, and treatment of psychopathology.

Sociocultural norms The beliefs and expectations of certain groups about what kinds of emotions, cognitions, and/or behaviors are undesirable or unacceptable.

Somatic management A main component of cognitive-behavioral therapy for anxiety disorders. It involves targeting the distressing physiological symptoms and is usually focused on relaxation and breathing techniques. In addition, children and adolescents learn how to predict and tolerate the anxiety that accompanies challenging and stressful events.

Somatization A term that refers to a variety of processes in which an individual experiences physical symptoms, such as pain or loss of function, for which a physical cause cannot be found or, if present, cannot fully account for the level of impairment.

Somatic symptom disorders Disorders characterized by the expression of anxiety through physical symptoms, such as headaches and abdominal pain, leading to clinically significant distress and impairment.

Specific learning disorder Disorders characterized by unexpected underachievement in reading, written expression, and mathematics.

Specific phobias A type of anxiety disorder characterized by particular fear of an object, situation, or person (e.g., animals, injury or blood, natural phenomena).

Specific risk Increased vulnerability to one particular disorder.

Stability The degree to which an individual characteristic or pattern is similar over time.

Standardized tests Measures such as intelligence tests and some personality tests, in which the data from a particular child can be compared to data gathered from large samples of children, including normally developing children and those with a variety of diagnoses.

Statistical deviance Compared to the distribution in a particular sample, statistical deviance refers to the relative infrequency of certain emotions, cognitions, and/or behaviors.

Stigmatization Negative attitudes (such as blaming or overconcern with dangerousness), emotions (such as shame, fear, or pity), and behaviors (such as ridicule or isolation) related to psychopathology and mental illness.

Strange Situation A carefully designed laboratory assessment in which toddlers are challenged to regulate themselves and use their caregivers or an unfamiliar adult for assistance and support. The child's emotional and behavioral patterns in response to these challenges are interpreted to reflect underlying attachment relationships that are classified as secure, insecure avoidant, insecure resistant, and disorganized.

Stress Physical and psychological response to adjustive demands that exceed coping resources.

Successive comorbidity When disorders are experienced sequentially, one after the other.

Suicidal ideation Involves a variety of cognitions from fleeting thoughts that life is not worth living to specific plans for killing oneself.

Suicidality A broad term that refers to the risk of suicidal ideation (thinking about suicide) as well as the risk for suicidal behavior (attempted or completed suicide).

Suicide The intentional taking of one's own life.

Surgency Extraversion; an individual characteristic described in current continuous, or dimensional, models of temperament.

Systematic desensitization A classic treatment for fears based on the principles of classical conditioning; involves teaching an anxious child how to relax and how to maintain relaxation when exposed to the feared stimulus. Exposure is done gradually (i.e., systematically, from stuffed dogs to videos of dogs to real dogs), building on the child's successes over time.

T

Temperament Variations in newborns' styles of reactivity (e.g., attention, activity, moods, and distress) and regulation of reactivity.

Tertiary prevention Interventions that are implemented for already present and clinically significant disorders.

Theory of mind The ability to attribute mental states to others.

Tolerance Occurs when the central nervous system (CNS) gradually becomes less responsive to stimulation by particular drugs; individuals then need to ingest higher and higher doses to achieve the same CNS effects.

Transactional model A recent revision and expansion of the coercion model that asserts that parent–child incompatibility is multiply determined, with multiple pathways to both externalizing and internalizing disorders, multiple interventions, and multiple outcomes.

Translational research Research designed, conducted, and interpreted with meaningful applications and social value in mind.

Tripartite model A model of anxiety and depression with three core concepts: (1) anxiety and depression share a common underlying factor of negative affectivity; (2) along with negative affectivity, low levels of positive affectivity are associated with depression; and (3) along with negative affectivity, high levels of physiological arousal are associated with anxiety.

Tripartite influence model of eating disorders A model of eating disorders that proposes that parent, peer, and media factors influence the development of body dissatisfaction and eating problems through two mechanisms: the internalization of the thin ideal and appearance comparison processes.

Two-factor model A model of ADHD emphasizing two distinct factors that underlie impairments: inattention and hyperactivity/impulsivity.

U

Underreactive regulatory disorder Clinically significant difficulties and/or impairment related to lack of interest and responsivity, limited exploration, and lagging skills in organizational processing.

Universal measures Prevention strategies, such as early child education programs, for attachment disorders in the general population.

Universal preventive measures Type of preventive measure provided for entire populations (e.g., mandatory immunizations for children).

V

Validity Measure of whether the classification gives us true-to-life, meaningful information.

W

Williams syndrome A developmental disorder caused by a microdeletion on chromosome 7, Williams syndrome is characterized by deficits in general cognitive function and visual–spatial skills, and relative strengths in language and music domains.

Withdrawal symptoms Noxious physical and psychological effects caused by reduction or cessation of substance intake (e.g., sleep disturbances, headaches, nausea and vomiting, tremors and restlessness, anxiety and depression); these symptoms can range from relatively mild to life threatening.

Worries Anxieties about possible future events.

References

Aaron, R., Joseph, A., Abraham, S., Muliyii, J., George, K., Prasad, J., et al. (2004). Suicides in young people in rural southern India. *Lancet, 363*(9415), 1117–1118.

Aarons, G. A., Brown, S. A., Garland, A. F., & Hough, R. L. (2004). Race/ethnic disparity and correlates of substance abuse service utilization and juvenile justice involvement among adolescents with substance use disorders. *Journal of Ethnicity in Substance Abuse, 3*, 47–64.

Abaied, J. L., & Rudolph, K. D. (2010). Parents as a resource in times of stress: Interactive contributions of socialization of coping and stress to youth psychopathology. *Journal of Abnormal Child Psychology, 38*, 273–289.

Abbeduto, L., Brady, N., & Kover, S. T. (2007). Language development and fragile X syndrome: Profiles, syndrome-related specificity, and within-syndrome differences. *Mental Retardation and Developmental Disabilities Research Reviews, 13*, 36–46.

Abbeduto, L., & Hagerman, R. J. (1997). Language and communication in fragile X syndrome. *Mental Retardation and Developmental Disabilities Research Reviews, 3*, 313–322.

Abbeduto, L., Warren, S. F., & Conners, F. A. (2007). Language development in Down syndrome: From the prelinguistic period to the acquisition of literacy. *Mental Retardation and Developmental Disabilities Research Reviews, 13*, 247–261.

Abel, E. L. (1998a). Prevention of alcohol abuse-related birth effects: I. Public education efforts. *Alcohol and Alcoholism, 33*, 411–416.

Abel, E. L. (1998b). Prevention of alcohol abuse-related birth effects: II. Targeting and pricing. *Alcohol and Alcoholism, 33*, 417–420.

Aber, J. L., Jones, S. M., & Raver, C. C. (2007). Poverty and child development: New perspectives on a defining issue. In J. L. Aber, S. J. Bishop-Josef, S. M. Jones, K. T. McLearn, & D. A. Phillips (Eds.), *Child Development and Social Policy: Knowledge for action* (pp. 149–166). Washington, DC: American Psychological Association.

Aberson, B., Shure, M.B., & Goldstein, S. (2007). Social problem-solving intervention can help children with ADHD. *Journal of Attention Disorders, 11*, 4–7.

Abosi, O. (2007). Educating children with learning disabilities in Africa. *Learning Disabilities Research & Practice, 22*, 196–201.

Abraham, H. D., & Fava, M. (1999). Order of onset of substance abuse and depression in a sample of depressed outpatients. *Comprehensive Psychiatry, 40*, 44–50.

Abroms, L., Simons-Morton, B., Haynie, D. L., & Chen, R. (2005). Psychosocial predictors of smoking trajectories during middle and high school. *Addiction, 100*, 852–861.

Achenbach, T. M. (1966). The classification of children's psychiatric symptoms: A factor-analytic study. *Psychological Monographs: General and Applied, 80*, 1–37.

Achenbach, T. M. (1982). *Developmental Psychopathology* (2nd ed.). New York: Wiley.

Achenbach, T. M. (1990). What is "developmental" about developmental psychopathology? In J. E. Rolf & A. S. Masten (Eds.), *Risk and protective factors in the development of psychopathology* (pp. 29–48). New York: Cambridge University Press.

Achenbach, T. M. (1991). The derivation of taxonomic constructs: A necessary stage in the development of developmental psychopathology. In D. Cicchetti & S. L. Toth (Eds.), *Rochester Symposium on Developmental Psychopathology,*

Vol. 3: Models and integrations (pp. 43–74). Rochester, NY: University of Rochester Press.

Achenbach, T. M. (1993). Taxonomy and comorbidity of conduct problems: Evidence from empirically based approaches. *Development and Psychopathology, 5*, 51–64.

Achenbach, T. M. (1995a). Diagnosis, assessment, and comorbidity in psychosocial treatment research. *Journal of Abnormal Child Psychology, 23*, 45–65.

Achenbach, T. M. (1995b). Empirically based assessment and taxonomy: Applications to clinical research. *Psychological Assessment, 7*, 261–274.

Achenbach, T. M., & Edelbrock, C. S. (1983). Behavioral problems and competencies reported by parents of normal and disturbed children aged four through sixteen. *Monographs of the Society for Research in Child Development, 46*, 1–82.

Achenbach, T. M., & Howell, C. T. (1993). Are American children's problems getting worse? A 13-year comparison. *Journal of the American Academy of Child and Adolescent Psychiatry, 32*, 1145–1154.

Achenbach, T. M., Howell, C. T., McConaughy, S. H., & Stanger, C. (1995b). Six-year predictors of problems in a national sample of children and youth: II. Signs of disturbance. *Journal of the American Academy of Child and Adolescent Psychiatry, 34*, 488–498.

Achenbach, T. M., Howell, C. T., McConaughy, S. H., & Stanger, C. (1995c). Six-year predictors of problems in a national sample of children and youth: III. Transitions to young adult syndromes. *Journal of the American Academy of Child and Adolescent Psychiatry, 34*, 658–669.

Achenbach, T. M., Howell, C. T., McConaughy, S. H., & Stanger,C. (1995a). Six-year predictors of problems in a national sample of children and youth: I. Cross-informant syndromes. *Journal of the American Academy of Child and Adolescent Psychiatry, 34*, 336–347.

Achenbach, T. M., Howell, C. T., Quay, H. C., & Conners, C. K. (1991). National survey of problems and competencies among four- to sixteen-year-olds: Parents' reports for normative and clinical samples. *Monographs of the Society for Research in Child Development, 56*, v–120.

Achenbach, T. M., & Rescorla, L. A. (2007). *Multicultural understanding of child and adolescent psychopathology.* New York: Guilford Press.

Ackard, D. M., & Neumark-Sztainer, D. (2002). Date violence and date rape among adolescents: Associations with disordered eating behaviors and psychological health. *Child Abuse and Neglect, 26*, 455–473.

Adams, R. E., Bukowski, W. M., & Bagwell, C. (2005). Stability of aggression during early adolescence as moderated by reciprocated friendship status and friend's aggression. *International Journal of Behavioral Development, 29*, 139–145.

Adams, R.E., Santo, J.B., & Bukowski, W.M. (2011). The presence of a best friend buffers the effects of negative experiences. *Developmental Psychology, 47*, 1786–1791.

Agrawal, A., Madden, P. A. F., Heath, A. C., Andrew, C., Lynskey,M. T., Bucholz, K. K., & Martin, N. G. (2005). Correlates of regular cigarette smoking in a population-based sample of Australian twins. *Addiction, 100*, 1709–1719.

Agrawal, A., Neale, M. C., Jacobson, K. C., Prescott, C. A., & Kendler, K. S. (2005). Illicit drug use and abuse/dependence: Modeling of two-stage variables using the CCC approach. *Addictive Behaviors, 30,* 1043–1048.

Agrawal, A., Neale, M. C., Prescott, C. A., & Kendler, K. S. (2004). Cannabis and other illicit drugs: Comorbid use and abuse/dependence in males and females. *Behavior Genetics, 34,* 217–228.

Ahmed, F.S., & Miller, S. (2011). Executive function mechanisms of theory of mind. *Journal of Autism and Developmental Disorders, 41,* 667–678.

Ahrano, J. (1997). Type III: Motor processing—Impulsive, motorically disorganized. In A. Lieberman, S. Wieder, & E. Fenichel (Eds.), *DC: 0–3 Casebook* (pp. 245–266). Washington, DC: Zero to Three: National Center for Infants, Toddlers, and Families.

Ainsworth, M. D. S. (1969). Object relations, dependency, and attachment: A theoretical view of the infant-mother relationship. *Child Development, 40,* 969–1025.

Ainsworth, M. D. S. (1979). Infant-mother attachment. *American Psychologist, 34,* 932–937.

Ainsworth, M. D. S., Bell, S. M., & Stayton, D. J. (1974). Infant-mother attachment and social development: Socialisation as a product of reciprocal responsiveness to signals. In M. J. M. Richards (Ed.), *The integration of a child into a social world* (pp. 99–135). London: Cambridge University Press.

Ainsworth, M. D. S., Blehar, M. C., Waters, E., & Wall, S. (1978). *Patterns of attachment: A psychological study of the strange situation.* Oxford, England: Erlbaum.

Alarcon, M., Plomin, R., Fulker, D. W., Corley, R., & DeFries, J.C. (1998). Multivariate path analysis of specific cognitive abilities date at 12 years of age in the Colorado Adoption Project. *Behavior Genetics, 28,* 255–264.

Alarcon, R. D., Bell, C. C., Kirmayer, L. J., Lin, K., Ustun, B., & Wisner, K. L. (2002). Beyond the funhouse mirrors: Research agenda on culture and psychiatric diagnosis. In D. J. Kupfer, M. B. First, & D. A. Regier (Eds.), *A research agenda for DSM-V* (pp. 219–282). Washington, DC: American Psychiatric Association.

Albano, A. M., Chorpita, B. F., & Barlow, D. H. (2003). Childhood anxiety disorders. In E. J. Mash & R. A. Barkley (Eds.), *Child psychopathology* (2nd ed., pp. 279–329). New York: Guilford Press.

Albano, A. M., & Hayward, C. (2004). Social anxiety disorder. In T. H. Ollendick & J. S. March (Eds.), *Phobic and anxiety disorders in children and adolescents: A clinician's guide to effective psychosocial and pharmacological interventions* (pp. 198–235). New York: Oxford University Press.

Albano, A. M., & Kendall, P. C. (2002). Cognitive behavioural therapy for children and adolescents with anxiety disorders: Clinical research advances. *International Review of Psychiatry, 14,* 129–134.

Albert, D., & Steinberg, L. (2011). Judgment and decision making in adolescence. *Journal of Research on Adolescence, 21,* 211–224.

Aldred, C., Green, J., & Adams, C. (2004). A new social communication intervention for children with autism: Pilot randomized controlled treatment study suggesting effectiveness. *Journal of Child Psychology and Psychiatry, 45,* 1420–1430.

Alegria, M., Carson, N.J., Goncalves, M., & Keefe, K. (2011). Disparities in treatment for substance use disorders and co-occuring disorders for ethnic/racial minority youth. *Journal of the American Academy of Child & Adolescent Psychiatry, 50,* 22–31.

Alfano, C. A., Beidel, D. C., & Turner, S. M. (2002). Cognition in childhood anxiety: Conceptual methodological and developmental issues. *Clinical Psychology Review, 22,* 1209–1238.

Alfano, C.A., & Gamble, A.L. (2009). The role of sleep in childhood psychiatric disorders. *Child Youth Care Forum, 38,* 327–340.

Allan, N.P., & Lonigan, C.J. (2011). Examining the dimensionality of effortful control in preschool children and its relation to academic and socioeconomic indicators. *Developmental Psychology, 47,* 905–915.

Allen, J. P., Moore, C., Kupermine, G., & Bell, K. (1998). Attachment and adolescent psychosocial functioning. *Child Development, 69,* 1406–1419.

Amaral, D.G., Schumann, C.M., & Nordhal, C.W. (2008). Neuroanatomy of autism. *Trends in Neurosciences, 3,* 137–145.

Amaro, H., Blake, S.M., Schwartz, P.M. & Flinchbaugh, L.J. (2001). Developing theory-based substance abuse prevention programs for young adolescent girls. *Journal of Early Adolescence, 21,* 256–293.

Amaya-Jackson, L., Reynolds, V., Murray, M. C., McCarthy, G., Nelson, A., Cherney, M. S., et al. (2003). Cognitive-behavioral treatment for pediatric posttraumatic stress disoders: Protocol and application in school and community settings. *Cognitive and Behavioral Practice, 10,* 204–213.

American Academy of Child & Adolescent Psychiatry (AACAP). (2010). Practice parameter for the assessment and treatment of children and adolescents with posttraumatic stress disorder. *Journal of the American Academy of Child & Adolescent Psychiatry, 49,* 414–430.

American Association on Mental Retardation/American Association on Intellectual and Developmental Disabilities. (2002). *Mental retardation: Definition, classification and systems of support.* Washington, DC: American Association on Intellectual and Developmental Disabilities.

American Psychiatric Association. (2013). *Diagnostic and statistical manual of mental disorders* (5th ed.). Washington, DC.

American Psychiatric Association Work Group on Eating Disorders. (2000). Practice guidelines for the treatment of patients with eating disorders (revision). *American Journal of Psychiatry, 157,* 1–39.

Ametller, L., Castro, J., Serrano, E., Martinez, E., & Toro, J. (2005). Readiness to recover in adolescent anorexia nervosa: Prediction of hospital admission. *Journal of Child Psychology and Psychiatry, 46,* 394–400.

Anagnostaras, S. G., Craske, M. G., & Fanselow, M. S. (1999). Anxiety: At the intersection of genes and experience. *Nature Neuroscience, 2,* 780–782.

Anders, T. E., & Dahl, R. (2007). Classifying sleep disorders in infants and toddlers. In W. E. Narrow, M. B. First, P. J. Sirovatka, & D. A. Regier (Eds.), *Age and gender considerations in psychiatric diagnosis: A research agenda for DSM-V* (pp. 215–226). Arlington, VA: American Psychiatric Publishing.

Anders, T. E., Goodlin-Jones, B., & Sadeh, A. (2000). Sleep disorders. In C. H. Zeanah, Jr. (Ed.), *Handbook of infant mental health* (2nd ed., pp. 326–338). New York: Guilford Press.

Andersen, S. L., & Navalta, C. P. (2004). Altering the course of neurodevelopment: A framework for understanding the enduring effects of psychotropic drugs. *International Journal of Developmental Neuroscience, 22,* 423–440.

Anderson, C. B., & Bulik, C. M. (2004). Gender differences in compensatory behaviors, weight, shape salience, and drive for thinness. *Eating Behaviors, 5,* 1–11.

Anderson, D. A., Lundgren, J. D., Shapiro, J. R., & Paulosky, C. A. (2004). Assessment of eating disorders: Review and recommendations for clinical use. *Behavior Modifi cation, 28,* 763–782.

Anderson, E. & Hope, D.A. (2008). A review of the tripartite model for understanding the link between anxiety and depression in youth. *Clinical Psychology Review, 28,* 275–287.

Anderson, G. (1998). Creating moral space in prenatal genetic services. *Qualitative Health Reasearch, 8,* 168–187.

Anderson, M. (1998). Mental retardation, general intelligence, and modularity. *Learning and Individual Differences, 10,* 159–178.

Anderson, M. (2001). Conceptions of intelligence. *Journal of Child Psychology and Psychiatry, 42,* 287–298.

Anderson, M. (2007). Biology and intelligence—The race/IQ controversy. In S. Della Sala (Ed.), *Tall Tales about the Mind & Brain: Separating fact from fiction* (pp. 123–147). New York: Oxford University Press.

Anderson, M. (2008). What can autism and dyslexia tell us about intelligence? *Quarterly Journal of Experimental Psychology, 61,* 116–128.

Anderson-Fye, E. P. (2004). A "Coca-Cola" shape: Cultural change, body image, and eating disorders in San Andres, Belize. *Culture, Medicine and Psychiatry, 28,* 561–595.

Angold, A., & Costello, E. J. (1996a). The relative diagnostic utility of child and parent reports of oppositional defiant behaviors. *International Journal of Methods in Psychiatric Research, 6,* 253–259.

Angold, A., Costello, E. J., & Erkanli, A. (1999). Comorbidity. *Journal of Child Psychology and Psychiatry and Allied Disciplines, 40,* 57–87.

Angold, A., Costello, E. J., Erkanli, A., & Worthman, C. M. (1999). Pubertal changes in hormone levels and depression in girls. *Psychological Medicine, 29,* 1043–1053.

Angold, A., Costello, E. J., & Worthman, C. M. (1998). Puberty and depression: The roles of age, pubertal status and pubertal timing. *Psychological Medicine, 28,* 51–61.

Angold, A., & Costello, E.J. (2009). Nosology and measurement in child and adolescent psychiatry. *Journal of Child Psychology and Psychiatry, 50,* 9–15.

Angold, A., & Costello, J. (1996b). Toward establishing an empirical basis for the diagnosis of oppositional defiant disorder. *Journal of the American Academy of Child and Adolescent Psychiatry, 35,* 1205–1212.

Angold, A., Erkanli, A., Costello, E. J., & Rutter, M. (1996). Precision, reliability and accuracy in the dating of symptom onsets in child and adolescent psychopathology. *Journal of Child Psychology and Psychiatry and Allied Disciplines, 37,* 657–664.

Angold, A., & Fisher, P. W. (1999). Interviewer-based interviews. In D. Shaffer & C. P. Lewis (Eds.), *Diagnostic assessment in child and adolescent psychopathology* (pp. 34–64). New York: Guilford Press.

Angold, A., Worthman, C., & Costello, E. J. (2003). Puberty and depression. In C. Hayward (Ed.), *Gender differences at puberty* (pp. 137–164). New York: Cambridge University Press.

Anthony, E. J. (1974). The syndrome of the psychologically invulnerable child. In E. J. Anthony & C. Koupernik (Eds.), *The child in his family: Children at psychiatric risk* (pp. 529–545). New York: Wiley.

Anthony, J. L., Lonigan, C. J., Hooe, E. S., & Phillips, B. M. (2002). An affect-based, hierarchical model of temperament and its relations with internalizing symptomatology. *Journal of Clinical Child and Adolescent Psychology, 31,* 480–490.

Antshel, K.M., & Barkley, R. (2008). Psychosocial interventions in attention deficit hyperactivity disorder. *Child and Adolescent Psychiatric Clinics of North America, 17,* 421–437.

Appleyard, K., Egeland, B., van Dulmen, M.H.M., & Sroufe, L.A. (2005). When more is not better: The role of cumulative risk in child behavior outcomes. *Journal of Child Psychology and Psychiatry, 46,* 235–245.

Apter, A. (2003). Biological factors influencing suicidal behavior in adolescents. In R. A. King & A. Apter (Eds.), *Suicide in children and adolescents* (pp. 118–149). New York: Cambridge University Press.

Apter, A., & Wasserman, D. (2003). Suicide in children and adolescents. In R. A. King & A. Apter (Eds.), *Suicide in children and adolescents* (pp. 63–85). New York: Cambridge University Press.

Archer, J. (2004). Sex differences in aggression in real-world settings: A meta-analytic review. *Review of General Psychology, 8,* 291–322.

Armitage, R., Hoffmann, R., Emslie, G., Rintelman, J., Moore, J., & Lewis, K. (2004). Rest-activity cycles in childhood and adolescent depression. *Journal of the American Academy of Child and Adolescent Psychiatry, 43,* 761–769.

Armitage, R., Hoffmann, R. F., Emslie, G. J., Weinberg, W. A., Mayes, T. L., & Rush, A. J. (2002). Sleep microarchitecture as a predictor of recurrence in children and adolescents with depression. *International Journal of Neuropsychopharmacology, 5,* 217–228.

Armstrong, T. D., & Costello, E. J. (2002). Community studies on adolescent substance use, abuse, or dependence and psychiatric comorbidity. *Journal of Consulting and Clinical Psychology, 70,* 1224–1239.

Arnett, J. J. (1999). Adolescent storm and stress, reconsidered. *American Psychologist, 54,* 317–326.

Arnett, J. J. (2000). Emerging adulthood: A theory of development from the late teens through the twenties. *American Psychologist, 55,* 469–480.

Arnett, J. J. (2007). *Adolescence and emerging adulthood: A cultural approach.* Upper Saddle River, NJ: Pearson/Prentice Hall.

Arnold, L. E., Chuang, S., Davies, M., Abikoff, H. B., Conners, C. K., Elliot, G. R., et al. (2004). Nine months of multicomponent behavioral treatment for ADHD and effectiveness of MTA fading procedures. *Journal of Abnormal Child Psychology, 32,* 39–51.

Arnold, L. E., Elliott, M., Sachs, L., Bird, H., Kraemer, H. C., Wells, K. C., et al. (2003). Effects of ethnicity on treatment attendance, stimulant response/dose, and 14-month outcome in ADHD. *Journal of Consulting and Clinical Psychology, 71,* 713–727.

Arnsten, A.F.T., Berridge, C.W., & McCracken, J.T. (2009). The neurobiological basis of attention-deficit/hyperactivity disorder. *Primary Psychiatry, 16,* 47–54.

Aro, M. & Wimmer, H. (2003). Learning to read: English in comparison to six more regular orthographies. *Applied Psycholinguistics 24,* 621–635.

Aronson, S. (2009). Am I my brother's keeper? Challenges for the siblings of autistic children. *Journal of Infant, Child, and Adolescent Psychotherapy, 8,* 49–56.

Arseneault, L., Kim-Cohen, J., Taylor, A., Caspi, A., & Moffit, T.E. (2005). Psychometric evaluation of 5- and 7-year old children's self-reports of conduct problems. *Journal of Abnormal Child Psychology, 33,* 537–550.

Arsenio, W.F., & Lemerise, E.A. (2001). Varieties of childhood bullying: Values, emotion processes, and social competence. *Social Development, 10,* 60–73.

Arsenio, W.F., & Lemerise, E.A. (2004). Aggression and moral development: Integrating social information processing and moral domain models. *Child Development, 75,* 987–1002.

Asarnow, J., Glynn, S., Pynoos, R. S., Nahum, J., Guthrie, D., Cantwell, D. P., et al. (1999). When the earth stops shaking: Earthquake sequelae among children diagnosed for pre-earthquake psychopathology. *Journal of the American Academy of Child and Adolescent Psychiatry, 38,* 1016–1023.

Asbury, K., Dunn, J.F., Pike, A. & Plomin, R. (2003). Non-shared environmental influences on individual differences in early behavioral development: A monozygotic twin differences study. *Child Development, 74,* 933–943.

Aschenbrand, S.G., Angelosante, A.G. & Kendall, P.C. (2005). Discriminant validity and clinical utility of the CBCL with anxiety-disordered youth. *Journal of Clinical Child and Adolescent Psychology, 34,* 735–746.

Ascherman, L.I., & Rubin, S. (2008). Current ethical issues in child and adolescent psychotherapy. *Child & Adolescent Psychiatry Clinics of North America, 17,* 21–35.

Asher, S.R. & Paquette, J.A. (2003). Loneliness and peer relations in childhood. *Current Directions in Psychological Science, 12,* 75–78.

Asherson, P., Kuntsi, J., & Taylor, E. (2005). Unravelling the complexity of attention-deficit hyperactivity disorder: A behavioral genomic approach. *British Journal of Psychiatry,187,* 103–105.

Ashman, S. B., Dawson, G., Panagiotides, H., Yamada, E., & Wilkinson, C. W. (2002). Stress hormone levels of children of depressed mothers. *Development and Psychopathology, 14,* 333–349.

Asperger, H. (1944/1991). Autistic psychopathy in childhood. In U. Frith (Ed.), *Asperger and his syndrome* (pp. 37–92). Cambridge: Cambridge University Press.

Astley, S. J., Bailey, D., Talbot, C., & Clarren, S. K. (2000). Fetal alcohol syndrome (FAS) primary prevention through FAS diagnosis: II A comprehensive profile of 80 birth mothers of children with FAS. *Alcohol and Alcoholism, 35,* 509–519.

Atkins, M.S., Hoagwood, K.E., Kutash, K., & Seidman, E. (2010). Toward the integration of education and mental health in schools. *Administration & Policy in Mental Health, 37,* 40–47.

Auerbach, J. G., Lerner, Y., Barasch, M., & Tepper, D. (1995). The identification in infancy of children at cognitive and behavioral risk: The Jerusalem Kindergarten Project. *Journal of Applied Developmental Psychology, 16,* 319–338.

August, G. J., Bloomquist, M. L., Lee, S. S., Realmuto, G. M., & Hektner, J. M. (2006). Can evidence-based prevention programs be sustained in community practice settings? The Early Risers' advanced stage effectiveness trial. *Prevention Science, 7,* 151–165.

August, G. J., Lee, S. S., Bloomquist, M. L., Realmuto, G. M., & Hektner, J. M. (2004). Dissemination of an evidence-based prevention innovation for aggressive children living in culturally diverse, urban neighborhoods: The Early Risers effectiveness study. *Prevention Science, 4,* 271–286.

Austin, A. A., & Chorpita, B. F. (2004). Temperament, anxiety, and depression: Comparisons across five ethnic groups of children. *Journal of Clinical Child Adolescent Psychology, 33,* 216–226.

Austin, A., & Wagner, E.F. (2010). Treatment attrition among racial and ethnic minority youth. *Journal of Social Work Practice in the Addicitons, 10,* 63–80.

Austin, S. B., & Gortmaker, S. L. (2001). Dieting and smoking initiation in early adolescent girls and boys: A prospective study. *American Journal of Public Health, 91,* 446–450.

Austin, S. B., Ziyadeh, N., Kahn, J. A., Camargo, C. A., Jr., Colditz, G. A., & Field, A. E. (2004). Sexual orientation, weight concerns, and eating disordered behaviors in adolescent boys and girls. *Journal of the American Academy of Child and Adolescent Psychiatry, 43,* 1115–1123.

Avenevoli, S., Knight, E., Kessler, R. C., & Merikangas, K. R. (2008). Epidemiology of depression in children and adolescents. In J. R. Z. Abela & B. L. Hankin (Eds.), *Handbook of depression in children and adolescents* (pp. 6–32). New York: Guilford Press.

Avramidis, E., Bayliss, P., & Burden, R. (2000). A survey into mainstream teachers' attitudes towards the inclusion of children with special educational needs in the ordinary school in one local education authority. *Educational Psychology, 20,* 191–211.

Avramidis, E., & Norwich, B. (2002). Teachers' attitudes towards integration/inclusion: A review of the literature. *European Journal of Special Needs Education, 17,* 129–147.

Axline, V. M. (1969). *Play Therapy.* New York: Ballantine.

Ayoub, C.C., O'Connor, E., Rappolt-Schlictmann, G., Fischer, K.W., Rogosch, F.A., Toth, S.L., & Cicchetti, D. (2006). Cognitive and emotional differences in young maltreated children: A translational application of dynamic skill theory. *Development and Psychopathology, 18,* 679–706.

Azar, S.T. (2002). Parenting and child maltreatment. In M.H. Bornstein (Ed.) *Handbook of parenting: Vol 4: Social conditions and applied parenting* (2nd ed.) (pp. 361–388). Mahwah, NJ: Erlbaum.

Azar, S.T.,Stevenson, M.T., Johnson, D.R. (2012). Intellectual disabilities and neglectful parenting: Preliminary findings on the role of cognition in parenting risk. *Journal of Mental Health Research in Intellectual Disabilities,5,* 94–129.

Babor, T. F., Higgins-Biddle, J., Dauser, D., Higgins, P., & Burleson, J. A. (2005). Alcohol screening and brief intervention in primary care settings: Implementation models and predictors. *Journal of Studies on Alcohol, 66,* 361–368.

Babor, T. F., Webb, C., Burleson, J. A., & Kaminer, Y. (2002). Subtypes for classifying adolescents with marijuana use disorders: Construct validity and clinical implications. *Addiction, 97,* 58–69.

Bae, S., Ye, R., Chen, S., Rivers, P. A., & Singh, K. P. (2005). Risky behaviors and factors associated with suicide attempt in adolescents. *Archives of Suicide Research, 9,* 193–202.

Bagwell, C. L., & Coie, J. D. (2004). The best friendships of aggressive boys: Relationship quality, conflict management, and rule-breaking behavior. *Journal of Experimental Child Psychology, 88,* 5–24.

Bailey, D. B., Jr., Hatton, D. D., & Skinner, M. (1998). Early developmental trajectories of males with fragile X syndrome. *American Journal on Mental Retardation, 103,* 29–39.

Bailey, J. A., & McCloskey, L. (2005). Pathways to adolescent substance use among sexually abused girls. *Journal of Abnormal Child Psychology, 33,* 39–53.

Bailey, S. (1999). Young people, mental illness and stigmatization. *Psychiatric Bulletin, 23,* 107–110.

Baird, G., Charman, T., Baron-Cohen, S., Cox, A., Swettenham, J., Wheelwright, S., et al. (2000). A screening instrument for autism at 18 months of age: A 6-year follow-up study. *Journal of the American Academy of Child and Adolescent Psychiatry, 39,* 694–702.

Baker, B. L. (1996). Parent training. In J. W. Jacobson & J. A. Mulick (Eds.), *Manual of diagnosis and professional practice in mental retardation* (pp. 289–299). Washington, DC: American Psychological Association.

Baker, B. L., Balcher, J., Crnic, K. A., & Edelbrock, C. (2002). Behavior problems and parenting stress in families of three-year-old children with and without developmental delays. *American Journal on Mental Retardation, 107*, 433–444.

Baker, T. B., Brandon, T. H., & Chassin, L. (2004). Motivational influences on cigarette smoking. *Annual Review of Psychology, 55*, 463–491.

Bakermans-Kranenburg, M. J., van IJzendoorn, M. H., & Juffer, F. (2003). Less is more: Meta-analysis of sensitivity and attachment interventions in early childhood. *Psychological Bulletin, 129*, 195–215.

Bakermans-Kranenburg, M.J., van IJzendoorn, M.H. (2007). Research review: Genetic vulnerability or differential susceptibility in child development: The case of attachment. *Journal of Child Psychology and Psychiatry, 48,* 1160–1173.

Bal, S., Crombez, G., De Bourdeaudhuij, I., & Van Oorst, P. (2009). Symptomatology in adolescents following initial disclosure of sexual abuse: The roles of crisis support, appraisals and coping. *Child Abuse & Neglect, 33,* 717–127.

Balch, G. I., Tworek, C., Barker, D. C., Sasso, B., Mermelstein, R. J., & Giovino, G. A. (2004). Opportunities for youth smoking cessation: Findings from a national focus group study. *Nicotine and Tobacco Research, 6*, 9–17.

Ballanti, C. J., Bierman, K. L., & Conduct Problems Prevention Research Group. (2000). Disentangling the impact of low cognitive ability and inattention on social behavior and peer relationships. *Journal of Clinical Child Psychology, 29*, 66–75.

Banaschewski, T., & Cagill, D. (2009). The genetics of attention-deficit/hyperactivity disorder. *Expert Review of Neurotherapeutics, 9,* 1547–1576.

Bandura, A. (1986). *Social Foundations of Thought and Action.* Englewood Cliffs, NJ: Prentice Hall.

Bandura, A., Pastorelli, C., Barbaranelli, C., & Caprara, G. V. (1999). Self-efficacy pathways to childhood depression. *Journal of Personality and Social Psychology, 76*, 258–269.

Baradon, T. (2002). Psychotherapeutic work with parents and infants: Psychoanalytic and attachment perspectives. *Attachment and Human Development, 4*, 25–38.

Barbe, R. P., Bridge, J. A., Birmaher, B., Kolko, D. J., & Brent, D. A. (2004). Lifetime history of sexual abuse, clinical presentation, and outcome in a clinical trial for adolescent depression. *Journal of Clinical Psychiatry, 65*, 77–83.

Barbe, R. P., Williamson, D. E., Bridge, J. A., Birmaher, B., Dahl, R. E., Axelson, D., et al. (2005). Clinical differences between suicidal and nonsuicidal depressed children and adolescents. *Journal of Clinical Psychiatry, 66*, 492–498.

Barber, B. L., Eccles, J. S., & Stone, M. R. (2001). Whatever happened to the jock, the brain, and the princess? Young adult pathways linked to adolescent activity involvement and social identity. *Journal of Adolescent Research, 16*, 429–455.

Barber, B. L., Stone, M. R., Hunt, J. E., & Eccles, J. S. (2005). Benefits of activity participation: The roles of identity affirmation and peer group norm sharing. In J. L. Mahoney, R. W. Larson, & J. S. Eccles (Eds.), *Organized activities as contexts of development: Extracurricular activities, after-school and community programs* (pp. 185–210). Mahwah, NJ: Erlbaum.

Barker, E. T., & Galambos, N. L. (2003). Body dissatisfaction of adolescent girls and boys: Risk and resources factors. *Journal of Early Adolescence, 23,* 141–165.

Barker, E.D., Tremblay, R.E., van Lier, P.A.C., Vitaro, F., Nagin, D.S., Assaad, J., Séguin, J.R. (2011). The neurocognition of conduct disorder behaviors: Specificity to physical aggression and theft after controlling for ADHD symptoms. *Aggressive Behavior, 37,* 63–72.

Barker, E.T., Hartley, S.L., Seltzer, M.M., Floyd, F.J., Greenberg, J.S., & Orsmond, G.I. (2011). Trajectories of emotional well-being in mothers of adolescents and adults with autism. *Developmental Psychology, 47,* 551–561.

Barkley, R. A. (1997a). *ADHD and the nature of self-control.* New York: Guilford Press.

Barkley, R. A. (1997b). Behavioral inhibition, sustained attention, and executive functions: Constructing a unifying theory of ADHD. *Psychological Bulletin, 121*, 65–94.

Barkley, R. A. (2004). Attention deficit/hyperactivity disorder and self-regulation: Taking an evolutionary perspective on executive functioning. From R. F. Baumeister & K. D. Vohs (Eds.), *Handbook of self-regulation: Research, theory and applications* (pp. 301–323). New York: Guilford Press.

Barkley, R. A., Cook, E. H., Dulcan, M., Campbell, S., Prior, M., Atkins, M., et al. (2002). Consensus statement on ADHD. *European Child and Adolescent Psychiatry, 11*, 96–98.

Barkley, R. A., Murphy, K. R., Dupaul, G. J., & Bush, T. (2002). Driving in young adults with attention deficit hyperactivity disorder: Knowledge, performance, adverse outcomes, and the role of executive functioning. *Journal of the International Neuropsychological Society, 8*, 655–672.

Barnes, G. M., Welte, J. W., Hoffman, J. H., & Dintcheff, B. A. (2005). Shared predictors of youthful gambling, substance use, and delinquency. *Psychology of Addictive Behaviors, 19*, 165–174.

Barnett, D., Hunt, K. H., Butler, C. M., McCaskill, J. W., Kaplan-Estrin, M., & Pipp-Siegel, S. (1999). Indices of attachment disorganization among toddlers with neurological and non-neurological problems. In J. Solomon & C. George (Eds.), *Attachment disorganization* (pp. 189–212). New York: Guilford Press.

Barnett, W. S. (1986). Definition and classification of mental retardation: A reply to Zigler, Balla, and Hodapp. *American Journal of Mental Deficiency, 91*, 111–116.

Baron-Cohen, S. (1989). The autistic child's theory of mind: A case of specific developmental delay. *Journal of Child Psychology and Psychiatry, 30*, 285–297.

Baron-Cohen, S. (1995). *Mindblindness: An essay on autism and theory of mind.* Cambridge, MA: MIT Press.

Baron-Cohen, S. (1997). *The maladapted mind: Classic readings in evolutionary psychopathology.* Hove, England: Psychology Press/Erlbaum.

Baron-Cohen, S. (2000). Is Asperger syndrome/high-functioning autism necessarily a disability? *Development and Psychopathology, 12*, 489–500.

Baron-Cohen, S. (2001). Theory of mind and autism: A review. In L. M. Glidden (Ed.), *International review of research in mental retardation: Autism* (pp. 169–184). San Diego, CA: Academic Press.

Baron-Cohen, S. (2002a). The extreme male brain theory of autism. *Trends in Cognitive Sciences, 6*, 248–254.

Baron-Cohen, S. (2002b). Is Asperger syndrome necessarily viewed as a disability? *Focus on Autism and Other Developmental Disabilities, 17*, 186–191.

Baron-Cohen, S. (2010). Autism and the empathizing-systemizing (E-S) theory. In In P.D. Zelazo, M. Chandler & E. Crone (Eds.) *Developmental Social Cognitive Neuroscience* (pp. 125–138). New York: Psychology Press.

Baron-Cohen, S., Jolliffe, T., Mortimore, C., & Robertson, M. (1997). Another advanced test of theory of mind: Evidence from very high functioning adults with autism or Asperger Syndrome. *Journal of Child Psychology and Psychiatry and Allied Disciplines, 38*, 813–822.

Baron-Cohen, S., Ring, H. A., Bullmore, E. T., Wheelwright, S., Ashwin, C., & Williams, S. C. R. (2000). The amygdala theory of autism. *Neuroscience and Biobehavioral Reviews, 24*, 355–364.

Baron-Cohen, S., & Wheelwright, S. (1999). Obsessions' in children with autism or Asperger syndrome: Content analysis in terms of core domains of cognition. *British Journal of Psychiatry, 175*, 484–490.

Baron-Cohen, S., Wheelwright, S., & Jolliffe, T. (1997). Is there a "language of the eyes"? Evidence from normal adults, and adults with autism or Asperger syndrome. *Visual Cognition, 4*, 311–31.

Baron-Cohen, S., Wheelwright, S., Lawson, J., Griffin, R., & Hill, J. (2002). The exact mind: Empathizing and systemizing in autism spectrum conditions. In U. Goswami (Ed.), *Blackwell handbook of childhood cognitive development* (pp. 491–508). Malden, MA: Blackwell.

Baron-Cohen, S., Wheelwright, S., Stone, V., & Rutherford, M. (1999). A mathematician, a physicist and a computer scientist with Asperger syndrome: Performance on folk psychology and folk physics tests. *Neurocase, 5*, 475–483.

Barrera, M., Biglan, A., Taylor, T. K., Gunn, B. K., Smolkowski, K., Black, C., et al. (2002). Early elementary school intervention to reduce conduct problems: A randomized trial with Hispanic and non-Hispanic children. *Prevention Science, 3*, 83–94.

Barrett, P., Healy-Farrell, L., & March, J. S. (2004). Cognitive-behavioral family treatment of childhood obsessive-compulsive disorder: A controlled trial. *Journal of the American Academy of Child and Adolescent Psychiatry, 43*, 46–62.

Barrett, P. M. (2000). Treatment of childhood anxiety: Developmental aspects. *Clinical Psychology Review, 20*, 479–494.

Barrett, P. M., Dadds, M. R., & Rapee, R. M. (1996). Family treatment of childhood anxiety: A controlled trial. *Journal of Consulting and Clinical Psychology, 64*, 333–342.

Barrett, P. M., & Healy, L. J. (2003). An examination of the cognitive processes involved in childhood obsessive-compulsive disorder. *Behaviour Research and Therapy, 41*, 285–299.

Barrett, P. M., & Shortt, A. L. (2003). Parental involvement in the treatment of anxious children. In A. E. Kazdin (Ed.), *Evidence-based psychotherapies for children and adolescents* (pp. 101–119). New York: Guilford Press.

Barrett, P., Shortt, A., & Healy, L. (2002). Do parent and child behaviours differentiate families whose children have obsessive-compulsive disorder from other clinic and non-clinic families? *Journal of Child Psychology and Psychiatry and Allied Disciplines, 43*, 597–607.

Barrett, P.M., Farrell, L., Pina, A.A., Peris, T.S., & Piacentini, J. (2008). Evidence-based psychosocial treatments for child and adolescent obsessive-compulsive disorder. *Journal of Clinical Child & Adolescent Psychology, 37*, 131–155.

Barrickman, L. (2003). Disruptive behavioral disorders. *Pediatric Clinics of North America, 50*, 1005–1017.

Barry, C. T., Frick, P. J., Grooms, T., McCoy, M. G., Ellis, M. L., & Loney, B. R. (2000). The importance of callous-unemotional traits for extending the concept of psychopathy to children. *Journal of Abnormal Psychology, 109*, 335–340.

Barry, R.A., Kochanska, G., & Philibert, R.A. (2008). G x E interaction in the organization of attachment: Mothers' responsiveness as a moderator of children's genotypes. *Journal of Child Psychology and Psychiatry, 49*, 1313–1320.

Bartlett, C. W., Gharani, N., Millonig, J. H., & Brzutowicz, L. M. (2005). Three autism candidate genes: A synthesis of human genetic analysis with other disciplines. *International Journal of Developmental Neuroscience, 23*, 221–234.

Barton, M.L. & Robins, D. (2000). Regulatory disorders. In C. H. Zeanah (Ed.), *Handbook of Infant Mental Health, 2nd ed) (pp. 311–325).* New York, NY: Guilford Press.

Bates, J.E., & Pettit, G.S. (2007). Temperament, parenting, and socialization. In J.E. Grusec & P.D. Hastings (Eds.), *Handbook of Socialization: Theory and Research* (pp. 153–177). New York: Guilford Press.

Bates, J.E., Schermerhorn, A.C., & Goodnight, J.A. (2010). Temperament and personality through the life span. In Lerner, M.E. Lamb & A.M. Freund (Eds.), *The Handbook of Life-Span Development, Vol. 2: Social and Emotional Development* (pp. 209–245). Hoboken, NJ: Wiley.

Battjes, R. J., Gordon, M. S., O'Grady, K. E., & Kinlock, T. W. (2004). Predicting retention of adolescents in substance abuse treatment. *Addictive Behaviors, 29*, 1021–1027.

Battjes, R. J., Gordon, M. S., O'Grady, K. E., Kinlock, T. W., & Carswell, M. A. (2003). Factors that predict adolescent motivation for substance abuse treatment. *Journal of Substance Abuse Treatment, 24*, 221–232.

Battjes, R. J., Gordon, M. S., O'Grady, K. E., Kinlock, T. W., Katz, E. C., & Sears, E. A. (2004). Evaluation of a group-based substance abuse treatment program for adolescents. *Journal of Substance Abuse Treatment, 27*, 123–134.

Battle, C.L., Shea, M.T., Johnson, D.M., Yen, S., Ziotnick, C., Zananni, M.C, Stanislow, C.A., Skodol, A.E., Gunderson, J.G., Griolo, C.M., McGlashan, T.H., & Morey, L.C. (2004). Childhood maltreatment associated with adult personality disorders: Findings from the collaborative longitudinal personality disorders study. *Journal of Personality Disorders, 18*, 193–211.

Bauermeister, J. J., Matos, M., Reina, G., Salas, C. C., Martinez, J. V., Cumba, E., et al. (2005). Comparison of the DSM-IV combined and inattentive types of ADHD in a school-based sample of Latino/Hispanic children. *Journal of Child Psychology and Psychiatry, 46*, 166–179.

Bauermeister, J. J., Shrout, P. E., Chavez, L., Rubio-Stipec, M., Ramirez, R., Padilla, L., et al. (2007). ADHD and gender: Are risks and sequela of ADHD the same for boys and girls? *Journal of Child Psychology and Psychiatry, 48*, 831–839.

Baum, S. M., & Olenchak, F. R. (2002). The alphabet children: GT, ADHD, and more. *Exceptionality, 10*, 77–91.

Bauman, M. L., & Kemper, T. L. (2005). Neuroanalytic observations of the brain in autism: A review and future directions. *International Journal of Developmental Neuroscience, 23*, 183–187.

Baumeister, A.A. & Baumeister, A.A. (1995). Mental retardation. In M. Hersen & R.T. Ammerman (Eds.), *Advanced Abnormal Child Psychology* (pp. 283–303). Hillsdale, NJ: Earlbaum.

Baumeister, R. F., Muraven, M., & Tice, D. M. (2000). Ego depletion: A resource model of volition, self-regulation, and controlled processing. *Social Cognition, 18*, 130–150.

Baumrind, D. (1971). Current patterns of parental authority. *Developmental Psychology, 4*, 1–103.

Bearman, S. K., Presnell, K., Martinez, E., & Stice, E. (2006). The skinny on body dissatisfaction: A longitudinal study of adolescent girls and boys. *Journal of Youth and Adolescence, 35,* 229–241.

Beauchaine, T. P. (2003). Taxometrics and developmental psychopathology. *Development and Psychopathology, 15,* 501–527.

Beauchaine, T.P., Gatzke-Kopp, L., & Mead, H.K. (2006). Polyvagal theory and developmental psychopathology: Emotion dysregulation and conduct problems from preschool to adolescence. *Biological Psychology, 74,* 174–184.

Beauchaine, T.P., Hinshaw, S. P., & Pang, K.L. (2010). Comorbidity of attention-deficit/hyperactivity disorder and early-onset conduct disorder: Biological, environmental, and developmental mechanisms. *Clinical Psychology Science and Practice, 17,* 327–336.

Beauchaine, T.P., Neuhaus, E., Brenner, S.L., & Gatzke-Kopp, L. (2008). Ten good reasons to consider biological processes in prevention and intervention research. *Development and Psychopathology, 20,* 745–774.

Beaver, B.R. (2008). A positive approach to children's internalizing problems. *Professional Psychology: Research and Practice, 39,* 129–136.

Beck, A. T. (1987). Cognitive models of depression. *Journal of Cognitive Psychotherapy, 1,* 5–37.

Beck, J. S., Liese, B. S., & Najavits, L. M. (2005). Cognitive therapy. In R. J. Frances, S. I. Miller, & A. H. Mack (Eds.), *Clinical textbook of addictive disorders* (3rd ed., pp. 474–501). New York: Guilford Press.

Becker, A. E. (2004). Television, disordered eating, and young women in Fiji: Negotiating body image and identity during rapid social change. *Culture, Medicine and Psychiatry, 28,* 533–559.

Becker, A.E., Eddy, K.T, & Perloe, A. (2009). Clarifying criteria for cognitive signs and symptoms for eating disorders in DSM-V. *International Journal of Eating Disorders, 42,* 611–619.

Becker, C. B., Bull, S., Schaumberg, K., Cauble, A., & Franco, A. (2008). Effectiveness of peer-led eating disorders prevention: A replication trial. *Journal of Consulting and Clinical Psychology, 76,* 347–354.

Becker, C. B., Smith., L. M., & Ciao, A. C. (2006). Peer-facilitated eating disorder prevention: A randomized effectiveness trial of cognitive dissonance and media advocacy. *Journal of Counseling Psychology, 53,* 550–555.

Becker, K. D., Stuewig, J., Herrera, V. M., & McCloskey, L. A. (2004). A study of firesetting and animal cruelty in children: Family influences and adolescent outcomes. *Journal of the American Academy of Child and Adolescent Psychiatry, 43,* 905–912.

Becker, K., & Schmidt, M. H. (2004). Internet chat rooms and suicide. *Journal of the American Academy of Child and Adolescent Psychiatry, 43,* 246–247.

Beesdo, K., Bittner, A., Pine, D.S., Stein, M.B., Höfler, M., Lieb, R., & Wittchen, H. (2007). Incidence of social anxiety disorder and the consistent risk for secondary depression in the first three decades of life. *Archives of General Psychiatry, 64,* 903–912.

Beesdo, K., Knappe, S., & Pine, D.S. (2009). Anxiety and anxiety disorders in children and adolescents: Developmental issues and implications for DSM-V. *Psychiatric Clinics of North America, 32,* 483–524.

Beitchman, J. H., Adlaf, E. M., Atkinson, L., Douglas, L., Massak, A., & Kenaszchuk, C. (2005). Psychiatric and substance use disorders in late adolescence: The role of risk and perceived social support. *American Journal on Addictions, 14,* 124–138.

Beitchman, J. H., Adlaf, E. M., Douglas, L., Atkinson, L., Young, A., Johnson, C. J., Escobar, M., & Wilson, B. (2001). Comorbidity of psychiatric and substance use disorders in late adolescence: A cluster analytic approach. *American Journal of Drug and Alcohol Abuse, 27,* 421–440.

Belenko, S., & Dembo, R. (2003). Treating adolescent substance abuse problems in the juvenile drug court. *International Journal of Law and Psychiatry. Specialty courts, 26,* 87–110.

Belfer, M.L. (2008). Child and adolescent mental disorders: The magnitude of the problem across the globe. *Journal of Child Psychology and Psychiatry, 49,* 226–236.

Bell, M. A., & Fox, N. A. (1996). Crawling experience is related to changes in cortical organization during infancy: Evidence from EEG coherence. *Developmental Psychobiology, 29,* 551–561.

Bell, M.A., & Deater-Deckard, K. (2007). Biological systems and the development of self-regulation: Integrating behavior, genetics, and psychophysiology. *Journal of Developmental and Behavioral Pediatrics, 28,* 409–420.

Belsky, J. (1980). Child maltreatment: An ecological integration. *American Psychologist, 35,* 320–335.

Belsky, J. (1993). Etiology of child maltreatment: A developmental ecological analysis. *Psychological Bulletin, 114,* 413–434.

Belsky, J. & Bakermans-Kranenburg, M.J. & van Ijzendoorn, M.H. (2007). For better and for worse: Differential susceptibility to environmental influences. *Current Directions in Psychological Science, 16,* 300–304.

Belsky, J., & Pluess, M. (2009). Beyond diathesis stress: Differential susceptibility to environmental influences. *Psychological Bulletin, 135,* 885–908.

Ben-Sasson, A., Hen, L., Fluss, R., Cermak, S.A., Engel-Yeger, B., & Gal, E. (2009). A meta-analysis of sensory modulation symptoms in individuals with autism spectrum disorders. *Journal of Autism and Developmental Disorders, 39,* 1–11.

Benard, B. (1999). Applications of resilience: Possibilities and promise. In M. D. Glantz & J. L. Johnson (Eds.), *Resilience and development: Positive life adaptations. Longitudinal research in the social and behavioral sciences* (pp. 269–277). Dordrecht, Netherlands: Kluwer Academic Publishers.

Benes, F. M. (1994). Developmental changes in stress adaptation in relation to psychopathology. *Development and Psychopathology, 6,* 723–739.

Bennett, R. L., Pettersen, B. J., Niendorf, K. B., & Anderson, R. R. (2003). Developing standard recommendations (Guidelines) for genetic counseling practice: A process of the National Society of Genetic Counselors. *Journal of Genetic Counseling, 12,* 287–295.

Bennett, T., Szatmari, P., Bryson, S., Volden, J., Zwaigenbaum, L., Vaccarella, L., et al. (2008). Differentiating autism and Asperger syndrome on the basis of language delay or impairment. *Journal of Autism and Developmental Disorders, 38,* 616–625.

Bennett-Gates, D., & Zigler, E. (1998). Resolving the developmental-difference debate: An evaluation of the triarchic and systems theory models. In J. A. Burack & R. M. Hodapp (Eds.), *Handbook of mental retardation and development* (pp. 115–131). New York: Cambridge University Press.

Benoit, D. (2009). Feeding disorders, failure to thrive, and obesity. In C. H. Zeanah (Ed.) *Handbook of Infant Mental Health* (pp. 377–391). New York, NY: Guilford Press.

Benoit, D., & Coolbear, J. (1998). Post-traumatic feeding disorders in infancy: Behaviors predicting treatment outcome. *Infant Mental Health Journal, 19,* 409–421.

Benson, B. A., & Valenti-Hein, D. (2001). Cognitive and social learning treatments. In A. Dosen & K. Day (Eds.), *Treating mental illness and behavior disorders in children and adults with mental retardation* (pp. 101–118). Washington, DC: American Psychiatric Publishing.

Berg-Nielsen, T. S., Vikan, A., & Dahl, A. A. (2002). Parenting related to child and parental psychopathology: A descriptive review of the literature. *Clinical Child Psychology and Psychiatry, 7,* 529–552.

Berge, J.M., Loth, K., Hanson, C. Croll-Lampert, J., & Neumark-Sztainer, D. (2012). Family life cycle transitions and the onset of eating disorders: A retrospective grounded theory approach. *Journal of Clinical Nursing,* 21, 1355–1363.

Berk, L. E. (2009). *Child Development* (4th ed.). Boston: Pearson. Berkson, G. (1993). *Children with handicaps: A review of behavioral research.* Hillsdale, NJ: Erlbaum.

Berkson, G. (1993). *Children with handicaps: A review of behavioral research.* Hillsdale, NJ: Earlbaum.

Berlin, L., Bohlin, G., Nyberg, L., & Janols, L. (2004). How well do measures of inhibition and other executive functions discriminate between children with ADHD and controls? *Child Neuropsychology, 10,* 1–13.

Berlin, L., Bohlin, G., & Rydell, A.-M. (2003). Relations between inhibition, executive functioning, and ADHD symptoms: A longitudinal study from age 5 to 8½ years. *Child Neuropsychology, 9,* 255–266.

Berlin, L. J., & Cassidy, J. (1999). Relations among relationships: Contributions from attachment theory and research. In J. Cassidy & P. R. Shaver (Eds.), *Handbook of attachment: Theory, research, and clinical applications* (pp. 688–712). New York: Guilford Press.

Berlin, L.J., Appleyard, K., & Dodge, K.A. (2011). Intergenerational continuity in child maltreatment: Mediating mechanisms and implications for prevention. *Child Development, 82,* 162–176.

Berman, S. L., Weems, C. F., Silverman, W. K., & Kurtines, W. M. (2000). Predictors of outcome in exposure-based cognitive and behavioral treatments for phobic and anxiety disorders in children. *Behavior Therapy, 31,* 713–731.

Berman, S.L., Silverman, W.K. & Kurtines, W.M. (2002). The effects of community violence on children and adolescents: Intervention and social policy. In B. L. Bottoms, M. B. Kovera & B.D. McAuliff (Eds.) *Children, Social Science, and the Law* (pp. 301–321). New York, NY: Cambridge University Press.

Bernabei, P., Camaioni, L., & Levi, G. (1998). An evaluation of early development in children with autism and pervasive developmental disorders from home movies: Preliminary findings. *Autism, 2,* 243–258.

Bernard, K., Dozier, M., Bick, J., Lewis-Morrarty, E., Lindhiem, O., & Carlson, E. (2012). Enhancing attachment organization among maltreated children: Results of a randomized clinical trial. *Child Development, 83,* 623–636.

Bernat, D. H., August, G. J., Hektner, J. M., & Bloomquist, M. L. (2007). The Early Risers preventive intervention: Testing for six-year outcomes and mediational processes. *Journal of Abnormal Child Psychology, 35,* 605–617.

Bernier, A., Carlson, S.M., Bordeleau, S., & Carrier, J. (2010). Relations between physiological and cognitive regulatory systems: Infant sleep regulation and subsequent executive functioning. *Child Development, 81,* 1739–1752.

Bernier, A., & Meins, E. (2008). A threshold approach to understanding the origins of attachment disorganization. *Developmental Psychology, 44,* 969–982.

Bernier, R., & Dawson, R. (2009). The role of mirror neuron dysfunction in autism. In J.A. Pineda (Ed.) *Mirror neuron systems: The role of mirroring processes in social cognition* (pp. 261–286). Totowa, NJ: Humana Press.

Bernstein, G. A., Borchardt, C. M., & Perwein, A. R. (1996). Anxiety disorders in children and adolescents: A review of the past 10 years. *Journal of the American Academy of Child and Adolescent Psychiatry, 35,* 1110–1119.

Bernstein, G.A., Layne, A.E., Egan, E.A. & Tennison, D.M. (2005). School-based interventions for anxious children. *Journal of the American Academy of Child & Adolescent Psychiatry, 44,* 1118–1127.

Berridge, K.C. (2007). The debate over dopamine's role in reward: the case for incentive salience. *Psychopharmacology, 191,* 391–431.

Berridge, K.C. (2009). "Liking" and "wanting" food rewards: Brain substrates and roles in eating disorders. *Physiology & Behavior, 97,* 537–550.

Bers, S. A., Blatt, S. J., & Dolinksy, A. (2004). The sense of self in anorexia-nervosa patients: A psychoanalytically informed method for studying self-representation. *Psychoanalytic Study of the Child, 59,* 294–315.

Berument, S. K., Rutter, M., Lord, C., Pickles, A., & Bailey, A. (1999). Autism screening questionnaire: Diagnostic validity. *British Journal of Psychiatry, 175,* 444–451.

Best, J.R., & Miller, P.H. (2010). A developmental perspective on executive function. *Child Development, 81,* 1641–1660.

Best, J.R., Miller, P.H., & Jones, L.J. (2009). Executive functions after age 5: Changes and correlates. *Developmental Review, 29,* 180–200.

Betancourt, T.S., Borisova, I.I., Williams, T.P., Brennan, R.T., Whitfield, T.H., de la Soudiere, M., Williamson, J., & Gilman, S.E. (2010). Sierra Leone's former child soldiers: A follow-up study of psychosocial adjustment and community reintegration. *Child Development, 81,* 1077–1095.

Bettelheim, B. (1967). *The empty fortress: Infantile autism and the birth of the self.* New York: The Free Press.

Beyer, J.F. (2009). Autism spectrum disorders and sibling relationships: research and strategies. *Education and training in developmental disabilities, 44,* 444–452.

Beyers, J. M., Bates, J. E., Pettit, G. S., & Dodge, K. A. (2003). Neighborhood structure, parenting processes, and the development of youths' externalizing behaviors: A multilevel analysis. *American Journal of Community Psychology, 31,* 35–53.

Bezdjian, S., Tuvblad, C., Raine, A., & Baker, J.A. (2011). The genetic and environmental covariation among personality traits, reactive and proactive aggression in childhood. *Child Development, 82,* 1267–1281.

Bhangoo, R. K., Dell., M. L., Towbin, K., Myers, F. S., Lowe, C. H., Pine, D. S., et al. (2003). Clinical correlates of episodicity in juvenile mania. *Journal of Child and Adolescent Psychopharmacology, 13,* 507–514.

Bhangoo, R. K., & Leibenluft, E. (2002). Affective neuroscience and the study of normal and abnormal emotion regulation. *Child and Adolescent Psychiatric Clinics of North America, 11,* 519–532.

Biederman, J., Faraone, S. V., Mick, E., Willamson, S., Wilens, T. E., Spencer, T. J., et al. (1999). Clinical correlates of ADHD in females: findings from a large group of girls ascertained from pediatric and psychiatric referral sources. *Journal of the American Academy of Child and Adolescent Psychiatry, 38,* 966–967.

Biederman, J., Faraone, S. V., Milberger, S., & Doyle, A. (1993). Diagnoses of attention-deficit hyperactivity disorder from parent reports predict diagnoses based on teacher reports. *Journal of the American Academy of Child and Adolescent Psychiatry, 32,* 315–317.

Biederman, J., Kwon, A., Aleardi, M., Chouinard, V., Marino, T., Cole, H., et al. (2005). Absence of gender effects on attention deficit hyperactivity disorder: Findings in nonreferred subjects. *American Journal of Psychiatry, 162,* 1083–1089.

Biederman, J., Mick, E. & Faraone, S.V. (2000). Age-dependent decline of symptoms of attention deficit hyperactivity disorder: Impact of remission definition and symptom type. *American Journal of Psychiatry, 157,* 816–818.

Biederman, J., Mick, E., Wozniak, J., Monuteaux, M. C., Galdo, M., & Faraone, S. V. (2003). Can a subtype of conduct disorder linked to bipolar disorder be identified? Integration of findings from the Massachusetts General Hospital Pediatric Psychopharmacology Research Program. *Biological Psychiatry, 53,* 952–960.

Biederman, J., Monuteaux, M. C., Doyle, A. E., Seidman, L. J., Wilens, T. E., Ferrero, F., et al. (2004). Impact of executive function deficits and attention-deficit/hyperactivity disorder (ADHD) on academic outcomes in children. *Journal of Consulting and Clinical Pscyhology, 72,* 757–766.

Biederman, J., Wilens, T., Mick, E., Faraone, S. V., Weber, W., Curtis, S., et al. (1997). Is ADHD a risk factor for psychoactive substance use disorders? Findings from a four-year prospective follow-up study. *Journal of the American Academy of Child and Adolescent Psychiatry, 36,* 21–30.

Bierman, K. L., Coie, J. D., Dodge, K. A., Foster, E. M., Greenberg, M. T., Lochman, J. E., et al. (2004). The effects of the fast track program on serious problem outcomes at the end of elementary school. *Journal of Clinical Child and Adolescent Psychology, 33,* 650–651.

Bierman, K. L., Coie, J. D., Dodge, K. A., Foster, E. M., Greenberg, M. T., Lochman, J. E., et al. (2007). Fast track randomized controlled trial to prevent externalizing psychiatric disorders: Findings from grades 3 to 9. *Journal of the American Academy of Child and Adolescent Psychiatry, 46,* 1250–1262.

Bierman, K. L., Coie, J. D., Dodge, K. A., Greenberg, M. T., Lochman, J. E., McMahon, R. J., et al. (2002). Using the Fast Track randomized prevention trial to test the early-starter model of the development of serious conduct problems. *Development and Psychopathology, 14,* 925–943.

Bierman, K. L., & Montminy, H. P. (1993). Developmental issues in social-skills assessment and intervention with children and adolescents. *Behavior Modification, 17,* 229–254.

Bierman, K. L., & Welsh, J. A. (2000). Assessing social dysfunction: The contributions of laboratory and performance-based measures. *Journal of Clinical Child Psychology, 29,* 526–539.

Bierut, L. J., Dinwiddie, S. H., Begleiter, H., Crowe, R. R., Hesselbrock, V., Nurnberger, J. I., Jr., et al. (1998). Familial transmission of substance dependence: Alcohol, marijuana, cocaine, and habitual smoking: A report from the collaborative study on the genetics of alcoholism. *Archives of General Psychiatry, 55,* 982–988.

Biggs, B., Vernberg, E., Little, T.D., Dill, E.J., Fonagy, P., & Twemlow, S.W. (2010). Peer victimization trajectories and their association with children's affect in late elementary school. *International Journal of Behavioral Development, 34,* 136–146.

Bina, M., Graziano, F., & Bonino, S. (2006). Risky driving and lifestyles in adolescence. *Accident Analysis and Prevention, 38,* 472–481.

Bird, H. R., Canino, G. J., Davies, M., Zhang, H., Ramirez, R., & Lahey, B. B. (2001). Prevalence and correlates of antisocial behaviors among three ethnic groups. *Journal of Abnormal Child Psychology, 29,* 465–478.

Birmaher, B., Axelson, D., Goldstein, B., Strober, M., Gill, M.K., Hunt, J., … Keller, M. (2009). Four-year longitudinal course of children and adolescents with bipolar spectrum disorders: The course and outcome of bipolar youth (COBY) study. *American Journal of Psychiatry, 166,* 795–804.

Birmaher, B., & Brent, D. (2002). Pharmacotherapy for depression in children and adolescents. In D. Shaffer & B. D. Waslick (Eds.), *Review of psychiatry: Vol. 21. The many faces of depression in children and adolescents* (pp. 73–103). Washington, DC: American Psychiatric Publishing.

Birmaher, B., Brent, D., Bernet, W., Bukstein, O., Walter, H., Benson, R. S., et al. (2007). Practice parameter for the assessment and treatment of children and adolescents with depressive disorder. *Journal of the American Academy of Child and Adolescent Psychiatry, 46,* 1503–1526.

Birmaher, B., & Heydl, P. (2001). Biological studies in depressed children and adolescents. *International Journal of Neuropsychopharmacology, 4,* 149–157.

Birmaher, B., Ryan, N. D., Williamson, D. E., Brent, D. A., & Kaufman, J. (1996a). Childhood and adolescent depression: A review of the past 10 years. Part II. *Journal of the American Academy of Child and Adolescent Psychiatry, 35,* 1575–1583.

Birmaher, B., Ryan, N. D., Williamson, D. E., Brent, D. A., Kaufman, J., Dahl, R. E., et al. (1996b). Childhood and adolescent depression: A review of the past 10 years. Part I. *Journal of the American Academy of Child and Adolescent Psychiatry, 35,* 1427–1439.

Birmaher, B., Williamson, D. E., Dahl, R. E., Axelson, D. A., Kaufman, J., Dorn, L. D., et al. (2004). Clinical presentation and course of depression in youth: Does onset in childhood differ from onset in adolescence? *Journal of the American Academy of Child and Adolescent Psychiatry, 43,* 63–70.

Birman D., Trickett, E., & Buchanan, R. M. (2005). A tale of two cities: Replication of a study on the acculturation and adaptation of immigrant adolescents from the former Soviet Union in a different community context. *American Journal of Community Psychology, 35,* 83–101.

Bittner, A., Egger, H.L., Erkanli, A., Costello, E.J., Foley, D.L., & Angold, A. (2007). What do childhood anxiety disorders predict? *Journal of Child Psychology and Psychiatry, 48,* 1174–1183.

Black, L. M. (1997). Type I: Hypersensitive. In A. Lieberman, S. Wieder, & E. Fenichel (Eds.), *DC: 0–3 Casebook* (pp. 195–218). Washington, DC: Zero to Three: National Center for Infants, Toddlers, and Families.

Blackman, G. L., Ostrander, R., & Herman, K. C. (2005). Children with ADHD and depression: A multisource, multimethod assessment of clinical, social, and academic functioning. *Journal of Attention Disorders, 8,* 195–207.

Blader, J. C., & Carlson, G. A. (2007). Increased rates of bipolar disorder diagnoses among U. S. child, adolescent, and adult inpatients 1996–2004. *Biological Psychiatry, 62,* 107–114.

Blair, C. (2002). School readiness: Integrating cognition and emotion in a neurobiological conceptualization of children's functioning at school entry. *American Psychologist, 57,* 111–127.

Blair, C. (2002).School readiness: Integrating cognition and emotion in a neurobiological conceptualization of children's functioning at school entry. *American Psychologist, 57,* 111–127.

Blair, C. (2010). Stress and the development of self-regulation in context. *Child Development Perspectives, 4,* 181–188.

Blair, C. (2011). Allostasis and allostatic load in the context of poverty in early childhood. *Development and Psychopathology, 23,* 845–857.

Blair, C., & Dennis, T. (2010). An optimal balance: The integration of emotion and cognition in context. In S. D. Calkins & M. A. Bell (Eds.), *Child development at theiIntersection of emotion and cognition* (pp. 17–35). Washington, DC: American Psychological Association.

Blair, C., & Peters, R. (2003). Physiological and neurocognitive correlates of adaptive behavior in preschool among children in Head Start. *Developmental Neuropsychology, 24,* 479–497.

Blair, R. J. R. (1997). Moral reasoning and the child with psychopathic tendencies. *Personality and Individual Differences, 22,* 731–739.

Blair, R. J. R. (2005). Applying a cognitive neuroscience perspective to the disorder of psychopathy. *Development and Psychopathology, 17,* 865–891.

Blandon, A.Y., Calkins, S.D., Kean, S.P., & O'Brien, M. (2010) Contributions of child's physiology and maternal behavior to children's trajectories of temperamental reactivity. *Developmental Psychology, 46,* 1089–1102.

Blasi, A. (1983). Moral cognition and moral action: A theoretical perspective. *Developmental Review, 3,* 178–210.

Blasi, A., & Milton, K. (1991). The development of the sense of self in adolescence. *Journal of Personality, 59,* 217–242.

Blatt, S.J., & Luyten, P. (2009). A structural-developmental psychodynamic approach to psychopathology: Two polarities of experience across the life span. *Development and Psychopathology, 21,* 793–814.

Bloch, J.S., & Weinstein, J.D. (2010). Families of young children with autism. *Social Work in Mental Health, 8,* 23–40.

Bloch, M.H., Panza, K.E., Landeros-Weisenberger, A., & Leckman, J.F. (2009). Meta-analysis: Treatment of attention-deficit/hyperactivity disorder in children with comorbid tic disorders. *Journal of the American Academy of Child & Adolescent Psychiatry, 48,* 884–893.

Block, J., & Block, J. H. (2006). Venturing a 30-year longitudinal study. *American Psychologist, 61,* 315–327.

Bloomquist, M. L., & Schnell, S. V. (2002). *Helping children with aggression and conduct problems: Best practices for intervention.* New York: Guilford Press.

Blum, R. W., Beuhring, T., Shew, M. L., Beringer, L. H., Sieving, R. E., & Resnick, M. D. (2000). The effects of race/ethnicity, income, and family structure on adolescent risk behaviors. *American Journal of Public Health, 90,* 1879–1884.

Bogels, S., & Phares, V. (2007). Fathers' role in the etiology, prevention and treatment of child anxiety: A review and new model. *Clinical Psychology Review, 28,* 539–558.

Bogels, S.M., van Dongen, L. & Muris, P. (2003). Family influences on dysfunctional thinking in anxious children. *Infant and Child Development, 12,* 243–252.

Bolton, P.F., Carcani-Rathwell, I., Hutton, J., Goode, S., Howlin, P., & Michael, R. (2011). Epilepsy in autism: Features and correlates. *The British Journal of Psychiatry, 198,* 289–294.

Bonanno, G. A. (2004). Loss, trauma, and human resilience: Have we underestimated the human capacity to thrive after extremely aversive events? *American Psychologist, 59,* 20–28.

Bonanno, G.A., & Mancini, A.D. (2008). The human capacity to thrive in the face of potential trauma. *Pediatrics, 121,* 369–375.

Bonanno, R.A., & Hymel, S. (2010). Beyond hurt feelings: Investigating why some victims of bullying are at greater risk for suicidal ideation. *Merrill-Palmer Quarterly: Journal of Developmental Psychology, 56,* 420–440.

Booth-LaForce, C., & Oxford, M.L. (2008). Trajectories of social withdrawal from grades 1 to 6: Prediction from early parenting, attachment, and temperament. *Developmental Psychology, 44,* 1298–1313.

Booze, R. M. (2004). Developmental aspects of addiction. *International Journal of Developmental Neuroscience, 22,* 241–245.

Bornholt, L., Brake, N., Thomas, S., Russel, L., Madden, S., Anderson, G., et al. (2005). Understanding affective and cognitive self-evaluations about the body for adolescent girls. *British Journal of Health Psychology, 10,* 485–503.

Bornstein, M. H. (2002). Toward a multiculture, multiage, multimethod science. *Human Development, 45,* 257–263.

Bornstein, M.H., Hahn, C., & Haynes, O.M. (2010). Social competence, externalizing, and internalizing behavioral adjustment from early childhood through early adolescence: Developmental cascades. *Development and Psychopathology, 22,* 717–735.

Bos, K., Zeanah, C.H., Fox, N.A., Drury, S.S., McLaughlin, K.A., Nelson, C.A. (2011). Psychiatric outcomes in young children with a history of institutionalization. *Harvard Review of Psychiatry, 19,* 15–24.

Botvin, G. J., Scheier, L. M., & Griffin, K. W. (2002). Preventing the onset and developmental progression of adolescent drug use: Implications for the gateway hypothesis. In D. B. Kandel (Ed.), *Stages and pathways of drug involvement: Examining the gateway hypothesis* (pp. 115–138). New York: Cambridge University Press.

Bower, M. A., Veach, P. M., Bartels, D. M., & LeRoy, B. S. (2002). A survey of genetic counselors' strategies for addressing ethical and professional challenges in practice. *Journal of Genetic Counseling, 11,* 163–186.

Bowes, L., Arseneault, L., Maughan, B., Taylor, A., Caspi, A., & Moffitt, T.E. (2009). School, neighborhood, and family factors are associated with children's bullying involvement: A nationally representative longitudinal study. *Journal of the American Academy of Child and Adolescent Psychiatry, 48,* 545–553.

Bowlby, J. (1953, 1982). *Attachment.* New York: Basic Books.

Bowlby, J. (1961). Separation anxiety: A critical review of the literature. *Journal of Child Psychology and Psychiatry, 1,* 251–269.

Bowlby, J. (1977). The making and breaking of affectional bonds:I. Actiology and psychopathology in the light of attachment theory. *British Journal of Psychiatry, 130,* 201–210.

Bowlby, J. (1980). *Attachment and loss.* New York: Basic Books.

Bowlby, J. (1982). Attachment and loss: Retrospect and prospect. *American Journal of Orthopsychiatry, 52,* 664–678.

Boxer, P., Guerra, N. G., Huesmann, L. R., & Morales, J. (2005). Proximal peer-level effects of a small-group selected prevention on aggression in elementary school children: An investigation of the peer contagion hypothesis. *Journal of Abnormal Child Psychology, 33,* 325–339.

Boyce, W. T. (2007). A biology of misfortune: Stress reactivity, social context, and the ontogeny of psychopathology in early life. In A. S. Masten (Ed.), *Multilevel Dynamics in Developmental Psychopathology, Minnesota Symposia on Child Psychology* (Vol. 34, pp. 45–82). Mahwah, NJ: Erlbaum.

Boyce, W. T., Frank, E., Jensen, P. S., Kessler, R. C., Nelson, C. A., & Steinberg, L. (1998). Social context in developmental psychopathology: Recommendations for future research from the MacArthur Network on Psychopathology and Development. *Development and Psychopathology, 10*, 143–164.

Boyd, B.A., Baranek, G.T., Sideris, J., Poe, M.D., Watson, L.R., Patten, E., & Miller, H. (2010). Sensory features and repetitive behaviors in children with autism and developmental delays. *Autism Research, 3*, 78–87.

Boylan, K., Vaillancourt, T., Boyle, M., & Szatmari, P. (2007). Comorbidity of internalizing disorders in children with oppositional defiant disorder. *European Child & Adolescent Psychiatry, 16*, 484–494.

Braddock, D. (2002). Public financial support for disability at the dawn of the 21st century. *American Journal on Mental Retardation, 107*, 478–489.

Braden, J. S., & Obrzut, J. E. (2002). Williams syndrome: Neuropsychological findings and implications for practice. *Journal of Development and Physical Disabilities, 14*, 203–213.

Bradley, B., Westen, D., Mercer, K.B., Binder, E.B., Jovanovic, T., Crain, D., Wingo, A., & Heim, C. (2011). Association between childhood maltreatment and adult emotional dysregulation in a low-income, urban, African American sample: Moderation by oxytocin receptor gene. *Development and Psychopathology, 23*, 439–452.

Bradshaw, C.P., Brown, J.S., & Hamilton, S.F. (2008). Bridging positive youth development and mental health services for youth with serious behavior problems. *Child Youth Care Forum, 37*, 209–226.

Branco, E. I., & Kaskutas, L. A. (2001). "If it burns going downÖ": How focus groups can shape fetal alcohol syndrome (FAS) prevention. *Substance Use and Misuse, 36*, 333–345.

Braswell, L. (1998). Self-regulation training for children with ADHD: Response to Harris and Schmidt. *The ADHD Report, 6*, 1–3.

Bratton, S.C., Ray, D., Rhine, T., & Jones, L. (2005). The efficacy of play therapy with children: A meta-analytic review of treatment outcomes. *Professional Psychology: Research and Practice, 36*, 376–390.

Brazelton, T. B. (1994, 2006). *Touchpoints: Birth to three.* Cambridge, MA: DaCapo Press.

Brazelton, T. B., & Greenspan, S. I. (2000). *The irreducible needs of children.* Cambridge, MA: Perseus.

Breda, C., & Heflinger, C. A. (2004). Predicting incentives to change among adolescents with substance abuse disorder. *American Journal of Drug and Alcohol Abuse, 30*, 251–267.

Breda, C., & Heflinger, C.A. (2004). Predicting incentives to change among adolescents with substance abuse disorder. *The American Journal of Drug and Alcohol Abuse, 30*, 251–267.

Brendgen, M., Vitaro, F., & Bukowski, W. M. (2000a). Deviant friends and early adolescents' emotional and behavioral adjustment. *Journal of Research on Adolescence, 10*, 173–189.

Brendgen, M., Viatro, F., & Bukowski, W. M. (2000b). Stability and variability of adolescents' affiliation with delinquent friends: Predictors and consequences. *Social Development, 9*, 205–225.

Brendgen, M., Wanner, B., Morin, A. J.S., & Vitaro, F. (2005). Relations with parents and with peers, temperament, and

trajectories of depressed mood during early adolescence. *Journal of Abnormal Psychology, 33*, 579.

Brent, D. A., Oquendo, M., Birmaher, B., Greenhill, L., Kolko, D., Stanley, B., et al. (2004). Familial transmission of mood disorders: Convergence and divergence with transmission of suicidal behavior. *Journal of the American Academy of Child and Adolescent Psychiatry, 43*, 1259–1266.

Brent, D.A., & Maalouf, F.T. (2009). Pediatric depression: is there evidence to improve evidence-based treatments? *Journal of Child Psychology and Psychiatry, 50*, 143–152.

Bretherton, I. (1990). Communication patterns, internal working models, and the intergenerational transmission of attachment relationships. *Infant Mental Health Journal, 11*, 237–252.

Bretherton, I., Ridgeway, D., & Cassidy, J. (1990). Assessing internal working models of the attachment relationship: An attachment story completion task for 3-year-olds. In M. T. Greenberg, D. Cicchetti, & E. M. Cummings (Eds.), *Attachment in the preschool years: Theory, research, and intervention* (pp. 273–308). Chicago: University of Chicago Press.

Bricker, J. B., Leroux, B. G., Peterson, A. V., Kealey, K. A., Sarason, I. G., Andersen, M. R., et al. (2003). Nine-year prospective relationship between parental smoking cessation and children's daily smoking. *Addiction, 98*, 585–593.

Bridge, J. A., & Axelson, D. A. (2008). The contribution of pharmacoepdemiology to the antidepressant-suicidality debate in children and adolescents. *International Review of Psychiatry, 20*, 209–214.

Bridge, J. A., Barbe, R. P., Birmaher, B., Kolko, D. J., & Brent, D. A. (2005). Emergent suicideality in a clinical psychotherapy trial for adolescent depression. *American Journal of Psychiatry, 162*, 2173–2175.

Bridge, J. A., Goldstein, T. R., & Brent, D. A. (2006). Adolescent suicide and suicidal behavior. *Journal of Child Psychology and Psychiatry, 47*, 372–394.

Bridge, J. A., Iyengar, S., Salary, C. B., Barbe, R. P., Birmaher, B., Pincus, H. A., et al. (2007). Clinical response and risk for reported suicidal ideation and suicide attempts in pediatric antidepressant treatment: A meta-analysis of randomized controlled trials. *Journal of the American Medical Association, 297*, 1683–1696.

Briggs-Gowan, M.J., Carter, A.S., Clark, R., Augustyn, M., Mc Carthy, K.J., & Ford, J.D. (2010). Exposure to potentially traumatic events in early childhood: differential links to emergent psychopathology. *Journal of Child Psychology and Psychiatry, 51*, 1132–1140.

Bringewatt, E.H. & Gershoff, E.T. (2010). Falling through the cracks: Gaps and barriers in the mental health system for America's disadvantaged children. *Children and Youth Services Review, 32*, 1291–1299.

Brocki, K. C., & Bohlin, G. (2004). Executive functions in children aged 6 to 13: A dimensional and developmental study. *Developmental Neuropsychology, 26*, 571–593.

Brody, G. H. (1998). Sibling relationship quality: Its causes and consequences. *Annual Review of Psychology, 49*, 1–24.

Brody, G. H. (2003). Parental monitoring: Action and reaction. In A. C. Crouter & A. Booth (Eds.), *Children's influence on family dynamics: The neglected side of family relationships* (pp. 163–169). Mahwah, NJ: Erlbaum.

Brody, G. H. (2004). Siblings' direct and indirect contributions to child development. *Current Directions in Psychological Science, 13*, 124–126.

Brody, G. H., Flor, D. L., Hollett-Wright, N., McCoy, J. K., & Donovan, J. (1999). Parent-child relationships, child temperament profiles and children's alcohol use norms. *Journal of Studies on Alcohol, 13,* 45–51.

Brody, G. H., Flor, D. L., Hollett-Wright, N., & McCoy, J. K. (1998). Children's development of alcohol use norms: Contributions fo parent and sibling norms, children's temperaments, and parent-child discussions. *Journal of Family Psychology, 12,* 209–219.

Brody, G. H., Ge, X., Kim, S. Y., Murry, V. M., Simons, R. L., Gibbons, F. X., et al. (2003). Neighborhood disadvantage moderates associations of parenting and older sibling problem attitudes and behavior with conduct disorders in African American children. *Journal of Consulting and Clinical Psychology, 71,* 211–222.

Brody, G. H., Kim, S., Murry, V. M., & Brown, A. C. (2004). Protective longitudinal paths linking child competence to behavioral problems among African American siblings. *Child Development, 75,* 455–467.

Brody, G. H., Murry, V. M., Gerrard, M., Gibbons, F. X., Molgaard, V., McNair, L., et al. (2004). The Strong African American Families program: Translating research into prevention programming. *Child Development, 75,* 900–917.

Broidy, L. M., Nagin, D. S., Tremblay, R. E., Bates, J. E., Brame, B., Dodge, K. A., et al. (2003). Developmental trajectories of childhood disruptive behaviors and adolescent delinquency: A six-site, cross-national study. *Developmental Psychology, 39,* 222–245.

Bronfenbrenner, U. (1986). Ecology of the family as a context for human development: Research perspectives. *Developmental Psychology, 22,* 723–742.

Bronson, G. W., & Pankey, W. B. (1977). On the distinction between fear and wariness. *Child Development, 48,* 1167–1183.

Brooks, R. B. (2002). Changing the mindset of adults with ADHD: Strategies for fostering hope, optimism, and resilience. In S. Goldstein & A. T. Ellison (Eds.), *Clinicians' guide to adult ADHD: Assessment and intervention* (pp. 127–146). San Diego, CA: Academic Press.

Brotman, L. M., Gouley, K. K., O'Neal, C., & Klein, R. G. (2004). Preschool-aged siblings of adjudicated youths: Multiple risk factors for conduct problems. *Early Education and Development, 15,* 387–406.

Brotman, L.M., Kamboukos, K., & Theise, R. (2008). Symptom-specific measures for disorders usually first diagnosed in infancy, childhood, or adolescence. In A. J. Rush, M.B First & D. Blacker (Eds.) *Handbook of psychiatric measures (2nd ed.)* (pp. 309–342). Arlington, VA: American Psychiatric Publishing.

Brotman, M. A., Schmajuk, M., Rich, B. A., Dickstein, D. P., Guyer, A. E., Costello, E. J., et al. (2006). Prevalence, clinical correlates, and longitudinal course of severe mood dysregulation in children. *Biological Psychiatry, 60,* 991–997.

Brown, E.J. & Goodman, R.F. (2005). Childhood traumatic grief: An exploration of the construct in children bereaved on September 11. *Journal of Clinical Child and Adolescent Psychology 34,* 248–259.

Brown, J. B., Winzelberg, A. J., Abascal, L. B., & Taylor, B. C. (2004). An evaluation of an Internet-delivered eating disorder prevention program for adolescents and their parents. *Journal of Adolescent Health, 35,* 290–296.

Brown, M. Z., Comtois, K. A., & Linehan, M. M. (2002). Reasons for suicide attempts and nonsuicidal self-injury in women with borderline personality disorder. *Journal of Abnormal Psychology, 111,* 198–202.

Brown, R. T., Freeman, W. S., Perrin, J. M., Stein, M. T., Amler, R. W., Feldman, H. M., et al. (2001). Prevalence and assessment of attention-deficit/hyperactivity disorder in primary care settings. *Pediatrics, 107,* E43.

Brown, R. T., & Sammons, M. T. (2002). Pediatric psychopharmacology: A review of new developments and recent research. *Professional Psychology: Research and Practice, 33,* 135–147.

Brown, S. A., & Tapert, S. F. (2004). Adolescence and the trajectory of alcohol use: Basic to clinical studies. In R. E. Dahl & L.P. Spear (Eds.), *Adolescent brain development: Vulnerabilities and opportunities. Annals of the New York Academy of Sciences* (Vol. 1021, pp. 234–244). New York: New York Academy of Sciences.

Brown, S.A., McGue, M., Maggs, J., Schulenberg, J., Hingson, R., Swartzwelder, S., Martin, C., … Murphy, S. (2008). A developmental perspective on alcohol and youths 16 to 20 years of age. *Pediatrics, 121,* S290–S310.

Brown, T.H., Mellman, T.A., Alfano, C.A., & Weems, C.F. (2011). Sleep fears, sleep disturbance, and PTSD symptoms in minority youth exposed to Hurricane Katrina. *Journal of Traumatic Stress, 24,* 575–580.

Bruce, J., Tarullo, A.R., & Gunnar, M.R. (2009). Disinhibited social behavior among internationally adopted children. *Development and Psychopathology, 21,* 157–171.

Bruce, J.E. & Boyce, W.T. (2008). Biological sensitivity to context. *Current Directions in Psychological Science, 17,* 183–187.

Bruch, H. (1973). *Eating disorders: Obesity, anorexia nervosa, and the person within.* New York: Basic Books.

Bruch, H. (1982). Anorexia nervosa: Therapy and theory. *American Journal of Psychiatry, 139,* 1531–1538.

Bruijnzeel, A. W., Repetto, M., & Gold, M. S. (2004). Neurobiological mechanisms in addictive and psychiatric disorders. *Psychiatric Clinics of North America, 27,* 661–674.

Bruinsma, Y., Koegel, R. L., & Koegel, L. K. (2004). Joint attention and children with autism: A review of the literature. *Mental Retardation and Developmental Disabilities Research Review, 10,* 169–173.

Brüne, M., & Brüne-Cohrs, U. (2006). Theory of mind-evolution, ontogeny, brain mechanisms and psychopathology. *Neuroscience and Biobehavioral Reviews, 30,* 437–455.

Bryant, A. L., Schulenberg, J. E., O'Malley, P. M., Bachman, J. G., & Johnston, L. D. (2003). How academic achievement, attitudes, and behaviors relate to the course of substance use during adolescence: A 6-year, multiwave, national longitudinal study. *Journal of Research on Adolescence, 13,* 361–397.

Bryant-Waugh, R. (2006). Pathways to recovery: Promoting change within a developmental-systemic framework. *Clinical Child Psychology and Psychiatry, 11,* 213–224.

Bryant-Waugh, R., Markham, L., Kreipe, R.E., & Walsh, B.T. (2009). Feeding and eating disorders in childhood. *International Journal of Eating Disorders, 43,* 1–14.

Bryson, S. E., Zwaigenbaum, L., Brian, J., Roberts, W., Szatmari, P., Rombough, V., et al. (2007). A prospective case series of high-risk infants who developed autism. *Journal of Autism and Developmental Disorders, 37,* 12–24.

Bryson, S. E., Zwaigenbaum, L., McDermott, C., Rombough, V., & Brian, J. (2008). The Autism Observation Scale for Infants: Scale development and reliability data. *Journal of Autism and Developmental Disorders, 38,* 731–738.

Buckholtz, J.W., & Meyer-Lindenberg, A. (2008). MAOA and the neurogenetic architecture of human aggression. *Trends in Neurosciences, 31,* 120–129.

Buckner, J. C., Mezzacappa, E., & Beardslee, W. R. (2003). Characteristics of resilient youths living in poverty: The role of self-regulatory processes. *Development and Psychopathology, 15,* 139–162.

Buell, M. J., Gamel-McCormick, M., & Hallam, R. (1999). Incusion in a childcare context: Experiences and attitudes of family childcare providers. *Topics in Early Childhood Special Education, 19,* 217–224.

Buell, M. J., Hallam, R., Gamel-McCormick, M., & Scheer, S. (1999). A survey of general and special education teachers' perceptions and inservice needs concerning inclusion. *International Journal of Disability, Development and Education, 46,* 143–156.

Bukowski, W. M. (2002). Peer Relationships. In M. H. Bornstein,L. Davidson, C. L. M. Keyes, & K. Moore (Eds.), *Well-Being: Positive development across the life course.* Mahwah, NJ: Erlbaum.

Bukowski, W. M., & Adams, R. (2005). Peer relationships and psychopathology: Markers, moderators, mediators, mechanisms, and meanings. *Journal of Clinical Child and Adolescent Psychology, 34,* 3–10.

Bulik, C. M., Klump, K. L., Thornton, L., Kaplan, A. S., Devlin, B., Fichter, M. M., et al. (2004). Alcohol use disorder comorbidity in eating disorders: A multicenter study. *Journal of Clinical Psychiatry, 65,* 1000–1006.

Bulik, C. M., & Reba, L. (2005). Anorexia nervosa: Defi nition, epidemiology and cycle of risk. *International Journal of Eating Disorders, 37,* S2–S9.

Bulik, C. M., Reba, L., Siega-Riz, A., & Reichborn-Kjennerud, T. (2002). Substance use in female adolescents with eating disorders. *Journal of Adolescent Health, 31,* 176–182.

Bulik, C. M., Sullivan, P. F., Tozzi, F., Furberg, H., Lichtenstein, P., & Pedersen, N. L. (2006). Prevalence, heritability, and prospective risk factors for anorexia nervosa. *Archives of General Psychiatry, 63,* 305–312.

Bullock, B. M., & Dishion, T. J. (2002). Sibling collusion and problem behavior in early adolescence: Toward a process model for family mutuality. *Journal of Abnormal Child Psychology, 30,* 143–153.

Burack, J. A. (1997). The study of atypical and typical populations in developmental psychopathology: The quest for a common science. In S. S. Luthar, J. A. Burack, D. Cicchetti, & J. R. Weisz (Eds.), *Developmental psychopathology: Perspectives on adjustment, risk, and disorder* (pp. 139–165). New York: Cambridge University Press.

Burack, J. A., Evans, D. W., Klaiman, C., & Iarocci, G. (2001). The mysterious myth of attention deficits and other defect stories: Contemporary issues in the developmental approach to mental retardation. In L. M. Glidden (Ed.), *International review of research in mental retardation* (Vol. 24, pp. 299–320). San Diego, CA: Academic Press.

Burke, J. D., Loeber, R., & Lahey, B. B. (2003). Course and outcomes. In C. A. Essau (Ed.), *Conduct and oppositional defiant disorders: Epidemiology, risk factors, and treatment* (pp. 61–94). Mahwah, NJ: Erlbaum.

Burke, J. D., Loeber, R., Lahey, B. B., & Rathouz, P. J. (2005). Developmental transitions among affective and behavioral disorders in adolescent boys. *Journal of Child Psychology and Psychiatry, 46,* 1200–1210.

Burke, J. D., Pardini, D. A., & Loeber, R. (2008). Reciprocal relationships between parenting behavior and disruptive psychopathology from childhood through adolescence. *Journal of Abnormal Child Psychology, 36,* 679–692.

Burke, J.D., Waldman, I., & Lahey, B.B. (2010). Predictive validity of childhood oppositional defiant disorder and conduct disorder: Implications for the *DSM-V. Journal of Abnormal Psychology, 119,* 739–751.

Burns, G. L., Walsh, J. A., Patterson, D. R., Holte, C. S., Sommers-Flanagan, R., & Parker, C. M. (1997). Internal validity of the disruptive behavior disorder symptoms: Implications from parent ratings for a dimensional approach to symptom validity. *Journal of Abnormal Child Psychology, 25,* 307–319.

Burt, S. A., M., DeMarte, J. A., Krueger, R. F., & Iacono, W. G. (2006). Timing of menarche and the origins of conduct disorder. *Archives of General Psychiatry, 63,* 890–896.

Burt, S. A., McGue, M., Krueger, R. F., & Iacono, W. G. (2005). How are parent-child conflict and childhood externalizing symptoms related over time? Results from a genetically informative cross-lagged study. *Development and Psychopathology, 17,* 145–165.

Burt, S. A., Krueger, R. F., McGue, M., & Iacono, W. (2003). Parent-child conflict and the comorbidity among childhood externalizing disorders. *Archives of General Psychiatry, 60,* 505–513.

Burt, S.A. (2009). Are there meaningful etiological differences within antisocial behavior? Results of a meta-analysis. *Clinical Psychology Review, 29,* 163–178.

Burt, S.A., Donnellan, M.B., Iacono, W.G., & McGue, M. (2011). Age-of-onset or behavioral sub-types? A prospective comparison of two approaches to characterizing the heterogeneity within antisocial behavior. *Journal of Abnormal Child Psychology, 39,* 633–644.

Burton, E, Stice, E., Bearman, S. K., & Rhode, P. (2007). Experimental test of the affect-regulation theory of bulimic symptoms and substance use: A randomized trial. *International Journal of Eating Disorders, 40,* 27–36.

Burwell, R.A., & Shirk, S.R. (2007). Subtypes of rumination in adolescence: Associations between brooding, reflection, depressive symptoms, and coping. *Journal of Clinical Child and Adolescent Psychology, 36,* 56–65.

Busatto, G.F., Zamignani, D.R., Buchpiguel, C.A., Garrido, G.E.J., Glabus, M.F., Rocha, E.T., Maia, A.F., Rasario-Campos, M.C., Castro, C.C., Furuie, S.S., Gutierrez, M.A., Mc-guire, P.K. & Miguel, E.C. (2000). A voxel-based investigation of regional cerebral blood flow abnormalities in obsessive-compulsive disorder using single photon emission computed tomography (SPECT). *Psychiatry Research: Neuroimaging, 99,* 15–27.

Bushman, J. B., & Anderson, C. A. (2001). Is it time to pull the plug on the hostile versus instrumental aggression dichotomy? *Psychological Review, 108,* 273–279.

Buss, K.A. (2011). Which fearful toddlers should we worry about? Context, fear regulation, and anxiety risk. *Developmental Psychology, 47,* 804–819.

Bussing, R., Gary, F.A., Mills, T.L., & Garvan, C.W. (2007). Cultural variations in parental health beliefs, knowledge, and information sources related to attention-deficit/hyperactivity disorder. *Journal of Family Issues, 28,* 291–318.

Butler, S., Baruch, G., Hickey, N., & Fonagy, P. (2011). A randomized controlled trial of multisystemic therapy and a statutory therapeutic intervention for young offenders. *Journal of the American Academy of Child Psychiatry, 50,* 1220–1235.

Butterworth, B., Varma, S., & Laurillard, D. (2011). Dyscalculia: From brain to education. *Science, 332,* 1049–1053.

Buttimer, J., & Tierney, E. (2005). Patterns of leisure participation among adolescents with a mild intellectual disability. *Journal of Intellectual Disabilities, 9,* 25–42.

Button, T.M.M, Scourfield, J., Neilson, M., Purcell, S., McGuffin, P. (2005). Family dysfunction interacts with genes in the causation of antisocial symptoms. *Behavior Genetics, 35,* 115–120.

Byrant, R.A., Salmon, K., Sinclair, E. & Davison, P. (2007). The relationship between acute stress disorder and posttraumatic stress disorder in injured children. *Journal of Traumatic Stress, 20,* 1075–1079.

Byrd, A.L., Loeber, R., & Pardini, D.A. (2012). Understanding desisting and persisting forms of delinquency: The unique contributions of disruptive behavior disorders and interpersonal callousness. *Journal of Child Psychology and Psychiatry, 53,* 371–380.

Cafri, G., Yamamiya, Y., Brannick, M., & Thompson, J. K. (2005). The influence of sociocultural factors on body image: A metaanalysis. *Clinical Psychology: Science and Practice, 12,* 421–433.

Cairney, S., Maruff, P., Burns, C., & Currie, B. (2002). The neurobehavioural consequences of petrol (gasoline) sniffing. *Neuroscience and Biobehavioral Reviews, 26,* 81–89.

Cairns, R. B., Cairns, B. D., Rodkin, P., & Xie, H. (1998). New directions in developmental research: Models and methods. In R. Jessor (Ed.), *New perspectives on adolescent risk behavior* (pp. 13–42). New York: Cambridge University Press.

Calkins, S. D., & Fox, N. A. (2002). Self-regulatory processes in early personality development: A multilevel approach to the study of childhood social withdrawal and aggression. *Development and Psychopathology, 14,* 477–498.

Calkins, S. D., & Hill, A. (2007). Caregiver influences on emerging emotion regulation: Biological and environmental transactions in early development. In J. J. Gross (Ed.), *Handbook of emotion regulation* (pp. 229–248). New York: Guilford Press.

Calkins, S. D., & Johnson, M. C. (1998). Toddler regulation of distress to frustrating events: Temperamental and maternal correlates. *Infant Behavior and Development, 21,* 379–395.

Calkins, S. D., & Marcovitch, S. (2010). Emotion regulation and executive functioning in early development: Integrated mechanisms of control supporting adaptive functioning. In S. D. Calkins & M. A. Bell (Eds.), *Child Development at the Intersection of Emotion and Cognition* (pp. 37–57). Washington, DC: American Psychological Association.

Calkins, S.D. (2009). Regulatory competence and early disruptive behavior problems: The role of physiological regulation. In S. Olson, A.J. Sameroff, (Eds.), *Biopsychosocial regulatory processes in the development of childhood behavioral problems* (pp. 86–115). New York: Cambridge University Press.

Calkins, S.D., Hungerford, A. & Dedmon, S.E. (2004). Mothers' interactions with temperamentally frustrated infants. *Infant Mental Health Journal, 25,* 219–239.

Calkins, S.D., & Keane, S.P. (2009). Developmental origins of early antisocial behavior. *Development and Psychopathology, 21,* 1095–1109.

Call, K. T., & Mortimer, J. T. (2001). *Arenas of comfort in adolescence: A study of adjustment in context.* Mahwah, NJ: Erlbaum.

Callaghan, R. C., Hathaway, A., Cunningham, J. A., Vettese, L. C., Wyatt, S., & Taylor, L. (2005). Does stage-of-change predict dropout in a culturally diverse sample of adolescents admitted to inpatient substance-abuse treatment? A test of the transtheoretical model. *Addictive Behaviors, 30,* 1834–1847.

Calvete, E., & Cardenoso, O. (2005). Gender differences in cognitive vulnerability to depression and behavior problems in adolescents. *Journal of Abnormal Child Psychology, 33,* 179–192.

Calzada, E. J., Eyberg, S. M., Rich, B., & Querido, J. G. (2004). Parenting disruptive preschoolers: Experiences of mothers and fathers. *Journal of Abnormal Child Psychology, 32,* 203–213.

Campbell, F.A., & Ramey, C.T. (2010). Carolina Abecedarian Project. In A.J. Reynolds, A.J. Rolnick, M.M. Englund, & J.A. Temple (Eds.), *Childhood Programs and Practices in the First Decade of Life: A Human Capital Integration* (pp. 76–98). New York: Cambridge University Press.

Campbell, S.B, Shaw, D.S. & Gilliom, M. (2000). Early externalizing behavior problems: Toddlers and preschoolers at risk for later maladjustment. *Development and Psychopathology, 12,* 467–488.

Campo, J. V., & Fritsch, S. L. (1994). Somatization in children and adolescents. *Journal of the American Academy of Child and Adolescent Psychiatry, 33,* 1223–1235.

Campo, J.V., Jansen-McWilliams, L., Comer, D.M., & Kelleher, K.J. (1999). Somatization in pediatric primary care: Association with psychopathology, functional impairment, and use of services. *Journal of the American Academy of Child & Adolescent Psychiatry, 38,* 1093–1101.

Campos, J. J., Frankel, C. B., & Camras, L. (2004). On the nature of emotion regulation. *Child Development, 75,* 377–394.

Canavera, K.E., Ollendick, T.H., May, J.T.E. & Pincus, D.B (2010). Clinical correlates of comorbid obsessive-compulsive disorder and depression in youth. *Child Psychiatry and Human Development, 41,* 583–594.

Canino, G., Shrout, P. E., Runio-Stipec, M., Bird, H. R., Bravo, M., Ramirez, R., et al. (2004). The DSM-IV rates of child and adolescent disorders in Puerto Rico. *Archives of General Psychiatry, 61,* 85–93.

Canitano, R., Luchetti, A., & Zappella, M. (2005). Epilepsy, electroencephalographic abnormalities, and regression in children with autism. *Journal of Child Neurology, 20,* 27–31.

Cannon, M.F., & Weems, C.F. (2010). Cognitive biases in childhood anxiety disorders: Do interpretive and judgment biases distinguish anxious youth from their non-anxious peers? *Journal of Anxiety Disorders, 24,* 751–758.

Canpolat, B. I., Orsel, S., Akdemir, A., & Ozbay, M. H. (2005). The relationship between dieting and body image, body ideal, self-perception and body mass in Turkish adolescents. *International Journal of Eating Disorders, 37,* 150–155.

Cantwell, D. P. (1985). Hyperactive children grown up. What have we learned about what happened to them? *Archives of General Psychiatry, 42,* 1026–1028.

Cantwell, D. P. (1996). Attention deficit disorder: A review of the past 10 years. *Journal of the American Academy of Child and Adolescent Psychiatry, 35,* 978–987.

Capaldi, D. M. (1991). Co-occurrence of conduct problems and depressive symptoms in early adolescent boys: I. Familial factors and general adjustment at grade 6. *Development and Psychopathology, 3,* 277–300.

Capaldi, D. M. (1992). Co-occurrence of conduct problems and depressive symptoms in early adolescent boys: II. A 2-year follow-up at Grade 8. *Development and Psychopathology, 4,* 125–144.

Capaldi, D. M. (1999). Co-occurrence of conduct problems and depressive symptoms in early adolescent boys: III. Prediction to young-adult adjustment. *Development and Psychopathology, 11*, 59–84.

Capaldi, D. M., & Stoolmiller, M. (1999). Co-occurrence of conduct problems and depressive symptoms in early adolescent boys: III. Prediction to young-adult adjustment. *Development and Psychopathology, 11*, 59–84.

Caparrotta, L., & Ghaffari, K. (2006). A historical overview of the psychodynamic contributions to the understanding of eating disorders. *Psychoanalytic Psychotherapy, 20*, 175–196.

Cappella, E., Frazier, S.L., Atkins, M.S., Schoenwald, S.K., & Glisson, C. (2008). Enhancing schools' capacity to support children in poverty: An ecological model of school-based mental health services. *Administration & Policy in Mental Health, 35*, 395–409.

Card, N. A., Stucky, B. D., Sawalani, G. M., & Little, T. D. (2008). Direct and indirect aggression during childhood and adolescence: A meta-analytic review of gender differences, intercorrelations, and relations to maladjustment. *Child Development, 79*, 1185–1229.

Card, N.A. (2011). Toward a relationship perspective on aggression among schoolchildren: Integrating social cognitive and interdependence theories. *Psychology of Violence, 1*, 188–201.

Card, N.A., Stucky, B.D., Sawalani, G.M., & Little, T.D. (2008). Direct and indirect aggression during childhood and adolescence: A meta-analytic review of gender differences, intercorrelations, and relations to maladjustment. *Child Development, 79*, 1185–1229.

Cardemil, E. V., Reivich, K. J., & Seligman, M. E. P. (2002, May 8). The prevention of depressive symptoms in low-income minority middle school students. *Prevention and Treatment, 5.* http://journals.apa.org/prevention/volume5/tocmay08–02.htm.

Carlson, C. L., & Miranda, M. (2002). Sluggish cognitive tempo predicts a different pattern of impairment in the attention deficit hyperactivity disorder, predominantly inattentive type. *Journal of Clinical Child and Adolescent Psychology, 31*, 123–129.

Carlson, C. L., Tamm, L., & Hogan, A. E. (1999). The child with oppositional defiant disorder and conduct disorder in the family. In H. C. Quay & A. E. Hogan (Eds.), *Handbook of disruptive behavior disorders* (pp. 337–352). Dordrecht, Netherlands: Kluwer Academic Publishers.

Carlson, E.A., Yates, T.M., & Sroufe, LA. (2009). Dissociation and development of the self. In P.F. Dell & J.A. O'Neil (Eds,) *Dissociation and the dissociative disorders: DSM-V and beyond* (pp. 39–52). New York: Routledge/Taylor & Francis Group.

Carlson, G. A. (1998). Mania and ADHD: Comorbidity or confusion. *Journal of Affective Disorders, 51*, 177–187.

Carlson, G. A., Jensen, P. S., Findling, R. L., Meyer, R. E., Calabrese, J., DelBello, M. P., et al. (2003). Methodological issues and controversies in clinical trials with child and adolescent patients with bipolar disorder: Report of a consensus conference. *Journal of Child and Adolescent Psychopharmacology,13*, 13–27.

Carlson, V., Cicchetti, D., Barnett, D., & Braunwald, K. (1989). Disorganized/disoriented attachment relationships in maltreated infants. *Developmental Psychology, 25*, 525–531.

Carpenter, L. L., Tyrka, A. R., McDouble, C. J., Malison, R. T., Owens, M. J., Nemeroff, C. B., et al. (2004). Cerebrospinal fluid and corticotropin-releasing factor and perceived early-life stress in depressed patients and healthy control subjects. *Neuropsychopharmacology, 29*, 777–784.

Carr, T., & Lord, C. (2009). Autism spectrum disorders. In C. Zeanah (Ed.), Handbook of Infant Mental Health (3rd ed.) (pp. 301–317). New York: Guilford Press.

Carrington, S., & Elkins, J. (2002). Bridging the gap between inclusive policy and inclusive culture in secondary schools. *Support for Learning, 17*, 51–57.

Carrion, V.G., Weems, C.F., & Reiss, A.L. (2007). Stress predicts brain changes in children: A pilot longitudinal study on youth stress, posttraumatic stress disorder, and the hippocampus. *Pediatrics, 119*, 509–516.

Carrion, V.G., Weems, C.F., Watson, C., Eliez, S., Menon, V., & Reiss, A.L. (2009). Converging evidence for abnormalities of the prefrontal cortex and evaluation of midsagittal structures in pediatric posttraumatic stress disorder: An MRI study. *Psychiatry Research: Neuroimaging, 172*, 226–234.

Carskadon, M. A., Acebo, C., & Jenni, O. G. (2004). Regulation of adolescent sleep: Implications for behavior. In R. E. Dahl & L. P. Spear (Eds.), *Adolescent brain development: Vulnerabilities and opportunities. Annals of the New York Academy of Sciences* (Vol. 1021, pp. 276–291). New York: New York Academy of Sciences.

Cartwright, K.L., Bitsakou, P., Daley, D., Gramzow, R.H., Psychogiou, L., Simonoff, E., … Sonuga-Barke, E.J.S. (2011). Disentangling child and family influences on maternal expressed emotion toward children with attention-deficit/hyperactivity disorder. *Journal of the American Academy of Child & Adolescent Psychiatry, 50*, 1042–1053.

Cartwright-Hatton, S., McNicol, K., & Doubleday, E. (2006). Anxiety in a neglected population: Prevalence of anxiety disorders in preadolescent children. *Clinical Psychology Review, 26*, 817–833.

Case, B.G., Olfson, M., Marcus, S.C., & Siegel, C. (2007). Trends in the inpatient mental health treatment of children and adolescents in US community hospitals between 1990 and 2000. *Archives of General Psychiatry, 64*, 89–96.

Casey, B.J., & Jones, R.M. (2010). Neurobiology of the adolescent brain and behavior: Implications for substance use disorders. *Journal of the American Academy of Child & Adolescent Psychiatry, 49*, 1189–1201.

Casey, B.J., Tottenham, N., Listen, C., & Durston, S. (2005). Imaging the developing brain: What have we learned about cognitive development? *Trends in Cognitive Sciences, 9*, 104–110.

Caspi, A., Harrington, H., Milne, B., Amell, J. W., Theodore, R. F., & Moffitt, T. E. (2003). Children's behavioral styles at age 3 are linked to their adult personality traits at age 26. *Journal of Personality, 71*, 495–513.

Caspi, A., Moffitt, T. E., Morgan, J., Rutter, M., Taylor, A., Arseneault, L., et al. (2004). Maternal expressed emotion predicts children's antisocial behavior problems: Using monozygotic-twin differences to identify environmental effects on behavioral development. *Developmental Psychology, 40*, 149–161.

Cassidy, J., & Shaver, P. R. (1999*). Handbook of attachment: Theory, research, and clinical applications.* New York: Guilford Press.

Cassin, S. E., & von Ranson, K. M. (2005). Personality and eating disorders: A decade in review. *Clinical Psychology Review, 25*, 895–916.

Castellanos, F. X. (1999). Stimulants and tic disorders: From dogma to data. *Archives of General Psychiatry, 56*, 337–338.

Castellanos, F.X., Sonuga-Barke, E.J.S., Milham, M.P., & Tannock, R. (2006). Characterizing cognition in ADHD: Beyond executive dysfunction. *Trends in Cognitive Sciences, 10*, 117–123.

Castle, L., Aubert, R.E., Verbrugge, R.R., Khalid, M., & Epstein, R.S. (2007). Trends in medication treatment for ADHD. *Journal of Attention Disorders, 10,* 335–342.

Castro-Fornieles, J., Gual, P., Lahortiga, F., Gila, A., Casula, V., Fuhrmann, C., et al. (2007). Self-oriented perfectionism in eating disorders. *International Journal of Eating Disorders, 40,* 562–568.

Catani, C., Gewirtz, E., Schauer, E. Elbert, T., & Neuner, F. (2010). Tsunami, war, and cumulative risk in the lives of Sri Lankan schoolchildren. *Child Development, 81,* 1176–1191.

Causton-Theoharis, J., Ashby, C., & Cosier, M. (2009). Islands of loneliness: Exploring social interaction through the autobiographies of individuals with autism. *Intellectual and Developmental Disabilities, 47,* 84–96.

Centers for Disease Control and Prevention. (2007). Autism Information Center. Retrieved July 6, 2009, from www.cdc.gov/ncbddd/autism/index.htm.

Centers for Disease Control and Prevention (2012). Prevalence of autism spectrum disorders—Autism and developmental disabilities monitoring network, 14 sites, Unites States, 2008. *Surveillance Summaries, 61,* 1–19.

Cerel, J., Roberts, T. A., & Nilsen, W. J. (2005). Peer suicidal behavior and adolescent risk behavior. *Journal of Nervous and Mental Disease, 193*(4), 237–243.

Chabrol, H., Massot, E., & Mullet, E. (2004). Factor structure of cannabis-related beliefs in adolescents. *Addictive Behaviors, 29,* 929–933.

Chakrabarti, S., & Fombonne, E. (2005). Pervasive developmental disorders in preschool children: Confirmation of high prevalence. *America Journal of Psychiatry, 162*(6), 1133–1141.

Chamay-Weber, C. Narring, F., & Michaud, P. (2005). Partial eating disorders among adolescents: A review. *Journal of Adolescent Health, 37,* 417–427.

Chamberlain, P., & Patterson, G. R. (1995). Discipline and child compliance in parenting. In M. H. Bornstein (Ed.), *Handbook of parenting: Vol. 4. Applied and practical parenting* (pp. 205–225). Mahwah, NJ: Erlbaum.

Chambers, D. A., Ringeisen, H., & Hickman, E. E. (2005). Federal, state, and foundation initiatives around evidence-based practices for child and adolescent mental health. *Child and Adolescent Psychiatric Clinics of North America, 14,* 307–327.

Chambers, R. A., & Potenza, M. N. (2003). Neurodevelopment, impulsivity, and adolescent gambling. *Journal of Gambling Studies, 19,* 53–84.

Chandana, S. R., Behen, M. E., Juhasz, C., Muzik, O., Rothermel, R. D., Mangner, T. J., et al. (2005). Significance of abnormalities in developmental trajectory and asymmetry of cortical serotonin synthesis in autism. *International Journal of Developmental Neuroscience, 23,* 171–182.

Chang, K., Karchemskiy, A., Barnea-Goraly, N., Garrett, A., Simeonova, D. I., & Reiss, A. (2005). Reduced amygdalar gray matter volume in familial pediatric bipolar disorder. *Journal of the American Academy of Child and Adolescent Psychiatry, 44,* 565–573.

Chao, R. K. (2000). Cultural explanations for the role of parenting in the school success of Asian-American children. In R. D. Taylor & M.Wang (Eds.), *Resilience across contexts: Family, work, culture, and community* (pp. 333–363). Mahwah, NJ: Erlbaum.

Charman, T., Baron-Cohen, S., Baird, G., Cox, A., Swettenham, J., Wheelwright, S., et al. (2002). Is 18 months too early for the CHAT? *Journal of the American Academy of Child and Adolescent Psychiatry, 41,* 235–236.

Charman, T., Swettenham, J., Baron-Cohen, S., Cox, A., Baird, G., & Drew, A. (1997). Infants with autism: An investigation of empathy, pretend play, joint attention, and imitation. *Developmental Psychology, 33,* 781–789.

Charman, T., Swettenham, J., Baron-Cohen, S., Cox, A., Baird, G., & Drew, A. (2000). An experimental investigation of social-cognitive abilities in infants with autism: Clinical implications. In D. Muir & A. Slater (Eds.), *Infant development: The essential readings. Essential readings in development psychology* (pp. 343–363). Malden, MA: Blackwell.

Chassin, L., Presson, C. C., Pitts, S. C., & Sherman, S. J. (2000). The natural history of cigarette smoking from adolescence to adulthood in a midwestern community sample: Multiple trajectories and their psychosocial correlates. *Health Psychology, 19,* 223–231.

Chassin, L., Presson, C. C., Rose, J., Sherman, S. J., Davis, M. J., & Gonzalez, J. L. (2005). Parenting style and smoking-specific parenting practices as predictors of adolescent smoking onset. *Journal of Pediatric Psychology, 30,* 334–344.

Chassin, L., Presson, C. C., & Sherman, S. J. (1989). "Constructive" vs. "destructive" deviance in adolescent health-related behaviors. *Journal of Youth and Adolescence, 18,* 245–262.

Chassin, L., Presson, C. C., & Sherman, S. J. (2005). Adolescent cigarette smoking: A commentary and issues for pediatric psychology. *Journal of Pediatric Psychology, 30,* 299–303.

Chatoor, I. (2002). Feeding disorders in infants and toddlers: Diagnosis and treatment. *Child and Adolescent Psychiatric Clinics of North America, 11,* 163–183.

Chatoor, I., & Ammaniti, M. (2007). Classifying feeding disorders of infancy and early childhood. In W. E. Narrow, M. B. First, P. J. Sirovatka, & D. A. Regier (Eds.), *Age and gender considerations in psychiatric diagnosis: A research agenda for DSM-V* (pp. 227–242). Arlington, VA: American Psychiatric Publishing.

Chatterji, P., Dave, D., Kaestner, R., & Markowitz, S. (2004). Alcohol abuse and suicide attempts among youth. *Economics and Human Biology, 2,* 159–180.

Chavez, M., & Insel, T.R. (2007). Eating disorders: National Institute of Mental Health's Perspective. *American Psychologist, 62,* 159–166.

Chavira, D. A., Stein, M. B., Bailey, K., & Stein, M. T. (2004). Child anxiety in primary care: Prevalent but untreated. *Depression and Anxiety, 20,* 155–164.

Chawarska, K., Paul, R., Klin, A., Hannigen, S., Dichtel, L. E., & Volkmar, F. (2007). Parental recognition of developmental problems in toddlers with autism spectrum disorders. *Journal of Autism and Developmental Disorders, 37,* 2007.

Chen, C., Greenberger, E., Lester, J., Dong, Q., & Guo, M.-S. (1998). A cross-cultural study of family and peer correlates of adolescent misconduct. *Developmental Psychology, 34,* 770–781.

Chess, S., & Thomas, A. (1984). *Origins and evolution of behavior disorders: From infancy to early adult life.* New York: Brunner/Mazel Publishers.

Chi, T. C., & Hinshaw, S. P. (2002). Mother-child relationships of children with ADHD: the role of maternal depressive symptoms and depression-related distortions. *Journal of Abnormal Child Psychology, 30,* 387–401.

Chisholm, K., Carter, M. C., Ames, E. W., & Morison, S. J. (1995). Attachment security and indiscriminately friendly behavior in children adopted from Romanian orphanages. *Development and Psychopathology, 7,* 283–294.

Choi, Y.Y., Shamosh, N.A., Cho, S.H., DeYoung, C.G., Lee, M.J., Lee, J., Kim, S.I., Cho, Z., Kim, K., Gray, J.R., & Lee, K.H. (2008). Multiple bases of human intelligence revealed by cortical thickness and neural activation. *Journal of Neuroscience, 28,* 10323–10329.

Chorpita, B. F., Brown, T. A., & Barlow, D. H. (1998). Perceived control as a mediator of family environment in etiological models of childhood anxiety. *Behavior Therapy, 29,* 457–476.

Chorpita, B. F., Yim, L. M., Donkervoet, J. C., Arensdorf, A., Amundsen, M. J., McGee, C., et al. (2002). Toward large-scale implementation of empirically supported treatments for children: A review and observations by the Hawaii Empirical Basis to Services Task Force. *Clinical Psychology: Science and Practice, 9,* 165–190.

Chorpita, B.F. (2001). Control and the development of negative emotion. In M. W. Vasey, & M.R. Dadds (Eds.) *The Developmental Psychopathology of Anxiety* (pp. 112–142). New York, NY: Oxford University Press.

Chorpita, B.F., Bernstein, A., & Daleiden, E.L. (2010). Empirically guided coordination of multiple evidence-based treatments: an illusion of relevance mapping in children's mental health services. *Journal of Consulting and Clinical Psychology, 79,* 470–480.

Chorpita, B.F., & Daleiden, E.L. (2009). Mapping evidence-based treatments for children and adolescents: application of the distillation and matching model to 615 treatments from 322 randomized trials. *Journal of Consulting and Clinical Psychology, 77,* 566–579.

Chowdhury, U., Gordon, I., Lask, B., Watkins, B., Watt, H., & Christie, D. (2003). Early-onset anorexia nervosa: Is there evidence of limbic system imbalance? *International Journal of Eating Disorders, 33,* 388–396.

Christie, K. A., Burke, J. D., Regier, D. A., Rae, D. S., Boyd, J. H., & Locke, B. Z. (1988). Epidemiologic evidence for early onset of mental disorders and higher risk of drug abuse in young adults. *American Journal of Psychiatry, 145,* 971–975.

Christophersen, E. R., & Mortweet, S. L. (2001). *Treatments that work with children: Empirically supported strategies for managing childhood problems.* Washington, DC: American Psychological Association.

Chugani, H. T. (1999). PET scanning studies of human brain development and plasticity. *Developmental Neuropsychology, 16,* 379–381.

Chung, H. L., & Steinberg, L. (2006). Relations between neighborhood factors, parenting behaviors, peer deviance, and delinquency among serious juvenile offenders. *Developmental Psychology, 42,* 319–331.

Cicchetti, D. (1984). The emergence of developmental psychopathology. *Child Development, 55,* 1–7.

Cicchetti, D. (1990a). A historical perspective on the discipline of developmental psychopathology. In J. E. Rolf, A. S. Masten, D. Cicchetti, K. H. Nuechterlein, & S. Weintraub (Eds.), *Risk and protective factors in the development of psychopathology* (pp. 2–28). New York: Cambridge University Press.

Cicchetti, D. (1990b). The organization and coherence of socio-motivational, cognitive, and representational development: Illustrations through a developmental psychopathology perspective of Down syndrome and child maltreatment. In R. A. Thompson (Ed.), *Socioemotional development. Current theory and research in motivation* (pp. 259–279). Lincoln: University of Nebraska Press.

Cicchetti, D. (1991). Fractures in the crystal: Developmental psychopathology and the emergence of self. *Developmental Review, 11,* 271–287.

Cicchetti, D. (2002). The impact of social experience on neuro-biological systems: Illustration from a constructivist view of child maltreatment. *Cognitive Development, 17,* 1407–1428.

Cicchetti, D. (2004). An odyssey of discovery: Lessons learned through three decades of research on child maltreatment. *American Psychologist, 59,* 731–741.

Cicchetti, D. (2010). Resilience under conditions of extreme stress: a multilevel perspective. *World Psychiatry, 9,* 145–154.

Cicchetti, D. (2011). Pathways to resilient functioning in maltreated children. In D. Cicchetti & G. I. Roisman (Eds.), *The Origins and Organization of Adaptation and Maladaptation, Minnesota Symposia on Child Psychology* (Vol. 36, pp. 459). New York: Wiley.

Cicchetti, D., & Dawson, G. (2002). Editorial: Multiple levels of analysis. *Development and Psychopathology, 14,* 417–420.

Cicchetti, D., & Ganiban, J. (1990). The organization and coherence of developmental processes in infants and children with Down syndrome. In R. M. Hodapp, J. A. Burack, & E. Zigler (Eds.), *Issues in the developmental approach to mental retardation* (pp. 169–225). New York: Cambridge University Press.

Cicchetti, D., & Garmezy, N. (1993). Prospects and promises in the study of resilience. *Development and Psychopathology, 5,* 497–502.

Cicchetti, D., & Gunnar, M.R. (2008). Integrating biological measures into the design and evaluation of preventative interventions. *Development and Psychopathology, 20,* 737–743.

Cicchetti, D., & Lynch, M. (1993). Toward an ecological/transactional model of community violence and child maltreatment: Consequences for children's development. *Psychiatry, 56,* 96–118.

Cicchetti, D., & Pogge-Hesse, P. (1982). Possible contributions of the study of organically retarded persons to developmental theory. In E. Zigler & D. Balla (Eds.), *Mental retardation: The developmental-difference controversy* (pp. 277–318). Hillsdale, NJ: Erlbaum.

Cicchetti, D., Rappaport, J., Sandler, I., & Weissberg, R. P. (2000). *The promotion of wellness in children and adolescents.* Washington, DC: Child Welfare League of America.

Cicchetti, D., & Rogosch, F. (1997). The role of self-organization in the promotion of resilience in maltreated children. *Development and Psychopathology, 9,* 797–815.

Cicchetti, D., & Rogosch, F. A. (1996). Equifinality and multifinality in developmental psychopathology. *Development and Psychopathology, 8,* 597–600.

Cicchetti, D., & Rogosch, F. A. (1999). Psychopathology as risk for adolescent substance use disorders: A developmental psychopathology perspective. *Journal of Clinical Child Psychology, 28,* 355–365.

Cicchetti, D., & Rogosch, F. A. (2002). A developmental psychopathology perspective on adolescence. *Journal of Consulting and Clinical Psychology, 70,* 6–20.

Cicchetti, D., & Rogosch, F. A. (2007). Personality, adrenal steroid hormones, and resilience in maltreated children: A multilevel perspective. *Development and Pscyhopathology, 19,* 787–809.

Cicchetti, D., Rogosch, F. A., & Toth, S. L. (1997). Ontogenesis, depressotypic organization, and the depressive spectrum. In S. Luthar, J. Burack, D. Cicchetti, & J. R. Weisz (Eds.), *Developmental psychopathology: Perspectives on adjustment, risk and disorder* (pp. 273–313). New York: Cambridge University Press.

Cicchetti, D., Rogosch, F. A., & Toth, S. L. (1998). Maternal depressive disorder and contextual risk: Contributions to the development of attachment insecurity and behavior problems in toddler-hood. *Development and Psychopathology, 10*, 283–300.

Cicchetti, D., Rogosch, F. A., & Toth, S. L. (2006). Fostering secure attachment in infants in maltreating families through preventive interventions. *Development and Psychopathology, 18*, 623–649.

Cicchetti, D., & Rogosch, F.A. (2012). Neuroendocrine regulation and emotional adaptation in the context of child maltreatment. *Monographs of the Society for Research in Child Development, 77*, 87–95.

Cicchetti, D., Rogosch, F.A., & Sturge-Apple, M.L. (2007). Interactions of child maltreatment and serotonin transporter and monoamine oxidase A polymorphisms: Depressive symptomatology among adolescents from low socioeconomic status backgrounds. *Development and Psychopathology, 19*, 1161–1180.

Cicchetti, D., Rogosch, F.A., Toth, S.L., & Sturge-Apple, M.L. (2011). Normalizing the development of cortisol regulation in maltreated infants through preventative interventions. *Development and Psychopathology, 23*, 789–800.

Cicchetti, D., & Serafica, F. C. (1981). Interplay among behavioral systems: Illustrations from the study of attachment, affiliation, and wariness in young children with Down's syndrome. *Developmental Psychology, 17*, 36–49.

Cicchetti, D., & Sroufe, L. A. (2000). The past as prologue to the future: The times, they've been a-changin'. *Development and Psychopathology, 12*, 255–264.

Cicchetti, D., & Toth, S. L. (1987). The application of a transactional risk model to intervention with multi-risk maltreating families. *Zero to Three, 7*, 1–8.

Cicchetti, D., & Toth, S. L. (1995). A developmental psychopathology perspective on child abuse and neglect. *Psychiatry, 34*, 541–565.

Cicchetti, D., & Toth, S. L. (1995). Developmental psychopathology and disorders of affect. In D. Cicchetti & D. J. Cohen (Eds.), *Developmental psychopathology, Vol. 2: Risk, disorder, and adaptation* (pp. 369–420). Oxford, England: Wiley.

Cicchetti, D., & Toth, S. L. (1998). The development of depression in children and adolescents. *American Psychologist, 53*, 221–241.

Cicchetti, D., & Toth, S. L. (2003). Child maltreatment: Past, present, and future perspectives. In R. P. Weissberg & H. J. Walberg (Eds.), *Long-term trends in the well-being of children and youth: Issues in children's and families lives* (pp. 181–205). Washington, DC: Child Welfare League of America.

Cicchetti, D., Toth, S. L., & Lynch, M. (1995). Bowlby's dream comes full circle: The application of attachment theory to risk and psychopathology. *Advances in Clinical Child Psychology, 17*, 1–65.

Cicchetti, D., Toth, S. L., & Rogosch, F. A. (2000). The development of psychological wellness in maltreated children. In D. Cicchetti & J. Rappaport (Eds.), *The promotion of wellness in children and adolescents* (pp. 395–426). Washington, DC: Child Welfare League of America.

Cicchetti, D., & Toth, S.L. (2009). The past achievements and future promises of developmental psychopathology: The coming of age of a discipline. *Journal of Child Psychology and Psychiatry, 50*, 16–25.

Cicchetti, D., & Valentino, K. (2006). An ecological-transactional perspective on child maltreatment: Failure of the average expectable environment and its influence on child development. In D. Cicchetti & D.J. Cohen (Eds.) *Developmental Psychopathology, Vol 3: Risk, disorder, and adaptation* (2nd ed.) (pp 129–201). Hoboken, NJ: Wiley.

Cicchetti, D., & Valentino, K. (2007). Toward the application of a multiple-levels-of-analysis perspective to research in development and psychopathology. In A. S. Masten (Ed.), *Multilevel dynamics in developmental psychopathology: Pathways to the future, Minnesota Symposia on Child Psychology* (Vol. 34, pp. 243–284). Mahwah, NJ: Erlbaum.

Cicchetti, D., & Walker, E. (2003). *Neurodevelopmental mechanisms in psychopathology*. New York: Cambridge University Press.

Claes, M. (1998). Adolescents' closeness with parents, siblings, and friends in three countries: Canada, Belgium, and Italy. *Journal of Youth and Adolescence, 27*, 165–184.

Clahsen, H., & Temple, C. (2003). Words and rules in children with Williams syndrome. In Y. Levy & J. Schaeffer (Eds.), *Language competence across populations: Toward a definition of specific language impairment* (pp. 323–352). Mahwah, NJ: Erlbaum.

Clark, C., Prior, M., & Kinsella, G. J. (2000). Do executive function deficits differentiate between adolescents with ADHD and oppositional defiant/conduct disorder? A neuropsychological study using the Six Elements Test and Hayling Sentence Completion Test. *Journal of Abnormal Child Psychology, 28*, 403–414.

Clark, D. B., Cornelius, J. R., Kirisci, L, & Tarter, R. E. (2005). Childhood risk categories for adolescent substance involvement: A general liability typology. *Drug and Alcohol Dependence, 77*, 13–21.

Clark, L. A. (2005). Temperament as a unifying basis for personality and psychopathology. *Journal of Abnormal Psychology, 114*, 505–521.

Clark, L. A., Watson, D., & Reynolds, S. (1995). Diagnosis and classification of psychopathology: Challenges to the current system and future directions. *Annual Review of Psychology, 46*, 121–153.

Clarren, S., & Astley, S. (1997). Development of the FAS Diagnostic and Prevention Network in Washington State. In A. Streissguth & J. Kanter (Eds.), *The challenge of fetal alcohol syndrome: Overcoming secondary disabilities* (pp. 40–51). Seattle: University of Washington Press.

Clay, D., Vignoles, V. L., & Dittmar, H. (2005). Body image and self-esteem among adolescent girls: Testing the influence of sociocultural factors. *Journal of Research on Adolescence, 15*, 451–477.

Clayton, R. R., Scutchfield, D., & Wyatt, S. W. (2000). Hutchinson Smoking Prevention Project: A new gold standard in prevention science requires new transdisciplinary thinking. *Journal of the National Cancer Institute, 92*, 1964–1965.

Cleary, C. (2000). Self-directed violence in adolescence: A psychotherapeutic perspective. In G. Boswell (Ed.), *Violent children and adolescents: Asking the question why* (pp. 91–103). Philadelphia: Whurr Publishers.

Clemmy, P., Payne, L., & Fishman, M. (2004). Clinical characteristics and treatment outcomes of adolescent heroin users. *Journal of Psychoactive Drugs, 36*, 85–94.

Cleveland, M. J., Gibbons, F. X., Gerrard, M., Pomery, E. A., & Brody, G. H. (2005). The impact of parenting on risk cognitions and risk behavior: A study of mediation and moderation in a panel of African American adolescents. *Child Development, 76*, 900–916.

Clingempeel, W. G., & Henggeler, S. W. (2003). Aggressive juvenile offenders transitioning into emerging adulthood: Factors discriminating persistors and desistors. *American Journal of Orthopsychiatry, 73,* 310–323.

Clinton, D. (2006). Affect regulation, object relations and the central symptoms of eating disorders. *European Eating Disorders Review, 14,* 203–211.

Cloninger, C. R., Bohman, M., & Sigvardsson, S. (1981). Inheritance of alcohol abuse: Cross-fostering analysis of adopted men.
Archives of General Psychiatry, 38, 861–868.

Coates, D. L., & Vietze, P. M. (1996). Cultural considerations in assessment, diagnosis, and intervention. In J. W. Jacobson & J. A. Mulick (Eds.), *Manual of diagnosis and professional practice in mental retardation* (pp. 243–256). Washington, DC: American Psychological Association.

Coffelt, N. L., Forehand, R., Olson, A. L., Jones, D. J., Gaffney, C. A., & Zens, M. S. (2006). A longitudinal examination of the link between parent alcohol problems and youth drinking: The moderating roles of parent and child gender. *Addictive Behaviors, 31,* 593–605.

Coghill, D. & Banaschewski, T. (2009). The genetics of attention-deficit/hyperactivity disorder. *Expert Review of Neurotherapeutics, 9,* 1547–1565.

Cohen, D. J., Volkmar, F. R., Anderson, G., & Klin, A. (1993). Integrating biological and behavioral perspectives in the study and care of autistic individuals: The future ahead. *Israel Journal of Psychiatry, 30,* 15–32.

Cohen, J.A., & Mannarino, A. P. (2008). Trauma-focused cognitive behavioural therapy for children and parents. *Child & Adolescent Mental Health, 13,* 158–162.

Cohen, J.A., Mannarino, A.P., Kliethermes, M., & Murray, L.A. (2012). Trauma-focused CBT for youth with complex trauma. *Child Abuse & Neglect, 36,* 528–541.

Cohen, J.A., Mannarino, A.P., Perel, J.M., & Stratton, V. (2007). A pilot randomized controlled trial of combined trauma-focused CBT and sertraline for childhood PSTD symptoms. *Journal of the American Academy of Child & Adolescent Psychiatry, 46,* 811–819.

Cohen, N.J., Muir, E., Parker, C.J., Brown, M., Lojkasek, M., Muir, R. & Barwick, M. (1999). Watch, wait and wonder: Testing the effectiveness of a new approach to mother-infant psychotherapy. *Infant Mental Health Journal, 20,* 429–451.

Cohen, P., Cohen, J., & Brook, J. (1993). An epidemiological study of disorders in late childhood and adolescence—II. Persistence of disorders. *Journal of Child Psychology and Psychiatry, 34,* 869–877.

Cohen, P., & Flory, M. (1998). Issues in the disruptive behavior disorders: Attention deficit disorder without hyperactivity and the differential validity of oppositional defiant and conduct disorders. In T. Widiger (Ed.), *DSM-IV Sourcebook, Vol. 4* (pp. 455–463). Washington, DC: American Psychiatric Press.

Coie, J. D., & Dodge, K. A. (1998). Aggression and antisocial behavior. In W. Damon & N. Eisenberg (Eds.), *Handbook of child psychology: Vol. 3. Social, emotional, and personality development* (5th ed., pp. 779–862). Hoboken, NJ: Wiley.

Coie, J. D., Dodge, K. A., & Coppotelli, H. (1982). Dimensions and types of social status: A cross-age perspective. *Developmental Psychology, 18,* 557–570.

Colby, S. M., Tiffany, S. T., Shiffman, S., & Niaura, R. S. (2000). Are adolescent smokers dependent on nicotine? A review of the evidence. *Drug and Alcohol Dependence, 59,* S83–S95.

Colder, C. R., & Chassin, L. (1999). The psychosocial characteristics of alcohol users versus problem users: Data from a study

of adolescents at risk. *Development and Psychopathology, 11,* 321–348.

Colder, C. R., Mehta, P., Balanda, K., Campbell, R. T., Mayhew, K. P., & Stanton, W. R. (2001). Identifying trajectories of adolescent smoking: An application of latent growth mixture model. *Health Psychology, 20,* 127–135.

Cole, D. A., Hoffman, K., Tram, J. M., & Maxwell, S. E. (2000). Structural differences in parent and child reports of children's symptoms of depression and anxiety. *Psychological Assessment, 12,* 174–185.

Cole, D. A., Martin, J. M., Powers, B., & Truglio, R. (1996). Modeling causal relations between academic and social competence and depression: A multitrait-multimethod longitudinal study of children. *Journal of Abnormal Psychology, 105,* 258–270.

Cole, D. A., Tram, J. M., Martin, J. M., Hoffman, K. B., Ruiz, M. D., Jacquez, F. M., et al. (2002). Individual differences in the emergence of depressive symptoms in children and adolescents: A longitudinal investigation of parent and child reports. *Journal of Abnormal Psychology, 111,* 156–165.

Cole, P. (1998). Developmental versus difference approaches to mental retardation: A theoretical extension to the present debate. *American Journal on Mental Retardation, 102,* 379–391.

Cole, P. M., & Hall, S. E. (2008). Emotion dysregulation as a risk factor for psychopathology. In T. P. Beauchaine & S. P. Hinshaw (Eds.), *Child and adolescent psychopathology* (pp. 265–298). Hoboken, NJ: Wiley.

Cole, P. M., Martin, S. E., & Dennis, T. A. (2004). Emotion regulation as a scientific construct: Methodological challenges and directions for child development research. *Child Development, 75,* 317–333.

Cole, P.M., & Deater-Deckard, K. (2009). Emotion regulation, risk, and psychopathology. *Journal of Child Psychology and Psychiatry, 50,* 1327–1330.

Cole, P.M., Hall, S.E., Radzioch, A.M. (2009). Emotional dysregulation and the development of serious misconduct. In S.L. Olson, A.J. Sameroff (Eds.), *Biopsychosocial Regulatory Processes in the Development of Childhood Behavioral Problems* (pp. 186–211). New York: Cambridge University Press.

Cole, P.M., Luby, J., & Sullivan, M.W. (2008). Emotions and the development of childhood depression: Bridging the gap. *Child Development Perspectives, 2,* 141–148.

Coleman, D., Walker, J.S., Lee, J., Friesen, B.J., & Squire, P.N. (2009). Children's beliefs about causes of childhood depression and ADHD: A study in stigmatization. *Psychiatric Services, 60,* 950–957.

Coleman, L., & Cater, S. (2005). Underage 'binge' drinking: A qualitative study into motivations and outcomes. *Drugs: Education, Prevention, & Policy, 12,* 125–136.

Coll, C.G. & Magnuson, K. (1999). Cultural influences on child development: Are we ready for a paradigm shift? In A. S. Masten (Ed.) *Cultural Processes in Child Development* (pp. 1–24). Mahwah, NJ: Erlbaum.

Collett, B. R., Ohan, J. L., & Myers, K. M. (2003). Ten-year review of rating scales. VI: Scales assessing externalizing behaviors. *Journal of the American Academy of Child and Adolescent Psychiatry, 42,* 1143–1170.

Colletti, C.J.M., Forehand, R., Garai, E., Rakow, A., McKee, L., Fear, J.M., & Compas, B.E. (2009). Parent depression and child anxiety: An overview of the literature with clinical implications. *Child Youth Care Forum, 38,* 151–160.

Collins, D.W., & Rourke, B.P. (2003). Learning-disabled brains: A review of the literature. *Journal of Clinical & Experimental Neuropsychology, 25,* 1011–1034.

Collins, R. L., & Ricciardelli, L. A. (2005). Assessment of eating disorders and obesity. In D. M. Donovan (Ed.), *Assessment of addictive behaviors* (pp. 305–333). New York: Guilford Press.

Collins, W.A., Maccoby, E.E., Steinberg, L., Hetherington, E.M. & Bornstein, M.H. (2000). Contemporary research on parenting: The case for nature and nurture. *American Psychologist, 55,* 218–232.

Collishaw, S., Maughan, B., Goodman, R., & Pickles, A. (2004). Time trends in adolescent mental health. *Journal of Child Psychology and Psychiatry, 45,* 1350–1362.

Collishaw, S., Pickles, A., Messer, J., Rutter, M., Shearer, C., & Maughan, B. (2007). Resilience to adult psychopathology following childhood maltreatment: Evidence from a community sample. *Child Abuse and Neglect, 31,* 211–229.

Comer, J. S., Kendall, P. C., Franklin, M. E., Hudson, J. L., & Pimentel, S. S. (2004). Obsessing/worrying about the overlap between obsessive-compulsive disorder and generalized anxiety disorder in youth. *Clinical Psychology Review, 24,* 663–683.

Comer, J.S., Furr, J.M., Beidas, R.S, Weiner, C.L., & Kendall, P.C. (2008).Children and terrorism-related news: Training parents in coping and media literacy. *Journal of Consulting and Clinical Psychology, 76,* 568–578.

Comer, J.S. & Kendall, P.C. (2004). A symptom-level examination of parent-child agreement in the diagnosis of anxious youths. *Journal of the American Academy of Child & Adolescent Psychiatry, 43,* 878–886.

Compas, B. E., Hinden, B. R., & Gerhardt, C. A. (1995). Adolescent development: Pathways and processes of risk and resilience. *Annual Review of Psychology, 46,* 265–293.

Compas, B. E., Malcarne, V. L., & Fondacaro, K. M. (1988). Coping with stressful events in older children and young adolescents. *Journal of Consulting and Clinical Psychology, 56,* 405–411.

Compas, B. E. (1987). Coping with stress during childhood and adolescence. *Psychological Bulletin, 101,* 393–403.

Compas, B. E. (2009). Coping, regulation, and development during childhood and adolescence. *New Directions for Child and Adolescent Development, 124,* 87–99.

Compton, S.N. (2002). Review of the evidence base for treatment of childhood psychopathology: Internalizing disorders. *Journal of Consulting and Clinical Psychology, 70,* 1240–1266.

Conduct Problems Prevention Research Group. (1999a). Initial impact of the FAST Track prevention trial for conduct problems: I. The high-risk sample. *Journal of Consulting and Clinical Psychology, 67,* 631–647.

Conduct Problems Prevention Research Group. (1999b). Initial impact of the FAST Track prevention trial for conduct problems: II. Classroom effects. *Journal of Consulting and Clinical Psychology, 67,* 648–657.

Conduct Problems Prevention Research Group. (2002). The implementation of the FAST Track Program: An example of a large-scale prevention science effi cacy trial. *Journal of Abnormal Child Psychology, 30,* 1–17.

Conduct Problems Prevention Research Group. (2003). Initial impact of the Fast Track Prevention Trial for Conduct Problems: II. Classroom effects. In M. E. Hertzig & E. A. Farber (Eds.), *Annual progress in child psychiatry and child development: 2000–2001* (pp. 605–628). New York: Brunner-Routledge.

Conduct Problems Prevention Research Group. (2007). The Fast Track randomized controlled trial to prevent externalizing psychiatric disorders. *Journal of the American Academy of Child and Adolescent Psychiatry, 46,* 1250–1262.

Conger, R.D., & Donnellan, M.B. (2007). An interactionist perspective on the socioeconomic context of human development. *Annual Review of Psychology, 58,* 175–199.

Conner, K. R., & Goldston, D. B. (2007). Rates of suicide among males increase steadily from age 11 to 21: Developmental framework and outline for prevention. *Aggression and Violent Behavior, 21,* 193–207.

Conner, K. R., Meldrum, S., Wieczorek, W. F., Duberstein, P. R., & Welte, J. W. (2004). The association of irritability and impulsivity with suicidal ideation among 15–20-year-old males. *Suicide and Life-Threatening Behavior, 34,* 363–373.

Conners-Burrow, N.A., Johnson, D.L., Whiteside-Mansell, L., McKelvey, L., Gargus, R.A. (2009). Adults matter: Protecting children from the negative impacts of bullying. *Psychology in the Schools, 46,* 593–604.

Constantino, M. J., Arnow, B. A., Blasey, C., & Agras, W. S. (2005). The association between patient characteristics and the therapeutic alliance in cognitive-behavioral and interpersonal therapy for bulimia nervosa. *Journal of Consulting and Clinical Psychology, 73,* 203–211.

Conway, A., & Stifter, C.A. (2012). Longitudinal antecedents of executive function in preschoolers. *Child Development, 83,* 1022–1036.

Conyers, C., Martin, T. L., Martin, G. L., & Yu, D. (2002). The 1983 AAMR manual, the 1992 AAMR manual, or the developmental disabilities act: Which do researchers use? *Education and Training in Mental Retardation and Developmental Disabilities, 37,* 310–316.

Cook, A., Spinazzola, J., Ford, J., Lanktree, C., Blaustein, M., Cloitre, M., DeRosa, R., Hubbard, R., Kagan, R., Liautaud, J., Mallah, K., Olafson, E. & van der Kolk, B. (2005). Complex trauma in children and adolescents. *Psychiatric Annals, 35,* 390–398.

Cooley, E., Toray, T., Wang, M. C., & Valdez, N. N. (2008). Maternal effects on daughters' eating pathology and body image. *Eating Behaviors, 9,* 52–61.

Coolidge, F.L., DenBoer, J.W. & Segal, D.L. (2002). Personality and neuropsychological correlates of bullying behavior. *Personality and Individual Differences, 36,* 1559–1569.

Cooper, M. J., Rose, K. S., & Turner, H. (2005). Core beliefs and the presence or absence of eating disorder symptoms and depressive symptoms in adolescent girls. *International Journal of Eating Disorders, 38,* 60–64.

Cooper, M. J., Rose, K. S., & Turner, H. (2006). The specific content of core beliefs and schema in adolescent girls high and low in eating disorder symptoms. *Eating Behaviors, 7,* 27–35.

Copel, J. A., & Bahado-Singh, R. O. (1999). Prenatal screening for Down's syndrome: A search for the family's values. *New England Journal of Medicine, 341,* 521–522.

Copeland, W. E., Keeler, G., Angold, A., & Costello, E. J. (2007). Traumatic events and posttraumatic stress in childhood. *Archives of General Psychiatry, 64,* 577–584.

Copeland, W., Keeler, G., Angold, A., & Costello, E.J. (2010). Posttraumatic stress without trauma in children. *American Journal of Psychiatry, 167,* 1059–1065.

Copeland, W., Shanahan, L., Costello, E. J., & Angold, A. (2011). Cumulative prevalence of psychiatric disorders by young adulthood: A prospective cohort analysis from the

Great Smoky Mountains study. *Journal of the American Academy of Child & Adolescent Psychiatry, 50,* 252–261.

Cornelius, J. R., Maisto, S. A., Pollock, N. K., Martin, C. S., Salloum, I. M., Lynch, K. G., et al. (2003). Rapid relapse generally follows treatment for substance use disorders among adolescents. *Addictive Behaviors, 28,* 381–386.

Cornell, A.H., & Frick, P.J. (2007). The moderating effects of parenting styles on the association between behavioral inhibition and parent-reported guilt and empathy in preschool children. *Journal of Clinical Child and Adolescent Psychology, 36,* 305–318.

Correia, L.M. & Martins, A.P.L. (2007). Specific learning disabilities and the Portuguese educational system. *Learning Disabilities Research & Practice, 22,* 189–195.

Corrigan, P. W. (2005). *On the stigma of mental illness: Practical strategies for research and social change.* Washington, DC: American Psychological Association.

Corrigan, P. W., Watson, A. C., & Barr, L. (2006). The self-stigma of mental illness: Implications for self-esteem and self-efficacy. *Journal of Social and Clinical Psychology, 25,* 875–884.

Corrigan, P. W., Watson, A. C., Otey, E., Westbrook, A. L., Gardner, A. L., Lamb, T. A., et al. (2007). How do children stigmatize people with mental illness? *Journal of Applied Social Psychology, 37,* 1405–1417.

Costa, F. M., Jessor, R., Turbin, M. S., Dong, Q., Zhang, H., & Wang, C. (2005). The role of social contexts in adolescence: Context protection and risk in the United States and China. *Applied Developmental Science, 9,* 67–85.

Costello, E. J., & Angold, A. (1996). Developmental psychopathology. In R. B. Cairns, G. H. Elder., & E. J. Costello (Eds.), *Developmental science. Cambridge studies in social and emotional development* (pp. 168–189). New York: Cambridge University Press.

Costello, E. J., & Angold, A. (2001). Bad behaviour: An historical perspective on disorders of conduct. In J. Hill & B. Maughan (Eds.), *Conduct disorders in childhood and adolescence. Cambridge child and adolescent psychiatry* (pp. 1–31). New York: Cambridge University Press.

Costello, E. J., Angold, A., Burns, B. J., Stangl, D. K., Tweed,

Costello, E. J., Egger, H. L., & Angold, A. (2005). The developmental epidemiology of anxiety disorders: Phenomenology, prevalence, and comorbidity. *Child and Adolescent Clinics of North America, 14,* 631–648.

Costello, E. J., Erkanli, A., & Angold, A. (2006). Is there an epidemic of child or adolescent depression? *Journal of Child Psychology and Psychiatry, 47,* 1263–1271.

Costello, E. J., Erkanli, A., & Angold, A. (2006). Is there an epidemic of child or adolescent depression? *Journal of Child Psychology and Psychiatry, 47,* 1263–1271.

Costello, E. J., Erkanli, A., Fairbank, J. A., & Angold, A. (2002). The prevalence of potentially traumatic events in childhood and adolescence. *Journal of Traumatic Stress, 15,* 99–112.

Costello, E. J., Erkanli, A., Federman, E., & Angold, A. (1999). Development of psychiatric comorbidity with substance abuse in adolescents: Effects of timing and sex. *Journal of Clinical Child Psychology, 28,* 298–311.

Costello, E. J., Mustillo, S., Erkanli, A., Keeler, G., & Angold, A. (2003). Prevalence and development of psychiatric disorders in childhood and adolescence. *Archives of General Psychiatry, 60,* 837–844.

Costello, E.J., & Angold, A. (2010). Developmental transitions to psychopathology: Are there prodromes of substance use disorders? *Journal of Child Psychology and Psychiatry, 51,* 526–532.

Costello, E.J., Egger, H., & Angold, A. (2005). 10-year research update review: The epidemiology of child and adolescent psychiatric disorders: I. Methods and public health burden. *Journal of American Academy of Child and Adolescent Psychiatry, 44,* 972–986

Costello, E.J., Foley, D.L., & Angold, A. (2006). 10-year research update review: The epidemiology of child and adolescent psychiatric disorders: II. Developmental Epidemiology. *Journal of American Academy of Child and Adolescent Psychiatry, 45,* 8–25.

Cottrell, D. (2003). Outcome studies of family therapy in child and adolescent depression. *Journal of Family Therapy, 25,* 406–416.

Courchesne, E., Campbell, K., & Solso, S. (2011). Brain growth across the life span in autism: Age-specific changes in anatomical pathology. *Brain Research, 1380,* 138–145.

Courchesne, E., Karns, C. M., Davis, H. R., Ziccardi, R., Carper, R. A., Tigue, Z. D., et al. (2001). Unusual brain growth patterns in early life in patients with autistic disorder: An MRI study. *Neurology, 57,* 245–254.

Courchesne, E., Mueller, R.-A., & Saitoh, O. (1999). Brain weight in autism: Normal in the majority of cases, megalencephalic in rare cases. *Neurology, 52,* 1057–1059.

Courchesne, E., & Pierce, K. (2005). Brain overgrowth in autism during a critical time in development: Implications for frontal pyramidal neuron and interneuron development and connectivity. *International Journal of Developmental Neuroscience, 23,* 153–170.

Courchesne, E., Redclay, E., Morgan, J. T., & Kennedy, D. P. (2005). Autism at the beginning: Microstructural and growth abnormalities underlying the cognitive and affective neuroscience and developmental psychopathology. *Development and Psychopathology, 17,* 577–597.

Couturier, J., & Lock, J. (2006). What is remission in adolescent anorexia nervosa? A review of various conceptualizations and quantitative analysis. *International Journal of Eating Disorders, 39,* 175–183.

Cowan, P. A., & Cowan, C. P. (2003). Normative family transitions, normal family processes, and healthy development. In F. Walsh (Ed.), *Normal Family Processes: Growing Diversity and Complexity* (3rd ed.). New York: Guilford Press.

Cowen, E. L. (1996). The ontogenesis of primary prevention: Lengthy strides and stubbed toes. *American Journal of Community Psychology, 24,* 235–249.

Cowen, E. L., & Durlak, J. A. (2000). Social policy and prevention in mental health. *Development and Psychopathology, 12,* 815–834.

Cox, A., Klein, K. Charman, T., Baird, G., Baron-Cohen, S., Swettenham, J., Drew, A., & Wheelwright, S. (1999). Autism spectrum disorders at 20 and 42 months of age: Stability of clinical and ADI-R diagnosis. *Journal of Child Psychology and Psychiatry and Allied Disciplines, 40,* 719–732.

Coyle, J.T., Pine, D.S., Charney, D.S., Lewis, L., Nemeroff, C.B, Carlson, C.A., Joshi, P.T., Reiss, D., Todd, R.D. & Hellander, M. (2003). Depression and bipolar support alliance consensus statement on the unment needs in diagnosis and treatment of mood disorders in children and adolescents. *Journal of the American Academy of Child & Adolescent Psychiatry, 42,* 1494–1503.

Craig, J., Baron-Cohen, S., & Scott, F. (2001). Drawing ability in autism: A window into the imagination. *Israel Journal of Psychiatry and Related Sciences, 38*, 242–253.

Cramer, A.O.J., Waldorp, L.J., van der Mass, H.L.J., & Borsboom, D. (2010). Comorbidity: A network perspective. *Behavioral and Brain Sciences, 33*, 137–193.

Craney, J. L., & Geller, B. (2003a). A prepubertal and early adolescent bipolar disorder-I phenotype: Review of phenomenology and longitudinal course. *Bipolar Disorders, 5*, 243–256.

Craney, J. L., & Geller, B. (2003b). Clinical implications of antidepressant and stimulant use on switching from depression to mania in children. *Journal of Child and Adolescent Psychopharmacology, 13*, 201–204.

Craske, M. G. (1997). Fear and anxiety in children and adolescents. *Bulletin of the Menninger Clinic, 61*, A4-A36.

Craske, M. G., Poulton, R., Tsao, J. C. I., & Plotkin, D. (2001). Paths to panic disorder/agoraphobia: An exploratory analysis from age 3 to 21 in an unselected birth cohort. *Journal of the American Academy of Child and Adolescent Psychiatry, 40*, 556–563.

Craske, M. G., & Zucker, B. G. (2001). Prevention of anxiety disorders: A model for intervention. *Applied and Preventive Psychology, 10*, 155–175.

Crawford, A. M., Pentz, M. A., Chou, C-P., Li, C., & Dwyer, J. H. (2003). Parallel developmental trajectories of sensation seeking and regular substance use in adolescents. *Psychology of Addictive Behaviors, 17*, 179–192.

Crick, N. R., & Dodge, K. A. (1994). A review and reformulation of social information processing mechanisms in children's social adjustment. *Psychological Bulletin, 115*, 74–101.

Crick, N. R., & Dodge, K. A. (1996). Social information-processing mechanisms in reactive and proactive aggression. *Child Development, 67*, 993–1002.

Crick, N. R., & Grotpeter, J. K. (1995). Relational aggression, gender, and social-psychological adjustment. *Child Development, 66*, 710–722.

Crick, N. R., & Zahn-Waxler, C. (2003). The development of psychopathology in females and males: Current progress and future challenges. *Development and Psychopathology, 15, 719*–742.

Crijen, A. A. M., Achenbach, T. M., & Verhulst, F. C. (1997). Comparisons of problems reported by parents of children in 12 cultures: Total problems, externalizing and internalizing. *Journal of the American Academy of Child and Adolescent Psychiatry, 36*, 1269–1277.

Crnic, K. A., Greenberg, M. T., & Slough, N. M. (1986). Early stress and social support influences on mothers' and high-risk infants' functioning in late infancy. *Infant Mental Health Journal, 7*, 19–33.

Crockenberg, S.C., Rutter, M., Bakermans-Kranenburg, M.J., van IJzendoorn, M.H., & Juffer, F. (2008). The effects of early social-emotional and relationship experiences on the development of young orphanage children. *Monographs of the Society for Research in Child Development, 73*, 1–293.

Crockett, L. J. (1997). Cultural, historical, and subcultural contexts of adolescence: Implications for health and development. In J. Schulenberg, J. L. Maggs, & K. Hurrelmann (Eds.), *Health risks and developmental transitions during adolescence* (pp. 23–53). New York: Cambridge University Press.

Croen, L. A., Grether, J. K., & Selvin, S. (2002). Descriptive epidemiology of autism in a California population: Who is at risk? *Journal of Autism and Developmental Disorders, 32*, 217–224.

Crosby, R.D., Wonderlich, S.A., Engel, S.G., Simonich, H., Smyth, J., & Mitchell, J.E. (2009). Daily mood patterns and bulimic behaviors in the natural environment. *Behavior Research and Therapy, 47*, 181–188.

Cross, C.P., Copping, L.T., & Campbell, A. (2011). Sex differences in impulsivity: A meta-analysis. *Psychological Bulletin, 137*, 97–130.

Crowley, T. J., Mikulich, S. K., Ehlers, K. M., Whitmore, E. A., & Macdonald, M. J. (2001). Validity of structured clinical evaluations in adolescents with conduct and substance problems. *Journal of the American Academy of Child and Adolescent Psychiatry, 40*, 265–273.

Crystal, D. S., Watanabe, H., Weinfurt, K., & Wu, C. (1998). Concepts of human differences: A comparison of American, Japanese, and Chinese children and adolescents. *Developmental Psychology, 34*, 714–722.

Cuellar, A. E., Markowitz, S., & Libby, A. M. (2004). Mental health and substance abuse treatment and juvenile crime. *Journal of Mental Health Policy and Economics, 7*, 59–68.

Cullen, D. (2004, April 20). The depressive and the psychopath. *Slate*, Article 2099203. Retrieved July 13, 2009, from http://www.slate.com/id/2099203.

Cullerton-Sen, C., Cassidy, A.R., Murray-Close, D., Cicchetti, D., Crick, N.R., & Rogosch, F.A. (2008). Childhood maltreatment and the development of relational and physical aggression: The importance of a gender-informed approach. *Child Development, 79*, 1736–1751.

Cummings, E. M. (1999). Some considerations on integrating psychology and health from a life-span perspective. In T. L. Whitman, T. V. Merluzzi, & R. D. White (Eds.), *Life-span perspectives on health and illness* (pp. 277–294). Mahwah, NJ: Erlbaum.

Cummings, E. M., & Davies, P. T. (1994). Maternal depression and child development. *Journal of Child Psychology and Psychiatry, 35*, 73–112.

Cummings, E. M., & Davies, P. T. (1995). The impact of parents on their children: An emotional security hypothesis. *Annals of Child Development, 10*, 167–208.

Cummings, E.M., Davies, P.T. & Campbell, S.B. (2000). Developmental Psychopathology and Family Process. New York, NY: Guilford Press.

Cummins, T. K., & Ninan, P. T. (2002). The neurobiology of anxiety in children and adolescents. *International Review of Psychiatry, 14*, 114–128.

Cunningham, P.B., Foster, S.L., Warner, S.E. (2010). Culturally relevant family-based treatment for adolescent delinquency and substance abuse: Understanding within-session processes. *Journal of Clinical Psychology, 66*, 830–846.

Curley, J.P., Jensen, C.L., Mashoodh, R., & Champagne, F. (2011). Social influences on neurobiology and behavior: Epigenetic effects during development. *Psychoneuroendochrinology, 36*, 352–371.

Curran, P. J., Stice, E. M., & Chassin, L. (1997). The relation between adole scent alcohol use and peer alcohol use: A longitudinal random coeffi cients model. *Journal of Consulting and Clinical Psychology, 65*, 130–140.

Curry, J., Rohde, P., Simons, A., Silva, S., Vitiello, B., Kratochvil, C., et al. (2006). Predictors and moderators of acute outcome in the Treatment for Adolescents with Depression Study (TADS). *Journal of the American Academy of Child and Adolescent Psychiatry, 45*, 1427–1439.

D. L., Erkanli, A., et al. (1996). The Great Smoky Mountains study of youth: Goals, design, methods, and the prevalence of DSM-III-R disorders. *Archives of General Psychiatry, 53,* 1129–1136.

D'Amico, E. J., Ellickson, P. L., Collins, R. L., Martino, S., & Klein, D. J. (2005). Processes linking adolescent problems to substance-use problems in late young adulthood. *Journal of Studies on Alcohol, 66,* 766–775.

D'Andrea, W, Ford, J., Stolbach, B., Spinazzola, J. & van der Kolk, B.A. (2012). Understanding interpersonal trauma in children: Why we need a developmentally appropriate trauma diagnosis. *American Journal of Orthopsychiatry, 82,* 187–200.

D'Eramo, K. S., Prinstein, M. J., Freeman, J. Grapentine, W. L., & Spirito, A. (2004). Psychiatric diagnoses and comorbidity in relation to suicidal behavior among psychiatrically hospitalized adolescents. *Child Psychiatry and Human Development, 35,* 21–35.

Daddis, D., & Smetana, J. (2005). Middle-class African American families' expectations for adolescents' behavioural autonomy. *International Journal of Behavioral Development, 29,* 371–381.

Dadds, M. R. (2002). Learning and intimacy in the families of anxious children. In R. J. McMahon & R. Peters (Eds.) *The effects of parental dysfunction on children* (pp. 87–104). New York: Kluwer Academic/Plenum Publishers.

Dadds, M.R. & Roth, J.H. (2008). Prevention of anxiety disorders: Results of a universal trial with young children. *Journal of Child and Family Studies, 17,* 320–335.

Dahl, R. E. (1996). The regulation of sleep and arousal: Development and psychopathology. *Development and Psychopathology, 8,* 3–27.

Dahl, R. E. (2004). Adolescent brain development: A period of vulnerabilities and opportunities. In R. E. Dahl & L. P. Spear (Eds.), *Adolescent brain development: Vulnerabilities and opportunities. Annals of the New York Academy of Sciences* (Vol. 1021, pp. 1–22). New York: New York Academy of Sciences.

Dahl, R. E., Birmaher, B., Williamson, D. E., Dorn, L., Perel, J., Kaufman, J., et al. (2000). Low growth hormone response to growth hormone–releasing hormone in child depression. *Biological Psychiatry, 48,* 981–988.

Dahl, R. E., & Lewin, D. S. (2002). Pathways to adolescent health: Sleep regulation and behavior. *Journal of Adolescent Health, 31,* 175–184.

Dale, K. L., & Baumeister, R. F. (1999). Self-regulation and psychopathology. In Robin M. Kowalski & M. R. Leary (Eds.), *The social psychology of emotional and behavioral problems: Interfaces of social and clinical psychology* (pp. 139–166). Washington, DC: American Psychological Association.

Dalgleish, T., Meiser-Stedman, R. & Smith, P. (2005). Cognitive aspects of posttraumatic stress reactions and their treatment in children and adolescents: An empirical review and some recommendations. *Behavioural and Cognitive Psychotherapy, 33,* 459–486.

Dammann, O., & Leviton, A. (1997). The role of perinatal brain damage in developmental disabilities: An epidemiologic perspective. *Mental Retardation and Developmental Disabilities Research Reviews, 3,* 12–21.

Damon, W., & Lerner, R. M. (1998). *Handbook of Child Psychology: Vol. 1. Theoretical Models of Human Development* (5th ed., pp. 635–684). Hoboken, NJ: Wiley.

Danckaerts, M., Sonuga-Barke, E.J.S., Banaschewski, T., Buitelaaar, J., Döpfner, M., Hollis, C., … Coghill, D. (2009) The quality of life of children with attention deficit/hyperactivity disorder: a systematic review. *European Child & Adolescent Pyschiatry, 19,* 83–105.

Dancyger, I., Fornari, V., Scionti, L., Wisotsky, W., & Sunday, S. (2005). Do daughters with eating disorders agree with their parents' perception of family functioning? *Comprehensive Psychology, 46,* 135–139.

Dancyger, I., Fornari, V., & Sunday, S. (2006). What may underlie differing perceptions of family functioning between mothers and their adolescent daughters with eating disorders? *International Journal of Adolescent Medicine and Health, 18,* 281–286.

Danese, A., & McEwen, B.S. (2012). Adverse childhood experiences, allostasis, allostatic load, and age-related disease. *Pysiology & Behavior, 106,* 29–39.

Danielson, C. K., de Arellano, M. A., Kilpatrick, D. G., Saunders, B. E., & Resnick, H. S. (2005). Child maltreatment in depressed adolescents: Differences in symptomology based on history of abuse. *Child Maltreatment, 10,* 37–48.

Danielson, C. K., Feeny, N. C., Findling, R. L., & Youngstrom, E.A. (2004). Psychosocial treatment of bipolar disorders in adolescence: A proposed cognitive-behavioral intervention. *Cognitive and Behavioral Practice, 11,* 283–297.

Das, J. P. (2004). Theories of intelligence: Issues and applications. In G. Goldstein, S. Beers, & M. Hersen (Eds.), *Comprehensive handbook of psychological assessment: Vol. 1. Intellectual and neurophysical assessment* (pp. 5–23). Hoboken, NJ: Wiley.

Dasinger, L. K., Shane, P. A., & Martinovich, Z. (2004). Assessing the effectiveness of community-based substance abuse treatment for adolescents. *Journal of Psychoactive Drugs, 36,* 27–33.

Daughton, J.M. & Kratochvil, C.J. (2009). Review of ADHD pharmacotherapies: Advantages, disadvantages, and clinical pearls. *Journal of the American Academy of Child & Adolescent Psychiatry, 48,* 240–248.

Davanzo, P., Yue, K., Thomas, M. A., Belin, T., Mintz, J., Venkatraman, T. N., et al. (2003). Proton magnetic resonance spectroscopy of bipolar disorder versus intermittent explosive disorder in children and adolescents. *American Journal of Psychiatry, 160,* 1442–1452.

Davidson, R. J. (2000). Affective style, psychopathology, and resilience: Brain mechanisms and plasticity. *American Psychologist, 55,* 1196–1214.

Davidson, R. J. (2000). Cognitive neuroscience needs affective neuroscience (and vice versa). *Brain and Cognition, 42,* 89–92.

Davidson, R. J., Abercrombie, H., Nitschke, J. B., & Putnam, K. (1999). Regional brain function, emotion and disorder of emotion. *Current Opinion in Neurobiology, 9,* 228–234.

Davidson, R. J., Jackson, D. C., & Kalin, N. H. (2000). Emotion, plasticity, context, and regulation: Perspectives from affective neuroscience. *Psychological Bulletin, 126,* 890–909.

Davies, S. (2004). A group-work approach to addressing friendship issues in the treatment of adolescents with eating disorders. *Clinical Child Psychology and Psychiatry, 9,* 519–531.

Davies, T., & Cicchetti, D. (2004). Toward an integration of family systems and developmental psychopathology approaches. *Development and Psychopathology, 16,* 477–481.

Davies, W.H., Satter, E., Berlin, K.S., Sato, A.F., Silverman, A.H., Fischer, E.A., … Rudolph, C.D. (2006). Reconceptualizing feeding and feeding disorders in interpersonal context: The case for a relational disorder. *Journal of Family Psychology, 20,* 409–417.

Davis, B., Sheeber, L., & Hops, H. (2002). Coercive family processes and adolescent depression. In J. B. Reid, G. R. Patterson, & J. Snyder (Eds.), *Antisocial behavior in children and adolescents: A developmental analysis and model for intervention* (pp. 173–192). Washington, DC: American Psychological Association.

Davis, T. E. & Ollendick, T.H. (2005). Empirically supported treatments for specific phobia in children: Do efficacious treatments address the components of a phobic response? *Clinical Psychology: Science and Practice, 12,* 144–160.

Davison, T., & McCabe, M. P. (2006). Adolescent body image and psychosocial functioning. *Journal of Social Psychology, 146,* 15–30.

Dawes, M. A., Antelman, S. M., Vanyukov, M. M., Giancola, P., Tarter, R. E., Susman, E. J., et al. (2000). Developmental sources of variation in liability to adolescent substance use disorders. *Drug and Alcohol Dependence, 61,* 3–14.

Dawes, M. A., & Johnson, B. A. (2004). Pharmacotherapeutic trials in adolescent alcohol use disorders: Opportunities and challenges. *Alcohol and Alcoholism, 39,* 166–177.

Dawson, D. A., & Grant, B. F. (1998). Family history of alcoholism and gender: Their combined effects on DSM-IV alcohol dependence and major depression. *Journal of Studies on Alcohol, 59,* 97–106.

Dawson, D. A., Grant, B. F., Stinson, F. S., & Chou, P. S. (2006). Maturing out of alcohol dependence: The impact of transitional life events. *Journal of Studies on Alcohol: 67,* 195–203.

Dawson, G. (2008). Early behavioral intervention, brain plasticity, and the prevention of autism spectrum disorder. *Development and Psychopathology, 20,* 775–803.

Dawson, G., Ashman, S. B., Panagiotides, H., Hessl, D., Self, J., Yamada, E., et al. (2003). Preschool outcomes of children of depressed mothers: Role of maternal behavior, contextual risk, and children's brain activity. *Child Development, 74*(4), 1158–1175.

Dawson, G. & Ashman, S.B. (2000). On the origins of a vulnerability to depression: The influence of the early social environment on the development of psychobiological systems related to risk of affective disorder. In C. A. Nelson (Ed.), *The Minnesota Symposia on Child Psychology, Vol. 31: The Effects of Early Adversity on Neurobehavioral Development* (pp. 245–279). Mahwah, NJ: Erlbaum.

Dawson, G., Carver, L., Meltzoff, A. N., Panagiotides, H., Mc-Partland, J., & Webb, S. J. (2002). Neural correlates of face and object recognition in young children with autism spectrum disorder, developmental delay and typical development. *Child Development, 73,* 700–717.

Dawson, G., Frey, K., Self, J., Panagiotides, H., Hessl, D., Yamada, E., & Rinaldi, J. (1999). Frontal brain electrical activity in infants of depressed and nondepressed mothers: Relation to variations in infant behavior. *Development and Psychopathology, 11,* 589–605.

Dawson, G., Munson, J., Estes, A., Osterling, J., McPartland, J., Toth, K., et al. (2002). Neurocognitive function and joint attention ability in young children with autism spectrum disorder versus developmental delay. *Child Development, 73,* 345–358.

Dawson, G., Toth, K., Abbott, R., Osterling, J., Munson, J., Estes, A., et al. (2004). Early social attention impairments in autism: Social orienting, joint attention, and attention to distress. *Developmental Psychology, 40,* 271–283.

Dawson, G., Webb, S. J., Wijsman, E., Schellenberg, G., Estes, A., Munson, J., et al. (2005) Neurocognitive and electrophysiological evidence of altered face processing in parents of children with autism: Implications for a model of abnormal development of social brain circuitry in autism. *Development and Psychopathology, 17,* 679–697.

Dawson, G., Webb, S.J. & McPartland, J. (2005). Understanding the nature of face processing impairment in autism: Insights from behavioral and electrophysiological studies. *Developmental Neuropsychology, 27,* 403–424.

Day, K., & Dosen, A. (2001). Treatment: An integrative approach. In A. Dosen & K. Day (Eds.), *Treating mental illness and behavior disorders in children and adults with mental retardation* (pp. 519–528). Washington, DC: American Psychiatric Publishing.

De Bellis, M. D. (2002). Developmental traumatology: A contributory mechanism for alcohol and substance use disorders. *Psychoneuroendocrinology, 27,* 155–170.

De Bellis, M.D. & Kuchibhatla, M. (2006). Cerebellar volumes in pediatric maltreatment-related posttraumatic stress disorder. *Biological Psychiatry, 60,* 697–703.

De Bellis, M.D., & Van Dillen, T. (2005). Childhood posttraumatic stress disorder: An overview. *Child & Adolescent Psychiatric Clinics of North America, 14,* 745–772.

de Bildt, A., Sytema, S., Ketelaars, C., Kraijer, D., Volkmar, F. & Minderaa, R. (2003). Measuring pervasive developmental disorders in children and adolescents with mental retardation: A comparison of two screening instruments used in a study of the total mentally retarded population from a designated area. *Journal of Autism and Developmental Disorders, 33,* 595–605.

de Bruin, G. O., Muris, P. & Rassin, E. (2007). Are there specific meta-cognitions associated with vulnerability to symptoms of worry and obsessional thoughts? *Personality and Individual Differences, 42,* 689–699.

De Los Reyes, A., & Kazdin, A. E. (2005). Informant discrepancies in the assessment of childhood psychopathology: A critical review, theoretical framework, and recommendations for further study. *Psychological Bulletin, 131,* 483–509.

de Miranda Correia, L., & Martins, A.P.L. (2007). Specific learning disabilities and the Portuguese educational system. *Learning Disabilities Research & Practice, 22,* 189–195.

De Wolff, M. S., & Van IJzendoorn, M. H. (1997). Sensitivity and attachment: A meta-analysis on parental antecedents of infant attachment. *Child Development, 68,* 571–591.

DeAngelis, T. (2007). A new diagnosis for childhood trauma. *Monitor on Psychology, 38,* 32–34.

Deas, D., St. Germaine, K., & Upadhyaya, H. (2006). Psychopathology in substance abusing adolescents: Gender comparisons. *Journal of Substance Use, 11,* 45–51.

Deas, D., & Thomas, S. E. (2001). An overview of controlled studies of adolescent substance abuse treatment. *American Journal on Addictions, 10,* 178–189.

Deas-Nesmith, D., Brady, K. T., Campbell, S. (1998). Comorbid substance use and anxiety disorders in adolescents. *Journal of Psychopathology and Behavioral Assessment, 20,* 139–148.

Deater-Deckard, K., & Dodge, K. A. (1997). Externalizing behavior problems and discipline revisited: Nonlinear effects and variation by culture, context, and gender. *Psychological Inquiry, 8,* 161–175.

Deater-Deckard, K., & Mullineaux, P. Y. (2010). Cognition and emotion: A behavioral genetic perspective. In S. D. Calkins & M. A. Bell (Eds.), *Child Development at the Intersection of*

Emotion and Cognition (pp. 133–152). Washington, DC: American Psychological Association.

Deblinger, E., Mannarino, A.P., Cohen, J.A. &. Steer, R.A (2006). A follow-up study of a multisite, randomized, controlled trial for children with sexual abuse-related PTSD symptoms. *Journal of the American Academy of Child & Adolescent Psychiatry, 45,* 1474–1484.

DeGangi, G. A., Breinbauer, C., Doussard Roosevelt, J., Porges, S., & Greenspan, S. (2000). Prediction of childhood problems at three years in children experiencing disorders of regulation during infancy. *Infant Mental Health Journal, 21,* 156–175.

DeGangi, G. A., Porges, S. W., Sickel, R. Z., & Greenspan, S. I. (1993). Four-year follow-up of a sample of regulatory disordered infants. *Infant Mental Health Journal, 14,* 330–343.

Degnan, K.A., Almas, A.N., & Fox, N.A. (2010). Temperament and the environment in the etiology of childhood anxiety. *Journal of Child Psychology and Psychiatry, 51,* 497–517.

DeJong, W., Schneider, S. K., Towvim, L. G., Murphy, M. J., Doerr, E. E., Simonson, N. R., et al. (2006). A multisite randomized trial of social norms marketing campaigns to reduce college student drinking. *Journal of Studies on Alcohol, 67,* 868–879.

Dekker, A. H., Estroff, T. W., & Hoffmann, N. G. (2001). Medical evaluation of substance-abusing adolescents. In Estroff, T. W. (Ed.), *Manual of adolescent substance abuse treatment* (pp. 91–98). Washington, DC: American Psychiatric Publishing.

DeKlyen, M. (1996). Disruptive behavior disorder and intergenerational attachment patterns: A comparison of clinic-referred and normally functioning preschoolers and their mothers. *Journal of Consulting and Clinical Psychology, 64,* 357–365.

DeKlyen, M., Biernbaum, M. A., Speltz, M. L., & Greenberg, M. T. (1998). Fathers and preschool behavior problems. *Developmental Psychology, 34,* 264–275.

DeKlyen, M. & Greenberg, M.T. (2008). Attachment and psychopathology in childhood. In J. Cassidy & P.R. Shaver (Eds.), *Handbook of Attachment: Theory, Research, and Clinical Applications (2nd ed.)* (pp. 637–665). New York, NY: Guilford Press.

Dekovic, M., Engels, R. C. M. E., Shirai, T., De Kort, G., & Anker, A. L. (2002). The role of peer relations in adolescent development in two cultures: The Netherlands and Japan. *Journal of Cross-Cultural Psychology, 33,* 577–595.

DelBello, M. P., Adler, C. M., & Strakowski, S. M. (2006). The neurophysiology of childhood and adolescent bipolar disorder. *CNS Spectrums, 11*), 298–311.

DelBello, M. P., Hanseman, D., Adler, C. M., Fleck, D. E., & Strakowski, S. M. (2007). Twelve-month outcome of adolescents with bipolar disorder following first hospitalization for a manic or mixed episode. *American Journal of Psychiatry, 164,* 582–590.

DelBello, M.P., Zimmerman, M.E., Mills N.P, Getz, G.E. & Strakowski, S.M. (2004). Magnetic resonance imaging analysis of amygdale and other subcortical brain regions in adolescents with bipolar disorder. *Bipolar Disorders 6,* 43–52.

Dell, M.L., Campo, J.V. (2011). Somatoform disorders in children and adolescents. *Psychiatric Clinics of North America, 34,* 643–660.

Delligatti, N., Akin-Little, A., & Little, S. G. (2003). Conduct disorder in girls: Diagnostic and intervention issues. *Psychology in the Schools, 40,* 183–192.

Delva, J., Wallace, J. M., Jr., O'Malley, P. M., Bachman, J. G., Johnston, L. D., & Schulenberg, J. E. (2005). The epidemiology of alcohol, marijuana, and cocaine use among Mexican American, Puerto Rican, Cuban American, and other Latin American eighth-grade students in the United States: 1991–2002. *American Journal of Public Health, 95,* 696–702.

Demaray, M. K., Schaefer, K., & Delong, L. K. (2003). Attention-deficit/hyperactivity disorder (ADHD): A national survey of training and current assessment practices in the schools. *Psychology in the Schools, 40,* 583–597.

Demb, H. B., & Noskin, O. (2001). The use of the term Multiple Complex Developmental Disorder in a diagnostic clinic serving young children with developmental disabilities: A report of 15 cases. *Mental Health Aspects of Developmental Disabilities, 4,* 4960.

Demetrious, A., & Raftopoulos, A. (1999). Modeling the developmental mind: From structure to change. *Developmental Review, 19,* 319–368.

Demir, M., & Urberg, K. A. (2004). Friendship and adjustment among adolescents. *Journal of Experimental Child Psychology, 88,* 68–82.

Denda, K., Sunami, T., Inoue, S., Sasaki, F., Sasaki, Y., Asakura, S., et al. (2002). Clinical study of early-onset eating disorders. *Japanese Journal of Child and Adolescent Psychiatry, 43,* 30–56.

Denham, S. A. (1998). *Emotional development in young children.* New York: Guilford Press.

Denham, S. A., Workman, E., Cole, P. M., Weissbrod, C., Kendziora, K. T., & Zahn-Waxler, C. (2000). Prediction of externalizing behavior problems from early to middle childhood: The role of parental socialization and emotion expression. *Development and Psychopathology, 12,* 23–45.

Denning, C. B., Chamberlain, J. A., & Polloway, E. A. (2000). An evaluation of state guidelines for mental retardation: Focus of definition and classification practices. *Education and Training in Mental Retardation and Developmental Disabilities, 35,* 226–232.

Dennis, M. (2000). Developmental plasticity in children: The role of biological risk, development, time, and reserve. *Journal of Communication Disorders, 3,* 321–332.

Denson, T.F., DeWall, C.N., & Finkel, E.J. (2012). Self-control and aggression. *Current Directions in Psychological Science, 21,* 20–25.

Deprey, L., & Ozonoff, S. (2009). Assessment of comorbid psychiatric conditions in autism spectrum disorders. In S. Goldstein, J.A. Naglieri & S. Ozonoff (Eds.) *Assessment of autism spectrum disorders* (pp. 290–317). New York: Guilford Press.

Depue, R. A., Collins, P. F., & Luciana, M. (1996). A model of neurobiology—Environment interaction in developmental psychopathology. *Frontiers of developmental psychopathology* (pp. 44–77). New York: Oxford University Press.

Derenne, J. L., & Beresin, E. V. (2006). Body image, media and eating disorders. *Academic Psychiatry, 30,* 257–261.

Derks, E. M., Dolan, C. V., Hudziak, J. J., Neale, M. C., & Boomsma, D. I. (2007). Assessment and etiology of attention deficit hyperactivity disorder and oppositional defiant disorder in boys and girls. *Behavior Genetics, 37,* 559–566.

DeRobertis, E.M. (2006). Deriving a humanistic theory of child development from the works of Carl R. Rogers and Karen Horney. *The Humanistic Psychologist, 34,* 177–199.

DeRoma, V. M., Lassiter, K. S., & Davis, V. A. (2004). Adolescent involvement in discipline decision making. *Behavior Modification, 28,* 420–437.

DeRosier, M. E., & Marcus, S. R. (2005). Building friendships and combating bullying: Effectiveness of S. S. GRIN at one-year follow-up. *Journal of Clinical Child and Adolescent Psychology, 34,* 140–150.

Derzon, J. H., Sale, E., Springer, J. F., & Brounstein, P. (2005). Estimating intervention effectiveness: Synthetic projection of field evaluation results. *Journal of Primary Prevention, 26,* 321–343.

Desai, R. A., Maciejewski, P. K., Pantalon, M. V., & Potenza, M. N. (2005). Gender differences in adolescent gambling. *Annals of Clinical Psychiatry, 17,* 249–258.

DeSantis, A., Harkins, D., Tronick, E., Kaplan, E., & Beeghly, M. (2011). Exploring an integrative model of infant behavior: What is the relationship among temperament, sensory processing, and neurobehavioral measures? *Infant Behavior and Development, 43,* 280–292.

DeWit, D. J., Adlaf, E. M., Offord, D. R., & Ogborne, A. C. (2000). Age at first alcohol use: A risk factor for the development of alcohol disorders. *American Journal of Psychiatry, 157,* 745–750.

DeYoung, C.G., Cicchetti, D., Rogosch, F.A., Gray, J.R., Eastman, M., & Grigorenko, E.L. (2011). Sources of cognitive exploration: Genetic variation in the prefrontal dopamine system predicts openness/intellect. *Journal of Research in Personality, 45,* 364–371.

Dhossche, D., van der Steen, F., & Ferdinand, R. (2002). Somatoform disorders in children and adolescents: A comparison with other internalizing disorders. *Annals of Clinical Psychiatry, 14,* 23–31.

Diamond, A., & Lee, K. (2011). Interventions shown to aid executive function development in children 4–12 years old. *Science, 333,* 959–964.

Dick, D. M. (2011). Developmental changes in genetic influences on alcohol use and dependence. *Child Development Perspectives, 5,* 223–230.

Dick, D.M., Viken, R.J., Kaprio, J., Pulkkinen, L. & Rose, R.J. (2005). Understanding the covariation among childhood externalizing symptoms: Genetic and environmental Influences on conduct disorder, attention deficit hyperactivity disorder, and oppositional defiant disorder symptoms. *Journal of Abnormal Child Psychology, 33,* 219–229.

Dickstein, D. P., Treland, J. E., Snow, J., McClure, E. B., Mehta, M. S., Towbin, K. E., et al. (2004). Neuropsychological performance in pediatric bipolar disorder. *Biological Psychiatry, 55,* 32–39.

Dieckstra, R. F. W. (1995). Depression and suicidal behaviors in adolescence: Sociocultural and time trends. In M. Rutter (Ed.), *Psychosocial disturbances in young people: Challenges for prevention* (pp. 214–243). New York: Cambridge University Press.

Diego, M. A., Field, T., Hernandez-Reif, M., Cullen, C., Schanberg, S., Kuhn, C., et al. (2004). Prepartum, postpartum, and chronic depression effects on newborns. *Psychiatry: Interpersonal Biological Processes, 67,* 63–80.

Dierker, L.C., Merikangas, K.R. & Szatmari, P. (1999). Influence of parental concordance for psychiatric disorders on psychopathology in offspring. *Journal of the American Academy of Child & Adolescent Psychiatry, 38,* 280–288.

Dierssen, M., & Ramakers, G. J.A. (2006). Dendritic pathology in mental retardation: From molecular genetics to neurobiology. *Genes, Brain and Behavior, 5,* 48–60.

DiLalla, L. F. (2002). Behavior genetics of aggression in children: Review and future directions. *Developmental Review, 22,* 593–622.

DiLalla, L. F., Kagan, J., & Reznick, J. S. (1994). Genetic etiology of behavioral inhibition among 2-year-old children. *Infant Behavior and Development, 17,* 405–412.

Diler, R.S., Birmaher, B., Brent, D.A., Axelson, D.A., Firinciogullari, S., Chiapetta, L., & Bridge, J. (2004). Phenomenology of panic disorder in youth. *Depression and Anxiety, 20,* 39–43.

Diniz, J.B., Rosario-Campos, M.C.,. Shavitt, R.G, Curi, M.,. Hounie, A.G, Brotto, S. A. & Miguel, E.C. (2004). Impact of age at onset and duration of illness on the expression of comorbidities in obsessive-compulsive disorder. *Journal of Clinical Psychiatry, 65,* 22–27.

Dishion, T. J., & Bullock, B. M. (2002). Parenting and adolescent problem behavior: An ecological analysis of the nurturance hypothesis. In J. G. Borkowski, & S. L. Ramey (Eds.), *Parenting and the child's world: Influences on academic, intellectual, and social-emotional development. Monographs in parenting* (pp. 231–249). Mahwah, NJ: Erlbaum.

Dishion, T. J., Bullock, B. M., & Granic, I. (2002). Pragmatism in modeling peer influence: Dynamics, outcomes and change processes. *Development and Psychopathology, 14,* 969–981.

Dishion, T. J., Capaldi, D., Spracklen, K. M., & Li, F. (1995). Peer ecology of male adolescent drug use. *Development and Psychopathology, 7,* 803–824.

Dishion, T. J., Eddy, M. Haas, E., & Li, F. (1997). Friendships and violent behavior during adolescence. *Social Development, 6,* 207–223.

Dishion, T. J., & Kavanagh, K. (2002). The Adolescent Transitions Program: A family-centered prevention strategy for schools. In J. B. Reid & G. R. Patterson (Eds.), *Antisocial behavior in children and adolescents: A developmental analysis and model for intervention* (pp. 257–272). Washington, DC: American Psychological Association.

Dishion, T. J., Kavanagh, K., Schneiger, A., Nelson, S., & Kaufman, N. K. (2002). Preventing early adolescent substance use: A family-centered strategy for the public middle school. *Prevention Science, 3,* 191–201.

Dishion, T. J., McCord, J., Poulin, F. (1999). When interventions harm: Peer groups and problem behavior. *American Psychologist, 54,* 755–764.

Dishion, T. J., & Medici Skaggs, N. (2000). An ecological analysis of monthly "bursts" in early adolescent substance use. *Applied Developmental Science, 4,* 89–97.

Dishion, T. J., Nelson, S. E., & Bullock, B. M. (2004). Premature adolescent autonomy: Parent disengagement and deviant peer process in the amplification of problem behaviour. *Journal of Adolescence, 27,* 515–530.

Dishion, T. J., & Owen, L. D. (2002). A longitudinal analysis of friendships and substance use: Bidirectional influence from adolescence to adulthood. *Developmental Psychology, 38,* 480–491.

Dishion, T. J., & Patterson, G. R. (1999). Model building in developmental psychopathology: A pragmatic approach to understanding and intervention. *Journal of Clinical Child Psychology, 28,* 502–512.

Dishion, T. J., & Stormshak, E. A. (2007). Child and adolescent intervention groups. In T. J. Dishion & E. A. Stormshak (Eds.), *Intervening in children's lives: An ecological, family-centered approach to mental health care* (pp. 201–215). Washington, DC: American Psychological Association.

Dishion, T.J., & Piehler, T.F. (2007). Peer dynamics in the development and change of child and adolescent problem behavior. In A. S. Masten (Ed.), *Multilevel Dynamics in Developmental Psychopathology: Pathways to the Future* (pp. 151–180). Mahwah, NJ: Erlbaum.

Dishion, T.J., Poulin, F. & Burraston, B (2001). Peer group dynamics associated with iatrogenic effects in group interventions with high-risk young adolescents. In D. W. Nangle & C.A. Erdley (Eds.) *The Role of Friendship in Psychological Adjustment* (pp. 79–92). San Francisco, CA: Jossey-Bass.

Dixon, R. S., Gill, J. M. W., & Adair, V. A. (2003). Exploring paternal influences on the dieting behavior of adolescent girls. *Eating Disorders: The Journal of Treatment and Prevention, 11,* 39–50.

Docherty, S.J., Davis, O.S.P., Kovas, Y., Meaburn, E.L., Dale, P.S., Petrill, S.A., Schalkwyk, E.L., & Plomin, R. (2010). A genome-wide association study identifies multiple loci associated with mathematics ability and disability. *Genes, Brain and Behavior, 9,* 234–247.

Docherty, S.J., Kovas, Y., & Plomin, R. (2011). Gene-environment interaction in the etiology of mathematical ability using SNP sets. *Behavioral Genetics, 41,* 141–154.

Dodge, K. A. (1991). The structure and function of reactive and proactive aggression. In D. J. Pepler & K. H. Rubin (Eds.), *The development and treatment of childhood aggression* (pp. 201–218). Hillsdale, NJ: Erlbaum.

Dodge, K. A. (2006). Translational science in action: Hostile attributional style and the development of aggressive behavior problems. *Development and Psychopathology, 18,* 791–814.

Dodge, K. A. (2007). Temperamental resistance to control increases the association between sleep problems and externalizing behavior development. *Journal of Family Psychology, 21,* 39–48.

Dodge, K. A., & Coie, J. D. (1987). Social-information-processing factors in reactive and proactive aggression in children's peer groups. *Journal of Personality and Social Psychology, 53,* 1146–1158.

Dodge, K. A., Dishion, T. J., & Lansford, J. E. (2006). The problem of deviant peer influence in public interventions. *Social Policy Report, 20,* 3–19.

Dodge, K. A., Lansford, J. E., Burks, V. S., Bates, J. E., Pettit, G. S., Fontaine, R., et al. (2003). Peer rejection and social information-processing factors in the development of aggressive behavior problems in children. *Child Development, 74,* 374–393.

Dodge, K. A., Malone, P. S., Lansford, J. E., Miller, S., Pettit, G. S., & Bates, J. E. (2009). A dynamic cascade model of the development of substance-use onset. *Monographs of the Society for Research in Child Development, 74,* Serial No. 294.

Dodge, K. A., & Pettit, G. S. (2003). A biopsychosocial model of the development of chronic conduct problems in adolescence. *Developmental Psychology, 39,* 349–371.

Dodge, K.A., Greenberg, M.T., Malone, P.S., & Conduct Problems Prevention Research Group. (2008). Testing an idealized dynamic cascade model of the development of serious violence in adolescence. *Child Development, 79,* 1907–1927.

Domino, M.e., Burns, B.J., Silva, S.G., Kratochvil, C.J., Vitiello, B., Reinecke, M.A., Mario, J., & March, J.S. (2008). Cost-effectiveness of treatments for adolescent depression: Results from TADS. *American Journal of Psychiatry, 165,* 588–596.

Donaldson, D., Spirito, A., & Esposito-Smythers, C. (2005). Treatment for adolescents following a suicide attempt: Results of a pilot trial. *Journal of the American Academy of Child and Adolescent Psychiatry, 44,* 113–120.

Donaldson, D., Spirito, A., & Overholser, J. (2003). Treatment of adolescent suicide attempters. In A. Spirito & J. C. Overholser (Eds.), *Evaluation and treating adolescent suicide attempters: From research to practice* (pp. 295–321). San Diego, CA: Academic Press.

Donovan, J. E., Leech, S. L., Zucker, R. A., Loveland-Cherry, C. J., Jester, J., Fitzgerald, H. E., et al. (2004). Really underage drinkers: Alcohol use among elementary students. *Alcoholism: Clinical and Experimental Research, 28,* 341–349.

Dorn, L. D., Campo, J. C., Thato, S., Dahl, R. E., Lewin, D., Chandra, R., et al. (2003). Psychological comorbidity and stress reactivity in children and adolescents with recurrent abdominal pain and anxiety disorders. *Journal of the American Academy of Child and Adolescent Psychiatry, 42,* 66–75.

Dorn, L. D., Dahl, R. W., Williamson, D. W., Birmaher, B., Axel-son, D., Perel, J., et al. (2003). Developmental markers in adolescence: Implications for studies of pubertal processes. *Journal of Youth and Adolescence, 32,* 315–324.

dos Reis, S., Barksdale, C.L., Sherman, A., Maloney, K., & Charach, A. (2010). Stigmatizing experiences of parents of children with a new diagnosis of ADHD. *Psychiatric Services, 61,* 811–816.

Dosen, A. (2001). Developmental-dynamic relationship therapy: An approach to more severely mentally retarded children. In A. Dosen & K. Day (Eds.), *Treating mental illness and behavior disorders in children and adults with mental retardation* (pp. 415–427). Washington, DC: American Psychiatric Publishing.

Dosen, A. (2001). Pharmacotherapy in mentally retarded children. In A. Dosen & K. Day (Eds.), *Treating mental illness and behavior disorders in children and adults with mental retardation* (pp. 429–450). Washington, DC: American Psychiatric Publishing.

Dougherty, L.R., Klein, D.N., Rose, S., & Laptook, R.S. (2011). Hypothalmic-pituitary-adrenal axis reactivity in the preschool-age offspring of depressed parents: Moderation by early parenting. *Psychological Science, 22,* 650–658.

Doyle, A. E., Faraone, S. V., Seidman, L. J., Willcutt, E. G., Nigg, J. T., Waldman, I. D., et al. (2005). Are endophenotypes based on measures of executive functions useful for molecular genetic studies of ADHD? *Journal of Child Psychology and Psychiatry, 46,* 778–803.

Doyle, P.M., Smyth, A., & le Grange, D.L. (2012). Child and adulthood: When do eating disorders start and do treatments differ? In J. Alexander & J. Treasure (Eds.) *A Collaborative Approach to Eating Disoders* (pp. 217–224). New York: Routledge/Taylor & Francis Group.

Drabick, D. A. G., Gadow, K. D., & Loney, J. (2007). Source-specific oppositional defiant disorder: Comorbidity and risk factors in referred elementary schoolboys. *Journal of the American Academy of Child and Adolescent Psychiatry, 46,* 92–101.

Draughton, J.M., & Kratochvil, C.J. (2009). Review of ADHD pharmacotherapies: Advantages, disadvantages, and clinical pearls. *Journal of the American Academy of Child & Adolescent Psychiatry, 48,* 240–248.

Drury, S.S., Gleason, M.M., Theall, K.P., Smyke, A.T., Nelson, C.A., Fox, N.A., & Zeanah, C.H. (2011). Genetic sensitivity to the caregiving context: The influence of 5httlpr and BDNF val66met on indiscriminate social behavior. *Physiology & Behavior* [serial online], http://dx.doi.org/10.1016/j.physbeh.2011.11.014.

Duarte, C.S., Bird, H.R., Shrout, P.E., Wu, P., Lewis-Fernandéz, R., Shen, S., & Canino, G. (2008). Culture and psychiatric symptoms in Puerto Rican children: Longitudinal results from one ethnic group in two contexts. *Journal of Psychology and Psychiatry, 49,* 563–572.

Duggal, S., Carlson, E. A., Sroufe, L. A., & Egeland, B. (2001). Depressive symptomatology in childhood and adolescence. *Development and Psychopathology, 13,* 143–164.

Duhig, A. M., Renk, K., Epstein, M. K., & Phares, V. (2000). Interparental agreement on internalizing, externalizing, and total behavior problems: A meta-analysis. *Clinical Psychology: Science and Practice, 7*, 435–453.

Dulcan, M.K. & Benson, R.S. (1997). Summary of the practice parameters for the assessment and treatment of children, adolescents, and adults with ADHD. *Journal of the American Academy of Child Psychiatry, 36*, 1311–1317.

Dumont-Mathieu, T., & Fein, D. (2005). Screening for autism in young children: The modified checklist for autism in toddlers (M-CHAT) and other measures. *Mental Retardation and Developmental Disabilities Research Review, 11*, 253–262.

Dunham, K. (2004). Young adults' support strategies when peers disclose suicidal intent. *Suicide and Life-Threatening Behavior, 34*, 56–65.

Dunn, J. (2004). Understanding children's family worlds: Family transitions and children's outcomes. *Merrill-Palmer Quarterly, 50*, 224–235.

Dunn, W. (1997). The impact of sensory processing abilities on the daily lives of young children and their families: A conceptual model. *Infants and Young Children, 9*, 23–35.

Dunn, W., & Westman, K. (1997). The sensory profile: The performance of a national sample of children without disabilities. *American Journal of Occupational Therapy, 51*, 25–34.

Dunne, J. E., Arnold, V., Benson, S., Bernet, W., Bukstein, O., Kinlan, J., et al. (1997). Summary of the practice parameters for the assessment and treatment of children, adolescents, and adults with ADHD. *Journal of the American Academy of Child and Adolescent Psychiatry, 36*, 1311–1317.

DuPaul, G. J., Anastopoulos, A. D., McGoey, K. E., Power, T. J., Reid, R., & Ikeda, M. J. (1998). Teacher ratings of attention deficit hyperactivity disorder symptoms: Factor structure and normative data. *Psychological Assessment, 9*, 436–444.

DuPaul, G. J., & Barkley, R. A. (2008). Attention defi cit hyperactivity disorder. From R. J. Morris & T. R. Kratochwill (Eds.), *The practice of child therapy* (4th ed., pp. 143–186). Mahwah, NJ: Erlbaum.

DuPaul, G.J., Helwig, J.R., & Slay, P.M. (2011). Classroom interventions for attention and hyperactivity. In M.A. Bray & T. J. Kehle (Eds.), *The Oxford Handbook of School Psychology* (pp. 428–441). New York: Oxford University Press.

Durand, V. M. (2001). Future directions for children and adolescents with mental retardation. *Behavior Therapy, 32*, 633–650.

Durbrow, E. H. (1999). Cultural processes in child competence: How rural Caribbean parents evaluate their children. In A. S. Masten (Ed.), *Cultural processes in child development* (pp. 97–121). Mahwah, NJ: Erlbaum.

Durbrow, E. H., Pena, L. F., Masten, A., Sesma, A., & Williamson, I. (2001). Mothers' conceptions of child competence in contexts of poverty: The Phillipines, St. Vincent, and the United States. *International Journal of Behavioral Development, 25*, 438–443.

Durkin, M. (2002). The epidemiology of developmental disabilities in low-income countries. *Mental Retardation and Developmental Disabilities Research Reviews, 8*, 206–211.

Durkin, S. J., Paxton, S. J., & Wertheim, E. H. (2005). How do adolescent girls evaluate body dissatisfaction prevention messages? *Journal of Adolescent Health, 37*, 381–390.

Durston, S., & Konrad, K. (2007). Integrating genetic, psychopharmacological and neuroimaging studies: A converging methods a roach to understanding the neurobiology of ADHD. *Developmental Review, 27*, 374–395.

Dyck, M. J., Ferguson, K., & Shochet, I. M. (2001). Do autism spectrum disorders differ from each other and from nonspectrum disorders on emotion recognition tests? *European Child and Adolescent Psychiatry, 10*, 105–116.

Dykens, E. M. (1997). Maladaptive behavior in children with Prader-Willi syndrome, Down syndrome, and nonspecific mental retardation. *American Journal on Mental Retardation, 102*, 228–237.

Dykens, E. M. (2000). Annotation: Psychopathology in children with intellectual disability. *Journal of Child Psychology and Psychiatry, 41*, 407–417.

Dykens, E. M. (2001). Intervention issues in persons with Williams syndrome. *Mental Health Aspects of Developmental Disabilities, 4*, 130–137.

Dykens, E. M. (2001). Personality and psychopathology: New insights from genetic syndromes. In H. N. Switzy (Ed.), *Personality and motivational differences in persons with mental retardation. The LEA series on special education and disability* (pp. 283–317). Mahwah, NJ: Erlbaum.

Dykens, E. M. (2003). Anxiety, fears, and phobias in persons with Williams syndrome. *Developmental Neuropsychology, 23*, 291–316.

Dykens, E. M. (2006). Toward a positive psychology of mental retardation. *American Journal of Orthopsychiatry, 76*, 185–193.

Dykens, E. M., & Hodapp, R. M. (1997). Treatment issues in genetic mental retardation syndromes. *Professional Psychology: Research and Practice, 28*, 263–270.

Dykens, E. M., & Hodapp, R. M. (1999). Behavioural phenotypes: Towards new understandings of people with developmental disabilities. In N. Bouras (Ed.), *Psychiatric and behavioural disorders in developmental disabilities and mental retardation* (pp. 96–108). New York: Cambridge University Press.

Dykens, E. M., & Hodapp, R. M. (2001). Research in mental retardation: Toward an etiologic approach. *Journal of Child Psychology and Psychiatry and Allied Disciplines, 42*, 49–71.

Dykens, E. M., Hodapp, R. M., & Evans, D. W. (1994). Profi les and development of adaptive behavior in children with Down syndrome. *American Journal on Mental Retardation, 98*, 580–587.

Dykens, E. M., Hodapp, R. M., & Finucane, B. M. (2000). *Genetics and mental retardation syndromes: A new look at behavior and interventions.* Baltimore: Paul H. Brookes Publishing.

Dykens, E. M., Hodapp, R. M., & Leckman, J. F. (1994). *Behavior and development in fragile X syndrome.* Thousand Oaks, CA: Sage.

Dykens, E. M., Hodapp, R. M., Walsh, K., & Nash, L. J. (1992). Adaptive and maladaptive behavior in Prader-Willi syndrome. *Journal of the American Academy of Child and Adolescent Psychiatry, 31*, 1131–1136.

Dykens, E. M., Shah, B., Sagun, J., Beck, T., & King, B. H. (2002). Maladaptive behavior in children and adolescents with Down's syndrome. *Journal of Intellectual Disability Research, 46*, 484–492.

Dykens, E.M. (2005). Happiness, well-being, and character strengths: Outcomes for families and siblings of persons with mental retardation. *Mental Retardation, 43*, 360–364.

DyKlyen, M., & Greenberg, M.T. (2008). Attachment and psychopathology in childhood. In J. Cassidy & P.R. Shaver (Eds.), *Handbook of attachment: Theory, research, and clinical applications* (2nd ed.) (pp. 637–335). New York: Guilford Press.

Earls, F., Raviola, G. J., & Carlson, M. (2008). Promoting child and adolescent mental health in the context of the

HIV/AIDS pandemic with a focus on sub-Saharan Africa. *Journal of Child Psychology and Psychiatry, 49,* 295–312.

Easterbrooks, M. A. (1989). Quality of attachment to mother and father: Effects of perinatal risk status. *Child Development, 60,* 825–830.

Eccles, J. S., & Barber, B. L. (1999). Student council, volunteering, basketball, or marching band: What kind of extracurricular involvement matters? *Journal of Adolescent Research, 14,* 10–43.

Eccles, J. S., Barber, B. L., Stone, M. R., & Templeton, J. L. (2002). Adolescence and emerging adulthood: The critical passage ways to adulthood. In M. H. Bornstein, L. Davidson, C. L. M. Keyes, & K. Moore (Eds.), *Well-Being: Positive development across the life course* (pp. 383–406). Mahwah, NJ: Erlbaum.

Eccles, J.S., Roeser, R., Vida, R., Fredericks, J., & Wigfield, A. (2006). Motivational and achievement pathways through middle childhood. In L. Balter & C.S. Tamis-LeMonda (Eds.) *Child Psychology: A handbook of contemporary issues* (2nd ed.) (pp. 325–355). New York: Psychology Press.

Eddy, K. T., Hennessey, M., & Thompson-Brenner, H. (2007). Eating pathology in East African women: The role of media exposure and globalization. *Journal of Nervous and Mental Disease, 195,* 196–202.

Edelson, M. G. (2005). A car goes in the garage like a can of peas goes into the refrigerator: Do deficits in real-world knowledge affect the assessment of intelligence in individuals with autism? *Focus on Autsim and Other Developmental Disabilities, 20,* 2–9.

Edelson, M. G. (2006). Are the majority of children with autism mentally retarded? A systematic evaluation of the data. *Focus on Autism and other Developmental Disabilities, 21,* 66–83.

Edelson, M. G., Schubert, D. T., & Edelson, S. M. (1998). Factors predicting intelligence scores on the TONI in individuals with autism. *Focus on Autism and Other Developmental Disabilities, 13,* 17–26.

Eder, R. A., & Mangelsdorf, S. C. (1997). The emotional basis of early personality development: Implications for the emergent self-concept. In R. Hogan, J. A. Johnson, et al. (Eds.), *Handbook of personality psychology* (pp. 209–240). San Diego, CA: Academic Press.

Egeland, B., Carlson, E., & Sroufe, L. A. (1993). Resilience as process. *Development and Psychopathology, 5,* 517–528.

Egger, H. L. (2011). Preschool temper tantrums: What they mean and when to worry. *Presentation to Children's Hospitals and Clinics of Minnesota,* May 12, 2011.

Egger, H. L., Costello, E. J., Erkanli, A., & Angold, A. (1999). Somatic complaints and psychopathology in children and adolescents: Stomachaches, musculoskeletal pains, and headaches. *Journal of the American Academy of Child and Adolescent Psychiatry, 38,* 852–860.

Egger, H.L., & Angold, A. (in press). Preschool temper tantrums and early childhood mental health. *Pediatrics.*

Egger, H.L., & Emde, R.N. (2011). Developmentally sensitive diagnostic criteria for mental health disorders in early childhood. *American Psychologist, 66,* 95–106.

Eggum, N.D., Eisenberg, N., Kao, K., Spinrad, T.L., Bolnick, R., Hofer, C., Kupfer, A.S., & Fabricius, W.V. (2011). Emotion understanding, theory of mind, and prosocial orientation: Relations over time in early childhood. *Journal of Positive Psychology, 6,* 4–16.

Ehlers, A. (2000). A cognitive model of posttraumatic stress disorder. *Behaviour Research and Therapy, 38,* 319–345.

Ehlers, A., R.A. Mayou & B. Byrant (2003). Cognitive predictors of posttraumatic stress disorder in children: Results of a prospective longitudinal study. *Behaviour Research and Therapy, 41,* 1–10.

Ehringer, M. A., Rhee, S. H., Young, S., Corley, R., & Hewitt, J. K. (2006). Genetic and environmental contributions to common psychopathologies of childhood and adolescence: A study of twins and their siblings. *Journal of Abnormal Child Psychology, 34,* 1–17.

Einfeld, S.L., Ellis, L.A., Doran, C.M., Emerson, E., Horstead, S.K., Madden, R.H., & Tonge, B.J. (2010). Behavior problems increase costs of care of children with intellectual disabilities. *Journal of Mental Health Research in Intellectual Disabilities, 3,* 202–209.

Einfield, S. L., Tonge, B. J., & Reese, V. W. (2001). Longitudinal course of behavioral and emotional problems in Williams syndrome. *American Journal on Mental Retardation, 106,* 73–81.

Eisen, A.R., Spasaro, S.A., Brien, L.K., Kearney, C.A. & Albano, A.M. (2004). Parental expectancies and childhood anxiety disorders: psychosomatic properties of the Parental Expectancies Scale. *Journal of Anxiety Disorers, 18,* 89–109.

Eisenberg, L., & Belfer, M. (2008). Prerequisites for global child and adolescent mental health. *Journal of Child Psychology and Psychiatry, 50,* 26–35.

Eisenberg, M. E., Neumark-Sztainer, D., Haines, J., & Wall, M. (2006). Weight teasing and emotional well-being in adolescents: Longitudinal findings from Project EAT. *Journal of Adolescent Health, 38,* 675–683.

Eisenberg, N. (2002). Emotion-related regulation and its relation to quality of social functioning. In W. Hartup & R. A. Weinberg (Eds.), *Child psychology in retrospect and prospect. The Minnesota symposia on child psychology* (Vol. 32, pp. 133–171). Mahwah, NJ: Erlbaum.

Eisenberg, N., & Fabes, R.A. (1992). Emotion, regulation, and the development of social competence. In M.S. Clark (Ed.), *Emotion and Social Behavior* (pp. 119–150). Thousand Oaks, CA: Sage Publications, Inc.

Eisenberg, N., Valiente, C., & Eggum, N.D. (2010). Self-regulation and school readiness. *Early Education and Development, 21,* 681–698.

Eisenberg, N., Valiente, C., Spinrad, T.L., Cumberland, A., Liew, J., Reiser, M., … Losoya, S.H. (2009). Longitudinal relations of children's effortful control, impulsivity, and negative emotionality to their externalizing, internalizing, and co-occurring behavior problems. *Developmental Psychology, 45,* 988–1008.

Eisenberg, N., Valiente, C., & Sulik, M.J. (2009). How the study of regulation can inform the study of coping. *New Directions for Child & Adolescent Development, 124,* 75–86.

Eisenberg, N., Zhou, Q., Losoya, S. H., Fabes, R. A., Shepard, S. A., Murphy, B. C., et al. (2003). The relations of parenting, effortful control, and ego control to children's emotional expressivity. *Child Development, 74,* 875–895.

El-Mallakh, R. S., Peters, C., & Waltrip, C. (2000). Antidepressant treatment and neural plasticity. *Journal of Child and Adolescent Psychopharmacology, 10,* 287–294.

El-Sheik, M., Kouros, C.D., Erath, S., Cummings, E.M., Keller, P., & Staton, L. (2009). Marital conflict and children's externalizing behavior: Interactions between parasympathetic and sympathetic nervous system activity. *Monographs of the Society for Research in Child Development, 74,* 1–99.

El-Sheikh, M., Buckhalt, J. A., Cummings, E. M., & Keller, P. (2007). Sleep disruptions and emotional insecurity are pathways of risk for children. *Journal of Child Psychology and Psychiatry, 48*, 88–96.

Elder, T.E. (2010). The importance of relative standards in ADHD diagnoses: Evidence based on exact birth dates. *Journal of Health Economics, 29,* 641–656.

Eleonora, E., King, N. J., & Ollendick, T. H. (2001). Self-reported anxiety in children and adolescents: A three-year follow-up study. *Journal of Genetic Psychology, 162,* 5–19.

Eley, T. C., & Stevenson, J. (1999a). Exploring the covariation between anxiety and depression symptoms: A genetic analysis of the effects of age and sex. *Journal of Child Psychology and Psychiatry and Allied Disciplines, 40,* 1273–1282.

Eley, T. C., & Stevenson, J. (1999b). Using genetic analyses to clarify the distinction between depressive and anxious symptoms in children. *Journal of Abnormal Child Psychology, 27,* 105–114.

Eley, T. C., & Stevenson, J. (2000). Specific life events and chronic experiences differentially associated with depression and anxiety in young twins. *Journal of Abnormal Child Psychology, 28,* 383–394.

Eley, T.C. (1999). Behavioral genetics as a tool for developmental psychology: Anxiety and depression in children and adolescents. *Psychological Disorders, 2,* 21–36.

Eley, T.C., Gregory, A.M., Clark, D.M., Ehlers, A. (2007). Feeling anxious: A twin study of panic/somatic ratings, anxiety sensitivity and heartbeat perception in children. *Journal of Child Psychology and Psychiatry, 48,* 1184–1191.

Eley, T.C., Striling, L., Ehlers, A., Gregory, A.M. & Clark, D.M. (2004). Heart-beat perception, panic/somatic symptoms and anxiety sensitivity in children. *Behaviour Research and Therapy, 42,* 439–448.

Elfhag, K., & Linne, Y. (2005). Gender differences in associations of eating pathology between mothers and their adolescent offspring. *Obesity Research, 13,* 1070–1076.

Eliot, A. O. (2004). A concept of self in eating disordered adolescent girls: A consideration of genetic factors. *Annals of the American Psychotherapy Association, 7,* 14–22.

Elizabeth, J., King, N., & Ollendick, T. H. (2004). Etiology of social anxiety disorder in children and youth. *Behaviour Change, 21,* 162–172.

Elkind, D. (1994). *Ties that stress.* Cambridge, MA: Harvard University Press.

Elkins, I. J., King, S. M., McGue, M., & Iacono, W. G. (2006). Personality traits and the development of nicotine, alcohol, and illicit drug disorders: Prospective links from adolescence to young adulthood. *Journal of Abnormal Psychology, 115,* 26–39.

Elkins, I. J., McGue, M., & Iacono, W. G. (1997). Genetic and environmental influences on parent-son relationships: Evidence for increasing genetic influence during adolescence. *Developmental Psychology, 33,* 351–363.

Elkins, R.M., McHugh, R.K., Santucci, L.C., & Barlow, D.H. (2011). Improving the transportability of CBT for internalizing disorders in children. *Clinical Child and Family Psychology Review, 14,* 161–173.

Ellenbogen, M. A., & Hodgins, S. (2004). The impact of high neuroticism in parents on children's psychosocial functioning in a population at high risk for major affective disorder: A family-environmental pathway of intergenerational risk. *Development and Psychopathology, 16,* 113–136.

Ellickson, P. L., Tucker, J. S., Klein, D. J., & Saner, H. (2004). Antecedents and outcomes of marijuana use initiation during adolescence. *Preventive Medicine: An International Journal Devoted to Practice and Theory, 39,* 976–984.

Ellis, B.J., & Boyce, T. (2008). Biological Sensitivity to Context. *Current Directions in Psychological Science, 17,* 183–187.

Ellis, B.J., Boyce, W.T., Belsky, J.,. Bakermans-Kranenburg, M.J & van IJzendoorn, M.H. (2011). Differential susceptibility to the environment: An evolutionary-neurodevelopmental theory. *Development and Psychopathology, 23,* 7–28.

Ellis, B.J., Jackson, J.J., & Boyce, W.T. (2006). The stress response systems: Universality and adaptive individual differences. *Developmental Review, 26,* 175–212.

Ellis, C. R., Singh, N. N., & Ruane, A. L. (1999). Nutritional, dietary, and hormonal treatments for individuals with mental retardation and developmental disabilities. *Mental Retardation and Developmental Disabilities Research Reviews, 5,* 335–341.

Else-Quest, N. M., Hyde, J. S., Goldsmith, H. H., & Van Hulle, C.A. (2006). Gender differences in temperament: A meta-analysis. *Psychological Bulletin, 132,* 33–72.

Emde, R. N. (1985). The affective self: Continuities and transformations from infancy. In J. Call & E. Galenson (Eds.), *Frontiers of infant psychiatry* (Vol. 2, pp. 38–54). New York: Basic Books.

Emde, R. N. (1992). Individual meaning and increasing complexity: Contributions of Sigmund Freud and Rene Spitz to developmental psychology. *Developmental Psychology, 28,* 347–359.

Emde, R. N., Bingham, R. D., & Harmon, R. J. (1993). Classification and the diagnostic process in infancy. In C. H. Zeanah (Ed.), *Handbook of Infant Mental Health* (pp. 225–235). New York: Guilford Press.

Emde, R. N., & Robinson, J. (2000). Guiding principles for a theory of early intervention: A developmental-psychoanalytic perspective. In J. P. Shonkoff & S. J. Meisels (Eds.), *Handbook of Early Childhood Intervention* (2nd ed., pp. 160–178). Cambridge: Cambridge University Press.

Eme, R.F. (2007). Sex differences in child-onset, life-course-persistent conduct disorder. A review of biological influences. *Clinical Psychology Review, 27,* 607–627.

Emery, R. E., & Kitzmann, K. M. (1995). The child in the family: Disruptions in family functions. In D. Cicchetti & D. J. Cohen (Eds.), *Developmental Psychopathology: Vol. 2. Risk, disorder, and adaptation* (pp. 3–31). Oxford, England: Wiley.

Emslie, G. J., Kennard, B. D., Mayes, T. L., Nightingale-Teresi, J., Carmody, T., Hughes, C. W., et al. (2008). Fluoxetine versus placebo in preventing relapse of major depression in children and adolescents. *American Journal of Psychiatry, 165,* 459–467.

Emslie, G. J., Mayes, T. L., Laptook, R. S., & Batt, M. (2003). Predictors of response to treatment in children and adolescents with mood disorders. *Psychiatric Clinics of North America, 26,* 435–456.

Emslie, G. J., Rush, J, Weinberg, W. A., Kowatch, R. A., Hughes, C. W., Carmody, T., et al. (1997). A double-blind, randomized, placebo-controlled trial of fluoxetine in children and adolescents with depression. *Archives of General Psychiatry, 54,* 1031–1037.

Eppright, T.D., Bradley, S., & Sanfacon, J.A. (1998). The diagnosis of infant psychopathology: Current challenges and recent contributions. *Child Psychiatry and Human Development, 28,* 213–222.

Erickson, C. A., Posey, D. J., Stigler, K. A., & McDougle, C. J. (2007). Pharmacotherapy of autism and related disorders. *Psychiatric Annals, 37,* 490–500.

Erickson, M. F., Korfmacher, J., & Egeland, B. (1992). Attachments past and present: Implications for therapeutic interventions with mother-infant dyads. *Development and Psychopathology, 4,* 495–507.

Erikson, E. H. (1968). *Identity: Youth and crisis.* Oxford, England: Norton.

Ernst, M., & Hardin, M. (2010). Neurodevelopment underlying adolescent behavior. In In P.D. Zelazo, M. Chandler & E. Crone (Eds.) *Developmental Social Cognitive Neuroscience* (pp. 165–189). New York: Psychology Press.

Esbensen, A.J., Bishop, S., Seltzer, M.M., Greenberg, J.S., & Taylor, J.L. (2010). Comparisons between individuals with autism spectrum disorders and individuals with Down syndrome in adulthood. *American Journal on Intellectual and Developmental Disabilities, 115,* 277–290.

Esbensen, A.J., Greenberg, J.S., Seltzer, M.M., & Aman, M.J. (2009). A longitudinal investigation of psychotropic and non-psychotropic medication use among adolescents and adults with autism spectrum disorders. *Journal of Autism & Developmental Disorders, 39,* 1339–1349.

Espelage, D. L., Mebane, S. E., & Adams, R. S. (2004). Empathy, caring, and bullying: Toward an understanding of complex associations. In D. L. Espelage & S. M. Swearer (Eds.), *Bullying in American schools: A social-ecological perspective on prevention and intervention* (pp. 37–61). Mahwah, NJ: Erlbaum.

Esposito, C., Spirito., A. Boergers, J., & Donaldson, D. (2003). Affective, behavioral, and cognitive functioning in adolescents with multiple suicide attempts. *Suicide and Life-Threatening Behavior, 33,* 389–399.

Esposito-Smythers, C. (2004). Adolescent substance use and suicidal behavior: A review with implications for treatment research. *Alcoholism: Clinical and Experimental Research, 28,* 77S–88S.

Esposito-Smythers, C. (2005). Adolescent substance abuse and comorbid conditions: An integrated treatment model. *DATA: The Brown University Digest of Addiction Theory and Application, 24,* 8–13.

Essau, C. A., Conradt, J., & Petermann, F. (2000). Frequency, comorbidity, and psychosocial impairment of specific phobia in adolescents. *Journal of Clinical Child Psychology, 29,* 221–231.

Essau, C. A., Conradt, J., & Petermann, F. (2002). Course and outcome of anxiety disorders in adolescents. *Journal of Anxiety Disorders, 16,* 67–81.

Essau, C. A., & Dobson, K. S. (1999). Epidemiology of depressive disorders. In C. A. Essau & F. Petermann (Eds.), *Depressive disorders in children and adolescents: Epidemiology, risk factors, and treatment* (pp. 69–103). Northvale, NJ: Jason Aronson, Inc.

Essau, C.A., Lewinsohn, P.M., Seeley, J.R., & Sasagawa, S. (2010). Gender differences in the developmental course of depression. *Journal of Affective Disorders, 127,* 185–190.

Evans, D. W., Gray, F. L., & Leckman, J. F. (1999). The rituals, fears, and phobias of young children: Insights from development, psychopathology, and neurobiology. *Child Psychiatry and Human Development, 29,* 261–276.

Evans, E., Hawton, K., & Rodham, K. (2005). Suicidal phenomena and abuse in adolescents: A review of epidemiological studies. *Child Abuse and Neglect, 29,* 45–58.

Evans, S.W., Schultz, B.K., DeMars, C.E., & Davis, H. (2011). Effectiveness of the challenging horizons after-school program for young adolescents with ADHD. *Behavior Therapy, 42,* 462–474.

Evans, W. D., Powers, A., Hersey, J., & Renaud, J. (2006). The influence of social environment and social image on adolescent smoking. *Health Psychology, 25,* 26–33.

Eyberg, S.M. (1988). Parent-child interaction therapy: Integration of traditional and behavioral concerns. *Child & Family Behavior Therapy, 10,* 33–46.

Eyberg, S.M. (2005). Tailoring and adapting parent-child interaction therapy for new populations. *Education and Treatment of Children, 28,* 197–201.

Eyberg, S.M., Nelson, M.M., & Boggs, S.R. (2008). Evidence-based psychosocial treatments for children and adolescents with disruptive behavior. *Journal of Clinical Child and Adolescent Psychology, 37,* 215–237.

Fabiano, G.A., Pelham, W.E., Coles, E.K., Gnagy, E.M., Chronis-Tuscano, A., O'Connor, B.C. (2009). A meta-analysis of behavioral treatments for attention-deficit/hyperactivity disorder. *Clinical Psychology Review, 29,* 129–140.

Fainsilber Katz, L., & Low, S. M. (2004). Marital violence, coparenting, and family-level processes in relation to children's adjustment. *Journal of Family Psychology, 18,* 372–382.

Fairburn, C. G., Agras, W. S., Walsh, B. T., Wilson, G. T., & Stice, E. (2004). Prediction of outcome in bulimia nervosa by early change in treatment. *American Journal of Psychiatry, 161,* 2322–2324.

Fairburn, C. G., Stice, E., Cooper, Z., Doll, H. A., Norman, P. A., & O'Connor, M. E. (2003). Understanding persistence in bulimia nervosa: A 5-year naturalistic study. *Journal of Consulting and Clinical Psychiatry, 71,* 103–109.

Fairburn, C.G. (2008). *Cognitive Behavior Therapy and Eating Disorders.* New York: Guilford Press.

Fairburn, C.G., & Cooper, Z. (2011). Eating disorders, DSM-5 and clinical reality. *The British Journal of Psychiatry, 198,* 8–10.

Fairburn, C.G., Cooper, Z., Doll, H.A., O'Connor, M.E., Bohn, K., Hawker, D.M., Wales, J.A., & Palmer, R.L. (2009). Transdiagnostic cognitive-behavioral therapy for patients with eating disorders: A two-site trial with 60-week follow-up. *American Journal of Psychiatry, 166,* 311–319.

Fairchild, G., Passamonti, L., Hurford, G., Hagan, C.C., von dem Hagen, E.A.H., van Goozen, S.H.M., … Calder, A.J. (2011). Brain structure abnormalities in early-onset and adolescent-onset conduct disorder. *American Journal of Psychiatry, 168,* 624–633.

Fairchild, G., van Goozen, S.H.M., Stollery, S.J., Aitken, M.R.F., Savage, J., Moore, S.C., Goodyer, I.M. (2009). Decision making and executive function in male adolescents with early-onset or adolescence-onset conduct disorder and control subjects. *Biological Psychiatry, 66,* 162–168.

Faraone, S. V., Althoff, R. R., Hudziak, J. J., Monuteaux, M., & Biederman, J. (2005). The CBCL predicts DSM bipolar disorder in children: A receiver operating characteristic curve analysis.*Bipolar Disorder, 7,* 518–524.

Faraone, S. V., Biederman, J., & Mick, E. (2006). The age-dependent decline of attention deficit hyperactivity disorder: A metaanalysis of follow-up studies. *Psychological Medicine, 36,* 159–165.

Faraone, S. V., Biederman, J., Spencer, T., Wilens, T., Larry, J., Mick, E, et al. (2000). Attention-deficit disorder in adults: an overview. *Biological Psychiatry, 48,* 9–20.

Faraone, S. V., Biederman, J., Weber, W., & Russell, R. L. (1998). Psychiatric, neuropsychological, and psychosocial features of DSM-IV subtypes of attention-defi cit/hyperactivity disorder: Results from a clinically referred sample. *Journal of the American Academy of Child and Adolescent Psychiatry, 37,* 185–193.

Faraone, S. V., Glatt, S. J., & Tsuang, M. T. (2003). The genetics of pediatric-onset bipolar disorder. *Biological Psychiatry, 53,* 970–977.

Faraone, S. V., Lasky-Su, J., Glatt, S. J., Van Eerdewegh, P., & Tsuang, M. T. (2006). Early onset bipolar disorder: Possible linkage to chromosome 9q34. *Bipolar Disorders, 8,* 144–151.

Faraone, S. V., Perlis, R. H., Doyle, A. E., Smoller, J. W., Goralnick, J. J., Holmgren, M., et al. (2005). Molecular genetics of attention-deficit/hyperactivity disorder. *Biological Psychiatry, 57,* 1313–1323.

Faraone, S. V., Pliszka, S. R., Olvera, R. L., Skolnik, R., & Biederman, J. (2001). Efficacy of Adderall and methylphenidate in attention deficit hyperactivity disorder: A reanalysis using drug-placebo and drug-drug response curve methodology. *Journal of Child and Adolescent Psychopharmacology, 11,* 171–180.

Faraone, S.V., Sergeant, J., Gillberg, C., & Biederman, J. (2003). The worldwide prevalence of ADHD: Is it an American condition? *World Psychiatry, 2,* 104–113.

Faris, P. L, Eckert, E. D., Kim, S. W., Meller, W. H. Pardo, J. V., Goodale, R. L., et al. (2006). Evidence for a vagal pathophysiology for bulimia nervosa and the accompanying depressive symptoms. *Journal of Affective Disorders, 92,* 79–90.

Farley, R.C. (2002). Attachment stability from infancy to adulthood: Meta-analysis and dynamic modeling of developmental mechanisms. *Personality and Social Psychology Review, 6,* 123–151.

Farmer, E. M.Z., Burns, B. J., Phillips, S. D., Angold, A., & Costello, E. J. (2003). Pathways into and through mental health services for children and adolescents. *Psychiatric Services, 54,* 60–66.

Farran, D. C. (2000). Another decade of intervention for children who are low income or disabled: What do we know now? In J. P. Shonkoff & S. J. Meisels (Eds.), *Handbook of early childhood intervention* (2nd ed., pp. 510–548). New York: Cambridge University Press.

Farrant, B.M., Devine, T.A.J., Maybery, M.T., Fletcher, J. (2012). Empathy, perspective taking and prosocial behavior: the importance of parenting practices. *Infant and Child Development, 21,* 175–188.

Farrell, L., Barrett, P., & Piacentini, J. (2006). Obsessive-compulsive disorder across the developmental trajectory: Clinical correlates in children, adolescents and adults. *Behavior Change, 23,* 103–120.

Farrington, D. P., & West, D. (1993). Criminal, penal, and life histories of chronic offenders: Risk and protective factors and early identifi cation. *Criminal Behaviour and Mental Health, 3,* 492–523.

Favaro, A., Zanetti, T., Tenconi, E., Degortes, D., Ronzan, A., Veronses, A., et al. (2005). The relationship between temperament and impulsive behaviors in eating disordered subjects. *Eating Disorders: The Journal of Treatment and Prevention, 13,* 61–70.

Fayyad, J., de Graaf, R., Kessler, R., Alonso, J., Angermeyer, M., Demyttenaere, K., et al. (2007). Cross-national prevalence and correlates of adult attention-deficit hyperactivity disorder. *British Journal of Psychiatry, 190,* 402–409.

Fearon, R.P., Bakermans-Kranenburg, M.J., van IJzendoorn, M.H., Lapsley, A., & Roisman, G.I. (2010). The significance of insecure attachment and disorganization in the development of children's externalizing behavior: A meta-analytic study. *Child Development, 81,* 435–456.

Feder, A., Coplan, J.D., Goetz, R.R., Mathew, S.J., Pine, D.S., Dahl, R.E., Ryan, N.D., Greenwald, S. & Weissman, M.M. (2004). Twenty-four-hour cortisol secretion patterns in prepubertal children with anxiety or depressive disorders. *Biological Psychiatry, 56,* 198–204.

Fehm, L., & Schmidt, K. (2006). Performance anxiety in gifted adolescent musicians. *Journal of Anxiety Disorders, 20,* 98–109.

Feinberg, I., & Campbell, I.G. (2010). Sleep EEG changes during adolescence: An index of a fundamental brain reorganization. *Brain and Cognition, 72,* 56–65.

Feinberg, M. E., & Kan, M. L. (2008). Establishing family foundations: Intervention effects on coparenting, parent/infant well-being, and parent-child relations. *Journal of Family Psychology, 22,* 253–263.

Feldman, M.B., & Meyer, I.H. (2010). Comorbidity and age of onset of eating disorders in gay men, lesbians, and bisexuals. *Psychiatry Research, 180,* 126–131.

Feldman, R. (2007). Maternal versus child risk and the development of parent-child and family relationships in five high-risk populations. *Development and Psychopathology, 19,* 293–312.

Fennig, S., Geva, K., Zalsman, G., Wietzman, A., Fenning, S., & Apter, A. (2005). Effect of gender on suicide attempters versus nonattempters in an adolescent inpatient unit. *Comprehensive Psychiatry, 46,* 90–97.

Ferdinand, R. F., van der Ende, J., & Verhulst, F. C. (2004). Parent-adolescent disagreement regarding psychopathology in adolescents from the general population as a risk factor for adverse outcome. *Journal of Abnormal Psychology, 113,* 198–206.

Ferguson vs. City of Charleston et al., 532 U.S. 67 (2001).

Ferrari, M. (1986). Fears and phobias in childhood: Some clinical and developmental considerations. *Child Psychiatry and Human Development, 17,* 75–87.

Fidler, D. J. (2006). The emergence of a syndrome-specifi c personality profile in young children with Down syndrome. *Down Syndrome: Research and Practice, 10,* 53–60.

Fidler, D. J., Hodapp, R. M., & Dykens, E. M. (2000). Stress in families of young children with Down syndrome, Williams syndrome, and Smith-Magenis syndrome. *Early Education and Development, 11,* 395–406.

Fidler, D. J., Hodapp, R. M., & Dykens, E. M. (2002). Behavioral phenotypes and special education: Parent report of educational issues for children with Down syndrome, Prader-Willi syndrome and Williams syndrome. *Journal of Special Education, 36,* 80–88.

Fidler, D. J., Most, D. E., Booth-LaForce, C., & Kelly, J. F. (2006). Temperament and behavior problems in young children with Down syndrome at 12, 30, and 45 months. *Down Syndrome Research and Practice, 10,* 23–29.

Field, A. E., Austin, S. B., Frazier, A. L., Gillman, M. W., Camarog, C. A., Jr., & Colditz, G. A. (2002). Smoking, getting drunk and engaging in bulimic behaviors: In which order are the behaviors adopted? *Journal of the American Academy of Child and Psychiatry, 41,* 846–853.

Field, A. E., Camargo, C. A., Taylor, C. B., Berkey, C. S., Frazier,L. Gillman, M. W., et al. (1999). Overweight, weight concerns, and bulimic behaviors among girls and boys. *Journal of the American Academy of Child and Adolescent Psychiatry, 38,* 754–760.

Field, A.P., Argyris, N.G. & Knowles, K.A. (2001). Who's afraid of the big bad wolf: A prospective paradigm to test Rachman's indirect pathways in children. *Behaviour Research and Therapy, 39,* 1259–1276.

Field, C. E., Nash, H. M., Handwerk, M. L., & Friman, P. C. (2004). A modification of the token economy for nonresponsive youth in family-style residential care. *Behavior Modification, 28*, 438–457.

Field, T. (2002). Infants' need for touch. *Human Development, 45*, 100–103.

Field, T. M., Hossain, Z., & Malphurs, J. (1999). "Depressed" fathers' interactions with their infants. *Infant Mental Health Journal, 20*, 322–332.

Fiese, B. H., Tomcho, T. J., Douglas, M., Josephs, K., Poltrock, S., & Baker, T. (2002). A review of 50 years of research on naturally occurring family routines and rituals: Cause for celebration? *Journal of Family Psychology, 16*, 381–390.

Fiese, B. H., Winter, M. A., Sliwinski, M., & Anbar, R. D. (2007). Nighttime waking in children with asthma: An exploratory study of daily functioning in family climate. *Journal of Family Psychology, 21*, 95–103.

Fiese, B.H., & Spagnola, M. (2007). The interior life of the family: Looking from the inside out and the outside in. In A.S. Masten (Ed.), *Multilevel Dynamics in Developmental Psychopathology: Pathways to the Future* (pp. 119–150). Mahwah, NJ: Erlbaum.

Figueroa, R. A. (1979). The system of multicultural pluralistic assessment. *School Psychology Review, 8*, 28–36.

Filipek, P. A. (1999). Neuroimaging in the developmental disorders: The state of the science. *Journal of Child Psychology and Psychiatry and Allied Disciplines, 40*, 113–128.

Filipek, P. A., Accardo, P. J., Baranek, G. T., Cook, E. H., Dawson, G., Gordon, B., et al. (1999). The screening and diagnosis of autistic spectrum disorders. *Journal of Autism and Developmental Disorders, 29*, 439–484.

Finkelhor, D., Ormrod, R., Turner, H., Holt, M. (2009). Pathways to poly-victimization. *Child Maltreatment, 14,* 316–329.

Finlay, W. M. L., & Lyons, E. (2001). Methodological issues in interviewing and using self-report questionnaires with people with mental retardation. *Psychological Assessment, 13*, 319–335.

Finn, P. R., Sharkansky, E. J., Brandt, K. M., & Turcotte, N. (2000). The effects of familial risk, personality, and expectancies on alcohol use and abuse. *Journal of Abnormal Psychology,109*, 122–133.

Fischer, K. W., Ayoub, C., Singh, I., Noam, G., Maraganore, A., & Raya, P. (1997). Psychopathology as adaptive development along distinctive pathways. *Development and Psychopathology, 9*, 749–779.

Fischer, P.A., et al. (2006). Effects of therapeutic interventions for foster children on behavioral problems, caregiver attachment, and stress regulatory neural systems. *Annals of the New York Academy of Sciences, 1094*, 215–225.

Fischer, P.A., Stoolmiller, M., Gunnar, M.R., & Burraston, B.O. (2007). Effects of a therapeutic intervention for foster preschoolers on diurnal cortisol activity. *Psychoendochrinology, 32*, 892–905.

Fishbein, D., Hyde, C., Coe, B., & Paschall, M. J. (2004). Neurocognitive and physiological prerequisites for prevention of adolescent drug abuse. *Journal of Primary Prevention, 24*, 471–495.

Fishbein, D., Hyde, C., Eldreth, D., Paschall, M. J., Hubal, R., Das, A., et al. (2006). Neurocognitive skills moderate urban male adolescents' responses to preventive intervention materials. *Drug and Alcohol Dependence, 82*, 47–60.

Fisher, C. B., Hoagwood, K., Boyce, C., Duster, T., Frank, D. A., Grisso, T., et al. (2002). Research ethics for mental health science involving ethnic minority children and youths. *American Psychologist, 57,* 1024–1040.

Fisher, C.B, Jackson, J.F. & Villaruel, F.A. (1998). The study of African American and Latin American children and youth. In W. Damon & R.M. Lerner (Eds.) *Handbook of child psychology: Volume 1: Theoretical models of human development (5th ed.)* (pp. 1145–1207). Hoboken, NJ, US: Wiley.

Fisher, L., Ames, E. W., Chisholm, K., & Savoie, L. (1997). Problems reported by parents of Romanian orphans adopted to British Columbia. *International Journal of Behavioral Development, 20*, 67–82.

Fisher, P. A., Gunnar, M. R., Chamberlain, P., & Reid, J. B. (2000). Preventive intervention for maltreated preschool children: Impact on children's behavior, neuroendocrine activity, and foster parent functioning. *Journal of the American Academy of Child and Adolescent Psychiatry, 39*, 1356–1364.

Fishman, M., Clemmey, P., & Adger, H. (2003). Mountain Manor Treatment Center: Residential adolescent addictions treatment program. In S. J. Stevens & A. R. Morral (Eds.), *Adolescent substance abuse treatment in the United States: Exemplary models from a national evaluation study* (pp. 135–154). New York: Haworth Press.

Flanagan, K. S., Bierman, K. L., Kam, C., Coie, J. D., Dodge, K. A., Foster, E. M., et al. (2003). Identifying at-risk children at school entry: The usefulness of multibehavioral problem profiles. *Journal of Clinical Child and Adolescent Psychology, 32*, 396–407.

Flannery-Schroeder, E., Suveg, C., Safford, S., Kendall, P. C., & Webb, A. (2004). Comorbid externalizing disorders and child anxiety treatment outcomes. *Behaviour Change, 21*, 14–25.

Flavell, J. H. (1982). On cognitive development. *Child Development, 53*, 1–10.

Flavell, J. H. (1982a). Structures, stages, and sequences of cognitive development. In W. A. Collins (Ed.), *The concept of development: The Minnesota symposia on child psychology* (pp. 1–27). Hillsdale, NJ: Erlbaum.

Flavell, J. H. (2004). Theory-of-mind development: Retrospect and prospect. *Merrill-Palmer Quarterly, 50*, 274–290.

Fletcher, J.M., Lyon, G.R., Fuchs, L.S., & Barnes, M.A. (2007). *Learning disabilities: From identification to intervention.* New York: Guilford Press.

Fletcher, J.M., & Vaughn, S. (2009). Response to intervention: Preventing and remediating academic difficulties. *Child Development Perspectives, 3*, 30–37.

Flewelling, R. L., Austin, D., Hale, K., LoPlante, M., Liebig, M., Piasecki, L., et al. (2005). Implementing research-based substance abuse prevention in communities: Effects of a coalition-based prevention initiative in Vermont. *Journal of Community Psychology, 33*, 333–353.

Flinn, M.V. (2006). Evolution and ontogeny of stress response to social challenges in the human child. *Developmental Review, 26*, 138–174.

Flores, E., Cicchetti, D., & Rogosch, F. (2005). Predictors of resilience in maltreated and nonmaltreated Latino children. *Developmental Psychology, 2*, 338–351.

Flynn, J. R. (1987). Massive IQ gains in 14 nations: What IQ tests really measure. *Psychological Bulletin, 101*, 171–191.

Flynn, J. R. (1998). IQ gains over time: Toward finding the causes. In U. Neisser (Ed.), *The Rising Curve: Long-term gains in IQ and related measures* (pp. 25–66). Washington, DC: American Psychological Association.

Flynn, J. R. (2007). *What is intelligence? Beyond the Flynn effect.* New York: Cambridge University Press.

Fombonne, E. (2003). The prevalence of autism. *Journal of the American Medical Association, 289,* 87–89.

Fombonne, E. (2007). Epidemiological surveys of pervasive developmental disorders. In F. R. Volkmar (Ed.), *Autism and pervasive developmental disorders* (2nd ed., pp. 33–68). New York: Cambridge University Press.

Fombonne, E., Wostear, G., Cooper, V., Harrington, R., & Rutter, M. (2001a). The Maudsley long-term follow-up of child and adolescent depression: Psychiatric outcomes in adulthood. *British Journal of Psychiatry, 179,* 210–217.

Fombonne, E., Wostear, G., Cooper, V., Harrington, R., & Rutter, M. (2001b). The Maudsley long-term follow-up of child and adolescent depression: 2. Suicidality, criminality and social dysfunction in adulthood. *British Journal of Psychiatry, 179,* 218–223.

Fonagy, P., & Target, M. (1996). Playing with reality: I. Theory of mind and the normal development of psychic reality. *International Journal of Psychoanalysis, 77,* 217–233.

Fonagy, P., & Target, M. (1997). Attachment and reflective function: Their role in self-organization. *Development and Psychopathology, 9*(4), 679–700.

Fonagy, P., Target, M., & Gergely, G. (2006). Psychoanalytic perspectives on developmental psychopathology. In D. Cicchetti & D.J. Cohen (Eds.), *Developmental Psychopathology, Vol. 1: Theory and Method* (2nd ed.) (pp. 701–749). Hoboken, NJ: John Wiley and Sons.

Fonseca, H., Ireland, M., & Resnick, M. D. (2002). Familial correlates of extreme weight control behaviors among adolescents. *International Journal of Eating Disorders, 32,* 441–448.

Fontes, L.A., & O'Neill-Arana, M.R. (2008). Assessing for child maltreatment in culturally diverse families. In L.A. Suzuki & J.G. Ponterotto (Eds.) *Handbook of multicultural assessment: Clinical, psychological and educational applications* (pp 627–650). San Francisco, CA: Jossey-Bass.

Forbes, E.E., Betocci, M.A., Gregory, A.M., Ryan, N.D., Birmaher, B., & Dahl, R.E. (2008). Objective sleep in pediatric anxiety disorders and major depressive disorder. *Journal of the American Academy of Child & Adolescent Psychiatry, 47,* 148–155.

Forbes, E.E., & Dahl, R.E. (2005). Neural systems of positive affect: Relevance to understanding child and adolescent depression? *Development and Psychopathology, 17,* 827–850.

Forbes, E.E., & Dahl, R.E. (2009). Pubertal development and behavior: Hormonal activation of social and motivational tendencies. *Brain and Cognition, 72,* 66–72.

Forbes, E.E., Phillips, M.L., Silk, J.S., Ryan, N.D., Dahl, R.E. (2011). Neural systems of threat processing in adolescents: Role of pubertal maturation and relation to measures of negative affect. *Developmental Neuropsychology, 36,* 429–452.

Ford, T., Goodman, R., & Meltzer, H. (2003). The British child and adolescent mental health survey 1999: The prevalence of DSM-IV disorders. *Journal of the American Academy of Child and Adolescent Psychiatry, 42,* 1203–1211.

Forgatch, M. S., & Patterson, G. R. (2010). Parent management training—Oregon Model: An intervention for antisocial behavior in children and adolescents. In J. R. Weisz & A. E. Kazdin (Eds.), *Evidence-Based Psychotherapies for Children and Adolescents* (2nd ed.) (pp. 159–178). New York: Guilford Press.

Foster, E. M., & Jones, D. E. (2005). The high costs of aggression: Public expenditures resulting from conduct disorder. *American Journal of Public Health, 95,* 1767–1772.

Foster, E. M., Olchowski, A. E., & Webster-Stratton, C. H. (2007). Is stacking intervention components cost-effective? An analysis of the Incredible Years program. *Journal of the American Academy of Child and Adolescent Psychiatry, 46,* 1414–1424.

Foster, J. D., Kuperminc, G. P., & Price, A. W. (2004). Gender differences in posttraumatic stress and related symptoms among inner-city minority youth exposed to community violence. *Journal of Youth and Adolescence, 33,* 59–69.

Fountain, C., Winter, A.S., & Bearman, P.S. (2011). Six developmental trajectories characterize children with autism. *Pediatrics, 129,* e1112–e1120.

Fowles, D.C., & Dindo, L. (2009). Temperament and psychopathy: A dual pathway model. *Current Directions in Psychological Science,18,* 179–183.

Fox, N. A., & Henderson, H. A. (1999). Does infancy matter? Predicting social behavior from infant temperament. *Infant Behavior and Development, 22,* 445–455.

Fox, N.A., Henderson, H.A., Marshall, P.J., Nichols, K.E., & Ghera, M.M. (2005). Behavioral inhibition: Linking biology and behavior within a developmental framework. *Annual Review of Psychology, 56,* 235–262.

Fox, S.E., Levitt, P., & Nelson, C.A. (2010). How the timing and quality of early experiences influence the development of brain architecture. *Child Development, 81,* 28–40.

Foy, J.M., & Earls, M.F. (2005). A process for developing community consensus regarding the diagnosis and management of attention-deficit/hyperactivity disorder. *Pediatrics, 115,* 97–104.

Foynes, M.M., Freyd, J.J., & DePrince, A.P. (2009). Child abuse: Betrayal and disclosure. *Child Abuse & Neglect, 33,* 209–217.

Fraiberg, S., Adelson, E., & Shapiro, V. (1980). *Ghosts in the nursery: A psychoanalytic approach.* New York: Basic Books.

Fraley, R.C. (2002). Attachment stability from infancy to adulthood: Metal-analysis and dynamic modeling of developmental mechanisms. *Personality and Social Psychology Review, 6,* 123–151.

Franco, X., Saavedra, L. M., & Silverman, W. K. (2007). External validation of comorbid patterns of anxiety disorders in children and adolescents. *Journal of Anxiety Disorders, 21,* 717–729.

Frank, G. K., Bailer, U. F., Henry, S., Wagner, A., & Kaye, W. H. (2004). Neuroimaging studies in eating disorders. *CNS Spectrums, 9,* 539–548.

Frank, G. K., Wagner, A., Achenbach, S., McConaha, C., Skovira, K., Aizenstein, H., et al. (2006). Altered brain activity in women recovered from bulimic-type eating disorders after a glucose challenge: A pilot study. *International Journal of Eating Disorders, 39,* 76–79.

Franko, D. L., Striegel-Moore, R. H., Barton, B. A., Schumann, B. C., Garner, D. M., Daniels, S. R., et al. (2004). Measuring eating concerns in black and white adolescent girls. *International Journal of Eating Disorders, 35,* 179–189.

Frazier, J. A., Ahn, M. S., DeJong, S., Bent, E. K., Breeze, J. L., & Giuliano, A. J. (2005). Magnetic resonance imaging studies in early-onset bipolar disorder: A critical review. *Harvard Review of Psychiatry, 13,* 125–140.

Frazier, S.L., Chacko, A., Van Gessel, C., O'Boyle, C., & Pelham, W.E. (2011). The summer treatment program meets the south side of Chicago: Bridging science and service in urban after-school programs. *Child & Adolescent Mental Health, 17,* 86–92.

Frazier, T.W., Youngstrom, E.A., Speer, L., Embacher, R., Law, P., Constantino, J., Findling, R.L., Hardan, A.Y., & Eng, C. (2012). Validation of proposed *DSM-5* criteria for autism spectrum disorder. *Journal of the American Academy of Child & Adolescent Psychiatry, 51,* 28–40.

Freedenthal, S., & Stiffman, A. R. (2004). Suicidal behavior in urban American Indian adolescents: A comparison with reservation youth in a southwestern state. *Suicide and Life-Threatening Behavior, 34,* 160–171.

Freud, A. (1946). *The Psycho-Analytical Treatment of Children.* International University Press.

Freud, A. (1966). A short history of child analysis. *Psychoanalytic Study of the Child, 21,* 7–14.

Frick, P. J. (1998). Classification of conduct disorders. In P. J. Frick (Ed.), *Conduct disorders and severe antisocial behavior* (pp. 20–39). New York: Plenum Press.

Frick, P. J. (1998). The nature of antisocial behaviors and conduct disorders. In P. J. Frick (Ed.), *Conduct disorders and severe antisocial behavior* (pp. 9–19). New York: Plenum Press.

Frick, P. J., Bodin, D., & Barry, C. T. (2000). Psychopathic traits and conduct problems in community and clinic-referred samples of children: Further development of the psychopathy screening device. *Psychological Assessment, 12,* 382–393.

Frick, P. J., & Loney, B. R. (2002). Understanding the association between parent and child antisocial behavior. In R. J. McMahon & R. Peters (Eds.), *The effects of parental dysfunction on children* (pp. 105–126). New York: Kluwer Academic/Plenum Publishers.

Frick, P. J., & Morris, A. S. (2004). Temperament and developmental pathways to conduct problems. *Journal of Clinical Child and Adolescent Psychology, 33,* 54–68.

Frick, P.J., Moffitt, T.E. (2010). *A proposal to the DSM-V childhood disorders and the ADHD and disruptive behavior disorders work groups to include a specifier to the diagnosis of conduct disorder based on the presence of callous-unemotional traits.* Arlington, VA: American Psychiatric Association.

Frick, P.J., & Viding, E. (2009). Antisocial behavior from a developmental psychopathology perspective. *Development and Psychopathology, 21,* 1111–1131.

Friedman, N.P., Miyake, A., Corley, R.P., Young, S.E., DeFries, J.C., & Hewitt, J.K. (2006). Not all executive functions are related to intelligence. *Psychological Science, 17,* 172–179.

Friedman, N.P., Miyake, A., Robinson, J.L., & Hewitt, J.K. (2011). Developmental trajectories in toddlers' self-restraint predict individual differences in executive functions 14 years later: A behavioral genetic analysis. *Developmental Psychology, 47,* 1410–1430.

Frilo, C. M. (2004). Subtyping female adolescent psychiatric inpatients with features of eating disorders along dietary restraint and negative affect dimensions. *Behavior Research and Therapy, 42,* 67–78.

Frimer, J.A., & Walker, L.J. (2009). Reconciling the self and morality: An empirical model of moral centrality development. *Developmental Psychology, 45,* 1669–1681.

Fristad, M. A., Goldberg-Arnold, J. S., & Gavazzi, S. M. (2002). Multifamily psychoeducation groups (MFPG) for families of children with bipolar disorder. *Bipolar Disorders, 4,* 254–262.

Fristad, M. A., Goldberg-Arnold, J. S., & Gavazzi, S. M. (2003). Multi-family psychoeducation groups in the treatment of children with disorders. *Journal of Marital and Family Therapy, 29,* 491–504.

Fristad, M. A., & Shaver, A. E. (2001). Psychosocial interventions for suicidal children and adolescents. *Depression and Anxiety, 14,* 192–197.

Fristad, M. A., Shaver, A. E., & Holderle, K. E. (2002). Mood disorders in childhood and adolescence. In D. T. Marsh & M. A. Fristad (Eds.), *Handbook of serious emotional disturbance in children and adolescents* (pp. 228–265). New York: Wiley.

Frith, C.D., & Frith, U. (2012). Mechanisms of social cognition. *Annual Review of Psychology, 63,* 287–313.

Frith, U., & Happe, F. (1994). Autism: Beyond "theory of mind." *Cognition, 50,* 115–132.

Fritz, G. K., Fritsch, S., & Hagino, O. (1997). Somatoform disorder in children and adolescents: A review of the past 10 years. *Journal of the American Academy of Child and Adolescent Psychiatry, 36,* 1329–1338.

Froehlich, T.E., Lanphear, B.P., Auinger, P., Hornung, R., Epstein, J.N., Bruan, J., & Kahn, R.S. (2009). Association of tobacco and lead exposures with attention-deficit/hyperactivity disorder. *Pediatrics, 124,* e1054-e1063.

Fuligni, A. J. (1997). The academic achievement of adolescents from immigrant families: The roles of family background, attitudes, and behavior. *Child Development, 68,* 351–363.

Fuligni, A. J. (1998a). The adjustment of children from immigrant families. *Current Directions in Psychological Science, 7,* 99–103.

Fuligni, A. J. (1998b). Authority, autonomy, and parent-adolescent conflict and cohesion: A study of adolescents from Mexican, Chinese, Filipino, and European backgrounds. *Developmental Psychology, 34,* 782–792.

Fuligni, A. J., Tseng, V., & Lam, M. (1999). Attitudes toward family obligations among American adolescents with Asian, Latin American, and European backgrounds. *Child Development, 70,* 1030–1044.

Fuligni, A. J., Witkow, M., & Garcia, C. (2005). Ethnic identity and the academic adjustment of adolescents from Mexican, Chinese, and European backgrounds. *Developmental Psychology, 41,* 799–811.

Funk, R. R., McDermeit, M., Godley, S. H., & Adams, L. (2003). Maltreatment issues by level of adolescent substance abuse treatment: The extent of the problem at intake and relationship to early outcomes. *Child Maltreatment: Journal of the American Professional Society on the Abuse of Children, 8,* 36–45.

Furman, W. (1999). Friends and lovers: The role of peer relationships in adolescent heterosexual relationships. In Collins, W. A., & Laursen, B. (Eds.), *The Minnesota symposia on child psychology: Vol. 29. Relationships as developmental constructs* (pp. 133–154). Hillsdale, NJ: Erlbaum.

Furman, W. & Shaffer, L. (2003). The role of romantic relationships in adolescent development. In P. Florsheim (Ed.), *Adolescent Romantic Relations and Sexual Behavior* (pp. 2–33). Mahwah, NJ: Erlbaum.

Furr, J.M., Comer, J.S., Edmunds, J.M., & Kendall, P.C. (2010). Disasters and youth: A meta-analytic examination of post-traumatic stress. *Journal of Consulting and Clinical Psychology, 78,* 765–780.

Furr-Holden, C. D. M., Ialongo, N. S., Anthony, J. C., Petras, H., & Kellam, S. G. (2004). Developmentally inspired drug prevention: Middle school outcomes in a school-based randomized prevention trial. *Drug Alcohol Dependence, 73,* 149–158.

Gabowitz, D., Zucker, M., & Cook, A. (2008). Neuropsychological assessment in clinical evaluation of children and adolescents with complex trauma. *Journal of Child and Adolescent Trauma, 1*, 163–178.

Gadow, K. D., Sprafkin, J., Carlson, G. A., Schneider, J., Nolan, E. E., Mattison, R. E., et al. (2002). A DSM-IV-referenced, adolescent self-report rating scale. *Journal of the American Academy of Child and Adolescent Psychiatry, 41*, 671–679.

Gadow, K.D. & Nolan, E.E. (2002). Differences between preschool children with ODD, ADHD and ODD + ADHD symptoms. *Journal of Child Psychology and Psychiatry, 43*, 191–201.

Gagne, J.R., & Saudino, K.J. (2009). Wait for it! A twin study of inhibitory control in early childhood. *Behavioral Genetics, 40*, 327–337.

Galambos, N., Leadbetter, B., & Barker, E. (2004). Gender differences in and risk factors for depression in adolescence: A 4-year longitudinal study. *International Journal of Behavioral Development, 28*, 16–25.

Galanter, C. A., & Leibenluft, E. (2008). Frontiers between attention deficit hyperactivity disorder and bipolar disorder. *Child and Adolescent Psychiatry Clinics of North America, 17*, 325–346.

Galanter, C.A., & Leibenluft, E. (2008). Frontiers between attention deficit hyperactivity disorder and bipolar disorder. *Child and Adolescent Psychiatric Clinics of North America, 17*, 325–346.

Gallay, L.S. & Flanagan, C.A. (2000). The well-being of children in a changing economy: time for a new social contract in America. In R. D. Taylor & W.C. Wang (Eds.) *Resilience Across Contexts: Family, Work, Culture, and Community* (pp. 3–33). Mahwah, NJ: Erlbaum.

Galvin, M. R., Stilwell, B. M., Shekhar, A., Kipta, S. M., & Goldfarb, S. M. (1997). Maltreatment, conscience functioning and dopamine beta hydroxylase in emotionally disturbed boys. *Child Abuse and Neglect, 21*, 83–92.

Ganiban, J.M., Ulbricht, J., Saudino, K.J., Reiss, D., & Neiderhiser, J.M. (2010). Understanding child-based effects on parenting: Temperament as a moderator of genetic and environmental contributions to parenting. *Developmental Psychology, 47*, 676–692.

Ganzel, B.L., & Morris, P.A. (2011). Allostasis and the developing human brain: Explicit consideration of implicit models. *Development and Psychopathology, 23*, 955–974.

Garb, H. N., Wood, J. M., Lilienfeld, S. O., & Nezworski, M. T. (2002). Effective use of projective techniques in clinical practice: Let the data help with selection and interpretation. *Professional Psychology: Research and Practice, 33*, 454–463.

Garber, J. (2007). Depression in youth: A developmental psychopathology perspective. In A.S. Masten (Ed.), *Multilevel dynamics in developmental psychopathology. The Minnesota Symposia on Child Psychology (Vol. 34)* (pp. 181–242). Mahwah, NJ: Laurence Erlbaum Associates.

Garber, J., Braafladt, N., & Weiss, B. (1995). Affect regulation in depressed and nondepressed children and young adolescents. *Development and Psychopathology, 7*, 93–115.

Garber, J., & Carter, J. S. (2006). Major depression. In R. T. Ammerman (Ed.), *Comprehensive handbook of personality and psychopathology* (Vol. 3, pp. 165–216). Hoboken, NJ: Wiley.

Garber, J. & Carter, J.S. (2006). Major depression. In R. T. Ammerman (Ed.), *Comprehensive Handbook of Personality and Psychopathology, Vol. 3* (pp. 165–216). Hoboken, NJ: Wiley.

Garber, J., & Cole, D.A. (2010). Intergenerational transmission of depression: A launch and grow model of change across adolescence. *Development and Psychopathology, 22*, 819–830.

Garber, J., & Kaminski, K. M. (2000). Laboratory and performance-based measures of depression in children and adolescents. *Journal of Clinical Child Psychology, 29*, 509–525.

Garber, J., Keiley, M. K., & Martin, N. C. (2002). Developmental trajectories of adolescents' depressive symptoms: Predictors of change. *Journal of Consulting and Clinical Psychology, 70*, 79–95.

Garber, J., & Little, S. (1999). Predictors of competence among offspring of depressed mothers. *Journal of Adolescent Research, 14*, 44–71.

Garber, J., & Martin, N. C. (2002). Negative cognitions in offspring of depressed parents: Mechanisms of risk. In S. H. Goodman & I. H. Gotlib (Eds.), *Children of depressed parents: Mechanisms of risk and implications for treatment* (pp. 121–153). Washington, DC: American Psychological Association.

Garcia Coll, C. (2001). Cultural influences on children's and families' well-being. In A. Thornton (Ed.), *The well-being of children and families: Research and data needs* (pp. 244–261). Ann Arbor: The University of Michigan Press.

Garcia, J. A., & Weisz, J. R. (2002). When youth mental health care stops: Therapeutic relationships problems and other reasons for ending youth outpatient treatment. *Journal of Consulting and Clinical Psychology, 70*, 439–443.

Garcia-Lopez, L. J., Olivares, J., Beidel, D., Albano, A. M., Turner, S., & Rosa, A. I. (2006). Efficacy of three treatment protocols for adolescents with social anxiety disorder: A 5-year follow-up assessment. *Journal of Anxiety Disorders, 20*, 175–191.

Gardner, H. (1983). Can Piaget and Lévi-Strauss be reconciled? *New Ideas in Psychology, 1*, 187–189.

Gardner, H. (1993). *Multiple intelligences.* New York: Basic Books.

Gardner, J., Carran, D. T., & Nudler, S. (2001). Measuring quality of life and quality of services through personal outcomes measures: Implication for public policy. In L. M. Glidden (Ed.), *International review of research in mental retardation* (Vol. 24, pp. 75–100). San Diego, CA: Academic Press.

Gardner, M., & Steinberg, L. (2005). Peer influence on risk taking, risk preference, and risky decision making in adolescence and adulthood: An experimental study. *Developmental Psychology, 41*, 625–635.

Gardner, W. I., Graeber-Whalen, J. L., & Ford, D. R. (2001). Behavioral therapies: Individualizing interventions through treatment formulations. In A. Dosen & K. Day (Eds.), *Treating mental illness and behavior disorders in children and adults with mental retardation* (pp. 69–100). Washington, DC: American Psychiatric Publishing.

Garfield, J. L., & Perry, T. (2001). Social cognition, language acquisition and the development of the theory of mind. *Mind and Language, 16*, 494–541.

Garmezy, N. (1974). The study of competence in children at risk for severe psychopathology. In E. J. Anthony & C. Koupernick (Eds.), *The child in his family: Children at psychiatric risk.* New York: Wiley.

Garmezy, N., Masten, A. S., & Tellegen, A. (1984). The study of stress and competence in children: A building block for developmental psychopathology. *Child Development, 55*, 97–111.

Garmezy, N., & Rutter, M. (1983). *Stress, coping and development in children.* Baltimore, MD: John Hopkins University Press.

Garralda, M.E. (2010). Unexplained physical complaints. *Child and Adolescent Psychiatric Clinics of North America, 19*, 199–209.

Garralda, M.E., & Raynaud, J. (2008). *Culture and conflict in child and adolescent mental health.* Lanham, MD: Jason Aronson.

Gartstein, M. A., Gonzalez, C., Carranza, J. A., Ahadi, S. A., Ye, R., Rothbart, M. K., et al. (2006). Studying cross-cultural differences in the development of infant temperament: People's Republic of China, the United States of America, and Spain. *Child Psychiatry Human Development, 37*, 145–161.

Gartstein, M.A., Slobodskaya, H.R., Zylicz, P.O., Gosztyla, D., & Nakagawa, A. (2010). A cross-cultural evaluation of temperament: Japan, USA, Poland and Russia. *International Journal of Psychology & Psychological Therapy, 10*, 55–75.

Gaub, M., & Carlson, C. L. (1997). Gender differences in ADHD: a meta-analysis and critical review. *Journal of the American Academy of Child and Adolescent Psychiatry, 36*, 1036–1045.

Gaughan, M. (2006). The gender structure of adolescent peer influence on drinking. *Journal of Health and Social Behavior, 47*, 47–61.

Gause, C., Morris, C., Vernekar, S., Pardo-Villamizar, C., Grados, M.A., & Singer, H.S. (2009). Antineuronal antibodies in OCD: Comparisons in children with OCD-only, OCD + chronic tics and OCD + PANDAS. *Journal of Neuroimmunology, 214*, 118–124.

Gaylor, E. E., Burnham, M. M., Goodlin-Jones, B. L., & Anders, T. F. (2005). A longitudinal follow-up study of young children's sleep patterns using a developmental classification system. *Behavioral Sleep Medicine, 3*, 44–61.

Ge, X., Brody, G. H., Conger, R. D., Simons, R. L., & Murry, V. M. (2002). Contextual amplification of pubertal transition effects on deviant peer affiliation and externalizing behavior among African American children. *Developmental Psychology, 38*, 42–54.

Ge, X., Kim, I. J., Brody, G. H., Conger, R. D., Simons, R. L., Gibbons, F. X., et al., (2003). It's about timing and change: Pubertal transition effects on symptoms of major depression among African American youths. *Developmental Psychology, 39*, 430–439.

Gelb, S. A. (1997). The problem of typological thinking in mental retardation. *Mental Retardation, 35*, 448–457.

Gelb, S. A. (2002). The dignity of humanity is not a scientific construct. *Mental Retardation, 40*, 55–56.

Geldhill, J., & Garralda, M.E. (2006). Functional symptoms and somatoform disorders in children and adolescents: the role of standardized measures in assessment. *Child and Adolescent Mental Health, 11*, 208–214.

Geller, B., Craney, J. L., Bolhofner, K., DelBello, M. P., Axelson, D., Luby, J. L., et al. (2003). Phenomenology and longitudinal course of children with a prepubertal and early adolescent bipolar disorder phenotype. In B. Geller & M. P. DelBello (Eds.), *Bipolar disorder in childhood and early adolescence* (pp. 25–50). New York: Guildford Press.

Geller, B., Craney, J. L., Bolhofner, K., Nickelsburg, M. J., Williams, M., & Zimerman, B. (2002). Two-year prospective follow-up of children with a prepubertal and early adolescent bipolar disorder phenotype. *American Journal of Psychiatry, 159*, 927–933.

Geller, B., & Luby, J. (1997). Child and adolescent bipolar disorder: A review of the past 10 years. *Journal of the American Academy of Child and Adolescent Psychiatry, 36*, 1168–1176.

Geller, B., Tillman, R., Craney, J. L., & Bolhofner, K. (2004). Four-year prospective outcome and natural history of mania in children with a prepubertal and early adolescent bipolar disorder phenotype. *Archives of General Psychiatry, 61*, 459–467.

Geller, B., Zimerman, B., Williams, M., Bolhofner, K., & Craney, J. L. (2001). Adult psychosocial outcome of prepubertal major depressive disorder. *Journal of the American Academy of Child and Adolescent Psychiatry, 40*, 673–677.

Geller, B., Zimerman, B., Williams, M., DelBello, M. P., Bolhofner, K., Craney, J. L., Frazier, J., Beringer, L., & Nickelsburg, M. J. (1997). Bipolar disorder at prospective follow-up of adults who had prepubertal major depressive disorder. *Journal of Child and Adolescent Psychiatry, 36*, 1168–1176.

Geller, D., Biederman, J., Jones, J., Park, K., Schwartz, S., Shapiro, S., et al. (1998). Is juvenile obsessive-compulsive disorder a developmental sub-type of the disorder? A review of the pediatric literature. *Journal of the American Academy of Child and Adolescent Psychiatry, 37*, 420–427.

George, C., Herman, K., & Ostrander, R. (2006). The family environment and developmental psychopathology: The unique and interactive effects of depression, attention, and conduct problems. *Child Psychiatry and Human Development, 37*, 163–177.

George, S., & Moselhy, H. (2005). "Gateway hypothesis"—A preliminary evaluation of variables predicting non-conformity. *Addictive Disorders and Their Treatment, 4*, 39–40.

Georgiades, K., Lewinsohn, P.M., Monroe, S.M., & Seeley, J.R. (2006). Major depressive disorder in adolescence: The role of subthreshold symptoms. *Journal of the American Academy of Child & Adolescent Psychiatry, 45*, 936–944.

Georgiades, S., Szatmari, P., Zwaigenbaum, L., Duku, E., Bryson, S., Roberts, W., et al. (2007). Structure of the autism symptom phenotype: A proposed multidimensional model. *Journal of the American Academy of Child and Adolescent Psychiatry, 46*, 188–196.

Georgiou, S. N. (2008). Parental style and child bullying and victimization experiences in school. *Social Psychology of Education, 11*, 213–227.

Gernsbacher, M. A., Stevenson, J. L., Khandakar, S., & Goldsmith, H. H. (2008). Why does joint attention look atypical in autism? *Society for Research in Child Development, 2*, 38–45.

Gershoff, E.T., Lansford, J.E., Zelli, A., Grogan-Kaylor, A., Chang, L., Dodge, K., & Deater-Deckard, K. (2010). Parent discipline practices in an international sample: Associations with child behaviors and moderation by perceived normativeness. *Child Development, 81*, 487–502.

Gerstein, E.D., Crnic, K.A. Blacher, J., & Baker, B.L. (2009). Resilience and the course of daily parenting stress in families of young children with intellectual disabilities. *Journal of Intellectual Disability Research, 53*, 981–997.

Gestsdottir, S., Lewin-Bizan, S., von Eye, A., Lerner, J.V., & Lerner, R.M. (2009). The structure and function of selection, optimization, and compensation in middle adolescence: Theoretical and applied implications. *Journal of Applied Developmental Psychology, 30*, 585–600.

Gewirtz, A.H., & August, G.J. (2008). Incorporating multifaceted mental health prevention services in community sectors-of-care. *Clinical Child & Family Psychology Review, 11*, 1–11.

Gewirtz, A.H., DeGarmo, D.S., & Medhanie, A. (2011). Effects of mother's parenting practices on child internalizing trajectories following partner violence. *Journal of Family Psychology, 29*–38.

Gewirtz, A.H., & Edleson, J.L. (2007). Young children's exposure to intimate partner violence: Towards a developmental risk and resilience framework for research and intervention. *Journal of Family Violence, 22*, 151–163.

Ghaziuddin, M., Ghaziuddin, N., & Greden, J. (2002). Depression in persons with autism: Implications for research and clinical care. *Journal of Autism and Developmental Disorders, 32,* 299–306.

Ghuman, J.K., Arnold,L.E. & Anthony, B.J. (2008). Psycho-pharmacological and other treatments in preschool children with attention-deficit/hyperactivity disorder: Current evidence and practice. *Journal of Child and Adolescent Psychopharmacology, 18,* 413–447.

Giaconia, R. M., Reinherz, H. Z., Paradis, A. D., & Stashwick, C. K. (2003). Comorbidity of substance use disorders and posttraumatic stress disorder in adolescents. In P. Ouimette & P. J. Brown (Eds.), *Trauma and substance abuse: Causes, consequences, and treatment of comorbid disorders* (pp. 227–242). Washington, DC: American Psychological Association.

Giannopoulou, I., Dikaiakou, A., & Yule, W. (2006). Cognitive-behavioural group intervention for PTSD symptoms in children following the Athens 1999 earthquake: A pilot study. *Clinical Child Psychology and Psychiatry, 11,* 543–553.

Giannopoulou, I., Strouthos, M., Smith, P., Dikaiakou, A., Galanopoulou, V., & Yule, W. (2006). Post-traumatic stress reactions of children and adolescents exposed to the Athens 1999 earthquake. *European Psychiatry, 21,* 160–166.

Giedd, J. N., Blumenthal, J., Jeffries, N. O., Castellano, F. Z., Liu, H., Zijdenbos, A., Paus, T., Evans, A. C., & Rapoport, J. L. (1999). Brain development during childhood and adolescence: A longitudinal MRI study. *Nature Neuroscience, 2,* 861–863.

Gifford-Smith, M., Dodge, K. A., Dishion, T. J., & McCord, J. (2005). Peer influence in children and adolescents: Crossing the bridge from developmental to intervention science. *Journal of Abnormal Child Psychology, 33,* 255–265.

Gil, A. G., Wagner, E. F., & Tubman, J. G. (2004). Culturally sensitive substance abuse intervention for Hispanic and African American adolescents: Empirical examples from the Alcohol Treatment Targeting Adolescents in Need (AT-TAIN) Project. *Addiction, 99,* 140–150.

Gilbert, G., & Blair, C. (2004). How early experience matters in intellectual development in the case of poverty. *Prevention Science, 5,* 245–252.

Gilbert, S. C. (2003). Eating disorders in women of color. *Clinical Psychology: Science and Practice, 10,* 444–455.

Gillham, J. E., & Reivich, K. (2004). Cultivating optimism in childhood and adolescence. *Annals of the American Academy of Political and Social Science, 591,* 146–163.

Gillham, J. E., & Reivich, K. J. (1999). Prevention of depressive symptoms in school children: A research update. *Psychological Science, 10,* 461–462.

Gillham, J. E., Reivich, K. J., Jaycox, L. H., & Seligman, M. E. P. (1995). Prevention of depressive symptoms in schoolchildren: Two-year follow-up. *Psychological Science, 6,* 343–351.

Gilliom, M., Shaw, D. S., Beck, J. E., Schonberg, M. A., & Lukon, J. L. (2002). Anger regulation in disadvantaged preschool boys: Strategies, antecedents, and the development of self-control. *Developmental Psychology, 38,* 222–235.

Ginsburg, G. S., Albano, A. M., Findling, R. L., Kratochvil, C., & Walkup, J. (2005). Integrating cognitive behavioral therapy and pharmacotherapy in the treatment of adolescent depression. *Cognitive and Behavioral Practice, 12,* 252–262.

Ginsburg, G. S., Riddle, M. A., & Davies, M. (2006). Somatic symptoms in children and adolescents with anxiety disorders. *Journal of the American Academy of Child and Adolescent Psychiatry, 45,* 1179–1187.

Ginsburg, G.S. & Schlossberg, M.C. (2002). Family-based treatment of childhood anxiety disorders. *International Review of Psychiatry, 14,* 143–154.

Girouard, P. C., Baillargeon, R. H., Tremblay, R. E., Glorieux, J., Lefebvre, F., & Robaey, P. (1998). Developmental pathways leading to externalizing behaviors in 5 year olds born before 29 weeks of gestation. *Journal of Developmental and Behavioral Pediatrcs, 19,* 244–253.

Giummarra, M. J., & Haslam, N. (2005). The lay concept of childhood mental disorder. *Child Psychiatry and Human Development, 35,* 265–280.

Gladstone, T. R. G., & Beardslee, W. R. (2002). Treatment, intervention, and prevention with children of depressed parents: A developmental perspective. In S. H. Goodman & I. H. Gotlib (Eds.), *Children of depressed parents: Mechanisms of risk and implications for treatment* (pp. 277–305). Washington, DC: American Psychological Association.

Glascoe, F. P. (1995). The role of parents in the detection of developmental and behavioral problems. *Pediatrics, 95,* 829–836.

Glascoe, F. P. (1997). Parents' concerns about children's development: Prescreening technique or screening test? *Pediatrics, 99,* 522–528.

Glascoe, F. P. (2000). Evidence-based approach to developmental and behavioral surveillance using parents' concerns. *Child: Care, Health and Development, 26,* 137–149.

Gleason, M.M., Fox, N.A., Drury, S., Smyke, A., Egger, H.L., Nelson, C.A., … Zeanah, C.H. (2011). Validity of evidence-derived criteria for reactive attachment disorder: Indiscriminately social/disinhibited and emotionally withdrawn/inhibited types. *Journal of the American Academy of Child & Adolescent Psychiatry, 50,* 216–231.

Gleaves, D. H., Brown, J. D., & Warren, C. S. (2004). The continuity/discontinuity models of eating disorders: A review of the literature and implications for assessment, treatment and prevention. *Behavior Modifcation, 28,* 739–762.

Gledhill, J. & Garralda, M.E. (2006). Functional symptoms and somatoform disorders in children and adolescents: The role of standardized measures in assessment. *Child and Adolescent Mental Health, 11,* 208–214.

Glidden, L. M. (2002). Parenting children with developmental disabilities: A ladder of influence. In J. G. Borowski, S. Landesman, & M. Bristol-Power (Eds.), *Parenting and the child's world: Influences on academic, intellectual, and social-emotional development. Monographs in Parenting* (pp. 329–344). Mahwah, NJ: Erlbaum.

Goenjian, A. K., Pynoos, R. S., Steinberg, A. M., Najarian, L. M., Asarnow, J. R., & Karayan, I., (1995). Psychiatric comorbidity in children after the 1988 earthquake in Armenia. *Journal of the American Academy of Child and Adolescent Psychiatry, 34,* 1174–1184.

Goenjian, A. K., Stilwell, B. M., Steinberg, A. M., Fairbanks,L. A., Galvin, M., Karayan, I., et al. (1999). Moral development among adolescents after trauma. *Journal of the American Academy of Child and Adolescent Psychiatry, 38,* 376–384.

Gogtay, N., Giedd, J. N., Lusk, L., Hayashi, K. M., Greenstein, D., Vaituzis, A. C., et al. (2004). Dynamic mapping of human cortical development during childhood through early adulthood. *Procedures of the National Academy of Science, 101,* 8174–8179.

Goin, R., & Myers, B. J. (2004). Characteristics of infantile autism: Moving toward earlier detection. *Focus on Autism and Other Developmental Disabilities, 19,* 5–12.

Goin-Kochel, R., & Myers, B. J. (2005). Parental report of early autistic symptoms: Differences in ages of detection and frequencies of characteristics among three autism-spectrum disorders. *Journal on Developmental Disabilities, 11,* 21–39.

Gold, M. S., Frost-Pineda, K., & Jacobs, W. S. (2003). Overeating, binge eating, and eating disorders as addictions. *Psychiatric Annals, 33,* 117–122.

Goldberg, S., Gotowiec, A., & Simmons, R. J. (1995). Infant-mother attachment and behavior problems in healthy and chronically ill preschoolers. *Development and Psychopathology, 7,* 267–282.

Goldberg-Arnold, J. S., & Fristad, M. A. (2003). Psychotherapy for children with bipolar disorder. In B. Geller & M. P. DelBello (Eds.), *Bipolar disorder in childhood and early adolescence* (pp. 272–294). New York: Guildford Press.

Goldman, D., Oroszi, G., & Ducci, F. (2005). The genetics of addictions: Uncovering the genes. *National Review of Genetics, 6,* 521–532.

Goldsmith, H. H., Lemery, K. S., Essex, M. J. (2004). Temperament as a liability factor for childhood behavioral disorders: The concept of liability. In L. F. DiLalla (Ed.), *Behavior genetics principles: Perspectives in development, personality, and psychopathology. Decade of behavior* (pp. 19–39). Washington, DC: American Psychological Association.

Goldstein, D.B., Daniel, S.S., Arnold, E.M (2006). Suicidal and nonsuicidal self-harm behaviors. In D. A. Wolfe & E.J. Mash (Eds.), *Behavioral and Emotional Disorders in Adolescents: Nature, Assessment, and Treatment* (pp. 343–380). New York, NY: Guilford Press.

Goldstein, D.B., Molock, S.D., Whitbeck, L.B., Murakami, J.L., Zayas, L.H., & Hall, G.C.N. (2008). Cultural considerations in adolescent suicide prevention and psychosocial treatment. *American Psychologist, 63,* 14–31.

Goldstein, G., Allen, D. N., Minshew, N. J., Williams, D. L., Volkmar, F., Klin, A., et al. (2008). The structure of intelligence in children and adults with high functioning autism. *Neuropsychology, 22,* 301–312.

Goldstein, R.B., Olfson, M., Wickramaratne, P.J. & Wolk, S.I. (2006). Use of outpatient mental health services by depressed and anxious children as they grow up. *Psychiatric Services, 5,* 966–975.,

Goldston, D. B. (2004). Conceptual issues in understanding the relationship between suicidal behavior and substance use during adolescence. *Drug and Alcohol Dependence, 76,* S79–S91.

Goodey, C. F. (2001). What is developmental disability? The origin and nature of our conceptual models. *Journal on Developmental Disabilities, 8,* 1–18.

Goodlin-Jones, B., Tang, K., Liu, J., & Anders, T.F. (2009). Sleep problems, sleepiness and daytime behavior in preschool-age children. *Journal of Child Psychology and Psychiatry, 50,* 1532–1540.

Goodlin-Jones, B.L., Tang, K., Liu, J., & Anders, T.F. (2008). Sleep patterns in preschool-age children with autism, developmental delay, and typical development. *Journal of the American Academy of Child & Adolescent Psychiatry, 47,* 930–938.

Goodman, A., Patel, V., & Leon, D.A. (2010). Why do British Indian children have an apparent mental health advantage? *Journal of Child Psychology and Psychiatry, 51,* 1171–1183.

Goodman, S. H., & Gotlib, I. H. (1999). Risk for psychopathology in the children of depressed mothers: A developmental model for understanding mechanisms of transmission. *Psychological Review, 106,* 458–490.

Goodman, S. H., & Gotlib, I. H. (2002). Transmission of risk to children of depressed parents: Integration and conclusions.

In S. H. Goodman & I. H. Gotlib (Eds.), *Children of depressed parents: Mechanisms of risk and implications for treatment* (pp. 307–326). Washington, DC: American Psychological Association.

Goodman, S.H., Rouse, M.H., Connell, A.M., Broth, M.R., Hall, C.M., & Heyward, D. (2010). Maternal depression and child psychopathology: A meta-analytic review. *Clinical Child & Family Psychology Review, 14,* 1–27.

Goodman, S.H., Rouse, M.H., Connell, A.M., Broth, M.R., Hall, C.M. & Heyward, D. (2011). Maternal depression and child psychopathology: A meta-analytic review. *Clinical Child and Family Psychology Review, 14,* 1–27.

Goodnight, J. A., Bates, J. E., Staples, A. D., Pettit, G. S., & Dodge, K. A. (2007). Temperamental resistance to control increases the association between sleep problems and externalizing behavior development. *Journal of Family Psychology, 21,* 39–48.

Goodnight, J.A., Lahey, B.B., Van Hulle, C.A., Rodger, J.L., Rathouz, P.J., Waldman, I.D., & D'Onofrio, B.M.D. (2011). A quasi-experimental analysis of the influence of neighborhood disadvantage on child and adolescent conduct problems. *Journal of Abnormal Psychology, 121,* 95–108.

Goodwin, R. D., Lieb, R., Hoefler, M., Pfister, H., Bittner, A., Beesdo, K., et al. (2004). Panic attack as a risk factor for severe psychopathology. *American Journal of Psychiatry, 161,* 2207–2214.

Gopnik, A., & Tenenbaum, J.B. (2007). Bayesian networks, Bayesian learning and cognitive development. *Developmental Science, 10,* 281–287.

Gordon, J., King, N., Gullone, E., Muris, P., & Ollendick, T. H. (2007). Nighttime fears of children and adolescents: Frequency, content, severity, harm expectations, disclosure, and coping behaviours. *Behaviour Research and Therapy, 45,* 2464–2472.

Gordon, J., King, N.J., Gullone, E., Muris, P., & Ollendick, T.H. (2007). Treatment of children's nighttime fears: The need for a modern randomized controlled trial. *Clinical Psychology Review, 27,* 98–113.

Gordon, K., Holm-Denoma, J. Smith, A., Fink, E., & Joiner, T. (2007). Taxometric analysis: Introduction and overview. *International Journal of Eating Disorders, 40,* S35–S39.

Gordon, R. (1983). An operational classification of disease prevention. *Public Health Reports, 98,* 107–109.

Gordon, R. (1987). An operational classification of disease prevention. In J. A. Steinberg & M. M. Silverman (Eds.), *Preventing Mental Disorders* (pp. 20–26). Rockville, MD: Department of Health and Human Services.

Gosch, E.A., Flannery-Schroeder, E., Mauro, C.F. & Compton, S.N. (2006). Principles of cognitive-behavioral therapy for anxiety disorders in children. *Journal of Cognitive Psychotherapy, 20,* 247–262.

Gothelf, D., Aharonovsky, O., Horesh, N., Carty, T., & Apter, A. (2004). Life events and personality factors in children and adolescents with obsessive-compulsive disorder and other anxiety disorders. *Comprehensive Psychiatry, 45,* 192–198.

Gotlib, I. H., & Sommerfeld, B. K. (1999). Cognitive functioning in depressed children and adolescents: A developmental perspective. In C. A. Essau & F. Petermann (Eds.), *Depressive disorders in children and adolescents: Epidemiology, risk factors, and treatment* (pp. 195–236). Northvale, NJ: Jason Aronson.

Gottlieb, G. (2003). On making behavioral genetics truly developmental. *Human Development, 46,* 337–355.

Gottlieb, G. (2007). Probabilistic epigenesist. *Developmental Science, 10,* 1–11.

Gottlieb, G. & Blair, C. (2004). How early experience matters in intellectual development in the case of poverty. *Prevention Science, 5,* 245–252.

Gould, M. S., Greenberg, T., Velting, D. M., & Shaffer, D. (2003). Youth suicide risk and preventive interventions: A review of the past 10 years. *Journal of the American Academy of Child and Adolescent Psychiatry, 42,* 386–405.

Gould, M. S., Velting, D., Kleinman, M., Lucas, C., Thomas, J. G., & Chung, M. (2004). Teenagers' attitudes about coping strategies and help-seeking behavior for suicidality. *Journal of the American Academy of Child and Adolescent Psychiatry, 43,*1124–1133.

Gowers, S., & Bryant-Waugh, R. (2004). Management of child and adolescent eating disorders: The current evidence base and future directions. *Journal of Child Psychology and Psychiatry, 45,* 63–83.

Gowers, S. G. (2006). Evidence based research in CBT with adolescent eating disorders. *Child and Adolescent Mental Health, 11,* 9–12.

Graber, J. A., Lewinsohn, P. M., Seeley, J. R., & Brooks-Gunn, J. (1997). Is psychopathology associated with the timing of pubertal development? *Journal of the American Academy of Child and Adolescent Psychiatry, 36,* 1768–1776.

Graber, J. A., Tyrka, A.R. & Brooks-Gunn, J. (2003). How similar are correlates of different subclinical eating problems and bulimia nervosa? *Journal of Child Psychology and Psychiatry, 44,* 262–273.

Graber, J.A. & Brooks-Gunn, J. (1996). Transitions and turning points: Navigating the passage from childhood through adolescence. *Developmental Psychology, 32,* 768–776.

Graham, J. E., Kennard, B. D., Mayes, T. L., Nightingale-Teresi, J., Carmody, T., Hughes, C. W., et al. (2008). Fluoxene versus placebo in preventing relapse of major depression in children and adolescents. *American Journal of Psychiatry, 165,* 459–467.

Graham, S., Bellmore, A. D., & Mize, J. (2006). Peer victimization, aggression, and their co-occurrence in middle school: Pathways to adjustment problems. *Journal of Abnormal Child Psychology, 34,* 363–378.

Granic, I., Hollenstein, T., Dishion, T.J. & Patterson, G.R. (2003). Longitudinal analysis of flexibility and reorganization in early adolescence: A dynamic systems study of family interactions. *Developmental Psychology, 39,* 606–617.

Granillo, T., Jones-Rodriguez, G., & Carvajal, S. C. (2005). Prevalence of eating disorders in Latina adolescents: Associations with substance use and other correlates. *Journal of Adolescent Health, 36,* 214–220.

Grant, B. F. (1997). Prevalence and correlates of alcohol use and DSM-IV alcohol dependence in the United States: Results of the National Longitudinal Alcohol Epidemiologic Survey. *Journal of Studies on Alcohol, 58,* 464–473.

Grant, B. F. (1998). The impact of a family history of alcoholism on the relationship between age at onset of alcohol use and DSM-IV alcohol dependence: Results from the National Longitudinal Alcohol Epidemiologic Survey. *Alcohol Health and Research World, 22,* 144–147.

Grant, B. F. (2000). Estimates of US children exposed to alcohol abuse and dependence in the family. *American Journal of Public Health, 90,* 112–115.

Grant, B. F., Stinson, F. S., & Harford, T. C. (2001). Age at onset of alcohol use and DSM-IV alcohol abuse and dependence: A 12year follow-up. *Journal of Substance Abuse, 13,* 493–504.

Gratz, K. L., Conrad, S. D., & Roemer, L. (2002). Risk factors for deliberate self-harm among college students. *American Journal of Orthopsychiatry, 72,* 128–140.

Gratz, K.L. (2007). Targeting emotion dysregulation in the treatment of self-injury. *Journal of Clinical Psychology: In Session, 63,* 1091–1103.

Gratz, K.L., Conrad, S.D. & Roemer, L. (2002). Risk factors for deliberate self-harm among college students. *American Journal of Orthopsychiatry, 72,* 128–140.

Gratz, K.L., Latzman, R.D., Young, J., Heiden, L.J., Damon, J., Hight, T., & Hull, M.T. (2012). Deliberate self-harm among underserved adolescents: The moderating roles of gender, race, and school-level and association with borderline personality features. *Personality Disorders: Theory, Research, and Treatment, 3,* 39–54.

Gray, J.R., & Thompson, P.M. (2004). Neurobiology of intelligence: Science and ethics. *Nature Reviews, 5,* 471–482.

Graziano, P.A., Keane, S.P., & Calkins, S.D. (2010). Maternal behavior and children's early emotion regulation skills differentially predict development of children's reactive control and later effortful control. *Infant and Child Development, 19,* 333–353.

Graziano, W. G., Jensen-Campbell, L. A., & Sullivan-Logan, G.M. (1998). Temperament, activity, and expectations for later personality development. *Journal of Personality and Social Psychology, 74,* 1266–1277.

Graziano, W. G., & Tobin, R. M. (2002). Emotional regulation from infancy through adolescence. In M H. Bornstein, L. Davidson, C. L. M. Keyes, C. L. M., & K. Moore (Eds.), *Well-Being: Positive development across the life course* (pp.139–154). Mahwah, NJ: Erlbaum.

Greenberg, M. T., Lengua, L. J., Coie, J. D., Pinderhughes, E. E., Bierman, K., Dodge, K. A., et al. (1999). Predicting developmental outcomes at school entry using a multiple-risk model: Four American communities. *Developmental Psychology, 35,* 403–417.

Greenberg, M. T., Weissberg, R. P., O'Brien, M. U., Fredericks, L., Resnik, H., & Elias, M. J. (2003). Enhancing school-based prevention and youth development through coordinated social, emotional, and academic learning. *American Psychologist, 58,* 466–474.

Greenberg, M.T., Speltz, M.L. & DeKlyen, M. (1993). The role of attachment in the early development of disruptive behavior problems. (1993). *Development and Psychopathology, 5,* 191–213.

Greene, R. W. (1996). Students with attention-deficit hyperactivity disorder and their teachers: Implications of a goodness-of-fit perspective. From T. H. Ollendick & R. J. Prinz (Eds.), *Advances in clinical child psychology* (Vol. 18, pp. 205–230). New York: Plenum Press.

Greene, R. W., Ablon, J. S., Goring, J. C., Raezer-Blakely, L., Markey, J., Monuteaux, M. C., et al., (2004). Effectiveness of collaborative problem solving in affectively dysregulated children with oppositional defiant disorder: Initial findings. *Journal of Consulting and Clinical Psychology, 72,* 1157–1164.

Greene, R. W., Beszterczey, S. K., Katzenstein, T., Park, K., & Goring, J. (2002). Are students with ADHD more stressful to teach? Patterns of teacher stress in an elementary school sample. *Journal of Emotional and Behavioral Disorders, 10,* 79–89.

Greene, R. W., Biederman, J., Faraone, S. V., Wilens, T. E., Mick, E., & Blier, H. K. (1999). Further validation of social impairment as a predictor of substance use disorders: Findings from a sample of siblings of boys with and without ADHD. *Journal of Clinical Child Psychology, 28*, 349–354.

Greene, R. W., Biederman, J., Zerwas, S., Monuteaux, M., Goring, J. C., & Faraone, S. V. (2002). Psychiatric comorbidity, family dysfunction, and social impairment in referred youth with oppositional defiant disorder. *American Journal of Psychiatry, 159*, 1214–1224.

Greene, R.W., A.J., Stuart, & Goring, J.C. (2003). A transactional model of oppositional behavior: Underpinnings of the collaborative problem solving approach. *Journal of Psychosomatic Research, 55*, 67–75.

Greene, R.W. & Doyle, A.E. (1999). Toward a transactional conceptualization of oppositional defiant disorder: Implications for assessment and treatment. *Clinical Child and Family Psychology Review, 2*, 129–148.

Greenfield, P.M., Keller, H., Fuligni, A., & Maynard, A. (2003). Cultural pathways through universal development. *Annual Review of Psychology, 54*, 461–490.

Greenfield, S. F., & Sugarman, D. E. (2001). The treatment and consequences of alcohol abuse and dependence during pregnancy. In K. Yonkers & B. Little (Eds.), *Management of Psychiatric Disorders in Pregnancy* (pp. 213–227). London: Oxford University Press.

Greenhill, L. L., Jensen, P. S., Abikoff, H., Blumer, J. L., De-Veaugh-Geiss, J., Fisher, C., et al. (2003). Developing strategies for psychopharmacological studies in preschool children. *Journal of the American Academy of Child and Adolescent Psychiatry, 42*, 406–414.

Greenhill, L. L., Posner, K., Vaughan, B. S., & Kratochvil, C. J. (2008). Attention deficit hyperactivity disorder in preschool children. *Child and Adolescent Psychiatric Clinics of North America, 17*, 347–366.

Greenough, W., Black, J., & Wallace, C. (1987). Experience and brain development. *Child Development, 58*, 539–559.

Greenough, W. T., & Black, J. E. (1992). Induction of brain structure by experience: Substrates for cognitive development. In M. R. Gunnar & C. A. Nelson (Eds.), *Developmental behavioral neuroscience. Minnesota Symposium on Child Psychology* (Vol. 24, pp.155–200). Hillsdale, NJ: Erlbaum.

Greenspan, S. I., & Weider, S. (1993). *The child with special needs: Encouraging intellectual and emotional growth.* Reading, MA: Addison-Wesley.

Griffin, R., & Baron-Cohen, S. (2002). The intentional stance: Developmental and neurocognitive perspectives. In A. Brook & D. Ross (Eds.), *Daniel Dennett. Contemporary philosophy in focus* (pp. 83–116). New York: Cambridge University Press.

Grillon, C., Warner, V., Hille, J., Merikagnas, K.R., Bruder, G.E., Tenke, C.E., Nomura, Y., Leite, P., Weissman, M.M. (2005). Families at high and low risk for depression: A three-generation startle study. *Biological Psychiatry, 57*, 953–960.

Grilo, C. M., Walker, M. L., Becker, D. F., Edell, W. S., & McGlashan, T. H. (1997). Personality disorders in adolescents with major depression, substance abuse disorders, and coexisting major depression and substance use disorders. *Journal of Consulting and Clinical Psychology, 65*, 328–332.

Groesz, L. M., Levine, M. P., & Murnen, S. K. (2002). The effect of experimental presentation of thin media images on body satisfaction: A meta-analytic review. *International Journal of Eating Disorders, 31*, 1–16.

Groh, A.M., Roisman, G.I., vanIJzendoorn, M.H., Bakermans-Kranenburg, M.J., & Fearon, R.P. (2012). The significance of insecure and disorganized attachment for children's internalizing symptoms: A meta-analytic study. *Child Development, 83*, 591–610.

Grolnick, W.S., & Pomerantz, E.M. (2009). Issues and challenges in studying parental control: Toward a new conceptualization. *Child Development Perspectives, 3*, 165–170.

Gross, J. J., & Thompson, R. A. (2007). Emotion regulation: Conceptual foundations. In J. J. Gross (Ed.), *Handbook of emotion regulation* (pp. 3–24). New York: Guilford Press.

Grossmann, K. E., & Grossmann, K. (Eds.). (2005). *The longitudinal studies of attachment.* New York: Guilford Press.

Grossmann, K. E., Grossmann, K., & Keppler, A. (2005). Universal and culture-specific aspects of human behavior: The case of attachment. In W. Friedlmeier, P. Chakkarath, & B. Schwarz (Eds.), *Culture and human development: The importance of cross-cultural research for the social sciences* (pp. 75–97). Hove, England: Psychology Press/Erlbaum (UK) Taylor and Francis.

Guerra, N. G., Huesmann, L. R., & Spindler, A. (2003). Community violence exposure, social cognition, and aggression among urban elementary school children. *Child Development, 74*, 1561–1576.

Guerra, V. S., Asher, S. R., & DeRosier, M. E. (2004). Effect of children's perceived rejection on physical aggression. *Journal of Abnormal Child Psychology, 32*, 551–563.

Guilamo-Ramos, V., Jaccard, J., Johansson, M., & Tunisi, R. (2004). Binge drinking among Latino youth: Role of acculturation-related variables. *Psychology of Addictive Behaviors, 18*, 135–142.

Gullone, E., King, N. J., & Ollendick, T. H. (2001). Self-reported anxiety in children and adolescents: A three-year follow-up study. *Journal of Genetic Psychology, 162*, 5–19.

Gumpel, T.P., & Sharoni, V. (2007). Current best practices in learning disabilities in Israel. *Learning Disabilities Research & Practice, 22*, 202–209.

Gunnar, M. R. (1994). Psychoendocrine studies of temperament and stress in early childhood: Expanding current models. In J. E. Bates & T. D. Wachs (Eds.), *Temperament: Individual differences at the interface of biology and behavior. APA science volumes* (pp. 175–198). Washington, DC: American Psychological Association.

Gunnar, M. R. (1998). Quality of early care and buffering of neuroendocrine stress reactions: Potential effects on the developing human brain. *Preventive Medicine: An International Journal Devoted to Practice and Theory, 27*, 208–211.

Gunnar, M. R. (2001). The role of glucocorticoids in anxiety disorders: A critical analysis. In M. W. Vasey & M. R. Dadds (Eds.), *The developmental psychopathology of anxiety* (pp. 143–159). London: Oxford University Press.

Gunnar, M. R. (2003). Integrating neurosciences and psychological approaches in the study of early experiences. In J. A. King, C. F. Ferris, & I. I. Lederhendler (Eds.), *Annals of the New York Academy of Sciences: Vol. 1008. Roots of mental illness in children* (pp. 238–247). New York: Academy of Sciences.

Gunnar, M. R., & Cicchetti, D. (2009). Meeting the challenge of translational research in child development: Opportunities and roadblocks. In D. Cicchetti & M. R. Gunnar (Eds.), *Meeting the Challenge of Translational Research in Child Psychology: The Minnesota Symposia on Child Psychology* (Vol. 35, pp. 1–27). Hoboken, NJ: Wiley.

Gunnar, M. R., & Donzella, B. (2002). Social regulation of the cortisol levels in early human development. *Psychoneuroendocrinology, 27,* 199–220.

Gunnar, M. R., & Loman, M. M. (2011). Early experience and stress regulation in human development. In D. P. Keating (Ed.), *Nature and Nurture in Early Child Development* (pp. 97–113). Cambridge: Cambridge University Press.

Gunnar, M. R., & Mangelsdorf, S. (1989). The dynamics of temperament-physiology relations: A comment on biological processes in temperament. In G. A. Kohnstamm & J. E. Bates (Eds.), *Temperament in childhood* (pp. 145–152). Oxford, England: Wiley.

Gunnar, M. R., Mangelsdorf, S., Larson, M., & Hertsgaard, L. (1989). Attachment, temperament, and adrenocortical activity in infancy: A study of psychoendocrine regulation. *Developmental Psychology, 25,* 355–363.

Gunnar, M. R., Porter, F. L., Wolf, C. M., & Rigatuso, J. (1995). Neonatal stress reactivity: Predictions to later emotional temperament. *Child Development, 66,* 1–13.

Gunnar, M.R., & Fischer, P.A. The Early Experience, Stress, and Prevention Network (2006). Bringing basic research on early experience and stress neurobiology to bear on preventative interventions for neglected and maltreated children. *Development and Psychopathology, 18,* 651–677.

Gunnar, M.R., & Quevedo, K. (2007). The neurobiology of stress and development. *Annual Review of Psychology, 58,* 145–173.

Guo, J., Collins, L. M., Hill, K. G., & Hawkins, J. D. (2000). Developmental pathways to alcohol abuse and dependence in young adulthood. *Journal of Studies on Alcohol, 61,* 799–808.

Gupta, A.R., & State, M.W. (2007). Recent advances in the genetics of autism. *Biological Psychiatry, 61,* 429–737.

Habermas, T., & Bluck, S. (2000). Getting a life: The emergence of the life story in adolescence. *Psychological Bulletin, 126,* 748–769.

Habeych, M. E., Charles, P. J., Sclabassi, R. J., Kirisci, L., & Tarter, R. E. (2005). Direct and mediated associations between P300 amplitude in childhood and substance use disorders outcome in young adulthood. *Biological Psychiatry, 57,* 76–82.

Hackett, R., & Hackett, L. (1999). Child psychiatry across cultures. *International Review of Psychiatry, 11,* 225–235.

Hadadian, A., & Merbler, J. (1995a). Fathers of young children with disabilities: How do they want to be involved? *Child and Youth Care Forum, 24,* 327–338.

Hadadian, A., & Merbler, J. (1995b). Parents of infants and toddlers with special needs: Sharing views of desired services. *Infant-Toddler Intervention, 5,* 141–152.

Hafen, C.A., & Laursen, B. (2009). More problems and less support: Early adolescent adjustment forecasts changes in perceived support from parents. *Journal of Family Psychology, 23,* 193–202.

Hagekull, B., & Bohlin, G. (2004). Predictors of middle childhood psychosomatic problems: An emotion regulation approach. *Infant and Child Development, 13,* 389–405.

Haines, J., & Neumark-Sztainer, D. (2006). Prevention of obesity and eating disorders: A consideration of shared risk factors. *Health Education Research, 21,* 770–782.

Halberstadt, A. G., Denham, S. A., & Dunsmore, J. C. (2001). Affective social competence. *Social Development, 10,* 79–119.

Hale, W.W., Raaijmakers, Q., Muris, P., van Hoof, A. & Meeus, W. (2008). Developmental trajectories of adolescent anxiety disorder symptoms: A 5-year prospective community study. *Journal of the American Academy of Child & Adolescent Psychiatry, 47,* 555–564.

Hall, W. A., Zubrick, S. R., Silburn, S. R., Parsons, D. E., & Kurinczuk, J. J. (2007). A model for predicting behavioural sleep problems in a random sample of Australian preschoolers. *Infant and Child Development, 16,* 509–523.

Hall, W. D., & Lynskey, M. (2005). Is cannabis a gateway drug? Testing hypotheses about the relationship between cannabis use and the use of other illicit drugs. *Drug and Alcohol Review, 24,* 39–48.

Halle, T. (2002). Emotional development. In M. H. Bornstein, L. Davidson, C. L. M. Keyes, & K. Moore (Eds.), *Well-being: Positive development across the life course.* Mahwah, NJ: Erlbaum.

Haller, M., Handley, E., Chassin, L., & Bountress, K. (2010). Developmental cascades: Linking adolescent substance use, affiliation with substance use promoting peers, and academic achievement to adult substance use disorders. *Development and Psychopathology, 22,* 899–916.

Hallfors, D. D., Waller, M. W., Ford, C. A., Halpern, C. T., Brodish, P. H., & Iritani, B. (2004). Adolescent depression and suicide risk: Association with sex and behavior. *American Journal of Preventative Medicine, 27,* 224–230.

Hallfors, D., & Van Dorn, R. A. (2002). Strengthening the role of two key institutions in the prevention of adolescent substance abuse. *Journal of Adolescent Health, 30,* 17–28.

Hallmayer, J., Cleveland, S., Torres, A., Phillips, J., Cohen, B., Torigoe, T., ... Risch, N. (2011). Genetic heritability and shared environmental factors among twin pairs with autism. *Archives of General Psychiatry, 68,* 1095–1102.

Halmi, K. A., Agras, W. S., Crow, S., Mitchell, J., Wilson, G. T., Bryson, S. W., et al. (2005). Predictors of treatment acceptance and completion in anorexia nervosa: Implications for future study designs. *Archives of General Psychiatry, 62,* 776–781.

Halmi, K. A., Agras, W. S., Mitchell, J., Wilson, G. T., Crow, S. Bryson, S. W., et al. (2002). Relapse predictors of patients with bulimia nervosa who achieved abstinence through cognitive behavioral therapy. *Archives of General Psychiatry, 59,* 1105–1109.

Halmi, K. A., Sunday, S. R., Klump, K. L., Strober, M., Leckman, J. F.-L., Fichter, M., et al. (2003). Obsessions and compulsions in anorexia nervosa subtypes. *International Journal of Eating Disorders, 33,* 308–319.

Halmi, K. A., Tozzi, F., Thornton, L. M., Crow, S., Fichter, M. M., Kaplan, A. S., et al. (2005). The relation among perfectionism, obsessive-compulsive personality disorder and obsessive-compulsive disorder in individuals with eating disorders. *International Journal of Eating Disorders, 38,* 371–374.

Halmi, K.A. (2009). Perplexities and provocations of eating disorders. *Journal of Child Psychology and Psychiatry, 50,* 163–169.

Halonen, A., Aunola, K., Ahonen, T., & Nurmi, J. (2006). The role of learning to read in the development of problem behavior: A cross-lagged longitudinal study. *British Journal of Educational Pscyhology, 72,* 517–534.

Halperin, J.M., Trampush, J.W., Miller, C.J., Marks, D.J., & Newcorn, J.H. (2008). Neuropsychological outcome in adolescents/young adults with childhood ADHD: Profiles of persisters, remitters and controls. *The Journal of Child Psychology and Psychiatry, 49,* 958–966.

Halpern, C. T., King, R. B., Oslak, S. G., & Udry, J. R. (2005). Body mass index, dieting, romance, and sexual activity in adolescent girls: Relationships over time. *Journal of Research on Adolescence, 15,* 535–559.

Hamada, R. S., Kameoka, V., Yanagida, E., & Chemtob, C. M. (2003). Assessment of elementary school children for disaster-related posttraumatic stress disorder symptoms: The Kauai recovery index. *Journal of Nervous and Mental Disease, 191,* 268–272.

Hamilton, A. F. de C., Brindley, R. M., & Frith, U. (2007). Imitation and action understanding in autistic spectrum disorders: How valid is the hypothesis of a deficit in the mirror neuron system? *Neuropsychologia, 45,* 1859–1868.

Hammen, C., Brennan, P.A., Keenan-Miller, D.K., Hazel, N.A., & Najman, J.M. (2010). Chronic and acute stress, gender, and serotonin transporter gene-environment interactions predicting depression symptoms in youth. *Journal of Child Psychology and Psychiatry, 51,* 180–187.

Hammen, C., & Rudolph, K. D. (1996). Childhood depression. In E. J. Mash & R. A. Barkley (Eds.), *Child psychopathology* (pp. 153–195). New York: Guilford Press.

Hammen, C., Shih, J. H., & Brennan, P. A. (2004). Intergenerational transmission of depression: Test of an interpersonal stress model in a community sample. *Journal of Consulting and Clinical Psychology, 72,* 511–522.

Hampe, E., Noble, H., Miller, L. C., & Barrett, C. L. (1973). Phobic children one and two years post treatment. *Journal of Abnormal Psychology, 82,* 446–453.

Hampson, S. E., Severson, H. H., Burns, W. J., Slovic, P., & Fisher, K. J. (2001). Risk perception, personality factors and alcohol use among adolescents. *Personality and Individual Differences, 30,* 167–181.

Hanish, L. D., & Guerra, N. G. (2002). A longitudinal analysis of patterns of adjustment following peer victimization. *Development and Psychopathology, 14,* 69–89.

Hanish, L. D., & Guerra, N. G. (2004). Aggressive victims, passive victims, and bullies: Developmental continuity or developmental change? *Merrill-Palmer Quarterly, 50,* 17–38.

Hankin, B. L., & Abramson, L. Y. (2001). Development of gender differences in depression: An elaborated cognitive vulnerability-transactional stress theory. *Psychological Bulletin, 127,* 773–796.

Hankin, B. L., Fraley, R. C., Lahey, B. B., & Waldman, I. D. (2005). Is depression best viewed as a continuum or discrete category? A taxometric analysis of childhood and adolescent depression in a population-based sample. *Journal of Abnormal Psychology, 114,* 96–110.

Hankin, B. L., Mermelstein, & R., Roesch, L. (2007). Sex differences in adolescent depression: Stress exposure and reactivity models. *Child Development, 78,* 279–295.

Hankin, B. L., Wetter, E., & Cheely, C. (2008). Sex differences in child and adolescent depression: A developmental psychopathological approach. In J. R. Z. Abela & B. L. Hankin (Eds.), *Handbook of depression in children and adolescents* (pp. 377–414). New York: Guilford Press.

Hankin, J. R. (2002). Fetal alcohol syndrome prevention research. *Alcohol Research and Health, 26,* 58–62.

Hanna, A. C., & Bond, M. J. (2006). Relationships between family conflict, perceived maternal verbal messages, and daughters' disturbed eating symptomology. *Appetite, 47,* 205–211.

Hanna, E. Z., & Grant, B. F. (1999). Parallels to early onset alcohol use in the relationship of early onset smoking with drug use and DSM-IV drug and depressive disorders: Findings from the National Longitudinal Epidemiologic Survey. *Alcoholism: Clinical and Experimental Research, 23,* 513–522.

Hardy, S.A., & Carlo, G. (2011). Moral identity: What it is, how does it develop, and is it linked to moral action? *Child Development Perspectives, 3,* 212–218.

Harford, T. C., Grant, B. F., Yi, H., & Chen, C. M. (2005). Patterns of DSM-IV alcohol abuse and dependence criteria among adolescents and adults: Results from the 2001 National Household Survey on Drug Abuse. *Alcoholism: Clinical and Experimental Research, 29,* 810–828.

Harmon, R. J. (2002). The administration of programs for infants and toddlers. *Child and Adolescent Psychiatric Clinics of North America, 11,* 1–21.

Harmon, R.J. (2002). The administration of programs for infants and toddlers. *Child and Adolescent Psychiatric Clinics of North America, 11,* 1–21.

Harold, R. D. (2000). *Becoming a family: Parents' stories and their implications for practice, policy and research.* Mahwah, NJ: Erlbaum.

Harpaz-Rotem, I., Leslie, D. L., Martin, A., & Rosenheck, R. A. (2005). Changes in child and adolescent inpatient psychiatric admission diagnoses between 1995 and 2000. *Social Psychiatry and Psychiatric Epidemiology, 40,* 642–647.

Harper, G., & Çetin, F.C. (2008). Child and adolescent mental health policy: Promise to provision. *International Review of Psychiatry, 20,* 217–224.

Harris, S.L. (1995). Educational strategies in autism. In E. Schopler & G.B. Mesibov (Eds.) *Learning and Cognition in Autism* (pp. 293–309). New York, NY: Plenum Press.

Harrison, A.M., & Tronick, E.Z. (2007). Contributions to understanding therapeutic change: Now we have a playground. *Journal of the American Psychoanalytic Association, 55,* 853–874.

Harrison, K. (2001). Ourselves, our bodies: Thin-ideal media, self-discrepancies, and eating disorder symptomatology in adolescents. *Journal of Social and Clinical Psychology, 20,* 289–323.

Harrison, K., & Hefner, V. (2008). Media, body image, and eating disorders. In S. L. Calvert & B. J. Wilson (Eds.), *The handbook of children, media, and development* (pp. 381–406). Malden, MA: Blackwell.

Hart, E.L., Lahey, B.B., Loeber, R. & Hanson, K.S. (1994). Criterion validity of informants in the diagnosis of disruptive behavior disorders in children: A preliminary study. *Journal of Consulting and Clinical Psychology, 62,* 410–414.

Harter, S. (1999). *The construction of the self: A developmental perspective.* New York: Guilford Press.

Harter, S. (2003). The development of self-representations during childhood and adolescence. In M. R. Leary & J. P. Tangney (Eds.), *Handbook of self and identity* (pp. 610–642). New York: Guilford Press.

Hartman, C. A., Willcutt, E. G., Rhee, S. H., & Pennington, B. F. (2004). The relation between sluggish cognitive tempo and DSM-IV ADHD. *Journal of Abnormal Child Psychology, 32,* 491–503.

Hartung, C. M., McCarthy, D. M., Milich, R., & Martin, C. A. (2005). Parent-adolescent agreement on disruptive behavior symptoms: A multitrait-multimethod model. *Journal of Psychopathology and Behavioral Assessment, 27,* 159–168.

Hartup, W. W. (2005). The development of aggression: Where do we stand? In R. E. Tremblay, W. W. Hartup, & J. Archer (Eds.), *Developmental origins of aggression* (pp. 3–22). New York: Guilford Press.

Hartup, W. W., & Laursen, B. (1999). Relationships as developmental contexts: Retrospective themes and contemporary issues. In W. A. Collins & B. Laursen (Eds.), *Relationships as developmental contexts: The Minnesota Symposia on Child Psychology* (Vol. 30, pp. 13–35). Mahwah, NJ: Erlbaum.

Hastings, P.D., Sullivan, C., McShane, K.E., Coplan, R.J., Utendale, W.T. & Vyncke, J.D. (2008). Parental socialization, vagal regulation, and preschoolers' anxious difficulties: Direct mothers and moderated fathers. *Child Development, 79,* 45–64.

Hawkins, E. H., Cummins, L. H., & Marlatt, G. A. (2004). Preventing substance abuse in American Indian and Alaska native youth: Promising strategies for healthier communities. *Psychological Bulletin, 130,* 304–323.

Hawkins, J. D., Hill, K. G., Guo, J., & Battin-Pearson, S. R. (2002). Substance use norms and transitions in substance use: Implications for the gateway hypothesis. In D. B. Kandel (Ed.), *Stages and pathways of drug involvement: Examining the gateway hypothesis* (pp. 42–64). New York: Cambridge University Press.

Hawley, K. M., & Weisz, J. R. (2003). Child, parent, and therapist (dis)agreement on target problems in outpatient therapy: The therapist's dilemma and its implications. *Journal of Consulting and Clinical Psychology, 71,* 62–70.

Hawley, P. & Vaughn, B.E. (2003). Aggression and adaptive functioning: The bright side to bad behavior. *Merrill-Palmer Quarterly, 49,* 239–242.

Haworth, C.M.A., Wright, M.J., Luciano, M., Martin, N.G., de Geus, E.J.C., van Beijsterveldt, C.E.M., Bartles, M., Posthuma, D., & Plomin, R. (2010). The heritability of general cognitive ability increases linearly from childhood to young adulthood. *Molecular Psychiatry, 15,* 1112–1120.

Hay, D. F., Pawlby, S., Sharp, D., Schmücker, G., Mills, A., Allen, H., et al. (1999). Parents' judgements about young children's problems: Why mothers and fathers might disagree yet still predict later outcomes. *Journal of Child Psychology and Psychiatry and Allied Disciplines, 40,* 1249–1258.

Hazler, R., & Mellin, E. (2004). The developmental origins and treatment needs of female adolescents with depression. *Journal of Counseling and Development, 82,* 18–24.

He, K., Kramer, E., Houser, R. F., Chomitz, V. R., & Hacker, K. A. (2004). Defining and understanding healthy lifestyles choices for adolescents. *Journal of Adolescent Health, 35,* 26–33.

Heal, L. W., Borthwick-Duffy, S. A., & Saunders, R. R. (1996). Assessment of quality of life. In J. W. Jacobson & J. A. Mulick (Eds.), *Manual of diagnosis and professional practice in mental retardation* (pp. 199–209). Washington, DC: American Psychological Association.

Heaton, P., Hermelin, B., & Pring, L. (1998). Autism and pitch processing: A precursor for savant musical ability. *Music Perception, 15,* 291–305.

Hechtman, L., Ectovitch, J., Platt, R., Arnold, L.E., Abikoff, H.B., Newcorn, J.H., … Wigal, T. (2005). Does multimodal treatment of ADHD decrease other diagnoses? *Clinical Neuroscience Research, 5,* 273–282.

Heflinger, C.A., & Hinshaw, S.P. (2010). Stigma in child and adolescent mental health services research: Understanding professional and institutional stigmatization of youth with mental health problems and their families. *Administration and Policy in Mental Health, 37,* 61–70.

Heim, C., & Nemeroff, C. B. (2001). The role of childhood trauma in the neurobiology of mood and anxiety disorders: Preclinical and clinical studies. *Biological Psychiatry, 49,* 1023–1039.

Heim, C., Newport, D. J., Heit, S, Graham, Y. P., Wilcox, M., Bonsall, R., et al. (2000). Pituitary-adrenal and autonomic responses to stress in women after sexual and physical abuse in childhood. *Journal of the American Medical Association, 284,* 592–597.

Heiman, T. (2000). Friendship quality among children in three educational settings. *Journal of Intellectual and Developmental Disability, 25,* 1–12.

Heiman, T. (2001). Inclusive schooling—Middle school teachers' perceptions. *School Psychology International, 22,* 451–462.

Heiman, T. (2002). Parents of children with disabilities: Resilience, coping, and future expectations. *Journal of Developmental and Physical Disabilities, 14,* 159–171.

Hellander, M. (2003). Pediatric bipolar disorder: The parent advocacy perspective. *Biological Psychiatry, 53,* 935–937.

Hellander, M., Sisson, D. P., & Fristad, M. A. (2003). Internet support for parents of children with early-onset bipolar disorder. In B. Geller & M. P. DelBello (Eds.), *Bipolar disorder in childhood and early adolescence* (pp.314–329). New York: Guilford Press.

Henggeler, S. W., Clingempeel, W. G., Brondino, M. J., & Pickrel, S. G. (2002). Four-year follow-up of multisystemic therapy with substance-abusing and substance-dependent juvenile offenders. *Journal of the American Academy of Child and Adolescent Psychiatry, 41,* 868–874.

Henggeler, S. W., Halliday-Boykins, C. A., Cunningham, P. B., Randall, J., Shapiro, S. B., & Chapman, J. E. (2006). Juvenile drug court: Enhancing outcomes by integrating evidence-based treatments. *Journal of Consulting and Clinical Psychology, 74,* 42–54.

Henggeler, S. W., & Lee, T. (2003). Multisystemic treatment of serious clinical problems. In A. E. Kazdin & J. R. Weisz (Eds.), *Evidence-based psychotherapies for children and adolescents* (pp. 301–322). New York: Guilford Press.

Henin, A., Mick, E., Biederman, J., Fried, R., Wozniak, J., Faraone, S. V., et al. (2007). Can bipolar disorder-specific neuropsychological impairments in children be identified? *Journal of Consulting and Clinical Psychology, 75,* 210–220.

Henningfield, J. E., Michaelides, T., & Sussman, S. (2000). Developing treatment for tobacco addicted youth—Issues and challenges. *Journal of Child and Adolescent Substance Abuse, 9,* 5–26.

Henry, B., Caspi, A., Moffitt, T. E., Harrington, H., & Silva, P.A. (1999). Staying in school protects boys with poor self-regulation in childhood from later crime: A longitudinal study. *International Journal of Behavioral Development, 23,* 1049–1073.

Hensley, L., & R.E. Varela (2008). PTSD symptoms and somatic complaints following hurricane Katrina: The roles of trait anxiety and anxiety sensitivity. *Journal of Clinical Child & Adolescent Psychology, 37,* 542–552.

Herman, K. C., Lambert, S. F., Ialongo, N. S., & Ostrander, R. (2007). Academic pathways between attention problems and depressive symptoms among urban African American children. *Journal of Abnormal Child Psychology, 35,* 265–274.

Herman, K. C., Ostrander, R., & Tucker, C. M. (2007). Do family environments and negative cognitions of adolescents with depressive symptoms vary by ethnic group? (2007). *Journal of Family Psychology, 21,* 325–330.

Hermelin, B. (2001). *Bright splinters of the mind: A personal story of research with autistic savants.* Philadelphia: Jessica Kingsley Publishers.

Hermes, S. F., & Keel, P. K. (2003). The influence of puberty and ethnicity on awareness and internalization of the thin ideal. *International Journal of Eating Disorders, 33,* 465–467.

Herring, M., & Kaslow, N. J. (2002). Depression and attachment in families: A child-focused perspective. *Family Process, 41*, 494–518.

Hesse, E., & Main, M. (2006). Frightened, threatening, and dissociative parental behavior in low-risk samples: Description, discussion, and interpretations. *Development and Psychopathology, 18*, 309–343.

Hetherington, E. M., Bridges, M., & Insabella, G. M. (1998). What matters? What does not? Five perspectives on the association between marital transitions and children's adjustment. *American Psychologist, 53*, 167–184.

Hewitt, A.S., Stancliffe, R.J., Sirek, A.J., Hall-Lande, J., Taub, S., Engler, J., Bershadsky, J., Fortune, J., &Moseley, C.R. (2012). Characteristics of adults with autism spectrum disorder who use adult developmental disability services: Results from 25 states. *Research in Autism Spectrum Disorders, 6*, 741–751.

Hewitt, J. K., Silberg, J. L., Rutter, M., Simonoff, E., Meyer, J. M., Maes, H., et al. (1997). Genetics and developmental psychopathology: 1. Phenotypic assessment in the Virginia Twin Study of Adolescent Behavioral Development. *Journal of Child Psychology and Psychiatry and Allied Disciplines, 38*, 943–963.

Heyman, I., Fombonne, E., Simmons, H., Ford, T., Meltzer, H., & Goodman, R. (2001). Prevalence of obsessive-compulsive disorder in the British nationwide survey of child mental health. *British Journal of Psychiatry, 179*, 324–329.

Heyne, D., King, N. J., Tonge, B. J., Rollings, S., Young, D., Pritchard, M., et al. (2002). Evaluation of child therapy and caregiver training in the treatment of school refusal. *Journal of the American Academy of Child and Adolescent Psychiatry, 41*, 687–695.

Higgins, E. T., Loeb, I., & Moretti, M. (1995). Self-discrepancies and developmental shifts in vulnerability: Life transitions in the regulatory significance of others. In D. Cicchetti & S. L. Toth (Eds.), *Emotion, cognition and representation* (pp. 191–230). Rochester, NY: University of Rochester Press.

Hilarski, C. (2004). Victimization history as a risk factor for conduct disorder behaviors: Exploring connections in a national sample of youth. *Stress, Trauma and Crisis: An International Journal, 7*, 47–59.

Hill, A.L., Degnan, K.A., Calkins, S.D. & Keane, S.P (2006). Profiles of externalizing behavior problems for boys and girls across preschool: The roles of emotion regulation and inattention. *Developmental Psychology, 42*, 913–928.

Hillegers, M. H. J., Burger, H., Wals, M., Reichart, C. G., Verhulst, F. C., Nolen, W. A., et al. (2004). Impact of stressful life events, familial loading and their interaction on the onset of mood disorders: Study in a high-risk cohort of adolescent offspring of parents with bipolar disorder. *British Journal of Psychiatry, 185*, 97–101.

Hilton, C.L. (2011). Sensory processing and motor issues in autism spectrum disorders. In J.L. Matson & P. Sturmey (Eds.) *International handbook of autism and pervasive developmental disorders* (pp. 175–193). New York: Springer Science & Business Media.

Hinshaw, S. P. (2005). The stigmatization of mental illness in children and parents: developmental issues, family concerns, and research needs. *Journal of Child Psychology and Psychiatry, 46*, 714–734.

Hinshaw, S.P. (2002). Intervention research, theoretical mechanisms and causal processes related to externalizing behavior patterns. *Development and Psychopathology, 14*, 789–818.

Hinshaw, S.P. (2007). Moderators and mediators of treatment outcome for youth with ADHD: Understanding for whom and how interventions work. *Journal of Pediatric Psychology, 32*, 664–675.

Hinshaw, S.P., Scheffler, R.M., Fulton, B.D., Aase, H., Banaschewski, T., Cheng, W. … Weiss, M.D. (2011). International variation in treatment procedures for ADHD: Social context and recent trends. *Psychiatric Services, 62*, 459–464.

Hipke, K., Wolchik, S. A., Sandler, I. N., & Braver, S. L. (2002). Predictors of children's intervention-induced resilience in a parenting program for divorced mothers. *Family Relations: Interdisciplinary Journal of Applied Family Studies, 51*, 121–129.

Hirsh, J.B., Galinsky, A.D., & Zhong, C. (2011). Drunk, powerful, and in the dark: How general processes of disinhibition produce both prosocial and antisocial behavior. *Perspectives on Psychological Science, 6*, 415–427.

Hirshberg, L. M. (1993). Clinical interviews with infants and their families. In C. H. Zeanah (Ed.), *Handbook of infant mental health* (pp. 173–190). New York: Guilford Press.

Hirshfeld-Becker, D. R., Biederman, J., Calltharp, S., Rosenbaum, E. D., Faraone, S. V., & Rosenbaum, J. F. (2003). Behavioral inhibition and disinhibition as hypothesized precursors to psychopathology: Implications for pediatric bipolar disorder. *Biological Psychiatry, 53*, 985–999.

Hirshfeld-Becker, D. R., Biederman, J., Faraone, S. V., Vioilette, H., Wrightsman, J., & Rosenbaum, J. F. (2002). Temperamental correlates of disruptive behavior disorders in young children: Preliminary fi ndings. *Biological Psychiatry, 51*, 563–574.

Hishinuma, E. S., Johnson, R. C., Kim, P., Nishimura, S. T., Makini Jr., G. K., Andrade, N. N., et al. (2005). Prevalence and correlates of misconduct among ethnically diverse adolescents of native Hawaiian/part-Hawaiian and non-Hawaiian ancestry. *International Journal of Social Psychiatry, 51*, 242–258.

Hjelmeland, H., & Groholt, B. (2005). A comparative study of young and adult deliberate self-harm patients. *Crisis: The Journal of Crisis Intervention and Suicide Prevention, 26*, 64–72.

Hoagwood, K. (2000). Commentary: The dose effect in children's mental health services. *Journal of the American Academy of Child and Adolescent Psychiatry, 39*, 172–175.

Hoagwood, K., & Jensen, P. S. (1997). Developmental psychopathology and the notion of culture: Introduction to the special section on "The fusion of cultural horizons: Cultural influences on the assessment of psychopathology in children and adolescents." *Applied Developmental Science, 1*, 108–112.

Hoagwood, K., Jensen, P. S., Petti, T., & Burns, B. J. (1996). A comprehensive conceptual model. *Journal of the American Academy of Child and Adolescent Psychiatry, 35*, 1055–1063.

Hoagwood, K.E., Cavaleri, M.A., Olin, S.S., Burns, B.J., Slaton, E., Gruttadaro, D., & Hughes, R. (2009). Family support in children's mental health: A review and synthesis. *Clinical Child & Family Psychology Review, 13*, 1–45.

Hobfoll, S.E., Watson, P., Bell, C.C., Bryant, R.A., Brymer, M.J., Friedman, M.F., … Ursano, R.J. (2007). Five essential elements of immediate and mid-term mass trauma intervention: Empirical evidence. *Psychiatry: Interpersonal and Biological Processes, 70*, 283–315.

Hobson, R. P. (1990). On the origins of self and the case of autism. *Development and Psychopathology, 2*, 163–181.

Hobson, R. P. (1991). What is autism? *Psychiatric Clinics of North America, 14*, 1–17.

Hobson, R. P. (1993). *Essays in developmental psychology.* Hillsdale, NJ: Erlbaum.

Hobson, R. P. (1999). Beyond cognition: A theory of autism. In P. Lloyd & C. Fernyhough (Eds.), *Lev Vygotsky: Critical assessments: Future directions* (Vol. IV, pp. 253–281). Florence, KY: Taylor & Francis/Routledge.

Hobson, R. P., & Lee, A. (1998). Hello and goodbye: A study of social engagement in autism. *Journal of Autism and Developmental Disorders, 28,* 117–127.

Hobson, R. P., & Lee, A. (1999). Imitation and identification in autism. *Journal of Child Psychology and Psychiatry and Allied Disciplines, 40,* 649–659.

Hobson, R. P., Ouston, J., & Lee, A. (1988). Emotion recognition in autism: Coordinating faces and voices. *Psychological Medicine, 18,* 911–923.

Hobson, R.P., Chidambi, G., Lee, A., & Meyer, J. (2006). Foundations for self-awareness: An exploration through autism. *Monographs of the Society for Research in Child Development, 71,* 1–190.

Hodapp, R. M. (2002). Parenting children with mental retardation. In M. H. Bornstein (Ed.), *Handbook of parenting: Vol. 1. Children and parenting* (2nd ed., pp. 355–381). Mahwah, NJ: Erlbaum.

Hodapp, R. M. (2004). A model for socialization studies in mental retardation? *Parenting: Science and Practice, 4,* 325–328.

Hodapp, R. M. (2006). Developmental approaches to children with mental retardation: A second generation? In D. Cicchetti & D. J. Cohen (Eds.), *Developmental psychopathology: Vol. 3. Risk, disorder, and adaptation* (2nd ed., pp. 235–267). Hoboken, NJ: Wiley.

Hodapp, R. M. (2007). Families of persons with Down syndrome: New perspectives, findings, and research and service needs. *Mental Retardation and Developmental Disabilities Research Reviews, 13,* 279–287.

Hodapp, R. M., & Burack, J. A. (2006). Developmental approaches to children with mental retardation: A second generation? In D. Cicchetti & D. J. Cohen (Eds.), *Developmental psychopathology, Vol. 3: Risk, disorder, and adaptation* (2nd ed., pp. 235–267). Hoboken, NJ: Wiley.

Hodapp, R. M., & DesJardin, J. L. (2002). Genetic etiologies of mental retardation: Issues for interventions and interventionists. *Journal of Developmental and Physical Disabilities, 14,* 323–338.

Hodapp, R. M., & Dykens, E. M. (2001). Strengthening behavioral research on genetic mental retardation syndromes. *American Journal on Mental Retardation, 106,* 4–15.

Hodapp, R. M., & Dykens, E. M. (2003). Mental retardation (intellectual disabilities). In E. J. Mash & R. A. Barkley (Eds.), *Child psychopathology* (2nd ed., pp. 486–519). New York: Guilford Press.

Hodapp, R. M., & Dykens, E. M. (2005). Measuring behavior in genetic disorders of mental retardation. *Mental Retardation and Developmental Disabilities Research Reviews, 11,* 340–346.

Hodapp, R. M., & Zigler, E. (1995). Past, present, and future issues in the developmental approach to mental retardation and developmental disabilities. In D. Cicchetti & D. J. Cohen (Eds.), *Developmental psychopathology: Vol. 2. Risk, disorder, and adaptation* (pp. 299–331). Oxford, England: Wiley.

Hodapp, R. M., & Zigler, E. (1997). New issues in the developmental approach to mental retardation. In W. E. MacLean (Ed.), *Ellis' handbook of mental deficiency, psychological theory and research* (3rd ed., pp. 115–136). Mahwah, NJ: Erlbaum.

Hodapp, R. M., & Zigler, E. (1999). Intellectual development and mental retardation—Some continuing controversies. In M. Anderson (Ed.), *The development of intelligence: Studies in developmental psychology* (pp. 295–308). Hove, England: Psychology Press/Taylor & Francis.

Hodapp, R.M., Urbano, R.C., & Burke, M.M. (2010). Adult female and male siblings of persons with disabilities: Findings from a national survey. *Intellectual and Developmental Disabilities, 48,* 52–62.

Hoek, H. W., & van Hoeken, D. (2003). Review of the prevalence and incidence of eating disorders. *International Journal of Eating Disorders, 34,* 383–396.

Hofacker, N. V., & Papousek, M. (1998). Disorders of excessive crying, feeding, and sleeping: The Munich interdisciplinary research and intervention program. *Infant Mental Health Journal, 19,* 180–201.

Hofflich, S. A., Hughes, A. A., & Kendall, P. C. (2006). Somatic complaints and childhood anxiety disorders. *International Journal of Clinical and Health Psychology, 6,* 229–242.

Hoge, E.A., Austin, E.D., & Pollack, M.H. (2007). Resilience: Research evidence and conceptual considerations for posttraumatic stress disorder. *Depression and Anxiety, 24,* 139–152.

Hogue, A., Dauber, S., Stambaugh, L. F., Cecero, J. J., & Liddle, H. A. (2006). Early therapeutic alliance and treatment outcome in individual and family therapy for adolescent behavior problems. *Journal of Consulting and Clinical Psychology, 74,* 121–129.

Hoksbergen, R. A. C., ter Laak, J., van Dijkum, C., Rijk, S., Rijk, K., & Stoutjesdijk, F. (2003). Posttraumatic stress disorder in children adopted from Romania. *American Journal of Orthopsychiatry, 73,* 255–265.

Holaway, R. M., Rodebaugh, T. L., & Heimberg, R. G. (2006). The epidemiology of worry and generalized anxiety disorder. In G. C. L. Davey & A. Wells (Eds.), *Worry and its psychological disorders: Theory, assessment and treatment* (pp. 3–20). Hoboken, NJ: Wiley.

Holburn, C. S. (2008). Detrimental effects of overestimating the occurrence of autism. *Intellectual and Developmental Disabilities, 46,* 243–246.

Holden, G.W. (2010). Childrearing and developmental trajectories: Positive pathways, off-ramps, and dynamic processes. *Child Development Perspectives, 4,* 197–204.

Holliday, J., Landau, S., Collier, D., & Treasure, J. (2006). Do illness characteristics and familiar risk differ between women with anorexia nervosa grouped on the basis of personality pathology? *Psychological Medicine, 36,* 529–538.

Hollins, S. (2001). Psychotherapeutic methods. In A. Dosen & K. Day (Eds.), *Treating mental illness and behavior disorders in children and adults with mental retardation* (pp. 27–44). Washington, DC: American Psychiatric Publishing.

Holm, S.M., Forbes, E.E., Ryan, N.D., Phillips, M.L., Tarr, J.A., Dahl, R.E. (2009). Reward-related brain function and sleep in pre/early pubertal and mid/late pubertal adolescents. *Journal of Adolescent Health, 45,* 326–334.

Holmbeck, G. N. (1997). Toward terminological, conceptual, and statistical clarity in the study of mediators and moderators: Examples from the child-clinical and pediatric psychology literatures. *Journal of Consulting and Clinical Psychology, 65,* 599–610.

Holmbeck, G. N., Colder, C., Shapera, W., Westhoven, V., Kenealy, L., & Updegrove, A. L. (2000). Working with adolescents: Guides from developmental psychology. In P. C. Kendall (Ed.),

Child and adolescent therapy: Cognitive-behavioral procedures (2nd ed., pp. 334–385). New York: Guilford Press.

Holmbeck, G. N., & Kendall, P. C. (2002). Introduction to the special section on clinical adolescent psychology: Developmental psychopathology and treatment. *Journal of Consulting and Clinical Psychology, 70,* 3–5.

Holtkamp, K., Herpertz-Dahlmann, B., Vloet, T., & Hagenah,U. (2005). Group psychoeducation for parents of adolescents with eating disorders: The Aachen Program. *Eating Disorders, 13,* 381–390.

Holtmann, M., Bolte, S., Goth, K., Dopfner, M., Pluck, J., Huss, M., et al. (2007). Prevalence of the child behavior checklist-pediatric bipolar disorder phenotype in a German general population sample. *Bipolar Disorders, 9,* 895–900.

Hooper, S.R. & Tramontana, M.G. (1997). Advances in the neuropsychological bases of child and adolescent psychopathology: Proposed models, findings, and ongoing issues. *Advances in Clinical Child Psychology, 19,* 133–175.

Hope, T. L., Adams, C., Reynolds, L., Powers, D., Perez, R. A., & Kelley, M. L. (1999). Parent vs. self-report: Contributions toward diagnosis of adolescent psychopathology. *Journal of Psychopathology and Behavioral Assessment, 21,* 349–363.

Horesch, N., Sever, J., & Apter, A. (2003). A comparison of life events between suicidal adolescents with major depression and borderline personality disorder. *Comprehensive Psychiatry, 44,* 277–283.

Horesch, N. Zalsman, G., & Apter, A. (2004). Suicidal behavior and self-disclosure in adolescent psychiatric inpatients. *Journal of Nervous and Mental Disease, 192,* 837–842.

Horowitz, J. L., Garber, J., Ciesla, J. A., Young, J. F., & Mufson, L. (2007). Prevention of depressive symptoms in adolescents: A randomized trial of cognitive-behavioral and interpersonal prevention programs. *Journal of Consulting and Clinical Psychology, 75,* 693–706.

Hosterman, S., DuPaul, G.J., & Jitendra, A.K. (2008). Teacher ratings of ADHD symptoms in ethnic minority students: Bias or behavioral difference? *School Psychology Quarterly, 23,* 418–435.

Howard, K.S., & Brooks-Gunn, J. (2009). The role of home-visiting programs in preventing child abuse and neglect. *The Future of Children, 19,* 119–146.

Howe, M.L., Cicchetti, D., & Toth, S.L. (2006). Children's basic memory processes, stress, and maltreatment. *Development and Psychopathology, 18,* 759–769.

Howerton, K., Fernandez, G., Touchette, P., Gurbani, S., Sandman, C. A., Ashurst, J., et al. (2002). Psychotropic mediations in community based individuals with developmental disabilities: Observations of an interdisciplinary team. *Mental Health Aspects of Developmental Disabilities, 5,* 78–86.

Howlin, P., Goode, S., Hutton, J., & Rutter, M. (2004). Adult outcome for children with autism. *Journal of Child Psychology and Psychiatry, 45,* 212–229.

Hoza, B., Gerdes, A., Mrug, S., Hinshaw, S.P., Bukowski, W.M., Gold, J.A., … Wigal, T. (2005). Peer-assessed outcomes in the multimodal treatment study of children with attention deficit hyperactivity disorder. *Journal of Clinical Child and Adolescent Psychology, 34,* 74–86.

Hoza, B., Gerdes, A.,C., Mrug, S., Hinshaw, S. P., Bukowski, W. M., Gold, J. A., et al. (2005). Peer-assessed outcomes in the multimodal treatment study of children with attention deficit hyperactivity disorder. *Journal of Clinical Child and Adolescent Psychology, 34,* 74–86.

Hoza, B., Kaiser, N., & Hurt, E. (2008). Evidence-based treatments for attention-deficit/hyperactivity disorder (ADHD). In R.G. Steele, T.D. Elkin, & M.C. Roberts (Eds.), *Handbook of evidence-based therapies for children and adolescents: Bridging science and practice* (pp. 197–219). New York: Springer.

Hoza, B., Mrug, S., Gerdes, A. C., Hinshaw, S. P., Bukowski, W. M., Gold, J. A., et al. (2005). What aspects of peer relationships are impaired in children with attention-defi cit/ hyperactivity disorder? *Journal of Consulting and Clinical Psychology, 73,* 411–423.

Hsia, R. Y., & Belfer, M.L. (2008). A framework for the economic analysis of child and adolescent mental disorders. *International Review of Psychiatry, 20,* 251–259.

Hsu, C., Chong, M., Yang, P., & Yen, C. (2002). Posttraumatic stress disorder among adolescent earthquake victims in Taiwan. *Journal of the American Academy of Child and Adolescent Psychiatry, 41,* 875–881.

Huang, L., Sadler, L., O'Riordan, M., & Robin, N. H. (2002). Delay in diagnosis of Williams syndrome. *Clinical Pediatrics, 41,* 257–261.

Huang, L., Stroul, B., Friedman, R., Mrazek, P., Friesen, B., Pires, S., & Mayberg, S. (2005). Transforming mental health care for children and their families. *American Psychologist, 60,* 615–627.

Hudenko, W.J., Stone, W., & Bachorowski, J. (2009). Laughter differs in children with autism: An acoustic analysis of laughs produced by children with and without the disorder. *Journal of Autism & Developmental Disorders, 39,* 1392–1400.

Hudson, J. I., Hiripi, E., Pope, H. G., & Kessler, R. C. (2007). The prevalence and correlates of eating disorders in the national comorbidity survey replication. *Biological Psychology, 61,* 348–358.

Hudson, J. I., Lalonde, J. K., Berry, J. M., Pindyck, L. J., Bulik, C. M., Crow, S. J., et al. (2006). Binge-eating disorder as a distinct familial phenotype in obese individuals. *Archives of General Pscyhology, 63,* 313–319.

Hudson, J. L., Kendall, P. C., Coles, M. E., Robin, J. A., & Webb, A. (2002). The other side of the coin: Using intervention research in child anxiety disorders to inform developmental psychopathology. *Development and Psychopathology, 14,* 819–841.

Huey, S. J. Jr., Henggeler, S. W., Brondno, M. J., & Pickrel, S. G. (2000). Mechanisms of change in multisystemic therapy: Reducing delinquent behavior through therapist adherence and improved family and peer functioning. *Journal of Consulting and Clinical Psychology, 68,* 451–467.

Hughes, A.A., Hedtke, K.A. & Kendall, P.C. (2008). Family functioning in families of children with anxiety disorders. *Journal of Family Psychology, 22,* 325–328.

Hughes, C., Cutting, A. L., & Dunn, J. (2001). Acting nasty in the face of failure? Longitudinal observations of "hard-to-manage" children playing a rigged competitive game with a friend. *Journal of Abnormal Child Psychology, 29,* 403–416.

Hughes, C. W., Emslie, G. J., Crismon, M. L., Posner, K., Birmaher, B., Neal, R., et al. (2007). Texas children's medication algorithm project: Update from Texas Consensus Conference Panel on Medication Treatment of Childhood Major Depressive Disorder. *American Academy of Child and Adolescent Psychiatry, 46,* 667–686.

Hughes, J.N., Cavall, T.A. & Prasad-Gaur, A. (2001). A positive view of peer acceptance in aggressive youth risk for future peer acceptance. *Journal of School Psychology, 39,* 239–252.

Hunsley, J. & Mash, E.J. (2007). Evidence-based assessment. *Annual Review of Clinical Psychology, 3,* 29–51.

Huprich, S. K., Stepp, S. D., Graham, A., & Johnson, L. (2004). Gender differences in dependency, separation, object relations and pathological eating behavior and attitudes. *Personality and Individual Differences, 36,* 801–811.

Husain, S.A., Allwood, M.A. & Bell, D.J. (2008). The relationship between PTSD symptoms and attention problems in children exposed to the Bosnian war. *Journal of Emotional and Behavioural Disorders, 16,* 52–62.

Hussong, A. M., Curran, P. J., Moffitt, T. E., Caspi, A., & Carrig, M. M. (2004). Substance abuse hinders desistance in young adults' antisocial behavior. *Development and Psychopathology, 16,* 1029–1046.

Hwang, C. P., Lamb, M. E., & Sigel, I. E. (1996). *Images of childhood.* Mahwah, NJ: Erlbaum.

Hyde, J.S., Mezulis, A.H., & Abramson, L.Y. (2008). The ABCs of depression: Integrating affective, biological and cognitive models to explain the emergence of the gender difference in depression. *Psychological Review, 115,* 291–313.

Iacono, W.G., Malone, S.M. & McGue, M. (2003). Substance use disorders, externalizing psychopathology, and P300 event-related potential amplitude. *International Journal of Psychophysiology, 48,* 147–178.

Iacono, W.G., Malone, S.M., McGue, Matt (2008). Behavioral disinhibition and the development of early-onset addiction. *Annual Review of Clinical Psychology, 4,* 325–348.

Ialongo, N., Edelsohn, G., Werthamer-Larsson, L., & Crockett, L. (1995). The significance of self-reported anxious symptoms in first grade children: Prediction to anxious symptoms and adaptive functioning in fifth grade. *Journal of Child Psychology and Psychiatry and Allied Disciplines, 36,* 427–437.

Ialongo, N., Edelsohn, G., Werthamer-Larsson, L., Crockett, L., & Kellam, S. (1996). Social and cognitive impairment in fi rstgrade children with anxious and depressive symptoms. *Journal of Clinical Child Psychology, 25,* 15–24.

Ialongo, N. S., Edelsohn, G., & Kellam, S. G. (2001). A further look at the prognostic power of young children's reports of depressed mood. *Child Development, 72,* 736–747.

Ialongo, N. S., Rogosch, F. A., Cicchetti, D., Toth, S. L., Buckley, J., Petras, H., & Neiderhiser, J. (2006). A developmental psychopathology approach to the prevention of mental health disorders. In D. Cicchetti & D. J. Cohen (Eds.), Developmental Psychopathology (Vol. 1): *Theory and Method* (2nd ed.) (pp. 968–1018). Hoboken, NJ: John Wiley & Sons.

Iarocci, G., & Burack, J. A. (2004). Intact covert orienting to periperhal cues among children with autism. *Journal of Autism and Developmental Disorders, 34,* 257–264.

Iervolino, A. C., Pike, A., Manke, B., Reiss, D., Hetherington, E. M., & Plomin, R. (2002). Genetic and environmental infl uences in adolescent peer socialization: Evidence from two genetically sensitive designs. *Child Development, 73,* 162–174.

Inderbitzen, H.M., K.S., Waltners, & Bukowski, A.L. (1997). The role of social anxiety in adolescent peer relations: Differences among sociometric status groups and rejected subgroups. *Journal of Clinical Child Psychology, 26,* 338–348.

Individuals with Disabilities Education Improvement Act of 2004 (IDEA), Pub. L. No. 108–446, 118 stat. 2647.

Ingber, S., & Dromi, E. (2002, April). *Family characteristics and mother's expectations from early intervention.* Poster presented at the Conference on Human Development, Charlotte, NC.

Ingersoll, B., Schreibman, L., & Tran. Q. H. (2003). Effect of sensory feedback on immediate object imitation in children with autism. *Journal of Autism and Developmental Disorders, 33,* 673–683.

Ingman, K. A., Ollendick, T. H., & Akande, A. (1999). Cross-cultural aspects of fears in African children and adolescents. *Behaviour Research and Therapy, 37,* 337–343.

Ivanova, M.Y., Achenbach, T.M., Dumenci, L., Rescorla, L.A., Almqvist, F., Weintraub, S., … Yang, H. (2007). Testing the 8-syndrome structure of the Child Behavior Checklist in 30 societies. *Journal of Clinical Child and Adolescent Psychology, 36,* 405–417.

Jaccard, J., Blanton, H., & Dodge, T. (2005). Peer influences on risk behavior: An analysis of the effects of a close friend. *Developmental Psychology, 41,* 135–147.

Jackson, K. M., Sher, K. J., Cooper, M., L., & Wood, P. K. (2002). Adolescent alcohol and tobacco use: Onset, persistence, and trajectories of use across two samples. *Addiction, 97,* 517–531.

Jacob, M.L., Morelen, D., Suveg, C., Jacobsen, A.M.B., & Whiteside, S.P. (2012). Emotional, behavioral, and cognitive factors that differentiate obsessive-compulsive disorder and other anxiety disorder in youth. *Anxiety, Stress & Coping: An International Journal, 25,* 229–237.

Jacob, T., & Johnson, S. L. (1997). Parent-child interaction among depressed fathers and mothers: Impact on child functioning. *Journal of Family Psychology, 11,* 391–409.

Jacobs, J. E., Bleeker, M. M., & Constantino, M. J. (2003). The self-system during childhood and adolescence: Development, influences, and implications. *Journal of Psychotherapy Integration, 13,* 33–65.

Jacobson, C. M., & Mufson, L. (2010). Treating adolescent depression using Interpersonal Psychotherapy. In J. R. Weisz & A. E. Kazdin (Eds.), *Evidence-Based Psychotherapies for Children and Adolescents* (2nd ed.) (pp. 140–155). New York: Guilford Press.

Jacques, H.A.K. & Mash, E.J. (2004). A test of the tripartite model of anxiety and depression in elementary and high school boys and girls. *Journal of Abnormal Child Psychology, 32,* 13–25.

Jaffe, S.R., Caspi, A., Moffitt, T.E., Dodge, K.A., Rutter, M., Taylor, A., & Tully, L.A. (2005). Nature × nurture: Genetic vulnerabilities interact with physical maltreatment to promote conduct problems. *Development and Psychopathology, 17,* 67–84.

Jaffee, S. R., Caspi, A., Moffitt, T. E., Dodge, K. A., Turrer, M., Taylor, A., et al. (2005). Nature × nurture: Genetic vulnerabilities interact with physical maltreatment to promote conduct problems. *Development and Psychopathology, 17,* 67–84.

Jaffee, S. R., Caspi, A., Moffitt, T. E., & Taylor, A. (2004). Physical maltreatment victim to antisocial child: Evidence of an environmentally mediated process. *Journal of Abnormal Psychology, 113,* 44–55.

Jaffee, S. R., Harrington, H., Cohen, P., & Moffitt, T. E. (2005). Cumulative prevalence of psychiatric disorder in youths. *Journal of the American Academy of Child and Adolescent Psychiatry, 44,* 406–407.

Jaffee, S.R., Moffitt, T.E. Avshalom, C. & Taylor, A. (2003). Life with (or without) father: The benefits of living with two biological parents depend on the father's antisocial behavior. *Child Development, 74,* 109–126.

Jairam, R., Srinath, S., Girimaji, S. C., & Seshadri, S. P. (2004). A prospective 4–5 year follow-up of juvenile onset bipolar disorder. *Bipolar Disorders, 6,* 386–394.

Jaycox, L. H., Asarnow, J. R., Sherbourne, C. D., Rea, M. M., LaBorde, A. P., & Wells, K. B. (2006). Adolescent primary care patients' preferences for depression treatment. *Administration and Policy in Mental Health and Mental Health Services Research, 33,* 198–207.

Jaycox, L. H., Reivich, K. J., Gillham, J., & Seligman, M. E. P. (1994). Prevention of depressive symptoms in school children. *Behaviour Research and Therapy, 32,* 801–816.

Jenkins, J., & Bisceglia, R. (2011). Understanding within-family variability in children's responses to environmental stress. In D.P. Keating (Ed.), *Nature and Nurture in Early Child Development* (pp. 143–168). New York: Cambridge University Press.

Jenni, O.G., & Carskadon, M.A. (2007). Sleep behavior and sleep regulation from infancy through adolescence: Normative aspects. *Sleep Medicine Clinics, 2,* 321–329.

Jennison, K. M. (2004). The short-term effects and unintended long-term consequences of binge drinking in college: A 10-year follow-up study. *American Journal of Drug and Alcohol Abuse, 30,* 659–684.

Jensen, P. S., Arnold, L. E., Swanson, J. M., Vitiello, B., Abikoff, H., Greenhill, L. L., et al. (2007). 3-year follow-up of the NIMH MTA study. *Journal of American Academy of Child and Adolescent Psychiatry, 46,* 989–1002.

Jensen, P. S., Hoagwood, K., & Petti, T. (1996). Literature review and application of a comprehensive model. *Journal of the American Academy of Child and Adolescent Psychiatry, 35,* 1064–1077.

Jensen, P. S., Knapp, P., & Mrazek, D. A. (2006). Toward a New Diagnostic System for Child Psychopathology: Moving Beyond the DSM. New York: Guilford Press.

Jensen, P. S., & members of the MTA Cooperative Group (2002). ADHD comorbidity findings from the MTA Study: New diagnostic subtypes and their optimal treatments. In J. E. Helzer & J. Hudziak (Eds.), *Defining psychopathology in the 21st century: DSM-V and beyond* (pp. 169–192). Washington, DC: American Psychiatric Publishing.

Jensen, P. S., Rubio-Stipec, M., Canino, G., Bird, H. R., Dulan, M. K., Schwab-Stone, M. E., et al. (1999). Parent and child contributions to diagnosis of mental disorder: Are both informants always necessary? *Journal of the American Academy of Child and Adolescent Psychiatry, 38,* 1569–1579.

Jensen, P.S., Garcia, J.A., Glied, S., Crowe, M., Foster, M., Schlander, M., … Wells, K. (2005). Cost-effectiveness of ADHD treatments: Findings from the Multimodal Treatment Study of Children with ADHD. *The America Journal of Psychiatry, 162,* 1628–1636.

Jent, J.F., Merrick, M.T., Dandes, S.K., Lambert, W.F, Haney, M.L., & Cano, N.M. (2009). Mulitdisciplinary assessment of child maltreatment: A multi-site pilot descriptive analysis of the Florida Child Protection Team model. *Children and Youth Services Review, 31,* 896–902.

Jessor, R. (1998). *New perspectives on adolescent risk behavior.* New York: Cambridge University Press.

Jessor, R., Turbin, M. S., & Costa, F. M. (1998). Protective factors in adolescent health behavior. *Journal of Personality and Social Psychology, 75,* 788–800.

Jessor, R., Turbin, M. S., & Costa, F. M. (1998). Risk and protection in successful outcomes among disadvantaged adolescents. *Applied Developmental Science, 2,* 194–208.

Jessor, R., Turbin, M. S., Costa, F. M., Dong, Q., Zhang, H., & Wang, C. (2003). Adolescent problem behavior in China and the United States: A cross-national study of psychosocial protective factors. *Journal of Research on Adolescence, 13,* 329–360.

Jester, J. M., Nigg, J. T., Adams, K., Fitzgerald, H. E., Puttler, L. I., Wong, M., et al. (2005). Inattention/hyperactivity and aggression from early childhood to adolescence: Heterogeneity of trajectories and differential influences on environment characteristics. *Development and Psychopathology, 17,* 99–125.

Jiménez, J.E., & de la Cadena, C.G. (2007). Learning Disabilities in Guatemala and Spain: A cross-national study of the prevalence and cognitive processes associated with reading and spelling disabilities. *Learning Disabilities Research and Practice, 22,* 161–169.

Jin, M.K., Jacobvitz, D., & Hazen, N. (2010). A cross-cultural study of attachment in Korea and the United States: Infant and maternal behavior during the Strange Situation. In P. Erdman & K. Ng (Eds.), *Attachment: Expanding the Cultural Connections* (pp. 143–156). New York: Routledge/Taylor and Francis Group.

Johansson, A., & Götestam, K. G. (2004). Internet addiction: Characteristics of a questionnaire and prevalence in Norwegian youth (12–18 years). *Scandinavian Journal of Psychology, 45,* 223–229.

Johnson, C. P., Myers, S. M., & the Council of Children with Disabilities. (2007). Identification and evaluation of children with autism spectrum disorders. *Pediatrics, 120,* 1183–1215.

Johnson, F., & Wardle, J. (2005). Dietary restraint, body disatisfaction, and psychological distress: A prospective analysis. *Journal of Abnormal Psychology, 114,* 119–125.

Johnson, J. G., Cohen, P., Kasen, S., & Brook, J. S. (2002). Eating disorders during adolescence and the risk for physical and mental disorders during early adulthood. *Archives of General Psychology, 59,* 545–552.

Johnson, K. D., Whitbeck, L. B., & Hoyt, D. R. (2005). Substance abuse disorders among homeless and runaway adolescents. *Journal of Drug Issues, 35,* 799–816.

Johnson, M. H. (1999). Cortical plasticity in normal and abnormal cognitive development: Evidence and working hypotheses. *Development and Pscyhopathogy, 11,* 419–437.

Johnson, M.H., Grossmann, T., & Kadosh, K.C. (2009). Mapping functional brain development: Building a social brain through interactive specialization. *Developmental Psychology, 45,* 151–159.

Johnston, C., & Freeman, W. (1997). Attributions for child behavior in parents of children without behavior disorders and children with attention deficit hyperactivity disorder. *Journal of Consulting and Clinical Psychology, 65,* 636–645.

Johnston, L. D., O'Malley, P. M., Bachman, J. G., & Schulenberg, J. W. (2008). Monitoring the Future: National Survey Results on Drug Use, 1975–2007. Volume 1: Secondary School Students (NIH Pub. No. 08–6418A). Bethesda, MD: National Institute on Drug Abuse.

Johnston, L. D., O'Malley, P. M., & Terry-McElrath, Y. M. (2004). Methods, locations, and ease of cigarette access for

American youth, 1997–2002. *American Journal of Preventive Medicine, 27,* 267–276.

Joiner, T. E. (2002). The trajectory of suicidal behavior over time. *Suicide and Life-Threatening Behavior, 32,* 33–41.

Joiner, T. E. (2005). *Why people die by suicide.* Cambridge: Harvard University Press.

Joiner, T. E., Brown, J. S., & Wingate, L. R. (2005). The psychology and neurobiology of suicidal behavior. *Annual Review of Psychology, 56,* 287–314.

Joiner, T. E., Conwell, Y., Fitzpatrick, K. K., Witte, T. K., Schmidt, N. B., Berlim, M. T., et al. (2005). Four studies on how past and current suicidality relate even when "everything but the kitchen sink" is covaried. *Journal of Abnormal Psychology, 114,* 291–303.

Jolliffe, T., & Baron-Cohen, S. (2001a). A test of central coherence theory: Can adults with high-functioning autism or Asperger syndrome integrate fragments of an object? *Cognitive Neuropsychiatry, 6,* 193–216.

Jolliffe, T., & Baron-Cohen, S. (2001b). A test of central coherence theory: Can adults with high-functioning autism or Asperger syndrome integrate objects in context? *Visual Cognition, 8,* 67–101.

Jones, C.R.G., Pickles, A., Falcaro, M., Marsden, A.J.S., Happé, F., Scott, S.K., … Charman, T. (2011). A multimodal approach to emotion recognition ability in autism spectrum disorders. *Journal of Child Psychology and Psychiatry, 52,* 275–285.

Jones, D. C. (2004). Body image among adolescent girls and boys: A longitudinal study. *Developmental Psychology, 40,* 823–835.

Jones, D. C., & Crawford, J. K. (2005) Adolescent boys and body image: Weight and muscularity concerns as dual pathways to body dissatisfaction. *Journal of Youth and Adolescence, 34,* 629–636.

Jones, D. C., Vigfusdottir, T. H., & Lee, Y. (2004). Body image and the appearance culture among adolescent girls and boys: An examination of friend conversations, peer criticism, appearance magazines, and the internalization of appearance ideals. *Journal of Adolescent Research, 19,* 323–339.

Jones, D., Dodge, K. A., Foster, E. M., Nix, R., & Conduct Problems Prevention Research Group. (2002). Early identification of children at risk for costly mental health service use. *Prevention Science, 3,* 247–256.

Jones, D. J., Forehand, R., Brody, G., & Armistead, L. (2003). Parental monitoring in African American, single mother-headed families: An ecological approach to the identification of predictors. *Behavior Modification, 27,* 435–457.

Jones, H.A., Epstein, J.N., Hinshaw, S.P., Owens, E.B., Chi, T.C., Arnold, L.E., … Wells, K.C. (2010). Ethnicity as a moderator of treatment effects on parent-child interaction for children with ADHD. *Journal of Attention Disorders, 13,* 592–600.

Jones, W., Bellugi, U., Lai, Z., Chiles, M., Reilly, J., Lincoln, A., et al. (2000). Hypersociability: The social and affective phenotype of Williams syndrome. *Journal of Cognitive Neuroscience, 12,* 30–46.

Jones, W., Hesselink, J., Courchesne, E., Duncan, T., Matsuda, K., & Bellugi, U. (2002). Cerebellar abnormalities in infants and toddlers with Williams syndrome. *Developmental Medicine and Child Neurology, 44,* 688–694.

Jose, P. E., D'Anna, C. A., Cafasso, L. L., Bryant, F. B., Chiker, V., Gein, N., et al. (1998). Stress and coping among Russian and American early adolescents. *Developmental Psychology, 34,* 757–769.

Joseph, R.M., Tager-Flusberg, H. & Lord, C. (2002). Cognitive profiles and social-communicative functioning in children with autism spectrum disorder. *Journal of Child Psychology and Psychiatry, 43,* 807–821.

Joshi, P. (2011, November 29). Finding good apps for children with autism. *New York Times.* Retrieved from http://gadgetwise.blogs.nytimes.com/2011/11/29/finding-good-apps-for-children-with-autism/.

Judge, B., & Billick, S. B. (2004). Suicidality in adolescence: Review and legal considerations. *Behavioral Sciences and the Law, 22,* 681–695.

Jung, D. Y. (2007). South Korean perspectives on learning disabilities. *Learning Disabilities Research & Practice, 22,* 183–188.

Jureidini, J., Doecke, C., Mansfield, P., Haby, M, Michelle, M., Menkes, D., et al. (2004). Efficacy and safety of antidepressants for children and adolescents. *British Medical Journal, 328,* 879–883.

Juster, R., Bizik, G., Picard, M., Arsenault-Lapierre, G., Sindi, S., Trepanier, L., … Lupien, S.J. (2011). A transdisciplinary perspective of chronic stress in relation to psychopathology throughout life span development. *Development and Psychopathology, 23,* 725–776.

Kagan, J. & Fox, N.A. (2006). Biology, culture, and temperamental biases. In N. Eisenberg, W. Damon & R.M. Lerner (Eds.) *Handbook of Child Psychology: Vol 3, Social, Emotional, and Personality Development (6th ed.) (pp.* 167–225). Hoboken, NJ: Wiley.

Kagan, J., Reznick, J. S., & Snidman, N. (1988). Biological bases of childhood shyness. *Science, 240,* 167–171.

Kagan, J., & Snidman, N. (1991). Temperamental factors in human development. *American Psychologist, 46,* 856–862.

Kagan, J., & Snidman, N. (1999). Early childhood predictors of adult anxiety disorders. *Biological Psychiatry, 46,* 1536–1541.

Kagan, J., Snidman, N., Arcus, D., & Reznick, J. S. (1994). *Galen's prophecy: Temperament in human nature.* New York: Basic Books.

Kagan, J., Snidman, N., McManis, M., & Woodward, S. (2001). Temperamental contributions to the affect family of anxiety. *Psychiatric Clinics of North America, 24,* 677–688.

Kail, R. (2000). Speed of information processing: Developmental change and links to intelligence. *Journal of School Psychology, 38,* 51–61.

Kail, R. V. (2003). Information processing and memory. In M. H. Bornstein, L. Davidson, C. L. M. Keyes, & A. Moore (Eds.), Well-being: Positive development across the life course (pp. 269–279). Mahwah, NJ: Erlbaum.

Kalachnik, J. E. (1999). Measuring side effects of psychopharmacologic medication in individuals with mental retardation and developmental disabilities. *Mental Retardation and Developmental Disabilities Research Reviews, 5,* 348–359.

Kalin, N.H., Shelton, S.E. & Davidson, R.J. (2007). Role of the primate orbitofrontal cortex in mediating anxious temperament. *Biological Psychiatry, 62),* 1134–1139.

Kalmanson, B. (1997). Type II: Underreactive. In A. Lieberman, S. Wieder, & E. Fenichel (Eds.), *DC: 0–3 Casebook* (pp. 233–244). Washington, DC: Zero to Three: National Center for Infants, Toddlers, and Families.

Kaltiala-Heino, R., Lintonen, T., & Rimpelä, A. (2004). Internet addiction? Potentially problematic use of the Internet in a population of 12–18 year-old adolescents. *Addiction Research and Theory, 12,* 89–96.

Kaminer, Y. (2005). Challenges and opportunities of group therapy for adolescent substance abuse: A critical review. *Addictive Behaviors, 30*, 1765–1774.

Kaminer, Y., & Bukstein, O. G. (2005). Treating adolescent substance abuse. In R. J. Frances, S. I. Miller & A. H. Mack (Eds.), *Clinical textbook of addictive disorders* (3rd ed., pp. 559–587). New York: Guilford Press.

Kaminski, R. A., Stormshak, E. A., Good, R. H., III, & Goodman, M. R. (2002). Prevention of substance abuse with rural head start children and families: Results of project STAR. *Psychology of Addictive Behaviors, 16*, S11–S26.

Kanaya, T., & Ceci, S. J. (2007). Are all IQ scores created equal? The differential costs of IQ cutoff scores for at-risk children. *Child Development Perspectives, 1*, 52–56.

Kanaya, T., Scullin, M. H., & Ceci, S. J. (2003). The Flynn effect and U. S. policies: The impact of rising IQ scores on American society via mental retardation diagnosis. *American Psychologist, 58,* 778–790.

Kandel, D. B. (2002). Examining the gateway hypothesis: Stages and pathways of drug involvement. In D. B. Kandel (Ed.), *Stages and pathways of drug involvement: Examining the gateway hypothesis* (pp. 3–15). New York: Cambridge University Press.

Kandel, D. B., & Yamaguchi, K. (2002). Stages of drug involvement in the U. S. population. In D. B. Kandel (Ed.), *Stages and pathways of drug involvement: Examining the gateway hypothesis* (pp. 65–89). New York: Cambridge University Press.

Kandel, E. R. (1999). Biology and the future of psychoanalysis: A new intellectual framework for psychiatry revisited. *American Journal of Psychiatry, 156*, 505–524.

Kane, P., & Garber, J. (2004). The relations among depression in fathers, children's psychopathology, and father-child conflict: A meta-analysis. *Clinical Psychology Review, 24*, 339–360.

Kanne, S.M., & Muzurek, M.O. (2011). Aggression in children and adolescents with ASK: Prevalence and risk factors. *Journal of Autism and Developmental Disorders, 41*, 926–937.

Kanner, L. (1943). Autistic disturbances of affective contact. *Nervous Child, 2*, 217–250.

Karmiloff-Smith, A. (2009). Nativism versus neuroconstructivism: Rethinking the study of developmental disorders. *Developmental Psychology, 45,* 56–63.

Karpenko, V., Owens, J.S., Evangelista, N.M., & Dodds, C. (2009). Clinically significant symptom change in children with attention-deficit/hyperactivity disorder: Does it correspond with reliable improvement in functioning? *Journal of Clinical Psychology, 65,* 76–93.

Karreman, A., van Tuijl, C., van Aken, M. A.G., & Dekovic, M. (2008). Parenting, coparenting and effortful control in preschoolers. *Journal of Family Psychology, 22*, 30–40.

Karreman, A., van Tuijl, C., van Aken, M.A.G., & Dekovi⊠, M. (2006). Parenting and self-regulation in preschoolers: A meta-analysis. *Infant and Child Development, 15,* 561–579.

Karreman, A., van Tuijl, C., van Aken, M.A.G., & Dekovi⊠, M. (2009). Predicting young children's externalizing problems: Interactions among effortful control, parenting, and child gender. *Merrill-Palmer Quarterly, 55,* 111–134.

Karver, M.S., Handelsman, J.B., Fields, S., & Bickman, L. (2005). A theoretical model of common process factors in youth and family therapy. *Mental Health Services Research, 7,* 35–51.

Kasari, C., Freeman, S., & Paparella, T. (2006). Joint attention and symbolic play in young children with autism: A randomized controlled intervention study. *Journal of Child Psychology and Psychiatry, 47*, 611–620.

Kasari, C., Paparella, T., Freeman, S., & Jahromi, L. B. (2008). Language outcome in autism: Randomized comparison of joint attention and play interventions. *Journal of Consulting and Clinical Psychology, 76*, 125–137.

Kaufman, J., & Charney, D. (2003). The neurobiology of child and adolescent depression: Current knowledge and future directions. In D. Cicchetti & E. Walker (Eds.), *Neurodevelopmental mechanisms in psychopathology* (pp. 461–490). New York: Cambridge University Press.

Kaufman, J., Plotsky, P. M., Nemeroff, C. B., & Charney, D. S. (2000). Effects of early adverse experiences on brain structure and function: Clinical implications. *Biological Psychiatry, 48,* 778–790.

Kaufman, J., Yang, B., Douglas-Palumberi, H., Grasso, D., Lipschitz, D., Houshyar, S., … Gelernter, J. (2006). Brain-derived neurotrophic factor-5-HHTLPR gene interactions and environmental modifiers of depression in children. *Biological Psychiatry, 59,* 673–680.

Kaufman, N. K., Rohde, P., Seeley, J. R., Clarke, G. N., & Stice, E. (2005). Potential mediators of cognitive-behavioral therapy for adolescents with comorbid major depression and conduct disorder. *Journal of Consulting and Clinical Psychology, 73*, 38–46.

Kavale, K. A. (2002). Mainstreaming to full inclusion: From orthogenesis to pathogenesis of an idea. *International Journal of Disability, Development and Education, 49*, 201–214.

Kavale, K. A., & Forness, S. R. (2000). History, rhetoric, and reality: Analysis of the inclusion debate. *Remedial and Special Education, 21*, 279–296.

Kaye, W. H., Bulik, C. M., Thornton, L., Barbarich, N., & Masters, K. (2004). Comorbidity of anxiety disorders with anorexia and bulimia nervosa. *American Journal of Psychiatry, 161*, 2215–2221.

Kaye, W. H., Devlin, B., Barbarich, B., Bulik, C. M., Thornton, L., Bacanu. S. A., et al. (2004). Genetic analysis of bulimia nervosa: Methods and sample description. *International Journal of Eating Disorders, 35*, 556–570.

Kazdin, A. (2005). *Parent management training: Treatment for oppositional, aggressive, and antisocial behavior in children and adolescents.* New York: Oxford University Press.

Kazdin, A. E., Holland, L., & Crowley, M. (1997). Family experience of barriers to treatment and premature termination from child therapy. *Journal of Consulting and Clinical Psychology, 65*, 453–463.

Kazdin, A. E., Marciano, P. L., & Whitley, M. K. (2005). The therapeutic alliance in cognitive-behavioral treatment of children referred for oppositional, aggressive, and antisocial behavior. *Journal of Consulting and Clinical Psychology, 73*, 726–770.

Kazdin, A. E., & Nock, M. K. (2003). Delineating mechanisms of change in child and adolescent therapy: Methodological issues and research recommendations. *Journal of Child Psychology and Psychiatry, 44*, 1116–1129.

Kazdin, A.E., & Blase, S.L. (2011). Rebooting psychotherapy research and practice to reduce the burden of mental illness. *Perspectives on Psychological Science, 6,* 21–37.

Kearney, C. A., & Albano, A. M. (2004). The functional profiles of school refusal behavior: Diagnostic aspects. *Behavior Modification, 28*, 147–161.

Keating, D.P. (2011). Society and early child development: developmental health disparities in the nature-and-nurture paradigm. In D.P. Keating (Ed.), *Nature and Nurture in Early Child Development* (pp. 245–291). New York: Cambridge University Press.

Keehn, B., Lincoln, A.J., Müller, R., & Townsend, J. (2010). Attentional networks in children and adolescents with autism spectrum disorder. *Journal of Child Psychology and Psychiatry, 51,* 1251–1259.

Keel, P. K., & Haedt, A. (2008). Evidence-based psychosocial treatments for eating problems and eating disorders. *Journal of Clinical Child and Adolescent Psychology, 37,* 39–61.

Keenan, K., Shaw, D., Delliquadri, E., Giovannelli, J., & Walsh, B. (1998). Evidence for the continuity of early problem behaviors: Application of a developmental model. *Journal of Abnormal Child Psychology, 26,* 441–452.

Keenan, K., Stouthamer-Loeber M., & Loeber, R. (2005). Developmental approaches to studying conduct problems in girls. In D.J. Pepler, K. C. Madsen, C. Webster, & K. S. Levene (Eds.), *The development and treatment of girlhood aggression* (pp. 29–46). Mahwah, NJ: Erlbaum.

Keenan, K., Wakschlag, L. S., Danis, B., Hill, C., Humphries, M., Duax, J., et al. (2007). Further evidence of the reliability and validity of DSM-IV ODD and CD in preschool children. *Journal of the American Academy of Child and Adolescent Psychiatry, 46,* 457–468.

Keery, H., Boutelle, K., van den Berg, P., & Thompson, J. K. (2005). The impact of appearance-related teasing by family members. *Journal of Adolescent Health, 37,* 120–127.

Keery, H., van den Berg, P., & Thompson, J. K. (2004). An evaluation of the Tripartite Influence Model of body dissatisfaction and eating disturbance with adolescent girls. *Body Image, 1,* 237–251.

Keil, F. C. (1999). Cognition, content and development. In M. Ben-net (Ed.), *Developmental psychology: Achievements and prospects* (pp. 165–184). Philadelphia: Psychology Press.

Keiley, M. K., Lofthouse, N., Bates, J. E., Dodge, K. A., & Pettit, G. S. (2003). Differential risks of covarying and pure components in mother and teacher reports of externalizing and internalizing behavior across ages 5 to 14. *Journal of Abnormal Child Psychology, 31,* 267–283.

Kelley, A. E., Schochet, T., & Landry, C. F. (2004). Risk taking and novelty seeking in adolescence: Introduction to part I. In R. E. Dahl & L. P. Spear (Eds.), *Adolescent brain development: Vulnerabilities and opportunities. Annals of the New York Academy of Sciences* (Vol. 1021, pp. 27–32). New York: New York Academy of Sciences.

Kelley, B. M., & Rowan, J. D. (2004). Long-term, low-level adolescent nicotine exposure produces dose-dependent changes in cocaine sensitivity and reward in adult mice. *International Journal of Developmental Neuroscience, 22,* 339–348.

Kelly, A. E., Schiltz, C. A., & Landry, C. F. (2005). Neural systems recruited by drug-and food-related cues: Studies of gene activation in corticolimbic regions. *Physiology and Behavior, 86,* 11–14.

Kelly, A. M., Wall, M., Eisenberg, M. E., Story, M., & Neumark-Sztainer, D. (2005). Adolescent girls with high body image satisfaction: Who are they and what can they teach us? *Journal of Adolescent Health, 37,* 391–396.

Kelly, J. F., Myers, M. G., & Brown, S. A. (2002). Do adolescents affiliate with 12-step groups? A multivariate process model of effects. *Journal of Studies on Alcohol, 63,* 293–304.

Kelly, T. M., Cornelius, J. R., & Clark, D. B. (2004). Psychiatric disorders and attempted suicide among adolescents with substance use disorders. *Drug and Alcohol Dependence, 73,* 87–97.

Kempton, W., & Kahn, E. (1991). Sexuality and people with intellectual disabilities: A historical perspective. *Sexuality and Disability, 9,* 93–111.

Kendall, P. C., & Southam-Gerow, M. A. (1996). Long-term follow-up of a cognitive-behavioral therapy for anxiety-disordered youth. *Journal of Consulting and Clinical Psychology, 64,* 724–730.

Kendall, P.C. (2012). *Child and adolescent therapy: Cognitive-behavioral procedures* (4th ed.). New York: Guilford Press.

Kendall, P.C., Pliafico, A.C., Barmish, A.J., Choudhury, M.S., Henin, A. & Treadwell, K.S. (2007). Assessing anxiety with the Child Behavior Checklist and the Teacher Report Form. *Journal of Anxiety Disorders, 21,* 1004–1015.

Kendler, K. S. (2005). "A gene for Ö": The nature of gene action in psychiatric disorders. *American Journal of Psychiatry, 162,* 1243–1252.

Kennard, B., Silva, S., Vitiello, B., Curry, J., Kratochvil, C., Simons, A., et al. (2006). Remission and residual symptoms after short-term treatment in the Treatment of Adolescents with Depression Study (TADS). *Journal of the American Academy of Child and Adolescent Psychiatry, 45,* 1404–1411.

Keren, M., Feldman, R., & Tyano, S. (2001). Diagnoses and interactive patterns of infants referred to a community-based infant mental health clinic. *Journal of the American Academy of Child and Adolescent Psychiatry, 40,* 27–35.

Kerr, D.C.R., Lopez, N.L., Olson, S.L., & Sameroff, A.J. (2004). Parental discipline and externalizing behavior problems in early childhood: the roles of moral regulation and child gender. *Journal of Abnormal Child Psychology, 32,* 369–383.

Kerwin, M. E. (1999). Empirically supported treatments in pediatric psychology: Severe feeding problems. *Journal of Pediatric Psychology, 24,* 193–214.

Kessler, R. C., Adler, L., Barkley, R., Biederman, J., Conners, C. K., Demler, O., et al. (2006). The prevalence and correlates of adult ADHD in the United States: Results from the National Comorbidity Survey replication. *American Journal of Psychiatry, 163* 716–723.

Kessler, R. C., Avenevoli, S., & Merikangas, K. R. (2001). Mood disorders in children and adolescents: An epidemiologic perspective. *Biological Psychiatry, 49,* 1002–1014.

Keyes, C. L.M. (2007). A complementary strategy for improving national mental health. *American Psychologist, 62,* 95–108.

Keyes, C.L.M. (2006). Mental health in adolescence: Is America's youth flourishing? *American Journal of Orthopsychiatry, 76,* 395–402.

Kichler, J., Luyster, R., Risi, S., Hsu, W., Dawson, G., Bernier, R., et al. (2006). Is there a ëregressive phenotype' of autism spectrum disorder associated with the measles-mumps-rubella vaccine? A CPEA study. *Journal of Autism and Developmental Disorders, 36,* 299–316.

Kieling, C., Kieling, R.R., Rohde, L.A., Frick, P.J., Moffitt, T., Nigg, J.T., … Castellanos, F.X. (2010). The age at onset of attention deficit hyperactivity disorder. *American Journal of Psychiatry, 167,* 14–16.

Kilmer, R. P., Cowen, E. L., Wyman, P. A., Work, W. C., & Magnus, K. B. (1998). Differences in stressors experienced by urban African American, White, and Hispanic children. *Journal of Community Psychology, 26,* 415–428.

Kilmer, R.P., Cook, J.R., Taylor, C., Kane, S.F., & Clark, L.Y. (2008). Siblings of children with severe emotional disturbances: Risks, resources and adaptations. *American Journal of Orthopsychiatry, 78,* 1–10.

Kim, E.Y. & Miklowitz, D.J. (2002). Childhood mania, attention deficit hyperactivity disorder and conduct disorder: A critical review of diagnostic dilemmas. *Bipolar Disorders, 4,* 215–225.

Kim, I. J., Ge, X., Brody, G. H., Conger, R. D., Gibbons, F. X., & Simons, R. L. (2003). Parenting behaviors and the occurrence and co-occurrence of depressive symptoms and conduct problems among African American children. *Journal of Family Psychology, 17,* 571–583.

Kim, I. J., Zane, N. W. S., & Hong, S. (2002). Protective factors against substance use among Asian American youth: A test of the peer cluster theory. *Journal of Community Psychology, 30,* 565–584.

Kim, J., & Cicchetti, D. (2010). Longitudinal pathways linking child maltreatment, emotion regulation, peer relations, and psychopathology. *Journal of Child Psychology and Psychiatry, 51,* 706–716.

Kim, S., Larson, S. A., & Lakin, K. C. (2001). Behavioural outcomes of deinstitutionalisation for people with intellectual disability: A review of US studies conducted between 1980 and 1999. *Journal of Intellectual and Developmental Disability, 26,* 35–50.

Kim-Cohen, J., & Gold, A.L. (2009). Measured gene-environment interactions and mechanisms promoting resilient development. *Current Directions in Psychological Science, 18,* 138–142.

Kim-Cohen, J., Moffitt, T. E., Caspi, A., & Taylor, A. (2004). Genetic and environmental processes in young children's resilience and vulnerability to socioeconomic deprivation. *Child Development, 75,* 651–668.

Kim-Cohen, J., Moffitt, T. E., Taylor, A., Pawlby, S. J., & Caspi, A. (2005). Maternal depression and children's antisocial behavior: Nature and nurture effects. *Archives of General Psychiatry, 62,* 173–181.

King, B. H., State, M. W., Shah, B., Davanzo, P., & Dykens, E. (1997). A review of the past 10 years. *Journal of the American Academy of Child and Adolescent, 36,* 1656–1663.

King, N. A., Eleonora, G., Tonge, B. J., & Ollendick, T. H. (1993). Self-reports of panic attacks and manifest anxiety in adolescents. *Behaviour Research and Therapy, 31,* 111–116.

King, N. J., Eleonora, E., & Ollendick, T. H. (1998). Etiology of childhood phobias: Current status of Rachman's three pathways theory. *Behaviour Research and Therapy, 36,* 297–309.

King, N. J., Heyne, D., Tonge, B. J., Mullen, P., Myerson, N., Rollings, S., et al. (2003). Sexually abused children suffering from post-traumatic stress disorder: Assessment and treatment strategies. *Cognitive Behaviour Therapy, 32,* 2–12.

King, N. J., Muris, P., & Ollendick, T. H. (2005). Childhood fears and phobias: assessment and treatment. *Child and Adolescent Mental Health, 10,* 50–56.

King, N. J., & Ollendick, T. H. (1997). Treatment of childhood phobias. *Journal of Child Psychology and Psychiatry and Allied Disciplines, 38,* 389–400.

King, N. J., Ollendick, T. H., Mattis, S. G., Yang, B., & Tonge, B. (1996). Nonclinical panic attacks in adolescents: Prevalece, symptomatology, and associated features. *Behaviour Change, 13,* 171–183.

King, N. J., Ollendick, T. H., & Murphy, G. C. (1997). Assessment of childhood phobias. *Clinical Psychology Review, 17,* 667–687.

King, N., Ollendick, T. H., Tonge, B. J., Heyne, D., Pritchard, M., Rollings, S., et al. (1998). School refusal: An overview. *Behaviour Change, 15,* 5–15.

King, N., Tonge, B. J., Heyne, D., Turner, S., Pritchard, M., Young, D., et al. (2001). Cognitive-behavioural treatment of school-refusing children: Maintenance of improvement at 3- to 5-year follow-up. *Scandinavian Journal of Behaviour Therapy, 30,* 85–89.

King, R., Nurcombe, B., Bickman, L., Hides, L., & Reid, W. (2003). Telephone counseling for adolescent suicide prevention: Changes in suicidality and mental state from beginning to end of a counseling session. *Suicide and Life-Threatening Behavior, 33,* 400–411.

King, S. M., Burt, A., Malone, S. M., McGue, M., & Iacono, W.G. (2005). Etiological contributions to heavy drinking from late adolescence to young adulthood. *Journal of Abnormal Psychology, 114,* 587–598.

King, S. M., Iacono, W. G., & McGue, M. (2004). Childhood externalizing and internalizing psychopathology in the prediction of early substance use. *Addiction, 99,* 1548–1559.

Kinniburge, K.J., Blaustein, M., Spinazzola, J. & van der Kolk, B.A. (2005). Attachment, self-regulation and competency. *Psychiatric Annals, 35,* 424–430.

Kinzie, J. D., Cheng, K., Tsai, J., & Riley, C. (2006). Traumatized refugee children: The case for individualized diagnosis and treatment. *Journal of Nervous and Mental Disease, 194,* 534–537.

Kirisci, L., Tarter, R. E., Reynolds, M., & Vanyukov, M. (2006). Individual differences in childhood neurobehavior disinhibition predict decision to desist substance use during adolescence and substance use disorder in young adulthood: A prospective study. *Addictive Behaviors, 31,* 686–696.

Kistner, J.A., David-Ferdon, C.F., Lopez, C.M., & Dunkel, S.B. (2007). Ethnic and sex differences in children's depressive symptoms. *Journal of Clinical Child and Adolescent Psychology, 36,* 171–181.

Kithakye, M., Morris, A.S., Terranova, A.M., & Myers, S.S. (2010). The Kenyan political conflict and children's adjustment. *Child Development 81,* 1114–1128.

Kjelsas, E., Bjornstrom, C., & Gotestam, K. G. (2004). Prevalence of eating disorders in female and male adolescents (14–15). *Eating Behaviors, 5,* 13–25.

Klahr, A.M., McGue, M., Iacono, W.G., & Burt, S.A. (2011). The association between parent-child conflict and adolescent conduct problems over time: Results from a longitudinal adoption study. *Journal of Abnormal Psychology, 120,* 46–56.

Klasen, H. (2000). A name, what's in a name? The medicalization of hyperactivity, revisited. *Harvard Review of Psychology, 7,* 334–344.

Klein, M. (1955). The psychoanalytic play technique. *American Journal of Orthopsychiatry, 25,* 223–237.

Klesges, R., Elliott, V., & Robinson, L. (1997). Chronic dieting and the belief that smoking controls body weight in a biracial population-based adolescent sample. *Tobacco Control, 6,* 89–94.

Klimes-Dougan, B., August, G.J., Lee, C.S., Realmuto, G.M., Bloomquist, M.L., Horowitz, J.L., Eisenberg, T.L. (2009). Practitioner and site characteristics that relate to fidelity of implementation: The Early Risers prevention program in a going-to-scale intervention trial. *Professional Psychology: Research and Practice, 40,* 467–475.

Klimes-Dougan, B., Long, J.D., Lee, C., S., Ronsaville, D.S., Gold, P.W., Martinez, P.E. (2010). Continuity and cascade in offspring of bipolar parents: A longitudinal study of externalizing, internalizing, and thought problems. *Development and Psychopathology, 22,* 849–866.

Klin, A. (1994). Asperger syndrome. *Child and Adolescent Psychiatry Clinics of North America, 3,* 131–148.

Klin, A. (2002). *Asperger syndrome: Clinical features, assessment, and intervention.* Clinical presentation to Minnesota Association of Child Psychologists, Minneapolis, MN.

Klin, A., Jones, W., Schultz, R., Volkmar, F., & Cohen, D. (2002a). Defining and quantifying the social phenotype in autism. *American Journal of Psychiatry, 159,* 909–916.

Klin, A., Jones, W., Schultz, R., Volkmar, F., & Cohen, D. (2002b). Visual fixation patterns during viewing of naturalistic social situations as predictors of social competence in individuals with autism. *Archives of General Psychiatry, 59,* 809–816.

Klin, A., Sparrow, S. S., Marans, W. D., Carter, A., & Volkmar, F. R. (2000). Assessment issues in Asperger syndrome. In A. Klin, F. R. Volkmar, & S. S. Sparrow (Eds.), *Asperger syndrome* (pp. 309–339). New York: Guilford Press.

Klin, A., Sparrow, S. S., Volkmar, F. R., Cicchetti, D. V., & Rourke, B. (1995). Asperger syndrome. In B. P. Rourke (Ed.), *Syndrome of nonverbal learning disabilities: Manifestations in neurological disease, disorder, and dysfunction* (pp. 93–118). New York: Guilford Press.

Klin, A., & Volkmar, F. R. (1994). The development of individuals with autism: Implications for the theory of mind hypothesis. In S. Baron-Cohen & H. Tager-Flusberg (Eds.), *Understanding other minds: Perspectives from autism* (pp. 317–331). London: Oxford University Press.

Klin, A., & Volkmar, F. R. (1997). Asperger's syndrome. In D. J. Cohen & F. R. Volkmar (Eds.), *Handbook of autism and pervasive developmental disorders* (2nd ed.). (pp. 94–122). New York: Wiley.

Klin, A., & Volkmar, F. R. (2000). Treatment and intervention guidelines for individuals with Asperger syndrome. In A. Klin, F. R. Volkmar, & S. S. Sparrow (Eds.), *Asperger syndrome* (pp. 340–366). New York: Guilford Press.

Klin, A., Volkmar, F. R., & Sparrow, S. S. (2000). *Asperger syndrome.* New York: Guilford Press.

Klin, A., Volkmar, F. R., Sparrow, S. S., & Cicchetti, D. V. (1995). Validity and neuropsychological characterization of Asperger syndrome: Convergence with nonverbal learning disabilities syndrome. *Journal of Child Psychology and Psychiatry and Allied Disciplines, 36,* 1127–1140.

Klinger, L. G., & Dawson, G. (2001). Prototype formation in autism. *Development and Psychopathology, 13,* 111–124.

Klomek, A. B., & Mufson, L. (2006). Interpersonal psychotherapy for depressed adolescents. *Child and Adolescent Psychiatric Clinics of North America, 15,* 959–975.

Knappe, S., Lieb, R., Beesdo, K., Fehm, L., Low, N.C.P., Gloster, A.T., & Wittchen, H. (2009). The role of parental psychopathology and family environment for social phobia in the first three decades of life. *Depression and Anxiety, 26,* 363–370.

Knopik, V. S., Heath, A. C., Madden, P. A. F., Bucholz, K. K., Slutske, W. S., Nelson, E. C., et al. (2004). Genetic effects on alcohol dependence risk: Re-evaluating the importance of psychiatric and other heritable risk factors. *Psychological Medicine, 34,* 1519–1530.

Ko, C-H., Yen, J-Y, Chen, C-C., Chen, S-H., & Yen, C-F. (2005). Gender differences and elated factors affecting online gaming addiction among Taiwanese adolescents. *Journal of Nervous and Mental Disease, 193,* 273–277.

Kochanska, G. (1995). Children's temperament, mother's discipline, and security of attachment: Multiple pathways to emerging internalization. *Child Development, 66,* 597–615.

Kochanska, G. (1997). Multiple pathways to conscience for children with different temperaments: From toddlerhood to age 5. *Developmental Psychology, 33,* 228–240.

Kochanska, G., & Aksan, N. (2004). Conscience in childhood: Past, present, and future. *Merrill-Palmer Quarterly, 50,* 299–310.

Kochanska, G., & Aksan, N. (2006). Children's conscience and self-regulation. *Journal of Personality, 74,* 1587–1617.

Kochanska, G., Barry, R.A., Aksan, N., & Boldt, L.J. (2008). A developmental model of maternal and child contributions to disruptive conduct: the first six years. *Journal of Child Psychology and Psychiatry, 49,* 1220–1227.

Kochanska, G., Barry, R.a., Jimenez, N.B., Hollatz, A.L., & Woodard, J. (2009). Guilt and effortful control: Two mechanisms that prevent disruptive developmental trajectories. *Journal of Personality and Social Psychology, 87,* 322–333.

Kochanska, G., Barry, R.A., Stellern, S.A., & O'Bleness, J.J. (2009). Early attachment organization moderates the parent-child mutually coercive pathway to children's antisocial conduct. *Child Development, 80,* 1288–1300.

Kochanska, G., Koenig, J.L., Barry, R.A., Kim, S., & Yoon, J.E. (2010). Children's conscience during toddler and preschool years, moral self, and a competent, adaptive developmental trajectory. *Developmental Psychology, 46,* 1320–1332.

Kochanska, G., Murray, K. T., & Harlan, E. T. (2000). Effortful control in early childhood: Continuity and change, antecedents, and implications for social development. *Developmental Psychology, 36,* 220–232.

Kochanska, G., Philibert, R.A., & Barry, R.A. (2009). Interplay of genes and early mother-child relationship in the development of self-regulation from toddler to preschool age. *Journal of Child Psychology and Psychiatry, 50,* 1331–1338.

Kochenderfer-Ladd, B. (2003). Identification of aggressive and asocial victims and the stability of their peer victimization. *Merrill-Palmer Quarterly, 49,* 401–425.

Kochman, F. J., Hantouche, E. G., Ferrari, P., Lancrenon, S., Bayart, D., & Akiskal, H. S. (2005). Cyclothymia temperament as a prospective predictor of bipolarity and suicidality in children and adolescents with major depressive disorder. *Journal of Affective Disorders, 85,* 181–189.

Kodjo, C. M., Auinger, P., & Ryan, S. A. (2004). Prevalence of, and factors associated with, adolescent physical fighting while under the influence of alcohol and drugs. *Journal of Adolescent Health, 35,* 11–16.

Koegl, C.J., Farrington, D.P., Augimeri, L.K., & Day, D.M. (2008). Evaluation of a targeted cognitive-behavioral program for children with conduct problems—The SNAP Under 12 Outreach Project: Service intensity, age and gender effects on short-and long-term outcomes. *Clinical Child Psychology and Psychiatry, 13,* 419–434.

Koenig, A. L., Ialongo, N., Wagner, B. M., Poduska, J., & Kellam, S. (2002). Negative caregiver strategies and psychopathology in urban, African-American young adults. *Child Abuse and Neglect, 26,* 1211–1233.

Kohen, D. E., Leventhal, T., Dahinten, V. S., & McIntosh, C. N. (2008). Neighborhood disadvantage: Pathways of effects for young children. *Child Development, 79,* 156–169.

Kohlberg, L. (1994). Stage and sequence: the cognitive-developmental approach to socialization. In B. Puka (Ed.), *Defining perspectives in moral development* (pp. 1–134). New York: Garland Publishing.

Kolevzon, A., Gross, R., & Riechenberg, A. (2007). Prenatal and perinatal risk factors for autism: A review and integration of findings. *Archives of Pediatrics & Adolescent Medicine, 61,* 326–333.

Kolko, D.J., & Pardini, D.A. (2010). ODD dimensions, ADHD and callous-unemotional traits as predictors of treatment response in children with disruptive behavior disorders. *Journal of Abnormal Psychology, 119,* 713–725.

Kollins, S.H. (2007). Abuse liability of medications used to treat attention-deficit/hyperactivity disorder (ADHD). *American Journal on Addictions, 16,* 35–44.

Komro, K. A., Perry, C. L., Veblen-Mortenson, S., Bosma, L. M., Dudovitz, B. S., Williams, C., et al. (2004). Brief report: The adaptation of Project Northland for urban youth. *Journal of Pediatric Psychology, 29,* 457–466.

Komro, K. A., & Toomey, T. L. (2002). Strategies to prevent underage drinking. *Alcohol Research and Health, 26,* 5–14.

Koob, G. F. (2002). Neurobiology of drug addiction. In D. B. Kandel (Ed.), *Stages and pathways of drug involvement: Examining the gateway hypothesis* (pp. 337–361). New York: Cambridge University Press.

Koob, G.F., & LeMoal, M. (1997). Drug abuse: Hedonic homeostatic dysregulation. *Science, 278,* 52–58.

Koocher, G.P. (2003). Ethical issues in psychotherapy with adolescents. *Journal of Clinical Psychology, 59,* 1247–1256.

Koops, W., & de Castro, B. O. (2004). The development of aggression and its linkages with violence and youth delinquency. *European Journal of Developmental Psychology, 1,* 241–269.

Kopp, C. B. (1982). Antecedents of self-regulation: A developmental perspective. *Developmental Psychology, 18,* 199–214.

Kopp, C. B. (1989). Regulation of distress and negative emotions: A developmental view. *Developmental Psychology, 25,* 343–354.

Kopp, C. B. (1997). Young children: Emotion management, instrumental control, and plans. In S. L. Friedman & E. K. Scholnick (Eds.), *The developmental psychology of planning: Why, how, and when do we plan?* (pp. 103–124). Mahwah, NJ: Erlbaum.

Kopp, C.B. (2009). Emotion-focused coping in young children: Self and self-regulatory processes. In E.A. Skinner & M.J. Zimmer-Gembeck (Eds.), *Coping and the Development of Regulation. New Directions for Child and Adolescent Development* (pp. 33–46). San Francisco: Jossey-Bass.

Kosten, T. R., George, T. P., & Kleber, H. D. (2005). The neurobiology of substance dependence: Implications for treatment. In R. J. Frances, S. I. Miller, & A. H. Mack (Eds.), *Clinical textbook of addictive disorders* (3rd ed.). New York: Guilford Press.

Kotler, L. A., Cohen, P., Davies, M., Pine, D. S., & Walsh, B. T. (2001). Longitudinal relationships between childhood, adolescent and adult eating disorders. *Journal of the American Academy of Child and Adolescent Psychiatry, 40,* 1434–1440.

Koukoui, S. D., & Chaudhuri, A. (2007). Neuroanatomical, molecular genetic, and behavioral correlates of fragile X syndrome. *Brain Research Reviews, 53,* 27–38.

Kovacs, M. (1985). The Children's Depression Inventory (CDI). *Psychopharmacology Bulletin, 21,* 995–998.

Kovacs, M. (1992). *Manual for the Children's Depression Inventory.* North Tonawanda, NJ: Multi-Health Systems.

Kovacs, M., Obrosky, D. S., & Sherrill, J. (2003). Developmental changes in the phenomenology of depression in girls compared to boys from childhood onward. *Journal of Affective Disorders, 74,* 33–48.

Kovas, Y., Haworth, C.M.A., Dale, P.S., Plomin, R., Weinberg, R.A., Thomson, J.M., & Fischer, K.W. (2007). The genetic and environmental origins of learning abilities and disabilities in the early school years. *Monographs of the Society for Research in Child Development, 72,* 124–144.

Kowatch, R. A., Fristad, M., Birmaher, B., Wagner, K. D., Findling, R., Hellander, M., et al. (2005). Treatment guidelines for children and adolescents with bipolar disorder. *American Academy of Child and Adolescent Psychiatry, 44,* 213–235.

Kowatch, R. A., Sethuraman, G., Hume, J. H., Kromelis, M., & Weinberg, W. A. (2003). Combination pharmacotherapy in children and adolescents with bipolar disorder. *Biological Psychiatry, 53,* 978–984.

Kowatch, R.A. & DelBello, M.P. (2005). Pharmacotherapy of children and adolescents with bipolar disorder. *Psychiatric Clinics of North America 28,* 385–397.

Krain, A.L., Kendall, P.C., Power, T.J. (2005). The role of treatment acceptability in the initiation of treatment for ADHD. *Journal of Attention Disorders, 9,* 425–434.

Krajewski, J. J., Hyde, M. S., & O'Keefe, M. K. (2002) Teen attitudes toward individuals with mental retardation from 1987 to 1998: Impact of respondent gender and school variables. *Education and Training in Mental Retardation and Developmental Disabilities, 37,* 27–39.

Krasny, L., Williams, B. J., Provencal, S., & Ozonoff, S. (2003). Social skills interventions for the autism spectrum: Essential ingredients and a model curriculum. *Child and Adolescent Psychiatric Clinics of North America, 12,* 107–122.

Kratochvil, C. J., Simons, A., Vitiello, B., Walkup, J., Emslie, G., Rosenberg, D., et al. (2005). A multisite psychotherapy and medication trial for depressed adolescents: Background and benefits. *Cognitive and Behavioral Practice, 12,* 159–165.

Krauss, M. W., Simeonsson, R., & Ramey, S. L. (Eds.). (1989). Research on families [Special issue]. *American Journal on Mental Retardation, 94.*

Kris, E. (1950). Notes on the development and on some current problems of psychoanalytic child psychology. *The Psychoanalytic Study of the Child, 5,* 24–46. New York: International Universities Press.

Kroes, M., Kalff, A. C., Kessels, A. G. H., Setaert, J., Feron, F. J. M., van Someren, A. J. W. G. M., et al. (2001). Child psychiatric diagnoses in a population of Dutch schoolchildren aged 6 to 8 years. *Journal of the American Academy of Child and Adolescent Psychiatry, 40,* 1401–1409.

Kroneman, L.M., Hipwell, A.E., Loeber, R., Koot, H.M., & Pardini, D.A. (2011). Contextual risk factors as predictors of disruptive behavior disorder trajectories in girls: the moderating effect of callous-unemotional features. *Journal of Child Psychology and Psychiatry, 52,* 167–175.

Kronenberg, M.E., Hansel, T.C., Brennan, A.M., Howard, H.J., Osofsky, J.D & Lawrason, B. (2010). Children of Katrina: Lessons learned about postdisaster symptoms and recovery patterns. *Child Development, 81,* 1241–1259.

Krueger, R. F., Hicks, B. M., Patrick, C. J., Carlson, S. R., Iacono, W. G., & McGue, M. (2002). Etiologic connections among substance dependence, antisocial behavior, and personality: modeling the externalizing spectrum. *Journal of Abnormal Psychology, 111,* 411–424.

Krueger, R. F., Silva, P. A., Avshalom, C., & Moffitt, T. E. (1998). The structure and stability of common mental disorders (DSMIII-R): A longitudinal-epidemiological study. *Journal of Abnormal Psychology, 107*, 216–227.

Krueger, R.F., Caspi, A., Moffitt, T.E. & Silva, P.A. (1998). The structure and stability of common mental disorders (DSM-III-R): A longitudinal-epidemiological study. *Journal of Abnormal Psychology, 107*, 216–227.

Kuhl, P. K., Coffey-Corina, S., Padden, D., & Dawson, G. (2005). Links between social and linguistic processing of speech in preschool children with autism: Behavioral and electrophysiological measures. *Developmental Science, 8*, F1–F12.

Kumar, R., O'Malley, P. M., & Johnston, L. D. (2005). School tobacco control policies related to students' smoking and attitudes toward smoking: National survey results, 1999–2000. *Health Education and Behavior, 32*, 780–794.

Kumpfer, K. L., & Alvarado, R. (2003). Family-strengthening approaches for the prevention of youth problem behaviors. *American Psychologist, 58*, 457–465.

Kumsta, R., Kreppner, J., Rutter, M., Beckett, C., Castle, J., Stevens, S., & Sonuga-Barke, E.J. (2010). Deprivation-specific psychological patterns. *Monographs of the Society for Research in Child Development, 75*, 48–78.

Kupersmidt, J.B. & DeRosier, M.E. (2004). How peer problems lead to negative outcomes: An integrative meditational model. In J. B. Kupersmidt & K.A. Dodge (Eds.), *Children's Peer Relations: From Development to Intervention* (pp. 119–138). Washington, DC: American Psychological Association.

Kuttner, L. (1997). Mind-body methods of pain management. *Child and Adolescent Psychiatric Clinics of North America, 6*, 783–796.

La Greca, A.M., & Silverman, W.K. (2009). Treatment and prevention of posttraumatic stress reactions in children and adolescents exposed to disasters and terrorism: What is the evidence? *Child Development Perpsectives, 3*, 4–10.

La Malfa, G., Lassi, S., Bertelli, M., Salvini, R., & Placidi, G. F. (2004). Autism and intellectual disability: A study of prevalence on a sample of the Italian population. *Journal of Intellectual Disability Research, 48*, 262–267.

Lacourse, E., Nagin, D., Tremblay, R. E., Vitaro, F., & Claes, M. (2003). Developmental trajectories of boys' delinquent group membership and facilitation of violent behaviors during adolescence. *Development and Psychopathology, 15*, 183–197.

Lahey, B. B., Applegate, B., Waldman, I. D., Loft, J. D., Hankin, B. L., & Frick, J. (2004). The structure of child and adolescent psychopathology: Generating new hypotheses. *Journal of Abnormal Psychology, 113*, 358–385.

Lahey, B. B., Flagg, E. W., Bird, H. R., Schwab-Stone, M. E., Canino, G., Dulcan, M. K., et al. (1996). The NIMH methods for the epidemiology of child and adolescent mental disorders (MECA) study: Background and methodology. *Journal of the American Academy of Child and Adolescent Psychiatry, 35*, 855–865.

Lahey, B. B., Gordon, R. A., Loeber, R., Stouthamer-Loeber, M., & Farrington, D. P. (1999). Boys who join gangs: A prospective study of predictors of first gang entry. *Journal of Abnormal Child Psychology, 27*, 261–276.

Lahey, B. B., & Loeber, R. (1997). Attention-deficit/hyperactivity disorder, oppositional defiant disorder, conduct disorder, and adult antisocial behavior: A life span perspective. In D. M. Stoff & J. Breiling (Eds.), *Handbook of antisocial behavior* (pp. 51–59). New York: Wiley.

Lahey, B. B., Loeber, R., Burke, J. D., & Applegate, B. (2005). Predicting future antisocial personality disorder in males from a clinical assessment in childhood. *Journal of Consulting and Clinical Psychology, 73*, 389–399.

Lahey, B. B., Loeber, R., Burke, J., Rathouz, P. J., & McBurnett, K. (2002). Waxing and waning in concert: Dynamic comorbidity of conduct disorder with other disruptive and emotional problems over 17 years among clinic-referred boys. *Journal of Abnormal Psychology, 111*, 556–567.

Lahey, B. B., & Waldman, I. D. (2003). A developmental propensity model of the origins of conduct problems during childhood and adolescence. In B. B. Lahey, T. E. Moffitt, & A. Caspi (Eds.), *Causes of conduct disorder and juvenile delinquency* (pp. 76–117). New York: Guilford Press.

Lahey, B.B., D'Onofrio, B.M., Waldman, I.D. (2009). Using epidemiologic methods to test hypothesis regarding causal influences on child and adolescent mental disorders. *Journal of Child Psychology and Psychiatry, 50*, 53–62.

Lahey, B.B., Pelham, W.E., Loney, J., Kipp, H., Ehrhardt, A., Lee, S.S., … Massetti, G. (2004). Three-year predictive validity of DSM-IV attention deficit hyperactivity disorder in children diagnosed at 4–6 years of age. *American Journal of Psychiatry, 161*, 2014–2020.

Lahey, B.B., Rathouz, P.J., Lee, S.S., Chronis-Tuscano, A., Pelham, W.E., Waldman, I.D., & Cook, E.H. (2011). Interactions between early parenting and a polymorphism of the child's dopamine transporter gene in predicting future child conduct disorder symptoms. *Journal of Abnormal Psychology, 120*, 33–45.

Lahey, B.B., Rathouz, P.J., Van Hulle, C., Urbano, R.C., Krueger, R.F., Applegate, B., … Waldman, I.D. (2008). Testing structural models of DSM-IV symptoms of common forms of child and adolescent psychopathology. *Journal of Abnormal Child Psychology, 36*, 187–206.

Lahey, B.B., Van Hulle, C.A., Singh, A.L., Waldman, I.D., & Rathouz, P.J. (2011). Higher-order genetic and environmental structure of prevalent forms of child and adolescent psychopathology. *Archives of General Psychiatry, 68*, 181–189.

Lahey, B.B., Van Hulle, C.A., Waldman, I.D., Rodgers, J.L., D'Onofrio, B.M.D., Pedlow, S., … Keenan, K. (2006). Testing descriptive hypotheses regarding sex differences in the development of conduct problems and delinquency. *Journal of Abnormal Child Psychology, 34*, 737–755.

Laing, E. (2002). Investigating reading development in atypical populations: The case of Williams syndrome. *Reading and Writing, 15*, 575–587.

Laird, R. D., Pettit, G. S., Dodge, K. A., & Bates, J. E. (2003). Change in parents' monitoring knowledge: Links with parenting, relationship quality, adolescent beliefs, and antisocial behavior. *Social Development, 12*, 401–419.

Lambert, N. (2005). The contribution of childhood ADHD, conduct problems, and stimulant treatment to adolescent and adult tobacco and psychoactive substance abuse. *Ethical Human Psychology and Psychiatry, 7*, 197–221.

Lambert, S.F., McCreary, B.T., Joiner, T.E., Schmidt, N.B. & Ialongo, N.S. (2004). Structure of anxiety and depression in urban youth: An examination of the tripartite model. *Journal of Consulting and Clinical Psychology, 72*, 904–908.

Landa, R. (2000). Social language use in Asperger syndrome and high-functioning autism. In A. Klin, F. R. Volkmar, &

S. S. Sparrow (Eds.), *Asperger syndrome* (pp. 125–155). New York: Guilford Press.

Langberg, J.M., Eugene, A.L., Flowers, A.M., Epstein, J.N., Epstein, J.N., Mekibib, A., ... Hechtman, L. (2010). Parent-reported homework problems in the MTA study: Evidence for sustained improvement with behavioral treatment. *Journal of Clinical Child and Adolescent Psychology, 39,* 220–233.

Langhinrichsen-Rohling, J., Rohde, P., Seeley, J. R., & Rohling, M. L. (2004). Individual, family, and peer correlates of adolescent gambling. *Journal of Gambling Studies, 20,* 23–46.

Langley, A. K., Bergman, R. L., McCracken, J., & Piacentini, J. C. (2004). Impairment in childhood anxiety disorders: Preliminary examination of the Child Anxiety Impact Scale—Parent Version. *Journal of Child and Adolescent Psychopharmacology, 14,* 105–114.

Langley, A.K., Lewin, A.B., Bergman, R.L., Lee, J.C., & Piacentini, J. (2010). Correlates of comorbid anxiety and externalizing disorders in childhood obsessive compulsive disorder. *European Child & Adolescent Psychiatry, 19,* 637–645.

Lansford, J. E., Chang, L., Dodge, K. A., Malone, P. S., Oburu, P., Palmérus, K., et al. (2005). Physical discipline and children's adjustment: Cultural normativeness as a moderator. *Child Development, 76,* 1234–1246.

Lansford, J. E., Deater-Deckard, K., Dodge, K. A., Bates, J. E., & Pettit, G. S. (2004). Ethnic differences in the link between physical discipline and later adolescent externalizing behaviors. *Journal of Child Psychology and Psychiatry, 45,* 801–812.

Lansford, J.E., Criss, M.M., Pettit, G.S., Dodge, K.A. & Bates, J.E. (2003). Friendship quality, peer group affiliation, and peer antisocial behavior as moderators of the link between negative parenting and adolescent externalizing behavior. *Journal of Research on Adolescence, 13,* 161–184.

Lansford, J.E., Erath, S., Yu, T., Pettit, G.S., Dodge, K.A., & Bates, J.E. (2008). The developmental course of illicit substance use from age 12 to 22: links with depressive, anxiety, and behavior disorders at age 18. *Journal of Child Psychology and Psychiatry, 49,* 877–885.

Lansford, J.E., Malone, P.S., Dodge, K.A., Pettit, G.S., & Bates, J.E. (2010). Developmental cascades of peer rejection, social information processing biases, and aggression during middle childhood. *Developmental and Psychopathology, 22,* 593–602.

Lansford, J.E., Miller-Johnson, S., Berlin, L.J., Dodge, K.A., Bates, J.E., Pettit, G.S. (2007). Early physical abuse and later violent delinquency: A prospective longitudinal study. *Child Maltreatment, 12,* 233–245.

Lansford, J.E., Wager, L.B., Bates, J.E., Dodge, K.A., & Pettit, G.S. (2012). Parental reasoning, denying privileges, yelling, and spanking: Ethnic differences and associations with child externalizing behavior. *Parenting: Science and Practice, 12,* 42–56.

Lanza, S. T., & Collins, L. M. (2002). Pubertal timing and the onset of substance use in females during early adolescence. *Prevention Science, 3,* 69–82.

Lapinski, M. K. (2006). StarvingforPerfect.com: A theoretically based content analysis of pro-eating disorder web sites. *Health Communication, 20,* 243–253.

Larkin, J., & Rice, C. (2005). Beyond "healthy eating" and "healthy weights": Harassment and the health curriculum in middle schools. *Body Image, 2,* 219–232.

Larkin, M. (1999). "Mozart effect" comes under strong fire. *The Lancet, 354,* 749.

Larson, R. W. (2000). Toward a psychology of positive youth development. *American Psychologist, 55,* 170–183.

Larue, R.H., Patel, M.R., Piazza, C.C., Stewart, V., Volkert, V.M., & Zeleny, J. (2011). Escape as reinforcement and escape extinction in the treatment of feeding problems. *Journal of Applied Behavior Analysis, 44,* 719–735.

Latendresse, S.J., Bates, J.E., Goodnight, J.A., Lansford, J.E., Budde, J.P., Goate, A., ... Dick, D.M. (2011). Differential susceptibility to adolescent externalizing trajectories: examining the interplay between CHRM2 and peer group antisocial behavior. *Child Development, 6,* 1797–1814.

Latzer, Y. (2003). Disordered eating behaviors and attitudes in diverse groups in Israel. In G. M. Ruggeiro (Ed.), *Eating disorders in the Mediterranean area: An exploration in transcultural psychology* (pp. 159–181). Hauppauge, NY: Nova Science Publishers.

Latzer, Y., & Gilat, I. (2000). Calls to the Israeli hotline from individuals who suffer from eating disorders: An epidemiological study. *Eating Disorders: The Journal of Treatment and Prevention, 8,* 31–42.

Laugesen, N., Dugas, M.J.& Bukowski, W.M. (2003). Understanding adolescent worry: The application of a cognitive model. *Journal of Abnormal Child Psychology, 31,* 55–64.

Laursen, B., & Bukowski, W. M. (1997). A developmental guide to the organization of close relationships. *International Journal of Behavioral Development, 21,* 747–770.

Laursen, B., & Collins, W.A. (2009). Parent-child relationships during adolescence. In R.M. Lerner & L. Steinberg (Eds.), *Handbook of adolescent psychology, Vol. 2: Contextual influences on adolescent development* (3rd ed.) (pp. 3–42). Hoboken, NJ: Wiley.

Laursen, B., Hafen, C.A., Kerr, M., & Stattin, H. (2012). Friend influence over adolescent problem behaviors as a function of relative peer acceptance: To be liked is to be emulated. *Journal of Abnormal Psychology, 121,* 88–94.

Laursen, B. Hafen, C.A., Rubin, K.H., Booth-LaForce, C., & Rose-Krasnor, L. (2010). The distinctive difficulties of disagreeable youth. *Merrill-Palmer Quarterly, 56,* 80–103.

Lawendowski, L. A. (1998). A motivational intervention for adolescent smokers. *Preventive Medicine: An International Journal Devoted to Practice and Theory, 27,* A39–A46.

Lawlor, D. A., Batty, G. D., Morton, S. M. B., Deary, I. J., Macintyre, S., Ronalds, G., et al. (2005). Early life predictors of childhood intelligence: Evidence from the Aberdeen children of the 1950s study. *Journal of Epidemiology and Community Health, 59,* 656–663.

Layne, C.M., Ippen, C.G., Strand, V., Stuber, M., Abramovitz., R., Reyes, G., ... Pynoos, R. (2011). The core curriculum on childhood trauma: A tool for training a trauma-informed workforce. *Psychological Trauma: Theory, Research, Practice, and Policy, 3,* 243–252.

Lazarus, R. S., & Folkman, S. (1984). *Coping and adaptation.* New York: Guilford Press.

Le Grange, D. (2004). Family-based treatment for adolescent anorexia nervosa: A promising approach? *Clinical Psychologist, 8,* 56–63.

Le Grange, D., Lock, J., Agras, W.S., Moye, A., Bryson, S.W., Jo, B., & Kraemer, H.C. (2012). Moderators and mediators of remission in family-based treatment and adolescent focused therapy for anorexia nervosa. *Behaviour Research and Therapy, 50,* 85–92.

Le Grange, D., Lock, J., Loeb, K., & Nicholls, D. (2010). Academy for eating disorders position paper: The role of the family in eating disorders. *International Journal of Eating Disorders, 43,* 1–5.

Le Grange, D., & Loeb, K.L. (2007). Early identification and treatment of eating disorders: Prodrome to syndrome. *Early Intervention in Psychiatry, 1,* 27–39.

Leary, M. R., & Springer, C. A. (2001). Hurt feelings: The neglected emotion. In R. M. Kowalski (Ed.), *Behaving badly: Aversive behaviors in interpersonal relationships* (pp. 151–175). Washington, DC: American Psychological Association.

Lebowitz, E.R., Vitulano, L.A., & Omer, H. (2011). Coercive and disruptive behaviors in pediatric obsessive compulsive disorder: A qualitative analysis. *Psychiatry, 74,* 362–371.

Leboyer, M., Henry, C., Paillere-Martinot, M., & Bellivier, F. (2005). Age at onset in bipolar affective disorders: A review. *Bipolar Disorders, 7,* 111–118.

Leckman, J.F., & Yazgan, M.Y. (2010). Editorial: Developmental transitions to psychopathology: from genomics and epigenomics to social policy. *Journal of Child Psychology and Psychiatry, 51,* 333–340.

LeDoux, J. E. (1995). Emotion: Clues from the brain. *Annual Review of Psychology, 46,* 209–235.

Lee, C.S., August, G.J., Realmuto, G.M., Horowitz, J.L., Bloomquist, M.L., & Klimes-Dougan, B. (2008). *Prevention Science, 9,* 215–229.

Lee, S.S., August, G.J., Gewirtz, A.H., Klimes-Dougan, B., Bloomquist, M.L., & Realmuto, G.M. (2010). Identifying unmet mental health needs in children of formerly homeless mothers living in a supportive housing community sector of care. *Journal of Abnormal Child Psychology, 38,* 421–432.

Lee, S.S., Lahey, B.B., Owens, E.B., & Hinshaw, S.P. (2008). Few preschool boys and girls with ADHD are well-adjusted during adolescence. *Journal of Abnormal Child Psychology, 36,* 373–383.

Lee, V., & Hoaken, P. N. (2007). Cognition, emotion, and neurobiological development: Mediating the relation between maltreatment and aggression. *Child Maltreatment, 12,* 281–298.

Leekam, S.R., Prior, M.R., & Uljarevic, M. (2011). Restricted and repetitive behaviors in autism spectrum disorders: A review of research in the last decade. *Psychological Bulletin, 137,* 562–593.

Leff, S. S., Costigan, T., & Power, T. J. (2004). Using participatory research to develop a playground-based prevention program. *Journal of School Psychology, 42,* 3–21.

Leffert, J. S., & Siperstein, G. N. (2002). Social cognition: A key to understanding adaptive behavior in individuals with mild mental retardation. In L. M. Glidden (Ed.), *International review of research in mental retardation* (Vol. 25, pp. 135–181). San Diego, CA: Academic Press.

Leffert, N., Benson, P. L., Scales, P. C., Sharma, A. R., Drake, D. R., & Blyth, D. (1998). Developmental assets: Measurement and prediction of risk behavior in adolescents. *Applied Developmental Science, 2,* 209–230.

Leibenluft, E. (2011). Severe mood dysregulation, irritability, and the diagnostic boundaries of bipolar disorder in youth. *American Journal of Psychiatry, 168,* 129–142.

Leibenluft, E., Charney, D. S., & Pine, D. S. (2003). Resesarching the pathophysiology of pediatric bipolar disorder. *Biological Psychiatry, 53,* 1009–1020.

Leonard, H., & Wen, X. (2002). The epidemiology of mental retardation: Challenges and opportunities in the new millennium. *Mental Retardation and Developmental Disabilities Research Reviews, 8,* 117–134.

Lépine, J-P., & Pélissolo, A. (2000). Why take social anxiety disorder seriously? *Depression and Anxiety, 11,* 87–92.

Leppanen, J.M., & Nelson, C.A. (2012). Early development of fear processing. *Psychological Science, 21,* 200–204.

Lerner, J., Safren, S. A., Henin, A., Warman, M., Heimberg, R. G., & Kendall, P. C. (1999). Differentiating anxious and depressive self-statements in youth: Factor structure of the Negative Affect Self-Statement Questionnaire among youth referred to an anxiety disorders clinic. *Journal of Clinical Child Psychology, 28,* 82–93.

Lerner, R. M. (1998). Theories of human development: Contemporary perspectives. In W. Damon & R. M. Lerner (Eds.), *Handbook of child psychology: Vol. 1. Theoretical models of human development* (5th ed., pp. 1–24). Hoboken, NJ: Wiley.

Lerner, R. M. (2001). Toward a democratic ethnotheory of parenting for families and policymakers: A developmental systems perspective. *Parenting: Science and Practice, 1,* 339–351.

Lerner, R. M., Villarruel, F. A., & Castellino, D. R. (1999). Adolescence. In W. K. Silverman & T. H. Ollendick (Eds.), *Developmental issues in the clinical treatment of children* (pp. 125–136). Boston: Allyn and Bacon.

Lerner, R.M., Lerner, J.V., von Eye, A., Bowers, E.P., & Lewin-Bizan, S. (2011). Individual and contextual bases of thriving in adolescence: A view of the issues. *Journal of Adolescence, 34,* 1107–1114.

Leslie, L. K., Plemmons, D., Monn, A. R., & Palinkas, L. A. (2007). Investigating ADHD treatment trajectories: Listening to families' stories about medication use. *Journal of Developmental and Behavioral Pediatrics, 28,* 179–188.

Levine, K., & Wharton, R. (2000). Williams syndrome and happiness. *American Journal on Mental Retardation, 105,* 363–371.

Levine, M. P., & Murnen, S. K. (2009). "Everybody knows that mass media are/are not (pick one) a cause of eating disorders": A critical review of evidence for a causal link between media, negative body image, and disordered eating in females. *Journal of Social and Clinical Psychology, 28,* 9–42.

Levine, S.Z., Laufer, A., Stein, E., Hamama-Raz, Y., & Solomon, Z. (2009). Examining the relationship between resilience and posttraumatic growth. *Journal of Traumatic Stress, 22,* 282–286.

Levitas, A. S., Hurley, A. D., & Pary, R. (2001). The mental status examination in patients with mental retardation and developmental disabilities. *Mental Health Aspects of Developmental Disabilities, 4,* 2–16.

Levitas, A. S., & Silka, V. R. (2001). Mental health clinical assessment of persons with mental retardation and developmental disabilities: History. *Mental Health Aspects of Developmental Disabilities, 4,* 31–42.

Levitin, D.J., Cole, K., Chiles, M., Lai, Z., Lincoln, A., & Bellugi, U. (2004). Characterizing the musical phenotype in individuals with Williams Syndrome. *Child Neuropsychology, 10,* 223–247.

Lewin, A. B., & Piacentini, J. (2010). Evidence-based assessment of child obsessive compulsive disorder: Recommendations for clinical practice and treatment research. *Child Youth Care Forum, 39,* 73–89.

Lewin, A.B., Caporino, N., Murphy, T.K., Geffken, G.R., & Storch, E.A. (2010). Understudied clinical dimensions in pediatric obsessive compulsive disorder. *Child Psychiatry & Human Development, 41,* 675–691.

Lewin, A.B., Chang, S., McCracken, J., McQueen, M., & Piacentini, J. (2010). Comparison of clinical features among youth with tic disorders, obsessive-compulsive disorder (OCD), and both conditions. *Psychiatry Research, 178,* 317–322.

Lewin-Bizan, S., Bowers, E.P., & Lerner, R.M. (2010). One good thing leads to another: Cascades of positive youth development among American adolescents. *Development and Psychopathology, 22,* 759–770.

Lewinsohn, P. M., Rohde, P., & Seeley, J. R. (1995). Adolescent psychopathology: III. The clinical consequences of comorbidity. *Journal of the American Academy of Child and Adolescent Psychiatry, 34,* 510–519.

Lewinsohn, P. M., Seeley, J. R., & Klein, D. N. (2003). Bipolar disorder in adolescents: Epidemiology and suicidal behavior. In B. Geller & M. P. DelBello (Eds.), *Bipolar disorder in childhood and early adolescence* (pp. 7–24). New York: Guilford Press.

Lewinsohn, P. M., Zinbarg, R., Seeley, J. R., Lewinsohn, M., & Sack, W. H. (1997). Lifetime comorbidity among anxiety disorders and between anxiety disorders and other mental disorders in adolescents. *Journal of Anxiety Disorders, 11,* 377–394.

Lewinsohn, P.M., & Essau, C.A. (2002). Depression in adolescents. In I.H. Gotlib & C.L. Hammen (Eds.) *Handbook of Depression* (pp. 541–559). New York: Guilford Press.

Lewis, M.D., Todd, R., & Xu, X. (2010). The development of emotion regulation: A neuropsychological perspective. In M.E. Lamb, A.M. Freund, R.M. Lerner (Eds.), *The handbook of life-span development, Vol. 2: Social and emotional development* (pp. 51–78). Hoboken, NJ: John Wiley & Sons, Inc.

Li, C., Pentz, M. A., & Chou, C-P. (2002). Parental substance use as a modifier of adolescent substance use risk. *Addiction, 97,* 1537–1550.

Li, Y., Hu. X., Ma, W., Wu, J., & Ma, G. (2005). Body image perceptions among Chinese children and adolescents. *Body Image, 2,* 91–103.

Li-Grining, C. P. (2007). Effortful control among low-income preschoolers in three cities: Stability, change, and individual differences. *Developmental Psychology, 43,* 208–221.

Li-Grining, C.P., Votruba-Drzal, E., Maldonado-Carreño, C., & Haas, K. (2010). Children's early approaches to learning and academic trajectories through fifth grade. *Developmental Psychology, 46,* 1062–1077.

Lieberman, A. F., and Pawl, J. H. (1993). Infant-parent psychotherapy. In C. H. Zeanah (Ed.), *Handbook of infant mental health* (pp. 427–442). New York: Guilford Press.

Lieberman, A. F., Wieder, S., & Fenichel, E. (1997). *The DC: 0–3 casebook: A guide to the use of 0 to 3's diagnostic classification of mental health and developmental disorders of infancy and early childhood in assessment and treatment planning.* Washington, DC: National Center for Infants, Toddlers and Families.

Lieberman, A. F., & Zeanah, C. H. (1999). Contributions of attachment theory to infant-parent psychotherapy and other interventions with infants and young children. In J. Cassidy & P. R. Shaver (Eds.), *Handbook of attachment: Theory, research, and clinical applications* (pp. 555–574). New York: Guilford Press.

Lieberman, A.F., Chu, A., Van Horn, P., & Harris, W.W. (2011). Trauma in early childhood: Empirical evidence and clinical implications. *Development and Psychopathology, 23,* 397–410.

Lieberman, A.F., & Van Horn, P. (2009). Child-parent psychotherapy: A developmental approach to mental health treatment in infancy and early childhood. In C.H. Zeanah *Handbook of Infant Mental Health,*(3rd ed.) (pp. 439–449). New York: Guilford Press.

Liebowitz, M. R., & Ginsberg, D. L. (2005). Integrating neurobiology and psychopathology into evidence-based treatment of social anxiety disorder. *CNS Spectrums, 10,* 1–5.

Liese, B. S., & Franz, R. A. (1996). Treating substance use disorders with cognitive therapy: Lessons learned and implications for the future. In P. M. Salkovskis (Ed.), *Frontiers of cognitive therapy* (pp. 470–508). New York: Guilford Press.

Lilienfeld, S. O., Waldman, I. D., & Israel, A. C. (1994). A critical examination of the use of the term and concept of comorbidity in psychopathology research. *Clinical Psychology: Science and Practice, 1,* 71–83.

Lim, M., Stormshak, E. A., & Dishion, T. J. (2005). A one-session intervention for parents of young adolescents: Videotape modeling and motivational group discussion. *Journal of Emotional and Behavioral Disorders, 13,* 194–199.

Lindeman, M., & Stark, K. (2000). Loss of pleasure, ideological food choice reasons and eating pathology. *Appetite, 35,* 263–268.

Lipscomb, S.T., Leve, L.D., Harold, G.T., Neiderhiser, J.M., Shaw, D.S., Ge, X., & Reiss, D. (2011). Trajectories of parenting and child negative emotionality during infancy and toddlerhood: A longitudinal analysis. *Child Development, 82,* 1661–1675.

Little, T. D., Jones, S. M., Henrich, C. C., & Hawley, P. H. (2003). Disentangling the "whys" from the "whats" of aggressive behaviour. *International Journal of Behavioral Development, 27,* 122–133.

Littleton, H. L., & Ollendick, T. (2003). Negative body image and disordered eating behavior in children and adolescents: What places youth at risk and how can these problems be prevented? *Clinical Child and Family Psychology Review, 6,* 51–66.

Liu, R.T., Alloy, L.B., Abramson, L.Y., Iacoviello, B.M., & Whitehouse, W.G. (2009). Emotional maltreatment and depression: Prospective prediction of depressive episodes. *Depression and Anxiety, 26,* 174–181.

Lloyd-Richardson, E. E., Papandonatos, G., Kazura, A., Stanton, C., & Niaura, R. (2002). Differentiating stages of smoking intensity among adolescents: Stage-specific psychological and social influences. *Journal of Consulting and Clinical Psychology, 70,* 998–1009.

Lochman, J. E., Boxmeyer, C. L., Powell, N. P., Barry, T. D., & Pardini, D. A. (2010). Anger control training for aggressive youths. In J. R. Weisz & A. E. Kazdin (Eds.), *Evidence-Based Psychotherapies for Children and Adolescents* (2nd ed.) (pp. 227–242). New York: Guilford Press.

Lochman, J. E., & van den Steenhoven, A. (2002). Family-based approaches to substance abuse prevention. *Journal of Primary Prevention, 23,* 49–114.

Lock, J., & Le Grange, D. (2005). Family-based treatment of eating disorders. *International Journal of Eating Disorders, 37,* S64–S67.

Lock, J., Le Grange, D., Agras, W.S., Moye, A., Byrson, S.W., & Jo, B. (2010). Randomized clinical trial comparing family-based treatment with adolescent-focused individual therapy for adolescents with anorexia nervosa. *Archives of General Psychiatry, 67,* 1025–1032.

Lock, J., Walker, L. R., Rickert, V. I., & Katzman, D. K. (2005). Suicidality in adolescents being treated with antidepressant medications and the black box label: Position paper of the Society for Adolescent Medicine. *Journal of Adolescent Health, 36,* 92–93.

Lock, S., & Barrett, P. M. (2003). A longitudinal study of developmental differences in universal preventive intervention for child anxiety. *Behaviour Change, 20,* 183–199.

Loe, I.M., & Feldman, H.M. (2007). Academic and educational outcomes of children with ADHD. *Journal of Pediatric Psychology, 32,* 643–654.

Loeb, K.L., Lock, J., Grief, R., & le Grange, D. (2010). Transdiagnostic theory and application of family-based treatment for youth with eating disorders. *Cognitive and Behavioral Practice, 19,* 17–30.

Loeber, R., Burke, J. D., Lahey, B. B., Winters, A., & Zera, M. (2000). Oppositional defiant and conduct disorder: A review of the past 10 years, Part I. *Journal of the American Academy of Child and Adolescent Psychiatry, 39,* 1468–1484.

Loeber, R., Burke, J., & Pardini, D.A. (2009). Perspectives on oppositional defiant disorder, conduct disorder, and psychopathic features. *Journal of Child Psychology and Psychiatry, 50,* 133–142.

Loeber, R., & Farrington, D. P. (2000). Young children who commit crime: Epidemiology, developmental origins, risk factors, early interventions, and policy implications. *Development and Psychopathology, 12,* 737–762.

Loeber, R., & Farrington, D. P. (Eds.). (1998). *Serious and violent juvenile offenders: Risk factors and successful interventions.* Thousand Oaks, CA: Sage.

Lofthouse, N., & Fristad, M. A. (2004). Psychosocial interventions for children with early-onset bipolar spectrum disorder. *Clinical Child Family Psychology Review, 7,* 71–88.

Lonigan, C. J., Phillips, B. M., & Hooe, E. S. (2003). Relations of positive and negative affectivity to anxiety and depression in children: Evidence from a latent variable longitudinal study. *Journal of Consulting and Clinical Psychology, 71,* 465–481.

Lord, C. (1994). The complexity of social behaviour in autism. In S. Baron-Cohen & H. Tager-Glusberg (Eds.), *Understanding other minds: Perspectives from autism* (pp. 292–316). London: Oxford University Press.

Lord, C., & Magill-Evans, J. (1995). Peer interactions of autistic children and adolescents. *Development and Psychopathology, 7,* 611–626.

Lord, C., & Paul, R. (1997). Language and communication in autism. In D. Cohen & F. Volkmar (Eds.), *Handbook of autism and pervasive developmental disorders* (2nd ed., pp. 707–729). New York: Wiley.

Lord, C., & Pickles, A. (1996). Language level and nonverbal social-communicative behaviors in autistic and language-delayed children. *Journal of the American Academy of Child and Adolescent Psychiatry, 35,* 1542–1550.

Lord, C., Pickles, A., McLennan, J., Rutter, M., Bregman, J., Folstein, S., et al. (1997). Diagnosing autism: Analyses of data from the Autism Diagnostic Interview. *Journal of Autism and Developmental Disorders, 27,* 501–517.

Lord, C., & Risi, S. (2000). Diagnosis of autism spectrum disorders in young children. In A. M. Wetherby & B. M. Prizant (Eds.), *Communication and language intervention series: Vol. 9. Autism spectrum disorders: A transactional developmental perspective* (pp. 11–30). Baltimore: Paul H. Brookes Publishing.

Lord, C., Risi, S., Lambrecht, L., Cook, E. H., Levethal, B. L., DiLavore, P. C., et al. (2000). The autism diagnostic observation schedule—generic: A standard measure of social and communication deficits associated with the spectrum of autism. *Journal of Autism and Developmental Disorders, 30,* 205–223.

Lord, C., Rutter, M., & LeCouteur, A. (1994). Autism diagnostic interview—revised: A revised version of a diagnostic interview for caregivers of individuals with possible pervasive developmental disorders. *Journal of Autism and Developmental Disorders, 24,* 659–685.

Lord, C., & Volkmar, F. (2002). Genetics of childhood disorders:XLII. Autism, Part 1: Diagnosis and assessment in autistic spectrum disorders. (Development and Neurobiology). *Journal of the American Academy of Child and Adolescent Psychiatry, 41,* 1134–1136.

Losh, M., & Capps, L. (2006). Understanding of emotional experience in autism: Insights from the personal accounts of high-functioning children with autism. *Developmental Psychology, 42,* 809–818.

Lott, D. A. (1998). Eating disorders and the family: controversies and questions. *Psychiatric Times, 15* www.psychiatrictimes.com/p980952.html.

Loukas, A., Zucker, R. A., Fitzgerald, H. E., & Krull, J. L. (2003). Developmental trajectories of disruptive behavior problems among sons of alcoholics: Effects of parent psychopathology, family conflict, and child undercontrol. *Journal of Abnormal Psychology, 112,* 119–131.

Lovaas, O. I. (1987). Behavioral treatment and normal educational and intellectual functioning in young autistic children. *Journal of Consulting and Clinical Psychology, 55,* 3–9.

Lovaas, O. I. (1993). The development of a treatment-research project for developmentally disabled and autistic children. *Journal of Applied Behavior Analysis, 26,* 617–630.

Lovaas, O. I. (2003). *Teaching individuals with developmental delays: Basic intervention techniques.* Austin, TX: PRO-ED.

Lovaas, O. I., & Buch, G. (1997). Intensive behavioral intervention with young children with autism. In N. N. Singh (Ed.), *Prevention and treatment of severe behavior problems: Models and methods in developmental disabilities* (pp. 61–86). Belmont, CA: Thomson.

Lowell, D.I., Carter, A.S., Godoy, L., Paulicin, B., & Briggs-Gowan, M.J. (2011). A randomized controlled trial of Child FIRST: A comprehensive home-based intervention translating research into early childhood practice. *Child Development, 82,* 193–208.

Lowenthal, B. (1999). Early childhood inclusion in the United States. *Early Childhood Development and Care, 150,* 17–32.

Loxton, N. J., & Dawe, S. (2006). Reward and punishment sensitivity in dysfunctional eating and hazardous drinking women: Associations with family risk. *Appetite, 47,* 361–371.

Lubell, K. M., & Vetter, J. B. (2006). Suicide and youth violence prevention: The promise of an integrated approach. *Aggression and Violent Behavior, 11,* 167–175.

Luby, J. L. (2000). Depression. In C. H. Zeanah (Ed.), *Handbook of infant mental health* (2nd ed., pp. 382–396). New York: Guilford Press.

Luby, J. L., Heffelfinger, A., Koenig-McNaught, A. L., Brown, K., & Spitznagel, E. (2004). The preschool feelings checklist: A brief and sensitive screening measure for depression in young children. *Journal of the American Academy of Child Adolescent Psychiatry, 43,* 708–717.

Luby, J., Todd, R. D., & Geller, B. (1996). Outcome of depressive syndromes: Infancy to adolescence. In K. I. Shulman & M. Tohen et al. (Eds.), *Mood disorders across the life span* (pp. 83–100). New York: Wiley-Liss.

Luby, J.L., Navsaria, N. (2010). Pediatric bipolar disorder: evidence for prodromal states and early markers. *Journal of Child Psychology and Psychiatry, 51,* 459–471.

Luckasson, R., & Reeve, A. (2001). Naming, defining, and classifying in mental retardation. *Mental Retardation, 39,* 47–52.

Luckasson, R., Schalock, R. L., Snell, M. E., & Spitalnik, D. M. (1996). The 1992 AAMR definition and preschool children: Response from the Committee on Terminology and Classification. *Mental Retardation, 34*, 247–253.

Luecken, L. J., & Lemery, K. S. (2004). Early caregiving and physiological stress responses. *Clinical Psychology Review, 24*, 171–191.

Lumley, V. A., & Scotti, J. R. (2001). Supporting the sexuality of adults with mental retardation: Current status and future directions. *Journal of Positive Behavior Interventions, 3*, 109–119.

Luna, B., Doll, S. K., Hegedus, S. J., Minshew, N. J., & Sweeney, J. A. (2007). Maturation of executive function in autism. *Biological Psychiatry, 61*, 474–481.

Luna, B., & Sweeney, J. A. (2004). Cognitive development: Functional magnetic resonance imaging studies. In M. S. Keshavan, J. L. Kennedy, & R. M. Murray (Eds.), *Neurodevelopment and schizophrenia* (pp. 45–68). New York: Cambridge University Press.

Lundström, S., Haworth, C.M.A., Carlström, E., Gillberg, C., Mill, J., Råstam, M., … Richenberg, A. (2010). Trajectories leading to autism spectrum disorders are affected by paternal age: findings from two nationally representative twin studies. *Journal of Child Psychology and Psychiatry, 51*, 850–856.

Lunsky, Y., & Konstantareas, M. M. (1998). The attitudes of individuals with autism and mental retardation towards sexuality. *Education and Training in Mental Retardation and Developmental Disabilities, 33*, 24–33.

Lupien, S.J., McEwen, B.S., Gunnar, M.R., & Heim, C. (2009). Effects of stress throughout the lifespan on the brain, behavior and cognition. *Nature, 10*, 434–445.

Lustig, D. C. (2002). Family coping in families with a child with a disability. *Education and Training in Mental Retardation and Developmental Disabilities, 27*, 14–22.

Lustig, D. C., & Strauser, D. R. (2002). An empirical typology of career thoughts of individuals with disabilities. *Rehabilitation Counseling Bulletin, 46*, 98–107.

Luthar, S. S., Cicchetti, D., & Becker, B. (2000). The construct of resilience: A critical evaluation and guidelines for future work. *Child Development, 71*, 543–562.

Luyster, R., Richler, J., Risi, S., Hsu, W., Dawson, G., Bernier, R., et al. (2005). Early regression in social communication in autism spectrum disorders: A CPA study. *Developmental Neuropsychology, 27*, 311–336.

Lynam, D. R., Caspi, A., Moffitt, T. E., Raine, A., Loeber, R., & Stouthamer-Loeber, M. (2005). Adolescent psychopathy and the Big Five: Results from two samples. *Journal of Abnormal Child Psychology, 33*, 431–443.

Lynam, D. R., Caspi, A., Moffitt, T. E., Wikstroem, P., Loeber, R., & Novak, S. (2000). The interaction between impulsivity and neighborhood context on offending: The effects of impulsivity are stronger in poorer neighborhoods. *Journal of Abnormal Psychology, 109*, 563–574.

Lynam, D. R., & Gudonis, L. (2005). The development of psychopathy. *Annual Review of Clinical Psychology, 1*, 381–407.

Lynch, M., & Cicchetti, D. (1998). Trauma, mental representation, and the organization of memory for mother-referent material. *Development and Psychopathology, 10*, 739–759.

Lynch, M., & Cicchetti, D. (1998). An ecological-transactional analysis of children and contents: The longitudinal interplay among child maltreatment, community violence, and children's symptomatology. *Development and Psychopathology, 10*, 235–257.

Lynch, W. C., & Eppers-Reynolds, K. (2005) Children's Eating Attitudes Test: Revised factor structure for adolescent girls. *Eating and Weight Disorders, 10*, 222–235.

Lynne-Landsman, S.D., Bradshaw, C.P., & Ialongo, N.S. (2010). Testing a developmental cascade model of adolescent substance use trajectories and young adult adjustment. *Development and Psychopathology, 22,* 933–948.

Lyons, M. J., Bar, J. L., Panizzon, M. S., Toomey, R., Eisen, S., Xian, H., et al. (2004). Neuropsychological consequences of regular marijuana use: A twin study. *Psychological Medicine, 34*, 1239–1250.

Lyons-Ruth, K. (1995). Broadening our conceptual frameworks: Can we reintroduce relational strategies and implicit representational systems to the study of psychopathology? *Developmental Psychology, 31*, 432–436.

Lyons-Ruth, K., Lyubchik, A., Wolfe, R., & Bronfman, E. (2002). Parental depression and child attachment: Hostile and helpless profiles of parent and child behavior among families at risk. In S. H. Goodman & I. H. Gotlib (Eds.), *Children of depressed parents: Mechanisms of risk and implications for treatment* (pp. 89–120). Washington, DC: American Psychological Association.

Lyons-Ruth, K., Wolfe, R., & Lyubchik, A. (2000). Depression and the parenting of young children: Making the case for early preventive mental health services. *Harvard Review of Psychiatry, 8*, 148–153.

Lyons-Ruth, K., Yellin, C., Melnick, S., & Atwood, G. (2005). Expanding the concept of unresolved mental states: Hostile/helpless states of mind on the adult attachment interview are associated with disrupted mother-infant communication and infant disorganization. *Development and Psychopathology, 17*, 1–23.

Lyons-Ruth, K., & Zeanah, C. H. (1993). The family context of infant mental health: I. Affective development in the primary caregiving relationship. In C. H. Zeanah, Jr. (Ed.), *Handbook of infant mental health* (pp. 14–37). New York: Guilford Press.

Ma, G. X., Toubbeh, J., Cline, J., & Chisholm, A. (1998a). Fetal alcohol syndrome among Native American adolescents: A model prevention program. *Journal of Primary Prevention, 19*, 43–55.

Ma, G. X., Toubbeh, J., Cline, J., & Chisholm, A. (1998b). The use of a qualitative approach in fetal alcohol syndrome prevention among American Indian youth. *Journal of Alcohol and Drug Education, 43*, 53–65.

Ma, G. X., Toubbeh, J., Cline, J., & Chisholm, A. (2002). A model for fetal alcohol syndrome prevention in Native American population. In G. Xuequin Ma & G. Henderson (Eds.), *Ethnicity and substance abuse: Prevention and intervention* (pp. 284–295). Springfield, IL: Charles C. Thomas.

MacDonald, M. (2000). Bewildered, blamed and broken-hearted: Parents' views of anorexia nervosa. In B. Lask (Ed.), *Anorexia nervosa and related eating disorders in childhood and adolescence* (pp. 11–24). Hove, England: Psychology Press/Taylor & Francis.

MacDonald, V. M., Tsiantis, J., Achenbach, T. M., Motti-Stefanidi, F., & Richardson, S. C. (1995). Competencies and problems reported by parents of Greek and American children, ages 6–11. *European Child and Adolescent Psychiatry, 4*, 1–13.

Macgowan, M. J. (2004). Psychosocial treatment of youth suicide: A systematic review of the research. *Research on Social Work Practice, 14*, 147–162.

Macgowen, M. J., & Wagner, E. F. (2005). Iatrogenic effects of group treatment on adolescents with conduct and substance use problems: A review of the literature and a presentation of a model. In C. Hilarski (Ed.), *Addiction, assessment, and treatment with adolescents, adults, and families* (pp. 79–90). Binghamton, NY: Haworth Social Work Practice Press.

Mackintosh, V. H., Myers, B. J., & Goin-Kochel, R. P. (2006). Sources of information and support used by parents of children with autism spectrum disorders. *Journal on Developmental Disabilities, 12*, 41–52.

MacLean, K. (2003). The impact of institutionalization on child development. *Development and Psychopathology, 15*, 853–884.

MacMaster, S. A., Holleran, L. K., & Chaffin, K. (2005). Empirical and theoretical support for the inclusion of non-abstinence-based perspectives in prevention services for substance using adolescents. In C. Hilarski (Ed.), *Addiction, assessment, and treatment with adolescents, adults, and families* (pp. 91– 111). Binghamton, NY: Haworth Social Work Practice Press.

Madsen, K. M., Hviid, A., Vestergaard, M., Schendel, D., Wohlfahrt, J., Thorsen, P., et al. (2002). A population-based study of measles, mumps, and rubella vaccination and autism. *New England Journal of Medicine, 347*, 1477–1482.

Madsen, K. M., Lauritsen, M. B., Pedersen, C. B., Thorsen, P., Plesner, A. M., Andersen, P. H., et al. (2003). Thimerosal and the occurrence of autism: Negative ecological evidence from Danish population-based data. *Pediatrics, 112*, 604–606.

Maestro, S., Muratori, F., Cesari, A., Pecini, C., Apicella, F., & Stern, D. (2006). A view to regressive autism through home movies. Is early development really normal? *Acta Psychiatrica Scandinavica, 113*, 68–72.

Magai, C. (1999). Affect, imagery, and attachment: Working models of interpersonal affect and the socialization of emotion. In J. Cassidy & P. R. Shaver (Eds.), *Handbook of attachment: Theory, research, and clinical applications* (pp. 787–802). New York: Guilford Press.

Maggs, J. L., & Schulenberg, J. E. (2004–2005). Trajectories of alcohol use during the transition to adulthood. *Alcohol Research and Health, 28*, 195–201.

Maggs, J. L., & Schulenberg, J. E. (2005). Initiation and course of alcohol consumption among adolescents and young adults. *Recent Developments in Alcoholism, 17*, 29-47.

Maguire, J., & Philadelphia Child Guidance Center. (1993). *Your child's emotional health: The middle years.* New York: Macmillan.

Magus, K.B., Cowen, E.L., Wyman, P.A., Fagen, D.B. & Work, W.C. (1999). Correlates of resilient outcomes among highly stressed African-American and White urban children. *Journal of Community Psychology, 27*, 473–488.

Maia, T.V., Cooney, R.E., & Peterson, B.S. (2008). The neural bases of obsessive-compulsive disorder in children and adults. *Development and Psychopathology, 20*, 1251–1283.

Main, M. (1996). Introduction to the special section on attachment and psychopathology: 2. Overview of the field of attachment. *Journal of Consulting and Clinical Psychology, 64*, 237–243.

Main, M., & Hesse, E. (1990). Parents' unresolved traumatic experiences are related to infant disorganized attachment status: Is frightened and/or frightening parental behavior the linking mechanism? In M. T. Greenberg, D. Cicchetti, & E. M. Cummings (Eds.), *Attachment in the preschool years: Theory, research, and intervention* (pp. 161–182). Chicago: University of Chicago Press.

Main, M., Kaplan, N., & Cassidy, J. (1985). Security in infancy, childhood, and adulthood: A move to the level of representation. *Monographs of the Society for Research in Child Development, 50*, 66–104.

Malloy, L.C., Brubacher, S.P., & Lamb, M.E. (2011). Expected consequences of disclosure revealed in investigative interviews with suspected victims of child sexual abuse. *Applied Developmental Science, 15,* 8–19.

Malone, R.P. (2000). Assessment and treatment of abnormal aggression in children and adolescents. In M. L. Cronwer (Ed.), *Understanding and Treating Violent Psychiatric Patients* (pp. 21–47). Washington, D.C.: American Psychiatric Association.

Malone, S. M., Iacono, W. G., & McGue, M. (2002). Drinks of the father: Father's maximum number of drinks consumed predicts externalizing disorders, substance use, and substance use disorders in preadolescent and adolescent offspring. *Alcoholism: Clinical and Experimental Research, 26*, 1823–1832.

Malone, S. M., Taylor, J., Marmorstein, N. R., McGue, M., & Iacono, W. G. (2004). Genetic and environmental infl uences on antisocial behavior and alcohol dependence from adolescence to early adulthood. *Development and Psychopathology, 16*, 943–966.

Manassis, K., Hudson, J.L., Webb, A. & Albano, A.M. (2004). Beyond behavioral inhibition: Etiological factors in childhood anxiety. *Cognitive and Behavioral Practice, 11*, 3–12.

Mancini, C., Van Ameringen, M., Bennett, M., Patterson, B., & Watson, C. (2005). Emerging treatments for child and adolescent social phobia: A review. *Journal of Child and Adolescent Psychopharmacology, 15*, 589–607.

Mandy, W.P.L., Charman, T., Skuse, D.H. (2012). Testing the construct validity of proposed criteria for *DSM-5* autism spectrum disorder. *Journal of the American Academy of Child & Adolescent Psychiatry, 51*, 41–50.

Mangione, P. L., & Speth, T. (1998). The transition to elementary school: A framework for creating early childhood continuity through home, school, and community partnerships. *The Elementary School Journal, 98*, 381–397.

Maniadaki, K, Sonuga-Barke, E., Kakouros, E., & Karaba, R. (2007). Parental beliefs about the nature of ADHD behaviors and their relationship to referral intentions in preschool children. *Child: Care, Health and Development, 33*, 188–195.

Manley, J., & Chavez, D. (2008). Child maltreatment parental assessments. In H.V. Hall (ed.) *Forensic Psychology and neuropsychology for criminal and civil cases* (pp. 621–646). Boca Raton, FL: CRC Press.

Mannering, A.M., Harold, G.T., Leve, L.D., Shelton, K.H., Shaw, D.S., Conger, R.D., ... Reiss, D. (2011). Longitudinal associations between marital instability and child sleep problems across infancy and toddlerhood in adoptive families. *Child Development, 82,* 1252–1266.

Mannuzza, S., Klein, R. G., Abikoff, H., & Moulton, J. L. (2004). Significance of childhood conduct problems to later development of conduct disorder among children with ADHD: A prospective follow-up study. *Journal of Abnormal Child Psychology, 32*, 565–573.

Mannuzza, S., Klein, R. G., Bessler, A., Malloy, P., & LaPadula, M. (1998). Adult psychiatric status of hyperactive boys grown up. *American Journal of Psychiatry, 155*, 493–498.

Mannuzza, S., Klein, R. G., & Moulton, J. L. (2003b). Persistence of attention-deficit/hyperactivity disorder into adulthood: What have we learned from the prospective follow-up studies? *Journal of Attention Disorders, 7,* 93–100.

Marcell, M. M., & Jett, D. A. (1985). Identification of vocally expressed emotions by mentally retarded and nonretarded individuals. *American Journal of Mental Deficiency, 89,* 537–545.

March, J., Silva, S., Petrycki, S., Curry, J., Wells, K., Fairanks, J., et al. (2004). Fluoxine, cognitive, behavioral therapy, and their combination for adolescents with depression: Treatment for Adolescents with Depression Study (TADS) randomized controlled trial. *Journal of the American Medical Association, 292,* 807–820.

March, J., Silva, S., & Vitiello, B. (2006). The Treatment for Adolescents with Depression Study (TADS): Methods and message at 12 weeks. *Journal of the American Academy of Child and Adolescent Psychiatry, 45,* 1393–1403.

March, J.S. (2009). The future of psychotherapy for mentally ill children and adolescents. *Journal of child Psychology and Psychiatry, 50,* 170–179.

March, J.S., Entusah, A.R., Rynn, M., Albano, A.M. & Tourian, K.A. (2007). A randomized controlled trial of venlafaxine ER versus placebo in pediatric social anxiety disorder. *Biological Psychiatry, 62,* 1149–1154.

Marcus, D.K., & Barry, T.D. (2011). Does attention-deficit/hyperactivity disorder have a dimensional latent structure? A taxometric analysis. *Journal of Abnormal Psychology, 120,* 427–442.

Margolin, G., & Vickerman, K. A. (2007). Posttraumatic stress in children and adolescents exposed to family violence: I. Overview and issues. *Professional Psychology: Research and Practice, 38,* 613–619.

Margolin, G., & Vickerman, K.A. (2011). Posttraumatic stress in children and adolescents exposed to family violence: I. Overview and issues. *Couple and Family Psychology: Research and Practice, 1,* 63–73.

Markey, C. N. (2004). Culture and the development of eating disorders: A tripartite model. *Eating Disorders: The Journal of Treatment and Prevention, 12,* 139–156.

Markowitz, S., Chatterji, P., & Kaestner, R. (2003). Estimating the impact of alcohol policies on youth suicides. *Journal of Mental Health Policy and Economics, 6,* 37–46.

Marks, A.K., & Coll, C.G. (2007). Psychological and demographic correlates of early academic skill development among American Indian and Alaska Native youth: A growth modeling study. *Developmental Psychology, 43,* 663–674.

Marmorstein, N. R., & Iacono, W. G. (2004). Major depression and conduct disorder in youth: Associations with parental psychopathology and parent-child conflict. *Journal of Child Psychology and Psychiatry, 45,* 377.

Mars, A. E., Mauk, J. E., & Dowrick, P. (1998). Symptoms of pervasive developmental disorders as observed in prediagnostic home videos of infants and toddlers. *Journal of Pediatrics, 132,* 500–504.

Marshall, M. F., Menikoff, J., & Paltrow, L. M. (2003). Perinatal substance abuse and human subjects research: Are privacy protections adequate? *Mental Retardation and Developmental Disabilities Research Reviews, 9,* 54–59.

Martel, M.M., Gremillion, M., Roberts, B., von Eye, A., & Nigg, J.T. (2010). The structure of childhood disruptive behaviors. *Psychological Assessment, 22,* 816–826.

Martin, A., Patzer, D. K., & Volkmar, F. R. (2000). Psychopharmacological treatment of higher-functioning pervasive developmental disorders. In A. Klin, F. R. Volkmar, & S. S. Sparrow (Eds.), *Asperger syndrome* (pp. 210–228). New York: Guilford Press.

Martin, G. C., Wertheim, E. H., Prior, M., Smart, D., Sanson, A., & Oberklaid, F. (2000). A longitudinal study of the role of childhood temperament in the later development of eating concerns. *International Journal of Eating Disorders, 27,* 150–162.

Martin, J. K., Pescosolido, B. A., Olafsdottir, S., & Mcleod, J. D. (2007). The construction of fear: Americans' preferences for social distance from children and adolescents with mental health problems. *Journal of Health and Social Behavior, 48,* 50–67.

Martin, M.J., Conger, R.D., Schofield, T.J., Dogan, S.J., Widaman, K.F., Donnellan, M.B., & Neppl, T.K. (2010). Evaluation of the interactionist model of socioeconomic status and problem behavior: A developmental cascade across generations. *Development and Psychopathology, 22,* 695–713.

Marvin, R. S., & Pianta, R. C. (1996). Mothers' reactions to their child's diagnosis: Relations with security of attachment. *Journal of Clinical Child Psychology, 25,* 436–445.

Mash, E. J., & Dozois, D. J. A. (1996). Child psychopathology: A developmental-systems perspective. In E. J. Mash & R. A. Barkley (Eds.), *Child psychopathology* (pp. 3–60). New York: Guilford Press.

Mash, E. J., & Hunsley, J. (2005). Evidence-based assessment of child and adolescent disorders: Issues and challenges. *Journal of Clinical Child and Adolescent Psychology, 34,* 362–379.

Mashburn, A.J., Pianta, R.C. (2006). Social relationships and school readiness. *Early Education and Development, 17,* 151–176.

Masi, G., Millepiedi, S., Mucci, M., Pascale, R. R., Perugi, G., & Akiskal, H. S. (2003). Phenomenology and comorbidity of dysthmic disorder in 100 consecutively referred children and adolescents: Beyond DSM-IV. *Canadian Journal of Psychiatry, 48,* 99–105.

Masi, G., Perugi, G., Toni, C., Millepiedi, S., Mucci, M., Bertini, N., & Akiskal, H. S. (2004). Obsessive-compulsive bipolar comorbidity: Focus on children and adolescents. *Journal of Affective Disorders, 78,* 175–183.

Masi, G., Toni, C., Perugi, G., Travierso, M. C., Millepiedi, S., Mucci, M., et al. (2003). Externalizing disorders in consecutively referred children and adolescents with bipolar disorder. *Comprehensive Psychiatry, 44,* 184–189.

Masia-Warner, C., Klein, R. G., Dent, H. C., Fisher, P. H., Alvir, J., Albano, A. M., et al. (2005). School-based intervention for adolescents with social anxiety disorder: Results of a controlled study. *Journal of Abnormal Child Psychology, 33,* 707–722.

Mason, W. A., Kosterman, R., Hawkins, J. D., Haggerty, K. P., & Spoth, R. L. (2003). Reducing adolescents' growth in substance use and delinquency: Randomized trial effects of a parent-training prevention intervention. *Prevention Science, 4,* 203–212.

Masten, A. S. (2001). Ordinary magic: Resilience processes in development. *American Psychologist, 56,* 227–238.

Masten, A. S. (2004). Regulatory processes, risk, and resilience in adolescent development. In R. E. Dahl & L. P. Spear (Eds.), *Adolescent brain development: Vulnerabilities and opportunities. Annals of the New York Academy of Sciences* (Vol. 1021, pp. 310–319). New York: New York Academy of Sciences.

Masten, A. S., Best, K. M., & Garmezy, N. (1990). Resilience and development: Contributions from the study of children who overcome adversity. *Development and Psychopathology, 2*, 425–444.

Masten, A. S., & Coatsworth, J. D. (1995). Competence, resilience, and psychopathology. In D. Cicchetti & D. J. Cohen (Eds.), *Developmental psychopathology: Vol. 2. Risk, disorder, and adaptation* (pp. 715–752). Oxford, England: Wiley.

Masten, A. S., & Coatsworth, J. D. (1998). The development of competence in favorable and unfavorable environments. *American Psychologist, 53*, 205–220.

Masten, A. S., Coatsworth, J. D., Neemann, J., Gest, S. D., Tellegen, A., & Garmezy, N. (1995). The structure and coherence of competence from childhood through adolescence. *Child Development, 66*, 1635–1659.

Masten, A. S., Hubbard, J. J., Gest, S. D., Tellegen, A., Garmezy, M., & Ramirez, M. (1999). Competence in the context of adversity: Pathways to resilience and maladaptation from childhood to late adolescence. *Development and Psychopathology, 11*, 143–169.

Masten, A. S., Morison, P., Pellegrini, D., & Tellegen, A. (1990). Competence under stress: Risk and protective factors. In J. E. Rolf & A. S. Masten (Eds.), *Risk and protective factors in the development of psychopathology* (pp. 236–256). New York: Cambridge University Press.

Masten, A. S., & Reed, M-G. J. (2002). Resilience in development. In C. R. Snyder & S. J. Lopez (Eds.), *Handbook of Positive Psychology* (pp. 74–88). New York: Oxford University Press.

Masten, A.S. (2011). Resilience in children threatened by extreme adversity: Frameworks for research, practice, and translational synergy. *Development and Psychopathology, 23*, 493–506.

Masten, A.S., & Cicchetti, D. (2010). Developmental cascades. *Development and Psychopathology, 22*, 491–495.

Masten, A.S., Faden, V.B., Zucker, R.A., & Spear, L.P. (2008). Underage drinking: A developmental framework. *Pediatrics, 121*, S235–S251.

Masten, A.S., & Narayan, A.J. (2012). Child development in the context of disaster, war, and terrorism: Pathways of risk and resilience. *Annual Review of psychology, 63*, 227–257.

Masten, A.S., & Obradovié, J. (2008). Disaster preparation and recovery: lessons from research on resilience in human development. *Ecology and Society, 13* http://ecologyandsociety.org/vol13/iss1/art9/.

Matson, J. L., Bamburg, J. W., Mayville, E. A., Pinkston, J., Bielecki, J., Kuhn, D., et al. (2000). Psychopharmacology and mental retardation: A 10 year review. *Research in Developmental Disabilities, 21*, 263–296.

Matson, J. L., & Smiroldo, B. B. (1999). Intellectual disorders. In W. K. Silverman & T. H. Ollendick (Eds.), *Developmental issues in the clinical treatment of children* (pp. 295–306). Needham Heights, MA: Allyn & Bacon.

Mattila, M., Kielinen, M., Linna, S., Jussila, K., Ebeling, H., Bloigu, R., … Moilanen, I. (2011). Autism spectrum disorders according to DSM-IV-TR and comparison with DSM-5 draft criteria: An epidemiological study. *Journal of the American Academy of Child & Adolescent Psychiatry, 50*, 583–592.

Mattison, R. E., Gadow, K. D., Sprafkin, J., & Nolan, E. E. (2002). Discriminant validity of a DSM-IV-based teacher checklist: Comparison of regular and special education students. *Behavioral Disorders, 27*, 304–316.

Mattison, R.E., & Mayes, S.D. (2012). Relationships between learning disability, executive function and psychopathology in Children with ADHD. *Journal of Attention Deficit Disorders, 16*, 138–146.

Matts, L., & Zionts, P. (1997). Implementing inclusion in a middle school setting. In P. Zionts (Ed.), *Inclusion strategies for students with learning and Behavioral Problems: Perspectives, experiences, and best practices,* (pp. 83–100). Austin, TX: PRO-ED.

Maughan, B., Iervolino, A. C., & Collishaw, S. Time trends in child and adolescent mental disorders. *Current Opinion in Psychiatry, 18*, 381–385.

Maughan, B., Rowe, R., Messer, J., Goodman, R., & Meltzer, H. (2004). Conduct disorder and oppositional defiant disorder in a national sample: Developmental epidemiology. *Journal of Child Psychology and Psychiatry, 45*, 609–621.

Maulik, P.K., Mascarenhas, M.N., Mathers, C.D., Dua, T., & Saxena, S. (2011). Prevalence of intellectual disability: A meta-analysis of population-based studies. *Research in Developmental Disabilities, 32*, 419–436.

Mawhood, L., Howlin, P., & Rutter, M. (2000). Autism and developmental receptive language disorder—A comparative follow-up in early adult life. I: Cognitive and language outcomes. *Journal of Child Psychology and Psychiatry and Allied Disciplines, 41*, 547–559.

Mayes, L. C., & Bornstein, M. H. (1996). The context of development for young children from cocaine-abusing families. In P. M. Kato & T. Mann (Eds.), *Handbook of diversity issues in health psychology. The Plenum series in culture and health* (pp. 69–95). New York: Plenum Press.

Mayes, R., Bagwell, C., & Erkulwater, J. (2008). ADHD and the rise in stimulant use among children. Harvard Review of Psychiatry, *16*, 151–166.

Mayes, S.D., & Calhoun, S.L. (2004). Frequency of reading, math, and writing disabilities in children with clinical disorders. *Learning and Individual Differences, 16*, 145–157.

Mayes, S.D., Calhoun, S.L., Aggarwal, R., Baker, C., Mathapati, S., Anderson, R., & Petersen, C. (2011). Explosive, oppositional, and aggressive behavior in children with autism compared to other clinical disorders and typical children. *Research in Autism Spectrum Disorders, 6*, 1–10.

Mazefsky, C.A., Pelphrey, K.A., & Dahl, R.E. (2012). The need for a broader approach to emotion regulation research in autism. *Child Development Perspectives, 6*, 92–97.

McArthur, L. H., Holbert, D., & Pena, M. An exploration of the attitudinal and perceptual dimensions of body image among male and female adolescents from six Latin American cities. *Adolescence, 40*, 801–813.

McCabe, L. A., & Brooks-Gunn, J. (2007). With a little help from my friends? Self-regulation in groups of young children. *Infant Mental Health, 28*, 584–605.

McCabe, M. P., & Ricciardelli, L. A. (2004a). A longitudinal study of pubertal timing and extreme body change behaviors among adolescent boys and girls. *Adolescence, 39*, 145–166.

McCabe, M. P., & Ricciardelli, L. A. (2004b). Body image dissatisfaction among males across the lifespan: A review of past literature. *Journal of Psychosomatic Research, 56*, 675–685.

McCall, J. N. (1999). Research on the psychological effects of orphanage care: A critical review. In R. B. McKenzie (Ed.), *Rethinking orphanages for the 21st century* (pp. 127–150). Thousand Oaks, CA: Sage.

McCarthy, D. M., Tomlinson, K. L., Anderson, K. G., Marlatt, G. A., & Brown, S. A. (2005). Relapse in alcohol- and drug-disordered adolescents with comorbid psychopathology: Changes in psychiatric symptoms. *Psychology of Addictive Behaviors, 19*, 28–34.

McCarty, C. A., Weisz, J. R., Wanitromanee, K., Eastman, K. L., Suwanlert, S., Chaiyasit, W., et al. (1999). Culture, coping, and context: Primary and secondary control among Thai and American youth. *Journal of Child Psychology and Psychiatry and Allied Disciplines, 40,* 809–818.

McCaughan, J. A., Carlson, R. G., Falck, R. S., & Siegel,H. A. (2005). From "candy kids" to "chemi-kids": A typology of young adults who attend raves in the midwestern United States. *Substance Use and Misuse, 40,* 1503–1523.

McCauley, E., Pavidis, K., & Kendall, K. (2001). Developmental precursors of depression. In I. Goodyer (Ed.), *The depressed child and adolescent: Developmental and clinical perspectives* (pp. 46–78). New York: Cambridge University Press.

McCleery, J.P., Allman, E., Carver, L.J., & Dobkins, K.R. (2007). Abnormal magnocellular pathway visual processing in infants at risk for autism. *Biological Psychiatry Special Issue: Autism and attention deficit hyperactivity disorder, 62,* 1007–1014.

McClellan, J. M., & Werry, J. S. (2000). Research psychiatric diagnostic interviews for children and adolescents. *Journal of the American Academy of Child and Adolescent Psychiatry, 39,* 19–99.

McClellan, J., McCurry, C., Ronnei, M., & Adams, J. (1997). Relationship between sexual abuse, gender, and sexually inappropriate behaviors in seriously mentally ill youths. *Journal of the American Academy of Child and Adolescent Psychiatry, 36,* 959–965.

McClelland, M. M., Cameron, C. E., Connor, C. M., Farris, C. L., Jewkes, A. M., & Morrison, F. J. (2007). Links between behavioral regulation and preschoolers' literacy, vocabulary, and math skills. *Developmental Psychology, 43,* 947–959.

McClure, E. G., Connell, A. M., Zucker, M., Griffith, J. R., & Kaslow, N. J. (2005). The Adolescent Depression Empowerment Project (ADEPT): A culturally sensitive family treatment for African American girls. In E. D. Hibbs & P. S. Jensen (Eds.), *Psychosocial treatments for child and adolescent disorders: Empirically based strategies for clinical practice* (2nd ed., pp. 149–164). Washington, DC: American Psychological Association.

McClure, E.B., Kubiszyn, T. & Kaslow, N.J. (2002). Advances in the diagnosis and treatment of childhood disorders. *Professional Psychology: Research and Practice, 33,* 125–134.

McConatha, J. T., & Huba, H. M. (1999). Primary, secondary, and emotional control across adulthood. *Current Psychology, 18,* 164–170.

McConaughy, S. H., & Achenbach, T. M. (1994). Comorbidity of empirically based syndromes in matched general population and clinical samples. *Journal of Child Psychology and Psychiatry and Allied Disciplines, 35,* 1141–1157.

McConkey, R., & Ryan, D. (2001). Experiences of staff in dealing with client sexuality in services for teenagers and adults with intellectual disability. *Journal of Intellectual Disability Research, 45,* 83–87.

McCracken, J. T., Walkup, J. T., & Koplewicz, H. S. (2002). Childhood and early-onset anxiety: Treatment and biomarker studies. *Journal of Clinical Psychiatry, 63,* 8–11.

McDonough, S.C. (1993). Interaction guidance: Understanding and treating early infant-caregiver relationship disturbances. In C. H. Zeanah (Ed.), *Handbook of Infant Mental Health* (pp. 414–126). New York: NY: Guilford Press.

McDougle, C. J. (1997). Psychopharmacology. In D. J. Cohen & F. R. Volkmar (Eds.), *Handbook of autism and pervasive developmental disorders* (2nd ed., pp. 707–729). New York: Wiley.

McElroy, S. L., Kotwal, R., Keck, P. E., & Akiskal, H. S. (2005). Comorbidity of bipolar and eating disorders: Distinct or related disorders with shared dysregulations? *Journal of Affective Disorders, 86,* 107–127.

McEwan, B.S. (2007). Physiology and neurobiology of stress and adaptation: Central role of the brain. *Psychological Review, 87,* 873–904.

McGee, R., Prior, M., Williams, S., Smart, D., & Sanson, A. (2002). The long-term significance of teacher-rated hyperactivity and reading ability in childhood: Findings from two longitudinal studies. *Journal of Child Psychology and Psychiatry and Applied Disciplines, 43,* 1004–1016.

McGilley, B. H. (2006). Group therapy for adolescents with eating disorders. *Group, 30,* 321–336.

McGough, J. J., & Barkley, R. A. (2004). Diagnostic controversies in adult attention deficit hyperactivity disorder. *American Journal of Psychiatry, 161,* 1948–1956.

McGue, M., Elkins, I., Walden, B., & Iacono, W. G. (2005). Perceptions of the parent-adolescent relationship: A longitudinal investigation. *Developmental Psychology, 41,* 971–984.

McGue, M., Elkins, I., Walden, B., & Iacono, W.G. (2005). Perceptions of the parent-adolescent relationship: A longitudinal investigation. *Developmental Psychology, 41,* 971–984.

McGue, M., & Iacono, W. G. (2004). The initiation of substance use in adolescence: A behavioral genetics perspective. In L. F. DiLalla (Ed.), *Behavior genetics principles: Perspectives in development, personality, and psychopathology. Decade of behavior* (pp. 41–57). Washington, DC: American Psychological Association.

McGuffin, P. (2004). Behavioral genomics: Where molecular genetics is taking psychiatry and psychology. In L. F. DiLalla (Ed.), *Behavior genetics principles: Perspectives in development, personality, and psychopathology. Decade of behavior* (pp. 191–204). Washington, DC: American Psychological Association.

McGuffin, P., Riley, B., & Plomin, R. (2001). Toward behavioral genomics. *Science, 291,* 1232–1249.

McGuire, S., & Shanahan, L. (2010). Sibling experiences in diverse family contexts. *Child Development Perspectives, 4,* 72–79.

McIntosh, V. V.W., Jordan, J., Carter, F. A., Luty, S. E., McKenzie, J. M., Bulik, C. M., et al. (2005). Three psychotherapies for anorexia nervosa: A randomized, controlled trial. *American Journal of Psychology, 162,* 741–747.

McKay, D., Piacentini, J., Greisberg, J., Graae, F., Jaffer, M., & Miller, J. (2006). The structure of childhood obsessions and compulsions: Dimensions in an outpatient sample. *Behavior Research and Therapy, 44,* 137–146.

McLaughlin, K. A., Hilt, L. M., & Nolen-Hoeksema, S. (2007). Racial/ethnic differences in internalizing and externalizing symptoms in adolescents. *Journal of Abnormal Child Psychology, 35,* 801–816.

McLaughlin, K.A., Zeanah, C.H., Fox, N.A., & Nelson, C.A. (2012). Attachment security as a mechanism linking foster care placement to improved mental health outcomes in previously institutionalized children. *Journal of Child Psychology and Psychiatry, 53,* 46–55.

McLean, K., & Pasupathi, M. (2010). *Narrative Development in Adolescence: Creating the storied self.* New York: Springer Science & Business Media.

McMahon, R. J., & Frick, P. J. (2005). Evidence-based assessment of conduct problems in children and adolescents. *Journal of Clinical Child and Adolescent Psychology, 34,* 477–505.

McMahon, R.J., Witkiewitz, K., Kotler, J.S., & The Conduct Problems Prevention Research Group. (2010). Predictive validity of callous-unemotional traits measured in early adolescence with respect to multiple antisocial outcomes. *Journal of Abnormal Psychology, 119,* 752–763.

McVey, G., Tweed, S., & Blackmore, E. (2007). Healthy Schools-Healthy Kids: A controlled evaluation of a comprehensive universal eating disorder prevention program. *Body Image, 4,* 115–136.

Meaney, M.J. (2010). Epigenetics and the biological definition of gene × environment interactions. *Child Development, 81,* 41–79.

Measelle, J. R., Stice, E., & Hogansen, J. M. (2006). Developmental trajectories of co-occurring depressive, eating, antisocial, and substance abuse problems in female adolescents. *Journal of Abnormal Psychology, 115,* 524–538.

Medeiros, D., Carlson, E., Surko, M., Munoz, N., Castillo, M., & Epstein, I. (2005). Adolescents' self-reported substance risks and need to talk about them in mental health counseling. In K. Peake, I. Epstein, & D. Medeiros (Eds.), *Clinical and research uses of an adolescent mental health intake questionnaire: What kids need to talk about* (pp. 171–189). Binghamton, NY: Haworth Social Work Practice Press.

MedlinePlus Medical Encyclopedia. (2009, January 20). Anorexia nervosa. Retrieved July 20, 2009, from http://www.nlm.nih.gov /medlineplus/ency/article/000362.htm.

Mednick, S. A., & Schulsinger, F. (1968). Some premorbid characteristics related to breakdown in children with schizophrenic mothers. *Journal of Psychiatric Research, 11,* 267–291.

Meesters, C., Muris, P. Ghys, A., Reumerman, T., & Rooijmans, M. (2003). The Children's Somatization Inventory: Further evidence for its reliability and validity in a pediatric sample and a community sample of Dutch children and adolescents. *Journal of Pediatric Psychology, 28,* 413–422.

Meijer, A. M., & van den Wittenboer, G. L. H. (2007). Contribution of infants' sleep and crying to marital relationship of first-time parent couples in the first year after childbirth. *Journal of Family Psychology, 21,* 49–57.

Meiser-Stedman, R. (2008). The posttraumatic stress disorder diagnosis in preschool-and elementary school-age children exposed to motor vehicle accidents. *The American Journal of Psychiatry, 165,* 1326–1337.

Melhem, N. M., Brent, D. A., Ziegler, M., Iyengar, S., Kolko, D., Oquendo, M., et al. (2007). Familial pathways to early-onset suicidal behavior: Familiar and individual antecedents of suicidal behavior. *American Journal of Psychiatry, 164,* 1364–1370.

Meltzer, L. J., & Mindell, J. A. (2006). Sleep and sleep disorders in children and adolescents. *Psychiatric Clinics of North America, 29,* 1059–1076.

Meltzoff, A.N. (2007). 'Like me': a foundation for social cognition. *Developmental Science, 10,* 126–134.

Mendola, P., Selevan, S. G., Gutter, S., & Rice, D. (2002). Environmental factors associated with a spectrum of neuro-developmental deficits. *Mental Retardation and Developmental Disabilities Research Reviews, 8,* 188–197.

Merikangas, K.R., He, J., Burstein, M., Swendsen, J., Avenevoli, S., Case, B., Georgiades, K., Heaton, L., Swanson, S., & Olfson, M. (2011). Service utilization for lifetime mental disorders in U.S. adolescents: Results of the National Comorbidity Survey—Adolescent Supplement (NCSA). *Journal of the American Academy of Child & Adolescent Psychiatry, 50,* 32–45.

Merikangas, K.R., & Risch, N. (2003). Will the genomics revolution revolutionize psychiatry? *American Journal of Psychiatry, 160,* 625–635.

Merkigangas, K.R., He, J., Brody, D., Fisher, P.W., Bourdon, K., & Koretz, D.S. (2009). Prevalence and treatment of mental disorders among US children in the 2001–2004 NHANES. *Pediatrics, 125,* 75–81.

Merline, A. C., O'Malley, P. M., Schulenberg, J. E., Bachman, J. G., & Johnston, L. D. (2004). Substance use among adults 35 years of age: Prevalence, adulthood predictors, and impact of adolescent substance use. *American Journal of Public Health, 94,* 96–102.

Mermelstein, R. (1999). Ethnicity, gender, and risk factors for smoking initiation: An overview. *Nicotine and Tobacco Research, 1,* 45–51.

Mermelstein, R. (1999). Explanations of ethnic and gender differences in youth smoking: A multi-site, qualitative investigation. *Nicotine and Tobacco Research, 1,* S91–S98.

Merrell, K.W., Guelder, B.A., Ross, S.W., & Isava, D.M. (2008). How effective are school bullying intervention programs? A meta-analysis of intervention research. *School Psychology Quarterly, 23,* 26–42.

Mervis, C.B., & Becerra, A.M. (2007). Language and communicative development in Williams Syndrome. *Mental Retardation and Developmental Disabilities Research Reviews, 13,* 3–15.

Meschke, L. L., Zweig, J. M., Barber, B. L., & Eccles, J. S. (2000). Demographic, biological, psychological, and social predictors of the timing of first intercourse. *Journal of Research on Adolescence, 10,* 315–338.

Mesibov, G. B. (1976). Mentally retarded people: 200 years in America. *Journal of Clinical Child Psychology, Winter,* 25–29.

Mesibov, G. B. (1986). A cognitive program for teaching social behaviors to verbal autistic adolescents and adults. In E. Schopler & G. B. Mesibov (Eds.), *High-functioning individuals with autism* (pp. 143–156). New York: Plenum Press.

Mesibov, G. B. (1992). Treatment issues with high-functioning adolescents and adults with autism. In E. Schopler & G. B. Mesibov (Eds.), *High-functioning individuals with autism: Current issues in autism* (pp. 143–155). New York: Plenum Press.

Mesibov, G. B. (1994). A comprehensive program for serving people with autism and their families: The TEACCH model. In J. L. Matson (Ed.), *Autism in children and adults: Etiology, assessment, and intervention* (pp. 85–97). Belmont, CA: Brooks/Cole Publishing.

Mesibov, G. B. (1995). Facilitated communication: A warning for pediatric psychologists. *Journal of Pediatric Psychology, 20,* 127–130.

Mesibov, G. B. (1997). Formal and informal measures on the effectiveness of the TEACCH programme. *Autism, 1,* 25–35.

Mesibov, G. B., Adams, L. W., & Schopler, E. (2000). Autism: A brief history. *Psychoanalytic Inquiry, 20,* 637–647.

Mesibov, G. B., & Shea, V. (1996). Full inclusion and students with autism. *Journal of Autism and Developmental Disorders, 26,* 337–346.

Messerlian, C., Derevensky, J., & Gupta, R. (2005). Youth gambling problems: A public health perspective. *Health Promotion International, 20,* 69–79.

Metrik, J., Frissell, K. C., McCarthy, D. M., D'Amico, E. J., & Brown, S. A. (2003). Strategies for reduction and cessation of alcohol use: Adolescent preferences. *Alcoholism: Clinical and Experimental Research, 27,* 74–80.

Meyer, S. E., Carlson, G. A., Wiggs, E. A., Martinez, P. E., Ronsaville, D. S., Klimes-Dougan, B., et al. (2004). A prospective study of the association among impaired executive functioning, childhood attentional problems, and the development of bipolar disorder. *Development and Psychopathology, 16,* 461–476.

Meyer, S.E., & Carlson, G.A. (2010). Development, age of onset, and phenomenology in bipolar disorder. In D.J. Miklowitz & D. Cicchetti (Eds.), *Understanding Bipolar Disorder: A developmental psychopathology perspective* (pp. 35–66). New York: Guilford Press.

Meyers, A. W., Klesges, R. C., Winders, S. E., & Ward, K. D. (1997). Are weight concerns predictive of smoking cessation? A prospective analysis. *Journal of Consulting and Clinical Psychology, 65,* 448–452.

Mezulis, A.H., Funasaki, K.S., Charbonneau, A.M. (2009). Gender differences in the cognitive vulnerability-stress model of depression in the transition to adolescence. *Cognitive Therapy Research, 34,* 501–513.

Micali, N., Simonoff, E., Stahl, E., & Treasure, J. (2010). Maternal eating disorders and infant feeding difficulties: maternal and child mediators in a longitudinal general population study. *Journal of Child Psychology and Psychiatry, 52,* 800–807.

Micklowitz, D. J., George, E. L., Axelson, D. A., Kim, E. Y., Birmaher, B., Schneck, C., et al. (2004). Family-focused treatment for adolescents with bipolar disorder. *Journal of Affective Disorders, 82,* S113–S128.

Mikko, A., & Wimmer, H. (2003). Learning to read: English in comparison to six more regular orthographies. *Applied Psycholinguistics, 24,* 621–635.

Mikton, C., & Butchart, A. (2009). Child maltreatment prevention: a systematic review of reviews. *Bulletin of the World Health Organization, 87,* 353–361.

Milan, S., Pinderhughes, E. E., & Conduct Problems Prevention Research Group (2006). Family instability and child maladjustment trajectories during elementary school. *Journal of Abnormal Child Psychology, 34,* 43–56.

Milan, S., Snow, S., & Belay, S. (2007). The context of preschool children's sleep: Racial/ethnic differences in sleep locations, routines, and concerns. *Journal of Family Psychology, 21,* 20–28.

Milich, R., Balentine, A. C., & Lynam, D. R. (2001). ADHD combined type and ADHD predominantly inattentive type are distinct and unrelated disorders. *Clinical Psychology: Science and Practice, 8,* 463–488.

Mill, J., & Petronis, A. (2008). Pre- and peri-natal environmental risks for attention-deficit hyperactivity disorder (ADHD): the potential role of epigenetic processes in mediating susceptibility. *Journal of Child Psychology and Psychiatry, 49,* 1020–1030.

Miller, A., Fox, N. A., Cohn, J. F., Forbes, E. E., Sherrill, J. T., & Kovacs, M. (2002). Regional patterns of brain activity in adults with a history of childhood depression: Gender differences and clinical variability. *American Journal of Psychiatry, 159,* 934–940.

Miller, F. G., & Lazowski, L. E. (2005). Substance Abuse Subtle Screening Inventory for Adolescents – second version. In T. Grisso, G. Vincent, & D. Seagrave (Eds.), *Mental health screening and assessment in juvenile justice* (pp. 139–151). New York: Guilford Press.

Miller, K. J., Fullmer, S. L., & Walls, R. T. (1996). Reflections on "A dozen years of mainstreaming literature: A content analysis." *Exceptionality, 6,* 129–131.

Miller, K.W., Melnick, M.J., Farrell, M.P., Sabo, D.F. & Barnes, G.M. (2006). Jocks, gender, binge drinking, and adolescent violence. *Journal of Interpersonal Violence 21,* 105–120.

Miller, M., Ho, J., & Hinshaw, S.P. (2012). Executive function in girls with ADHD followed prospectively into young adulthood. *Neuropsychology, 26,* 278–287.

Miller, P. M., Smith, G. T., & Goldman, M. S. (1990). Emergence of alcohol expectancies in childhood: A possible critical period. *Journal of Studies on Alcohol, 51,* 343–349.

Miller, S. M., & Green, M. L. (1985) Coping with stress and frustration: Origins, nature, and development. In M. Lewis & C. Saarni (Eds.), *The socialization of emotions* (pp. 263–314). New York: Plenum Press.

Miller, T.W., Nigg, J.T., Miller, R.L. (2009). Attention deficit hyperactivity disorder in African American children: What can be concluded from the past ten years? *Clinical Psychology Review, 29,* 77–86.

Minde, K. (2002). Sleep disorders in infants and young children. In J. M. Maldonado-Duran (Ed.), *Infant and toddler mental health: Models of clinical intervention with infants and their families* (pp. 269–307). Arlington, VA: American Psychiatric Publishing.

Mineka, S. & Zinbarg, R. (2006). A contemporary learning theory perspective on the etiology of anxiety disorders: It's not what you thought it was. *American Psychologist, 61,* 10–26.

Minnis, H., Reekie, J., Young, D., O'Connor, T., Ronald, A., Gray, A., & Plomin, R. (2007). Genetic, environmental and gender influences on attachment disorder behaviors. *British Journal of Psychiatry, 190,* 490–495.

Minshew, N. J., & Williams, D. L. (2007). The new neurobiology of autism: Cortex, connectivity, and neuronal organization. *Archives of Neurology, 64*(7), 945–950.

Mintz, S. (2006). *Huck's raft: A history of American childhood.* Cambridge, MA: Belknap Press.

Minuchin, S. (1974). *Families and family therapy.* Oxford, England: Harvard University Press.

Minuchin, S., Rosman, S., & Baker, L. (1978). *Psychosomatic families.* Cambridge, MA: Harvard University Press.

Miodrag, N., & Hodapp,R.M. (2010). Chronic stress and health among parents of children with intellectual and developmental disabilities. *Current Opinion in Psychiatry, 23,* 407–411.

Mirsky, J. (1997). Psychological distress among immigrant adolescents: Culture-specific factors in the case of immigrants from the former Soviet Union. *International Journal of Psychology, 32,* 221–230.

Mischel, W., Ayduk, O., Berman, M.G., Casey, B.J., Gotlib, I.H., Jonides, J., ... Shoda, Y. (2011). "Willpower" over the life span: decomposing self-regulation. *SCAN, 6,* 252–256.

Mitchell, C.M., Croy, C., Spicer, P., Frankel, K., & Emde, R.N. (2011). Trajectories of cognitive development among American Indian young children. *Developmental Psychology, 47,* 991–999.

Miyake, A., Friedman, N.P, Emerson, M.J., Witzki, A.H., & Howerter, A. (2000). The unity and diversity of executive functions and their contributions to complex "frontal lobe" tasks: a latent variable analysis. *Cognitive Psychology, 41,* 49–100.

Miyake, A., & Friendman, N.P. (2012). The nature and organization of individual differences in executive functions: four general conclusions. *Current Directions in Psychological Sciences, 21,* 8–14.

Modell, J., & Elder, G. H. (2002). Children develop in history: So what's new? In W. Hartup & R. A. Weinberg (Eds.), *Child psychology in retrospect and prospect: In celebration of the*

75th anniversary of the Institute of Child Development. The Minnesota symposia on child psychology (Vol. 32, pp. 173–205). Mahwah, NJ: Erlbaum.

Moehler, E., Kagan, J., Oeklers-Ax, R., Brunner, R., Poustka, L., Haffner, J. & Resc,h F. (2008). Infant predictors of behavioural inhibition. *British Journal of Developmental Psychology, 26,* 145–150.

Moffitt, T. E. (2003). Life-course-persistent and adolescence-limited antisocial behavior: A 10-year research review and a research agenda. In B. B. Lahey, T. E. Moffitt, & A. Caspi (Eds.), *Causes of conduct disorder and juvenile delinquency* (pp. 49–75). New York: Guilford Press.

Moffitt, T. E. (2005). The new look of behavioral genetics in developmental psychopathology: Gene-environment interplay in antisocial behaviors. *Psychological Bulletin, 131,* 533–554.

Moffitt, T. E., & Caspi, A. (2001). Childhood predictors differentiate life-course persistent and adolescence-limited antisocial pathways among males and females. *Development and Psychopathology, 13,* 355–375.

Moffitt, T. E., & Melchior, M. (2007). Why does worldwide prevalence of childhood attention deficit hyperactivity disorder matter? *American Journal of Psychiatry, 164,* 856–858.

Moffitt, T.E., Arseneault, L., Belsky, D., Dickson, N., Hancox, R.J., Harrington, H., ... Thomson, W.M. (2011). A gradient of childhood self-control predicts health, wealth, and public safety. *Proceedings of the National Academy of Sciences, 108,* 2693–2698.

Moffitt, T.E., Caspi, A., & Rutter, M. (2006). Measured gene-environment interactions in psychopathology. *Perspectives on Psychological Science, 1,* 5–27.

Mohahan, K.C., Steinberg, L., & Cauffman, E. (2009). Affiliation with antisocial peers, susceptibility to peer influence, and antisocial behavior during the transition to adulthood. *Developmental Psychology, 45,* 1520–1530.

Molina, B.S.G., Hinshaw, S.P., Swanson, J.M., Eugene, A.L., Vitiello, B., Jensen, P.S., Houck, P.R. (2009). The MTA at 8 years: Prospective follow-up of children treated for combined-type ADHD in a multisite study. *Journal of the American Academy of Child & Adolescent Psychiatry, 48,* 484–500.

Monahan, K.C., Steinberg L. & Cauffman E. (2009). Affiliation with antisocial peers, susceptibility to peer influence, and antisocial behavior during the transition to adulthood. *Developmental Psychology, 45,* 1520–1530.

Monk, C.S. (2008). The development of emotion-related neural circuitry in health and psychopathology. *Development and Psychopathology, 20,* 1231–1250.

Monks, C.P., Smith, P.K., Naylor, P., Barter, C., Ireland, J.L., & Coyne, I. (2008). Bullying in different contexts: Commonalities, differences and the role of theory. *Aggression and Violent Behavior, 14,* 146–156.

Moore, C. M., Biederman, J., Wozniak, J., Mick, E., Aleardi, M., Wardrop, M., et al. (2006). Differences in brain chemistry in children and adolescents with attention deficit hyperactivity disorder with and without comorbid bipolar disorder: A proton magnetic resonance spectroscopy study. *American Journal of Psychiatry, 163,* 316–318.

Moore, D. G. (2001). Reassessing emotion recognition performance in people with mental retardation: A review. *American Journal on Mental Retardation, 106,* 481–502.

Moore, K. A., & Keyes, C. L. M. (2002). A brief history of well-being: In children and adults. In M. H. Bornstein, L. Davidson, C. L. M. Keyes, & K. Moore (Eds.), *Well-Being:*

Positive development across the life course (pp. 1–12). Mahwah, NJ: Erlbaum.

Moore, K.W., & Varela, R.E. (2009). Correlates of long-term post-traumatic stress symptoms in children following Hurricane Katrina. *Child Psychiatry and Human Development, 41,* 239–250.

Moorhead, D. J., Stashwick, C. K., Reinhertz, H. Z., Gianconia, R. M., Striegel-Moore, R. M., & Paradis, A. D. (2003). Child and adolescent predictors for eating disorders in a community population of young adult women. *International Journal of Eating Disorders, 33,* 1–9.

Morales, J. R., & Guerra, N. G. (2006). Effects of multiple context and cumulative stress on urban children's adjustment in elementary school. *Child Development, 77,* 907–923.

Moran, P. B., Vuchinich, S., & Hall, N. K. (2004). Associations between types of maltreatment and substance use during adolescence. *Child Abuse and Neglect, 28,* 565–574.

Moreno, C., Laje, G., Blanco, C., Huiping, J., Schmidt, A.B., & Olfson, M. (2007). National trends in the outpatient diagnosis and treatment of bipolar disorder in youth. *Archives of General Psychiatry, 64,* 1032–1039.

Moreno, C., Laje, G., Blanco, C., Jiang, H., Schmidt, A. B., & Olfson, M. (2007). National trends in the outpatient diagnosis and treatment of bipolar disorder in youth. *Archive of General Psychology, 64,* 1032–1039.

Morgan, P.L., Farkas, G., & Wu, Q. (2011). Kindergarten children's growth trajectories in reading and mathematics: Who falls increasingly behind? *Journal of Learning Disabilities, 44,* 472–488.

Morgos, D., Worden, J.W. & Gupta, L. (2008). Psychosocial effects of war experiences among displaced children in Southern Darfur. *Omega: Journal of Death and Dying, 56,* 229–253.

Morison, S. J., & Ellwood, A. L. (2000). Resiliency in the aftermath of deprivation: A second look at the development of Romanian orphanage children. *Merrill-Palmer Quarterly, 46,* 717–737.

Morral, A. R., McCaffrey, D. F., & Paddock, S. M (2002). Reassessing the marijuana gateway effect. *Addiction, 97,* 1493–1504.

Morrell, J., & Steele, H. (2003). The role of attachment security, temperament, maternal perception, and care-giving behavior in persistent infant sleeping problems. *Infant Mental Health Journal, 24,* 447–468.

Morris, C. D., Miklowitz, D. J., & Waxmonsky, J. A. (2007). Family-focused treatment for bipolar disorder in adults and youth. *Journal of Clinical Psychology, 63,* 433–445.

Morris, J., Belfer, M., Daniels, A., Flisher, A., Villé, L., Lora, A., & Saxena, S. (2011). Treated prevalence of and mental health services received by children and adolescents in 42 low-and-middle income countries. *Journal of Child Psychology and Psychiatry, 52,* 1239–1246.

Morris, R. J., & Kratochwill, T. R. (1998). *The practice of child therapy.* Needham Heights, MA: Allyn & Bacon.

Morrison, F. J., Ponitz, C. C., & McClelland, M. M. (2010). Self-regulation and academic achievement in the transition to school. In S. D. Calkins & M. A. Bell (Eds.), *Child Development at the Intersection of Emotion and Cognition* (pp. 203–224). Washington, DC: American Psychological Association.

Morrison, T. G., Kalin, R., & Morrison, M. A. (2004). Body-image evaluation and body-image investment among adolescents: A test of sociocultural and social comparison theories. *Adolescence, 39,* 571–572.

Moses, T. (2009). Stigma and self-concept among adolescents receiving mental health treatment. *American Journal of Orthopsychiatry, 79*, 261–274.

Moss, H. B., Lynch, K. G., & Hardie, T. L. (2003). Affiliation with deviant peers among children of substance-dependent fathers from pre-adolescence into adolescence: Associations with problem behaviors. *Drug and Alcohol Dependence, 71*, 117–125.

Motti, F., Cicchetti, D., & Sroufe, L. A. (1983). From infant affect expression to symbolic play: The coherence of development in Down syndrome children. *Child Development, 54*, 1168–1175.

Mottron, L., Dawson, M., Soulieres, I., Hubert, B., & Burack, J. (2006). Enhanced perceptual functioning in autism: An update, and eight principles of autistic perception. *Journal of Autism and Developmental Disorders, 36*, 27–43.

Mrug, S., & Windle, M. (2010). Prospective effects of violence exposure across multiple contexts on early adolescents' internalizing and externalizing problems. *Journal of Child Psychology and Psychiatry, 51*, 953–961.

Muehlenkamp, J. J. (2005). Self-injurious behavior as a separate clinical syndrome. *American Journal of Orthopsychiatry, 75*, 324–333.

Muehlenkamp, J. J., & Gutierrez, P. M. (2004). An investigation of differences between self-injurious behavior and suicide attempts in a sample of adolescents. *Suicide and Life-Threatening Behavior, 34*, 12–23.

Mufson, L., Dorta, K. P., Wickramaratne, P., Nomura, Y., Olfson, M., & Myrna, M. W. (2004). A randomized effectiveness trial of interpersonal therapy for depressed adolescents. *Archives of General Psychiatry, 61*, 577–584.

Mufson, L., Gallagher, T., Dorta, K. P., & Young, J. F. (2004). A group adaptation of interpersonal therapy for depressed adolescents. *American Journal of Psychotherapy, 58*, 220–237.

Muise, A. M., Stein, D. G., & Arbess, G. (2003). Eating disorders in adolescent boys: A review of the adolescent and young adult literature. *Journal of Adolescent Health, 33*, 427–435.

Mukolo, A., Heflinger, C.A., & Wallston, K.A. (2010). The stigma of childhood mental disorders: A conceptual framework. *Journal of the American Academy of Child & Adolescent Psychiatry, 49*, 92–103.

Mullett-Hume, E., Anshel, D., Guevara, V., & Cloitre, M. (2008). Cumulative trauma and posttraumatic stress disorder among children exposed to the 9/11 World Trade Center attack. *American Journal of Orthopsychiatry, 78*, 103–108.

Multimodal Treatment Study of Children with ADHD Cooperative Group (2004). National Institute of Mental Health multimodal treatment study of ADHD follow-up: 24-month outcomes of treatment strategies for attention-deficit/hyperactivity disorder. *Pediatrics, 113*, 754–761.

Multimodal Treatment Study of Children with ADHD Cooperative Group, US. (1999). A 14-month randomized clinical trial of treatment strategies for attention-deficit/hyperactivity disorder. *Archives of General Psychiatry, 56*, 1073–1086.

Mulveen, R., & Hepworth, J. (2006). An interpretive phenomenological analysis of participation in a pro-anorexia Internet site and its relationship with disordered eating. *Journal of Health Psychology, 11*, 283–296.

Mundy, P., & Jarrold, W. (2010). Infant joint attention, neural networks and social cognition. *Neural Networks, 23*, 985–997.

Muphy, R., Straebler, S., Basden, S., Cooper, Z., & Fairburn, C.G. (2012). Interpersonal psychotherapy for eating disorders. *Clinical Psychology & Psychotherapy, 19*, 150–158.

Muralidharan, A., Yoo, D., Ritschel, L.A., Simeonova, D.I., & Craighead, W.E. (2010). Development of emotion regulation in children of bipolar parents: putative contributions of socioemotional and familial risk factors. *Clinical Psychology: Science and Practice, 17*, 169–186.

Muratori, F., & Maestro, S. (2007). Early signs of autism in the first year of life. In S. Acquarone (Ed.), *Signs of autism in infants: Recognition and early intervention* (pp. 46–62). London: Karnac Books.

Muraven, M., & Baumeister, R. F. (2000). Self-regulation and depletion of limited resources: Does self-control resemble a muscle? *Psychological Bulletin, 126*, 247–259.

Muris, P. (2006). The pathogenesis of childhood anxiety disorders: Considerations from a developmental psychopathology perspective. *International Journal of Behavioral Development, 30*, 5–11.

Muris, P., Bodden, D., Merckelbach, H., Ollendick, T. H., & King, N. (2003). Fear of the beast: A prospective study on the effects of negative information on childhood fear. *Behaviour Research and Therapy, 41*, 195–208.

Muris, P & Dietvorst, R. (2006). Underlying personality characteristics of behavioral inhibition in children. *Child Psychiatry and Human Development, 36*, 437–445.

Muris, P., Mayer, B., Bartelds, E., Tierney, S., & Bogie, N. (2001). The revised version of the Screen for Child Anxiety Related Emotional Disorders (SCARED-R): Treatment sensitivity in an early intervention trial for childhood anxiety disorders. *British Journal of Clinical Psychology, 40*, 323–336.

Muris, P., Mayer, B., Vermeulen, L. & Hiemstra, H. (2007). Theory-of-mind, cognitive development, and children's interpretation of anxiety-related physical symptoms. *Behaviour Research and Therapy, 45*, 2121–2132.

Muris P., & Meesters, C. (2002). Symptoms of anxiety disorders and teacher-reported school functioning of normal children. *Psychological Reports, 91*, 588–590.

Muris, P., Meesters, C., Merckelbach, H., Sermon, A., & Zwakhalen, S. (1998). Worry in normal children. *Journal of the American Academy of Child and Adolescent Psychiatry, 37*, 703–710.

Muris, P., & Merckelbach, H. (2000). The parent's point of view. *Behaviour Research and Therapy, 38*, 813–818.

Muris, P., Merckelbach, H., & Collaris, R. (1997). Common childhood fears and their origins. *Behaviour Research and Therapy, 35*, 929–937.

Muris, P., Merckelbach, H., Meesters, C., & van den Brand, K. (2002). Cognitive development and worry in normal children. *Cognitive Therapy and Research, 26*, 775–785.

Muris, P., Merckelbach, H., Ollendick, T., King, N., & Bogie, N. (2002). Three traditional and three new childhood anxiety questionnaires: Their reliability and validity in a normal adolescent sample. *Behaviour Research and Therapy, 40*, 753–772.

Muris, P., Merckelbach, H., Wessel, I., & van de Ven, M. (1999). Psychopathological correlates of self-reported behavioural inhibition in normal children. *Behaviour Research and Therapy, 37*, 575–576.

Muris, P., & Ollendick, T. H. (2005). The role of temperament in the etiology of child psychopathology. *Clinical Child and Family Psychology Review, 8*, 271–289.

Murphy, K. R., Barkley, R. A., & Bush, T. (2002). Young adults with attention deficit hyperactivity disorder: Subtype differences in comorbidity, educational and clinical history. *Journal of Nervous and Mental Disease, 190*, 147–157.

Murphy, L. B. (1962). *The widening world of childhood.* New York: Basic Books.

Murphy, L. B. (1974). *Growing up in Garden Court.* Oxford, England: Child Welfare League of America.

Murphy, L. B., & Moriarty, A. E. (1976). *Vulnerability, coping and growth from infancy to adolescence.* Oxford, England: Yale University Press.

Murphy, R., Stradbler, S., Basden, S., Cooper, Z. & Fairburn, C.G. (2012). Interpersonal psychotherapy for eating disorders. *Clinical Psychology &Psychotherapy, 19,* 150–158.

Murphy-Brennan, M. G., & Oei, T. P.S. (1999). Is there evidence to show that fetal alcohol syndrome can be prevented? *Journal of Drug Education, 29,* 5–24.

Murray, K. T., & Kochanska, G. (2002). Effortful control: Factor structure and relation to externalizing and internalizing behaviors. *Journal of Abnormal Child Psychology, 30,* 503–514.

Murray-Close, D., Hoza, B., Hinshaw, S.P., Arnold, L.E., Swanson, J., Jensen, P.S., … Wells, K. (2010). Developmental processes in peer problems of children with attention-deficit/hyperactivity disorder in The Multimodal Treatment Study of Children with ADHD: Developmental cascades and vicious cycles. *Development and Psychopathology, 22,* 785–802.

Musser, E.D., Backs, R.W., Schmitt, C.F., Ablow, J.C., Measelle, J.R., & Nigg, J.T. (2011). Emotion regulation via the autonomic nervous system in children with attention-deficit/hyperactivity disorder (ADHD). *Journal of Abnormal Child Psychology, 39,* 841–852.

Nachmias, M., Gunnar, M. R., Mangelsdorf, S., Parritz, R. H., & Buss, K. (1996). Behavioral inhibition and stress reactivity: The moderating role of attachment security. *Child Development, 67,* 508–522.

Nadeau, K. G. (1998). Psychotherapy for adults with ADHD: A call to training. *The ADHD Report, 6,* 9–11.

Nadeem, E., & Jensen, P.S. (2009). Teacher consultation research in attention deficit hyperactivity disorder: A cause for congratulation or consolation? *School Psychology Review, 38,* 38–44.

Nagel, B.J., Bathula, D., Herting, M., Schmitt, C., Kroenke, C.D., Fair, D., & Nigg, J.T. (2011). Altered white matter microstructure in children with attention-deficit/hyperactivity disorder. *Journal of the American Academy of Child & Adolescent Psychiatry, 50,* 283–292.

Nation, M., Crusto, C., Wandersman, A., Kumpfer, K. L., Seybolt, D., Morrissey-Kane, E., et al. (2003). What works in prevention: Principles of effective prevention programs. *American Psychologist, 58,* 449–456.

National Child Traumatic Stress Network (NCTSN). (2011). NCTSN national and community partners report 2011. Retrieved from www.nctsn.org.

National Institute of Diabetes and Digestive and Kidney Diseases. (2008, June). Binge eating disorders (NIH Publication No. 04–3589), http://win.niddk.nih. gov/publications/binge.htm.

National Institute of Mental Health. (2004). *Preventing child and adolescent mental disorders: Research roundtable on economic burden and cost effectiveness.* Rockville, MD., www.nimh.nih.gov/scientificmeetings/economicroutable.cfm.

National Institute of Mental Health. (2008). The numbers count: Mental disorders in America. Retrieved July 20, 2009, from http://nimh. nih.gov/health/publications/the-numbers-count-mental-disordersin-america/index.shtml#Eating.

National Institute on Alcohol Abuse and Alcoholism (NIAAA). (2005). Underage drinking and related risk behaviors among youth. http://www.niaaa.nih.gov/Resources/DatabaseResources/QuickFacts/Youth/default.htm.

National Institute on Drug Abuse (NIDA) (1995). *Epidemiology of inhalant abuse: An international perspective* (Research Monograph #148). Bethesda, MD.

National Institute on Drug Abuse (NIDA). (2001a). *Hallucinogens and dissociative drugs: Including LSD, PCP, ketamine, dextromethorphan* (Research Report Series, NIH Pub. No. 01–4209). Bethesda, MD.

National Institute on Drug Abuse (NIDA). (2001b). Nicotine addiction. (Research Report Series, NIH Pub. No. 01–4342). Bethesda, MD.

National Institute on Drug Abuse (NIDA). (2002). *Methamphetamine: Abuse and addiction* (Research Report Series, NIH Pub. No. 02–4210). Bethesda, MD.

National Institute on Drug Abuse (NIDA). (2004). *Cocaine: Abuse and addiction* (Research Report Series, NIH Pub. No. 99–4342). Bethesda, MD.

National Institute on Drug Abuse (NIDA). (2005a). *Heroin: Abuse and addiction* (Research Report Series, NIH Pub. No. 05–4165). Bethesda, MD.

National Institute on Drug Abuse (NIDA). (2005b). Inhalant abuse. (Research Report Series, NIH Pub. No. 05–3818). Bethesda, MD.

National Institute on Drug Abuse (NIDA). (2005c). Marijuana abuse. (Research Report Series, NIH Pub. No. 05–3859). Bethesda, MD.

National Institute on Drug Abuse (NIDA). (2006). *MDMA (ecstasy) abuse* (Research Report Series, NIH Pub. No. 06–4728). Bethesda, MD.

National Institute on Drug Abuse (NIDA). (2012). Drug Facts: High School and Youth Trends. Retrieved from www.nida.gov

National Institute on Druge Abuse (NIDA). (2000). Anabolic steroid abuse. (Research Report Series, NIH Pub. No. 00–3721). Bethesda, MD.

National Institutes of Health (1994). Attention deficit hyperactivity disorder. NIH Publication No. 96–3572.

National Institutes of Health. (1998). Diagnosis and treatment of attention deficit hyperactivity disorder [Electronic version]. *NIH Consensus Statement Online, 16*(2): 1–37. Available at: consensus.nih.gov/1998/1998AttentionDefi citHyperactivity Disorder110PDF.pdf

Nauta, M.H., Scholing, A., Rapee, R.M., Abbott, M., Spence, S.H. & Waters, A. (2004). A parent-report measure of children's anxiety: Psychometric properties and comparison with child-report in a clinic and normal sample. *Behaviour Research and Therapy, 42,* 813–839.

Neal, D. J., & Carey, K. B. (2004). Developing discrepancy within self-regulation theory: Use of personalized normative feedback and personal strivings with heavy-drinking college students. *Addictive Behaviors, 29,* 281–297.

Neale, B.M., Medland, S.E., Ripke, S., Asherson, P., Franke, B., Lesche, K., … Nelson, S. (2010). Meta-analysis of genome-wide association studies of attention-deficit/hyperactivity disorder. *Journal of the American Academy of Child & Adolescent Psychiatry, 49,* 884–897.

Neiderhiser, J. M., Reiss, D., Hetherington, E. M., & Plomin, R. (1999). Relationships between parenting and adolescent adjustment over time: Genetic and environmental contributions. *Developmental Psychology, 35,* 680–692.

Neiderhiser, J. M., Reiss, D., Pedersen, N. L., Lichtenstein, P., Spotts, E. L., Hansson, K., et al. (2004). Genetic and environmental influences on mothering of adolescents: A comparison of two samples. *Developmental Psychology, 40*, 335–351.

Neisser, U., Boodoo, G., Bouchard, T.J., Boykin, A.W., Brody, N., Ceci, S.J., … Urbina, S. (1996). Intelligence: Knowns and unknowns. *American Psychologist, 51*, 77–101.

Nelson, C. A. (2000). Neural plasticity and human development: The role of early experience in sculpting memory systems. *Developmental Science, 3*, 115–136.

Nelson, C. A. (2007). A neurobiological perspective on early human deprivation. *Child Development Perspectives, 1*, 13–18.

Nelson, C. A., Bloom, F. E., Cameron, J. L., Amaral, D., Dahl, R. E., & Pine, D. (2002). An integrative, multidisciplinary approach to the study of brain-behavior relations in the context of typical and atypical development. *Development and Psychopathology, 14*, 499–520.

Nelson, C. A., Zeanah, C. H., & Fox, N. A. (2007). The effects of early deprivation on brain-behavioral development: The Bucharest early intervention project. In D. Romner & E. F. Walker (Eds.), *Adolescent psychopathology and the developing brain: Integrating brain and prevention science* (pp. 197–215). New York: Oxford University Press.

Nelson, C. A., Zeanah, C. H., Fox, N. A., Marshall, P. J., Smyke, A. T., & Guthne, D. (2007). Cognitive recovery in socially deprived young children: The Bucharest early intervention project. *Science, 318*, 1937–1940.

Nelson, C.A. (2011). Neural development and lifelong plasticity. In D.P. Keating (Ed.), *Nature and Nurture in Early Child Development* (pp. 45–69). New York: Cambridge University Press.

Nelson, C.A., Zeanah, C.H., Fox, N.A., Marshall, P.J., Smyke, A. T., & Guthrie, D. (2007). Cognitive recovery in socially deprived young children: The Bucharest Early Intervention Project. t*Science, 318*, 1937–1940.

Nelson-LeGall, S. (1981). Help-seeking: An understudied problem-solving skill in children. *Developmental Review, 1*, 224–246.

Neumark-Sztainer, D, Levine, M. P., Paxton, S. J., Smolak, L., Piran, N., & Wertheim, E. H. (2006). Prevention of body dissatisfaction and disordered eating: What next? *Eating Disorders: The Journal of Treatment and Prevention, 14*, 265–285.

Newcombe, N.S. (2011). What is Neoconstructivism? In S.P. Johnson (Ed.), *Neoconstructivism: The New Science of Cognitive Development* (pp. 157–160). New York: Oxford University Press.

Newes-Adeyi, G., Chen, C. M., Williams, G. D., & Faden, V. B. (2005). *Surveillance Report #74: Trends in underage drinking in the United States, 1991–2003.* Bethesda, MD: National Institute on Alcohol Abuse and Alcoholism.

Nichols, S. L., & Waschbusch, D. A. (2004). A review of the validity of laboratory cognitive tasks used to assess symptoms of ADHD. *Child Psychiatry and Human Development, 34*, 297–315.

Nickels, K. C., Katusic, S. K., Colligan, R. C., Weaver, A. L., Voight, R. G., & Barbaresi, W. J. (2008). Stimulant medication treatment of target behaviors in children with autism: A population-based study. *Journal of Developmental and Behavioral Pediatrics, 29*, 75–81.

Nigg, J. T. (2006). Temperament and developmental psychopathology. *Journal of Child Psychology and Psychiatry, 47*, 395–422.

Nigg, J. T., Glass, J. M., Wong, M. M., Poon, E., Jester, J. M., Fitzgerald, H., et al. (2004). Neuropsychological executive functioning in children at elevated risk for alcoholism: Findings in early adolescence. *Journal of Abnormal Psychology, 113*, 302–314.

Nigg, J. T., Martel, M. M., Nikolas, M., & Casey, B. J. (2010). Intersection of emotion and cognition in developmental psychopathology. In S. D. Calkins & M. A. Bell (Eds.), *Child Development at the Intersection of Emotion and Cognition* (pp. 225–245). Washington, DC: American Psychological Association.

Nigg, J.T. (2004). Neuropsychologic theory and findings in attention deficit/hyperactivity disorder: the state of the field and salient challenges for the coming decade. *Biological Psychiatry, 57*, 1424–1435.

Nigg, J.T. (2006). Temperament and developmental psychopathology. *Journal of Child Psychology and Psychiatry, 47*, 395–422.

Nigg, J.T. (2011). Where to with treatment for ADHD? *Current Medical Research and Opinion, 27*, 1–3.

Nigg, J.T., Nikolas, M., & Burt S.A. (2010). Measured gene-by-environment interaction in relation to attention-deficit /hyperactivity disorder. *Journal of the American Academy of Child & Adolescent Psychiatry, 49*, 863–873.

Nigg, J.T., Nikolas, M., Knottnerus, G.M., Cavanagh, K., & Friderici, K. (2010). Confirmation and extension of association of blood lead with attention-deficit/hyperactivity disorder (ADHD) and ADHD symptom domains at population-typical exposure levels. *Journal of Child Psychology and Psychiatry, 51*, 58–65.

Nikolas, M.A., & Burt, S.A. (2010). Genetic and environmental influences on ADHD symptom dimensions of inattention and hyperactivity: A meta-analysis. *Journal of Abnormal Psychology, 119*, 1–17.

Nikulina, V., Widom, C.S., & Brzustowicz, L.M. (2012). Child abuse and neglect, MAOA, and mental health outcomes: A prospective examination. *Biological Psychiatry, 71*, 350–357.

Nilsson, K., Sundbom, E., & Hägglöf, B. (2008). A longitudinal study of perfectionism in adolescent onset anorexia nervosa-restricting type. *European Eating Disorders Review, 16*, 386–394.

Nishimura, S. T., Goebert, D. A., Ramisetty-Mikler, S., & Caetano, R. (2005). Adolescent alcohol use and suicide indicators among adolescents in Hawaii. *Cultural Diversity and Ethnic Minority Psychology, 11*, 309–320.

Nishina, A., Ammon, N. Y., Bellmore, A. D., & Graham, S. (2006). Body disatisfaction and physical development among ethnic minority adolescents. *Journal of Youth and Adolescence, 35*, 189–201.

Nix, R. L., Pinderhughes, E. E., Bierman, K. L., Maples, J. J., & Conduct Problems Prevention Research Group. (2005). Decoupling the relation between risk factors for conduct problems and the receipt of intervention services: Participation across multiple components of a prevention program. *American Journal of Community Psychology, 36*, 307–325.

Nobakht, M., & Dezhkam, M. (2000). An epidemiological study of eating disorders in Iran. *International Journal of Eating Disorders, 28*, 265–271.

Nock, M. K., & Kazdin, A. E. (2005). Randomized controlled trial of a brief intervention for increasing participation in parent management training. *Journal of Consulting and Clinical Psychology, 73*, 872–879.

Nock, M. K., Kazdin, A. E., Hiripi, E., & Kessler, R. C. (2007). Lifetime prevalence, correlates, and persistence of oppositional defiant disorder: Results from the National

Comorbidity Study replication. Journal of Child Psychology and Psychiatry, 48, 703–713.

Nock, M. K., & Prinstein, M. J. (2004). A functional approach to the assessment of self-mutilative behavior. *Journal of Consulting and Clinical Psychology, 72*, 885–890.

Nock, M. K., & Prinstein, M. J. (2005). Contextual features and behavioral functions of self-mutilation among adolescents. *Journal of Abnormal Psychology, 114*, 140–146.

Nock, M.K., Kazdin, A.E., Hiripi, E., & Kessler, R.C. (2007), Lifetime prevalence, correlates, and persistence of oppositional defiant disorder: results from the National Comorbidity Survey Replication. *Journal of Child Psychology and Psychiatry, 48,* 703–713.

Nolan, S. A., Flynn, C., & Garber, J. (2003). Prospective relations between rejection and depression in young adolescents. *Journal of Personality and Social Psychology, 85*, 745–755.

Nolen-Hoeksema, S. (1998). Ruminative coping with depression. In J. Heckhausen & C. S. Dweck (Eds.), *Motivation and self-regulation across the life span* (pp. 237–256). New York: Cambridge University Press.

Nolen-Hoeksema, S. (1998). The other end of the continuum: The costs of rumination. *Psychological Inquiry, 9*, 216–219.

Nolen-Hoeksema, S. (2002). Gender differences in depression. In I. H. Gotlib & C. L. Hammen (Eds.), *Handbook of depression* (pp. 492–509). New York: Guilford Press.

Nolen-Hoeksema, S., & Girgus, J. S. (1994). The emergence of gender differences in depression during adolescence. *Psychological Bulletin, 115*, 424–443.

Nolen-Hoeksema, S., Girgus, J. S., & Seligman, M. E. (1992). Predictors and consequences of childhood depressive symptoms: A 5-year longitudinal study. *Journal of Abnormal Psychology, 101*, 405–422.

Nolte, T., Guiney, J., Fonagy, P., Mayes, L.C., & Luyten, P. (2011). Interpersonal stress regulation and the development of anxiety disorders: an attachment-based developmental framework. *Frontiers in Behavioral Neuroscience, 5*, 1–21.

Nottelmann, E. D., & Jensen, P. S. (1995). Comorbidity of disorders in children and adolescents: Developmental perspectives. In T. H. Ollendick & R. J. Prinz (Eds.), *Advances in Clinical Child Psychology* (Vol. 17, pp. 109–155). New York: Plenum Press.

Nowicki, E. A., & Sandieson, R. (2002). A meta-analysis of school-age children's attitudes towards persons with physical or intellectual disabilities. *International Journal of Disability, Development and Education, 49*, 243–265.

Nugent, N.R., Tyrka, A.R., Carpenter, L.L., & Price, L.H. (2011). Gene-environment interactions: Early life stress and risk for depressive and anxiety disorders. *Psychopharmacology, 214*, 175–196.

O'Brien, C. P., Charney, D. S., Lewis, L., Cornish, J., Post, R., Woody, G. et al. (2004). Priority actions to improve the care of persons with co-occurring substance abuse and other mental disorders: A call to action. *Biological Psychiatry, 56*, 703–713.

O'Brien, G. V. (1999). Protecting the social body: Use of the organism metaphor in fighting the "menace of the feeble-minded." *Mental Retardation, 37*, 188–200.

O'Connor, N., & Hermelin, B. (1994). Two autistic savant readers. *Journal of Autism and Developmental Disorders, 24*, 501–515.

O'Connor, T. G., McGuire, S., Reiss, D., & Hetherington, E. M. (1998). Co-occurrence of depressive symptoms and antisocial behavior in adolescence: A common genetic liability. *Journal of Abnormal Pscyhology, 107*, 27–37.

O'Connor, T. G., & Zeanah, C. H. (2003). Attachment disorders: Assessment strategies and treatment approaches. *Attachment and Human Development, 5*, 223–244.

O'Donnell, L., O'Donnell, C., Wardlaw, D. M., & Stueve, A. (2004). Risk and resiliency factors influencing suicidality among urban African American and Latino youth. *American Journal of Community Psychology, 33*, 37–49.

O'Hearn, K., Asato, M., Ordaz, S., & Luna, B. (2008). Neurodevelopment and executive function in autism. *Development and Psychopathology, 20*, 1103–1132.

O'Leary, T. A., Brown, S. A., Colby, S. M., Cronce, J. M., D'Amico, E. J., Fader, J. S., et al. (2002). Treating adolescents together or individually? Issues in adolescent substance abuse interventions. *Alcoholism: Clinical and Experimental Research, 26*, 890–899.

O'Leary Tevyaw, T., & Monti, P. M. (2004). Motivational enhancement and other brief interventions for adolescent substance abuse: Foundations, applications and evaluations. *Addiction, 99*, 63–75.

O'Malley, P. M., & Johnston, L. D. (2003). Unsafe driving by high school seniors: National trends from 1976 to 2001 in ticket and accidents after use of alcohol, marijuana and other illegal drugs. *Journal of Studies on Alcohol, 64*, 305–312.

Oberklaid, F., Prior, M., Nolan, T., & Smith, P. (1986). Temperament in infants born prematurely. *Annual Progress in Child Psychiatry and Child Development, 6*, 386–396.

Obradović, J., & Boyce, W.T. (2009). Individual differences in behavioral, psychological, and genetic sensitivities to contexts: Implications for development and adaptation. *Developmental Neuroscience, 31*, 300–308.

Obradović, J., Burt, K.B., & Masten, A.S. (2010). Testing a dual cascade model linking competence and symptoms over 20 years from childhood to adulthood. *Journal of Clinical Child & Adolescent Psychology, 39,* 90–102.

Obradović, J., Bush, N.R. & Boyce, W.T. (2011). The interactive effect of marital conflict and stress reactivity on externalizing and internalizing symptoms: The role of laboratory stressors. *Development and Psychopathology, 23*,101–114.

Obradović, J., Pardini, D.A., Long, J.D., & Loeber, R. (2007). Measuring interpersonal callousness in boys from childhood to adolescence: An examination of longitudinal invariance and temporal stability. *Journal of Clinical Child and Adolescent Psychology, 36*, 276–292.

Ochsner, K.N., & Gross, J.J. (2008). Cognitive emotion regulation: Insights from social cognitive and affective neuroscience. *Current Directions in Psychological Science, 17,* 153–158.

Offer, D. (1999). Normality and the boundaries of psychiatry. In S. Weissman & M. Sabshin (Eds.), *Psychiatry in the new millennium* (pp. 67–77). Washington, DC: American Psychiatric Association.

Offit, P. A. (2008). *Autism's false prophets.* New York: Columbia University Press.

Offord, D. R., Boyle, M. H., Racine, Y., Szatmari, P., Fleming, J. E., Sanford, M., et al. (1996). Integrating assessment data from multiple informants. *Journal of the American Academy of Child and Adolescent Psychiatry, 35*, 1078–1085.

Ogawa, J. R., Sroufe, L. A., Weinfield, N. S., Carlson, E. A., & Egeland, B. (1997). Development and the fragmented self: Longitudinal study of dissociative symptomatology in a nonclinical sample. *Development and Psychopathology, 9*, 855–879.

Ohannessian, C. M., Hesselbrock, V. M., Kramer, J., Kuperman, S., Bucholz, K. K., Schuckit, M. A., et al. (2004). The relationship between parental alcoholism and adolescent psychopathology: A systematic examination of parental comorbid psychopathology. *Journal of Abnormal Child Psychology, 32*, 519–533.

Ohannessian, C. M., Hesselbrock, V. M., Kramer, J., Kuperman, S., Bucholz, K. K., Schuckit, M. A., et al. (2005). The relationship between parental psychopathology and adolescent psychopathology: An examination of gender patterns. *Journal of Emotional and Behavioral Disorders, 13*, 67–76.

Okasha, A. (2002). The new ethical context of psychiatry. In N. Sartorius & W. Gaebel (Eds.), *Psychiatry in society* (pp. 101–130). New York: Wiley.

Oldehinkel, A. J., Hartman, C. A., Ferdinand, R. F., Verhulst, F. C., & Ormel, J. (2007). Effortful control as modifier of the association between negative emotionality and adolescents'mental health problems. *Development and Psychopathology,19*, 523–539.

Olfson, M., Gameroff, M. H., Marcus, S. C., & Waslick, B. D. (2003). Outpatient treatment of child and adolescent depression in the United States. *Archives of General Psychiatry, 60*, 1236–1242.

Ollendick, T. H., Birmaher, B., & Mattis, S. G. (2004). Panic disorder. In T. L. Morris & J. S. March (Eds.), *Anxiety disorders in children and adolescents* (2nd ed., pp. 189–211). New York: Guilford Press.

Ollendick, T. H., & King, N. J. (1998). Empirically supported treatments for children with phobic and anxiety disorders: Current status. *Journal of Clinical Child Psychology, 27*, 156–167.

Ollendick, T. H., King, N. J., & Muris, P. (2002). Fears and phobias in children: Phenomenology, epidemiology, and aetiology. *Child and Adolescent Mental Health, 7*, 98–106.

Ollendick, T. H., Matson, J. L., & Helsel, W. J. (1985). Fears in children and adolescents: Normative data. *Behaviour Research and Therapy, 23*, 465–467.

Ollendick, T. H., Shortt, A. L., & Sander, J. B. (2005). Internalizing disorders of childhood and adolescence. In J. E. Maddux & B. A. Winstead (Eds.), *Psychopathology: Foundations for a contemporary understanding* (pp. 353–376). Mahwah, NJ: Erlbaum.

Ollendick, T. H., & Vasey, M. W. (1999). Developmental theory and the practice of clinical child psychology. *Journal of Clinical Child Psychology, 28*, 457–466.

Ollendick, T.H., Seligman, L.D., Goza, A.B., Byrd, D.A., Singh, K. (2003). Anxiety and depression in children and adolescents: A factor-analytic examination of the tripartite model. *Journal of Child and Family Studies, 12,* 157–170.

Olson, H. C. (2002). Helping children with fetal alcohol syndrome and related conditions: A clinician's overview. In R. J. McMahon & R. D. Peters (Eds.), *The effects of parental dysfunction on children* (pp. 147–177). New York: Kluwer Academic /Plenum Press.

Olweus, D. (2005). A useful evaluation design, and effects of the Olweus Bullying Prevention Program. *Psychology, Crime and Law, 11*, 389–402.

Omigbodun, O. (2008). Developing child mental health services in resource-poor countries. *International Review of Psychiatry, 20*, 225–235.

Oosterman, M., De Schipper, J.C., Fisher, P., Dozier, M., & Schuengel, C. (2010). Autonomic reactivity in relation to attachment and early adversity among foster children. *Development and Psychopathology, 22*, 109–118.

Oppenheim, D. (2006). Child, parent, and parent-child emotion narratives: Implications for developmental psychopathology. *Development and Psychopathology, 18,* 771–790.

Oquendo, M., Brent, D. A., Birmaher, B., Greenhill, L., Kolko, D., Stanley, B., et al. (2005). Posttraumatic stress disorder comorbid with major depression: Factors mediating the association with suicidal behavior. *American Journal of Psychiatry, 162*, 560–566.

Orlando, M., Tucker, J. S., Ellickson, P. L., & Klein, D. J. (2004). Developmental trajectories of cigarette smoking and their correlates from early adolescence to young adulthood. *Journal of Consulting and Clinical Psychology, 72*, 400–410.

Orlando, M., Tucker, J. S., Ellickson, P. L., & Klein, D. J. (2005). Concurrent use of alcohol and cigarettes from adolescence to young adulthood: An examination of developmental trajectories and outcomes. *Substance Use and Misuse, 40*, 1051–1069.

Ornoy, A. (2002). The effects of alcohol and illicit drugs on the human embryo and fetus. *Israel Journal of Psychiatry and Related Sciences, 39*, 120–132.

Orpinas, P., & Horne, A. M. (2006). *Bullying prevention: Creating a positive school climate and developing social competence.* Washington, DC: American Psychological Association.

Orsmond, G.I., & Seltzer, M.M. (2007). Siblings of individuals with autism or Down syndrome: Effects on adult lives. *Journal of Intellectual Disability Research, 51,* 682–696.

Osborne, L., & Pober, B. (2001). Genetics of childhood disorders:XXVII. Genes and cognition in Williams syndrome. *Journal of the American Academy of Child and Adolescent Psychiatry, 40,* 732–735.

Osborne, M. S., & Kenny, D. T. (2005). Development and validation of a music performance anxiety inventory for gifted adolescent musicians. *Journal of Anxiety Disorders, 19,* 725–751.

Osborne, M. S., Kenny, D. T., & Holsomback, R. (2005). Assessment of music performance anxiety in late childhood: A validation study of the Music Performance Anxiety Inventory for Adolescents (MPAI-A). *International Journal of Stress Management, 12*, 312–330.

Osofsky, J. D. (2003). Prevalence of children's exposure to domestic violence and child maltreatment: Implications for prevention and intervention. *Clinical Child and Family Psychology Review, 6,* 161–170.

Osterling, J. A., & Dawson, G. (1994). Early recognition of children with autism: A study of first birthday home videotapes. *Journal of Autism and Developmental Disorders, 24*, 247–257.

Osterling, J. A., Dawson, G., & Munson, J. A. (2002). Early recognition of 1-year-old infants with autism spectrum disorder versus mental retardation. *Development and Psychopathology, 14*, 239–251.

Ostrowski, S.A., Christopher, N.C. & Delahanty, D.L. (2007). Brief report: The impact of maternal posttraumatic stress disorder symptoms and child gender on risk for persistent posttraumatic stress disorder symptoms in child trauma victims. *Journal of Pediatric Psychology, 32*, 338–342.

Owens, E.B., Hinshaw, S.P., Kramer, H.C., Arnold, L.E., Abikoff, H.B., Cantwell, D.P., ... Wigal, T. (2003). Which treatment for whom for ADHD? Moderators of treatment response in the MTA. *Journal of Consulting and Clinical Psychology, 71,* 540–52.

Owens J. S., & Hoza, B. (2003). Diagnostic utility of DSM-IV-TR symptoms in the prediction of DSM-IV-TR ADHD subtypes and ODD. *Journal of Attention Disorders, 7*, 11–27.

Owens, P. L., Hoagwood, K., Horwitz, S. M., Leaf, P. J., Poduska, J. M., Kellam, S. G., et al. (2002). Barriers to children's mental health services. *Journal of the American Academy of Child & Adolescent Psychiatry, 41*, 731–738.

Owens, P.L., Hoagwood, K., Horwitz, S.M., Leaf, P.J., Poduska, J.M., Kellam, S.G., & Ialongo, N.S. (2002). Barriers to children's mental health services. *Journal of the American Academy of Child & Adolescent Psychiatry, 41,* 731–738.

Ozonoff, S. (1997). Components of executive function in autism and other disorders. In J. Russell (Ed.), *Autism as an executive disorder* (pp. 179–211). New York: Oxford University Press.

Ozonoff, S. (1998). Assessment and remediation of executive dysfunction in autism and Asperger syndrome. In E. Schopler, G. Mesibov & L. J. Kunce (Eds.), *Asperger syndrome or high functioning autism?* (pp. 263–289). New York: Plenum Press.

Ozonoff, S., Iosif, A., Baguio, F., Cook, I.C., Hill, M.M., Hutman, T., … Young, G.S. (2010). A prospective study of the emergence of early behavioral signs of autism. *Journal of the American Academy of Child & Adolescent Psychiatry, 49,* 256–266.

Ozonoff, S., Williams, B.J., & Landa, R. (2005). Parental report of the early development of children with regressive autism: The delays-plus-regression phenotype. *Autism, 9,* 461–486.

Page, R. M., Lee, C., & Miao, N. (2005). Self-perception of body weight among high school students in Taipei, Taiwan. *International Journal of Adolescent Medicine and Health, 17,* 123–136.

Pajer, K., Chung, J., Leininger, L., Wang, W., Gardner, W., & Yeates, K. (2008). Neuropsychological function in adolescent girls with conduct disorder. *Journal of the American Academy of Child & Adolescent Psychiatry, 47,* 416–425.

Palmer, D. S., Borthwick-Duffy, S. A., Widaman, K., & Best, S. J. (1998). Influences on parent perceptions of inclusive practices for their children with mental retardation. *American Journal on Mental Retardation, 103,* 272–287.

Panksepp, J. (1998). Attention deficit hyperactivity disorders, psychostimulants, and intolerance of childhood playfulness: A tragedy in the making. *American Psychological Society, 7,* 91–98.

Papadakis, A. A., Prince, R. P., Jones, N. P., & Strauman, T. J. (2006). Self-regulation, rumination, and vulnerability to depression in adolescent girls. *Development and Psychopathology, 18,* 815–829.

Papezova, H, Yamamotova, A., & Uher, R. (2005). Elevated pain threshold in eating disorders: Physiological and psychological factors. *Journal of Psychiatric Research, 39,* 431–438.

Pappadopulos, E., Jensen, P.S., Chait, A.R., Arnold, L.E., Swanson, J.M., Greenhill, L.L., … Newcorn, J.H. (2009). Medication adherence in the MTA: Saliva methylphenidate samples versus parent report and mediating effect of concomitant behavioral treatment. *Journal of the American Academy of Child & Adolescent Psychiatry, 48,* 501–510.

Pardini, D., Stepp, S., Hipwell, A., Stouthamer-Loeber, M., & Loeber, R. (2012). The clinical utility of the proposed DSM-5 callous-unemotional subtype of conduct disorder in young girls. *Journal of the American Academy of Child Psychiatry, 51,* 62–73.

Parent, S., Normandeua, S., & Larivée, S. (2000). A quest for the holy grail in the new millennium: In search of a unified theory of cognitive development. *Child Development, 71,* 860–861.

Parikh, M. S., Kolevzon, A., & Hollander, E. (2008). Psychopharmacology of aggression in children and adolescents with autism: A critical review of efficacy and tolerability. *Journal of Child and Adolescent Psychopharmacology, 18,* 157–178.

Park, C.C. (1995). *The Siege A Family's Journey into the World of an Autistic Child.* New York: Little, Brown and Company.

Parke, R. D. (2004a). Development in the family. *Annual Review of Psychology, 55,* 365–399.

Parke, R. D. (2004b). Fathers, families, and the future: A plethora of plausible predictions. *Merrill-Palmer Quarterly, 50,* 456–470.

Parker, J. G., Rubin, K. H., Price, J. M., & DeRosier, M. E. (1995). Peer relationships, child development, and adjustment: A developmental psychopathology perspective. In D. Cicchetti & D. J. Cohen (Eds.), *Developmental psychopathology: Vol. 2. Risk, disorder, and adaptation* (pp. 96–161). New York: Wiley.

Parker, L. S., & Gettig, E. (1997). Ethical issues in genetic screening and testing, gene therapy, and scientific conduct. In K. Blum & E. P. Noble (Eds.), *Handbook of Psychiatric Genetics,* (pp. 469–478). Boca Raton, FL: CRC Press.

Parmelee, A. H. (1986). Children's illnesses: Their beneficial effects on behavioral development. *Child Development, 57,* 1–10.

Patel, N. C., DelBello, M. P., Cecil, K. M., Adler, C. M., Bryan, H. S., Stanford, K. E., et al. (2006). Lithium treatment effects on myo-inositol in adolescents with bipolar depression. *Biological Psychiatry, 60,* 998–1004.

Patel, V., Flisher, A.J., Nikapota, A., & Malhotra, S. (2007). Promoting child and adolescent mental health in low and middle income countries. *Journal of Child Psychology and Psychiatry, 49,* 313–334.

Patrick, C.J., Fowles, D.C., & Krueger, R.F. (2009). Triarchic conceptualization of psychopathology: Developmental origins of disinhibition, boldness, and meanness. *Development and Psychopathology, 21,* 913–938.

Patterson, G. R., DeGarmo, D. S., & Knutson, N. (2000). Hyperactivity and antisocial behaviors: Comorbid or two points in the same process? *Development and Psychopathology, 12,* 91–106.

Patterson, G. R., Dishion, T. J., & Yoerger, K. (2000). Adolescent growth in new forms of problem behavior: Macro- and micro-peer dynamics. *Prevention Science, 1,* 3–13.

Patterson, G. R., & Fisher, P. A. (2002). Recent developments in our understanding of parenting: Bidirectional effects, causal models, and the search for parsimony. In M. H. Bornstein (Ed.), *Handbook of parenting: Vol. 5. Practical issues in parenting* (2nd ed., pp. 59–88). Mahwah, NJ: Erlbaum.

Patterson, G. R., Reid, J. B., & Eddy, J. M. (2002). A brief history of the Oregon model. In J. B. Reid & G. R. Patterson (Eds.), *Antisocial behavior in children and adolescents: A developmental analysis and model for intervention* (pp. 3–20). Washington, DC: American Psychological Association.

Patterson, G. R., & Yoerger, K. (2002). A developmental model for early- and late-onset delinquency. In J. B. Reid & G. R. Patterson (Eds.) *Antisocial behavior in children and adolescents: A developmental analysis and model for intervention* (pp. 147–172). Washington, DC: American Psychological Association.

Patterson, G.R., Forgatch, M.S., & DeGarmo, D.S. (2010). Cascading effects following intervention. *Development and Psychopathology, 22,* 949–970.

Patton, G. C., Coffey, C., & Sawyer, S. M. (2003). The outcome of adolescent eating disorders: Findings from the Victorian adolescent health cohort study. *European Child and Adolescent Psychiatry, 12,* 125–129.

Paul, R. (2003). Promoting social communication in high functioning individuals with autistic spectrum disorders. *Child and Adolescent Psychiatric Clinics of North America, 12,* 87–106.

Pauletti, R.E., Menon, M., Tobin, D.D., & Perry, D.G. (2012). Narcissism and adjustment in preadolescence. *Child Development, 83,* 831–837.

Paulson, J. F., Buermeyer, C., & Nelson-Gray, R. O. (2005). Social rejection and ADHD in young adults: An analogue experiment. *Journal of Attention Disorders, 8,* 127–135.

Pavuluri, M. N., Graczyk, P. A., Henry, D. B., Carbray, J. A., Heidenreich, J., & Miklowitz, D. J. (2004). Child- and family-focused cognitive-behavioral therapy for pediatric bipolar disorder: Development and preliminary results. *Journal of the American Academy of Child Adolescent Psychiatry, 43*, 528–537.

Pavuluri, M. N., Janicak, P. G., Naylor, M. W., & Sweeney, J. A. (2003). Early recognition and differentiation of pediatric schizophrenia and bipolar disorder. In L. T. Flaherty (Ed.), *Adolescent psychiatry: Developmental and clinical studies* (pp. 117–134). New York: Analytic Press/Taylor & Francis Group.

Paxton, S. J., Norris, M., Wertheim, E. H., Durkin, S. J., & Anderson, J. (2005). Body dissatisfaction, dating, and the importance of thinness to attractiveness in adolescent girls. *Sex Roles, 53,* 663–675.

Pearce, M. J., Jones, S. M., Schwab-Stone, M.E., & Ruchkin, V. (2003). The protective effects of religiousness and parent involvement on the development of conduct problems among youth exposed to violence. *Child Development, 74,* 1682–1696.

Pearlman-Avnion, S., & Eviatar, Z. (2002). Narrative analysis in developmental social and linguistic pathologies: Dissociation between emotional and informational language use. *Brain and Cognition, 49,* 494–499.

Pears, K.C., Bruce, J., Fisher, P.A., & Kim, H.K. (2010). Indiscriminate friendliness in maltreated foster children. *Child Maltreatment, 15,* 64–75.

Peat, C., Mitchell, J.E., Hoek, H.W., & Wonderlich, S.A. (2009). Validity and utility of subtyping anorexia nervosa. *International Journal of Eating Disorders, 42,* 590–594.

Pedersen, W., Mastekaasa, A., & Wichstrom, L. (2001). Conduct problems and early cannabis initiation: A longitudinal study of gender differences. *Addiction, 96,* 415–431.

Pelham, W. E., Gnagy, E. M., Greiner, A. R., Waschbusch, D. A., Fabiano, G. A., & Burrows-MacLean, L. (2010). Summer treatment programs for attention-deficit/hyperactivity disorder. In J. R. Weisz & A. E. Kazdin (Eds.), *Evidence-Based Psychotherapies for Children and Adolescents* (2nd ed.) (pp. 277–292). New York: Guilford Press.

Pelham, W. E., Hoza, B., Pillow, D. R., Gnagy, E. M., Kipp, H. L., Greiner, A. R., et al. (2002). Effects of methyphenidate and expectancy on children with ADHD: Behavior, academic performance, and attributions in a summer treatment program and regular classroom settings. *Journal of Consulting and Clinical Psychology, 70,* 320–335.

Pelham, W.E., & Fabiano, G.A. (2008). Evidence-based psychosocial treatments for attention-deficit/hyperactivity disorder. *Journal of Clinical Child & Adolescent Psychology, 37,* 184–214.

Pelkonen, M., Marttunen, M., Henriksson, M., & Lonnqvist, J. (2005). Suicidality in adjustment disorder: Clinical characteristics of adolescent outpatients. *European Child and Adolescent Psychiatry, 14,* 174–180.

Pelletier, S., & Dorval, M. (2004). Predictive genetic testing raises new professional challenges of psychologists. *Canadian Psychology, 45,* 16–30.

Pennington, B. F. (2002). *The development of psychopathology: Nature and nurture.* New York: Guilford Press.

Pennington, B. F., Moon, J., Edgin, J., Stedron, J., & Nadel, L. (2003). The neuropsychology of Down syndrome: Evidence for hippocampal dysfunction. *Child Development, 74,* 75–93.

Pennington, B.F. (2006). From single to multiple deficit models of developmental disorders. *Cognition, 101,* 385–413.

Pennington, B.F. (2009). How neuropsychology informs our understanding of developmental disorders. *Journal of Child Psychology and Psychiatry, 50,* 72–78.

Pennington, B.F., McGrath, L.M., & Smith, S.D. (2009). Genetics of dyslexia: Cognitive analysis candidate genes, comorbidities, and etiologic interactions. In T.E. Goldberg, D.R. Weinberger (Eds.), *The Genetics of Cognitive Neuroscience* (pp. 177–193). Cambridge, MA: MIT Press.

Pentz, M. A. (2003). Evidence-based prevention: Characteristics, impact, and future. *Journal of Psychoactive Drugs, 35,* 143–152.

Pentz, M. A., Mares, D., Schinke, S., & Rohrbach, L. A. (2004). Political science, public policy, and drug use prevention. *Substance Use and Misuse, 39,* 1821–1865.

Pepler, D., Jiang, D., Craig, W., & Connolly, J. (2008). Developmental trajectories of bullying and associated factors. *Child Development, 79,* 325–338.

Pepler, D.J., Craig, W.M., Connolly, J.A., Yuile, A., McMaster, L., & Jiang, D. (2006). A developmental perspective on bullying. *Aggressive Behavior, 32,* 376–384.

Perez, M, Joiner, T. E., & Lewinsohn, P. M. (2004). Is major depressive disorder or dysthymia more strongly associated with bulimia nervosa? *International Journal of Eating Disorders, 36,* 55–61.

Peris, T.S., Sugar, C.A., Bergman, R.L., Change,S., Langley, A. & Piacentini, J. (2012). Family factors predict treatment outcome for pediatric obsessive-compulsive disorder. *Journal of Consulting and Clinical Psychology, 80,* 255–263.

Perkins, D. F., & Jones, K. R. (2004). Risk behaviors and resiliency within physically abused adolescents. *Child Abuse and Neglect, 28,* 547–563.

Perkins, D. F., Luster, T., & Jank, W. (2002). Protective factors, physical abuse, and purging from community-wide surveys of female adolescents. *Journal of Adolescent Research, 17,* 377–400.

Perkonigg, A., Pfister, H., Stein, M. B., Höfler, M., Lieb, R., Maercker, A., et al. (2005). Longitudinal course of posttraumatic stress disorder and posttraumatic stress disorder symptoms in a community sample of adolescents and young adults. *American Journal of Psychiatry, 162,* 1320–1327.

Perlman, S.B., Hudac, C.M., Pegors, T., Minshew, N.J., & Pelphrey, K.A. (2011). Experimental manipulation of face-evoked activity in the fusiform gyrus of individuals with autism. *Social Neuroscience, 6,* 22–30.

Perlman, S.B., Wyk, B.C.V., & Pelphrey, K.A. (2010). Brain mechanisms in the typical and atypical development of social cognition. In P.D. Zelazo, M. Chandler & E. Crone (Eds.) *Developmental Social Cognitive Neuroscience* (pp. 99–124). New York: Psychology Press.

Perren, S., & Alsaker, F. D. (2006). Social behavior and peer relationship of victims, bully-victims, and bullies in kindergarten. *Journal of Child Psychology and Psychiatry, 47,* 45–57.

Perris, T.S., Sugar, C.A., Bergman, R.L., Chang, S., Langley, A., & Piacentini, J. (2012). Family factors predict treatment outcome for pediatric obsessive-compulsive disorder. *Journal of Consulting and Clinical Psychology, 80,* 255–263.

Perry, A. C., Rosenblatt, E. B., & Wang, X. (2004). Physical, behavioral, and body image characteristics in a tri-racial group of adolescent girls. *Obesity Research, 12,* 1670–1679.

Pérusse, D., & Gendreau, P. L. (2005). Genetics and the development of aggression. In R. E. Tremblay, W. W. Hartup, & J. Archer (Eds.), *Developmental origins of aggression* (pp. 220–241). New York: Guilford Press.

Pervanidou, P., Kolaitis, G., Charitaki, S., Lazaropoulou, C., Papassotiriou, I., Hindmarsh, P., Bakoula, C., Tsiantis, J. & Chrousos, G. P. (2007). The natural history of neuroendocrine changes in pediatric posttraumatic stress disorder (PTSD) after motor vehicle accidents: Progressive divergence of noradrenaline and cortisol concentrations over time. *Biological Psychiatry, 62,* 1095–1102.

Pescosolido, B. A. (2007). Culture, children, and mental health treatment: Special section on the National Stigma Study—Children. *Psychiatric Services, 58,* 611–612.

Pescosolido, B.A., Jensen, P.s., Martin, J.K., Perry, B.L., Olafsdottir, S., & Fettes, D. (2008). Public health and assessment of child mental health problems: Findings from the national stigma study—children. *Journal of the American Academy of Child and Adolescent Psychiatry, 47,* 339–349.

Peterson, A. V., Kealey, K. A., Mann, S. L., Marek, P. M., & Sarason, I. G. (2000). Hutchinson Smoking Prevention Project: Long-term randomized trial in school-based tobacco use prevention—Results on smoking. *Journal of the National Cancer Institute, 92,* 1979–1991.

Peterson, C.B., Crow, S.J., Swanson, S.A., Crosby, R.D., Wonderlich, S.A., Mitchell, J.E., ... Halmi, K.A. (2011). Examining the stability of DSM-IV and empirically derived eating disorder classification: Implications for DSM-5. *Journal of Consulting and Clinical Psychology, 79,* 777–783.

Peterson, C.B., Swanson, S.A., Crow, S.J., Mitchell, J.E., Agras, W.S., Halmi, K.A., ... Berg, K.C. (2012). Longitudinal stability of binge-eating type in eating disorders. *International Journal of Eating Disorders, 45,* 664–669.

Peterson, C.B., Thuras, P., Ackard, D.M., Mitchell, J.E., Berg, K., Sandager, N., ... Crow, S.J. (2010). Personality dimensions in bulimia nervosa, binge eating disorder, and obesity. *Comprehensive Psychiatry, 51,* 31–36.

Peterson, C.C., Wellman, H.M., & Slaughter, V. (2012). The mind behind the message: Advancing theory-of-mind scales for typically developing children, and those with deafness, autism, or asperger syndrome. *Child Development, 83,* 469–485.

Petot, D., Petot, J., & Achenbach, T.M. (2008). Behavioral and emotional problems of Algerian children and adolescents as reported by parents. *European Child and Adolescent Psychiatry, 17,* 200–208.

Petrill, S. A., Lipton, P. A., Hewitt, J. K., Plomin, R., Cherny, S. A., Corley, R., et al. (2004). Genetic and environmental contributions to general cognitive ability through the first 16 years of life. *Developmental Psychology, 40,* 805–812.

Petrill, S.A., & Justice, L.M. (2007). Bridging the gap between genomics and education. *Mind, Brian, and Education, 1,* 153–161.

Petry, N. M. (2005). Prevention: Focus on gambling in youth and young adults. In Petry, N. M. *Pathological gambling: Etiology, comorbidity, and treatment* (pp. 269–278). Washington, DC: American Psychological Association.

Petti, T., Reich, W., Todd, R. D., Joshi, P., Galvin, M., Reich, T., et al. (2004). Psychosocial variables in children and teens of extended families identified through bipolar affective disorder probands. *Bipolar Disorders, 6,* 106–114.

Pettit, G. S., & Dodge, K. A. (2003). Violent children: Bridging development, intervention, and public policy. *Developmental Psychology, 39,* 187–188.

Pfeifer, M., Goldsmith, H.H., Davidson, R.J., Rickman, M. (2002). Continuity and change in inhibited and uninhibited children. *Child Development, 73,* 1474–1485.

Phares, V., Steinberg, A. R., & Thompson, J. K. (2004). Gender differences in peer and parental influences: Body image disturbance, self-worth, and psychological functioning in preadolescent children. *Journal of Youth and Adolescence, 33,* 421–429.

Philadelphia Child Guidance Center. (1993). *Your child's emotional health: The middle years.* New York: Macmillan.

Pickens, R. W., Svikis, D. S., McGue, M., & LaBuda, M. C. (1995). Common genetic mechanisms in alcohol, drug, and mental disorder comorbidity. *Drug and Alcohol Dependence, 39,* 129–138.

Pike, A., Reiss, D., Hetherington, E. M., & Plomin, R. (1996). Using MZ differences in the search for nonshared environmental effects. *Journal of Psychology and Psychiatry and Allied Disciplines, 37,* 695–704.

Pillow, D. R., Pelham, W. E., Hoza, B., Molina, B. S. G., & Stultz,C. H. (1998). Confirmatory factor analyses examining attention deficit hyperactivity disorder symptoms and other childhood disruptive behaviors. *Journal of Abnormal Child Psychology, 26,* 293–309.

Pina, A. A., & Silverman, W. K. (2004). Clinical phenomenology, somatic symptoms, and distress in Hispanic/Latino and European American youths with anxiety disorders. *Journal of Clinical Child and Adolescent Psychology, 33,* 227–236.

Pinderhughes, E. E., Nix, R., Foster, E. M., Jones, D., & Conduct Problems Prevention Research Group. (2001). Parenting in context: Impact of neighborhood poverty, residential stability, public services, social networks, and danger on parental behaviors. *Journal of Marriage and the Family, 63,* 941–953.

Pine, D. S. (1999). Pathophysiology of childhood anxiety disorders. *Biological Psychiatry, 46,* 1555–1566.

Pine, D. S. (2002). Treating children and adolescents with selective serotonin reuptake inhibitors: How long is appropriate? *Journal of Child and Adolescent Psychopharmacology, 12,* 189–203.

Pine, D. S. (2003). Developmental psychobiology and response to threats: Relevance to trauma in children and adolescents. *Biological Psychiatry, 53,* 796–808.

Pine, D. S. (2009). A social neuroscience approach to adolescent depression. In M. De Haan & M. R. Gunnar (Eds.), *Handbook of Developmental Social Neuroscience* (pp. 399–418). New York: Guilford Press.

Pine, D. S., Alegria, M., Cook, E. H., Costello, E. J., Dahl, R. E., Koretz, D., et al. (2002). Advances in developmental sciences and DSM-V. In D. J. Kupfer, M. B. First, & D. A. Regier (Eds.), *A research agenda for DSM-V.* Washington, DC: American Psychiatric Association.

Pine, D. S., Grun, J., & Peterson, B. S. (2001). Use of magnetic resonance imaging to visualize circuits implicated in developmental disorders: The examples of attention-deficit/ hyperactivity disorder and anxiety. In D. D. Dougherty & S. L. Rauch (Eds.), *Psychiatric neuroimaging research: Contemporary strategies* (pp. 335–365). Washington, DC: American Psychiatric Publishing.

Pine, D. S., Walkup, J. T., Labellarte, M. J., Riddle, M. A., Green-hill, L., Klein, R., et al. (2001). Fluvoxamine for the treatment of anxiety disorders in children and adolescents. *New England Journal of Medicine, 344,* 1279–1285.

Pine, D.S. (2007). Research Review: A neuroscience framework for pediatric anxiety disorders. *Journal of Child Psychology and Psychiatry, 48,* 631–648.

Pine, K. J. (2001). Children's perceptions of body shape: A thinness bias in preadolescent girls and associations with femininity. *Clinical Child Psychology and Psychiatry, 6,* 519–536.

Pinker, S. (2002). *The blank slate: The modern denial of human nature.* New York: Viking.

Piper, M. E., Piasecki, T. M., Federman, E. B., Bolt, D. M., Smith, S. S., Fiore, M. C., et al. (2004). A multiple motives approach to tobacco dependence: The Wisconsin Inventory of Smoking Dependence Motives (WISDM-68). *Journal of Consulting and Clinical Psychology, 72*, 139–154.

Pipp-Siegel, S., Siegel, C. H., & Dean, J. (1999). Neurological aspects of the disorganized/disoriented attachment classification system: Differentiating quality of the attachment relationship from neurological impairment. *Monographs of the Society for Research in Child Development, 64*, 25–44.

Pirkle, E. C., & Richter, L. (2006). Personality, attitudinal and behavioral risk profiles of young female binge drinkers and smokers. *Journal of Adolescent Health, 38*, 44–54.

Pitre, N., Stewart, S., Adams, S., Bedard, T., & Landry, S. (2007). The use of puppets with elementary school children in reducing stigmatizing attitudes towards mental illness. *Journal of Mental Health, 16*, 415–429.

Pliszka, S. R., Lopez, M., Crismon, M. L., Toprac, M. G., Hughes,C. W., Emslie, G. J., et al. (2003). A feasibility study of the Children's Medication Algorithm Project (CMAP) algorithm for the treatment of ADHD. *Journal of the American Academy of Child and Adolescent Psychiatry, 42*, 279–287.

Pliszka, S.R. (2009). *Treating ADHD and Comorbid disorders: Psychosocial and Psychopharmacological Interventions.* New York: Guilford Press.

Plomin, R. (2002). Individual differences in a postgenomic era. *Personality and Individual Differences, 33*, 909–920.

Plomin, R. (2004). Genetics and developmental psychology. *Merrill-Palmer Quarterly, 50*, 341–352.

Plomin, R., & Davis, O.S.P. (2009). The future of genetics in psychology and psychiatry: microarrays, genome-wide association, and non-coding RNA. *Journal of child Psychology and Psychiatry, 50,* 63–71.

Plomin, R., DeFries, J. C., Craig, I. W., & McGuffin, P. (2003). Behavioral genomics. In R. Plomin & J. DeFries (Eds.), *Behavioral genetics in the postgenomic era* (pp. 531–540). Washington, DC: American Psychological Association.

Plomin, R., & Kovas, Y. (2005). Generalist genes and learning disabilities. *Psychological Bulletin, 131*, 592–617.

Plomin, R., & McGuffin, P. (2003). Psychopathology in the postgenomic era. *Annual Review of Psychology, 54*, 205–228.

Plunkett, J. W., Meisels, S. J., Steifel, G. S., & Pasik, P. L. (1986). Patterns of attachment among preterm infants of varying biological risk. *Journal of the American Academy of Child Psychiatry, 25*, 794–800.

Polak-Toste, C. P., & Gunnar, M. R. (2006). Temperamental exuberance: Correlates and consequences. In P. J. Marshall & N. A. Fox (Eds.), *The development of social engagement: Neurobiological perspectives* (pp. 19–45). New York: Oxford University Press.

Polanczyk, G., de Lima, M. S., Horta, B. L., Biederman, J., & Rohde, L. A. (2007). The worldwide prevalence of ADHD: A systematic review and metaregression analysis. *American Journal of Psychiatry, 164*, 942–948.

Polanczyk, G., de Lima, M.S., Horta, B.L., Biederman, J., & Rohde, L.A. (2007). The worldwide prevalence of ADHD: A systematic review and metaregression analysis. *American Journal of Psychiatry, 164,* 942–948.

Pollak, S.D. (2008). Mechanisms linking early experience and the emergence of emotions. *Current Directions in Psychological Science, 17,* 370–375.

Pollard, E. L., & Rosenberg, M. L. (2002). The strength-based approach to child well-being: Let's begin with the end in mind. In M. H. Bornstein, L. Davidson, C. L. M. Keyes, & K. Moore (Eds.), *Well-being: Positive development across the life course.* Mahwah, NJ: Erlbaum.

Pomerantz, E. M., & Altermatt, E. R. (1999). Considering the role of development in self-regulation. In R. S. Wyer (Ed.), *Perspectives on behavioral self-regulation* (pp. 175–192). Mahwah, NJ: Erlbaum.

Pomerantz, E. M., & Eaton, M. M. (2001). Maternal intrusive support in the academic context: Transactional socialization processes. *Developmental Psychology, 37*, 174–186.

Pomerantz, E.M., Thompson, R.A. (2008). Parents' role in children's personality development: The psychological resource principle. In O.P. John, R.W., Robins & L.A. Pervin (Eds.) *Handbook of personality: Theory and research* (3rd ed.) (pp 351–374). New York: Guilford Press.

Pomeroy, J. C., & Gadow, K. D. (1998). An overview of psychopharmacology for children and adolescents. In R. J. Morris & T.R. Kratochwill (Eds.), *The practice of child therapy* (3rd ed., pp. 419–470). Needham Heights, MA: Allyn & Bacon.

Pomery, E. A., Gibbons, F. X., Gerrard, M., Cleveland, M. J., Brody, G. H., & Wills, T. A. (2005). Families and risk: Prospective analyses of familial and social influences on adolescent substance use. *Journal of Family Psychology, 19*, 560–570.

Porter, C.L., Hart, C.H., Chongming, Y., Robinson, C.C., Olsen, S.F., Zeng, Q., … Jin, S. (2005). A comparative study of child temperament and parenting in Beijing, China and the western United States. *International Journal of Behavioral Development, 29*, 541–551.

Posada, G., & Jacobs, A. (2001). Child-mother attachment relationships and culture. *American Psychologist, 56*, 821–822.

Posner, J., Nagel, B.J., Maia, T.V., Mechling, A., Oh, M., Wang, Z., & Peterson, B.S. (2011). Abnormal amygdalar activation and connectivity in adolescents with attention-deficit/hyperactivity disorder. *Journal of the American Academy of Child & Adolescent Psychiatry, 50,* 828–837.

Posner, J., Russell, J.A., & Peterson, B.S. (2005). The circumplex model of affect: An integrative approach to affective neuroscience, cognitive development, and psychopathology. *Development and Psychopathology, 17,* 715–734.

Posner, M. I., & Rothbart, M. K. (1980). The development of attentional mechanisms. *Nebraska Symposium on Motivation* (Vol. 28, pp. 1–52). Lincoln: University of Nebraska Press.

Posner, M.I., & Rothbart, M.K. (2007). Research on attention networks as a model for the integration of psychological science. *Annual Review of Psychology, 58,* 1–23.

Potash, J. B., Toolan, J., Steele, J., Miller, E. B., Pearl, J., Zandi, P. P., et al. (2007). The bipolar disorder phenome database: A resource for genetic studies. *American Journal of Psychiatry, 164,* 1229–1237.

Poulin, F., & Chan, A. (2009). Friendship stability and change in childhood and adolescence. *Developmental Review, 30,* 257–272.

Poulin, F., Dishion, T. J., & Haas, E. (1999). The peer influence paradox: Friendship quality and deviancy training within male adolescent friendships. *Merrill-Palmer Quarterly, 45*, 42–61.

Poulton, R., Milne, B. J., Craske, M. G., & Menzies, R. G. (2001). A longitudinal study of the etiology of separation anxiety. *Behaviour Research and Therapy, 39*, 1395–1410.

Power, T. J., Costigan, T. E., Eiraldi, R. B., & Leff, S. S. (2004). Variations in anxiety and depression as a function of ADHD subtypes defined by DSM-IV: Do subtype differences exist or not? *Journal of Abnormal Child Psychology, 32,* 27–37.

Power, T. J., Shapiro, E. D., & DuPaul, G. J. (2003). Preparing psychologists to link systems of care in managing and preventing children's health problems. *Journal of Pediatric Psychology, 28,* 147–155.

Power, T.J., Mautone, J.A., Soffer, S.L., Clarke, A.T., Marshall, S.A., Sharman, J., ... Jawad, A.F. (2012). A family-school intervention for children with ADHD: Results of a randomized clinical trial. *Journal of Consulting and Clinical Psychology, 80,* 611–623.

Powers, A.D., & Westen, D. (2010). Personality subtypes in adolescents with panic disorder. *Clinical Child Psychology and Psychiatry, 16,* 551–565.

Prescott, C. A., Cross, R. J., Kuhn, J. W., Horn, J. L., & Kendler,K. S. (2004). Is risk for alcoholism mediated by individual differences in drinking motivations? *Alcoholism: Clinical and Experimental Research, 28,* 29–39.

Prescott, C. A., Maes, H. H., & Kendler, K. S. (2005). Genetics of substance use disorders. In K. S. Kendler & L. J. Eaves (Eds.), *Review of psychiatry series: Vol. 24, no. 1. Psychiatric genetics* (pp. 167–196). Washington, DC: American Psychiatric Publishing.

Presnell, K., Bearman, S. K., & Stice, E. (2004). Risk factors for body dissatisfaction in adolescent boys and girls. *International Journal of Eating Disorders, 36,* 389–401.

Pring, L., & Hermelin, B. (2002). Numbers and letters: Exploring an autistic savant's unpractised ability. *Neurocase, 8,* 330–337.

Pring, L., Hermelin, B., Buhler, M., & Walker, I. (1997). Native savant talent and acquired skill. *Autism, 1,* 199–214.

Prins, P. J. M., & Ollendick, T. H. (2003). Cognitive change and enhanced coping: Missing mediational links in cognitive behavior therapy with anxiety-disordered children. *Clinical Child and Family Psychology Review, 6,* 87–105.

Proal, E., Reiss, P.T., Klein, R.G., Mannuzza, S., Gotimer, K., Ramos-Olazagasti, M.A., ... Castellanos, F.X. (2011). Brain gray matter deficits at 33-year follow-up in adults with attention-deficit/hyperactivity disorder established in childhood. *Archives of General Psychiatry, 68,* 1122–1134.

Pry, R., Petersen, A., & Baghdadli, A. (2005). The relationship between expressive language level and psychological development in children with autism 5 years of age. *Autism, 9,* 179–189.

Punamäki, R., Qouta, S., El Sarraj, E. & Montgomery, E. (2006). Psychological distress and resources among siblings and parents exposed to traumatic events. *International Journal of Behavioral Development, 30,* 385–397.

Putnam, F.W. (2003). Ten-year research update review: Child sexual abuse. *Journal of the American Academy of Child & Adolescent Psychiatry, 42,* 269–278.

Putnins, A. L. (2006). Substance use among young offenders: Thrills, bad feelings, or bad behavior? *Substance Use and Abuse, 41,* 415–422.

Pynoos, R. S., Steinberg, A. M., & Piacentini, J. C. (1999). A developmental psychopathology model of childhood traumatic stress and intersection with anxiety disorders. *Biological Psychiatry, 46,* 1542–1554.

Quintana, S.M., Chao, R.K., Cross, W.E., Hughes, D., Nelson-Le-Gall, S., Aboud, F.E., Contreras-Grau, J., Hudley, C., Liben, L.S., & Vietze, D.L. (2006). Race, ethnicity, and culture in child development: Contemporary research and future directions. *Child Development, 77,* 1129–1141.

Rachman, S. (1977). The conditioning theory of fear-acquisition: A critical examination. *Behaviour Research and Therapy, 15,* 375–387.

Radke-Yarrow, M., & Klimes-Dougan, B. (1997). Children of depressed mothers: A developmental and interactional perspective. In S. Luthar, J. Burack, D. Cicchetti, & J. R. Weisz (Eds.), *Developmental psychopathology: Perspectives on adjustment, risk and disorder* (pp. 374–389). New York: Cambridge University Press.

Raffaelli, M., & Crockett, L. J. (2003). Sexual risk taking in adolescence: The role of self-regulation and attraction to risk. *Developmental Psychology, 39,* 1036–1046.

Raine, A., Moffitt, T. E., Caspi, A., Loeber, R., Stouthamer-Loeber, M., & Lynam, D. (2005). Neurocognitive impairments in boys on the life-course persistent antisocial path. *Journal of Abnormal Psychology, 114,* 38–49.

Rajan, K. B., Leroux, B. G., Peterson, A. V., Jr., Bricker, J. B., Andersen, M. R., Kealey, K. A., & Sarason, I. G. (2003). Nine-year prospective association between older siblings' smoking and children's daily smoking. *Journal of Adolescent Health, 33,* 25–30.

Ramey, C. T., Campbell, F. A., & Blair, C. (1998). Enhancing the life course for high risk children: Results from the Abecedarian Project. In J. Crane (Ed.), *Social programs that work* (pp. 163–183). New York: Russell Sage Foundation.

Ramisetty-Mikler, S., & Caetano, R. (2004). Ethnic differences in the estimates of children exposed to alcohol problems and alcohol dependence in the United States. *Journal of Studies on Alcohol, 65,* 593–599.

Ramisetty-Mikler, S., Caetano, R., Goebert, D., & Nishimura, S. (2004). Ethnic variation in drinking, drug use, and sexual behavior among adolescents in Hawaii. *Journal of School Health, 74,* 16–22.

Ramsey, S. E., Strong, D. R., Stuart, G. L., Weinstock, M. C., Williams, L. A., Tarnoff, G., et al. (2003). Substance use and diagnostic characteristics that differentiate smoking and nonsmoking adolescents in a psychiatric setting. *Journal of Nervous and Mental Disease, 191,* 759–762.

Randall, J., Henggeler, S. W., Cunningham, P. B., Rowland, M. D., & Swenson, C. C. (2001). Adapting multisystemic therapy to treat adolescent substance abuse more effectively. *Cognitive and Behavioral Practice, 8,* 359–366.

Rao, R., & Georgieff, M. K. (2000). Early nutrition and brain development. In C. A. Nelson (Ed.), *The effects of early adversity on neurobehavioral development. The Minnesota symposium on child psychology* (Vol. 30, pp. 1–30). Mahwah, NJ: Erlbaum.

Rao, U., Dahl, R.E., Ryan, N.D., Birmaher, B., Williamson, D.E., Rao, R. & Kaufman, J. (2002). Heterogeneity in EEG sleep findings in adolescent depression: Unipolar versus bipolar clinical course. *Journal of Affective Disorders, 70,* 273–280.

Rapee, R. M. (2002). The development and modification of temperamental risk for anxiety disorders: Prevention of a lifetime of anxiety? *Biological Psychiatry, 52,* 947–957.

Rapee, R. M., & Sweeney, L. (2005). Social phobia in children and adolescents: Nature and assessment. In W. R. Crozier & L. E. Alden (Eds.), *The essential handbook of social anxiety for clinicians* (pp. 133–151). New York: Wiley.

Rapee, R.M. (2008). Prevention of mental disorders: Promises, limitations, and barriers. *Cognitive and Behavioral Practice, 15,* 47–52.

Rapee, R.M., Kennedy, S.J., Ingram, M., Edwards, S.L., & Sweeney, L. (2010). Altering the trajectory of anxiety in at-risk young children. *American Journal of Psychiatry, 167,* 1518–1525.

Rapee, R.M., Schniering, C.A., & Hudson, J.L. (2009). Anxiety disorders during childhood and adolescence: origins and treatment. *Annual Review of Clinical Psychology, 5,* 311–341.

Rapport, M. (1995). Attention deficit hyperactivity disorder. In M. Hersen & R. T. Ammerman (Eds.), *Advanced abnormal child psychology* (pp. 353–373). Hillsdale, NJ: Erlbaum.

Rapport, M. D., Denney, C. B., Chung, K.-M., & Hustace, K. (2001). Internalizing behavior problems and scholastic achievement in children: Cognitive and behavioral pathways as mediators of outcome. *Journal of Clinical Child Psychology, 30,* 536–551.

Rassin, E., Cougle, J. R., & Muris, P. (2007). Content difference between normal and abnormal obsessions. *Behaviour Research and Therapy, 45,* 2800–2803.

Raver, C. C. (2004). Placing emotional self-regulation in sociocultural and socioeconomic contexts. *Child Development, 75,* 346–353.

Raver, C.C., Jones, S.M., Li-Grining, C., Zahi, F., Bub, K., & Pressler, E. (2011). CSRP's impact on low-income preschoolers' preacademic skills: Self-regulation as a mediating mechanism. *Child Development, 82,* 362–378.

Reba, L., Thornton, L., Tozzi, F., Klump, K., Brandt, H., Crawford, S., et al. (2005). Relationships between features associated with vomiting in purging-type disorders. *International Journal of Eating Disorders, 38,* 287–294.

Reddy, V. (2001). Positively shy! Developmental continuities in the expression of shyness, coyness, and embarrassment. In W. R. Crozier & L. E. Alden (Eds.), *International handbook of social anxiety: Concepts, research and interventions relating to the self and shyness* (pp. 77–99). New York: Wiley.

Reddy, V., Williams, E., & Vaughan, A. (2001). Sharing laughter: The humor of pre-school children with Down syndrome. *Down Syndrome: Research and Practice, 7,* 125–128.

Redfield Jamison, K. (1999). *Night falls fast: Understanding suicide.* New York: Knopf.

Redmond, C., Spoth, R., Shin, C., & Hill, G. J. (2004). Engaging rural parents in family-focused programs to prevent youth substance abuse. *Journal of Primary Prevention, 24,* 223–242.

Reese, L., Kroesen, K., & Gallimore, R. (2000). Agency and school performance among urban Latino youth. In R. D. Taylor & M. Wang (Eds.), *Resilience across contexts: Family, work, culture, and community* (pp. 295–332). Mahwah, NJ: Erlbaum.

Reid, G.J., Huntley, E.,D., & Lewin, D.S. (2009). Insomnias of childhood and adolescence. *Child and Adolescent Psychiatric Clinics of North America, 18,* 979–1000.

Reid, J. B., Patterson, G. R., & Snyder, J. J. (Eds.). (2003). Antisocial behavior in children and adolescents: A developmental analysis and model for intervention. *American Journal of Psychiatry, 160,* 805.

Reid, M. J., Webster-Stratton, C., & Hammond, M. (2007). Enhancing a classroom social competence and problem-solving curriculum by offering parent training to families of moderate- to high-risk elementary school children. *Journal of Clinical Child and Adolescent Psychology, 36,* 605–620.

Reid, M., Landesman, S., Treder, R., & Jaccard, J. (1989). "My family and friends": Six-to twelve-year-old children's perceptions of social support. *Child Development, 60,* 896–910.

Reid, R., DuPaul, G. J., Power, T. J., Anastopoulos, A. D., Rogers-Adkinson, D., Noll, M., et al. (1998). Assessing culturally different students for attention deficit hyperactivity disorder using behavior rating scales. *Journal of Abnormal Child Psychology, 26,* 187–198.

Reijonen, J. H., Pratt, H. D., Patel, D. R., & Greydanus, D. E. (2003). Eating disorders in the adolescent population: An overview. *Journal of Adolescent Research, 18,* 209–222.

Rende, R., Birmaher, B., Axelson, D., Strober, M., Gill, M. K., Valeri, S., et al. (2007). Childhood-onset bipolar disorder: Evidence for increased familial loading of psychiatric illness. *Journal of the American Academy of Child and Adolescent Psychiatry, 46,* 197–204.

Renk, K., Liljequist, L, Simpson, J.E., & Phares, V. (2005). Gender and age differences in the topics of parent-adolescent conflict. *The Family Journal: Counseling and Therapy for Couples and Families, 13,* 139–149.

Renouf, A. G., Kovacs, M., & Mukerji, P. (1997). Relationship of depressive, conduct, and comorbid disorders and social functioning in childhood. *Journal of the American Academy of Child and Adolescent Psychiatry, 36,* 998–1004.

Repacholi, B.M., & Meltzoff, A.N. (2007). Emotional eavesdropping: Infants selectively respond to indirect emotional signals. *Child Development, 78,* 503–521.

Repetti, R. L., Taylor, S. E., & Seeman, T. E. (2002). Risky families: Family social environments and the mental and physical health of offspring. *Psychological Bulletin, 128,* 330–366.

Repetti, R.L., Robles, T.F., & Reynolds, B. (2011). Allostatic processes in the family. *Development and Psychopathology, 23,* 921–938.

Repetti, R.L., Taylor, S.K., & Seeman, T. E. (2002). Risky families: Family social environments and the mental and physical health of offspring. *Psychological Bulletin, 128,* 330–366.

Reschly, D. J. (1981). Evaluation of the effects of SOMPA measures on classification of students as mildly mentally retarded. *American Journal of Mental Deficiency, 86,* 16–20.

Rezvani, A. H., & Levin, E. D. (2004). Adolescent and adult rats respond differently to nicotine and alcohol: Motor activity and body temperature. *International Journal of Developmental Neuroscience, 22,* 349–354.

Rhodes, R. (1993). Mental retardation and sexual expression: An historical perspective. *Journal of Social Work and Human Sexuality, 8,* 1–27.

Ribases, M., Gratacos, M., Badia, A., Badia, A., Jeminez, L., Solano, R., et al. (2005). Contribution of NTRK2 to the genetic susceptibility to anorexia nervosa, harm avoidance and minimum body mass index. *Molecular Psychiatry,10,* 851–860.

Ricciardelli, L. A., & McCabe, M. P. (2004). A biopsychosocial model of disordered eating and the pursuit of muscularity in adolescent boys. *Psychological Bulletin, 130,* 179–205.

Ricciardelli, L. A., McCabe, M. P., Ball, K., & Mellor, D. (2004). Sociocultural influences on body image concerns and body change strategies among indigenous and non-indigenous Australian adolescent girls and boys. *Sex Roles, 51,* 731–741.

Ricciardelli, L. A., McCabe, M. P., Williams, R. J., & Thompson, J.K. (2007). The role of ethnicity and culture in body image and disordered eating among males. *Clinical Psychology Review, 27,* 582–606.

Rice, C. (2001). Making moral decisions: Comparing two theories. *Mental Retardation, 39,* 155–157.

Rich, B.A., Carver, F.W., Holroyd, T., Rosen, H.R., Mendoza, J.K., Cornwell, B.R., ... Leibenluft, E. (2011). Different neural pathways to negative affect in youth with pediatric bipolar disorder and severe mood dysregulation. *Journal of Psychiatric Research, 45,* 1283–1294.

Richards, J. M., & Gross, J. (1999). Composure at any cost? The cognitive consequences of emotion suppression. *Personality and Social Psychology Bulletin, 25,* 1033–1044.

Richards, M. H., Larson, R., Miller, B. V., Luo, Z., Sims, B., Parrella, D. P., et al. (2004). Risky and protective contexts and exposure to violence in urban African American young adolescents. *Journal of Clinical Child and Adolescent Psychology, 33,* 138–148.

Richardson, A. S., Bergen, H. A., Martin, G., Roeger, L., & Allison, S. (2005). Perceived academic performance as an indicator of risk of attempted suicide in young adolescents. *Archives of Suicide Research, 9,* 163–167.

Richert, K.A., Carrion, V.G., Karchemskiy, A. & Reiss, A.L. (2006). Regional differences of the prefrontal cortex in pediatric PTSD: An MRI study. *Depression and Anxiety, 23,* 17–25.

Richler, J., Heurta, M., Bishop, S.L., & Lord, C. (2010). Developmental trajectories of restricted and repetitive behaviors in children with autism spectrum disorders. *Development and Psychopathology, 22,* 55–69.

Richler, J., Luyster, R., Risi, S., Hsu, W., Dawson, G., Bernier, R., et al., (2006). Is there a "regressive phenotype" of autism spectrum disorder associated with the measles-mumps-rubella vaccine? A CPEA study. *Journal of Autism and Developmental Disorders, 36,* 299–316.

Riedel, B. W., Blitstein, J. L., Robinson, L. A., Murray, D. M., & Klesges, R. C. (2003). The reliability and predictive value of adolescents' reports of initial reactions to smoking. *Nicotine and Tobacco Research, 5,* 553–559.

Rieppi, R., Greenhill, L. L., Ford, R. E., Chuang, S., Wu, M., Davies, M., et al. (2002). Socioeconomic status as a moderator of ADHD treatment outcomes. *Journal of the American Academy of Child and Adolescent Psychiatry, 41,* 269–277.

Rierdan, J., & Koff, E. (1997). Weight, weight-related aspects of body image, and depression in early adolescent girls. *Adolescence, 32,* 615–624.

Riley, E. P., Guerri, C., Calhoun, F., Charness, M. E., Foroud, T. M., Li, T., et al. (2003). Prenatal alcohol exposure: Advancing knowledge through international collaborations. *Alcoholism: Clinical and Experimental Research, 27,* 118–135.

Rind, B., Tromovitch, P., & Bauserman, R. (1998). A meta-analytic examination of assumed properties of child sexual abuse using college samples. *Psychological Bulletin, 124,* 22–53.

Ristic, J., Mottron, L., Friesen, C. K., Iarocci, G., Burack, J. A., & Kingstone, A. (2005). Eyes are special but not for everyone: The case of autism. *Cognitive Brain Research, 24,* 715–718.

Rizzolatti, G., Fogassi, L., & Gallese, V. (2009). The mirror neuron system: A motor-based mechanism for action and intention understanding. In M.S. Gazzaniga, E. Bizzi, L.M. Chalupa, S.T. Grafton, T.F. Heatherton, C. Koch, J.E., LeDoux, S.J. Luck, G.R. Mangan, J.A. Movshon, H. Neville,... B.A. Wandell (Eds.), *The cognitive neuroscience,* (4th ed.) (pp. 625–640). Cambridge, MA: Massachusetts Institute of Technology.

Robb, A. S., & Dadson, M. J. (2002). Eating disorders in males. *Child and Adolescent Psychiatric Clinics of North America, 11,* 399–418.

Roberts, C., Kane, R., Thomson, H., Bishop, B., & Hart, B. (2003). The prevention of depressive symptoms in rural school children: A randomized controlled trial. *Journal of Consulting and Clinical Psychology, 71,* 622–628.

Roberts, E., Bornstein, M. H., Slater, A. M., & Barrett, J. (1999). Early cognitive development and parental education. *Infant and Child Development, 8,* 49–62.

Roberts, E.M. (2006). Deriving a humanistic theory of child development from the works of Carl. R. Rogers and Karen Horney. *The Humanistic Psychologist, 34,* 177–199.

Roberts, J. E., Boccia, M. L., Hatton, D. D., Skinner, M. L., & Sideris, J. (2006). Temperament and vagal tone in boys with fragile X syndrome. *Journal of Developmental and Behavioral Pediatrics, 27,* 193–201.

Roberts, R. E., Phinney, J. S., Masse, L. C., Chen, Y. R., Roberts,C. R., & Romero, A. (1999). The structure of ethnic identity of young adolescents from diverse ethnocultural groups. *Journal of Early Adolescence, 19,* 301–322.

Roberts, R. E., Roberts, C. R., & Chen, Y. (1997). Ethnocultural differences in prevalence of adolescent depression. *American Journal of Community Psychology, 25,* 95–110.

Roberts, T. A., Auinger, P., & Ryan, S. A. (2004). Body piercing and high-risk behavior in adolescents. *Journal of Adolescent Health, 34,* 224–229.

Robin, J. A., Puliafico, A. C., Creed, T. A., Comer, J. S., Hofflich,S. A., Barmish, A. J., et al. (2006). Generalized anxiety disorder. In R. T. Ammerman (Ed.), *Comprehensive handbook of personality and psychopathology* (Vol. 3, pp. 117–134). Hoboken, NJ: Wiley.

Robins, D.L. (2008). Screening for autism spectrum disorders in primary care settings. *Autism, 12,* 537–556.

Robins, L. (1966). *Deviant children grown up.* Philadelphia: Williams & Wilkins.

Robins, L. N. (1995). The epidemiology of aggression. In E. Hollander & D. J. Stein (Eds.), *Impulsivity and aggression* (pp. 43–55). Oxford, England: Wiley.

Robins, L.N. (1999). A 70-year history of conduct disorder: Variations in definition, prevalence, and correlates. In P. Cohen, C. Slomkowski & L.N. Robins (Eds.), *Historical and Geographical Influences on Psychopathology (pp.* 37–56). Mahwah, NJ: Erlbaum.

Robins, R. W., John, O. P., Caspi, A., Moffitt, T. E., & Stouthamer-Loeber, M. (1996). Resilient, overcontrolled, and undercontrolled boys: Three replicable personality types. *Journal of Personality and Social Psychology, 70,* 157–171.

Robins, R. W., & Trzesniewski, K. H. (2005). Self-esteem development across the lifespan. *Current Directions in Psychological Science, 14,* 158–162.

Rodgers, J., Riby, D.M., Janes, E., Connolly, B., & McConachie, H. (2012). Anxiety and repetitive behaviours in autism spectrum disorders and Williams syndrome: A cross-syndrome comparison. *Journal of Autism and Developmental Disorders, 42,* 175–180.

Rodgers, R., Chabrol, H., & Paxton, S.J. (2011). An exploration of the tripartite influence model of body dissatisfaction and disordered eating among Australian and French college women. *Body Image, 8,* 208–215.

Rodham, K., Hawton, K., & Evans, E. (2004). Reasons for self-harm: Comparison of self-poisoners and self-cutters in a community sample of adolescents. *Journal of the American Academy of Child and Adolescent Psychiatry, 43,* 80–87.

Rodriguez, R., Marchand, E., Ng, J., & Stice, E. (2008). Effects of a cognitive dissonance-based eating disorder prevention program are similar for Asian American,

Hispanic, and White participants. *International Journal of Eating Disorders, 41*, 618–625.

Roffman, J.L., & Gerber, A.J. (2009). Neural models of psychodynamic concepts and treatments: Implications for psychodynamic psychotherapy. In R.A. Levy & J.S. Ablon (Eds.), *Handbook of Evidence-based Psychodynamic psychotherapy: Bridging the gap between science and practice* (pp. 305–338). Totowa, NJ: Humana Press.

Rogers, S., & DiLalla, D. (1991). A comparative study of the effects of a developmentally based instructional model on young children with autism and young children with other disorders of behavior and development. *Topics in Early Childhood Special Education, 11*, 29–47.

Rogers, S., & Lewis, H. (1988). An effective day treatment model for young children with pervasive developmental disorders. *Journal of the American Academy of Child and Adolescent Psychiatry, 28*, 207–214.

Rogosch, F.A., Dackis, M.N., & Cicchetti, D. (2011). Child maltreatment and allostatic load: Consequences for physical and mental health in children from low-income families. *Development and Psychopathology, 23*, 1107–1124.

Rogosch, F.A., Oshri, A., & Cicchetti, D. (2010). From child maltreatment to adolescent cannabis abuse and dependence: A developmental cascade model. *Development and Psychopathology, 22*, 883–897.

Rohde, L. A., Szobot, C., Polanczyk, G., Schmitz, M., Martins, S., & Tramontina, S. (2005). Attention-deficit/hyperactivity disorder in a diverse culture: Do research and clinical findings support the notion of a cultural construct for the disorder? *Biological Psychiatry, 57*, 1436–1441.

Rohde, P. (2009). Comorbidities with adolescent depression. In S. Nolen-Hoeksema & L.M. Hilt (Eds.), *Handbook of Depression in Adolescents* (pp. 139–177). New York, NY: Routledge/Taylor & Francis Group.

Rohde, P., Lewinsohn, P. M., Clarke, G. N., Hops, H., & Seeley, J. R. (2005). The Adolescent Coping with Depression Course: A cognitive-behavioral approach to the treatment of adolescent depression. In E. D. Hibbs & P. S. Jensen (Eds.), *Psychosocial treatments for child and adolescent disorders: Empirically based strategies for clinical practice* (2nd ed., pp. 219–237). Washington, DC: American Psychological Association.

Rohde, P., Lewinsohn, P.M., Kahler, C.W., Seeley, J.R. & Brown, R.A. (2001). Natural course of alcohol use disorders from adolescence to young adulthood. *Journal of the American Academy of Child & Adolescent Psychiatry, 40*, 83–90.

Roid, G. H. (2003). *Stanford-Binet Intelligence Scale* (5th ed.). Itasca, IL: Riverside.

Roisman, G. I., Masten, A. S., Coatsworth, J. D., & Tellegen, A. (2004). Salient and emerging developmental tasks in the transition to adulthood. *Child Development, 75*, 123–133.

Rojo-Moreno, L., Livianos-Aldana, L., Conesa-Burguet, L., & Cava, G. Dysfunctional rearing in community and clinic based populations with eating problems: Prevalence and mediating role of psychiatric morbidity. *European Eating Disorders Review, 14*, 32–42.

Romanczyk, R. G., Gillis, J. M., Noyes-Grosser, D. M., Holland,J. P., Holland, C. L., & Lyons, D. (2005). Clinical clues, developmental milestones, and early identification/assessment of children with disabilities: Practical applications and conceptual considerations. *Infants and Young Children, 18*, 212–221.

Rome, E. S., & Ammerman, S. (2003). Medical complications of eating disorders: An update. *Journal of Adolescent Health, 33*, 418–426.

Romeo, R.D., & McEwen, B.S. (2006). Stress and the adolescent brain. *Annals of the New York Academy of Sciences, 1094*, 202–14.

Rommelse, N.N.J., Altink, M.E., Fliers, E.A., Martin, N.C., Buschgens, C.J.M., Hartman, C.A., … Oosterlaan, J. (2009). Comorbid problems in ADHD: Degree of association, shared endophenotypes, and formation of distinct subtypes. Implications for a future *DSM. Journal of Abnormal Child Psychology, 37*, 793–804.

Ronk, M.J., Hund, A.M., & Landau, S. (2011). Assessment of social competence of boys with attention-deficit/hyperactivity disorder: Problematic peer entry, host responses, and evaluations. *Journal of Abnormal Child Psychology, 39*, 829–840.

Rose, A. J., Swenson, L. P., & Carlson, W. (2004). Friendships of aggressive youth: Considering the influences of being disliked and of being perceived as popular. *Journal of Experimental Child Psychology, 88*, 24–45.

Rose, A.J., & Rudolph, K.D. (2006). A review of sex differences in peer relationship process: Potential trade-offs for the emotional and behavioral development of girls and boys. *Psychological Bulletin, 132*, 98–131.

Rose, L. T., & Fischer, K.W. (2009). Dynamic development: A neo-Piagetian approach. In U. Muller & J.I. M. Carpendale (Eds.), *The Cambridge Companion to Piaget* (pp. 400–421). New York: Cambridge University Press.

Rose, R. J., Dick, D. M., Viken, R. J., Pulkkinen, L., & Kaprio, J. (2001). Drinking or abstaining at age 14? A genetic epidemiological study. *Alcoholism: Clinical and Experimental Research, 25*, 1594–1604.

Rose, R. J., Dick, D. M., Viken, R. J., Pulkkinen, L., & Kaprio, J. (2004). Genetic and environmental effects on conduct disorder and alcohol dependence symptoms and their covariation at age 14. *Alcoholism: Clinical and Experimental Research, 28*, 1541–1548.

Rose, R. J., & Ditto, W. B. (1983). A developmental-genetic analysis of common fears from early adolescence to early adulthood. *Child Development, 54*, 361–368.

Rose, R. J., Viken, R. J., Dick, D. M., Bates, J. E., Pulkkinen, L., & Kaprio, J. (2003) It does take a village: Nonfamilial environments and children's behavior. *Psychological Science, 14*, 273–277.

Rose-Krasnor, L. (1997). The nature of social competence: A theoretical review. *Social Development, 6*, 111–135.

Rosenfield, S., Lennon, M. C., & White, H. R. (2005). The self and mental health: Self-salience and the emergence of internalizing and externalizing problems. *Journal of Health and Social Behavior, 46*, 323–340.

Rosenzweig, M. R., & Bennett, E. L. (1996). Psychobiology of plasticity: Effects of training and experience on brain and behavior. *Behavioural Brain Research, 78*, 57–65.

Rosner, B. A., Hodapp, R. M., Fidler, D. J., Sagun, J. N., & Dykens, E. M. (2004). Social competence in persons with Prader-Willi, Williams, and Down's syndromes. *Journal of Applied Research in Intellectual Disabilities, 17*, 209–217.

Rossello, J., & Bernal, G. (2005). New developments in cognitive-behavioral and interpersonal treatments for depressed Puerto Rican adolescents. In E. D. Hibbs & P. S. Jensen (Eds.), *Psychosocial treatments for child and adolescent disorders:*

Empirically based strategies for clinical practice (2nd ed., pp. 187–217). Washington, DC: American Psychological Association.

Rossow, I., Groholt, B., & Wichstrom, L. (2005). Intoxicants and suicidal behavior among adolescents: Changes in levels and associations from 1992–2002. *Addiction, 100,* 79–88.

Roth, J., Brooks-Gunn, J., Murray, L., & Foster, W. (1998). Promoting healthy adolescents: Synthesis of youth development program evaluations. *Journal of Research on Adolescence, 8,* 423–459.

Rothbart, M. K. (1991). Temperament: A developmental framework. In J. Strelau & A. Angleitner (Eds.), *Explorations in temperament: International perspectives on theory and measurement* (pp. 61–74). New York: Plenum Press.

Rothbart, M. K. (2007). Temperament, development, and personality. *Current Directions in Psychological Science, 16,* 207–212.

Rothbart, M. K., Ellis, L. K., Rueda, M. R., & Posner, M. (2003). Developing mechanisms of temperamental effortful control. *Journal of Personality, 71,* 1113–1143.

Rothbart, M. K., & Hwang, J. (2002). Measuring infant temperament. *Infant Behavior and Development, 25,* 113–116.

Rothbart, M. K., & Jones, L. B. (1999). Temperament: Developmental perspectives. In R. Gallimore, L. P. Bernheimer, D. L. MacMillan, D. L. Speece, & S. Vaughn (Eds.), *Developmental perspectives on children with high-incidence disabilities* (pp. 33–53). Mahwah, NJ: Erlbaum.

Rothbart, M.K., & Bates, J.E. (2006). Temperament. In N. Eisenberg, W. Damon, & R.M. Lerner (Eds.), *Handbook of Child Psychology: Vol. 3 Social, emotional, and personality development (6th ed.)* (pp. 99–166). Hoboken, NJ: John Wiley & Sons.

Rothbaum, F., Kakinuma, M., Nagaoka, R., & Azuma, H. (2007). Attachment and AMAE: Parent-child closeness in the United States and Japan. *Journal of Cross-Cultural Psychology, 38,* 465–486.

Rothbaum, F., Weisz, J. R., & Snyder, S. S. (1982). Changing the world and changing the self: A two-process model of perceived control. *Journal of Personality and Social Psychology, 42,* 5–37.

Rotheram-Fuller, E., Kasari, C., Chamberlain, B., & Locke, J. (2010). Social involvement of children with autism spectrum disorders in elementary school classrooms. *Journal of Child Psychology and Psychiatry, 51,* 1227–1234.

Rotthaus, W. (2001). Systemic therapy. In A. Dosen & K. Day (Eds.), *Treating mental illness and behavior disorders in children and adults with mental retardation* (pp. 167–180). Washington, DC: American Psychiatric Publishing.

Rowe, R., Costello, E.J., Angold, A., Copeland, W.E., & Maughan, B. (2010). Developmental Pathways in oppositional defiant disorder and conduct disorder. *Journal of Abnormal Psychology, 119,* 726–738.

Rowe, R., Maughan, B., Costello, E. J., & Angold, A. (2005). Defining oppositional defi ant disorder. *Journal of Child Psychology and Psychiatry, 46,* 1309–1316.

Rubinstein, M. L., Halpern-Felsher, B. L., Thompson, P. J., & Millstein, S. G. (2003). Adolescents discriminate between types of smokers and related risks: Evidence from nonsmokers. *Journal of Adolescent Research, 18,* 651–663.

Rudd, M. D., Joiner, T. E., & Rumzek, H. (2004). Childhood diagnoses and later risk for multiple suicide attempts. *Suicide and Life-Threatening Behavior, 34,* 113–125.

Rudolph, K. D., & Asher, S. R. (2000). Adaptation and maladaptation in the peer system: Developmentall processes and outcomes. In A. J. Sameroff, M. Lewis, & S. M. Miller (Eds.), *Handbook of developmental psychopathology* (2nd ed.) (pp. 157–175). Dordrecht, Netherlands: Kluwer Academic Publishers.

Russo, M. F., & Beidel, D. C. (1994). Comorbidity of childhood anxiety and externalizing disorders: Prevalence, associated characteristics, and validation issues. *Clinical Psychology Review, 14,* 199–221.

Rutter, M. (1979). Maternal deprivation, 1972–1978: New findings, new concepts, new approaches. *Child Development, 50,* 283–305.

Rutter, M. (1987). Psychosocial resilience and protective mechanisms. *American Journal of Orthopsychiatry, 57,* 316–331.

Rutter, M. (1990). Psychosocial resilience and protective mechanisms. In J. E. Rolf & A. S. Masten (Eds.), *Risk and protective factors in the development of psychopathology* (pp. 181–214). New York: Cambridge University Press.

Rutter, M. (1996). Transitions and turning points in developmental psychopathology: As applied to the age span between childhood and mid-adulthood. *International Journal of Behavioral Development, 19,* 603–626.

Rutter, M. (2000). Genetic studies of autism: From the 1970s into the millennium. *Journal of Abnormal Child Psychology, 28,* 3–14.

Rutter, M. (2009). Understanding and testing risk mechanisms for mental disorders. *Journal of Child Psychology and Psychiatry, 50,* 44–52.

Rutter, M. (2011). Biological and experiential influences on psychological development. In D.P. Keating (Ed.), *Nature and nurture in early child development* (pp. 7–44). New York: Cambridge University Press.

Rutter, M., Kim-Cohen, J., & Maughan, B. (2006). Continuities and discontinuities in psychopathology between childhood and adult life. *Journal of Child Psychology and Psychiatry, 47,* 276–295.

Rutter, M., Kreppner, J., & Sonuga-Barke, E. (2009). Emanuel Miller Lecture: Attachment insecurity, disinhibited attachment, and attachment disorders: where do research findings leave the concepts? *Journal of Child Psychology and Psychiatry, 50,* 529–543.

Rutter, M., Maughan, B., Meyer, J., Pickles, A., Silberg, J., Simonoff, E., et al. (1997). Heterogeneity of antisocial behavior: Causes, continuities, and consequences. In D. W. Osgood (Ed.), *Motivation and delinquency. Nebraska symposium on motivation, vol. 44* (pp. 45–118). Lincoln: University of Nebraska Press.

Rutter, M., O'Connor, T. G., & English and Romanian Adoptees (ERA) Study Team (2004). Are there biological programming effects for psychological development? Findings from a study of Romanian adoptees. *Developmental Psychology, 40,* 81–94.

Rutter, M., Sonuga-Barke, E.J., & Castle, J. (2010). Investigating the impact of early institutional deprivation on development: Background and research strategy of the English and Romanian adoptees (ERA). *Monographs of the Society for Research in Child Development, 75,* 1–20.

Rutter, M., & Sroufe, L. A. (2000). Developmental psychopathology: Concepts and challenges. *Development and Psychopathology, 12,* 265–296.

Rutter, P. A., & Behrendt, A. E. (2004). Adolescent suicide risk: Four psychosocial factors. *Adolescence, 39,* 295–302.

Rutz, E. M., & Wasserman, D. (2004). Trends in adolescent suicide mortailty in the WHO European region. *European Child and Adolescent Psychiatry, 13*, 321–331.

Ryan, N. D., Puig-Antich, J., Ambrosini, P., Rabinovich, H., et al. (1987). The clinical picture of major depression in children and adolescents. *Archives of General Psychiatry, 44*, 854–861.

Ryan, W., & Smith, J.D. (2009). Antibullying programs in schools: How effective are evaluation practices? *Prevention Science, 10,* 248–259.

Saarni, C. (1999). *The development of emotional competence.* New York: Guilford Press.

Saavedra, L. M., & Silverman, W. K. (2002). Classification of anxiety disorders in children: What a difference two decades make. *International Review of Psychiatry, 14,* 87–101.

Sadeh, A., Flint-Ofir, E., Tirosh, T., & Tidotzky, L. (2007). Infant sleep and parental sleep-related cognitions. *Journal of Family Psychology, 21,* 74–87.

Safford, S. M., Kendall, P. C., Flannery-Shroeder, E., Webb, A., & Sommer, H. (2005). A longitudinal look at parent-child diagnostic agreement in youth treated for anxiety disorders. *Journal of Clinical Child and Adolescent Psychology, 34,* 747–757.

Safren, S.A., Horner, K.J., Leung, A.W., Heimberg, R.G. & Juster, H.R. (2000). Anxiety in ethnic minority youth: Methodological and conceptual issues and review of the literature. *Behavior Modification, 24,* 147–183.

Sagrestano, L. M., Paikoff, R. L., Holmbeck, G. N., & Fendrich, M. (2003). A longitudinal examination of familial risk factors for depression among inner-city African American adolescents. *Journal of Family Psychology, 17,* 108–120.

Sahin, N. H., Batigun, A. D., & Yilmaz, B. (2007). Psychological symptoms of Turkish children and adolescents after the 1999 earthquake: Exposure, gender, location, and time duration. *Journal of Traumatic Stress, 20,* 335–345.

Sakai, J. T., Mikulich-Gilbertson, S. K., & Crowley, T. J. (2006). Adolescent inhalant use among male patients in treatment for substance and behavior problems: Two-year outcome. *American Journal of Drug and Alcohol Abuse, 32,* 29–40.

Sale, E., Sambrano, S., Springer, J. F., Pena, C., Pan, W., & Kasim, R. (2005). Family protection and prevention of alcohol use among Hispanic youth at high risk. *American Journal of Community Psychology, 36,* 195–205.

Salekin, R.T., Leistico, A.R., Trobst, K.K., Schrum, C.L. & Lochman, J.E. (2005). Adolescent psychopathology and personality theory—the interpersonal circumplex: Expanding evidence of a nomological net. *Journal of Abnormal Child Psychology, 33,* 445–460.

Saling, M., Ricciardelli, L. A., & McCabe, M. P. (2005). A prospective study of individual factors in the development of weight and muscle concerns among preadolescent children. *Journal of Youth and Adolescence, 34,* 651–661.

Sameroff, A. J. (1993). Models of development and developmental risk. In C. H. Zeanah (Ed.), *Handbook of infant mental health* (pp. 3–13). New York: Guilford Press.

Sameroff, A. J. (2000). Developmental systems and psychopathology. *Development and Psychopathology, 12,* 297–312.

Sameroff, A. J., Seifer, R., Baldwin, A., & Baldwin, C. (1993). Stability of intelligence from preschool to adolescence: The influence of social and family risk factors. *Child Development, 64,* 80–97.

Samuel, V. J., George, P., Thornell, A., Curtis, S., Taylor, A., Brome, D., et al. (1999). A pilot controlled family study of DSM-III-R and DSM-IV ADHD in African American children. *Journal of the American Academy of Child and Adolescent Psychiatry, 38,* 34–39.

Sanches, M., Roberts, R. L., Sassi, R. B., Axelson, D., Nicoletti, M., Brambilla, P.,et al. (2005). Developmental abnormalities in striatum in young bipolar patients: A preliminary study. *Bipolar Disorders, 7,* 153–158.

Sanders, S.J., Murtha, M.T., Gupta, A.R., Murdoch, J.D., Raubeson, M.J., Willsey, A.J., … State, M.W. (2012). *De novo* mutations revealed by whole-exome sequencing are strongly associated with autism. *Nature, 485,* 237–241.

Sansone, R. A., & Levitt, J. L. (2002). Self-harm behaviors among those with eating disorders: An overview. *Eating Disorders: The Journal of Treatment and Prevention, 10,* 205–213.

Sansone, R. A., Levitt, J. L., & Sansone, L. A. (2005). The prevalence of personality disorders among those with eating disorders. *Eating Disorders: The Journal of Treatment and Prevention, 13,* 7–21.

Santalahti, P., Hemminki, E., Latikka, A., & Ryynaenen, M. (1998). Womens' decision-making in prenatal screening. *Social Science and Medicine, 46,* 1067–1076.

Saunders, B., & Chambers, S. M. (1996). A review of the literature on attention-deficit hyperactivity disorder children: Peer interactions and collaborative learning. *Psychology in the Schools, 33,* 333–340.

Saveanu, R.V., & Nemeroff, C.B. (2012). Etiology of depression: Genetic and environmental factors. *Psychiatric Clinics of North America, 35,* 51–71.

Sawyer, M. G., Arney, F. M., Baghurst, P. A., Clark, J. J., Graetz, B. W., Kosky, R. J., et al. (2001). The mental health of young people in Australia: Key findings from the child and adolescent component of the national survey of mental health and well-being. *Australian and New Zealand Journal of Psychiatry, 35,* 806–814.

Sbarra, D. A., & Pianta, R. C. (2001). Teacher ratings of behavior among African American and Caucasian children during the first two years of school. *Psychology in the Schools, 38,* 229–238.

Scarr, S. (1997). The development of individual differences in intelligence and personality. In H. W. Reese & M. D. Franzen (Eds.), *Biological and neuropsychological mechanisms: Life-span developmental psychology* (pp. 1–22). Hillsdale, NJ: Erlbaum.

Scarr, S. (1998). How do families affect intelligence? Social environmental and behavior genetic predictions. In J. J. McArdle & R. W. Woodcock (Eds.), *Human cognitive abilities in theory and practice* (pp. 113–136). Mahwah, NJ: Erlbaum.

Schafer, I., Barkmann, C., Riedesser, P., & Schulte-Markwort, M. (2006). Posttraumatic syndromes in children after road traffic accidents: A prospective cohort study. *Psychopathology, 39,* 159–164.

Schalock, R. L. (1996). The quality of children's lives. In A. H. Fine & N. M. Fine (Eds.), *Therapeutic recreation for exceptional children: Let me in, I want to play,* (2nd ed., pp. 83–94). Springfield, IL: Charles C. Thomas.

Schalock, R. L. (1997). The conceptualization and measurement of quality of life: Current status and future considerations. *Journal on Developmental Disabilities, 5,* 1–21.

Schalock, R. L. (2000). Three decades of quality of life. *Focus on Autism and Other Developmental Disabilities, 15,* 116–127.

Scheeringa, M. S., & Gaensbauer, T. J. (2000). Posttraumatic stress disorder. In C. H. Zeanah (Ed.), *Handbook of infant mental health* (2nd ed., pp. 369–381). New York: Guilford Press.

Scheeringa, M.S., Weems, C.F., Cohen, J.A., Amaya-Jackson, L., Guthrie, D. (2011). Trauma-focused cognitive-behavioral therapy for posttraumatic stress disorder in three-through six year-old children: A randomized clinical trial. *Journal of Child Psychology and Psychiatry, 52*, 853–860.

Scheeringa, M.S., Zeanah, C.H., & Cohen, J.A. (2011). PTSD in children and adolescents: Toward an empirically based algorithm. *Depression and Anxiety, 28*, 770–782.

Schelble, J.L., Franks, B.A., & Miller, M.D. (2010). Emotion dysregulation and academic resilience in maltreated children. *Child Youth Care Forum, 39*, 289–303.

Schellenberg, G. D., Dawson, G., Sung, Y. G., Estes, A., Muson, J., Rosenthal, E., et al. (2006). Evidence for genetic linkage of autism to chromosomes 7 and 4. *Molecular Psychiatry, 11*, 979.

Schenk, S. (2002). Sensitization as a process underlying the progression of drug use via gateway drugs. In D. B. Kandel (Ed.), *Stages and pathways of drug involvement: Examining the gateway hypothesis* (pp. 318–336). New York: Cambridge University Press.

Scherff, A. R., Eckert, T. L., & Miller, D. N. (2005). Youth suicide prevention: A survey of public school superintendents' acceptability of school-based programs. *Suicide and Life-Threatening Behavior, 35*, 154–169.

Schneider, B. H. (1998). Cross-cultural comparison as doorkeeper in research on the social and emotional adjustment of children and adolescents. *Developmental Psychology, 34*, 793–797.

Schneider-Rosen, K., & Cicchetti, D. (1984). The relationship between affect and cognition in maltreated infants: Quality of attachment and the development of visual self-recognition. *Child Development, 55*, 648–658.

Schock, A. M., Gavazzi, S. M., Fristad, M. A., & Goldberg-Arnold,J. S. (2002). The role of father participation in the treatment of childhood mood disorders. *Family Relations: Interdisciplinary Journal of Applied Family Studies, 51*, 230–237.

Scholtz, S., Hill, L.S., & Lacey, H. (2010). Eating disorders in older women: does late onset anorexia nervosa exist? *International Journal of Eating Disorders, 43*, 393–397.

Schopler, E. (1998). Prevention and management of behavior problems: The TEACCH approach. In E. Sanavio (Ed.), *Behavior and cognitive therapy today: Essays in honor of Hans J. Eysenck* (pp. 249–259). Oxford, England: Elsevier Science.

Schopler, E., & Mesibov, G. B. (2000). Cross-cultural priorities in developing autism services. *International Journal of Mental Health, 29*, 3–21.

Schopler, E., Mesibov, G. B., & Hearsey, K. (1995). Structured teaching in the TEACCH system. In E. Schopler & G. B. Mesibov (Eds.), *Learning and cognition in autism* (pp. 243–268). New York: Plenum Press.

Schopler, E., Reichler, R. J., & Renner, B. R. (1988). The Childhood Autism Rating Scale. Los Angeles: Western Psychological Services.

Schopler, E., Yirmiya, N., Shulman, C., & Marcus, L. M. (Eds.). (2001). *The research basis for autism intervention*. New York: Kluwer Academic/Plenum Publishers.

Schore, A. N. (1994). *Affect regulation and the origin of the self: The neurobiology of emotional development*. Hillsdale, NJ: Erlbaum.

Schore, A. N. (2001). Effects of a secure attachment relationship on right brain development, affect regulation and infant mental health. *Infant Mental Health Journal, 22*, 7–66.

Schreibman, L. (2005). *The science and fiction of autism*. Cambridge, MA: Harvard University Press.

Schreibman, L., & Koegel, R. L. (2005). Training for parents of children with autism: Pivotal responses, generalization, and individualization of interventions. In E. Hibbs & P. Jensen (Eds.), *Psychological treatments for child and adolescent disorders: Empirically based strategies for clinical practice* (2nd ed., pp. 605–631). Washington, DC: American Psychological Association.

Schulenberg, J. E., Merline, A. C., Johnston, L. D., O'Malley, P. M., Bachman, J. G., & Laetz, V. B. (2005). Trajectories of marijuana use during the transition to adulthood: The big picture based on national panel data. *Journal of Drug Issues, 35*, 255–280.

Schulenberg, J., Maggs, J. L., Long, S. W., Sher, K. J., Gotham, H. J., Baer, J. S., et al. (2001). The problem of college drinking: Insights from a developmental perspective. *Alcoholism: Clinical and Experimental Research, 25*, 473–477.

Schulenberg, J., Maggs, J. L., Steinman, K. J., & Zucker, R. A. (2001). Developmental matters: Taking the long view on substance abuse etiology and intervention during adolescence. In P. M. Monti & S. M. Colby (Eds.), *Adolescents, alcohol, and substance abuse: Reaching teens through brief interventions* (pp. 19–57). New York: Guilford Press.

Schultz, R. T. (2005). Developmental deficits in social perception in autism: The role of the amygdale and fusiform face area. *International Journal of Developmental Neuroscience, 23*, 125–141.

Schultz, R. T., Grelotti, D. J., Klin, A., Kleinman, J., Van der Gaag, C., Marois, R., et al. (2003). The role of the fusiform face area in social cognition: Implications for the pathobiology of autism. In U. Frith & E. Hill (Eds.), *Autism: Mind and brain* (pp.267–293). New York: Oxford University Press.

Schumann, C. M., Buonocore, M. H., & Amaral, D. G. (2001). Magnetic resonance imaging of the post-mortem autistic brain. *Journal of Autism and Developmental Disorders, 31*, 561–568.

Schwarte, A. R. (2008). Fragile X syndrome. *School Psychology Quarterly, 23*, 290–300.

Schwartz, C. E., Snidman, N., & Kagan, J. (1999). Adolescent social anxiety as an outcome of inhibited temperament in childhood. *Journal of the American Academy of Child and Adolescent Psychiatry, 38*, 1008–1015.

Schwartz, D., Dodge, K. A., Pettit, G. S., Bates, J. E., & Conduct Problems Prevention Research Group. (2000). Friendship as a moderating factor in the pathway between early harsh home environment and later victimization in the peer group. *Developmental Psychology, 36*, 646–662.

Scime, M., Cook-Cottone, C., Kane, L., & Watson, T. (2006). Group prevention of eating disorders with fifth-grade females: Impact on body dissatisfaction, drive for thinness, and media influence. *Eating Disorders: The Journal of Treatment and Prevention 14*, 143–155.

Sciutto, M. J., Nolfi, C. J., & Bluhm, C. (2004). Effects of gender and symptom type on referrals for ADHD by elementary school teachers. *Journal of Emotional and Behavioral Disorders, 12*, 247–253.

Scorgie, K., Wilgosh, L., & McDonald, L. (1996). A qualitative study of managing life when a child has a disability. *Developmental Disabilities Bulletin, 24*, 68–90.

Scott, M. M., & Deneris, E. S. (2005). Making and breaking serotonin neurons and autism. *International Journal of Developmental Neuroscience, 23*, 277–285.

Scotti, J. R., Morris, T. L., McNeil, C. B., & Hawkins, R. P. (1996). DSM-IV and disorders of childhood and adolescence: Can structural criteria be functional? *Journal of Consulting and Clinical Psychology, 64,* 1177–1191.

Scourfield, J., Rice, F., Thapar, A., Gordon, T., Martin, N., & McGuffin, P. (2003). Depressive symptoms in children and adolescents: Changing aetiological influences with development. *Journal of Child Psychology and Psychiatry, 44,* 968–976.

Sebanz, N., Knoblich, G., Stumpf, L., & Prinz, W. (2005). Far fromaction-blind: Representation of others' actions in individuals with autism. *Cognitive Neuropsychology, 22,* 433–454.

Seeds, P.M., Harkness, K.L., & Quilty, L.C. (2010). Parental maltreatment, bullying, and adolescent depression: Evidence for the mediating role of perceived social support. *Journal of Clinical Child & Adolescent Psychology, 39,* 681–692.

Seidman, L. J., Biederman, J., Monuteaux, M. C., Valera, E., Doyle, A. E., & Faraone, S. V. (2005). Impact of gender and age on executive functioning: Do girls and boys with and without attention deficit hyperactivity disorder differ neuropsychologically in preteen and teenage years? *Developmental Neuropsychology, 27,* 79–105.

Seifer, R., & Dickstein, S. (2000). Parental mental illness and infant development. In C. H. Zeanah (Ed.), *Handbook of infant mental health* (2nd ed., pp. 145–160). New York: Guilford Press.

Seiffge-Krenke, I. (1998). Chronic disease and perceived developmental progression in adolescence. *Developmental Psychology, 34,* 1073–1084.

Seiffge-Krenke, I. (2003). Testing theories of romantic development from adolescence to young adulthood: Evidence of a developmental sequence. *International Journal of Behavioral Development, 27,* 519–531.

Seligman, M. E. P., & Csikszentmihalyi, M. (2000). Positive psychology: An introduction. *American Psychologist, 55,* 5–14.

Seligman, M.E. (1975). *Helplessness: On depression, development, and death.* Oxford, England: W. H. Freeman.

Sellinger, M. H., Hodapp, R. M., & Dykens, E. M. (2006). Leisure activities of individuals with Prader-Willi, Williams, and Down syndromes. *Journal of Developmental and Physical Disabilities, 18,* 59–71.

Seltzer, M.M., Floyd, F., Song, J., Greenberg, J., & Hong, J. (2011). Midlife and aging parents of adults with intellectual and developmental disabilities: Impacts of lifelong parenting. *American Association on Intellectual and Developmental Disabilities, 116,* 479–499.

Seltzer, M.M., Greenberg, J.S., Orsmond, G.I., & Lounds, J. (2005). Life course studies of siblings of individuals with developmental disabilities. *Mental Retardation, 43,* 354–359.

Semel, E., & Rosner, S. R. (2003). *Understanding Williams syndrome: Behavioral patterns and interventions.* Mahwah, NJ: Erlbaum.

Serafucam F. C., & Cicchetti, D. (1976). Down's syndrome children in a strange situation: Attachment and exploration behaviors. *Merrill-Palmer Quarterly, 22,* 137–150.

Seroczynski, A. D., Cole, D. A., & Maxwell, S. E. (1997). Cumulative and compensatory effects of competence and incompetence on depressive symptoms in children. *Journal of Abnormal Psychology, 106,* 586–597.

Servan-Schreiber, D., Lin, B. L., & Birmaher, B. (1998). Prevalence of posttraumatic stress disorder and major depressive disorder in Tibetan refugee children. *Journal of the American Academy of Child and Adolescent Psychiatry, 37,* 874–879.

Sessa, F. M., Avenevoli, S., Steinberg, L., & Morris, A. S. (2001). Correspondence among informants on parenting: Preschool children, mothers, and observers. *Journal of Family Psychology, 25,* 53–68.

Sewitch, M. J., Blais, R., Rahme, E., Bexton, B., & Galarneau, S. (2005). Pharmacologic response to depressive disorders among adolescents. *Psychiatric Services, 56,* 1089–1097.

Shaw, D. S., Dishion, T. J., Supplee, L., Gardner, F., & Arends, K. (2006). Randomized trial of a family-centered approach to the prevention of early conduct problems: 2-Year effects of the family check-up in early childhood. *Journal of Consulting and Clinical Psychology, 74,* 1–9.

Shaw, D.S., Gilliom, M., Ingoldsby, E.M. & Nagin, D.S. (2003). Trajectories leading to school-age conduct problems. *Developmental Psychology, 39,* 189–200.

Shaw, H., Ramirez, L., Trost, A., Randall, P., & Stice, E. (2004). Body image and eating disturbances across ethnic groups: More similarities than differences. *Psychology of Addictive Behaviors, 18,* 12–18.

Shaw, P., Eckstrand, K., Sharp, W., Blumenthal, J., Lerch, J.P., Greenstein, D., ... Rapport, J.L. (2007). Attention-deficit/hyperactivity disorder is characterized be a delay in cortical maturation. *Proceedings of the National Academy of Sciences, 104,* 19649–19654.

Shaw, P., Greenstein, D., Lerch, J., Clasen, L., Lenroot, R., Gogtay, N., ... Giedd, J. (2006). Intellectual ability and cortical development in children and adolescents. *Nature, 440,* 676–679.

Shaw, P., Kabani, N.J., Lerch, J.P., Eckstrand, K., Lenroot, R., Gogtay, N., ... Wise, S.P. (2008). Neurodevelopmental trajectories of the human cerebral cortex. *Journal of Neuroscience, 28,* 3586–3594.

Shaw, P., Lalonde, F., Lepage, C., Rabin, C., Eckstrand, K., Sharp, W., ... Rapoport, J. (2009). Development of cortical asymmetry in typically developing children and its disruption in attention-deficit/hyperactivity disorder. *Archives of General Psychiatry, 66,* 888–896.

Shea, A., Walsh, C., MacMillan, H. & Steiner, M. (2005). Child maltreatment and HPA axis dysregulation: Relationship to major depressive disorder and post traumatic disorder in females. *Psychoneuroendochrinology, 30,* 162–178.

Sheeber, L., Biglan, A., Metzler, C. W., & Taylor, T. K. (2002). Promoting effective parenting practices. In L. A. Jason & D. S. Glenwick (Eds.), *Innovative strategies for promoting health and mental health across the life span* (pp. 63–84). New York: Springer.

Sheffield, J. K., Spence, S. H., Rapee, R. M., Kowalenko, N., Wignall, A., Davis, A., et al. (2006). Evaluation of universal, indicated, and combined cognitive-behavioral approaches to the prevention of depression among adolescents. *Journal of Consulting and Clinical Psychology, 74,* 66–79.

Shelef, K., Diamond, G. M., Diamond, G. S., & Liddle, H. A. (2005). Adolescent and parent alliance and treatment outcome in multidimensional family therapy. *Journal of Consulting and Clinical Psychology, 73,* 689–698.

Sher, L., & Zalsman, G. (2005). Alcohol and adolescent suicide. *International Journal of Adolescent Medicine and Helath 17,* 197–203.

Sherer, M. R., & Schreibman, L. (2005). Individual behavioral profiles and predictors of treatment effectiveness for children with autism. *Journal of Consulting and Clinical Psychology, 73,* 525–538.

Sherrill, J. T., & Kovacs, M. (2002). Nonsomatic treatment of depression. *Child and Adolescent Psychiatric Clinics of North America, 11*, 579–594.

Sherwood, N. E., & Neumark-Sztainer, D. (2001). Internalization of the sociocultural ideal: Weight-related attitudes and dieting behaviors among young adolescent girls. *American Journal of Health Promotion, 15*, 228–231.

Sherwood, N. E., Neumark-Sztainer, D, Story, M. Beuhring, T., & Resnick, M. D. (2002). Weight-related sports involvement in girls: Who is at risk for disordered eating? *American Journal of Health Promotion, 16*, 341–344.

Shields, A., Dickstein, S., Seifer, R., Giusti, L. Magee, K. D., & Spritz, B. (2001). Emotional competence and early school adjustment: A study of preschoolers at risk. *Early Education and Development, 12*, 73–96.

Shih, J. H., Eberhart, N. K., Hammen, C. L., & Brennan, P. A. (2006). Differential exposure and reactivity to interpersonal stress predict sex differences in adolescent depression. *Journal of Clinical Child and Adolescent Psychology, 35*, 103–115.

Shin, J. Y. (2002). Social support for families of children with mental retardation: Comparison between Korea and the United States. *Mental Retardation, 40*, 103–118.

Shiner, R., & Caspi, A. (2003). Personality differences in childhood and adolescence: measurement, development, and consequences. *Journal of Child Psychology and Psychiatry, 44*, 2–32.

Shirk, S. R., & Saiz, C. C. (1992). Clinical, empirical, and developmental perspectives on the therapeutic relationship in child psychotherapy. *Development and Psychopathology, 4*, 713–728.

Shonkoff, J. P., & Meisels, S. J. (2000). *Handbook of early childhood intervention.* New York: Cambridge University Press.

Shonkoff, J. P., & Phillips, D. A. (Eds.). (2000). *From neurons to neighborhoods: The science of early childhood development.* Washington, DC: National Academy Press.

Shonkoff, J.P. (2010). Building a new biodevelopmental framework to guide the future of early childhood policy. *Child Development, 81*, 357–367.

Shonkoff, J.P. (2011). Protecting brains, not simply stimulating minds. *Science, 333*, 982–983.

Shonkoff, J.P., & Bales, S.N. (2011). Science does not speak for itself: translating child development research for the public and its policymakers. *Child Development, 82*, 17–32.

Shoval, G., Zalsman, G., Polakevitch, J., Shtein, N., Sommerfeld, E., & Apter, A. (2005). Effect of the broadcast of a television documentary about a teenage suicide in Israel on suicidal behavior and methods. *Crisis: The Journal of Crisis Intervention and Suicide Prevention, 26*, 20–24.

Shroff, H., Reba, L., Thornton, L. M., Tozzi, F., Klump, K. L., Berrettini, W. H., et al. (2006). Features associated with excessive exercise in women with eating disorders. *International Journal of Eating Disorders, 39*, 454–461.

Shroff, H., & Thompson, J. K. (2004). Body image and eating disturbance in India: Media and interpersonal influences. *International Journal of Eating Disorders, 35*, 198–203.

Shroff, H., & Thompson, J. K. (2006). The Tripartite Influence Model of body image and eating disturbance: A replication with adolescent girls. *Body Image, 3*, 17–23.

Shumow, L., Vandell, D. L., & Posner, J. (1999). Risk and resilience in the urban neighborhood: Predictors of academic performance among low-income elementary school children. *Merrill-Palmer Quarterly, 45*, 309–331.

Siegler, R. S. (2003). Thinking and intelligence. In M. H. Bornstein, L. Davidson, C. L. M. Keyes, & A. Moore (Eds.), *Well-being: Positive development across the life course* (pp. 311–320). Mahwah, NJ: Erlbaum.

Sigman, M., & Ruskin, E. (1999). Continuity and change in the social competence of children with autism, Down syndrome, and developmental delays. *Monographs of the Society for Research in Child Development, 64*, 1–139.

Sigvardsson, S., Bohman, M., & Clonginger, C. R. (1996). Replication of the Stockholm Adoption Study of alcoholism: Confirmatory cross-fostering analysis. *Archives of General Psychiatry, 53*, 681–687.

Silberg, J. L., & Bulik, C. M. (2005). The developmental association between eating disorders symptoms and symptoms of depression and anxiety in juvenile twin girls. *Journal of Child Psychology and Psychiatry, 46*, 1317–1326.

Silberg, J., Pickles, A., Rutter, M., Hewitt, J., Simonoff, E., Maes, J., et al. (1999). The influence of genetic favors and life stress on depression among adolescent girls. *Archives of General Psychology, 56*, 225–232.

Silk, J. S., Sessa, F. M., Sheffield Morris, A., Steinberg, L., & Avenevoli, S. (2004). Neighborhood cohesion as a buffer against hostile maternal parenting. *Journal of Family Psychology, 18*, 135–146.

Silk, J.S., Vanderbilt-Adriance, E., Shaw, D.S., Forbes, E.E., Whalen, D.J., Ryan, N.D., Dahl, R.E. (2007). Resilience among children and adolescents at risk for depression: Mediation and moderation across social and neurobiological context. *Development and Psychopathology, 19*, 841–865.

Silverman, W. K., Kurtines, W. M., Ginsburg, G. S., Weems, C. F., Lumpkin, P. W., & Carmichael, D. H. (1999). Treating anxiety disorders in children with group cognitive-behavioral therapy: A randomized clinical trial. *Journal of Consulting and Clinical Psychology, 67*, 995–1003.

Silverman, W. K., La Greca, A. M., & Wasserstein, S. (1995). What do children worry about? Worries and their relation to anxiety. *Child Development, 66*, 671–686.

Silverman, W. K., & Moreno, J. (2005). Specific phobia. *Child and Adolescent Psychiatric Clinics of North America, 14*, 819–843.

Silverman, W. K., & Ollendick, T. H. (2005). Evidence-based assessment of anxiety and its disorders in children and adolescents. *Journal of Clinical Child and Adolescent Psychology, 34*, 380–411.

Silverman, W.K., Pina, A.A., Viswesvaran, C. (2008). Evidence-based psychosocial treatments for phobic and anxiety disorders in children and adolescents. *Journal of Clinical Child and Adolescent Psychology, 37*, 105–130.

Silverthorn, P., & Frick, P. J. (1999). Developmental pathways to antisocial behavior: The delayed-onset pathway in girls. *Development and Psychopathology, 11*, 101–126.

Sim, L., & Zeman, J. (2004). Emotion awareness and identification skills in adolescent girls with bulimia nervosa. *Journal of Clinical Child and Adolescent Psychology, 33*, 760–771.

Simmerman, S., & Baker, B. L. (2001). Fathers' and mothers' perceptions of father involvement in families with young children with a disability. *Journal of Intellectual and Developmental Disability, 26*, 325–338.

Simmons, R. G. (2001). Comfort with the self. In T. J. Owens, S. Stryker, & N. Goodman (Eds.), *Extending self-esteem theory and research: Sociological and psychological currents* (pp. 198–222). New York: Cambridge University Press.

Simmons, R. G., & Blyth, D. A. (1987). *Moving into adolescence: The impact of pubertal change and school context.* Hawthorne, NY: Aldine de Gruyter.

Simonoff, E., Bolton, P., & Rutter, M. (1996). Mental retardation: Genetic findings, clinical implications and research agenda. *Journal of Child Psychology and Psychiatry, 37,* 259–280.

Simons-Morton, B. (2004). Prospective association of peer influence, school engagement, drinking expectancies, and parent expectations with drinking initiation among sixth graders. *Addictive Behaviors, 29,* 299–309.

Simons-Morton, B., & Chen, R. (2005). Latent growth curve analyses of parent influences on drinking progression among early adolescents. *Journal of Studies on Alcohol, 66,* 5–13.

Simons-Morton, B. G. (2004). The protective effect of parental expectations against early adolescent smoking initiation. *Health Education Research, 19,* 561–569.

Simons-Morton, B. G., Hartos, J. L., Leaf, W. A., & Preusser, D. F. (2006). Increasing parent limits on novice young drivers: Cognitive mediation of the effect of persuasive messages. *Journal of Adolescent Research, 21,* 83–105.

Simons-Morton, B. G., & Haynie, D. L. (2003). Growing up drug free: A developmental challenge. In M. H. Bornstein & L. Davidson (Eds.), *Well-being: Positive development across the life course* (pp. 109–122). Mahwah, NJ: Erlbaum.

Simons-Morton, B. G., Lerner, N., & Singer, J. (2005). The observed effects of teenage passengers on the risky driving behavior of teenage drivers. *Accident Analysis & Prevention, 37,* 973–982.

Simpson, G.A., Cohen, R., Pastor, P.N., & Reuben, C. (2008). *Use of mental health services in the past 12 months by children aged 4–17 years: United States, 2005–2006* (NCHS Data Brief, No. 8). Hyattsville, MD: National Center for Health Statistics.

Simpson, R. L., Myles, B. S., & Simpson, J. D. (1997). Inclusion of students with disabilities in general education settings: Structuring for successful management. In P. Zionts (Ed.), *Inclusion strategies for students with learning and behavioral problems: Perspectives, experiences, and best practices* (pp. 171–196). Austin, TX: PRO-ED.

Singer, G. H.S., Gert, B., & Koegel, R. L. (1999). A moral framework for analyzing the controversy over aversive behavioral interventions for people with severe mental retardation. *Journal of Positive Behavior Interventions, 1,* 88–100.

Singh, I. (2008). Beyond polemics: science and ethics of ADHD. *Nature Reviews, 9,* 957–964.

Singh, M. K., DelBello, M. P., Adler, C. M., Stanford, K. E., & Strakowski, S. M. (2008). Neuroanatomical characterization of child offspring of bipolar patients. *Journal of the American Academy of Child and Adolescent Psychiatry, 47,* 526–531.

Singh, N.N., Oswald, D.P. & Ellis, C.R. (1998). Mental retardation. In T. H. Ollendick & M. Hersen (Eds.), *Handbook of Child Psychopathology (3rd ed)* (pp. 91–116). New York, NY: Plenum Press.

Sivberg, B. (2002). Family system and coping behaviors: A comparison between parents of children with autistic spectrum disorders and parents with non-autistic children. *Autism, 6,* 397–409.

Skara, S., & Sussman, S. (2003). A review of 25 long-term adolescent tobacco and other drug use prevention program evaluations. *Preventive Medicine: An International Journal Devoted to Practice and Theory, 37,* 451–474.

Skowron, E., & Reinemann, D.H.S. (2005). Effectiveness of psychological interventions for child maltreatment: a meta-analysis. *Psychotherapy: Theory, Research, Practice, Training, 42,* 52–71.

Slesnick, N., & Waldron, H. B. (1997). Interpersonal problem-solving interactions of depressed adolescents and their parents. *Journal of Family Psychology, 11,* 234–245.

Slof-Op't, Landt, M. C. T., van Furth, E. F., Meulenbelt, I., Slag-boom, P. E., Bartels, M., Boomsma, D. I., et al. (2005). Eating disorders: From twin studies to candidate genes and beyond. *Twin Research and Human Genetics, 8,* 467–482.

Slonim-Nevo, V., Sharaga, Y., Mirsky, J., Petrovsky, V., & Borodenko, M. (2006). Ethnicity versus migration: Two hypotheses about the psychosocial adjustment of immigrant adolescents. *International Journal of Social Psychiatry, 52,* 41–53.

Slovic, P. (2000). What does it mean to know a cumulative risk? Adolescents' perceptions of short-term and long-term consequences of smoking. *Journal of Behavioral Decision Making, 13,* 259–266.

Slutske, W. S., Caspi, A., Moffitt, T. E., & Poulton, R. (2005). Personality and problem gambling: A prospective study of a birth cohort of young adults. *Archives of General Psychiatry, 62,* 769–775.

Smalley, N., Scourfield, J., & Greenland, K. (2005). Young people, gender, and suicide: A review of research on the social context. *Journal of Social Work, 5,* 133–154.

Smetana, J. G., & Gettman, D. C. (2006). Autonomy and relatedness with parents and romantic development in African American adolescents. *Developmental Psychology, 42,* 1347–1351.

Smith, B. H., Pelham, W. E., Gnagy, E., & Yudell, R. S. (1998). Equivalent effects of stimulant treatment for attention-deficit hyperactivity disorder during childhood and adolescence. *Journal of the American Academy of Child and Adolescent Psychiatry, 37,* 314–321.

Smith, B.H., Pelham, W.E., Gnagy, E., Molina, B. &Evans, S. (2000). The reliability, validity, and unique contributions of self-report by adolescents receiving treatment for attention-deficit/hyperactivity disorder. *Journal of Consulting and Clinical Psychology, 68,* 489–499.

Smith, C. A., & Farrington, D. P. (2004). Continuities in antisocial behavior and parenting across three generations. *Journal of Child Psychology and Psychiatry, 45,* 230–247.

Smith, I. M. (2000). Motor functioning in Asperger syndrome. In A. Klin, F. R. Volkmar, & S. S. Sparrow (Eds.), *Asperger syndrome* (pp. 97–124). New York: Guilford Press.

Smith, J. D. (2002). The myth of mental retardation: Paradigm shifts, dissaggregation, and developmental disabilities. *Mental Retardation, 40,* 62–64.

Smith, J., & Prior, M. (1995). Temperament and stress resilience in school-age children: A within-families study. *Journal of the American Academy of Child and Adolescent Psychiatry, 34,* 168–179.

Smith, R.L., & Rose, A.J. (2011). The "cost of caring" in youths' friendships: Considering associations among social perspective taking, co-rumination, and empathetic distress. *Developmental Psychology, 47,* 1792–1803.

Smith, T. (2010). Early and intensive behavioral intervention in autism. In J. R. Weisz & A. E. Kazdin (Eds.), *Evidence-Based Psychotherapies for Children and Adolescents* (2nd ed.) (pp. 312–326). New York: Guilford Press.

Smorti, A., Menesini, E., & Smith, P.K. (2003). Parents' definitions of children's bullying in a five=country comparison. *Journal of Cross-Cultural Psychology, 34,* 417–432.

Smyke, A.T., Zeanah, C.H., Fox, N.A., & Nelson, C.A. (2009). A new model of foster care for young children: The Bucharest Earl Intervention Project. *Child and Adolescent Psychiatric Clinics of North America, 18,* 721–734.

Snell, M. E., & Janney, R. E. (2000). Teachers' problem-solving about children with moderate and severe disabilities in elementary classrooms. *Exceptional Children, 66,* 472–490.

Snidman, N., Kagan, J., Riordan, L., & Shannon, D. C. (1995). Cardiac function and behavioral reactivity during infancy. *Psychophysiology, 32,* 199–207.

Snyder, A. R. (2006). Risky and casual sexual relationships among teens. In A. C. Crouter & A. Booth (Eds.), *Romance and sex in adolescence and emerging adulthood: Risks and opportunities. The Penn State University family issues symposia series* (pp. 161–169). Mahwah, NJ: Erlbaum.

Snyder, J., Schreperman, L., McEachern, A., Barner, S., Johnson, K., & Provines, J. (2008). Peer deviancy training and peer coercion: Dual processes associated with early-onset conduct problems. *Child Development, 79,* 252–268.

Snyder, J., Schreperman, L., McEachern, A., Barner, S., Johnson, K., & Provines, J. (2008). Peer deviancy training and peer coercion: Dual processes associated with early-onset conduct problems. *Child Development, 79,* 252–268.

Sobanski, E., & Schmidt, M. H. (2000). Body dysmorphic disorder: A review of the current knowledge. *Child Psychology and Psychiatry Review, 5,* 17–24.

Södersten, P., Bergh, C., & Zandian, M. (2006). Understanding eating disorders. *Hormones and Behavior, 50,* 572–578.

Sokol, R. J., Delaney-Black, V., & Nordstrom, B. (2003). Fetal alcohol spectrum disorder. *Journal of the American Medical Association, 290,* 2996–2999.

Soldz, S., Huyser, D. J., & Dorsey, E. (2003). The cigar as a drug delivery device: Youth use of blunts. *Addiction, 98,* 1379–1386.

Solomon, J., & George, C. (1999a). The measurement of attachment security in infancy and childhood. In J. Cassidy & P. R. Shaver (Eds.), *Handbook of attachment: Theory, research, and clinical applications* (pp. 287–316). New York: Guilford Press.

Solomon, J., & George, C. (1999b). The place of disorganization in attachment theory: Linking classic observations with contemporary findings. In J. Solomon & C. George (Eds.), *Attachment disorganization* (pp. 3–32). New York: Guilford Press.

Solomon, Z. & Lavi, T. (2005). Israeli youth in the second Intifada: PTSD and future orientation. *Journal of the American Academy of Child & Adolescent Psychiatry, 44,* 1167–1175.

Sommers-Flanagan, J., Richardson, B.G., & Sommers-Flanagan, R. (2011). A multi-theoretical, evidence-based approach for understanding and managing adolescent resistance to psychotherapy. *Journal of Contemporary Psychotherapy, 41,* 69–80.

Songua-Barke, E.J.S., Kumsta, R., Schlotz, W., Lasky-Su, J., Marco, R., Miranda, A., … Faraone, S.V. (2011). A functional variant of the serotonin transporter gene (SLC6A4) moderates impulsive choice in attention-deficit/hyperactivity disorder boys and siblings. *Biological Psychiatry, 70,* 230–236.

Sonuga-Barke, E. J. S. (1998). Categorical models of childhood disorder: A conceptual and empirical analysis. *Journal of Child Psychology and Psychiatry, 39,* 115–133.

Sonuga-Barke, E. J. S., Minocha, K., Taylor, E. A., & Sandberg, S. (1993). Inter-ethnic bias in teacher's ratings of childhood hyperactivity. *British Journal of Developmental Psychology, 11,* 187–200.

Sonuga-Barke, E.J.S., Coghill, D., Wigal, T., DeBacker, M., & Swanson, J. (2009). Adverse reactions to methylphenidate treatment for attention-deficit/hyperactivity disorder: Structure and associations with clinical characteristics and symptom control. *Journal of Child and Adolescent Psychopharmacology, 19,* 683–690.

Sonuga-Barke, E.J.S., & Halperin, J.M. (2010). Developmental phenotypes and causal pathways in attention deficit/hyperactivity disorder: potential targets for early intervention? *Journal of Child Psychology and Psychiatry, 51,* 368–389.

Sonuga-Barke, E.J.S., Oades, R.D., Psychogiou, L., Chen, W., Franke, B., Buitelaar, J., … Faraone, S.V. (2009). Dopamine and serotonin transporter genotypes moderate sensitivity to maternal expressed emotion: The case of conduct and emotional problems in attention deficit hyperactivity disorder. *Journal of Child Psychology and Psychiatry, 50,* 1052–1063.

Sonuga-Barke, J.S. (2010). Editorial: "It's the *environment* stupid!" On epigenetics, programming and plasticity in child mental health. *Journal of Child Psychology and Psychiatry, 51,* 113–115.

Soodak, L. C., Podell, D. M., & Lehman, L. R. (1998). Teacher, student, and school attributes as predictors of teachers' responses to inclusion. *Journal of Special Education, 31,* 480–497.

South, M., Ozonoff, S., & McMahon, W. M. (2007). The relationship between executive functioning, central coherence, and repetitive behaviors in the high-functioning autism spectrum. *Autism, 11,* 437–451.

Southam-Gerow, M., A., & Kendall, P. C. (2002). Emotion regulation and understanding: Implications for child psychopathology and therapy. *Clinical Psychology Review, 22,* 189–222.

Southam-Gerow, M.A. & Chorpita, B.F. (2007). Anxiety in children and adolescents. In E. J. Mash & R.A. Barkley (Eds.), *Assessment of Childhood Disorders (4th ed.)* (pp. 347–397). New York, NY: Guilford Press.

Sparrow, S. S., Cicchetti, D. V., & Balla, D. A. (2005). *Vineland-II: Vineland adaptive behavior scales* (2nd ed). Circle Pines, MN: AGS Publishing.

Spear, L. P. (2002a). Alcohol's effects on adolescents. *Alcohol Research and Health, 26,* 287–291.

Spear, L. P. (2002b). The adolescent brain and the college drinker: Biological basis of propensity to use and misuse alcohol. *Journal of Studies on Alcohol, 14,* 71–81.

Spear, L. P. (2011). Adolescent neurobehavioral characteristics, alcohol sensitivities, and intake: Setting the stage for alcohol use disorders? *Child Development Perspectives, 5,* 231–238.

Speltz, M. L., DeKlyen, M., Calderon, R., Greenberg, M. T., & Fisher, P. A. (1999). Neuropsychological characteristics and test behaviors of boys with early onset conduct problems. *Journal of Abnormal Psychology, 108,* 315–325.

Spence, S.H., Holmes, J.M., March, S., Lipp, O.V. (2006). The feasibility and outcome of clinic plus Internet delivery of cognitive-behavior therapy for childhood anxiety. *Journal of Consulting and Clinical Psychology, 74,* 614–621.

Spencer, M. B., Cole, S. P., DuPree, D., Glymph, A., & Pierre, P. (1993). Self-efficacy among urban African American early adolescents: Exploring issues of risk, vulnerability, and resilience. *Development and Psychopathology, 5,* 719–739.

Spencer, T., Biederman, J., Kerman, K., & Steingard, R. (1993). Desipramine treatment of children with attention-deficit hyperactivity disorder and tic disorder or Tourette's syndrome. *Journal of the American Academy of Child and Adolescent Psychiatry, 32,* 354–360.

Spencer, T., Biederman, J., Wilens, T. & Harding, M., et al. (1996). Pharmacotherapy of attention-deficit hyperactivity disorder across the life cycle. *Journal of the American Academy of Child & Adolescent Psychiatry, 35,* 409–432.

Spencer, T. J., Biederman, J., Wozniak, J., Faraone, S. V., Wilens, T. E., & Mick, E. (2001). Parsing pediatric bipolar disorder from its associated comorbidity with the disruptive behavior disorders. *Biological Psychiatry, 49,* 1062–1070.

Spiker, D., Boyce, G. C., & Boyce, L. K. (2002). Parent-child interactions when young children have disabilities. In L. M. Glidden (Ed.), *International review of research in mental retardation,* Vol. 25 (pp. 35–70). San Diego, CA: Academic Press.

Spinazzola, J., Blaustein, M., & van der Kolk M.A. (2005). Post-traumatic stress disorder treatment outcome research: The study of unrepresentative samples? *Journal of Traumatic Stress, 18,* 425–436.

Spinrad, T.L., Eisenberg, N., Silva, K.M., Eggum, N.D., Reiser, M., Edwards, A., Roopa, I., Kupfer, A.S., Hofer, C., Smith, C.L., Hayashi, A., & Gaertner, B.M. (2012). Longitudinal relations among maternal behaviors, effortful control and young children's committed compliance. *Developmental Psychology, 48,* 552–566.

Spirito, A., Boergers, J., Donaldson, D., Bishop, D., & Lewander, W. (2002). An intervention trial to improve adherence to community treatment by adolescents after a suicide attempt. *Journal of the American Academy of Child and Adolescent Psychiatry, 41,* 435–442.

Spirito, A., Kurkjian, J., & Donaldson, D. (2003). Case examples. In A. Spirito & J. C. Overholser (Eds.), *Evaluating and treating adolescent suicide attempters: From research to practice* (pp. 277–294). San Diego, CA: Academic Press.

Spirito, A., Valeri, S., Boergers, J., & Donaldson, D. (2003). Predictors of continued suicidal behavior in adolescents following a suicide attempt. *Journal of Clinical Child and Adolescent Psychology, 32,* 284–289.

Spitz, R. (1946). Anaclitic depression: An inquiry into the genesis of psychiatric conditions in early childhood. *The Psychoanalytic Study of the Child, I,* 47–53.

Spitz, R. A. (1945). Hospitalism: An inquiry into the genesis of psychiatric conditions. *Psychoanalytic Study of the Child, 1,* 53–74.

Spitz, R. A., & Wolf, K. M. (1946). Anaclitic depression: An inquiry into the genesis of psychiatric conditions in early childhood. *Psychoanalytic Study of the Child, 2,* 313–342.

Sprung, M., & Harris, P.L. (2010). Intrusive thoughts and young children's knowledge about thinking following a natural disaster. *Journal of Child Psychology and Psychiatry, 51,* 1115–1124.

Srinath, S., Kandasamy, P., & Golhar, T.S. (2010). Epidemiology of child and adolescent mental health disorders in Asia. *Current Opinion in Psychiatry, 23,* 330–336.

Sroufe, L. A. (1977). Attachment as an organizational construct. *Child Development, 48,* 1184–1199.

Sroufe, L. A. (1979). Socioemotional development. In *Handbook of Infant Development* (pp. 462–516). New York: Wiley.

Sroufe, L. A. (1979). The coherence of individual development: Early care, attachment, and subsequent developmental issues. *American Psychologist, 34,* 834–841.

Sroufe, L. A. (1982). The organization of emotional development. *Psychoanalytic Inquiry, 1,* 575–599.

Sroufe, L. A. (1983). Infant-caregiver attachment and patterns of adaptation in preschool: The roots of maladaptation and competence. In M. Perlmutter (Ed.), *Minnesota symposium on child psychology* (Vol. 16, pp. 41–81). Minneapolis: University of Minnesota Press.

Sroufe, L. A. (1986). Appraisal: Bowlby's contribution to psychoanalytic theory and developmental psychology. *Journal of Child Psychology and Psychiatry, 27,* 841–849.

Sroufe, L. A. (1995). *Emotional development: The organization of emotional life in the early years.* Cambridge: Cambridge University Press.

Sroufe, L. A. (1997). Psychopathology as an outcome of development. *Development and Psychopathology, 9,* 251–268.

Sroufe, L. A., Carlson, E. A., Levy, A. K., & Egeland, B. (1999). Implications of attachment theory for developmental psychopathology. *Development and Psychopathology, 11,* 1–13.

Sroufe, L. A., & Fleeson, J. (1986). Attachment and the construction of relationships. In W. W. Hartup & Z. Rubin (Eds.), *Relationships and development* (pp. 51–71). Mahwah, NJ: Erlbaum.

Sroufe, L. A., & Rutter, M. (1984). The domain of developmental psychopathology. *Child Development, 55,* 17–29.

Sroufe, L. A., Schork, E., Motti, F., Lawroski, N., & LaFreniere, P. (1984). The role of affect in social competence. In C. E. Izard, J. Kagan, & R. B. Zajonc (Eds.), *Emotions, cognition and behavior* (pp. 289–319). Cambridge: Cambridge University Press.

Sroufe, L. A., & Waters, E. (1977). Attachment as an organizational construct. *Child Development, 48,* 1184–1199.

Sroufe, L.A. (2005). Attachment and development: A prospective, longitudinal study from birth to adulthood. *Attachment & Human Development, 7,* 349–367.

Sroufe, L.A. (2009). The concept of development in developmental psychopathology. *Child Development Perspectives, 3,* 178–183.

Stack, S. (2005). Suicide in the media: A quantitative review of the studies based on nonfictional stories. *Suicide and Life-Threatening Behavior, 35,* 121–133.

Staff, J., Schulenberg, J.E., Maslowsky, J., Bachman, J.G., O'Malley, P.M., Maggs, J.L., & Johnston, L.D. (2010). *Development and Psychopathology, 22,* 917–932.

Stainton, T. (2003). Identity, difference and the ethical politics of parental testing. *Journal of Intellectual Disability Resarch, 47,* 533–539.

Stainton, T., & McDonagh, P. (2001). Chasing shadows: The historical construction of developmental disability. *Journal on Developmental Disabilities, 8,* ix–xvi.

Stallard, P. & Smith, E. (2007). Appraisals and cognitive coping styles associated with chronic post-traumatic symptoms in child road traffic accident survivors. *Journal of Child Psychology and Psychiatry, 48,* 194–201.

Stang, J., & Story, M. (2005). Adolescent growth and development. In J. Stang & M. Story (Eds.), *Guidelines for Adolescent Nutrition Services,* from http://www.epi.umn.edu/let/pubs/adol _book.shtm.

Stanton, C., Spirito, A., Donaldson, D., & Boergers, J. (2003). Risk-taking behavior and adolescent suicide attempts. *Suicide and Life-Threatening Behavior, 33,* 74–79.

Stanton, W. R., Flay, B. R., Colder, C. R., & Mehta, P. (2004). Identifying and predicting adolescent smokers' developmental trajectories. *Nicotine and Tobacco Research, 6,* 843–852.

Stark, K. D., Ballatore, M., Hamff, A., Valdez, C., & Selvig, L. (2001). Childhood depression. In H. Orvaschel, J. Faust, & M. Hersen (Eds.), *Handbook of conceptualization and treatment of child psychopathology* (pp.107–132). Amsterdam: Pergamon/Elsevier Science.

Stark, K. D., Hoke, J., Ballatore, M., Valdez, C., Scammaca, N., & Griffin, J. (2005). Treatment of child and adolescent depressive disorders. In E. D. Hibbs, & P. S. Jensen (Eds.), *Psychosocial treatments for child and adolescent disorders: Empirically based strategies for clinical practice* (2nd ed., pp. 239–265). Washington, DC: American Psychological Association.

State, M.W., King, B.H. & Dykens, E. (1997). Mental retardation: A review of the past 10 years: II. *Journal of the American Academy of Child & Adolescent Psychiatry, 36,* 1664–1671.

Staudinger, U. M., Marsiske, M., & Baltes, P. B. (1993). Resilience and levels of reserve capacity in later adulthood: Perspectives from life-span theory. *Development and Psychopathology, 5,* 541–566.

Steiger, H. (2004). Eating disorders and the serotonin connection: State, trait and developmental effects. *Journal of Psychiatry and Neuroscience, 29,* 20–29.

Stein, D., Orbach, I., Shani-Sela, M., Har-Even, D., Yaruslasky, A., Roth, D., et al. (2003). Suicidal tendencies and body image and experience in anorexia nervosa and suicidal female adolescent inpatients. *Psychotherapy and Psychosomatics, 72,* 16–25.

Steinberg, A. B., & Phares, V. (2001). Family functioning, body image, and eating disturbances. In J. K. Thompson (Ed.), *Body image, eating disorders, and obesity in youth: Assessment, prevention, and treatment* (pp. 127–141). Washington, DC:American Psychological Association.

Steinberg, L. (2004). Risk taking in adolescence: What changes, and why? In R. E. Dahl & L. P. Spear (Eds.), *Adolescent brain development: Vulnerabilities and opportunities. Annals of the New York Academy of Sciences* (Vol. 1021, pp. 51–58). New York: New York Academy of Sciences.

Steinberg, L. (2007). Risk taking in adolescence: New perspectives from brain and behavioral science. *Current Directions in Psychological Science, 16,* 55–59.

Steinberg, L. & Avenevoli, S. (1998). Disengagement from school and problem behavior in adolescence: A developmental-contextual analysis of the influences of family and part-time work. In R. Jessor (Ed.), *New Perspectives on Adolescent Risk Behavior* (pp. 392–424). New York, NY: Cambridge University Press.

Steinberg, L., Blatt-Eisengart, I., & Cauffman, E. (2006). Patterns of competence and adjustment among adolescents from authoritative, authoritarian, indulgent, and neglectful homes: A replication in a sample of serious juvenile offenders. *Journal of Research on Adolescence, 16,* 47–58.

Steiner, A.M. (2011). A strength-based approach to parent education for children with autism. *Journal of Positive Behavior Interventions, 13,* 178–190.

Steiner, H., Kwan, W., Shaffer, T. G., Walker, S., Miller, S., Sagar, A., et al. (2003) Risk and protective factors for juvenile eating disorders. *European Child and Adolescent Psychiatry, 12,* 138–146.

Steinhausen, H. C., Boyadjieva, S, Griogoroiu-Serbanescu, M., & Neumarker, K. J. (2003). The outcome of adolescent eating disorders: Finds from an international collaborative study. *European Child and Adolescent Pyschiatry, 12,* 191–198.

Sterba, S.K., Copeland, W., Egger, H.L., Costello, E.J., Erkanli, A., & Angold, A. (2010). Longitudinal dimensionality of adolescent psychopathology: testing the differentiation hypothesis. *Journal of Child Psychology and Psychiatry, 51,* 871–884.

Stern, D. N. (1985). *The interpersonal world of the infant.* New York: Basic Books.

Stern, D. N. (1995). *The motherhood constellation: A unified view of parent-infant psychotherapy.* New York: Basic Books.

Stevens, S. J., & Morral, A. R. (Eds.). (2003). *Adolescent substance abuse treatment in the United States: Exemplary models from a national evaluation study.* New York: Haworth Press.

Stewart, S. E., Manion, I. G., & Davidson, S. (2002). Emergency management of the adolescent suicide attemptor: A review of the literature. *Journal of Adolescent Health, 30,* 312–325.

Stewart, S. M., Kennard, B. D., Lee, P. W. H., Hughes, C. W., Mayes, T. L., Emslie, G. J., et al. (2004). A cross-cultural investigation of cognitions and depressive symptoms in adolescents. *Journal of Abnormal Psychology, 113,* 248–257.

Stewart, S. M., Kennard, B. D., Lee, P. W.H., Mayes, T., Hughes, C., & Emslie, G. (2005). Hopelessness and suicidal ideation among adolescents in two cultures. *Journal of Child Psychology and Psychiatry, 46,* 364–372.

Stewart, S. M., Lewinsohn, P. M., Lee, P. W.H., Ho, L. M., Kennard, B., Hughes, C., et al. (2002). Symptom patterns in depression and "subthreshold" depression among adolescents in Hong Kong and the United States. *Journal of Cross-Cultural Psychology, 33,* 559–576.

Stewart, S.E., Geller, D.A., Jenike, M., Pauls, D., Shaw, D., Mullin, B., & Faraone, S.V. (2004). Long-term outcome of pediatric obsessive-compulsive disorder: A meta-analysis and qualitative review of the literature. *Acta Psychiatrica Scandinavica, 110,* 4–13.

Stewart, T. M. (2004). Light on body image treatment: Acceptance through mindfulness. *Behavior Modification, 28,* 783–811.

Stewart, T. M., & Williamson, D. A. (2004). Multidisciplinary treatment of eating disorders—part I: Structure and costs of treatment. *Behavior Modification, 28,* 812–830.

Stewart, T. M., & Williamson, D. A. (2004). Multidisciplinary treatment of eating disorders—part II: Primary goals and content of treatment. *Behavior Modification, 28,* 831–853.

Stewart-Sabin, C., & Chaffin, M. (2003). Culturally competent substance abuse treatment for American Indian and Alaska native youths. In S. J. Stevens & A. R. Morral (Eds.), *Adolescent substance abuse treatment in the United States: Exemplary models from a national evaluation study* (pp. 155–182). New York: Haworth Press.

Stice, E. (2002). Risk and maintenance factors for eating pathology: A meta-analytic review. *Psychology Bulletin, 128,* 825–848.

Stice, E. (2003). Puberty and body image. In C. Hayward (Ed.), *Gender differences at puberty* (pp. 61–76). New York: Cambridge University Press.

Stice, E., Burton, E. M., & Shaw, H. (2004). Prospective relations between bulimic pathology, depression, and substance abuse: Unpacking comorbidity in adolescent girls. *Journal of Consulting and Clinical Psychology, 72,* 62–71.

Stice, E., Fisher, M., & Martinez, E. (2004). Eating disorder diagnostic scale: Additional evidence of reliability and validity. *Psychological Assessment, 16,* 60–71.

Stice, E., Martinez, E. E., Presnell, K., & Groesz, L. M. (2006). A prospective study of adolescent girls. *Health Psychology, 25,* 274–281.

Stice, E., Maxfield, J., & Wells, T. (2003). Adverse effects of social pressure to be thin on young women: An experimental investigation of "fat talk." *International Journal of Eating Disorders, 34,* 108–117.

Stice, E., Presnell, K., Groesz, L., & Shaw, H. (2005). Effects of a weight maintenance diet on bulimic symptoms in adolescent girls: An experimental test of the dietary restraint theory. *Health Psychology, 24,* 402–412.

Stice, E., & Shaw, H. (2003). Prospective relations of body image, eating, and affective disturbances to smoking onset in adolescent girls: How Virginia slims. *Journal of Consulting and Clinical Psychology, 71,* 129–135.

Stice, E., & Shaw, H. (2004). Eating disorder prevention programs: A meta-analytic review. *Psychological Bulletin, 130,* 206–227.

Stice, E., Shaw, H., Burton, E., & Wade, E. (2006). Dissonance and healthy weight eating disorder prevention programs: A randomized efficiency trial. *Journal of Consulting and Clinical Psychology, 74,* 263–275.

Stice, E., & Whitenton, K. (2002). Risk factors for body dissatisfaction in adolescent girls: A longitudinal investigation. *Developmental Psychology, 38,* 339–378.

Stiffman, A., Striley, C., Brown, E., Limb, G., & Ostmann, E. (2003). American Indian youth: Who southwestern urban and reservation youth turn to for help with mental health or addictions. *Journal of Child and Family Studies, 12,* 319–333.

Stifter, C. A. (2002). Individual differences in emotion regulation in infancy: A thematic collection. *Infancy, 3,* 129–132.

Stifter, C.A., Cipriano, E., Conway, A., & Kelleher, R. (2008). Temperament and the development of conscience: the moderating role of effortful control. *Social Development, 18,* 353–374.

Stiles, J. (2009). On genes, brains, and behavior: Why should developmental psychologists care about brain development? *Child Development Perspectives, 3,* 196–202.

Stock, S. L., Goldberg, E., Corbett, S., & Katzman, D. K. (2002). Substance use in female adolescents with eating disorders. *Journal of Adolescent Health, 31,* 176–182.

Storch, E.A., Jones, A.M., Lack, C.W., Ale, C.M., Sulkowski, M.L., Lewin, A.B., … Murphy, T.K. (2012). Rage attacks in pediatric obsessive-compulsive disorder: Phenomenology and clinical correlates. *Journal of the American Academy of Child & Adolescent Psychiatry, 51,* 582–592.

Storch, E.A., Ledley, D.R., Lewin, A.B., Murphy, T.K., Johns, N.B., Goodman, W.K., & Geffken, G.R. (2006). Peer victimization in children with obsessive-compulsive disorder: Relations with symptoms of psychopathology. *Journal of Clinical Child and Adolescent Psychology, 35,* 446–455.

Storch, E.A., & McKay, D. (2010). Introduction to the special issue: Recent developments in childhood obsessive compulsive disorder. *Child Youth Care Forum, 39,* 69–71.

Storch, E.A., Murphy, T.K., Lack, C.W., Geffken, G.R., Jacob, M.L., & Goodman, W.K. (2008). Sleep-related problems in pediatric obsessive-compulsive disorder. *Journal of Anxiety Disorders, 22,* 877–885.

Stormshak, E. A., Bierman, K. L., McMahon, R. J., Lengua, L. J., & Conduct Problems Prevention Research Group. (2000). Parenting practices and child disruptive behavior problems in early elementary school. *Journal of Clinical Child Psychology, 29,* 17–29.

Stormshak, E.A., Connell, A.M., Véronneau, M., Myers, M.W., Dishion, T.J., Kavanagh, K., & Caruthers, A.S. (2011). An ecological approach to promoting early adolescent mental health and social adaptation: Family-centered intervention in public middle-schools. *Child Development, 82,* 209–225.

Storvoll, E. E., Strandbu, A., & Wichstrom, L. (2005). A cross-sectional study of changes in Norwegian adolescents' body image from 1992–2002. *Body Image, 2,* 5–18.

Story, T. J., Zucker, B. G., & Craske, M. G. (2004). Secondary prevention of anxiety disorders. In D. J. A. Dozois & K. S. Dobson (Eds.), *The prevention of anxiety and depression: Theory, research, and practice* (pp. 131–160). Washington, DC: American Psychological Association.

Stouthamer-Loeber, M., Loeber, R., Wei, E., Farrington, D. P., & Wikstroem, P-O. H. (2002). Risk and promotive effects in the explanation of persistent serious delinquency in boys. *Journal of Consulting and Clinical Psychology, 70,* 111–123.

Stovall, K. C., & Dozier, M. (2000). The development of attachment in new relationships: Single subject analyses for 10 foster infants. *Development and Psychopathology, 12,* 133–156.

Stover, C.S. & Berkowitz, S. (2005). Assessing violence exposure and trauma symptoms in young children: A critical review of measures. *Journal of Traumatic Stress, 18,* 707–717.

Strada, M. J., Donohue, B., & Lefforge, N. L. (2006). Examination of ethnicity in controlled treatment outcome studies involving adolescent substance abusers: A comprehensive literature review. *Psychology of Addictive Behaviors, 20,* 11–27.

Strakowski, S. M., Shang-Ying, T., DelBello, M. P., Chiao-Chicy, C., Fleck, D. E., Adler, C. M., et al. (2007) Outcome following a first manic episode: Cross-national US and Taiwan comparison. *Bipolar Disorders, 9,* 820–827.

Strand, V.C., Sarmiento, T.L. & Pasquale, L.E. (2005). Assessment and screening tools for trauma in children and adolescents: A review. *Trauma, Violence & Abuse 6,* 55–78.

Street., H., Nathan, P., Durkin, K., Morling, J., Dzahari, M. A., Carson, J., et al. (2004). Understanding the relationships between well-being, goal-setting and depression in children. *Australian and New Zealand Journal of Psychiatry, 38,* 155–161.

Striegel-Moore, R. H., Fairburn, C. G., Wilfley, D. E., Pike, K. M., Dohm, F., & Kraemer, H. C. (2005). Toward an understanding of risk factors for binge-eating disorder in black and white women: A community-based case-control study. *Psychological Medicine, 35,* 907–917.

Striegel-Moore, R. H., Seeley, J. R., & Lewinsohn, P. M. (2003). Psychosocial adjustment in young adulthood of women who experienced an eating disorder during adolescence. *Journal of the American Academy of Child and Adolescent Psychiatry, 42,* 587–593.

Stringaris, A. (2011). Irritability in children and adolescents: a challenge for DSM-5. *European Child & Adolescent Psychiatry, 20,* 61–66.

Stringaris, A., & Goodman, R. (2009). Three dimensions of oppositionality in youth. *Journal of Child Psychology and Psychiatry, 50,* 216–223.

Stringaris, A., Maughan, B., & Goodman, R. (2010). What is a disruptive disorder? Temperamental antecedents of oppositional defiant disorder: Findings from the Avon Longitudinal Study. *Journal of the American Academy of Child & Adolescent Psychiatry, 49,* 474–483.

Stromme, P., Bjornstad, P. G., & Ramstad, K. (2002). Prevalence estimation of Williams syndrome. *Journal of Child Neurology, 17,* 269–271.

Stronach, E.P., Toth, S.L., Rogosch, F., Oschri, A., Manly, J.T., & Cicchetti, D. (2011). Child maltreatment, attachment security, and internal representations of mother and mother-child relationships. *Child Maltreatment, 16,* 137–145.

Stueve, A., & O'Donnell, L. N. (2005). Early alcohol initiation and subsequent sexual and alcohol risk behaviors among urban youths. *American Journal of Public Health, 95,* 887–893.

Suarez-Morales, L. & Bell, D. (2006). Relation of childhood worry to information-processing factors in an ethnically diverse community sample. *Journal of Clinical Child and Adolescent Psychology, 35,* 136–147.

Suárez-Orozco, C., Todorova, I., & Qin, D. B. (2006). The well-being of immigrant adolescents: A longitudinal perspective on risk and protective factors. In F. A. Villarruel & ?, T. Luster (Eds.), *The crisis in youth mental health: Critical issues and effective programs, Vol. 2: Disorders in adolescence* (pp. 58–83). Westport, CT: Praeger Publishers/Greenwood Publishing Group.

Substance Abuse and Mental Health Services Administration. (2011). Results from the 2010 National Survey on Drug Use and Health: Summary of national findings. *NSDUH Series H-41, HHS Publication No. (SMA) 11–4658.* Rockville, MD: Substance Abuse and Mental Health Services Administration.

Suitor, J.J., Sechrist, J., Plikuhn, M., Pardo, S.T., & Pillemer, K. (2008). Within-family differences in parent-child relations across the life course. *Current Directions in Psychological Science, 17,* 334–338.

Suizzo, M-A. (2000). The social-emotional and cultural contexts of cognitive development: Neo-Piagetian perspectives. *Child Development, 71,* 846–849.

Sulik, M.J., Eisenberg, N., Lemery-Chalfant, K., Spinrad, T.L., Silva, K.M., Eggum, N.D., ... Verrelli, B.C. (2011). Interactions between serotonin transporter gene haplotypes and quality of mothers' parenting predict the development of children's noncompliance. *Developmental Psychology, 48,* 740–754.

Sullivan, H. S. (1953). *The interpersonal theory of psychiatry.* New York: Norton.

Sullivan, M. L. (1998). Integrating qualitative and quantitative methods in the study of developmental psychopathology in context. *Development and Psychopathology, 10,* 377–393.

Sundram, C. J., & Stavis, P. F. (1994). Sexuality and mental retardation: Unmet challenges. *Mental Retardation, 32,* 255–264.

Sung, M., Erkanli, A., Angold, A., & Costello, E. J. (2004). Effects of age at first substance use and psychiatric comorbidity on the development of substance use disorders. *Drug and Alcohol Dependence, 75,* 287–299.

Suominen, K., Isometsa, E., Martunnen, M., Ostamo, A., & Lonnqvist, J. (2004). Health care contacts before and after attempted suicide among adolescent and young adult versus older suicide attempters. *Psychological Medicine, 34,* 313–321.

Sussman, S., Stacy, A. W., Johnson, C. A., Pentz, M. A., & Robertson, E. (2004). A transdisciplinary focus on drug abuse prevention: An introduction. *Substance Use and Misuse, 39,* 1441–1456.

Sutton, J., Smith, P.K., & Swettenham, J. (1999). Social cognition and bullying: Social inadequacy or skilled manipulation? *British Journal of Developmental Psychology, 17,* 435–450.

Suveg, C., Aschenbrand, S. G., & Kendall, P. C. (2005). Separation anxiety disorder, panic disorder, and school refusal. *Child and Adolescent Psychiatric Clinics of North America, 14,* 773–795.

Suveg, C., Southam-Gerow, M.A., Goodman, K.L. & Kendall, P.C. (2007). The role of emotion theory and research in child therapy development. *Clinical Psychology: Science and Practice, 14,* 358–371.

Suveg, C., & Zeman, J. (2004). Emotion regulation in children with anxiety disorders. *Journal of Clinical Child and Adolescent Psychology, 33,* 750–759.

Suveg, C., Zeman, J., Flannery-Schroeder, E. & Cassano, M. (2005). Emotion socialization in families of children with an anxiety disorder. *Journal of Abnormal Child Psychology, 33,* 145–155.

Svanberg, P. O. G. (1998). Attachment, resilience and prevention. *Journal of Mental Health, 7,* 543–578.

Swahn, M. H., & Donovan, J. E. (2005). Predictors of fighting attributed to alcohol use among adolescent drinkers. *Addictive Behaviors, 30,* 1317–1334.

Swain, J. E., Lorberbaum, J. P., Kose, S., & Strathearn, L. (2007). Brain basis of early parent-infant interactions: Psychology, physiology, and in vivo functional neuroimaging studies. *Journal of Child Psychology and Psychiatry, 48,* 262–287.

Swami, V., Frederick, D.A., Aavik, T., Alcalay, L., Allik, J., Anderson, D., ... Zivcic-Becirevic, I. (2009). The attractive female body weight and female body dissatisfaction in 26 countries across 10 world regions: Results of the International Body Project I. *Personality and Social Psychology Bulletin, 36,* 309–325.

Swanson, J.M., Elliot, G.R., Greenhill, L.L., Wigal, T., Arnold, L.E., Vitiello, B., ... Volkow, N.D. (2007). Effects of stimulant medication on growth rates across 3 years in the MTA follow-up. *Journal of the American Academy of Child & Adolescent Psychiatry, 46,* 1015–1027.

Sweeney, L., & Rapee, R. M. (2005). Social phobia in children and adolescents: Psychological treatments. In W. R. Crozier & L. E. Alden (Eds.), *The essential handbook of social anxiety for clinicians* (pp. 153–165). New York: Wiley.

Szalacha, L.A., Marks, A.K., Lamarre, M., & Coll, C.G. (2005). Academic pathways and children of immigrant families. *Research in Human Development, 2,* 179–211.

Szatmari, P., Georgiades, S., Bryson, S., Zwaigenbaum, L., Roberts, W., Mahoney, W., Goldberg, J., & Tuff, L. (2006). Investigating the structure of the restricted, repetitive behaviors and interests domain of autism. *Journal of Child Psychology and Psychiatry, 47,* 582–590.

Szatmari, P., Jones, M. B., Zwaigenbaum, L., & MacLean, J. E. (1998). Genetics of autism: Overview and new directions. *Journal of Autism and Developmental Disorders, 28,* 351–368.

Szyf, M., McGowan, P.O., Turecki, G., & Meaney, M.J. (2010). The social environment and the epigenome. In C.M. Worthman, P.M. Plotsky, D.S. Schechter, & C. Cummings (Eds.), *Formative experiences: The interaction of caregiving, culture, and developmental psychobiology* (pp. 53–81). New York: Cambridge University Press.

Szymanski, L., King, B. H., Bernet, W., Dunne, J. E., Adair, M., Arnold, V., et al. (1999). Practice parameters for the assessment and treatment of children, adolescents, and adults with mental retardation and comorbid mental disorders. *Journal of the American Academy of Child and Adolescent Psychiatry, 38,* 5S–31S.

Tackett, J.L. (2010). Toward and externalizing spectrum in *DSM-V:* Incorporating developmental concerns. *Child Development Perspectives, 4,* 161–167.

Tager-Flusberg, H., & Dominick, K.C. (2011). Comorbid disorders. In E. Hollander, A. Kolevzon & J.T. Coyle (Eds.) *Textbook of autism spectrum disorders* (pp. 209–218). Arlington, VA: American Psychiatric Publishing, Inc.

Tammet, D. (2006). *Born on a blue day: Inside the extraordinary mind of an autistic savant.* New York: Free Press.

Tanguay, P. E., Robertson, J., & Derrick, A. (1998). A dimensional classification of autism spectrum disorder by social communication domains. *Journal of the American Academy of Child and Adolescent Psychiatry, 37,* 271–277.

Tantam, D. (2000). Psychological disorder in adolescents and adults with Asperger syndrome. *Autism, 4,* 47–62.

Tantam, D. (2003). The challenge of adolescents and adults with Asperger syndrome. *Child and Adolescent Psychiatric Clinics of North America, 12,* 143–163.

Tarrier, N., Taylor, K., & Gooding, P. (2008). Cognitive-behavioral interventions to reduce suicide behavior: A systematic review and meta-analysis. *Behavior Modification, 32,* 77–108.

Tarter, R. E. (2005). Psychological evaluation of substance use disorders in adolescents and adults. In R. J. Frances, S. I. Miller, & A. H. Mack (Eds.), *Clinical textbook of addictive disorders* (3rd ed., pp. 37–62). New York: Guilford Press.

Tarter, R. E., Kirisci, L., Reynolds, M., & Mezzich, A. (2004). Neurobehavior disinhibition in childhood predicts suicide potential and substance use disorder by young adulthood. *Drug and Alcohol Dependence, 76,* S45–S52.

Tarter, R. E., Vanyukov, M., Giancola, P., Dawes, M., Blackson, T., Mezzich, A., et al. (1999). Etiology of early age onset substance use disorder: A maturational perspective. *Development and Psychopathology, 11,* 657–683.

Tarullo, A.R., & Gunnar, M.R. (2006). Child maltreatment and the developing HPA axis. *Hormones and Behavior, 50,* 632–639.

Taylor, C. S., Smith, P. R., Taylor, V. A., von Eye, A., Lerner, R. M., Balsano, A. B., et al. (2005). Individual and ecological assets and thriving among African American adolescent male gang and community-based organization members: A report from Wave 3 of the "Overcoming the Odds" study. *Journal of Early Adolescence, 25,* 72–93.

Taylor, H. G., & Alden, J. (1997). Age-related differences in outcomes following childhood brain insults: An introduction and overview. *Journal of the International Neuropsychological Society, 3,* 555–567.

Taylor, J.L., & Seltzer, M.M. (2011). Changes in the mother-child relationship during the transition to adulthood for youth with autism spectrum disorders. *Journal of Autism & Developmental Disorders, 41,* 1397–1410.

Taylor, L.K., & Weems, C.F. (2011). Cognitive-behavior therapy for disaster-exposed youth with posttraumatic stress: results from a multiple-baseline examination. *Behavior Therapy, 42,* 349–363.

Taylor, R. D., Jacobson, L., Rodriguez, A., Dominguez, A., Cantic, R., Doney, J., et al. (2000). Stressful experiences and the psychological functioning of African-American and Puerto Rican families and adolescents. In R. D. Taylor & M. C. Wang (Eds.), *Resilience across contexts: Family, work, culture, and community* (pp. 35–53). Mahwah, NJ: Erlbaum.

Tedeschi, R.G., & Calhoun, L.G. (2004). Posttraumatic growth: Conceptual foundations and empirical evidence. *Psychological Inquiry, 15,* 1–18.

Teicher, M., Ito, Y., Glod, C. A., Andersen, S. L., Dumont, N., & Ackerman, E. (1997). Preliminary evidence for abnormal cortical development in physically and sexually abused children using EEG coherence and MRI. *Annual New York Academy of Science, 821,* 160–175.

Temple, C. M., Almazan, M., & Sherwood, S. (2002). Lexical skills in Williams syndrome: A cognitive neuropsychological analysis. *Journal of Neurolinguistics, 15,* 463–495.

Tetzlaff, B. T., Kahn, J. H., Godley, S. H., Godley, M.D., Diamond, G. S., & Funk, R. R. (2005). Working alliance, treatment satisfaction, and patterns of posttreatment use among adolescent substance users. *Psychology of Addictive Behaviors, 19,* 199–207.

Thabet, A. A. M., Abed, Y., & Vostanis, P. (2004). Comorbidity of PTSD and depression among refugee children during war conflict. *Journal of Child Psychology and Psychiatry, 45,* 533–542.

Thabet, A.A., Tawahina, A.A., El Sarraj, E. & Vostanis, P. (2008). Exposure to war trauma and PTSD among parents and children in the Gaza strip. *European Child & Adolescent Psychiatry, 17,* 191–199.

Thoits, P. A. (1999). Self, identity, stress, and mental health. In C. S. Aneshensel & J. C. Phelan (Eds.), *Handbook of sociology of mental health* (pp. 345–368). Dordrecht, Netherlands: Kluwer Academic Publishers.

Thomas, A., & Chess, S. (1977). *Temperament and development.* New York: Brunner/Mazel.

Thomas, C. R. (2006). Evidence-based practice for conduct disorder symptoms. *Journal of the American Academy of Child and Adolescent Psychiatry, 45,* 109–114.

Thomas, M.S.C., & Johnson, M.H. (2008). New advances in understanding sensitive periods in brain development. *Current Directions in Psychological Science, 17,* 1–5.

Thomas, R., & Zimmer-Gembeck, M.J. (2011). Accumulating evidence for parent-child interaction therapy in prevention of child maltreatment. *Child Development, 82,* 177–192.

Thompson, P.H. (1994). Obsessive-compulsive disorder in children and adolescents: A 6–22-year follow-up study: Clinical descriptions of the course and continuity of obsessive-compulsive symptomatology. *European Child & Adolescent Psychiatry, 3,* 82–96.

Thompson, J. R., Hughes, C., Schalock, R. L., Silverman, W., Tasse, M. J., Bryant, B., et al. (2002). Integrating supports in assessment and planning. *Mental Retardation, 40,* 390–405.

Thompson, R. A. (1997). Sensitivity and security: New questions to ponder. *Child Development, 68,* 595–597.

Thompson, R. A. (1998). Early sociopersonality development. In W. Damon & N. Eisenberg (Eds.), *Handbook of child psychology* (5th ed.): *Vol. 3. Social, emotional, and personality development* (pp. 25–104). Hoboken, NJ: Wiley.

Thompson, R. A. (1999). Early attachment and later development. In J. Cassidy & P. R. Shaver (Eds.), *Handbook of attachment: Theory, research, and clinical applications* (pp. 265–286). New York: Guilford Press.

Thompson, R. A. (2001). Childhood anxiety disorders from the perspective of emotion regulation and attachment. In M. W. Vasey & M. R. Dadds (Eds.), *The developmental psychopathology of anxiety* (pp. 160–182). New York: Oxford University Press.

Thompson, R. A., & Meyer, S. (2007). Socialization of emotion regulation in the family. In J. J. Gross (Ed.), *Handbook of emotion regulation* (pp. 249–268). New York: Guilford Press.

Thompson, R.A., Lewis, M.D., & Calkins, S.D. (2008). Reassessing emotion regulation. *Child Development Perspectives, 2,* 124–131.

Thompson, S. H., Rafiroiu, A. C., & Sargent, R. G. (2003). Examining gender, racial, and age differences in weight concern among third, fifth, eighth, and eleventh graders. *Eating Behaviors, 3,* 307–323.

Thompson, S. J., Pomeroy, E. C., & Gober, K. (2005). Family-based treatment models targeting substance use and high-risk behaviors among adolescents: A review. In Hilarski, C. (Ed.), *Addiction, assessment, and treatment with adolescents, adults, and families* (pp. 207–233). Binghamton, NY: Haworth Social Work Practice Press.

Thomsen, P. H. (1994). Obsessive-compulsive disorder in children and adolescents: A review of the literature. *European Child and Adolescent Psychiatry, 3*, 138–158.

Thuppal, M., Carlson, G. A., Sprafkin, J., & Gadow, K. D. (2002). Correspondence between adolescent report, parent report and teacher report of manic symptoms. *Journal of Child and Adolescent Psychopharmacology, 12*, 27–35.

Thurston, I. B., & Phares, V. (2008). Mental health service utilization among African American and Caucasian mothers and fathers. *Journal of Consulting and Clinical Psychology, 76*, 1058–1067.

Thygesen, R. (2007). Students with learning disabilities: An update on Norwegian educational policy, practice, and research. *Learning Disabilities Research & Practice, 22*, 176–182.

Tierney, S., & Wyatt, K. (2005). What works for adolescents with AN: A systematic review of psychosocial interventions. *Eating and Weight Disorders, 10*, 66–75.

Tiet, Q. Q., Bird, H. R., Hoven, C. W, Moore, R., Wu, P., Wicks, J., et al. (2001). Relationship between specific adverse life events and psychiatric disorders. *Journal of Abnormal Child Psychology, 29*, 153–164.

Tiet, Q. Q., Bird, H. R., Hoven, C. W., Wu, P., Moore, R., & Davies, M. (2001). Resilience in the face of maternal psychopathology and adverse life events. *Journal of Child and Family Studies, 10*, 347–363.

Tillman, R., & Geller, B. (2005). A brief screening tool for a prepubertal and early adolescent bipolar disorder phenotype. *American Journal of Psychiatry, 162*, 1214–1216.

Tillman, R., Geller, B., Bolhofner, K., Craney, J. L., Williams, M., & Zimerman, B. (2003). Ages of onset and rates of syndromal and subsyndromal comorbid DSM-IV diagnoses in a prepubertal and early adolescent bipolar disorder phenotype. *Journal of the American Academy of Child and Adolescent Psychiatry, 42*, 1486–1493.

Tillman, R., Geller, B., Craney, J. L., Bolhofner, K., Williams, M., & Zimerman, B. (2004). Relationship of parent and child informants to prevalence of mania symptoms in children with a prepubertal and early adolescent bipolar disorder phenotype. *American Journal of Psychiatry, 161*, 1278–1284.

Timimi, S. (2009). The commercialization of children's mental health in the era of globalization. *International Journal of Mental Health, 38*, 5–27.

Tirosh, E., Bendrian, S. B., Golan, G., Tamir, A., & Dar, M. C. (2003). Regulatory disorders in Israeli infants: Epidemiologic perspective. *Journal of Child Neurology, 18*, 748–754.

Titus, J. C., Dennis, M. L., White, W. L., Scott, C. K., & Funk, R.R. (2003). Gender differences in victimization severity and outcomes among adolescents treated for substance abuse. *Child Maltreatment, 8*, 19–35.

Tizard, B., & Hodges, J. (1978). The effect of early institutional rearing on the development of eight year old children. *Journal of Child Psychology and Psychiatry, 19*, 99–118.

Tizard, B., & Rees, J. (1975). The effect of early institutional rearing on the behaviour problems and affectional relationships of four-year-old children. *Journal of Child Psychology and Psychiatry, 16*, 61–73.

Todd, R. D., Rasmussen, E. R., Wood, C., Levy, F., & Hay, D. A. (2004). Should sluggish cognitive tempo symptoms be included in the diagnosis of attention-deficit/hyperactivity disorder? *Journal of the American Academy of Child and Adolescent Psychiatry, 43*, 588–597.

Toga, A.W., Thompson, P.M., & Sowell, E.R. (2006). Mapping brain maturation. *Trends in Neurosciences, 29,* 148–159.

Tolan, P. H., & Dodge, K. A. (2005). Children's mental health as a primary care and concern: A system for comprehensive support and service. *American Psychologist, 60*, 601–614.

Tolan, P.H., & Dodge, K.A. (2005). Children's mental health as a primary care and concern. *American Psychologist, 60*, 601–614.

Tolan, P.H., & Titus, J.A. (2009). Therapeutic jurisprudence in juvenile justice. In B.L. Bottoms, C.J. Najdowski, & G.S. Goodman (Eds.), *Children as victims and offenders: Psychological science and the law* (pp. 313–333). New York: Guilford Press.

Tomoe, K., & Ceci, S. J. (2007). Are all IQ scores created equal? The differential costs of IQ cutoff scores for at-risk children. *Child Development Perspectives, 1*, 52–56.

Toth, S. L., Pianta, R. C., & Erickson, M. F. (2011). From research to practice: Developmental contributions to the field of prevention science. In D. Cicchetti & G. I. Roisman (Eds.), *The Origins and Organization of Adaptation and Maladaptation, The Minnesota Symposia on Child Psychology* (Vol. 36, pp. 323–377). Hoboken, NJ: Wiley.

Toth, S.L., Manly, J.T., & Nilsen, W.J. (2008). From research to practice: Lessons learned. *Journal of Applied Developmental Psychology, 29*, 317–325.

Toth, S.L., Munson, J., Meltzoff, A.N., & Dawson, G. (2006). Early predictors of communication development in young children with autism spectrum disorder: Joint attention, imitation, and toy play. *Journal of Autism & Developmental Disorders, 36*, 993–1005.

Toumbourou, J. W., Williams, J., Waters, E., & Patton, G. (2005). What do we know about preventing drug-related harm through social developmental intervention with children and young people? In T. Stockwell, P. J. Gruenewald, J. W. Toumbourou, & W. Loxley (Eds.), *Preventing harmful substance use: The evidence base for policy and practice* (pp. 87–100). New York: Wiley.

Towers, H., Spotts, E. L., & Neiderhiser, J. M. (2001). Genetic and environmental influences on parenting and marital relationships: Current findings and future directions. *Marriage and Family Review, 33*, 11–29.

Tozzi, F., Aggen, S. H., Neale, B. M., Anderson, C. B., Mazzeo, S. E., Neale, M. C., et al. (2004). The structure of perfectionism: A twin study. *Behavior Genetics, 34,* 483–494.

Tozzi, F., Thornton, L. M., Klump, K. L., Fichter, M. M., Halmi, K. A., Kaplan, A. S., et al. (2005). Symptom fluctuation in eating disorders: Correlates of diagnostic crossover. *American Journal of Psychology, 162*, 732–740.

Tozzi, F., Throngon, L. M., Mitchell, J., Fichter, M. M., Klump, K. L., Lilenfeld, L. R., et al. (2006). Features associated with laxative abuse in individuals with eating disorders. *Psychosomatic Medicine, 68*, 470–477.

Tram, J. M., & Cole, D. M. (2000). Self-perceived competence and the relation between life events and depressive symptoms in adolescence: Mediator or moderator? *Journal of Abnormal Psychology, 109*, 753–760.

Trickett, P.K., Noll, J.G., & Putnam, F.W. (2011). The impact of sexual abuse on female development: Lessons from a multigenerational, longitudinal research study. *Development and Psychopathology, 23*, 453–476.

Triplett, R., & Payne, B. (2004). Problem solving as reinforcement in adolescent drug use: Implications for theory and policy. *Journal of Criminal Justice, 32*, 617–630.

Tronick, E. Z., & Gianino, A. F. (1986). The transmission of maternal disturbance to the infant. *New Directions for Child Development, 34*, 5–11.

Troy, M. (2003). Structure of psychopathology: Childhood conduct problems. Presentation on June 20, 2003 for Children's Hospitals and Clinics, Psychological Services, St. Paul, MN.

Troy, M. F. (1989). Antecedents, correlates, and continuity of ego-control and ego-resiliency in a high-risk sample of preschool children. *Dissertation Abstracts International, 49*(9-B), 4028.

Troy, M., & Sroufe, L. A. (1987). Victimization among preschoolers: Role of attachment relationship history. *Journal of the American Academy of Child and Adolescent Psychiatry, 26*, 166–172.

Troy, M., & Walker, J. (2003). Identifying and treating childhood conduct problems. Presentation on June 17 and 19, 2003 for Children's Hospitals and Clinics, Psychological Services, St.Paul, MN.

Tsao, J.C.I., Mystkowski, J.L., Zucker, B.G. & Craske, M.G. (2005). Impact of cognitive-behavioral therapy for panic disorder on comorbidity: A controlled investigation. *Behaviour Research and Therapy, 43*, 959–970.

Tsatsanis, K. D., Rourke, B. P., Klin, A., Volkmar, F. R., Cicchetti, D., & Schultz, R. T. (2003). Reduced thalamic volume in high-functioning individuals with autism. *Biological Psychiatry, 53*, 121–129.

Tsuang, M. T., Lyons, M. J., Harley, R. M., Xian, H., Eisen, S., Goldberg, J., et al. (1999). Genetic and environmental influences on transitions in drug use. *Behavior Genetics, 29*, 473–479.

Tsuang, M. T., Lyons, M. J., Meyer, J. M., Doyle, T., Eisen, S. A., Goldberg, J., et al. (1998). Co-occurrence of abuse of different drugs in men: The role of drug-specific and shared vulnerabilities. *Archives of General Psychiatry, 55*, 967–972.

Tucker, C. J., Barber, B. L., & Eccles, J. S. (1997). Advice about life plans and personal problems in late adolescent sibling relationships. *Journal of Youth and Adolescence, 26*, 63–76.

Tucker, J. S., Ellickson, P. L., Orlando, M., Martino, S. C., & Klein, D. J. (2005). Substance use trajectories from early adolescence to emerging adulthood: A comparison of smoking, binge drinking, and marijuana use. *Journal of Drug Issues, 35*, 307–332.

Tullis, L. M., DuPont, R., Frost-Pineda, K., & Gold, M. S. (2003). Marijuana and tobacco: A major connection? *Journal of Addictive Diseases, 22*, 51–62.

Turbin, M. S., Jessor, R., & Costa, F. M. (2000). Adolescent cigarette smoking: Health-related behavior or normative transgression? *Prevention Science, 1*, 115–124.

Turkheimer, E., & Waldron, M. (2000). Nonshared environment: A theoretical, methodological, and quantitative review. *Psychological Bulletin, 126*, 78–108.

Turner, C. M., & Barrett, P. M. (2003). Does age play a role in structure of anxiety and depression in children and youths? An investigation of the tripartite model in three age cohorts. *Journal of Consulting and Clinical Psychology, 71*, 826–833.

Turner, L., Mermelstein, R., & Flay, B. (2004). Individual and contextual influences on adolescent smoking. In R. E. Dahl & L.P. Spear (Eds.), *Adolescent brain development: Vulnerabilities and opportunities. Annals of the New York Academy of Sciences* (Vol. 1021, pp. 175–197). New York: New York Academy of Sciences.

Turner, L. R., & Mermelstein, R. (2004). Motivation and reasons to quit: Predictive validity among adolescent smokers. *American Journal of Health Behavior, 28*, 542–550.

Turner, L. R., Mermelstein, R., Berbaum, M. L., & Veldhuis,C. B. (2004). School-based smoking cessation programs for adolescents: What predicts attendance? *Nicotine and Tobacco Research, 6*, 559–568.

Twenge, J. M., & Nolen-Hoeksema, S. (2002). Age, gender, race, socioeconomic status, and birth cohort differences on the children's depression inventory: A meta-analysis. *Journal of Abnormal Psychology, 111*, 578–588.

Tyrer, S., & Hill, S. (2001). Psychopharmacological approaches. In A. Dosen & K. Day (Eds.), *Treating mental illness and behavior disorders in children and adults with mental retardation* (pp. 45–67). Washington, DC: American Psychiatric Publishing.

Tzeng, S. (2007). Learning disabilities in Taiwan: A Case of cultural constraints on the education of students with disabilities. *Learning Disabilities Research & Practice, 22*, 170–175.

Uher, R., Caspi, A., Renate, H., Sugden, K., Williams, B., Richie, P., & Moffitt, T.E. (2011). Serotonin transporter gene moderates childhood maltreatment's effects on persistent but not single-episode depression: Replications and implications for resolving inconsistent results. *Journal of Affective Disorders, 135*, 56–65.

Uher, R., Murphy, T, Brammer, M. J., Brammer, M. J., Dalgleish, T., Phillips, M. L., et al. (2004). Medial prefrontal cortex activity associate with symptom provocation in eating disorders. *American Journal of Psychiatry, 161*, 1238–1246.

Underwood, M. K. (2003a). The comity of modest manipulation, the importance of distinguishing among bad behaviors. *Merrill-Palmer Quarterly, 49*, 373–389.

Underwood, M. K. (2003b). *Social aggression among girls.* New York: Guilford Press. Underwood, M. K. (2004a). Gender and peer relations: Are the two gender cultures really all that different? In J. B. Kupersmidt & K. A. Dodge (Eds.), *Children's peer relations: From development to intervention. Decade of behavior* (pp. 21–36). Washington, DC: American Psychological Association.

Underwood, M. K. (2004b). III. Glares of contempt, eye rolls of disgust and turning away to exclude: Non-verbal forms of social aggression among girls. *Feminism and Psychology, 14*, 371–375.

Underwood, M.K., Galen, B.R. & Paquette, J.A. (2001). Top ten challenges for understanding gender and aggression in children: Why can't we all just get along? *Social Development, 10*, 248–266.

Ungar, M. (2005). Pathways to resilience among children in child welfare, corrections, mental health and educational settings: Navigation and negotiation. *Child & Youth Care Forum, 34*, 423–444.

Ungar, M. (2005). Resilience among children in child welfare, corrections, mental health and educational settings: Recommendations for service. *Child & Youth Care Forum, 34*, 445–464.

Ungar, M. (2010). Families as navigators and negotiators: Facilitating culturally and contextually specific expressions. *Family Process, 49*, 421–435.

Ungar, M. (2011). Community resilience for youth and families: facilitative physical and social capital in contexts of adversity. *Children and Youth Services Review, 33*, 1742–1748.

Ungar, M., Barter, K., McConnell, S.M., Tutty, L.M., & Fairholm, J. (2009). Patterns of abuse disclosure among youth. *Qualitative Social Work: Research and Practice, 8*, 341–356.

Ungar, M., Tutty, L.M., McConnell, S., Barter, K., & Fairholm, J. (2009). What Canadian youth tell us about disclosing abuse. *Child Abuse & Neglect, 33,* 699–708.

U.S. Census Bureau. (2000). Percent of people in poverty by definition of income and selected characteristics: 1998. Available: http://www.census.gov/hhes/poverty/poverty98/table5.html.

U.S. Department of Health and Human Services. (2000). *Report of the Surgeon General's Conference on Children's Mental Health: A National Action Agenda.* Washington, DC.

U.S. Department of Health and Human Services. (2002). *Closing the gap: A national blueprint to improve the health of persons with mental retardation.* Report of the Surgeon General's Conference on Health Disparities and Mental Retardation, Rockville, MD.

U.S. Department of Health and Human Services. (2007). Administration on Children, Youth and Families. *Child Maltreatment 2005.* Washington, DC: U.S. Government Printing Office.

U.S. Food and Drug Administration: Antidepressant Use in Children, Adolescents, and Adults, 2004. http://www.fda.gov/cder/drug/antidepressants/default.htm.

Vachon, J., Vitaro, F., Wanner, B., & Tremblay, R. E. (2004). Adolescent gambling: Relationships with parent gambling and parenting practices. *Psychology of Addictive Behaviors, 18,* 398–401.

Valenti-Hein, D., & Dura, J. R. (1996). Sexuality and sexual development. In J. W. Jacobson & J. A. Mulick (Eds.), *Manual of diagnosis and professional practice in mental retardation* (pp. 301–310). Washington, DC: American Psychological Association.

Valentiner, D. P., Mounts, N. S., & Deacon, B. J. (2004). Panic attacks, depression and anxiety symptoms, and substance use behaviors during late adolescence. *Journal of Anxiety Disorders, 18,* 573–585.

Valentino, K., Toth, S.L., & Cicchetti, D. (2009). Autobiographical memory functioning among abused, neglected, and non-maltreated children: The overgeneral memory effect. *Journal of Child Psychology and Psychiatry, 50,* 1029–1038.

Valle, J.W. (2011). Down the rabbit hole: A commentary about research on parents and special education. *Learning Disability Quarterly, 34,* 183–190.

Van Bourgondien, M. E., Reichle, N. C., & Schopler, E. (2003). Effects of a model treatment approach on adults with autism. *Journal of Autism and Developmental Disorders, 33,* 131–140.

van der Kolk, B. A., Roth, S., Pelcovitz, D., Sunday, S., & Spinazzola, J. (2005). Disorders of extreme stress: The empirical foundation of a complex adaptation to trauma. *Journal of Traumatic Stress, 18,* 389–399.

Van der Kolk, B.A. (2007). The developmental impact of childhood trauma. In L. J. Kirmayer, R. Lemelson, & M. Barad (Eds.), *Understanding Trauma: Integrating Biological, Clinical, and Cultural Perspectives* (pp. 224–221). New York, NY: Cambridge University Press.

van Furth, E. F., van Strein, D. C., Martin, L. M. L., van Son, M. J. M, Hendrickx, J. P., & van Engeland, H. (1996). Expressed emotion and the prediction of outcome in adolescent eating disorders. *International Journal of Eating Disorders, 20,* 19–31.

van Goozen, S.H.M., Fairchild, G., & Harold, G.T. (2006). The role of neurobiological deficits in childhood antisocial behavior. *Current Directions in Psychological Science, 17,* 224–228.

van Harmelen, A., de Jong, K.A., Spinhoven, P., Penninx, B.W. J.H., & Elzinga, B.M. (2010). Child abuse and negative explicit and automatic self-associations: The cognitive scars of emotional maltreatment. *Behavior Research and Therapy, 48,* 486–494.

van Hoeken, D., Veling, W., Sinke, S., Mitchell, J.E., & Hoek, H.W. (2009). The validity and utility of subtyping bulimia nervosa. *International Journal of Eating Disorders, 42,* 595–602.

Van Hulle, C.A., Waldman, I.D., D'Onofrio, B.M., Rodgers, J.L., Rathouz, P.J., & Lahey, B.B. (2009). Developmental structure of genetic influences on antisocial behavior across childhood and adolescence. *Journal of Abnormal Psychology, 118,* 711–721.

van IJzendoorn, M. (1995). Adult attachment representations, parental responsiveness, and infant attachment: A meta-analysis on the predictive validity of the Adult Attachment Interview. *Psychological Bulletin, 117,* 387–403.

van IJzendoorn, M. H., Goldberg, S., Kroonenberg, P. M., & Frenkel, O. J. (1992). The relative effects of maternal and child problems on the quality of attachment: A meta-analysis in clinical samples. *Child Development, 63,* 840–858.

van IJzendoorn, M. H., Schuengel, C., & Bakermans-Kranenburg, M. J. (1999). Disorganized attachment in early childhood: Meta-analysis of precursors, concomitants, and sequelae. *Development and Psychopathology, 11,* 225–249.

van IJzendoorn, M.H. (1995). Adult attachment representations, parental responsiveness, and infant attachment: A meta-analysis on the predictive validity of the adult attachment interview. *Psychological Bulletin, 117,* 387–403.

van IJzendoorn, M.H. & Bakermans-Kranenburg, M.J. (1996). Attachment representations in mothers, fathers, adolescents, and clinical groups: A meta-analytic search for normative data. *Journal of Consulting and Clinical Psychology, 64,* 8–21.

Van Lier, P. A. C., van der Ende, J., Koot, H. M., & Verhulst, F. C. (2007). Which better predicts conduct problems? The relationships of trajectories of conduct problems with ODD and ADHD symptoms from childhood into adolescence. *Journal of Child Psychology and Psychiatry, 48,* 601–608.

Van Lier, P. A. C., Vitaro, F., Wanner, B., Vuijk, P., & Crijnen,A. A. M. (2005). Gender differences in developmental links among antisocial behavior, friends' antisocial behavior, and peer rejection in childhood: Results from two cultures. *Child Development, 76,* 841–855.

Van Lier, P. A. C., Vuijk, P., & Crijnen, A. A. M. (2005). Understanding mechanisms of change in the development of antisocial behavior: The impact of a universal intervention. *Journal of Abnormal Child Psychology, 33,* 521–535.

Van Lier, P.A.C., & Koot, H.M. (2010). Developmental cascades of peer relations and symptoms of externalizing and internalizing problems from kindergarten to fourth-grade elementary school. *Development and Psychopathology, 22,* 569–582.

van Lieshout, C.F.M., De Meyer, R.E., Curfs, L.M.G. & Fryns, J. (1998). Family contexts, parental behavior, and personality profiles of children and adolescents with Prader-Willi, fragile-X, or Williams syndrome. *Journal of Child Psychology and Psychiatry, 39,* 699–710.

Van Orden, K. A., Witte, T. K., Selby, E. A., Bender, T. W., & Joiner, T. E. (2008). Suicidal behavior in youth. In J. R.Z. Abela & B. L. Hankin (Eds.), *Handbook of depression in children and adolescents* (pp. 441–461). New York: Guilford Press.

Vanderlinden, J, Grave, R. D., Fernandez, F, Vandereycken, W., Pieters, G., & Noorduin, C. (2004). Which factors do provoke binge eating? An exploratory study in eating disorder patients. *Eating and Weight Disorders, 9,* 300–305.

Vandrey, R., Budney, A. J., Kamon, J. L., & Stanger, C. (2005). Cannabis withdrawal in adolescent treatment seekers. *Drug and Alcohol Dependence, 78,* 205–210.

VanFleet, R. (2000). Understanding and overcoming parent resistance to play therapy. *International Journal of Play Therapy, 9,* 35–46.

VanFleet, R., Ryan, S. D., & Smith, S. K. (2005). Filial therapy: A critical review. In L. A. Reddy, T. M. Files-Hall, & C. E. Schaefer (Eds.), *Empirically based play interventions for children* (pp. 241–264). Washington, DC: American Psychological Association.

Vanyukov, M. M., Kirisci, L., Tarter, R. E., Simkevitz, H. F., Kirillova, G. P., Maher, B. S., et al. (2003). Liability to substance use disorders: 2. A measurement approach. *Neuroscience and Biobehavioral Reviews, 27,* 517–526.

Vanyukov, M. M., Tarter, R. E., Kirisci, L., Kirillova, G. P., Maher,B. S., & Clark, D. B. (2003). Liability to substance use disorders: 1. Common mechanisms and manifestations. *Neuroscience and Biobehavioral Reviews, 27,* 507–515.

Varela, R.E., & Hensley-Maloney, L. (2009). The influence of culture on anxiety in Latino youth: A review. Clinical Child & Family Psychology Review, *12,* 217–233.

Varela, R.E. Sanchez-Sosa, J.J., Biggs, B.K., & Luis, T.M. (2009). Parenting strategies and socio-cultural influences in childhood anxiety: Mexican, Latin American descent, and European American families. *Journal of Anxiety Disorders, 23,* 609–616.

Vasey, M. W., & Dadds, M. R. (Eds.) (2001). *The developmental psychopathology of anxiety.* London: Oxford University Press.

Vaughn, B. E., Egeland, B. R., Sroufe, L. A., & Waters, E. (1979). Individual differences in infant-mother attachment at twelve and eighteen months: Stability and change in families under stress. *Child Development, 50,* 971–975.

Vazsonyi, A. T., Chen, P., Jenkins, D. D., Burcu, E., Torrente, G., & Sheu, C-J. (2010). Jessor's Problem Behavior Theory: Cross-national evidence from Hungary, the Netherlands, Slovenia, Spain, Switzerland, Taiwan, Turkey, and the United States. *Developmental Psychology, 46,* 1779–1791.

Veach, P. M., Bartels, D. M., & LeRoy, B. S. (2002). Commentary on genetic counseling—A profession in search of itself. *Journal of Genetic Counseling, 11,* 187–191.

Vedder, P., & Virta, E. (2005). Language, ethnic identity, and the adaptation of Turkish immigrant youth in the Netherlands and Sweden. *International Journal of Intercultural Relations, 29,* 317–337.

Vega, W. A., Aguilar-Gaxiola, S., Andrade, L., Bijl, R., Borges, G., Caraveo-Anduaga, J. J., et al. (2002). Prevalence and ages of onset for drug use in seven international sites: Results from the International Consortium of Psychiatric Epidemiology. *Drug and Alcohol Dependence, 68,* 285–297.

Velting, O. N., Setzer, N. J., & Albano, A. M. (2004). Update on and advances in assessment and cognitive-behavioral treatment of anxiety disorders in children and adolescents. *Professional Psychology: Research and Practice, 35,* 42–54.

Vendlinski, M., Silk, J.S., Shaw, D.S., & Lane, T.J. (2006). Ethnic differences in relations between family process and child internalizing problems. *Journal of Child Psychology and Psychiatry, 47,* 960–969.

Verduin, T. L., & Kendall, P. C. (2003). Differential occurrence of comorbidity within childhood anxiety disorders. *Journal of Clinical Child and Adolescent Psychology, 32,* 290–295.

Verhulst, F. C., & Achenbach, T. M. (1995). Empirically based assessment and taxonomy of psychopathology: Cross-cultural applications: A review. *European Child and Adolescent Psychiatry, 4,* 61–76.

Verhulst, F. C., Dekker, M. C., & van der Ende, J. (1997). Parent, teacher and self-reports as predictors of signs of disturbance in adolescents: Whose information carries the most weight? *Acta Psychiatrica Scandinavica, 96,* 75–81.

Verhulst, F. C., & van der Ende, J. (1997). Factors associated with child mental health service use in the community. *Journal of the American Academy of Child and Adolescent Psychiatry, 36,* 901–909.

Verhulst, F. C., Van der Ende, J., Ferdinand, R. F., & Kasius, M. C. (1997). The prevalence of DSM-III-R diagnoses in a national sample of Dutch adolescents. *Archives of General Psychiatry, 54,* 329–336.

Verlinden, S., Hersen, M., & Thomas, J. (2000). Risk factors in school shootings. *Clinical Psychology Review, 20,* 3–56.

Vermetten, E. & Bremner, J.D. (2002). Circuits and systems in stress. I. Preclinical studies. *Depression and Anxiety, 15,* 126–147.

Vermetten, E. & Bremner, J.D. (2002). Circuits and systems in stress: II. Applications to neurobiology and treatment in post-traumatic stress disorder. *Depression and Anxiety, 16,* 14–38.

Vernberg, E. M., Routh, D. K., & Koocher, G. P. (1992). The future of psychotherapy with children: Developmental psychotherapy. *Psychotherapy, 29,* 72–80.

Vicari, S., Caselli, M. C., Gagliardi, C., Tonucci, F., & Volterra, V. (2002). Language acquisition in special populations: A comparison between Down and Williams syndrome. *Neuropsychologia, 40,* 2461–2470.

Vickerman, K. A., & Margolin, G. (2007). Posttraumatic stress in children and adolescents exposed to family violence: II. Treatment. *Professional Psychology: Research and Practice, 38,* 620–628.

Vila, M., Kramer, T., Hickey, N., Dattani, M., Jefferis, H., Singh, M., & Garraida, M.E. (2009). Assessment of somatic symptoms in British secondary school children using the Children's Somatization Inventory (CSI). *Journal of Pediatric Psychology, 34,* 989–998.

Villalba, R., & Harrington, C. (2003). Repetitive self-injurious behavior: The emerging potential of psychotropic intervention. *Psychiatric Times, 20,* 66–70.

Vitiello, B. (2008). An international perspective on pediatric psychopharmacology. *International Review of Psychiatry, 20,* 121–126.

Volkmar, F. R., Chawarska, K., & Klin, A. (2005). Autism in infancy and early childhood. *Annual Review of Psychology, 56,* 315–336.

Volkmar, F. R., & Klin, A. (1994). Social development in autism: Historical and clinical perspectives. In S. Baron-Cohen & H. Tager-Flusberg (Eds.), *Understanding other minds: Perspectives from autism* (pp. 40–55). London: Oxford University Press.

Volkmar, F. R., & Klin, A. (2000). Diagnostic issues in Asperger syndrome. In A. Klin, F. R. Volkmar, & S. S. Sparrow (Eds.), *Asperger syndrome* (pp. 25–71). New York: Guilford Press.

Volkmar, F. R., & Klin, A. (2001). Asperger's disorder and higher functioning autism: Same or different? In L. M. Glidden (Ed.), *International review of research in mental retardation: Autism* (Vol. 23, pp. 83–110). San Diego, CA: Academic Press.

Volkmar, F. R., Klin, A., Marans, W., & Cohen, D. J. (1996). The pervasive developmental disorders: Diagnosis and assessment. *Child and Adolescent Psychiatric Clinics of North America, 5,* 963–977.

Volkmar, F. R., & Lord, C. (1998). Diagnosis and definition of autism and other pervasive developmental disorders. In F. R. Volkmar (Ed.), *Autism and pervasive developmental disorders: Cambridge monographs in child and adolescent psychiatry* (pp. 1–31). New York: Cambridge University Press.

Volkmar, F.R., State, M., & Klin, A. (2009). Autism and autism spectrum disorders: Diagnostic issues for the coming decade. *Journal of Child Psychology and Psychiatry, 50,* 108–115.

Volkow, N.D. Wang, G.J., Newcom, J.H., Kollins, S.H., Wiga, T.L., Telang, F., … Swanson, J.M. (2011). Motivation deficit in ADHD is associated with dysfunction of the dopamine reward pathway. *Molecular Psychiatry, 16,* 1147–1154.

Volterra, V., Capirci, O., & Caselli, M. C. (2001). What atypical populations can reveal about language development: The contrast between deafness and Williams syndrome. *Language and Cognitive Processes, 16,* 219–239.

Von Korff, M. R., Eaton, W. W., & Keyl, P. M. (1985). The epidemiology of panic attacks and panic disorder. *American Journal of Epidemiology, 122,* 970–981.

Von Salisch, M. (2001). Children's emotional development: Challenges in their relationships to parents, peers, and friends. *International Journal of Behavioral Development, 25,* 310–319.

Von Salisch, M., & Saarni, C. (2001). Introduction to the Special Section: Emotional development in interpersonal relationships. *International Journal of Behavioral Development, 25,* 289.

von Stauvffenberg, C., & Campbell, S.B. (2007). Predicting the early developmental course of symptoms of attention deficit hyperactivity disorder. *Journal of Applied Developmental Psychology, 28,* 536–552.

Vostanis, P. (2012). Mental health services for children in public care and other vulnerable groups: Implications for international collaboration. *Clinical Child Psychology and Psychiatry, 15,* 555–571.

Vungkhanching, M., Sher, K. J., Jackson, K. M., & Parra, G. R. (2004). Relation of attachment style to family history of alcoholism and alcohol use disorders in early adulthood. *Drug and Alcohol Dependence, 75,* 47–53.

Vythilingam, M., Heim, C., Newport, J., Miller, A. H., Anderson, E., Bronen, R., et al. (2002). Childhood trauma associated with smaller hippocampal volume in women with major depression. *The American Journal of Psychiatry, 159,* 2072–2080.

Waaddegaard, M., & Petersen, T. (2002). Dieting and desire for weight loss among adolescents in Denmark: A questionnaire survey. *European Eating Disorders Review, 10,* 329–346.

Wade, T. D., Bulik, C. M., Prescott, C. A., & Kendler, K. S. (2004). Sex influences on shared risk factors for bulimia nervosa and other psychiatric disorders. *Archives of General Pyschiatry, 61,* 251–256.

Wagenaar, A. C., Lenk, K. M., & Toomey, T. L. (2006). Policies to reduce underage drinking. In M. Galanter (Ed.), *Alcohol problems in adolescents and young adults: Epidemiology, neurobiology, prevention, and treatment* (pp. 275–297). New York: Springer Science and Business Media.

Wagenaar, A. C., Toomey, T. L., & Erickson, D. J. (2005). Preventing youth access to alcohol: Outcomes from a multicommunity time-series trial. *Addiction, 100,* 335–345.

Wagner, B. M., Silverman, M. A.C., & Martin, C. E. (2003). Family factors in youth suicidal behaviors. *American Behavioral Scientist, 46,* 1171–1191.

Wagner, E. F., Brown, S. A., Monti, P. M., Myers, M. G., & Waldron, H. B. (1998). Innovations in adolescent substance abuse intervention. *Alcoholism: Clinical and Experimental Research, 23,* 236–249.

Wahl, O. F. (2002). Children's views of mental illness: A review of the literature. *Psychiatric Rehabilitation Skills, 6,* 134–158.

Wahl, S. K., Turner, L. R., Mermelstein, R. J., & Flay, B. R. (2005). Adolescents' smoking expectancies: Psychometric properties and prediction of behavior change. *Nicotine and Tobacco Research, 7,* 613–623.

Wakefield, J. C. (1992). The concept of mental disorder: On the boundary between biological facts and social values. *American Psychologist, 47,* 373–388.

Wakefield, J. C. (1997). When is development disordered? Developmental psychopathology and the harmful dysfunction analysis of mental disorder. *Development and Psychopathology, 9,* 269–290.

Wakefield, J. C. (2002). Values and the validity of diagnostic criteria: Disvalued versus disordered conditions of childhood and adolescence. In J. Z. Sadler (Ed.), *Descriptions and prescriptions: Values, mental disorders and the DSMs* (pp. 148–164). Baltimore, MD: Johns Hopkins University Press.

Wakefield, M., Kloska, D. D., O'Malley, P. M., Johnston, L. D., Chaloupka, F., Pierce, J., et al. (2004). The role of smoking intentions in predicting future smoking among youth: Findings from Monitoring the Future data. *Addiction, 99,* 914–922.

Wakschlag, L.S., Tolan, P.H., & Leventhal, B.L. (2010). "Ain't misbehaving": Towards a developmentally-specified nosology for preschool disruptive behavior. *Journal of Child Psychology and Psychiatry, 51,* 3–22.

Walden, B., McGue, M., Iacono, W. G., Burt, S. A., & Elkins, I. (2004). Identifying shared environmental contributions to early substance use: The respective roles of peers and parents. *Journal of Abnormal Psychology, 113,* 440–450.

Waldman, I. D., & Lilienfeld, S. O. (2001). Applications of taxometric methods to problems of comorbidity: Perspectives and challenges. *Clinical Psychology: Science and Practice, 8,* 520–527.

Waldman, I.D., Tackett, J.L., Van Hulle, C.A., Applegate, B., Pardini, D., Frick, P.J., & Lahey, B.B. (2011). Child and adolescent conduct disorder substantially shares genetic influences with three socioemotional dispositions. *Journal of Abnormal Psychology, 120,* 57–70.

Waldron, H. B., & Kaminer, Y. (2004). On the learning curve: The emerging evidence supporting cognitive-behavioral therapies for adolescent substance abuse. *Addiction, 99,* 93–105.

Walker, D. R., Thompson, A., Zwaigenbaum, L., Goldberg, J., Bryson, S. E., Mahoney, W. J., et al. (2004). Specifying PDD-NOS: A comparison of PDD-NOS, Asperger syndrome, and autism.*Journal of the American Academy of Child and Adolescent Psychiatry, 43,* 172–780.

Walker, L. S., Claar, R. L., & Garber, J. (2002). Social consequences of children's pain: When do they encourage symptom maintenance? *Journal of Pediatric Psychology, 27,* 680–698.

Walkup, J. T., & Ginsburg, G. S. (2002). Anxiety disorders in children and adolescents. *International Review of Psychiatry, 14,* 85–86.

Walkup, J.T., Albano, A.M., Piacentini, J., Birmaher, B., Compton, S.N., Sherrill, J.T., Ginsburg, G.S., … Kendall, P.C. (2008). Cognitive behavioral therapy, sertraline, or a combination in childhood anxiety. *The New England Journal of Medicine, 359,* 2753–2766.

Wallace, J. M., Jr., & Muroff, J. R. (2002). Preventing substance abuse among African American children and youth: Race differences in risk factor exposure and vulnerability. *Journal of Primary Prevention, 22*, 235–261.

Wallace, K.S., & Rogers, S.J. (2010). Intervening in infancy: implications for autism spectrum disorders. *Journal of Child Psychology and Psychiatry, 51*, 1300–1320.

Waller, M., Hallfors, D., Halpern, C., Iritani, B., Ford, C., & Cuo,G. (2006). Depressive symptoms and patterns of substance use and risky sexual behavior among nationally representative samples of U. S. adolescents, *Archives of Women's Mental Health, 9*, 139–150.

Wallis, A., Rhodes, P., Kohn, M., & Madden, S. (2007). Five years of family based treatment for anorexia nervosa: The Maudsley model at the Children's Hospital at Westmead. *International Journal of Adolescent Medicine and Health, 19*, 277–283.

Wang, M. Q., Matthew, R. F., Bellamy, N., & James, S. (2005). A structural model of the substance use pathways among minority youth. *American Journal of Health Behavior, 29*, 531–541.

Wang, S. S., Houshyar, S., & Prinstein, M. J. (2006). Adolescent girls' and boys' weight-related health behaviors and cognitions: Associations with reputation- and preference-based peer status. *Health Psychology, 25,* 358–663.

Wang, Z., Byrne, N. M., Kenardy, J. A., & Hills, A. P. (2005). Influences of ethnicity and socioeconomic status on the body dissatisfaction and eating behavior of Australian children and adolescents. *Eating Behaviors, 6,* 23–33.

Wanner, B., Vitaro, F., Ladouceur, R., Brendgen, M., & Tremblay, R. E. (2006). Joint trajectories of gambling, alcohol and marijuana use during adolescence: A person- and variable-centered developmental approach. *Addictive Behaviors, 31*, 566–580.

Wardle, K. A., Robb, F. J., Griffith, J., Brunner, E., Power, C., & Tovee, M. (2004). Socioeconomic variation in attitudes to eating and weight in female adolescents. *Health Psychology, 23,* 275–282.

Warren, S. L., Emde, R., & Sroufe, L. A. (2000). Internal representations: Predicting anxiety from children's play narratives. *Journal of the American Academy of Child and Adolescent Psychiatry, 39*, 100–107.

Warren, S.L., Huston, L., Egeland, B. & Sroufe, L.A. (1997). Child and adolescent anxiety disorders and early attachment. *Journal of the American Academy of Child & Adolescent Psychiatry, 36*, 637–644.

Waschbusch, D. A. (2002). A meta-analytic examination of co-morbid hyperactive-impulsive-attention problems and conduct problems. *Psychological Bulletin, 128*, 118–150.

Waschbusch, D. A., & Hill, G. P. (2003). Empirically supported, promising, and unsupported treatments for children with attention-deficit/hyperactivity disorder. From S. O. Lilienfeld & S. J. Lynn (Eds.), *Science and pseudoscience in clinical psychology* (pp. 333–362). New York: Guilford Press.

Waschbusch, D. A., Pelham, W. E. Jr., Jennings, J. R., Greiner, A. R., Tarter, R. E., & Moss, H. B. (2002). Reactive aggression in boys with disruptive behavior disorders: Behavior physiology, and affect. *Journal of Abnormal Child Psychology, 30*, 641–656.

Waschbusch, D. A., Porter, S., Carrey, N., Kazmi, S. O., Roach, K. A., & D'Amico, D. A. (2004). Investigation of the heterogeneity of disruptive behaviour in elementary-age children. *Canadian Journal of Behavioural Science, 36*, 97–112.

Waschbusch, D. A., Walsh, T. M., Andrade, B. F., King, S., & Carrey, N. J. (2007). Social problem solving, conduct problems, and callous-unemotional traits in children. *Child Psychiatry and Human Development, 37*, 293–305.

Waters, E. (1995). Attachment Q-Set (Appendix A). *Monographs of the Society for Research in Child Development, 60*, 234–346.

Waters, E., Merrick, S., Treboux, D., Crowell, J., & Albersheim, L. (2000). Attachment security in infancy and early adulthood: A twenty-year longitudinal study. *Child Development, 71*, 684–689.

Waters, E., & Sroufe, L. A. (1983). Social competence as a developmental construct. *Developmental Review, 3*, 79–97.

Waters, T. L., & Barrett, P. M. (2000). The role of the family in childhood obsessive-compulsive disorder. *Clinical Child and Family Psychology Review, 3,* 173–184.

Watson, A. C., Miller, F. E., & Lyons, J. S. (2005). Adolescent attitudes toward serious mental illness. *Journal of Nervous and Mental Disease, 193*, 769–772.

Watson, A. C., Otey, E., Westbrook, A. L., Gardner, A. L., Lamb, T. A., Corrigan, P. W., et al. (2004). Changing middle schoolers' attitudes about mental illness through education. *Schizophrenia Bulletin, 30*, 563–572.

Watson, A. C., Painter, K. M., & Bornstein, M. H. (2001). Longitudinal relations between 2-year-olds' language and 4-year-olds' theory of mind. *Journal of Cognition and Development, 2*, 449–457.

Watson, D., & Clark, L. A. (1984). Negative affectivity: The disposition to experience aversive emotional states. *Psychological Bulletin, 96*, 465–490.

Watters, E. (2010). *Crazy Like Us: The Globalization of the American Psyche.* New York: Free Press.

Webster-Stratton, C. (2005). The Incredible Years: A training program for the prevention and treatment of conduct problems in young children. In E. D. Hibbs & P. S. Jensen (Eds.), *Psychosocial treatments for child and adolescent disorders: Empirically based strategies for clinical practice* (2nd ed., pp. 507–555). Washington, DC: American Psychological Association.

Webster-Stratton, C., & Herman, K.C. (2010). Disseminating incredible years series early-intervention programs: Integrating and sustaining services between school and home. *Psychology in the Schools, 47,* 36–54.

Webster-Stratton, C., & Reid, M. J. (2006). Treatment and prevention of conduct problems: Parent training interventions for young children (2–7 years old). In K. McCartney & D. Phillips (Eds.), *Blackwell handbook of early childhood development* (pp. 616–641). Malden, MA: Blackwell.

Webster-Stratton, C., & Reid, M. J. (2007). Incredible Years parents and teachers training series: A Head Start partnership to promote social competence and prevent conduct problems. In P. Tolan, J. Szapocznik, & S. Sambrano (Eds.), *Preventing youth substance abuse: Science-based programs for children and adolescents* (pp. 67–88). Washington, DC: American Psychological Association.

Webster-Stratton, C., Reid, M. J., & Stoolmiller, M. (2008). Preventing conduct problems and improving school readiness: Evaluation of the Incredible Years teacher and child training programs in high-risk schools. *Journal of Child Psychology and Psychiatry, 49*, 251–263.

Webster-Stratton, C., & Taylor, T. (2001). Nipping early risk factors in the bud: Preventing substance abuse, delinquency, and violence in adolescence through interventions targeted at young children (0 to 8 years). *Prevention Science, 2*, 165–192.

Wechsler, D. (2003). *Wechsler Intelligence Scale for Children, 4th ed. (WISC-IV)*. San Antonio, TX: The Psychological Corporation.

Wechsler, H., & Wuethrich, B. (2002*). Dying to drink: Confronting binge drinking on college campuses*. Emmaus, PA: Rodale Press.

Weems, C.F. (2006). An integrative model of control: Implications for understanding emotion regulation and dysregulation in childhood anxiety. *Journal of Affective Disorders, 91,* 113–124.

Weems, C.F. (2008). Developmental trajectories of childhood anxiety: Identifying continuity and change in anxious emotion. *Developmental Review, 28,* 488–502.

Weems, C.F. (2009). Developmental psychopathology, positive psychology, and knowledge development in child and youth care: Editorial hopes and aspirations for the forum. *Child and Youth Care Forum, 38,* 1–4.

Weems, C.F. (2011). Anxiety sensitivity as a specific form of distress tolerance in youth: Developmental assessment, origins, and applications. In M.J. Zvolensky, A. Bernstein & A.A. Vujanovic (Eds.), *Distress tolerance: Theory, research, and clinical applications* (pp. 28–51). New York: Guilford Press.

Weems, C.F. & Silverman, W.K. (2006). An integrative model of control: Implications for understanding emotion regulation and dysregulation in childhood anxiety. *Journal of Affective Disorders, 91,* 113–124.

Weems, C.F., Taylor, L.K., Marks, A.B., & Varela, R.E. (2010). Anxiety sensitivity in childhood and adolescence: Parent reports and factors that influence associations with child reports. *Cognitive Therapy and Research, 34,* 303–315.

Weersing, V. R., & Weisz, J. R. (2002). Community clinic treatment of depressed youth: Benchmarking usual care against CBT clinical trials. *Journal of Consulting and Clinical Psychology, 70,* 299–310.

Wei, E. H., Loeber, R., & White, H. R. (2004). Teasing apart the developmental associations between alcohol and marijuana use and violence. *Journal of Contemporary Criminal Justice, 20,* 166–183.

Weil, J. (2003). Psychosocial genetic counseling in the postnondirective era: A point of view. *Journal of Genetic Counseling, 12,* 199–211.

Weine, A. M., Phillips, J. S., & Achenbach, T. M. (1995). Behavioral and emotional problems among Chinese and American children: Parent and teacher reports for ages 6 to 13. *Journal of Abnormal Child Psychology, 23,* 619–639.

Weiner, M. D., Pentz, M. A., Skara, S. N., Li, C., Chou, C-P., & Dwyer, J. H. (2004). Relationship of substance use and associated predictors of violence in early, middle, and late adolescence. *Journal of Child and Adolescent Substance Abuse, 13,* 97–117.

Weis, R., Whitemarsh, S. M., & Wilson, N. L. (2005). Military-style residential treatment for disruptive adolescents: Effective for some girls, all girls, when, and why? *Psychological Services, 2,* 105–122.

Weis, R., Wilson, N. L., & Whitemarsh, S. M. (2005). Evaluation of a voluntary, military-style residential treatment program for adolescents with academic and conduct problems. *Journal of Clinical Child and Adolescent Psychology, 34,* 692–705.

Weiser, M., Reichenberg, A., Grotto, I., Yasvitzky, R., Rabinowitz, J., Lubin, G., et al. (2004). Higher rates of cigarette smoking in male adolescents before the onset of schizophrenia: A historical-prospective cohort study. *American Journal of Psychiatry, 161,* 1219–1223.

Weisner, T. S. (2005). Attachment as a cultural and ecological problem with pluralistic solution. *Human Development, 48,* 89–94.

Weiss, B., & Garber, J. (2003). Developmental differences in the phenomenology of depression. *Development and Psychopathology, 15,* 403–430.

Weiss, E.L., Longhurst, J.G. & Mazure, C.M. (1999). Childhood sexual abuse as a risk factor for depression in women: Psychosocial and neurobiological correlates. *The American Journal of Psychiatry, 156,* 816–828.

Weiss, G., & Hechtman, L. T. (1999). *ADHD in adulthood: A guide to current theory, diagnosis and treatment*. Baltimore: Johns Hopkins University.

Weiss, K., & Wertheim, E. H. (2005). An evaluation of a prevention program for disordered eating in adolescent girls: Examining responses of high- and low-risk girls. *Eating Disorders: The Journal of Prevention and Treatment, 13,* 143–156.

Weisz, J. R. (2004). *Psychotherapy for children and adolescents: Evidence-Based treatments and case examples*. New York: Cambridge University Press.

Weisz, J. R., Chaiyasit, W., Weiss, B., Eastman, K. L., & Jackson, E. W. (1995). A multimethod study of problem behavior among Thai and American children in school: Teacher reports versus direct observations. *Child Development, 66,* 402–415.

Weisz, J. R., Doss, A. J., & Hawley, K. M. (2005). Youth psychotherapy outcome research: A review and critique of the evidence base. *Annual Review of Psychology, 56,* 337–363.

Weisz, J. R., & Eastman, K. L. (1995). Cross-national research on child and adolescent psychopathology. In F. C. Verhulst (Ed.), *The epidemiology of child and adolescent psychopathology* (pp. 42–65). London: Oxford University Press.

Weisz, J. R., & Hawley, K. M. (2002). Developmental factors in the treatment of adolescents. *Journal of Consulting and Clinical Psychology, 70,* 21–43.

Weisz, J. R., & Kazdin, A. E. (2010). Evidence-Based Psychotherapies for Children and Adolescents (2nd ed.). New York: Guilford Press.

Weisz, J. R., & McCarty, C. A. (1999). Can we trust parent reports in research on cultural and ethnic differences in child psychopathology? Using the bicultural family design to test parental culture effects. *Journal of Abnormal Psychology, 108,* 598–603.

Weisz, J. R., McCarty, C. A., Eastman, K. L., Chaiyasit, W., & Suwanlert, S. (1997). Developmental psychopathology and culture: Ten lessons from Thailand. In S. Luthar, J. A. Burack, D. Cicchetti, & J. R. Weisz (Eds.), *Developmental psychopathology: Perspectives on adjustment, risk, and disorder* (pp. 568–592). New York: Cambridge University Press.

Weisz, J. R., McCarty, C. A., & Valeri, S. M. (2006). Effects of psychotherapy for depression in children and adolescents: A meta-analysis. *Psychological Bulletin, 132,* 132–149.

Weisz, J. R., Sandler, I. N., Durlak, J. A., & Anton, B. S. (2005). Promoting and protecting youth mental health through evidence-based prevention and treatment. *American Psychologist, 60,* 628–648.

Weisz, J. R., Sigman, M., Weiss, B., & Mosk, J. (1993). Parent reports of behavioral and emotional problems among children in Kenya, Thailand, and the United States. *Child Development, 64,* 98–109.

Weisz, J. R., Southam-Gerow, M. A., Gordis, E. B., & Connor-Smith, J. (2003). Primary and secondary control enhancement training for youth depression: Applying the deployment-focused model of treatment development and testing. From

A. E. Kazdin & J. R. Weisz (Eds.), *Evidence-based psycho-therapies for children and adolescents* (pp. 165–182). New York: Guilford Press.

Weisz, J. R., Suwanlert, S., Chaiyasit, W., Weiss, B., Walter, B. R., & Anderson, W. W. (1988). Thai and American perspectives on over- and undercontrolled child behavior problems: Exploring the threshold model among parents, teachers, and psychologists. *Journal of Consulting and Clinical Psychology, 56*, 601–609.

Weisz, J. R., Suwanlert, S., Chaiyasit, W., Weiss, B., Walter, B.R., & Anderson, W. W. (1991). Adult attitudes toward over- and undercontrolled child problems: Urban and rural parents and teachers from Thailand and the United States. *Journal of Child Psychology and Psychiatry and Allied Disciplines, 32*, 645–654.

Weisz, J. R., Sweeney, L., Proffitt, V., & Carr, T. (1993). Control-related beliefs and self-reported depressive symptoms in late childhood. *Journal of Abnormal Psychology, 102*, 411–418.

Weisz, J.R., Weiss, B., Suwanlert, S., & Chaiyasit, W. (2006). Culture and youth psychopathology: Testing the syndromal sensitivity model in Thai and American Adolescents. *Journal of Consulting and Clinical Psychology, 74*, 1098–1107.

Weller, E. B., Calvert, S. M., & Weller, R. A. (2003). Bipolar disorder in children and adolescents: Diagnosis and treatment. *Current Opinion in Psychiatry, 16*, 383–388.

Weller, E. B., Danielyan, A. K., & Weller, R. A. (2002). Somatic treatment of bipolar disorder in children and adolescents. *Child and Adolescent Psychiatric Clinics of North America, 11*, 595–618.

Weller, E. B., Weller, R. A., & Fristad, M. A. (1995). Bipolar disorder in children: Misdiagnosis, underdiagnosis, and future directions. *Journal of the American Academy of Child and Adolescent Psychiatry, 34*, 709–714.

Wellman, H. M., Baron-Cohen, S., Caswell, R., Gomez, J. C., Swettenham, J., Toye, E. et al. (2002). Thought bubbles help children with autism acquire an alternative to a theory of mind. *Autism, 6*, 343–363.

Wells, J. E., Horwood, L. J., & Fergusson, D. M. (2004). Drinking patterns in mid-adolescence and psychosocial outcomes in late adolescence and early adulthood. *Addiction, 99*, 1529–1541.

Wells, K. C., & Albano, A. M. (2005). Parent involvement in CBT treatment of adolescent depression: Experiences in the Treatment for Adolescents with Depression Study (TADS). *Cognitive and Behavioral Practice, 12*, 209–220.

Wentworth, N., & Witryol, S. L. (2003). Curiosity, exploration, and novelty seeking. In M. H. Bornstein, L. Davidson, C. L. M. Keyes, & A. Moore (Eds.), Well-being: Positive development across the life course (pp. 281–294). Mahwah, NJ: Erlbaum.

Werner, E., & Dawson, G. (2005). Validation of the phenomenon of autistic regression using home videotapes. *Archives of General Psychiatry, 62,* 889–895.

Werner, E., Dawson, G., Muson, J., & Osterling, J. (2005). Variation in early developmental course in autism and its relation with behavioral outcome at 3–4 years of age. *Journal of Autism and Developmental Disorders, 35*, 337–350.

Werner, E., Dawson, G., Osterling, J., & Dinno, N. (2000). Recognition of autism spectrum disorder before one year of age: A retrospective study based on home videotapes. *Journal of Autism and Developmental Disorders, 30*, 157–162.

Werner, E. E. (1993). Risk, resilience and recovery: Perspectives from the Kauai longitudinal study. *Development and Psychology, 5*, 503–515.

Werner, E. E., & Smith, R. S. (1977). *Kauai's Children Come of Age*. Honolulu: University of Hawaii Press.

Werner, E. E., & Smith, R. S. (1982, 1989). Vulnerable but invincible: A study of resilient children. New York: McGraw-Hill.

Werner, N. E., & Crick, N. R. (2004). Maladaptive peer relationships and the development of relational and physical aggression during middle childhood. *Social Development, 13*, 495–514.

Wertheim, E. H., Martin, G., Prior, M., Sanson, A., & Smart, D. (2002). Parent influences in the transmission of eating- and weight-related values and behaviors. *Eating Disorders: The Journal of Treatment and Prevention, 10*, 321–334.

West, A., Henry, D. B., & Pavuluri, M. (2007). Maintenance model of integrated psychosocial treatment in pediatric bipolar disorder: A pilot feasibility study. *Journal of the American Academy of Child and Adolescent Psychiatry, 46*, 205–212.

West, A.E. & Newman, D.L. (2007). Childhood behavioral inhibition and the experience of social anxiety in American Indian adolescents. *Cultural Diversity and Ethnic Minority Psychology, 13*, 197–206.

Westen, D. (1998). The scientific legacy of Sigmund Freud: Toward a psychodynamically informed psychological science. *Psychological Bulletin, 124*, 333–371.

Westenberg, P. M., Drewes, M. J., Goedhart, A. W., Siebelink,B. M., & Treffers, P. D. (2004). A developmental analysis of self-reported fears in late childhood through mid-adolescence: Social-evaluative fears on the rise? *Journal of Child Psychology and Psychiatry, 45*, 481–495.

Wetherby, A. M. (1986). Ontogeny of communicative functions in autism. *Journal of Autism and Developmental Disorders, 16*, 157–162.

Wetter, D. W., Kenford, S. L., Welsch, S. K., Smith, S. S., Fouladi, R. T., Fiore, M. C., et al. (2004). Prevalence and predictors of transitions in smoking behavior among college students. *Health Psychology, 23*, 168–177.

Whalen, C., & Schreibman, L. (2003). Joint attention training for children with autism using behavior modification procedures. *Journal of Child Psychology and Psychiatry, 44*, 456–468.

Whalen, C., Schreibman, L., & Ingersoll, B. (2006). The collateral effects of joint attention training on social initiations, positive affect, imitation, and spontaneous speech for young children with autism. *Journal of Autism and Developmental Disorders, 36*, 655–664.

Wheeler, H. A., Wintre, M. G., & Polivy, J. (2003). The association of low parent-adolescent reciprocity, a sense of incompetence, and identity confusion with disordered eating. *Journal of Adolescent Research, 18*, 405–429.

Whitaker-Azmitia, PM. (2005). Behavioral and cellular consequences of increasing serotonergic activity during brain development: A role in autism? *International Journal of Developmental Neuroscience, 23*, 75–83.

White, H. R., Pandina, R. J., & Chen, P-H. (2002). Developmental trajectories of cigarette use from early adolescence into young adulthood. *Drug and Alcohol Dependence, 65*, 167–178.

White, H. R., Tice, P. C., Loeber, R., & Stouthamer-Loeber, M. (2002). Illegal acts committed by adolescents under the influence of alcohol and drugs. *Journal of Research in Crime and Delinquency, 39*, 131–152.

White, H. R., Xie, M., Thompson, W., Loeber, R., & Stouthamer-Loeber, M. (2001). Psychopathology as a predictor of adolescent drug use trajectories. *Psychology of Addictive Behaviors, 15*, 210–218.

White, M. A., Kohlmaier, J. R., Varnado-Sullivan, P., & Williamson, D. A. (2003). Racial/ethnic differences in weight concerns: Protective and risk factors for the development of eating disorders and obesity among adolescent females. *Eating and Weight Disorders, 8,* 20–25.

Whitfield, J. B., Zhu, G., Madden, P. A., Neale, M. C., Heath, A. C., & Martin, N. G. (2004). The genetics of alcohol intake and of alcohol dependence. *Alcoholism: Clinical and Experimental Research, 28,* 1153–1160.

Wicker, A. W. (1992). Making sense of environments. In W. B. Walsh & K. H. Craik (Eds.), *Person-environment psychology: Models and perspectives* (pp. 157–192). Hillsdale, NJ: Erlbaum.

Wiers, R. W., Gunning, W. B., & Sergeant, J. A. (1998). Do young children of alcoholics hold more positive or negative alcohol-related expectancies than controls? *Alcoholism: Clinical and Experimental Research, 22,* 1855–1863.

Wiersema, J.R., & Roeyers, H. (2009). ERP correlates of effortful control in children with varying levels of ADHD symptoms. *Journal of Child Psychology, 37,* 327–336.

Wiggins, L. D., Baio, J., & Rice, C. (2006). Examination of the time between first evaluation and first autism spectrum diagnosis in a population-based sample. *Journal of Developmental and Behavioral Pediatrics, 27,* S79–S87.

Wilburn, V. R., & Smith, D. E. (2005). Stress, self-esteem, and suicidal ideation in late adolescents. *Adolescence, 40,* 33–45.

Wild, L. G., Flisher, A. J., & Lombard, C. (2004). Suicidal ideation and attempts in adolescents: Association with depression and six domains of self-esteem. *Journal of Adolescence, 27,* 611–624.

Wilens, T. E., Biederman, J., Kwon, A., Ditterline, J., Forkner, P., Moore, H., et al. (2004). Risk of substance use disorders in adolescents with bipolar disorder. *Journal of the American Academy of Child and Adolescent Psychiatry, 43,* 1380–1386.

Wilens, T. E., Faraone, S. V., & Biederman, J. (2006). Attention-deficit/hyperactivity disorder in adults. *Journal of the American Medical Association, 292,* 619–623.

Willcutt, E.G., Doyle, A.E., Nigg, J.T., Faraone, S.V., & Pennington, B.F. (2005). Validity of the executive function theory of attention-deficit/hyperactivity disorder: A meta-analytic review. *Biological Psychiatry, 57,* 1336–1346.

Willcutt, E.G., Nigg, J.T., Pennington, B.F., Soanto, M.V., Rohde, L.A., Tannock, R., … Lahey, B.B. (2012). Validity of DSM-IV attention deficit/hyperactivity disorder symptom dimensions and subtypes. *The Journal of Abnormal Psychology, Advance online publication,* doi: 10.1037/a0027347.

Wille, D. E. (1991). Relation of preterm birth with quality of infant-mother attachment at one year. *Infant Behavior and Development, 14,* 227–240.

Willem, L., Bijttebier, P., Claes, L., Sools, J., Vandenbussche, I., & Nigg, J.T. (2011). Temperamental characteristics of adolescents with substance abuse and/or dependence: A case-control study. *Personality and Individual Differences, 50,* 1094–1098.

Williams, C., Alderson, P., & Farsides, B. (2002). 'Drawing the line' in prenatal screening and testing: Health practitioners' discussions. *Health, Risk and Society, 4,* 61–75.

Williams, D. L., Goldstein, G., & Minshew, N. J. (2006a). Neuropsychologic functioning in children with autism: Further evidence for disordered complex information-processing. *Child Neuropsychology, 12,* 279–298.

Williams, D. L., Goldstein, G., Minshew, N. J. (2006b). The profile of memory function in children with autism. *Neuropsychology, 20,* 21–29.

Williams, J., Mark, G., Barnhofer, T., Crane, C., Herman, D., Raes, F., … Dalgleish, T. (2007). Autobiographical memory specificity and emotional disorder. *Psychological Bulletin, 133,* 122–148.

Williams, K. R., & Guerra, N. G. (2007). Prevalence and predictors of internet bullying. *Journal of Adolescent Health, 41,* S14–S21.

Williams, P. G., Holmbeck, G. N., & Greenley, R. N. (2002). Adolescent health psychology. *Journal of Consulting and Clinical Psychology, 70,* 828–842.

Williamson, D. A., Marney, A, York-Crowe, E., & Stewart, T. M. (2004). Cognitive-behavior theories of eating disorders. *Behavior Modification, 28,* 711–738.

Williamson, D. E., Birmaher, B., Brent, D. A., Balach, L., Dahl, R. E., & Ryan, N. D. (2000). Atypical symptoms of depression in a sample of depressed child and adolescent outpatients. *Journal of the American Academy of Child and Adolescent Psychiatry, 39,* 1253–1259.

Williamson, D.A. (2007). Does the evidence point to a binge eating phenotype?: Comment on Gordon et al. (2007) and Wonderlich et al. (2007). *International Journal of Eating Disorders, 40,* S72-S75.

Williamson, D.A., White, M.A., York-Crowe, E. & Stewart, T.M. (2004). Cognitive-behavioral theories of eating disorders. *Behavior Modification, 28,* 711–738.

Williford, A. P., Calkins, S. D., & Keane, S. P. (2007). Predicting change in parenting stress across early childhood: Child and maternal factors. *Journal of Abnormal Child Psychology, 35,* 251–263.

Willner, P. (2001). A view through the gateway: Expectancies as a possible pathway from alcohol to cannabis. *Addiction, 96,* 691–703.

Willner, P., & Hart, K. (2001). Adolescents' reports of their illicit alcohol purchases. *Drugs: Education, Prevention and Policy, 8,* 233–242.

Willner, P., James, D., & Morgan, M. (2005). Excessive alcohol consumption and dependence on amphetamine are associated with parallel increases in subjective ratings of both 'wanting' and 'liking'. *Addiction, 100,* 1487–1495.

Willoughby, T., Chalmers, H., & Busseri, M. A. (2004). Where is the syndrome? Examining co-occurrence among multiple problem behaviors in adolescence. *Journal of Consulting and Clinical Psychology, 72,* 1022–1037.

Wills, K. (2007). Remediating specific learning disabilities. In S. Hunter & J. Donders (Eds.), *Pediatric Neuropsychological Intervention* (pp. 224–253). New York: Cambridge.

Wills, T. A., & Cleary, S. D. (1999). Peer and adolescent substance use among 6th–9th graders: Latent growth analyses of influence versus selection mechanisms. *Health Psychology, 18,* 453–463.

Wills, T. A., Resko, J. A., Ainette, M. G., & Mendoza, D. (2004). Role of parent support and peer support in adolescent substance use: A test of mediated effects. *Psychology of Addictive Behaviors, 18,* 122–134.

Wills, T. A., Sandy, J. M., & Yaeger, A. (2000). Temperament and adolescent substance use: An epigenetic approach to risk and protection. *Journal of Personality, 68,* 1127–1151.

Wills, T. A., Sandy, J. M., Yaeger, A., & Shinar, O. (2001). Family risk factors and adolescent substance use: Moderation effects for temperament dimensions. *Developmental Psychology, 37,* 283–297.

Wills, T. A., Sandy, J. M., Yeager, A. M., Cleary, S. D., & Shinar, O. (2001). Coping dimensions, life stress, and adolescent substance use: A latent growth analysis. *Journal of Abnormal Psychology, 110,* 309–323.

Wilson, G. T. (2005). Psychological treatment of eating disorders. *Annual Review of Clinical Psychology, 1,* 439–465.

Windle, M. (2003). Alcohol use among adolescents and young adults. *Alcohol Research and Health, 27,* 79–85.

Windle, M., Mun, E. Y., & Windle, R. C. (2005). Adolescent-to-young adulthood heavy drinking trajectories and their prospective predictors. *Journal of Studies on Alcohol, 66,* 313–322.

Windle, M., & Wiesner, M. (2004). Trajectories of marijuana use from adolescence to young adulthood: Predictors and outcomes. *Development and Psychopathology, 16,* 1007–1027.

Windle, M., & Windle, R. C. (2001). Depressive symptoms and cigarette smoking among middle adolescents: Prospective associations and intrapersonal and interpersonal infl uences. *Journal of Consulting and Clinical Psychology, 69,* 215–226.

Windle, M., & Windle, R. C. (2006). Alcohol consumption and its consequences among adolescents and young adults. In M. Galanter (Ed.), *Alcohol problems in adolescents and young adults: Epidemiology, neurobiology, prevention, and treatment* (pp. 67–83). New York: Springer.

Wing, L. (1991). Mental retardation and the autistic continuum. In P. E. Bebbington (Ed.), *Social psychiatry: Theory, methodology, and practice* (pp. 113–138). New Brunswick, NJ: Transaction Publishers.

Wing, L. (1991). The relationship between Asperger's syndrome and Kanner's autism. In U. Firth (Ed.), *Autism and Asperger syndrome* (pp. 93–121). New York: Cambridge University Press.

Wing, L. (1993). The definition and prevalence of autism: A review. *European Child and Adolescent Psychiatry, 2,* 61–74.

Wing, L. (1997). The history of ideas on autism. *Autism, 1,* 13–23.

Wing, L. (1998). The history of Asperger syndrome. In E. Schopler & G. B. Mesibov (Eds.), *Asperger syndrome or high-functioning autism? Current issues in autism* (pp. 11–28). New York: Plenum Press.

Wing, L., & Potter, D. (2009). The epidemiology of autism spectrum disorders: Is the prevalence rising? In S. Goldstein, J.A. Naglieri & S. Ozonoff (Eds.) *Assessment of autism spectrum disorders* (pp. 18–54). New York: Guilford Press.

Wing, L., & Wing. J. K. (1971). Multiple impairments in early childhood autism. *Journal of Autism and Childhood Schizophrenia, 1,* 256–266.

Winnepenninckx, B., Rooms, L., & Kooy, R. F. (2003). Mental retardation: A review of the genetic causes. *British Journal of Developmental Disabilities, 49,* 29–44.

Winters, K. C., Latimer, W. W., & Stinchfield, R. (2001). Assessing adolescent substance use. In E. F. Wagner & H. B. Waldron (Eds.), *Innovations in adolescent substance abuse interventions* (pp. 1–29). Amsterdam: Pergamon/Elsevier Science.

Winters, K. C., Stinchfield, R. D., Botzet, A., & Slutske, W. S. (2005). Pathways of youth gambling problem severity. *Psychology of Addictive Behaviors, 19,* 104–107.

Winters, N. C., Myers, K., & Proud, L. (2002). Ten-year review of rating scales. III: Scales assessing suicidality, cognitive style, and self esteem. *Journal of the American Academy of Child and Adolescent Pyschiatry, 41,* 1150–1181.

Wintersteen, M. B., Mensinger, J. L., & Diamond, G. S. (2005). Do gender and racial differences between patient and therapist affect therapeutic alliance and treatment retention in adolescents? *Professional Psychology: Research and Practice, 36,* 400–408.

Wiseman, C. V., Peltzman, B., Halmi, K., A., & Sunday, S. R. (2004). Risk factors for eating disorders: Surprising similarities between middle school boys and girls. *Eating Disorders: The Journal of Treatment and Prevention, 12,* 315–320.

Wiseman, C. V., Sunday, S. R., & Becker, A. E. (2005). Impact of the media on adolescent body image. *Child and Adolescent Psychiatric Clinics of North America, 14,* 453–471.

Wliksch, S. M., Durbridge, M. R., & Wade, T. D. (2008). A preliminary controlled comparison of programs designed to reduce risk of eating disorders targeting perfectionism and media literacy. *Journal of the American Academy of Child and Adolescent Psychiatry, 47,* 939–947.

Wodrich, D. L., Pfeiffer, S. I., & Landau, S. (2008). Contemplating the new DSM-V: Considerations from psychologists who work with school children. *Professional Psychology: Research and Practice, 39,* 626–632.

Wolf, E. M., & Sefferino, M. R. (2008). Group treatments of eating disorders with children and adolescents. In L. VandeCreek & J. B. Allen (Eds.), *Innovations in clinical practice: Focus on group, couples, and family therapy* (pp. 29–45). Sarasota, FL: Professional Resource Press/ Professional Resource Exchange.

Wonderlich, S.A., Crosby, R.D., Mitchell, J.E., & Engel, S.G. (2007). Testing the validity of eating disorder diagnoses. *International Journal of Eating Disorders, 40,* S40–S45.

Wonderlich, S.A., Gordon, K.H., Mitchell, J.E., Crosby, R.D., & Engel, S.G. (2009). The validity and clinical utility of binge eating disorder. *International Journal Eating Disorders, 42,* 687–705.

Wood, J.J., Piacentini, J.C., Southam-Gerow M., Chu, B.C. & Sigman, M. (2006). Family cognitive behavioral therapy for child anxiety disorders. *Journal of the American Academy of Child & Adolescent Psychiatry, 45,* 314–321.

Wozniak, J. Spencer, T., Biederman, J., Kwon, A., Monuteaux, M., Rettew, J., et al. (2004). The clinical characteristics of unipolar versus bipolar major depression in ADHD youth. *Journal of Affective Disorders, 82,* S59–S69.

Wren, F. J. Berg, E. A., Heiden, L. A., Kinnamon, C. J., Ohlson, L. A., Bridge, J. A., et al. (2007). Childhood anxiety in a diverse primary care population: Parent-child reports, ethnicity and SCARED factor structure. *Journal of the American Academy of Child and Adolescent Psychiatry, 46,* 332–340.

Wren, F.J., Bridge, J.A. & Birmaher, B. (2004). Screening for childhood anxiety symptoms in primary care: Integrating child and parent reports. *Journal of the American Academy & Adolescent Psychiatry 43,* 1364–1371.

Wright, F. D., Beck, A. T., Newman, C. F., & Liese, B. S. (1993). Cognitive therapy of substance abuse: Theoretical rationale. *NIDA Research Monograph, 137,* 123–146.

Wunderlich, S. A., Connolly, K. M., & Stice, E. (2004). Impulsivity as a risk factor for eating disorder behavior: Assessment implications with adolescents. *International Journal of Eating Disorders, 36,* 172–182.

Yamamiya, Y., Shroff, H., & Thompson, J. K. (2008). The Tripartite Influence Model of body image and eating disturbance: A replication with a Japanese sample. *Eating Behaviors, 41,* 88–91.

Yates, T. M. (2004). The developmental psychopathology of self-injurious behavior: Compensatory regulation in posttraumatic adaptation. *Clinical Psychology Review, 24,* 35–74.

Yates, T. M., Egeland, B., & Sroufe, L. A. (2003). Rethinking resilience: A developmental process perspective. In S. S. Luthar (Ed.), *Resilience and vulnerability: Adapatation in the context of childhood adversities* (pp. 243–266). New York: Cambridge University Press.

Yates, T. M., & Masten, A. S. (2004). Fostering the future: Resilience theory and the practice of positive psychology. In P. A. Linsley & S. Joseph (Eds.), *Positive Psychology in practice* (pp. 521–539). Hoboken, NJ: Wiley.

Yates, T.M. (2009). Developmental pathways from child maltreatment to nonsuicidal self-injury. In M.K. Nock (Ed.) *Understanding nonsuicidal self-injury: Origins, assessment, and treatment* (pp. 117–137). Washington, DC: American Psychological Association.

Yates, T.M., Burt, K.B., & Troy, M.F. (2011). A developmental approach to clinical research, classification, and practice. In D. Cicchetti & G. Roisman (Eds.), *MN Symposium on Child Psychology: The Origins and Organization of Adaptation & Maladaptation, vol. 36.* (pp. 197–201). Hoboken, NJ: Wiley.

Yates, T.M., Carlson, E.A., & Egeland, B. (2008). A prospective study of child maltreatment and self-injurious behavior in a community sample. *Development and Psychopathology, 20,* 651–671.

Yau, J., & Smetana, J. (2003). Adolescent-parent conflict in Hong Kong and Shenzen: A comparison of youth in two cultural contexts. *International Journal of Behavioral Development, 27,* 201–211.

Yearwood, E. L., Crawford, S., Kelly, M., & Moreno, N. (2007). Immigrant youth at risk for disorders of mood: Recognizing complex dynamics. *Archives of Psychiatric Nursing, 21,* 162–171.

Yeh, M., McCabe, K., Hough, R.L., Lau, A., Fakhry, F., & Garland, A. (2005). Why bother with beliefs? Examining relationships between race/ethnicity, parental beliefs about causes of child problems, and mental health service use. *Journal of Consulting and Clinical Psychology, 73,* 800–807.

Yeh, M., & Weisz, J. R. (2001). Why are we here at the clinic? Parent-child (dis)agreement on referral problems at outpatient treatment entry. *Journal of Consulting and Clinical Psychology, 69,* 1018–1025.

Ying, Z., & Hong, C. (2005). Physical self-satisfaction of adolescents from Han, Tibet and Yi nationalities. *Chinese Mental Health Journal, 19,* 796–797.

Yirmiya, N., & Charman, T. (2010). The prodrome of autism: early behavioral and biological signs, regression, peri-and post-natal development and genetics. *Journal of Child Psychology and Psychology, 51,* 432–458.

Yirmiya, N., Erel, O., Shaked, M., & Solomonica-Levi, D. (1998). Meta-analyses comparing theory of mind abilities of individuals with autism, individuals with mental retardation, and normally developing individuals. *Psychological Bulletin, 124,* 283–307.

Young, J. F., Mufson, L., & Davies, M. (2006). Efficacy of interpersonal psychotherapy-adolescent skills training: An indicated preventive intervention for depression. *Journal of Child Psychology and Psychiatry, 47,* 1254–1262.

Young, S.E., Friedman, N.P, Miyake, A., Willcutt, E.G., Corley, R.P., Haberstick, B.C., & Hewitt, J.K. (2009). Behavioral disinhibition: liability for externalizing spectrum disorders and its genetic and environmental relation to response inhibition across adolescence. *Journal of Abnormal Psychology, 118,* 117–130.

Youngstrom, E. A., Findling, R. L., & Calabrese, J. R. (2004). Effects of adolescent manic symptoms on agreement between youth, parent, and teacher ratings of behavior problems. *Journal of Affective Disorders, 82,* S5–S16.

Youngstrom, E. A., Findling, R. L., Calabrese, J. R., Gracious, B. L., Demeter, C., Bedoya, D. D., et al. (2004). Comparing the diagnostic accuracy of six potential screening instruments for bipolar disorder in youths aged 5 to 17 years. *Journal of the American Academy of Child and Adolescent Psychiatry, 43,* 847–858.

Youngstrom, E., Findling, R. L., & Calabrese, J. R. (2003). Who are the comorbid adolescents? Agreement between psychiatric diagnosis, youth, parent, and teacher report. *Journal of Abnormal Psychology, 31,* 231–246.

Youngstrom, E., Loeber, R., & Stouthamer-Loeber, M. (2000). Patterns and correlates of agreement between parent, teacher, and male adolescent ratings of externalizing and internalizing problems. *Journal of Consulting and Clinical Psychology, 68,* 1038–1050.

Yu, M., Stiffman, A. R., & Freedenthal, S. (2005). Factors affecting American Indian adolescent tobacco use. *Addictive Behaviors, 30,* 889–904.

Zahn-Waxler, C. (2000). The development of empathy, guilt, and internalization of distress. In R. Davidson (Ed.), *Wisconsin Symposium on Emotion: Vol. 1. Anxiety, depression and emotion* (pp. 222–265). New York: Oxford University Press.

Zahn-Waxler, C., Cole, P., Welsh, J., & Fox, N. (1995). Psychophysiological correlates of empathy and prosocial behavior in preschool children with behavior problems. *Development and Psychopathology, 7,* 27–48.

Zahn-Waxler, C., Klimes-Dougan, B. & Slattery, M.J. (2000). Internalizing problems of childhood and adolescence: Prospects, pitfalls, and progress in understanding the development of anxiety and depression. *Development and Psychopathology 12,* 443–466.

Zayas, L. H., Lester, R. J., Cabassa, L. J., & Fortuna, L. R. (2005). Why do so many Latina teens attempt suicide? A conceptual model of research. *American Journal of Orthopsychiatry, 75,* 275–287.

Zeanah, C. H., Scheeringa, M., Boris, N. W., Heller, S. S., Smyke, A. T., & Trapani, J. (2004). Reactive attachment disorder in maltreated toddlers. *Child Abuse and Neglect, 28,* 877–888.

Zeanah, C. H., Smyke, A. T., Koga, S. F., & Carlson, E. (2005). Attachment in institutionalized and community children in Romania. *Child Development, 76,* 1015–1028.

Zeanah, C.H. (2009). *Handbook of Infant Mental Health* (3rd ed.) New York: Guilford Press.

Zeanah, C.H., Egger, H.L., Smyke, A.T., Nelson, C.A., Fox, N.A., Marshall, P.J., & Guthrie, D. (2009). Institutional rearing and psychiatric disorders in Romanian preschool children. *American Journal of Psychiatry, 166,* 777–785.

Zeanah, C.H., & Smyke, A.T. (2009). Attachment disorders. In C. H. Zeanah (Ed.), *Handbook of Infant Mental Healt,* (3rd ed.) (pp. 421–434). New York: Guilford Press.

Zelazo, P.D., & Müller, U. (2011). Executive function in typical and atypical development. In U. Goswami (Ed.), *The Wiley-Blackwell handbook of childhood cognitive development* (2nd ed.) (pp. 574–603). Hoboken, NJ: Wiley-Blackwell.

Zerbe, K. J. (2003a). Eating disorders in middle and late life: A neglected problem. *Primary Psychiatry, 10,* 80–82.

Zerbe, K. J. (2003b). Eating disorders over the life cycle: Diagnosis and treatment. *Primary Psychiatry, 10,* 28–29.

Zero to Three Association. (1994, 2005). *Diagnostic classification of mental health and developmental disorders of infancy and early childhood.* Washington, DC: Zero to Three: National Center for Infants, Toddlers, and Families.

Zhou, Q., Lengua, L.J., & Wang, Y. (2009). The relations of temperament reactivity and effortful control to children's adjustment problems in China and the United States. *Developmental Psychology, 45,* 724–739.

Zigler, E. (1969). Developmental versus difference theories of mental retardation and the problem of motivation. American Journal of Mental Deficiency, 73, 536–556.

Zigler, E. (1971). The retarded child as a whole person. In H. E. Adams & W. K. Boardman III (Eds.), Advances in experimental clinical psychology (Vol. 1, pp. 47–121). New York: Pergamon Press.

Zigler, E. (1999). The individual with mental retardation as a whole person. In E. Zigler & D. Bennett-Gates (Eds.), *Personality development in individuals with mental retardation* (pp. 1–16).New York: Cambridge University Press.

Zigler, E., Balla, D., & Hodapp, R. (1984). On the definition and classification of mental retardation. *American Journal of Mental Deficiency, 89*, 215–230.

Zigler, E., & Bennett-Gates, D. (Eds.), (1999). *Personality development in individuals with mental retardation.* New York: Cambridge University Press.

Zigman, W. B., Schupf, N., Devenny, D. A., Miezejeski, C., Ryan, R., Urv, T. K., et al. (2004). Incidence and prevalence of dementia in elderly adults with mental retardation without Down syndrome. *American Journal on Mental Retardation, 109,* 126–141.

Zimmer-Gembeck, M. J., Geiger, T. C., & Crick, N. R. (2005). Relational and physical aggression, prosocial behavior, and peer relations: Gender moderation and bidirectional associations. *Journal of Early Adolescence, 25*, 421–452.

Zimmer-Gembeck, M.J., & Skinner, E.A. (2011). The development of coping across childhood and adolescence: An integrative review and critique of research. *International Journal of Behavioral Development, 35,* 1–17.

Zucker, N. L., Marcus, M., & Bulik, C. A group parent-training program: A novel approach for eating disorder management. *Eating and Weight Disorders, 11,* 78–82.

Zucker, R. A., Heitzeg, M. M., & Nigg, J. T. (2011). Parsing the undercontrol-disinhibition pathway to substance use disorders: A multilevel developmental problem. *Child Development Perspectives, 5*, 248–255.

Zwaigenbaum, L., Bryson, S., Lord, C., Rogers, S., Carter, A., Carver, L., … Yirmiya, N. (2012). Clinical assessment and management of toddlers with suspected autism spectrum disorder: Insights from studies of high-risk infants. *Pediatrics, 123,* 1383–1391.

Zwaigenbaum, L., Bryson, S., Rogers, T., Roberts, W., Brian, J., & Szatmari, P. (2005). Behavioral manifestations of autism in the first year of life. *International Journal of Developmental Neuroscience, 23*, 143–152.

Name Index

Subject Index